Psychology

Psychology

Fourth Edition

Robin Kowalski Clemson University

Drew Westen Emory University

WILEY

John Wiley & Sons, Inc.

Dedication

To my sweet little boys, Noah and Jordan.
I love you more than you could ever know,
    and
To my parents, Randolph and Frances Kowalski.
Thank you for being such great parents, role models, and friends.
    RMK

To Laura and Mackenzie.
    DW

EXECUTIVE EDITOR	Ryan Flahive
DEVELOPMENT EDITOR	Johnna Barto
MARKETING MANAGER	Kate Stewart
SENIOR PRODUCTION EDITOR	Patricia McFadden
SENIOR DESIGNER	Kevin Murphy
COVER AND INTERIOR DESIGN	Laura Ierardi
SENIOR ILLUSTRATION EDITOR	Sandra Rigby
ILLUSTRATIONS	Fourth Edition updated by Hadel Studio
SENIOR PHOTO EDITOR	Sara Wight
PHOTO RESEARCHER	Mary Ann Price
COVER PHOTO	© Robert Silvers/Runaway Technology, Inc.
FREELANCE PRODUCTION MANAGEMENT	Ingrao Associates
EDITORIAL ASSISTANT	Deepa Chungi
MEDIA EDITOR	Thomas Kulesa

This book was set in 10/12 Palatino Light by LCI Design and printed and bound by Von Hoffmann, Inc. The cover was printed by Von Hoffmann, Inc.

This book is printed on acid-free paper. ∝

To order books or for customer service please, call 1(800)-CALL-WILEY (225-5945).

ISBN 0-471-44757-9
WIE 0-471-65244-X

Printed in the United States of America

10 9 8 7 6 5 4 3 2 1

Preface

From the moment I enrolled in my first psychology course—a college transfer class in high school—I was hooked. I loved the content of the course, but I also remember two other very specific things about the class. First, the professor, Dr. John Pellew, was a superb teacher and thus was instrumental in my becoming the psychologist I am today. Second, the textbook was user-friendly, interesting, and even enjoyable. I still have the book and, suffice it to say, high school was many years ago.

Stemming from that early experience, my philosophy of teaching and my philosophy of writing an introductory psychology book are similar. I love interactions with students, either directly in the classroom, or indirectly through writing or email contacts. I want my students to enjoy the process of learning, to be exposed to the story of psychology in a way that captures their attention, and to see applications of what they learn in introductory psychology to their everyday lives. As a teacher I try to accomplish these goals by establishing good relationships with my students, by maintaining my own excitement and energy for the subject matter, and by using many stories and illustrations as I teach them the concepts of psychology.

As the new author of this edition, I have pursued similar goals. My expertise is in the area of social psychology, with secondary emphases in health psychology and gender. My primary research interests focus on aversive interpersonal behaviors, such as complaining and teasing, that occur frequently in the context of people's ongoing interactions with one another. I also conduct research on organ donation and transplantation within the field of health psychology. Given my areas of expertise, it won't surprise you to learn that the fourth edition of *Psychology* includes more extensive coverage of research related to gender. Furthermore, a separate chapter is now devoted to health psychology, one of the most rapidly growing subdisciplines within psychology.

I hope that my enthusiasm for psychology is apparent as you proceed through the text. And I encourage you to contact me (rkowals@clemson.edu) regarding what it is that you like and dislike, what is immediately clear, and what you find confusing. As a student, you are the primary means of improving this book.

The overall vision for *Psychology* is that it is the "thinking student's introduction to psychology." The goal is that you as students are drawn into the material in such a way that you begin to ask probing questions about the information and begin to see psychology at work in your everyday lives. The aim from the start of this revision has also been to give you a sense of the "big picture," that is, of how we human beings think, feel, and behave, and how our evolving science continually addresses and re-addresses the key questions that brought most of us into the field—questions about the relation between psychological events and their neural underpinnings, between cognition and emotion, between cultural processes and human evolution, between nature and nurture, and so forth. Introductory psychology is probably the last time most students—and psychologists—get a broad overview of the depth and breadth of our field. In fact, one of the greatest personal benefits for those of us who teach introductory psychology is that we are continually exposed to new information, often in domains far from our own areas of expertise, that stretch and challenge our imaginations.

As the "thinking student's introduction to psychology," I wrote this edition of *Psychology* to tell the "story of psychology." As a teacher and writer, I try to make use of one of the most robust findings in psychology: that memory and understanding are enhanced when target information is associated with vivid and personally relevant material. Thus, each chapter begins with an experiment, a case, or an event that lets you know why the topic is important and why anyone might be excited about it. None of the cases is invented; each is a real story. Chapter 2, for example, begins with the case of a young woman who lost her entire family in a car accident and found herself suddenly contracting one minor ailment after another until finally starting to talk about the event with a psychologist. I then juxtapose this with an experiment by James Pennebaker on the influence of emotional expression on physical health to show how a researcher can take a striking phenomenon or philosophical question (the relation between mind and body) and turn it into a researchable question.

Writing a textbook is always a balancing act, with each addition adjusting scales that were tipped a bit too far in one direction in the previous one. Probably the most difficult balance to achieve in writing an introductory text is how to cover what we know (at least for now) and what's on the cutting edge without making an encyclopedia, particularly when the field of psychology is moving forward so rapidly. Another balancing act involves helping those of you who might desire more structure to learn the material, without placing roadblocks in the path of students who would find most pedagogical devices contrived and distracting. A final balancing act involves presenting solid research in a manner that is accessible, lively, and thought-provoking. I believe that this edition of *Psychology* successfully achieves the balance across these different issues.

New Features of the Fourth Edition

Finding the Take Home Message: "The Big Questions"

Wherever possible, this book and its previous editions have tried to delineate some of the links across topics that our best intellectual efforts often obscure. For example, Chapter 7 presents connectionist models in some detail, linking them to concepts of association described in Chapter 1, Chapter 5 on associative learning, and Chapter 6 on associative memory. Multiple chapters revisit connectionist models, such as research on psychomotor slowing in Chapter 13 and research on stereotype activation and prejudice in Chapter 17. Similarly, in various places throughout the book, I present avenues of integration across theoretical perspectives, showing the roles that biological, psychological, *and* social factors play in behavior. Chapter 6 on memory concludes by linking the expanded understanding of memory characteristic of the last decade to research from multiple traditions that can now be incorporated under the larger tent of cognitive neuroscience. Students are challenged to consider the link between classical and operant conditioning and implicit and procedural memory and to consider the evolutionary challenge to the concept of an all-purpose, general processing brain.

In the fourth edition, I have taken this integrative approach one step further. Particularly with a comprehensive course such as introductory psychology, students are often left wondering what the take-home message is. What are the key elements or big picture questions that unify all of the different topics covered? To provide you with this take-home message, new to this edition of *Psychology* is the introduction of eight philosophical questions central to the study of psychology—the "Big Picture Questions."

Many contemporary questions that psychologists raise were debated among early philosophers. However, psychologists do not tackle philosophical issues such as free will versus determinism directly. Rather, classic philosophical questions reverberate through many contemporary psychological discussions. These are the questions on which much, if not most, psychological theory and research are predicated, as will become evident as you read subsequent chapters of this book. Some of the questions are beginning to be answered as theorists and researchers examine the roots of human self-understanding. Others remain unanswered, yet they still guide current theory and research. These questions are addressed throughout the text where you see the symbol (φ) followed by the Big Picture Question most relevant to the constructs being discussed at that point in the chapter. Although the following list is not all inclusive, it gives a sense of the overriding questions guiding psychological research today.

(φ) Question 1: To what extent can mental processes be reduced to the brain or body? Although hard-core behaviorists argue that mental processes are outside the purview of research and theory, most other psychologists argue that at least part of our mental processes can be reduced to the brain or body. For example, one application of this question might be to ask "Can we understand the loss of a loved one by mapping the neural networks? Or when we hold a phone number in mind briefly as we reach for the phone, are we using different neural 'hardware' than when we store that number 'for keeps'?

(φ) Question 2: What is the relationship between reason and desire or, more precisely, between cognition and affect? For example, to what extent should people choose their mates based on "gut" feelings? Should they carefully weigh a potential partner's costs and benefits if they want to have a happy, long-lasting marriage? For that matter, to what extent do people's thoughts actually determine how they feel?

(φ) Question 3: To what extent is human psychology continuous with the psychology of other animals? For example, to what extent can studying fear responses in rats inform humans about their own fear responses? Or, conversely, to what extent do current theories of altruism derived from research with humans apply also to animals? Can we understand people's relationships with animals by examining their patterns of relationship with other humans?

(φ) Question 4: To what extent is human nature particular versus universal? In other words, to what extent is human nature relatively invariant as opposed to culturally variable? Is logical reasoning universal, for example, or do people use different kinds of "logic" in different cultures? Do children follow similar patterns of language development throughout the world?

(φ) Question 5: To what extent are psychological processes the same in men and women? For example, to what extent do gender differences in linguistic and spatial problem solving reflect differential evolutionary selection pressures? Why might men and women make different attributions for their own successes and failures? Are men and women similarly affected by a partner's infidelity?

(φ) Question 6: What is the relation between nature and nurture in shaping psychological processes? For example, how can we understand that the likelihood of getting killed in an accident is heritable? To what extent is intelligence inherited? How do we account for data showing remarkable similarities between identical twins who have been reared apart?

(φ) Question 7: To what extent are psychological processes conscious or unconscious—that is, explicit versus implicit? Can, for example, amnesiacs show cognitive dissonance effects, even when they cannot remember having performed a prior act involved in the production of dissonance? Similarly, can people describe themselves accurately or are they unaware of the contents of their minds and the causes of their behavior?

(φ) Question 8: To what extent can we inform our knowledge through reason or through observation—that is, rationalism versus empiricism? Relatedly, to what extent are humans passive recipients of, or active constructors of, their understanding? When an air traffic controller notices an anomalous and potentially dangerous "blip" on the radar screen, to what extent is this an active process of construction and decision making or a passive process of sensations inevitably producing perceptions?

General Organization

The fourth edition of *Psychology* has been organized in a way that should be convenient for most instructors and that follows a coherent design. Of course, different instructors organize things differently, but I do not think many will find the organization idiosyncratic. Following an introductory chapter (Chapter 1) and a chapter on the primary research methods used in psychology (Chapter 2), the content moves on to physiological psychology (Chapter 3), sensation and perception (Chapter 4), learning (Chapter 5), memory (Chapter 6), thought and language (Chapter 7), and intelligence (Chapter 8). Following this, attention is given to consciousness (Chapter 9), motivation and emotion (Chapter 10), and health, stress, and coping (Chapter 11). I then discuss topics related to personality (Chapter 12), developmental psychology (Chapter 13 and Chapter 14), clinical psychology (Chapter 15 and Chapter 16), and social psychology (Chapter 17 and Chapter 18).

Teaching the material in the order presented is probably optimal, for chapters do build on each other. For example, Chapter 9 on consciousness presupposes knowledge of the distinction posed in Chapter 6 between implicit and explicit memory. However, if instructors want to rearrange the order of chapters, they can certainly do so, as material mentioned from a previous chapter is cross-referenced so that students can easily find any information they need.

Research Focus

This book is about psychological science. A student should come out of an introductory psychology class not only with a sense of the basic questions and frameworks for answering them but also with an appreciation for how to obtain psychological knowledge. Thus, Chapter 2 is devoted to research methods, and the style reflects an effort to engage, not intimidate, so that you can see how methods actually make a difference. The statistical supplement that immediately followed this methodological presentation as an appendix in the third edition is now included in the body of the text. Thus, you can more easily see which statistics are most relevant to particular research designs. From start to finish, you will read about specific studies so that you can learn about the logic of scientific investigation.

Cutting Edge Information

Many of the changes to the fourth edition of *Psychology* involved updating information that had either become outdated or the substance of which had changed. Additions were made to reflect some of the newer and more cutting edge research within the field of psychology, in large part to align the book with my vision of *Psychology* as the "thinking student's introduction to psychology." Some of the highlights in this edition are as follows.

- Chapter 1, "Psychology: The Study of Mental Processes and Behavior," introduces you to the Big Picture Questions that provide a unifying theme for the entire book.
- Chapter 2, "Research Methods in Psychology," provides a more integrative perspective of research methods and statistics. Special sections, entitled "Focus on

Methodology," have been added to facilitate your thinking about research methods.

- Chapter 3, "Biological Bases of Mental Life and Behavior," includes an expanded coverage of genetics and evolution, as well as new information on genetic engineering and psychoneuroimmunology.

- Chapter 4, "Sensation and Perception," examines the paradoxical role of Capsaicin, the active ingredient in hot peppers, as a treatment for pain.

- Chapter 5, "Learning," includes new information directly comparing and contrasting classical and operant conditioning.

- Chapter 6, "Memory," includes new information on the relationship between emotional arousal and memory.

- Chapter 7, "Thought and Language," explores several new applications of research on thought and language such as the fact that many hearing-impaired individuals show reasoning deficits, particularly in the areas of inductive reasoning and cognitive flexibility, and the finding that people who are multilingual generate different thoughts depending on the language they are speaking.

- Chapter 8, "Intelligence," addresses many interesting and, at times, controversial issues, including the relationship between emotional intelligence and intelligence as measured by an IQ test, gender differences and similarities in intelligence, and the use of "virtual twins" to tease apart genetic and environmental contributions to intelligence.

- Chapter 9, "Consciousness," examines the various forms of consciousness and unconsciousness, including new information related to the growing abuse of legal prescription drugs such as Oxycontin.

- Chapter 10, "Motivation and Emotion," represents a reorganization of emotion with motivation in a single chapter. Specifically, the chapter addresses the role of thoughts, feelings, and arousal in affecting motivation.

- Chapter 11, "Health, Stress, and Coping," includes new information about health psychology, one of the fastest growing areas within psychology today. Attention is given to the biological, psychological, and social factors involved in health and illness.

- Chapter 12, "Personality," discusses different approaches to the study and measurement of personality, including, most recently, the Five Factor Model of Personality.

- Chapter 13, "Physical and Cognitive Development," provides cutting edge research related to Alzheimer's disease.

- Chapter 14, "Social Development," includes a discussion of attachment in childhood and adulthood, including the problems associated with attachment or the lack thereof, such as that demonstrated by "feral" children.

- Chapter 15, "Psychological Disorders," addresses the role of prenatal trauma as a possible risk factor for schizophrenia. Could exposure to malnutrition, maternal infection during pregnancy, and birth trauma contribute to the onset of schizophrenia later in life?

- Chapter 16, "Treatment of Psychological Disorders," includes cutting edge information on virtual reality therapy (VRT), a technologically innovative technique for helping patients, most recently survivors of 9/11, cope with fears, phobias, and posttraumatic stress disorder.

- Chapter 17, "Social Cognition," gives expanded coverage to the "Self," including recent research on self-esteem and self-presentation.

- Chapter 18, "Interpersonal Processes," takes a new look at the darker side of relationships, with a particular focus on the types of aversive behaviors that people perpetrate in their relationships with family and friends on a regular basis. This chapter also examines everyday social influence tactics to which we all fall victim.

Making Connections

In many respects, schizophrenia is a disorder of consciousness, in which the normal monitor and control functions of consciousness are suspended (Chapter 9). People with schizophrenia have trouble keeping irrelevant associations out of consciousness and controlling to the contents of their consciousness to solve problems. In fact, multiple studies have found deficits in focusing and maintaining attention and in using working memory effectively in patients with schizophrenia (Cornblatt & Kelip, 1994; Gold et al., 1997).

Apply and Discuss

A recent article in the medical journal *The Lancet* stated that teens who watch movies in which the actors smoke are three times more likely to smoke than those who don't watch those same movies.

▪ Do you agree with the journal's finding?

▪ What other factors might be involved that could possibly distort the findings obtained in this study? How many people do you know who started smoking because of someone they had seen smoking in the movies?

Key Pedagogical Features: An Integrated Package

Consistent with the goal of providing you, the student, with a more integrative perspective on psychology, and with the goal of creating "the thinking student's introduction to psychology," the fourth edition of *Psychology* again includes an integrated study package built into the structure of the text, without cluttering the margins and distracting from the narrative.

In this edition, I continue to integrate photos with the text in a way that fosters critical thinking and helps you to see the connections between concepts presented in different chapters. Instead of using photos primarily to brighten the color of the book or provide interesting diversions (both lofty aims, of course), I have used the photos to *link concepts and visual images*, through the two pedagogical features called **Making Connections** and **Apply & Discuss**.

Making Connections illustrates and links material from different chapters, so that you can see the threads that tie the discipline together. For example, as you consider the fact that schizophrenia is a disorder of consciousness (Chapter 15), you are reminded of the role and function of consciousness discussed in Chapter 9.

Apply and Discuss combines visual imagery with critical thinking to challenge you to apply what you have just learned. For example, in discussing variables that influence teens to smoke (Chapter 11), you will see a photograph of an actor in a movie smoking. You will be asked to think about the extent to which teens are influenced by such media images of a health-compromising behavior, and to generate other factors that might be involved in teen smoking. The visual example pulls you in, while the questions require you to apply what you have just learned about facilitators and inhibitors of health-compromising behaviors, such as smoking.

Key words are **boldfaced** in the text, and the *definitions of those words are italicized* in the text where they appear, so that you can readily understand every term introduced. Each chapter ends with a list of **Key Terms** with page numbers, so that you, the student, can be certain that you understand all the major terms introduced in the chapter.

Key Conceptual Features

Several key conceptual features remain from the third edition that give *Psychology* its distinctive "signature." They arose from five objectives in creating this book:

▪ To focus on both the biological basis of psychology and the role of culture in shaping basic psychological processes;

▪ To provide a conceptual orientation that would capture the excitement and tensions in the field;

▪ To help students understand the logic of scientific discovery and hypothesis testing as applied to psychological questions;

▪ To suggest ways of integrating psychological theories and knowledge across subfields; and

▪ To employ language that would be sophisticated but engaging.

Biology and Culture: A Micro to Macro Approach

A consistent theme of the book, introduced in the first chapter, is that biology and culture form the boundaries of psychology. Understanding people means attending simultaneously to biological processes, psychological experience, and cultural and historical context. The focus on biological and neural underpinnings echoes one of the major trends in contemporary psychological science, as technological developments allow progressively more sophisticated understanding of the neural substrates of psychological experience. The focus on culture has been a central feature of *Psychology* since publication of the first edition.

Each chapter of this book contains at least two extended discussions that show the way psychological experience is situated between the nervous system and cultural experience.

From Brain to Behavior focuses on concepts and findings from biopsychology and the neurosciences, providing a detailed discussion of a specific issue, such as psychoneuroimmunology (Chapter 3), the neural basis of classical conditioning (Chapter 5), or individual differences in IQ (Chapter 8; see below). One of the key features of this text, however, is the integration of neuroscientific research into the fabric of the narrative.

Individual Differences in IQ | From Brain to Behavior

The influence of both nature and nurture on individual differences in intelligence is well established (see Sternberg, 1997b, 2000a). With respect to environmental effects, as we saw in Chapter 3, early enrichment of the environments of rats not only makes them better learners but actually increases their brain mass (see Bors & Forrin, 1996). In humans, some of the best predictors of a child's performance on tests of IQ and language in the toddler and preschool years include an enriched home environment, positive mother–child interactions that foster interest and exploration, and maternal knowledge about child rearing and child development (Bee, 1982; Benasich & Brooks-Gunn, 1996; Hart & Risley, 1992; Landau & Weissler, 1993).

A **Global Vista** uses ethnographic material and cross-cultural studies to explore psychological phenomena in other cultures, with an eye to addressing the universality or culture-specificity of psychological theories and observations. For example, menopause has a very different meaning, and hence different symptoms, in a Mayan village than it does in North America (Chapter 13), and the concept of "the self" differs across individualistic and collectivistic cultures (Chapter 17). Like research in the neurosciences, cross-cultural research is integrated into the structure of each chapter, so that students do not isolate cross-cultural issues as distinct from the "psychology of white people" but instead ask cross-cultural questions from the start.

Culture and Self | A Global Vista

The notion that people have a self-concept and some core of selfhood that distinguish them from others seems intuitively obvious to people living in twenty-first century Western societies. This view would not, however, be commonsensical to people in most cultures in most historical epochs (Geertz, 1974; Markus & Kitayama, 1991; Shweder & Bourne, 1982). That the term "the individual" is synonymous with "the person" in contemporary usage demonstrates how the individualism of our culture is reflected in its language. Not coincidentally, the prefix "self-," as in "self-esteem" or "self-representation," did not evolve in the English language until around the time of the Industrial Revolution.

Learning Aids

Given the breadth of information that is included within an introductory psychology book, students often find it beneficial to have learning aids. The learning aids from the last edition that were most effective in helping students learn were retained in the present edition: *Interim Summaries*, a feature called *One Step Further*, and *Chapter Summaries*.

Interim Summaries. At the end of major sections, **Interim Summaries** recap the "gist" of what has been presented, not only to help you consolidate your knowledge of what you have read but also to alert you if you failed to "get" something important (see below). The inclusion of these summaries reflects both feedback from professors and the results of research suggesting that distributing conceptual summaries throughout a chapter and presenting them shortly after students have read the material is likely to optimize learning.

INTERIM SUMMARY

Myriad reasons exist to account for why people continue to engage in negative health behaviors and why they fail to engage in positive health behaviors. A useful way of compartmentalizing these reasons is to group them into four barriers to health promotion: individual barriers, family barriers, health system barriers, and community barriers. However, as with most things in life, barriers can be overcome, and the barriers to health promotion presented here are no exception.

One Step Further. This edition, like the last, includes a feature called **One Step Further**. Like the other recurring features in the book, these discussions flow naturally from the text but are highlighted in color. Generally, these are advanced discussions of some aspect of the topic, usually with a strong methodological or conceptual focus. These sections are intended to be assigned by professors who prefer a high-level text, or to be read by students who find the topic intriguing and want to learn more about it even if it isn't assigned. Highlighting these sections gives professors—and students—some choice about what to read or not to read.

For example, in Chapter 5, the **One Step Further** section addresses why reinforcers are reinforcing (see below). In Chapter 6, this feature describes research tracking down the neuropsychology of working memory, linking primate studies, basic laboratory research with humans, and the latest neuroimaging research.

One Step Further	## Why Are Reinforcers Reinforcing?
	Learning theorists aim to formulate general laws of behavior that link behaviors with events in the environment. Skinner and others who called themselves "radical behaviorists" were less interested in theorizing about the mechanisms that produced these laws, since these mechanisms could not really be observed. Other theorists within and without behaviorism, however, have asked, "What makes a reinforcer reinforcing or a punisher punishing?" No answer has achieved widespread acceptance, but three are worth considering.

Chapter Summaries. Each chapter concludes with a summary of the major points, which are organized under the headings in which they were presented. These summaries provide an outline of the chapter.

Summary

Health

1. Health psychology examines the psychological and social influences on how people stay healthy, why they become ill, and how they respond when they do get ill.

2. Although the field has taken off only in the last two decades, it has a rich heritage in the fields of medicine and philosophy. This history began with the early theorists and the practice of trephination, continued through the humoral theory of illness, and the Renaissance, and received one of its major boosts from Freud and the field of psychosomatic medicine.

Stress

10. Stress refers to a challenge to a person's capacity to adapt to inner and outer demands, which may be physiologically arousing and emotionally taxing and call for cognitive and behavioral responses. Stress is a psychobiological process that entails a transaction between a person and her environment. Selye proposed that the body responds to stressful conditions with a general adaptation syndrome consisting of three stages: alarm, resistance, and exhaustion.

12. Events that often lead to stress are called stressors. Stressors include life events, catastrophes, and daily hassles.

Coping

14. The ways people deal with stressful situations are known as strategies for coping; these coping mechanisms are in part culturally patterned. People cope by trying to change the situation directly, changing their perception of it, or changing the emotions it elicits.

Supplementary Materials

Psychology, Fourth Edition, features a full line of teaching and learning resources developed to help professors create a more dynamic and innovative learning environment.

These resources—including print, software, and Web-based materials—are integrated with the text and take an active learning approach to help build students' ability to think clearly and critically.

For Students

Study Guide. Written by Alastair Younger of the University of Ottawa, the *Study Guide* offers students a comprehensive way to review materials from the text and test their knowledge. Each chapter in the text has a corresponding chapter in the *Study Guide.* Six tools help students master the material: chapter outlines, learning objectives, key terms, fill-in exercises, critical thinking exercises, and sample test questions with answers.

Kowalski *Psychology 4e* Web Site at www.wiley.com/college/kowalski. Students have access to the following supplements to help them succeed in the course.

- **Vocabulary Flash Cards.** This interactive module gives students the opportunity to test their knowledge of vocabulary terms. In addition, students can take self-tests and monitor their progress throughout the semester.
- **Interactive Animations.** Prepared by Marvin Lee of Shenandoah University and Margaret Olimpieri of Westchester Community College, the interactive modules help students understand concepts featured in the text. Each interactive animation includes a preface and a summary to reinforce students' understanding of the module.

For Instructors

Instructor's Manual. Prepared by Paul J.Wellman of Texas A&M University, this comprehensive resource includes for each text chapter an outline, student learning objectives, outline/lecture organizer (referenced to text pages), lecture topic extensions, in-class demonstrations and discussion questions, out-of-class student exercises, website resources, suggested Web links, software, videos, PowerPoint presentations, and numerous student handouts.

Instructor's Resource CD-ROM. This multiplatform CD-ROM is an invaluable resource for in-class lectures and out-of-class preparation. It includes:

- The entire **Instructor's Manual**
- The student **Study Guide**
- The **Computerized Test Bank**
- **PowerPoints**

PowerPoint Presentation Slides and Lecture Notes. This includes 450 original lecture slides and 215 art slides that can be sequenced and customized by instructors to fit any lecture. The PowerPoint slides contain a combination of key concepts, images, and problems from the textbook for use in the classroom. Designed according to the organization of the material in the textbook, this series of electronic transparencies can be used to illustrate concepts visually and graphically.

Web CT and Blackboard Courses. Web CT and Blackboard courses, prepared by John S. Conklin of Camosun College, are available with this edition of the textbook. This powerful Web program allows professors to set up their own online course with chat rooms, bulletin boards, quizzing, and student tracking. These course-management systems are tools that facilitate the organization and delivery of course materials on the Web. Easy to use, these tools help broaden communication and provide in-depth content for easy and flexible course administration and sophisticated online testing and diagnostic systems.

Computerized Test Bank. Prepared by Michael Russell of Washburn University, this multiplatform CD-ROM has nearly 2000 test items, which have been meticulously proofread and reviewed. Each multiple-choice question has been linked to the text's learning objectives, coded "Factual" or "Applied," and referenced to its source in the text. The easy-to-use test-generation program fully supports graphics, print tests, student answer sheets, and answer keys quickly and easily. The software's advanced features allow you to create an exam to your exact specifications, with an easy-to-use interface.

Transparencies. Full-color traditional acetate transparencies of every single illustration from the text are available for professors who cannot or do not wish to use the slides available on the *Instructor's Resource CD-ROM*.

Video Library. A number of the videotapes available to adopters of the text are new to this edition. Please contact your local Wiley representative for details of this rich resource.

Kowalski *Psychology 4e* Web Site at www.wiley.com/college/kowalski. Our on-line resources add a rich, interactive learning experience designed to give professors the tools they need to teach and students the tools and foundations needed to grasp concepts and expand their critical thinking skills. The Kowalski *Psy-*

chology 4e website provides instructors with the following: Instructor's Manual, Test Bank, Student Study Guide, Discussion Questions, Chapter Summaries, Interactive Animations, Web Links, PowerPoint Slides and Lecture Notes, Additional Reading Suggestions, and Supplementary Content.

Acknowledgments

This project began many years ago—in 1987—and several people have played important roles at different points in the endeavor. Jean Stein, a talented writer, helped write the first draft of the first half of the first edition. Several other people also contributed in earlier stages, notably Judy Block, Colleen Coffey, Dr. Alfred Kellam, Dr. Carol Holden, Dr. Lauren Korfine, Dr. Barbara Misle, Dr. Patricia Harney, and Karen Schenkenfeldter. Like Jean, they helped lay the foundations, and their efforts, too, are greatly appreciated. Appreciation also goes to multiple talented research assistants, including (but not limited to) Michelle Levine, Samantha Glass, Chad Lakey, and Holly Payne. Chad and Holly did most of the leg work required to update information presented in the fourth edition.

Reviewers

Over the past eighteen years, this book has been shaped by the insightful comments of dozens of colleagues and would look nothing like it does now without their tireless efforts. From prior editions , I would like to thank Walt Lonner of Western Washington University, who gave advice on cross-cultural coverage for many chapters and gave feedback on others, and Paul Watson of the University of Tennessee for his uncanny ability throughout the years to give advice as to the general coverage and prose of the text. Several other professors have provided invaluable feedback on multiple chapters of the new and prior editions.

Reviewers for the Fourth Edition

Gordon Atlas, *Alfred University*
Richard Bowen, *Loyola University, Chicago*
Robin Bowers, *College of Charleston*
John Broida, *University of Southern Maine*
James Calhoun, *University of Georgia*
Tim Cannon, *University of Scranton*
Dennis Cogan, *Texas Tech University*
Kevin Corcoran, *University of Cincinnati*
Joanne Davis, *University of Tulsa*

Eric De Vos, *Saginaw Valley State University*
Sosimo Fabian, *Hunter College*
Perry Fuchs, *University of Texas at Arlington*
Ronald Gandleman, *Rutgers University*
Doug Hodge, *Dyersburg State Comm. College*
Mark Hoyert, *Indiana University Northwest*
Joan Ingram, *Northwestern*
Shelia Kennison, *Oklahoma State*
Gretchen Lovas, *UC Davis*
David MacDonald, *University of Missouri, Columbia*
Michael McCall, *Ithaca College*
Bill McKeachie, *University of Michigan*
Stephen Meier, *University of Idaho*
Katherine Perez-Rivera
David Pittenger, *University of Tennessee, Chattanooga*
Don Polzella, *University of Dayton*
Lauretta Reeves, *University of Texas, Austin*
Tom Swan, *Siena College*
Susan Tammaro, *Regis College*
Anre Venter, *Notre Dame*
Benjamin Walker, *Georgetown*
Robert Weiskopf, *Indiana University*
Larry Wichlinski, *Carleton*
Stephen Wurst, *SUNY Oswego*

Reviewers for Prior Editions

Millicent H. Abel, *Western Carolina University*; George Adler, *University College of the Cariboo*; Eugene Aidman, *University of Ballarat*; Gary Allen, *University of South Carolina*; Gordon Allen, *Miami University*; Harvard L. Armus, *University of Toledo*; Elaine Baker, *Marshall University*; Robert Batsell, *Southern Methodist University*; Carol M. Batt, *Sacred Heart University*; Col. Johnson Beach, *United States Military Academy-West Point*; Richard Belter, *University of West Florida*; John B. Best, *Eastern Illinois University*; Kathleen Bey, *Palm Beach Community College*; Paul Bloom, *University of Arizona*; Toni L. Blum, *Stetson University*; Joanna Boehnert, *University of Guelph*; John D. Bonvillian, *University of Virginia*; Douglas A. Bors, *University of Toronto-Scarborough*; Robert B. Branstrom, *United Behavioral Health*; Bruce Bridgeman, *University of California, Santa Cruz*; Nathan Brody, *Wesleyan University*; John P. Broida, *University of Southern Maine*; Robert Brown, *Georgia State University*; Adam Butler, *University of Northern Iowa*; James Butler, *James Madison University*; Simone Buzwell, *Swinburne University of Technology*; Mark Byrd, *University of Canterbury (New Zealand)*; Susan Calkins,

University of North Carolina-Greensboro; Barbara K. Canaday, *Southwestern College;* Kelly B. Cartwright, *Christopher Newport University;* George A. Cicala, *University of Delaware;* Toon Cillessen, *University of Connecticut;* John M. Clark, *Macomb Community College;* Margaret Cleek, *University of Wisconsin-Madison;* Dennis Cogan, *Texas Tech University;* Patricia Colby, *Skidmore College;* Ken Cramer, *University of Windsor;* James Dalziel, *University of Sidney;* Hank Davis, *University of Guelph;* Daniel L. C. DeNeui, *Elon College;* Peter Ditto, *Kent State University;* Allen Dobbs, *University of Alberta;* Mark Dombeck, *Idaho State University;* William Domhoff, *University of California, Santa Cruz;* Eugene B. Doughtie, *University of Houston;* Richard Eglsaer, *Sam Houston State University;* Joseph R. Ferrari, *DePaul University;* J. Gregor Fetterman, *Arizona State University;* Oney D. Fitzpatrick, Jr., *Lamar University;* Sandra P. Frankmann, *University of Southern Colorado;* Nelson Freedman, *Queens University;* Jennifer J. Freyd, *University of Oregon;* Herbert Friedman, *College of William and Mary;* Mauricio Gaborit, S. J., *St. Louis University;* Adrienne Ganz, *New York University;* Wendi Gardner, *Northwestern University;* Mark Garrison, *Kentucky State University;* Nellie Georgiou, *Monash University;* Marian Gibney, *Phoenix College;* William E. Gibson, *Northern Arizona University;* Marvin Goldfried, *State University of New York-Stony Brook;* Mary Alice Gordon, *Southern Methodist University;* Charles R. Grah, *Austin Peay State University;* Leonard Green, *Washington University;* Mary Banks Gregerson, *George Washington University;* Joseph Guido, *Providence College;* Robert Guttentag, *University of North Carolina-Greensboro;* Richard Halgin, *University of Massachusetts-Amherst;* Larry Hawk, *University at Buffalo;* Thomas Herrman, *University of Guelph;* Douglas Herrmann, *Indiana State University;* Julia C. Hoigaard, *University of California, Irvine;* Linda Hort, *Griffith University;* Julia Jacks, *University of North Carolina-Greensboro;* Timothy Jay, *North Adams State College;* James Johnson, *Illinois State University;* Lance K. Johnson, *Pasadena City College;* Robert Johnston, *College of William and Mary;* Kevin Kennelly, *University of North Texas;* Norman E. Kinney, *Southeast Missouri State University;* Lynne Kiorpes, *New York University;* Stephen B. Klein, *Mississippi State University;* Keith Kluender, *University of Wisconsin-Madison;* James M. Knight, *Humboldt State University;* James Kopp, *University of Texas-Arlington;* Emma Kraidman, *Franciscan Children's Hospital, Boston;* Philip Langer, *University of Colorado-Boulder;* Randy J. Larsen, *Washington University;* Len Lecci, *University of North Carolina-Wilmington;* Peter Leppmann, *University of Guelph;* Alice Locicero, *Lesley College;* Karsten Look, *Columbus State Community College;* Stephen Madigan, *University of Southern California;* Matthew Margres, *Saginaw Valley State University;* Richard M. Martin, *Gustavus Adolphus College;* Donald McBurney, *University of Pittsburgh;* Ann Meriwether, *University of Michigan;* Eleanor Midkiff, *Eastern Illinois University;* David Mitchell, *Southern Methodist University;* Robert F. Mosher, *Northern Arizona University;* David I. Mostofsky, *Boston University;* J. L. Mottin, *University of Guelph;* John Mullennix, *Wayne State University;* Andrew Neher, *Cabrillo College;* John B. Nezlek, *College of William and Mary;* William H. Overman, *University of North Carolina at Wilmington;* Constance Pilkington, *College of William and Mary;* Dorothy C. Pointkowski, *San Francisco State University;* Donald J. Polzella, *University of Dayton;* Felicia Pratto, *University of Connecticut;* J. Faye Pritchard, *La Salle University;* David Rabiner, *University of North Carolina-Greensboro;* Freda Rebelsky, *Boston University;* Bradley C. Redburn, *Johnson County Community College;* Laura Reichel, *Metropolitan State College of Denver;* Paul Roberts, *Murdoch University;* Hillary R. Rodman, *Emory University;* Daniel Roenkert, *Western Kentucky University;* Lawrence Rosenblum, *University of California-Riverside;* Alexander Rothman, *University of Minnesota;* Kenneth W. Rusiniak, *Eastern Michigan University;* Michael K. Russell, *Bucknell University;* Robert DeBrae Russell, *University of Michigan-Flint;* Ina Samuels, *University of Massachusetts-Boston;* Karl E. Scheibe, *Wesleyan University;* Richard Schiffman, *Rutgers University;* David A. Schroeder, *University of Arkansas;* Alan Searlman, *St. Lawrence University;* Robert Sekuler, *Brandeis University;* Norm Simonson, *University of Massachusetts;* Steven Sloman, *Brown University;* J. Diedrick Snoek, *Smith College;* Sheldon Solomon, *Skidmore College;* Paul Stager, *York University;* Margo A. Storm, *Temple University;* Chehalis Strapp, *Western Oregon University;* Angela D.Tigner, *Nassau Community College;* Perry Timmermans, *San Diego City College;* David Uttal, *Northwestern University;* D. Rene Verry, *Millikin University;* Malcolm Watson, *Brandeis University;* Paul J.Watson, *University of Tennessee-Chattanooga;* Paul Waxer, *York University;* Russell H.Weigel, *Amherst College;* Joel Weinberger, *Adelphi University;* Cheryl Weinstein, *Harvard Medical School;* Robert W. Weisberg, *Temple University;* Cara Wellman, *Indiana University;* Paul J. Wellman, *Texas A&M University;* Macon Williams, *Illinois State University;* Jeremy M.Wolfe, *Massachusetts Institute of Technology;* Billy Wooten, *Brown University;* David M.Wulff, *Wheaton College;* Todd Zakrajsek, *Southern Oregon State College;* and Thomas Zentall, *University of Kentucky.*

Student Reviews

I have also benefitted considerably from students' comments in reviews and in focus groups. Thanks to the students who provided their feedback as they used the text and/or evaluated the new pedagogy, as well as to the following faculty members and graduate students who coordinated focus groups and reviews.

Harvey Pines, *Canisius College*
Joseph Ferrari, *DePaul University*
Tody Klinger, *Johnson County Community College*
Alexis Collier, *Ohio State University Faculty*
Gordon Pitz, *Southern Illinois University-Carbondale*
Gail Peterson, *University of Minnesota-Minneapoli*
Robert J. Sutherland, *University of New Mexico-Albuquerque*
Adam Butler, *University of Northern Iowa*
Richard Reardon, *University of Oklahoma-Norman*
Sandra P. Frankmann, *University of Southern Colorado*
William H. Calhoun, *University of Tennessee-Knoxville*
Wendy Domjan, *University of Texas-Austin*

Finally, I would like to offer my deep appreciation to the extraordinary team at Wiley. I truly don't think I could have found a more supportive or encouraging team, and it has been a pleasure to work with all of them. I am deeply indebted to my editor, Ryan Flahive, and to Vice President of Higher Education, Anne Smith, both of whose vision and dedication have helped to shape the book into what it is today. Both Ryan and Anne offered encouragement and advice just when it was most needed. I admire their vision and drive. (They are also responsible for many firsts in the lives of my children—first plane trip, first trip to New York, first trip to Washington, D.C., first cab ride, and first ferris wheel ride. For that, they will also always be remembered and appreciated.) Johnna Barto and Barbara Conover served as developmental editors for this edition, and to both of them I owe my gratitude. Barbara guided every stage of this revision, taught me lessons about writing, helped me work on my hang-up with passive voice, and provided a listening ear when I got frustrated. Suzanne Ingrao did an exceptional job with production and with handling my many queries when reviewing the page proofs. I always looked forward to getting her replies to my emails because they were always encouraging. Kate Stewart, the Marketing Manager for this book, was also a source of great encouragement. I spent a lot of time on the phone with Kate and appreciate her guidance, her sense of humor, and her support. My thanks also go to Trish McFadden, the Production Editor, and Mary Savel, the Production Assistant. Harry Nolan supervised the design with great creativity, Tom Kulesa deserves recognition as the Media Editor, Sara Wight as the Senior Photo Editor, and Mary Ann Price as the Photo Researcher. Finally, I am grateful to Lauren Sartori, the Marketing Assistant, and Aliyah Avinkoo, Justin Bow, and Christine Cordek, Editorial Assistants at Wiley. Without the input of all of these individuals, the book could never have been created.

Robin Kowalski
Clemson University

Contents in Brief

Contents

About the Authors

Robin Kowalski is Professor of Psychology in the Department of Psychology at Clemson University. She received her B.A. at Furman University, an M.A. in General Psychology at Wake Forest University, and her Ph.D. in Social Psychology at the University of North Carolina at Greensboro. Robin spent the first 13 years of her career at Western Carolina University in Cullowhee, North Carolina. While there, she received the Botner Superior Teaching Award and the University Teaching-Research Award. She is also an active researcher who is on the editorial board for the *Journal of Social and Clinical Psychology* and the *Journal of Social Psychology*. She has written or edited six books, and has published in many professional journals, including *Psychological Bulletin* and the *Journal of Experimental Social Psychology*.

Robin has two primary research interests. The first focuses on aversive interpersonal behaviors, specifically complaining and teasing. Her research on complaining has received international attention, including an appearance on NBC's *Today Show*. Most recently, her book, *Complaining, Teasing, and Other Annoying Behaviors*, was featured on National Public Radio's *All Things Considered*, and in an article in *USA Weekend*. Her second research focus is health psychology, with a particular focus on organ donation and transplantation.

Robin is married to another social psychologist, Thomas Britt, and they have three-year-old twin boys, Noah and Jordan.

Drew Westen is Professor in the Department of Psychology and Department of Psychiatry and Behavioral Sciences at Emory University. He received his B.A. at Harvard University, an M.A. in Social and Political Thought at the University of Sussex (England), and his Ph.D. in Clinical Psychology at the University of Michigan, where he subsequently taught for six years. While at the University of Michigan, he was honored two years in a row by the *Michigan Daily* as the best teaching professor at the university, and was the recipient of the first Golden Apple Award for outstanding undergraduate teaching. More recently, he was selected as a G. Stanley Hall Lecturer by the American Psychological Association. Professor Westen is an active researcher who is on the editorial boards of multiple journals, including *Clinical Psychology: Science and Practice*, *Psychological Assessment*, and the *Journal of Personality Disorders*. His major areas of research are personality disorders, eating disorders, emotion regulation, implicit processes, psychotherapy effectiveness, and adolescent psychopathology. His series of videotaped lectures on abnormal psychology, called *Is Anyone Really Normal?*, was published by the Teaching Company, in collaboration with the Smithsonian Institution. He also provides psychological commentaries on political issues for *All Things Considered* on National Public Radio. His main loves outside of psychology are his wife, Laura, and his baby daughter, Mackenzie. He also writes comedy music, has performed as a stand-up comic in Boston, and has performed and directed improvisational comedy for the President of the United States.

Chapter 1

Psychology: The Study of Mental Processes and Behavior

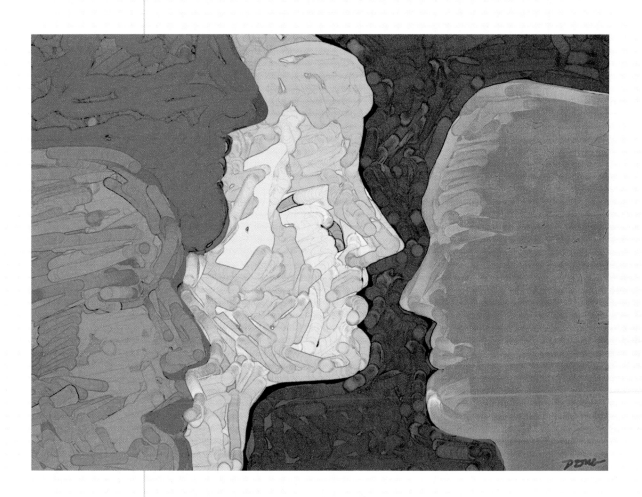

35-year-old woman named Jenny worked for a manufacturing plant where she was known as an efficient but quiet worker (Feldman & Ford, 1994). Rarely did she form close personal relationships with co-workers, relying instead on her fiancé of a year for affection and companionship. That is, until the day when, for no apparent reason, her fiancé announced that their relationship was over. Forced to leave the apartment she had shared with him, Jenny moved back home to live with her mother. To occupy the free time that she had once devoted to the man she loved, Jenny began sewing costumes for the drama club at the elementary school where her mother worked. However, this task wasn't enough to allow Jenny to find meaning in life or to feel connected with other people. Jenny felt hurt, betrayed, and alone.

After several months of leading a relatively solitary existence, Jenny went to work

and reported to her co-workers that she was dying of cancer. Suddenly, this relatively unassuming co-worker became the center of attention as people showered her with friendship and support. Having spent time with a neighbor who was suffering from breast cancer, Jenny was well aware of the course of a terminal illness, including treatment regimens, hair loss, and weight loss. To simulate hair loss, Jenny began cutting her hair and leaving hair remnants in the bathroom sink for her mother to find. Eventually, she shaved her head, the hair loss ostensibly the result of the chemotherapy she told everyone she was receiving. She went on a diet to lose weight, often a side effect of the treatment. She even joined a support group for women with breast cancer so that she could acquire even more of the attention and support she desperately desired. The students at her mother's elementary school raised money to help her pay for medical treatments.

Although a few eyebrows were raised when the months passed and Jenny continued to report to work, few co-workers questioned the status of her illness. However, suspicions began to arise in the breast cancer support group. Needing information about Jenny, the support group leaders attempted to contact one of the doctors Jenny had claimed was treating her for her illness. Of course, there was no such doctor, so their attempts were futile. After one attempt after another failed to allow the support group leaders to contact Jenny's doctors, they confronted her with the belief that she was faking the illness. Once confronted, Jenny confessed that they were right and the entire illness had been a fabrication!

How could Jenny have created such a preposterous ruse? What could have motivated a seemingly normal individual to do this? The answer: Munchausen's syndrome, a psychological illness that falls within the spectrum of factitious illnesses, in which people actually fabricate or induce illness in themselves. Compared to the lengths to which some people go, enduring repeated hospitalizations and unnecessary surgeries, Jenny's case was relatively mild. Imagine the woman who stuck pins in her eyes to "blind" herself to the sexual abuse she was experiencing at home. Or, the woman who cut her tonsils out with scissors. Relatively speaking, Jenny's case was at the less extreme end of the continuum. (For a more complete rendering of these and other stories, refer to Feldman & Ford, 1994.) In fact, some people perpetrate Munchausen's syndrome by proxy, in which they fabricate or induce illness in others. Typically a mother does this to her child. Although the actual cause of Munchausen's remains unknown, researchers believe it is motivated in part by a desire for attention.

In Jenny's case, an external or environmental event—her fiancé's calling off their engagement—created a psychological illness that in some individuals can have fatal results. Unlike many perpetrators of Munchausen's syndrome, Jenny immediately entered therapy and never experienced any problems of this nature again.

Perhaps because the true cause remains elusive, many questions are raised by Munchausen's syndrome or Munchausen's by proxy. Are these people mentally ill? Are their brains the same as those of other people? Does an environmental stimulus, such as a broken engagement, activate neural pathways in the brain that lead to such behavior? Did the stress of losing her romantic partner affect Jenny's brain in ways that produced behavioral manifestations of the stress in the form of factitious illness? Is this phenomenon limited to Western cultures or do other cultures display similar types of bizarre behavior? Jenny's case; as well as those of others who perpetrate factitious illness; illustrates a central issue that has vexed philosophers for over two millennia and psychologists for over a century—the relation between mental and physical events, between meaning and mechanism.

Humans are complex creatures whose psychological experience lies at the intersection of biology and culture. To paraphrase one theorist, Erik Erikson (1963), psychologists must practice "triple bookkeeping" to understand an individual at any given time, simultaneously tracking biological events, psychological experience, and the cultural and historical context. Had Jenny's fiancé not broken the engagement, perhaps she would not have perpetrated Munchausen's syndrome. Many people have had their engagements called off yet do not go to the lengths that Jenny did. Her actions suggest that in addition to the specific environmental trigger of the broken engagement, Jenny had some underlying psychological issues and needs that remained unresolved.

At the intersection of biology and culture lies **psychology**, *the scientific investigation of mental processes (thinking, remembering, feeling, etc.) and behavior*. All psychological processes occur through the interaction of cells in the nervous system, and all human action occurs in the context of cultural beliefs and values that render it meaningful. Psychological understanding thus requires a constant movement between the microlevel of biology and the macrolevel of culture.

This chapter begins by exploring the biological and cultural boundaries and borders that frame human psychology. We then examine the theoretical perspectives that have focused, and often divided, the attention of the scientific community for a century. We close the chapter with an examination of "The Big Picture Questions," questions on which many, if not most, psychological theory and research are predicated. Where appropriate, these questions will be revisited throughout the remainder of the book.

INTERIM SUMMARY

Psychology is the scientific investigation of mental processes (thinking, remembering, feeling, etc.) and behavior. Understanding a person requires attention to the individual's biology, psychological experience, and cultural context.

The Boundaries and Borders of Psychology

Biology and culture establish both the possibilities and the constraints within which people think, feel, and act. On the one hand, the structure of the brain sets the parameters, or limits, of human potential. Most 10-year-olds cannot solve algebra problems because the neural circuitry essential for abstract thought has not yet matured. Similarly, the capacity for love has its roots in the innate tendency of infants to develop an emotional attachment to their caretakers. These are biological givens.

On the other hand, most adults throughout human history would find algebra problems as mystifying as would a preschooler because their culture never provided the groundwork for this kind of reasoning. And though love may be a basic potential, the way people love depends on the values, beliefs, and practices of their society. In some cultures, people seek and expect romance in their marriages, whereas in others, they do not select a spouse based on affection or attraction at all.

From Brain to Behavior   The Boundary with Biology

The biological boundary of psychology is the province of **biopsychology** (or **behavioral neuroscience**), which *investigates the physical basis of psychological phenomena* such as memory, emotion, or stress. Instead of studying thoughts, feelings, or fears, behavioral neuroscientists (some of whom are physicians or biologists rather than psychologists) investigate the electrical and chemical processes in the nervous system that underlie these mental events. Their aim is to link mind and body, psyche and brain.

The connection between brain and behavior became increasingly clear during the nineteenth century, when doctors began observing patients with severe head injuries. These patients often showed deficits in language and memory, or dramatic changes in their personality. One of the most famous cases was that of Phineas Gage who worked as a foreman on a railroad construction site. After Gage accidentally set off an explosion on September 13, 1848, the tamping iron he had been using went straight through his head, crushing his jawbone and exiting at the top of his skull behind his eye. As you can see in the photograph, this tamping iron was no small piece of equipment, measuring 3 feet 7 inches long and weighing over three pounds. Although Gage survived the accident (and is believed to have never lost consciousness!), the damage to his brain was so severe and the change in his personality so marked that people said he was no longer the same person. He became very irreverent and used profanity regularly. He was rude, uncivil, and incapable of resuming his work responsibilities.

Such observations led researchers to experiment by *producing* lesions surgically in different neural regions in animals to observe the effects on behavior. This method is still in use today, as in research on emotion, which has begun to identify the neural pathways involved in fear reactions (LeDoux, 1995). In this research, psychologists lesion one brain structure at a time along pathways they hypothesize are involved when rats learn to fear an object associated with pain. When a lesion disrupts learning, the researcher knows that the lesioned area, or other areas connected to it, is involved in fear.

Since its origins in the nineteenth century, one of the major issues in behavioral neuroscience has been **localization of function,** or *the extent to which different*

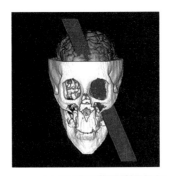

Tamping iron that went through Phineas Gage's head and the trajectory the iron took.

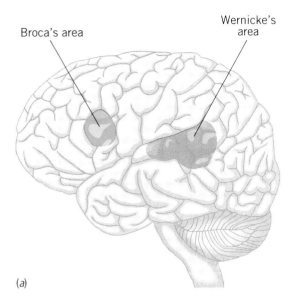

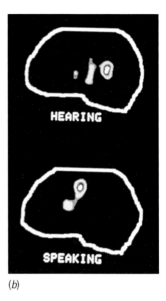

FIGURE 1.1 Broca's and Wernicke's areas. (*a*) Broca's aphasia involves difficulty producing speech, whereas Wernicke's aphasia typically involves difficulty comprehending language. (*b*) Positron emission tomography (PET) is a computerized imaging technique that allows researchers to study the functioning of the brain as the person responds to stimuli. The PET scans here show activity in Wernicke's area (top) and Broca's area (bottom).

parts of the brain control different aspects of functioning. In 1836, a physician named Marc Dax presented a paper suggesting that lesions on the left side of the brain were associated with *aphasia*, or language disorders. The notion that language was localized to the left side of the brain (the left hemisphere) developed momentum with new discoveries linking specific language functions to specific regions of the left hemisphere. Paul Broca (1824–1880) discovered that brain-injured people with lesions in the front section of the left hemisphere were often unable to speak fluently but could comprehend language. Carl Wernicke (1848–1904) showed that damage to an area a few centimeters behind the section Broca had discovered could lead to another kind of aphasia. These individuals can speak fluently and follow rules of grammar, but they can neither understand language nor speak in a way that is comprehensible to others (Figure 1.1).

Individuals with this form of aphasia might speak fluently, apparently following rules of grammar, but their words make little sense (e.g., "I saw the bats and cuticles as the dog lifted the hoof, the pauser"). One of the metaphors that underlies neuropsychological thinking compares the brain to an electronic device with a complex series of circuits. Particular experiences or behaviors reflect patterns or sequences of activated cells that are "wired" together. Just as no single point on a television screen means anything on its own, because each pixel or dot can be used in millions of different configurations, the *pattern* in which that dot is activated gives it meaning. Similarly, the pattern of firing cells determines the meaning of a neural event.

Contemporary neuroscientists no longer believe that complex psychological functions "happen" exclusively in a single localized part of the brain. Rather, the circuits for psychological events, such as emotions or thoughts, are distributed throughout the brain, with each part contributing to the total experience. A man who sustains lesions to one area may be unable consciously to distinguish his wife's face from the face of any other woman—a disabling condition indeed—but may react physiologically to her face with a higher heart rate or pulse (Bruyer, 1991; Young, 1994). Technological advances over the last two decades have allowed researchers to pinpoint lesions precisely, and even to watch computerized portraits of the brain light up with activity (or fail to light up, in cases of neural damage) as people perform psychological tasks (Chapter 2). In large part as a result of these technological advances, psychology has become increasingly biological over the last decade, as behavioral neuroscience has extended into virtually all areas of psychology.

A Global Vista   The Boundary with Culture

Margaret Mead was a leading figure among anthropologists and psychologists trying to understand the relation between personality and culture. Here she is pictured among the Manus of Micronesia in the late 1920s.

Apply & Discuss

■ How do parents in an industrial society teach their children to value punctuality? What aspects of life—at home, in school, and later in life—foster a belief in the value of being on time? Do these all require intentional teaching or do some "just happen" as the child goes through the course of a day?

■ Why are some people chronically late?

Humans are not only collections of cells; they are also themselves the "cells" of larger groups, such as tribes or nations, which similarly impose their stamp on psychological functioning. The emergence of agriculture and cities, generally known as *civilization*, occurred less than ten thousand years ago. Before that time, and until well into the twentieth century in much of this planet's southern hemisphere, humans lived in small bands composed largely of their kin. Several bands often joined together into larger tribes in order to trade mates, protect territory, wage war on other groups, or participate in communal rituals.

The anthropologists who first studied these "exotic" cultures in Africa, Australia, North America, and elsewhere were struck by their differentness from their own cultures. Their observations raised a central issue that psychology has been slow to address: To what extent do cultural differences create psychological differences? What can we make of someone who becomes terrified because he believes that a quarrel with kin has offended the forest and may bring disaster upon his family? Does he share our psychological nature, or does each society produce its own psychology?

The first theorists to address this issue were psychologically sophisticated anthropologists like Margaret Mead and Ruth Benedict, who were interested in the relation between culture and personality (Bock, 2001; LeVine, 1982). They argued that individual psychology is fundamentally shaped by cultural values, ideals, and ways of thinking. As children develop, they learn to behave in ways that conform to cultural standards. The openly competitive, confident, self-interested style generally rewarded in North American society, an individualistic society, is unthinkable in Japan, a collectivist society, where communal sentiments are much stronger. Until recently, Japanese manufacturing companies did not lay off workers during economic downturns as did their North American and European counterparts because they believed corporations are like families and should treat their employees accordingly.

In the middle of the twentieth century, **psychological anthropologists**, who *study psychological phenomena in other cultures by observing people in their natural settings* (see Shimizu & LeVine, 2001; Suarez-Orozco et al., 1994), began studying the way economic realities shape child-rearing practices, which in turn mold personality (Kardiner, 1945; Whiting & Child, 1953). Then, as now, people in less industrialized cultures were leaving their ancestral homelands seeking work in large cities. Working as a laborer in a factory requires attitudes toward time, mobility, and individuality different from those for farming or foraging. A laborer must punch a time clock, move where the work is, work for wages, and spend all day away from kin (see Inkeles & Smith, 1974). Notions we take for granted—such as arriving at work within a prescribed span of minutes—are not "natural" to human beings. Punctuality is necessary for shift-work in a factory or for changing from class to class in a modern school, and we consider it an aspect of character or personality. Yet punctuality was probably not even recognized as a dimension of personality in most cultures before the contemporary era and was certainly not a prime concern of parents in rearing their children.

After the 1950s, interest in the relation between culture and psychological attributes waned for decades. Within psychology, however, a small group of researchers developed the field of **cross-cultural psychology**, which *tests psychological hypotheses in different cultures* (Berry et al., 1992, 1997; Lonner & Malpass, 1994a,b; Shweder, 1999; Triandis, 1980, 1994). Interest in cross-cultural psychology has blossomed recently as issues of diversity have come to the fore. Psychologists are now pondering the extent to which decades of research on topics such as memory, motivation, psychological disorders, or obedience have yielded results about *people* or about a particular *group* of people. Do individuals in all cultures experience depression? Do toddlers learn to walk and talk at the same rate cross-culturally? Do people dream in all cultures, and if so, what is the function of dreaming? Only cross-cultural comparisons can distinguish between universal and culturally specific psychological processes.

INTERIM SUMMARY

Biopsychology (or **behavioral neuroscience**) examines the physical basis of psychological phenomena such as motivation, emotion, and stress. Although different neural regions perform different functions, the neural circuits that underlie psychological events are distributed throughout the brain and cannot be "found" in one location. At one other boundary of psychology, cross-cultural investigation tries to distinguish universal psychological processes from those that are specific to particular cultures.

From Philosophy to Psychology

Questions about human nature, such as whether psychological attributes are the same everywhere, were once the province of philosophy. Early in the twentieth century, however, philosophers entered a period of intense self-doubt, wrestling with the limitations of what they could know about topics like morality, justice, and the nature of knowledge. At the same time, psychologists began to apply the methods and technologies of natural science to psychological questions. They reasoned that if physicists can discover the atom and industrialists can mass produce automobiles, then psychological scientists could uncover basic laws of human and animal behavior.

Philosophical Roots of Psychological Questions   The fact that psychology was born from the womb of philosophy is of no small consequence. Many issues at the heart of contemporary psychological research and controversy are classic philosophical questions, a point we will return to near the end of this chapter. One of these is whether human action is the product of **free will** or **determinism**—that is, *do we freely choose our actions or is our behavior caused—determined—by things outside our control?*

Champions of free will follow in the footsteps of seventeenth-century French philosopher René Descartes (1596–1650), who contended that human action follows from human intention—that people choose a course of action and act on it. Proponents of determinism, from the Greek philosopher Democritus onward, assert, however, that behavior follows lawful patterns like everything else in the universe, from falling rocks to orbiting planets. Psychological determinists believe that the actions of humans and other animals are determined by physical forces—internally by genetic processes and externally by environmental events.

This debate has no easy resolution. Subjectively, we have the experience of free will. I could choose to stop writing—or you to stop reading—at this very moment. Yet here we are, continuing into the next sentence. Why? What determined our decision to forge ahead? And how can mental processes exercise control over physical processes such as moving a pen or turning a page?

Humans are material beings, part of nature, like birds, plants, and water. When we choose to move, our limbs exert a force that counters gravity and disturbs molecules of air. How can a nonmaterial force—will—displace material forces? No one has ever proposed a satisfactory solution to the **mind–body problem**, *the question of*

Apply & Discuss

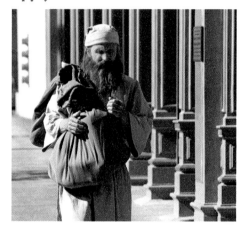

Brian David Mitchell, who calls himself Immanuel, abducted Elizabeth Smart at knifepoint from her bedroom in the early morning hours of June 5, 2002. A reading of his religious manifesto suggests to most people that Brian David Mitchell was a religious fanatic with psychological problems. His ex-wife referred to him as abusive and controlling. His stepdaughter admitted on national television that he had sexually abused her.

■ To the degree that Mr. Mitchell indeed suffers from mental illness, how responsible is he for his actions?

■ Was he more responsible than a person who has a heart attack while driving and consequently kills a pedestrian? What are the reasons for your answer?

Wilhelm Wundt is often called the father of psychology for his pioneering laboratory research. This portrait was painted in Leipzig, where he founded the first psychological laboratory.

how mental and physical events interact. However, psychological phenomena put the mind–body problem in a new light by drawing attention to the way psychological meaning can be transformed into mechanism).

From Philosophical Speculation to Scientific Investigation   Philosophical arguments have thus set the agenda for many issues confronting psychologists, and in our lifetimes, psychological research may shed light on questions that have seemed unanswerable for 2500 years. The fact that psychology emerged from philosophy, however, has had another monumental influence on the discipline. Philosophers searched for answers to questions about the nature of thought, feeling, and behavior in their minds, using logic and argumentation. By the late nineteenth century an alternative approach emerged: If we want to understand the mind and behavior, we should investigate it scientifically, just as physicists study the nature of light or gravity through systematic observation and experimentation. Thus, in 1879, Wilhelm Wundt (1832–1920), often described as the "father of psychology," founded the first psychological laboratory in Leipzig, Germany.

Wundt's Scientific Psychology   Wundt hoped to use scientific methods to uncover the elementary units of human consciousness that combine to form more complex ideas, much as atoms combine into molecules in chemistry. Foremost among the methods he and his students used was **introspection**, *the process of looking inward and reporting on one's conscious experience*. The kind of introspection Wundt had in mind, however, was nothing like the introspection of philosophers, who speculated freely on their experiences and observations. Instead, Wundt trained observers to report verbally everything that went through their minds when they were presented with a stimulus or task. By varying the objects presented to his observers and recording their responses, he concluded that the basic elements of consciousness are sensations (such as colors) and feelings. These elements can combine into more meaningful perceptions (such as of a face or a cat), which can combine into still *more* complex ideas if one focuses attention on them and mentally manipulates them.

Wundt never believed that experimentation was the *only* route to psychological knowledge. He considered it essential for studying the basic elements of mind, but other methods—such as the study of myths, religion, and language in various cultures—were essential for understanding higher mental processes. The next generation of experimental psychologists, however, took a different view, motivated by their wish to divorce themselves from philosophical speculation and establish a fully scientific psychology.

Structuralism and Functionalism   Wundt's student, Edward Titchener (1867–1927), advocated the use of introspection in experiments with the hope of devising a periodic table of the elements of human consciousness, much like the periodic table developed by chemists. *Because of his interest in studying the structure of consciousness, the school of thought Tichener initiated was known as* **structuralism**. Unlike Wundt, Titchener believed that experimentation was the only appropriate method for a science of psychology and that concepts such as "attention" implied too much free will to be scientifically useful (see Figure 1.2). As we will see, the generation of experimental psychologists who followed Titchener went even further, viewing the study of consciousness itself as unscientific because the data—sensations and feelings—could not be observed by anyone except the person reporting them

Structuralism was one of two schools of thought that dominated psychology in its earliest years. The other was functionalism. Instead of focusing on the *contents* of the mind, **functionalism** *emphasized the role—or function—of psychological processes in helping individuals adapt to their environment*. A functionalist would not be content to state that the idea of running comes into consciousness in the presence of a bear showing its teeth. From a functionalist perspective, it is no accident

HOW TO FAIL IN LABORATORY SCIENCE

- Do not accept any general explanation, under any circumstances. Cherish the belief that your mind is different, in its ways of working, from all other minds.

- See yourself in everything. If the Instructor begins an explanation, interrupt him with a story of your childhood which seems to illustrate the point he is making.

- Call upon the Instructor at the slightest provocation. If he is busy, stroll about the laboratory until he can attend to you. Do not hesitate to offer advice to other students, who are already at work.

- Tell the Instructor that the science is very young, and that what holds of one mind does not necessarily hold of another. Support your statement by anecdotes.

- Work as noisily as possible. Converse with your partner, in the pauses of the experiment, upon current politics or athletic records.

- Explain when you enter the laboratory, that you have long been interested in experimental psychology…. Describe the telepathic experiences or accounts that have aroused your interest.

- Make it a rule always to be a quarter of an hour late for the laboratory exercises. In this way you throw the drudgery of preliminary work upon your partner, while you can still take credit to yourself for the regularity of your class attendance.

(a)   (b)

FIGURE 1.2   At the time that Titchener (*a*) came to America, American students were being trained in the essentials of methodology and experimentation in what were referred to as drill courses. To aid instructors of these courses, Titchener wrote a manual titled *Experimental Psychology: A Manual of Laboratory Practice.* One part of the manual was a guide to students on how to fail in laboratory psychology. Part (*b*) presents the specific issues that Titchener wanted his students to avoid in order to receive a passing grade in the lab. The advice is still useful today. (Reprinted from Goodwin, 1999, p. 187.)

that this particular idea enters consciousness when a person sees a bear but not when he sees a flower.

One of the founders of functionalism, Harvard psychologist William James (1842–1910), penned the first textbook in psychology in 1890. James believed that knowledge about human psychology could come from many sources, including not only introspection and experimentation but also the study of children, other animals (whose introspective reports may not be very useful), and people whose minds do *not* function adequately (such as the mentally ill). James thought the structuralists' efforts to catalog the elements of consciousness were not only misguided but profoundly boring! Consciousness exists because it serves a function, and the task of the psychologist is to understand that function. James was interested in explaining, not simply describing, the contents of the mind. As we will see, functionalism bore the imprint of Charles Darwin's evolutionary theory, which a century later has again come to play a central role in psychological thought.

Structuralism and functionalism were two early "camps" in psychology that attracted passionate advocates and opponents. But they were not the last.

INTERIM SUMMARY

Although many contemporary psychological questions derive from age-old philosophical questions, by the end of the nineteenth century psychology emerged as a discipline that aimed to answer questions about human nature through scientific investigation. Two prominent early schools of thought were **structuralism** and **functionalism**. Structuralism attempted to uncover the basic elements of consciousness through **introspection**. Functionalism attempted to explain psychological processes in terms of the role, or function, they serve.

Perspectives in Psychology

Thomas Kuhn, a philosopher of science, studied the history of science and found some remarkable convergences across disciplines in the way schools of thought come and go and knowledge is generated. Kuhn (1970) observed that science does not progress, as many believe, primarily through the accumulation of "facts." Rather, scientific progress depends as much or more on the development of better and better paradigms.

A **paradigm** is *a broad system of theoretical assumptions that a scientific community uses to make sense of their domain of study*. A paradigm has several components. First, it includes a set of theoretical assertions that provide a *model*, or abstract picture, of the object of study. Chemists, for example, have models of the way atoms combine to form molecules—something the structuralists hoped to emulate, by identifying basic "elements" of consciousness and discovering the ways they combine into thoughts and perceptions. Second, a paradigm includes a set of shared metaphors that compare the object under investigation to something else that is readily apprehended (such as "the mind is like a computer"). Metaphors provide mental models for thinking about a phenomenon in a way that makes the unfamiliar seem familiar. Third, a paradigm includes a set of methods that members of the scientific community agree will, if properly executed, produce valid and useful data. Astronomers, for example, agree that telescopic investigation provides a window to events in space. According to Kuhn, the social sciences and psychology differ from the older natural sciences (like physics and biology) in that they lack an accepted paradigm upon which most members of the scientific community agree. Instead, he proposes, these young sciences are still splintered into several *schools of thought*, or what we will call **perspectives**.

In this chapter and throughout the book, we shall examine four perspectives that guide current psychological thinking, offering sometimes competing and sometimes complementary points of view on phenomena ranging from antisocial personality disorder to the way people make decisions when choosing a mate. The four psychological perspectives we consider offer the same kind of broad, orienting approach as a scientific paradigm, and they share its three essential features. Focusing on these particular perspectives does not mean that other less comprehensive approaches have not contributed to psychological knowledge, or that nothing can be studied without them. A researcher interested in a specific question, such as whether preschool programs for economically disadvantaged children will improve their functioning later in life (Reynolds et al., 1995; Zigler & Styfco, 2000), does not need to employ a broader outlook. But perspectives generally guide psychological investigations.

In the following sections, we examine the psychodynamic, behaviorist, cognitive, and evolutionary perspectives. The order in which the perspectives are presented reflects their chronology rather than their relative importance. In many respects, these perspectives have evolved independently, and at the center of each are phenomena the others tend to ignore.

INTERIM SUMMARY

A **paradigm** is a broad system of theoretical assumptions employed by a scientific community that includes shared models, metaphors, and methods. Psychology lacks a unified paradigm but has a number of schools of thought, or **perspectives**, that can be used to understand psychological events.

The Psychodynamic Perspective

A friend has been dating a man for five months and has even jokingly tossed around the idea of marriage. Suddenly, her boyfriend tells her he has found someone else. She is shocked and angry and cries uncontrollably but a day later declares that "he didn't mean that much to me anyway." When you try to console her about the rejection she must be feeling, she says, "Rejection? Hey, I don't know why I put up with him as long as I did," and jokes that "bad character is a genetic abnormality carried on the Y chromosome." You know she really cared about him, and you conclude that she is being defensive—that she really feels rejected. You draw these conclusions because you have grown up in a culture influenced by the psychoanalytic theory of Sigmund Freud.

In the late nineteenth century, Sigmund Freud (1856–1939), a Viennese physician, developed a theory of mental life and behavior and an approach to treating psychological disorders known as *psychoanalysis*. Since then, many psychologists have continued Freud's emphasis on **psychodynamics**, or *the dynamic interplay of mental forces*. The **psychodynamic perspective** rests on three key premises. First, *people's actions are determined by the way thoughts, feelings, and wishes are connected in their minds.* Second, *many of these mental events occur outside of conscious awareness.* And third, *these mental processes may conflict with one another*, leading to compromises among competing motives. Thus, people are unlikely to know precisely the chain of psychological events that leads to their conscious thoughts, intentions, feelings, or behaviors.

As we will see, Freud and many of his followers failed to take seriously the importance of using scientific methods to test and refine their hypotheses. As a result, many psychodynamic concepts that could have been useful to researchers, such as ideas about unconscious processes, remained outside the mainstream of psychology until brought into the laboratory by contemporary researchers (Westen, 1998; Wilson et al., 2000a). In this book, we will emphasize those aspects of psychodynamic thinking for which the scientific evidence is strongest.

Origins of the Psychodynamic Approach   Freud originated his theory in response to patients whose symptoms, although real, were not based on physiological malfunctioning. At the time, scientific thinking had no way to explain patients who were preoccupied with irrational guilt after the death of a parent or were so paralyzed with fear that they could not leave their homes. Freud made a deceptively simple deduction, but one that changed the face of intellectual history: If the symptoms were not consciously created and maintained, and if they had no physical basis, only one possibility remained—their basis must be unconscious.

Just as people have conscious motives or wishes, Freud argued, they also have powerful unconscious motives that underlie their conscious intentions. The reader has undoubtedly had the infuriating experience of waiting for half an hour as traffic crawls on the highway, only to find that nothing was blocking the road at all—just an accident in the opposite lane. Why do people slow down and gawk at accidents on the highway? Is it because they are concerned? Perhaps. But Freud would suggest that people derive an unconscious titillation or excitement, or at least satisfy a morbid curiosity, from viewing a gruesome scene, even though they may deny such socially unacceptable feelings.

Many have likened the relationship between conscious awareness and unconscious mental forces to the visible tip of an iceberg and the vast, submerged hulk that lies out of sight beneath the water. For example, one patient, a graduate student in economics, came to see a psychologist because of a pattern of failing to turn in papers. She would spend hours researching a topic, write two-thirds of the paper, and then suddenly find herself unable to finish. She was perplexed by her own behavior because she consciously wanted to succeed.

What *did* lie beneath the surface? The patient came from a very traditional working-class family, which expected girls to get married, not to develop a career. She had always outshone her brothers in school but had had to hide her successes because of the discomfort this caused in the family. When she would show her report card to her mother, her mother would glance anxiously around to make sure her brothers did not see it; eventually she learned to keep her grades to herself.

Apply & Discuss

Recent experimental research finds that homophobic men—men who report particularly negative attitudes toward homosexuality—show more sexual arousal when viewing photos of homosexual intercourse than do their less homophobic peers (Adams et al., 1996).

■ How might a psychodynamic psychologist explain this?

Sigmund Freud poring over a manuscript in his home office in Vienna around 1930.

Years later, finding herself succeeding in a largely male graduate program put her back in a familiar position, although she did not realize the link. The closer she came to success, the more difficulty she had finishing her papers. She was caught in a conflict between her conscious desire to succeed and her unconscious association of discomfort with success. Recent research confirms that most psychological processes occur outside awareness and that many of the associations between feelings and behaviors or situations that guide our behavior are expressed implicitly or unconsciously (Bargh, 1997; Westen, 1998; Wilson et al., 2000a).

Methods and Data of the Psychodynamic Perspective   The methods used by psychodynamic psychologists flow from their aims. Psychodynamic understanding seeks to *interpret meanings*—to infer underlying wishes, fears, and patterns of thought from an individual's conscious, verbalized thought and behavior. Accordingly, a psychodynamic clinician observes a patient's dreams, fantasies, posture, and subtle behavior toward the therapist. The psychodynamic perspective thus relies substantially on the *case study* method, which entails in-depth observation of a small number of people (Chapter 2).

The data of psychoanalysis can be thoughts, feelings, and actions that occur anywhere, from a vice president jockeying for power in a corporate boardroom to a young child biting his brother for refusing to vacate a Big Wheels tricycle. The use of any and all forms of information about a person reflects the psychodynamic assumption that people reveal themselves in everything they do.

Psychodynamic psychologists have typically relied primarily on clinical data to support their theories. Because clinical observations are open to many interpretations, many psychologists have been skeptical about psychodynamic ideas. In recent years, however, a number of researchers who are both committed to the scientific method and interested in psychodynamic concepts have been subjecting them to experimental tests and trying to integrate them with the body of scientific knowledge in psychology (see Fisher & Greenberg, 1985, 1996; Shedler et al., 1993; Westen & Gabbard, 1999). For example, several studies have documented that people who avoid conscious awareness of their negative feelings are at increased risk for a range of health problems such as asthma, heart disease, and cancer (Weinberger, 1990). Similarly, psychodynamic explanations have been offered and tested for their relevance to binge drinking (Blandt, 2002), attention-deficit hyperactivity disorder (ADHD; Rafalovich, 2001), and deadly acts of aggression, such as the shootings at Columbine High School (Stein, 2000).

Criticisms of Psychodynamic Theory   Although elements of psychodynamic theory pervade our language and our lives, no theory has been criticized more fervently. The criticisms leveled against psychodynamic theory have been so resounding that many theorists and researchers question why any attention is devoted to the theory in textbooks and courses. Indeed, behaviorist John B. Watson referred to psychodynamic theory as "voodooism." The failure of psychodynamic theory to be scientifically grounded, its violation of the **falsifiability criterion**, or *the ability of a theory to be proven wrong as a means of advancing science*, and its reliance on retrospective accounts are just a few of the criticisms that have been leveled against psychodynamic theory.

Psychodynamic theorists argue, however, that the failure to focus on empirical methods is one of the redeeming features of the theory. Rather than investigating specific variables that reflect only a fraction of an individual's personality or behavior, psychodynamic theorists focus on the entire person (Westen, 1998) and the whole of human experience. In addition, by not relying on empirical methods whose focus is limited to "solvable problems," psychodynamic theorists study phenomena not amenable to more traditional experimental methods. For example, a psychodynamic theorist might study why certain people are drawn to horror stories and movies (Tavris & Wade, 2001; see also Skal, 1993).

INTERIM SUMMARY

The **psychodynamic perspective** proposes that people's actions reflect the way thoughts, feelings, and wishes are associated in their minds; that many of these processes are unconscious; and that mental processes can conflict with one another, leading to compromises among competing motives. Although their primary method has been the analysis of case studies, reflecting the goal of interpreting the meanings hypothesized to underlie people's actions, psychodynamic psychologists are increasingly making use of experimental methods to try to integrate psychodynamic thinking with scientific psychology. This growing use of experimental methods should alleviate some of the criticism that has traditionally been leveled against psychodynamic theorists for being nonempirical and for using unreliable measures and approaches.

The Behaviorist Perspective

You are enjoying an intimate dinner at a little Italian place on Main Street when your partner springs on you an unexpected piece of news: The relationship is over. Your stomach turns and you leave in tears. One evening a year or two later, your new flame suggests dining at that same restaurant. Just as before, your stomach turns and your appetite disappears.

One of the broad perspectives that developed in psychology early in this century was behaviorism, which argues that the aversion to that quaint Italian cafe, like many reactions, is the result of *learning*—changes in behavior based on experience—in this case, instant, one-trial learning. The **behaviorist** (or **behavioral**) **perspective**, also called **behaviorism**, *focuses on the way objects or events in the environment (stimuli) come to control behavior through learning*. Thus, the behaviorist perspective focuses on the relation between *external* (environmental) events and observable behaviors. Indeed, John Watson (1878–1958), a pioneer of American behaviorism, considered mental events entirely outside the province of a scientific psychology, and B. F. Skinner (1904–1990), who developed behaviorism into a full-fledged perspective years later, stated, "There is no place in a scientific analysis of behavior for a mind or self" (1990, p. 1209).

Origins of the Behaviorist Approach   Early in the twentieth century, Ivan Pavlov (1849–1936), a Russian physiologist, was conducting experiments on the digestive system of dogs. During the course of his experiments, Pavlov made an important and quite accidental discovery: Once his dogs became accustomed to hearing a particular sound at mealtime, they began to salivate automatically whenever they heard it, much as they would salivate if food were presented. The process that had shaped this new response was learning. Behaviorists argue that human and animal behaviors—from salivation in Pavlov's laboratory to losing one's appetite upon hearing the name of a restaurant associated with rejection—are largely acquired by learning. Indeed, psychologists today have begun to identify biochemical changes in brain cells and neural circuits involved in learning (Martinez & Derrick, 1996).

The behaviorist perspective, particularly as it developed in the United States, sought to do away with two ideas propounded by the philosopher Descartes. Descartes stressed the role of reason in human affairs; he believed that thought can generate knowledge that is not derived from experience. To be human is to reflect upon one's experience, and to reflect is to create new insights about oneself and the world. Descartes also proposed a dualism of mind and body, in which mental events and physical events can have different causes. The mind, or soul, is free to think and choose, while the body is constrained by the laws of nature.

Behaviorists asserted that the behavior of humans, like other animals, can be understood entirely without reference to internal states such as thoughts and feelings. They therefore attempted to counter **Cartesian dualism** (*the doctrine of dual spheres of mind and body*) by demonstrating that human conduct follows laws of behavior, just as the law of gravity explains why things fall down instead of up. The task for behaviorists was to discover how environmental events, or *stimuli,* control behavior. John Locke (1632–1704), a seventeenth-century British philosopher had contended that at birth the mind is a *tabula rasa,* or blank slate, upon which experience writes its story. In a similar vein, John Watson later claimed that if he were given 12 healthy infants at birth, he could turn them into whatever he wanted, doctors or thieves, regardless of any innate dispositions or talents, simply by controlling their environments (Watson, 1925).

The Environment and Behavior   The dramatic progress of the natural sciences in the nineteenth century led many psychologists to believe that the time had come to wrest the study of human nature away from philosophers and put it into the hands of scientists. For behaviorists, psychology is the *science of behavior,* and the proper procedure for conducting psychological research should be the same as for other sciences—rigorous application of the scientific method, particularly experimentation.

Scientists can directly observe a rat running a maze, a baby sucking on a plastic nipple to make a mobile turn, and even the increase in a rat's heart rate at the sound of a bell that has previously preceded a painful electric shock. But no one can directly observe unconscious motives. Science, behaviorists argued, entails making observations on a reliable and calibrated instrument that others can use to make precisely the same observations. According to behaviorists, psychologists cannot even study *conscious* thoughts in a scientific way because no one has access to them except the person reporting them.

Structuralists like Titchener had used introspection to understand the way conscious sensations, feelings, and images fit together. But behaviorists like Watson questioned the scientific value of this research, because the observations on which it relied could not be independently verified. They proposed an alternative to introspective methods: Study observable behaviors and environmental events and build a science around the way people and animals *behave.* Hence the term *behaviorism.* Today, many behaviorists acknowledge the existence of mental events but do not believe these events play a *causal* role in human affairs. Rather, from the behaviorist perspective, mental processes are by-products of environmental events.

Probably the most systematic behaviorist approach was developed by B. F. Skinner. Building on the work of earlier behaviorists, Skinner observed that the behavior of organisms can be controlled by environmental consequences that either increase (*reinforce*) or decrease (*punish*) their likelihood of occurring. Subtle alterations in these conditions, such as the timing of an aversive consequence, can have dramatic effects on behavior. Most dog owners can attest that swatting a dog with a rolled-up newspaper after it grabs a piece of steak from the dinner table can be very useful in suppressing the dog's unwanted behavior, but not if the punishment comes an hour later.

Behaviorist researchers have discovered that this kind of learning by consequences can be used to control some very unlikely behaviors in humans. For example, by giving people feedback on their biological or physiological processes (*biofeedback*), psychologists can help them learn to control "behaviors" such as headaches, chronic pain, and blood pressure (Carmagnani & Carmagnani, 1999; Lisspers & Ost, 1990; Nakao et al., 1999).

Metaphors, Methods, and Data of Behaviorism   A primary metaphor of behaviorism is that humans and other animals are like machines. Just as pushing a button starts the coffee pot, presenting food triggered an automatic or reflexive response in Pavlov's dogs. Similarly, opening this book probably triggered the learned behavior of underlining and note taking. Some behaviorists are interested in mental processes that mediate stimulus response connections but are not convinced that these are accessible to scientific investigation with current technologies. Consequently, they prefer to study what they *can* observe—the relation between what goes in and what comes out.

B. F. Skinner offered a comprehensive behaviorist analysis of topics ranging from animal behavior to language development in children. In Walden Two, he even proposed a utopian vision of a society based on behaviorist principles.

The primary method of behaviorism is experimental. The experimental method entails framing a hypothesis, or prediction, about the way certain environmental events will affect behavior and then creating a laboratory situation to test that hypothesis. Consider two rats placed in simple mazes shaped like the letter T. The two mazes are identical in all respects but one: Pellets of food lie at the end of the left arm of the first rat's maze but not of the second. After a few trials (efforts at running through the maze), the rat that obtains the reward will be more likely to turn to the left and run the maze faster. The experimenter can now systematically modify the situation, again observing the results over several trials. What happens if the rat is rewarded only every third time? Every fourth time? Will it run faster or slower? Because they can measure these data quantitatively, experimenters can test the accuracy of their predictions, and they can apply them to practical questions, such as how an employer can maximize the rate at which employees produce a product.

Behaviorism was the dominant perspective in psychology, particularly in North America, from the 1920s to the 1960s. In its purest forms it has lost favor in the last two decades as psychology has once again become concerned with the study of mental processes. Many psychologists have come to believe that thoughts *about* the environment are just as important in controlling behavior as the environment itself (Bandura, 1977a,b, 1999; Mischel, 1990; Mischel & Shoda, 1995; Rotter, 1966, 1990). Some contemporary behaviorists even define behavior broadly to include thoughts as private behaviors. Nevertheless, traditional behaviorist theory continues to have widespread applications, from helping people quit smoking or drinking to enhancing children's learning in school.

INTERIM SUMMARY

The **behaviorist perspective** focuses on learning and studies the way environmental events control behavior. According to behaviorists, scientific knowledge comes from using experimental methods to study the relationship between environmental events and behavior.

The Cognitive Perspective

In the past 30 years psychology has undergone a "cognitive revolution." Today the study of **cognition**, or *thought*, dominates psychology in the same way that the study of behavior dominated in the middle of the twentieth century. When chairpersons of psychology departments were asked to rank the ten most important contemporary psychologists, eight were cognitive psychologists (Korn et al., 1991). Indeed, one could view the history of psychology as a series of shifts: from the "philosophy of the mind" of the Western philosophers, to the "science of the mind" in the work of the structuralists, to the "science of behavior" in the research of the behaviorists, to the "science of behavior and mental processes" in contemporary, cognitively informed psychology. (Importantly, because behaviorism was a distinctly American perspective, even during the heyday of behaviorism cognitive psychologists were still active in other parts of the world. One of the most notable examples is Jean Piaget, whose ideas had a significant influence on studies of child development; Goodwin, 1999.)

The **cognitive perspective** *focuses on the way people perceive, process, and retrieve information*. Cognitive psychology has roots in experiments conducted by Wundt and others in the late nineteenth century that examined phenomena such as the influence of attention on perception and the ability to remember lists of words.

In large measure, though, the cognitive perspective owes its contemporary form to a technological development—the computer. Many cognitive psychologists use the metaphor of the computer to understand and model the way the mind works. From this perspective, thinking is **information processing**: *The environment provides inputs, which are transformed, stored, and retrieved using various mental "programs," leading to specific response outputs*. Just as the computer database of a

FIGURE 1.3   Response time in naming drawings 48 weeks after initial exposure. This graph shows the length of time participants took to name drawings they saw 48 weeks earlier ("old" drawings) versus similar drawings they were seeing for the first time. Response time was measured in milliseconds (thousandths of a second). At 48 weeks—nearly a year—participants were faster at naming pictures they had previously seen. *Source:* Cave, 1997.

Making Connections

How do people recognize this abstract object as a dog, given that it does not look anything like a real dog? According to cognitive psychologists, people categorize an object that resembles a dog by comparing it to examples of dogs, generalized knowledge about dogs, or defining features of dogs stored in memory (Chapter 6).

bookstore codes its inventory according to topic, title, author, and so forth, human memory systems encode information in order to store and retrieve it. The coding systems we use affect how easily we can later access information. Thus, most people would find it hard to name the forty-second president of the United States (but easy to tell which president was linked with Afghanistan and Iraq) because they do not typically code presidents numerically.

To test hypotheses about memory, researchers need ways of measuring it. One way is simple: Ask a question like, "Do you remember seeing this object?" A second method is more indirect: See how quickly people can name an object they saw some time ago. Our memory system evolved to place frequently used and more recent information at the front of our memory "files" so that we can get to it faster. This makes sense, since dusty old information is less likely to tell us about our immediate environment. Thus, *response time* is a useful measure of memory.

For example, one investigator used both direct questions and response time to test memory for objects seen weeks or months earlier (Cave, 1997). In an initial session, she rapidly flashed over 100 drawings on a computer screen and asked participants to name them as quickly as they could. That was the participants' only exposure to the pictures. In a second session, weeks or months later, she mixed some of the drawings in with other drawings the students had *not* seen and asked them either to tell her whether they recognized them from the earlier session or to name them.

When asked directly, participants were able to distinguish the old pictures from new ones with better-than-chance accuracy as many as 48 weeks later; that is, they correctly identified which drawings they had seen previously more than half the time. Perhaps more striking, as Figure 1.3 shows, almost a year later they were also faster at naming the pictures they had seen previously than those they had not seen. Thus, exposure to a visual image appears to keep it toward the front of our mental files for a very long time.

The cognitive perspective is useful not only in examining memory but also in understanding processes such as decision making. When people enter a car showroom, they have a set of attributes in their minds: smooth ride, sleek look, good gas mileage, affordable price, and so forth. At the same time, they must process a great deal of new information (the salesperson's description of one car as a "real steal," for instance) and match it with stored linguistic knowledge. They can then comprehend the meaning of the dealer's speech, such as the connotation of "real steal" (from both his viewpoint and theirs). In deciding which car to buy, they must somehow integrate information about multiple attributes and weigh their importance. As we will see, some of these processes are conscious or explicit, whereas others happen through the silent whirring of our neural "engines."

Origins of the Cognitive Approach   The philosophical roots of the cognitive perspective lie in a series of questions about where knowledge comes from that were first raised by the ancient Greek philosophers and then were pondered by British and European philosophers over the last four centuries (see Gardner, 1985). Descartes, like Plato, reflected on the remarkable truths of arithmetic and geometry and noted that the purest and most useful abstractions—such as a circle, a hypotenuse, pi, or a square root—could never be observed by the senses. Rather, this kind of knowledge appeared to be generated by the mind itself. Other philosophers, beginning with Aristotle, emphasized the role of experience in generating knowledge. Locke proposed that complex ideas arise from the mental manipulation of simple ideas and that these simple ideas are products of the senses, of observation. The behaviorists roundly rejected Descartes's view of an active, reasoning mind that can arrive at knowledge independent of experience. Cognitive psychologists, in contrast, are interested in many of the questions raised by Descartes and other **rationalist philosophers,** *who emphasized the role of reason in creating knowledge*. For example, cognitive psychologists have studied the way people form abstract concepts or categories. These concepts are derived in part from experience, but they often differ from any particular instance the person has ever perceived—that is, they must be mentally constructed (Medin & Heit, 1999; Smith, 1995). Children can recognize that a bulldog is a dog, even if they have never seen one before, because they have formed an abstract concept of "dog" that goes beyond the details of any specific dogs they have seen.

Metaphors, Methods, and Data of Cognitive Psychology   Both the cognitive and behaviorist perspectives view organisms as machines that respond to environmental input with predictable output. Some cognitive theories even propose that a stimulus evokes a series of miniresponses inside the head, much like the responses that behaviorists study outside the head (Anderson, 1983). However, most cognitive psychologists rely on different metaphors than their behaviorist colleagues.

Recently, cognitive psychologists have begun using the brain itself as a metaphor for the mind (e.g., Burgess & Hitch, 1999; McClelland, 1995; Rumelhart et al., 1986). According to this view, an idea is a network of brain cells that are activated together. Thus, whenever a person thinks of the concept "bird," a certain set of nerve cells becomes active. When he or she is confronted with a stimulus that resembles a bird, part of the network is activated; if enough of the network becomes active, the person concludes that the animal is a bird. A person is likely to recognize a robin as a bird quickly because it resembles most other birds and hence immediately activates most of the "bird" network. Correctly classifying a penguin takes longer because it is less typically "birdlike" and activates less of the network.

As with behaviorism, the primary method of the cognitive perspective is experimental—with one important difference: Cognitive psychologists use experimental procedures to infer mental processes at work. For example, when people try to retrieve information from a list (such as the names of states), do they scan all the relevant information in memory until they hit the right item?

One way psychologists have explored this question is by presenting subjects with a series of word lists of varying lengths to memorize, such as those in Figure 1.4. Then they ask the participants in the study if particular words were on the lists. If participants take longer to recognize that a word was *not* on a longer list—which they do—they must be scanning the lists sequentially (i.e., item by item), because additional words on the list take additional time to scan (Sternberg, 1975).

Cognitive psychologists primarily study processes such as memory and decision making. In recent years, however, some have attempted to use cognitive concepts and metaphors to explain a much wider range of phenomena (Cantor & Kihlstrom, 1987; Sorrentino & Higgins, 1996). Cognitive research on emotion, for example, documents that the way people think about events plays a substantial role in generating emotions (Ferguson, 2000; Lazarus, 1999a,b; Roseman et al., 1995; Chapter 10).

List A	List B
Nevada	Texas
Arkansas	Colorado
Tennessee	Missouri
Texas	South Carolina
North Dakota	Alabama
Nebraska	California
Michigan	Washington
Rhode Island	Idaho
Massachusetts	
Idaho	
New York	
Pennsylvania	

FIGURE 1.4 Two lists of words used in a study of memory scanning. Giving participants in a study two lists of state names provides a test of the memory scanning hypothesis. Iowa is not on either list. If an experimenter asks whether Iowa was on the list, participants take longer to respond to list A than to list B because they have to scan more items in memory.

INTERIM SUMMARY

The **cognitive perspective** focuses on the way people perceive, process, and retrieve information. Cognitive psychologists are interested in how memory works, how people solve problems and make decisions, and similar questions. The primary metaphor originally underlying the cognitive perspective was the mind as computer. In recent years, many cognitive psychologists have turned to the brain itself as a source of metaphors. The primary method of the cognitive perspective is experimental.

The Evolutionary Perspective

- The impulse to eat in humans has a biological basis.
- The sexual impulse in humans has a biological basis.
- Caring for one's offspring has a biological basis.

- The fact that most males are interested in sex with females, and vice versa, has a biological basis.
- The higher incidence of aggressive behavior in males than in females has a biological basis.
- The tendency to care more for one's own offspring than for the offspring of other people has a biological basis.

Most people fully agree with the first of these statements, but many have growing doubts as the list proceeds. *The degree to which inborn processes determine human behavior* is a classic issue in psychology, called the **nature–nurture controversy**. Advocates of the "nurture" position maintain that behavior is primarily learned and not biologically ordained. Other psychologists, however, point to the similarities in behavior between humans and other animals, from chimpanzees to birds, and argue that some behavioral similarities are so striking that they must reflect shared tendencies rooted in biology. Indeed, anyone who believes the behavior of two male teenagers "duking it out" behind the local high school for the attention of a popular girl is distinctively human should observe the behavior of rams and baboons. As we will see, many, if not most, psychological processes reflect an *interaction* of nature and nurture. Biological and genetic factors predispose people and other animals to certain physical and psychological experiences. It is the environment, however, that often determines the degree to which these predispositions actually manifest themselves.

The **evolutionary perspective** argues that *many behavioral tendencies in humans, from the need to eat to concern for our children, evolved because they helped our ancestors survive and rear healthy offspring*. Why, for example, are some children devastated by the absence of their mother during childhood? From an evolutionary perspective, a deep emotional bond between parents and children prevents them from straying too far from each other while children are immature and vulnerable. Breaking this bond leads to tremendous distress.

Like the functionalists at the turn of the century, evolutionary psychologists believe that most enduring human attributes at some time served a function for humans as biological organisms (Buss, 1991, 2000). They argue that this is as true for physical traits—such as the presence of two eyes (rather than one), which allows us to perceive depth and distance—as for cognitive and emotional tendencies such as a child's distress over the absence of her caregivers or a child's development of language. The implication for psychological theory is that understanding human mental processes and behaviors requires insight into their evolution.

Origins of the Evolutionary Perspective   The evolutionary perspective is rooted in the writings of Charles Darwin (1872). Darwin did not invent the concept of

Apply & Discuss

Humans, like other animals, take care of their young.

- Is this behavior instinctive?
- How might a behaviorist explain the same phenomenon?

 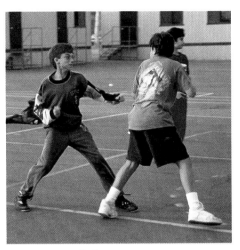

Similar behavior in humans and other animals may suggest common evolutionary roots.

evolution, but he was the first to propose a mechanism that could account for it—**natural selection**. Darwin argued that *natural forces select traits in organisms that are adaptive and are likely to be passed on to their offspring*. **Adaptive traits** *are characteristics that help organisms adjust and survive in their environment*. Selection of organisms occurs "naturally" because organisms that are not endowed with features that help them adapt to their particular environmental circumstances, or *niche*, are less likely to survive and reproduce. In turn, they have fewer offspring to survive and reproduce.

A classic example of natural selection occurred in Birmingham, Liverpool, Manchester, and other industrial cities in England (Bishop & Cook, 1975). A light-colored variety of peppered moth that was common in rural areas of Britain also populated most cities. But as England industrialized in the nineteenth century, light-colored moths became scarce in industrial regions and dark-colored moths predominated. How did this happen? With industrialization, the air became sooty, darkening the bark of the trees on which these moths spent much of their time. Light-colored moths were thus easily noticed and eaten by predators. Before industrialization, moths that had darker coloration were selected *against* by nature because they were conspicuous on light-colored bark. Now, however, they were *better* able to blend into the background of the dark tree trunks. As a result, they survived to pass on their coloration to the next generation. Over decades, the moth population changed to reflect the differential selection of light and dark varieties. Since England has been cleaning up its air through more stringent pollution controls in the past 30 years, the trend has begun to reverse.

Similar evolutionary adaptations have been observed in rock pocket mice. Normally sandy in color, these mice typically dwell in light-colored outcrops (Yoon, 2003). Lava flows in some areas, however, changed a once beige-colored landscape into dark-colored rock. Rock pocket mice in these lava-covered areas are black (see Figure 1.5). This mutation allowed the mice to survive in their "darker" environment.

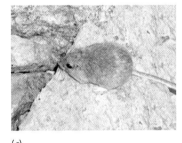 

(*a*)   (*b*)

FIGURE 1.5   The natural selection of rock pocket mice color. As environmental conditions changed in the desert Southwest, so, too, did the rock pocket mouse population. In (*a*), a lighter colored mouse resting on light rock outcrops is better camouflaged than a darker mouse would be. In contrast, (*b*) shows a blackened rock resulting from ancient lava flows, where the dark mouse is very hard to see and hence better able to evade its predators (Yoon, 2003, p. 3).

The peppered moth and rock pocket mice stories highlight a crucial point about evolution: Because adaptation is always relative to a specific niche, evolution is not synonymous with progress. A trait or behavior that is highly adaptive can suddenly become maladaptive in the face of even a seemingly small change in the environment. A new insect that enters a geographical region can eliminate a flourishing crop, just as the arrival of a warlike tribe (or nation) in a previously peaceful region can ren-

Charles Darwin revolutionized human self-understanding in 1859 by rewriting the family tree.

der prior attitudes toward war and peace maladaptive. People have used Darwinian ideas to justify racial and class prejudices ("people on welfare must be naturally unfit"), but sophisticated evolutionary arguments contradict the idea that adaptation or fitness can ever be absolute.

Ethology, Sociobiology, and Evolutionary Psychology   If Darwin's theory of natural selection can be applied to characteristics such as the color of a moth, can it also apply to behaviors? It stands to reason that certain behaviors, such as the tendency of moths to rest on trees in the first place, evolved because they helped members of the species survive. In the middle of the twentieth century the field of **ethology**, which *studies animal behavior from a biological and evolutionary perspective* (Hinde, 1982), began to apply this sort of evolutionary approach to understanding animal behavior.

For example, several species of birds emit warning cries to alert their flock about approaching predators; some even band together to attack. Konrad Lorenz, an ethologist who befriended a flock of black jackdaws, was once attacked by the flock while carrying a wet black bathing suit. Convinced that the birds were not simply offended by the style, Lorenz hypothesized that jackdaws have an inborn, or *innate*, tendency to become distressed whenever they see a creature dangling a black object resembling a jackdaw, and they respond by attacking (Lorenz, 1979).

If scientists can explain animal behaviors by their adaptive advantage, can they apply the same logic to human behavior? Just over two decades ago, Harvard biologist E. O. Wilson (1975) christened a new and controversial field called **sociobiology**, which *explores possible evolutionary and biological bases of human social behavior*. Sociobiologists and **evolutionary psychologists**, who *apply evolutionary thinking to a wide range of psychological phenomena*, propose that genetic transmission is not limited to physical traits such as height, body type, or vulnerability to heart disease. Parents also pass on to their children behavioral and mental tendencies. Some of these are universal, such as the need to eat and sleep or the capacity to perceive certain wavelengths of light. Others differ from individual to individual. Attention to the evolutionary origins of many behaviors is increasing to the point that even behaviors such as grief, which might seem at first blush out of the purview of evolutionary psychology, are now being investigated as adaptive in nature (Archer, 2001).

As we will see in later chapters, recent research in **behavioral genetics**—a field that *examines the genetic and environmental bases of differences among individuals on psychological traits*—suggests that heredity is a surprisingly strong determinant of many personality traits and intellectual skills. The tendencies to be outgoing, aggressive, or musically talented, for example, are all partially under genetic control (Bjorklund & Pellegrini, 2001; Loehlin, 1992; Plomin et al., 1997).

Perhaps the fundamental concept in all contemporary evolutionary theories is that evolution selects traits that maximize organisms' reproductive success. **Reproductive success** refers to *the capacity to survive and produce offspring*. Over many generations, organisms with greater reproductive success will have many more descendants because they will survive and reproduce more than other organisms, including other members

Although there are wide variations in the languages that are spoken throughout the world, Darwin and many current researchers believe that the capacity to learn language is innate in humans. Language is believed to have been adaptive in providing our ancestors a way of communicating succinctly and precisely with one another.

of their own species. Central to evolutionary psychology is the notion that the human brain, like the eye or the heart, has evolved modules through natural selection to solve certain problems associated with survival and reproduction, such as selecting mates, using language, competing for scarce resources, and cooperating with kin and neighbors who might be helpful in the future (Tooby & Cosmides, 1992). For example, current evolutionary psychologists argue that, through the process of natural selection, a "fear" module has evolved that is automatically activated in the presence of fear-producing stimuli (Oehman & Mineka, 2001). Neuroscientists can then conduct brain mapping, tracing neural paths of activation to see what other areas of the brain are associated with activation of the fear module.

As a more personal example, we take for granted that people usually tend to care more about, and do more for, their children, parents, and siblings than for their second cousins or nonrelatives. Most readers have probably received more financial support from their parents in the last five years than from their aunts and uncles. This seems natural—and we rarely wonder about it—but *why* does it seem so natural? And what are the causes of this behavioral tendency?

From an evolutionary perspective, individuals who care for others who share their genes will simply have more of their genes in the gene pool generations later. Thus, evolutionary theorists have expanded the concept of reproductive success to encompass **inclusive fitness**, which *refers not only to an individual's own reproductive success but also to his or her influence on the reproductive success of genetically related individuals* (Daly & Wilson, 1988; Hamilton, 1964).

According to the theory of inclusive fitness, natural selection favors animals whose concern for kin is proportional to their degree of biological relatedness. In other words, animals should devote more resources and offer more protection to close relatives than to more distant kin. The reasons for this preference are strictly mathematical. Imagine you are sailing with your brother or sister and with your cousin, and the ship capsizes. Neither your sibling nor your cousin can swim, and you can save only one of them. Whom will you save?

Most readers, after perhaps a brief, gleeful flicker of sibling rivalry, opt for the sibling because first-degree relatives such as siblings share much more genetic material than more distant relatives such as cousins. Siblings share half their genes, whereas cousins share only one-eighth. In crass evolutionary terms, two siblings are worth eight cousins. Evolution selects the neural mechanisms that make this preference feel natural—so natural that psychologists have rarely even thought to explain it.

At this point the reader might object that the real reason for saving the sibling over the cousin is that you know the sibling better; you grew up together, and you have more bonds of affection. This poses no problem for the evolutionary theorist, since familiarity and bonds of affection are probably the psychological mechanisms selected by nature to help you in your choice. When human genes were evolving, close relatives typically lived together. People who were familiar and loved were more often than not relatives. Humans who protected others based on familiarity and affection would be more prevalent in the gene pool thousands of years later because more of their genes would be available.

Metaphors, Methods, and Data of the Evolutionary Perspective   Darwin's theory of natural selection is part of a tradition of Western thought since the Renaissance that emphasizes individual self-interest and competition for scarce resources. Perhaps the major metaphor underlying the evolutionary perspective is borrowed from another member of that tradition, sixteenth-century philosopher Thomas Hobbes (1588–1679). According to Hobbes, wittingly or unwittingly, we are all runners in a race, competing for survival, sexual access to partners, and resources for our kin and ourselves.

Evolutionary methods are frequently deductive; that is, they begin with an observation of something that already exists in nature and try to explain it with logical arguments. For instance, evolutionists might begin with the fact that people care for their kin and will try to deduce an explanation. This method is very different from experimentation, in which investigators create circumstances in the laboratory and test the impact of changing these conditions on behavior. Many psychologists have challenged the deductive methods of evolutionary psychologists. They argue that predict-

It is seldom that I laugh at an animal, and when I do, I usually find out afterwards that it was at myself, at the human being whom the animal has portrayed in a more or less pitiless caricature, that I have laughed. We stand before the monkey house and laugh, but we do not laugh at the sight of a caterpillar or a snail, and when the courtship antics of a lusty greylag gander are so incredibly funny, it is only [because] our human youth behaves in a very similar fashion.

(LORENZ, 1979, P. 39)

ing behavior in the laboratory is much more difficult and convincing than explaining what has already happened.

One of the most distinctive features of evolutionary psychology in recent years has been its application of experimental and other procedures that involve *prediction* of behavior in the laboratory, rather than after-the-fact explanation (Buss et al., 1992). For example, two recent studies, one from the United States and one from Germany, used evolutionary theory to predict the extent to which grandparents will invest in their grandchildren (DeKay, 1998; Euler & Weitzel, 1996). According to evolutionary theory, one of the major problems facing males in many animal species, including our own, is paternity uncertainty—the lack of certainty that their presumed offspring are really theirs. Female primates (monkeys, apes, and humans) are always certain that their children are their own because they bear them. Males, on the other hand, can never be certain of paternity because their mate could have copulated with another male. (Psychological language is typically precise but not very romantic.)

If a male is going to invest time, energy, and resources in a child, he wants to be certain that the child is his own. Not surprisingly, males of many species develop elaborate ways to minimize the possibility of accidentally investing in another male's offspring, such as guarding their mates during fertile periods and killing off infants born too close to the time at which they began copulating with the infants' mother. In humans, infidelity (or suspicion of infidelity) is one of the major causes of spouse battering and homicide committed by men cross-culturally (Daly & Wilson, 1988).

Evolutionary psychologists have used the concept of paternity uncertainty to make some very specific and novel predictions about patterns of *grandparental* investment in children. As shown in Figure 1.6a, the father's father is the least certain of all grandparents that his grandchildren are really his own, since he did not bear his son,

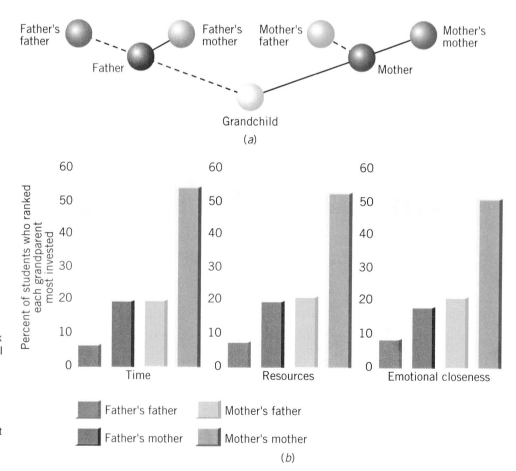

FIGURE 1.6 (a) Certainty of genetic relatedness. Dashed lines indicate uncertainty of genetic relatedness, whereas solid lines indicate certainty. As can be seen, the father's father is least certain that his presumed grandchild is his own (dashed lines between both himself and his son and his son and the son's child), whereas the mother's mother is most certain. Each of the other two grandparents is sure of one link but unsure of the other. (b) Rankings of grandparental investment. This graph shows the percent of participants in the study who ranked each grandparent the highest of all four grandparents on investment (measured two ways) and on emotional closeness. Students ranked their maternal grandmothers most invested and close and their paternal grandfathers least invested and close on all three dimensions (based on DeKay, 1998).

who did not bear *his* child. The mother's mother is the most certain of all grandparents because she is sure that her daughter is hers, and her daughter is equally certain that she is the mother of *her* children. The other two grandparents (father's mother and mother's father) are intermediate in certainty. This analysis leads to a hypothesis about the extent to which grandparents will invest in their grandchildren: The greatest investment should be seen in maternal grandmothers, the least in paternal grandfathers, and intermediate levels in paternal grandmothers and maternal grandfathers.

To test this hypothesis, one study asked U.S. college students to rank their grandparents on a number of dimensions, including emotional closeness and amount of time and resources their grandparents invested in them (DeKay, 1998). On each dimension, the pattern was as predicted: Maternal grandmothers, on the average, were ranked most invested of all four grandparents and paternal grandfathers least invested. Figure 1.6*b* shows the percent of college students who ranked each grandparent a 1—that is, most invested or most emotionally close. A similar pattern emerged in a German study (Euler & Weitzel, 1996). Although a critic could generate alternative explanations, these studies are powerful because the investigators tested hypotheses that were not intuitively obvious or readily predictable from other perspectives.

INTERIM SUMMARY

The **evolutionary perspective** argues that many human behavioral tendencies evolved because they helped our ancestors survive and reproduce. Psychological processes have evolved through the natural selection of traits that help organisms adapt to their environment. Evolution selects organisms that maximize their reproductive success, defined as the capacity to survive and reproduce as well as to maximize the reproductive success of genetically related individuals. Although the methods of evolutionary theorists have traditionally been deductive and comparative, evolutionary psychologists are increasingly using experimental methods.

Putting Psychological Perspectives in Perspective

Commentary

A tale is told of several blind men in India who came upon an elephant. They had no knowledge of what an elephant was, and, eager to understand the beast, they reached out to explore it. One man grabbed its trunk and concluded, "An elephant is like a snake." Another touched its ear and proclaimed, "An elephant is like a leaf." A third, examining its leg, disagreed: "An elephant," he announced, "is like the trunk of a tree." Psychologists are in some ways like those blind men, struggling with imperfect instruments to try to understand the beast we call human nature, and typically touching only part of the animal while trying to grasp the whole. So why don't we just look at "the facts," instead of relying on perspectives that lead us to grasp only the trunk or the tail? Because we are cognitively incapable of seeing reality without imposing some kind of order on what otherwise seems like chaos.

Consider Figure 1.7. Does it depict a vase? The profiles of two faces? The answer depends on one's perspective on the whole picture. Were we not to impose some perspective on this figure, we would see nothing but patches of black and white. This picture was used by a German school of psychology in the early twentieth century, known as **Gestalt psychology**. The Gestalt psychologists argued that perception is not a passive experience akin to taking photographic snapshots. Rather, ***perception is an active experience of imposing order on an overwhelming panorama of details by seeing them as parts of larger wholes (or gestalts)***.

The same premise is true of the complex perceptual and cognitive tasks that constitute scientific investigation. The way psychologists and other scientists un-

FIGURE 1.7 An ambiguous figure. The indentation in the middle could be either an indentation in a vase or a nose. In science, as in everyday perception, knowledge involves understanding "facts" in the context of a broader interpretive framework.

derstand any phenomenon depends on their interpretation of the whole—on their paradigms or perspectives. Perspectives are like imperfect lenses through which we view some aspect of reality. Often they are too convex or too concave, leaving their wearers blind to data on the periphery of their understanding. But without them, we are totally blind.

We have seen that what psychologists study, how they study it, and what they observe reflect not only the reality "out there" but also the conceptual lenses they wear. In many cases adherents of one perspective know very little—and may even have stereotypic views or misconceptions—about other perspectives. Many readers will no doubt be tempted to conclude that a particular perspective is the right one. This condition unfortunately afflicts most of us who make our careers wearing one set of theoretical lenses and then forgetting that we wear glasses. In fact, the different perspectives often contribute in unique ways depending on the object being studied. (For a sampling of the different subdisciplines within psychology and the diversity of topics they study, see Table 1.1.) Deciding that one perspective is valid in all situations is like choosing to use a telescope instead of a microscope without knowing whether the objects of study are amoebas or asteroids. Although psychologists disagree on the merits of the different perspectives, each has made distinctive contributions.

Consider the behaviorist perspective. Among its contributions are two that we cannot overestimate. The first is its focus on learning and its postulation of a *mechanism* for many kinds of learning: reward and punishment. Behaviorists offer a fundamental insight into the psychology of humans and other animals that can be summarized in a simple but remarkably important formula: *Behavior follows its*

Table 1.1   ■ ■   Major Subdisciplines in Psychology

Subdiscipline	Examples of Questions Asked
Biopsychology: investigates the physical basis of psychological phenomena such as thought, emotion, and stress	How are memories stored in the brain? Do hormones influence whether an individual is heterosexual or homosexual?
Developmental psychology: studies the way thought, feeling, and behavior develop through the life span, from infancy to death	Can children remember experiences from their first year of life? Do children in daycare tend to be more or less well adjusted than children reared at home?
Social psychology: examines interactions of individual psychology and group phenomena; examines the influence of real or imagined others on the way people behave	When and why do people behave aggressively? Can people behave in ways indicating racial prejudice without knowing it?
Clinical psychology: focuses on the nature and treatment of psychological processes that lead to emotional distress	What causes depression? What impact does childhood sexual abuse have on later functioning?
Cognitive psychology: examines the nature of thought, memory, sensation perception, and language	What causes amnesia, or memory loss? How are people able to drive a car while engrossed in thought about something else?
Personality psychology: examines people's enduring ways of responding in different kinds of situations and the ways individuals differ in the ways they tend to think, feel, and behave	To what extent does the tendency to be outgoing, anxious, or conscientious reflect genetic and environmental influences?
Industrial/organizational (I/O) psychology: examines the behavior of people in organizations and attempts to help solve organizational problems	Are some forms of leadership more effective than others? What motivates workers to do their jobs efficiently?
Educational psychology: examines psychological processes in learning and applies psychological knowledge in educational settings	Why do some children have trouble learning to read? What causes some teenagers to drop out of school?
Health psychology: examines psychological factors involved in health and disease	Are certain personality types more vulnerable to disease? What factors influence people to take risks with their health, such as smoking or not using condoms?

consequences. The notion that the consequences of our actions shape the way we behave has a long philosophical history, but the behaviorists were the first to develop a sophisticated, scientifically based set of principles that describe the way environmental events shape behavior. The second major contribution of the behaviorist approach is its emphasis on **empiricism**—*the belief that the path to scientific knowledge is systematic observation and, ideally, experimental observation*.

The cognitive perspective focuses on the *reason* pole of the reason–passion dichotomy. Much of what is distinctive about *Homo sapiens*—and what lent our species its name (*sapiens* means "knowledge" or "wisdom")—is our extraordinary capacity for thought and memory. This capacity allows actors to perform a two-hour play without notes, three-year-old children to create grammatical sentences they have never before heard, and scientists to develop vaccines for viruses that they cannot see with the naked eye. In only three decades since the introduction of the first textbook on cognition (Neisser, 1967), the cognitive perspective has transformed our understanding of thought and memory in a way that 2500 years of philosophical speculation could not approach. Like the behaviorist perspective, the contributions of the cognitive perspective reflect its commitment to empiricism and experimental methods.

The evolutionary perspective asks a basic question about psychological processes that directs our attention to phenomena we might easily take for granted: *Why* do we think, feel, or behave the way we do as opposed to some other way? Although many psychological attributes are likely to have developed as accidental by-products of evolution with little adaptive significance, the evolutionary perspective forces us to examine *why* we feel jealous when our lovers are unfaithful, *why* we are so skillful at recognizing others' emotions just by looking at their faces, and *why* children are able to learn new words so rapidly in their first six years that if they were to continue at that pace for the rest of their lives they would scoff at *Webster's Unabridged*. In each case, the evolutionary perspective suggests a single and deceptively simple principle: We think, feel, and behave in these ways because they helped our ancestors adapt to their environments and hence to survive and reproduce.

Finally, the psychodynamic perspective has made its own unique contributions. Philosophers have long speculated about the relative value of "reason" and "passion" in human life. The psychodynamic perspective focuses above all on the passionate—on motivation and emotion. Recent research has begun to support some basic psychodynamic hypotheses about the emotional sides of human psychology, such as the view that our attitudes toward ourselves and others are often contradictory and ambivalent and that what we feel and believe consciously and unconsciously often differ substantially (e.g., Cacioppo et al., 1997; Wilson et al., 2000a). Indeed, the most important legacy of the psychodynamic perspective is its emphasis on unconscious processes. As we have seen, the existence of unconscious processes is now widely accepted, as new technologies have allowed the scientific exploration of cognitive, emotional, and motivational processes outside conscious awareness (Bargh, 1997; Schacter, 1999; Westen, 1998).

INTERIM SUMMARY

Although the different perspectives offer radically different ways of approaching psychology, each has made distinctive contributions. These perspectives have often developed in mutual isolation, but efforts to integrate aspects of them are likely to continue to be fruitful, particularly in clinical psychology.

The Big Picture Questions

Earlier in this chapter, we talked about the philosophical origins of psychology, highlighting that many contemporary questions that psychologists raise were debated among early philosophers. However, psychologists do not tackle philosophical issues such as free will versus determinism directly. Rather, classic philosophical questions reverberate through many contemporary psychological discussions.

Research into the genetics of personality and personality disturbances provides an intriguing, if disquieting, example. People with antisocial personality disorder have minimal conscience and a tendency toward aggressive or criminal behavior. In an initial psychiatric evaluation one man boasted that he had terrorized his former girl friend for an hour by brandishing a knife and telling her in exquisite detail the ways he intended to slice her flesh. This man could undoubtedly have exercised his free will to continue or discontinue his behavior at any moment and hence was morally (and legally) responsible for his acts. He knew what he was doing, he was not hearing voices commanding him to behave aggressively, and he thoroughly enjoyed his victim's terror. A determinist, however, could offer an equally compelling case. Like many violent men, he was the son of violent, alcoholic parents who had beaten him severely as a child. Both physical abuse in childhood and parental alcoholism (which can exert both genetic and environmental influences) render an individual more likely to develop antisocial personality disorder (see Cadoret et al., 1995; Zanarini et al., 1990). In the immediate moment, perhaps, he had free will, but over the long run, he may have had no choice but to be the person he was.

Other philosophical questions set the stage for psychology and are central to contemporary psychological theory and research. Many of these questions, like free will versus determinism, take the apparent form of choices between polar opposites, neither of which can be entirely true. Does human behavior reflect nature (biology) or nurture (environmental influence)? Does knowledge come from observing the world or from thinking about it?

Throughout the chapters of this book, the text will refer to philosophical questions such as these as "The Big Picture Questions." These are the questions on which much, if not most, psychological theory and research are predicated, as will become evident as you read subsequent chapters of this book. Some of the questions are beginning to be answered as theorists and researchers examine the roots of human self-understanding. Others remain unanswered, yet they still guide current theory and research. These questions will be addressed throughout the text and noted in the margins where appropriate. Although the list provided below is not all inclusive, it will give you a sense of the overriding questions guiding psychological research today. As you read these, you might begin to generate your own thoughts and answers.

φ **Question 1: To what extent can mental processes be reduced to the brain or body?** Although hard-core behaviorists argue that mental processes are outside the purview of research and theory, most other psychologists argue that at least part of our mental processes can be reduced to the brain or body. For example, one application of this question might be to ask "Can we understand the loss of a loved one by mapping the neural networks?" Or, when we hold a phone number in mind briefly as we reach for the phone, are we using different neural "hardware" than when we store that number "for keeps"?

φ **Question 2: What is the relationship between reason and desire or, more precisely, between cognition and affect?** For example, to what extent should people choose their mates based on "gut" feelings? Should they carefully weigh a potential partner's costs and benefits if they want to have a happy, long-lasting marriage? For that matter, to what extent do people's thoughts actually determine how they feel?

φ **Question 3: To what extent is human psychology continuous with the psychology of other animals?** For example, to what extent can studying fear responses in rats inform humans about their own fear responses? Or, conversely, to what extent do current theories of altruism derived from research with humans apply also to animals? Can we understand people's relationships with animals by examining their patterns of relationship with other humans?

φ **Question 4: To what extent is human nature particular versus universal?** In other words, to what extent is human nature relatively invariant as opposed to culturally variable? Is logical reasoning universal, for example, or do people use different kinds of "logic" in different cultures? Do children follow similar patterns of language development throughout the world?

φ **Question 5: To what extent are psychological processes the same in men and women?** For example, to what extent do gender differences in linguistic and spatial problem solving reflect differential evolutionary selection pressures? Why might men and women make different attributions for their own successes and failures? Are men and women similarly affected by a partner's infidelity?

φ **Question 6: What is the relation between nature and nurture in shaping psychological processes?** For example, how can we understand that the likelihood of getting killed in an accident is heritable? To what extent is intelligence inherited? How do we account for data showing remarkable similarities between identical twins who have been reared apart?

φ **Question 7: To what extent are psychological processes conscious or unconscious—that is, explicit versus implicit?** Can, for example, amnesiacs show cognitive dissonance effects, even when they have cannot remember having performed a prior act involved in the production of dissonance? Similarly, can people describe themselves accurately or are they unaware of the contents of their minds and the causes of their behavior?

φ **Question 8: To what extent can we inform our knowledge through reason or through observation—that is, rationalism versus empiricism?** Relatedly, to what extent are humans passive recipients of, or active constructors of, their understanding? When an air traffic controller notices an anomalous and potentially dangerous "blip" on his or her radar screen, to what extent is this an active process of construction and decision making or a passive process of sensations inevitably producing perceptions?

INTERIM SUMMARY

Because of its philosophical roots, psychology not surprisingly grapples with some difficult questions including the dichotomy between free will and determinism, and the nature–nurture controversy. Regardless of the specific psychological topic under investigation, such Big Picture Questions are behind much of the theory and research that you will read about in this text.

Summary

The Boundaries and Borders of Psychology

1. **Psychology** is the scientific investigation of mental processes and behavior. Understanding a person means practicing "triple bookkeeping"—simultaneously examining the person's biological makeup, psychological experience and functioning, and cultural and historical moment.

2. **Biopsychology** (or **behavioral neuroscience**) examines the physical basis of psychological phenomena such as motivation, emotion,

and stress. **Cross-cultural psychology** tests psychological hypotheses in different cultures. Biology and culture form the boundaries, or constraints, within which psychological processes operate.

3. A classic question inherited from philosophy is whether human action is characterized by **free will** or **determinism**, that is, whether people freely choose their actions or whether behavior follows lawful patterns. A related issue is the **mind–body problem**—the question of how mental and physical events interact.

4. The field of psychology began in the late nineteenth century as experimental psychologists attempted to wrest questions about the mind from philosophers. Most shared a strong belief in the scientific method as a way of avoiding philosophical debates about the way the mind works. Among the earliest schools of thought were structuralism and functionalism. **Structuralism**, developed by Edward Titchener, attempted to use introspection to uncover the basic elements of consciousness and the way they combine with one another into ideas (that is, the *structure* of consciousness). **Functionalism** looked for explanations of psychological processes in their role, or *function*, in helping the individual adapt to the environment.

Perspectives in Psychology

5. A **paradigm** is a broad system of theoretical assumptions employed by a scientific community to make sense of a domain of experience. Psychology lacks a unified paradigm but has a number of schools of thought, or **perspectives**, which are broad ways of understanding psychological phenomena. A psychological perspective, like a paradigm, includes theoretical propositions, shared metaphors, and accepted methods of observation.

6. **The psychodynamic perspective** originated with Sigmund Freud. From a psychodynamic perspective, most psychological processes that guide behavior are unconscious. Thus, consciousness is like the tip of an iceberg. Because a primary aim is to interpret the meanings or motives of human behavior, psychodynamic psychologists have relied primarily on case study methods. Although heavily criticized for, among other things, its violation of the **falsifiability criterion**, psychodynamic theory is benefitting

from ongoing efforts to apply more rigorous methods to psychodynamic concepts. These efforts are likely to prove fruitful in integrating these concepts into scientific psychology.

7. The **behaviorist perspective** focuses on the relation between environmental events (or **stimuli**) and the responses of the organism. Skinner proposed that all behavior can ultimately be understood as learned responses and that behaviors are selected on the basis of their consequences. A primary metaphor underlying behaviorism is the machine; many behaviorists also consider the "mind" an unknowable black box because its contents cannot be studied scientifically. The primary method of behaviorists is laboratory experimentation.

8. The **cognitive perspective** focuses on the way people process, store, and retrieve information. **Information processing** refers to taking input from the environment and transforming it into meaningful output. A metaphor underlying the cognitive perspective is the mind as computer, complete with software. In recent years, however, many cognitive psychologists have used the brain itself as a metaphor for the way mental processes operate. The primary method of the cognitive perspective is experimental.

9. The **evolutionary perspective** argues that many human behavioral proclivities exist because they helped our ancestors survive and produce offspring that would likely survive. **Natural selection** is the mechanism by which natural forces select traits in organisms that are adaptive in their environmental niche. The basic notion of evolutionary theory is that evolution selects organisms that maximize their **reproductive success**, defined as the capacity to survive and reproduce and maximize the reproductive success of genetically related individuals. The primary methods are deductive and comparative, although evolutionary psychologists are increasingly relying on experimental methods.

10. Although the four major perspectives largely developed independently, each has made distinctive contributions.

11. Much theory and research in psychology are predicated on certain critical or Big Picture Questions. Among these questions are the extent to which mental processes can be reduced to the brain or body, and the extent to which psychological processes are the same in men and women.

Key Terms

Research Methods in Psychology

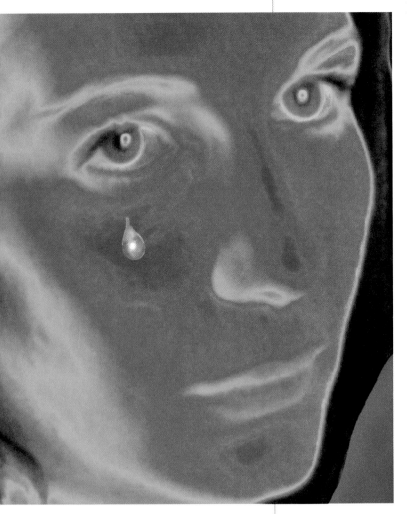

licia was 19 years old when she received a call that would change her life forever. Her parents and only brother had been killed in a car accident. Initially, Alicia reacted with shock and tremendous grief, but over the course of the next year, she gradually regained her emotional equilibrium. About a year after the accident, though, Alicia noticed that she was constantly ill with one cold, sore throat, or bout with flu after another. After a few trips to the health service, an astute doctor asked her if anything out of the ordinary had happened in the last year. When she mentioned the death of her family, the doctor recommended she see a psychologist. She did—and was free from physical illness from the day she entered the psychologist's office until more than a year later.

Was it coincidence that Alicia's health improved just as she began expressing her feelings about the loss of her family? Research by James Pennebaker and his colleagues (1997) suggests not.

In one study, the researchers examined a stressful experience much less calamitous than Alicia's: the transition to college. For most people, entering college is an exciting event, but it can also be stressful, since it often means leaving home, breaking predictable routines, finding a new group of friends, and having to make many more decisions independently. To assess the impact of emotional expression on health, Pennebaker and his colleagues assigned college freshmen to one of two groups. Students in the first group were instructed to write for 20 minutes on three consecutive days about "your very deepest thoughts and feelings about coming to college, including your emotions and thoughts about leaving your friends or your parents—or even about your feelings of who you are or what you want to become." Students in the other group were asked to describe in detail "what you have done since you woke up this morning" and were explicitly instructed *not* to mention their emotions, feelings, or opinions.

The results were dramatic (Figure 2.1). Students in the emotional expression group made significantly fewer visits to the health service in the following two to three months than those who simply described what they had done that day. The effect largely wore off by the fourth month, but it was remarkable given how seemingly minor the intervention had been.

Philosophers have speculated for centuries about the relation between mind and body. Yet here, psychologists were able to demonstrate *empirically*—that is, through systematic observation—how a psychological event (in this case, simply expressing feelings about a stressful experience) can affect the body's ability to protect itself from infection. In this chapter we address the ways psychologists use the scientific method to try to separate the scientific

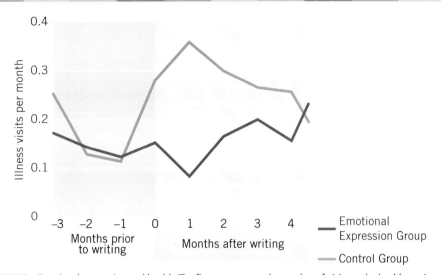

FIGURE 2.1 Emotional expression and health. The figure compares the number of visits to the health service of students writing about either emotionally significant or trivial events. Students who wrote about emotionally significant events had better health for the next four months, after which the effect wore off. *Source:* Adapted from Pennebaker et al., 1990, p. 533.

wheat from the speculative chaff—that is, to develop theories and answer practical questions using sound scientific procedures.

We begin by discussing the features of good psychological research. How do researchers take a situation like the sudden improvement in Alicia's health after seeing a psychologist and turn it into a researchable question? How do they know when the findings apply to the real world? Then, we will consider three major types of research: descriptive, experimental, and correlational. Finally, we will examine how to distinguish a good research study from a bad one.

Characteristics of Good Psychological Research

The tasks of a psychological researcher trying to understand human nature are in some respects similar to the tasks we all face in our daily lives as we try to predict other people's behavior. For example, a student named Elizabeth is running behind on a term paper. She wants to ask her professor for an extension but does not want to risk his forming a negative impression of her. Her task, then, is one of prediction: How will he behave?

To make her decision, she can rely on her observations of the way her professor normally behaves, or she can "experiment," by saying something and seeing how he responds. Elizabeth has observed her professor on many occasions, and her impression—or theory—about him is that he tends to be rigid. She has noticed that when students arrive late to class he looks angry and that when they ask to meet with him outside the class he often seems inflexible in scheduling appointments. She thus expects —hypothesizes—that he will not give her an extension.

Not sure, however, that her observations are accurate, she tests her hypothesis by speaking with him casually after class one day. She mentions a "friend" who is having trouble finishing the term paper on time, and she carefully observes his reaction—his facial expressions, his words, and the length of time he takes to respond. The professor

A THEORETICAL FRAMEWORK	A STANDARDIZED PROCEDURE	GENERALIZABILITY	OBJECTIVE MEASUREMENT
Systematic way of organizing and explaining observations	Procedure that is the same for all subjects except where variation is introduced to test a hypothesis	Sample that is representative of the population	Measures that are reliable (that produce consistent results)
Hypothesis that flows from the theory or from an important question		Procedure that is sensible and relevant to circumstances outside the laboratory	Measures that are valid (that assess the dimensions they purport to assess)

FIGURE 2.2 Characteristics of good psychological research. Studies vary tremendously in design, but most good research shares certain attributes.

surprises her by smiling and advising her that her "friend" can have an extra week. In this scenario, Elizabeth is doing exactly what psychologists do: observing a psychological phenomenon (her professor's behavior), constructing a theory, using the theory to develop a hypothesis, measuring psychological responses, and testing the hypothesis.

Psychologists are much more systematic in applying scientific methods, and they have more sophisticated tools, but the logic of investigation is basically the same. Like carpenters, researchers attempting to lay a solid empirical foundation for a theory or hypothesis have a number of tools at their disposal. Just as a carpenter would not use a hammer to turn a screw or loosen a bolt, a researcher would not rely exclusively on any single method to lay a solid empirical foundation for a theory. Nevertheless, most of the methods psychologists use—the tools of their trade—share certain features: a theoretical framework, standardized procedures, generalizability, and objective measurement (Figure 2.2). We examine each of these in turn.

Theoretical Framework

Psychologists study some phenomena because of their practical importance. They may, for example, research the impact of divorce on children (Kalter, 1990; Wallerstein & Corbin, 1999) or the effect of poverty on children's psychological development (Duncan & Brooks, 2000). In most cases, however, they firmly ground their research in theory.

A **theory** is *a systematic way of organizing and explaining observations*, which includes a set of propositions, or statements, about the relations among various phenomena. For example, a psychologist might theorize that a pessimistic attitude promotes poor physical health, for two reasons: Pessimists do not take good care of themselves, and pessimism taxes the body's defenses against disease by keeping the body in a constant state of alarm.

People frequently assume that a theory is simply a fact that has not yet been proven. As suggested in Chapter 1, however, a theory is always a mental construction, an imperfect rendering of reality by a scientist or community of scientists, which can have more or less evidence to support it. The scientist's thinking is the mortar that holds the bricks of reality in place. Without that mortar, the entire edifice would crumble.

In most research, theory provides the framework for the researcher's specific hypothesis. A **hypothesis** is *a tentative belief about the relationship between two or more variables*. A **variable** is *any phenomenon that can differ, or vary, from one situation to another or from one person to another*; in other words, a variable is a characteristic that can take on different values (such as IQ scores of 115 or 125).

For example, a research team interested in the links between optimism and health decided to test the hypothesis that optimism (variable 1) is related to speed of recovery from heart surgery (variable 2). Their theory suggested that optimism should be related to health in general; their specific hypothesis focused on heart disease in particular. In fact, the researchers found that patients undergoing coronary artery bypass operations who are optimistic recover more quickly than patients who are pessimistic (Scheier & Carver, 1993).

Making Connections

Optimism and pessimism are linked to mental as well as physical health (Chapter 15).

▪ To what extent is pessimism a cause or consequence of depression? Do people who are pessimistic become depressed more easily, or do people who are in a depressed mood just feel pessimistic because they are depressed?

▪ How might a researcher test the hypothesis that a pessimistic style predisposes people to later episodes of depression?

In this case, optimism and health are variables, because different people are more or less optimistic (they vary as to degree of optimism) and recover more or less quickly (they vary as to recovery rate). *A variable that can be placed on a continuum*—such as degree of optimism, intelligence, shyness, or rate of recovery—is called a **continuous variable**. In contrast, a **categorical variable** *is comprised of groupings or categories*, such as gender, species, or whether or not a person has had a heart attack. A categorical variable cannot easily be placed on a continuum; people are either male or female and cannot usually be located on a continuum between the two.

Focus on Methodology
Getting Research Ideas

As you read the chapters of this text, you may wonder where scientists derived the ideas for their research studies. The number of sources for research are as varied as the number of ideas themselves, but a few are prevalent. You can use these sources yourself as tips for getting ideas if you need to design your own research project.

- **Reading the research literature in an area you find interesting.** One of the first lessons of research is that you conduct research in an area that you find interesting. If you find a particular topic interesting, read the literature in that area and you will likely find many unanswered questions that will generate fruitful hypotheses for research.

- **Derive hypotheses from an existing theory.** Using this traditional way of generating research ideas, researchers read about a particular theory and then derive a series of hypotheses from that theory. Because theories themselves are somewhat abstract, researchers usually cannot test a particular theory. Rather, they test hypotheses that they derive from these theories.

- **Imagine what would happen if a particular variable were reduced to zero.** What would happen, for example, if people didn't care about what anyone thought of them? Would they work as hard to maintain their weight or to refrain from engaging in breaches of propriety, such as belching in public?

- **Investigate an area that you find personally interesting.** Many research studies stem from the personal interest of researchers and may even reflect personal experiences that they have had. For example, someone who was raised in foster care may decide to examine the implications of foster care for physical and mental health. Another individual who was sexually abused as a child may decide as an adult to conduct research in the area of sexual abuse. My (RMK) own research on complaining stemmed from my personal curiosity about why people complain as much as they do (and perhaps from the fact that maybe I, too, am a complainer!).

- **Apply an old theory to a new phenomenon.** A given theory can be used as a source for hypotheses about any number of different topics. Thus, a theory that has traditionally been thought of as being associated with a particular area of study can be applied to a completely new area.

- **Observe everyday interactions and ask yourself questions about why that behavior occurs.** Some of the best research ideas happen somewhat accidentally when a person simply observes the behavior of other individuals. A contemporary example is a study the hypothesis of which was generated from a song by Mickey Gilley, "The Girls Get Pretty at Closing Time" (Pennebaker et al., 1979). Do they? And, if so, why?

- **Reverse the direction of causality for a hypothesis.** Here, a researcher takes an existing hypothesis and reverses the direction of causality. For example, although most people would say that they blush when they are embarrassed, is it also possible that people are embarrassed because they blush?

(ADAPTED FROM LEARY, 2001)

Standardized Procedures

In addition to being grounded in theory, good psychological research uses **standardized procedures**, *which expose the participants in a study to as similar procedures as possible*. For example, in the study of emotional expression and health that opened this chapter, the experimenters instructed students in both groups to write for 20 minutes a day for three days. If instead they had let the students write as long as they wanted, students in one group might have written more, and the experimenters would not have been able to tell whether differences in visits to the health service reflected the *content* of their writing or simply the *quantity*.

Generalizability from a Sample

Psychological research typically studies the behavior of a subset of people in order to learn about *a larger group to whom research findings should be applicable*, called a **population**. The population might be as broad as all humans or as narrow as preschool children with working mothers. A **sample** is *a subgroup of the population that is likely to be* **representative** of the population as a whole—that is, *similar enough to other members of the population that conclusions drawn from the sample are likely to be true of the rest of the population. The individuals who participate in a study* are called **participants** or **subjects**.

A representative sample contributes to the generalizability of a study's conclusions. **Generalizability** refers to *the applicability of the findings to the entire population of interest to the researcher*. Often researchers intend their findings to be generalizable to people as a whole. At other times, however, they are interested in generalizing to specific subgroups, such as people over 65, married couples, or women.

For a study to be generalizable, its *procedures must be sound*, or **valid**. To be valid, a study must meet two criteria. First, it must employ *methods that convincingly test the hypothesis*; this is called **internal validity**—validity of the design itself. A study with low internal validity does not allow a researcher to convincingly make any inferences regarding cause and effect. If a study has fatal flaws—such as an unrepresentative sample or nonstandardized aspects of the design that affect the way participants respond—its internal validity is jeopardized. Similarly, if researchers have failed to control for extraneous variables that could account for their findings, the internal validity of the study is called into question.

Second, the study must establish **external validity**—that is, *the findings can be generalized to situations outside, or external to, the laboratory*. Does expressing feelings on paper for three days in a laboratory simulate what happens when people express feelings in their diary or to a close friend? The problem is that often researchers must strike a balance between internal and external validity, because the more tightly a researcher controls what participants experience, the less the situation may resemble life outside the laboratory. *This trade-off between internal and external validity* is referred to as the **experimenter's dilemma**. Whether a researcher opts for more internal than external validity or vice versa depends on his or her research hypothesis. A researcher conducting applied research would place more emphasis on external validity. A researcher focused more on advancing knowledge or increasing our understanding of a particular phenomenon might place more emphasis on internal validity.

INTERIM SUMMARY

Psychological research is generally guided by a **theory**—a systematic way of organizing and explaining observations. The theory helps generate a **hypothesis**, or tentative belief about the relationship between two or more variables. **Variables** are phenomena that differ or change across circumstances or individuals; they can be either **continuous** or **categorical**, depending on whether they form a continuum or are comprised of categories.

Standardized procedures expose participants in a study to as similar procedures as possible. Although psychologists are typically interested in knowing something about a **population**, to do so they usually study a **sample**, or subgroup, that is likely to be **representative** of the population. To be **generalizable**, a study must have both **internal validity** (a valid design) and **external validity** (applicability to situations outside the laboratory). Unfortunately, the researcher typically has to choose whether to place more emphasis on internal or on external validity, a trade-off referred to as the **experimenter's dilemma**.

Objective Measurement

As in all scientific endeavors, objectivity is an important ideal in psychological research. Otherwise, the results of a study might simply reflect the experimenter's subjective impression. Researchers must therefore devise ways to quantify or categorize variables so they can be measured.

Consider a study in which the researchers hoped to challenge popular beliefs and theories about children's popularity (Rodkin et al., 2000). Rather than viewing all popular children as "model citizens," the researchers theorized that some popular children (in this study, boys) are actually aggressive kids who impress others with their "toughness" more than with their good nature.

So how might researchers turn a seemingly subjective variable such as "popularity" in elementary school boys into something that they can measure? One way is through quantifying teachers' observations. Contrary to many students' beliefs, teachers often have a keen eye for what is going on in their classrooms, and they tend to know which kids are high or low on the school yard totem pole. Thus, in this study, teachers filled out an 18-item questionnaire that asked them to rate each boy in their class on items such as "popular with girls," "popular with boys," and "lots of friends." (Teachers also rated items about the boys' scholastic achievement, athletic ability, and other variables.)

Using statistical techniques that can sort people who are similar to each other and different from others into groups—in this case, sorting boys into groups based on their teachers' descriptions of them—the researchers discovered two kinds of boys who are popular. One kind was indeed the model citizen type—high in academic achievement, friendly, good looking, and good at sports. The other kind, however, differed from the first type in one respect: These boys, too, were good looking and good at sports, but their other most striking quality was that they were *aggressive*.

To study a variable such as popularity, then, a researcher must first devise a technique to **measure** it. A measure is *a concrete way of assessing a variable*, a way of bringing an often abstract concept down to earth. In this study, the investigators used a *rating scale*—that is, a measure that assesses a variable on a numerical scale, such as 1–7, where 1 = not true and 7 = very true, to assess popularity. As a general measure of popularity, they actually took the average of each child's rating on three items (popularity with boys, popularity with girls, and having many friends). In the study of emotional expression and health, the investigators obtained records of visits from the campus health service as a rough measure of illness. This was a better measure than simply asking students how often they got sick, because people may not be able to remember or report illness objectively. For example, one person's threshold for being "sick" might be much lower than another's.

For some variables, measurement is not a problem. Researchers typically have little difficulty distinguishing males from females. However, for some characteristics, such as popularity, health, or optimism, measurement is much more complex. In these cases, researchers need to know two characteristics of a measure: whether it is reliable and whether it is valid.

Reliability   **Reliability** refers to *a measure's ability to produce consistent results*. Using a measure is like stepping on a scale: The same person should not register 145 pounds one moment and 152 a few minutes later. Similarly, a reliable psychological measure does not fluctuate substantially despite the presence of random factors that may influence results, such as whether the participant had a good night's sleep or who coded the data.

Reliability in this technical sense is not altogether different from reliability in its everyday meaning: A test is unreliable if we cannot count on it to behave consistently, just as a plumber is unreliable if we cannot count on him consistently to show up when he says he will. An unreliable measure may sometimes work, just as an unreliable plumber may sometimes work, but we can never predict when either will perform adequately.

Three kinds of reliability are especially important (Figure 2.3). **Test-retest reliability** refers to *the tendency of a test to yield relatively similar scores for the same individual over time*. The researchers interested in boys' popularity examined the test-retest reliability of their measure by readministering it three weeks later; they found that boys rated as popular or aggressive initially were rated very similarly three weeks later—a confirmation of the measure's reliability.

Another kind of reliability is **internal consistency** or **interitem reliability**. This refers to the consistency of participants' responses across items on a scale. A measure is internally consistent if *several ways of asking the same question yield similar results*. Thus, if being high on popularity with boys did not predict being high on popularity with girls, averaging these two items would not yield an internally consistent measure.

A third kind of reliability is **interrater reliability**—*if two different interviewers rate an individual on some dimension, both should give the person similar scores*. In the study of popularity, for example, one way to assess interrater reliability would have been to ask two different teachers who knew the same children to rate them and to see if their ratings were similar. Although some variables can be rated quite easily with relatively high reliability, others, such as optimism as assessed from people's diaries, require the development of detailed *coding manuals* to guarantee that different raters are similarly "calibrated," like two thermometers recording temperature in the same room.

Validity   A study can be valid only if the measures it relies on are themselves valid. When the term **validity** is *applied to a psychological measure, it refers to the measure's ability to assess the variable it is supposed to assess*. For example, IQ tests are supposed to measure intelligence. One way psychologists have tried to demonstrate the validity of IQ test scores is to show that they consistently predict other phenomena that require intellectual ability, such as school performance. As we will see in Chapter 8, IQ tests and similar tests such as the Scholastic Aptitude Test (the SAT) are, in general, highly predictive of school success (Anastasi & Urbina, 1997). Some of the measures people intuitively use in their daily lives have much less certain validity, as when Elizabeth initially presumed that her professor's inflexibility in arranging meetings with students was a good index of his general flexibility (rather than, say, a tight schedule).

Just as there were different types of reliability, so, too, are there different types of validity (Figure 2.3). As you will see, some types of validity are more important than others. One type, the least important one, is **face validity**, or *whether or not the measure ap-*

FIGURE 2.3 Psychometric characteristics of good measures. To be valid, studies must contain measures that are both reliable and valid. The figure depicts the different types of reliability and validity that researchers must consider.

RELIABILITY	VALIDITY
Test-retest–consistency across time	Face validity
	Construct validity
Interitem reliability–consistency across items	Convergent validity
	Discriminant validity
Interrater reliability–consistency across people	Criterion validity

pears, just by looking at it, as though it measures what it purports to measure. Many researchers go out of their way to assure that their scale in fact does *not* have face validity. Concerned with the fact that participants may alter their responses if they discern the researcher's purpose, experimenters may try to disguise the true purpose of their measure.

More important is **construct validity**, or *the degree to which a measure actually assesses what it claims to measure*. Construct validity is determined in one of two ways. Measures that are high in construct validity should correlate with related measures, a type of construct validity referred to as *convergent validity*. Thus, a measure of social anxiety should correlate with other existing measures of social anxiety or related constructs, such as fear of negative evaluation or public self-consciousness. At the same time, a measure that has construct validity should not correlate with unrelated measures, a type of construct validity known as *discriminant validity*. A given measure should be distinct from unrelated measures.

A third type of validity, **criterion validity**, refers to *the degree to which a measure allows a researcher to distinguish among groups on the basis of certain behaviors or responses*. The SAT test mentioned earlier is assessed for its criterion validity or the extent to which, in fact, it distinguishes among students who do versus do not perform well in college approximately a year after they take the test.

Similarly, the teacher report measure used to assess children's popularity, aggressiveness, academic achievement, and other variables predicted children's functioning as many as eight years later (e.g., rates of school drop out and teenage pregnancy). Showing that a measure of children's achievement, popularity, and adjustment can predict how well they will do socially and academically several years later provides strong evidence for the criterion validity of a measure.

Multiple Measures   One of the best ways to obtain an accurate assessment of a variable is to employ multiple measures of it. *Multiple measures* or *converging operations* are important because no psychological measure is perfect. A measure that assesses a variable accurately 80 percent of the time is excellent—but it is also inaccurate 20 percent of the time. In fact, built into every measure is a certain amount of **error**, or *discrepancy between the phenomenon as measured and the phenomenon as it really is*. For example, IQ is a good predictor of school success *most* of the time, but for some people it overpredicts or underpredicts their performance. Multiple measures therefore provide a safety net for catching errors.

Virtually all good psychological studies share the ingredients of psychological research outlined here: a theoretical framework, standardized procedures, generalizability, and objective measurement. Nevertheless, studies vary considerably in design and goals. The following sections examine three broad types of research (Table 2.1): descriptive, experimental, and correlational. In actuality, the lines separating these types are not hard and fast. Many studies categorized as descriptive include experimental components, and correlational questions are often built into experiments. The aim in designing research is scientific rigor and practicality, not purity; the best strategy is to use whatever systematic empirical methods are available to explore the hypothesis and to see if different methods and designs converge on similar findings—that is, to see if the finding is "reliable" with different methods.

Making Connections

Sometimes musical geniuses are brilliant in other realms, and sometimes they are not.

■ If an IQ test can predict school success but not musical genius, is it a valid measure of intelligence?

■ What assumptions about the meaning of intelligence underlie the use of paper-and-pencil IQ tests (Chapter 8)?

INTERIM SUMMARY

Just as researchers take a sample of a population, they similarly take a "sample" of a variable—that is, they use a **measure** of the variable, which provides a concrete way of assessing it. A measure is **reliable** if it produces consistent results—that is, if it does not show too much random fluctuation. A measure is **valid** if it accurately assesses or "samples" the construct it is intended to measure. Because every measure includes some degree of error, researchers often use *multiple measures* (in order to assess more than one sample of the relevant behavior).

Table 2.1 ■ ■ Comparison of Research Methods

Method	Description	Uses and Advantages	Potential Limitations
Experimental	Manipulation of variables to assess cause and effect	• Demonstrates causal relationships • Replicability: study can be repeated to see if the same findings emerge • Maximizes control over relevant variables	• Generalizability outside the laboratory • Some complex phenomena cannot be readily tested using pure experimental methods
Descriptive			
Case study	In-depth observation of a small number of cases	• Describes psychological processes as they occur in individual cases • Allows study of complex phenomena not easily reproduced experimentally • Provides data that can be useful in framing hypotheses	• Generalizability to the population • Replicability: study may not be repeatable • Researcher bias • Cannot establish causation
Naturalistic observation	In-depth observation of a phenomenon as it occurs in nature	• Reveals phenomena as they exist outside the laboratory • Allows study of complex phenomena not easily reproduced experimentally • Provides data that can be useful in framing hypotheses	• Generalizability to the population • Replicability • Observer effects: the presence of an observer may alter the behavior of the participants • Researcher bias • Cannot establish causation
Survey research	Asking people questions about their attitudes, behavior, etc.	• Reveals attitudes or self-reported behaviors of a large sample of individuals • Allows quantification of attitudes or behaviors	• Self-report bias: people may not be able to report honestly or accurately • Cannot establish causation
Correlational	Examines the extent to which two or more variables are related and can be used to predict one another	• Reveals relations among variables as they exist outside the laboratory • Allows quantification of relations among variables	• Cannot establish causation

Descriptive Research

The first major type of research, **descriptive research**, *attempts to describe phenomena as they exist* rather than to manipulate variables. Do people in different cultures use similar terms to describe people's personalities, such as "outgoing" or "responsible" (McCrae et al., 1998a; Paunonen et al., 1992)? Do members of other primate species compete for status and form coalitions against powerful members of the group whose behavior is becoming oppressive? To answer such questions, psychologists use a variety of descriptive methods, including case studies, naturalistic observation, and survey research. Table 2.1 summarizes the major uses and limitations of these descriptive methods as well as the other methods psychologists use.

Case Study Methods

A **case study** is *an in-depth observation of one person or a small group of individuals*. Case study methods are useful when trying to learn about complex psychological phenomena that are not yet well understood and require exploration or that are difficult to produce experimentally. For example, one study used the case of a four-year-old girl who had witnessed her mother's violent death three years earlier as a way of trying to explore the issue of whether, and if so in what ways, children can show effects of traumatic incidents they cannot explicitly recall (Gaensbauer et al., 1995). Single-case designs can also be used in combination with quantitative or experimental procedures (Blampied, 1999; Kazdin & Tuma, 1982). For example, researchers studying patients with severe seizure disorders who have had the connecting tissue between two sides of their brains surgically cut have presented information to one side of the brain to see whether the other side of the brain can figure out what is going on (Chapters 3 and 9).

Psychologists who take an *interpretive* (or *hermeneutic*) *approach* to methodology often use case studies; their aim is to examine the complex meanings that may underlie human behavior (Martin & Sugarman, 1999; Messer et al., 1988). One person may commit suicide because he feels he is a failure; another may kill herself to get back at a relative or spouse; another may seek escape from intense or chronic psychic pain; and still another may take his life because cultural norms demand it in the face of a wrongdoing or humiliation. From an interpretive point of view, explaining a behavior such as suicide means understanding the subjective meanings behind it. Interpreting meanings of this sort typically requires in-depth interviewing.

One major limitation of case study methods is sample size. Because case studies examine only a small group of participants, generalization to a larger population is always uncertain. An investigator who conducts intensive research on one or several young women with anorexia and finds that their self-starvation behavior appears tied to their wishes for control (in this case, demonstrating to themselves that they have complete control over their most intense desires) might be tempted to conclude that control issues are central to this disorder (e.g., Bruch, 1973). They may well be, but they may also be idiosyncratic to this particular study.

One way to minimize this limitation is to use a multiple-case-study method (Rosenwald, 1988), extensively examining a small sample of people individually and drawing generalizations across them. Another way is to follow up case studies with more systematic studies using other designs. Several studies have now shown, for example, that patients with anorexia *do* tend to be preoccupied with control, a finding initially discovered through the careful analysis of individual cases (Serpell et al., 1999).

A second limitation of case studies is their susceptibility to researcher bias. Investigators tend to see what they expect to see. A psychotherapist who believes that anorexic patients have conflicts about sexuality will undoubtedly see such conflicts in his anorexic patients because they are operative in virtually everyone. In writing up the case, he may select examples that demonstrate these conflicts and miss other issues that might be just as salient to another observer. Because no one else is privy to the data of a case, no other investigator can examine the data directly and draw different conclusions unless the therapy sessions are videotaped; the data are always filtered through the psychologist's theoretical lens.

Case studies are probably most useful at either the beginning or the end of a series of studies that employ quantitative methods with larger samples. Exploring individual cases can be crucial in deciding what questions to ask or what hypotheses to test because they allow the researcher to immerse herself in the phenomenon as it appears in real life. A case study can also flesh out the meaning of quantitative findings by providing a detailed analysis of representative examples.

Naturalistic Observation

A second descriptive method, **naturalistic observation**, is *the in-depth observation of a phenomenon in its natural setting*, such as Jane Goodall's well-known studies of apes in the wilds of Africa. For example, Frans de Waal, like Goodall, has spent years both in the wild and at zoos observing the way groups of apes or monkeys behave. De Waal (1989) describes an incident in which a dominant male chimpanzee in captivity made an aggressive charge at a female. The troop, clearly distressed by the male's behavior, came to the aid of the female and then settled into an unusual si-

Making Connections

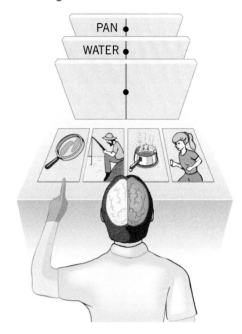

Case studies are often useful when large numbers of subjects are not available, either because they do not exist or because obtaining them would be extremely difficult. For example, extensive case studies of patients who have undergone surgery to sever the tissue connecting the right and left hemispheres of the brain (in order to control severe epileptic seizures) have yielded important information about the specific functions of the two hemispheres (Chapters 3 and 9).

Naturalistic observation can lead to novel insights, such as the importance of peacemaking in primates.

lence. Suddenly, the room echoed with hoots and howls, during which two of the chimps kissed and embraced. To de Waal's surprise, the two chimps were the same ones who had been involved in the fight that had set off the episode! After several hours of pondering the incident, de Waal suddenly realized that he had observed something he had naively assumed was unique to humans: reconciliation. This observation led him to study the way primates maintain social relationships despite conflicts and acts of aggression. His research led him to conclude that for humans, as for our nearest neighbors, "making peace is as natural as making war" (p. 7).

Psychologists also observe humans "in the wild" using naturalistic methods, as in some classic studies of Genevan school children by the Swiss psychologist Jean Piaget (1926). Piaget and his colleagues relied heavily on experimental methods, but they also conducted naturalistic research in playgrounds and classrooms, taking detailed notes on who spoke to whom, for how long, and on what topics (Chapter 13). Piaget found that young children often speak in "collective monologues," talking all at once; they may neither notice whether they are being listened to nor address their comments to a particular listener. An advantage of naturalistic observation over experimental methods to be discussed shortly is that its findings are clearly applicable outside the laboratory.

In fact, however, the awareness of being watched may alter people's "natural" behavior in real-world settings. Researchers try to minimize this problem in one of two ways. One is simply to be as inconspicuous as possible—"to blend into the woodwork." The other is to become a *participant–observer*, interacting naturally with subjects in their environment, much as Goodall did once she came to "know" a troop of apes over months or years. Similarly, researchers interested in doomsday groups whose members believe that they know when the world will end often join the groups so that their presence appears natural and unobtrusive.

No matter how inconspicuous the researcher makes herself to the participants, researcher bias can pose limitations since observers' theoretical biases can influence what they look for and therefore what they see. As with case studies, this limitation can be minimized by observing several groups of participants or by videotaping interactions, so that more than one judge can independently rate the data. Finally, like other descriptive studies, naturalistic observation primarily *describes* behaviors; it cannot explain *why* they take place. Based on extensive observation, a psychologist can make a convincing *argument* about the way one variable influences another, but this method does not afford the luxury of doing something to participants and seeing what they do in response, as in experimental designs.

Survey Research

A third type of descriptive research, **survey research**, involves *asking a large sample of people questions, usually about their attitudes or behaviors*. For example, a large corporation might call in an organizational psychologist to try to help understand why morale is declining among workers in the factory. The psychologist begins by interviewing a small sample of employees, from executives to workers on the line, and then designs a survey, which is completed by a random sample of workers in randomly selected plants around the country. The survey asks workers to rate a series of statements, such as "My job does not pay well," "I do not receive enough vacation time," and "I feel I am not learning anything on the job," on a seven-point scale (where 1 = strongly disagree and 7 = strongly agree). *The two most frequently used tools of survey researchers are* **interviews**, in which *researchers ask questions using a standard format*, usually to a large sample of participants; and **questionnaires**, which *participants fill out by themselves*

Selecting the sample is extremely important in survey research. For example, pollsters conducting voter exit interviews must be sure that their sample reflects a large and heterogeneous population if they are to predict election results accurately.

Researchers typically want a **random sample**, *a sample selected from the general population in a relatively arbitrary way that does not introduce any systematic bias*. The organizational psychologist seeking a random sample of factory workers in a company, for instance, might choose names randomly selected from payroll or personnel records.

Random selection, however, does not always guarantee that a sample will accurately reflect the *demographic characteristics* (qualities such as gender, race, and socioeconomic status) of the population in which the researcher is interested. A survey sent to a random sample of workers in a company may, for example, lead to biased results if unhappy workers are afraid to answer, or if workers who are unhappy have higher absentee rates (and hence are not at work when the form arrives). Similarly, a political poll that randomly samples names from the phone book may overrepresent people who happen to be home answering the phone during the day, such as older people, and may underrepresent poor people who do not have a phone.

Where proportional representation of different subpopulations is important, researchers use a stratified random sample. A **stratified random sample** *specifies the percentage of people to be drawn from each population category (age, race, etc.) and then randomly selects participants from within each category*. Researchers often use census data to provide demographic information on the population of interest and then match this information as closely as possible in their sample. Thus, they may stratify a sample along a number of lines, such as age, sex, race, marital status, geographical region, and education, to make sure that they provide an accurate picture of the population.

The major problem with survey methods is that they rely on participants to report on themselves truthfully and accurately, and even minor wording changes can sometimes dramatically alter their responses (Schwarz, 1999). For example, most people tend to describe their behaviors and attitudes in more flattering terms than others would use to describe them (Campbell & Sedikides, 1999; John & Robins, 1994). How many people are likely to admit their addiction to *Baywatch* or *Seinfeld* reruns? In part, people's answers may be biased by conscious efforts to present themselves in the best possible light. However, they may also shade the truth without being aware of doing so because they want to feel intelligent or psychologically healthy (Shedler et al., 1993). In addition, participants may honestly misjudge themselves, or their conscious attitudes may differ from attitudes they express in their behavior (Chapter 17). Measuring people's attitudes toward the disabled by questionnaire typically indicates much more positive attitudes than measuring how far they *sit* from a disabled person when entering a room (see Greenwald & Banaji, 1995; Wilson et al., 2000b). People who sit farther away convey more negative attitudes than do those who sit closer.

Finally, some participants may simply not know their own minds. In other words, they may not know what they think about particular issues or why they behave in particular ways, yet they will provide a response on a survey when called to do so. Thus, the answers that they provide will not necessarily reflect actual attitudes or behaviors because the participants are unaware of those attitudes and behaviors or have simply not devoted any attention to thinking about them.

Regardless of the particular type of descriptive research someone decides to use, the researcher is faced with the dilemma of how to summarize the responses that are provided by individuals or groups through observations or in response to surveys or interviews. Perhaps the most important descriptive statistics are measures of central tendency, which provide an index of the way a typical participant responded on a measure. The three most common measures of central tendency are the mean, the mode, and the median.

Focus on Methodology
What to Do with
Descriptive Research

Table 2.2 ■ ■ ■ Distribution of Test Scores on a Midterm Examination

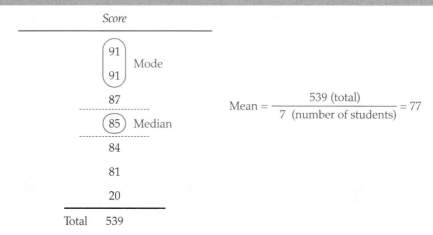

Score

91	Mode
91	
87	
85	Median
84	
81	
20	

Total   539

$$\text{Mean} = \frac{539 \ (\text{total})}{7 \ (\text{number of students})} = 77$$

The **mean** is simply *the statistical average of the scores of all participants, computed by adding up all the participants' scores and dividing by the number of participants*. The mean is the most commonly reported measure of central tendency and is the most intuitively descriptive of the average participant.

Sometimes, however, the mean may be misleading. For example, consider the table of midterm exam scores presented in Table 2.2. The mean grade is 77. Yet the mean falls below 6 of the 7 scores on the table. In fact, most students' scores fall somewhere between 81 and 91.

Why is the mean so low? It is pulled down by a single student's score—an outlier—who probably did not study. In this case, the median would be a more useful measure of central tendency, because a mean can be strongly influenced by extreme and unusual scores in a sample. The **median** refers to *the score that falls in the middle of the distribution of scores*, with half scoring below and half above it. Reporting the median essentially allows one to ignore extreme scores on each end of the distribution that would bias a portrait of the typical participant. In fact, the median in this case—85 (which has 3 scores above and 3 below it)—makes more intuitive sense, in that it seems to capture the middle of the distribution, which is precisely what a measure of central tendency is supposed to do.

In other instances, a useful measure of central tendency is the **mode** (or **modal score**), which is *the most common (i.e., most frequent) score observed in the sample*. In this case, the mode is 91, because two students received a score of 91, whereas all other scores had a frequency of only 1. The problem with the mode in this case is that it is also the highest score, which is not a good estimate of central tendency.

Another important descriptive statistic is a measure of the **variability of scores**, that is, *how much participants' scores differ from one another*. Variability influences the choice of measure of central tendency. The simplest measure of variability is the **range**, which *shows the difference between the highest and lowest value observed on the variable.*

The range can be a biased estimate of variability, however, in much the same way as the mean can be a biased estimate of central tendency. Scores do range considerably in this sample, but for the vast majority of students, variability is minimal (ranging from 81 to 91). Hence, a more useful measure is the **standard deviation (SD)**, which again is just what it sounds like: *the amount the average participant deviates from the mean of the sample*. Table 2.3 shows how to compute a standard deviation, using five students' scores on a midterm exam as an illustration.

Apply & Discuss

In Peru, as in much of Latin America, many people are very poor, whereas a small number are extremely wealthy.

■ How might the mean, median, and mode for family income provide realistic or misleading measures of central tendency in describing how poor or wealthy the average Peruvian is?

Table 2.3   The Standard Deviation

Score	Deviation from the Mean (D)	D²	
91	91 – 87.6 = 3.4	11.56	
91	91 – 87.6 = 3.4	11.56	Mean = $\frac{\Sigma}{N}$ = 438/5 = 87.6
87	87 – 87.6 = –.6	.36	
85	85 – 87.6 = -2.6	6.76	SD = $\sqrt{\frac{\Sigma D^2}{N}}$ = $\sqrt{\frac{43.2}{5}}$ = 2.94
84	84 – 87.6 = -3.6	12.96	
Σ = Sum = 438		0 43.20	

Note: Computing a standard deviation (SD) is more intuitive than it might seem. The first step is to calculate the mean score, which in this case is 87.6. The next step is to calculate the difference, or deviation, between each participant's score and the mean score, as shown in column 2. The standard deviation is meant to capture the average deviation of participants from the mean. The only complication is that taking the average of the deviations would always produce a mean deviation of zero because the sum of deviations is by definition zero (see the total in column 2). Thus, the next step is to square the deviations (column 3). The standard deviation is then computed by taking the square root of the sum (Σ) of all the squared differences divided by the number of participants (N).

INTERIM SUMMARY

Descriptive research describes phenomena as they already exist rather than manipulates variables. A **case study** is an in-depth observation of one person or a group of people. Case studies are useful in generating hypotheses, exploring complex phenomena that are not yet well understood or difficult to examine experimentally, fleshing out the meaning of quantitative findings, and interpreting behaviors with complex meanings. **Naturalistic observation** is the in-depth observation of a phenomenon in its natural setting. It is useful for describing complex phenomena as they exist outside the laboratory. **Survey research** involves asking a large sample of people questions, usually about their attitudes or behavior, through **interviews** or **questionnaires**. **Random** and **stratified random samples** allow psychologists to gather substantial information about the population by examining representative samples. However, descriptive methods cannot unambiguously establish causation. To summarize participants' responses obtained in descriptive research, researchers often use a measure of central tendency: the **mean**, **median**, or **mode**.

Experimental Research

In **experimental research**, *investigators manipulate some aspect of a situation and examine the impact on the way participants respond*. Experimental methods are important because they can establish cause and effect—*causation*—directly. An experiment can demonstrate causation by proving that manipulating one variable leads to predicted changes in another. The researchers studying the impact of emotional expression on health can be confident that writing emotionally about a stressful experience *caused* better health because participants who did so were subsequently healthier than those who did not.

The emphasis on experimentation as a way of understanding nature derives in part from Sir Francis Bacon (1561–1626), a British philosopher who was writing as England took its first steps into the modern age in the sixteenth century. According to Bacon, the best way to test our understanding of nature is to bend it to do something it normally does not do (Smith, 1992). Scientists who understand the laws of physics—or behavior—ought to be able to "bend nature" in a laboratory to do something scientifically interesting or practically useful. College students do not typically write for 20 minutes a day for three consecutive days about the experience of beginning college, but when researchers bent nature in this way, they found some very practical, and theoretically interesting, impacts on physical health.

The Logic of Experimentation

The logic of experimentation is much more straightforward and intuitive than many people think. (Elizabeth used it implicitly when she tested her professor's flexibility, as we all do multiple times a day in one situation after another.) *An experimenter manipulates variables*, called **independent variables**, *which are outside the participants' control (i.e., independent of their actions)*. The aim is to assess the impact of these manipulations on the way participants subsequently respond. Because participants' responses depend on their exposure to the independent variable, these responses are known as **dependent variables**. The independent variable, then, is the variable the experimenter manipulates; *the dependent variable is the response the experimenter measures to see if the experimental manipulation had an effect*.

To assess cause and effect, experimenters present participants with *different possible variations*, or **conditions**, *of the independent variable* and study the way participants react. In the study of emotional expression and health that opened this chapter, the experimenters used an independent variable (emotional expression) with two conditions (express or do not express). They then tested the impact on health (dependent variable). Consider a series of classic studies conducted in the 1950s by Harry Harlow and his colleagues (Harlow & Zimmerman, 1959). They were interested in determining which of two theories better explained why infant monkeys become emotionally attached to their mothers. One theory proposed that the basis for this attachment was the mother's role as the source of food. An alternative theory suggested that infant monkeys are drawn by the security and comfort mothers provide.

To compare these two theories, the researchers conducted an experiment in which infant monkeys were separated from their mothers and raised in social isolation. Each monkey shared its cage with two surrogate (replacement) "mothers," one made of wire and the other also made of wire but covered with terrycloth (and hence softer and more "maternal" to the touch).

The independent variable—the variable manipulated by the researchers—was the placement of the milk bottle. In one experimental condition, a bottle was attached to the wire mother, whereas in the other condition it was attached to the cloth mother (Figure 2.4). The dependent variable was the infant monkeys' response, notably the amount of time they spent holding onto each of the two mothers, and which mother they turned to when frightened. The researchers tested the hypothesis that the infant monkeys would cling to the terrycloth mother regardless of which mother held the bottle.

In fact, as predicted, whether the wire or the cloth surrogate was the source of milk did not matter: The infants showed a clear preference for the cloth surrogate. Harlow and Zimmerman (1959) concluded that security and comfort were more important than simple nourishment in the development of attachment (Chapter 14).

FIGURE 2.4 Surrogate mother in Harlow's monkey studies. Monkeys were separated from birth from their mothers and given the choice of spending time with a wire mother or a terrycloth mother. Regardless of which "mother" fed the baby monkey, it preferred the soft terrycloth mother, suggesting that security, not nourishment, is the basis of attachment in monkeys.

INTERIM SUMMARY

In **experimental research**, psychologists manipulate some aspect of a situation (the **independent variables**) and examine the impact on the way participants respond (the **dependent variables**). By comparing results in different experimental **conditions**, researchers can assess cause and effect.

Steps in Conducting an Experiment

Experiments vary widely in both their designs and their goals, but the steps in conceiving and executing them are roughly the same, from the starting point of framing a hypothesis to the ultimate evaluation of findings (Figure 2.5). Although these steps relate specifically to the experimental method, many apply to descriptive and correlational methods as well.

Step 1: Framing a Hypothesis　Suppose a researcher wants to investigate how mood influences memory. Most of us recognize that when we are sad, we tend to recall sad memories, and when we are happy, we remember good times. Gordon Bower (1981, 1989) and his associates developed a cognitive theory to account for this, based on the idea that having an emotion similar to an emotion one has previously experienced tends to "dredge up" (i.e., activate in memory) ideas previously associated with that feeling (Chapter 6).

To conduct an experiment, a researcher must first frame a hypothesis that predicts the relationship between two or more variables. Usually that hypothesis is derived from a theory. Thus, Bower and his colleagues hypothesized that people who are in a positive mood while learning new information will be more likely to remember pleasant aspects of that information. Conversely, people in a negative mood while learning will be more likely to remember negative information. This hypothesis states a relationship between two variables: *mood state* when learning material (the independent variable) and later ability to *recall* that material (the dependent variable).

Step 2: Operationalizing Variables　The second step in experimental research is to operationalize the variables. **Operationalizing** means *turning an abstract concept into a concrete variable defined by some set of actions, or operations*. Bower (1981) operationalized the independent variable, mood state, by hypnotizing participants to feel either happy or sad (the two conditions of the independent variable). He then had participants read a psychiatric patient's descriptions of various happy and

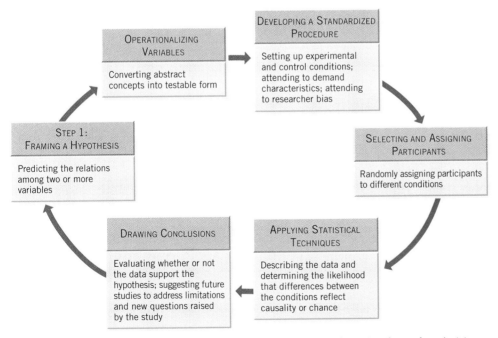

FIGURE 2.5　Conducting an experiment requires systematically going through a series of steps, from the initial framing of a hypothesis to drawing conclusions about the data. The process is circular, as the conclusion of one study is generally the origin of another.

Apply & Discuss

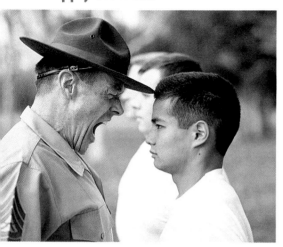

How might a researcher operationalize a variable such as the need for power? To what extent can we trust what people say about themselves when asked?

sad memories. Bower operationalized the dependent variable—the ability to recall either positive or negative information—as the number of positive and negative memories the participant could recall 20 minutes later.

Step 3: Developing a Standardized Procedure   The next step in constructing an experiment is to develop a standardized procedure, so that the only things that vary from participant to participant are the independent variables and participants' performance on the dependent variables. Standardized procedures maximize the likelihood that any differences observed in participants' behavior can be attributed to the experimental manipulation, allowing the investigator to draw inferences about cause and effect.

In Bower's study, the experiment would have been *contaminated* (i.e., ruined) if different participants had heard different stories or varying numbers of positive and negative memories. These differences might have influenced the number of positive and negative memories participants would later recall. Bower's method of inducing happy or sad mood states also had to be standardized. If the experimenter induced a negative mood in one participant by hypnotizing him and in another by asking him to try to imagine that his mother was dying, differences in recall could stem from the different ways mood was induced.

Control Groups   Experimental research typically involves dividing participants into groups who experience different conditions of the independent variable and then comparing the responses of the different groups. In Bower's experiment, one group consisted of participants who were hypnotized to be in a happy mood and another of participants hypnotized to be in a sad mood. Experiments often include another kind of group or condition, called a **control group**. *Instead of being exposed to the experimental manipulation, participants in the control group experience a neutral condition.*

Although Bower's experiment did not have a control group, a control condition for this experiment could have been a group of participants who were brought under hypnosis but not given any mood induction. By comparing participants who were induced to feel sad while reading the story with those who were not induced to feel anything, Bower could have seen whether sad participants recall more sad memories (or fewer happy ones) than neutral participants. Examining the performance of participants who have not been exposed to the experimental condition gives researchers a clearer view of the impact of the experimental manipulation.

Protecting Against Bias   Researchers try to anticipate and offset the many sources of bias that can affect the results of a study. At the most basic level, investigators must ensure that participants do not know too much about the study, because this knowledge could influence their performance. Some participants try to respond in the way they think the experimenter wants them to respond. (They are nice people but lousy participants.) They try to pick up on **demand characteristics** or *cues in the experimental situation that reveal the experimenter's purpose.* To prevent these demand characteristics from biasing results, psychologists conduct **blind studies**, *in which participants (and often the researchers themselves) are kept unaware of, or blind to, important aspects of the research.* (For example, if participants in the study of emotional expression and health had known why their subsequent health records were important, they might have avoided the doctor as long as possible if they were in the experimental group. If they believed the hypothesis, they might even have been less likely to *notice* when they were sick.)

Blind studies are especially valuable in researching the effects of medication on psychological symptoms. Participants who think they are taking a medication often find that their symptoms disappear after they have taken what is really an inert, or inactive, substance such as a sugar pill (a placebo). *Simply believing that a treatment is effective can sometimes prove as effective as the drug itself*, a phenomenon called the **placebo effect**. In a **single-blind study**, *participants are kept blind to crucial information, such as the condition to which they are being exposed* (here, placebo versus medication). In this case, the participant is blind, but the experimenter is not.

The design of an experiment should also guard against researcher bias. Experimenters are usually committed to the hypotheses they set out to test, and, being human, they might be predisposed to interpret their results in a positive light. An experimenter who expects an antianxiety medication to be more effective than a placebo may inadvertently overrate improvement in participants who receive the medication. Experimenters may also inadvertently communicate their expectations to participants—by probing for improvement more in the medication group than in the control group, for example. The best way to avoid the biases of both participants and investigators is to perform a **double-blind study**. In this case, *both participants and the researchers who interact with them are blind to who has been exposed to which experimental condition until the research is completed.* Thus, in a study assessing the efficacy of a medication for depression, an interviewer who assesses participants for depression before and after treatment should have no idea which treatment they received.

Step 4: Selecting and Assigning Participants Having developed standardized procedures, the researcher is now ready to find participants who are representative of the population of interest. Experimenters typically place participants randomly in each of the experimental conditions (such as sad mood, happy mood, or neutral mood). Random assignment is essential for internal validity, because it minimizes the chance that participants in different groups will differ in some systematic way (e.g., gender or age) that might influence their responses and lead to mistaken conclusions about cause and effect. If all participants in the sad condition were male and all those in the happy condition were female, Bower could not tell whether his participants' responses were determined by mood or by sex. In this case the sex of the participants would be a **confounding variable**, *a variable that could produce effects that are confused, or confounded, with the effects of the independent variable.* The presence of confounding variables compromises the internal validity of a study by making inferences about causality impossible.

Step 5: Applying Statistical Techniques to the Data Having selected participants and conducted the experiment, an investigator is ready to analyze the data. Analyzing data involves two tasks: The first consists of *describing the findings in a way that summarizes their essential features* (**descriptive statistics**). The second involves *drawing inferences from the sample to the population as a whole* (**inferential statistics**). Descriptive statistics, such as those discussed earlier in this chapter, are a way of taking what may be a staggeringly large set of observations, sometimes made over months or years, and putting them into a summary form that others can comprehend in a table or graph. Almost *any* time two groups are compared, differences will appear between them simply because no two groups of people are exactly alike. Determining whether the differences are meaningful or simply random is the job of inferential statistics, which yield tests of statistical significance (see Focus on Methodology: Testing the Hypothesis—Inferential Statistics).

In experimental research, the goal of inferential statistics is to test for differences between groups or conditions—to see if the independent variable really had an impact on the way participants responded. Figure 2.6 shows the results of Bower's study on mood and memory. The average number of positive and negative memories participants recalled did vary according to mood: Happy participants recalled almost 8 happy incidents but fewer than 6.5 sad ones, whereas sad participants recalled over 8 sad but fewer than 6 happy incidents. (Knowing whether those differences really mean anything requires knowing something about statistics, because a difference of 1.5 memories could be random. In this case, however, the difference was statistically significant, suggesting that it did not just occur by chance.)

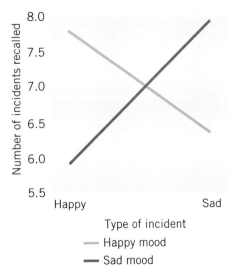

FIGURE 2.6 The influence of mood on memory. Happy participants stored and later retrieved more happy incidents, whereas sad participants were more likely to recall sad incidents. *Source:* Bower, 1981.

Step 6: Drawing Conclusions   The final step in experimental research, drawing conclusions, involves evaluating whether or not the hypothesis was supported—that is, whether the independent and dependent variables were related as predicted. Researchers also try to interpret their findings in light of the broader theoretical framework and assess their generalizability outside the laboratory.

Researchers and their theories tend to be like dogs and bones: They do not part with them easily. Although scientists try to maintain their commitment to objectivity, they typically do not spend months or years conducting an experiment testing a hypothesis they do not strongly believe. Thus, if the findings do not turn out the way they expect, they might conclude that their theory was wrong, but they are just as likely to conclude that they made some kind of error in operationalizing the variables, testing the hypothesis, or deriving the hypothesis from the broader theory. Part of drawing conclusions means figuring out what worked, what did not, and where to go from here. Thus, most published research reports conclude by acknowledging their limitations and point toward future research that might address unanswered questions. In fact, Bower and others discovered over time that some of their findings held up when they tried to replicate them and others did not. For example, negative mood states not only facilitate retrieval of negative memories, but they also motivate people to search for positive memories as a way of bringing their mood back up (Chapter 10).

INTERIM SUMMARY

The first step in conducting an experiment is to frame a hypothesis that predicts the relations among two or more variables. The second is to **operationalize** variables—to turn abstract ideas or constructs into concrete form defined by a set of actions or operations. The third step is to develop a standardized procedure so that only the variables of interest vary. In experimental research, researchers often divide participants into different groups, who experience different conditions of the independent variable. Some participants may be assigned to a **control group**—a neutral condition against which participants in various experimental conditions can be compared. The fourth step is to select samples that are as representative as possible of the population of interest. The fifth step is to analyze the data using statistical techniques. The final step is to conclude from the data whether the hypothesis was supported and whether the results are generalizable. Although these steps are best exemplified in experimental studies, most of them apply to other research designs as well.

Limitations of Experimental Research

Because experimenters can manipulate variables one at a time and observe the effects of each manipulation, experiments provide the "cleanest" findings of any research method in psychology. No other method can determine cause and effect so unambiguously. Furthermore, experiments can be *replicated*, or repeated, to see if the same findings emerge with a different sample; the results can thus be corroborated or refined.

Experimental methods do, however, have their limitations. First, for both practical and ethical reasons, many complex phenomena cannot be tested in the laboratory. A psychologist who wants to know whether divorce has a negative impact on children's intellectual development cannot manipulate people into divorcing in order to test the hypothesis. Researchers frequently have to examine phenomena as they exist in nature.

When experiments are impractical, psychologists sometimes employ **quasi-experimental designs**, which *share the logic and many features of the experimental method, but do not allow as much control over all relevant variables* (Campbell & Stanley, 1963). An experimenter interested in the impact of divorce on memory, for example, might compare the ability of children from divorced and nondivorced families to retrieve positive and negative memories. In this case, the independent variable (divorced or nondivorced) is not really something the experimenter manipulates; it is a *subject characteristic* that she uses to predict the dependent variable (memory). Because researchers have to "take subjects as they find them" in quasi-experimental designs, they have to be particularly careful to test to be sure the groups do not differ on other variables that might influence the results, such as age, gender, or socioeconomic status (social class).

Quasi-experimental designs cannot provide the degree of certainty about cause-and-effect relationships that experiments offer. Because participants cannot be randomly assigned to divorced and nondivorced groups, experimenters can only observe differences, rather than create differences by "bending nature."

A second limitation of the experimental method regards external validity. Researchers can never be certain how closely a phenomenon observed in a laboratory parallels its real-life counterparts. In some instances, such as the study that opened this chapter, the implications seem clear: If briefly writing about stressful events can improve health, imagine what talking about them with a professional over time might do. And, in fact, research shows that people who get help for *psychological* problems through psychotherapy tend to make fewer trips to the doctor for *medical* problems (Gabbard & Atkinson, 1996). In other cases, external validity is more problematic. For example, do the principles that operate in a laboratory study of decision making apply when a person decides whether to stay in a relationship (Ceci & Bronfenbrenner, 1991; Neisser, 1976a; Rogoff & Lave, 1984)?

Despite its limitations, the experimental method is the bread and butter of psychology. No research method is more definitive than a well-executed experiment. Nevertheless, few of us would desire a steady diet of bread and butter, and scientific investigation is nourished by multiple methods and many sources of data.

INTERIM SUMMARY

Experimentation is the only research method in psychology that allows researchers to draw unambiguous conclusions about cause and effect. Limitations include the difficulty of bringing some complex phenomena into the laboratory and the question of whether results apply to phenomena outside the laboratory.

Focus on Methodology
Testing the Hypothesis—Inferential Statistics

When researchers find a difference between the responses of participants in one condition and another, they must infer whether these differences likely occurred by chance or reflect a true causal relationship. Similarly, if they discover a correlation between two variables, they need to know the likelihood that the two variables simply correlated by chance.

As the philosopher David Hume (1711–1776) explained more than two centuries ago, we can never be entirely sure about the answer to questions like these. If someone believes that all swans are white and observes 99 swans that are white and none that are not, can the person conclude with certainty that the hundredth swan will also be white? The issue is one of probability: If the person has observed a representative sample of swans, what is the likelihood that, given 99 white swans, a black one will appear next?

Psychologists typically deal with this issue in their research by using tests of statistical significance, which help determine whether the results of a study are likely to have occurred simply by chance (and thus cannot be meaningfully generalized to a population) or whether they reflect true properties of the population. We should not confuse statistical significance with practical or theoretical significance. A researcher may demonstrate with a high degree of certainty that, on the average, females spend less time watching football than males, but who cares? Statistical significance means only that a finding is unlikely to be an accident of chance.

Table 2.4 ▪ ▪ Children's Prosocial Response to Another Person's Distress during the Second Year of Life			
	Percentage of Episodes in Which the Child Behaved Prosocially		
Type of Incident	Time 1	Time 2	Time 3
Witnessed distress	9	21	49
Caused distress	7	10	52

Source: Adapted from Zahn-Waxler et al., 1992a.

Big Picture φ Question 7

To what extent are psychological processes conscious or unconscious—explicit versus implicit?

Making Connections

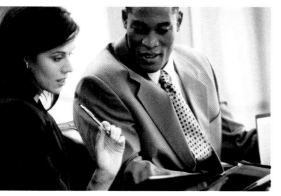

Many people think they believe in equal treatment of men and women in the workplace. However, "implicit" attitudes often show up in their behavior—as when they assign women smaller offices than men with the same level of seniority or accomplishment. The recognition that people may be of "two minds" in their attitudes toward women and men, ethnic minorities, and even themselves has led to new technologies for measuring attitudes people cannot easily report (Chapter 17).

Beyond describing the data, then, the researcher's second task is to draw inferences from the sample to the population as a whole. Inferential statistics help sort out whether or not the findings of a study really show anything. Researchers usually report the likelihood that their results mean something in terms of a **probability value** (or ***p*-value**). A p-value represents *the probability that any positive findings obtained with the sample* (such as differences between two experimental conditions) *were just a matter of chance*. In other words, a *p*-value is an index of the probability that positive findings obtained would not apply to the population and instead reflect only the peculiar characteristics of the particular sample.

To illustrate, one study tested the hypothesis that children increasingly show signs of morality and empathy during their second year (Zahn-Waxler et al., 1992a). The investigators trained 27 mothers to tape-record reports of any episode in which their one-year-olds either witnessed distress (e.g., seeing the mother burn herself on the stove) or caused distress (e.g., pulling the cat's tail or biting the mother's breast while nursing). The mothers dictated descriptions of these events over the course of the next year; each report included the child's response to the other person's distress. Coders then rated the child's behavior using categories such as prosocial behavior, defined as efforts to help the person in distress.

Table 2.4 shows the average percentage of times the children behaved prosocially during these episodes at each of three periods: time 1 (13 to 15 months of age), time 2 (18 to 20 months), and time 3 (23 to 25 months). As the table shows, the percentage of times children behaved prosocially increased dramatically over the course of the year, regardless of whether they witnessed or caused the distress. When the investigators analyzed the changes in rates of prosocial responses over time to both types of distress (witnessed and caused), they found the differences statistically significant. A jump from 9 to 49 prosocial behaviors in 12 months was thus probably not a chance occurrence.

Nevertheless, researchers can never be certain that their results are true of the population as a whole; a black swan could always be swimming in the next lake. Nor can they be sure that if they performed the study with 100 different participants they would not obtain different findings. This is why replication—repeating a study to see if the same results occur again—is extremely important in science.

Correlational Research

Correlational research *attempts to determine the degree to which two or more variables are related*, so that knowing the value (or score) on one variable allows prediction of the other. Although correlational analyses can be applied to data from any kind of study, most often correlational designs rely on survey data such as self-report questionnaires.

For example, for years psychologists have studied the extent to which personality in childhood predicts personality in adulthood (Block, 1971; Caspi, 1998). Are we the same person at age 30 as we were at age 4? In one study, researchers followed up children whose personalities were first assessed around age 9, examining their personalities again 10 years later (Shiner, 2000). They then correlated childhood person-

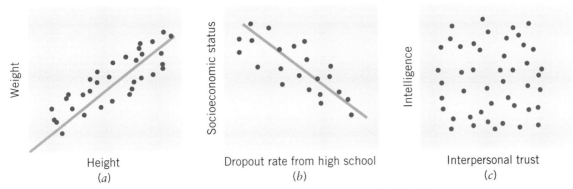

FIGURE 2.7 (*a*) Positive, (*b*) negative, and (*c*) zero correlations. A correlation expresses the relation between two variables. The panels depict three kinds of correlations on hypothetical scatterplot graphs, which show the way data points fall (are scattered) on two dimensions. Panel (*a*) shows a positive correlation, between height and weight. A comparison of the dots (which represent individual participants) on the right with those on the left shows that those on the left are lower on both variables. The dots scatter around the line that summarizes them, which is the correlation coefficient. Panel (*b*) shows a negative correlation, between socioeconomic status and drop out rate from high school. The higher the socioeconomic status, the lower the drop out rate. Panel (*c*) shows a zero correlation, between intelligence and the extent to which an individual believes people can be trusted. Being high on one dimension predicts nothing about whether the participant is high or low on the other.

ality variables with personality characteristics in late adolescence. ***To correlate two variables means to assess the extent to which being high or low on one measure predicts being high or low on the other.*** The statistic that allows a researcher to do this is called a correlation coefficient. A **correlation coefficient** *measures the extent to which two variables are related* (literally, *co-related*, or related to each other).

A correlation can be either positive or negative. A **positive correlation** means that *the higher individuals measure on one variable, the higher they are likely to measure on the other.* This also means, of course, that the lower they score on one variable, the lower they will score on the other. A **negative correlation** means that *the higher participants measure on one variable, the lower they will measure on the other.* Correlations can be depicted on *scatterplot graphs,* which show the scores of every participant along two dimensions (Figure 2.7).

Correlation coefficients vary between +1.0 and −1.0. A strong correlation—one with a value close to either positive or negative 1.0—means that a psychologist who knows a person's score on one variable can confidently predict that person's score on the other. For instance, one might expect a high positive correlation between childhood aggressiveness at age 9 and social problems at age 19 (i.e., the higher the aggressiveness, the higher the person's score on a measure of social dysfunction). One might equally expect a high *negative* correlation between childhood aggressiveness and adult academic success. A weak correlation (say, between childhood agreeableness and adult height) hovers close to zero, either on the positive or the negative side.

Importantly, variables can actually be related to one another, yet the correlation coefficient does not reflect that relationship. Correlation is an index of the linear relationship between variables. As shown in Figure 2.6, a straight line can be drawn that captures many of the data points when two variables are related in a linear fashion. Alternatively, however, variables may be related to one another in a curvilinear fashion, yet the correlation coefficient does not reflect this relationship. As shown in Figure 2.8, the relationship between arousal and performance is curvilinear, a suggestion that there is clearly a relationship between these two variables. However, because the relationship is not linear, the correlation between the two variables approaches zero.

Table 2.5 shows the correlations among three childhood personality variables—extraversion (sociability), agreeableness, and achievement motivation—and three measures of functioning in late adolescence—academic achievement, conduct (e.g.,

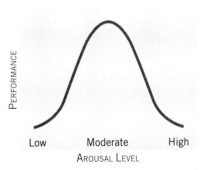

FIGURE 2.8 The relationship between arousal and performance is curvilinear. Because correlation assesses only linear relationships, the correlation coefficient reflecting the relationship between arousal and performance is close to zero.

Table 2.5 ■ ■ The Relation between Childhood Personality and Late Adolescent Functioning			
	Late Adolescent Functioning		
Childhood Personality Trait	*Academic*	*Conduct*	*Social*
Extraversion	−.07	−.14	.35
Agreeableness	.23	.33	.19
Achievement motivation	.37	.26	.25

Source: Adapted from R. L. Shiner, 2000. Linking childhood personality with adaptation: Evidence for continuity and change across time in late adolescence. *Journal of Personality and Social Psychology* 78, p. 316.

Apply & Discuss

In 1986 the Meese Commission, established by President Ronald Reagan, reviewed the evidence linking pornography to violence, particularly crimes against women. Relying primarily on correlational evidence (that men who rape tend to read pornography), the Commission concluded that pornography leads to rape.

■ What might be the problems with this conclusion?

■ What third variable might account for both rape and a preoccupation with pornography?

■ If many people read pornography but only some commit rape, what might be the relation between these two variables?

not breaking rules or committing crimes), and social functioning. These correlations are arrayed as a **correlation matrix**—*a table presenting the correlations among a number of variables.* As the table shows, childhood extraversion is not a strong predictor of academic functioning and conduct in late adolescence (in fact, if anything, extraverted kids become rowdier adolescents; the correlation coefficient, denoted by the letter *r*, = −.14). However, extraverted children do tend to become socially well-adapted adults (*r* = .35). Childhood agreeableness and achievement motivation both tend to predict positive functioning in all three domains in late adolescence.

In psychological research, theoretically meaningful correlations tend to hover around .3, and correlations above .5 are considered large (Cohen, 1988). Sometimes, however, seemingly tiny correlations can be very meaningful. For example, a study of the impact of aspirin on heart disease in a sample of roughly 20,000 subjects had to be discontinued on ethical grounds when researchers found a −.03 correlation between use of a single aspirin a day and risk of death by heart attack (Rosenthal, 1996)! This correlation translates to 15 out of 1000 people dying if they do not take an aspirin a day as a preventive measure.

The virtue of correlational research is that it allows investigators to study a whole range of phenomena that vary in nature—from personality characteristics to attitudes —but cannot be produced in the laboratory. Like other nonexperimental methods, however, correlational research can only *describe* relationships among variables (which is why it is actually sometimes categorized as a descriptive method, rather than placed in its own category). When two variables correlate with each other, the researcher must *infer* the relation between them: Does one cause the other, or does some *third variable* explain the correlation?

Media reports on scientific research often disregard or misunderstand the fact that *correlation does not imply causation.* If a study shows a correlation between drug use and poor grades, the media often report that "scientists have found that drug use leads to bad grades." That *may* be true, but an equally likely hypothesis is that some underlying aspect of personality (such as alienation) or home environment (such as poor parenting, abuse, or neglect) produces both drug use *and* bad grades (Shedler & Block, 1990).

INTERIM SUMMARY

Correlational research assesses the degree to which two variables are related; a **correlation coefficient** quantifies the association between two variables, and ranges from −1.0 to +1.0. A correlation of 0 means that two variables are not related to one another in a linear fashion, whereas a high correlation (either positive or negative) means that subjects' scores on one variable are good predictors of their scores on the other. Correlational research can shed important light on the relations among variables, but *correlation does not imply causation.*

Researching the Brain | From Brain to Behavior

The research methods psychologists use are only as powerful as the technologies and statistical tools that support them. For example, the development of a seemingly simple mathematical device—the correlation coefficient—sets the stage for psychologists to begin answering questions about the influence of heredity on traits such as intelligence, anxiety, and shyness that were previously mere topics of speculation.

In the last three decades, a powerful new set of technologies for studying the brain has revolutionized our understanding of human thought and memory (Posner & Raichle, 1996). Advances in these technologies are proceeding at such a bewildering rate that the next decade may well yield as much new knowledge about the basic mechanisms of thought, feeling, and behavior as humans have accumulated since the dawn of civilization.

Scientists began studying the functioning of the brain over a century ago by examining patients who had sustained damage or disease (lesions) to particular neural regions (Chapter 3). A major advance came in the 1930s, with the development of the **electroencephalogram**, or **EEG**, which *measures electrical activity toward the surface of the brain* (near the skull). The EEG capitalizes on the fact that every time a nerve cell fires it produces electrical activity. Researchers can measure this activity in a region of the brain's outer layers by placing electrodes on the scalp. The EEG is frequently used to diagnose disorders such as epilepsy as well as to study neural activity during sleep. It has also been used to examine questions such as whether the two hemispheres of the brain respond differently to stimuli that evoke positive versus negative emotions—and they do (Davidson, 1995).

A technological breakthrough that is revolutionizing our understanding of brain and behavior occurred when scientists discovered ways to use X-ray technology and other methods to produce pictures of soft tissue (rather than the familiar bone X-rays), such as the living brain. **Neuroimaging techniques** *use computer programs to convert the data taken from brain-scanning devices into visual images of the brain. One of the first neuroimaging techniques to be developed was* **computerized axial tomography**, *commonly known as a* **CT scan** *or* **CAT scan**. A CT scanner rotates an X-ray tube around a person's head, producing a series of X-ray pictures. A computer then combines these pictures into a composite visual image. Computerized tomography scans can pinpoint the location of abnormalities such as neuronal degeneration and abnormal tissue growths (tumors). A related technology, **magnetic resonance imaging (MRI)**, is *a neuroimaging technique that produces similar results without using X-rays.*

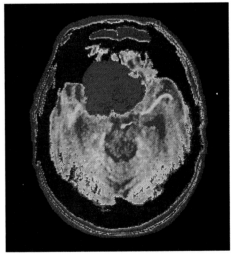

A CT scan of a patient with a tumor (shown in purple).

It was only a matter of time before scientists developed two imaging techniques that actually allow researchers to observe the brain in action rather than simply detect neural damage. These techniques rely on properties of cells in the brain that can be measured, such as the amount of blood that flows to cells that have just been activated. Thus, researchers can directly observe what occurs in the brain as participants solve mathematical problems, watch images, or retrieve memories.

Positron emission tomography (PET) is *a neuroimaging method that requires injection of a small quantity of radioactive glucose* (too small a dose to be dangerous) *into the bloodstream*. Nerve cells use glucose for energy, and they replenish their supply from the bloodstream. As these cells use glucose that has been radioactively "tagged," a computer produces a color portrait of the brain, showing which parts are active. The results of such investigations are changing our understanding of diseases such as schizophrenia, as researchers can administer tasks to patients and find the neural pathways on which they diverge from individuals without the disorder (e.g., Andreasen, 1999; Heckers et al., 1999; Spence et al., 2000).

Another technique, called **functional magnetic resonance imaging (fMRI)**, *uses MRI to watch the brain as an individual carries out tasks* such as solving

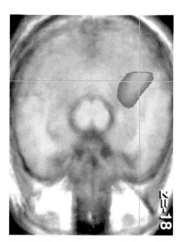

FIGURE 2.9 An averaged view of the working brain using fMRI. The red and yellow show the areas of the brain that were significantly more active while participants were forming mental images than when they were performing a control task.

mathematical problems or looking at emotionally evocative pictures (Rickard et al., 2000; Puce et al., 1996). Functional MRI works by exposing the brain to pulses of a phenomenally strong magnet (strong enough to lift a truck) and measuring the response of chemicals in blood cells going to and from various regions, which become momentarily "lined up" in the direction of the magnet.

For example, one research team used fMRI to study the parts of the brain that are active when people generate mental images, such as of a horse, an apple, or a house (D'Esposito et al., 1997). When we conjure up a picture of a horse in our minds, do we activate different parts of the brain from those when we simply hear about an object but do not picture it? In other words, how are memories *represented* in our brains? Do we actually form visual images or do we really think in words?

The investigators set out to answer this question by asking seven participants to carry out two tasks with their eyes closed, while their heads were surrounded by the powerful magnet of the MRI scanner. In the first experimental condition, participants listened to 40 concrete words and were asked to try to picture them in their minds. In the second condition, they listened to 40 words that are difficult to picture (such as "treaty" and "guilt") and were asked simply to listen to them. (This is called a *within-subjects* experimental design, because instead of placing each subject in one condition or the other, each subject is exposed to *both* conditions. Differences in the way subjects respond to the two conditions are then compared within, rather than across, subjects.)

The experimenters then used fMRI to measure whether the same or different parts of the brain were activated under the two conditions. They hypothesized that when people actually picture objects, their brains would show activity in regions involved in forming and remembering visual images and their meanings, regions that are also activated when people actually see an object, such as a horse. In contrast, when people just hear words, these vision centers should not be active—the finding of the investigators, as can be seen in Figure 2.9.

Researchers are still a long way from mapping the microdetails of the brain. The *resolution*, or sharpness, of the images produced by most scanning techniques is still too fuzzy to allow psychologists to pinpoint, for example, the different neural networks activated when a person feels guilty versus sad or angry. Further, people's brains differ, so that a single map will not work precisely for every person; averaging the responses of several participants can thus sometimes lead to imprecise results. Nevertheless, if progress made in the last decade is any indication, imaging techniques will continue to increase in precision at a dazzling pace, and so will our knowledge of brain and behavior.

A Global Vista · Cross-Cultural Research

To some degree, human nature is the same everywhere because the brain and its genetic blueprints are so similar. But the *expression* of those blueprints can be as varied as an adobe hut and a high-rise apartment. Determining the extent to which psychological findings in one culture apply to people around the globe presents challenges as important and difficult as brain mapping.

Many cross-cultural investigations in psychology involve naturalistic observation supplemented with quantitative methods. For example, when Western researchers wanted to explore the origins of social behavior in infants reared in a culture very different from their own, they studied Efe pygmies in the tropical rain forests of Zaire, who survive by hunting, gathering food, and trading with neighboring agricultural peoples (Tronick et al., 1992). The Efe establish camps composed of huts arranged in a semicircle, usually consisting of about 20 people. Researchers armed with laptop computers recorded minute-by-minute observations of the social life of Efe infants and toddlers in the camps. They found that, unlike Western children, who are groomed for independence, Efe children are surrounded by other people virtually every hour of their lives, preparing them well for a communal lifestyle as adults.

Other researchers rely on correlational and experimental methods to investigate psychological phenomena across cultures. For example, psychologists have used experimental procedures in other countries to test whether the findings of Western studies replicate cross-culturally, such as studies of perception and obedience to authority (see Berry et al., 1992, 1997; Triandis, 1994).

Psychologists interested in the cross-cultural validity of their theories face many difficulties, however, in transporting research from one culture to another. The same stimulus may mean very different things to people in different cultures. How might the Efe, who have had minimal exposure to photographs, respond to a study asking them to judge what emotion people are feeling from pictures of faces? Creating an equivalent experimental design often requires using a *different* design, but then is it really the same experiment?

Similarly, when employing a questionnaire cross-culturally, researchers must be very careful about translation because even minor changes or ambiguities could make cross-cultural comparisons invalid. To minimize distortions in translation, researchers use a procedure called *back-translation*, in which a bilingual speaker translates the items into the target language, and another bilingual speaker translates it back into the original language (usually English). The speakers then repeat the process until the translation back into English matches the original. Even this procedure is not always adequate; sometimes concepts simply differ too much across cultures to make the items equivalent. Asking a participant to rate the item "I have a good relationship with my brother" would be inappropriate in Japan, where speakers distinguish between older and younger brothers and lack a general term to denote both (Brislin, 1986).

Once again reality poses obstacles to research, but we have to try to hurdle them if we want to make generalizations about *people* rather than particular *peoples*.

Life among the Efe people.

INTERIM SUMMARY

Researchers study the relation between mental and neural processes using a number of methods, including case studies of patients with brain damage, experimental lesion studies with animals, **EEGs**, and computerized **neuroimaging techniques** that allow researchers to study the brain in action, such as **CT, PET**, and **fMRI**. Cross-cultural research attempts to assess the extent to which psychological processes vary across cultures. Researchers studying psychological phenomena cross-culturally use various methods, including naturalistic observation, correlational studies linking one cultural trait to another, and experiments.

How to Evaluate a Study Critically

Having explored the major research designs, we now turn to the question of how to be an informed consumer of research. In deciding whether to "buy" the results of a study, the same maxim applies as in buying a car: *caveat emptor*—let the buyer beware. The popular media often report that "researchers at Harvard have found…" followed by conclusions that are tempting to take at face value. In reality, most studies have their limitations. To evaluate a study critically, the reader should examine the research carefully and attempt to answer seven broad questions.

1. **Does the theoretical framework make sense?** This question encompasses a number of others. Does the specific hypothesis make sense, and does it flow logically from the broader theory? Are terms defined logically and consistently? For example, if the study explores the relation between social class and intelligence, does the article explain why social class and intelligence should have some relationship to each other? Are the two terms defined the same way throughout the study?

2. **Is the sample adequate and appropriate?** A second question is whether the sample represents the population of interest. If researchers want to know about emotional expression and health in undergraduates, then a sample of undergraduates is perfectly appropriate. If they truly want to generalize to other populations, however, they may need additional samples, such as adults drawn from the local community, or people from Bali, to see if the effects hold. Another question is *sample size*: To test a hypothesis, the sample has to be large enough to determine whether the results are meaningful or accidental. A sample of six rolls of the dice that twice produces "snake eyes" is not sufficient to conclude that the dice are loaded because the "results" could easily happen by chance.

3. **Are the measures and procedures adequate?** Once again, this question encompasses a number of issues. Do the measures assess what they were designed to assess? Were proper control groups chosen to rule out alternative explanations and to assure the validity of the study? Did the investigators carefully control for confounding variables? For example, if the study involved interviews, were some of the interviewers male and some female? If so, did the gender of the interviewer affect how participants responded?

4. **Are the data conclusive?** The central question here is whether the data demonstrate what the author claims. Typically, data in research articles are presented in a section entitled "Results," usually in the form of graphs, charts, or tables. To evaluate a study, a researcher must carefully examine the data presented in these figures and ask whether any alternative interpretations could explain the results as well as or better than the researcher's explanation. Often, data permit many interpretations, and the findings may fit a pattern that the researcher rejected or did not consider.

5. **Are the broader conclusions warranted?** Even when the results "come out" as hypothesized, researchers have to be careful to draw the right conclusions, particularly as they pertain to the broader theory or phenomenon. A researcher who finds that children who watch aggressive television shows are more likely to hit other children can conclude that the two are correlated, but not that watching aggressive shows causes violence. An equally plausible hypothesis is that violent children prefer to watch violent television shows—or perhaps that violent television shows trigger actual violence only in children who are already predisposed to violence.

6. **Does the study say anything meaningful?** This is the "so what?" test. Does the study tell us anything we did not already know? Does it lead to questions for future research? The meaningfulness of a study depends in part on the importance, usefulness, and adequacy of the theoretical perspective from which it derives. Important studies tend to produce findings that are in some way surprising or help choose between opposing theories (Abelson, 1995).

7. **Is the study ethical?** Finally, if the study uses human or animal subjects, does it treat them humanely, and do the ends of the study—the incremental knowledge it produces—justify the means? Individual psychologists were once free to make

ethical determinations on their own. Today, however, the American Psychological Association (APA) publishes guidelines that govern psychological research practices (APA, 1973, 1997), and universities and other institutions have *institutional review boards* that review proposals for psychological studies, with the power to reject them or ask for substantial revisions to protect the welfare of participants. In fact, most people would be surprised to learn just how much effort is involved in getting institutional approval for the most benign studies, such as studies of memory or mathematical ability.

Ethical Questions Come in Shades of Gray

One Step Further

The ethical issues involved in research are not always black and white. Two central issues concern the use of deception and the use of animals in research. Both relate to the issue of **informed consent**—*the participant's ability to agree (or refuse) to participate in an informed manner*.

Deception in Psychological Research

Many studies keep participants blind to the aims of the investigation until the end; some go further by giving participants a "cover story" to make sure they do not "catch on" to the hypothesis being tested. For example, in one experiment researchers wanted to study the conditions under which people can be induced to make false confessions (Kassin & Kiechel, 1996). They led college student participants to believe that they would be taking a typing test with another participant, who was really an accomplice, or *confederate*, of the experimenters. The experimenters explicitly instructed the participants not to touch the ALT key on the computer, since that would allegedly make the computer crash, and all data would be lost. Sixty seconds into the task, the computer seemed to stop functioning, and the experimenter rushed into the room accusing the participant of having hit the forbidden key.

To assess whether false incriminating evidence could convince people that they had actually done something wrong, in one condition the confederate (allegedly simply waiting to take the test herself) "admitted" having seen the participant hit the ALT key. In a control condition, the accomplice denied having seen anything. The striking finding was that in the experimental condition about half of the participants came to believe that they *had* hit the key and destroyed the experiment. Obviously, if they had known what the experiment was really about, the experiment would not have worked.

Only a small proportion of experiments actually involve deception, and APA guidelines permit deception only if a study meets four conditions: (1) The research is of great importance and cannot be conducted without deception; (2) participants can be expected to find the procedures reasonable once they are informed after the experiment; (3) participants can withdraw from the experiment at any time; and (4) experimenters *debrief* the participants afterward, explaining the purposes of the study and removing any stressful aftereffects. Many universities address the issue of deception by asking potential participants if they would object to being deceived temporarily in a study. That way, any participant who is deceived by an experimenter has given prior consent to be deceived.

Ethics and Animal Research

A larger ethical controversy concerns the use of nonhuman animals for psychological research (Bersoff, 1999; Petrinovich, 1999; Ulrich, 1991). By lesioning a region of a rat's brain, for example, researchers can sometimes learn a tremendous

Apply & Discuss

■ Is it possible to obtain informed consent from people who are seriously disturbed or mentally retarded? If not, should we suspend all research on these populations, even if this research could lead to substantial improvements in their quality of life?

■ What about research with children, who cannot be expected to understand the implications of participating or not participating?

amount about the function of similar regions in the human brain. Such experiments, however, have an obvious cost to the animal, raising questions about the moral status of animals, that is, whether they have rights (Plous, 1996; Regan, 1997). Again the issue is how to balance costs and benefits: To what extent do the costs to animals justify the benefits to humans? The problem, of course, is that, unlike humans, animals cannot give informed consent.

To what extent humans can use other sentient creatures (i.e., animals who feel) to solve human problems is a difficult moral question. Some animal rights groups argue that animal research in psychology has produced little of value to humans, especially considering the enormous suffering animals have undergone. Most psychologists, however, disagree (King, 1991; Miller, 1985). Animal research has led to important advances in behavior therapy, treatments for serious disorders such as Alzheimer's disease (a degenerative brain illness that leads to loss of mental functions and ultimately death), and insight into nearly every area of psychological functioning, from stress and emotion to the effects of aging on learning and memory. The difficulty lies in balancing the interests of humans with those of other animals and advancing science while staying within sensible ethical boundaries (Bowd, 1990). Accordingly, institutional review boards examine proposals for experiments with nonhuman animals as they do with human participants and similarly veto or require changes in proposals they deem unethical.

INTERIM SUMMARY

To evaluate a study, a critical reader should ask a number of questions regarding the theoretical framework, the sample, the measures and procedures, the results, the broader conclusions drawn, and the ethics of the research.

Summary

Characteristics of Good Psychological Research

1. Good psychological research is characterized by a theoretical framework, standardized procedures, generalizability, and objective measurement.

2. A **theory** is a systematic way of organizing and explaining observations that includes a set of propositions about the relations among various phenomena. A **hypothesis** is a tentative belief or educated guess that purports to predict or explain the relationship between two or more variables; **variables** are phenomena that differ or change across circumstances or individuals. A variable that can be placed on a continuum is a **continuous variable**. A variable comprised of groupings or categories is a **categorical variable**.

3. A **sample** is a subgroup of a **population** that is likely to be **representative** of the population as a whole. **Generalizability** refers to the applicability of findings based on a sample to the entire population of interest. For a study's findings to be generalizable, its methods must be sound, or **valid**.

4. A **measure** is a concrete way of assessing a variable. A good measure is both reliable and valid. **Reliability** refers to a measure's ability to produce consistent results. The **validity** of a measure refers to its ability to assess the construct it is intended to measure.

Descriptive Research

5. **Descriptive research** cannot unambiguously demonstrate cause and effect because it describes phenomena as they already exist rather than manipulates variables to test the effects. Descriptive methods include case studies, naturalistic observation, and survey research.

6. A **case study** is an in-depth observation of one person or a small group of people. **Naturalistic observation** is the in-depth observation of a phenomenon in its natural setting. Both case studies and naturalistic observation are vulnerable to researcher bias—the tendency of investigators to see what they expect to see. **Survey research** involves asking a large sample of people questions, often about attitudes or behaviors, using **questionnaires** or **interviews**.

Experimental Research

7. In **experimental research**, investigators manipulate some aspect of a situation and examine the impact on the way participants respond in order to assess cause and effect. **Independent variables** are the variables the experimenter manipulates; **dependent variables** are the participants' responses, which indicate if the manipulation had an effect.

8. Conducting an experiment—or most other kinds of research—entails a series of steps: framing a hypothesis, operationalizing variables, developing a standardized procedure, selecting participants, testing the results for statistical significance, and drawing conclusions. **Operationalizing** means turning an abstract concept into a concrete variable defined by some set of actions, or operations.

9. A **control group** is a neutral condition of an experiment in which participants are not exposed to the experimental manipulation. Researchers frequently perform **blind studies**, in which participants are kept unaware of, or "blind" to, important aspects of the research. In a **single-blind study**, only participants are kept blind; in **double-blind studies**, participants and researchers alike are blind.

10. A **confounding variable** is a variable that could produce effects that might be confused with the effects of the independent variable.

11. Experimental studies provide the strongest evidence in psychology because they can establish cause and effect. The major limitations of experimental studies include the difficulty bringing some important phenomena into the laboratory and issues of external validity (applicability of the results to phenomena outside the laboratory).

Correlational Research

12. **Correlational research** assesses the degree to which two variables are related, in an effort to see whether knowing the value of one can lead to prediction of the other. A **correlation coefficient** measures the extent to which two variables are related. A **positive correlation** between two variables means that the higher individuals measure on one variable, the higher they are likely to measure on the other. A **negative correlation** means that the higher individuals measure on one variable, the lower they will measure on the other, and vice versa. *Correlation does not demonstrate causation.*

13. Researchers studying the relation between mental and neural processes use a number of methods, including case studies of patients with brain damage, experimental lesion studies with animals, **EEGs**, and computerized **neuroimaging techniques**, such as **CT, PET**, and **fMRI**.

14. Researchers studying psychological phenomena cross-culturally use studies linking one cultural trait to another, and experiments.

How to Evaluate a Study Critically

15. To evaluate a study, a critical reader should answer several broad questions: (a) Does the theory make sense, and do the hypotheses flow sensibly from it? (b) Is the sample adequate and appropriate? (c) Are the measures and procedures valid and reliable? (d) Are the data conclusive? (e) Are the broader conclusions warranted? (f) Does the study say anything meaningful? (g) Is the study ethical?

Key Terms

blind studies   46
case study   38
categorical variable   33
computerized axial tomographs
    (CT or CAT scans)   53
conditions   44
confounding variable   47
construct validity   37
continuous variable   33
control group   46
correlate   51
correlational research   50
correlation coefficient   51
correlation matrix   52
criterion validity   37
demand characteristics   46
dependent variables   44
descriptive research   38
descriptive statistics   47

double-blind study   47
electroencephalogram
    (EEG)   53
error   37
experimental research   43
experimenter's dilemma   34
external validity   34
face validity   36
functional magnetic resonance
    imaging (fMRI)   53
generalizability   34
hypothesis   32
independent variables   44
inferential statistics   47
informed consent   57
interitem reliability   36
internal consistency   36
internal validity   34
interrater reliability   36

interviews   40
magnetic resonance imaging
    (MRI)   53
mean   42
measure   35
median   42
mode   42
modal score   42
naturalistic observation   39
negative correlation   51
neuroimaging techniques   53
operationalizing   45
participants *or* subjects   34
placebo effect   47
population   34
positive correlation   51
positron emission tomography
    (PET)   53
probability value (p-value)   50

quasi-experimental designs   48
questionnaires   40
random sample   41
range   42
reliability   36
representative   34
sample   34
single-blind study   47
standard deviation   42
standardized procedures   34
stratified random sample   41
survey research   40
test-retest reliability   36
theory   32
valid   34
validity   36
variability of scores   42
variable   32

Biological Bases of Mental Life and Behavior

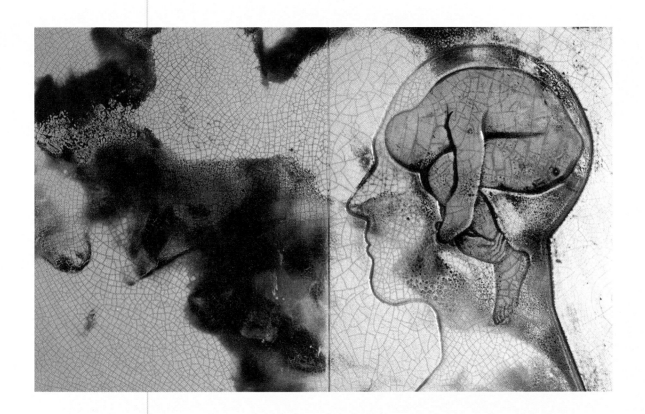

n 1917, an epidemic broke out in Vienna that quickly spread throughout the world. The disease was a mysterious sleeping sickness called *encephalitis lethargica. Encephalitis* refers to an inflammation of the central nervous system that results from infection. (*Lethargica* simply referred to the fact that extreme lethargy, or lack of energy, was a defining feature of the disease.) The infection that led to the disease was thought to be viral, although the viral agent was never discovered. The epidemic disappeared as unexpectedly as it appeared—but not until 10 years had passed and 5 million people had fallen ill to it (Cheyette & Cummings, 1995; Sacks, 1993).

The acute phase of the illness (when symptoms were most intense) was characterized by extreme states of arousal. Some patients were so underaroused that they seemed to sleep for weeks; others became so hyperaroused that they could not sleep at all (Sacks, 1973). Roughly one-third of the victims died during the acute phase, but those who seemingly recovered had no idea what would affect them in the future. Delayed-onset symptoms typically arose 5 to 10 years later and were remarkably diverse, including severe depression, mania (a state of extreme grandiosity, extraordinarily high energy, and little need for sleep), sexual perversions, abnormal twitching movements, sudden episodes in which the person would shout obscenities, and, in children, severe conduct problems (Cheyette & Cummings, 1995).

For most of the survivors of the epidemic, the most striking and tragic symptom was brain deterioration in the years following the acute phase of the illness, leaving many in a virtual state of sleep for almost 40 years. These survivors were aware of their surroundings, but they did not seem to be fully awake. They were motionless and speechless, without energy, motivation, emotion, or appetite. And they remained in that stuporous state until the development of a new drug in the 1960s. The drug, L-dopa, suddenly awakened many from their slumbers by restoring a chemical in the brain that the virus had destroyed. (Their story was the basis of a movie, *Awakenings*, based on the book by neurologist Oliver Sacks, 1973.)

Ms. B contracted a severe form of *encephalitis lethargica* when she was 18. Although she recovered in a few months, she began to show signs of the post-encephalitic disorder four years later. For almost half a century she was unable—for long periods of time—to perform any voluntary movements, speak, or even blink. Ms. B was not in a coma. She was somewhat aware of the events around her but could not react to them physically or emotionally.

Ms. B began to come alive within days of receiving L-dopa. After one week, she started to speak. Within two weeks she was able to write, stand up, and walk between parallel bars. Eventually her emotions returned, and she reestablished contact with her family—or what was left of it. She had "fallen asleep" a vibrant young woman of 22. She "awakened" a woman of 67.

To comprehend Ms. B's experience requires an understanding of the **nervous system**—*the interacting network of nerve cells that underlies all psychological activity*. We begin by examining the neuron, or nerve cell, and the way neurons communicate with one another to produce thought, feeling, and behavior. After briefly exploring the hormones that work together with chemicals in the nervous system to create psychological experience, we then consider the extraordinary organization of the billions of neurons in the central nervous system (the brain and spinal cord) and in the peripheral nervous system (neurons in the rest of the body). We conclude with a brief discussion of the role of genetics and evolution in understanding human mental processes and behavior.

Throughout, we wrestle with some thorny questions about the way these physical mechanisms are translated into psychological meanings. Indeed, a question that runs throughout this chapter is the extent to which we can separate the mental and the physical. Can we study psychological processes—thoughts, feelings, wishes, hopes, and dreams—as if they were independent of the brain that embodies them? Alternatively, can we reduce the pain of a jilted lover or a grieving widow to the neural circuits that regulate emotion? Is our subjective experience little more than a shadow cast by our neurons, hormones, and genes?

Big Picture φ Question 1

To what extent can mental processes be reduced to the brain or body?

Neurons: Basic Units of the Nervous System

The fundamental unit of the nervous system is the **neuron**. These cells are specialized for electrical and chemical communication, thereby helping to coordinate all of the functions of the body. Appreciating a sunset, swaying to music, pining for a lover 500 miles away, or praying for forgiveness— all of these acts reflect the coordinated action of thousands or millions of neurons. We do not, of course, *experience* ourselves as systems of interacting nerve cells, any more than we experience hunger as the depletion of sugar in the bloodstream. We think, we feel, we hurt, we want. But we do all these things through the silent, behind-the-scenes activity of neurons, which carry information from cell to cell within the nervous system as well as to and from muscles and organs. No one knows how many neurons are in the nervous system; the best estimates range from 10 to 100 billion in the brain alone (Stevens, 1979). Some neurons connect with as many as 30,000 neurons, although the average neuron transmits information to about 1000 (Damasio, 1994).

The nervous system is comprised of three kinds of neurons: sensory neurons, motor neurons, and interneurons. **Sensory neurons** (also called **afferent neurons**) *transmit information from sensory cells in the body, called receptors* (i.e., cells that *receive* sensory information) *to the brain* (either directly or by way of the spinal cord). Thus, sensory neurons might send information to the brain about the sensations perceived as a sunset or a sore throat. **Motor neurons** (also called **efferent neurons**) *transmit information to the muscles and glands of the body, most often through the spinal cord*. Motor neurons carry out both voluntary actions, such as grabbing a glass of water, and vital bodily functions, such as digestion and heartbeat. **Interneurons** *pass information between the various sensory and motor neurons*. The vast majority of neurons in the brain and spinal cord are interneurons.

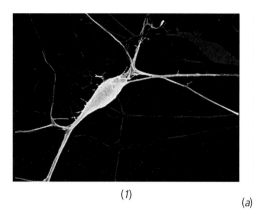

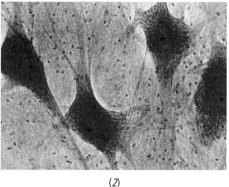

(1)

(2)

(a)

FIGURE 3.1 The anatomy of a neuron. (*a*) Neurons differ in their shape throughout the nervous system. Photo (*1*) shows a neuron in the most evolutionarily recent part of the brain, the cerebral cortex, which is involved in the most complex psychological processes. Photo (*2*) shows neurons in the spinal cord, which is a much older structure. (These images were magnified using an electron microscope.) (*b*) The dendrites receive neural information from other neurons and pass it down the axon. The terminal buttons then release neurotransmitters, chemicals that transmit information to other cells.

Anatomy of a Neuron

A single neuron has no function if there are no other neurons with which to communicate. Nevertheless each neuron has a characteristic structure that optimizes its function of communication. *Branchlike extensions of the neuron*, called **dendrites** (Figure 3.1), *receive inputs from other cells*. The **cell body** *includes a nucleus that contains the genetic material of the cell* (the *chromosomes*). The nucleus, with its genetic blueprints, is the "brains" of the operation, which determines how that particular neuron will manipulate the input from the dendrites. If a neuron receives enough stimulation through its dendrites and cell body, it passes the manipulated input to the dendrites of other neurons through its axon. The **axon** is *a long extension from the cell body*—occasionally as long as several feet—*whose central function is to transmit information to other neurons*. Axons often have two or more offshoots, or collateral branches.

The axons of most neurons in the nervous system are covered with a **myelin sheath**, *a tight coat of cells composed primarily of lipids* (fats) *that facilitates transmission of information to other neurons*. Myelinated axons give some portions of the brain a white appearance (hence the term "white matter"). The "gray matter" of the brain gets its color from cell bodies, dendrites, and unmyelinated axons.

The myelin sheath, derived from **glial cells**, insulates the axon from chemical and physical stimuli that might interfere with the transmission of nerve impulses, much as the coating of a wire prevents electrical currents from getting crossed. The myelin sheath also dramatically increases the speed of transmission of messages (Stevens & Field, 2000). It does this by capitalizing on the fact that between the cells that form the sheath are small spaces of "bare wire" called *nodes of Ranvier*. When a neuron fires (is activated enough to send information to other neurons), the electrical impulse is rapidly conducted from node to node.

Not all axons are myelinated at birth. The transmission of impulses along these axons is slow and arduous—an explanation of why babies have such poor motor control. As myelination occurs in areas of the nervous system involved in motor action, an infant becomes capable of reaching and pointing. Such developmental achievements can be reversed in *demyelinating* diseases such as multiple sclerosis. In these disorders, degeneration of the myelin sheath on large clusters of axons can cause jerky, uncoordinated movement, although for reasons not well understood the disease often goes into remission and the symptoms temporarily disappear. Multiple sclerosis and other diseases that progressively strip axons of their myelin (such as Lou Gehrig's disease) may be fatal, particularly if they strike the neurons that control basic life-support processes such as the beating of the heart.

At the end of an axon are **terminal buttons**, *which send signals from a neuron to adjacent cells*. These signals are triggered by the electrical impulse that has traveled down the axon and been received by the dendrites or cell bodies of other neu-

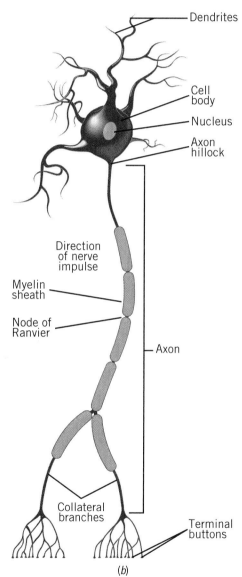

Dendrites

Cell body

Nucleus

Axon hillock

Direction of nerve impulse

Myelin sheath

Node of Ranvier

Axon

Collateral branches

Terminal buttons

(b)

rons. *Connections between neurons occur at* **synapses**. Two cells do not actually touch at a synapse; instead, a space exists between the two neurons, called the *synaptic cleft*. (Not all synapses work quite the same way. For example, in the brain, many synapses are located on parts of the cell other than the dendrites. Elsewhere in the nervous system, neurons may send their signals to glands or muscles rather than to other neurons.) The synapse is the most important functional unit of the nervous system (LeDoux, 2000), as attested to by the fact that the earliest stages of Alzheimer's disease involve dysfunction of synapses in areas of the brain related to memory (Selkoe, 2002).

INTERIM SUMMARY

The nervous system is the interacting network of nerve cells that underlies all psychological activity. **Neurons** are the basic units of the nervous system. **Sensory (afferent) neurons** carry sensory information from sensory receptors to the central nervous system. **Motor (efferent) neurons** transmit commands from the brain to the glands and muscles of the body. **Interneurons** connect neurons with one another. Neurons generally have a **cell body, dendrites** (branchlike extensions of the cell body), and an **axon** that carries information to other neurons. Neurons connect at **synapses**.

Firing of a Neuron

Most neurons communicate at the synapse through a process that involves the conversion of the electrical charge in one neuron to a chemical "message." When this message is released into the synapse, it alters the electrical charge of the next neuron. Most neurons receive inputs from many other neurons and provide output to many neurons as well. The overall pattern of neural activation distributed across many thousands of neurons gives rise to the changes we experience in our thoughts and feelings. Before we can hope to understand this cavalcade of neural fireworks, we must examine the events that energize a single resting neuron so that it fires off a chemical message to its neighbors.

The Resting Potential   When a neuron is "at rest," its membrane is *polarized*, like two sides of a battery: The inside of the cell membrane is negatively charged relative to the fluid outside of the neuron, which has a positive charge. As the name **resting potential** implies, this is *the potential when the neuron is at rest—that is, when it is not communicating but is ready to communicate when needed*. (It is called a *potential* because the cell has a stored-up source of energy, which has the potential to be used.) In fact, at rest, the electrical difference between the inside and the outside of the axon is –70 millivolts (mV). (A volt is a standard unit of electricity, and a millivolt is one-thousandth of a volt.) Researchers discovered this by inserting tiny electrodes (materials that conduct electricity) on the inside and the outside of the cell membrane of animals with the largest neurons they could find (giant squid neurons) and measuring the electrical potential across the membrane.

The membrane is kept in this state of readiness as a function of specific membrane-bound proteins (sometimes called "pumps") that keep sodium ions (Na^+) and chloride ions (CL^-) outside the cell and keep potassium ions (K^+) inside the cell. (An ion is an atom or small molecule that carries an electrical charge.) Naturally, these ions want to be equally distributed inside and outside the cell. However, the cell membrane of a neuron is typically not permeable to positively charged sodium ions—that is, these ions cannot easily get through the membrane—so they tend to accumulate outside the neuron. The membrane is also completely impermeable to a variety of negatively charged protein ions inside the cell that are involved in carrying out its basic functions. As a result, the electrical charge is normally more negative on the inside than on the outside of the cell. Without the sodium–potassium pump, the ions would reach a state of equilibrium in which they were equally distributed. In fact, this is what happens when the dentist numbs your mouth with Novocaine. The Novocaine interrupts the ability of the membrane to keep the unequal balance of sodium and potassium. Without this imbalance, the nerves that tell your brain that there is pain in your mouth do not work, even though the tissue is being irritated. Because the nerves are not doing their job, your brain doesn't know about the pain.

Graded Potentials   When a neuron is stimulated by another neuron, one of two things can happen. The stimulation can reduce the membrane's polarization, decreasing the voltage discrepancy between the inside and the outside. For instance, the resting potential might move from –70 to –60 mV. This movement *excites* the neuron—that is, with further stimulation renders it more likely to fire. Alternatively, stimulation from another neuron can increase polarization. This inhibits the neuron—that is, renders it less likely to fire.

Typically, a decrease in polarization—called *depolarization*—stems from an influx of positive sodium ions. As a result, the charge inside the cell membrane becomes less negative, making it more likely to fire if it is further stimulated. The opposite state—increasing the electrical difference between the inside and outside of the cell—is called *hyperpolarization*. This condition usually results from an outflow of potassium ions, which are also positively charged, or an influx of negatively charged chloride ions; as a result, the potential across the membrane becomes even more negative, making the neuron less likely to fire.

Most of these brief voltage changes occur at synapses along the neuron's dendrites and cell body; they then spread down the cell membrane like ripples on a pond. These **spreading voltage changes, which occur when the neural membrane receives a signal from another cell**, are called **graded potentials**. Graded potentials have two notable characteristics. First, their strength diminishes as they travel along the cell membrane away from the source of the stimulation, just as the ripples on a pond grow smaller with distance from a tossed stone's point of impact. Second, graded potentials are cumulative, or additive. If a neuron is simultaneously depolarized by +2 mV at one point on a dendrite and hyperpolarized by –2 mV at an adjacent point, the two graded potentials add up to zero and essentially cancel each other out. In contrast, if the membrane of a neuron is depolarized at multiple points, a progressively greater influx of positive ions occurs, producing a "ripple" all the way down the cell body to the axon.

Action Potentials   If this cumulative electrical "ripple" crosses a certain threshold, depolarizing the membrane at the axon from its resting state of –70 mV to about –50 mV, a sudden change occurs. For an instant, the membrane is totally permeable to positive sodium ions, which have accumulated outside the membrane. These ions pour in, changing the potential across the membrane to about +40 mV (Figure 3.2). Thus, the charge on the inside of the cell momentarily becomes positive. An outpouring of positive potassium ions then rapidly restores the neuron to its resting potential, rendering the charge inside the cell negative once again. This entire electrochemical process typically takes less than 2 milliseconds (msec, or thousandths of a second).

The shift in polarity across the membrane and subsequent restoration of the resting potential is called an **action potential**, or **the "firing" of the neuron**. The action potential rapidly spreads down the length of the axon to the terminal buttons, as ions pour in and out (Figure 3.2*a*). Unlike a graded potential, an action potential (or nerve impulse) is not cumulative. Instead, it has an all-or-none quality: The action potential either occurs or does not. In this sense, the firing of a neuron is like the firing of a gun. Unless the trigger is pulled hard enough, the amount of pressure placed on the trigger below that threshold does not matter. Once the threshold is crossed, however, the trigger gives way, the gun fires, and the trigger springs back, ready to be pulled once more. Although action potentials seem more dramatic, in many ways the prime movers behind psychological processes are graded potentials. Graded potentials cre-

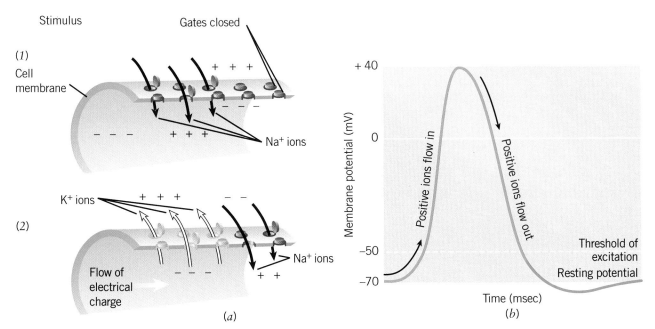

FIGURE 3.2   An action potential. (*a*) Initially, when the axon is depolarized at a specific locus (*1*), the "floodgates" open, and sodium ions (Na+) come rushing in. Immediately afterward (*2*), the gates close to those ions, and potassium ions (K+) come rushing back out, restoring the potential to its resting negative state. This process, however, leads to depolarization of the next segment of the cell's membrane, spreading down the axon. (*b*) This graph depicts the firing of a neuron as recorded by nearby electrodes. When a neuron is depolarized to about −50 mV (the threshold of excitation), an influx of positively charged ions briefly creates an action potential. An outpouring of positive ions then contributes to restoring the neuron to its resting potential. (This outpouring actually overshoots the mark briefly, so that for a brief instant after firing the potential across the membrane is slightly more negative than −70 mV.)

ate new information at the cellular level by allowing the cell to integrate signals from multiple sources (multiple synapses). Action potentials, in contrast, can only pass along already collected information without changing it.

INTERIM SUMMARY

When a neuron is at rest (its **resting potential**), it is polarized, with a negative charge inside the cell membrane and a positive charge outside. When a neuron is stimulated by another neuron, its cell membrane is either depolarized or hyperpolarized. The spreading voltage changes along the cell membrane that occur as one neuron is excited by other neurons are called **graded potentials**. If the cell membrane is depolarized by enough graded potentials, the neuron will fire. This process is called an **action potential**, or nerve impulse.

Transmission of Information between Cells

When a nerve impulse travels down an axon, it sets in motion a series of events that can lead to transmission of information to other cells (Table 3.1). Figure 3.3 presents a simplified diagram of a synaptic connection between two neurons. The neuron that is sending an impulse is called the *presynaptic neuron* (i.e., *before* the synapse); the cell receiving the impulse is the *postsynaptic neuron*.

Neurotransmitters and Receptors   Within the terminal buttons of a neuron are small sacs called *synaptic vesicles*. These sacs contain **neurotransmitters**, *chemicals that transmit information from one cell to another*. When the presynaptic neuron fires, the synaptic vesicles in its terminal buttons move toward the cell's membrane (the presynaptic membrane). Some of them adhere to the membrane and break open, releasing neurotransmitters into the synaptic cleft.

Table 3.1 ■ ■ Communication from One Neuron to Another

Stage	What happens
1. Resting state	Na$^+$ cannot enter, or is actively pumped out of, the neuron; the cell is negatively charged.
2. Depolarization	Na$^+$ enters dendrites and cell body, making the cell less negatively charged.
3. Graded potential	Change in cell voltage is passed down dendrites and cell body.
4. Action potential	If the change in axon voltage surpasses a threshold, the axon suddenly lets in a surge of Na$^+$.
5. Neurotransmitter release	The action potential causes terminal buttons to release neurotransmitters into the synaptic cleft.
6. Chemical message transmitted	Depending on the facilitating or inhibitory nature of the neurotransmitter released, the voltage of the cell membrane receiving the message becomes depolarized or hyperpolarized, and the process repeats.

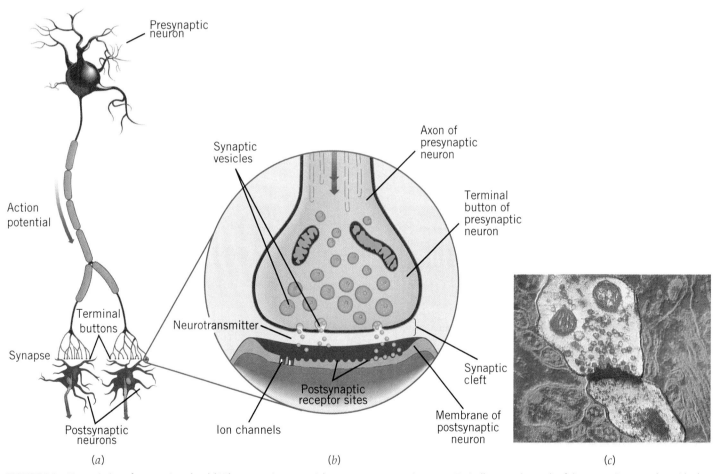

(a)   (b)   (c)

FIGURE 3.3   Transmission of a nerve impulse. (*a*) When an action potential occurs, the nerve impulse travels along the axon until it reaches the synaptic vesicles. The synaptic vesicles release neurotransmitters into the synaptic cleft.(*b*) The neurotransmitters then bind with postsynaptic receptors and produce a graded potential on the membrane of the postsynaptic neuron. Receptors are strings of amino acids (the building blocks of proteins) suspended in the fatty membrane of the postsynaptic neuron. Typically, several strands of these proteins extend outside the cell into the synapse, where they detect the presence of neurotransmitters and may transport them through the membrane. Other strands remain on the inside of the cell and send information to the nucleus of the cell, alerting it, for example, to open or close channels in the membrane (called ion channels) in order to let various ions in or out. (*c*) An electron micrograph of a synapse.

Once in the synaptic cleft, some of these neurotransmitters then bind with *protein molecules in the postsynaptic membrane that receive their chemical messages*; these molecules are called **receptors**. Receptors act like locks that can be opened only by particular keys. In this case, the keys are neurotransmitters in the synaptic cleft. When a receptor binds with the neurotransmitter that fits it—in both molecular structure and electrical charge—the chemical and electrical balance of the postsynaptic cell membrane changes, producing a graded potential—a ripple in the neuronal pond.

The Effects of Neurotransmitters   Neurotransmitters can either increase or decrease neural firing. *Excitatory neurotransmitters* depolarize the postsynaptic cell membrane, making an action potential more likely. (That is, they excite the neuron.) In contrast, *inhibitory neurotransmitters* hyperpolarize the membrane (increase its polarization); this action reduces the likelihood that the postsynaptic neuron will fire (or inhibits firing). Excitatory neurotransmitters thus grease the wheels of neural communication, whereas inhibitory neurotransmitters put on the brakes. A neuron can also release more than one neurotransmitter, affecting the cells to which it is connected in various ways.

Aside from being excitatory or inhibitory, neurotransmitters differ in another important respect. Some, like the ones we have been describing, are released into a specific synapse and only affect the neuron at the other end of the synaptic cleft (the postsynaptic neuron). Others have a much wider radius of impact and remain active considerably longer. Once released, they find their way into multiple synapses, where they can affect any neuron within reach that has the appropriate chemicals in its membrane. The primary impact of these transmitter substances, called *modulatory neurotransmitters* (or *neuromodulators*), is to increase or decrease (i.e., modulate) the impact of other neurotransmitters released into the synapse.

Types of Neurotransmitters   Researchers have discovered at least 75 chemical substances that can transmit messages between neurons. Although knowledge remains incomplete, let us now briefly examine six of the best understood neurotransmitters: glutamate, GABA, dopamine, serotonin, acetylcholine, and endorphins (Table 3.2).

Table 3.2   Partial List of Neurotransmitters

Transmitter Substance	Some of Its Known Effects
Glutamate	Excitation of neurons throughout the nervous system
GABA (gamma-aminobutyric acid)	Inhibition of neurons in the brain
Glycene	Inhibition of neurons in the spinal cord and lower brain
Dopamine	Emotional arousal, pleasure, and reward; voluntary movement; attention
Serotonin	Sleep and emotional arousal; aggression; pain regulation; mood
Acetylcholine (ACh)	Learning and memory
Endorphins and enkephalins	Pain relief and elevation of mood
Epinephrine and norepinephrine	Emotional arousal, anxiety, and fear

Note: The effect of a neurotransmitter depends on the type of receptor it fits. Each neurotransmitter can activate different receptors, depending on where in the nervous system the receptor is located. Thus, the impact of any neurotransmitter depends less on the neurotransmitter itself than on the receptor it unlocks. In fact, some neurotransmitters can have an excitatory effect at one synapse and an inhibitory effect at another.

Glutamate and GABA   **Glutamate** (*glutamic acid*) is *a neurotransmitter that can excite nearly every neuron in the nervous system*, as they are used by the interneurons that modulate neuronal activity. Glutamate is involved in many psychological processes; however, it appears to play a particularly important role in learning (Blokland, 1997; Izquierdo & Medina, 1997). Some people respond to the MSG (monosodium glutamate) in Chinese food with neurological symptoms such as tingling and numbing because this ingredient activates glutamate receptors.

GABA (*gamma-aminobutyric acid*) has the opposite effect in the brain: It is *a neurotransmitter that plays an inhibitory role*. Roughly one-third of all the neurons in the brain use GABA for synaptic communication (Petty, 1995). GABA is particularly important in regulating anxiety. Drugs like valium and alcohol that bind with its receptors tend to reduce anxiety (Chapter 9).

Dopamine   **Dopamine** is *a neurotransmitter that has wide-ranging effects in the nervous system, involving thought, feeling, motivation, and behavior*. Some neural pathways that rely on dopamine are involved in emotional arousal, the experience of pleasure, and the association of particular behaviors with reward (Schultz, 1998). Drugs ranging from marijuana to heroin increase the release of dopamine in some of these pathways and may play a part in addictions (Robbins & Everitt, 1999). Other dopamine pathways are involved in movement, attention, decision making, and various cognitive processes. Abnormally high levels of dopamine in some parts of the brain have been linked to schizophrenia (Chapter 15).

Dopamine is synthesized by a part of the brain called the *substantia niagra*, or "black substance." There are two major dopaminergic pathways leading to different brain areas, each with its own function. The pathway that terminates in the *nucleus accumbens* is essential for feelings of pleasure and reward. Normally when a person enjoys her food, falls in love, or listens to his favorite music, dopamine is released. When a person abuses drugs or alcohol, the dopaminergic neurons are excited even more than for nondrug stimuli. Although this gives an extraordinary (but temporary) sense of pleasure, it also takes a toll on the dopaminergic neurons in the substantia niagra. The neurons fire so intensely that they run out of energy and die. More and more of the drug is necessary to produce a sense of heightened pleasure, leading to *tolerance* (i.e., the same amount of the drug produces a weaker effect) and *addiction* (dependence on the drug to function normally).

The second major pathway from the substantia nigra goes to the basal ganglia. The *basal ganglia* are necessary for normal control of the muscles. Degeneration of the dopamine-producing cells of the substantia nigra causes **Parkinson's disease**, *a disorder characterized by uncontrollable tremors and difficulty in both initiating behavior* (such as standing up) *and stopping movements already in progress* (such as reaching for a glass of water). Other symptoms can include depression, reduced facial displays of emotion, and a general slowing of thought that parallels the slowing of behavior (Rao et al., 1992; Tandberg et al., 1996).

Because the victims of encephalitis lethargica described at the beginning of this chapter showed Parkinsonian symptoms, physicians tried treating them with L-dopa, a chemical that readily converts to dopamine and had recently proven effective in treating Parkinson's disease. Dopamine itself cannot be administered because it cannot cross the *blood–brain barrier*, which normally protects the brain from foreign substances in the blood. The blood–brain barrier exists because the cells in the blood vessels of the brain tend to be so tightly packed that large molecules have difficulty entering. The effects of the L-dopa on the victims of encephalitis lethargica were remarkable. For example, Ms. B. was able to speak and walk: she was "awakened."

More recently, in an unusual "epidemic" of bad heroin in San Francisco in the 1990s, several apparently paralyzed individuals showed up in the emergency room (Langston & Palfreman, 1995). These "frozen zombies" were subjected to all sorts of testing, some of it painful (such as prolonged immersion of their hands in ice water),

Making Connections

Dopamine overactivity in certain parts of the brain has been implicated in the hallucinations and delusions seen in schizophrenia (Chapter 15). Medications that block dopamine receptors can reduce these symptoms. Because dopamine is also involved in movement, however, these drugs can have side effects, such as jerky movements or tics (Chapter 16).

Making Connections

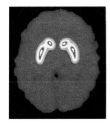
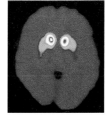

Normal   Severe Parkinson's disease

Developments in neuroimaging—taking computerized images of a live functioning nervous system—have revolutionized our understanding of the brain (Chapter 2). These PET scans contrast the brain of a normal volunteer (left) with that of a patient with Parkinson's disease (right). Brighter areas indicate more activity. Areas of the brain that normally use dopamine and control movement are less active in the Parkinsonian brain.

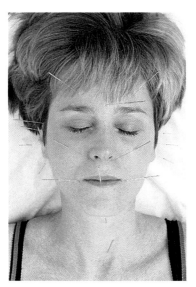

Stimulation of endorphins may be responsible in part for the pain-killing effects of acupuncture.

Apply & Discuss

Many plants in addition to the opium poppy produce psychological effects in humans and other animals. Deadly nightshade produces atropine (the substance that the eye doctor uses to dilate the eyes); coffee produces caffeine, a stimulant; marijuana produces a mellow state, stimulates appetite, and reduces glaucoma.

to try to elicit movement. Finally, doctors determined that the bad heroin had essentially destroyed the dopamine-producing cells of the substantia nigra. L-dopa was administered, and as in the Parkisonism patients, there was a remarkable recovery.

The blood–brain barrier is a double-edged sword. On the one hand, it serves an adaptive function, preventing toxic substances from disrupting neural functioning. On the other hand, the blood-brain barrier rejects medications that could treat brain diseases. Because of its chemical structure, only a small percentage of even L-dopa gets past the blood–brain barrier. The rest, affecting other cells throughout the body, causes side effects such as nausea, vomiting, and shortness of breath. The L-dopa that does make its way into the brain can also have unwanted consequences because the brain uses dopamine for neural transmission in many regions and for different purposes. The L-dopa can thus reduce Parkinsonian symptoms, but it can also produce disordered thinking (such as hallucinations) or movement disorders other than Parkinson's. For example, Ms. B, the victim of the 1917 encephalitis epidemic, developed a "touching tic," whereby she had to touch everything she passed. For many patients, however, symptoms such as tics were a minor price to pay for reawakening.

Serotonin Serotonin *is a neurotransmitter involved in the regulation of mood, sleep, eating, arousal, and pain.* Decreased serotonin in the brain is common in severe depression, which often responds to medications that increase serotonin activity. The short-hand chemical nomenclature for these medications, which include Zoloft, Paxil, and Prozac, is SSRIs (*selective serotonin reuptake inhibitors*). **SSRI's *increase the duration of action of serotonin in the synapse by blocking its reuptake into the presynaptic membrane.*** It is becoming evident that many individuals who suffer from depression (and anxiety) have insufficient serotonin activity in the parts of their brains that regulate mood. Serotonin usually plays an inhibitory role, affecting, for example, neural circuits involved in aggression, antisocial behavior, and other forms of social behavior (Altamura et al., 1999; Chung et al., 2000).

Acetylcholine The *neurotransmitter* **acetylcholine (ACh)** is *involved in learning and memory*. Experiments show increased ACh activity while rats are learning to discriminate one stimulus from another (Butt et al., 1997). A key piece of evidence linking ACh to learning and memory is the fact that patients with Alzheimer's disease, which destroys memory, show depleted ACh (Perry et al., 1999).

Knowing about the functions of acetylcholine holds out the possibility that scientists can eventually transplant neural tissue rich in this neurotransmitter into the brains of patients with Alzheimer's disease. Some promising animal research along these lines is ongoing. For example, old rats with neural transplants perform substantially better on learning tasks than same-aged peers without the transplants (Bjorklund & Gage, 1985).

Endorphins Endorphins are *chemicals that elevate mood and reduce pain*. They have a range of effects, from the numbness people often feel immediately after tearing a muscle (which wears off once these natural pain killers stop flowing) to the "runner's high" athletes sometimes report after a prolonged period of exercise (see Hoffman, 1997).

The word endorphin comes from *endogenous* (meaning "produced within the body") and *morphine* (a chemical substance derived from the opium poppy that elevates mood and reduces pain). Opium and similar narcotic drugs kill pain and elevate mood because they stimulate receptors in the brain specialized for endorphins. Essentially, narcotics "pick the locks" normally opened by endorphins.

INTERIM SUMMARY

Within the terminal buttons of the presynaptic neuron are **neurotransmitters**, such as **glutamate, GABA, dopamine, serotonin, acetylcholine**, and **endorphins**. Neurotransmitters transmit information from one neuron to another as they are released into the synapse from the synaptic vesicles. They bind with receptors in the membrane of the postsynaptic neuron, which produces graded potentials that can either excite or inhibit the postsynaptic neuron from firing.

The Endocrine System

Neurotransmitters are not the only chemicals that transmit psychologically significant messages. The **endocrine system** is *a collection of glands that secrete chemicals directly into the bloodstream*. (Figure 3.4). These chemicals are called **hormones**. Like neurotransmitters, *hormones bind with receptors in cell membranes, but because they travel through the bloodstream they can simultaneously activate many cells all over the body*.

The chemical structure of some hormones is similar or even identical to that of some neurotransmitters. For example, the *hormones* **adrenalin** *and* **noradrenalin** *trigger physiological arousal, particularly in potential danger situations*. These two hormones are actually the same chemicals as the neurotransmitters *epinephrine* and *norepinephrine*, respectively, which are involved in anxiety, fear, and emotional arousal. Similarly, another chemical, oxytocin, increases nurturing behaviors when it is released in the brain as a neurotransmitter. Oxytocin that is released into the body as a hormone facilitates breast milk production (Mendoza & Mason, 1997).

The endocrine system is thus a second system for intercellular communication, but it does not rely on the kind of intricate "wiring" between cells used by the nervous system. The difference between the methods of communication used by the two systems is like the difference between word of mouth—which requires transmission from one person to the next—and mass media—which can communicate information to millions of people at once. The endocrine system "broadcasts" its signals by releasing hormones into the bloodstream. Its messages are less specific but are readily "heard" throughout the body.

The **pituitary gland**, an oval structure in the brain that is about the size of a pea, is *often described as the "master gland" because many of the hormones it releases stimulate and regulate the other glands*. The pituitary is connected more directly to the central nervous system than any of the other endocrine glands.

The **thyroid gland**, located in the neck, *releases hormones that control growth and metabolism* (transformation of food into energy). The thyroid gland also affects energy levels and mood (Hahn et al., 1999). People with hypothyroidism, or an underactive thyroid (hypo means "under"), sometimes require artificial replacement of thyroid hormones to relieve sluggishness and depression. In fact, roughly 10 percent of people who complain of depression actually have undiagnosed hypothyroidism (Gold & Pearsall, 1983).

The **adrenal glands** are located above the kidneys. (The Latin *ad renal* means "toward the kidney.") *These glands secrete adrenalin (epinephrine) and other hormones during emergencies*. Most people are familiar with the effects of adrenalin: a racing heart, increased respiration rate, piloerection (your hair stands up), a flushed face, and pupil dilation. When these effects are severe, you may experience a panic attack (Chapter 15). The function of these changes is to prepare you either to run from danger or to fight for your life, the *fight-or-flight reaction*. Another endocrine gland, the *pancreas*, is located near the stomach and the adrenal glands and produces hormones that control blood-sugar level.

Baltimore Orioles pitcher Steve Bechler died as a consequence of heat exhaustion after his body temperature reached 108 degrees. His organs failed and he went into a coma. It was discovered that he had been taking excessive amounts of a diet pill that contained ephedra, a form of epinephrine.

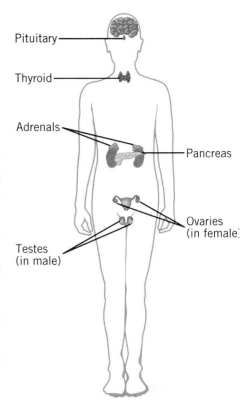

FIGURE 3.4 The major endocrine glands. The endocrine system is a series of glands that rely on hormonal communication to activate cells throughout the body.

Making Connections

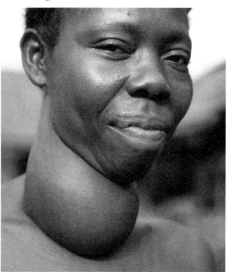

In the 1930s, many people in the Midwestern United States developed goiter. A goiter is an enlargement of the thyroid gland, causing swelling of the neck. The cause of the goiter was a lack of iodine, necessary for the production of thyroid hormone in the diet. In the absence of iodine, the thyroid gland initiates the production of thyroid hormone but cannot finish its development and the gland swells with incomplete thyroid hormone. To treat goiter, nutritionists suggested adding iodine to table salt, a treatment that led to the eradication of goiter (Chapter 11). A similar dietary strategy is being used in Africa where beta-carotene (vitamin A) deficiency is endemic in some communities. "Golden rice" has been genetically engineered so that beta-carotene is inserted into the rice The rice gets its golden color from the beta-carotene (which also makes carrots yellow-orange).

Apply & Discuss

At menopause women experience many changes in their physiology. Hormone replacement therapy is often recommended to reverse the effects of low estrogen and progesterone.

▪ What does this suggest about the normal role of estrogen and progesterone in the premenopausal woman?

The **gonads** are *endocrine glands that influence sexual development and behavior.* The *male gonads,* or *testes, are located in the testicles. The most important hormone they produce is* **testosterone. Estrogens** are *hormones produced by the female gonads* (*ovaries*). In both sexes, these hormones control not only sex drive but also the development of secondary sex characteristics such as growth of breasts in females, deepened voice in males, and pubic hair in both sexes.

INTERIM SUMMARY

The **endocrine system** is a collection of glands that control various bodily functions through the secretion of **hormones**. The endocrine system complements the cell-to-cell communication of the nervous system by sending global messages through the bloodstream. Hormones are like neurotransmitters, except that they travel through the bloodstream and can thus activate many cells simultaneously.

From Brain to Behavior   Psychoneuroimmunology

Psychoneuroimmunology *is the study of the interactions among behavior, the nervous system, the endocrine system, and the immune system* (Leonard & Song, 2002). The newly revived field of psychoneuroimmunology crosses traditional boundaries to achieve a more holistic view of how we function (Damasio et al., 2002).

How does the immune system communicate with the nervous system? The immune cells (cytokines, T cells, macrophages, etc.) do not cross the blood–brain barrier. However, they do affect at least one of the cranial nerves, the vagus nerve (cranial nerve X), which has receptors for a specific cytokine—interleukin-1. When you are sick and have elevated levels of interleukin-1, the vagal receptors signal the brain that the immune system is activated. Maier (2003) cut the vagus nerve of rats that he then made sick. Although the rats responded physically to the infection, they did not display behavioral symptoms of being sick. *Immunological synapses* (between nerves and immune cells) also have been identified (Vander et al., 2002).

A second avenue by which the nervous system affects the immune system is via the effect of stress on the hippocampus. The psychological state of stress increases the likelihood of illness, perhaps because stress interferes with immune functioning. And, in fact, studies have shown that rats subjected to sustained stress have reduced immunological functioning (Watkins & Maier, 2000). Maier (2003) calls this syndrome the *sickness pattern*.

Under sustained levels of stress hormones, specialized cells of the hippocampus die. These cells are critical for activation of the immune system in times of stress (McEwen, 2003; Sapolsky, 1996). Depression can cause similar destruction of hippocampal neurons (MacQueen et al., 2003). Clearly, the relationship between brain, behavior, and immunology is not only important, but more complex than previously thought. These relationships may explain some autoimmune diseases and may play a critical role in the complex of symptoms exhibited by AIDS victims (McEwen, 2002). Psychoneuroimmunology may also one day explain how such alternative medicine practices as acupuncture, meditation, and prayer work.

The Peripheral Nervous System

Although the endocrine system plays an important role in psychological functioning, the center of our psychological experience is the nervous system. The nervous system has two major divisions, the central nervous system and the peripheral nervous system (Figures 3.5 and 3.6). The **central nervous system (CNS)** *consists of the brain and spinal cord*. The **peripheral nervous system (PNS)** *consists of neurons that convey messages to and from the central nervous system*. The CNS and PNS can

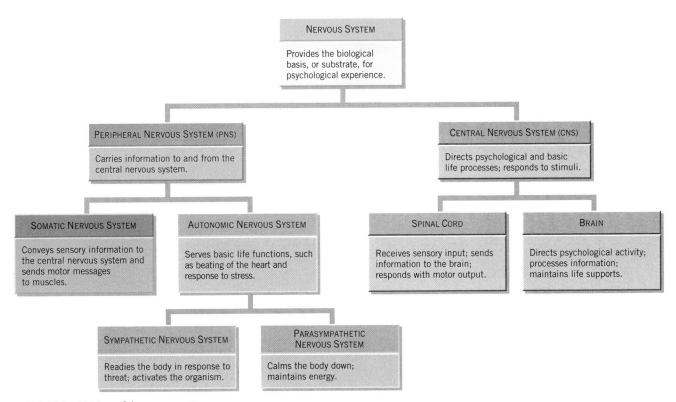

FIGURE 3.5 Divisions of the nervous system.

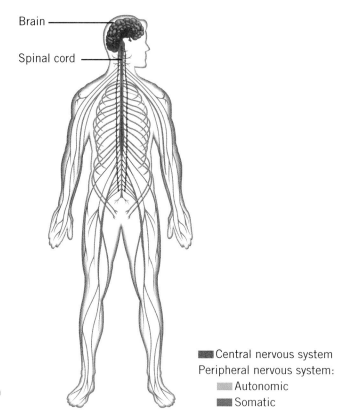

Brain

Spinal cord

▬ Central nervous system
Peripheral nervous system:
    ▬ Autonomic
    ▬ Somatic

FIGURE 3.6 The nervous system. The nervous system consists of the brain, the spinal cord, and the neurons of the peripheral nervous system that carry information to and from these central nervous system structures.

Apply & Discuss

Have you ever noticed that when you stub your toe on the sofa leg, you know that you have done this before you feel the pain? Because the nerves that send the pain information are unmyelinated, they are slower than the fibers that convey the sensation of touch and pressure as your toe connects with the sofa leg.

▪ What might be the evolutionary advantage of having a delayed pain response?

be further broken down into functional units. We begin with the peripheral nervous system, which has two subdivisions: the somatic and the autonomic nervous systems.

The Somatic Nervous System

The **somatic nervous system** *transmits sensory information to the central nervous system and carries out its motor commands*. Sensory neurons receive information through receptors in the eyes, ears, tongue, skin, muscles, and other parts of the body. Motor neurons direct the action of skeletal muscles. Because the somatic nervous system is involved in intentional actions, such as standing up or shaking someone's hand, it is sometimes called the *voluntary nervous system*. However, the somatic nervous system also directs some involuntary or automatic actions, such as adjustments in posture and balance. For example, when your hand touches a hot stove, sensory receptors in your skin trigger an *afferent* (sensory) neural signal to the spinal cord. The information is integrated via interneurons in the gray matter of the spinal cord which trigger action potentials in the *efferent* (motor) neurons to cause your arm muscles to contract and thus to withdraw your hand from the stove. In reality, this action takes place much more quickly than it took to read about how it happens! In addition, information about the heat and pain is relayed up the spinal cord to the central nervous system.

The Autonomic Nervous System

The **autonomic nervous system** *conveys information to and from internal bodily structures that carry out basic life processes such as digestion and respiration. It consists of* two parts: *the sympathetic and the parasympathetic nervous systems*. Although these systems work together, their functions are often opposed or complementary. In broadest strokes, you can think of the sympathetic nervous system as an emergency system and the parasympathetic nervous system as a "business-as-usual"

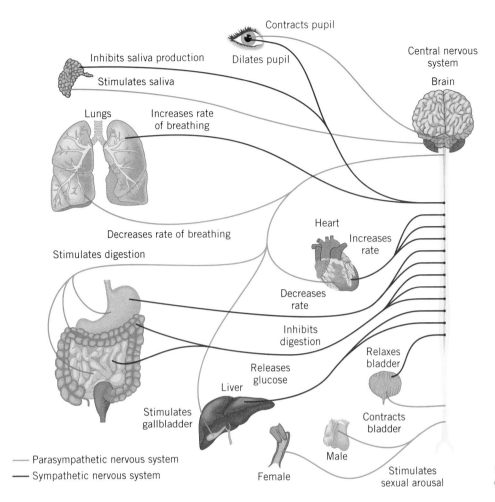

Contracts pupil

Inhibits saliva production   Dilates pupil

Central nervous system

Brain

Stimulates saliva

Lungs   Increases rate of breathing

Decreases rate of breathing

Stimulates digestion

Heart   Increases rate

Decreases rate

Inhibits digestion

Relaxes bladder

Releases glucose

Liver

Stimulates gallbladder

Contracts bladder

Male

—— Parasympathetic nervous system
—— Sympathetic nervous system

Female

Stimulates sexual arousal

FIGURE 3.7   The sympathetic and parasympathetic divisions of the autonomic nervous system.

system (Figure 3.7). The **sympathetic nervous system** *is typically activated in response to threats*. Its job is to ready the body for fight or flight, which it does in several ways. It stops digestion, diverting blood away from the stomach and redirecting it to the muscles, which may need extra oxygen for an emergency response. It increases heart rate, dilates the pupils, and causes hairs on the body and head to stand erect.

By preparing the organism to respond to emergencies, the sympathetic nervous system serves an important adaptive function. Sometimes, however, the sympathetic cavalry comes to the rescue when least wanted. A surge of anxiety, tremors, sweating, dry mouth, and a palpitating heart may have helped prepare our ancestors to flee from a hungry lion, but they are less welcome when we are trying to deliver a speech.

The **parasympathetic nervous system** *supports more mundane, or routine, activities that maintain the body's store of energy*, such as regulating blood-sugar levels, secreting saliva, and eliminating wastes. It also participates in functions such as regulating heart rate and pupil size. The relationship between the sympathetic and parasympathetic nervous systems is in many ways a balancing act: When an emergency has passed, the parasympathetic nervous system resumes control, reversing sympathetic effects and returning to the normal business of storing and maintaining resources.

INTERIM SUMMARY

The nervous system consists of the **central nervous system (CNS)** and the **peripheral nervous system (PNS)**. Neurons of the PNS carry messages to and from the CNS. The

PNS has two subdivisions: the somatic nervous system and the autonomic nervous system. The **somatic nervous system** consists of sensory neurons that carry sensory information to the brain and motor neurons that direct the action of skeletal muscles. The **autonomic nervous system** controls basic life processes such as the beating of the heart, workings of the digestive system, and breathing. It consists of two parts, the **sympathetic nervous system**, which is activated primarily in response to threats (but is also involved in general emotional arousal), and the **parasympathetic nervous system**, which is involved in more routine activities such as maintaining the body's energy resources and restoring the system to an even keel following sympathetic activation.

The Central Nervous System

The peripheral nervous system reflects a complex job of neural wiring, but the human central nervous system is probably the most remarkable feat of electrical engineering ever accomplished. Before discussing the major structures of the central nervous system, an important caveat, or caution, is in order. A central debate since the origins of modern neuroscience in the nineteenth century has centered on the extent to which certain functions are localized to specific parts of the brain. One of the most enlightening things about watching a brain scan in action as a person performs even a simple task is just how much of the brain actually "lights up." Different regions are indeed specialized for different functions; a severe blow to the head that damages the back of the cortex is more likely to disrupt vision than speech. Knowing that a lesion at the back of the cortex can produce blindness thus suggests that this region is involved in visual processing. With that caveat in mind, we now turn to the main features of the central nervous system.

The Spinal Cord

As in all vertebrates, neurons in the human spinal cord produce reflexes, as sensory stimulation activates rapid, automatic motor responses. In humans, however, an additional, and crucial, function of the spinal cord is to transmit information between the brain and the rest of the body. Thus, the spinal cord is the anatomical location where peripheral information "shakes hands" with the central nervous system. The **spinal cord** *sends information from sensory neurons in various parts of the body to the brain, and it relays motor commands back to muscles and organs* (such as the heart and stomach) via motor neurons.

The spinal cord is segmented, with each segment controlling a different segment of the body. By and large, the upper segments control the upper parts of the body and the lower segments the lower body (Figure 3.8). As in the earliest vertebrates, sensory information enters one side of the spinal cord (toward the back of the body), and motor impulses exit the other (toward the front).

Outside the cord, bundles of axons from these sensory and motor neurons join together to form 31 pairs (from the two sides of the body) of *spinal nerves*; these nerves carry information to and from the spinal cord to the periphery. Inside the spinal cord, other bundles of axons (*spinal tracts*, which comprise much of the white matter of the cord) send impulses to and from the brain, relaying sensory messages and motor commands. (Outside the central nervous system, bundles of axons are usually called *nerves*; within the brain and spinal cord, they are called *tracts*.) When the spinal cord is severed, the result is loss of feeling and paralysis at all levels below the injury because the tracts of communication within the brain are interrupted. Even with less severe lesions, physicians can often pinpoint the location of spinal damage from patients' descriptions of their symptoms alone.

Making Connections

Whereas the spinal cord has 31 paired nerves, *the brain has 12 pairs of specialized nerves* called the **cranial nerves**. By convention, the nerves are numbered with Roman numerals. Each of the 12 nerves serves a special function. For example, cranial nerve I is necessary for our sense of smell. The trigeminal, or cranial nerve V, conveys information about irritation (hot peppers) and pain (a toothache). We have four cranial nerves devoted to vision: one for the sensory information (II, optic) and three for three sets of muscles that control our eye movement (III, oculomotor; IV, trochlear; and VI, abducens). Medical students have to memorize all of the nerves and their order. To help, someone came up with a rather silly *mneumonic* (memory device, Chapter 6): On Old Olympus Towering Tops a Fin and German Viewed Some Hops. If you write down the first letter of every word (even the "a's") you will have the first letter of each of the cranial nerves in order.

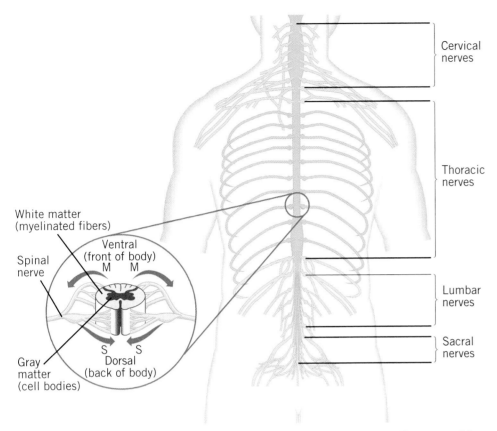

White matter
(myelinated fibers)

Ventral
(front of body)
M   M

Spinal
nerve

Gray
matter
(cell bodies)

S   S
Dorsal
(back of body)

Cervical
nerves

Thoracic
nerves

Lumbar
nerves

Sacral
nerves

FIGURE 3.8   The spinal cord. Segments of the spinal cord relay information to and from different parts of the body. Sensory fibers (S) relay information to the back of the spine (dorsal), and motor neurons (M) transmit information from the front of the spinal cord (ventral) to the periphery.

INTERIM SUMMARY

The central nervous system (CNS) consists of the brain and spinal cord. The **spinal cord** carries out reflexes (automatic motor responses), transmits sensory information to the brain, and transmits messages from the brain to the muscles and organs. Each of its 31 paired segments controls sensation and movement in a different part of the body.

The Hindbrain

Directly above and connected to the spinal cord are several structures that comprise the **hindbrain:** *the medulla oblongata, cerebellum, and parts of the reticular formation* (Figure 3.9). Another small hindbrain region, the pons, is not yet well understood. The hindbrain is the most primitive but essential part of our nervous system. As in other animals, hindbrain structures sustain life by controlling the supply of air and blood to cells in the body and regulate arousal level. Damage to this part of the brain is likely to be instantly fatal. With the exception of the cerebellum, which sits at the back of the brain and has a distinct appearance, the structures of the hindbrain merge into one another and perform multiple functions as information passes from one structure to the next on its way to and from higher brain regions.

Medulla Oblongata   Anatomically, *the lowest brain stem structure,* **the medulla oblongata** (*or simply* **medulla**), *is actually an extension of the spinal cord that links the spinal cord to the brain.* Although quite small—about an inch and a half long and three-fourths of an inch wide at its broadest part—the medulla is essential to

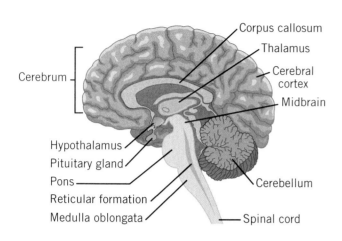

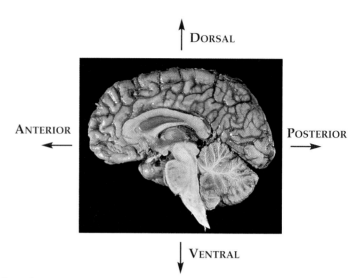

FIGURE 3.9   Cross section of the human brain. The drawing and accompanying photo show a view of the cerebral cortex and the more primitive structures below the cerebellum. (Not shown here are the limbic system and the basal ganglia, which are structures within the cerebrum.) Also marked on the photo are common terms used to describe location in the brain. For example, a structure toward the front of the brain is described as *anterior* (*ante* means "before"). Not shown are two other directions: *lateral* ("toward the left or right side") and *medial* ("toward the middle"). Thus, a neural pathway through the upper sides of the brain might be described as *dorsolateral*—*dorsal* meaning "toward the top of the head" and *lateral* meaning "toward the side."

life, controlling such vital physiological functions as heartbeat, circulation, and respiration. Neither humans nor other animals can survive destruction of the medulla.

The medulla is the link between the spinal cord (and hence much of the body) and the rest of the brain. Here, many bundles of axons cross over from each side of the body to the opposite side of the brain. As a result, most of the sensations experienced on the right side of the body, as well as the capacity to move the right side, are controlled by the left side of the brain, and vice versa. Thus, if a person has weakness in the left side of the body following a stroke, the damage to the brain was likely on the right side of the brain.

Reticular Activating System   The **reticular activating system (RAS)** is *a diffuse network of neurons that extends from the lowest parts of the medulla in the hindbrain to the upper end of the midbrain*. The RAS sends axons to many parts of the brain and to the spinal cord. *Its major functions are to maintain consciousness, regulate arousal levels, and modulate the activity of neurons throughout the central nervous system*. When our RAS is less active, we go to sleep. The RAS also appears to help direct higher brain centers to focus on information from different neural pathways (such as sounds and associated images) by calling attention to their simultaneous activation (Munk et al., 1996). Many general anesthetics exert their effects by reducing the activity of the RAS. Damage to the RAS is a major cause of coma. In fact, humans can lose an entire side (or hemisphere) of the cerebrum—about 50 billion cells—without losing the capacity for consciousness, whereas lesions to the reticular formation can render all the information in the cortex useless (Baars, 1995).

Cerebellum   The **cerebellum** (Latin for "little cerebrum"), *a large structure at the back of the brain, is involved in movement and fine motor learning, as well as other functions*. For decades researchers believed that the cerebellum was exclusively involved in coordinating smooth, well-sequenced movements (such as riding a bike) and in maintaining balance and posture. Slurred speech and staggering after a few too many drinks stem in large part from the effects of alcohol on cerebellar functioning. More recently, researchers using positron emission tomography (PET) and functional magnetic resonance imaging (fMRI) scans have found the cerebellum to be involved in other psychological processes as well. Among the most important are sensory and cognitive processes, such as learning to associate one stimulus with another (Drepper et al., 1999).

The Midbrain

The **midbrain** *consists of the tectum and tegmentum*. The **tectum** *includes structures involved in vision and hearing*. These structures largely help humans orient to visual and auditory stimuli with eye and body movements. When higher brain structures are lesioned, people can often still sense the presence of stimuli, but they cannot identify them. For example, people may think they are blind but can actually respond to visual stimuli. The **tegmentum**, *which includes parts of the RAS and other neural structures, serves a variety of functions, many related to movement*, such as orienting the body and eyes toward sensory stimuli. The *substantia nigra* (the site of the dopamine producing neurons of the body) is also located in this part of the brain.

INTERIM SUMMARY

The **hindbrain** includes the **medulla oblongata**, the **cerebellum**, and parts of the **reticular activating system**. The **medulla** regulates vital physiological functions, such as heartbeat, circulation, and respiration, and forms a link between the spinal cord and the rest of the brain. The **cerebellum** is the brain structure involved in movement (in particular, fine motor movements) but parts of it also appear to be involved in learning and sensory discrimination. The **RAS** is most centrally involved in consciousness and arousal. The **midbrain** consists of the tectum and tegmentum. The **tectum** is involved in orienting to visual and auditory stimuli. The **tegmentum** is involved, among other things, in movement and arousal.

The Subcortical Forebrain

The **subcortical forebrain** (*sub*, or *below*, the cortex), *which is involved in complex sensory, emotional, cognitive, and behavioral processes, consists of the hypothalamus, thalamus, limbic system, and basal ganglia*. These areas are responsible for recognizing emotions, initiating voluntary movements, and regulating everyday homeostasis for temperature, body weight, water and salt balance, and sex drive.

Hypothalamus Situated in front of the midbrain and adjacent to the pituitary gland is the **hypothalamus**. Although the hypothalamus accounts for only 0.3 percent of the brain's total weight, this tiny structure *helps regulate behaviors ranging from eating and sleeping to sexual activity and emotional experience*.

In nonhuman animals, the hypothalamus is involved in species-specific behaviors, such as responses to predators. For example, electrical stimulation of the hypothalamus in cats can produce rage attacks—filled with hissing, growling, and biting (Bandler, 1982; Lu et al., 1992; Siegel et al., 1999).

The hypothalamus works closely with the pituitary gland and provides a key link between the nervous system and the endocrine system, largely by activating pituitary hormones. When people undergo stressful experiences (such as taking an exam or getting into a heated argument), the hypothalamus activates the pituitary, which in turn puts the body on alert by sending out hormonal messages. One of the most important functions of the hypothalamus is homeostasis—keeping vital processes such as body temperature, blood-sugar (glucose) level, and metabolism (use and storage of energy) within a fairly narrow range (Chapter 10). For example, as people ingest food, the hypothalamus detects a rise in glucose level and responds by shutting off hunger sensations. Chemically blocking glucose receptors (cells that detect glucose levels) in cats can produce ravenous eating, as the hypothalamus attempts to maintain homeostasis in the face of misleading information (Batuev & Gafurov, 1993; Berridge & Zajonc, 1991; Hagan et al., 1998).

Thalamus

The **thalamus** is *a set of nuclei located above the hypothalamus*. Its various nuclei perform a number of functions. ***One of its most important functions is to process sensory information as it arrives and transmit this information to higher brain centers***. In some respects the thalamus is like a switchboard for routing information from neurons connected to visual, auditory, taste, and touch receptors to appropriate regions of the brain. However, the thalamus plays a much more active role than a simple switchboard. Its function is not only to route messages to the appropriate structures but also to filter them, highlighting some and deemphasizing others.

The thalamus also receives input from the reticular activating system, which "highlights" neural messages of potential importance. Recent studies using PET and other techniques suggest that the reticular activating system and thalamus may be anatomically "lower" sections of a neural circuit that directs attention and consciousness toward potentially significant events (Fiset et al., 1999; Kinomura et al., 1996).

The Limbic System   The **limbic system** is *a set of structures with diverse functions involving emotion, motivation, learning, and memory*. Its name comes from the Greek word for "belt" or "circuit," which reflects the circular anatomy of the various areas of the brain that constitute the limbic system. The limbic system includes the septal area, the amygdala, and the hippocampus (Figure 3.10). The role of the *septal area* is only gradually becoming clear, but it appears to be involved in some forms of emotionally significant learning. Early research linked it to the experience of pleasure: Stimulating a section of the septal area is such a powerful reinforcer for rats that they will walk across an electrified grid to receive the stimulation (Milner, 1991; Olds & Milner, 1954).

More recent research suggests that, like most brain structures, different sections of the septal area likely have distinct, though related, functions. For example, one part of the septal area appears to be involved in relief from pain and unpleasant emotional states (Yadin & Thomas, 1996). Another part seems to help animals learn to avoid sit-

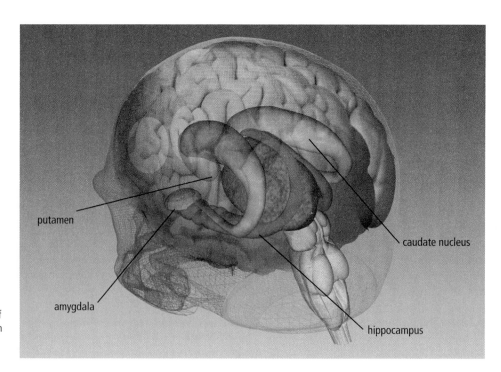

FIGURE 3.10   Subcortical areas of the brain. The hippocampus and amygdala are part of the limbic system. The putamen and caudate nucleus are part of the basal ganglia. (The temporal lobes are included in this photograph to illustrate the location of these subcortical structures.)

uations that lead to aversive experiences, since injecting chemicals that temporarily block its functioning makes rats less able to learn to avoid stimuli associated with pain (Rashidy-Pour et al., 1995). These regions receive projections from midbrain and thalamic nuclei involved in learning.

The **amygdala** is an almond-shaped structure (*amygdala* is Latin for "almond") *involved in many emotional processes, especially learning and remembering emotionally significant events* (Aggleton, 1992; LeDoux, 2002). One of its primary roles is to attach emotional significance to events. The amygdala appears to be particularly important in fear responses. Lesioning the amygdala in rats, for example, inhibits learned fear responses—that is, the rats no longer avoid a stimulus they had previously connected with pain (LaBar & LeDoux, 1996).

The amygdala is also involved in recognizing emotion, particularly fearful emotion, in other people. One study using PET technology found that presenting pictures of fearful rather than neutral or happy faces activated the left amygdala and that the amount of activation strongly correlated with the amount of fear displayed in the pictures (Morris et al., 1996). From an evolutionary perspective, these findings suggest that humans have evolved particular mechanisms for detecting fear in others and that these "fear detectors" are anatomically connected to neural circuits that produce fear. This hypothesis makes sense, since fear in others is likely a signal of danger to oneself. In fact, infants as young as 9 to 12 months show distress when they see distress on their parents' faces (Campos et al., 1992). Remarkably, the amygdala can respond to threatening stimuli even when the person has no awareness of seeing them. If researchers present a threatening stimulus so quickly that the person cannot report seeing it, the amygdala may nevertheless be activated, a suggestion that it is detecting some very subtle cues for danger (Morris et al., 1998).

The **hippocampus** is *particularly important for storing new information in memory so that the person can later consciously remember it* (see, e.g., Eldridge et al., 2000; Squire & Zola-Morgan, 1991). This was demonstrated dramatically in a famous case study by Brenda Milner and her colleagues (Milner et al., 1968; Scoville & Milner, 1957). A man identified as H. M. underwent surgery to control life-threatening epileptic seizures. The surgeon removed sections of his cortex and some underlying structures. Unfortunately, one of those structures was the hippocampus, and although H. M. was now free of seizures, he was also "free" of the capacity to remember new information.

Actually, that is only half the story, and the other half has, in the last two decades, changed our understanding of memory. H. M. did lose his memory in the sense that psychologists and laypeople alike have traditionally understood memory. For example, every time he met Dr. Milner, who studied him over 20 years, he had to be reintroduced; invariably, he would smile politely and tell her it was a pleasure to make her acquaintance. But, as we will see in Chapter 6, we now know that certain kinds of memory do not involve the hippocampus, and H. M. retained those capacities. For example, on one occasion H. M.'s father took him to visit his mother in the hospital. Afterward, H. M. did not remember anything of the visit, but he "expressed a vague idea that something might have happened to his mother" (Milner et al., 1968, p. 216). Amazingly, despite a lack of explicit knowledge of his mother's death, H. M. never responded to reminders of this event with the emotional response that would be expected when someone first heard this news (Hirst, 1994). He did not "remember" his mother's death, but it registered nonetheless.

The Basal Ganglia The **basal ganglia** are *a set of structures located near the thalamus and hypothalamus that are involved in a wide array of functions, particularly movement and judgments requiring minimal conscious thought*. Damage to structures in the basal ganglia can affect posture and muscle tone or cause abnormal movements. The basal ganglia have been implicated in Parkinson's disease and in the epidemic of encephalitis lethargica that struck millions early in the twentieth century (including Ms. B; see opening vignette). The dopamine-rich neurons of the sub-

Making Connections

Learning a complex piece of music at first requires the involvement of some of our most advanced cortical circuits. However, over time, the basal ganglia come to regulate the movement of the fingers. In fact, we can "remember" with our fingers far faster than we can consciously think about what our fingers are doing (Chapters 6 and 7).

stantia nigra (in the midbrain) normally project to the basal ganglia. When these neurons die, as in Parkinson's, they stop sending signals to the basal ganglia, which in turn cease functioning properly. Some neural circuits involving the basal ganglia appear to inhibit movement, whereas others initiate it, since lesions in different sections of the basal ganglia can either release movements (leading to twitches or jerky movements) or block them (leading to Parkinsonian symptoms).

Damage to the basal ganglia can also lead to a variety of emotional, social, and cognitive impairments (Knowlton et al., 1996; Lieberman, 2000; Postle & D'Esposito, 1999). For example, people with basal ganglia damage sometimes have difficulty making rapid, automatic judgments about how to classify or understand the meaning of things they see or hear. Thus, a person with damage to certain regions of the basal ganglia may have difficulty recognizing that a subtle change in another person's tone of voice reflects sarcasm—the kind of judgment the rest of us make without a moment's thought.

INTERIM SUMMARY

The **subcortical forebrain** consists of the **hypothalamus, thalamus**, the **subcortical structures** of the cerebrum, the **limbic system**, and the **basal ganglia**. The hypothalamus helps regulate a wide range of behaviors, including eating, sleeping, sexual activity, and emotional experience. Among its other functions, the thalamus processes incoming sensory information and transmits this information to higher brain centers. The **limbic system** includes the septal area, **amygdala**, and **hippocampus**. The precise functions of the septal area are unclear, although it appears to be involved in learning to act in ways that avoid pain and produce pleasure. The amygdala is crucial to the experience of emotion. The hippocampus plays an important role in committing new information to memory. **Basal ganglia** structures are involved in the control of movement and also play a part in "automatic" responses and judgments that may normally require little conscious attention.

The Cerebral Cortex

The cerebral cortex (from the Latin for "bark") consists of a 3-millimeter-thick layer of densely packed interneurons; it is grayish in color and highly convoluted (i.e., filled with twists and turns). The convolutions appear to serve a purpose: Just as crumpling a piece of paper into a tight wad reduces its size, the folds and wrinkles of the cortex allow a relatively large area of cortical cells to fit into a compact region within the skull. The hills of these convolutions are known as *gyri* (plural of *gyrus*) and the valleys as *sulci* (plural of *sulcus*). The cerebral cortex is the largest part of the human brain, comprising 80 percent of the brain's mass (Kolb & Whishaw, 2001).

In humans, the **cerebral cortex** performs three functions. First, it *allows the flexible construction of sequences of voluntary movements involved in activities such as changing a tire or playing a piano concerto*. Second, *it permits subtle discriminations among complex sensory patterns*; without a cerebral cortex, the words gene and gem would be indistinguishable. Third, *it makes possible symbolic thinking*—the ability to use symbols such as words or pictorial signs (like a flag) to represent an object or concept with a complex meaning. The capacity to think symbolically enables people to have conversations about things that do not exist or are not presently in view; it is the foundation of human thought and language (Finlay & Darlington, 1995).

Primary and Association Areas   The cortex consists of regions specialized for different functions, such as vision, hearing, and body sensation. Each of these areas can be divided roughly into two zones, called primary and association cortex. The **primary areas** *of the cortex process raw sensory information or (in one section of the brain, the frontal lobes) initiate movement. The* **association areas** *are involved in complex mental processes such as forming perceptions, ideas, and plans*; they were given this name in the nineteenth century because scientists believed that higher mental functioning revolved around the association of one idea with another.

The primary areas are responsible for the initial cortical processing of sensory information. Neurons in these zones receive sensory information, usually via the thalamus, from sensory receptors in the ears, eyes, skin, and muscles. When a person sees a safety pin lying on a dresser, the primary or sensory areas receive the simple visual sensations that make up the contours of the safety pin. Activation of circuits in the visual association cortex enables the person to recognize the object as a safety pin rather than a needle or a formless shiny object.

Neurons in the primary areas tend to have more specific functions than neurons in association cortex. Many of these neurons are wired to register very basic, and very specific, attributes of a stimulus. For example, some neurons in the primary visual cortex respond to horizontal lines but not to vertical lines; other neurons respond only to vertical lines (Hubel & Wiesel, 1963). Some neurons in the association cortex are equally specific in their functions, but many develop their functions through experience. The brain may be wired from birth to detect the contours of objects like safety pins, but a person must learn what a safety pin is and does. From an evolutionary perspective, this combination of "hard-wired" and "flexible" neurons is very important: It guarantees that we have the capacity to detect features of any environment that are likely to be relevant to adaptation, but we can also learn the features of the specific environment in which we find ourselves.

Lobes of the Cerebral Cortex   *The cerebrum is divided into two roughly symmetrical halves*, or **cerebral hemispheres**, which are separated by the *longitudinal fissure*. (A *fissure* is a deep sulcus, or valley.) *A band of neural fibers called the* **corpus callosum** *connects the right and left hemispheres*. Each hemisphere consists of four regions, or lobes: occipital, parietal, frontal, and temporal. Thus, a person has a right and left occipital lobe, a right and left parietal lobe, and so forth (Figure 3.11).

The Occipital Lobes   The **occipital lobes**, *located in the rear portion of the cortex, are specialized for vision*. Primary areas of the occipital lobes receive visual input from the thalamus. The thalamus, in turn, receives information from the receptors in the retina via the optic nerve. The primary areas respond to relatively simple features of a visual stimulus, and the association areas organize these simple characteristics into more complex maps of features of objects and their position in space. Damage to the primary areas leads to partial or complete blindness.

The visual association cortex, which actually extends into neighboring lobes, projects (i.e., sends axons carrying messages) to several regions throughout the cortex that receive other types of sensory information, such as auditory or tactile (touch). Areas that receive information from more than one sensory system are called *polysensory areas*. The existence of polysensory areas at various levels of the brain (including subcortical levels) helps us, for example, to associate the sight of a car stopping suddenly with the sound of squealing tires.

The Parietal Lobes   The **parietal lobes** *are located in front of the occipital lobes. They are involved in several functions, including the sense of touch, detecting movement in the environment, locating objects in space, and experiencing one's own body as it moves through space*. A person with damage to the primary area of the parietal lobes may be unable to feel a thimble on her finger, whereas damage to the association area could render her unable to recognize the object she was feeling as a thimble or to understand what the object does.

The primary area of the parietal lobe, called the **somatosensory cortex**, lies directly behind the *central fissure*, which divides the parietal lobe from the frontal lobe.

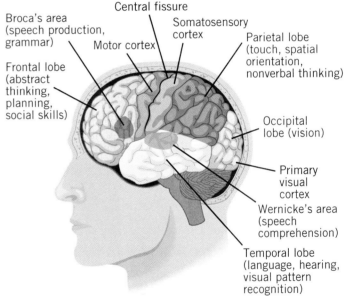

FIGURE 3.11   The lobes of the cerebral cortex. The cortex has four lobes, each specialized for different functions and each containing primary and association areas.

Somatosensory cortex

Motor cortex

Forearm   Arm   Head
Hand   Elbow   Neck
Fingers   Hip
Thumb   Trunk
Jaw
Teeth   Leg
Gums
Lips   Toes
Face
Nose   Genitals
Eye
Tongue
Pharynx
Intra-abdominal

Cross section of the somatosensory cortex
(just behind, or *posterior* to, the central fissure)

FIGURE 3.12   The motor and somatosensory cortex. (*a*) The motor cortex initiates movement. The somatosensory cortex receives sensory information from the spinal cord, largely via the thalamus. (*b*) Both the motor and the somatosensory cortex devote space according to the importance, neural density (number of neurons), and complexity of the anatomical regions to which they are connected. Here we see a functional map of the somatosensory cortex; the motor cortex adjacent to it is similarly arranged. *Source:* Adapted from Penfield and Rasmussen, 1978.

Apply & Discuss

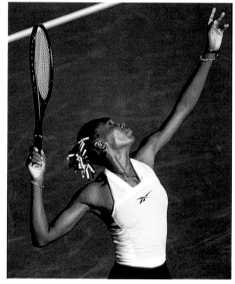

The players are tied at two sets apiece, and Venus Williams is about to serve.

■ Trace what is happening in her nervous system as she experiences the emotion of the moment. What cortical and subcortical circuits are activated as she considers the meaning of the situation and as she feels the pressure?

■ Trace what is happening in her nervous system as she plans and executes her serve. What parts of the cortex become active first? How do her intentions actually get carried out by her muscles?

Different sections of the somatosensory cortex receive information from different parts of the body (Figure 3.12). Thus, one section registers sensations from the hand, another from the foot, and so forth. The parietal lobes are also involved in complex visual processing, particularly the posterior (back) regions nearest to the occipital lobes.

The Frontal Lobes   The **frontal lobes** *are involved in a number of functions, including movement, attention, planning, social skills, abstract thinking, memory, and some aspects of personality* (see Goldman-Rakic, 1995; Russell & Roxanas, 1990). Just as there is a sensory homunculus in the parietal lobe, there is a motor homunculus in the **motor cortex**, *the primary zone of the frontal lobe* (Figure 3.12). Through its projections to the basal ganglia, cerebellum, and spinal cord, the motor cortex initiates voluntary movement. The motor cortex and the adjacent somatosensory cortex send and receive information from the same parts of the body.

As Figure 3.12 indicates, the amount of space devoted to different parts of the body in the motor and somatosensory cortexes is not directly proportional to their size. Parts of the body that produce fine motor movements or have particularly dense and sensitive receptors take up more space in the motor and somatosensory cortexes. These body parts tend to serve important or complex functions and thus require more processing capacity. In humans, the hands, which are crucial to exploring objects and using tools, occupy considerable territory, whereas a section of the back of similar size occupies only a fraction of that space. Other species have different cortical "priorities"; in cats, for example, input from the whiskers receives considerably more space than does input from "whiskers" on the face of human males.

In the frontal lobes, the primary area is motor rather than sensory. The association cortex is involved in planning and putting together sequences of behavior. Neurons in the primary areas then issue specific commands to motor neurons throughout the body.

Damage to the frontal lobes can lead to a wide array of problems, from paralysis to difficulty in thinking abstractly, focusing attention efficiently, coordinating complex sequences of behavior, and adjusting socially (Adolphs, 1999; Damasio, 1994). Lesions in other parts of the brain that project to the frontal lobes can produce similar symptoms because the frontal lobes fail to receive normal activation. For example, the victims of encephalitis lethargica could not initiate movements even though their frontal lobes were intact because projections from the basal ganglia that normally activate the frontal lobes were impaired by dopamine depletion.

In most individuals, the left frontal lobe is also involved in language. **Broca's area**, *located in the left frontal lobe at the base of the motor cortex, is specialized for movements of the mouth and tongue necessary for speech production. It also plays a pivotal role in the use and understanding of grammar*. Damage to Broca's area causes *Broca's aphasia*, characterized by difficulty speaking, putting together grammatical sentences, and articulating words, even though the person remains able to comprehend language. Individuals with lesions to this area occasionally have difficulty comprehending complex sentences if subjects and objects cannot be easily recognized from context. For example, they might have difficulty decoding the sentence "The cat, which was under the hammock, chased the bird, which was flying over the dog."

The frontal lobes are also suspected to be the site of neural dysfunction that underlies schizophrenia. Several lines of evidence support this assertion. First, PET scans reveal abnormal neural activity in the frontal lobes of schizophrenics. Second, schizophrenic symptoms do not begin to emerge until later in the teen years. The frontal lobes are not only the most recent evolutionarily areas of the brain, but they are also the last areas to fully mature. Normally, only when the frontal lobes mature is schizophrenia revealed. In a treatment no longer performed, some especially violent and irrational psychiatric patients had their prefrontal lobes surgically disconnected in a procedure called *prefrontal lobotomy* (i.e., the lobes of the prefrontal cortex were disconnected from the rest of the brain). After recovery the patients were indeed less violent: they did not exhibit *any* emotion or voluntary behaviors. This was the fate of the lead character in the novel and movie *One Flew over the Cuckoo's Nest*.

The Temporal Lobes The **temporal lobes**, *located in the lower side portions of the cortex, are particularly important in audition (hearing) and language, although they have other functions as well*. The connection between hearing and language makes evolutionary sense because language, until relatively recently, was always spoken (rather than written). The primary cortex receives sensory information from the ears, and the association cortex breaks the flow of sound into meaningful units (such as words). Cells in the primary cortex respond to particular frequencies of sound (i.e., to different tones) and are arranged anatomically from low (toward the front of the brain) to high frequencies (toward the back).

For most people the left hemisphere of the temporal lobe is specialized for language, although some linguistic functions are shared by the right hemisphere. **Wernicke's area**, *located in the left temporal lobe, is important in language comprehension*. Damage to Wernicke's area may produce *Wernicke's aphasia*, characterized by difficulty understanding what words and sentences mean. Patients with Wernicke's aphasia often produce "word salad": They may speak fluently and expressively, as if their speech were meaningful, but the words are tossed together so that they make little sense. In contrast, right temporal damage typically results in nonverbal deficits, such as difficulty recognizing songs, faces, or paintings.

Although psychologists once believed that hearing and language were the primary functions of the temporal lobes, more recent research suggests that the temporal lobes have multiple sections and that these different sections serve different functions (Rodman, 1997). For example, regions toward the back (posterior) of the temporal lobes respond to concrete visual features of objects such as color and shape, whereas regions toward the front respond to more abstract knowledge (such as memory for objects, or the meaning of the concept democracy) (Graham et al., 1999; Ishai et al., 1999; Srinivas et al., 1997). In general, information processed toward the back of temporal lobes is more concrete and specific, whereas information processed toward the front is more abstract and integrated.

Making Connections

Circuits in the frontal lobes make possible some of the most extraordinary feats of the human intellect, from solving equations to understanding complex social situations (Chapters 6 and 7).

INTERIM SUMMARY

The **cerebral cortex** includes **primary areas**, which usually process raw sensory data (except in the frontal lobes), and **association areas**, which are involved in complex mental processes such as perception and thinking. The cortex consists of two hemispheres, each of which has four lobes. The **occipital lobes** are involved in vision. The **parietal lobes** are involved in the sense of touch, perception of movement, and location of objects in space. The **frontal lobes** serve a variety of functions, such as coordinating and initiating movement, attention, planning, social skills, abstract thinking, memory, and aspects of personality. Sections of the **temporal lobes** are important in hearing, language, and recognizing objects by sight.

Cerebral Lateralization   We have seen that the left frontal and temporal lobes tend to play a more important role in speech and language than their right-hemisphere counterparts. This raises the question of whether other cortical functions are **lateralized**, that is, *localized to one or the other side of the brain*.

Global generalizations require caution because most functions that are popularly considered to be lateralized are actually represented on both sides of the brain in most people. However, some division of labor between the hemispheres does exist, with each side dominant for (i.e., in more control of) certain functions.

In general, at least for right-handed people, the left hemisphere tends to be dominant for language, logic, complex motor behavior, and aspects of consciousness (particularly verbal aspects). Many of these left-hemisphere functions are analytical; they break down thoughts and perceptions into component parts and analyze the relations among them. The right hemisphere tends to be dominant for nonlinguistic functions, such as forming visual maps of the environment. Studies indicate that it is involved in the recognition of faces, places, and nonlinguistic sounds such as music.

The right hemisphere's specialization for nonlinguistic sounds seems to hold in nonhuman animals as well: Japanese macaque monkeys, for example, process vocalizations from other macaques on the left but other sounds in their environment on the right (Petersen et al., 1984). Recent research indicates that the region of the brain that constitutes Wernicke's area of the left temporal lobe in humans may have special significance in chimpanzees as well, since this region is larger in the left than in the right hemisphere in chimps, as in humans (Gannon et al., 1998).

Split-Brain Studies   A particularly important source of information about cerebral lateralization has been case studies of **split-brain** *patients—individuals whose corpus callosum has been surgically cut, blocking communication between the two hemispheres*. Severing this connective tissue is a radical treatment for severe epileptic seizures that spread from one hemisphere to another and cannot be controlled by other means.

In their everyday behavior, split-brain patients generally appear normal (Sperry, 1984). However, their two hemispheres can actually operate independently, and each may be oblivious to what the other is doing. Under certain experimental circumstances, the disconnection between the two minds housed in one brain becomes apparent.

To understand the results of these experiments, bear in mind that the left hemisphere, which is dominant for most speech functions, receives information from the right visual field and that the right hemisphere receives information from the left. Normally, whether the right or left hemisphere receives the information makes little difference because once the message reaches the brain, the two hemispheres freely pass information between them via the corpus callosum. Severing the corpus callosum, however, blocks this sharing of information (Gazzaniga, 1967).

Figure 3.13*a* depicts a typical split-brain experiment. A patient is seated at a table, and the surface of the table is blocked from view by a screen so the individual cannot

Cartoon by Sidney Harris.

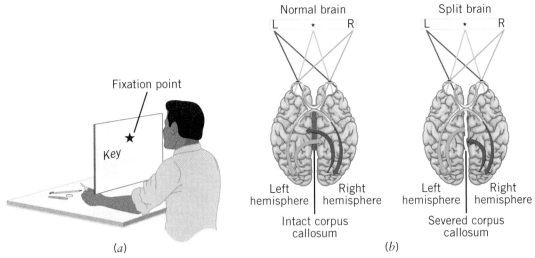

FIGURE 3.13 A split-brain experiment. In a typical split-brain study (*a*), a patient sees the word key flashed on the left portion of the screen. Although he cannot name what he has seen, because speech is lateralized to the left hemisphere, he is able to use his left hand to select the key from a number of objects because the right hemisphere, which has "seen" the key, controls the left hand and has some language skills. Part (*b*) illustrates the way information from the left and right visual fields is transmitted to the brain in normal and split brains. When participants focus their vision on a point in the middle of the visual field (such as the star in the diagram), anything on the left of this fixation point (for instance, point L) is sensed by receptors on the right half of each eye. This information is subsequently processed by the right hemisphere. In the normal brain, information is readily transmitted via the corpus callosum between the two hemispheres. In the split-brain patient, because of the severed neural route, the right and left hemispheres "see" different things. *Source:* Part (a) adapted from Gazzaniga, 1967.

see objects on it. The experimenter asks the person to focus on a point in the center of the screen. A word (here, key) is quickly flashed on the left side of the screen (which is therefore processed in the right hemisphere). When information is flashed for only about 150 milliseconds, the eyes do not have time to move, ensuring that the information is sent to only one hemisphere. The patient is unable to identify the word verbally because the information never reached his left hemisphere, which is dominant for speech. He can, however, select a key with his left hand from the array of objects hidden behind the screen because the left hand receives information from the right hemisphere, which "saw" the key. Thus, the right hand literally does not know what the left hand is doing, and neither does the left hemisphere. Figure 3.13b illustrates the way visual information from the left and right visual fields is transmitted to the brain in normal and split-brain patients.

This research raises an intriguing question: Can a person with two independent hemispheres be literally of two minds, with two centers of conscious awareness, like Siamese twins joined at the cortex? Consider the case of a 10-year-old boy with a split brain (LeDoux et al., 1977). In one set of tests, the boy was asked about his sense of himself, his future, and his likes and dislikes. The examiner asked the boy questions in which a word or words were replaced by the word blank. The missing words were then presented to one hemisphere or the other. For example, when the boy was asked, "Who _____?" the missing words "are you" were projected to the left or the right hemisphere. Not surprisingly, the boy could answer verbally only when inquiries were made to the left hemisphere. The right hemisphere could, however, answer by spelling out words with letter tiles with the left hand (because the right hemisphere is usually not entirely devoid of language) when the question was flashed to the right hemisphere. Thus, the boy could describe his feelings or moods with both hemispheres.

Big Picture φ Question 5

To what extent are psychological processes the same in men and women?

Many times the views expressed by the right and left hemispheres overlapped, but not always. One day, when the boy was in a pleasant mood, his hemispheres tended to agree (both, for example, reporting high self-esteem). Another day, when the boy seemed anxious and behaved aggressively, the hemispheres were in disagreement. In general, his right-hemisphere responses were consistently more negative than those of the left, as if the right hemisphere tended to be in a worse mood.

Researchers using other methods have also reported that the two hemispheres differ in their processing of positive and negative emotions and that these differences may exist at birth (Davidson, 1995; Fox, 1991b). Left frontal regions are generally more involved in processing positive feelings that motivate approach toward objects in the environment, whereas right frontal regions are more related to negative emotions that motivate avoidance or withdrawal.

Sex Differences in Lateralization Psychologists have long known that females typically score higher on tests of verbal fluency, perceptual speed, and manual dexterity than males, whereas males tend to score higher on tests of mathematical ability and spatial processing, particularly geometric thinking (Casey et al., 1997; Maccoby & Jacklin, 1974). In a study of students under age 13 with exceptional mathematical ability (measured by scores of 700 or above on the SAT), boys outnumbered girls 13 to 1 (Benbow & Stanley, 1983). On the other hand, males are much more likely than females to develop learning disabilities with reading and language comprehension.

Although most of these sex differences are not particularly large (Caplan et al., 1997; Hyde, 1990), they have been documented in several countries and have not consistently decreased over the last two decades despite social changes encouraging equality of the sexes (see Bradbury, 1989; Randhawa, 1991). Psychologists have thus debated whether such discrepancies in performance might be based in part on innate differences between the brains of men and women.

Some data suggest that women's and men's brains may indeed differ in ways that affect cognitive functioning. At a hormonal level, research with human and nonhuman primates indicates that the presence of testosterone and estrogen in the bloodstream early in development influences aspects of brain development (Clark & Goldman-Rakic, 1989; Gorski & Barraclough, 1963). One study found that level of exposure to testosterone during the second trimester of pregnancy predicted the speed with which children could rotate mental images in their minds at age 7 (Grimshaw et al., 1995). Some evidence even suggests that women's spatial abilities on certain tasks are lower during high-estrogen periods of the menstrual cycle, whereas motor skills, on which females typically have an advantage, are superior during high-estrogen periods (Kimura, 1987).

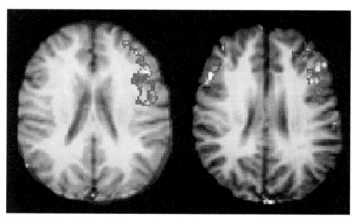

FIGURE 3.14 Gender differences in cortical activation during a rhyming task. The photo on the left shows that for males, rhyming activated only Broca's area in the left frontal lobe. For females (right), this task activated the same region in both hemispheres. (From the angle at which these images were taken, left activation appears on the right.) *Source:* Shaywitz et al., 1995. NMR/Yale Medical School.

Perhaps the most definitive data on gender differences in the brain come from recent research using fMRI technology (Shaywitz et al., 1995). In males, a rhyming task activated Broca's area in the left frontal lobe. The same task in females produced frontal activation in both hemispheres (Figure 3.14). Thus, in females, language appears less lateralized.

INTERIM SUMMARY

Some psychological functions are **lateralized**, or processed primarily by one hemisphere. In general, the left hemisphere is more verbal and analytic, and the right is specialized for nonlinguistic functions. Although the differences tend to be relatively small, males and females tend to differ in cognitive strengths, which appear to be related in part to differences between their brains, including the extent of lateralization of functions such as language

The issue of how, and in what ways, cultural practices and beliefs influence cognitive abilities raises an intriguing question: Because all abilities reflect the actions of neural circuits, can environmental and cultural factors actually affect the circuitry of the brain?

We have little trouble imagining that biological factors can alter the brain. Tumors, or abnormal tissue growths, can damage regions of the brain by putting pressure on them, leading to symptoms as varied as blurred vision, searing headaches, or explosive emotional outbursts. High blood pressure or diseases of the blood vessels can lead to strokes, in which blood flow to regions of the brain is interrupted. If the interruption occurs for more than about 10 minutes, the cells in that area die; the result can be paralysis, loss of speech, or even death if the stroke destroys neural regions vital for life support such as the medulla or hypothalamus. Trauma to the nervous system caused by automobile accidents, blows to the head, or falls that break the neck can have similar effects, as can infections caused by viruses, bacteria, or parasites.

But what about psychological blows to the head, or, conversely, experiences that enrich the brain or steer it in one direction or another? Research suggests that social and environmental processes can indeed alter the structure of the brain. A fascinating line of research indicates that early sensory enrichment or deprivation can affect the brain in fundamental ways (Heritch et al., 1990; Rosenzweig et al., 1972). In one series of studies, young male rats were raised in one of two conditions: an enriched environment, with 6 to 12 rats sharing an open-mesh cage filled with toys, or an impoverished one, in which rats lived alone without toys or companions (Cummins et al., 1977). Days or months later, the experimenters weighed the rats' forebrains. The brains of enriched rats tended to be heavier than those of the deprived rats, an indication that different environments can alter the course of neural development.

Is the same true of humans? And can cultural differences become translated into neurological differences? The human brain triples in weight in the first two years and quadruples to its adult weight by age 14 (Winson, 1985). Thus, social, cultural, and other environmental influences can become *built into* the brain (Shore, 1995), particularly into the more evolutionarily recent cortical regions involved in complex thought and learning (Damasio, 1994).

For instance, many native Asian language speakers have difficulty distinguishing *la* from *ra* because Asian languages do not distinguish these units of sound. One study found that Japanese people who heard sound frequencies between *la* and *ra* did not hear them as *either la or ra*, as do Americans (Goto, 1971). If children do not hear certain linguistic patterns in the first few years of life (such as the *la–ra* distinction, the French *r*, or the Hebrew *ch*), they may lose the capacity to do so. These patterns may then have to be laid down with different and much less efficient neural machinery later on (Lenneberg, 1967).

Big Picture φ Question 1

To what extent can mental processes be reduced to the brain or the body?

Genetics and Evolution

Having described the structure and function of the nervous system, we conclude this chapter with a brief discussion of the influence of genetics and evolution on psychological functioning. Few people would argue with the view that hair and eye color are heavily influenced by genetics or that genetic vulnerabilities contribute to heart disease, cancer, and diabetes. Is the same true of psychological qualities or disorders?

FIGURE 3.15   A magnified photograph of human chromosomes.

The Influence of Genetics on Psychological Functioning

Psychologists interested in genetics study the influence of genetic blueprints, or genotypes, on observable psychological attributes or qualities, or phenotypes. The phenotypes that interest psychologists are characteristics such as quickness of thought, extroverted behavior, and the tendency to become anxious or depressed. The **gene** *is the unit of hereditary transmission*. Although a single gene may control eye color, genetic contributions to most complex phenomena, such as intelligence or personality, reflect the action of many genes.

Genes are encoded in the DNA (deoxyribonucleic acid) contained within the nucleus of every cell in the body. Genes are arranged along **chromosomes**—*strands of paired DNA that spiral around each other* (Figure 3.15). Each individual gene has two **alleles**, *forms of the gene*, which can be either dominant or recessive. For any given characteristic—for example, brown-eyed or blue-eyed—the dominant allele is referred to with a capital letter ("R" for brown) and the recessive allele is referred to with the lower case of the dominant allele ("r" for blue). As the names suggest, the dominant allele "trumps" or overwhelms the recessive allele. The characteristics of the offspring depend on which pair of alleles for a given gene are inherited from the parents. For two brown-eyed parents with both alleles (that is Rr) there are four possible combinations of alleles for their offspring: RR, Rr, rR, and rr. Given that the brown-eyed form is dominant, three out of every four offspring should have brown eyes (the RR, Rr, and rR combinations of the parental alleles). The fourth offspring should have blue eyes (rr).

Both the RR and rr genotypes are called **homozygous**; *both alleles are the same*. The Rr and rR genotypes are **heterozygous**; *the two alleles are different*. At first it was thought that the only time the recessive allele was expressed (i.e., evident in the offspring) was when the alleles were homozygous recessive. The bigger picture turns out to be more complicated, however. For some genes there is **incomplete dominance** of the alleles and the heterozygous state is intermediate between the recessive and the dominant alleles. For example, not everyone has brown eyes or blue eyes. Some people's eyes are hazel.

Determining which genes are most closely tied to particular psychological or physical problems is a daunting task. *One of the methods frequently used by researchers to locate particular genes* is **linkage studies**. Researchers first examine genetic markers, segments of DNA that show wide variability across individuals and whose location along a chromosome is already known (Tavris & Wade, 2001). "They then look for patterns of inheritance of these markers in large families in which a condition—say, depression or impulsive violence—is common. If a marker tends to exist only in family members who have the condition, then it can be used as a genetic landmark: The gene involved in the condition is apt to be located nearby on the chromosome, so researchers have some idea where to search for it" (Tavris & Wade, 2001, p. 77).

One of the most momentous occasions in the history of science occurred in the first months of the twenty-first century, as scientists working on the Human Genome Project, an international collaborative effort, mapped the genetic structure of all 46 human chromosomes. Although in many respects the most important work lies ahead, mapping the human genome is beginning to allow researchers to discover genes that lead to abnormal cellular responses and contribute to a variety of diseases, from cancer to schizophrenia.

Behavioral Genetics

Human cells have 46 chromosomes, except sperm cells in males and egg cells in females, each of which has 23. The union of a sperm and an egg creates a cell with 46 chromosomes, half from the mother and half from the father. Children receive a somewhat random selection of half the genetic material of each parent, which means that the probability that a parent and child will share any particular gene that varies in the population (such as genes for eye color) is 1 out of 2, or .50.

The probability of sharing genes among relatives is termed the **degree of relatedness**. Table 3.3 shows the degree of relatedness for various relatives. The fact that relatives differ in degree of relatedness enables researchers to tease apart the relative contributions of heredity and environment to phenotypic differences between individuals. If the similarity between relatives on attributes such as intelligence or conscientiousness varies with their degree of relatedness, this suggests genetic influence, especially if the relatives did not share a common upbringing (such as siblings adopted into different families).

A subfield called *behavioral genetics* has made rapid advances in our understanding of the relative roles of genetics and environment in shaping mental processes and behavior (Chapter 1). Genetic influences are far greater than once believed in a number of domains, including personality, intelligence, and mental illness (Gottesman, 1991; McGue et al., 1993; Plomin et al., 1997).

Particularly important for research on the genetic basis of behavioral differences are identical and fraternal twins who typically share similar environments but differ in their degree of relatedness. **Monozygotic (MZ, or identical) twins** *develop from the union of the same sperm and egg*. Because they share the same genetic makeup, their degree of genetic relatedness is 1.0. In contrast, **dizygotic (DZ, or fraternal) twins** *develop from the union of two sperm with two separate eggs*. Like other siblings, their degree of relatedness is .50, since they have a 50 percent chance of sharing the same gene for any characteristic. Thus, if a psychological attribute is genetically influenced, MZ twins should be more likely than DZ twins and other siblings to share it.

This method is not free of bias; identical twins may receive more similar treatment than do fraternal twins, because they look the same. Thus, behavioral geneticists also compare twins reared together in the same family with twins who were adopted separately and reared apart (Loehlin, 1992; Lykken et al., 1992; Tellegen et al., 1988).

Findings from these studies have allowed psychologists to estimate the extent to which differences among individuals on psychological dimensions such as intelligence and personality are inherited or heritable. A **heritability coefficient** *quantifies the extent to which variation in the trait across individuals* (such as high or low levels of conscientiousness) *can be accounted for by genetic variation*. A coefficient of 0 indicates no heritability at all, whereas a coefficient of 1.0 indicates that a trait is completely heritable. Studies of personality traits across many different cultures have found heritability estimates as high as .60; that is, 60 percent of the variance in those traits within a group of people can be attributed to genetics.

An important point—and one that is often misunderstood—is that **heritability** refers to *genetic influences on variability among individuals*; it says nothing about the extent to which a trait is genetically determined. An example makes this point clear. The fact that humans have two eyes is genetically determined. For all practical purposes, however, humans show no variability in the expression of the trait of two-eyedness because virtually all humans are born with two eyes. Thus, the heritability of two-eyedness is 0; genetic variability is not correlated with phenotypic or observed variability because almost no variability exists. In contrast, the trait of eye *color* has a very high degree of heritability (approaching 1.0) in a heterogeneous population. Thus, heritability refers to the proportion of variability among individuals on an observed trait (phenotypic variance) that can be accounted for by variability in their genes (genotypic variance).

Genes influence both intellectual functioning (Chapter 8) and personality (Chapter 12). Several studies of the personality characteristics of twins have produced heritability estimates from .15 to .50 (i.e., up to 50 percent heritability) on a broad spectrum of traits, including conservatism, neuroticism, nurturance, assertiveness, and aggressiveness (Plomin et al., 1997). Some findings have been very surprising and counterintuitive. For example, identical twins reared apart, who may never have even met each other, tend to have very similar vocational interests and levels of job satisfaction (Arvey

Apply & Discuss

Genetic testing can predict whether a person will get breast cancer, Huntington's chorea, or Alzheimer's. Such applications are good, as they help to start early treatment and may also affect a person's choice of whether to have children (i.e., whether to pass the gene on). At the same time, however, genetic testing gives information to insurance companies, which may refuse to cover treatment for the genetic disease.

■ How should we use such genetic information?

Big Picture φ Question 6

What is the relation between nature and nurture in shaping psychological processes?

Table 3.3 ■■ Degree of Relatedness among Selected Relatives

Relation	Degree of Relatedness
Identical (MZ) twin	1.0
Fraternal (DZ) twin	.50
Parent/child	.50
Sibling	.50
Grandparent/grandchild	.25
Half-sibling	.25
First cousin	.125
Nonbiological parent/adopted child	0.0

Jerry Levey and Mark Newman, separated from birth, met when a colleague did a double-take at a fire-fighters convention.

et al., 1994; Moloney et al., 1991). Researchers have even found a genetic influence on religious attitudes, beliefs, and values (Waller et al., 1990). Remarkably, the likelihood of divorce is influenced by genetics, since personality traits such as the tendency to be unhappy are partly under genetic control and influence life events such as divorce (Jockin et al., 1996). Heritability estimates for IQ are over .50 (McGue & Bouchard, 1998).

In interpreting findings such as these, it is important to remember, as emphasized by leading behavioral geneticists but too readily forgotten, that heritability in the range of 50 percent means that environmental factors are equally important—they account for the other 50 percent (Kandel, 1998). Equally important in understanding heritability is that many genes require environmental input to "turn them on"; otherwise, they are never expressed. Thus, even though a trait may be highly heritable, whether it even "shows up" in behavior may actually depend on the environment. As we will see throughout the book, in most domains psychologists have become less interested in parceling out the relative roles of genes and environment than in understanding the way genetic and environmental variables interact.

A Global Vista   Genetic Homogeneity

It is a curious observation that *Homo sapiens* is represented by a single species (Smith & Layton, 1989). For most genuses, there are many if not thousands of species. Given that humans have conquered a vast variety of environments, each demanding different specializations to ensure survival, how did speciation not occur?

While each race has a distinct culture, language, and physical appearance, the respective gene pools have not drifted far enough apart to prevent viable offspring from interbreeding. (A definition of **speciation** is that *members of a previously common gene pool have become separated and over time genetic drift has acted to such an extent that the two subpopulations can no longer interbreed*.) In fact, any given population of humans contains 80 percent of the human genome (Owens & King, 1999). Within a continent there is only a 4 percent difference in the gene pool, and even across continents the difference is only 6 percent.

Several contributing factors for this limited difference have been proposed. First, historical migrations, to find better food or to escape harsh conditions, have helped to maintain the homogeneity of the human gene pool (Owens & King, 1999). Second, the development of symbolic culture (language, customs, beliefs, etc.) make environmental pressures toward speciation less likely (Smith & Layton, 1989). Third, there is cross-cultural as well as cross-generational transmission of knowledge. Because of trade, such as food exchange, groups are not as tied to one locale. Through barter and marriage alliances, groups maintain genetic homogeneity. The result: a rich gene pool, which maintains our adaptability.

Further, as humans evolve and take more control of their environment our gene pool is less influenced by natural selection. As we become more dependent on learning and on social transmission of information, as our ability to manipulate not only our environment but also our genome increases, natural selection has less and less influence on our evolution. And, it is more influenced by our actions, our medical advances, and our increasing impact on the world. This increased involvement may pose a problem for us…evolution has no foresight. It is a combination of genetic diversity and of changing environmental selective pressures. If we reduce our genetic diversity (through bioengineering, see below) and we continue to try to control our environ-

Big Picture φ Question 6

What is the relation between nature and nurture in shaping psychological processes?

ment (i.e., through use of pesticides, bioengineering, or selective breeding–domestication), we are attempting to have foresight. Species survive because of the interactions
of genes and environment. We control both, to some degree at least, but will we be the
instruments of our own extinction? Evolution works best without foresight, and, by in-
terfering with this, as Pogo said "We have met the enemy and he is us!" (Kelly, 1971).

INTERIM SUMMARY

Psychologists interested in genetics study the influence of genetic blueprints (*genotypes*)
on observable qualities (*phenotypes*). Research in behavioral genetics suggests that a surprisingly large percent of the variation among individuals on psychological attributes
such as intelligence and personality reflects genetic influences, which interact with environmental variables in very complex ways. **Heritability** refers to the proportion of variability among individuals on an observed characteristic (phenotypic variance) that can be
accounted for by genetic variability (genotypic variance).

Evolution

Whereas genetics focus on the heritability of genes that account for individual variations
in physical and psychological characteristics, evolution focuses on traits common to a
particular species that contribute to the survival and reproductive fitness of members of
that species. **Evolution** has been defined as "*a change in gene frequencies within a
given population over many generations*. As particular genes become more common
in the population or less common, so do the characteristics they influence" (Tavris &
Wade, 2001, p. 78). **Evolutionary theory**, *which examines the adaptive significance of
human and animal behavior*, is one of the most recent theories of behavior and is
arousing more and more attention and interest among researchers and theorists.

The person most associated with evolutionary theory is the British naturalist
Charles Darwin. In his book *The Origin of Species*, Darwin outlined his principle of
natural selection, his explanation for why animals had changed over the course of
history. Darwin postulated not only evolution, but also the mechanisms by which
evolution worked. First, he speculated that natural selection accounted for changes in
the appearance and behavior of organisms over time. Second, he postulated traits of
inheritance or what we now call genes. (It would not be until several years later, that
Gregor Mendel would publish his work on breeding peas and his hypothetical "units
of inheritance.") Third, Darwin suggested that more offspring are produced than will
survive. That is, because of sexual reproduction (receiving a random 50 percent of the
genes from each parent), the offspring varied from each other and only some were
best equipped to survive. Fourth, to the degree that particular traits increase an organism's ability to survive and reproduce, organisms with those traits should continue to reproduce and pass on those traits. Thus, the prevalence of the adaptive traits
should increase, whereas the prevalence of less adaptive traits in terms of survival and
reproduction should decrease.

Evolutionary psychologists take a retrospective look at behaviors that, over time,
proved to be adaptive to human survival and reproduction. They suggest that the
human mind is composed of a number of very specific information-processing modules, each designed to solve a certain problem with adaptation (Kurzban & Leary,
2001; Tooby & Cosmides, 1992). For example, recently researchers have suggested
that **stigmatization** or *the process by which people with some discrediting feature
(e.g., mental illness, psoriasis, or AIDS) are excluded from social interactions* has
evolved to allow nondiscredited individuals to increase their chances for survival and
reproduction (Kurzban & Leary, 2001). Specifically, by stigmatizing individuals with
less than desired qualities, stigmatizers ensure that they will avoid social interactions
with people who might compromise their own reproductive fitness. In addition, not
only do stigmatizers increase their own reproductive fitness, but, by ostracizing stig-

Big Picture φ Question 1

To what extent can mental processes be
reduced to the brain or the body?

matized individuals, the likelihood that these people will, over time, survive and reproduce decreases.

At the same time that people are excluding those they see as contributing little if anything to their own reproductive fitness, they go to great lengths to increase their own likelihood of being included by others. Evidence for the adaptive significance of inclusionary-seeking behaviors can be seen in babies who smile and coo as a means of drawing other individuals to them. As adults, people do and don't do certain behaviors in order to maintain the degree to which they are included by others. Emotions, such as jealousy, are experienced when a person believes his inclusionary status with another is threatened. Some researchers have even suggested that social anxiety (anxiety experienced in social interactions with other people) evolved as an interrupt mechanism to alert the socially anxious individual to behaviors that are threatening her inclusionary status with others (Baumeister & Tice, 1990).

The development of language, too, seems to stem from an evolved information-processing module within the brain. Early language theorists and behaviorists within psychology believed that children acquired language by imitating other people and through the process of reinforcement. A leading American linguist, Noam Chomsky (1959, 1986), suggested, however, that children could not possibly learn the rules of grammar and acquire an immense vocabulary within a few short years, simply through reinforcement. Children effortlessly use grammatical rules far earlier than they can learn less complicated mental operations, such as multiplication, or even less complicated behaviors, such as opening a door. Further, they acquire language in similar ways and at a similar pace across cultures, despite different learning environments. Deaf children show similar developmental patterns in learning sign language as well (Bonvillian, 1999).

According to Chomsky, humans are born with a **language acquisition device (LAD)**, *an innate set of neural structures for acquiring language*. Through the operation of this device, children are born "knowing" the features that are universal to language, and language learning in childhood "sets the switches" so that children speak their native tongue rather than some others. As evidence, Chomsky noted that children routinely follow implicit rules of grammar to produce utterances they have never heard before. For example, most English-speaking four-year-olds use the pronoun *hisself* instead of *himself*, even though this usage has never been reinforced (Brown, 1973). Children essentially invent "hisself" by applying a general rule of English grammar. In fact, children exposed to language without proper grammar will infuse their language with grammatical rules they have never been taught.

Additional evidence for innate linguistic capacities comes from individuals with *dyslexia*, a language-processing impairment that makes tasks such as spelling and arithmetic difficult. The specific left-hemisphere regions activated during certain linguistic tasks (such as rhyming) in nondyslexic people are not activated in people with the disorder, a suggestion that certain innate circuits are not functioning normally (Paulesu et al., 1996; Shaywitz et al., 1998). This problem is apparent, however, only if the person grows up in a literate culture. Otherwise, the deficit would likely never be expressed, because people with dyslexia do not differ intellectually in other ways from other people (and are often highly intelligent, although the disorder often makes them feel incompetent, particularly in elementary school).

INTERIM SUMMARY

Evolution refers to a change in gene frequencies over many generations. **Evolutionary theory** examines the adaptive significance of human and animal behavior. Known for his conceptualization of evolutionary theory, Charles Darwin discussed the mechanisms through which evolution occurred. As evolutionary theory has taken root, its applications to a number of phenomena within social psychology (e.g., **stigmatization**), cognitive psychology (e.g., language), and other areas within psychology have flourished.

Evolution of the Central Nervous System

If an engineer were to design the command center for an organism like ours from scratch, it would probably not look much like the human central nervous system. The reason is that, at every evolutionary juncture, nature has had to work with the structures (collections of cells that perform particular functions) already in place. The modifications made by natural selection have thus been sequential, one building on the next. For example, initially no organisms had color vision; the world of the ancestors of all contemporary sighted organisms was like a black-and-white movie. Gradually the capacity to perceive certain colors emerged in some species, conferring an adaptive advantage to organisms that could now, for instance, more easily distinguish one type of plant from another. The human central nervous system, like that of all animals, is like a living fossil record: The further down one goes (almost literally, from the upper layers of the brain down to the spinal cord), the more one sees ancient structures that evolved hundreds of millions of years ago and were shared—and continue to be shared—by most other vertebrates (animals with spinal cords).

It is tempting to think of nature's creatures as arranged on a scale from simple to complex, beginning with organisms like amoebas, then moving up the ladder perhaps to pets and farm animals, and on to the highest form of life, ourselves (see Butler & Hodos, 1996). And in a sense, there is something to this hypothesis; after all, we can dissect the brain of a frog, but a frog cannot return the favor.

We must always remember, however, that natural selection is a process that favors adaptation to a niche, and different niches require different adaptations. I would not trade my brain for that of my dog, no matter how endearing he might be, because I would rather be the one throwing than fetching. But my dog has abilities I lack, either because we humans never acquired them or because over time we lost them as our brains evolved in a different direction. My dog can hear things I cannot hear, and he does not need to call out in the dark, "Who's there?" because his nose tells him.

The Evolution of Vertebrates Our understanding of the evolution of the human nervous system still contains heavy doses of guesswork, but a general outline looks something like the following (Butler & Hodos, 1996; Healy, 1996; Kolb & Whishaw, 1996; MacLean, 1982, 1990). The earliest precursors to vertebrate animals were probably fishlike creatures whose actions were less controlled by a central "executive" like the human brain than by "local" reactions at particular points along the body. These organisms were likely little more than stimulus–response machines whose actions were controlled by a simple fluid-filled tube of neurons that evolved into the spinal cord. Sensory information from the environment entered the upper side of the cord, and neurons exiting the underside produced *automatic responses* called **reflexes**.

Through evolution, the front end of the spinal cord became specialized to allow more sophisticated processing of information and more flexible motor responses (Figure 3.16). Presumably this end developed because our early ancestors moved forward, head first—which is why our brains are in our heads instead of our feet. The primitive vertebrate brain, or brain stem, appears to have had three parts. The foremost section, called the forebrain, was specialized for sensation at a very immediate level—smell and eventually taste. The middle region, or midbrain, controlled sensation for distant stimuli—vision and hearing. The back of the brain stem, or hindbrain, was specialized for movement, particularly for balance (Sarnat & Netsky, 1974).

The hindbrain was also the connecting point between the brain and spinal cord, allowing messages to travel between the two. This rough division of labor in the primitive central nervous system still applies in the spinal cord and brain stem of humans. For example, many human reflexes occur precisely as they did, and do, in the simplest vertebrates: Sensory information enters one side of the spinal cord (toward the back of the body in humans, who stand erect), and motor impulses exit from the other.

Big Picture φ Question 3

To what extent is human psychology continuous with the psychology of other animals?

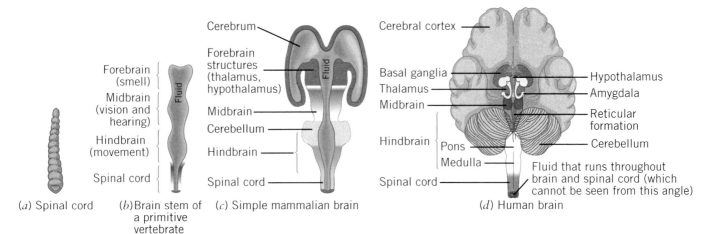

(a) Spinal cord   (b) Brain stem of   (c) Simple mammalian brain   (d) Human brain
                            a primitive
                            vertebrate

FIGURE 3.16   Evolution of the human brain. (*a*) The earliest central nervous system in the ancestors of contemporary vertebrates was likely a structure similar to the contemporary spinal cord. (*b*) The primitive brain, or brainstem, allowed more complex sensation and movement in vertebrates. (*c*) Among the most important evolutionary developments of mammals was the cerebrum. (*d*) The human brain is a storehouse of knowledge packed in a remarkably small container, the human skull. *Source:* Adapted from Kolb and Whishaw, 1996.

As animals, and particularly mammals, evolved, the most dramatic changes occurred in the hindbrain and forebrain. The hindbrain sprouted an expanded cerebellum, which increased the animal's capacity to put together complex movements and make sensory discriminations. The forebrain also evolved many new structures, most notably those that comprise the **cerebrum**, *the part of the brain most involved in complex thought*, which greatly expanded the capacity for processing information and initiating movement (see Finlay & Darlington, 1995). Of particular significance is the evolution of *the many-layered surface of the cerebrum* known as the **cortex** (from the Latin word for "bark"), which makes humans so "cerebral." In fact, 80 percent of the human brain's mass is cortex (Kolb & Whishaw, 1996).

The Human Nervous System   Although the human brain and the brains of its early vertebrate and mammalian ancestors differ dramatically, most of the differences are the result of additions to, rather than replacement of, the original brain structures. Two very important consequences flow from this.

First, many neural mechanisms are the same in humans and other animals; others differ across species that have evolved in different directions from common ancestors. Generalizations between humans and animals as seemingly different as cats or rats are likely to be more appropriate at lower levels of the nervous system, such as the spinal cord and brain stem, because these lower neural structures were already in place before these species diverged millions of years ago. The human brain stem (which includes most of the structures below the cerebrum) is almost identical to the brain stem of sheep (Kolb & Whishaw, 1996), but the two species differ tremendously in the size, structure, and function of their cortex. Much of the sheep's cortex is devoted to processing sensory information, whereas a greater part of the human cortex is involved in forming complex thoughts, perceptions, and plans for action.

The second implication is that human psychology bears the distinct imprint of the same relatively primitive structures that guide motivation, learning, and behavior in other animals. This is a sobering thought. It led Darwin to place species on our family tree that we might consider poor relations; Freud to view our extraordinary capacities to love, create, and understand ourselves and the universe as a thin veneer (only a few millimeters thick, in fact) over primitive structures that motivate

Big Picture φ Question 3

To what extent is human psychology continuous with the psychology of other animals?

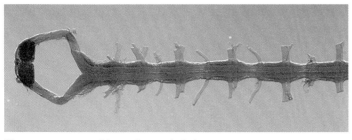

The nervous system of the earthworm includes a spinal cord and a small, simple brain.

our greatest achievements and our most "inhuman" atrocities; and Skinner to argue that the same laws of learning apply to humans as to other animals.

The human nervous system is thus a set of hierarchically organized structures built layer upon layer over millions of years of evolution. The most primitive centers send information to, and receive information from, higher centers; these higher centers are in turn integrated with, and regulated by, still more advanced areas of the brain. Behavioral and cognitive precision progressively increases from the lower to the higher and more recently evolved structures (Luria, 1973). Thus, the spinal cord can respond to a prick of the skin with a reflex without even consulting the brain, but more complex cognitive activity simultaneously occurs as the person makes sense of what has happened. We reflexively withdraw from a pinprick, but if the source is a vaccine injection, we inhibit our response—though often milliseconds later, since information traveling to and from the brain takes neural time. Responding appropriately requires the integrated functioning of structures from the spinal cord up through the cortex.

In our discussion of the central nervous system, we described a series of structures as if they were discrete entities. In reality, evolution did not produce a nervous system with neat boundaries. Distinctions among structures are not, of course, simply the whims of neuroanatomists; they are based on qualities such as the appearance, function, and cellular structure of adjacent regions. Nevertheless, where one structure ends and another begins is to some extent arbitrary. Axons from the spinal cord synapse with neurons far into the brain, so that parts of the brain could actually be called spinal. Similarly, progress in the understanding of the brain has led to increased recognition of different functions served by particular clumps of neurons or axons within a given structure. Whereas researchers once asked questions such as "What does the cerebellum do?" today they are more likely to ask about the functions of specific parts of the cerebellum.

INTERIM SUMMARY

The design of the human nervous system, like that of other animals, reflects its evolution. Early precursors to the first vertebrates (animals with spinal cords) probably reacted with reflexive responses to environmental stimulation at specific points of their bodies. The most primitive vertebrate brain, or brain stem, included a forebrain (specialized for sensing nearby stimuli, notably smells and tastes), a midbrain (specialized for sensation at a distance, namely vision and hearing), and a hindbrain (specialized for control of movement). This rough division of labor persists in contemporary vertebrates, including humans. The forebrain of humans and other contemporary vertebrates includes an expanded **cerebrum**, with a rich network of cells comprising its outer layers or **cortex**, which allows much more sophisticated sensory, cognitive, and motor processes.

The Future: Genetic Engineering

The classic science fiction novel *Brave New World* (1932) proposed that in the future we can produce any type of human that we want—for example, the alphas of the story are thinkers, the deltas are workers. The human race has come under complete genetic control. This future is less unlikely now that we can clone mammals. Dolly, the first sheep to be cloned, generated intense scrutiny over the morality of cloning: in particular, what if we could clone ourselves? What if when you needed a kidney or a new heart, you just made a clone of yourself and harvested the needed organ?

At least two attempts at cloning humans have been made; neither was successful. Failure here may be related to the failure to clone a nonhuman primate, the chimpanzee (Vogel, 2003). Apparently, in vitro (i.e., not in the body but in a test tube) the DNA fails to continue replicating. This finding suggests that for primates, factors of the uterine environment may be necessary for the development of the embryo to continue. Dolly recently was put to sleep (2003) because of health problems. Cloning of mammals is now possible, but the technique is certainly not perfected.

Clearly we have a lot to learn about cloning, and we also need to engage in discussion of the ethical issues of creating life. Perhaps it is fortunate that we do not have this "power" yet. Recall the eugenic program of the Nazis in which millions of non-Arayans were to be put to death, to purify a "master race." And, here in the United States, at one time many individuals of low mental ability were sterilized so that their genes would be eradicated from the population. On the other hand, we must consider the possibility that many troubling diseases such as cystic fibrosis and Huntington's chorea may be able to be "cured" by gene therapy.

A second argument against cloning is the ensuing reduction of genetic diversity for the cloned species. This is already a problem with our domesticated animals. Turkeys have been bred (by public demand) to have more white meat—a larger breast. In fact, the breast is now so large that the male turkeys cannot physically make critical contact with the female turkey and artificial insemination must be used. If a turkey were lucky enough to escape, it would never pass on its genes: it has lost its ability to reproduce. Many mares used for breeding race horses lack maternal behavior. Many purebred dogs, which have been bred to have particular characteristics, also have unwanted characteristics such as hip dysplasia and narcolepsy (a sleep disorder, see Chapter 9).

Among humans, genetic engineering raises critical questions such as whether couples should be allowed to choose the sex, eye color, intelligence level, hair color, etc., of their child. Should couples who conceive a fetus that does not have the desired features be allowed to abort that child? As strange as some of this may seem, just such an ethical issue is being raised in medical fields at the present time. For example, should parents with a child who needs a bone marrow transplant conceive children (aborting those fetuses that do not have the needed bone marrow type) until they get one who is a perfect match? What about selective reduction in which women who are carrying multiple fetuses abort some of the fetuses that may not have desired characteristics? (Importantly, sometimes selective reduction is a medical necessity, a situation we are not referring to here.) What effect would all of these examples of genetic engineering have on human evolution?

Summary

Neurons: Basic Units of the Nervous System

1. The firing of billions of nerve cells provides the physiological basis for psychological processes.

2. **Neurons**, or nerve cells, are the basic units of the nervous system. **Sensory neurons** carry sensory information from sensory receptors to the central nervous system. **Motor neurons** transmit commands from the brain to the glands and muscles of the body. **Interneurons** connect neurons with one another

3. A neuron typically has a **cell body, dendrites** (branchlike extensions of the cell body), and an **axon** that carries information to other neurons. Axons are often covered with **myelin** for more efficient electrical transmission. Located on the axons are **terminal buttons**, which contain **neurotransmitters**, chemicals that transmit information across the **synapse** (the space between neurons through which they communicate).

4. The "resting" voltage at which a neuron is not firing is called the **resting potential**. When a neuron stimulates another neuron, it either depolarizes the membrane (reducing its polarization) or hyperpolarizes it (increasing its polarization). The spreading voltage changes that occur when the neural membrane receives signals from other cells are called **graded potentials**. If enough depolarizing graded potentials accumulate to cross a threshold, the neuron will fire. This **action potential**, or nerve impulse, leads to the release of neurotransmitters (such as glutamate, GABA, dopamine, serotonin, and acetylcholine). These chemical messages are received by **receptors** in the cell membrane of other neurons, which in turn can excite or inhibit those neurons. Modulatory neurotransmitters can increase or reduce the impact of other neurotransmitters released into the synapse.

The Endocrine System

5. The **endocrine system** is a collection of glands that control various bodily functions through the secretion of **hormones**. The endocrine system complements the cell-to-cell communication of

the nervous system by sending global messages through the bloodstream.

The Peripheral Nervous System

6. The **peripheral nervous system (PNS)** consists of neurons that carry messages to and from the central nervous system. The peripheral nervous system has two subdivisions: the somatic nervous system and the autonomic nervous system. The **somatic nervous system** consists of the sensory neurons that receive information through sensory receptors in the skin, muscles, and other parts of the body, such as the eyes, and the motor neurons that direct the action of skeletal muscles. The **autonomic nervous system** controls basic life processes such as the beating of the heart, workings of the digestive system, and breathing. It consists of two parts, the **sympathetic nervous system**, which is activated in response to threats, and the **parasympathetic nervous system**, which returns the body to normal and works to maintain the body's energy resources.

The Central Nervous System

7. The **central nervous system (CNS)** consists of the brain and spinal cord.

8. The **spinal cord** transmits sensory information to the brain and transmits messages from the brain to the muscles and organs.

9. Several structures comprise the **hindbrain**. The **medulla oblongata** controls vital physiological functions, such as heartbeat, circulation, and respiration, and forms a link between the spinal cord and the rest of the brain. The **cerebellum** appears to be involved in a variety of tasks, including learning, discriminating stimuli from one another, and coordinating smooth movements. The **reticular activating system** maintains consciousness and helps regulate activity and arousal states throughout the central nervous system, including sleep cycles.

10. The **midbrain** consists of the tectum and tegmentum. The **tectum** includes structures involved in orienting to visual and auditory stimuli as well as others involved in linking unpleasant feelings to behaviors that can help the animal escape or avoid them. The **tegmentum** includes parts of the reticular formation and other nuclei with a variety of functions, of which two are particularly important: movement, and the linking of pleasure to behaviors that help the animal obtain reward.

11. The **forebrain** consists of the hypothalamus, thalamus, and cerebrum. The **hypothalamus** is involved in regulating a wide range of behaviors, including eating, sleeping, sexual activity, and emotional experience. The **thalamus** is a complex of nuclei that perform a number of functions; one of the most important is to process arriving sensory information and transmit this information to higher brain centers.

12. The **cerebrum** includes a number of **subcortical structures** as well as an outer layer, or **cortex**. The subcortical structures are the limbic system and the basal ganglia. Structures of the **limbic system** (the septal area, **amygdala**, and **hippocampus**) are involved in emotion, motivation, learning, and memory. **Basal ganglia** structures are involved in movement, mood, and memory.

13. In humans, the **cerebral cortex** allows the flexible construction of sequences of voluntary movements, enables people to discriminate complex sensory patterns, and provides the capacity to think symbolically. The **primary areas** of the cortex receive sensory information and initiate motor movements. The **association areas** are involved in putting together perceptions, ideas, and plans.

14. The right and left hemispheres of the cerebral cortex are connected by the **corpus callosum**. Each hemisphere consists of four sections or lobes. The **occipital lobes** are specialized for vision. The **parietal lobes** are involved in a number of functions, including the sense of touch, movement, and the experience of one's own body and other objects in space. The functions of the **frontal lobes** include coordination of movement, attention, planning, social skills, conscience, abstract thinking, memory, and aspects of personality. Sections of the **temporal lobes** are important in hearing, language, and visual object recognition. Some psychological functions are **lateralized**, or primarily processed by one hemisphere.

Genetics and Evolution

15. Environment and genes interact in staggeringly complex ways that psychologists are just beginning to understand. Psychologists interested in genetics study the influence of genetic blueprints (genotypes) on observable psychological attributes or qualities (phenotypes). Studies in behavioral genetics suggest that a substantial portion of the variation among individuals on many psychological attributes such as intelligence and personality are **heritable**. Heritability refers to the proportion of variability among individuals on an observed trait (phenotypic variance) that can be accounted for by variability in their genes (genotypic variance).

16. **Evolution** examines changes in gene frequencies over several generations. Evolutionary psychologists examine behaviors that, over time, proved to be adaptive to human survival and reproduction. The central nervous system in humans is hierarchically organized, with an overall structure that follows its evolution. Evolutionarily more recent centers regulate many of the processes that occur at lower levels.

The Future: Genetic Engineering

17. Advances in technology and genetic mapping have provided humans with the possibility of cloning and selecting desired traits in offspring. Not surprisingly, many ethical issues surround this wave of the future.

Key Terms

acetylcholine (ACh) 70
action potential 65
adrenal glands 71
adrenaline 71
afferent neurons 62
alleles 90
amygdala 81
association areas 82
autonomic nervous system 74
axon 63
basal ganglia 81
Broca's area 85

Sensation and Perception

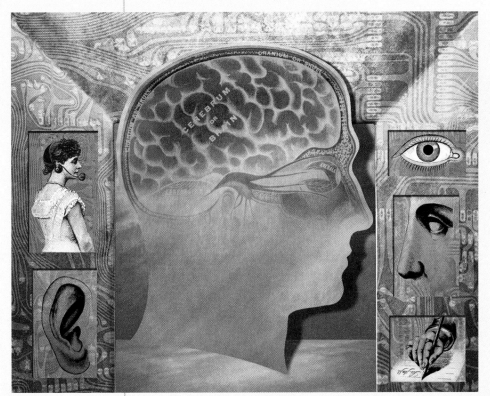

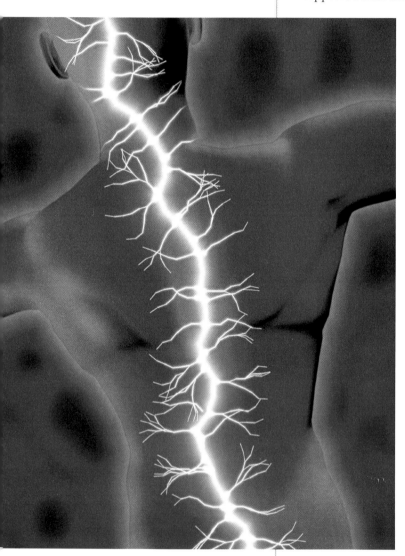

𝒜 woman in her early twenties damaged her knee in a fall. Following surgery, she experienced sharp, burning pain so excruciating that she could not eat or sleep. The pain ran from her ankle to the middle of her thigh, and the slightest touch—even a light brush with a piece of cotton—provoked a feeling of intense burning. Surgical attempts to relieve her pain gave her no relief or only temporary relief followed by even more severe pain (Gracely et al., 1992). Another case had a happier ending. A 50-year-old man whose chronic back pain failed to respond to exercise and medication finally underwent surgery. Like roughly 1 percent of patients who undergo this procedure (Sachs et al., 1990), he, too, developed severe burning pain and extraordinary sensitivity to any kind of stimulation of the skin. Fortunately, however, the pain disappeared after three months of treatment. These patients suffered from a disorder called painful neuropathy, which literally means a painful illness of the neurons. Painful neuropathy—caused by either an accident or surgery—results when the brain interprets as excruciating pain signals from receptors in the skin or joints that normally indicate only light touch, pressure, or movement.

This syndrome raises some intriguing questions about the way the nervous system translates information about the world into psychological experience. Does the intensity of sensory experience normally mirror the intensity of physical stimulation? In other words, when pain increases or the light in a theater seems extremely bright following a movie, how much does this reflect changes in reality versus changes in our perception of reality? And if neurons can become accidentally rewired so that touch is misinterpreted as burning pain, could attaching neurons from the ear to the primary cortex of the occipital lobes produce visual images of sound?

Questions such as these are central to the study of sensation and perception. **Sensation** refers to *the process by which the sense organs gather information about the environment and transmit this information to the brain for initial processing.* **Perception** is *the process by which the brain organizes and interprets these sensations*. Sensations are immediate experiences of qualities—red, hot, bright, and so forth—whereas perceptions are experiences of objects or events that appear to have form, order, or meaning (Figure 4.1). The distinction between sensation and perception is useful, though somewhat artificial, since sensory and perceptual processes form an integrated whole, translating physical reality into psychological reality.

Why do sensation and perception matter? In part because of individual differences in sensation and perception. If I am color blind, my sensory world is different

FIGURE 4.1 From sensation to perception. Take a careful look at this picture before reading further, and try to figure out what it depicts. When people first look at this photo, their eyes transmit information to the brain about which parts of the picture are white and which are black; this is sensation. Sorting out the pockets of white and black into a meaningful picture is perception. The photograph makes little sense until you recognize a Dalmatian, nose to the ground, walking toward a tree in the upper left corner.

from yours. If I am depressed or schizophrenic, my perceptual world is different from yours. To understand the behavior of individuals, we need to have an appreciation of the varieties of sensory and perceptual experiences. To understand psychological disturbances, we need to have an understanding of the complexity and limitations of the sensory systems and the role of perception in correcting or distorting our sensations. Sensation and perception are the gateway from the world to our imagination.

Memory involves the mental reconstruction of past experience—but what would we remember if we could not sense, perceive, and store images or sounds to recreate in our minds? Or consider love. What would love be if we could not feel another person's skin against ours? Could lovers experience the sense of comfort and security they feel when they mold into each other's arms if the skin were not laden with pressure detectors? Without our senses, we are literally senseless—without the capacity to know or feel. And without knowledge or feeling, there is little left to being human.

We begin the chapter with sensation, exploring basic processes that apply to all the senses (or *sensory modalities*—the different senses that provide ways of knowing about stimuli).We then discuss each sense individually, focusing on the two that allow sensation at a distance, vision and hearing (or *audition*), and more briefly exploring smell (*olfaction*), taste (*gestation*), touch, and *proprioception* (the sense of the body's position and motion). Next we turn to perception, beginning with the way the brain organizes and interprets sensations and concluding with the influence of experience, expectations, and needs on the way people make sense of sensations.

INTERIM SUMMARY

Sensation is the process by which sense organs gather information about the environment and transmit it to the brain for initial processing. **Perception** is the related process by which the brain selects, organizes, and interprets sensations.

Basic Principles

Throughout this discussion, three general principles repeatedly emerge. First, *there is no one-to-one correspondence between physical and psychological reality*. What is "out there" is not directly reproduced "in here." Of course, the relation between physical stimuli and our psychological experience of them is not random; as we will see, it is actually so orderly that it can be expressed as an equation.

Apply & Discuss

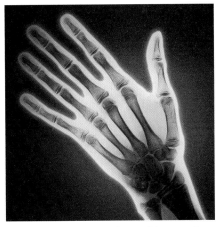

■ To what extent are we born with ways of viewing reality or have to discover them through experience?

■ Do people learn to organize visual sensations into three-dimensional shapes or do our brains automatically experience the world in three dimensions?

■ Does an X-ray of a finger actually give rise to different sensations or perceptions for a radiologist from those experienced by a patient, or does the radiologist just notice aspects of the X-ray that the patient is not trained to see as meaningful?

Sensation is an active process in which humans, like other animals, focus their senses on potentially important information.

Big Picture φ Question 8

To what extent can we inform our knowledge through reason or through observation—rationalism versus empiricism?

Yet the inner world is not simply a photograph of the outer. The degree of pressure or pain experienced when a pin presses against the skin—even in those of us *without* painful neuropathy—does not precisely match the actual pressure that is exerted. Up to a certain point, light pressure is not experienced at all, and pressure feels like pain only when it crosses a certain threshold. The inexact correspondence between physical and psychological reality is one of the fundamental findings of **psychophysics**, *the branch of psychology that studies the relation between attributes of the physical world and our psychological experience of them*.

Second, *sensation and perception are active processes*. Sensation may seem passive—images are cast on the retina at the back of the eye; pressure is imposed on the skin. Yet sensation is first and foremost an act of translation, converting external energy into an internal version, or *representation*, of it. People also orient themselves to stimuli to capture sights, sounds, and smells that are relevant to them. We turn our ears toward potentially threatening sounds to magnify their impact on our senses, just as we turn our noses toward the smell of baking bread. We also selectively focus our consciousness on parts of the environment that are particularly relevant to our needs and goals (Chapter 9).

Like sensation, perception is an active process: It organizes and interprets sensations. The world as subjectively experienced by an individual—the *phenomenological world*—is a joint product of external reality and the person's creative efforts to understand and depict it mentally. People often assume that perception is like photographing a scene or tape recording a sound and that they need only open their eyes and ears to capture what is "really" there. In fact, perception is probably more like stitching a quilt than taking a photograph. We must construct the phenomenological world from sensory experience, just as the quilt maker creates something whole from thread and patches.

If perception is a creative, constructive process, to what extent do people perceive the world in the same way? Does red appear to one person as it does to another? If one person loves garlic and another hates it, are the two loving and hating the same taste, or does garlic have a different taste to each? To what extent do people see the world the way it really is?

The third general principle is that *sensation and perception are adaptive*. From an evolutionary perspective, the ability to see, hear, or touch is the product of millions of adaptations that left our senses exquisitely crafted to serve functions that facilitate survival and reproduction (Tooby & Cosmides, 1992). Frogs have "bug detectors" in their visual systems that automatically fire in the presence of a potential meal. Similarly, humans have neural regions specialized for the perception of faces and facial expressions (Adolphs et al., 1996; Phillips et al., 1997). Human infants have an innate tendency to pay attention to forms that resemble the human face, and over the course of their first year they become remarkably expert at reading emotions from other people's faces (Chapter 13).

INTERIM SUMMARY

Three basic principles apply across all the senses: There is no one-to-one correspondence between physical and psychological reality; sensation and perception are active, not passive; and sensory and perceptual processes reflect the impact of adaptive pressures over the course of evolution.

Sensing the Environment

Although each sensory system is attuned to particular forms of energy, all the senses share certain common features. First, they must translate physical stimulation into sensory signals. Second, they all have thresholds below which a person does not sense anything despite external stimulation. Children know about this limitation threshold intuitively when they tiptoe through a room to "sneak up" on someone—who may suddenly hear them and turn around. The tiptoeing sounds increase gradually in intensity as the child approaches, but the person senses nothing until the sound crosses a threshold.

Third, sensation requires constant decision making, as the individual tries to distinguish meaningful from irrelevant stimulation. We are unaware of most of these sensory "decisions" because they occur rapidly and unconsciously. Alone at night, people often wonder, "Did I hear something?" Their answers depend not only on the intensity of the sound but also on their tendency to attach meaning to small variations in sound.

Fourth, sensing the world requires the ability to detect changes in stimulation, to notice when a bag of groceries has gotten heavier or a light has dimmed. Fifth and finally, efficient sensory processing means "turning down the volume" on information that is redundant; the nervous system tunes out messages that continue without change. We examine each of these processes in turn.

Transduction

Sensation requires converting energy in the world into internal signals that are psychologically meaningful. The more the brain processes these signals—from sensation to perception to cognition—the more meaningful they become. Sensation typically begins with an environmental stimulus, a form of energy capable of exciting the nervous system. We actually register only a tiny fraction of the energy surrounding us, and different species have evolved the capacity to process different types of information. Honeybees, for example, can sense the earth's magnetic field and essentially relocate important landmarks, such as places they have found food, by their compass coordinates (Collett & Baron, 1994).

Creating a Neural Code   *Specialized cells in the nervous system*, called **sensory receptors**, *transform energy in the environment into neural impulses* that can be interpreted by the brain (Loewenstein, 1960; Miller et al., 1961). Receptors respond to different forms of energy and generate action potentials in sensory neurons adjacent to them. In the eye, receptors respond to wavelengths of light; in the ear, to the movement of molecules of air.

The process of converting physical energy or stimulus information into neural impulses is called **transduction**. The brain then interprets the impulses generated by sensory receptors as light, sound, smell, taste, touch, or motion. It essentially reads a neural code—a pattern of neural firing—and translates it into a psychologically meaningful "language."

In 1826, Johannes Müller proposed the *doctrine of specific nerve energies*, which suggests that whether a neural message is experienced as light, sound, or some other sensation results less from differences in stimuli than from the particular neurons excited by them. Müller's hypothesis is bolstered by reports of syndromes such as painful neuropathy. If a cotton ball produces a sensation of burning instead of a light touch, sensory receptors may have been rewired to different neural fibers.

Extending and revising Müller's doctrine, psychologists now recognize that the nature of a sensation depends on the pathways in the brain that it activates. Electrical stimulation of the primary visual cortex produces visual sensations as surely as shining a light in the eye, whereas electrical stimulation of the auditory cortex produces sensations experienced as sound. The stimulus may be the same—electrical current—but the pathways are different.

Coding for Intensity and Quality of the Stimulus   For each sense, the brain codes sensory stimulation for intensity and quality. The neural code for *intensity*, or strength, of a sensation varies by sensory modality but usually involves the number of

Big Picture φ Question 3

To what extent is human psychology continuous with the psychology of other animals?

Apply & Discuss

In what ways might an innate (inborn) tendency to pay attention to faces foster adaptation in human infants?

Apply & Discuss

Some years ago, the media had a field day with claims that messages, such as "eat popcorn" were being presented subliminally to movie theater patrons. Others claimed that the word sex was being presented subliminally in advertisements to encourage people to buy particular products. Is there such a thing as subliminal perception? Can we actually hear sounds or see words or other stimuli that fall below our absolute threshold? The answer to these questions appears to be yes based on research evidence showing that words presented subliminally can prime participants to respond later to related words (e.g., presenting the word "cake" subliminally may allow the participant to more easily say icing later; Bar & Biederman, 1998; Bornstein & Pittman, 1992). However, subliminal presentation of stimuli does not appear to have the persuasive effects on people's attitudes and behavior that it was once thought to have.

sensory neurons that fire, the frequency with which they fire, or some combination of the two. The neural code for *quality* of the sensation (such as color, pitch, taste, or temperature) is often more complicated, relying on both the specific type of receptors involved and the pattern of neural impulses generated. For example, some receptors respond to warmth and others to cold, but a combination of both leads to the sensation of extreme heat. Remarkably, the brain synthesizes millions of simple on–off decisions (made by sensory neurons that receive information from receptors and either fire or do not fire) to perceive the lines and shapes of a Cézanne landscape or words on a printed page. It does this so quickly and automatically that we are unaware of anything but the end product.

INTERIM SUMMARY

Sensation begins with an environmental stimulus; all sensory systems have specialized cells called **sensory receptors** that respond to environmental stimuli and typically generate action potentials in adjacent sensory neurons. The process of converting stimulus information into neural impulses is called **transduction**. Within each sensory modality, the brain codes sensory stimulation for intensity and quality.

Absolute Thresholds

Even if a sensory system has the capacity to respond to a stimulus, the individual may not experience the stimulus if it is too weak. *The minimum amount of physical energy needed for an observer to notice a stimulus* is called an **absolute threshold**. One way psychologists measure absolute thresholds is to present a particular stimulus (light, sound, taste, odor, pressure) at varying intensities and determine the level of stimulation necessary for the person to detect it about 50 percent of the time.

For example, a psychologist trying to identify the absolute threshold for sound of a particular pitch would present subjects with sounds at that pitch, some so soft they would never hear them and others so loud they would never miss them. In between would be sounds they would hear some or most of the time. The volume at which most subjects hear the sound half the time but miss it half the time is defined as the absolute threshold; above this point, people sense stimulation most of the time. The absolute thresholds for many senses are remarkably low, such as a small candle flame burning 30 miles away on a clear night (Table 4.1).

Despite the "absolute" label, absolute thresholds vary from person to person and situation to situation. One reason for this variation is the presence of *noise*, which technically refers to irrelevant, distracting information (not just to sounds but to flashing lights, worries about a sick child, etc.). Some noise is external; to pick out the ticking of a watch at a concert is far more difficult than in a quiet room. Other noise,

Table 4.1 ▪ Examples of Absolute Thresholds	
Sense	*Threshold*
Vision	A candle flame 30 miles away on a dark, clear night
Hearing	A watch ticking 20 feet away in a quiet place
Smell	A drop of perfume in a six-room house
Taste	A teaspoon of sugar in 2 gallons of water
Touch	A wing of a fly falling on the cheek from a height of 1 centimeter

Source: Adapted from Brown et al., 1962.

created by the random firing of neurons, is internal. Psychological events such as expectations, motivation, stress, and level of fatigue can also affect the threshold at which a person can sense a low level of stimulation (see Fehm-Wolfsdorf et al., 1993; Pause et al., 1996). Someone whose home has been burglarized, for example, is likely to be highly attuned to nighttime sounds and to "hear" suspicious noises more readily, whether or not they actually occur.

Signal Detection

One Step Further

Is the absolute threshold, then, really absolute? Or perhaps sensation at low levels of stimulation actually requires the detection of a stimulus against a background of noise (Greene & Swets, 1966; Swets, 1992). According to *signal detection theory*, sensation is not a passive process that occurs when the amount of stimulation exceeds a critical threshold; rather, experiencing a sensation means making a *judgment* about whether a stimulus is present or absent.

Does a noise downstairs, a blip on a radar screen, or a small irregularity on a brain scan signal something dangerous? According to signal detection theory, two distinct processes are at work in detection tasks of this sort. The first is an initial sensory process, reflecting the observer's *sensitivity* to the stimulus—how well the person sees, hears, or feels the stimulus. The second is a decision process, reflecting the observer's **response bias** (or *decision criterion*); that is, **the individual's readiness to report detecting a stimulus when he is uncertain**.

Assessing Response Bias
To assess response bias, signal detection researchers present participants with stimuli at low intensities, as in the traditional procedure for measuring absolute thresholds, but they add trials with no stimulus presented. What participants experience on each trial is some mixture of stimulus energy (the signal), which may or may not be present, and noise, which randomly waxes and wanes. Sometimes the noise alone is enough to lead the person to say she heard or saw something because its effect crosses the decision criterion. At other times, the signal is present but too weak to be detected, and the noise level is too low to augment it. At still other times, noise, when added to a signal, increases the intensity of the signal enough to lead the participant to report a sensation.

Participants in signal detection experiments can make two kinds of errors. They may respond with a *false alarm*, reporting a stimulus when none was presented, or they may fail to report an actual stimulus (a *miss*). Similarly, they may give two kinds of correct response. They may *hit*, reporting an actual stimulus, or they may declare a *correct negative*, reporting no stimulus when none was presented. Accuracy in sensing a signal involves a trade-off between sensitivity to stimuli that are presented and vulnerability to reporting stimuli that have not been presented. Thus, an observer who tends to overreport sensations will have a high number of hits but also a high number of false alarms. An observer who tends to underreport will have a lower number of hits but also a lower number of false alarms.

Factors Affecting Response Bias
Whether a person has a low or high response bias for reporting "yes" depends on many factors. One is expectations: If a patient complains of heart pain, shooting pain in his legs, and shortness of breath, his doctor is more likely to hear an irregular heartbeat. Another factor that influences response bias is motivation. Two neurologists who review the MRI scan of a woman experiencing blinding headaches may come to different conclusions about a possible irregularity. The

HERMAN®

"My mistake! I thought I heard a noise down here."

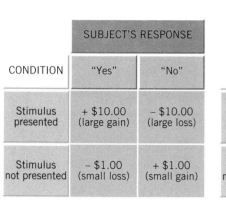

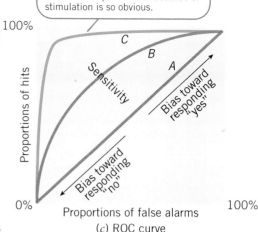

Note that at high stimulus intensities, a "no" response bias does not appreciably diminish the number of hits because presence or absence of stimulation is so obvious.

(a) Matrix that will produce a "yes" bias   (b) Matrix that will produce a "no" bias   (c) ROC curve

FIGURE 4.2   Signal detection. Two payoff matrices, one that leads to a "yes" bias (a), and the other to a "no" bias (b). To assess sensitivity to a stimulus (c), researchers plot the proportion of hits against the proportion of false alarms on an ROC curve. If the signal is so low that it is imperceptible (line A), the proportion of hits will equal the proportion of false alarms because the receiver's responses are essentially random. At a somewhat higher stimulus intensity (line B) subjects have a better ratio of hits to false alarms because their responses are influenced by the presence of a detectable signal, so they are no longer just guessing. At very high signal intensities (line C), people rarely give wrong answers. The sensitivity of the observer to different signal intensities (e.g., how well the person can hear) is represented by the dashed line, which shows how far the receiver's ROC curve diverges from the diagonal, which represents random responding.

Apply & Discuss

▪ To what extent does a perceiver skilled in detecting the presence of enemy missiles actually perceive what a lay person would not see?

▪ How does the skilled perceiver recognize the signal in a sea of noise? What changes with perceptual practice and learning?

neurologist who recently lost a patient by mistaking a tumor for noise will have a low threshold for reporting "yes" because the psychological cost of setting it higher is too great. The other, who recently performed exploratory surgery when in fact no tumor was present and accidentally left the patient with partial blindness, will have a much higher threshold for reporting a "hit."

To distinguish the relative contributions of sensitivity and response bias, psychologists experimentally manipulate the costs and benefits of over- or underreporting stimulation by paying participants different amounts for different types of correct or incorrect responses (Figure 4.2). These consequences can be described in a payoff matrix, which shows the costs and benefits of each type of response. Researchers then plot the proportion of hits against the proportion of false alarms on a *receiver operating characteristic (ROC) curve*, which literally shows the way the receiver of the signal operates at different signal intensities. This allows the researcher to determine how well the subject can actually sense the stimulus, independent of response bias.

Difference Thresholds

Thus far, we have focused on absolute thresholds, the lowest level of stimulation required to sense that a stimulus is present. Another important kind of threshold is the **difference threshold**—*the lowest level of stimulation required to sense that a change in stimulation has occurred*. In other words, the difference threshold is the difference in intensity between two stimuli that is necessary to produce a **just noticeable difference** (or **jnd**), such as the difference between two light bulbs of slightly different wattage. (The absolute threshold is actually a special case of the difference threshold, in which the difference is between no intensity and a very weak stimulus.)

The jnd depends not only on the intensity of the new stimulus but also on the level of stimulation already present. The more intense the existing stimulus, the larger the change must be to be noticeable. A person carrying a 2-pound backpack will easily notice the addition of a half-pound book, but adding the same book to a 60-pound backpack will not make the pack feel any heavier; that is, it will not produce a jnd.

Weber's Law   In 1834, the German physiologist Ernst Weber recognized not only this lack of a one-to one relationship between the physical and psychological worlds but also the existence of a consistent relationship between them. ***Regardless of the magnitude of two stimuli, the second must differ from the first by a constant proportion for it to be perceived as different.*** This relationship is called **Weber's law** (Figure 4.3*a*). That constant proportion—the ratio of change in intensity required to produce a jnd compared to the previous intensity of the stimulus—can be expressed as a fraction, called the *Weber fraction*. Weber was the first to show not only that subjective sensory experience and objective sensory stimulation were related but also that one could be predicted from the other mathematically. To put it another way, Weber was hot on the trail of a science of consciousness.

The Weber fraction varies depending on the individual, stimulus, context, and sensory modality. For example, the Weber fraction for perceiving changes in heaviness is 1/50. This means that the average person can perceive an increase of 1 pound if added to a 50-pound bag, 2 pounds added to 100 pounds, and so forth. The Weber fraction for a sound around middle C is 1/10, which means that a person can hear an extra voice in a chorus of 10 but would require 2 voices to notice an increase in loudness in a chorus of 20.

Fechner's Law   Weber's brother-in-law, Gustav Fechner, took the field a "just noticeable step" further in 1860 with the publication of his *Elements of Psychophysics*. He broadened the application of Weber's law by linking the subjective experience of intensity of stimulation with the actual magnitude of a stimulus. In other words, using Weber's law, Fechner was able to estimate precisely how intensely a person would report experiencing a sensation based on the amount of stimulus energy actually present. He assumed that for any given stimulus, all jnd's are created equal; that is, each additional jnd feels subjectively like one incremental (additional) unit in intensity.

Using Weber's law, he then plotted these subjective units against the actual incremental units of stimulus intensity necessary to produce each jnd (Figure 4.3b). He recognized that at low stimulus intensities, only tiny increases in stimulation are required to produce subjective effects as large as those produced by enormous increases in stimulation at high levels of intensity. As Figure 4.3*b* shows, the result is a logarithmic function—that is, as one variable (in this case, subjective intensity) increases arithmetically (1, 2, 3, 4, 5…), the other variable (in this case, objective intensity) increases geometrically (1, 2, 4, 8, 16…). ***The logarithmic relation between subjective and objective stimulus intensity*** became known as **Fechner's law**. Fechner's law means, essentially, that people experience only a small percentage of actual increases in stimulus intensity but that this percentage is predictable.

Stevens's Power Law   Fechner's law held up for a century but was modified by S. Stevens (1961, 1975) because it did not quite apply to all stimuli and senses. For example, the relation between perceived pain and stimulus intensity is the opposite of most other psychophysical relations: The greater the pain, the *less* additional intensity is required for a jnd. This law makes adaptive sense, since increasing pain means increasing danger and therefore demands *heightened* attention.

In part on a dare from a colleague, Stevens (1956) set out to prove that people can accurately rate subjective intensity on a numerical scale. He instructed participants to listen to a series of tones of differing intensity and simply assign numbers to the tones to indicate their relative loudness. What he discovered was a lawful relation between

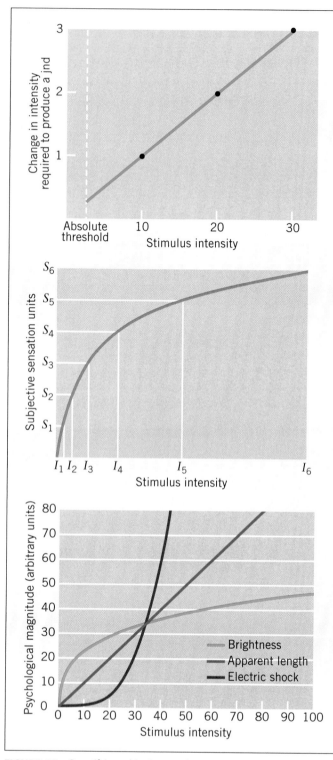

(a) Weber's Law

Weber's law states that regardless of the magnitude of two stimuli, the second must differ from the first by a constant proportion for it to be perceived as different. Expressed mathematically,

$$\Delta I / I = k$$

where I = the intensity of the stimulus, ΔI = the additional intensity necessary to produce a jnd at that intensity, and k = a constant. To put it still another way, the ratio of change in intensity to initial intensity required to produce a jnd—expressed as a fraction, such as one unit of change for every ten units—is a constant for a given sensory modality. This constant is known as a Weber fraction. This can be seen in the accompanying graph, where the constant is the slope of the line (in this case, 1/10), plotting ΔI (the y-axis) as a function of I (the x-axis).

(b) Fechner's Law

Starting with Weber's law, Fechner realized that as the experienced sensation increases one unit of perceived intensity at a time, the actual intensity of the physical stimulus is increasing logarithmically. Fechner's law thus holds that the subjective magnitude of a sensation (S) grows as a proportion (k) of the logarithm of the objective intensity of the stimulus (I), or

$$S = k \log I$$

This can be readily seen in the accompanying graph: Subjective units of sensation (S_1, S_2, ...) increase by increments of one, as objective units (I_1, I_2, ...) increase geometrically (i.e., by a factor of more than 1). This leads to a logarithmic curve. *Source:* Adapted from Guilford, 1954, p. 38.

(c) Stevens's Power Law

Stevens's power law states that subjective intensity (S) grows as a proportion (k) of the actual intensity (I) raised to some power (b). Expressed mathematically,

$$S = k I^b$$

As the graph shows, Stevens's power law plots subjective magnitude of stimulation as an exponential function of stimulus magnitude. Here, these functions are shown for brightness (where the exponent is 0.33), apparent length (where the exponent is 1.0, so the function is linear), and electric shock (where the exponent is 3.5). *Source:* Stevens, 1961, p. 11.

FIGURE 4.3   Quantifying subjective experience: From Weber to Stevens.

self-reports and stimulus intensity across a much wider range of sensory modes and intensities than Fechner's law could accommodate.

According to **Stevens's power law** (Figure 4.3*c*), *as the perceived intensity of a stimulus grows arithmetically, the actual magnitude of the stimulus grows exponentially*; that is, by some power (squared, cubed, etc.). The exponent varies for different senses but is constant within a sensory system.

Although our understanding of the relationships between stimulus and perception has become more precise, the message from Weber, Fechner, and Stevens is fundamentally the same: Sensation bears an orderly, predictable relation to physical stimulation, but psychological experience is not a photograph, tape recording, or wax impression of external reality.

Sensory Adaptation

A final process shared by all sensory systems is adaptation. You walk into a crowded restaurant, and the noise level is overwhelming, yet within a few minutes, you do not even notice it. Driving into an industrial city, you notice an unpleasant odor that smells like sulfur and wonder how anyone tolerates it; a short time later, you are no longer aware of it. These are examples of **sensory adaptation**—*the tendency of sensory receptors to respond less to stimuli that continue without change*.

Sensory adaptation makes sense from an evolutionary perspective. Constant sensory inputs provide no new information about the environment, so the nervous system essentially ignores them. Given all the stimuli that bombard an organism at any particular moment, an animal that paid as much notice to constant stimulation as to changes that might be adaptively significant would be at a disadvantage. By reducing its perceived intensity to a manageable level, sensory adaptation also performs the function of "turning down the volume" on information that would overwhelm the brain.

Although sensory adaptation generally applies across senses, the nervous system is wired to circumvent it in some important instances. For example, the visual system has ways to keep its receptors from adapting; otherwise, stationary objects would disappear from sight. The eyes are constantly making tiny quivering motions, which guarantees that the receptors affected by a given stimulus are constantly changing. The result is a steady flow of graded potentials on the sensory neurons that synapse with those receptors. Similarly, although we may adapt to mild pain, we generally do not adapt to severe pain (Miller & Kraus, 1990), an evolutionarily sensible design feature of a sensory system that responds to body damage.

INTERIM SUMMARY

The **absolute threshold** is the minimum amount of energy needed for an observer to sense that a stimulus is present. The **difference threshold** is the lowest level of stimulation required to sense that a change in stimulation has occurred. According to **Weber's law**, regardless of the magnitude of two stimuli, the second must differ by a constant proportion from the first for it to be perceived as different. According to **Fechner's law**, the magnitude of a stimulus grows logarithmically as the subjective experience of intensity grows arithmetically, so that people subjectively experience only a fraction of actual increases in stimulation. According to **Stevens's power law**, subjective intensity increases in a linear fashion as actual intensity grows exponentially. **Sensory adaptation** is the tendency of sensory systems to respond less to stimuli that continue without change.

Vision

Throughout this chapter we will use vision as our major example of sensory processes because it is the best understood of the senses. We begin by discussing the form of energy (light) transduced by the visual system. We then examine the organ responsible for transduction (the eye) and trace the neural pathways that take raw information from receptors and convert it into sensory knowledge.

The Nature of Light

Light is just one form of electromagnetic radiation, but it is the form to which the eye is sensitive. That humans and other animals respond to light is no accident, since cycles of light and dark have occurred over the course of five billion years of evolution. These cycles, and the mere presence of light as a medium for sensation, have shaped virtually every aspect of our psychology, from the times of day at which we are conscious to the way we choose mating partners (using visual appearance as a cue).

Indeed, light is so useful for tracking prey, avoiding predators, and "checking out" potential mates that a structure resembling the eye has apparently evolved independently over 40 times in different organisms (Feral, 1996). Other forms of electromagnetic radiation, to which humans are blind, include infrared, ultraviolet, radio, and X-ray radiation.

Electromagnetic energy travels in repeating, rhythmic waves of different frequencies. Different forms of radiation have *waves of different lengths*, or **wavelengths**. Their particles oscillate more or less frequently, that is, with higher or lower frequency. Some of these wavelengths, such as gamma rays, are as short or shorter than the diameter of an atom; others are quite long, such as radio waves, which may oscillate once in a mile. Wavelengths are measured in nanometers (nm), or billionths of a meter (Figure 4.4). The receptors in the human eye are tuned to detect only a very restricted portion of the electromagnetic spectrum, from roughly 400 to 700 nm. This span represents the colors that are in the rainbow: red, orange, yellow, green, blue, indigo, and violet. Other organisms are sensitive to different regions of the spectrum. For example, many insects (such as ants and bees) and some vertebrate animals (such as iguanas and some bird species) see ultraviolet light (Alberts, 1989; Goldsmith, 1994).

The physical dimension of wavelength translates into the psychological dimension of color, just as the physical *intensity* of light is related to the subjective sensation of brightness. Light is a useful form of energy to sense for a number of reasons (see Sekuler & Blake, 1994). Like other forms of electromagnetic radiation, light travels very quickly (186,000 miles, or roughly 300,000 kilometers, per second), so sighted organisms can see things almost immediately after they happen. As light also travels in straight lines, it preserves the geometric organization of the objects it illuminates; the image an object casts on the retina resembles its actual structure. Perhaps most importantly, light interacts with the molecules on the surface of many objects and is either absorbed or reflected. The light that is reflected reaches the eyes and creates a visual pattern. Objects that reflect a lot of light appear bright, whereas those that absorb much of the light that hits them appear dark.

Big Picture φ Question 1

To what extent can mental processes be reduced to the brain or body?

Big Picture φ Question 3

To what extent is human psychology continuous with the psychology of other animals?

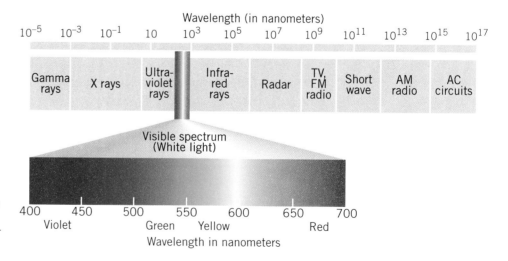

FIGURE 4.4 The electromagnetic spectrum. Humans sense only a small portion of the electromagnetic spectrum (enlarged in the figure), light. Light at different wavelengths is experienced as different colors.

The Eye

Two basic processes occur in the eyes (Figure 4.5). First, the cornea, pupil, and lens focus light on the retina. Next, the retina transduces this visual image into neural impulses that are relayed to and interpreted by the brain.

Focusing Light   Light enters the eye through the **cornea**, *a tough, transparent tissue covering the front of the eyeball*. Under water, people cannot see clearly because the cornea is constructed to bend (or refract) light rays traveling through air, not water. That is why a diving mask allows clearer vision: It puts a layer of air between the water and the cornea.

From the cornea, light passes through a chamber of fluid called *aqueous humor*, which supplies oxygen and other nutrients to the cornea and lens. Unlike blood, which performs this function in other parts of the body, the aqueous humor is a clear fluid, so that light can pass through it. Next, light travels through the **pupil**, an *opening in the center of the* **iris** *(the pigmented tissue that gives the eye its blue, green, or brown color)*. Muscle fibers in the iris cause the pupil to expand (dilate) or constrict to regulate the amount of light entering the eye.

The next step in focusing light occurs in the **lens**, *an elastic, disc-shaped structure* about the size of a lima bean which is *involved in focusing the eyes*. Muscles attached to cells surrounding the lens alter its shape to focus on objects at various distances. *The lens flattens for distant objects and becomes more rounded or spherical for closer objects, a process known as* **accommodation**. The light is then projected through the vitreous humor (a clear, gelatinous liquid) onto the **retina**, *a light-sensitive layer of tissue at the back of the eye that transduces light into visual sensations*. The retina receives a constant flow of images as people turn their heads and eyes or move through space.

The Retina   The eye is like a camera, insofar as it has an opening to adjust the amount of incoming light, a lens to focus the light, and the equivalent of photosensitive film—the retina. (The analogy is incomplete, of course, because the eye, unlike a camera, works best when it is moving.) The retina translates light energy from illuminated objects into neural impulses, transforming a pattern of light reflected off objects into psychologically meaningful information.

Structure of the Retina   The retina is a multilayered structure about as thick as a sheet of paper (Figure 4.6). The innermost layer (at the back of the retina) contains *two types of light receptors*, or *photoreceptors* ("photo" is from the Greek word for light), called **rods** and **cones**, which were named for their distinctive shapes. Each retina contains approximately 120 million rods and 8 million cones.

When a rod or cone absorbs light energy, it generates an electrical signal, stimulating the neighboring **bipolar cells**. These cells *combine the information from many receptors and produce graded potentials on* **ganglion cells**, *which integrate infor-*

Making Connections

Nearsightedness and farsightedness result when the lens of the eye focuses light rays either in front of or behind the retina. A person who is nearsighted has more difficulty viewing distant than near objects because the images are being projected in front of the retina. A farsighted person sees distant objects better than those that are close because the image is being focused behind the retina rather than on the retina. As people age the lens loses its elasticity and its ability to accommodate, so the likelihood of becoming farsighted and needing reading glasses increases (Chapter 13).

Making Connections

The size of the pupils changes not only with changes in light but also with changes in emotional state, such as fear, excitement, interest, and sexual arousal. A skilled gambler (or Don Juan) may literally be able to read other people's hands from their eyes. Interestingly, he may be able to do this even though he has no conscious awareness that he is making use of pupil size as a cue (Chapter 9).

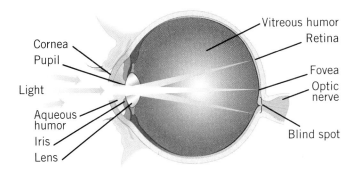
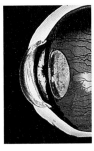

FIGURE 4.5   Anatomy of the human eye. The cornea, pupil, and lens focus a pattern of light onto the retina, which then transduces the retinal image into neural signals carried to the brain by the optic nerve.

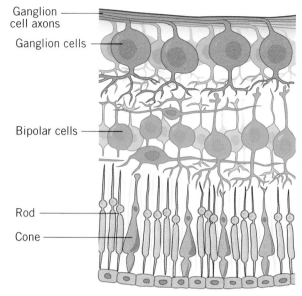
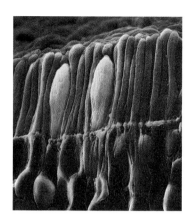

Ganglion cell axons

Ganglion cells

Bipolar cells

Rod

Cone

FIGURE 4.6 The retina. Light passes through layers of neurons to reach photoreceptors, called rods and cones, which respond to different wavelengths of light. These receptors in turn connect to bipolar cells, which pass information to the ganglion cells, whose axons form the optic nerve. The photo shows rods and cones magnified thousands of times, along with bipolar cells.

mation from multiple bipolar cells. The long axons of these ganglion cells bundle together to form the **optic nerve***, which carries visual information to the brain.*

The central region of the retina, the **fovea**, is most sensitive to small detail, so vision is sharpest for stimuli directly at this site on the retina. In contrast, the **blind spot** (or *optic disk*), *the point on the retina where the ganglion cell axons leave the eyes has no receptor cells.*

People are generally unaware of their blind spots for several reasons. Different images usually fall on the blind spots of the two eyes so one eye sees what the other does not. In addition, the eyes are always moving, providing information about the missing area. To avoid perceiving an empty visual space, the brain also automatically uses visual information from the rest of the retina to fill in the gap. (To see the effects of the blind spot in action, see Figure 4.7.)

Rods and Cones Rods and cones have distinct functions. Rods are more sensitive to light than cones, allowing vision in dim light. Rods only produce visual sensations in black, white, and gray. Cones are, evolutionarily speaking, a more recent development than rods and respond to color as well as black and white. They require more light to be activated, however, which is why we humans see little or no color in dim light. Nocturnal animals such as owls have mostly rods, whereas animals that sleep at night (including most other birds) have mostly cones (Schiffman, 1996).

FIGURE 4.7 The blind spot. Close your left eye, fix your gaze on the plus, and slowly move the book toward and away from you. The circle will disappear when it falls in the blind spot of the right retina.

Rods and cones also differ in their distribution on the retina and in their connections to bipolar cells. Cones are concentrated in the fovea, and decrease in density with increasing distance from the retina. Thus, in bright light, we can see an object best if we look at it directly, focusing the image on the fovea. Rods are concentrated off the center of the retina. Thus, in dim light, objects are seen most clearly by looking slightly away from them. (You can test this yourself tonight by looking at the stars. Fix your eyes directly on a bright star and then focus your gaze slightly off to the side of it. The star will appear brighter when the image is cast away from the fovea.)

Transforming Light into Sight   Both rods and cones contain photosensitive pigments that change chemical structure in response to light (Rushton, 1962; Weld, 1968). This process is called *bleaching* because the pigment breaks down when exposed to light and the photoreceptors lose their characteristic color. When photoreceptors bleach, they create graded potentials in the bipolar cells connected to them, which may then fire. Bleaching must be reversed before a photoreceptor is restored to full sensitivity. Pigment regeneration takes time, which is why people often have to feel their way around the seats when entering a dark theater on a bright day.

Adjusting to a dimly illuminated setting is called *dark adaptation*. The cones adapt relatively quickly, usually within about 5 minutes, depending on the duration and intensity of light to which the eye was previously exposed. Rods, in contrast, take about 15 minutes to adapt. Because they are especially useful in dim light, vision may remain less than optimal in the theater for some time. *Light adaptation,* the process of adjusting to bright light after exposure to darkness, is much faster; readapting to bright sunlight upon leaving a theater takes only about a minute (Marlin, 1983).

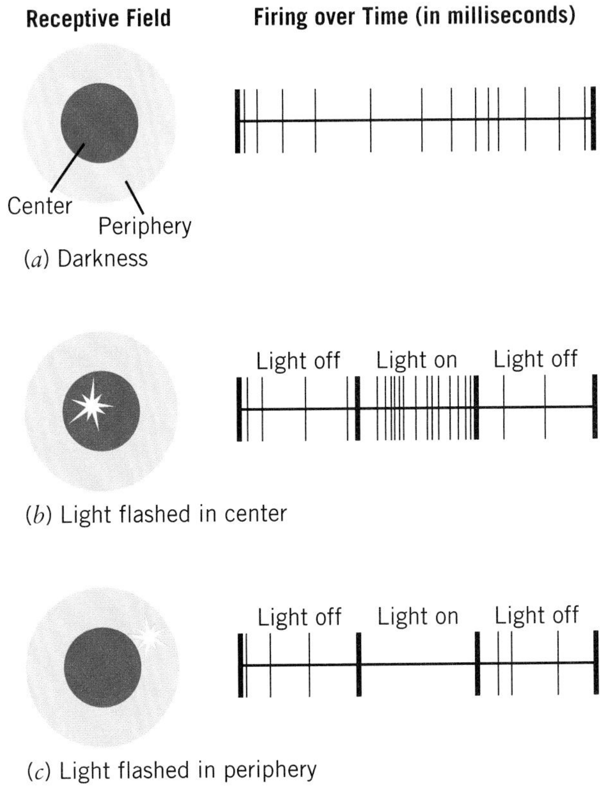

Receptive Fields   Once the rods and cones have responded to patterns of light, the nervous system must somehow convert these patterns into a neural code to allow the brain to reconstruct the scene. This is truly a remarkable process: Waves of light reflected off, say, your friend's face, pass through the eye to the rods and cones of the retina. The pattern of light captured by those receptor cells translates your friend's face into a pattern of nerve impulses that the brain can "read" with such precision that you know precisely whom you are seeing.

This process begins with the ganglion cells. Each ganglion cell has a receptive field. A **receptive field** is *a region within which a neuron responds to appropriate stimulation* (i.e., in which it is *receptive* to stimulation) (Hartline, 1938). Neurons at higher levels of the visual system (in the brain) also have receptive fields; at higher and higher levels of processing, the visual system keeps creating maps of the scenes the eye has observed. The same basic principles apply in other sensory systems, as when neurons from the peripheral nervous system all the way up through the cortex map precisely where a mosquito has landed on the skin.

Psychologists have learned about receptive fields in ganglion cells through a technique called single-cell recording. In single-cell recording, researchers insert a tiny electrode into the brain or retina of an animal, close enough to a neuron to detect when it fires. Then, holding the animal's head still, they flash light to different parts of the visual field to see what kind of stimulation leads the ganglion cell to fire. By placing electrodes in many places, psychologists can map the receptive fields of the ganglion cells of the retina.

Using this method, researchers discovered that the receptive fields of some ganglion cells have a center and a surrounding area, like a target (Figure 4.8). Presenting light to the center of the receptive field turns the cell "on" (i.e., excites the cell), whereas presenting light within the receptive field but outside the center turns the

Receptive Field   **Firing over Time (in milliseconds)**

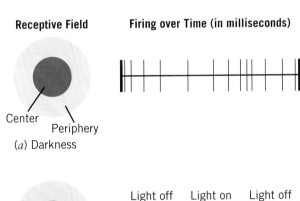

Center   Periphery
(a) Darkness

(b) Light flashed in center

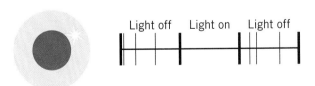

(c) Light flashed in periphery

FIGURE 4.8   Single-cell recording. In (*a*), the neuron spontaneously fires (indicated by the thin vertical lines) randomly in darkness. In (*b*), it fires repeatedly when light is flashed to the center of its receptive field. In (*c*), firing stops when light is flashed in the periphery of its receptive field; that is, light outside the center inhibits firing. *Source:* Adapted from Sekuler & Blake, 1994, p. 68.

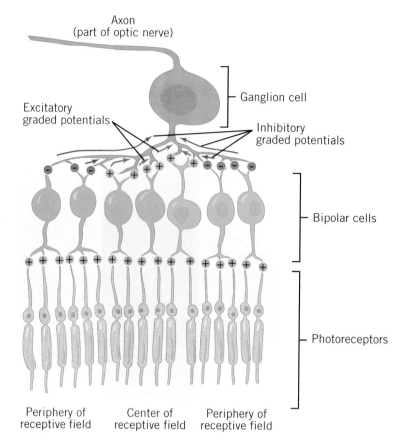

FIGURE 4.9   Activation of a center-on/periphery-off ganglion cell. Transduction begins as photoreceptors that respond to light in the center of the ganglion cell's receptive field excite bipolar cells, which in turn generate excitatory graded potentials (represented here by a +) on the dendrites of the ganglion cell. Photoreceptors that respond to light in the periphery of the ganglion cell's receptive field inhibit firing of the ganglion cell (represented by a –). If enough light is present in the center, and little enough in the periphery of the receptive field, the excitatory graded potentials will depolarize the ganglion cell membrane. The axon of the ganglion cell is part of the optic nerve, which will then transmit information about light in this particular visual location to the brain.

cell "off" (Muffler, 1953). For other ganglion cells the pattern is just the opposite: Light in the center inhibits neural firing, whereas light in the periphery excites the neuron. The process by which adjacent visual units inhibit or suppress each other's level of activity is called *lateral inhibition*. Figure 4.9 illustrates the way excitatory and inhibitory graded potentials from bipolar cells may be involved in this process.

Why do receptive fields have this concentric circular organization, with on and off regions that inhibit each other? As described at the beginning of the chapter, our sensory systems are attuned to changes and differences. The target-like organization of ganglion cells allows humans and other animals to perceive edges and changes in brightness and texture that signal where one surface ends and another begins. A neuron that senses light in the center of its receptive field will fire rapidly if the light is bright and covers much of the center. To the extent that light is also present in the periphery of the receptive field, however, neural firing will be inhibited, essentially transmitting the information that the image is continuous in this region of space, with no edges.

Lateral inhibition appears to be responsible in part for the phenomenon seen in *Hermann grids* (Figure 4.10), in which the intersections of white lines in a dark grid appear gray and the intersections of black lines in a white grid appear gray (Spillman, 1994). Essentially, white surrounded by white on all four sides (i.e., no contrast so no lateral inhibition) appears darker than white surrounded by black on two sides, and vice versa. The receptive fields of neurons in the fovea tend to be very small, allowing for high visual acuity, whereas receptive fields increase in size with distance from the center of the retina (Wiesel & Hubel, 1960). This is why looking straight at the illusory patches of darkness or lightness in Hermann grids makes them disappear: Receptive fields of neurons in the fovea can be so small that the middle of each line is surrounded primarily by the same shade regardless of whether it is at an intersection.

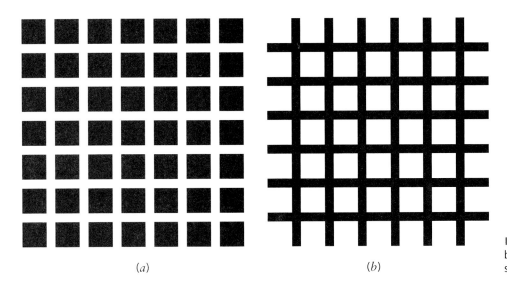

FIGURE 4.10 Hermann grids. White lines against a black grid appear to have gray patches at their intersections (*a*), as do black lines against a white grid (*b*).

(*a*)   (*b*)

INTERIM SUMMARY

Two basic processes occur in the eyes: Light is focused on the **retina** by the **cornea, pupil,** and **lens**, and the retina transduces this visual image into a code that the brain can read. The retina includes two kinds of photoreceptors: **rods** (which produce sensations in black, white, and gray and are very sensitive to light) and **cones** (which produce sensations of color). Rods and cones excite **bipolar cells**, which in turn excite or inhibit **ganglion cells**, whose axons constitute the **optic nerve**. Ganglion cells, like sensory cells higher up in the nervous system, have **receptive fields**, areas that are excited or inhibited by the arriving sensory information.

Neural Pathways

Transduction in the eye, then, starts with the focusing of images onto the retina. When photoreceptors respond to light stimulation, they excite bipolar cells, which in turn cause ganglion cells with particular receptive fields to fire. The axons from these ganglion cells comprise the optic nerve, which transmits information from the retina to the brain.

From the Eye to the Brain   Impulses from the optic nerve first pass through the *optic chiasm* (*chiasm* comes from the Greek word for "cross"), where the optic nerve splits (Figure 4.11*a*). Information from the left half of each retina (which comes from the right visual field) goes to the left hemisphere, and vice versa. Once past the optic chiasm, combined information from the two eyes travels to the brain via the *optic tracts*, which are simply a continuation of the axons from ganglion cells that constitute the optic nerve. From there, visual information flows along two separate pathways within each hemisphere (Figure 4.11*a*).

The first pathway projects to the *lateral geniculate nucleus* of the thalamus and then to the primary visual cortex in the occipital lobes. Neurons in the lateral geniculate nucleus preserve the map of visual space in the retina. That is, neighboring ganglion cells transmit information to thalamic neurons next to each other, which in turn transmit this retinal map to the cortex. Neurons in the lateral geniculate nucleus have the same kind of concentric (target-like) receptive fields as retinal neurons. They also receive input from the reticular activating system, which means that the extent to which an animal is attentive, aroused, and awake may modulate the transmission of impulses from the thalamus to the visual cortex (Burke & Cole, 1978; Munk et al., 1996).

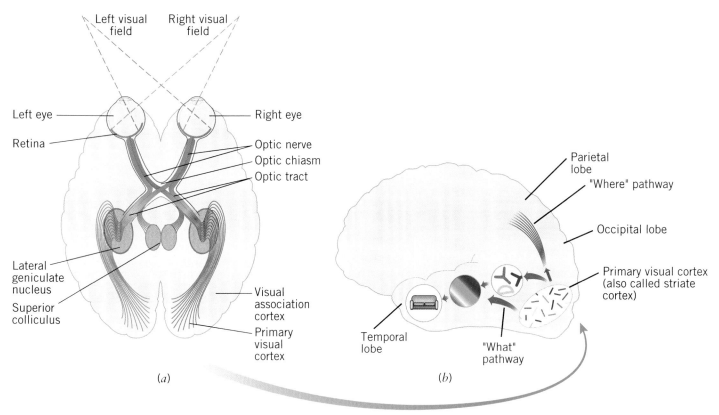

FIGURE 4.11   Visual pathways. The optic nerve carries visual information from the retina to the optic chiasm, where the optic nerve splits. The brain processes information from the right visual field in the left hemisphere and vice versa because of the way some visual information crosses and some does not cross over to the opposite hemisphere at the optic chiasm. At the optic chiasm, the optic nerve be- comes the optic tract (because bundles of axons within the brain itself are called tracts, not nerves). A small pathway from the optic tract carries information simultaneously to the superior colliculus. The optic tract then carries information to the lateral geniculate nucleus of the thalamus, where neurons project to the primary visual cortex.

Making Connections

The primary visual cortex in the occipital lobes lights up on a PET scan when people actively view words, in contrast to when their eyes are closed or they stare continuously at a black dot (Chapter 3).

A second, short pathway projects to a clump of neurons in the midbrain known as the *superior colliculus*, which in humans is involved in controlling eye movements. Its neurons respond to the presence or absence of visual stimulation in parts of the visual field but cannot identify specific objects. Neurons in the superior colliculus also integrate input from the eyes and the ears, so that weak stimulation from the two senses together can orient the person toward a region in space that neither sense alone could detect (Stein & Meredith, 1990).

The presence of two visual pathways from the optic nerve to the brain appears to be involved in an intriguing phenomenon known as **blindsight**, *in which individuals are unaware of their capacity to see* (Sahraie et al., 1997; Weiskrantz et al., 1974). Pursuing observations made by neurologists in the early part of the twentieth century, researchers have studied a subset of patients with lesions to the primary visual cortex, which receives input from the second visual pathway (through the lateral geniculate nucleus). These patients are, for all intents and purposes, blind: If shown an object, they deny that they have seen it. Yet if asked to describe its geometric form (e.g., triangle or square) or give its location in space (to the right or left, up or down), they do so with accuracy far better than chance—frequently protesting all the while that they cannot do the task because they cannot see! Visual processing in the superior colliculus, and perhaps at the level of the lateral geniculate nucleus, apparently leads to visual responses that can guide behavior outside of awareness.

Visual Cortex   From the lateral geniculate nucleus, visual information travels to the primary visual cortex in the occipital lobes. The primary visual cortex is sometimes called the *striate cortex* because of its striated (striped) appearance; visual pathways outside the striate cortex to which its neurons project are thus called *extrastriate cortex* (because they are outside, or extra to, the striate cortex).

Primary Visual Cortex   The size of a brain region that serves a particular function (in this case, vision) is a rough index of the importance of that function to the organism's adaptation over the course of evolution. Once again this characteristic simply reflects the "logic" of natural selection: If vision were particularly useful for survival and reproduction in our primate ancestors, those animals with larger visual processing centers would be at an adaptive advantage, and larger and more sophisticated visual "modules" would be likely to evolve over time. In fact, in many monkey species whose visual systems resemble those of humans, over half the cortex is devoted to visual processing (Van Essen et al., 1992).

Within a sensory system, such as the visual system, the same principle also holds true. For example, in humans as in other primates, the primary visual cortex does not give "equal time" to all regions of the person's visual field. Approximately 25 percent of the striate cortex is devoted to information from the central 2 percent of the visual field (Carlson, 1999; Drasdo, 1977), just as the somatosensory cortex in the parietal lobes overrepresents regions such as the hands, which have many receptors and transmit especially important information (Chapter 3). Additionally, much of the visual cortex is organized in such a way that adjacent groups of visual neurons receive inputs from adjacent areas of the retina (see Figure 4.12).

The striate cortex is the "first stop" in the cortex for all visual information. Neurons in this region begin to "make sense" of visual information, in large measure through the action of neurons known as feature detectors. **Feature detectors**, discovered by Nobel Prize winners David Hubel and Thorsten Wiesel (1959, 1979; see also Ferster & Miller, 2000), are *neurons that fire only when stimulation in their receptive field matches a very specific pattern*.

Simple cells are feature detectors that respond most vigorously to lines of a particular orientation, such as horizontal or vertical, in an exact location in the visual field (Figure 4.13). *Complex cells* are feature detectors that generally cover a larger receptive field and respond when a stimulus of the proper orientation falls anywhere within their receptive field, not just at a particular location. They may also fire only when the stimulus moves in a particular direction. Still other cells, called *hypercomplex cells*, require that a stimulus be of a specific size or length to fire. Other neurons in the primary visual cortex respond selectively to color, contrast, and texture (Engel et al., 1997; Livingstone & Hubel, 1988). This combination of cells allows us to recognize a

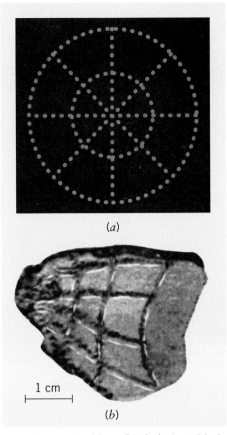

(*a*)

1 cm

(*b*)

FIGURE 4.12   Visual "maps" in the brain. Activity in the visual cortex mirrors the spatial organization of visual information in the world. Here, researchers injected a monkey with a substance that would allow them to see which parts of its brain were active when presented with the image shown in (*a*). Part (*b*) shows the parts of the monkey's brain that were active in the right hemisphere. Remarkably, the neuroimage— the map of activity in the brain—roughly resembles the shape of the stimulus. *Source:* Tootell et al., 1982.

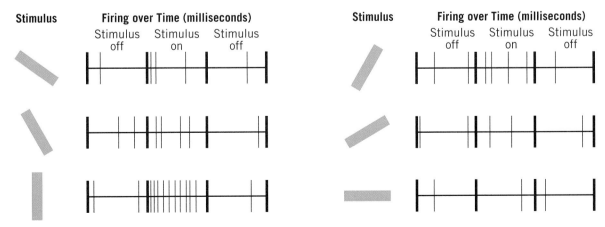

FIGURE 4.13   Feature detectors. A simple cell that responds maximally to vertical lines will show more rapid firing the closer a visual image in its receptive field matches its preferred orientation. *Source:* Sekuler & Blake, 1994, p. 199.

Big Picture φ Question 3

To what extent is human psychology continuous with the psychology of other animals?

Making Connections

Some patients with prosopagnosia, who cannot even recognize their spouse, nevertheless "feel" different upon seeing their husband or wife. This sensitivity suggests that some neural circuits are detecting that here is a familiar and loved person, even though these circuits have no direct access to consciousness (Chapter 9).

vertical line as a vertical line despite its size and ultimately allows us to distinguish a pencil from an antenna, even though both may be vertical.

The What and the Where Pathways From the primary visual cortex, visual information appears to flow along two pathways, or *processing streams* (Figure 4.11b) (Shapley, 1995; Ungerleider & Haxby, 1994; Van Essen et al., 1992). Much of what we know about these pathways comes from the study of macaque monkeys, although recent imaging studies using PET and fMRI confirm that the neural pathways underlying visual perception in the human and the macaque are very similar.

Researchers have labeled these visual streams the "what" and the "where" pathways. The **what pathway**, which runs from the striate cortex in the occipital lobes through the lower part of the temporal lobes (or the *inferior temporal cortex*), ***is involved in determining what an object is***. In this pathway, primitive features from the striate cortex (such as lines) are integrated into more complex combinations (such as cones or squares). At other locations along the pathway, the brain processes features of the object such as color and texture. All of these processes occur simultaneously, as the striate cortex routes shape information to a shape-processing module, color information to a color-processing module, and so forth.

Although some "cross-talk" occurs among these different modules, each appears to create its own map of the visual field, such as a shape map and a color map. Not until the information has reached the front, or anterior, sections of the temporal lobes does a fully integrated percept appear to exist. At various points along the stream, however, polysensory areas bring visual information in contact with information from other senses. For example, when a person shakes hands with another person, he not only sees the other's hand but also feels it, hears the person move toward him, and feels his own arm moving through space. This perception requires integrating information from all of the lobes of the cortex.

The second stream, the **where pathway**, ***is involved in locating the object in space, following its movement, and guiding movement toward it***. (Researchers could just as easily have labeled this the "where and how" pathway because it guides movement and hence offers information on "how to get there from here.") This pathway runs from the striate cortex through the middle and upper (superior) regions of the temporal lobes and up into the parietal lobes.

Lesions that occur along these pathways produce disorders that would seem bizarre without an understanding of the neuroanatomy. For example, patients with lesions at various points along the *what* pathway may be unable to recognize or name objects, to recognize colors, or to recognize familiar faces (prosopagnosia). Patients with lesions in the *where* pathway, in contrast, typically have little trouble recognizing or naming objects, but they may constantly bump into things, have trouble grasping nearby objects, or fail to respond to objects in a part of their visual field, even including their own limbs (a phenomenon called *visual neglect*). Interestingly, this neglect may occur even when they are picturing a scene from memory: When asked to draw a scene, patients with neglect may simply leave out an entire segment of the scene and have no idea that it is missing.

Anatomically, the location of these two pathways makes sense as well. Recognition of objects ("what") is performed by modules in the temporal lobes directly below those involved in language, particularly in naming objects. Knowing where objects are in space and tracking their movements, however, is important for guiding one's own movement toward or away from them. Circuits in the parietal lobes, adjacent to the "where" pathway, process information about the position of one's own body in space.

INTERIM SUMMARY

From the optic nerve, visual information travels along two pathways. One is to the superior colliculus in the midbrain, which in humans is particularly involved in eye movements. The other is to the lateral geniculate nucleus in the thalamus and on to the visual cortex. **Feature detectors** in the primary visual cortex respond only when stimulation in their receptive field matches a particular pattern or orientation. Beyond the primary visual cortex, visual information flows along two pathways, the **what pathway** (involved in determining what an object is) and the **where pathway** (involved in locating the object in space, following its movement, and guiding movement toward it).

Perceiving in Color

"Roses are red, violets are blue…."Well, not exactly. Color is a psychological property, not a quality of the stimulus. Grass is not green to a cow because cows lack color receptors; in contrast, most insects, reptiles, fish, and birds have excellent color vision (Nathans, 1987). As Sir Isaac Newton demonstrated in research with prisms in the sixteenth century, white light (such as sunlight and light from common indoor lamps) is composed of all the wavelengths that constitute the colors in the visual spectrum. A rose appears red because it absorbs certain wavelengths and reflects others, and humans have receptors that detect electromagnetic radiation in that range of the spectrum. Actually, color has three psychological dimensions: hue, saturation, and lightness (Sewall & Wooten, 1991). **Hue** is *what people commonly mean by color*, that is, whether an object appears blue, red, violet, and so on. *Saturation* is a color's purity (the extent to which it is diluted with white or black, or "saturated" with its own wavelength, like a sponge in water). *Lightness* is the extent to which a color is light or dark.

People of all cultures appear to perceive the same colors or hues, although cultures vary widely in the number of their color labels (Chapter 7). In the West, color also appears to be gendered (i.e., to differ between the two genders): Few men would pass a test requiring them to label colors such as bone, taupe, and magenta, despite their mastery of the English language.

Retinal Transduction of Color   How does the visual system translate wavelength into the subjective experience of color? The first step occurs in the retina, where cones with different photosensitive pigments respond to varying degrees to different wavelengths of the spectrum. In 1802, a British physician named Thomas Young proposed that human color vision is trichromatic, that is, the colors we see reflect blends of three colors to which our retinas are sensitive. Developed independently 50 years later by Hermann von Helmholtz, the **Young–Helmholtz** (or **trichromatic**) **theory of color** *holds that the eye contains three types of receptors, each maximally sensitive to wavelengths of light that produce sensations of blue, green, or red*.

Another century later, Nobel Prize winner George Wald and others confirmed the existence of three different types of cones in the retina (Brown & Wald, 1964; Schnapf et al., 1989). Each cone responds to a range of wavelengths but responds most persistently to waves of light at a particular point on the spectrum (Figure 4.14).

To what extent can we say that "roses are red"?

Big Picture φ Question 4

To what extent is human nature particular versus universal?

Big Picture φ Question 5

To what extent are psychological processes the same in men and women?

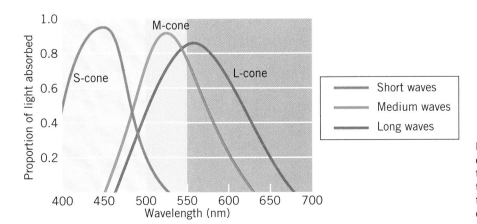

FIGURE 4.14   Cone response curves. All three kinds of cones respond to a range of frequencies—that is, they absorb light waves of many lengths, which contributes to bleaching—but they are maximally sensitive at particular frequencies and thus produce different color sensations.

FIGURE 4.15 Afterimage. Stare at the yellow and red globe for three minutes, centering your eyes on the white dot in the middle, and then look at the white space on the page below it. The afterimage is the traditional blue and green globe, reflecting the operation of antagonistic color-opponent cells in the lateral geniculate nucleus.

Big Picture φ Question 3

To what extent is human psychology continuous with the psychology of other animals?

Short-wavelength cones (S-cones) are most sensitive to wavelengths of about 420 nm, which are perceived as blue. Middle-wavelength cones (M-cones), which produce the sensation of green, are most sensitive to wavelengths of about 535 nm. Long-wavelength cones (L-cones), which produce red sensations, are most sensitive to wavelengths of about 560 nm (Brown & Wald, 1964). Mixing these three primary colors of light—red, green, and blue—produces the thousands of color shades humans can discriminate and identify.

This list of primary colors differs from the list of primary colors children learn in elementary school from mixing paints (blue, red, and yellow). The reason is that mixing paint and mixing light alter the wavelengths perceived in different ways, one *subtracting* and the other *adding* parts of the spectrum. Mixing paints is called *subtractive color mixture* because each new paint added actually blocks out, or subtracts, wavelengths reflected onto the retina. For example, yellow paint appears yellow because its pigment absorbs most wavelengths and reflects only those perceived as yellow; the same is true of blue paint. When blue and yellow paints are mixed, only the wavelengths not absorbed by *either* the blue or yellow paint reach the eye; the wavelengths left are the ones we perceive as green.

Subtractive color mixture, then, mixes wavelengths of light before they reach the eye. In contrast, *additive color mixture* takes place in the eye itself, as light of differing wavelengths simultaneously strikes the retina and thus expands (adds to) the perceived section of the spectrum. Newton discovered additive color mixture by using two prisms to funnel two colors simultaneously into the eye. Color television works on an additive principle. A television picture is composed of tiny blue, green, and red dots, which the eye blends from a distance. When struck by an electron beam inside the set, the spots light up. From a distance, the spots combine to produce multicolored images, although the dots can be seen at very close range.

Processing Color in the Brain   The trichromatic theory accurately predicted the nature of retinal receptors, but it was not a complete theory of color perception. For example, the physiologist Ewald Hering noted that trichromatic theory could not alone explain a phenomenon that occurs with *afterimages*, visual images that persist after a stimulus has been removed. Hering (1878, 1920) wondered why the colors of the afterimage were different in predictable ways from those of the original image (Figure 4.15). He proposed a theory, modified substantially by later researchers, known as opponent-process theory (DeValois & DeValois, 1975; Hurvich & Jameson, 1957). **Opponent-process theory** *argues that all colors are derived from three antagonistic color systems: black–white, blue–yellow, and red–green.* The black–white system contributes to brightness and saturation; the other two systems are responsible for hue.

Hering proposed his theory in opposition to trichromatic theory, but subsequent research suggests that the two theories are actually complementary. Trichromatic theory applies to the retina, where cones are, in fact, particularly responsive to red, blue, or green. Opponent-process theory applies at higher visual centers in the brain. Researchers have found that some neurons in the lateral geniculate nucleus of monkeys, whose visual system is similar to that of humans, are color-opponent cells, excited by wavelengths that produce one color but inhibited by wavelengths of the other member of the pair (DeValois & DeValois, 1975). For example, some red–green neurons increase their activity when wavelengths experienced as red are in their receptive fields and decrease their activity when exposed to wavelengths perceived as green; others are excited by green and inhibited by red. The pattern of activation of several color-opponent neurons together determines the color the person senses (Abramov & Gordon, 1994).

Opponent-process theory neatly explains afterimages. Recall that in all sensory modalities the sensory system adapts, or responds less, to constant stimulation. In the visual system, adaptation begins with bleaching in the retina. Photoreceptors take time to resynthesize their pigments once they have bleached and thus cannot respond continuously to constant stimulation. During the period in which their pigment is returning, they cannot send inhibitory signals; this period of resynthesis facilitates sensation of the opponent color. The afterimage of yellow therefore appears blue (and vice versa), red appears green, and black appears white.

Opponent-process and trichromatic theory together explain another phenomenon that interested Hering: color blindness (or, more accurately, color deficiency). Few people are entirely blind to color; those who are (because of genetic abnormalities that leave them with only one kind of cone) can detect only brightness, not color. Most color-deficient people confuse red and green (Figure 4.16). Red—green color blindness is sex linked, over 10 times more prevalent in males than females. It generally reflects a deficiency of either M- or L-cones, which makes red–green distinctions impossible at higher levels of the nervous system (Weale, 1982; Wertenbaker, 1981).

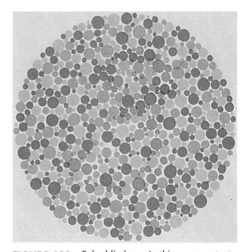

INTERIM SUMMARY

Two theories together explain what is known about color vision. According to the **Young–Helmholtz, or trichromatic, theory**, the eye contains three types of receptors, which are most sensitive to wavelengths experienced as red, green, or blue. According to **opponent-process theory**, the colors we experience (and the afterimages we perceive) reflect three antagonistic color systems—a blue–yellow, red–green, and black–white system. Trichromatic theory operates at the level of the retina, and opponent-process theory at higher neural levels.

FIGURE 4.16 Color blindness. In this common test for color blindness, a green 3 is presented against a background of orange and yellow dots. The pattern of stimulation normally sent to the lateral geniculate nucleus by S-, M-, and L-cones allows discrimination of these colors. People who are red–green color blind see only a random array of dots.

Hearing

If a tree falls in a forest, does it make a sound if no one hears it? To answer this question requires an understanding of *hearing*, or **audition**, and the physical properties it reflects. Like vision, hearing allows sensation at a distance and is thus of tremendous adaptive value. Hearing is also involved in the richest form of communication, spoken language. As with our discussion of vision, we begin by considering the stimulus energy underlying hearing—sound. Next we examine the organ that transduces it, the ear, and the neural pathways for auditory processing.

The Nature of Sound

When a tree falls in the forest, the crash produces vibrations in adjacent air molecules, which in turn collide with one another. A guitar string being plucked, a piece of paper rustling, or a tree falling to the ground all produce sound because they create vibrations in the air. Like ripples on a pond, these *rhythmic pulsations of acoustic energy (sound) spread outward from the vibrating object* as **sound waves**. Sound waves grow weaker with distance, but they travel at a constant speed, roughly 1130 feet (or 340 meters) per second.

Sound differs from light in a number of respects. Sound travels more slowly, the reason why fans in center field sometimes hear the crack of a bat after seeing the batter hit the ball, or why thunder often appears to follow lightning even when the two occur at the same time. At close range, however, the difference between the speed of light and the speed of sound is imperceptible.

Unlike light, sound also travels through most objects, which explains why sound is more difficult to shut out. Like light, sound waves can be reflected off or absorbed by objects in the environment, but the impact on hearing is different from the impact on vision. When sound is reflected off an object, it produces an echo; when it is absorbed by an object, such as carpet, it is muffled. Everyone sounds like the great Italian tenor Luciano Pavarotti in the shower because tile absorbs so little sound, creating echoes and resonance that give fullness to even a mediocre voice.

People see an airplane from a distance before they hear it because light travels faster than sound.

Apply & Discuss

Contemporary jazz would have been musically in-comprehensible to Mozart, just as hip-hop is senseless noise to people (like parents) who grew up with rock and roll.

▪ What makes some patterns of sound pleasur-able and others "noise?"

Big Picture φ Question 3

To what extent is human psychology continuous with the psychology of other animals?

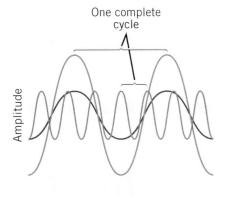

— High frequency, low amplitude (soft tenor or soprano)
— Low frequency, low amplitude (soft bass)
— Low frequency, high amplitude (loud bass)

FIGURE 4.17 Frequency and amplitude. Sound waves can differ in both frequency (pitch) and ampli-tude (loudness). A cycle can be represented as the length of time or the distance between peaks of the curve.

Frequency   Acoustic energy has three important properties: frequency, complexity, and amplitude. When a person hits a tuning fork, the prongs of the fork move rapidly inward and outward, putting pressure on the air molecules around them, which col-lide with the molecules next to them. *Each round of expansion and contraction of the distance between molecules of air* is known as a **cycle**.

The number of cycles per second determines the sound wave's frequency. **Fre-quency** is just what it sounds like—a measure of *how often (i.e., how frequently) a wave cycles*. Frequency is expressed in **hertz**, or **Hz** (named after the German physicist Heinrich Hertz). *One hertz equals one cycle per second*, so a 1500-Hz tone has 1500 cy-cles per second. The frequency of a simple sound wave corresponds to the psychological property of **pitch** *(the quality of a tone, from low to high)*. Generally, the higher the frequency, the higher the pitch. When frequency is doubled—that is, when the number of cycles per second is twice as frequent—the pitch perceived is an octave higher.

The human auditory system is sensitive to a wide range of frequencies. Young adults can hear frequencies from about 15 to 20,000 Hz, but as with most senses, ca-pacity diminishes with aging. Frequencies used in music range from the lowest note on an organ (16 Hz) to the highest note on a grand piano (over 4000 Hz). Human voices range from about 100 Hz to about 3500 Hz, and our ears are most sensitive to sounds in that frequency range. Other species are sensitive to different ranges. Dogs hear frequencies ranging from 15 to 50,000 Hz, the reason why they are responsive to "silent" whistles whose frequencies fall above the range humans can sense. Elephants can hear ultralow frequencies over considerable distances.

So, does a tree falling in the forest produce a sound? It produces sound waves, but the waves only become perceptible as "a sound" if creatures in the forest have re-ceptors tuned to them.

Complexity   Sounds rarely consist of waves of uniform frequency. Rather, most sounds are a combination of sound waves, each with a different frequency. **Complex-ity** refers to *the extent to which a sound is composed of multiple frequencies*, and corresponds to the psychological property of **timbre**, or *texture of the sound*. People recognize each other's voices, as well as the sounds of different musical instruments, from their characteristic timbre. The dominant part of each wave produces the pre-dominant pitch, but overtones (additional frequencies) give a voice or musical instru-ment its distinctive timbre. (Synthesizers imitate conventional instruments by elec-tronically adding the right overtones to pure frequencies.) The sounds instruments produce, whether in a rock band or a symphony, are music to our ears because we learn to interpret particular temporal patterns and combinations of sound waves as music. What people hear as music and as random auditory noise depends on their culture (as generations of teenagers have discovered while trying to get their parents to appreciate the latest musical "sensation").

Amplitude   In addition to frequency and complexity, sound waves have ampli-tude. **Amplitude** refers to *the height and depth of a wave*, that is, the difference be-tween its maximum and minimum pressure level (Figure 4.17). *The amplitude of a sound wave corresponds to the psychological property* of **loudness**; the greater the amplitude, the louder the sound. *Amplitude is measured in* **decibels (dB)**. Zero decibels is the absolute threshold above which most people can hear a 1000-Hz tone.

Like the visual system, the human auditory system has an astonishing range, handling energy levels that can differ by a factor of 10 billion or more (Bekesy & Rosenblith, 1951). The decibel scale is logarithmic, condensing a huge array of inten-sities into a manageable range, just as the auditory system does. A loud scream is 100,000 times more intense than a sound at the absolute threshold, but it is only 100 dB different.

Conversation is usually held at 50 to 60 dB. Most people experience sounds over 130 dB as painful, and prolonged exposure to sounds over about 90 dB, such as subway cars rolling into the station or amplifiers at a rock concert, can produce permanent hearing loss or ringing in the ears (Figure 4.18).

INTERIM SUMMARY

Sound travels in **waves**, which occur as a vibrating object sets air particles in motion. The sound wave's **frequency**, which is experienced as **pitch**, refers to the number of times those particles oscillate per second. Most sounds are actually composed of waves with many frequencies, which gives them their characteristic texture, or **timbre**. The loudness of a sound reflects the height and depth, or **amplitude**, of the wave.

The Ear

Transduction of sound occurs in the ear, which consists of an outer, middle, and inner ear (Figure 4.19). The outer ear collects and magnifies sounds in the air; the middle ear converts waves of air pressure into movements of tiny bones; and the inner ear transforms these movements into waves in fluid that generate neural signals.

The Outer Ear   The hearing process begins in the outer ear, which consists of the pinna and the auditory canal. Sound waves are funneled into the ear by the *pinna*, the skin-covered cartilage that protrudes from the sides of the head. The pinna is not essential for hearing, but its irregular shape helps locate sounds in space, which bounce off its folds differently when they come from various locations (Batteau, 1967). Just inside the skull is the *auditory canal*, a passageway about an inch long. As sound waves resonate in the auditory canal, they are amplified by up to a factor of 2.

The Middle Ear   At the end of the auditory canal is a thin, flexible membrane known as the **eardrum**, or **tympanic membrane**. The eardrum marks the outer boundary of the middle ear. When sound waves reach the eardrum, they set it in motion. The movements of the eardrum are extremely small—0.00000001 centimeter, in response to a whisper (Sekuler & Blake, 1994).

The eardrum essentially reproduces the cyclical vibration of the object that created the noise on a microcosmic scale. This only occurs, however, if air pressure on

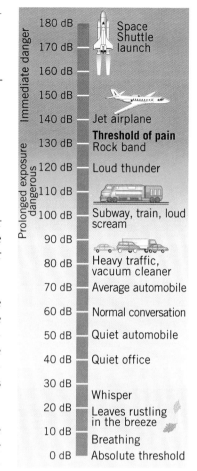

FIGURE 4.18 Loudness of various common sounds at close range, in decibels.

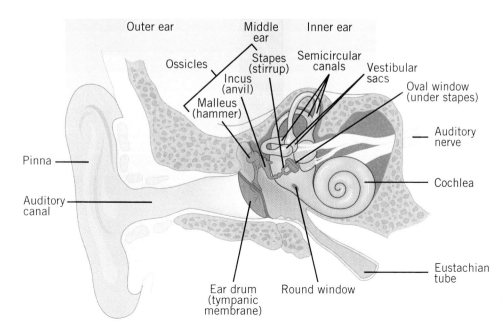

FIGURE 4.19 The ear consists of outer, middle, and inner sections, which direct the sound, amplify it, and turn mechanical energy into neural signals.

both sides of it (in the outer and middle ear) is roughly the same. When an airplane begins its descent and a person's head is blocked by a head cold, the pressure is greater on the inside, which blunts the vibrations of the eardrum. The normal mechanism for equalizing air pressure is the *Eustachian tube*, which connects the middle ear to the throat but can become blocked by mucus.

When the eardrum vibrates, it sets in motion three tiny bones in the middle ear, called *ossicles*. These bones, named for their distinctive shapes, are called the *malleus*, *incus*, and *stapes*, which translate from the Latin into hammer, anvil, and stirrup, respectively. The ossicles further amplify the sound two or three times before transmitting vibrations to the inner ear. The stirrup vibrates against a membrane called the oval window, which forms the beginning of the inner ear.

The Inner Ear   The inner ear consists of two sets of fluid-filled cavities hollowed out of the temporal bone of the skull: the semicircular canals (involved in balance) and the cochlea (involved in hearing). The temporal bone is the hardest bone in the body and serves as natural soundproofing for its vibration-sensitive cavities. Chewing during a meeting sounds louder to the person doing the chewing than to those nearby because it rattles the temporal bone and thus augments the sounds from the ears.

The **cochlea** (Figure 4.20) is *a three-chambered tube in the inner ear shaped like a snail and involved in transduction of sound*. When the stirrup vibrates against the oval window, the oval window vibrates, causing pressure waves in the cochlear fluid. These waves disturb the basilar membrane, which separates two of the cochlea's chambers. Damage to the receptors on the cochlea, through illness or age, for example, reduces or completely impairs an individual's impulses that are transmitted to the brain.

Attached to the basilar membrane are the ear's 15,000 receptors for sound, called **hair cells** (because they terminate in tiny bristles, or cilia). Above the hair cells is another membrane, the *tectorial membrane*, which also moves as waves of pressure travel through the cochlear fluid. The cilia bend as the basilar and tectorial membranes move in different directions. This triggers action potentials in sensory neurons forming the **auditory nerve**, *which transmits auditory information to the brain*. Thus, mechanical energy—the movement of cilia and membranes—is transduced into neural energy.

Sensory deficits in hearing, as in other senses, can arise from problems either with parts of the sense organ that channel stimulus energy or with the receptors and

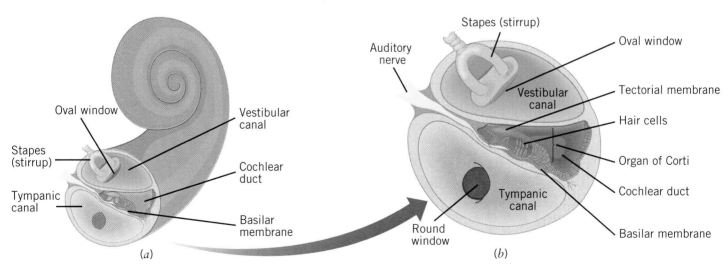

FIGURE 4.20   The anatomy of hearing. (*a*) The cochlea's chambers (the vestibular canal, the cochlear duct, and the tympanic canal) are filled with fluid. When the stirrup vibrates against the oval window, the window vibrates, causing pressure waves in the fluid of the vestibular canal. These pressure waves spiral up the vestibular canal and down the tympanic canal, flexing the basilar membrane and, to a lesser extent, the tectorial membrane. (*b*) Transduction occurs in the organ of Corti, which includes these two membranes and the hair cells sandwiched between them. At the end of the tympanic canal is the round window, which pushes outward to relieve pressure when the sound waves have passed through the cochlea.

neural circuits that convert this energy into psychological experience. Failure of the outer or middle ear to conduct sound to the receptors in the hair cells is called *conduction loss*; failure of receptors in the inner ear or of neurons in any auditory pathway in the brain is referred to as *sensorineural loss*.

The most common problems with hearing result from exposure to noise or reflect changes in the receptors with aging; similar age-related changes occur in most sensory systems (Chapter 13). A single exposure to an extremely loud noise, such as a firecracker, an explosion, or a gun firing at close range, can permanently damage the hair cell receptors in the inner ear. Many musicians who have spent years in front of loud amplifiers are functionally deaf or have lost a large portion of their hearing.

Sensing Pitch   Precisely how does auditory transduction transform the physical properties of sound frequency and amplitude into the psychological experiences of pitch and loudness? Two theories, both proposed in the nineteenth century and once considered opposing explanations, together appear to explain the available data.

The first, **place theory**, *holds that different areas of the basilar membrane are maximally sensitive to different frequencies* (Bekesy, 1959, 1960; Helmholtz, 1863). Place theory was initially proposed by Herman von Helmholtz (of trichromatic color fame), who had the wrong mechanism but the right idea. A Hungarian scientist named Georg von Bekesy discovered the mechanism a century after Helmholtz by recognizing that when the stapes hits the oval window, a wave travels down the basilar membrane like a carpet being shaken at one end (Figure 4.21). Shaking a carpet rapidly (i.e., at high frequency) produces an early peak in the wave of the carpet, whereas shaking it slowly produces a peak in the wave toward the other end of the carpet. Similarly, high-frequency tones, which produce rapid strokes of the stapes, produce the largest displacement of the basilar membrane close to the oval window, whereas low-frequency tones cause a peak in basilar movement toward the far end of the membrane. Peak vibration leads to peak firing of hair cells at a particular location. Hair cells at different points on the basilar membrane thus transmit information about different frequencies to the brain, just as rods and cones transduce electromagnetic energy at different frequencies.

There is one major problem with place theory. At *very* low frequencies the entire basilar membrane vibrates fairly uniformly; thus, for very low tones, location of maximal vibration cannot account for pitch. The second theory of pitch, **frequency theory**, overcomes this problem. It *proposes that the more frequently a sound wave cycles, the more frequently the basilar membrane vibrates and its hair cells fire*. Thus, pitch perception is probably mediated by two neural mechanisms: a place code at high frequencies and a frequency code at low frequencies. Both mechanisms likely operate at intermediate frequencies (Goldstein, 1989).

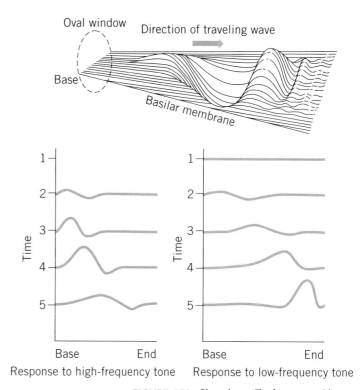

FIGURE 4.21   Place theory. The frequency with which the stapes strikes the oval window affects the location of peak vibration on the basilar membrane. The lower the tone, the farther the maximum displacement on the membrane is from the oval window. *Source:* Adapted from Sekuler & Blake, 1994, p. 315.

INTERIM SUMMARY

Sound waves travel through the auditory canal to the **eardrum**, which in turn sets the ossicles in motion, amplifying the sound. When the stirrup (one of the ossicles) strikes the oval window, it creates waves of pressure in the fluid of the **cochlea. Hair cells** attached to the basilar membrane then transduce the sound, triggering firing of the sensory neurons whose axons comprise the **auditory nerve**. Two theories, once considered opposing, explain the psychological qualities of sound. According to **place theory**, which best explains transduction at high frequencies, different areas of the basilar membrane respond to different frequencies. According to **frequency theory**, which best explains transduction at low frequencies, the rate of vibration of the basilar membrane transforms frequency into pitch.

Neural Pathways

Sensory information transmitted along the auditory nerves ultimately finds its way to the auditory cortex in the temporal lobes, but it makes several stops along the way (Figure 4.22). The auditory nerve from each ear projects to the medulla, where the majority of its fibers cross over to the other hemisphere. (Recall from Chapter 3 that the medulla is where sensory and motor neurons cross from one side of the body to the other.) From the medulla, bundles of axons project to the midbrain (to the *inferior colliculus*, just below the superior colliculus, which is involved in vision) and on to the thalamus (to the *medial geniculate nucleus*, just toward the center of the brain from its visual counterpart, the lateral geniculate nucleus). The thalamus transmits information to the auditory cortex in the temporal lobes, which has sections devoted to different frequencies.

Just as the cortical region corresponding to the fovea is disproportionately large, so, too, is the region of the primary auditory cortex tuned to sound frequencies in the middle of the spectrum—the same frequencies involved in speech (Schreiner et al., 2000). Indeed, in humans and other animals, some cortical neurons in the left temporal lobe respond exclusively to particular sounds characteristic of the "language" of the species, whether monkey calls or human speech.

Sound Localization　　Humans use two main cues for **sound localization**, which means *identifying the location of a sound in space*: differences between the two ears in loudness and timing of the sound (Feng & Ratnam, 2000; King & Carlile, 1995; Stevens & Newman, 1934). Particularly for high-frequency sounds, relative loudness in the ear closer to the source provides information about its location because the head blocks some of the sound from hitting the other ear. At low frequencies, localization

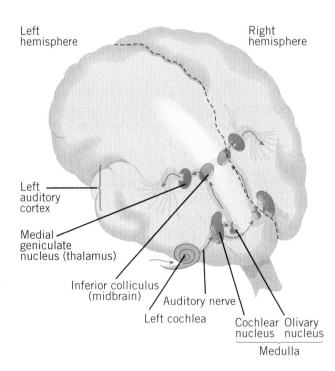

FIGURE 4.22　Auditory pathways. The drawing shows how the brain processes sensory information entering the left ear. Axons from neurons in the inner ear project to the cochlear nucleus in the medulla. From there, most cross over to a structure called the olivary nucleus on the opposite side, although some remain uncrossed. At the olivary nucleus, information from the two ears begins to be integrated. Information from the olivary nucleus then passes to a midbrain structure (the inferior colliculus) and on to the medial geniculate nucleus in the thalamus before reaching the auditory cortex.

Left hemisphere

Right hemisphere

Left auditory cortex

Medial geniculate nucleus (thalamus)

Inferior colliculus (midbrain)

Left cochlea

Auditory nerve

Cochlear nucleus　Olivary nucleus

Medulla

relies less on loudness and more on the split-second difference in the arrival time of the sound at the two ears. Moving the head toward sounds is also crucial.

Neurologically, the basis for sound localization lies in *binaural neurons,* neurons that respond to relative differences in the signals from two ears. Binaural neurons exist at nearly all levels of the auditory system in the brain, from the brain stem up through the cortex (King & Carlile, 1995). At higher levels of the brain, this information is connected with visual information about the location and distance of objects, which allows joint mapping of auditory and visual information.

Researchers have studied this process of "coordinating maps" in the barn owl, an animal whose brain localizes sound primarily through timing differences between the arrival of the sound at each ear (Feldman et al., 1996; Konishi, 1995). When these owls are raised wearing glasses that use prisms to distort the perceived location of objects, their auditory map essentially becomes linked to a visual map with different coordinates —leading to difficulty connecting what the eyes know with what the ears know.

INTERIM SUMMARY

From the auditory nerve, sensory information passes through the inferior colliculus in the midbrain and the medial geniculate nucleus of the thalamus on to the auditory cortex in the temporal lobes. **Sound localization**—identifying the location of a sound in space— depends on binaural neurons that respond to relative differences in the loudness and timing of sensory signals transduced by the two ears.

Other Senses

Vision and audition are the most highly specialized senses in humans, occupying the greatest amount of brain space and showing the most cortical evolution. Our other senses, however, play important roles in adaptation as well. These include smell, taste, the skin senses (pressure, temperature, and pain), and the proprioceptive senses (body position and motion).

Smell

Smell (**olfaction**) serves a number of functions in humans. It enables us to detect danger (e.g., the smell of something burning), discriminate palatable from unpalatable or spoiled foods, and recognize familiar odors, such as your mother's perfume. Smell plays a less important role in humans than in most other animals, who rely heavily on olfaction to mark territory and track other animals. Many species communicate through **pheromones** (Chapter 10), *scent messages detected through an auxiliary olfactory system* that regulate the sexual behavior of many animals and direct a variety of behaviors in insects (Carolsfeld et al., 1997; Sorensen, 1996). This pheromonal system acts more in the way of hormones than smells. In fact, many pheromones have no detectable odor, yet produce changes in the behavior and physiology of other members of the same species. Vestiges of this ancient reproductive mechanism remain. Humans appear both to secrete and sense olfactory cues related to reproduction. Experiments using sweaty hands or articles of clothing have shown that people can identify the gender of another person by smell alone with remarkable accuracy (Doty et al., 1982; Russell, 1976; Wallace, 1977). The synchronization of menstrual cycles of women living in close proximity also appears to occur through smell and may reflect ancient pheromonal mechanisms (McClintock, 1971; Preti et al., 1986; Stern & McClintock, 1998).

Transduction   The environmental stimuli for olfaction are invisible molecules of gas emitted by substances and suspended in the air. The thresholds for recognizing

Apply & Discuss

One of the hallmarks of schizophrenia is hearing "voices."

How might this happen in the absence of external sensory stimulation?

Big Picture φ Question 3

To what extent is human psychology continuous with the psychology of other animals?

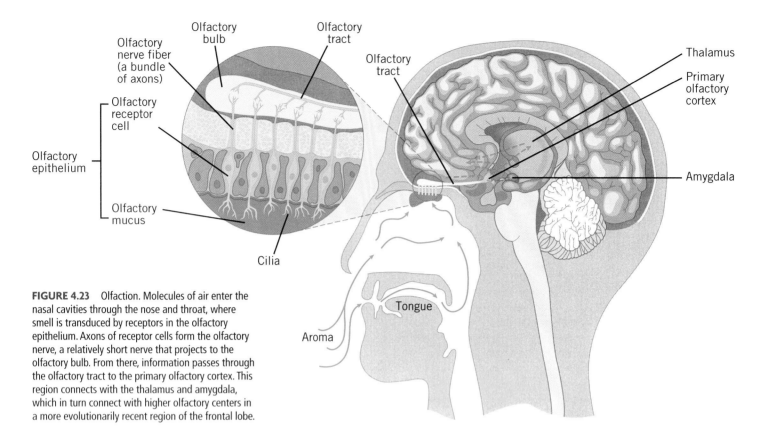

FIGURE 4.23 Olfaction. Molecules of air enter the nasal cavities through the nose and throat, where smell is transduced by receptors in the olfactory epithelium. Axons of receptor cells form the olfactory nerve, a relatively short nerve that projects to the olfactory bulb. From there, information passes through the olfactory tract to the primary olfactory cortex. This region connects with the thalamus and amygdala, which in turn connect with higher olfactory centers in a more evolutionarily recent region of the frontal lobe.

most odors are remarkably low—as low as one molecule per 50 *trillion* molecules of air for some odors (Geldard, 1972). Although the nose is the sense organ for smell, the vapors that give rise to olfactory sensations can enter the *nasal cavities*—the region hollowed out of the bone in the skull that contains smell receptors—through either the nose or the mouth (Figure 4.23). When food is chewed, vapors travel up the back of the mouth into the nasal cavity; this process actually accounts for much of the flavor.

Transduction of smell occurs in the **olfactory epithelium**, a thin pair of structures (one on each side) less than a square inch in diameter at the top of the nasal cavities. Chemical molecules in the air become trapped in the mucus of the epithelium, where they make contact with olfactory receptor cells that transduce the stimulus into olfactory sensations. Humans have approximately 10 million olfactory receptors (Engen, 1982), in comparison with dogs, whose 200 million receptors enable them to track humans and other animals with their noses (Marshall & Moulton, 1981).

Psychologists have long debated whether a small number of receptors coding different qualities combine to produce complex smells or whether the olfactory epithelium contains hundreds or thousands of receptors that bind only with very specific molecules. Recent research on the genes that produce proteins involved in smell transduction suggests that many receptors are responsive to chemicals with very specific molecular structures (Bartoshuk & Beauchamp, 1994; Breer et al., 1996).

Neural Pathways *The axons of olfactory receptor cells form the* **olfactory nerve**, which transmits information to the *olfactory bulbs*, multilayered structures that combine information from receptor cells. Olfactory information then travels to the primary olfactory cortex, a primitive region of the cortex deep in the frontal lobes. Unlike other senses, smell is not relayed through the thalamus on its way to the cortex; however, the olfactory cortex has projections to both the thalamus and the limbic system, so that smell is connected to both taste and emotion.

Many animals that respond to pheromonal cues have a second, or accessory, olfactory system that projects to the amygdala and on to the hypothalamus, which helps regulate reproductive behavior. Although the data at this point are conflicting, some studies suggest that humans may have a similar secondary olfactory system, which, if operative, has no links to consciousness and thus influences reproductive behavior without our knowing it (Bartoshuk & Beauchamp, 1994; Stern & McClintock, 1998).

INTERIM SUMMARY

The environmental stimuli for smell are gas molecules suspended in the air. These molecules flow through the nose into the **olfactory epithelium**, where they are detected by hundreds of different types of receptors. The axons of these receptor cells comprise the **olfactory nerve**, which transmits information to the olfactory bulbs and on to the primary olfactory cortex deep in the frontal lobes.

Taste

The sense of smell is sensitive to molecules in the air, whereas *taste* (**gustation**) is sensitive to molecules soluble in saliva. At the dinner table, the contributions of the nose and mouth to taste are indistinguishable, except when the nasal passages are blocked so that food loses much of its flavor.

From an evolutionary perspective, taste serves two functions: to protect the organism from ingesting toxic substances and to regulate intake of nutrients such as sugars and salt. For example, toxic substances often taste bitter, and foods high in sugar (which provides the body with energy) are usually sweet. The tendency to reject bitter substances and to ingest sweet ones is present even in newborns, despite their lack of experience with taste (Bartoshuk & Beauchamp, 1994).

***Transduction of taste occurs in the* taste buds** (Figure 4.24). Roughly 10,000 taste buds are distributed throughout the mouth and throat (Miller, 1995), although most are located in the bumps on the surface of the tongue called *papillae* (Latin for "pimple"). Soluble chemicals that enter the mouth penetrate tiny pores in the papillae and stimulate the taste receptors. Each taste bud contains between 50 and 150 receptor cells (Margolskee, 1995). Taste receptors, unlike sensory receptors in the eye or ear, wear out and are replaced every 10 or 11 days (Graziadei, 1969). Regeneration is essential, or a burn to the tongue would result in permanent loss of taste.

Taste receptors stimulate neurons that carry information to the medulla and pons and then along one of two pathways. The first leads to the thalamus and primary gustatory cortex and allows us to identify tastes. The second pathway is more primitive and has no access to consciousness. This pathway leads to the limbic system and pro-

Apply & Discuss

■ What senses do humans and other animals use in choosing mates?

■ Do species differ in the senses they favor in picking a potential "lover"?

■ How might such differences have evolved?

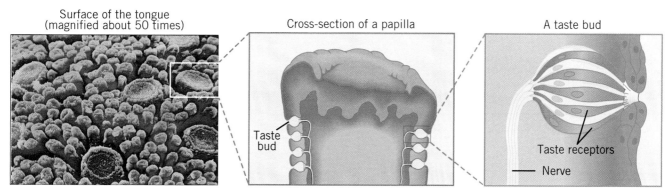

FIGURE 4.24 Taste buds. The majority of taste buds are located on the papillae of the tongue (shown in purple). Taste buds contain receptor cells that bind with chemicals in the saliva and stimulate gustatory neurons. (The cells shown in blue are support cells.)

Surface of the tongue (magnified about 50 times)

Cross-section of a papilla

Taste bud

A taste bud

Taste receptors

Nerve

Making Connections

Within the last few years, researchers believe they have discovered a gene for taste (Bartoshuk, 2000; Zhao et al., 2003). People who have two recessive alleles (Chapter 3) are nontasters, that is, they are not overly sensitive to taste and can consume very spicy foods. People with two dominant alleles are "supertasters." They are highly sensitive to taste and typically consume bland foods. People with one dominant and one recessive allele tend to perceive many foods as bitter. They are medium tasters. More women than men appear to be supertasters, and cross-cultural variations have also been observed. For example, a high percentage of Asians are supertasters.

Big Picture φ Question 4

To what extent is human nature particular versus universal?

duces immediate emotional and behavioral responses, such as spitting out a bitter substance or a substance previously associated with nausea. As in blindsight, people with damage to the first (cortical) pathway cannot identify substances by taste, but they react with appropriate facial expressions to bitter and sour substances if this second, more primitive pathway is intact.

The gustatory system responds to four basic tastes: sweet, sour, salty, and bitter. Different receptors are most sensitive to one of these tastes, at least at low levels of stimulation. This appears to be cross-culturally universal: People of different cultures diverge in their taste preferences and beliefs about basic flavors, but they vary little in identifying substances as sweet, sour, salty, or bitter (Laing et al., 1993).

More than one receptor, however, can produce the same sensation, at least for bitterness. Apparently, as plants and insects evolved toxic chemicals to protect against predation, animals that ate them evolved specific receptors for detecting these substances. The nervous system, however, continued to rely on the same sensation, bitterness, to discourage snacking on them (Bartoshuk & Beauchamp, 1994).

INTERIM SUMMARY

Taste occurs as receptors in the **taste buds** transduce chemical information from molecules soluble in saliva into neural information, which is integrated with olfactory sensations in the brain. Taste receptors stimulate neurons that project to the medulla and pons in the hindbrain. From there, the information is carried along two neural pathways, one leading to the primary gustatory cortex, which allows identification of tastes, and the other leading to the limbic system, which allows initial gut-level reactions and learned responses to tastes. The gustatory system responds to four tastes: sweet, sour, salty, and bitter.

Skin Senses

The approximately 18 square feet of skin covering the human body constitutes a complex, multilayered organ. The skin senses help protect the body from injury, aid in identifying objects, help maintain body temperature, and facilitate social interaction through hugs, kisses, holding, and handshakes.

What we colloquially call the sense of touch is actually a mix of at least three qualities: pressure, temperature, and pain. Approximately five million touch receptors in the skin respond to different aspects of these qualities, such as warm or cold or light or deep pressure (Figure 4.25). Receptors are specialized for different qualities, but most skin sensations are complex, reflecting stimulation across many receptors.

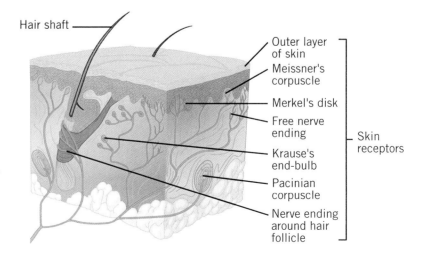

FIGURE 4.25 The skin and its receptors. Several different types of receptors transduce tactile stimulation, such as Meissner's corpuscles, which respond to brief stimulation (as when a ball of cotton moves across the skin); Merkel's disks, which detect steady pressure; and the nerve endings around hair follicles, why plucking eyebrows or pulling tape off the skin can be painful.

The qualities that sensory neurons convey to the nervous system (such as soft pressure, warmth, and cold) depend on the receptors to which they are connected. Thus, when receptors reattach to the wrong nerve fibers, as appears to occur in some cases of painful neuropathy, sensory information can be misinterpreted. Like neurons in other sensory systems, those involved in touch also have receptive fields, which distinguish both where and how long the stimulation occurred on the skin.

Sensory neurons synapse with spinal interneurons that stimulate motor neurons, allowing animals to respond with rapid reflex actions. Sensory neurons also synapse with neurons that carry information up the spinal cord to the medulla, where neural tracts cross over. From there, sensory information travels to the thalamus and is subsequently routed to the primary touch center in the brain, the somatosensory cortex (Chapter 3).

Phantom Limbs   As we have seen in the case of painful neuropathy described in the chapter opener, damage to the sensory systems that control tactile (touch) sensations can reorganize those systems in ways that lead to an altered experience of reality. Another syndrome that dramatically demonstrates what can happen when those systems are disrupted involves **phantom limbs**—*misleading "sensations" from missing limbs*. People who have had a limb amputated, for example, often awaken from the operation wondering why the surgeon did not operate, because they continue to have what feels like full sensory experiences from the limb (Katz & Melzack, 1990). Alternatively, they may experience *phantom limb pain*— pain felt in a limb that no longer exists, typically similar to the pain experienced before the limb was amputated. Even if the stump is completely anesthetized, the pain typically persists (Hill, 1999; Melzack, 1970).

Phantom limbs have some fascinating implications for our understanding of the way the brain processes sensory information. For example, although the experience of a phantom limb tends to be most pronounced in people who have more recently lost a limb, phantom experiences of this sort can occur even in people who lost a limb very early in life or were even born without it (Melzack, 1993). These findings suggest that certain kinds of sensory "expectations" throughout the body may be partly innate.

Another aspect of phantom limbs has begun to lead neuroscientists to a better understanding of how the brain reorganizes after damage to a sensory system (Ramachandran & Hirstein, 1998). If a hand has been amputated, the person often experiences a touch of the face or shoulder as sensation in the fingers of the missing hand. The locations of sensations that occur with phantom limbs tend to be precise, forming a map of the hand on the face and shoulders—so that touching a specific part of the face may repeatedly lead to feelings in a particular part of the missing hand (Figure 4.26).

What causes these feelings? Recall from Chapter 3 that the primary sensory cortex in the parietal lobes (the somatosensory cortex) contains a map of the body, with each part of the somatosensory cortex representing a specific part of the body. In fact, areas of the somatosensory cortex adjacent to the hand and arm are the *face and shoulder*. Because stimulation is no longer coming from the hand, these other areas begin to respond to input from the body to adjacent areas (Jones, 2000).

Although phantom limb phenomena certainly seem dysfunctional, the mechanism that produces them probably is not. The brain tends to make use of sensory tissue, and over time, unused cortex is more likely to be "annexed" than thrown away. For instance, individuals born blind show activity in the visual cortex when reading Braille with their fingers (Hamilton & Pascual-Leone, 1998). Essentially, because the "fingers" region of the parietal lobes is not large enough to store all the information necessary to read with the fingers, areas of the visual cortex usually involved in the complex sensory discriminations required in reading simply take on a different function. Lesions to the primary visual cortex can, in turn, impair the ability to read Braille (Pascual-Leone et al., 2000).

Transducing Pressure, Temperature, and Pain   Each of the skin senses transduces a distinct form of stimulation. Pressure receptors transduce mechanical energy (like the receptors in the ear). Temperature receptors respond to thermal en-

Making Connections

Recent research in the treatment of phantom limb pain has suggested a role for the somatosensory cortex (Chapter 3) in the perception of phantom limb pain or itch. Ramachandran and Hirstein (1998) have devised a way of tricking the brain into thinking that the intact limb (e.g., the right arm) is the missing left arm. Then, when the individual sees the "left arm" being exercised or scratched to relive itching, the brain interprets it as relief from the phantom limb. How is the brain tricked? It's all done with mirrors! The mirrors are arranged in such a way that the participant perceives the right limb to be the missing phantom limb.

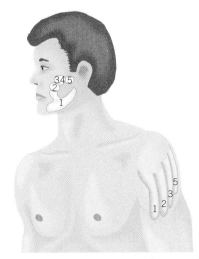

FIGURE 4.26   Reorganization of neurons after amputation of an arm and hand. Touching the face and shoulder of this patient led to reports that the phantom hand was being touched. Each of the numbered areas corresponds to sensations in one of the fingers on the phantom hand (1 = thumb). *Source:* Ramachandran & Hirstein, 1998, p. 1612.

ergy (heat). Pain receptors do not directly transform external stimulation into psychological experience; rather, they respond to a range of internal and external bodily states, from strained muscles to damaged skin.

Pressure   People experience pressure when the skin is mechanically displaced, or moved. Sensitivity to pressure varies considerably over the surface of the body (Craig & Rollman, 1999). The most sensitive regions are the face and fingers, the least sensitive the back and legs, as reflected in the amount of space taken by neurons representing these areas in the somatosensory cortex (see Chapter 3).

The hands are the skin's "foveas," providing tremendous sensory acuity and the ability to make fine discriminations (e.g., between a coin and a button). The primary cortex thus devotes substantial space to the hands (see Johnson & Lamb, 1981). The hands turn what could be a passive sensory process—responding to indentations produced in the skin by external stimulation—into an active process. As the hands move over objects, pressure receptors register the indentations created in the skin and hence allow perception of texture. Just as eye movements allow people to read written words, finger movements allow blind people to read the raised dots that constitute Braille. In other animals, the somatosensory cortex emphasizes other body zones that provide important information for adaptation, such as whiskers in cats (Kaas, 1987).

Temperature   When people sense the temperature of an object, they are largely sensing the difference between the temperature of the skin and the object, which is why a pool of 80-degree water feels warm to someone who has been standing in the cold rain but chilly to someone lying on a hot beach. Temperature sensation relies on two sets of receptors, one for cold and one for warmth. Cold receptors, however, not only detect coolness but also are involved in the experience of extreme temperatures, both hot and cold. Subjects who grasp two pipes twisted together, one containing warm water and the other cold, experience intense heat (Figure 4.27). Different neural circuits are, in fact, activated by the combination of cold and warm water than by either cold or warm alone (Craig et al., 1996).

Pain   People spend billions of dollars a year fighting pain, but pain serves an important function: preventing tissue damage. Indeed, people who are insensitive to pain because of nerve damage or genetic abnormalities are at serious risk of injury and infection. Young children with congenital (inborn) pain insensitivity have bitten off their tongues, chewed off the tips of their fingers, and been severely burned leaning against hot stoves or climbing into scalding bathwater (Jewesbury, 1951). Persistent pain, however, can be debilitating. Some estimates suggest that as many as one-third of North Americans suffer from persistent or recurrent pain. The cost in suffering, lost productivity, and dollars is immense (Miller & Kraus, 1990).

In contrast to other senses, pain has no specific physical stimulus; the skin does not transduce "pain waves." Sounds that are too loud, lights that are too bright, pressure that is too intense, temperatures that are too extreme, and other stimuli can all elicit pain. Although pain transduction is not well understood, the most important receptors for pain in the skin appear to be the *free nerve endings*. According to one prominent theory, when cells are damaged, they release chemicals that stimulate the free nerve endings, which in turn transmit pain messages to the brain (Price, 1988).

One such chemical involved in pain sensation is *substance P (for pain)*. In one study, researchers found that pinching the hind paws of rats led to the release of substance P in the spinal cord (Beyer et al., 1991). The concentration of substance P increased with the amount of painful stimulation and returned to baseline when the stimulation stopped. In another study, rats injected with substance P responded with biting, scratching, and distress vocalizations, which are all indicative of painful stimulation (DeLander & Wahl, 1991).

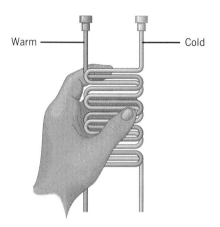

Warm ——————— Cold

FIGURE 4.27   Experiencing intense heat. Warm and cold receptors activated simultaneously produce a sensation of intense heat.

Making Connections

Capsaicin, the active ingredient in hot peppers, creates its burning sensation via substance P receptors. Further, excessive amounts of capsaicin actually destroy the substance P receptors. Thus, a treatment for pain, such as experienced with shingles, is topical application of a capsaicin cream.

Experiencing Pain   Of all the senses, pain is probably the most affected by beliefs, expectations, and emotional state and the least reducible to level of stimulation (Sternbach, 1968). (The next time you have a headache or a sore throat, try focusing your consciousness on the minute details of the sensation, and you will notice that you can momentarily kill the pain by "reframing" it.) Anxiety can increase pain, whereas intense fear, stress, or concentration on other things can inhibit it (al Absi & Rokke, 1991; Melzack & Wall, 1983).

Cultural norms and expectations also influence the subjective experience and behavioral expression of pain (Bates, 1987; Zatzick & Dimsdale, 1990). For example, on the island of Fiji, women of two subcultures appear to experience labor pain quite differently (Morse & Park, 1988). The native Fijian culture is sympathetic to women in labor and provides both psychological support and herbal remedies for labor pain. In contrast, an Indian subculture on the island considers childbirth contaminating and hence offers little sympathy or support. Women from the Indian group rate the pain of childbirth significantly lower than native Fijians. Apparently, cultural recognition of pain influences the extent to which people recognize and acknowledge it.

Pain Control   Because mental as well as physiological processes contribute to pain, treatment may require attention to both mind and matter—to both the psychology and neurophysiology of pain. The Lamaze method of childbirth, for example, teaches women to relax through deep breathing and muscle relaxation and to distract themselves by focusing their attention elsewhere.

These procedures can be quite effective: Lamaze-trained women tend to experience less pain during labor (Leventhal et al., 1989), and they show a general increase in pain tolerance. For example, experiments show that they are able to keep their hands submerged in ice water longer than women without the training, especially if their coach provides encouragement (Whipple et al., 1990; Worthington et al., 1983). Many other techniques target the cognitive and emotional aspects of pain. Though not a panacea, distraction is generally a useful strategy for increasing pain tolerance (Christenfeld, 1997; McCaul & Malott, 1984). Health care professionals often chatter away while giving patients injections in order to distract and relax them.

Something as simple as a pleasant view can affect pain tolerance as well. In one study, surgery patients whose rooms overlooked lush plant life had shorter hospital stays and required less medication than patients whose otherwise identical rooms looked out on a brick wall (Ulrich, 1984). When I (RMK) was in labor with my twins, my room looked out on beautiful mountains and a perfect sunrise. In theory, at least, that should have alleviated some of the pain. Environmental psychologists, who apply psychological knowledge to building and landscape design, use such information to help architects design hospitals (Saegert & Winkel, 1990).

Big Picture φ Question 4

To what extent is human nature particular versus universal?

Making Connections

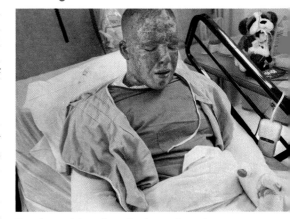

Experimental data show that hypnosis can be extremely helpful to burn victims, whose bandages must be constantly removed and replaced to avoid infection—a process so painful that the strongest narcotics can often barely numb the pain (Patterson et al., 1992) (Chapter 9).

Personality and Pain | From Brain to Behavior

If mental states can affect pain sensation, are some people vulnerable to chronic pain by virtue of their personalities? Despite long-standing controversy in this area, researchers have identified a personality style that appears to be shared by many chronic pain patients (Keller & Butcher, 1991). These patients often blame their physical condition for all life's difficulties and deny any emotional or interpersonal problems. They tend to have difficulty expressing anger and to be anxious, depressed, needy, and dependent.

The difficulty in studying such patients, however, is distinguishing the causes from the effects of chronic pain, since unending pain could produce many of these personality traits (Gamsa, 1990). A team of researchers addressed this methodological problem by studying patients at risk for developing chronic pain before they actually developed it (Dworkin et al., 1992; see also Mogil et al., 2000). The patients suffered from herpes zoster (shingles), a viral infection caused by reactivation of chicken pox virus. The nature and duration of pain associated with herpes zoster vary widely, but some patients experience disabling chronic pain.

To see if they could predict which patients would develop chronic pain, the investigators gave a sample of recently diagnosed herpes zoster patients a series of questionnaires and tests, including measures of depression, anxiety, life stress, attitudes toward their illness, and pain severity. Physicians provided data on the severity of the patients' initial outbreak of the disease. The researchers recontacted the patients several times over the next year to distinguish those who reported ongoing pain three months after the acute outbreak from those who did not.

Although the two groups did not differ in the initial severity of their symptoms, they did differ significantly on a number of psychological dimensions assessed at the time of their initial diagnosis. Fitting the description of the "chronic pain personality," those patients who would later experience continued pain were initially more depressed and anxious and less satisfied with their lives than patients without pain. They were also more likely to dwell on their illness and resist physicians' reassurances.

Chronic pain is by no means "all in the head." In many cases it likely reflects an interaction of psychological factors, physiological vulnerabilities, and disease or injury. But this research suggests that the way people experience themselves and the world affects their vulnerability to their own sensory processes.

INTERIM SUMMARY

Touch includes three senses: pressure, temperature, and pain. Sensory neurons synapse with spinal interneurons that stimulate motor neurons (producing reflexes) as well as with neurons that carry information up the spinal cord to the medulla. From there, nerve tracts cross over, and the information is conveyed through the thalamus to the somatosensory cortex, which contains a map of the body. The function of pain is to prevent tissue damage; the experience of pain is greatly affected by beliefs, expectations, emotional state, and personality.

Without the capacity to sense position of the body in space and position of the limbs relative to each other, this skier would be on his way to the hospital rather than the lodge.

Proprioceptive Senses

Aside from the five traditional senses—vision, hearing, smell, taste, and touch—two additional senses, called **proprioceptive senses**, *register body position and movement*. The first, the **vestibular sense**, *provides information about the position of the body in space by sensing gravity and movement*. The ability to sense gravity is a very early evolutionary development found in nearly all animals. The existence of this sense again exemplifies the way psychological characteristics have evolved to match characteristics of the environment that impact on adaptation. Gravity affects movement, so humans and other animals have receptors to transduce it, just as they have receptors for light.

The vestibular sense organs are in the inner ear, above the cochlea (see Figure 4.19). Two organs transduce vestibular information: the semicircular canals and the vestibular sacs. The semicircular canals sense acceleration or deceleration in any direction as the head moves. The vestibular sacs sense gravity and the position of the head in space. Vestibular receptors are hair cells that register movement, much as hair cells in the ear transduce air movements. The neural pathways for the vestibular sense are not well understood, although impulses from the vestibular system travel to several regions of the hindbrain, notably the cerebellum, which is involved in smooth movement, and to a region deep in the temporal cortex.

The other proprioceptive sense, **kinesthesia**, *provides information about the movement and position of the limbs and other parts of the body relative to one another*. Kinesthesia is essential in guiding every complex movement, from walking, which requires instantaneous adjustments of the two legs, to drinking a cup of coffee. Some receptors for kinesthesia are in the joints; these cells transduce information about the position of the bones. Other receptors, in the tendons and muscles, transmit messages about muscle tension that signal body position (Neutra & Leblond, 1969).

The vestibular and kinesthetic senses work in tandem to communicate different aspects of movement and position. Proprioceptive sensations are also integrated with messages from other sensory systems, especially touch and vision. For example, even when the proprioceptive senses are intact, walking can be difficult if tactile stimulation from the feet is shut off, as when a person's legs "fall asleep." (To see the importance of vision to balance, try balancing on one foot while raising the other foot as high as you can, first with your eyes closed and then with your eyes open.)

INTERIM SUMMARY

The **proprioceptive senses** register body position and movement. The **vestibular sense** provides information on the position of the body in space by sensing gravity and movement. **Kinesthesia** provides information about the movement and position of the limbs and other parts of the body relative to one another.

Perception

The line between sensation and perception is thin, and we probably have already crossed it in discussing the psychology of pain. The hallmarks of perception are organization and interpretation. (Many psychologists consider attention a third aspect of perception, but since attention is also involved in memory, thought, and emotion, we address it in Chapter 9 on consciousness.)

Perception *organizes* a continuous array of sensations into meaningful units. When we speak, we produce, on average, a dozen distinct units of sounds (called phonemes) per second (e.g., all the vowel and consonant sounds in a simple word, such as fascination) and are capable of understanding up to 40 phonemes per second (Pinker, 1994). This requires organization of sensations into units. Beyond organization, we must *interpret* the information organized. A scrawl on a piece of paper is not just a set of lines of particular orientation but a series of letters and words.

In this final section, we again emphasize the visual system, since the bulk of work in perception has used visual stimuli, but the same principles largely hold for all the senses. We begin by considering several ways in which perception is organized and then examine the way people interpret sensory experiences.

Organizing Sensory Experience

If you put this book on the floor, it does not suddenly look like part of the floor; if you walk slowly away from it, it does not seem to diminish in size. These are examples of perceptual organization. **Perceptual organization** *integrates sensations into percepts (meaningful perceptual units, such as images of particular objects), locates them in space, and preserves their meaning as the perceiver examines them from different vantage points*. Here we explore four aspects of perceptual organization: form perception, depth or distance perception, motion perception, and perceptual constancy.

FIGURE 4.28   An ambiguous figure. Whether the perceiver forms a global image of a young or an old woman determines the meaning of each part of the picture; what looks like a young woman's nose from one perspective looks like a wart on an old woman's nose from another. The perception of the whole even leads to different inferences about the coat the woman is wearing: In one case, it appears to be a stylish fur, whereas in the other, it is more likely to be interpreted as an old overcoat. *Source:* Boring, 1930, p. 42.

Form Perception   **Form perception** refers to *the organization of sensations into meaningful shapes and patterns.* When you look at this book, you do not perceive it as a patternless collection of molecules. Nor do you perceive it as part of your leg, even though it may be resting in your lap, or think a piece of it has disappeared simply because your hand or pen is blocking your vision of it.

Gestalt Principles   The first psychologists to study form perception systematically were the gestalt psychologists of the early twentieth century. As noted in Chapter 1, gestalt is a German word that translates loosely to "whole" or "form." Proponents of the Gestalt approach argued that in perception the whole (the percept) is greater than the sum of its sensory parts.

Consider the ambiguous picture in Figure 4.28, which some people see as an old woman with a scarf over her head and others see as a young woman with a feather coming out of a stylish hat. Depending on the perceiver's gestalt, or whole view of the picture, the short black line in the middle could be either the old woman's mouth or the young woman's necklace.

Based on experiments conducted in the 1920s and 1930s, the Gestalt psychologists proposed a small number of basic perceptual rules the brain automatically and unconsciously follows as it organizes sensory input into meaningful wholes (Figure 4.29).

Figure–ground perception: *People inherently distinguish between figure* (the object they are viewing) *and ground* (or background), such as words in black ink against a white page.

Similarity: *The brain tends to group similar elements together,* such as the circles that form the letter R in Figure 4.29*a*.

Proximity (nearness): *The brain tends to group together objects that are close to one another.* In Figure 4.29*b*, the first six lines have no particular organization, whereas the same six lines arranged somewhat differently in the second part of the panel are perceived as three pairs.

Good continuation: If possible, *the brain organizes stimuli into continuous lines or patterns* rather than discontinuous elements. In Figure 4.29*c*, the figure appears to show an X superimposed on a circle, rather than pieces of a pie with lines extending beyond the pie's perimeter.

Simplicity: *People tend to perceive the simplest pattern possible.* Most people perceive Figure 4.29*d* as a heart with an arrow through it because that is the simplest interpretation.

Closure: Where possible, *people tend to perceive incomplete figures as complete.* If part of a familiar pattern or shape is missing, perceptual processes complete the pattern, as in the triangle shown in Figure 4.29*e*. The second part of Figure 4.29*e* demonstrates another type of closure (sometimes called *illusory contour*) (Albert, 1993; Kanizsa, 1976). People see two overlapping triangles, but in fact, neither one exists; the brain simply fills in the gaps to perceive familiar pat-

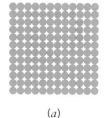

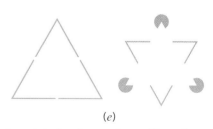

(*a*)   (*b*)   (*c*)   (*d*)   (*e*)

FIGURE 4.29   Gestalt principles of form perception. The Gestalt psychologists discovered a set of laws of perceptual organization, including (*a*) similarity, (*b*) proximity, (*c*) good continuation, (*d*) simplicity, and (*e*) closure. *Source:* Part (*e*) adapted from Kanizsa, 1976.

terns. Covering the notched yellow circles reveals that the solid white triangle is entirely an illusion. The brain treats illusory contours as if they were real because illusory contours activate the same areas of early visual processing in the visual cortex as real contours (Mendola et al., 1999).

Although Gestalt principles are most obvious with visual perception, they apply to other senses as well. For example, the figure–ground principle applies when people attend to the voice of a server in a noisy restaurant; her voice becomes figure and all other sounds, ground. In music perception, good continuation allows people to hear a series of notes as a melody; similarity allows them to recognize a melody played on a violin while other instruments are playing; and proximity groups notes played together as a chord.

From an evolutionary perspective, the Gestalt principles exemplify the way the brain organizes perceptual experience to reflect the regularities of nature. In nature, the parts of objects tend to be near one another and attached. Thus, the principles of proximity and good continuation are useful perceptual rules of thumb. Similarly, objects often partially block, or occlude, other objects, as when a squirrel crawls up the bark of a tree. The principle of closure leads humans and other animals to assume the existence of the part of the tree that is covered by the squirrel's body.

Combining Features   More recent research has focused on the question of how the brain combines the simple features detected in primary areas of the cortex (particularly primary visual cortex) into larger units that can be used to identify objects. *Object identification* requires matching the current stimulus array against past percepts stored in memory to determine the identity of the object (such as a ball, a chair, or a particular person's face). Imaging studies and research on patients and animals with temporal lobe lesions suggest that this process occurs along the "what" visual pathway.

One prominent theory of how the brain forms and recognizes images was developed by Irving Biederman (1987, 1990; Bar & Biederman, 1998). Consider the following common scenario. It is late at night, and you are channel surfing—rapidly pressing the television remote control in search of something to watch. From less than a second's glance, you can readily perceive what most shows are about and whether they might be interesting. How does the brain, in less than a second, recognize a complex visual array on a television screen in order to make such a rapid decision?

Biederman and his colleagues have shown that we do not even need a *half* a second to recognize most scenes; 100 milliseconds—a tenth of a second—will typically do. Lieberman's theory, called **recognition-by-components**, asserts that *we perceive and categorize objects in our environment by breaking them down into component parts and then matching the components and the way they are arranged against similar "sketches" stored in memory*. According to this theory, the brain combines the simple features extracted by the primary cortex (such as lines of particular orientations) into a small number of elementary geometrical forms (called *geons*, for "geometric ions"). From this geometrical "alphabet" of 20 to 30 geons, the outlines of virtually any object can be constructed, just as millions of words can be constructed from an alphabet of 26 letters. Figure 4.30 presents examples of some of these geons.

Biederman argues that combining primitive visual sensations into geons not only allows rapid identification of objects but also explains why we can recognize objects even when parts of them are blocked or missing. The reason is that the Gestalt princi-

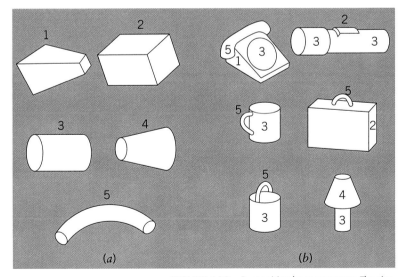

FIGURE 4.30   Recognition by components. The simple geons in (*a*) can be used to create thousands of different objects (*b*) simply by altering the relations among them, such as their relative size and placement. *Source:* Biederman, 1990, p. 49.

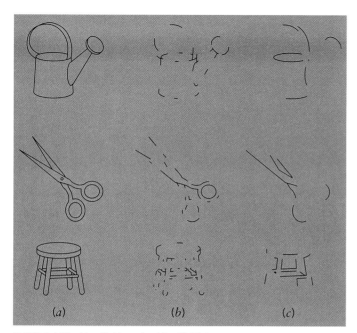

FIGURE 4.31 Identifiable and unidentifiable images. People can rapidly identify objects (*a*) even if many parts of them are missing, as long as the relations among their components, or geons, remain clear (*b*). When they can no longer tell where one geon ends and another begins (*c*), the ability to identify the objects will disappear. *Source:* Biederman, 1987, p. 135.

ples, such as good continuation, apply to perception of geons. In other words, the brain fills in gaps in a segment of a geon, such as a blocked piece of a circle. The theory predicts, and research supports the prediction, that failures in identifying objects should occur if the lines where separate geons connect are missing or ambiguous, so that the brain can no longer tell where one component ends and another begins (Figure 4.31).

Recognition-by-components is not a complete theory of form perception. It was intended to explain how people make relatively rapid initial determinations about what they are seeing and what might be worth closer inspection. More subtle discriminations require additional analysis of qualities such as color, texture, and movement, as well as the integration of these different mental "maps" (Ullman, 1995). For example, subjects asked to find a triangle in a large array of geometric shapes can do so very quickly, whether the triangle is one of 10 or 50 other shapes (Triesman, 1986). If they are asked to find the *red* triangle, not only does their response time increase, but the length of time required is directly proportional to the number of other geometric shapes in view. Apparently, making judgments about the *conjunction* of two attributes—in this case, shape and color—requires not only consulting two maps (one of shape and the other of color) but also superimposing one on the other. That we can carry out such complex computations as quickly as we can is remarkable.

Perceptual Illusions   Sometimes the brain's efforts to organize sensations into coherent and accurate percepts fail. This is the case with **perceptual illusions**, *in which normal perceptual processes produce perceptual misinterpretations*. Impossible figures are one such type of illusion; they provide conflicting cues for three-dimensional organization, as illustrated in Figure 4.32. Recognizing the impossibility of these figures takes time because the brain attempts to impose order by using principles such as simplicity on data that allow no simple solution. Each portion of an impossible figure is credible, but as soon as the brain organizes sensations in one way, another part of the figure invalidates it.

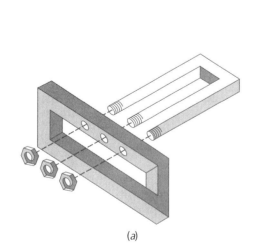

(*a*)

(*b*)

FIGURE 4.32   Impossible figures. The brain cannot form a stable percept because each time it does, another segment of the figure renders the percept impossible. Escher, who painted the impossible figure in (*b*), made use of perceptual research.

Perception involves the organization and interpretation of sensory experience. **Form perception** refers to the organization of sensations into meaningful shapes and patterns (**percepts**). The Gestalt psychologists described several principles of form perception. More recently, a theory called **recognition-by-components** has argued that people perceive and categorize objects by first breaking them down into elementary units. The brain's efforts to organize percepts can sometimes produce **perceptual illusions**.

Depth Perception   A second aspect of perceptual organization is **depth** or **distance perception**, *the organization of perception in three dimensions*. You perceive this book as having height, width, and breadth and being at a particular distance; a skilled athlete can throw a ball 15 yards into a small hoop not much bigger than the ball. We make three-dimensional judgments such as these based on a two-dimensional retinal image—and do so with such rapidity that we have no awareness of the computations our nervous system is making.

Although we focus again on the visual system, other sensory systems provide cues for depth perception as well, such as auditory cues and kinesthetic sensations about the extension of the body. Two kinds of visual information provide particularly important information about depth and distance: **binocular cues** (*visual input integrated from the two eyes*) and **monocular cues** (*visual input from one eye*).

Binocular Cues   Because the eyes are in slightly different locations, all but the most distant objects produce a different image on each retina, or a *retinal disparity*. To see this in action, hold your finger about 6 inches from your nose and alternately close your left and right eye. You will note that each eye sees your finger in a slightly different position. Now, do the same for a distant object; you will note only minimal differences between the views. Retinal disparity is greatest for close objects and diminishes with distance.

How does the brain translate retinal disparity into depth perception? Most cells in the primary visual cortex are **binocular cells**; that is, they *receive information from both eyes*. Some of these cells respond most vigorously when the same input arrives from each eye, whether the input is a vertical line, a horizontal line, or a line moving in one direction. Other binocular cells respond to disparities between the eyes.

Like many cells receptive to particular orientations, binocular cells require environmental input early in life to assume their normal functions. Researchers have learned about binocular cells by allowing kittens to see with only one eye at a time, covering one eye or the other on alternate days. As adults, these cats are unable to use binocular cues for depth (Blake & Hirsch, 1975; Crair et al., 1998; Packwood & Gordon, 1975).

Another binocular cue, *convergence*, is actually more kinesthetic than visual. When looking at a close object (such as your finger 6 inches in front of your face), the eyes converge, whereas distant objects require ocular divergence. Convergence of the eyes toward each other thus creates a distance cue produced by muscle movements in the eyes.

Monocular Cues   Although binocular cues are extremely important for depth perception, people do not crash their cars whenever an eyelash momentarily gets into one eye, because they can still rely on monocular cues. The photograph of the Taj Mahal in Figure 4.33 illustrates the main monocular depth cues involved even when we look at a nonmoving scene:

Interposition: When one object blocks part of another, the obstructed object is perceived as more distant.

Elevation: Objects farther away are higher on a person's plane of view and thus appear higher up toward the horizon.

Texture gradient: Textured surfaces, such as cobblestones or grained wood, appear coarser at close range, and finer and more densely packed at greater distances.

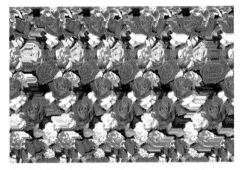

A 3-D Magic Eye image that, like most such images, capitalizes on the concept of retinal disparity. Place the picture close to your eyes and gradually move it away. You should see a 3-dimensional image emerge. Hint: This would be an appropriate picture to put on a Valentine's Day card.

FIGURE 4.33 Monocular depth cues. The photo of the Taj Mahal in India illustrates all of the monocular cues to depth perception: interposition (the trees blocking the sidewalk and the front of the building), elevation (the most distant object seems to be the highest), texture gradient (the relative clarity of the breaks in the walkways closer to the camera), linear perspective (the convergence of the lines of the walkways surrounding the water), shading (the indentation of the arches toward the top of the building), aerial perspective (the lack of the detail of the bird in the distance), familiar size (the person standing on the walkway who seems tiny), and relative size (the diminishing size of the trees as they are further away).

Big Picture ϕ Question 4

To what extent is human nature particular versus universal?

Linear perspective: Parallel lines appear to converge in the distance.

Shading: The brain assumes that light comes from above and hence interprets shading differently toward the top or the bottom of an object.

Aerial perspective: Since light scatters as it passes through space, and especially through moist or polluted air, objects at greater distances appear fuzzier than those nearby.

Familiar size: People tend to assume an object is its usual size and therefore perceive familiar objects that appear small as distant.

Relative size: When looking at two objects known to be of similar size, people perceive the smaller object as farther away.

Artists working in two-dimensional media rely on monocular depth cues to represent a three-dimensional world. Thus, people have used interposition and elevation to convey depth for thousands of years. Other cues, however, such as linear perspective, were not discovered until as late as the fifteenth century; as a result, art before that time appears flat to the modern eye (Figure 4.34). Although some monocular cues appear to be innate, cross-cultural research suggests that perceiving three dimensions in two-dimensional drawings is partially learned. For example, people in technologically less developed cultures who have never seen photography often initially have difficulty recognizing even their own images in two-dimensional form (Berry et al., 1992).

A final monocular depth cue arises from movement. **When people move, images of nearby objects sweep across their field of vision faster than objects farther away. This disparity in apparent velocity produces a depth cue** called **motion parallax**. The relative motion of nearby versus distant objects is particularly striking when we look out the window of a moving car or train. Nearby trees appear to speed by, whereas distant objects barely seem to move.

Motion Perception From an evolutionary perspective, just as important as identifying objects and their distance is identifying motion. A moving object is potentially a dangerous object—or, alternatively, a meal, a mate, or a friend or relative in distress. Thus, it is no surprise that humans, like other animals, developed the capacity for **motion perception**—*the perception of movement in objects*.

Motion perception occurs in multiple sensory modes. People can perceive the movement of a fly on the skin through touch, just as they can perceive the fly's trajec-

(a)

(b)

FIGURE 4.34   Artistic use of monocular cues for depth perception has developed tremendously since Giotto's *Flight into Egypt* painted in the fifteenth century (*a*). In the Cyclorama exhibit in Atlanta (*b*), which depicts the Battle of Atlanta during the U.S. Civil War, the artists had such mastery of monocular cues for depth perception that visitors cannot easily tell where actual three-dimensional objects (soldiers, trees, etc.) end and a painted background begins.

tory through space by the sounds it makes. We focus here again, however, on the visual system.

Neural Pathways   The visual perception of movement begins in the retina itself, with **ganglion cells** called **motion detectors** *that are particularly sensitive to movement.* These cells tend to be concentrated outside the fovea, to respond (and stop responding) very quickly, and to have large receptive fields. These characteristics make adaptive sense. An object in the fovea is one we are already "keeping a close eye on" through attention to it; motion detectors in the periphery of our vision, in contrast, provide an early warning system to turn the head or the eyes toward something potentially relevant. Without relatively quick onset and offset of motion-detecting neurons, many objects could escape detection by moving faster than these neurons could fire. Large receptive fields cover a large visual landscape, maximizing the likelihood of detecting motion (Schiffman, 1996).

With each "stop" along the processing stream in the brain, the receptive fields of neurons that detect motion grow larger. Several ganglion cells project to each motion-detecting neuron in the thalamus. Several of these thalamic neurons may then feed into motion-sensitive neurons in the primary visual cortex. From there, information travels along the where pathway through a region in the temporal lobes called *area MT* (for *medial temporal*) and finally to the parietal lobes (see Barinaga, 1997; Rodman & Albright, 1989; Tootell et al., 1995b). In area MT, receptive fields are even larger than in the primary visual cortex, and many neurons are direction sensitive, firing vigorously only if an object is moving in the direction to which the neuron is tuned. Area MT can be activated by still photos that contain cues suggesting movement, such as a runner in midstride (Kourtzi & Kanwisher, 2000b).

Two Systems for Processing Movement   Tracking an object's movement is a tricky business because the perceiver may be moving as well. Thus, accurate perception requires distinguishing the motion of the perceiver from the motion of the perceived.

Consider the perceptual task of a tennis player awaiting a serve. Most tennis players bob, fidget, or move from side to side as they await a serve; thus the image on their retina is changing every second, even before the ball is in the air. Once the ball is

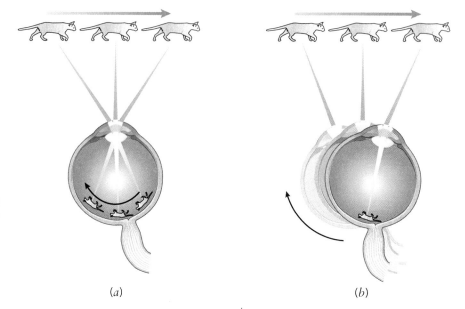

FIGURE 4.35 Two systems for processing movement. In (*a*), a stationary eye detects movement as an object moves across the person's visual field, progressively moving across the retina. In (*b*), the eye moves along with the object, which casts a relatively constant retinal image. What changes are the background and signals from the brain that control the muscles that move the eyes. *Source:* Adapted from Gregory, 1970, and Schiffman, 1996.

served, its retinal image becomes larger and larger as it approaches, and the brain must compute its distance and velocity as it moves through space. Making matters more complex, the perceiver is likely to be running, all the while trying to keep the ball's image on the fovea. And the brain must integrate these cues—the size of the image on the retina, its precise location on the retina, the movement of the eyes, and the movement of the body—all in a split second.

Two systems appear to be involved in motion perception (Gregory, 1978). The first computes motion from the changing image projected by the object on the retina (Figure 4.35*a*). This system operates when the eyes are relatively stable, as when an insect darts across the floor so quickly that the eyes cannot move fast enough to track it. In this case, the image of the insect moves across the retina, and motion detectors then fire as adjacent receptors in the retina bleach one after another in rapid succession.

The second system makes use of commands from the brain to the muscles in the eye that signal the presence of eye movements. This mechanism operates when people move their head and eyes to follow an object, as when fans watch a runner sprinting toward the finish line. In this case, the image of the object remains at roughly the same place on the retina; what moves is the position of the eyes (Figure 4.35*b*). The brain computes movement from a combination of the image on the retina and the movement of eye muscles. Essentially, if the eyes are moving but the object continues to cast the same retinal image, the object must be moving. (A third system, less well understood, likely integrates proprioceptive and other cues to offset the impact of body movements on the retinal image.)

Perceptual Constancy   A fourth form of perceptual organization, **perceptual constancy**, refers to *the perception of objects as relatively stable despite changes in the stimulation of sensory receptors*. As your friend walks away from you, you do not perceive her as shrinking, even though the image she casts on your retina is steadily decreasing in size. You similarly recognize that a song on the radio is still the same even though the volume has been turned down. Here we examine three types of perceptual constancy, again focusing on vision: color, shape, and size constancy.

Color Constancy   **Color constancy** refers to *the tendency to perceive the color of objects as stable despite changing illumination*. An apple appears the same color in the kitchen as it does in the sunlight, even though the light illuminating it is very different. A similar phenomenon occurs with achromatic color (black and white):

Snow in moonlight appears whiter than coal appears in sunlight, even though the amount of light reflected off the coal may be greater (Schiffman, 1996).

In perceiving the brightness of an object, neural mechanisms adjust for the amount of light illuminating it. For chromatic colors, the mechanism is more complicated, but color constancy does not work if the light contains only a narrow band of wavelengths. Being in a room with only red light bulbs causes even familiar objects to appear red.

A recent case study of a patient who lacked color constancy shed light on the neural circuits involved in color constancy. The patient had damage to an area at the border of the occipital and temporal lobes that responds to changing illumination and thus plays a central role in color constancy (Zeki et al., 1999). The patient could see colors, but as the illumination surrounding objects changed, so did the patient's perception of the object's color.

Shape Constancy   **Shape constancy**, a remarkable feat of the engineering of the brain, means ***we can maintain constant perception of the shape of objects despite the fact that the same object typically produces a new and different impression on the retina (or on the receptors in our skin) every time we encounter it.*** The brain has to overcome several substantial sources of noise to recognize, for example, that the unkempt beast in the mirror whose hair is pointing in every direction is the same person you happily called "me" the night before. When people see an object for the second time, they are likely to see it from a different position, with different lighting, in a different setting (e.g., against a different background), with different parts of it blocked from view (such as different locks of hair covering the face), and even in an altered shape (such as a body standing up versus one on the couch) (see Ullman, 1995).

Recognition-by-components (geon) theory offers one possible explanation: As long as enough of the geons that define the form of the object remain the same, the object ought to be identifiable. Thus, if a person views a bee on a flower and then as it flies around her face, she will still recognize the insect as a bee as long as it still looks like a tube with a little cone at the back and thin waferlike wings flapping at its sides.

Other theorists, however, argue that geons are not the whole story. Some propose that each time we view an object from a different perspective, we form a mental image of it from that point of view. Each new viewpoint provides a new image stored in memory. The next time we see a similar object, we rotate it in our minds so that we can "see" it from a previously seen perspective to determine if it looks like the same object, or we match it against an image generalized from our multiple "snapshots" of it.

Recent research suggests, in fact, that the more different a scene is from the way a person saw it before (e.g., if the image is 90 rather than 15 degrees off the earlier image), the longer the person will take to recognize it (DeLoache et al., 1997; Tarr et al., 1997; Ullman, 1989). Thus, shape constancy does, to some extent, rely on rotating mental images (probably of both geons and finer perceptual details) and comparing them against perceptual experiences stored in memory.

Size Constancy   A third type of perceptual constancy is **size constancy**: *Objects do not appear to change in size when viewed from different distances.* The closer an object is, the larger an image it casts on the retina. A car 10 feet away will cast a retinal image five times as large as the same car 50 feet away, yet people do not wonder how the car 50 feet away can possibly carry full-sized passengers. The reason is that the brain corrects for the size of the retinal image based on cues such as the size of objects in the background.

Helmholtz (1909) was the first to recognize that the brain adjusts for distance when assessing the size of objects, just as it adjusts for color and brightness. He called this process *unconscious inference*, because people have no consciousness of the computations involved. Although these computations generally lead to accurate inferences, they can also give rise to perceptual illusions. A classic example is the moon illusion, in which the moon seems larger on the horizon than at its zenith (Figure 4.36). This illusion appears to result from the visual system interpreting objects on the

FIGURE 4.36   The moon illusion. The moon appears larger against a city skyline than high in the sky, where among other things, no depth cues exist. The retinal image is the same size in both cases, but in one case, depth cues signal that it must be further away.

horizon as farther away than objects overhead (Kaufman & Rock, 1989). For most objects, like birds and clouds, this is a good inference. Astronomical objects, including the moon and sun, are the only phenomena we encounter that occur both overhead and on the horizon without varying in distance.

INTERIM SUMMARY

Depth perception is the organization of perception in three dimensions; it is based on **binocular** and **monocular visual cues. Motion perception**, the perception of movement, relies on motion detectors from the retina through the cortex. It appears to involve two systems: The first computes motion from the changing image on the retina, and the second uses information from eye muscles about the movement of the eyes. **Perceptual constancy** refers to the organization of changing sensations into percepts that are relatively stable. Three types of perceptual constancy are **color, shape**, and **size constancy**.

A Global Vista | Culture and Perceptual Illusions

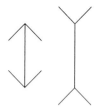

FIGURE 4.37 The Müller–Lyer illusion. The line on the right appears longer than the line on the left, when in fact they are exactly the same size.

Size constancy, like other processes of perceptual organization, can sometimes produce perceptual illusions. This is likely the case with the **Müller–Lyer illusion,** *in which two lines of equal length appear to differ in size* (Figure 4.37). According to one theory, the angled lines provide linear perspective cues that make the vertical line appear closer or farther away (Gregory, 1978). The brain then adjusts for distance, interpreting the fact that the retinal images of the two vertical lines are the same size as evidence that the line on the right is longer.

If the Müller–Lyer illusion relies on depth cues such as linear perspective that are not recognized in all cultures, are people in some cultures more susceptible to the illusion than others? That is, does vulnerability to an illusion depend on culture and experience, or is it rooted entirely in the structure of the brain? In the 1960s, a team of psychologists and anthropologists set out to answer these questions in what has become a classic study (Segall et al., 1966).

Two hypotheses that guided the investigators are especially relevant. The first, called the *carpentered world hypothesis*, holds that the nature of architecture in a culture influences the tendency to experience particular illusions. People reared in cultures without roads that join at angles, rectangular buildings, and houses with angled roofs lack experience with the kinds of cues that give rise to the Müller–Lyer illusion and hence should be less susceptible to it. The second hypothesis posits that individuals from cultures that do not use sophisticated two-dimensional cues (such as linear perspective) to represent three dimensions in pictures should also be less vulnerable to perceptual illusions of this sort.

The researchers presented individuals from 14 non-Western and three Western societies with several stimuli designed to elicit perceptual illusions. They found that Westerners were consistently more likely to experience the Müller–Lyer illusion than non-Westerners, but they were no more likely to experience other illusions unrelated to angles and sophisticated depth cues. Subsequent studies have replicated these findings with the Müller–Lyer illusion (Pedersen & Wheeler, 1983; Segall et al., 1990). Teasing apart the relative impact of architecture and simple exposure to pictures is difficult, but the available data support both hypotheses (Berry et al., 1992).

Size constancy is involved in another famous illusion, the *Ponzo illusion*, which also appears to be influenced by culture and experience (Figure 4.38). Linear perspective cues indicate that the upper bar is larger because it seems farther away. Cross-culturally, people who live in environments in which lines converge in the distance (such as railroad tracks and long, straight highways) appear to be more susceptible to this illusion than people from environments with relatively few converging lines (Brislin & Keating, 1976).

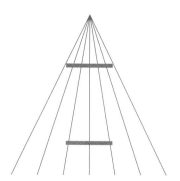

FIGURE 4.38 The Ponzo illusion. Converging lines lead to the perception of the upper red bar as larger since it appears to be farther away. The bars are actually identical in length.

(a)

(b)

People from this African village (a) are less susceptible to illusions involving straight lines than people who live in "carpentered worlds," such as Paris (b), who are familiar with angled buildings and streets.

Interpreting Sensory Experience

The processes of perceptual organization we have examined—form perception, depth perception, motion perception, and perceptual constancy—organize sensations into stable, recognizable forms. These perceptions do not, however, tell us what an object is or what its significance to us might be. ***Generating meaning from sensory experience*** is the task of **perceptual interpretation**. The line between organization and interpretation is not, of course, hard and fast. The kind of object identification tasks studied by Biederman, for example, involve both, and in everyday life, organizing perceptual experience is simply one step on the path to interpreting it.

Perceptual interpretation lies at the intersection of sensation and memory, as the brain interprets current sensations in light of past experience. These can occur at a very primitive level—reacting to a bitter taste, recoiling from an object coming toward the face, responding emotionally to a familiar voice—without either consciousness or cortical involvement. Much of the time, however, interpretation involves classifying stimuli—a moving object is a dog; a pattern of tactile stimulation is a soft caress. In this final section, we examine how experience, expectations, and motivation shape perceptual interpretation.

The Influence of Experience To what degree do our current perceptions rely on our past experience? This question leads back to the nature–nurture debate that runs through nearly every domain of psychology.

The German philosopher Immanuel Kant argued that humans innately experience the world using certain categories, such as time, space, and causality. For example, when a person slams a door and the door frame shakes, she naturally infers that slamming the door caused the frame to shake. According to Kant, people automatically infer causality, prior to any learning.

Direct Perception Whereas Kant emphasized the way the mind orders perception of the world, psychologist James Gibson (1966, 1979) emphasized the way the world organizes perception, so that we detect the order that exists in nature. Gibson championed a theory known as **direct perception**, which holds that ***the meaning of stimuli is often immediate and obvious, even to the "untrained eye."*** For example, we automatically perceive depth in an object that has patterned texture (such as a snake), because when the elements of the texture (in this case, the scales on the back of the

Big Picture φ Question 6

What is the relation between nature and nurture in shaping psychological processes?

Big Picture φ Question 8

To what extent can we inform our knowledge through reason or through observation—rationalism versus empiricism?

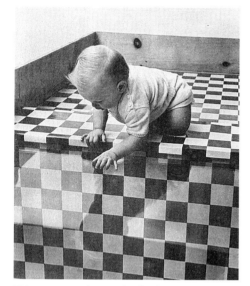

FIGURE 4.39 The visual cliff. Infants are afraid to crawl over the "cliff" even when they have recently begun to crawl and therefore have little experience leading them to fear it.

Big Picture φ Question 6

What is the relation between nature and nurture in shaping psychological processes?

snake) diminish in size, the brain interprets the change as a depth cue (Goodenough & Gillam, 1997).

Gibson's theory is essentially evolutionary: The senses evolved to respond to aspects of the environment relevant to adaptation. An object coming rapidly toward the face is dangerous; food with a sweet taste affords energy; a loud, angry voice is threatening. In this view, we do not construct our reality; we perceive it directly. And we can often perceive reality with little experience.

Laboratory evidence of direct perception comes from studies using the visual cliff. The **visual cliff** *is a clear table with a checkerboard directly beneath it on one side and another checkerboard that appears to drop off like a cliff on the other* (Figure 4.39). Infants are reluctant to crawl to the side of the table that looks deep even when they have recently begun crawling and have had little or no relevant experience with falling off surfaces (Gibson & Walk, 1960). In other words, the perceptual systems of infants are already adapted to make sense of the important features of the world before they have had an opportunity to learn what falling means (see Bertenthal, 1996). The infant directly perceives that certain situations signal danger.

As we have seen, specific parts of the brain do appear to have evolved to allow some very specific kinds of perception. Some regions, for example, respond solely to faces (Critchley et al., 2000; Kanwisher et al., 1997). One area of the brain seems to be so specialized that it responds selectively to movements of the eyes and mouth that are involved in interpreting facial expressions, but not to faces in general (Puce et al., 1998).

When Nurture Activates Nature Although the nervous system has certain innate potentials—such as seeing in depth or recognizing meaningful facial movements—most of these potentials require environmental input to develop. Where psychologists once asked, "Which is more important, nature or nurture?" today they often ask, "How do certain experiences activate certain innate potentials?"

In one set of studies, researchers reared kittens in darkness for their first five months except for five hours each day, during which time they placed the kittens in a cylinder with either horizontal or vertical stripes (Blakemore & Cooper, 1970). The kittens saw *only* the stripes, since they wore a big collar that kept them from seeing even their own bodies (Figure 4.40). As adults, kittens reared in horizontal environments were unable to perceive vertical lines, and they lacked cortical feature detectors responsive to vertical lines; the opposite was true of kittens reared in a vertical environment. Although these cats were genetically programmed to have both vertical and horizontal feature detectors, their brains adapted to a world without certain features to detect.

James and Eleanor Gibson, who pioneered the theory of direct perception.

Other studies have outfitted infant kittens and monkeys with translucent goggles that allow light to pass through but only in a blurry, diffuse, unpatterned form. When the animals are adults and the goggles are removed, they are able to perform simple perceptual tasks without difficulty, such as distinguishing colors, brightness, and size. However, they have difficulty with other tasks; for example, they are unable to distinguish objects from one another or to track moving objects (Riesen, 1960; Wiesel, 1982).

Similar findings have emerged in studies of humans who were born blind but subsequently became sighted in adulthood through surgery (Gregory, 1978; Sacks, 1993; von Senden, 1960). Most of these individuals can tell figure from ground, sense colors, and follow moving objects, but many never learn to recognize objects they previously knew by touch and hence remain functionally blind. What these studies suggest, like studies described in Chapter 3, is that the brain has evolved to "expect" certain experiences, without which it will not develop normally.

Early experiences are not the only ones that shape the neural system's underlying sensation and perception. In one study, monkeys who were taught to make fine-pitch discriminations showed increases in the size of the cortical regions responsive to pitch (Recanzone et al., 1993). Intriguing research with humans finds that practice at discriminating letters manually in Braille produces changes in the brain. A larger region of the cortex of Braille readers is devoted to the fingertips, with which they read (Pascual-Leone & Torres, 1993). Thus, experience can alter the structure of the brain, making it more or less responsive to subsequent sensory input.

FIGURE 4.40   Kittens reared in a vertical world lose their "innate" capacity to see horizontal lines.

Bottom-Up and Top-Down Processing   We have seen that experience can activate innate mechanisms or even affect the amount of cortical space devoted to certain kinds of sensory processing. But when we come upon a face that looks familiar or an animal that resembles one we have seen, does our past experience actually alter the way we perceive it, or do we only begin to categorize the face or the animal once we have identified its features? Similarly, does wine taste different to a wine connoisseur—does his knowledge about wine actually alter his perceptions —or does he just have fancier words to describe his experience after the fact?

Psychologists have traditionally offered two opposing answers to questions such as these, which now, as in many classic debates about sensation and perception, appear to be complementary. One view emphasizes the role of sensory data in shaping perception, whereas the other emphasizes the influence of prior experience. **Bottom-up processing** refers to *processing that begins "at the bottom" with raw sensory data that feed "up" to the brain*. A bottom-up explanation of visual perception argues that the brain forms perceptions by combining the responses of multiple feature detectors in the primary cortex, which themselves integrate input from neurons lower in the visual system.

Top-down processing, in contrast, *starts "at the top," with the observer's expectations and knowledge*. Theorists who favor a top-down processing explanation typically work from a cognitive perspective. They maintain that the brain uses prior knowledge to begin organizing and interpreting sensations as soon as the information starts coming in, rather than waiting for percepts to form based on sequential (step-by-step) analysis of their isolated features. Thus, like Gestalt theorists, these researchers presume that as soon as the brain has detected features resembling eyes, it begins to expect a face and thus to look for a nose and mouth.

Studies Demonstrating Bottom-Up and Top-Down Processing   Both approaches have empirical support. Research on motion perception provides an example of bottom-up processing. Psychologists trained monkeys to report the direction in which a display of dots moved. The researchers then observed the response of individual neurons previously identified as feature detectors for movement of a particular speed and direction while the monkeys performed the task (Newsome et al., 1989). They discovered that the "decisions" made by individual neurons about the direction the dots moved were as accurate as—and sometimes even *more* accurate than—the decisions of the monkeys!

Big Picture φ Question 6

What is the relation between nature and nurture in shaping psychological processes?

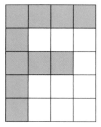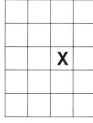

Perception   Imagery

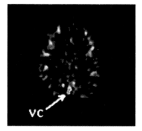

FIGURE 4.41 Visual imagery activates primary visual cortex. Participants viewed one of two stimulus patterns (left and center). In one, they actually saw a letter on a grid along with a black X. In another, they had to imagine the letter to decide whether the X would fall on the letter. In a control condition, participants simply watch the X appear and disappear. As can be seen from the small area of bright activation (marked "vc") in the brain (right), the imaging condition activated primary visual cortex, just as looking at the actual letter did.

Perceptual decisions on simple tasks of the sort given to these monkeys may require little involvement of higher mental processes. On the other hand, reading these words provides a good example of top-down processing, since reading would be incredibly cumbersome if people had to detect every letter of every word from the bottom up rather than expecting and recognizing patterns.

Recent evidence of top-down processing comes from studies using PET technology. In one study, participants viewed block letters presented in a grid, as in Figure 4.41 (Kosslyn et al., 1993). Then they were shown the same grid without the letter and asked to decide whether the letter would cover an X placed in one of the boxes of the grid. This task required that they create a mental image of the letter in the grid and locate the X on the imaginary letter. Next, they performed the same task, except this time the block letter was actually present in the grid, so they could perceive it instead of having to imagine it. Participants in a control condition performed a simple task that essentially involved viewing the empty grid with and without an X.

The study relied on a "method of subtraction" used in many imaging studies: The investigators measured the amount of neuronal activity in the imagery and perception conditions and subtracted out the amount of brain activity seen in the control condition. The logic is to have the experimental and control conditions differ in as few respects as possible, so that what is left in the computerized image of brain activity after subtraction is a picture of only the neural activity connected with the operation that is being investigated (in this case, mental imagery and perception).

Predictably, both perception and mental imagery activated many parts of the visual system, such as visual association cortex. However, the most striking finding was that the mental imagery condition activated the same areas of primary visual cortex activated by actual perception of the letters—normally believed to reflect bottom-up processing of sensory information (Figure 4.41). In fact, the primary cortex was even more active during mental imagery than during actual perception! Although these findings are controversial (D'Esposito et al., 1997), if they hold up with future replications, they suggest that when people picture an image in their minds, they actually create a visual image using the same neural pathways involved when they view a visual stimulus—a completely top-down activation of brain regions normally activated by sensory input.

Resolving the Paradox: Simultaneous Processing in Perception   Trying to explain perception by either bottom-up or top-down processes alone presents a paradox. You would not be able to identify the shapes in Figure 4.42*a* unless you knew they were part of a dog. Yet you would not recognize Figure 4.42*b* as a dog unless you could process information about the parts shown in the first panel. Without bottom-up processing, external stimuli would have no effect on perception; we would hallucinate rather than perceive. Without top-down processing, experience would have no effect on perception. How, then, do people ever recognize and classify objects?

According to current thinking, both types of processing occur simultaneously (Pollen, 1999; Rumelhart et al., 1986). For example, features of the environment create patterns of stimulation in the primary visual cortex. These patterns in turn stimulate neural circuits in the visual association cortex that represent various objects, such as a friend's face. If the perceiver expects to see that face or if a large enough component of the neural network representing the face becomes activated, the brain essentially forms a "hypothesis" about an incoming pattern of sensory stimulation, even though all the data are not yet in from the feature detectors. It may even entertain multiple hypotheses simultaneously, which are each tested against new incoming data until one hypothesis "wins out" because it seems to provide the best fit to the data.

(*a*)

(*b*)

FIGURE 4.42 Top-down and bottom-up processing. In isolation (perceiving from the bottom up), the designs in (*a*) would have no meaning. Yet the broader design in (*b*), the dog, cannot be recognized without recognizing component parts.

INTERIM SUMMARY

Perceptual interpretation means generating meaning from sensory experience. According to the theory of **direct perception**, the meaning or adaptive significance of a percept is often obvious, immediate, and innate. Trying to distinguish the relative roles of nature and nurture in perception may in some ways be asking the wrong question, because the nervous system has innate potentials that require environmental input to develop. Perception simultaneously involves **bottom-up processing**, which begins with raw sensory data that feed "up" to the brain, and **top-down processing**, which begins with the observer's expectations and knowledge.

Expectations and Perception   Experience with the environment thus shapes perception by creating perceptual expectations, an important top-down influence on perception. These expectations, called *perceptual set* (i.e., the setting, or context, for a given perceptual "decision"), make certain interpretations more likely. Two aspects of perceptual set are the current context and enduring knowledge.

Context   Context plays a substantial role in perceptual interpretation. Consider, for example how readily you understood the meaning of *substantial role* in the last sentence. Had someone uttered that phrase in a bakery, you would have assumed they meant "substantial roll," unless the rest of the sentence provided a context suggesting otherwise. Context is important in perceiving spoken language (Chapter 7) because even the most careful speaker drops syllables, slurs sounds, or misses words altogether, and many words (such as *role* and *roll*) have the same sound but different meanings.

Context is just as important with tactile sensations (touch). A hug from a relative or from a stranger may have entirely different meanings and may immediately elicit very different feelings, even if the pattern of sensory stimulation is identical. Figure 4.43 illustrates the importance of context in the visual mode.

Schemas   Not only the immediate context but a person's enduring beliefs and expectations affect perceptual interpretation. One way knowledge is organized in memory is in **schemas**—*patterns of thinking about a domain that render the environment relatively predictable* (Neisser, 1976a). We have schemas (organized knowledge) about

Making Connections

Recent research suggests that many psychological processes—perception, thought, and memory—occur through the simultaneous activation of multiple neural circuits. The perception or solution to a problem that "comes to mind," in this view, is the one that best fits the data. We are typically not even aware that we have considered and ruled out multiple competing hypotheses; we are only aware of the "conclusion" (Chapter 7).

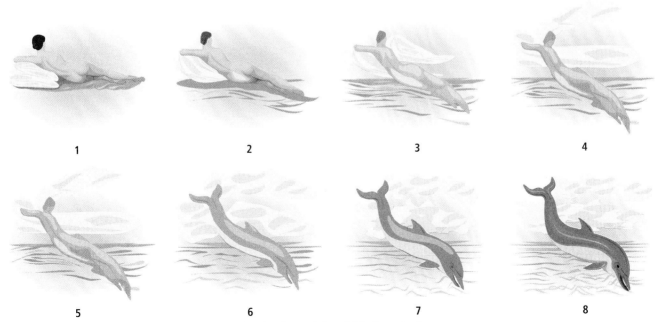

FIGURE 4.43   The impact of context on perception. Look at drawings 1, 2, 3, and 4, in that order (top row, left to right). Now look at drawings 5, 6, 7, and 8, in reverse order (bottom row, right to left). Drawing 4 most likely seems to be a woman's body and drawing 5, a porpoise, yet drawings 4 and 5 are identical. The same pattern of stimulation can be interpreted in many ways depending on context.

(a)

(b)

(c)

FIGURE 4.44   Schemas. Subjects had no trouble identifying and remembering objects in (a), a photo of a normal Chinatown street, because the scene activates a "city street schema" that guides perception and memory. In contrast, without a schema to help interpret what they were seeing (b), they had much more difficulty.

Schemas can also lead to perceptual failures. Before reading further, look briefly at (c). People rarely notice the unexpected object toward the right (the fire hydrant) because it is incongruent with their activated "restaurant schema."

objects (such as chairs and dogs), people (such as introverts and ministers), and situations (such as funerals and restaurants). The fact that people generally sit on chairs instead of on other people reflects their schemas about what chairs and people do.

Because schemas allow individuals to anticipate what they will encounter, they increase both the speed and efficiency of perception. For example, people process information extremely quickly when shown photographs of real-world scenes, such as a kitchen, a city street, or a desk top. In one study, subjects could recall almost half the objects in familiar scenes after viewing them for only one-tenth of a second (Biederman et al., 1973). In contrast, subjects who viewed the same scenes cut into six equal pieces and randomly reassembled had difficulty both identifying and remembering the objects in the picture (Figures 4.44a and b). Schemas can also induce perceptual errors, however, when individuals fail to notice what they do not expect to see (Figure 4.44c), such as a new pothole in the street (Biederman et al., 1981, 1982).

Motivation and Perception   As we have seen, expectations can lead people to see what they expect to see and hear what they expect to hear. But people also frequently hear the words they want to hear as well. In other words, motivation, like cognition, can exert a top-down influence on perception. This was the argument of a school of perceptual thought in the late 1940s called the *New Look* in perception, which focused on the impact of emotion, motivation, and personality on perception (Dixon, 1981; Erdelyi, 1985). Many of the issues raised by New Look researchers are receiving renewed attention a half century later (see, e.g., Bargh, 1997; Bruner, 1992).

One classic experiment examined the effects of food and water deprivation on identification of words (Wispe & Drambarean, 1953). The experimenters placed participants in one of three groups. Some went without food for 24 hours prior to the experiment; some ate nothing for 10 hours; and others ate just beforehand. The researchers then flashed two kinds of words on a screen so rapidly that they were barely perceptible: neutral words (e.g., *serenade* and *hunch*) and words related to food (e.g., *lemonade* and *munch*).

The three groups did not differ in their responses to the neutral words. However, both of the deprived groups perceived the need-related words more readily (i.e., when flashed more briefly) than nondeprived controls. A similar phenomenon occurs outside the laboratory: People are often intensely aware of the aroma of food outside a restaurant when they are hungry but oblivious to it when their stomachs are full.

Based on psychodynamic ideas, New Look researchers were also interested in the way emotional factors influence perception, as in the everyday experience of "failing to see what we don't want to see" (see Broadbent, 1958; Dixon, 1971, 1981; Erdelyi, 1985). In one study, the researcher exposed participants to neutral and taboo words so quickly that they could barely recognize even a flash of light (Blum, 1954). (In the 1950s, obscenities were viewed as taboo and were not used in movies, music, and so on. This experiment might be hard to replicate today!) When asked which stimuli seemed more salient—that is, which ones "caught their eye"more—participants consistently chose the taboo words, even though they had no idea what they had seen. Yet when presented with words at speeds that could just barely allow recognition of them, participants could identify the neutral words more quickly and easily than the taboo ones. These findings suggest that more emotionally evocative taboo words attract attention even below the threshold of consciousness but are harder to recognize consciously than neutral words. Subsequent research has replicated and extended these findings (Erdelyi, 1985; Shevrin et al., 1996).

What the New Look fundamentally showed was that perception is not independent of our *reasons* for perceiving. Evolution has equipped humans with a nervous system remarkably attuned to stimuli that matter. If people did not need to eat or to worry about what they put in their mouths, they would not have a sense of taste. If they did not need to find food, escape danger, and communicate, they would not need to see and hear. And if their skin were not vulnerable to damage, they would not need to feel pain.

INTERIM SUMMARY

Expectations based on both the current context and enduring knowledge structures (schemas) influence the way people interpret ongoing sensory experience. Motives can also influence perception, including motives to avoid perceiving stimuli with uncomfortable content.

Summary

Basic Principles

1. **Sensation** refers to the process by which sense organs gather information about the environment and transmit it to the brain for initial processing. **Perception** refers to the closely related process by which the brain selects, organizes, and interprets sensations.

2. Three basic principles apply across all the senses. First, there is no one-to-one correspondence between physical and psychological reality, a fundamental finding of **psychophysics**. Second, sensation and perception are active, not passive. Third, sensation and perception are adaptive.

Sensing the Environment

3. Sensation begins with an environmental stimulus; all sensory systems have specialized cells called **sensory receptors** that respond to environmental stimuli and typically generate action potentials in adjacent sensory neurons. This process is called **transduction**. Within each sensory modality, the brain codes sensory stimulation for intensity and quality.

4. The **absolute threshold** refers to the minimum amount of stimulation needed for an observer to notice a stimulus. The **difference** threshold refers to the lowest level of stimulation required to sense that a change in stimulation has occurred (a **just noticeable difference**, or **jnd**).

5. **Weber's law** states that regardless of the magnitude of two stimuli, the second must differ by a constant proportion from the first for it to be perceived as different. **Fechner's law** holds that the physical magnitude of a stimulus grows logarithmically as the subjective experience of intensity grows arithmetically; in other words, people only subjectively experience a small percentage of actual increases in stimulus intensity. **Stevens's power law** states that subjective intensity grows as a proportion of the actual intensity raised to some power, that is, that sensation increases in a linear fashion as actual intensity grows exponentially.

6. **Sensory adaptation** is the tendency of sensory systems to respond less to stimuli that continue without change.

Vision

7. The eyes are sensitive to a small portion of the electromagnetic spectrum called light. In vision, light is focused on the **retina** by the **cornea, pupil**, and **lens. Rods** are very sensitive to light, allowing vision in dim light; cones are especially sensitive to partic-

ular wavelengths, producing the psychological experience of color. **Cones** are concentrated at the **fovea**, the region of the retina most sensitive to detail.

8. The **ganglion cells** of the retina transmit visual information via the **optic nerve** to the brain. Ganglion cells, like other neurons involved in sensation, have **receptive fields**, a region of stimulation to which the neuron responds. **Feature detectors** are specialized cells in the cortex that respond only when stimulation in their receptive field matches a particular pattern or orientation, such as horizontal or vertical lines.

9. From the primary visual cortex, visual information flows along two pathways, or *processing streams*, called the "what" and the "where" pathways. The **what pathway** is involved in determining what an object is; this network runs from the primary visual cortex in the occipital lobes through the lower part of the temporal lobes (the inferior temporal cortex). The second stream, the **where pathway**, is involved in locating the object in space, following its movement, and guiding movement toward it. This pathway runs from the primary visual cortex through the middle and upper regions of the temporal lobes and up into the parietal lobes.

10. The property of light that is transduced into color is **wavelength**. The **Young–Helmholtz, or trichromatic, theory** proposes that the eye contains three types of sensory receptors, sensitive to red, green, or blue. **Opponent-process theory** argues for the existence of pairs of opposite primary colors linked in three systems: a blue–yellow system, a red–green system, and a black–white system. Both theories appear to be involved in color perception; trichromatic theory is operative at the level of the retina and opponent-process theory at higher neural levels.

Hearing

11. Hearing, or **audition**, occurs as a vibrating object sets air particles in motion. Each round of expansion and contraction of the air is known as a **cycle**. The number of cycles per second determines a sound wave's **frequency**, which corresponds to the psychological property of **pitch**. Most sounds are composed of waves with many frequencies, giving them their distinctive texture or **timbre**. **Amplitude** refers to the height and depth of the wave and corresponds to the psychological property of **loudness**.

12. Sound waves travel through the auditory canal to the eardrum, where they are amplified. Transduction occurs by way of hair cells attached to the basilar membrane that respond to vibrations in the fluid-filled **cochlea**. This mechanical process triggers action potentials in the **auditory nerve**, which are then transmitted to the brain.

13. Two theories, once considered opposing, explain the psychological qualities of sound. **Place theory**, which holds that different areas of the basilar membrane respond to different frequencies, appears to be most accurate for high frequencies. **Frequency theory**, which asserts that the basilar membrane's rate of vibration reflects the frequency with which a sound wave cycles, explains sensation of low-frequency sounds.

14. **Sound localization** refers to the identification of the location of a sound in space.

Other Senses

15. The environmental stimuli for smell, or **olfaction**, are invisible molecules of gas emitted by substances and suspended in the air.

As air enters the nose, it flows into the **olfactory epithelium**, where hundreds of different types of receptors respond to various kinds of molecules, producing complex smells. The axons of olfactory receptor cells constitute the **olfactory nerve**, which transmits information to the olfactory bulbs under the frontal lobes and on to the primary olfactory cortex, a primitive region of the cortex deep in the frontal lobes.

16. Taste, or **gustation**, is sensitive to molecules soluble in saliva. Much of the experience of flavor, however, is really contributed by smell. Taste occurs as receptors in the **taste buds** on the tongue and throughout the mouth transduce chemical information into neural information, which is integrated with olfactory information in the brain.

17. Touch actually includes three senses: pressure, temperature, and pain. The human body contains approximately five million touch receptors of at least seven different types. Sensory neurons synapse with spinal interneurons that stimulate motor neurons, allowing reflexive action. They also synapse with neurons that carry information up the spinal cord to the medulla, where nerve tracts cross over. From there, sensory information travels to the thalamus and is subsequently routed to the primary touch center in the brain, the somatosensory cortex, which contains a map of the body.

18. Pain is greatly affected by beliefs, expectations, and emotional state.

19. The **proprioceptive senses** provide information about the body's position and movement. The **vestibular sense** provides information on the position of the body in space by sensing gravity and movement. **Kinesthesia** provides information about the movement and position of the limbs and other parts of the body relative to one another.

Perception

20. The hallmarks of perception are organization and interpretation. **Perceptual organization** integrates sensations into meaningful units, locates them in space, tracks their movement, and preserves their meaning as the perceiver observes them from different vantage points. **Form perception** refers to the organization of sensations into meaningful shapes and patterns (**percepts**). The Gestalt psychologists described several principles of form perception, including figure–ground perception, similarity, proximity, good continuation, simplicity, and closure. A more recent theory, called **recognition-by-components**, asserts that we perceive and categorize objects in the environment by breaking them down into component parts, much like letters in words.

21. **Depth perception** is the organization of perception in three dimensions. Depth perception organizes two-dimensional retinal images into a three-dimensional world, primarily through **binocular** and **monocular visual cues**.

22. **Motion perception** refers to the perception of movement. Two systems appear to be involved in motion perception. The first computes motion from the changing image projected by the object on the retina; the second makes use of commands from the brain to the muscles in the eye that signal eye movements.

23. **Perceptual constancy** refers to the organization of changing sensations into percepts that are relatively stable in size, shape, and color. Three types of perceptual constancy are **size, shape**, and **color constancy**, which refer to the perception of unchanging

size, shape, and color despite momentary changes in the retinal image. The processes that organize perception leave perceivers vulnerable to **perceptual illusions**, some of which appear to be innate and others of which depend on culture and experience.

24. Perceptual interpretation involves generating meaning from sensory experience. Perceptual interpretation lies at the intersection of sensation and memory, as the brain interprets current sensations in light of past experience. Perception is neither entirely innate nor entirely learned. The nervous system has certain innate potentials, but these potentials require environmental input to develop. Experience can alter the structure of the brain, making it more or less responsive to subsequent sensory input. According

to the theory of direct perception, the meaning or adaptive significance of a percept is obvious, immediate, and innate.

25. **Bottom-up processing** refers to processing that begins "at the bottom," with raw sensory data that feeds "up" to the brain. **Top-down processing** starts "at the top," from the observer's expectations and knowledge. According to current thinking, perception proceeds in both directions simultaneously.

26. Experience with the environment shapes perceptual interpretation by creating perceptual expectations called perceptual set. Two aspects of perceptual set are current context and enduring knowledge structures called **schemas**. Motives, like expectations, can influence perceptual interpretation.

Key Terms

absolute threshold 106
accommodation 113
amplitude 124
audition 123
auditory nerve 126
binocular cells 141
binocular cues 141
bipolar cells 113
blindsight 118
blind spot 114
bottom-up processing 149
closure 138
cochlea 126
color constancy 144
complexity 124
cones 113
cornea 113
cycle 124
decibels (dB) 124
depth or distance perception 141
difference threshold 108
direct perception 147
eardrum or tympanic
   membrane 125

feature detectors 119
Fechner's law 109
figure–ground perception 138
form perception 138
fovea 114
frequency 124
frequency theory 127
ganglion cells 113
good continuation 138
gustation 131
hair cells 126
hertz (Hz) 124
hue 121
iris 113
just noticeable difference
   (jnd) 108
kinesthesia 137
lens 113
loudness 124
monocular cues 141
motion detectors 143
motion parallax 142
motion perception 142
Müller–Lyer illusion 146

olfaction 129
olfactory epithelium 130
olfactory nerve 130
opponent-process theory 122
optic nerve 114
perception 102
percepts 137
perceptual constancy 144
perceptual illusions 140
perceptual interpretation 147
perceptual organization 137
phantom limbs 133
pheromones 129
pitch 124
place theory 127
proprioceptive senses 136
proximity 138
psychophysics 104
pupil 113
receptive field 115
recognition-by-components
   139
response bias 107
retina 113

rods 113
schemas 151
sensation 102
sensory adaptation 111
sensory receptors 105
shape constancy 145
similarity 138
simplicity 138
size constancy 145
sound localization 128
sound waves 123
Stevens's power law 110
taste buds 131
timbre 124
top-down processing 149
transduction 105
vestibular sense 136
visual cliff 148
wavelengths 112
Weber's law 109
what pathway 120
where pathway 120
Young–Helmholtz or trichromatic
   theory of color 121

Chapter 5

Learning

*a*n experiment by John Garcia and his colleagues adds a new twist to all the stories ever told about wolves and sheep. The researchers fed a wolf a muttonburger (made of the finest sheep flesh) laced with odorless, tasteless capsules of lithium chloride, a chemical that induces nausea. Displaying a natural preference for mutton, the animal wolfed it down but half an hour later became sick and vomited (Garcia & Garcia y Robertson, 1985; Gustavson et al., 1976).

Several days later, the researchers introduced a sheep into the wolf's compound. At the sight of one of its favorite delicacies, the wolf went straight for the sheep's throat. But on contact, the wolf abruptly drew back. It slowly circled the sheep. Soon it attacked from another angle, going for the hamstring. This attack was as short-lived as the first. After an hour in the compound together, the wolf still had not attacked the sheep—and in fact, the sheep had made a few short charges at the wolf! Lithium chloride seems to have been the real wolf in sheep's clothing

Although the effects of a single dose of a toxic chemical do not last forever, Garcia's research illustrates the powerful impact of **learning**, which refers to any *enduring change in the way an organism responds based on its experience*. In humans, as in other animals, learning is central to adaptation. Knowing how to distinguish edible from inedible foods, or friends from enemies or predators, is essential for survival. The range of possible foods or threats is simply too great to be prewired into the brain. Learning is essentially about *prediction*—predicting the future from past experience, and using these predictions to guide behavior. For example, even the simplest organisms respond to the environment with reflexes. A **reflex** is *a behavior that is elicited automatically by an environmental stimulus*, such as the knee-jerk reflex elicited by a doctor's rubber hammer. (A **stimulus** is *something in the environment that elicits a response*.) In perhaps the simplest form of learning, habituation, organisms essentially learn what they can ignore. **Habituation** refers to the *decreasing strength of a response after repeated presentations of the stimulus*. For instance, I used to live very close to an airport and at first noticed every plane as it approached the runway. Within about a month, however, with repeated exposures to the sounds of the plane, I hardly reacted to them anymore. As we saw in Chapter 4, this kind of simple sensory learning makes sense, because it helps us screen out information that does not predict anything useful to us.

Theories of learning generally share three assumptions. The first is that experience shapes behavior. Particularly in complex organisms such as humans, the vast majority of responses are learned rather than innate. The migration patterns of Pacific salmon may be instinctive, but the migration of college students to Daytona Beach

Big Picture φ Question 3

To what extent is human psychology continuous with the psychology of other animals?

Big Picture φ Question 6

What is the relation between nature and nurture in shaping psychological processes?

Big Picture φ Question 1

To what extent can mental processes be reduced to the brain or body?

during spring break is not. Second, learning is adaptive. Just as nature eliminates organisms that are not well suited to their environments, the environment naturally selects those behaviors in an individual that are adaptive and weeds out those that are not (Skinner, 1977). Behaviors useful to the organism (such as avoiding fights with larger members of its species) will be reproduced because of their consequences (safety from bodily harm). A third assumption is that careful experimentation can uncover laws of learning, many of which apply to human and nonhuman animals alike.

Learning theory is the foundation of the behaviorist perspective, and the bulk of this chapter explores the behavioral concepts of classical and operant conditioning (known together as *associative learning*). The remainder examines cognitive approaches that emphasize the role of thought and social experience in learning. What unites these two approaches is a common philosophical ancestor: the concept of *association*. Twenty-five hundred years ago, Aristotle proposed a set of **laws of association**—*conditions under which one thought becomes connected, or associated, with another*—to account for learning and memory. The most important was the *law of contiguity*, which proposes that two events will become connected in the mind if they are experienced close together in time (such as thunder and lightning). Another was the *law of similarity*, which states that objects that resemble each other (such as two people with similar faces) are likely to become associated.

The philosophical school of thought called *associationism* built upon the work of Aristotle, asserting that our most complex thoughts—which allow us to use equations, program computers, and write symphonies—are ultimately nothing but elementary perceptions that become associated and then recombined in the mind. As we will see in the next few chapters, principles of association are fundamental to behaviorist theories of learning as well as to cognitive theories of memory, and neuroscientists have now begun to understand their neural basis—all the way down to changes at the synapse.

Throughout this chapter, you should keep in mind three of the Big Picture Questions raised in Chapter 1: First, to what extent are humans like other animals in the way they learn? Second, what constraints and possibilities has evolution placed on what we can learn? Has natural selection "wired" us to learn some things more readily than others? And if so, to what degree can experience override innate tendencies? Third, to what extent can we understand learning without reference to mental processes? As we saw in Chapter 1, a fundamental aspect of the behaviorist agenda was to rid psychology of terms such as "thoughts" and "motives." The aim was to create a *science of behavior* that focuses on what we can directly observe. As we will see, decades of behavioral research have produced extraordinary progress in our understanding of learning, as well as substantial challenges to some of the assumptions that generated that research.

INTERIM SUMMARY

Learning refers to any enduring change in the way an organism responds based on its experience. Learning theories assume that experience shapes behavior, that learning is adaptive, and that only systematic experimentation can uncover laws of learning. Principles of association are fundamental to most accounts of learning.

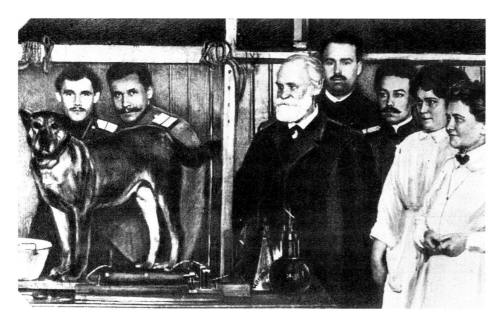

FIGURE 5.1 Pavlov's dog experiments. Pavlov's research with dogs documented the phenomenon of classical conditioning. Actually, his dogs became conditioned to salivate in response to many aspects of the experimental situation and not just to bells or tuning forks; the sight of the experimenter and the harness, too, could elicit the conditioned response.

Classical Conditioning

Classical conditioning (sometimes called *Pavlovian* or *respondent conditioning*) was *the first type of learning to be studied systematically*. In the late nineteenth century, the Russian physiologist Ivan Pavlov (1849–1936) was studying the digestive systems of dogs (research for which he won a Nobel Prize in physiology and medicine). During the course of his work, he noticed a peculiar phenomenon. Like humans and other animals, dogs normally salivate when presented with food, which is a simple reflex. Pavlov noticed that if a stimulus, such as the ringing of a bell or a tuning fork, repeatedly occurred just as a dog was about to be fed, the dog would start to salivate when it heard the bell, even if food were not presented. As Pavlov understood it, the dog had learned to associate the bell with food, and because food produced the reflex of salivation, the bell also came to produce the reflex.

Pavlov's Model

An innate reflex such as salivation to food is an unconditioned reflex. **Conditioning** is *a form of learning*; hence, an **unconditioned reflex** is *a reflex that occurs naturally, without any prior learning. The stimulus that produces the response in an unconditioned reflex* is called an **unconditioned stimulus (UCS)**. In this case the UCS was food. An unconditioned stimulus activates a reflexive response without any learning having taken place; thus, the reflex is unlearned, or unconditioned. An **unconditioned response (UCR)** is *a response that does not have to be learned*. In Pavlov's experiment, the UCR was salivation.

Pavlov's basic experimental setup is illustrated in Figure 5.1. Shortly before presenting the UCS (the food), Pavlov presented a *neutral stimulus*—a stimulus (in this case, ringing a bell) that normally does not elicit the response in question. After the bell had been paired with the unconditioned stimulus (the food) several times, the sound of the bell alone came to evoke a conditioned response, salivation (Figure 5.2). A **conditioned response (CR)** is *a response that has been learned*. By pairing the UCS (the food) with the sound of a bell, the bell became a **conditioned stimulus (CS)**—*a stimulus that, through learning, has come to evoke a conditioned response*. Figure 5.3 summarizes the classical conditioning process.

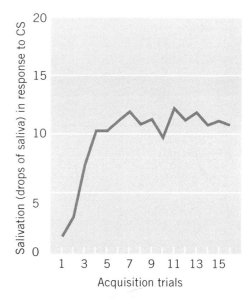

FIGURE 5.2 Acquisition of a classically conditioned response. Initially, the dog did not salivate in response to the sound of the bell. By the third conditioning trial, however, the conditioned stimulus (the bell) had begun to elicit a conditioned response (salivation), which was firmly established by the fifth or sixth trial. *Source:* Pavlov, 1927.

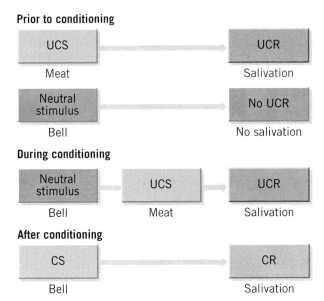

Prior to conditioning

UCS
Meat

UCR
Salivation

Neutral stimulus
Bell

No UCR
No salivation

During conditioning

Neutral stimulus
Bell

UCS
Meat

UCR
Salivation

After conditioning

CS
Bell

CR
Salivation

FIGURE 5.3 Classical conditioning. In classical conditioning, an initially neutral stimulus comes to elicit a conditioned response.

Why did such a seemingly simple discovery earn Pavlov a central place in the history of psychology? The reason is that classical conditioning can explain a wide array of learned responses outside the laboratory as well. For example, a house cat that was repeatedly sprayed with flea repellent squinted reflexively as the repellent got in its eyes. Eventually it came to squint and meow piteously (CR) whenever its owner used an aerosol spray (CS). The same cat, like many household felines, also came to associate the sound of an electric can opener with the opening of its favorite delicacies and would dash to the kitchen counter and meow whenever its owner opened any can, whether cat food or green beans.

If you are beginning to feel somewhat superior to the poor cat wasting all those meows and squints on cans of deodorant and vegetables, consider whether you have ever been at your desk, engrossed in work, when you glanced at the clock and discovered that it was dinner time. If so, you probably noticed some physiological responses—mouth watering, feelings of hunger—that had not been present seconds earlier. Through repeated pairings of stimuli associated with a particular time of day and dinner, you have been classically conditioned to associate a time of day indicated on a clock (the CS) with food (the UCS).

Conditioned Responses

Pavlov was heavily influenced by Darwin and recognized that the ability to learn new associations is crucial to adaptation. Conditioned aversions to particular tastes help us avoid foods that could poison us. Conditioned emotional responses lead us to approach or avoid objects, people, or situations associated with satisfaction or danger— as when an infant learns to associate feelings of warmth, security, and pleasure with his parents' presence. Here we will explore three kinds of conditioned responses— and see how learning can produce both adaptive and maladaptive responses.

Conditioned Taste Aversions   The case of the wolf and the muttonburger which opened this chapter is an example of a *conditioned taste aversion*—a learned aversion to a taste associated with an unpleasant feeling, usually nausea. Ask any woman who has ever been pregnant or who is currently expecting, and she can tell you a lot about conditioned taste aversions. Sometimes, several years after pregnancy, the smell of eggs or coffee is enough to trigger nausea in a woman. From an evolutionary perspective, connecting tastes with nausea or other unpleasant visceral ("gut") experiences is crucial to survival for an animal that forages for its meals. The capacity to learn taste aversions appears to be hundreds of millions of years old and is present in some very simple invertebrates, like slugs (Garcia et al., 1985; Schafe & Bernstein, 1996). As further evidence of its ancient roots, conditioned taste aversions do not require cortical involvement in humans or other vertebrates. Rats with their cortex removed can still learn taste aversions, and even animals that are *completely anesthetized* while nausea is induced can learn taste aversions, as long as they are conscious during presentation of the CS.

Although conditioned taste aversions normally protect an organism, anyone who has ever developed an aversion to a food eaten shortly before getting the flu knows how irrational—and long lasting—these aversions can sometimes be. Cancer patients undergoing chemotherapy often develop aversions to virtually all food (and may lose dangerous amounts of weight) because a common side effect of chemotherapy is nausea. To put this in the language of classical conditioning, chemotherapy is a UCS that leads to nausea, a UCR; the result is an inadvertent association of any food eaten (CS) with nausea (the CR). This conditioned response can develop rapidly, with only one or two exposures to the food paired with nausea (Bernstein, 1991), much as Garcia's wolf took little time to acquire an aversion to the taste of sheep. Some patients even begin to feel nauseous at the sound of a nurse's voice, the sight of the clinic, or the thought of treatment, although acquisition of these CRs generally requires repeated exposure (Bovbjerg et al., 1990).

Conditioned Emotional Responses   One of the most important ways classical conditioning affects behavior is in the conditioning of emotional responses. Consider the automatic smile that comes to a person's face when hearing a special song, or the sweaty palms, pounding heart, and feelings of anxiety that arise when an instructor walks into a classroom and begins handing out a test. Think of the chills that go through most people when they hear "Taps." *Conditioned emotional responses* occur when a formerly neutral stimulus is paired with a stimulus that evokes an emotional response (either naturally or through prior learning).

Perhaps the most famous example of the classical conditioning of emotional responses is the case of little Albert. The study was performed by John Watson, the founder of American behaviorism, and his colleague, Rosalie Rayner (1920). The study was neither methodologically nor ethically beyond reproach, but its provocative findings served as a catalyst for decades of research.

Albert was nine months old when Watson and Rayner presented him with a variety of objects, including a dog, a rabbit, a white rat, a Santa Claus mask, and a fur coat. Albert showed no fear of these objects; in fact, he played regularly with the rat— a budding behaviorist, no doubt. A few days later, Watson and Rayner tested little Albert's response to a loud noise (the UCS) by banging on a steel bar directly behind his head. Albert reacted by jumping, falling forward, and whimpering.

About two months later, Watson and Rayner selected the white rat to be the CS in their experiment and proceeded to condition a fear response in Albert. Each time Albert reached out to touch the rat, they struck the steel bar, creating the same loud noise that had initially startled him. After only a few pairings of the noise and the rat, Albert learned to fear the rat.

Studies since Watson and Rayner's time have proposed classical conditioning as an explanation for some human **phobias**, that is, *irrational fears of specific objects or situations* (Ost, 1991; Wolpe, 1958). For example, through exposure to injections in childhood, many people develop severe emotional reactions (including fainting) to hypodermic needles. Knowing as an adult that injections are necessary and relatively painless usually has little impact on the fear, which

Through classical conditioning, little Albert developed a fear of rats and other furry objects—even Santa's face (an unfortunate phobia for a child, indeed). Courtesy of Benjamin Harris.

Big Picture φ Question 1

To what extent can mental processes be reduced to the brain or body?

is elicited automatically. Athletes such as football players often amuse nurses in student health centers with their combination of fearlessness on the field and fainting at the sight of a tiny needle. Many such fears are acquired and elicited through the activation of subcortical neural pathways (pathways below the level of the cortex; Chapter 3) between the visual system and the amygdala (LeDoux, 1995). Adult knowledge may be of little use in counteracting them because the crucial neural circuits are outside cortical control and are activated before the cortex even gets the message.

Importantly, however, positive emotions can be classically conditioned as easily as negative emotions. In one study, researchers showed participants a slide of either a blue pen or a beige pen. While participants were viewing the slide, the researchers played either American music (whose familiarity was hypothesized to be associated with positive feelings) or non-American music (the unfamiliarity of which was hypothesized to elicit negative feelings). Following the presentation, participants were allowed to take either a blue or a beige pen. Results indicated that almost three-fourths of those who had heard the American music chose the pen that matched the pen presented to them on the slide. Conversely, approximately three-fourths of participants who heard the non-American music selected the pen of the opposite color of that they had seen in the slide (Gorn, 1982). Needless to say, advertisers who want to elicit positive reactions to the products they are marketing make good use of research such as this, choosing to associate the advertised product with stimuli that elicit positive feelings in the viewer.

Conditioned Immune Responses   Classical conditioning can even influence the **immune system**, *the system of cells throughout the body that fight disease* (Abrous et al., 1999; Ader & Cohen, 1985). For example, aside from causing nausea, chemotherapy for cancer has a second unfortunate consequence: It decreases the activity of cells in the immune system that normally fight off infection. Can stimuli associated with chemotherapy, then, become CSs that suppress cell activity?

One study tested this possibility by comparing the functioning of immune cells in cancer patients at two different times (Bovbjerg et al., 1990). The first time was a few days prior to chemotherapy; the second was the morning the patient checked into the hospital for treatment. The investigators hypothesized that exposure to hospital stimuli associated with prior chemotherapy experiences (CS) would suppress immune functioning (CR), just as chemotherapy (UCS) reduces the activity of immune cells (UCR). They were right: Blood taken the morning of hospitalization showed weakened immune functioning when exposed to germs. Researchers are now trying to see whether they can actually *strengthen* immune functioning by using classical conditioning (Alvarez-Borda et al., 1995; Ramirez-Amaya & Bermudez-Rattoni, 1999).

INTERIM SUMMARY

In **classical conditioning**, an environmental stimulus leads to a learned response, through pairing of an **unconditioned stimulus** with a previously neutral **conditioned stimulus**. The result is a **conditioned response**, or learned reflex. *Conditioned taste aversions* are learned aversions to a taste associated with an unpleasant feeling (usually nausea). *Conditioned emotional responses*, including positive feelings you associate with particular situations, events, or people, occur when a conditioned stimulus is paired with a stimulus that evokes an emotional response. *Conditioned immune responses* can occur when a conditioned stimulus is paired with a stimulus that evokes a change in the functioning of the **immune system** (the system of cells in the body that fights disease).

Stimulus Generalization and Discrimination

Once an organism has learned to associate a CS with a UCS, it may respond to stimuli that resemble the CS with a similar response. This phenomenon, called **stimulus generalization**, is related to Aristotle's principle of similarity. For example, you are at a sporting event and you stand for the national anthem. You suddenly well up with pride in your country (which you now, of course, recognize as nothing but a classically conditioned emotional response). But the song you hear, familiar as it may sound, is not *exactly* the same stimulus you heard the last time you were at a game. It is not in the same key, and this time the tenor took a few liberties with the melody. So how do you know to respond with the same emotion? To return to little Albert, the poor child learned to fear not only the rat but also other furry or hairy objects, including the rabbit, the dog, the fur coat, and even Santa's face! In other words, Albert's fear of the rat *generalized* to other furry objects.

Many years ago researchers demonstrated that the more similar a stimulus is to the CS, the more likely generalization will occur (Hovland, 1937). In a classic study, the experimenters paired a tone (the CS) with a mild electrical shock (the UCS). With repeated pairings, subjects produced a conditioned response to the tone known as a **galvanic skin response**, *or* **GSR** *(an electrical measure of the amount of sweat on the skin, associated with arousal or anxiety)*. The experimenter then presented tones of varying frequencies that had not been paired with shock and measured the resulting GSR. Tones with frequencies similar to the CS evoked the most marked GSR, whereas dissimilar tones evoked progressively smaller responses (Figure 5.4).

A major component of adaptive learning is knowing when to generalize and when to be more discriminating. Maladaptive patterns in humans often involve inappropriate generalization from one set of circumstances to others, as when a person who has been frequently criticized by a parent responds negatively to all authority figures.

Much of the time, in fact, we are able to discriminate among stimuli in ways that foster adaptation. **Stimulus discrimination** is *the learned tendency to respond to a restricted range of stimuli or only to the stimulus used during training*. In many ways, stimulus discrimination is the opposite of stimulus generalization. Pavlov's dogs did not salivate in response to just *any* sound, and people do not get hungry when the clock reads four o'clock even though it is not far from six o'clock. Organisms learn to discriminate between two similar stimuli when these stimuli are not consistently associated with the same UCS.

Extinction

In the *acquisition*, or initial learning, of a conditioned response, each pairing of the CS and UCS is known as a *conditioning trial*. What happens later, however, if the CS repeatedly occurs *without* the UCS? For example, suppose Watson and Rayner (1920) had, on the second, third, and all subsequent trials, exposed little Albert to the white rat without the loud noise?

Albert's learned fear response would eventually have been *extinguished*, or eliminated, from his behavioral repertoire. **Extinction** *in classical conditioning refers to the process by which a CR is weakened by presentation of the CS without the UCS*. If a dog has come to associate the sounding of a bell with food, it will eventually stop salivating at the bell tone if the bell rings enough times without the presentation of food. The association is weakened—but not obliterated. If days later the dog once more hears the bell, it is likely to salivate again. This is known as **spontaneous recovery**—*the reemergence of a previously extinguished conditioned response*. The spontaneous recovery of a CR is typically short-lived, however, and will rapidly extinguish again without renewed pairings of the CS and UCS.

INTERIM SUMMARY

Stimulus generalization occurs when an organism learns to respond to stimuli that resemble the CS with a similar response. **Stimulus discrimination** occurs when an organism learns to respond to a restricted range of stimuli. **Extinction** occurs when a CR is weakened by presentation of the CS without the UCS. Previously extinguished responses may reappear through a process known as **spontaneous recovery**.

Apply & Discuss

■ What are some ways a person might develop a fear of thunderstorms?

■ Could a fear of thunderstorms arise in some other way?

■ Can such fears all be explained through principles of classical conditioning?

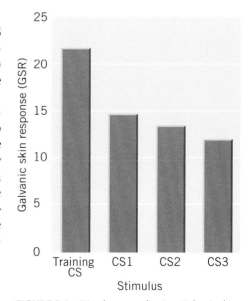

FIGURE 5.4 Stimulus generalization. Galvanic skin response (a measure of physiological arousal) varies according to the similarity of the CS to the training stimulus. In this case, the training stimulus was a tone of a particular frequency. CS1 is most similar to the training stimulus; CS3 is least similar to it. *Source:* Hovland, 1937.

Factors Affecting Classical Conditioning

Classical conditioning does not occur every time a bell rings, a baby startles, or a wolf eats some tainted lamb chops. Several factors influence the extent to which classical conditioning will occur. These include the interstimulus interval, the individual's learning history, and the organism's preparedness to learn (see Wasserman & Miller, 1997).

Interstimulus Interval   The **interstimulus interval** is *the time between presentation of the CS and the UCS*. Presumably, if too much time passes between the presentation of these two stimuli, the animal is unlikely to associate them, and conditioning is less likely to occur. For most responses, the optimal interval between the CS and UCS is very brief, usually a few seconds or less. The optimal interval depends, however, on the stimulus and tends to bear the imprint of natural selection (Hollis, 1997). A CS that occurs about a half a second before a puff of air hits the eye has the maximum power to elicit a conditioned eyeblink response in humans (Ross & Ross, 1971). This makes evolutionary sense because we usually have very little warning between the time we see or hear something and the time debris reaches our eyes.

At the other extreme, conditioned taste aversions do not occur when the interstimulus interval is *less than* 10 seconds, and learning often occurs with intervals up to several hours (Schafe & Bernstein, 1996). Given that nausea or stomach pain can develop hours after ingesting a toxic substance, the capacity to associate tastes with feelings in the gut minutes or hours later clearly fosters survival. Just as in perception (Chapter 4), our brains appear to be attuned to the patterns that exist in nature.

The temporal order of the CS and the UCS—that is, which one comes first—is also crucial (Figure 5.5). Maximal conditioning occurs when the CS precedes the UCS. This timing, too, makes evolutionary sense: A CS that consistently occurs after a UCS offers little additional information, whereas a CS that precedes a UCS allows the organism to "predict" and hence to prepare.

The Individual's Learning History   Another factor that influences classical conditioning is the individual's learning history. An extinguished response is usually easier to learn the second time around, presumably because the stimulus was once associated with the response. A previously extinguished nausea response to the taste of bacon can be easily reinstated—and difficult to extinguish—if bacon and nausea ever occur together again. Thus, neuronal connections established through learning may diminish in strength when the environment no longer supports them, but they do not entirely disappear. Later learning can build on old "tracks" that have been covered up but not obliterated.

In other circumstances, prior learning can actually *hinder* learning. Suppose a dog has learned to salivate at the sound of a bell (conditioned stimulus 1, or CS1). The re-

---

Forward (trace) conditioning

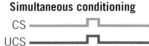

The CS is presented and terminated before the USC is presented. This type of conditioning is most effective if the time period between the presentation of the CS and the UCS is relatively brief. Applied to Pavlov's study, forward trace conditioning would have involved ringing the bell, and, then, at some time interval after the bell had ceased ringing, presenting the food.

Simultaneous conditioning

As the name implies, with simultaneous conditioning, the CS and the UCS are presented at the same time. This type of conditioning is considered to be less effective in producing a CR than either delayed conditioning or forward trace conditioning. An example of simultaneous conditioning would have been Pavlov ringing the bell and presenting the food at the same time.

Backward conditioning

The UCS is presented and stopped before the CS is presented. For example, had Pavlov used backward conditioning he would have presented the food, let the dog eat, and then rung the bell. Most researchers find this to be the least effective type of conditioning.

FIGURE 5.5   Several procedures can be used in pairing the UCS and the CS. These procedures differ in the temporal ordering of the two stimuli.

searcher now wants to teach the dog to associate food with a flash of light as well (CS2). If the bell continues to sound even occasionally in learning trials pairing the light (CS2) with food (the UCS), the dog is unlikely to produce a conditioned response to the light. This phenomenon is known as blocking. **Blocking** refers to *the failure of a stimulus* (such as a flash of light) *to elicit a CR when it is combined with another stimulus that already elicits the response* (Fanselow, 1998; Kamin, 1969). If a bell is already associated with food, a flashing light is of little consequence unless it provides additional, nonredundant information.

A similar phenomenon occurs in **latent inhibition**, in which *initial exposure to a neutral stimulus without a UCS slows the process of later learning the CS–UCS association and developing a CR* (Lubow & Gewirtz, 1995). Thus, if a bell repeatedly sounds without presentation of meat, a dog may be slower to learn the connection after the bell *does* start to signal mealtime. Similarly, people often take a while to change their attitude toward a colleague who has previously been relatively silent but suddenly starts making useful comments as he becomes more comfortable speaking his mind.

Preparedness to Learn: An Evolutionary Perspective   A third influence on classical conditioning is the organism's readiness to learn certain associations. Many early behaviorists, such as Watson, believed that the laws of classical conditioning could link virtually any stimulus to any response. Yet subsequent research has shown that some responses can be conditioned much more readily to certain stimuli than to others.

This preparedness to learn was demonstrated in a classic study by Garcia and Koelling (1966). The experimenters used three conditioned stimuli: light, sound, and taste (flavored water). For one group of rats, these stimuli were paired with the UCS of radiation, which produces nausea. For the other group, the stimuli were paired with a different UCS, electric shock. The experimenters then exposed the rats to each of the three conditioned stimuli to test the strength of the conditioned response to each.

The results are shown in Figure 5.6. Rats that experienced nausea after exposure to radiation developed an aversion to the flavored water but not to the light or sound cues. In contrast, rats exposed to electric shock avoided the audiovisual stimuli but not the taste cues. In other words, the rats learned to associate sickness in their stomachs with a taste stimulus and an aversive tactile stimulus (electrical shock) with audiovisual stimuli.

Prepared learning refers to *the biologically wired readiness to learn some associations more easily than others* (Ohman et al., 1995; Seligman, 1971). From an evolutionary perspective, natural selection has favored organisms that more readily associate stimuli that tend to be associated in nature and whose association is related to survival or reproduction. An animal lucky enough to survive after eating a poisonous caterpillar is more likely to survive thereafter if it can associate nausea with the right stimulus. For most land-dwelling animals, a preparedness to connect taste with nausea allows the animal to bypass irrelevant associations to the hundreds of other stimuli it might have encountered between the time it dined on the offending caterpillar and the time it got sick hours later.

In contrast, most birds do not have well-developed gustatory systems and thus cannot rely heavily on taste to avoid toxic insects. In support of the evolutionary hypothesis, research on quail and other birds finds that, unlike rats, they are more likely to associate nausea with visual than gustatory stimuli (Hollis, 1997). Garcia and colleagues (1985) theorize that vertebrate animals have evolved two defense systems, one attending to defense of the gut (and hence favoring associations between nausea and sensory cues relevant to food) and the other attending to defense of the skin (and usually predisposing the animal to form associations between pain and sights and sounds that signal dangers such as predators).

Making Connections

Many people have irrational fears—of dogs, spiders, public speaking, and so forth.

▪ How could psychologists use their understanding of classical conditioning to help people extinguish irrational fears (Chapter 16)?

Unconditioned stimulus (UCS)	Conditioned stimulus (CS)		
	Light	Sound	Taste
Shock (pain)	Avoidance	Avoidance	No avoidance
X-rays (nausea)	No avoidance	No avoidance	Avoidance

FIGURE 5.6   Preparedness to learn. Garcia and Koelling's experiment examined the impact of biological constraints on learning in rats exposed to shock or X-rays. Rats associated nausea with a taste stimulus rather than with audiovisual cues; they associated an aversive tactile event with sights and sounds rather than with taste stimuli. The results demonstrated that animals are prepared to learn certain associations more readily than others in classical conditioning. *Source:* Adapted from Garcia & Koelling, 1966.

Big Picture φ Question 3

To what extent is human psychology continuous with the psychology of other animals?

Humans show some evidence of biological preparedness as well. Phobias of spiders and snakes are more common than phobias of flowers or telephones (Marks, 1969; Ohman et al., 1976). Readers of this book, for example, are much more likely to have snake or spider phobias than automobile phobias, despite the fact that they are 10,000 times more likely to die at the wheel of a car than at the mouth of a spider—or to have experienced a car accident rather than a snakebite.

Biological preparedness, of course, has its limits, especially in humans, whose associative capacities are *almost* limitless (McNally, 1987). One study, for example, found people equally likely to develop a fear of handguns as of snakes (Honeybourne et al., 1993). Where biological predispositions leave off, learning begins as a way of naturally selecting adaptive responses.

What Do Organisms Learn in Classical Conditioning?

In some ways, contrasting innate with learned responses is setting up a false dichotomy, because the capacity to learn—to form associations—is itself a product of natural selection. Precisely what organisms learn when they are classically conditioned, however, has been a topic of considerable debate.

Most theorists would agree that organisms learn associations, but associations between what? According to Watson and other early behaviorists, the organism learns a *stimulus–response*, or *S–R*, association. In other words, the organism learns to associate the CR with the CS. Pavlov, in contrast, argued that the organism learns to associate the CS with the UCS—a *stimulus–stimulus*, or *S–S*, association. Pavlov (1927) hypothesized that in classical conditioning the CS essentially becomes a *signal* to an organism that the UCS is about to occur. Although both kinds of processes probably occur, the weight of the evidence tends to favor Pavlov's theory (Rescorla, 1973).

Another question is just how far we can take Aristotle's law of contiguity, which, as we have seen, proposes that organisms should associate stimuli that repeatedly occur together in time. Data from animal learning studies suggest that this principle is not quite right, although it was a monumental step in the right direction. If contiguity were the whole story, order of presentation of the UCS and CS would not matter—yet as we have seen, a CS that precedes a UCS produces more potent learning than a CS that follows or occurs simultaneously with the UCS. Similarly, if contiguity were all there were to learning, blocking would not occur: If two stimuli occur together frequently enough, it should make no difference whether some other CS is "coming along for the ride"—the organism should still associate the new CS with the UCS or CR.

On the basis of these and other findings, Rescorla and Wagner (1972) proposed the *law of prediction* to replace the law of contiguity. This law states that a CS–UCS association will form to the extent that the presence of the CS predicts the appearance of the UCS. As we will see, this law moved the field substantially in a cognitive direction, suggesting that animals are not blindly making connections between any two stimuli that come along. Rather—and in line with evolutionary theory as well—rats, humans, and other animals are making connections between stimuli in ways that are likely to guide adaptive responding. Recent research suggests, in fact, that animals learn not only about the *connection* between stimuli in classical conditioning but about their timing (Gallistel & Gibbon, 2000). Thus, a dog in a Pavlovian experiment learns not only that meat will follow the toll of a bell but also *how long* after the bell the meat (and hence salivation) is likely to occur. Rescorla (1988) summed it up well when he said "Pavlovian conditioning is not a stupid process by which the organism willy-nilly forms associations between any two stimuli that happen to co-occur. Rather, the organism is better seen as an information seeker using logical and perceptual relations among events, along with its own preconceptions, to form a sophisticated representation of its world."

A third question is the extent to which the CR and UR are really the same response. According to Pavlov, following classical conditioning, the organism responds

Apply & Discuss

- Why are public speaking phobias so common?
- Does this reflect prepared learning? Or does it simply reflect people's unpleasant experiences with public speaking?

to the CS as if it *were* the UCS and hence produces the same response. Pavlov proposed a neurological mechanism for this, hypothesizing that repeated pairings of the UCS and the CS lead to connections between them in the brain, so that the two stimuli eventually trigger the same response. Although Pavlov was probably right in broad strokes, subsequent research suggests that the CR and the UCR, though usually similar, are rarely identical. Dogs typically do not salivate as much in response to a bell as to the actual presentation of food, which means that the CS is not triggering the exact same response as the UCS.

Sometimes the CR is even the opposite of the UCR, as in *paradoxical conditioning*, in which the CR is actually the body's attempt to counteract the effects of a stimulus that is about to occur. For example, the sight of drug paraphernalia in heroin addicts can activate physiological reactions that reduce the effect of the heroin they are about to inject (Caggiula et al., 1991; Siegel, 1984). These produce a *conditioned tolerance*, or decreased sensitivity, to the drug with repeated use as the body counteracts dosages that were previously effective.

This CR may be involved in the processes that force addicts to take progressively higher doses of a drug to achieve the same effect. One study of paradoxical conditioning in opiate addicts compared the effects of self-injection, which involved exposure to drug paraphernalia (the CS), with an intravenous injection provided by the researchers, which did not (Ehrman et al., 1992). Only the bodies of addicts who self-injected showed efforts to counteract the drug.

The Neural Basis of Classical Conditioning From Brain to Behavior

Research *has* confirmed Pavlov's speculation that classical conditioning alters the action of neurons that ultimately link stimuli with responses (Bailey & Kandel, 1995; Martinez & Derrick, 1996). For years Eric Kandel and his colleagues have studied the cellular basis of learning in the marine snail, *Aplysia*. This simple and seemingly unremarkable organism is ideally suited to the study of associative learning because reflex learning in *Aplysia* involves a very small number of large neurons. Thus, researchers can actually observe what is happening at all the relevant synapses as *Aplysia* learns. (In humans, in comparison, thousands or millions of neurons may be activated in a simple instance of classical conditioning.)

Learning at the Synapse
In *Aplysia*, classical conditioning and similar forms of learning occur through changes at synapses that link sensory neurons (activated by the CS) to neurons that trigger a motor reflex. Changes occur in both the presynaptic neuron, which releases neurotransmitters more readily with additional conditioning trials, and the postsynaptic neuron, which becomes more easily excited with additional trials. A small number of trials produces changes that last minutes or hours, whereas a larger number of trials can produce changes that last for days.

Kandel and his colleagues have discovered some differences at the cellular level between short-term and longer term learning of this sort. For example, in short-term learning, the presynaptic neuron uses proteins already available within the cell to facilitate release of neurotransmitters. More frequent pairings of the CS and UCS, however, generate *new* proteins that lead to the sprouting of new dendritic connections between the presynaptic and postsynaptic neuron. This strengthens the connections between the two cells, creating a long-lasting neural association. (Kandel won the Nobel Prize for his research on *Aplysia*.)

Other researchers have studied a similar phenomenon called long-term potentiation in more complex animals (Bliss & Lomo, 1973; Jeffery, 1997; Guzowski et al., 2000). **Long-term potentiation (LTP)** refers to *the tendency of a group of neurons to fire more readily after consistent stimulation from other neurons*, as presum-

Big Picture φ Question 1

To what extent can mental processes be reduced to the brain or body?

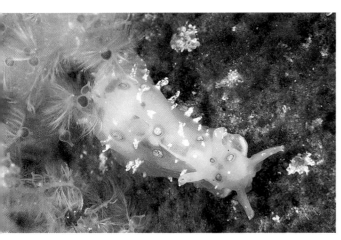

The marine snail, Aplysia, *has afforded researchers the opportunity to study the molecular basis of learning.*

ably occurs in classical conditioning. Its name refers to a heightened *potential* for neural firing ("potentiation") that lasts much longer than the initial stimulus. Thus, even after the CS is no longer present, cellular changes at the synapse *are*. To what extent LTP is involved in various forms of learning is currently a topic of debate among neuroscientists.

Like the work on *Aplysia*, research on LTP supports a hypothesis proposed by the neurologist Donald Hebb (1949) years before the technologies existed to test it: "When an axon of cell A is near enough to excite cell B and repeatedly or persistently take part in firing it, some…process…takes place in one or both cells such that A's efficiency, as one of the cells firing B, is increased." In other words, when the activation of one set of neurons repeatedly leads to activation of another, the strength of the connection between the two neurons increases—a neural translation of the principles of association first formulated by Aristotle.

Neural Circuits and Classical Conditioning

While Kandel and others have made great strides in understanding learning at the synaptic level, other researchers are focusing on the larger neural circuits that allow humans and other animals to learn conditioned responses. By selectively damaging rats' brains, researchers have been able to determine which parts of the brain are involved in different aspects of fear conditioning. As we will see in Chapter 10 on emotion, perhaps the most important discovery has been circuits involving the amygdala that play a central role in the capacity to associate fear with a new stimulus, which is crucial for survival (Fanselow & LeDoux, 1999; LeDoux, 2000).

Unlike lesions of the amygdala, lesions of the hippocampus, which plays a key role in memory (Chapter 6), do not disrupt simple fear conditioning—but they do have a very specific effect on learning to fear. In classical conditioning experiments, animals often learn not only the simple association between a CS and a US, such as the association between a tone and shock, but also that being in the experimental chamber (rather than their own cage) predicts shock. This additional learning is called *contextual learning* (learning about the *context*). Hippocampal lesions disrupt contextual learning—as if the rat can no longer remember the broader context in which negative events happen because it cannot remember the specific events at all (Fanselow, 1998; Kim & Fanselow, 1992; LeDoux, 1998).

The distinction between the kinds of learning disrupted by damage to the amygdala and to the hippocampus in animals such as rats appears to have a clear parallel in humans. Humans with lesions to the amygdala have difficulty learning to fear a novel stimulus at all—even if they consciously *know* that every time a tone sounded they received a shock. They can "talk the talk," but they cannot "walk the walk." In contrast, patients with lesions to the hippocampus respond with fear to a conditioned stimulus—even if they cannot remember having ever seen it before (Bechara et al., 1995). Their intact amygdala produces the fear response, even though they have no idea why it is there.

INTERIM SUMMARY

Several factors influence classical conditioning, including the **interstimulus interval** (the time between presentation of the CS and the UCS), the degree to which the presence of the CS is predictive of the US, the individual's learning history (such as prior associations between the stimulus and other stimuli or responses), and **prepared learning** (the evolved tendency of some associations to be learned more readily than others). Precisely what organisms learn in classical conditioning is a matter of debate. Research on the marine snail *Aplysia* and on **long-term potentiation** in more complex animals suggests that learning occurs through changes in the strength of connections between neurons. Research on fear conditioning implicates neural circuits involving the amygdala.

Operant Conditioning

In 1898, Edward Thorndike placed a hungry cat in a box with a mechanical latch and then placed food in full view just outside the box. The cat meowed, paced back and forth, and rubbed against the walls of the box. In so doing, it happened to trip the latch. Immediately, the door to the box opened, and the cat gained access to the food. Thorndike repeated the experiment, and with continued repetitions the cat became more adept at tripping the latch. Eventually, it was able to leave its cage almost as soon as food appeared.

Thorndike proposed a law of learning to account for this phenomenon, which he called the **law of effect**: *An animal's tendency to reproduce a behavior depends on that behavior's effect on the environment and the consequent effect on the animal*. If tripping the latch had not helped the cat reach the food, the cat would not have learned to keep brushing up against the latch. More simply, the law of effect states that *behavior is controlled by its consequences*.

Thorndike's cat exemplifies a second form of conditioning, known as instrumental or operant conditioning. Thorndike used the term *instrumental conditioning* because the behavior is instrumental to achieving a more satisfying state of affairs. B. F. Skinner, who spent years experimenting with the ways in which behavior is controlled by the environment, called it **operant conditioning**—that is, *learning to operate on the environment to produce a consequence*.

Although the lines between operant and classical conditioning are not always hard and fast, the major distinction regards which comes first, something in the environment or some behavior from the organism. In classical conditioning an environmental stimulus initiates a response, whereas in operant conditioning a behavior (or operant) *produces* an environmental response. **Operants** are *behaviors that are emitted (spontaneously produced) rather than elicited by the environment*.

Thorndike's cat spontaneously emitted the behavior of brushing up against the latch, which resulted in an effect that conditioned future behavior. Skinner emitted the behaviors of experimenting and writing about his results, which brought him the respect of his colleagues and hence influenced his future behavior. Had his initial experiments failed, he probably would not have persisted, just as Thorndike's cats did not continue emitting behaviors with neutral or aversive environmental effects. In operant conditioning—whether the animal is a cat or a psychologist—the behavior *precedes* the environmental event that conditions future behavior. By contrast, in classical conditioning, an environmental stimulus (such as a bell) precedes a response.

The basic idea behind operant conditioning, then, is that behavior is controlled by its consequences. In this section, we explore two types of environmental consequence that produce operant conditioning: **reinforcement**, *which increases the probability that a response will occur*, and **punishment**, *which diminishes its likelihood*.

Reinforcement

Reinforcement means just what the name implies: Something in the environment fortifies, or reinforces, a behavior. A **reinforcer** is *an environmental consequence that occurs after an organism has produced a response and makes the response more likely to recur*. Psychologists distinguish two kinds of reinforcement, positive and negative.

Positive Reinforcement   **Positive reinforcement** is *the process whereby presentation of a stimulus* (a reward or payoff) *after a behavior makes the behavior more likely to occur again*. For example, in experimental procedures pioneered by B. F. Skinner (1938, 1953), a pigeon was placed in a cage with a target mounted on one side (Figure 5.7). (Pigeons and rats were Skinner's favorite—that is, most reinforc-

FIGURE 5.7 Apparatus for operant conditioning. (*a*) A pigeon is placed in a cage with a target on one side, which can be used for operant conditioning. (*b*) B. F. Skinner experiments with a rat placed in a Skinner box, with a similar design, in which pressing a bar may result in reinforcement.

(*a*)

(*b*)

Big Picture φ Question 3

To what extent is human psychology continuous with the psychology of other animals?

"Oh, not bad. The light comes on, I press the bar, they write me a check. How about you?"

ing—subjects.) The pigeon spontaneously pecked around in the cage. This behavior was not a response to any particular stimulus; pecking is simply innate avian behavior. If, by chance, the pigeon pecked at the target, however, a pellet of grain dropped into a bin. If the pigeon happened to peck at the target again, it was once more rewarded with a pellet. The pellet is a **positive reinforcer**—*an environmental consequence that, when presented, strengthens the probability that a response will recur*. The pigeon would thus start to peck at the target more frequently because this operant became associated with the positive reinforcer.

Positive reinforcement is not limited to pigeons. In fact, it controls much of human behavior. Students learn to exert effort studying when they are reinforced with praise and good grades, salespeople learn to appease obnoxious customers and laugh at their jokes because this behavior yields them commissions, and people learn to go to work each day because they receive a paycheck. Animals learn to sit and lie down because they are reinforced with treats for the behavior.

Although positive reinforcement (and operant conditioning more generally) usually leads to adaptive responding, nothing guarantees that organisms make the "right" connections between behaviors and their consequences. Just as humans and other animals can develop phobias by forming idiosyncratic associations, they can also *erroneously associate an operant and an environmental event*, a phenomenon Skinner (1948) labeled **superstitious behavior**. For example, in one study, pigeons received grain at regular time intervals, no matter what behavior the pigeons happened to perform. As a result, each pigeon developed its own idiosyncratic response. One turned counterclockwise about the cage, another repeatedly thrust its head in an upper corner of the cage, and a third tossed its head as if lifting an invisible bar (Skinner, 1948). Skinner compared these behaviors to human actions such as wearing a lucky outfit to a basketball game or tapping home plate three times when up to bat in baseball. According to Skinner, such behaviors develop because the delivery of a reinforcer strengthens whatever behavior an organism is engaged in at the time.

Negative Reinforcement   Just as *presenting* an animal with a rewarding environmental consequence can reinforce a behavior, so, too, can *eliminating* an aversive consequence. This is known as **negative reinforcement**—*the process whereby termination of an aversive stimulus makes a behavior more likely to occur*. **Negative reinforcers** are *aversive or unpleasant stimuli that strengthen a behavior by their removal*. Hitting the snooze button on an alarm clock is negatively reinforced by the termination of the alarm; cleaning the kitchen is negatively reinforced by the elimination of unpleasant sights, smells, and whining by roommates.

Negative reinforcement occurs in both escape learning and avoidance learning. In **escape learning**, *a behavior is reinforced by the elimination of an aversive state of affairs that already exists*; that is, the organism escapes an aversive situation. For example, a rat presses a lever and terminates an electric shock or an overzealous sunbather applies lotion to her skin to relieve sunburn pain. **Avoidance learning** occurs as *an organism learns to prevent an expected aversive event from happening*. In this case, avoidance of a potentially aversive situation reinforces the operant. For example, a rat jumps a hurdle into a safe chamber when it hears a tone that signals that a shock is about to occur, and the sunbather puts on sunscreen before going out in the sun to avoid a sunburn.

As any parent with more than one child can attest, what is reinforcing to one person may not be reinforcing to another—at least not in the same way. Even for one individual, stimuli that are positively rewarding at one time may not be at another. For example, my young sons love hot dogs. Against my better judgment, we cook hot dogs a lot in our home. Most of the time, hot dogs are positive reinforcers for the boys. If, however, I serve them when they are tired of them or simply not hungry, the removal of the hot dogs becomes a negative reinforcer. To make matters more complicated, at any given meal a hot dog may be positively reinforcing to one of my sons whereas the removal of the hot dog may be negatively reinforcing to the other. Clearly, individual differences play a role in determining people's conceptions of reward and punishment (Timberlake, Farmer et al., 1991).

Punishment

Reinforcement is one type of environmental consequence that controls behavior through operant conditioning; the other is punishment (Figure 5.8). Whereas reinforcement always *increases* the likelihood of a response, either by the presentation of a reward or the removal of an aversive stimulus, punishment *decreases* the probability that a behavior will recur. Thus, if Skinner's pigeon received an electric shock each time it pecked at the target, it would be less likely to peck again because this operant resulted in an aversive outcome. Parents intuitively apply this behavioral technique when they "ground" a teenager for staying out past curfew. The criminal justice system also operates on a system of punishment, attempting to discourage illicit behaviors by imposing penalties.

Like reinforcement, punishment can be positive or negative. "Positive" and "negative" here do not refer to the feelings of the participants, who rarely consider punishment a positive experience. Positive simply means something is presented, whereas negative means something is taken away. In *positive punishment*, such as spanking, exposure to an aversive event following a behavior reduces the likelihood of the operant recurring. *Negative punishment* involves losing, or not obtaining, a reinforcer as a consequence of behavior, as when an employee fails to receive a pay increase because of frequent lateness. Bjorn Borg, one of the greats in men's tennis, provides an excellent example of the power of negative punishment. Known for his quiet demeanor on the tennis court, Borg so rarely questioned calls by umpires that on the few occasions when he did people were stunned. He presented a sharp contrast to John McEnroe, known for his on-court temper tantrums and racquet throwing. But, according to Borg himself, he was not always the antithesis of McEnroe. "Once I was like John.

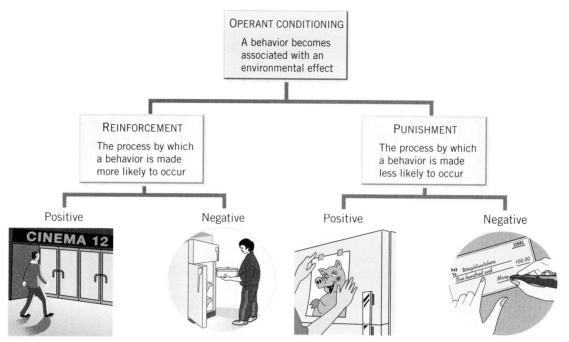

FIGURE 5.8   Types of reinforcement and punishment. Imagine that you are trying to lose weight. To facilitate your achievement of weight loss, you may choose to use either reinforcement or punishment. Whether you choose reinforcement or punishment, you may choose to use either positive or negative variants of each. Positive reinforcement: Positive reinforcement involves giving yourself something positive. Thus, prior to beginning your diet, you set up a program such that for every 10 pounds that you lose, you treat yourself to a movie at the theater. Negative reinforcement: Negative reinforcement involves taking something aversive away. Should you opt for this type of reward, you would allow yourself to remove that many pounds of lard stored in your refrigerator. (Anyone who watched Oprah after she lost a significant amount of weight will recall the wagon full of lard she wheeled out on stage.) Positive punishment: Positive punishment involves giving yourself something aversive in order to decrease the probability of a particular response. Applied to weight loss, when you fail to lose a particular amount of weight within a specified period of time, you would post pictures of Miss Piggy around the house. Negative punishment: Negative punishment involves removing something positive or rewarding. Assuming that money is rewarding to most people, when you fail to lose a particular amount of weight, you would give an amount of money corresponding to the pounds that you failed to lose to someone else or to some organization, such as Weight Watchers.

Worse. Swearing and throwing rackets. Real bad temper.… Then, when I was 13, my club suspended me for six months. My parents locked up my racket in a cupboard for six months. Half a year I could not play. It was terrible.… But it was a very good lesson. I never opened my mouth on the court again. I still get really mad, but I keep my emotions inside" (Collins, 1981).

Punishment is commonplace and essential in human affairs, because reinforcement alone does not inhibit many undesirable behaviors, but punishment is frequently applied in ways that render it ineffective (Chance, 1988; Laub & Sampson, 1995; Skinner, 1953). One problem in using punishment with animals and young children is that the learner may have difficulty distinguishing which operant is being punished. People who yell at their dog for coming after they have called it several times are actually punishing good behavior—coming when called. The dog is more likely to associate the punishment with its action than its inaction—and is likely to adjust its behavior accordingly, by becoming even *less* likely to come when called!

A second and related problem associated with punishment is that the learner may come to fear the person meting out the punishment (via classical conditioning) rather than the action (via operant conditioning). A child who is harshly punished by his father may become afraid of his father instead of changing his behavior.

Third, punishment may not eliminate existing rewards for a behavior. In nature, unlike the laboratory, a single action may have multiple consequences, and behavior can be controlled by any number of them. A teacher who punishes the class clown may not have much success if the behavior is reinforced by classmates. Sometimes, too, punishing one behavior (such as stealing) may inadvertently reinforce another (such as lying).

Fourth, people typically use punishment when they are angry, which can lead both to poorly designed punishment (from a learning point of view) and to the potential for abuse. An angry parent may punish a child for misdeeds just discovered but that occurred a considerable time earlier. The time interval between the child's action and the consequence may render the punishment ineffective because the child does not adequately connect the two events. Parents also frequently punish depending more on their mood than on the type of behavior they want to discourage, making it difficult for the child to learn what behavior is being punished, under what circumstances, and how to avoid it.

Finally, aggression that is used to punish behavior often leads to further aggression. The child who is beaten typically learns a much deeper lesson: that problems can be solved with violence. In fact, the more physical punishment parents use, the more aggressively their children tend to behave at home and at school (Bettner & Lew, 2000; Deater-Deckard et al., 1996; Dodge et al., 1995, 1997; Straus & Mouradian, 1998; Weiss et al., 1992). Correlation does not, of course, prove causation; aggressive children may provoke punitive parenting. Nevertheless, the weight of evidence suggests that violent parents tend to create violent children. Adults who were beaten as children are more likely than other adults to have *less* self-control, lower self-esteem, more troubled relationships, more depression, and a greater likelihood of abusing their own children and spouses (Rohner, 1975b, 1986; Straus & Kantor, 1994).

Punishment can, however, be used effectively and is essential for teaching children to control inappropriate outbursts, manipulative behavior, disruptive behavior, and so forth. Punishment is most effective when it is accompanied by reasoning—even with two- and three-year-olds (Larzelere et al., 1996). It is also most effective when the person being punished is also reinforced for an alternative, acceptable behavior. Explaining helps a child correctly connect an action with a punishment, and having other positively reinforced behaviors to draw on allows the child to generate alternative responses.

Extinction

As in classical conditioning, learned operant responses can be extinguished. Extinction occurs if enough conditioning trials pass in which the operant is not followed by the consequence previously associated with it. A child may study less if hard work no longer leads to reinforcement by parents (who may, for example, start taking good grades for granted and only comment on weaker grades), just as a manufacturer may discontinue a product that is no longer profitable.

Knowing how to extinguish behavior is important in everyday life, particularly for parents. Consider the case of a 21-month-old boy who had a serious illness requiring around-the-clock attention (Williams, 1959). After recovering, the child continued to demand this level of attention. At bedtime, he screamed and cried—sometimes for up to two hours—unless a parent sat with him until he fell asleep.

Relying on the principle that unreinforced behavior will be extinguished, the parents, with some help from a psychologist, began a new bedtime regimen. In the first trial of the extinction series, they spent a relaxed and warm good night session with their son, closed the door when they left the room, and refused to respond to the wails and screams that followed. After 45 minutes, the boy fell asleep, and he fell asleep immediately on the second trial (Figure 5.9). The next several bedtimes were accompanied by tantrums that steadily decreased in duration, so that by the 10th trial, the parents fully enjoyed the sound of silence.

As in classical conditioning, spontaneous recovery (in which a previously learned behavior recurs without renewed reinforcement) sometimes occurs. In fact, the boy cried and screamed again one night when his aunt attempted to put him to bed. She inadvertently reinforced this behavior by returning to his room; as a result, his parents had to repeat their extinction procedure.

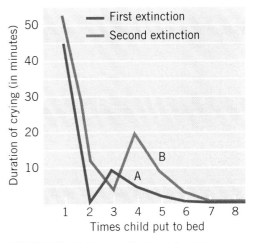

FIGURE 5.9 Extinction of tantrum behavior in a 21-month-old child. As shown in curve A, the child initially cried for long periods of time, but very few trials of nonreinforced crying were required to extinguish the behavior. In curve B, the behavior was again quickly extinguished following its spontaneous recovery. *Source:* Williams, 1959, p. 269.

INTERIM SUMMARY

Operant conditioning means learning to operate on the environment to produce a consequence. **Operants** are behaviors that are emitted rather than elicited by the environment. **Reinforcement** refers to a consequence that increases the probability that a response will recur. **Positive reinforcement** occurs when the environmental consequence (a reward or payoff) makes a behavior more likely to occur again. **Negative reinforcement** occurs when termination of an aversive stimulus makes a behavior more likely to recur. Whereas reinforcement increases the probability of a response, **punishment** decreases the probability that a response will recur. Punishment is frequently applied in ways that render it ineffective. Extinction in operant conditioning occurs if enough trials pass in which the operant is not followed by the consequence previously associated with it.

Operant Conditioning of Complex Behaviors

Thus far we have discussed relatively simple behaviors controlled by their environmental consequences—pigeons pecking, rats pressing, and people showing up at work for a paycheck. In fact, operant conditioning offers one of the most comprehensive explanations for the range of human and animal behavior ever produced.

Schedules of Reinforcement   In the examples described so far, an animal is rewarded or punished every time it performs a behavior. This situation, in which *the consequence is the same each time the animal emits a behavior*, is called a **continuous reinforcement schedule** (because the behavior is *continuously* reinforced). A child reinforced for altruistic behavior on a continuous schedule of reinforcement would be praised every time she shares, just as a rat might receive a pellet of food each time it presses a lever. Such consistent reinforcement, however, rarely occurs in nature or in human life. More typically, an action sometimes leads to reinforcement but other times does not. Such reinforcement schedules are known as **partial** or **intermittent schedules of reinforcement** because *the behavior is reinforced only part of the time, or intermittently*. (These are called schedules of *reinforcement*, but the same principles apply with punishment.)

Intuitively, we would think that continuous schedules would be more effective. Although this tends to be true during the initial learning (acquisition) of a response—presumably because continuous reinforcement makes the connection between the behavior and its consequence clear and predictable—partial reinforcement is usually superior for maintaining learned behavior. For example, suppose you have a relatively new car, and every time you turn the key, the engine starts. If, however, one day you try to start the car 10 times and the engine will not turn over, you will probably give up and call a towing company. Now suppose, instead, that you are the proud owner of a rusted-out 1972 Chevy and are accustomed to 10 turns before the car finally cranks up. In this case, you may try 20 or 30 times before enlisting help. Thus, behaviors maintained under partial schedules are usually more resistant to extinction (Rescorla, 1999).

Intermittent reinforcement schedules may be either ratio schedules or interval schedules (Ferster & Skinner, 1957; Skinner, 1938). In **ratio schedules**, *payoffs are tied to the number of responses emitted*; only a fraction of "correct" behaviors receive reinforcement, such as one out of every five. In **interval schedules**, *rewards (or punishments) are delivered only after some interval of time, no matter how many responses the organism emits*. Figure 5.10 illustrates the four reinforcement schedules we will now describe: fixed ratio, variable ratio, fixed interval, and variable interval.

Fixed-Ratio Schedules   In a **fixed-ratio (FR) schedule** *an organism receives reinforcement for a fixed proportion of the responses it emits*. Piecework employment uses a fixed-ratio schedule of reinforcement: A worker receives payment for every bushel of apples picked (an FR-1 schedule) or for every 10 scarves woven (an FR-10 schedule). Workers weave the first 9 scarves without reinforcement; the payoff occurs when the 10th scarf is completed. As shown in Figure 5.10, FR schedules are characterized by rapid responding, with a brief pause after each reinforcement.

Variable-Ratio Schedules In **variable-ratio (VR) schedules**, *an animal receives a reward for some percentage of responses, but the number of responses required before reinforcement is unpredictable* (i.e., variable). Variable-ratio schedules specify an *average* number of responses that will be rewarded. Thus, a pigeon on a VR-5 schedule may be rewarded on its 4th, 7th, 13th, and 20th responses, averaging one reward for every five responses. Variable-ratio schedules generally produce rapid, constant responding and are probably the most common in daily life (Figure 5.10).

Fixed-Interval Ratios In a **fixed-interval (FI) schedule**, *an animal receives reinforcement for its responses only after a fixed amount of time*. On an FI-10 schedule, a rat gets a food pellet whether it presses the bar 100 times or one time during that 10 minutes, just as long as it presses the bar at some point during each 10-minute interval. An animal on an FI schedule of reinforcement will ultimately learn to stop responding except toward the end of each interval, producing the scalloped cumulative response pattern shown in Figure 5.10. Fixed-interval schedules affect human performance in the same way. For example, workers whose boss comes by only at two o'clock are likely to relax the rest of the day. Schools rely heavily on FI schedules; as a result, some students procrastinate between exams and pull "all-nighters" when reinforcement (or punishment) is imminent.

Variable-Interval Schedules A **variable-interval (VI) schedule** *ties reinforcement to an interval of time, but unlike a fixed-interval schedule, the animal cannot predict how long that time interval will be*. Thus, a rat might receive reinforcement for bar pressing, but only at five, six, 20 and 40 minutes (a VI-10 schedule—a reinforcer that occurs, on average, every 10 minutes). In the classroom, pop quizzes make similar use of VI schedules. Variable-interval schedules are more effective than fixed-interval schedules in maintaining consistent performance. Random, unannounced governmental inspections of working conditions in a plant are much more effective in getting management to maintain safety standards than are inspections at fixed intervals.

Whichever type of reinforcement schedule is used, when the reward or the punishment is presented, it should be delivered as soon as possible after the performance of the behavior. If the time interval between the behavior and the reward or punishment is too great, too many other behaviors will have occurred, so that the human or animal will be uncertain as to which behavior they are being reinforced or punished for. This is one reason why telling a child "You just wait till your parents get home" when the child has misbehaved is not adaptive. The child continues to behave (even positively) in the interim before the parents return. If the parents subsequently punish the child, he or she may be confused as to which behavior is actually being punished.

Discriminative Stimuli In everyday life, then, rarely does a response receive continuous reinforcement. Making matters even *more* complicated for learners is that a single behavior can lead to different effects in different situations. Professors receive a paycheck for lecturing to their classes, but if they lecture new acquaintances at a cocktail party, the environmental consequences are not the same. Similarly, domestic cats learn that the dining room table is a great place to stretch out and relax—except when their owners are home.

In some situations, then, a connection might exist between a behavior and a consequence (called a response *contingency*, because the consequence is dependent, or *contingent*, on the behavior). In other situations, however, the contingencies might be

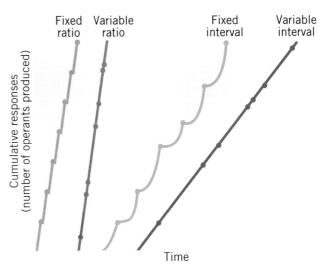

FIGURE 5.10 Schedules of reinforcement. An instrument called a cumulative response recorder graphs the total number of responses that a subject emits at any point in time. As the figure shows, different schedules of reinforcement produce different patterns of responding.

Apply & Discuss

▪ What kind of reinforcement schedule is involved in gambling, and why is it so effective?

different, so the organism needs to be able to discriminate circumstances under which different contingencies apply. *A stimulus that signals the presence of particular contingencies of reinforcement* is called a **discriminative stimulus (SD)**. In other words, an animal learns to produce certain actions only in the presence of the discriminative stimulus. For the professor, the classroom situation signals that lecturing behavior will be reinforced. For the cat on the dinner table, the presence of humans is a discriminative stimulus signaling punishment. For the rats in one study, reinforcement occurred if they turned clockwise when they were placed in one chamber but counterclockwise when placed in another (Richards et al., 1990).

Stimulus discrimination is one of the keys to the complexity and flexibility of human and animal behavior. Behavior therapists, who apply behaviorist principles to maladaptive behaviors (Chapter 16), use the concept of stimulus discrimination to help people recognize and alter some very subtle triggers for maladaptive responses, particularly in relationships (Kohlenberg & Tsai, 1994). For example, one couple was on the verge of divorce because the husband complained that his wife was too passive and indecisive, and the wife complained that her husband was too rigid and controlling. A careful behavioral analysis of their interactions suggested some complex contingencies controlling their behavior. At times, the woman would detect a particular "tone" in her husband's voice that she had associated with his getting angry; upon hearing this tone, she would "shut down" and become more passive and quiet. Her husband found this passivity infuriating and would then begin to push her for answers and decisions, which only intensified her "passivity" and his "controlling" behavior. She was not, in fact, always passive, and he was not always controlling. Easing the tension in the marriage thus required isolating the discriminative stimuli that controlled each of their responses.

INTERIM SUMMARY

In everyday life, **continuous reinforcement schedules** (in which the consequence is the same each time an animal emits a behavior) are far less common than **partial or intermittent reinforcement schedules** (in which reinforcement occurs in some ratio or after certain intervals). A **discriminative stimulus** signals that particular contingencies of reinforcement are in effect, so that the organism only produces the behavior in the presence of the discriminative stimulus.

Context   Thus far, we have treated operants as if they were isolated behaviors, produced one at a time in response to specific consequences. In fact, however, learning usually occurs in a broader context (see Herrnstein, 1970; Premack, 1965).

Costs and Benefits of Obtaining Reinforcement   In real life, reinforcement is not infinite, and attaining one reinforcer may affect both its future availability and the availability of other reinforcers. Researchers studying the way animals forage in their natural habitats note that reinforcement schedules change because of the animal's own behavior: By continually eating fruit from one tree, an animal may deplete the supply, so that it must retain the remaining fruit with more work (Stephens & Krebs, 1986).

Psychologists have simulated this phenomenon by changing contingencies of reinforcement based on the number of times rats feed from the same "patch" in the laboratory (Collier et al., 1998; Shettleworth, 1988). Thus, a rat may find that the more it presses one lever, the smaller the reward it receives at that lever but not at another. Researchers using this kind of experimental procedure have found that rats make "choices" about how long to stay at a patch depending on variables such as its current rate of reinforcement, the average rate of reinforcement they could obtain elsewhere, and the amount of time required to get to a new "patch." Rats, it turns out, are good economists.

Apply & Discuss

Whether in relationships with close friends or significant others, people engage in a number of aversive behaviors with one another. They complain, tease, induce guilt, spread rumors, intentionally embarrass, and the list goes on and on. How are such behaviors learned and why do people continue to engage in such behaviors in their relationships even though they know the consequences may be aversive?

Obtaining one reinforcer may also adversely affect the chances of obtaining another. An omnivorous animal merrily snacking on some foliage must somehow weigh the benefits of its current refreshments against the cost of pursuing a source of protein it notices scampering nearby. Similarly, a person at a restaurant must choose which of many potential reinforcers to pursue, knowing that each has a cost and that eating one precludes eating the others.

The cost–benefit analysis involved in operant behavior has led to an approach called *behavioral economics*, which weds aspects of behavioral theory with economics (Bickel et al., 1995; Green & Freed, 1993; Rachlin et al., 1976). For example, some reinforcers, such as two brands of soda, are relatively substitutable for each other, so that as the cost of one goes down, its consumption goes up and the consumption of the other decreases. Other reinforcers are complementary, such as bagels and cream cheese, so that if the cost of bagels skyrockets, consumption of cream cheese will decrease.

Psychologists have studied principles of behavioral economics in some ingenious ways in the laboratory using rats and other animals as subjects. For example, they put animals on a "budget" by only reinforcing them for a certain number of lever presses per day; thus, the animals had to "conserve" their lever presses to purchase the "goods" they preferred (Rachlin et al., 1976). Decreasing the "cost" of Tom Collins mix (by reducing the number of bar presses necessary to obtain it) led rats to shift their natural preference from root beer to Tom Collins—a finding the liquor industry would likely find heartening. In contrast, decreasing the cost of food relative to water had much less effect on consumption. In the language of economics, the demand for water is relatively "inelastic"; that is, it does not change much, regardless of the price.

Social and Cultural Context   We have spoken thus far as if reinforcement and punishment were unilateral techniques, in which one person (a trainer) conditions another person or animal (a learner). In fact, in human social interactions, each partner continuously uses operant conditioning techniques to mold the behavior of the other. When a child behaves in a way his parents find upsetting, the parents are likely to punish the child. But the parents' behavior is itself being conditioned: The operant of punishing the child will be *negatively reinforced* if it causes the child's bad behavior to cease. Thus, the child is negatively reinforcing the parents' use of punishment just as the parents are punishing the child's behavior! From this point of view, people reinforce and punish each other in nearly all their interactions (Homans, 1961).

The reliance on different operant procedures varies considerably cross-culturally. In part, this reflects the dangers that confront a society. The Gusii of Kenya, with a history of tribal warfare, face threats not only from outsiders but also from natural forces, including wild animals. Gusii parents tend to rely more on punishment and fear than on rewards in conditioning social behavior in their children. Caning, food deprivation, and withdrawing shelter and protection are common forms of punishment. One Gusii mother warned her child, "If you don't stop crying, I shall open the door and call a hyena to come and eat you!" (LeVine & LeVine, 1963, p. 166). Death from wild animals is a real fear, so this threat gains compliance from Gusii children. In Judeo-Christian cultures, parents have often instilled the "fear of God" in children to keep their behavior in line.

Characteristics of the Learner   An additional set of factors that increase the complexity of operant conditioning has to do less with the environment than with the learner. Environmental contingencies operate on an animal that already has behaviors in its repertoire, enduring ways of responding, and species-specific learning patterns.

Capitalizing on Past Behaviors: Shaping and Chaining   The range of behaviors humans and other animals can produce is made infinitely more complex by the fact that existing behaviors often serve as the raw material for novel ones. This occurs as the environment subtly refines them or links them together into sequences.

Big Picture φ Question 4

To what extent is human nature particular versus universal?

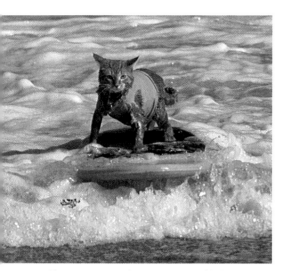

Shaping can introduce some unusual behaviors into an animal's repertoire.

A procedure used by animal trainers, called **shaping**, *produces novel behavior by reinforcing closer and closer approximations to the desired response*. The key is to begin by reinforcing a response the animal can readily produce. Skinner (1951) described a shaping procedure that can be used to teach a dog to touch its nose to a cupboard door handle. The first step is to bring a hungry dog (in behavioral terms, a dog that has been deprived of food for a certain number of hours) into the kitchen and immediately reward him with food any time he happens to face the cupboard; the dog will soon face the cupboard most of the time. The next step is to reward the dog whenever it moves toward the cupboard, then to reward it when it moves its head so that its nose comes closer to the cupboard, and finally to reward the dog only for touching its nose to the cupboard handle. This shaping procedure should take no more than five minutes, even for a beginner.

With humans, shaping occurs in all kinds of teaching. Through an applied behavioral analysis program, psychologists have used shaping with considerable success in helping autistic children (who tend to be socially unresponsive and uncommunicative and seem to "live in their own worlds") speak and act in more socially appropriate ways (Lovaas, 1977). The psychologist begins by initially rewarding the child for *any* audible sounds. Over time, however, the reinforcement procedure is refined until the child receives reinforcement only for complex language and behavior. In one study, over 40 percent of autistic children achieved normal scores on IQ tests following this shaping procedure, in comparison to 2 percent of children in a control group (Lovaas, 1987).

Shaping can allow psychologists to condition responses that most people would never think of as "behaviors." In **biofeedback**, *psychologists feed information back to patients about their biological processes, allowing them to gain operant control over autonomic responses* such as heart rate, body temperature, and blood pressure. As patients monitor their physiological processes on an electronic device or computer screen, they receive reinforcement for changes such as decreased muscle tension or heart rate.

Biofeedback can help patients reduce or sometimes eliminate problems such as high blood pressure, headaches, and chronic pain (Arena & Blanchard, 1996; Gauthier et al., 1996; Nakao et al., 1997). For example, patients treated for chronic back pain with biofeedback in one study showed substantial improvement compared to control subjects, and they maintained these benefits at follow-up over two years later (Flor et al., 1986).

Whereas shaping leads to the progressive modification of a specific behavior to produce a new response, **chaining** involves *putting together a sequence of existing responses in a novel order*. A psychologist tells the story of his brother using a variant of chaining to get the cat to wake him up every morning. For several weeks, the brother awakened at four o'clock in the morning and, while everyone else slept soundly, trained the family cat to wake his brother by licking his face. This trick does not come naturally to most felines and required several steps to accomplish. The cat already knew how to climb, jump, and lick, so the goal was to get the cat to perform these behaviors in a particular sequence. First, the "trainer" placed pieces of cat food on the stairs leading up to his brother's bedroom. After several trials, the cat learned to climb the stairs. To reinforce the operant of jumping onto the bed, the trainer again used a few judiciously placed bits of cat food. The same reward, placed gently in the proper location, was enough to train the cat to lick the brother's face. Once this occurred several times, the cat seemed to be reinforced simply by licking the brother's cheek. The same principles of chaining are used by animal trainers to get animals in circus acts or at Sea World, for example, to perform complex behaviors that rely on modifying a sequence of behaviors and linking them together.

Enduring Characteristics of the Learner   Not only do prior learning experiences influence operant conditioning, but so, too, do enduring characteristics of the learner. In humans as in other species, individuals differ in the ease with which they can be conditioned (Corr et al., 1995; Eysenck, 1990; Hooks et al., 1994). Individual rats vary, for example, in their tendency to behave aggressively or to respond with fear or avoidance in the face of aversive environmental events (e.g., Ramos et al., 1997). Rats can also be selectively bred for their ability to learn mazes (Innis, 1992; van der Staay & Blokland, 1996).

The role of the learner is especially clear in an experiment that attempted to teach three octopi (named Albert, Bertram, and Charles) to pull a lever in their saltwater tanks to obtain food (Dews, 1959). The usual shaping procedures worked successfully on Albert and Bertram, who were first rewarded for approaching the lever, then for touching it with a tentacle, and finally for tugging at it. With Charles, however, things were different. Instead of *pulling* the lever to obtain food, Charles tugged at it with such force that he broke it. Charles was generally a surly subject, spending much of his time "with eyes above the surface of the water, directing a jet of water at any individual who approached the tank" (p. 62).

Species-Specific Behavior and Preparedness Operant conditioning is influenced not only by characteristics of the individual but also by characteristics of the species. Just as some stimulus–response connections are easier to acquire in classical conditioning, certain behaviors are more readily learned by some species in operant conditioning—or may be emitted despite learning to the contrary. This species-specific behavior was vividly illustrated in the work of Keller and Marian Breland (1961), who worked with Skinner for a time. The Brelands went on to apply operant techniques in their own animal training business but initially with mixed success. In one case, they trained pigs to deposit wooden coins in a large "piggy bank" in order to obtain food. After several months, however, the pig would lose interest in the trick, preferring to drop the coin, root it along the way with his snout, toss it in the air, root it, drop it, root it, and so on. This pattern occurred with pig after pig. The pigs' rooting behavior eventually replaced the conditioned behavior of depositing coins in the bank so completely that the hungry pigs were not getting enough food (Young et al., 1994).

The Brelands had similar experiences with cats that stalked their food slots and raccoons that tried to wash the tokens they were to deposit in banks. All these operants were more closely related to instinctive, species-specific behaviors than the operants the Brelands were attempting to condition. Species-specific behavioral tendencies, like prepared learning in classical conditioning, make sense from an evolutionary perspective: Pigs' rooting behavior normally allows them to obtain food from the ground, and cats in the wild do not usually find their prey in bowls (Young et al, 1994).

INTERIM SUMMARY

Learning occurs in a broader context than one behavior at a time. Humans and other animals learn that attaining one reinforcer may affect attainment of others. Cultural factors also influence operant conditioning, as different cultures rely on different operant procedures. Characteristics of the learner influence operant conditioning, such as prior behaviors in the animal's repertoire, enduring characteristics of the learner (such as the tendency to respond with fear or avoidance in the face of aversive environmental events), and species-specific behavior (the tendency of particular species to produce particular responses).

Making Connections

Humans, like other animals, differ in their "conditionability." Many individuals with antisocial personality disorder, who show a striking disregard for society's standards, are relatively unresponsive to punishment. Their lack of anxiety when confronted with potential punishment renders them less likely to learn to control behaviors that other people learn to inhibit (Chapter 15).

Big Picture φ Question 4

To what extent is human nature particular versus universal?

Why Are Reinforcers Reinforcing?

One Step Further

Learning theorists aim to formulate general *laws of behavior* that link behaviors with events in the environment. Skinner and others who called themselves "radical behaviorists" were less interested in theorizing about the mechanisms that produced these laws, since these mechanisms could not be readily observed. Other theorists within and without behaviorism, however, have asked, "What makes a reinforcer reinforcing or a punisher punishing?" No answer has achieved widespread acceptance, but three are worth considering.

Reinforcers as Drive Reducers

One theory relies on the concept of **drive**, *a state that impels, or "drives," the organism to act*. Clark Hull (1943, 1952) used the term to refer to unpleasant tension states caused by deprivation of basic needs such as food and water. He proposed a **drive-reduction theory**, which *holds that stimuli that reduce drives are reinforcing*. This theory makes intuitive sense and explains why an animal that is not hungry will not typically work hard to receive food as reinforcement. However, the theory does not explain why behaviors related to basic needs may be learned even when drives are not currently activated. Lions can learn to hunt in packs, even when their stomachs are full (Smith, 1984). In fact, optimal learning does not typically occur under intense arousal.

Primary and Secondary Reinforcers

Drives help explain why some stimuli such as food, sex, and water are reinforcing. Hull and others called such stimuli **primary reinforcers** because they *innately reinforce behavior without any prior learning*. A **secondary reinforcer** is *an originally neutral stimulus that becomes reinforcing by being paired repeatedly with a primary reinforcer*. For example, children often hear phrases like "good girl!" while receiving other forms of reinforcement (such as hugs), so that the word "good" becomes a secondary reinforcer.

Most secondary reinforcers are culturally defined. Good grades, gold medals for athletic performance, thank-you notes, and cheering crowds are all examples of secondary reinforcers in many cultures. Children learn to associate coins and bills with many reinforcers in cultures that use money. In noncash economies, alternative forms of "currency" acquire secondary reinforcement value. In the Gusii community in Kenya, for example, cattle and other livestock are the primary form of economic exchange. Cattle, rather than cash, are thus associated with marriage, happiness, and social status (LeVine & LeVine, 1963), and the smell of the barnyard carries very different connotations than it does for most Westerners.

The Role of Feelings

Another explanation of reinforcement stresses the role of feelings. Consider the example of a student who cheats on a test and is lavishly praised for his performance by his unaware teacher. The more she praises him, the guiltier he feels. Paradoxically, the student may be *less* likely to cheat again following this apparent reinforcement. Why?

The explanation harkens back to Thorndike's law of effect: Feelings—including emotions such as sadness or joy as well as sensory experiences of pleasure or pain—provide a basis for operant conditioning (see Dollard & Miller, 1950; Mowrer, 1960; Wachtel, 1977; Westen, 1985, 1994). An operant that is followed by a pleasurable feeling will be reinforced, whereas one followed by unpleasant feelings will be less likely to recur. Thus, the teacher's praise—normally a positive reinforcer—is punishing because it evokes guilt, which in turn decreases the probability of future cheating. This third theory is incompatible with the goal of many behaviorists to avoid mentalistic explanations, but it fits with an intuitive understanding of operant conditioning: Positive reinforcement occurs because a consequence *feels good*, negative reinforcement occurs because termination of an unpleasant event *feels better*, and punishment occurs because a consequence *feels bad*.

Big Picture φ Question 2

What is the relationship between reason and desire or, more precisely, between cognition and affect?

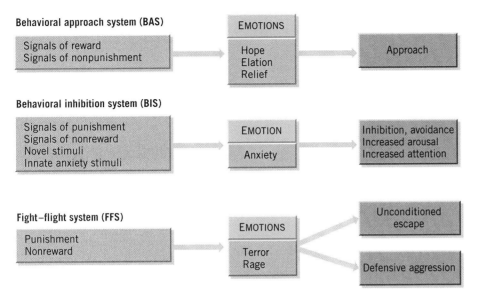

FIGURE 5.11   Gray's three behavioral systems. The behavioral approach system (BAS) orients the person (or animal) to stimuli associated with reward; approach is motivated by the positive emotions of hope, elation, and relief. The behavioral inhibition system (BIS) orients the person to avoidance and vigilance against threat. The BIS addresses potential dangers and involves anxiety. The fight–flight system (FFS) is a more evolutionarily primitive system that orients the person to escape currently punishing stimuli. It is associated with terror and rage. *Source:* Adapted from Gray, 1987, pp. 278–279.

Neuropsychological data support the proposition that feelings play a central role in operant conditioning. Gray (1987, 1990) has demonstrated the role of anatomically distinct pathways in the nervous system, each related to distinct emotional states that lead to approach and avoidance (Figure 5.11). **The behavioral approach system (BAS)** *is associated with pleasurable emotional states and is responsible for approach-oriented operant behavior.* This system appears to be primarily involved in positive reinforcement (Gomez & Gomez, 2002).

The **behavioral inhibition system (BIS)** *is associated with anxiety and is involved in negative reinforcement and punishment.* Dopamine is the primary neurotransmitter involved in transmitting information along BAS pathways (see also Schultz et al., 1997), whereas norepinephrine (known to be related to fear and anxiety) plays a more important role in the synapses involved in the BIS. Gray also describes a third, more evolutionarily primitive system, the **fight–flight system (FFS)** which *is associated with unconditioned escape (fleeing from something threatening) and defensive aggression and involves the emotions of rage and terror.* This system leads to species-specific responses such as the characteristic ways rats will crouch or freeze when threatened.

Evidence for these distinct pathways comes from numerous sources, such as experiments using EEG to measure electrical activity in the frontal lobes (Davidson, 1995; Sutton & Davidson, 1997). Left frontal activation tends to be more associated with pleasurable feelings and behavioral approach, whereas right frontal activation tends to be associated with unpleasant feelings and behavioral inhibition.

Psychodynamic conceptions have largely been aversive stimuli to learning theorists, but someday we may have an integrated account of learning that includes some psychodynamic concepts as well (Dollard & Miller, 1950; Wachtel, 1997). For example, one psychotherapy patient was unable to recall any events within a four-year period surrounding her parents' divorce. From a psychodynamic viewpoint, this likely reflects the patient's desire to avoid the unpleasant feelings associated with that period of his life. A conditioning explanation would similarly suggest that these memories are associated with emotions such as anxiety and sadness, so that recalling them elicits a conditioned emotional response. This CR is so unpleasant that it evokes avoidance or escape responses, one of which is to avoid retrieving or attending to the memories. If this mental "operant" reduces un-

Big Picture φ Question 1

To what extent can mental processes be reduced to the brain or body?

Apply and Discuss

Although research has shown that reinforcement and punishment can be effective in modifying behavior, their effects are not all good.

▪ What might be some of the costs associated with both reinforcement and punishment?

▪ Is it possible that reinforcing certain behaviors could actually reduce an individual's intrinsic interest in performing the behavior? Why or why not?

pleasant emotion, it will be negatively reinforced—strengthened by the removal of an aversive emotional state—and hence likely to be maintained or used again. Similar ideas have been proposed by leading behavioral researchers to account for "emotional avoidance" of unpleasant feelings (Hayes & Wilson, 1994).

Cognitive–Social Theory

By the 1960s, many researchers and theorists had begun to wonder whether a psychological science could be built strictly on observable behaviors without reference to thoughts. Most agreed that learning is the basis of much of human behavior, but some were not convinced that classical and operant conditioning could explain *everything* people do. From behaviorist learning principles thus emerged **cognitive–social theory** (sometimes called *cognitive–social learning* or *cognitive–behavioral theory*), which *incorporates concepts of conditioning but adds two new features: a focus on cognition and a focus on social learning*.

Learning and Cognition

According to cognitive–social theory, the way an animal *construes* the environment is as important to learning as actual environmental contingencies. That is, humans and other animals are always developing mental images of, and expectations about, the environment, and these cognitions influence their behavior.

Latent Learning　Some of the first research to question whether a science of behavior could completely dispense with thought was conducted by the behaviorist Edward Tolman. In a paper entitled "Cognitive Maps in Rats and Men," Tolman (1948) described learning that occurred when rats were placed in a maze without any reinforcement, similar to the kind of learning that occurs when people learn their way around a city while looking out the window of a bus. In one experiment, Tolman let rats wander through a maze in 10 trials on 10 consecutive days without any reinforcement (Tolman & Honzik, 1930). A control group spent the same amount of time in the maze, but these rats received food reinforcement on each trial.

The rats that were reinforced learned quite rapidly to travel to the end of the maze with few errors; not surprisingly, the behavior of the unreinforced rats was less predictable. On the 11th day, however, Tolman made food available for the first time to the previously unreinforced rats and recorded the number of errors they made. As Figure 5.12 shows, his findings were striking: These rats immediately took advantage of their familiarity with the maze and obtained food just as efficiently as the rats who had previously received reinforcement. A third group of rats who still received no reinforcement continued to wander aimlessly through the maze.

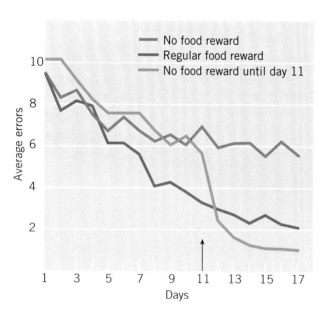

FIGURE 5.12　Latent learning. Rats that were not rewarded until the 11th trial immediately performed equally with rats that had been rewarded from the start. This suggests that they were learning the maze prior to reinforcement and were forming a cognitive map that allowed them to navigate it as soon as they received reinforcement. *Source:* Tolman & Honzik, 1930, p. 267.

To explain what had happened, Tolman suggested that the rats who were familiar with the maze had formed **cognitive maps**—*mental representations or images*—of the maze, even though they had received no reinforcement. Once the rats were reinforced, their learning became observable. Tolman called *learning that has occurred but is not currently manifest in behavior* **latent learning**. To cognitive–social theorists, latent learning is evidence that knowledge or beliefs about the environment are crucial to the way animals behave.

Conditioning and Cognition   Many learning phenomena have been reinterpreted from a cognitive perspective. For example, in classical fear conditioning, why does an organism respond to a previously neutral stimulus with a conditioned response? A cognitive explanation suggests that the presence of the CS alerts the animal to prepare for a UCS that is likely to follow. In other words, as suggested earlier, the CS *predicts* the presence of the UCS. If a CS does *not* routinely predict a UCS, it will not likely draw a CR. Thus, when a UCS (such as electric shock) frequently occurs in the absence of a CS (a tone), rats are unlikely to develop a conditioned fear response to the CS, regardless of the number of times the CS has been paired with the UCS (Rescorla, 1988; Rescorla & Holland, 1982; Rescorla & Wagner, 1972).

In cognitive language, rats will not become afraid of a stimulus unless it is highly predictive of an aversive event. Of course, rats are not *conscious* of these predictions; their nervous systems are making these predictions. In fact, this argument was offered by Pavlov himself, who described these predictions as "unconscious" (see excerpts of Pavlov, 1927). From a cognitive point of view, stimulus discrimination and generalization similarly reflect an animal's formation of a concept of what "counts" as a particular type of stimulus, which may be relatively general (any furry object) or relatively specific (a white rat).

Operant conditioning phenomena can also be reinterpreted from a cognitive framework. Consider the counterintuitive finding that intermittent reinforcement is more effective than continuous reinforcement in maintaining behavior. From a cognitive standpoint, exposure to an intermittent reinforcement schedule (such as that old car that starts after 5 or 10 turns of the ignition) produces the expectation that reinforcement will only come intermittently. As a result, lack of reinforcement over several trials does not signal a change in environmental contingencies. In contrast, when the owner of a new car suddenly finds the engine will not turn over, he has reason to stop trying after only three or four attempts because he has come to *expect* continuous reinforcement.

Insight in Animals   **Insight** is *the sudden understanding of the relation between a problem and a solution*. For most of the twentieth century, researchers debated whether animals other than humans have the capacity for insight or whether other animals must always learn associations slowly through operant and classical conditioning (Boysen & Himes, 1999; Kohler, 1925; Thorndike, 1911).

Research with a chimpanzee named Sheba suggests that insight may not be restricted to humans. In one study, Sheba was shown into a room with four pieces of furniture that varied in kind and color (Kuhlmeier et al., 1999). Upon leaving the room, Sheba was shown a small-scale model of the room that contained miniature versions of the furniture, each in its appropriate location. The experimenter then allowed Sheba to watch as a miniature soda can was hidden behind a miniature piece of furniture in the model. Upon returning to the full-sized room, Sheba went quickly to where the soda can had been in the model and retrieved the real soda that had been hidden there. Sheba had immediately formed the insight that changes in the model might reflect changes in the real room.

In another study, Sheba was shown a clear plastic tube with a piece of candy inside (Limongelli et al., 1995). The tube had holes at both ends as well as a hole in the middle of the tube on the bottom surface. Sheba was given a stick to poke the candy out of the tube, but if the candy passed over the hole in the middle, it fell into a box and could not be retrieved. The trick, then, was to put the stick in the end of the tube that was farther from the candy.

For the first several days, Sheba randomly put the stick in one side or the other. But on the eighth day, Sheba apparently had an insight, because from this point forward she solved the problem correctly 99 percent of the time. Her improvement was

Making Connections

Although much of the research on latent learning has been conducted with non-human animals, people demonstrate latent learning on a regular basis. Think of all of the things that a child can do as he or she grows that were actually learned through observation much earlier in life, things such as setting a table or finding their way around a city when they get their driver's license. (Chapter 14).

not gradual at all, as might be expected if it resulted from simple conditioning processes; rather, she went from poor performance to virtually perfect performance in an instant. As we will see, research using neuroimaging implicates the frontal lobes in this kind of "thoughtful" mental activity in both apes and humans (Chapters 6 and 7).

Expectancies Cognitive–social theory proposes that an individual's *expectations, or* **expectancies**, *about the consequences of a behavior are what render the behavior more or less likely to occur*. If a person expects a behavior to produce a reinforcing consequence, she is likely to perform it as long as she has the competence or skill to do so (Mischel, 1973).

Expectancies can create a **self-fulfilling prophecy**. In other words, *our expectations about the likelihood of particular outcomes lead us to engage in behavior that actually produces those outcomes*. Thus, if you predict that someone will be friendly, you will approach that individual in a manner that actually elicits the friendly behavior.

Julian Rotter (1954), one of the earliest cognitive–social theorists, distinguished expectancies that are specific to concrete situations ("If I ask this professor for an extension, he will refuse") from those that are more generalized ("You can't ask people for anything in life—they'll always turn you down"). Rotter was particularly interested in **generalized expectancies**—*expectancies that influence a broad spectrum of behavior*. He used the term **locus of control of reinforcement** (or simply *locus of control*) to refer to *the generalized expectancies people hold about whether or not their own behavior can bring about the outcomes they seek* (Rotter, 1954, 1990). *Individuals with an* **internal locus of control** *believe they are the masters of their own fate. People with an* **external locus of control** *believe their lives are determined by forces outside (external to) themselves*. Figure 5.13 shows items in Rotter's questionnaire for assessing locus of control. People who believe they control their own destiny are more likely to learn to do so, in part simply because they are more inclined to make the effort.

Cultural differences in locus of control have been observed with concomitant effects on health. One study examined death rates among over 28,000 Chinese-American individuals and over 412,000 white individuals (Phillips, et al., 1993). Chinese mythology suggests that certain birth years are more ill-fated than others, particularly if people born during those years contract particular illnesses, such as heart disease. Not surprisingly, then, people who endorse Chinese tradition (and, therefore, an external locus of control) would be expected to expect bad fortune more than those born in "good" years. In the comparison of the Chinese-Americans and whites, the researchers found that Chinese-Americans born during ill-fated years were significantly more likely to die at a younger age than white individuals born in the same year who had exactly the same illness. Importantly, participants in the two groups had been matched on all relevant variables. Furthermore, the more traditional-minded the Chinese-American individual, the sooner they died.

Learned Helplessness and Explanatory Style The powerful impact of expectancies on the behavior of nonhuman animals was dramatically demonstrated in a series of studies by Martin Seligman (1975). Seligman harnessed dogs so that they could not escape electric shocks. At first the dogs howled, whimpered, and tried to escape the shocks, but eventually they gave up; they would lie on the floor without struggle, showing physiological stress responses and behaviors resembling human depression. A day later Seligman placed the dogs in a shuttlebox from which they could easily escape the shocks. Unlike dogs in a control condition who had not been previously exposed to inescapable shocks, the dogs in the experimental condition made no effort to escape and generally failed to learn to do so even when they occasionally *did* escape. The dogs had come to expect that they could not get away; they had learned to be help-

Big Picture φ Question 2

What is the relationship between reason and desire or, more precisely, between cognition and affect?

I more strongly believe that

1. Promotions are earned through hard work and persistence.	**OR**	Making a lot of money is largely a matter of getting the right breaks.
2. In my experience I have noticed that there is usually a direct connection between how hard I study and the grades I get.	**OR**	Many times the reactions of teachers seem haphazard to me.
3. I am the master of my fate.	**OR**	A great deal that happens to me is probably a matter of chance.

FIGURE 5.13 Items from Rotter's locus-of-control questionnaire, called the Internal–External Scale. The scale presents subjects with a series of choices between two responses, one of which is internal and the other external. *Source:* Rotter, 1971.

less. **Learned helplessness** consists of *the expectancy that one cannot escape aversive events and the motivational and learning deficits that result from this belief*.

Seligman argued that learned helplessness is central to human depression as well. In humans, however, learned helplessness is not an automatic outcome of uncontrollable aversive events. Seligman and his colleagues observed that some people have a positive, active coping attitude in the face of failure or disappointment, whereas others become depressed and helpless (Peterson, 2000; Peterson & Seligman, 1984). They demonstrated in dozens of studies that **explanatory style**—*the way people make sense of bad events*—plays a crucial role in whether or not they become, and remain, depressed.

Individuals with a depressive or **pessimistic explanatory style** *blame themselves for the bad things that happen to them*. In the language of helplessness theory, pessimists believe the causes of their misfortune are *internal* rather than external, leading to lowered self-esteem. They also tend to see these causes as *stable* (unlikely to change) and *global* (broad, general, and widespread in their impact). When a person with a pessimistic style does poorly on a biology exam, he may blame it on his own stupidity—an explanation that is internal, stable, and global. Most people, in contrast, would offer themselves explanations that permit hope and encourage further effort, such as "I didn't study hard enough" or "The exam was ridiculous."

Whether optimists or pessimists are more *accurate* in these inferences is a matter of debate. Several studies suggest that pessimistic people are actually more accurate than optimists in recognizing when they lack control over outcomes. According to this view, people who maintain *positive illusions* about themselves and their ability to control their environment are less accurate but tend to be happier and report fewer psychological symptoms such as depression and anxiety (Taylor & Brown, 1988; Taylor et al., 2000).

Other researchers have challenged these findings, however, showing that people who deny their problems or substantially overestimate their positive qualities tend to be more poorly adjusted socially than people who see themselves as others see them (Colvin et al., 1995; Shedler et al., 1993). Optimism and positive illusions about the self are probably useful up to a point, because confidence can spur action. However, when optimism verges on denial of obvious realities, it is likely to be neither healthy nor useful.

Whether or not pessimists are accurate in their beliefs, they clearly pay a price for their explanatory style: Numerous studies document that pessimists have a higher incidence of depression and lower achievement in school than optimists (Bennett & Elliott, 2002; Isaacowitz & Seligman, 2001). As we will see (Chapter 11), pessimists are also more likely to become ill and to die earlier than people who find other ways of making meaning out of bad events.

Big Picture φ Question 3

To what extent is human psychology continuous with the psychology of other animals?

Making Connections

People's expectancies—about what they can and cannot accomplish, about societal barriers to their goals (e.g., prejudice), and so forth—influence all aspects of their lives, from how hard they work to whether they feel hopeful or depressed (Chapter 10, 12, and 15).

■ What kind of expectancies may motivate suicide bombers to deliberately kill themselves?

■ What about the terrorists in the planes that crashed into the World Trade Center towers and the Pentagon?

INTERIM SUMMARY

Cognitive–social theory incorporates concepts of conditioning from behaviorism but adds cognition and social learning. Many learning phenomena can be reinterpreted from a cognitive perspective. For example, intermittent reinforcement is more effective than continuous reinforcement because of the expectations, or **expectancies**, humans and other animals develop. In humans, **locus of control** (generalized beliefs about their ability to control what happens to them) and **explanatory style** (ways of making sense of bad events) play important roles in the way people behave and make sense of events.

Optimism, Pessimism, and Expectancies of Control in Cross-Cultural Perspective   A Global Vista

Expectancies arise within a social and cultural context. Cultural belief systems offer individuals ways of interpreting experience that influence their beliefs in what they can and cannot control as well as their reactions to unpleasant events. For example, in

Big Picture φ Question 4

To what extent is human nature particular versus universal?

Making Connections

■ To what extent does watching aggressive television shows make children more aggressive?

■ Do you think that watching aggression on television makes children behave aggressively or is it possible that aggressive children are more likely to watch violent shows?

■ How could a psychologist design a study to find out? What kind of practical and ethical obstacles might the psychologist face (Chapter 18)?

the United States, people from fundamentalist religious backgrounds (both Christian and Jewish) tend to have more optimistic explanatory styles than nonfundamentalists (Sethi & Seligman, 1993). They believe their fate is in God's hands, which can be extremely comforting in the face of illness or death.

People also share common experiences that lead to shared beliefs and expectancies. We often speak of "culture" as if it were a single variable. However, cultural beliefs and practices only influence individual thought and action through specific shared experiences (Sapir, 1949; Strauss & Quinn, 1997).

Studies comparing people from East and West Berlin before the fall of the Berlin Wall demonstrate the impact of social, political, and cultural factors on expectancies of control and optimism (Baltes & Staudinger, 2000; Oettingen & Seligman, 1990; Oettingen et al., 1994). Berliners shared a common culture until 1945, when the city was divided. Thereafter, West Berliners lived in an affluent, thriving country, in which individual initiative was rewarded through free enterprise. East Berliners, under Soviet domination, were much poorer and had fewer freedoms. Inefficient bureaucracies controlled many aspects of their daily lives, from the clothes that were available to the books they were allowed to read. These realities were reflected in a more pessimistic explanatory style and more external locus of control among East Berliners, patterns that could be observed as early as the school years.

Other studies document substantial cultural differences in expectancies. One study compared white American, Chinese-American, and mainland Chinese college students (Lee & Seligman, 1997). The mainland Chinese were much more pessimistic than white Americans; Chinese-Americans were intermediate between the other two groups. White Americans tended to attribute their successes to themselves and their failures to others. Although obviously biased, this self-serving way of interpreting events is probably useful for people who live in a technologically developed, capitalist society that emphasizes competition and achievement, because it keeps people going through the tough times. In contrast, mainland Chinese tended to attribute both positive and negative events to forces outside their control—a pattern much more common cross-culturally (Knowles et al., 2001).

These results likely reflect both recent Chinese history, with its emphasis on communal work and communal values, as well as long-standing cultural differences between China and the United States. For hundreds of years of Chinese history, people have lived with their families in densely populated agricultural areas. In such environments, as elsewhere in Asia, excessive pride and self-centeredness are considered disruptive and are discouraged. Attributing successes to one's personal characteristics is likely to be neither adaptive nor accurate, since much of labor in agricultural societies is communal, and families and villagers tend to share much of their fate. Chinese who immigrated to the United States appear to have begun to acquire more typically American patterns while retaining some of their cultural heritage in their explanatory style.

Social Learning

As this discussion suggests, learning does not occur in an interpersonal vacuum. Cognitive–social theory proposes that *individuals learn many things from the people around them, with or without reinforcement*, through **social learning** mechanisms other than classical and operant conditioning.

A major form of social learning is **observational learning**—*learning by observing the behavior of others*. The impact of observational learning in humans is enormous—from learning how to feel and act when someone tells an inappropriate joke, to learning what kind of clothes, haircuts, or foods are fashionable. Albert Bandura (1967), one of the major cognitive–social theorists, provides a tongue-in-cheek example of observational learning in the story of a lonesome farmer who bought a parrot to keep him company. The farmer spent many long hours trying to teach the parrot to repeat the phrase, "Say uncle," but to no avail. Even hitting the parrot with a stick whenever it failed to respond correctly had no effect. Finally, the farmer gave up; in disgust, he relegated the parrot to the chicken coop. Not long afterward, the farmer was walking by the chicken coop when he heard a terrible commotion. Looking in, he saw his parrot brandishing a stick at the chickens and yelling, "Say uncle! Say uncle!" The moral of the story is that the lesson intended in observational learning is not always the lesson learned.

Observational learning in which a person learns to reproduce behavior exhibited by a model is called **modeling** (Bandura, 1967). The most well-known modeling studies were done by Bandura and his colleagues (1961, 1963) on children's aggressive behavior. In these studies, children observed an adult model interacting with a large inflatable doll named Bobo. One group of children watched the model behave in a subdued manner, while other groups observed the model verbally and physically attack the doll in real life, on film, or in a cartoon. A control group observed no model at all. Children who observed the model acting aggressively displayed nearly twice as much aggressive behavior as those who watched the nonaggressive model or no model at all (Figure 5.14). The likelihood that a person will imitate a model depends on a number of factors, such as the model's prestige, likeability, and attractiveness.

Whether an individual actually *performs* modeled behavior also depends on the behavior's likely outcome. This outcome expectancy is, itself, often learned through an observational learning mechanism known as vicarious conditioning. In **vicarious conditioning**, *a person learns the consequences of an action by observing its consequences for someone else*. For example, adolescents' attitudes toward high-risk behaviors such as drinking and having unprotected sex are influenced by their perceptions of the consequences of their older siblings' risk-taking behavior (D'Amico & Fromme, 1997).

In a classic study of vicarious conditioning, Bandura and his colleagues (1963) had nursery school children observe an aggressive adult model named Rocky. Rocky took food and toys that belonged to someone named Johnny. In one condition, Johnny punished Rocky; in the other, Rocky packed all of Johnny's toys in a sack, singing, "Hi ho, hi ho, it's off to play I go" as the scene ended. Later, when placed in an analogous situation, the children who had seen Rocky punished displayed relatively little aggressive behavior. In contrast, those who had seen Rocky rewarded behaved much more aggressively. Because Rocky's aggressive behavior exemplified what the children had previously learned was bad behavior, however, even those who followed his lead displayed some ambivalence when they saw his behavior rewarded. One girl voiced strong disapproval of Rocky's behavior but then ended the experimental session by asking the researcher, "Do you have a sack?"

In Bandura's classic Bobo studies, children learned by observation.

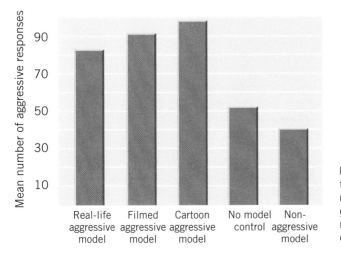

FIGURE 5.14 Social learning of aggressive behavior through modeling. This figure shows the average number of aggressive responses made by children after observing an adult model playing with an inflatable doll in each of five experimental conditions: real-life aggressive model, filmed aggressive model, cartoon aggressive model, no model control, and nonaggressive model. As can be seen, children tend to perform the behaviors of adult models. *Source:* Bandura, 1967, p. 45.

Apply and Discuss

Although clearly there are biological differences between boys and girls and men and women, many of the differences we observe between the sexes reflect learned behaviors.

■ How might the different perspectives on learning that you have read about in this chapter account for sex differences?

Another form of social learning is direct **tutelage**—*teaching concepts or procedures primarily through verbal explanation or instruction*. This is a central mechanism involved in formal education—and is (hopefully) occurring at this very moment. At times, conditioning processes, direct tutelage, and observational learning can influence behavior in contradictory ways. For example, most children receive the direct message that smoking is harmful to their health (tutelage). At the same time, they learn to associate smoking with positive images through advertising (classical conditioning) and may see high-status peers or parents smoking (modeling). In many cases, however, social learning processes, such as learning from a textbook (tutelage), work in tandem with conditioning processes. Most readers have been reinforced for completing reading assignments—and may also be reinforced by noticing that this chapter is just about over.

INTERIM SUMMARY

Social learning refers to learning that occurs through social interaction. **Observational learning** occurs as individuals learn by watching the behavior of others. Learning to reproduce behavior exhibited by a model is called **modeling. Vicarious conditioning** means learning by observing the consequences of a behavior for someone else. **Tutelage** occurs when people learn through direct instruction.

Summary

1. **Learning** refers to any enduring change in the way an organism responds based on its experience. Learning theories assume that experience shapes behavior, that learning is adaptive, and that uncovering laws of learning requires systematic experimentation.

Classical Conditioning

2. **Conditioning** is a type of learning studied by behaviorists. **Classical conditioning** refers to learning in which an environmental stimulus produces a response in an organism. An innate reflex is an **unconditioned reflex**. The stimulus that produces the response in an unconditioned reflex is called an **unconditioned stimulus**, or **UCS**. An **unconditioned response (UCR)** is a response that does not have to be learned. A **conditioned response (CR)** is a response that has been learned. A **conditioned stimulus (CS)** is a stimulus that, through learning, has come to evoke a conditioned response.

3. Once an organism has learned to produce a CR, it may respond to stimuli that resemble the CS with a similar response. This phenomenon is called **stimulus generalization. Stimulus discrimination** is the learned tendency to respond to a very restricted range of stimuli or to only the one used during training. **Extinction** in classical conditioning refers to the process by which a CR is weakened by presentation of the CS without the UCS; that is, the response is *extinguished*

4. Factors that influence classical conditioning include the **interstimulus interval** (the time between presentation of the CS and the UCS), the individual's learning history, and **prepared learning**.

5. Neuroscientists have begun to track down the neural processes involved in classical conditioning. Research on the marine snail *Aplysia* and on **long-term potentiation (LTP)** in more complex animals suggests that learning involves an increase in the strength of synaptic connections through changes in the presynaptic neuron (which more readily releases neurotransmitters), changes in the postsynaptic neuron (which becomes more excitable), and probably an increase in dendritic connections between the two.

Operant Conditioning

6. Thorndike's **law of effect** states that an animal's tendency to produce a behavior depends on that behavior's effect on the environment. Skinner elaborated this idea into the concept of **operant conditioning**—that is, learning to operate on the environment to produce a consequence. **Operants** are behaviors that are emitted rather than elicited by the environment. A consequence is said to lead to **reinforcement** if it increases the probability that a response will recur. A **reinforcer** is an environmental consequence that occurs after an organism has produced a response, which makes the response more likely to recur.

7. **Positive reinforcement** is the process whereby presentation of a stimulus (a reward or payoff) after a behavior makes the behavior more likely to occur again. A **positive reinforcer** is an environmental consequence that, when presented, strengthens the probability that a response will recur.

8. **Negative reinforcement** is the process whereby termination of an aversive stimulus (a negative reinforcer) makes a behavior

more likely to recur. **Negative reinforcers** are aversive or unpleasant stimuli that strengthen a behavior by their removal. Whereas the presentation of a positive reinforcer rewards a response, the removal of a negative reinforcer rewards a response.

9. Reinforcement always increases the probability that a response will recur. In contrast, **punishment** decreases the probability of a response, through either exposure to an aversive event following a behavior (positive punishment) or losing or failing to obtain reinforcement previously associated with behavior (negative punishment). Punishment is commonplace in human affairs but is frequently applied in ways that render it ineffective.

10. Extinction in operant conditioning occurs if enough conditioning trials pass in which the operant is not followed by its previously learned environmental consequence.

11. Four phenomena in particular help explain the power of operant conditioning: schedules of reinforcement, **discriminative stimuli** (stimuli that signal to an organism that particular contingencies of reinforcement are in effect), the behavioral context, and characteristics of the learner.

12. In a **continuous schedule of reinforcement**, the environmental consequence is the same each time an animal emits a behavior. In an **intermittent schedule of reinforcement**, reinforcement does not occur every time the organism emits a particular response. In a **fixed-ratio (FR) schedule of reinforcement**, an organism receives reinforcement at a fixed rate, according to the number of operant responses emitted. As in the fixed-ratio schedule, an animal on a **variable-ratio (VR) schedule** receives a reward for some percentage of responses, but the number of responses required before each reinforcement is unpredictable. In a **fixed-interval (FI) schedule**, an animal receives reinforcement for its responses only after a fixed amount of time. In a **variable-interval (VI) schedule**, the animal cannot predict how long that time interval will be.

13. The operant conditioning of a given behavior occurs in the context of other environmental contingencies (such as the impact of obtaining one reinforcer on the probability of obtaining another) and broader social and cultural processes. Characteristics of the learner also influence operant conditioning, such as prior behaviors in the animal's repertoire, enduring characteristics of the learner, and species-specific behavior.

14. Operant and classical conditioning share many common features, such as extinction, prepared learning, discrimination, generalization, and the possibility of maladaptive associations. Although operant conditioning usually applies to voluntary behavior, it can also be used in techniques such as **biofeedback** to alter autonomic responses, which are usually the domain of classical conditioning. In everyday life, operant and classical conditioning are often difficult to disentangle because most learned behavior involves both.

Cognitive–Social Theory

15. **Cognitive–social theory** incorporates concepts of conditioning from behaviorism but adds two additional features: a focus on cognition and on social learning. Tolman demonstrated that rats formed **cognitive maps** or mental images of their environment and that these were responsible for **latent learning**—learning that has occurred but is not currently manifest in behavior. Many classic learning phenomena have been reinterpreted from a cognitive perspective, including stimulus discrimination and generalization.

16. According to cognitive–social theory, the way an animal *construes* the environment is as important to learning as actual environmental contingencies. Cognitive–social theory proposes that expectations or **expectancies** of the consequences of behaviors are what render behaviors more or less likely to occur. **Locus of control** refers to the generalized expectancies people hold about whether or not their own behavior will bring about the outcomes they prefer. **Learned helplessness** involves the expectancy that one cannot escape aversive events and the motivational and learning deficits that accrue from it. **Explanatory style** refers to the way people make sense of bad events. Individuals with a depressive or **pessimistic explanatory style** see the causes of bad events as internal, stable, and global. Expectancies such as locus of control and explanatory style differ across cultures, since cultural belief systems offer people ready-made ways of interpreting events, and people who live in a society share common experiences (such as work and schooling) that lead to shared beliefs and expectancies.

17. Psychologists have studied several kinds of **social learning** (learning that takes place as a direct result of social interaction), including **observational learning** (learning by observing the behavior of others) and **tutelage** (direct instruction). Observational learning in which a human (or other animal) learns to reproduce behavior exhibited by a model is called **modeling**. In **vicarious conditioning**, a person learns the consequences of an action by observing its consequences for someone else.

Key Terms

Memory

*J*immie, healthy and handsome forty-nine-year-old, was a fine-looking man, with curly gray hair. He was cheerful, friendly, and warm.

"Hi, Doc!" he said. "Nice morning! Do I take this chair here?"

He was a genial soul, very ready to talk and to answer any question I asked him. He told me his name and birth date, and the name of the little town in Connecticut where he was born.... He recalled, and almost relived, his war days and service, the end of the war, and his thoughts for the future....

With recalling, Jimmie was full of animation; he did not seem to be speaking of the past but of the present.... A sudden, improbable suspicion seized me.

"What year is this, Mr. G.?" I asked, concealing my perplexity in a casual manner.

"Forty-five, man. What do you mean?" He went on, "We've won the war, FDR's dead, Truman's at the helm. There are great times ahead."

"And you, Jimmie, how old would you be?"

Oddly, uncertainly, he hesitated a moment as if engaged in calculation.

"Why, I guess I'm nineteen, Doc. I'll be twenty next birthday."

Sachs, 1970, pp. 21–23

Jimmie was decades behind the times: He was nearly 50 years old. His amnesia, or memory loss, resulted from Korsakoff's syndrome, a disorder related to chronic alcoholism in which subcortical structures involved in memory deteriorate. Jimmie had no difficulty recalling incidents from World War II, but he could not remember anything that had happened since 1945.

Curiously, though, amnesics like Jimmie are still able to form certain kinds of new memories (Knott & Marlsen-Wilson, 2001; Nadel et al., 2000; Schacter, 1995a; Squire & Zola-Morgan, 1991). If asked to recall a seven-digit phone number long enough to walk to another room and dial it, they have no difficulty doing so. A minute after completing the call, however, they will not remember having picked up the phone.

Or suppose Jimmie, who grew up before the days of computers, were to play a computer game every day for a week. Like most people, he would steadily improve at it, demonstrating that he was learning and remembering new skills. Yet each day he would likely greet the computer with, "Gee, what's this thing?"

Case studies of neurologically impaired patients and experimental studies of normal subjects have demonstrated that memory is not a single function that a person can have or lose. Rather, memory is composed of several systems. Just how many systems, and how independently they function, are questions at the heart of contemporary research.

The previous chapter was dominated by the behaviorist perspective; this one and the next focus primarily on the cognitive perspective. We begin by considering some of the basic features of memory and an evolving model of information processing that has guided research on memory for over three decades. We then explore the memory systems that allow people to store information temporarily and permanently, and examine why people sometimes forget and misremember. Along the way, we consider the implications of memory research for issues such as the accuracy of eyewitness testimony in court and the existence of repressed memories in victims of childhood sexual abuse.

Two questions form the backdrop of this chapter. The first is deceptively simple: What does it mean to remember? Is memory simply the recollection of "facts"? Or does memory extend to the activation (or reactivation) of goals, emotions, and behaviors—as when we effortlessly "remember" how to drive, even while deeply engrossed in conversation? Second, what is the relation between the kind of learning described in the last chapter, which emphasized behaviors and emotional responses, and memory?

Memory and Information Processing

Memory is so basic to human functioning that we take it for granted. Consider what was involved the last time you performed the seemingly simple task of remembering a friend's phone number. Did you bring to mind a visual image (a picture of the number), an auditory "image" (pronouncing a series of numbers out loud in your mind), or simply a pattern of motor movements as you punched the numbers on the phone? How did you bring to mind this particular number, given that you likely have a dozen other numbers stored in memory? Once a number was in your mind, how did you know it was the right one? And were you aware as you reached for the phone that you were remembering at that very moment how to use a phone, what phones do, how to lift an object smoothly to your face, how to push buttons, and who your friend is?

This example suggests how complex the simplest act of memory is. Memory involves taking something we have observed, such as a written phone number, and converting it into a form we can store, retrieve, and use. We begin by briefly considering the various ways the brain can preserve the past—the "raw material" of memory —and an evolving model of information processing that has guided psychologists' efforts to understand memory for the last quarter of a century.

Mental Representations

For a sound, image, or thought to return to mind when it is no longer present, it has to be represented in the mind—literally, *re*-presented, or presented again—this time without the original stimulus. As we saw in Chapter 4, *a mental representation* is a psychological version or mental model of a stimulus or category of stimuli. In neuropsychological terms, it is the patterned firing of a network of neurons that forms the neural "code" for an object or concept, such as "dog" or "sister."

Representational modes are like languages that permit conversation within the mind (see Jackendoff, 1996). The content of our thoughts and memories—a bird, an angry friend, a beautiful sunset—can be described or translated into many "languages"—images, sounds, words, and so forth—but some languages cannot capture

Making Connections

Although olfactory memory is less "accurate" than visual memory, it is far more emotionally charged. The smell of freshly cut grass can evoke powerful emotional memories from childhood. The scent of Chanel #5 may elicit recognition from grandmother, even in the last stages of Alzheimer's. Thus, smell (Chapter 4) and emotion (Chapter 10) are strongly linked by memory.

certain experiences the way others can. Fortunately, we are all "multilingual" and frequently process information simultaneously using multiple representational codes (Chapter 3).

Some kinds of representation are difficult to conceptualize and have received less attention from researchers. For example, people store memories of *actions*, such as how to press the buttons on a phone or how to squeeze the last drops of ketchup out of the bottle, which suggests the existence of *motoric representations*, or stored memories of muscle movements. The most commonly studied representations are sensory and verbal.

Sensory Representations   **Sensory representations** *store information in a sensory mode*, such as the sound of a dog barking or the image of a city skyline. The cognitive maps discovered in rats running mazes (Chapter 5) probably include visual representations. People rely on visual representations to recall where they left their keys last night or to catch a ball that is sailing toward them through the air. Visual representations are like pictures that can be mentally scrutinized or manipulated (Kosslyn, 1983).

The auditory mode is also important for encoding information (Thompson & Paivio, 1994). Some forms of auditory information are difficult to represent in any other mode. For instance, most readers would be able to retrieve a tune by Jewel or Celine Dion with little difficulty, but would have much more trouble describing the melody than "hearing" it in their minds.

Other types of sensory information have their own mental codes as well. People can identify many objects by smell, a finding that suggests that they are comparing current sensory experience with olfactory knowledge (Schab & Crowder, 1995). Olfactory representations in humans are, however, far less reliable than visual representations in identifying even common objects (de Wijk et al., 1995). For example, if exposed to the smell of a lemon, people often misidentify it as an orange, whereas people with an intact visual system rarely confuse the two fruits visually.

Verbal Representations   Although many representations are stored in sensory modes, much of the time people think using **verbal representations**, *information stored in words*. Try to imagine what "liberty" or "mental representation" means without thinking in words. Other experiences, in contrast, are virtually impossible to describe or remember verbally, such as the smell of bacon. In fact, using words to describe things about which one has little verbal knowledge can actually disrupt sensory-based memory.

Neuroimaging studies confirm that verbal representations are in fact distinct from sensory representations. Consider what happens when researchers present subjects with a string of X's versus a word (Menard et al., 1996). Both stimuli lead to activation of the visual cortex, since both are processed visually. Presentation of the word, however, leads to additional activation of a region at the juncture of the left occipital, parietal, and temporal lobes that appears to be involved in transforming the visual representation into a verbal or semantic one.

INTERIM SUMMARY

For information to come back to mind after it is no longer present, it has to be represented. **Sensory representations** store information in a sensory mode; **verbal representations** store information in words. People also store knowledge about actions as motoric representations.

Information Processing: An Evolving Model

Psychologists began studying memory in the late nineteenth century, although interest in memory waned under the influence of behaviorism until the "cognitive revolu-

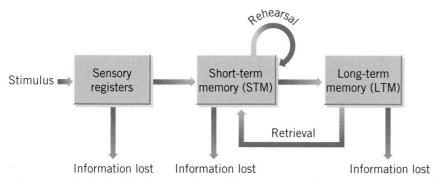

FIGURE 6.1 Standard model of memory. Stimulus information enters the sensory registers. Some information enters STM and is then passed on for storage in LTM. Information can be lost from any of the sensory stores, usually if it is not very important or if a traumatic event has occurred that interferes with memory consolidation or retrieval.

tion" of the 1960s. In 1890, William James proposed a distinction between two kinds of memory, which he called primary and secondary memory. *Primary memory* is immediate memory for information momentarily held in consciousness, such as a telephone number. *Secondary memory* is the vast store of information that is unconscious except when called back into primary memory, such as the 10 or 20 phone numbers a person could bring to mind if he wanted to call various friends, family members, stores, and so forth. James's distinction is embodied in what we will call the *standard model of memory*. This model has guided research on memory and cognition since the 1960s (Atkinson & Shiffrin, 1968; Healy & McNamara, 1996).

The standard model is predicated on the metaphor of the mind as a computer, which places information into different memory stores (the system's "hardware") and retrieves and transforms it using various programs ("software"). According to this model (Figure 6.1), memory consists of three stores: sensory registers, short-term memory (James's primary memory), and long-term memory (James's secondary memory). Storing and retrieving memories involve passing information from one store to the next and then retrieving the information from long-term memory.

Sensory Registers   Suppose you grab a handful of quarters (say, six or seven) from your pocket at the laundromat and, while looking away, stretch out your hand so that all of the coins are visible. If you then glance for a second at your hand but look away before counting the change, you are still likely to be able to report accurately the number of coins in your hand because the image is held momentarily in your visual sensory register. **Sensory registers** *hold information about a perceived stimulus for a fraction of a second after the stimulus disappears*, allowing a mental representation of it to remain in memory briefly for further processing (see Figure 6.2) (Sperling, 1960).

Most research has focused on visual and auditory sensory registration. The term **iconic storage** describes *momentary memory for visual information*. For a brief pe-

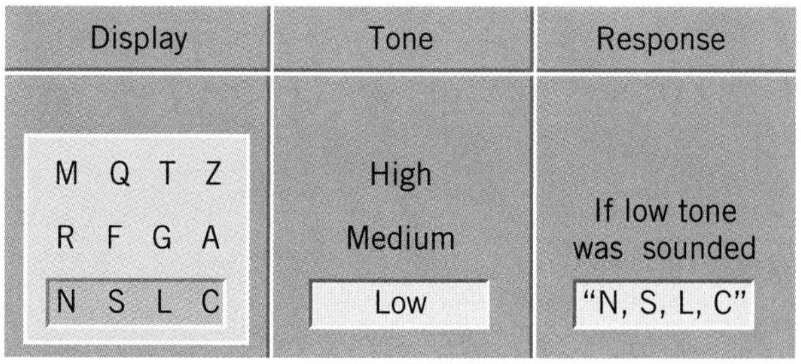

FIGURE 6.2 Visual sensory register. In a classic experiment, participants briefly viewed a grid of 12 letters and then heard a tone after a short delay. They had been instructed to report the top, middle, or low row, depending on whether a high, medium, or low tone sounded. If the tone sounded within half a second, they were 75 percent accurate, by reading off the image in their mind (iconic storage). If the tone sounded beyond that time, their accuracy dropped substantially because the visual image had faded from the sensory register. *Source:* Sperling, 1960.

Apply & Discuss

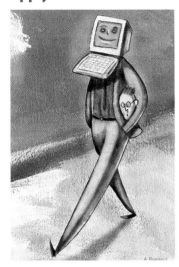

A Runzieri

▪ In what ways is the mind like a computer?

▪ In what ways does the computer metaphor fail to capture important aspects of human psychological functioning?

(a) **7 6 3 8 8 2 6**

(b) 7 6 3 8 8 2 6 (20 seconds later)

(c) **9 1 8** 8 8 2 6 (25 seconds later)

FIGURE 6.3 Short-term memory. In an experimental task, the subject is presented with a string of seven digits (a). Without rehearsal, 20 seconds later, the representations of the digits have begun to fade but are still likely to be retrievable. (b). At 25 seconds, however, the experimenter introduces three more digits, which "bump" the earliest of the still-fading digits (c).

riod after an image disappears from vision, people retain a mental image (or "icon") of what they have seen. This visual trace is remarkably accurate and contains considerably more information than people can report before it fades (Baddeley & Patterson, 1971). The duration of icons varies from approximately half a second to two seconds, depending on the individual, the content of the image, and the circumstances (Neisser, 1976a). The auditory counterpart of iconic storage is called **echoic storage**, *momentary memory for auditory information* (Battacchi et al., 1981; Neisser, 1967).

Short-Term Memory   According to the standard model, then, the first stage of memory is a brief sensory representation of a stimulus. Many stimuli that people perceive register for such a short time that they drop out of the memory system without further processing, as indicated in Figure 6.1 ("information lost"). Other stimuli make a greater impression. Information about them is passed on to **short-term memory (STM)**, *a memory store that holds a small amount of information in consciousness*—such as a phone number—*for roughly 20 to 30 seconds*, unless the person makes a deliberate effort to maintain it longer by repeating it over and over (Waugh & Norman, 1965).

Limited Capacity   Short-term memory has *limited capacity*—that is, it does not hold much information. To assess STM, psychologists often measure subjects' *digit span*, that is, how many numbers they can hold in mind at once. On the average, people can remember about seven pieces of information at a time, with a normal range of from five to nine items (Miller, 1956). That phone numbers in most countries are five to seven digits is no coincidence.

Hermann Ebbinghaus (1885) was the first to note the seven-item limit to STM. Ebbinghaus pioneered the study of memory using the most convenient and agreeable subject he could find—himself—with a method that involved inventing some 2300 nonsense syllables (such as *pir* and *vup*). Ebbinghaus randomly placed these syllables in lists of varying lengths and then attempted to memorize the lists; he used nonsense syllables rather than real words to try to control the possible influence of prior knowledge on memory. Ebbinghaus found that he could memorize up to seven syllables, but no more, in a single trial. The limits of STM seem to be neurologically based, as they are similar in other cultures, including those with very different languages (Yu et al., 1985).

Because of STM's limited capacity, psychologists often liken it to a lunch counter (Bower, 1975). If only seven stools are available at the counter, some customers will have to get up before new customers can be seated. Similarly, new information "bumps" previous information from consciousness. Figure 6.3 illustrates this bumping effect.

Rehearsal   Short-term memory is not, however, a completely passive process of getting bumped off a stool. People can control the information stored in STM. For example, after looking up a phone number, most people will *repeat the information over and over in their minds*—a procedure termed **rehearsal**—to prevent it from fading until they have dialed the number. This kind of *mental repetition in order to maintain information in STM* is called **maintenance rehearsal**.

Rehearsal is also important in transferring information to long-term memory, a finding that will not surprise anyone who has ever memorized a poem or a math formula by repeating it over and over. As we will see, however, maintenance rehearsal is not as useful for storing information in long-term memory as *actively thinking about the information while rehearsing*, a procedure known as **elaborative rehearsal**. Remembering the words to a poem, for example, is much easier if the person really understands what it is about, rather than just committing each word to memory by rote.

The standard model of memory is predicated on the metaphor of the mind as a computer. It distinguishes three memory stores: sensory memory (or sensory registers), short-term memory, and long-term memory. **Sensory registers** hold information about a perceived stimulus for a split second after the stimulus disappears. From the sensory registers, information is passed on to a limited-capacity **short-term memory (STM)**, which holds up to seven pieces of information in consciousness for roughly 20 to 30 seconds unless the person makes a deliberate effort to maintain it by repeating it over and over (**maintenance rehearsal**). **Elaborative rehearsal**, which involves actually thinking about the material while committing it to memory, is more useful for long-term than for short-term storage.

Long-Term Memory   Just as relatively unimportant information drops out of memory after brief sensory registration, the same is true after storage in STM. An infrequently called phone number is not worth cluttering up the memory banks. More important information, however, goes on to **long-term memory (LTM)**, in which *representations of facts, images, thoughts, feelings, skills, and experiences may reside for as long as a lifetime*. According to the standard model, the longer information remains in STM, the more likely it is to make a permanent impression in LTM. *Recovering information from LTM*, known as **retrieval**, involves bringing it back into STM (which is often used in information-processing models as a synonym for consciousness).

Why did researchers distinguish short-term from long-term memory? One reason was simple: Short-term memory is brief, limited in capacity, and quickly accessed, whereas LTM is enduring, virtually limitless, but more difficult to access (as anyone knows who has tried to recall a person's name or term on an exam without success).

Another reason emerged as psychologists tested memory using free-recall tasks. In *free-recall tasks*, the experimenter presents subjects with a list of words, one at a time, and then asks them to recall as many as possible. When the delay between presentation of the list and recall is short, participants demonstrate a phenomenon known as the **serial position effect**: *a tendency to remember information toward the beginning and end of a list rather than in the middle* (Figure 6.4).

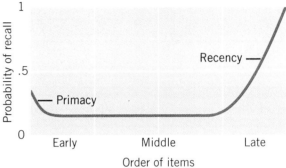

FIGURE 6.4   Serial position effect. Items earlier in a list and those at the end show a heightened probability of recall in comparison to those in the middle. *Source:* Atkinson & Shiffrin, 1968.

Evolution of the Model   Although the standard model provides a basic foundation for thinking about memory, in the last decade it has evolved in four major respects. First, the standard model is a *serial processing model*: It proposes a series of stages of memory storage and retrieval that occur one at a time *(serially)* in a particular order, with information passing from the sensory registers to STM to LTM. For information to get into LTM, it must first be represented in each of the prior two memory stores, and the longer it stays in STM, the more likely it is to receive permanent storage in LTM.

Subsequent research suggests that a serial processing model cannot provide a full account of memory. Most sensory information is never processed consciously (i.e., placed in STM), but it can nevertheless be stored and retrieved—an explanation for the familiar experience of finding oneself humming a tune that was playing in the background at a store without your ever having noticed consciously that it was playing.

Further, the process of selecting which sensory information to store in STM is actually influenced by LTM; that is, LTM is often activated *before* STM rather than after it. The function of STM is to hold important information in consciousness long enough to use it to solve problems and make decisions. But how do we know what information is important? The only way to decide which information to bring into STM is to compare incoming data with information stored in LTM that indicates its potential significance (Logie, 1996). Thus, LTM must actually be engaged *before* STM to figure out how to allocate conscious attention (Chapter 9).

Apply and Discuss

At times, we all have trouble remembering certain things, such as a phone number we wish to dial. But, what about remembering to remember? If I put a shirt in the dryer to dry for only 20 minutes, I need to remember in a short time to take the shirt out of the dryer.

■ What part of the memory system do you think is related to remembering to remember?

■ During the 20-minute interval that the shirt is drying, do most people constantly rehearse in their minds that they need to take the shirt out? Do they use external memory aids, such as a timer?

■ How successful are you at remembering to remember?

Big Picture φ Question 1

To what extent can mental processes be reduced to the brain or body?

A second major shift is that researchers have come to view memory as involving a set of **modules**—*discrete but interdependent processing units responsible for different kinds of remembering*. These modules operate simultaneously (i.e., *parallel*), rather than serially (one at a time) (Fodor, 1983; Rumelhart et al., 1986). This view fits with neuropsychological theories suggesting that the central nervous system consists of coordinated but autonomously functioning systems of neurons.

For instance, when people simultaneously hear thunder and see lightning, they identify the sound using auditory modules in the temporal cortex and identify the image as lightning using visual modules in the occipital and lower (inferior) temporal lobes (the "what" pathway), and pinpoint the location of the lightning using a visual–spatial processing module (the "where" pathway) that runs from the occipital lobes through the upper (superior) temporal and parietal lobes (Chapter 4). When they remember the episode, however, all three modules are activated at the same time, so they have no awareness that these memory systems have been operating in parallel.

Similarly, researchers have come to question whether STM is really a single memory store. As we will see shortly, experimental evidence suggests, instead, that STM is part of a *working memory* system that can briefly keep at least three different kinds of information in mind simultaneously so that the information is available for conscious problem solving (Baddeley, 1992, 1995).

Third, researchers once focused exclusively on conscious recollection of word lists, nonsense syllables, and similar types of information. Cognitive psychologists now recognize other forms of remembering that do not involve retrieval into consciousness. An amnesic like Jimmie (whose case opened this chapter) who learns a new skill, or a child who learns to tie a shoe, is storing new information in LTM. When this information is remembered, however, it is expressed directly in skilled behavior rather than retrieved into consciousness or STM. Further, researchers are now paying closer attention to the kinds of remembering that occur in everyday life, as when people remember emotionally significant events or try to remember to pick up several items at the grocery store on the way back home from work.

The fourth change is a shift in the metaphor underlying the model. Researchers in the 1960s were struck by the extraordinary developments in computer science that were just beginning to revolutionize technology, and they saw in the computer a powerful metaphor for the most impressive computing machine ever designed: the human mind. Today, after a decade of similarly extraordinary progress in unraveling the mysteries of the brain, cognitive scientists have turned to a different metaphor: mind as brain.

In the remainder of this chapter we will explore the major components of this evolving model. We begin with working memory (the current version of STM) and then examine the variety of memory processes and systems that constitute LTM.

INTERIM SUMMARY

In **long-term memory (LTM)**, representations of facts, images, thoughts, feelings, skills, and experiences may reside for as long as a lifetime. Recovering information from LTM, or **retrieval**, involves bringing it back into STM. The **serial position effect** is a tendency to remember information toward the beginning and end of a list rather than from the middle. Although the standard model still provides a foundation for thinking about memory, in the last decade it has evolved in four major ways. First, the assumption that a serial processing model can account for all of memory no longer seems likely. Second and related, researchers have come to view memory as involving a set of **modules**—discrete but interdependent processing units responsible for different kinds of remembering that operate simultaneously (in parallel) rather than sequentially (one at a time). Third, the standard model overemphasizes conscious memory for relatively neutral facts and underemphasizes other forms of remembering, such as skill learning and everyday remembering. Fourth, the underlying metaphor has changed, from *mind as computer to mind as brain*.

Working Memory

Because people use STM as a "workspace" to process new information and to call up relevant information from LTM, many psychologists now think of STM as a component of working memory. **Working memory** refers to *the temporary storage and processing of information that can be used to solve problems, to respond to environmental demands, or to achieve goals* (see Baddeley, 1992, 1995; Richardson, 1996a,b).

Working memory is *active* memory: Information remains in working memory only as long as the person is consciously processing, examining, or manipulating it. Like the older concept of STM, working memory includes both a temporary memory store and a set of strategies, or *control processes*, for mentally manipulating the information momentarily held in that store. These control processes can be as simple as repeating a phone number over and over until we have finished dialing it—or as complex as trying to solve an equation in our heads.

Researchers initially believed that these two components of working memory—temporary storage and mental control—competed for the limited space at the lunch counter. In this view, rehearsing information is an active process that itself uses up some of the limited capacity of STM. Researchers also tended to view STM as a single system that could hold a maximum of about seven pieces of information of *any* kind, whether numbers, words, or images.

More recent research suggests, instead, that working memory consists of multiple systems and that its storage and processing functions do not compete for limited space. According to one prominent model, working memory consists of three memory systems: a visual memory store, a verbal memory store, and a "central executive" that controls and manipulates the information these two short-term stores hold in mind (Baddeley, 1992, 1995). We begin by discussing the central executive and then examine the memory stores at its disposal.

Making Connections

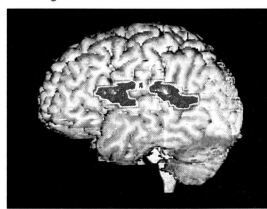

Psychologists once viewed memory as a warehouse for stored ideas. Today, however, many cognitive neuroscientists believe that memory involves the activation of a previously activated network to create a similar experience. Because the activated network is never identical to the original one, however, multiple opportunities for error exist (Chapter 7).

Processing Information in Working Memory: The Central Executive

In 1994, Alan Baddeley and Graham Hitch challenged the view of a single all-purpose working memory by presenting subjects with two tasks simultaneously, one involving recall of a series of digits and the other involving some kind of thinking, such as reasoning or comprehending the meaning of sentences. They reasoned that if working memory is a single system, trying to remember seven or eight digits would fill the memory store and eliminate any further capacity for thinking.

The investigators *did* find that performing STM and reasoning tasks simultaneously slowed down subjects' ability to think. In one study, holding a memory load of four to eight digits increased the time participants took to solve a reasoning task (Figure 6.5). However, a memory load of three items had no effect at all on reasoning speed, despite the fact that it should have consumed at least three of the "slots" in STM. Further, performing the two tasks simultaneously had no impact on the number of *errors* subjects made on the thinking task, suggesting that carrying out processes such as reasoning and rehearsal does not compete with storing digits for "workspace" in a short-term store.

These and other data led Baddeley and his colleagues to propose that storage capacity and processing capacity are two separate aspects of working memory. Processes such as rehearsal, reasoning, and making decisions about how to balance two tasks simultaneously are the work of a *central executive* system that has its own limited capacity, independent of the information it is storing or holding momentarily in mind. Other researchers have found that working memory as a whole does seem to have a limited capacity—people cannot do and remember too many things at the

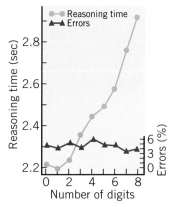

FIGURE 6.5 Speed and accuracy of reasoning as a function of number of digits to remember. Having to remember up to eight digits slowed the response time of participants as they tried to solve a reasoning task, but it did not lead to more errors. Keeping one to three digits in mind had minimal impact on reasoning time or speed. *Source:* Baddeley, 1995.

Apply & Discuss

Originally, researchers used the term *short-term memory* (which eventually became working memory) and *consciousness* as synonyms.

■ Are there aspects of consciousness that are not represented in working memory?

■ Is everything of which we are consciously aware held in working memory?

■ Are there aspects of working memory that are not conscious?

Big Picture φ Question 1

To what extent can mental processes be reduced to the brain or body?

same time—but working memory capacity varies across individuals and is related to their general intellectual ability (Chapter 8) (Daneman & Merikle, 1996; Just & Carpenter, 1992; Logie, 1996).

Visual and Verbal Storage

Most contemporary models of working memory distinguish between at least two kinds of temporary memory: a visual store and a verbal store (Baddeley, 1995; Baddeley et al., 1998). Evidence that these are indeed distinct components comes from several lines of research (Figure 6.6).

The visual store (also called the *visuospatial sketchpad*) is like a temporary image the person can hold in mind for 20 or 30 seconds. It momentarily stores visual information such as the location and nature of objects in the environment, so that, for example, a person turning around to grab a mug at the sink will remember where she placed a tea bag a moment before. Images in the visual store can be mentally rotated, moved around, or used to locate objects in space that have momentarily dropped out of sight.

The verbal (or *phonological*) store is the familiar short-term store studied using tasks such as digit span. Verbal working memory is relatively shallow: Words are stored in order, based primarily on their sound (*phonology*), not their meaning.

Researchers learned about the "shallowness" of verbal working memory by studying the kinds of words that interfere with each other in free-recall tasks (Baddeley, 1986). A list of similar-sounding words (such as *man, mat, cap,* and *map*) is more difficult to recall than a list of words that do not sound alike. Similarity of meaning (e.g., *large, big, huge, tall*) does not similarly interfere with verbal working memory, but it *does* interfere with LTM. These findings suggest that verbal working memory and LTM have somewhat different ways of storing information.

INTERIM SUMMARY

Many psychologists now refer to STM as **working memory**—the temporary storage and processing of information that can be used to solve problems, respond to environmental demands, or achieve goals. Working memory includes both a storage capacity and a processing capacity. According to the model proposed by Baddeley and his colleagues, processes such as rehearsal, reasoning, and making decisions about how to balance two tasks simultaneously are the work of a limited-capacity central executive system. Most contemporary models distinguish between at least two kinds of temporary memory—a visual store (the visuospatial sketchpad) and a verbal store.

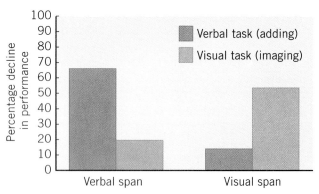

FIGURE 6.6   Independence of verbal and visual working memory storage. In one task, participants had to memorize briefly a sequence of letters ("verbal span"), whereas in another they had to remember the location of an extra gray block on a grid ("visual span"). At the same time, they either had to perform a verbal task (adding) or a visual one (imaging). As can be seen, the visual task interfered primarily with visual span, whereas the verbal task interfered primarily with verbal span. *Source:* Adapted from Logie, 1996.

The Neuropsychology of Working Memory

Recently researchers have begun tracking down the neuropsychology of working memory. The emerging consensus is that working memory is "orchestrated," or directed, by the *prefrontal cortex*, a region of the brain long known to be involved in the most high-level cognitive functions (Kane & Engle, 2002). When information is temporarily stored and manipulated, the prefrontal cortex is activated along with whichever posterior regions (i.e.,. regions toward the back of the brain) normally process the kind of information being held in memory, such as words or images (D'Esposito et al., 1997; Faw, 2003; Goldman-Rakic, 1996; Smith, 2000).

Activation of the prefrontal cortex seems to provide access to *consciousness* to representations normally processed in other parts of the cortex, so that the person can temporarily hold the information in mind and manipulate it. Evidence for the pivotal role of the prefrontal cortex began to accumulate when researchers designed working memory tasks for monkeys and observed the activity of neurons in this region (Fuster, 1989, 1997; Goldman-Rakic, 1995).

Similar studies have now been conducted with humans. In one study, the researchers used fMRI (functional magnetic resonance imaging) to study the activation of different cortical regions while participants tried to remember faces or scrambled faces (a meaningless visual stimulus) (Courtney et al., 1997). The results were striking (Figure 6.7). Relatively meaningless visual information activated posterior regions of the occipital lobes involved in the early stages of processing visual

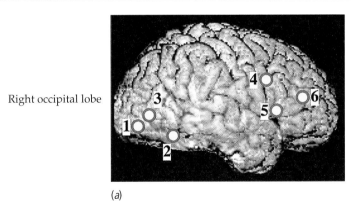

(a)

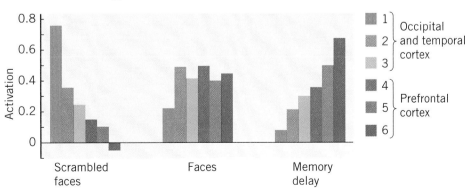

(b)

FIGURE 6.7   Working memory for faces and scrambled faces. Researchers used fMRI to study working memory for meaningful stimuli, in this case faces. The top part of the figure (a) shows the parts of the brain that were activated at different times by presentation of a meaningless stimulus (scrambled faces), a meaningful stimulus (faces), and the delay period in which participants had to hold images in working memory. As can be seen in (b), different regions of the brain showed distinct functions, with the prefrontal cortex involved in holding images in mind after they were no longer present. *Source:* Courtney et al., 1997.

stimuli. Facial stimuli activated areas of the visual cortex in the occipital and temporal lobes involved in processing and identifying meaningful visual stimuli (and perhaps faces in particular). Anterior regions of the frontal lobes, that is, the prefrontal cortex, were most active during the delay period in which the faces and scrambled faces were removed and had to be held in working memory.

Research also demonstrates the independence of different *components* of working memory. For example, neuroimaging studies confirm that verbal and visual working memory activate different cortical regions (Smith et al., 1996). Studies even document the existence of two distinct kinds of *visual* working memory, processed in different areas of the prefrontal cortex: memory for location and memory for objects (Courtney et al., 1998; Rao et al., 1997). This finding makes sense in light of research described in Chapter 4 that distinguishes between two visual pathways involved in perception, the "what" pathway (involved in identifying what objects are) and the "where" pathway (involved in identifying where they are in space). Researchers have even begun tracking down the anatomical location of the central executive.

Using fMRI, one team of researchers identified a region of the prefrontal cortex that may be involved in functions such as managing the demands of two simultaneous tasks (D'Esposito et al., 1997). The researchers presented subjects with two tasks that do not involve short-term storage, one verbal (making simple decisions about some words) and the other visual (mentally rotating images).

As expected, the verbal task activated the left temporal cortex, whereas the visual task activated the occipital and parietal cortex. Neither task alone activated the prefrontal cortex. However, when subjects had to complete both tasks at the same time, regions of the prefrontal cortex became active—a suggestion that prefrontal working memory circuits are indeed activated when people have to make "executive decisions" about how to manage the limited workspace in working memory (see also Adcock et al., 2000; Bunge et al., 2000).

The Relation between Working Memory and Long-Term Memory

What can we conclude from these various studies about working memory? First, consistent with the original concept of STM, working memory appears to be a system for temporarily storing and processing information, a way of holding information in mind long enough to use it. Second, working memory includes a number of limited-capacity component processes, including a central executive system, a verbal storage system, and at least one and probably two or three visual storage systems (one for location, one for identification of objects, and perhaps another that stores both simultaneously). Third, working memory is better conceived as a conscious workspace for accomplishing goals than as a way station or gateway to storage in LTM, because information can be stored in LTM without being represented in consciousness, and information in LTM is often accessed prior to its representation in working memory (Logie, 1996).

How Distinct Are Working Memory and Long-Term Memory?   Are working memory and LTM really distinct? In many ways, yes. As we have seen, working memory is rapidly accessed and severely limited in capacity. Imagine if our LTM allowed us to remember only seven pieces of verbal information, seven objects or faces, and seven locations!

Some of the strongest evidence for a distinction between working memory and LTM is neurological. Patients like Jimmie with severe amnesia can often store and manipulate information for momentary use with little trouble. They may be able, for example, to recall seven digits and keep them in mind by rehearsing them. The moment they stop rehearsing, however, they may forget that they were even trying to recall digits, an indication of a severe impairment in LTM. Researchers have also observed patients with the opposite problem: severe working memory deficits (such as a memory span of only two digits) but intact LTM (Caplan & Waters, 1990; Shallice & Warrington, 1970).

Interactions of Working Memory and Long-Term Memory   Working memory and LTM may be distinct, but much of the time they are so intertwined that they can be difficult to distinguish. For example, when people are asked to recall a sequence of words after a brief delay, their performance is better if the words are semantically related (such as *chicken* and *duck*), presumably because they recognize the link between them and can use the memory of one to cue the memory of the other from LTM (Wetherick, 1975). Similarly, words are more easily remembered than nonsense syllables (Hulme et al., 1991). These findings suggest that working memory involves the conscious activation of knowledge from LTM, since without accessing LTM, the person could not tell the difference between words and nonwords.

Indeed, from a neuroanatomical standpoint, working memory appears to become engaged when neural networks in the frontal lobes become activated along with (and linked to) networks in the occipital, temporal, and parietal lobes that represent various words or images. These mental representations of words or images themselves reflect an interaction between current sensory data and stored knowledge from LTM, such as matching a visual pattern with a stored image of a particular person's face. In this sense, working memory in part involves a special kind of activation of information stored in LTM (see Cowan, 1994; Ericsson & Kintsch, 1995).

Chunking   Perhaps the best example of the interaction between working memory and LTM in daily life is a strategy people use to expand the capacity of their working memory in particular situations (Erickson & Kintsch, 1995). We have noted that the brain holds a certain number of units of information in consciousness at a time. But what constitutes a unit? A letter? A word? Perhaps an entire sentence or idea?

Consider the working memory capacity of a skilled server in a restaurant. How can a person take the order of eight people without the aid of a notepad, armed only with a *mental* sketchpad and a limited-capacity verbal store? One way is to use **chunking**, *a memory technique that uses knowledge stored in LTM to group information in larger units than single words or digits*. Chunking is essential in everyday life, particularly in cultures that rely upon literacy, because people are constantly called upon to remember telephone numbers, written words, and lists.

Now consider the following sequence of letters: DJIBMNYSEWSJSEC. This string would be impossible for most people to hold in working memory, unless they are interested in business and recognize some meaningful chunks: DJ for Dow Jones, *IBM* for International Business Machines, *NYSE* for New York Stock Exchange, *WSJ* for *Wall Street Journal*, and *SEC* for Securities and Exchange Commission. In this example, chunking effectively reduces the number of pieces of information in working memory from 15 to 6, by putting two or three customers on each stool. People tend to use chunking most effectively in their areas of expertise, such as servers who know a menu "like the back of their hands." Similarly, knowledge of area codes allows people to store 10 or 11 digits at a time, since 202 (the area code for Washington, D.C.) or 212 (one of the area codes for Manhattan in New York City) can become a single chunk rather than three "slots" in verbal working memory.

Big Picture φ Question 1

To what extent can mental processes be reduced to the brain or body?

INTERIM SUMMARY

Working memory and LTM are distinct from one another in both their functions and neuroanatomy because patients with brain damage can show severe deficits on one but not the other. Working memory appears to occur as frontal lobe neural networks become activated along with and linked to networks in the occipital, temporal, and parietal lobes that represent various words or images. Working memory clearly interacts with LTM systems, as occurs in **chunking**—using knowledge stored in LTM to group information in larger units than single words or digits and hence to expand working memory capacity in specific domains.

Varieties of Long-Term Memory

Most readers have had the experience of going into the refrigerator looking for a condiment such as ketchup. Our first pass at "remembering" where the ketchup is seems more like habit than memory—we automatically look in a particular place, such as the side door, where we have found it many times. If the bottle is not there, we typically employ one of two strategies. The first is to think about where we *usually* put it, drawing on our general knowledge about what we have done in the past—do we usually put it on the door or on the top shelf? The second is to try to remember a specific episode, namely the last time we used the ketchup.

This simple example reveals something not so simple: that LTM comes in multiple forms, such as automatic "habits," general knowledge, and memory for specific episodes. Researchers do not yet agree on precisely how many systems constitute LTM, but developments in neuroimaging over the last decade have made clear that the three different ways of finding the ketchup represent three very different kinds of memory, each with its own neuroanatomy. In this section, we explore some of the major types of LTM.

Declarative and Procedural Memory

In general, people store two kinds of information, declarative and procedural. **Declarative memory** refers to *memory for facts and events*, much of which can be stated or "declared" (Squire, 1986). **Procedural memory** refers to *"how to" knowledge of procedures or skills.*

When we think of memory, we usually mean declarative memory: knowledge of facts and events. Remembering that Abraham Lincoln was the 16th president of the United States, or calling up a happy memory from the past, requires access to declarative memory.

Declarative memory can be semantic or episodic (Tulving, 1972, 1987). **Semantic memory** refers to *general world knowledge or facts*, such as the knowledge that summers are hot in Katmandu or that NaCl is the chemical formula for table salt (Tulving, 1972). The term is somewhat misleading because *semantic* implies that general knowledge is stored in words, whereas people know many things about objects, such as their color or smell, that are encoded as sensory representations. For this reason, many psychologists now refer to *semantic memory* as **generic memory**.

Episodic memory consists of *memories of particular events*, rather than general knowledge. Episodic memory allows people to travel mentally through time, to remember thoughts and feelings (or in memory experiments, word lists) from the recent or distant past, or to imagine the future (Wheeler et al., 1997).

In everyday life, episodic memory is often *autobiographical*, as when people remember what they did on their 18th birthday or what they ate yesterday (see Howe, 2000). It is also closely linked to semantic memory, since when people experience similar episodes over time (such as 180 days a year in school or hundreds of thousands of interactions with their father), they gradually develop generic memories of what those situations were like (e.g., "I used to love weekends with my father").

Declarative memory is the most obvious kind of memory, but another kind of memory is equally important in daily life: **procedural memory**, also referred to as *skill* or **habit memory**. People are often astonished to find that even though they have not skated for 20 years, the skills are reactivated easily, almost as if their use had never been interrupted. When people put a backspin on a tennis ball, speak grammatically, or drive a car, they are drawing on procedural memory. Other procedural skills are less obvious, such as reading, which involves a set of complex procedures for decoding strings of letters and words.

Although procedural memories often form without conscious effort (as in conditioning procedures with rats, who presumably do not carefully think out their next move in a maze), at other times, procedural memories are "residues" of prior conscious knowledge and strategies, which have become automatic and highly efficient. For example, when we first learn to type, we study the layout of the keyboard, trying to form declarative memories. As we are typing our first words, we also hold in working memory the sequence of keys to hit and knowledge about which fingers to use for each key. Over time, however, our speed and accuracy improve, while conscious effort diminishes. This process reflects the formation of procedural memory for typing. In the end, we think only of the words we want to type and would have difficulty describing the layout of the keyboard (declarative memory), even though our fingers "remember." As we will see, this shift from conscious, effortful memory to automatic procedural memory occurs as regions of the cortex "pass the torch" of memory to subcortical regions in the basal ganglia.

Explicit and Implicit Memory

For much of the last century psychologists studied memory by asking subjects to memorize word lists, nonsense syllables, or connections between pairs of words and then asking them to recall them. These tasks all tap **explicit memory**, or *conscious recollection*. Recently, however, psychologists have recognized another kind of memory: implicit memory (Graf & Schacter, 1987; Roediger, 1990; Schacter & Buckner, 1998). **Implicit memory** refers to *memory that is expressed in behavior but does not require conscious recollection*, such as tying a shoe.

Some psychologists use explicit and implicit memory as synonyms for declarative and procedural memory. Although there is clearly some overlap, the declarative–procedural dichotomy refers more to the *type of knowledge* that is stored (facts versus skills), whereas the explicit–implicit distinction refers more to the *way this knowledge is retrieved and expressed* (with or without conscious awareness). As we will see, people's knowledge of facts (declarative knowledge) is often expressed without awareness (implicitly). Figure 6.8 provides a model of the different dimensions of LTM.

Big Picture φ Question 7

To what extent are psychological processes conscious or unconscious—explicit versus implicit?

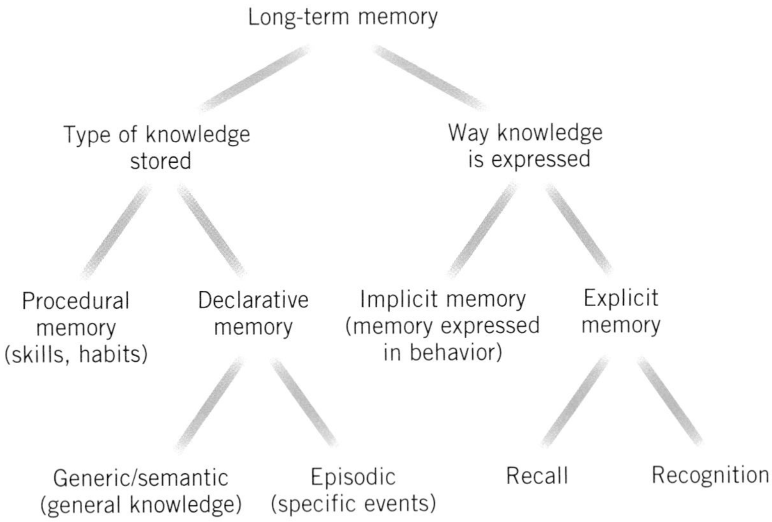

FIGURE 6.8 Key distinctions in long-term memory.

Making Connections

THE MAN ON THE LEFT IS 75 TIMES MORE LIKELY TO BE STOPPED BY THE POLICE WHILE DRIVING THAN THE MAN ON THE RIGHT.

It happens every day on America's highways. Police stop drivers based on their skin color rather than for the way they are driving. For example, in Florida 80% of those stopped and searched were black and Hispanic, while they constituted only 5% of all drivers. These humiliating and illegal searches are violations of the Constitution and must be fought. Help us defend your rights. Support the ACLU.

american civil liberties union
125 Broad Street, 18th Floor, NY, NY 10004 www.aclu.org

Researchers have recently learned that the distinction between explicit and implicit processes applies to virtually all areas of psychological functioning. For example, a person may hold explicitly neutral or positive attitudes toward ethnic minority groups while implicitly behaving in ways suggesting prejudice, such as giving stiffer jail sentences to blacks convicted of crimes (Chapter 17).

An expert guitarist like Eric Clapton can improvise much faster than he can consciously choose the notes he is going to play.

Explicit Memory   Explicit memory involves the conscious retrieval of information. Researchers distinguish between two kinds of explicit retrieval: recall and recognition. **Recall** is *the spontaneous conscious recollection of information from LTM*, as when a person brings to mind memories of her wedding day or the name of the capital of Egypt. Neuroimaging studies show that recall activates parts of the brain that are also activated during working memory tasks involving the central executive (Nolde et al., 1998). This makes sense given that recall requires conscious effort.

Although recall occurs spontaneously, it generally requires effortful use of strategies for calling the desired information to mind. When efforts at recall fail, people sometimes experience the **tip-of-the-tongue phenomenon**, in which *the person knows the information is "in there" but is not quite able to retrieve it* (Brown & McNeill, 1966). Recent research suggests that this phenomenon stems from problems linking the sounds of words (which are arbitrary—a *table* could just as easily have been called a *blah*) with their meanings (Merriman et al., 2000). Thus, using the word "prognosticate" in a conversation with someone who has the word "pontificate" on the tip of his tongue can lead to sudden recall (and a feeling of relief!).

Recognition refers to *the explicit sense or recollection that something currently perceived has been previously encountered or learned*. Researchers often test recognition memory by asking participants whether a word was on a list they saw the previous day. Recognition is easier than recall (as any student knows who has answered multiple-choice items that simply require recognition of names or concepts), because the person does not have to *generate* the information, just to make a judgment about it.

Implicit Memory   Implicit memory is evident in skills, conditioned learning, and associative memory (i.e., associations between one representation and another). It can be seen in skills such as turning the wheel in the correct direction when the car starts to skid in the snow (which skilled drivers in cold regions do before they have even formed the thought "I'm skidding") as well as in responses learned through classical and operant conditioning, such as avoiding a food that was once associated with nausea, whether or not the person has any explicit recollection of the event.

Implicit associative memory emerges in experiments on **priming effects**, in which *prior exposure to a stimulus (the prime) facilitates or inhibits the processing of new information*. Participants in memory experiments show priming effects even when they do not consciously remember being exposed to the prime (Bowers & Schacter, 1990; Tulving et al., 1982). For example, they might be exposed to a list of words that are relatively rarely used in everyday conversation, such as *assassin*. A week later, they may have no idea whether *assassin* was on the list (a test of explicit recognition memory), but if asked to fill in the missing letters of a word fragment such as *A–A–IN*, they are more likely to complete it with the word *assassin* than control subjects who studied a different list the week earlier. Priming effects appear to rely on activation of information stored in LTM, even though the person is unaware of what has been activated.

INTERIM SUMMARY

Types of LTM can be distinguished by kind of knowledge stored (facts versus skills) and the way this knowledge is retrieved and expressed (with or without conscious awareness). People store two kinds of information, declarative and procedural. **Declarative memory** refers to memory for facts and events; it can be **semantic** (general world knowledge or facts) or **episodic** (memories of particular events). **Procedural memory** refers to "how to" knowledge of procedures or skills. Knowledge can be retrieved explicitly or implicitly. **Explicit memory** refers to conscious recollection, whereas **implicit memory** refers to memory that is expressed in behavior. Researchers distinguish between two kinds of explicit retrieval: **recall** (the spontaneous retrieval of material from LTM) and **recognition** (memory for whether something currently perceived has been previously encountered or learned). Implicit memory is evident in skills, conditioned learning, and associative memory (associations between one representation and another).

The Neuropsychology of Long-Term Memory | From Brain to Behavior

How distinct are these varieties of long-term memories? Are researchers simply splitting hairs, or are they really "carving nature at its joints," making distinctions where distinctions truly exist?

Some of the most definitive data supporting distinctions among different types of memory are neuroanatomical studies, including case studies of patients with neurological damage, brain imaging with normal and brain-damaged patients, and experimental studies with animals (Gabrieli, 1998; Gluck & Myers, 1997; Squire, 1992, 1995). Researchers discovered the distinction between implicit and explicit memory in part by observing amnesic patients who have trouble storing and retrieving new declarative information (such as their age or the name or face of their doctor) but show minimal impairment on implicit tasks (Schacter, 1995a). Consider the case of H. M., who had most of his *medial temporal lobes* (the region in the middle of the temporal lobes, including the hippocampus and amygdala) removed because of uncontrollable seizures (Figure 6.9). Following the operation, H. M. had one of the deepest, purest cases of amnesia ever recorded, leading to the conclusion that medial temporal structures play a central role in the *consolidation* (i.e., encoding and "solidification") of new explicit memories. Despite his inability to store new memories, however, H. M. was able to learn new procedural skills, such as writing words upside down. Each new time H. M. was asked to perform this task, his speed improved, but he had no recollection that he had ever performed it before.

Over the last decade, lesion research with monkeys and imaging research with humans have demonstrated that the hippocampus and adjacent regions of the cortex are central to the consolidation of explicit memories (Eichenbaum, 1997; McGaugh, 2000; Squire & Zola, 1991). In contrast, the fact that amnesics like H. M. often show normal skill learning and priming effects suggests that the hippocampus is not central to implicit memory.

In daily life, of course, implicit and explicit memory are often intertwined. For example, people learn through conditioning to fear and avoid stimuli that are painful, but they are also frequently aware of the connection between various stimuli or behaviors and their effects. Thus, a child might learn by touching a stove that doing so is punishing (conditioning) but also might be able explicitly to recall the connection between the two events: "If I touch the stove, I get an ouchie!"

Neurologically speaking, however, implicit and explicit memory rely on separate mechanisms (Bechara et al., 1995). For example, fear conditioning and avoidance learning require an intact amygdala. In a classical conditioning procedure in which a particular sound (the conditioned stimulus) is paired with an electric shock (the unconditioned stimulus), patients with an intact hippocampus but a damaged amygdala can explicitly state the connection between the CS and the UCS–that is, they consciously know that the tone is associated with shock. However, their nervous system shows no signs of autonomic arousal (e.g., increased heart rate) or behavioral expressions of fear when exposed to the CS. They *know* the connection but cannot *feel* it. In contrast, patients with an intact amygdala but a damaged hippocampus may have no conscious idea that the CS is associated with electric shock—in fact, they may have no recollection of ever having encountered the stimulus before—but nonetheless they show a conditioned fear response to it, including autonomic arousal (see Chapters 3 and 5).

Subsystems of Implicit and Explicit Memory

Implicit and explicit memory are themselves broad categories that include neurologically distinct phenomena. The two kinds of explicit memory, semantic and episodic, rely on

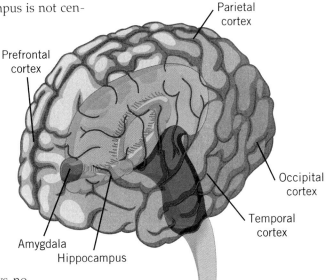

FIGURE 6.9 Anatomy of memory. The medial temporal region (inside the middle of the temporal lobes), particularly the hippocampus, plays a key role in consolidation of explicit, declarative information. The frontal lobes play a more important role in working memory, procedural memory, and aspects of episodic memory, such as dating memories for the time at which they occurred. Posterior regions of the cortex (occipital, parietal, and temporal cortex) are involved in memory just as they are in perception, by creating mental representations.

different neural mechanisms. Patients with damage to the frontal lobes have little trouble retrieving semantic knowledge but often show deficits in episodic memory (Shimamura, 1995; Wheeler et al., 1995, 1997). They may, for example, have trouble remembering the order of events in their lives (Swain et al., 1998), or they may vividly recall events that never occurred because they have difficulty distinguishing true from false memories of events (Schacter, 1997). PET studies show greater activation of prefrontal regions when recalling episodic rather than semantic information (Nyberg, 1998).

Implicit memory also likely comprises at least two systems. Patients with damage to the cortex caused by Alzheimer's disease may have normal procedural memory but impaired performance on priming tasks. In contrast, patients with Huntington's disease, a fatal, degenerative condition that affects the basal ganglia, show normal priming but impaired procedural learning (Butters et al., 1990).

Recent brain imaging data on normal subjects have provided insight into the way knowledge that at first requires considerable effort becomes procedural, as the brain essentially transfers the processing of the task from one network to another (see Poldrack et al., 1998). For example, after practice at reading words backward in a mirror, people show *decreased* activity in visual pathways but *increased* activity in verbal pathways in the left temporal lobe. This switch suggests that they are more rapidly moving from the visual task of mentally turning the word around to the linguistic task of understanding its meaning.

INTERIM SUMMARY

Implicit and explicit memory are neuroanatomically distinct. The hippocampus and adjacent regions of the cortex are centrally involved in consolidating explicit memories. Amnesics with hippocampal damage often show normal skill learning, conditioning, and priming effects, suggesting that the hippocampus is not central to implicit memory. Different kinds of explicit memory, notably episodic and semantic, also appear to constitute distinct memory systems. The same is true of two types of implicit memory, procedural and associative.

Everyday Memory

In designing studies, researchers have to strike a balance between the often conflicting goals of maximizing internal validity—creating a study whose methods are sound and rigorous and can lead to clear causal inferences—and external validity—making sure the results generalize to the real world (Chapter 2). Since Ebbinghaus's studies in the late nineteenth century, memory research has tended to emphasize internal validity, by measuring subjects' responses as they memorize words, nonsense syllables, and pairs of words, to try to learn about basic memory processes. Increasingly, however, researchers have begun to argue for the importance of studying **everyday memory** as well, that is, *memory as it occurs in daily life* (Ceci & Bronfenbrenner, 1991; Herrmann et al., 1996; Koriat et al., 2000; Rogoff & Lave, 1984).

In the laboratory, the experimenter usually supplies the information to be remembered, the reason to remember it (the experimenter asks the person to), and the occasion to remember it (immediately, a week later, etc.). Often the information to be remembered has little intrinsic meaning, such as isolated words on a list. In contrast, in daily life, people store and retrieve information because they need to for one reason or another, the information is usually meaningful and emotionally significant, and the context for retrieval is sometimes a future point in time that itself must be remembered, as when a person tries to remember to call a friend later in the day. Thus, researchers have begun to study everyday memory in its naturalistic setting—such as people's memory for appointments (Andrzejewski et al., 1991)—as well as to devise ways to bring it into the laboratory.

Everyday Memory Is Functional Memory   In their daily lives, people typically remember for a purpose, to achieve some goal (Anderson, 1996; Gruneberg et al., 1988). Memory, like all psychological processes, is *functional*. Of all the things we could commit to memory over the course of a day, we tend to remember those that bear on our needs and interests.

The functional nature of memory was demonstrated in a set of studies that examined whether men and women would have better recall for stereotypically masculine and feminine memory tasks (Herrmann et al., 1992). In one study, the investigators asked participants to remember a shopping list and a list of travel directions. As predicted, women's memory was better for the shopping list, whereas men had better memory for the directions.

Does this mean that women are born to shop and men to navigate? A second study suggested otherwise. This time, some participants received a "grocery list" to remember whereas others received a "hardware list." Additionally, some received directions on "how to make a shirt" whereas others received directions on "how to make a workbench." In reality, the grocery and hardware lists were identical, as were the two lists of "directions." For example, the shopping list included items such as *brush, oil, chips, nuts*, and *gum* that could just as easily be interpreted as goods at a grocery store as hardware items. The "directions" were so general that they could refer to almost anything (e.g., "First, you rearrange the pieces into different groups. Of course, one pile may be sufficient…").

As predicted, women were more likely to remember details about shirt making and grocery lists. The biases in recall for directions for men were particularly strong (Figure 6.10). Apparently, "real men" do not make shirts. These findings demonstrate the importance of noncognitive factors such as motivation and interest in everyday memory: What men define as not relevant, not interesting, or threatening to their masculinity does not make a lasting impression on their memory (Colley et al., 2002).

Recent research links some forms of everyday memory to the hippocampus. Researchers tested London taxi drivers' knowledge of the streets of their city. Drivers showed more activation in the hippocampus for a navigation task that required their expertise than for several other memory tasks (Maguire et al., 1997). In fact, the size of the activated regions of the hippocampus was strongly correlated with the number of years they had been driving, a suggestion that the brain devotes more "room" in the hippocampus for frequently used information, just as it does in the cortex (Maguire et al., 2000).

Prospective Memory   Most studies of memory have examined **retrospective memory**, that is, *memory for things from the past*, such as a list of words encountered 20 minutes earlier. In everyday life, an equally important kind of memory is **prospective memory**, or *memory for things that need to be done in the future*, such as picking up some items at the store after work (Brandimonte et al., 1996; Einstein & McDaniel, 1990; McDaniel et al., 1998; Smith, 2003). Prospective memory has at least two components: remembering *to* remember ("be sure to stop at the store after work") and remembering *what* to remember (e.g., a loaf of bread and a sponge). In other words, prospective memory requires memory of *intent* as well as *content* (Kvavilashvili, 1987; Marsh et al., 1998). Experimental studies suggest that intending to carry out certain acts in the future leads to their heightened activation in LTM (Goschke & Kuhl, 1993, 1996).

Although prospective memory is probably not itself a memory "system" with its own properties, it does have elements that distinguish it from other kinds of memory (see McDaniel, 1995). One is its heavy emphasis on time. Part of remembering an intention is remembering *when* to remember it such as at a specific time (e.g., right after work) or an interval of time (tonight, tomorrow, sometime over the next few days).

Another unique feature of remembered intentions is that the person has to remember whether they have been performed so they can be "shut off." This facet of prospective memory is more important with some tasks than with others. Inadver-

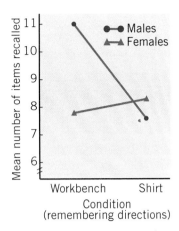

FIGURE 6.10   Gender and everyday memory. The figure shows men and women's memory, following a distracter task, for a list of directions that they thought were for making either a workbench or a shirt. Women recalled slightly more items when they thought they were remembering sewing instructions. Men's performance was dramatically different in the two conditions: Men were much more likely to remember the "manly" instructions for the workbench. *Source:* From Herrmann et al., 1992.

tently checking out the same video you already watched a month ago is clearly less harmful than taking medication you didn't remember taking an hour earlier.

INTERIM SUMMARY

Everyday memory refers to memory as it occurs in daily life. Everyday memory is functional, focused on remembering information that is meaningful. One kind of everyday memory is **prospective memory**, memory for things that need to be done in the future.

Encoding and Organization of Long-Term Memory

We have now completed our tour of the varieties of memory. But how does information find its way into LTM in the first place? And how is information organized in the mind so that it can be readily retrieved? In this section we explore these two questions. The focus is on the storage and organization of declarative knowledge, since it has received the most empirical attention.

Encoding

For information to be retrievable from memory, it must be **encoded**, or *cast into a representational form, or "code," that can be readily accessed*. The manner of encoding—how, how much, and when the person tries to learn new information—has a substantial influence on its *accessibility* (ease and ability of retrieval—i.e., how readily it can be *accessed*).

Levels of Processing   Anyone who has ever crammed for a test knows that rehearsal is important for storing information in LTM. As noted earlier, however, the simple, repetitive rehearsal that maintains information momentarily in working memory is not optimal for LTM. Usually, a more effective strategy is to attend to the *meaning* of the stimulus and form mental connections between it and previously stored information.

Some encoding is deliberate, such as studying for an exam, learning lines for a play, or trying to remember a joke. However, much of the time encoding simply occurs as a by-product of thought and perception—a reason why people can remember incidents that happened to them 10 years ago even though they were not trying to commit them to memory.

Deep and Shallow Processing   The degree to which information is elaborated, reflected upon, and processed in a meaningful way during memory storage is referred to as the *depth* or **level of processing** (Craik & Lockhart, 1972; Lockhart & Craik, 1990). Information may be processed at a shallow, structural level (focusing on physical characteristics of the stimulus); at a somewhat deeper, phonemic level (focusing on simple characteristics of the language used to describe it); or at the deepest, semantic level (focusing on the meaning of the stimulus).

For example, at a shallow, structural level, a person may walk by a restaurant and notice the typeface and colors of its sign. At a phonemic level, she may read the sign to herself and notice that it sounds Spanish. Processing material deeply, in contrast, means paying attention to its meaning or significance, noticing, for instance, that this is the restaurant a friend has been recommending for months.

Different levels of processing activate different neural circuits. As one might guess, encoding that occurs as people make judgments about the meaning of words (such as whether they are concrete or abstract) leads to greater activation of the left

Making Connections

As the philosopher of science Thomas Kuhn argued, a paradigm (or perspective in psychology) includes a set of propositions that constitute a model, an underlying metaphor, and a set of agreed-upon methods (Chapter 1). In the last few years, all of these have changed in cognitive psychology. We have moved from three sequential memory stores to multiple-memory systems operating in parallel; from a computer metaphor to a brain metaphor; and from a set of methods (such as memorizing word pairs) that tended to study memory divorced from meaning to more diverse methods, including those that can examine memory in its natural habitat—everyday life.

temporal cortex, which is involved in language comprehension, than if they attend to qualities of the printed words, such as whether they are in upper- or lowercase letters (Gabrieli et al., 1996). *Deliberate* use of strategies to remember (such as remembering to buy bread and bottled water by thinking of a prisoner who is fed only bread and water) activates regions of the prefrontal cortex involved in other executive functions such as manipulating information in working memory (Kapur et al., 1996). Recent research has even shown that the amount of activity in the prefrontal and temporal cortex predicts the extent to which subjects are likely to remember studied material successfully (Brewer et al., 1998; Wagner et al., 1998).

Encoding Specificity   Advocates of depth-of-processing theory originally thought that deeper processing is always better. Although this is *generally* true, subsequent research shows that the best encoding strategy depends on what the person later needs to retrieve (see Anderson, 1995). If a person is asked to recall shallow information (such as whether a word was originally presented in capital letters), shallow encoding tends to be more useful.

The fact that ***ease of retrieval depends on the match between the way information is encoded and later retrieved*** is known as the **encoding specificity principle** (Tulving & Thompson, 1973). For example, a student who studies for a multiple-choice test by memorizing definitions and details without trying to understand the underlying concepts may be in much more trouble if the professor decides to include an essay question, because the student has encoded the information at too shallow a level.

Why does the match between encoding and retrieval influence the ease with which people can access information from memory? According to several theorists, memory is not really a process distinct from perception and thought; rather, it is a by-product of the normal processes of perceiving and thinking, which automatically lay down traces of an experience as it is occurring. When people remember, they simply reactivate the same neural networks that processed the information in the first place (Crowder, 1993; Lockhart & Craik, 1990). If the circumstances at encoding and retrieval are similar, the memory is more easily retrieved because more of the neural network that represents it is activated. To put it another way, a new thought, feeling, or perception is like a hiker who has to create a new trail through the woods. Each time another traveler takes that path, that is, each time a similar event occurs, the trail becomes more defined and easier to locate.

Context and Retrieval   According to the encoding specificity principle, the *contexts* in which people encode and retrieve information can also affect the ease of retrieval. One study presented scuba divers with different lists of words, some while the divers were under water and others while they were above (Godden & Baddeley, 1975). The divers had better recall for lists they had encoded under water when they were under water at retrieval; conversely, lists encoded above water were better recalled above water. Another study of Russian immigrants to the United States found that they were more likely to remember events in their lives from Russia when interviewed in Russian, and more likely to remember events from their new lives in the United States when interviewed in English (Marian & Neisser, 2000). They retrieved few memories from the period shortly following their immigration, when they were "changing over" languages.

The same phenomenon appears to occur with people's *emotional state* at encoding and retrieval, a phenomenon called *state-dependent memory*: Being in a similar mood at encoding and retrieval (e.g., angry while learning a word list and angry while trying to remember it) can facilitate memory, as long as the emotional state is not so intense that it inhibits memory in general (see Bower, 1981; Keenly, 1997). Having the same context during encoding and retrieval facilitates recall because the context provides **retrieval cues**, ***stimuli or thoughts that can be used to facilitate recollection***.

Spacing   Another encoding variable that influences memory is of particular importance in educational settings: the interval between study sessions. Students intuitively

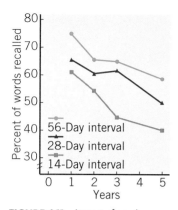

FIGURE 6.11 Impact of spacing on memory retention over five years. Longer intervals between rehearsal sessions for English–foreign language word pairs predicted higher long-term retention of the information one, two, three, and five years after the last training session. *Source:* Bahrick et al., 1993.

know that if they cram the night before a test, the information is likely to be available to them when they need it the next day. They also tend to believe that *massed* rehearsal (i.e., studying in one long session or several times over a short interval, such as a day) is more effective than *spaced,* or *distributed,* rehearsal over longer intervals (Zechmeister & Shaughnessy, 1980). But is this strategy really optimal for long-term retention of the information?

In fact, it is not (Bruce & Bahrick, 1992; Dempster, 1996; Ebbinghaus, 1885). Massed rehearsal *seems* superior because it makes initial acquisition of memory slightly easier, since the material is at a heightened state of activation in a massed practice session. Over the long run, however, research on the **spacing effect**—*the superiority of memory for information rehearsed over longer intervals*—demonstrates that spacing study sessions over longer intervals tends to double long-term retention of information.

In one study, the Bahrick family tested the long-term effects of spaced rehearsal on the study of 300 foreign language vocabulary words (Bahrick et al., 1993). The major finding was that, over a five-year period, 13 training sessions at intervals of 56 days apart increased memory retention rates compared to 26 sessions spaced at 14-day intervals (Figure 6.11). These results are robust across a variety of memory tasks, even including implicit memory (Perruchet, 1989; Toppino & Schneider, 1999).

These and related findings have important implications for students and teachers (Bruce & Bahrick, 1992; Rea & Modigliani, 1988). Students who want to remember information for more than a day or two after an exam should space their studying over time and avoid cramming. Medical students, law students, and others who intend to practice a profession based on their course work should be particularly wary of all-nighters.

Moreover, much as students might protest, cumulative exams over the course of a semester are superior to exams that test only the material that immediately preceded them. Cumulative exams require students to relearn material at long intervals, and the tests themselves constitute learning sessions in which memory is retrieved and reinforced. In fact, research on spacing is part of what led the authors of this text to include both interim summaries and a general summary at the end of each chapter, since learning occurs best with a combination of immediate review and spaced rehearsal.

Representational Modes and Encoding   The ability to retrieve information from LTM also depends on the modes used to encode it. In general, the more ways a memory can be encoded, the greater the likelihood that it will be accessible for later retrieval. Storing a memory in multiple representational modes—such as words, images, and sounds—provides more retrieval cues to bring it back to mind (see Paivio, 1991).

For instance, many people remember phone numbers not only by memorizing the digits but also by forming a mental map of the buttons they need to push and a motoric (procedural) representation of the pattern of buttons to push that becomes automatic and is expressed implicitly. When pushing the buttons, they may even be alerted that they have dialed the wrong number by hearing a sound pattern that does not match the expected pattern, suggesting auditory storage as well.

INTERIM SUMMARY

For information to be retrievable from memory, it must be **encoded**, or cast into a representational form that can be readily accessed from memory. The degree to which information is elaborated, reflected upon, and processed in a meaningful way during memory storage is referred to as the *depth* or **level of processing**. Although deeper processing tends to be more useful for storing information for the long term, ease of retrieval depends on the match between the way information is encoded and the way it is later retrieved, a phenomenon known as the **encoding specificity principle**. Similar contexts during encoding and retrieval provide **retrieval cues**—stimuli or thoughts that can be used to facilitate recollection. Aside from level of processing, two other variables influence accessibility of memory, the **spacing** of study sessions and the use of multiple representational modes.

Mnemonic Devices

The principles of encoding we have just been describing help explain the utility of many **mnemonic devices**—*systematic strategies for remembering information* (named after the Greek word *mneme*, which means "memory"). People can use external aids (such as note taking or asking someone else) to enhance their memory, or they can rely on internal aids, such as rehearsal and various mnemonic strategies (Harris, 1980). Most mnemonic devices draw on the principle that the more retrieval cues that can be created and the more vivid these cues are, the better memory is likely to be. Generally, mnemonic devices are most useful when the to-be-remembered information lacks clear organization.

Method of Loci One mnemonic strategy is the **method of loci**, which *uses visual imagery as a memory aid*. The ancient Roman writer Cicero attributed this technique to the Greek poet Simonides, who was attending a banquet when he was reportedly summoned by the gods from the banquet hall to receive a message. In his absence, the roof collapsed, killing everyone. The bodies were mangled beyond recognition, but Simonides was able to identify the guests by their physical placement around the banquet table. He thus realized that images could be remembered by fitting them into an orderly arrangement of locations (Bower, 1970).

To use the method of loci, you must first decide on a series of "snapshot" mental images of familiar locations. For instance, locations in your bedroom might be your pillow, your closet, the top of your dresser, and under the bed. Now, suppose that you need to do the following errands: pick up vitamin C, buy milk, return a book to the library, and make plans with one of your friends for the weekend. You can remember these items by visualizing each in one of your loci, making the image as vivid as possible to maximize the likelihood of retrieving it. Thus, you might picture the vitamin C pills as spilled all over your pillow, a bottle of milk poured over the best outfit in your closet, the book lying on top of your dresser, and your friend hiding under your bed until Friday night. Often, the more ridiculous the image, the easier it is to remember. While you are out doing your errands, you can mentally flip through your imagined loci to bring back the mental images.

SQ3R Method A strategy specifically developed to help students remember information in textbooks is called the **SQ3R method**, for *the five steps involved in the method: survey, question, read, recite, and review* (Martin, 1985; Robinson, 1961). The SQ3R method fosters active rather than passive learning while reading. In brief, the steps of this method are as follows:

- *Survey* Page through the chapter, looking at headings and the summary. This will help you organize the material more efficiently as you encode.
- *Question* When you begin a section, turn the heading into a question; this orients you to the content and makes reading more interesting. For example, for the subheading, "Long-Term Memory Systems," you might ask yourself, "What evidence could demonstrate the existence of separate memory systems? Could patients with different brain lesions have one kind of LTM intact and another disrupted?"
- *Read* As you read, try to answer the questions you posed.
- *Recite* Mentally (or orally) answer your questions and rehearse relevant information before going on to the next section.

Apply & Discuss

- What are the best ways to study material so that it "sinks in"?
- What forms of rehearsal and spacing are likely to lead to long-term retention of information?
- Are the same methods useful in procedural learning? What methods would be most useful in remembering a new tennis serve, or learning to type?

▪ *Review* When you finish the chapter, recall your questions and relate what you have learned to your experiences and interests.

INTERIM SUMMARY

Mnemonic devices are systematic strategies for remembering information. The **method of loci** associates new information with a visual image of a familiar place. The **SQ3R method** helps students study textbook material efficiently by encouraging them to survey, question, read, recite, and review.

Networks of Association

One of the reasons mnemonics can be effective is that they connect new information with information already organized in memory. This makes the new information easier to access because a "trail" blazed in the neural woods by prior knowledge can be more easily spotted than a new, barely worn path. As William James proposed over a century ago (1890, p. 662, italics deleted):

The more other facts a fact is associated with in the mind, the better possession of it our memory retains. Each of its associates becomes a hook to which it hangs, a means to fish it up by when sunk beneath the surface. Together, they form a network of attachments by which it is woven into the entire tissue of our thought. The "secret of a good memory" is thus the secret of forming diverse and multiple associations with every fact we care to retain.

James's comments bring us back once again to the concept of *association*, which, as we saw in Chapter 5, is central to many aspects of learning. Associations are crucial to remembering because the pieces of information stored in memory form **networks of association**, *clusters of interconnected information*. For example, for most people the word *dog* is associatively linked to characteristics such as barking and fetching (Figure 6.12). It is also associated, though less strongly, with *cat* because cats and dogs are both household pets. The word or image of a dog is also linked to more idiosyncratic personal associations, such as an episodic memory of being bitten by a dog in childhood.

Each piece of information along a network is called a **node**. Nodes may be thoughts, images, concepts, propositions, smells, tastes, memories, emotions, or any other piece of information. That one node may have connections to many other nodes

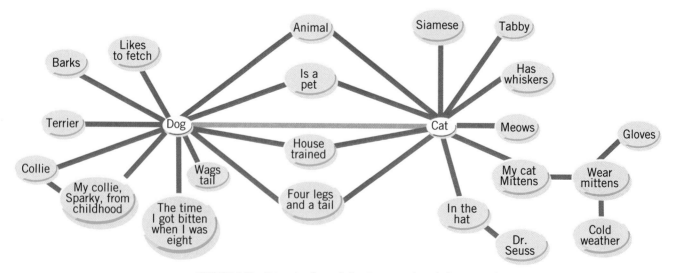

FIGURE 6.12   Networks of association. Long-term knowledge is stored in networks of association, ideas that are mentally connected with one another by repeatedly occurring together.

leads to tremendously complex networks of association. One way to think of a node is as a set of neurons distributed throughout the brain that fire together (see Chapter 3). Their joint firing produces a representation of an object or category such as *dog*, which integrates visual, tactile, auditory, verbal, and other information stored in memory. To search through memory means you go from node to node until you locate the right information. In this sense, nodes are like cities, which are connected to each other (associated) by roads (Reisberg, 1997).

Not all associations are equally strong; *dog* is more strongly connected to *barks* than to *cat* or *animal*. To return to the cities analogy, some cities are connected by superhighways, which facilitate rapid travel between them, whereas others are connected only by slow, winding country roads. Other cities have no direct links at all, which means that travel between them requires an intermediate link. The same is true of associative networks: In Figure 6.12 *cat* is not directly associated to *cold weather*, but it is through the intermediate link of *my cat Mittens*, which is semantically related to *wear mittens*, which is in turn linked to the *cold weather* node.

From a neuropsychological perspective, if two nodes without a direct link become increasingly associated through experience, a "road" between them is built; and if the association continues to grow, that road will be "widened" to ensure rapid neural transit between one and the other. If, on the other hand, a neural highway between two nodes falls into disuse because two objects or events stop occurring together (such as the link between the word *girlfriend* and a particular girlfriend months after the relationship has ended), the highway will fall into disrepair and be less easily traveled. The old road will not likely disappear completely: Occasionally a traveler may wander off the main road down the old highway, as when a person accidentally calls his new girlfriend by his old girlfriend's name.

Spreading Activation One theory that attempts to explain the workings of networks of association involves spreading activation (Collins & Loftus, 1975; Collins & Quillian, 1969). According to **spreading activation theory**, *activating one node in a network triggers activation in closely related nodes*. In other words, presenting a stimulus that leads to firing in the neural circuits that represent that stimulus spreads activation, or energy, to related information stored in memory.

Spreading activation does not always start with a stimulus such as a spoken word. Activation may also begin with a thought, fantasy, or wish, which in turn activates other nodes. For example, a psychotherapy patient trying to decide whether to divorce his wife found the song "Reunited and It Feels So Good" coming to mind on days when he leaned toward reconciliation. On days when he was contemplating divorce, however, he found himself inadvertently singing a different tune, "Fifty Ways to Leave Your Lover."

Considerable research supports the theory of spreading activation. In one study, the experimenters presented participants with word pairs to learn, including the pair *ocean–moon* (see Nisbett & Wilson, 1977). Later, when asked to name a laundry detergent, participants in this condition were more likely to respond with *Tide* than control subjects, who had been exposed to a different list of word pairs.

The researchers offered an intriguing explanation (Figure 6.13): The network of associations that includes *ocean* and *moon* also includes *tide*. Priming with *ocean–moon* thus activated other nodes on the network, spreading activation to *tide*, which was associated with another network of associations, laundry detergents.

According to many contemporary models, each time a thought or image is perceived, primed, or retrieved from memory, the level of activation of the neural networks that represent it increases. Thus, two kinds of information are likely to be at a high state of activation at any given moment: *recently activated information* (such as a

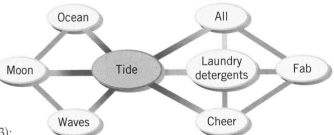

FIGURE 6.13 Spreading activation. Tide stands at the intersection of two activated networks of association and is thus doubly activated. In contrast, other brands only receive activation from one network. (This experiment, of course, only works in North America and other places where Tide has a substantial market share. I once tried demonstrating it in a lecture in Australia, where the only thing I demonstrated was my ethnocentrism.)

news story seen a moment ago on television) and *frequently activated information* (such as a physician's knowledge about disease). For example, a person who has just seen a documentary on cancer is likely to identify the word *leukemia* faster than someone who tuned in to a different channel; a doctor is similarly likely to identify the word quickly because *leukemia* is at a chronically higher state of activation.

Hierarchical Organization of Information   Although activating a *dog* node can trigger some idiosyncratic thoughts and memories, networks of association are far from haphazard jumbles of information. Efficient retrieval requires some degree of organization of information so that the mind can find its way through dense networks of neural trails.

Some researchers have compared LTM to a filing cabinet, in which important information is kept toward the front of the files and less important information is relegated to the back of our mental archives or to a box in the attic. The filing cabinet metaphor also suggests that some information is filed *hierarchically*; that is, broad categories are composed of narrower subcategories, which in turn consist of even more specific categories.

For example, a person could store information about *animals* under the subcategories *pets, farm animals*, and *wild animals*. Under *farm animals* are *cows, horses*, and *chickens*. At each level of the hierarchy, each node will have features associated with it (such as knowledge that chickens squawk and lay eggs) as well as other associations to it (such as roasted chicken, which is associated with a very different smell than is the generic "chickens").

Hierarchical storage is generally quite efficient, but it can occasionally lead to errors. For instance, when asked, "Which is farther north, Seattle or Montreal?" most people say Montreal (Stevens & Coupe, 1978). In fact, Seattle is farther north. People mistakenly assume that Montreal is north of Seattle because they go to their general level of knowledge about Canada and the United States and remember that Canada is north of the United States. In reality, some parts of the United States are farther north than many parts of Canada. A better strategy in this case would be to visualize a map of North America and scan it for Seattle and Montreal.

INTERIM SUMMARY

Knowledge stored in memory forms **networks of association**—clusters of interconnected information. Each piece of information along a network is called a **node**. According to **spreading activation theory**, activating one node in a network triggers activation in closely related nodes. Some parts of networks are organized hierarchically, with broad categories composed of narrower subcategories, which in turn consist of even more specific categories.

Schemas

The models of associative networks and spreading activation we have been discussing go a long way toward describing the organization of memory, but they have limits. For example, psychologists have not yet agreed on how to represent propositions like "The dog chased the cat" using network models, since if *dog* and *cat* are nodes how is the link between them (*chased*) represented? Further, activation of one node can actually either increase or *inhibit* activation of associated nodes, as when a person identifies an approaching animal as a dog and not a wolf and hence "shuts off" the *wolf* node.

Psychologists have argued for over a century about the adequacy of principles of association in explaining memory (Bahrick, 1985). Some have argued that we do not associate isolated bits of information with each other but instead store and remember the "gist" of facts and events. They note that when people remember passages of prose rather than single words or word pairs, they typically remember the general meaning of the passage rather than a verbatim account.

Now is the time for all good men to to come to the aid of their countrymen.

The extra "to" at the beginning of the second line is easily overlooked because of the schema-based expectation that it is not there. Students often fail to notice typographical errors in their papers for the same reason.

According to this view, when confronted with a novel event people match it against *schemas* stored in memory. Schemas are patterns of thought, or organized knowledge structures, that render the environment relatively predictable. When students walk into a classroom on the first day of class and a person resembling a professor begins to lecture, they listen and take notes in a routine fashion. They are not surprised that one person has assumed control of the situation and begun talking because they have a schema for events that normally transpire in a classroom. Proponents of schema theories argue that memory is an active process of *reconstruction* of the past. Remembering means combining bits and pieces of what we once perceived with general knowledge that helps us fill in the gaps. In this view, memory is not like taking snapshots of an event; it is more like *taking notes*.

Schemas affect the way people remember in two ways: by influencing the information they encode and by shaping the way they reconstruct data that they have already stored (Davidson, 1995; Rumelhart, 1984).

Schemas and Encoding   Schemas influence the way people initially understand the meaning of an event and thus the manner in which they encode it in LTM. Harry Triandis (1994) relates an account of two Englishmen engaged in a friendly game of tennis in nineteenth-century China. The two were sweating and panting under the hot August sun. As they finished their final set, a Chinese friend sympathetically asked, "Could you not get two servants to do this for you?" Operating from a different set of schemas, their Chinese friend encoded this event rather differently than would an audience at Wimbledon.

Schemas and Retrieval   Schemas not only provide hooks on which to hang information during encoding, but they also provide hooks for fishing information out of LTM. Many schemas have "slots" for particular kinds of information (Minsky, 1975). A person shopping for a compact disc player who is trying to recall the models she saw that day is likely to remember the names Sony and Pioneer but not Frank Sylvester (the salesman at one of the stores). Unlike Sony, Frank Sylvester does not fit into the slot "brand names of compact disc players."

The slots in schemas often have *default values,* standard answers that fill in missing information the person did not initially notice or bother to store. When asked if the cover of this book gives the authors' names, you are likely to report that it does (default value = *yes*) even if you never really noticed because the authors' names normally appear on a book cover. In fact, people are generally unable to tell which pieces of information in a memory are truly remembered and which reflect the operation of default values.

One classic study demonstrated the reconstructive role of schemas using a visual task (Brewer & Treyens, 1981). The experimenter instructed college student subjects to wait (one at a time) in a "graduate student's office" similar to the one depicted in Figure 6.14 while he excused himself to check on something. The experimenter returned in 35 seconds and led the student to a different room. There, he asked the subject either to write down a description of the graduate student's office or to draw a picture of it, including as many objects as could be recalled.

The room contained a number of objects (e.g., bookshelves, coffeepot, desk) that would fit most subjects' schema of a graduate student's office. Several objects, however, were conspicuous—or rather, inconspicuous—in their absence, such as a filing cabinet, a coffee cup, books on the shelves, a window, pens and pencils, and curtains. Many subjects assumed the pres-

FIGURE 6.14   Influence of schemas on memory. Subjects asked to recall this graduate student's office frequently remembered many items that actually were not in it but were in their office schemas. *Source:* Brewer & Treyens, 1981.

ence of these default items, however, and "remembered" seeing them even though they had not actually been present.

Without schemas, life would seem like one random event after another, and efficient memory would be impossible. Yet as the research just described shows, schemas can lead people to misclassify information, to believe they have seen what they really have not seen, and to fail to notice things that might be important.

INTERIM SUMMARY

One way psychologists describe the organization of LTM is in terms of schemas, organized knowledge about a particular domain. Proponents of schema theories argue that memory involves reconstruction of the past, by combining knowledge of what we once perceived with general knowledge that helps fill in the gaps. Schemas influence both the way information is encoded and the way it is retrieved.

A Global Vista ─ Cross-Cultural Variation in Memory—Better, Worse, or Just Different?

Big Picture φ Question 4

To what extent is human nature particular versus universal?

The account of memory presented thus far is based almost exclusively on studies of subjects in Western, technologically advanced societies. Do the general principles of memory from these samples apply cross-culturally, or do memory and thought differ depending on the cultural, historical, and ecological context?

Memory and Adaptation

Studies comparing memory processes across cultures (such as large industrial versus small tribal societies) often produce inconsistent findings, largely because people tend to do better on tasks that resemble the demands of their everyday lives (see Cole et al., 1967). Thus, members of hunter-gatherer societies are better at remembering the location of edible berries than people in industrial societies, who have superior recall for strings of digits (e.g., phone numbers).

Not everyone in a culture is the same, however, and different subgroups confront different ecological or environmental demands. For example, a study in Zambia (Africa)

In preliterate societies, oral tradition shapes the way people think and serves as an archive for collective memories.

compared the ability of urban schoolboys and rural women to recall information from stories relevant to *time* (Deregowski, 1970). Whereas the day of a Zambian schoolboy is precisely structured by the clock (as in the West), the daily life of rural Zambian women is regulated primarily by cycles of night and day and is not driven by specific units of time. The experimenters found no differences between the two groups in their ability to recall information in general. However, the schoolboys were significantly more likely to recall aspects of the stories related to *when* things happened. Across and within cultures, people tend to remember information that matters to them, and they organize information in memory to match the demands of their environment.

A particularly important influence on memory that varies across cultures is literacy. Literacy increases the role played by verbal representations, since it converts many visual experiences to verbal experiences. In preliterate societies, the human brain is the means of storing memories, and people rely on oral history and tradition, such as storytelling, to pass on collective knowledge. Literate societies, on the other hand, store information in many ways that extend the limits of memory, from magazines, textbooks, and computers, to simple devices such as lists, which can expand memory capacity exponentially (Goody, 1977).

Cultural Models

Throughout this chapter, we have described memory as if it occurs in isolated information processors (see Cole, 1975). However, **cultural models**, or *shared cultural concepts*, organize knowledge and shape the way people think and remember (D'Andrade, 1992; Moore & Mathews, 2001; Strauss & Quinn, 1997). Imagine, for example, how much more difficult the task of remembering how a neuron works might be for someone whose culture lacked the concept of *cells*.

Years ago, Frederic Bartlett (1932) demonstrated the impact of cultural models on retrieval. British subjects read a North American Indian folk tale, waited 15 minutes, and then attempted to reproduce it verbatim. Their errors were systematic: Subjects omitted or reworked unfamiliar details to make the story consistent with their own culturally shaped schemas.

INTERIM SUMMARY

Across and within cultures, people tend to remember information that matters to them, and they organize information in memory to match the demands of their environment. Shared cultural concepts, or **cultural models**, also shape the way people think and remember.

Remembering, Misremembering, and Forgetting

We could not do without our memories, but sometimes we wish we could. According to Daniel Schacter (1999), who has spent his life studying memory, human memory systems evolved through natural selection, but the same mechanisms that generally foster adaptation can regularly cause memory failures. He describes "seven sins of memory" that plague us all:

- *transience* (the fact that memories fade);
- *absent-mindedness* (the failure to remember something when attention is elsewhere);
- *misattribution* (misremembering the source of a memory—something advertisers rely on when they tell half-truths about competing brands and people remember the half-truth but forget its source);
- *suggestibility* (thinking we remember an event that someone actually implanted in our minds);
- *bias* (distortions in the way we recall events that often tell the story in a way we would *rather* remember it); and
- *persistence* (memories we wish we could get rid of but which keep coming back).

Although at first glance these "sins" all seem maladaptive, many stem from adaptive memory processes that can go awry. For example, if memory were not transient or temporary, our minds would overflow with irrelevant information.

Perhaps the cardinal sin of memory is **forgetting**, *the inability to remember*. Over a century ago, Ebbinghaus (1885) documented a typical pattern of forgetting that occurs with many kinds of declarative knowledge: rapid initial loss of information after initial learning and only gradual decline thereafter (Figure 6.15). More recently, researchers have refined Ebbinghaus's forgetting curve slightly to make it more precise—finding, in fact, that the relation between memory decline and length of time between learning and retrieval is logarithmic and hence predictable by a very precise mathematical function (Wixted & Ebbesen, 1991). This logarithmic relationship is very similar to the Stevens' power law for sensory stimuli (Chapter 4).

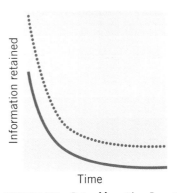

FIGURE 6.15 Rate of forgetting. Forgetting follows a standard pattern, with rapid initial loss of information followed by more gradual later decline. Increasing initial study time (the dotted line) increases retention, but forgetting occurs at the same rate. In other words, increased study shifts the curve upward but does not change the rate of forgetting or eliminate it.

This forgetting curve seems to apply whether the period of time is hours or years. For example, the same curve emerged when researchers studied people's ability to remember the names of old television shows: They rapidly forgot the names of shows canceled within the last seven years, but the rate of forgetting trailed off after that (Squire, 1989).

How Long Is Long-Term Memory?

When people forget, is the information no longer stored or is it simply no longer easy to retrieve? And is some information permanent, or does the brain eventually throw away old boxes in the attic if it has not used them for a number of years?

The first question is more difficult to answer than the second. Psychologists often distinguish between the *availability* of information in memory—whether it is still "in there"—and its *accessibility*—the ease with which it can be retrieved. The tip-of-the-tongue phenomenon, like the priming effects shown by amnesics, is a good example of information that is available but inaccessible.

In large part, accessibility reflects level of activation, which diminishes over time but remains for much longer than most people would intuitively suppose. Memory for a picture flashed briefly on a screen a year earlier continues to produce some activation of the visual cortex, which is expressed implicitly even if the person has no conscious recollection of it (Cave, 1997). And most people have vivid recollections from their childhood of certain incidents that occurred once, such as the moment they heard the news that a beloved pet died. But what about the other hundreds of millions of incidents that they cannot retrieve? To what degree these memories are now unavailable, rather than just inaccessible, is unknown.

Studies of very long term memory suggest, however, that if information is consolidated through spacing over long learning intervals, it will last a lifetime, even if the person does not rehearse it for half a century (Bahrick & Hall, 1991). Eight years after having taught students for a single semester, college professors will forget the names and faces of most of their students (sorry!), but 35 years after graduation people still recognize 90 percent of the names and faces from their high school yearbook.

The difference is in the spacing: The professor teaches a student for only a few months, whereas high school students typically know each other for at least three or four years. Similarly, people who take college mathematics courses that require them to use the knowledge they learned in high school algebra show nearly complete memory for algebra 50 years later even if they work as artists and never balance their checkbook. People who stop at high school algebra remember nothing of it decades later.

How Accurate Is Long-Term Memory?

Aside from the question of *how long* people remember is the question of *how accurately* they remember. The short answer is that memory is both functional and reconstructive, so that most of the time it serves us well, but it is subject to a variety of errors and biases.

For example, the normal associative processes that help people remember can also lead to memory errors (see Robinson & Roediger, 1997; Schacter et al., 1998). In one set of studies the researchers presented participants with a series of words (such as *slumber, nap,* and *bed*) that were all related to a single word that had *not* been presented (*sleep*). This essentially primed the word "sleep" repeatedly (Roediger & McDermott, 1995). Not only did most participants remember having heard the multiply primed word, but the majority even remembered which of two people had read the word to them. Some participants refused to believe that the word had not been presented even after hearing an audiotape of the session!

Emotional factors can also bias recall. The investigators in one study asked college student participants to recall their math, science, history, English, and foreign language grades from high school and then compared their recollections to their high school transcripts (Bahrick et al., 1996). Students recalled 71 percent of their grades correctly, which is certainly impressive.

More interesting, however, was the pattern of their errors (Figure 6.16). Participants rarely misremembered their A's, but they rarely *correctly* remembered their D's. In fact, a D was twice as likely to be remembered as a B or C than as a D. Approximately 80 percent of participants tended to inflate their remembered grades, whereas only 6 percent reported grades lower than they had actually achieved. (The remaining 14 percent tended to remember correctly.)

Flashbulb Memories   If remembering is more like consulting an artist's sketch than a photograph, what do we make of **flashbulb memories**, that is, *vivid memories of exciting or highly consequential events* (Brown & Kulik, 1977; Conway, 1995; Winograd & Neisser, 1993)? Many people can recall precisely where and when they first heard the news of the space shuttle Columbia disaster in 2003, almost as if a camera had recorded that moment in time. People report similarly vivid memories of the verdict in the OJ Simpson murder trial in 1995, as well as personal events such as the death of a loved one or a romantic encounter (Rubin & Kozin, 1984).

Flashbulb memories are so clear and vivid that we tend to think of them as totally accurate; however, considerable evidence suggests that they are often not of snapshot clarity or accuracy and can even be entirely incorrect (Neisser, 1991). For example, on the day following the Challenger disaster in 1986, people reported where they were when they heard the space shuttle had disintegrated. Three years later when they were again asked where they were, not a single person recalled with complete accuracy where they had been, and a third of the respondents were completely incorrect in their recall (McCloskey et al., 1988; Neisser & Harsch, 1992).

Eyewitness Testimony   Research on the accuracy of memory has an important real-life application in the courtroom: How accurate is eyewitness testimony (see Schacter, 1995b; Sporer et al., 1996)? Numerous studies have explored this question experimentally, usually by showing participants a short film or slides of an event such as a car accident (Wells & Loftus, 1984; Zaragosta & Mitchell, 1996). The experimenter then asks subjects specific questions about the scene, sometimes introducing information that was not present in the actual scene, asking leading questions, or contradicting what participants saw.

These studies show that seemingly minor variations in the wording of a question can determine what participants remember from a scene. One study simply substituted the definite article *the* for the indefinite article *a* in the question "Did you see the/a broken headlight?" Using *the* instead of *a* increased both the likelihood that participants would recall seeing a broken headlight and their certainty that they had, even if they never actually observed one (Loftus & Palmer, 1974; Loftus & Zanni, 1975).

These findings have clear implications both in the courtroom and in the way police interrogate witnesses. However, individuals vary in their susceptibility to misleading information (Loftus et al., 1992). Further, some aspects of a memory may be more reliable than others. The emotional stress of witnessing a traumatic event can lead to heightened processing of (and hence better memory for) core details of the event but less extensive processing of peripheral details (Christianson, 1992). A sharp attorney could thus attack the credibility of a witness's entire testimony by establishing that her memory of peripheral details is faulty even though she clearly remembers the central aspects of the event.

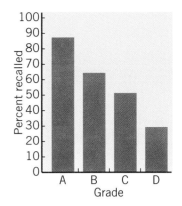

FIGURE 6.16   Distortion in memory for high school grades. The lower the grade, the less memorable it seems to be, demonstrating the impact of motivation and emotion on memory. *Source:* Adapted from Bahrick et al., 1996.

INTERIM SUMMARY

The flipside of memory is **forgetting**. Many kinds of declarative knowledge show a similar forgetting curve, which is initially steep and then levels off. Psychologists often distinguish between the availability of information in memory—whether it is still "in there"—and its accessibility—the ease with which it can be retrieved. People tend to make memory errors for a variety of reasons, some cognitive and some emotional. **Flashbulb memories**—vivid memories of exciting or highly consequential events—are sometimes extremely accurate but sometimes completely mistaken. Eyewitness testimony is also subject to many biases and errors.

From Brain to Behavior   Emotional Arousal and Memory

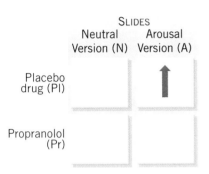

FIGURE 6.17   In an investigation of the relationship between emotional arousal and memory, researchers found that memory was higher for participants in the arousal condition who had not received propranolol, relative to the other three conditions.

In trying to understand "flashbulb" memories, Cahill et al. (1994) designed an elegant experiment that manipulated both the emotional content of the material to be remembered and adrenalin (the fight-or-flight hormone, Chapter 3). First, they developed two series of 12 slides depicting a little boy leaving for school, having an unusual experience, and then returning home. In the middle section of slides, the unusual experience differed for the two series. In the *control* or neutral condition, the little boy goes on a field trip to the hospital and sees a disaster drill. In the *experimental* or arousal condition, the little boy is in a tragic accident in which his feet are severed from his legs and a concussion leads to bleeding in the brain. Miraculously, the doctors are able to reattach the boy's feet and control the brain bleeding.

Half of the subjects were shown the neutral slide series; the other half were shown the arousal slide series. The second manipulation, that of adrenalin activity, was created by giving a drug that antagonizes the actions of adrenalin (propranolol) to half of the subjects in each group. The propranolol blocked any effect of adrenalin that the arousal slides produced. In this *two-by-two design*, two factors were studied: (1) neutral or arousal slide versions, and (2) placebo drug or the adrenalin antagonist propranolol. Thus, there were four groups (see Figure 6.17: NPl: Neutral, placebo drug; NPr: Neutral, propranolol; APl: Arousal, placebo drug; and APr: Arousal, propranolol.

The researchers hypothesized that the memory for all groups, when tested one week later, would be the same, *except for* the APl group, for which memory of the middle set of slides (when the boy was in the accident) would be better than the other groups. That is, they hypothesized that the emotionally arousing slides, which triggered adrenalin release, would lead to enhanced memory of those slides. Neither of the neutral groups would have any adrenalin release (thus, the propranolol would not have any adrenalin to antagonize) and the arousal group whose adrenalin activity was antagonized by propranolol would not have enhanced memory, even though they saw the arousing slides. The results supported their hypothesis.

These results support the notion that our "flashbulb" memories for emotionally arousing events are dependent on the fight-or-flight hormone, adrenalin. It is important to note that memory was enhanced *only* for the arousal slide, not for the neutral beginning and ending slides. Thus, emotional arousal, via adrenalin activity in the brain, leads to enhanced memory.

Apply and Discuss

Most people cannot explicitly remember events before about age 4, a phenomenon known as childhood amnesia.

■ What is your earliest memory?

■ Why might we be unable to retrieve memories from before age 3 or 4? What aspects of the way we represent, store, and retrieve information might impact our capacity to recall early memories?

■ What neurological factors might limit access to early episodic memories?

Why Do People Forget?

The reconstructive nature of remembering—the fact that we have to weave together a memory from patches of specific and general knowledge—leaves memory open to a number of potential errors and biases. But why do people sometimes forget things entirely? Psychologists have proposed several explanations, including decay, interference, and motivated forgetting.

Decay Theory   **Decay theory** *explains forgetting as a result of a fading memory trace*. Having a thought or perception produces changes in synaptic connections, which in turn create the *potential* for remembering if the neural circuits that were initially activated are later reactivated. According to decay theory, these neurophysiological changes fade with disuse, much as a path in the forest grows over unless repeatedly trodden.

The decay theory is difficult to corroborate or disprove empirically. However, it fits with many observed memory phenomena. Further, some studies do show a pattern of rapid and then more gradual deactivation of neural pathways in the hippocampus (which is involved in memory consolidation), which suggests a possible physiological basis for decay (see Anderson, 1995).

Interference Theory   A prime culprit in memory failure is **interference**, *the intrusion of similar memories on each other*, as when students confuse two theories they learned around the same time or two similar-sounding words in a foreign language. Finding the right path in the neural wilderness is difficult if two paths are close together and look alike. Or to use the filing cabinet metaphor, storing too many documents under the same heading makes finding the right one difficult.

Cognitive psychologists distinguish two kinds of interference. **Proactive interference** refers to *the interference of previously stored memories with the retrieval of new information*, as when a person calls a new romantic partner by the name of an old one (a common but dangerous memory lapse). In **retroactive interference**, *new information interferes with retrieval of old information*, as when people have difficulty recalling their home phone numbers from past residences. One reason children take years to memorize multiplication tables, even though they can learn the names of cartoon characters or classmates with astonishing speed, is the tremendous interference that is involved, because every number is paired with so many others (Anderson, 1995).

Motivated Forgetting   Another cause of forgetting is **motivated forgetting**, or *forgetting for a reason*. People often explicitly instruct themselves or others to forget, as when a person stops in the middle of a sentence and says, "Oops—forget that. That's the wrong address. The right one is…" (Bjork & Bjork, 1996). At other times, the intention to forget is implicit, as when a person who parks in a different parking space every day implicitly *remembers to forget* where she parked the day before so it does not interfere with memory for where she parked today (Bjork et al., 1998).

Experimental evidence suggests that goal-directed forgetting requires active inhibition of the forgotten information, which remains available but inaccessible. Researchers have demonstrated this by using *directed forgetting* procedures: Participants learn a list of words but are told midway to forget the words they just learned and remember only the last part of the list. This procedure reduces recall for the words in the first part of the list and decreases proactive interference from them, so that participants can more easily remember words in the last half of the list. This outcome suggests that the procedure is in fact inhibiting retrieval of the to-be-forgotten words. On the other hand, this procedure does *not* decrease recognition of, or implicit memory for, the to-be-forgotten words, and they remain available, just less accessible.

Other studies show that instructing a person not to think about something can effectively keep the information from consciousness, but that deliberately suppressing information in this way creates an automatic, unconscious process that "watches out" for the information and hence keeps it available (Wegner, 1992). For example, when people are instructed to suppress an exciting thought about sex, they remain physiologically aroused even while the thought is outside awareness. In fact, they remain just as aroused as subjects instructed to *think about* the sexual thought (Wegner et al., 1990). In a sense, goal-directed forgetting is like a form of prospective memory, in which the intention is to forget something in the future rather than to remember it. In this situation, forgetting is actually a form of remembering!

In real life, people often try to inhibit unpleasant or anxiety-provoking thoughts or feelings (Chapter 12). They often forget things they do not want to remember, such as "overlooking" a dentist appointment. If dentists were handing out $100 bills instead of filling teeth, few people would forget their appointments.

An accident can become more severe if a lawyer asks the right questions, such as, "How fast were the cars going when they smashed [rather than 'hit'] each other?"

…AND, AS YOU GO OUT INTO THE WORLD, I PREDICT THAT YOU WILL, GRADUALLY AND IMPERCEPTIBLY, FORGET ALL YOU EVER LEARNED AT THIS UNIVERSITY."

Drawing by Sidney Harris

Commentary

Repressed Memories of Sexual Abuse

The concept of repression has always been controversial in psychology (Holmes, 1990), but it is now the centerpiece of controversy. It is at the heart of claims of childhood sexual abuse and counterclaims of false memories raised by alleged perpetrators. The alleged perpetrators claim that the charges of sexual abuse against them have been invented by incompetent clinicians who have convinced their patients of the existence of events that never occurred (Delmonte, 2001; Howe, 2000; Pezdek & Banks, 1996).

The question of implanting false memories is exceedingly difficult to address scientifically for a number of reasons. First, distinguishing true from false allegations is difficult in all legal circumstances, but it is even more difficult when the events may have occurred 15 years ago. Second, a cardinal feature of sexual abuse is that the perpetrator does everything possible to maintain secrecy (including threatening the victim) and to discredit the victim if she or he ever tells the story—a situation not unlike what often occurs with rape, political torture, and genocide (Herman, 1992). Third, some number of innocent people are unfairly accused: Divorcing parents sometimes accuse former spouses as a tactic in custody disputes, and some poorly trained therapists look for (and "find") abuse whenever an adult female patient steps into their office complaining of anxiety or depression (Loftus, 1993).

Evidence of False Memories

Data from numerous laboratory studies suggest that people can sometimes be led to create compelling memories of things that did not happen (Loftus, 1997a; Payne et al., 1997). As we have seen, presenting people with a series of words semantically related to a target word that was *not* presented can produce high rates of false recognition of the target, and people can be quite firm in their beliefs about these false memories. Women reporting a recovered memory of childhood sexual abuse are more likely than other women to recognize a target word (*sweet*) mistakenly as having been present in an earlier list of related words (*sugar, candy, honey*) (Clancy et al., 2000). Women who report remembering abuse all along (as opposed to recovering it) do not show this bias.

In another experimental design that bears on false memories, researchers obtain detailed information from parents of college students about events that actually occurred when their children were younger and then present the students with several real memories and one false one, such as getting lost in a mall at age 5 and being found by an elderly woman (Loftus, 1997b). The investigators then interview participants about each event, ask them if they remember it, and ask them to recall what they remember. In these studies, roughly 15 to 25 percent of participants can be induced to recall a false memory over the course of two or three interviews.

For most people, however, the vulnerability to recall false memories is not without limit. When one researcher tried to induce memories more like those of sexual abuse victims (in this case, memory of a rectal enema in childhood), *none* of the subjects created a false memory (Pezdek, cited in Loftus, 1997b). There is obviously a need for caution in extending the findings of these experimental studies to the creation of false memories of sexual abuse, a highly traumatic and evocative event.

Evidence of Repressed Memories

Other studies call into question the charge that most psychotherapy patients who believe they have been sexually abused invent these memories. The majority of victims of repeated or severe sexual abuse in childhood have at least some memories of the abuse prior to psychotherapy, although their memories are often fragmented

(Herman, 1992). Their recollection of childhood events tends to have gaps of months or years, and the memories of traumatic experiences they do recall frequently come to them in flashbacks, in physical forms (such as the sensation of gagging that initially attended the experience of being forced to perform oral sex), or in nightmares.

Several studies document that periods of amnesia for sexual abuse are common (see Loftus et al., 1994; Briere & Conte, 1993), just as in other traumatic events such as combat or rape (Arrigo & Pezdek, 1997). Perhaps the clearest empirical evidence for repressed memories comes from a study that tracked down women who had been treated at a hospital for sexual molestation when they were children (Williams, 1994). Seventeen years after their documented abuse, 38 percent were amnesic for the incident. When asked if any family members had ever gotten into trouble for their sexual behavior, one subject, who denied sexual abuse, reported that before she was born an uncle had apparently molested a little girl and was stabbed to death by the girl's mother. Examination of newspaper reports 17 years earlier found that the subject herself had been one of the uncle's two victims and that the mother of the other victim had indeed stabbed the perpetrator.

Perhaps the moral of the story is that psychologists should always attend both to the phenomenon they are studying—in this case, repressed memories—and to their own needs, fears, and cognitive biases. For example, research demonstrates that people with abuse histories are more likely to see or hear themes of abuse in ambiguous situations (Nigg et al., 1992). Thus, clinicians with painful childhood histories of their own childhood should be particularly careful to avoid jumping to conclusions or subtly influencing patients with leading questions.

On the other hand, researchers who may have had little or no exposure to real sexual abuse victims should be circumspect about overstepping the limits of their vantage point. Researchers and clinicians alike need to look carefully at their own cognitive and motivational biases before attempting to rewrite—or write off—the life histories of others.

INTERIM SUMMARY

The **decay theory** explains forgetting as a result of a fading memory trace; disuse of information leads to a gradual decrease in the strength of neural connections. **Interference** of similar information is another cause of forgetting. **Proactive interference** refers to the interference of previously stored memories with the retrieval of new information, whereas **retroactive interference** refers to the interference of new information with retrieval of old information. Another cause of forgetting is **motivated forgetting**, or forgetting for a reason. The final word has not yet been written about repressed memories of childhood sexual abuse, although the data suggest caution on both sides: Memories recovered in therapy cannot be assumed to be accurate, but they also cannot be routinely dismissed as false.

Summary

Memory and Information Processing

1. Case studies of neurologically impaired patients and experimental studies of normal subjects have demonstrated that memory is composed of several systems.

2. For information to return to mind after it is no longer present, it has to be put into a mental code, or representation. The major forms of representations studied by psychologists are **sensory representations** and **verbal representations**. People also store memory for actions as motoric representations.

3. The standard model of memory views the mind as a computer, which stores, transforms, and retrieves information processing. It includes three sequential memory stores or stages of memory. The first is the **sensory register**, the split-second mental representation of a perceived stimulus that remains very briefly after that stimulus disappears. **Iconic storage** describes visual sensory registration; **echoic storage** describes auditory sensory registration.

4. **Short-term memory (STM)** stores information for roughly 20 to 30 seconds, unless the information is maintained through **rehearsal** (repeating the information again and again). This form of rehearsal, which merely maintains information in STM, is called **maintenance rehearsal. Elaborative rehearsal**—thinking about and elaborating on the information's meaning—tends to be superior for storing information in long-term memory.

5. Important information is passed along to **long-term memory (LTM)**, where representations may last as long as a lifetime. Recovering information from LTM, or **retrieval**, brings it back into STM, or consciousness.

6. In recent years this model has been changing substantially. Instead of viewing memory exclusively in terms of serial processing (which assumes that information passes through a series of stages, one at a time and in order), researchers now view memory as involving a set of **modules** that operate simultaneously (in parallel) rather than sequentially (one at a time). Researchers now recognize that not all remembering is expressed by retrieving information into consciousness, or STM, and they rely less on the metaphor of mind as computer than mind as brain.

Working Memory

7. Psychologists now refer to STM as **working memory**, the temporary storage and processing of information that can be used to solve problems, respond to environmental demands, or achieve goals. According to one prominent model, control processes such as rehearsal, reasoning, and making decisions about how to balance two tasks simultaneously are the work of a limited capacity central executive system; whereas storage involves at least two limited-capacity systems, a visual store (also called the visuospatial sketchpad) and a verbal store.

8. The existence of neurological patients who show deficits in either working memory or LTM but not both suggests that these memory systems are neurologically distinct, although in everyday life they work together, as frontal working memory networks provide a special form of activation to networks in the posterior parts of the cortex that represent current perceptions and information stored in LTM. One way to expand the capacity of working memory in particular domains is **chunking**, that is, grouping information into larger units than single words or digits. The roughly seven pieces of information stored in visual or auditory working memory can represent larger, more meaningful pieces of information.

Varieties of Long-Term Memory

9. Types of long-term memory can be distinguished by the kind of knowledge stored and the way this knowledge is retrieved and expressed. People store two kinds of information, declarative and procedural. **Declarative memory** refers to memory for facts and events and is subdivided into **semantic** or **generic memory** (general world knowledge or facts) and **episodic memory**

(memories of particular events). **Procedural memory** refers to "how to" knowledge of procedures or skills.

10. Information can be retrieved either explicitly or implicitly. **Explicit memory** refers to conscious recollection, expressed through **recall** (the spontaneous retrieval of material from LTM) or **recognition** (memory for whether something currently perceived has been previously encountered or learned). **Implicit memory** is expressed in behavior rather than consciously retrieved.

11. Neurological data suggest that different kinds of memory form discrete memory systems. The hippocampus and adjacent regions of the cortex are central to the consolidation of explicit memories but do not appear to play an important role in either implicit memory or working memory.

12. **Everyday memory**—memory as it occurs in daily life—tends to be functional (focused on remembering information that is meaningful) and emotionally significant. **Prospective memory** is memory for things that need to be done in the future.

Encoding and Organization of Long-Term Memory

13. For information to be retrievable from memory, it must be **encoded**, or cast into a representational form, or "code," that can be readily accessed from memory.

14. Among the factors that influence later accessibility of memory are the degree to which information is elaborated, reflected upon, and processed in a meaningful way during encoding (**level of processing**); the presence of **retrieval cues** (stimuli or thoughts that can be used to facilitate recollection); the **spacing** of study sessions (with longer intervals between rehearsal sessions tending to be more effective); and the use of multiple and redundant representational modes to encode the information, which provides more cues for its retrieval. **Mnemonic devices**, or systematic strategies for remembering information, can also be useful for remembering, as can external memory aids such as notes.

15. Information stored in memory forms networks of association—clusters of interconnected units of information called **nodes**. According to spreading activation theory, activating one node in a network triggers activation in closely related nodes. Some information is organized hierarchically, with broad categories composed of narrower subcategories, which in turn consist of even more specific categories.

16. Schemas are organized knowledge about a particular domain. According to schema theory, memory is an active, reconstructive process that involves reactivation of both the initial representations of an event and general knowledge that helps fill in the gaps. Schemas facilitate memory by organizing information at both encoding and retrieval.

17. Many schemas are shaped by culture, from beliefs about foods that are appropriate to eat to beliefs about the meaning of life. Across cultures, people tend to remember what matters to them.

Remembering, Misremembering, and Forgetting

18. Ebbinghaus discovered a forgetting curve that applies to many kinds of declarative memory, in which considerable information is initially lost but **forgetting** then tapers off.

19. Memory is a reconstructive process that mingles representations of actual experiences with general knowledge. Although memory

is functional and tends to work well most of the time, misremembering is common, even in **flashbulb memories** (vivid memories of exciting or highly consequential events) and eyewitness testimony, which can be biased by even seemingly minor changes in the way questions are asked.

20. Three theories attempt to account for forgetting: **decay theory** (which explains forgetting as a result of a fading memory trace); **interference** of new and old information with retrieval of the other; and **motivated forgetting** (forgetting for a reason, which leads to inhibition of retrieval).

Key Terms

Thought and Language

Y ou are sitting in a café with your closest friend, and she tells you tearfully, "I think my relationship with Brett has hit a dead end. Things have been pretty bumpy for a while, but I had no idea how bad. He says he loves me, but I can tell he's really putting on the brakes, and I think he just wants to bail out. Every time we try to talk about it, we just end up spinning our wheels. It's hard to see how we can move forward."

You have no trouble understanding your friend. You are not confused by her metaphors—the relationship hitting a *dead end*, things being *bumpy*, her boyfriend *putting on the brakes* and wanting to *bail out*, the two of them *spinning their wheels* and having trouble *moving forward*. Your friend is not a poet, yet she communicates her problem through a single controlling metaphor that you understand implicitly: Lovers are like travelers on a journey trying to reach a common destination, and their relationship is the vehicle for this journey. With the exception of *bailing out* (an aeronautical metaphor), your friend is describing her relationship as a car traveling on a bumpy road and reaching a dead end, and she is unsure whether the vehicle can go forward under these circumstances (Lakoff, 1985, 1989, 1997).

Several features of this scenario in the café are striking. First, your friend is not Shakespeare—"love is a car" would probably not have played well at the Globe Theatre. Yet both of you understand what she is saying because you share a metaphor rooted in your culture.

Second, in transforming her experience into words, she is manipulating representations—knowledge about cars and relationships—and mapping one knowledge domain onto another (a rough time in a relationship is a bumpy road; feeling "stuck" in a relationship despite efforts to talk is like spinning your wheels trying to get out of a snowbank). She is speaking in highly evocative poetry—and you are able to understand it— without a second's thought and without any likely awareness on your part or hers of the metaphor guiding your thinking.

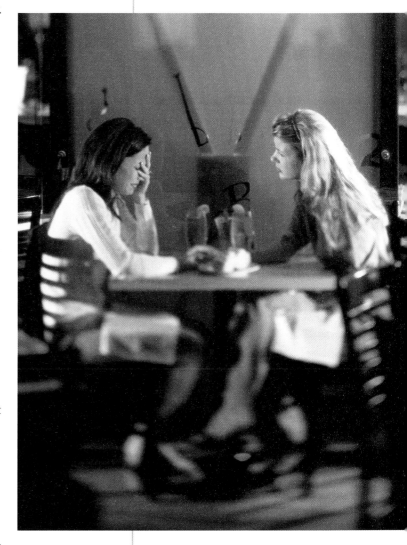

Finally, and perhaps most importantly, through words, a set of thoughts and feelings in one person's mind enters another's.

This chapter is about thought and language—the ways we transform and manipulate mental representations to navigate our way through life (another journey metaphor) and interact with others using words. We begin by exploring the basic units of thought, such as mental images and concepts, and the way people manipulate these units to reason, to solve problems, and to make decisions. Next we examine implicit and everyday thinking, exploring how people solve problems and make judgments outside awareness, often relying on emotion as well as cognition. Then we turn to language, the system of symbols that forms the medium for much of human thought and communication. Could we think in metaphor without language? When we have an idea, do we *translate* it into language, or are complex thoughts inherently linguistic? Finally, we examine the way children learn language, and address the question of whether evolution has created a brain specifically attuned to linguistic information.

Units of Thought

In many ways, thought is simply an extension of perception and memory. When we perceive, we form a mental representation. When we remember, we try to bring that representation to mind. When we think, we use representations to try to solve a problem or answer a question. **Thinking** means *manipulating mental representations for a purpose.*

Manipulating Mental Representations

People can manipulate virtually any kind of representation in their minds. You may not have realized it, but the last time you sniffed the milk and decided it was spoiled, you were thinking with your nose (actually, with olfactory representations). Or consider what happens when people harmonize while singing along with the radio.

Although their companions in the car may not appreciate it, they are engaged in an impressive act of musical thinking, unconsciously manipulating auditory representations and using sophisticated rules of harmonic structure, probably with no awareness whatsoever.

Thinking in Words and Images Much of the time humans think using words and images. When people try to figure out whether they have enough money with them to buy an extra bag of pretzels or how to tell an unwanted suitor they are not interested, they usually think in words. At other times they rely on **mental images**, *visual representations* such as the image of a street or a circle.

Psychologists once disagreed about whether people actually think in images or whether they convert visual questions into verbal questions in order to solve them. For example, to figure out how to carry a large desk through a narrow doorway, do people somehow rotate a visual image of the desk in their minds, or do they convert the problem into statements (e.g., "the desk won't fit if it isn't turned sideways")?

A classic study addressed this question by showing subjects pictures of a stimulus such as a capital *R*, rotated between 0 and 360 degrees (Figure 7.1). The subject had to decide whether the letter was shown normally or in mirror image. The results were clear: The amount of time subjects took to answer varied directly with the degree of rotation from upright. In other words, the more the rotation, the longer the reaction time. This finding indicated that subjects were actually mentally rotating an image of the letter to come to a conclusion (Cooper, 1976; Cooper & Shepard, 1973). Supporting these findings, recent PET studies show that perceiving, remembering, and mentally manipulating visual scenes all involve activation of the visual cortex (Farah, 2000; Kosslyn et al., 1993).

As we saw in Chapter 5, humans are not the only animals that use mental images or mental maps. In fact, other animals seem to understand geometry! In one

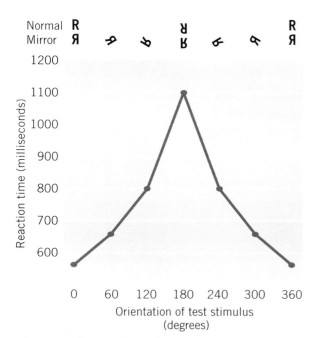

FIGURE 7.1 The manipulation of visual representations. The investigators asked participants to determine whether the "R" they saw at different degrees of rotation was forward or backward. The dependent variable was the amount of time required to accomplish the task. The figure graphs reaction time as a function of degree of rotation. As you can see, the more that subjects had to rotate the letter mentally, the longer they took to complete the task. Peak reaction time was at 180 degrees, which requires the furthest rotation. *Source:* Adapted from Cooper & Shepard, 1973.

study, the investigators consistently hid birdseed midway between two pipes on a wall, but they moved the pipes different distances from each other so that nutcrackers flying around the room had to keep finding the new midpoint (Kamil & Jones, 1997). Remarkably, the birds were consistently able to locate the midpoint to find the seed.

They also appeared to be mentally drawing a straight line between the two pipes, which were always placed one above the other, since they tended to land right on the line that intersected them rather than to the right or left.

Mental Models   People also frequently think by using **mental models**, *representations that describe, explain, or predict the way things work* (Johnson-Laird, 1999; Johnson-Laird et al., 2000). Mental models may be simple, like most people's understanding of automobiles ("If the car doesn't start, there's a problem somewhere under the hood") or a child's understanding of what a "cavity" is (a bad thing in the mouth that requires a trip to the dentist). On the other hand, they can be complex, such as the mental models used by mechanics to troubleshoot a car or a dentist's conception of the processes that produce cavities.

Although mental models often include visual elements (such as the dentist's visual representations of different kinds of teeth and what erosion in a tooth looks like), they always include descriptions of the *relations* among elements. For example, the dentist may have a *causal* model of how buildup of food residues leads to bacteria that eats away at a tooth.

INTERIM SUMMARY

Thinking means manipulating mental representations for a purpose. Much of the time people think using words, **mental images** (visual representations), and **mental models** (representations that describe, explain, or predict the way things work).

Concepts and Categories

Before people can think about an object, they usually have to *classify* it so that they know what it is and what it does. An approaching person is a friend or a stranger; a piece of fruit on the table is an apple or an orange.

People and things fall into *groupings based on common properties* called **categories**. A **concept** is *a mental representation of a category*, that is, an internal portrait of a class of objects, ideas, or events that share common properties (Goldstone & Kersten, 2003; Murphy & Medin, 1985; Smith, 1995). Some concepts can be visualized, but a concept is broader than its visual image. For example, the concept *car* stands for a class of vehicles with four wheels, seating space for at least two people, and a generally predictable shape. Other concepts, like *honest*, defy visualization or representation in any other sensory mode, although they may have visual associations (such as an image of an honest face).

The process of identifying an object as an instance of a category—recognizing its similarity to some objects and dissimilarity to others—is called **categorization**. Categorization is essential to thinking, because it allows people to make inferences about objects. For example, if I classify the drink in my glass as an alcoholic beverage, I am likely to make assumptions about how many I can drink and what I will feel like afterward.

Defining Features and Prototypes   For years, philosophers and psychologists have wrestled with the question of how people categorize objects or situations (Medin et al., 2000; Medin & Smith, 1981). How do they decide that a crab is not a spider, even though crabs look like big hairless tarantulas?

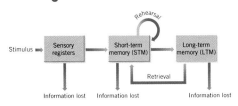

Making Connections

The standard model of memory described in Chapter 6 is an example of a mental model.

- To what extent is it visual?
- What nonvisual elements does the model include?

Apply & Discuss

■ At what point does an animal become categorized as human?

■ What principles do we use to make that decision? Does the concept human have defining features?

Defining Features   One possibility is that people compare the features of objects with a list of **defining features**—*qualities that are essential, or necessarily present, in order to classify the object as a member of the category*. For some concepts this strategy could work. Concepts like salt, water, or triangle are **well-defined concepts**—they *have properties clearly setting them apart from other concepts*. A triangle can be defined as a two-dimensional geometric figure with three sides and three angles, and anything that does not fit this definition is not a triangle.

Most of the concepts used in daily life, however, are not easily defined (Rosch, 1978). Consider the concept *good*. This concept takes on different meanings when applied to a meal or a person: Few of us look for tastiness in a person or honesty and sensitivity in a meal. Similarly, the concept *adult* is fuzzy around the edges, at least in Western cultures: At what point does a person stop being an adolescent and become an adult? Is a person an adult at voting age? At drinking age? At marriage?

Prototypes   Even where concepts are well defined, consulting a list of defining features is, in psychological time (i.e., milliseconds), a rather slow procedure. As we saw in Chapter 4, a person flipping through television stations with a remote control can recognize scenes and classify the objects in them far faster than anyone could possibly go through a list of defining features.

People typically classify objects rapidly by judging their *similarity* to concepts stored in memory (Estes, 1994; Robertson et al., 1999; Tversky, 1977). For example, if asked whether Windsor, Ontario, is a city, most people compare it with their image of a crowded, bustling, typical example of a city, such as New York City, or with a generalized portrait extracted from experience with several cities, such as Los Angeles, Toronto, New York, and London.

Researchers have learned how people use similarity in classification by measuring their speed of responding to visual and verbal categorization tasks. In visual categorization tasks, the experimenter states the name of a target category (e.g., *bird*) and then presents a picture and asks whether it is a member of the category. In verbal categorization tasks, the target category is followed by a word instead of a picture (e.g., *sparrow*); the task for the subject is to judge whether the second word is an instance of the category. People rapidly recognize that a robin is a bird but take 100 to 200 milliseconds longer to classify a penguin (see Smith, 1995). The reason is that a robin is a more *prototypical* bird; that is, it shares more of the characteristic features of the concept (Rosch, 1978).

A **prototype** is *an abstraction across many instances of a category* (such as robins, bluebirds, and sparrows). When people construct a prototype in their minds, they essentially abstract out the most important common features of the objects in a category. Thus, the prototype of a bird does not look exactly like any particular bird

People readily recognize robins as birds. Categorizing penguins takes a little more thought—and hence measurably more time.

Shape	Defining features	Characteristic features	Exemplars
	• Electronic device • Has a particular architecture, or operating design • Uses digital processor to perform computations	• Has a keyboard • Has a screen • Can be used for word processing • Can store information on hard drive or disks	• IBM Pentium • Macintosh

FIGURE 7.2 Multiple ways concepts can represent information.

the person has ever seen; it is more like an airbrushed photograph that smoothes out idiosyncratic features.

When people judge similarity in visual tasks, they rely primarily on shape. When they judge similarity verbally, they tend to rely on *characteristic* or *prototypical features*, that is, qualities typically found in members of a category. For example, most birds fly, sing, and lay eggs. People classify robins quickly because they do all three. Penguins take longer to classify because they lay eggs but do not share many other features of birds, except for having wings (see Malt & Smith, 1984).

Most concepts include both visual information and information about characteristic features, so that in everyday categorization, people often use some combination of the two. People may also compare an object to an *exemplar*, a particularly good example of the category (such as a robin), rather than an abstract prototype (Medin & Schaffer, 1978; Smith, 1998).

Categorization Is Functional   Are these two views of categorization—one based on defining features and the other on similarity—irreconcilable? People probably represent information in multiple ways that they use flexibly in different categorization tasks (Figure 7.2). As with other psychological processes, categorization is *functional*. Rapid, implicit categorization usually relies primarily on similarity. However, if a person has difficulty implicitly classifying a novel object based on similarity or if the classification task is complex, she may switch to explicit categorization based on defining features (or on features that may not be defining but are nevertheless *useful* or *diagnostic*).

Complex classification tasks generally require careful, explicit evaluation of the data. A doctor will not diagnose appendicitis in a patient whose symptoms appear similar to a textbook case of appendicitis (a prototype) or cases she has seen before (exemplars) unless a laboratory test shows an abnormal white blood cell count. The symptoms of appendicitis are similar to those of food poisoning and the flu, so that rapid similarity judgments may not be precise enough to start sharpening the scalpel.

The strategies people use to categorize also depend on what they are told and what they think will be most useful. For example, when given an instruction (e.g., "sort the stones into light and dark"), people tend to use rule-based (defining features) categorization, but in the absence of a rule, they tend to rely on similarity judgments (Allen & Brooks, 1991). Neuroimaging studies confirm that people often carry out both kinds of categorization and that these two types activate different neural circuits (Smith et al., 1998).

Big Picture φ Question 7

To what extent are psychological processes conscious or unconscious—that is, explicit versus implicit?

INTERIM SUMMARY

A **concept** is a mental representation of a class of objects, ideas, or events that share common properties. **Categorization** is the process of identifying an object as an instance of a category. Although people sometimes categorize objects by comparing them with a list of **defining features**, people typically classify objects rapidly by judging their similarity to **prototypes** (abstract representations of a category) stored in memory.

Hierarchies of Concepts   Many concepts are hierarchically ordered, with subconcepts at varying levels of abstraction. We categorize all pets that pant, slobber, and bark as dogs, but we can further subdivide the concept *dog* into more specific categories such as *collie* and *poodle*. Similarly, *dog* itself is a member of larger, more general categories such as *mammal* and *vertebrate* (Figure 7.3).

Efficient thinking requires choosing the right level of abstraction. A woman walking down the street in a bright purple raincoat belongs to the categories *mammal, vertebrate*, and *human* just as clearly as she belongs to the category *woman*. Yet we are more likely to say "Look at that woman in the purple raincoat" than "Look at that vertebrate in brightly colored apparel."

The Basic Level of Categorization   The level people naturally tend to use in categorizing objects is known as the **basic level**: *the broadest, most inclusive level at which objects share common attributes that are distinctive of the concept* (i.e., attributes that "stand out") (Rosch, 1978). The basic level is the level at which people categorize most quickly; it is thus the "natural" level to which the mind gravitates. Thus, *woman* is a basic-level category; so are *dinner, car*, and *bird*.

At times, however, people categorize at the **subordinate level**, *the level of categorization below the basic level in which more specific attributes are shared by members of a category*. Thus, people on a nature hike distinguish between robins and wrens. The natural level at which people tend to classify an *unusual* instance of a category, such as penguin, is often the subordinate level (Jolicoeur, Gluck & Kosslyn 1984).

People also sometimes classify objects at the **superordinate level**, *an abstract level in which members of a category share few common features*. A farmer, for example, may ask, "are the animals in the barn?" rather than running down a list including chickens, horses, and so forth. The superordinate level is one level more abstract than the basic level, and members of this class share fewer specific features (Figure 7.3).

The metaphors people use tend to be mapped at the superordinate, rather than the basic, level (Lakoff, 1997). In the example that opened this chapter, the underlying metaphor was that *love is a journey*, and hence a *relationship is a vehicle*. Since the richest, most evocative information is stored at the basic level, using the superordinate level allows the mapping of *multiple* rich concepts onto the current situation. Thus, the listener was not surprised when the woman talking about her relationship seemingly mixed metaphors in likening her relationship to a car but throwing in a metaphor based on a different kind of vehicle, an airplane ("he just wants to *bail out*"). She could also have used the metaphor of a boat: Initially the relationship had been *smooth sailing*, but now it is *on the rocks* or has *gotten off course*.

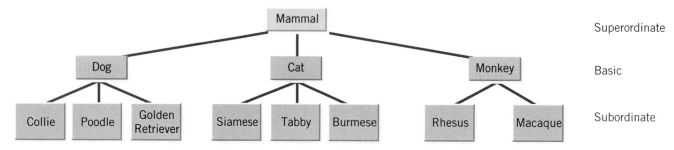

FIGURE 7.3   Superordinate, basic, and subordinate levels of categorization.

Neuroimaging research suggests that categorizing at different levels actually activates different cognitive processes and neural networks. In one study the experimenters presented participants with line drawings of objects followed by a word (Kosslyn et al., 1995). The participant was to decide whether the object was an instance of the category. Some of the words were at the basic level (such as *shirt*), whereas others were subordinate (*dress shirt*) or superordinate (*clothing*).

The researchers reasoned that identifying an object at the superordinate level requires a memory search using language (e.g., mentally "looking up" whether a shirt is a kind of clothing). In contrast, an object at a subordinate level requires a perceptual search of the object to see if it has particular features (e.g., does the shirt have the characteristic collar of a dress shirt?).

The results were as hypothesized: Categorizing at the superordinate level activated a region of the *left* prefrontal cortex involved in verbal memory retrieval. In contrast, categorizing at the subordinate level activated the *right* prefrontal cortex along with circuits involved in paying visual attention to the object.

One Person's Basic May Be Another's Subordinate   Although the basic level shows surprising similarity across people and cultures, the more a person knows about a particular domain, the more likely she is to use more specific rather than basic-level terms (Mervis & Rosch, 1981; Tanaka & Taylor, 1991). For example, clinical psychologists do not use words like *nut* to describe a psychotic patient or say that a person "has problems," as people do in everyday discourse. Instead, they make a more specific diagnosis that identifies precisely what the problem is.

The basic level of categorization also changes according to the situation. During the workday, furniture makers may refer to chairs according to specific types (for instance, an oak ladder-back reproduction), but when the day ends and they are ready to rest their feet, *chair* will suffice (Holland et al., 1986).

Basic-level categories also vary to some extent across cultures (Medin et al., 2002; Robertson, et al., 2002). While *love* is a basic-level concept for most Westerners, the Native American Utku have two basic level concepts for love: love-for-those-who-need-protection and love-for-those-who-are-charming-or-admired (J. A. Russell, 1994).

Making Connections

The self-concept, like other concepts, appears to be hierarchically organized. For example, we often have a general view of ourselves but more specific views of what we are like with our friends and with our parents (which might include subordinate concepts of self-with-mother and self-with-father) (Chapter 17).

Big Picture φ Question 4

To what extent is human nature particular versus universal?

Culture and Categorization   A Global Vista

To a large extent, culture shapes not only the categories people consider basic but also the way they group things together (Lopez et al., 1997; Mishra, 1997). One tribe of Australian aborigines includes women, fire, and dangerous things in one category (Lakoff, 1985). This category would make little sense to members of other societies, but to the aborigines it seems perfectly natural. In their mythology, the sun—a woman—is the wife of the moon. Because the sun gives off heat, it is associated with fire, and since fire is dangerous, both the sun and women are linked to dangerous things. Although this way of classifying may seem peculiar to the Western ear, consider the difficulty a Christian might have explaining to an aboriginal Papuan how Jesus could simultaneously be a man, a god, a spirit, and the Son of God.

One study examined the influence of culture on categorization, comparing 100 college students from New Mexico with 80 illiterate Manu farmers from a small village in Liberia, Africa (Irwin et al., 1974). To assess people's ability to categorize and think abstractly, psychologists in the West often use card-sorting tasks. The psychologist presents participants with a deck of cards showing different geometric forms (squares, triangles, etc.). The geometric forms vary in color and number. The task is to figure out the three dimensions on which the cards vary and sort them by category (i.e., by form, color, and number). The subject has a certain amount of time (in this study, five minutes) in which to sort the cards in all three correct ways. Previous studies had found

Table 7.1 ■ ■ Sorting Performance of U.S. and Manu Subjects Using Cards and Rice				
	Mean Number of Correct Sorts		Mean Time Taken to Perform Sorts (sec)	
Sample	Cards	Rice	Cards	Rice
United States	2.92	1.82	11.42	27.80
Manu	1.42	2.10	49.40	42.43

U.S. subjects performed better with cards, a familiar stimulus.

Manu subjects performed better with rice, a familiar stimulus.

Source: Adapted from Irwin et al., 1974.

Apply & Discuss

Recently, scientists have discovered that some nonhuman animals also have a sense of self. For example, both dolphins and chimpanzees who have learned to identify themselves in a mirror, notice (and try to remove) marks placed on their foreheads.

■ To what extent do these findings indicate that dolphins and chimpanzees can "think" about the self?

■ To what extent is self-identification a characteristic of humans, and why do so few other animals share it?

that preliterate people often did poorly on this task, which psychologists attributed to their lack of formal education.

The experimenters in this study wondered, however, whether the apparent superiority of Western subjects on this task would disappear if the task involved materials more familiar to the Manu. An extremely familiar object in Manu culture is rice, which comes in different forms that the Manu readily distinguish. Thus, the experimenters adapted the sorting task to fit Manu experience by presenting subjects with bowls of rice. The bowls varied in amount of rice, type (long grain and short grain), and texture (polished versus unpolished). The task, then, was to sort the rice using each of these three categories. The researchers hypothesized that Manu subjects would do better on the rice task, whereas North American subjects would do better on the card sort task.

In fact, North American subjects performed much better and faster on the card-sorting task, which is more familiar to them, than on rice sorting (Table 7.1). The opposite was true for the Manu, whose performance was substantially better when sorting rice than sorting cards. Interestingly, however, Western subjects were faster on both tasks than the Manu, and their performance was generally superior. This result likely reflects both the effects of education, which teaches children to think in systematic ways, and greater exposure to tests, particularly timed ones.

Culture can also affect the extent to which people rely on similarity or defining features in categorizing objects. East Asians tend to use exemplar- and prototype-based categorization relying on similarity. North Americans are more likely to look for rules (Nisbett et al., 2001). This difference is consistent with a general tendency in Eastern cultures to favor holistic over analytical thinking (Peng & Nisbett, 1999). Whether it reflects primarily a cultural difference or the longer history of industrialization in the West (which requires breaking things down into their component parts, as in creating an assembly line or software program) is not yet clear.

Thus, to what extent do principles of categorization vary across cultures? Categorization is constrained by the nature of reality, which leads to cross-cultural universals. People everywhere group some things together simply because that is the way they are. At the same time, people tend to categorize in ways that help them solve problems (Medin et al., 1997), and these problems differ across cultures and individuals.

INTERIM SUMMARY

Many concepts are hierarchically ordered. The level people naturally tend to use in categorizing objects is known as the **basic level**. One level up is the **superordinate** level, and one level down is the **subordinate** level. Culture shapes not only the categories people consider basic but also the way they group things together. Categorization, like most cognitive processes, is functional, so that people tend to categorize in ways that help them solve problems.

Reasoning, Problem Solving, and Decision Making

Mental images, mental models, and concepts are the building blocks of thought. In the next several pages, we explore how people manipulate these elementary units of thought to reason, solve problems, and make decisions.

Reasoning

Reasoning refers to *the process by which people generate and evaluate arguments and beliefs* (Anderson, 1985; Holyoak & Spellman, 1993). Philosophers have long distinguished two kinds of reasoning: inductive and deductive. We examine each separately here, although as we shall see, psychologists have begun to question whether induction and deduction are really distinct *psychological* processes (Rips, 1990). We then explore one of the most powerful mechanisms people use to make inferences, particularly about novel situations: reasoning by analogy.

Inductive Reasoning   Kissing and casual contact (such as handshakes) do not transmit HIV, which leads to AIDS. How do we know this? Early in the epidemic, scientists interviewed a large number of people who had casual contact with HIV-positive individuals. Whereas people who had sexual intercourse with people with HIV had an increased likelihood of testing positive, those who had not did not. Thus, scientists concluded that casual contact does not, as a rule, cause HIV infection. This kind of thinking is called **inductive reasoning**—*reasoning from specific observations to more general propositions* (Holland et al., 1986).

Inductive reasoning relies on probabilities. An inductive conclusion is not *necessarily* true because its underlying premises are only probable, not certain. A few people who reported kissing a person with HIV did come down with AIDS, but whether they had contracted the virus some other way or had been unwilling to admit more than kissing was not absolutely certain.

Inductive reasoning is clearly fallible. One four-year-old child, for example, used inductive reasoning to reinforce her fear of the bogeyman: If Santa can come down the chimney, she reasoned, so can the bogeyman! Nevertheless, inductive reasoning is essential in daily life. Every time we categorize an object, we are using a form of inductive reasoning. When we classify a novel animal as a cat, we assume that a particular body shape, whiskers, and feline body movements imply "cat-hood." In reality, the animal could turn out to be an unusual rabbit or a species with which we are unfamiliar.

Deductive Reasoning   **Deductive reasoning** is *logical reasoning that draws a conclusion from a set of assumptions, or premises*. In contrast to inductive reasoning, it starts with an idea rather than an observation. In some ways, deduction is the flipside of induction: Whereas induction starts with specifics and draws general conclusions, deduction starts with general principles and makes inferences about specific instances. For example, if you understand the general premise that all dogs have fur and you know that Barkley is a dog, then you can deduce that Barkley has fur, even though you have never made Barkley's acquaintance.

This kind of deductive argument is referred to as a syllogism. A **syllogism** consists of *two premises that lead to a logical conclusion*. If it is true that

(A) all dogs have fur and

(B) Barkley is a dog,

then there is no choice but to accept the conclusion that

(C) Barkley has fur.

Unlike inductive reasoning, deductive reasoning can lead to *certain* rather than simply *probable* conclusions, as long as the premises are correct and the reasoning is logical.

The Influence of Content on Deductive Reasoning   Although deductive reasoning seems completely "logical," in everyday life both the form (abstract or concrete) and content of deductive reasoning problems influence how easily people solve them

Apply & Discuss

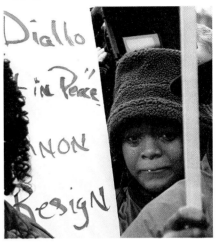

When four New York City police officers saw Amidou Diallo reach for his wallet, they shot him—40 times—believing he was reaching for a gun.

■ What factors might have influenced their induction that when he reached, he was reaching for a gun?

■ What factors might have influenced the protestors who expressed outrage when a jury acquitted the officers of murder?

FIGURE 7.4   Card selection task. If each card has a number on one side and a letter on the other, which cards must be turned over to verify or disprove the rule, "If a card has an A on one side, then it has a 3 on the other"? *Source:* Wason, 1968.

In a crackdown against drunk drivers, Massachusetts law enforcement officials are revoking liquor licenses left and right. You are a bouncer in a Boston bar, and you'll lose your job unless you enforce the following law:

> If a person is drinking beer, then he or she must be at least 21 years old.

In front of you are four cards belonging to four patrons of your bar. Each card has the person's age on one side and what she or he is drinking on the other. Which cards must you turn over to ensure that the law is being followed?

Answer: 1 and 3

FIGURE 7.5   Card selection task with familiar content. *Source:* Adapted from Griggs and Cox, 1982.

(Cosmides, 1989; Thompson et al., 2003; Wilkins, 1982). Consider the card problem presented in Figure 7.4 . Participants are shown four cards and told that each card has a letter on one side and a number on the other. They are also told that the cards conform to the following rule: *If a card has an A on one side, then it has a 3 on the other side.* The task: Turn over only those cards necessary to discover whether the rule is true or false (Johnson-Laird et al., 1972; Wason, 1968).

While most people correctly conclude that they must turn over the card with the *A* on it (a number other than 3 would falsify the rule), few also realize that they must turn over the 2 card: Finding an *A* on the opposite side of this card would disprove the rule just as surely as would turning over the *A* card and finding something other than a 3. Most subjects also think they have to turn over the 3 card, which is irrelevant: If an *A* is not on the other side, it has no bearing on the rule *If A, then 3*. (If your self-esteem has just plummeted, take heart, I did not get this right on the first try, either.) If the same problem is posed with more familiar contents, deductive reasoning is much easier (Figure 7.5).

If deductive reasoning depends in part on the content of the premises, do people really solve deductive problems by mentally manipulating abstract propositions? According to one theory, deduction is actually less about formal rules of inference (about *A*s and *B*s) than about forming mental models of each of the premises, which allows the person to draw reasonable judgments about the conclusion (Johnson-Laird, 1995).

For example, if asked to solve a syllogism of the form, "If *A* is on the left of *B*, and *B* is on the left of *C*, then…," people typically *visualize* the scene, creating a mental model that combines the premises. According to this view, people make both inductive and deductive inferences by imagining scenarios or scenes and the relations among their elements and then imagining what they are, could be, or could not be like.

Are Deduction and Induction Really Distinct Processes?   Because the content of a syllogism can influence the ability to solve it, some psychologists now question whether induction and deduction are really different forms of reasoning (Rips, 1990, 1995). If people can reason more accurately about the properties of Barkley the dog and fur than about *A*'s and *B*'s, perhaps they are really intermingling deduction and induction—using mental models about the world that emerged inductively to draw deductive conclusions. At the very least, maybe they are using their inductive knowledge about reality to *check* their logical deductions (Johnson-Laird, 1996, 1999; Oakhill et al., 1989). Further, where do the premises of deductive logic come from, such as the proposition that all dogs have fur? Usually from induction—from seeing several dogs and noticing that they all have fur.

Some fascinating neurological data bear on this issue. In a series of studies, researchers tested syllogistic reasoning in psychiatric patients just before and after treatment with electroconvulsive therapy (ECT, or "shock therapy") (Deglin & Kinsbourne, 1996). Electroconvulsive therapy is sometimes used to treat depression when other methods have proven ineffective (Chapter 16). Because jarring the brain with electric shocks temporarily disrupts cognitive functioning, the procedure is typically applied to only one hemisphere.

Patients with right-hemisphere ECT, who had to rely on their left hemisphere (the "analytical" side of the brain), solved syllogisms using formal, theoretical reasoning. When given syllogisms with false premises, they did not seem to notice and continued to test the logic of the syllogism. In contrast, patients with left-hemisphere ECT, who had to rely on their right hemispheres, tried to reason from their knowledge and personal experience. When given syllogisms with unfamiliar content or obviously false premises, they often refused to respond. These data suggest that the right and left hemispheres may contribute differently to deductive reasoning, with the left hemisphere evaluating the "pure" logic and the right hemisphere responding to the content.

Is Deductive Reasoning Universal? Deductive reasoning seems like it would follow similar principles everywhere. However, recent research suggests that Eastern and Western cultures may follow somewhat different rules of logic—or at least have different levels of tolerance for certain kinds of inconsistency (Norenzayan & Nisbett, 2000; Peng & Nisbett, 1999). The tradition of logic in the West, extending from ancient Greece to the present, places an enormous premium on the law of noncontradiction: Two statements that contradict each other cannot both be true. This law is central to solving syllogisms.

In the East, in contrast, people often view contradictions with much more acceptance, and often believe them to contain great wisdom—like principles of *ying* and *yang*. Consider the statements, "People are the same over time," and "People are never the same from one moment to the next." Each statement has considerable truth. In the West, the law of noncontradiction leads us to try to resolve paradoxes such as these—to find ways to resolve the contradiction, by qualifying one statement or the other, integrating the two, or deciding that one is not true after all. In the East, in contrast, the focus is instead on finding the truth that each statement provides—relishing rather than resolving paradox.

Reasoning by Analogy Deductive and inductive reasoning are central to human intelligence. So is reasoning by analogy—**analogical reasoning**—*the process by which people understand a novel situation in terms of a familiar one* (Gentner & Holyoak, 1997). Thus, to a cognitive psychologist, the mind is like a computer or a network of neurons; to a premedical student primarily studying physics, biology, and organic chemistry, a literature course may be "a breath of fresh air."

People use analogies to categorize novel situations, make inferences, and solve problems. They also try to influence the inferences other people will make and the conclusions they will reach by using analogies that suit their own goals. For example, during the Gulf War, former U.S. President George Bush compared Saddam Hussein to Hitler. If we accept this premise, then Iraq's invasion of Kuwait was like Germany's invasion of its neighbors at the start of World War II, an implication that Saddam must be stopped immediately before becoming a danger to the world (Spellman & Holyoak, 1992). Similarly, Saddam compared Bush and the United States to Satan, an implication that fighting the enemy was a holy war.

A key aspect of analogies of this sort is that the familiar situation and the novel situation must each contain a system of elements that can be mapped onto one another (Gentner, 1983; Gentner & Markman, 1997). For an analogy to take hold, the two situations need not *literally* resemble each other; Saddam did not look much like Hitler (although each sported a distinctive mustache), and Iraq was not a mighty power like Germany. However, the elements of the two situations must relate to one another in a way that explains how the elements of the novel situation are related. If we accepted the analogy that Saddam was like Hitler, then his behavior could be understood as the actions of a ruthless, power-hungry megalomaniac who must be stopped before he took over any more of his neighbors.

The analogies people use can be highly influenced by emotionally significant events. World War II played a central role in determining the analogies that shaped foreign policy in the West for three decades. When communist governments began coming to power in Asia in the late 1940s and 1950s, policy makers in the West had the analogy of prewar Germany squarely in mind: To "lose" another country to communism was like letting another country fall to Hitler.

As a consequence, in the 1960s, the United States entered into a war against the communists in North Vietnam. That war, however, led to disastrous consequences for the United States—60,000 dead soldiers and nothing to show for it—and created a

Apply & Discuss

Research has indicated that hearing-impaired individuals show reasoning deficits, particularly in the areas of inductive reasoning and cognitive flexibility (Passig & Eden, 2003).

▪ Why would this be?

▪ What role would different sensory modalities play in one's ability to think?

Big Picture φ Question 4

To what extent is human nature particular versus universal?

new analog as powerful to a younger generation of Americans as World War II had been to their elders. Thus, whenever an aggressor nation attacked one of its neighbors, opponents of intervention likened the situation to "another Vietnam."

INTERIM SUMMARY

Reasoning is the process by which people generate and evaluate arguments and beliefs. **Inductive reasoning** means reasoning from specific observations to more general propositions that seem likely to be true. **Deductive reasoning** means drawing a conclusion from a set of assumptions that is true if the premises are true. Both the form (abstract or concrete) and content of deductive reasoning problems such as syllogisms influence how easily people solve them. **Analogical reasoning** is the process by which people understand a novel situation in terms of a familiar one. Analogical reasoning is influenced by the similarity of the situations, the ease of mapping of their elements, and the reasoner's goals.

Problem Solving

Life is a series of problems to solve. How much should you tip the waiter? How are you going to be able to afford a new car? How do you decide what your college major will be?

Problem solving refers to *the process of transforming one situation into another to meet a goal* (Gilhooly, 1989; Greeno, 1978). The aim is to move from a current, unsatisfactory state (the *initial state*) to a state in which the problem is resolved (the *goal state*) (Figure 7.6). To get from the initial state to the goal state, the person uses *operators*, mental and behavioral processes aimed at transforming the initial state until it eventually approximates the goal (Miller et al., 1960; Newell & Simon, 1972).

In **well-defined problems**, *the initial state, goal state, and operators are easily determined*. Math problems are examples of well-defined problems (Kintsch & Greeno, 1985). Few problems are so straightforward in real life, however. **Ill-defined problems** occur when *both the information needed to solve them and the criteria for determining when the goal has been met are vague* (Schraw et al., 1995; Simon, 1978). For example, a manager trying to raise morale among his employees faces an ill-defined problem, since he may not know the extent of the problem or whether his efforts to solve it have been successful. (This is why business executives often call in organizational psychologists as consultants, to help them identify and measure problems, goal states, strategies for solving them, and criteria for assessing change.)

Solving a problem, once it has been clarified, can be viewed as a four-step process (Newell, 1969; Reiman & Chi, 1989). The first step is to compare the initial state with the goal state to identify precise differences between the two. Thus, if the initial state is that the person sitting next to you on a flight from Chicago to Melbourne, Australia, has decided that you are the perfect person to hear his life story (the problem), the goal state is to be free of his charming discourse.

The second step is to identify possible operators and select the one that seems most likely to reduce the differences. In this case, one possible strategy is to pull out a book and start reading. Another is to tell him how much you enjoy talking with people about your profession, theoretical mathematics.

The third step is to apply the operator or operators, responding to challenges or roadblocks by establishing **subgoals**—*minigoals on the way to achieving the broader goal*. For example, if your seatmate does not take the hint when you pull out a book and announce with great fanfare that you have to finish reading it by the end of the trip, you may determine that your only means of escape is to change seats. This subgoal then creates a search for operators (and flight attendants) that might help you attain it. The final step is to continue using operators until all differences between the initial state and the goal state are eliminated.

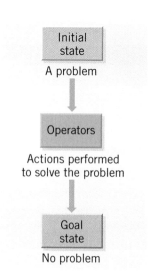

FIGURE 7.6 The problem-solving process. Problem solving means transforming an initial problem state, using operators, to attain a goal state.

Problem-Solving Strategies Problem solving would be impossible if people had to try every potential operator in every situation until they found one that worked. Instead, they employ **problem-solving strategies**, *techniques that serve as guides for solving a problem* (Demorest, 1986; Reimann& Chi, 1989).

For example, **algorithms** are *systematic procedures that inevitably produce a solution to a problem* (Anderson, 1995). Computers use algorithms in memory searches, as when a spell-check command compares every word in a file against an internal dictionary. Humans also use algorithms to solve some problems, such as counting the number of guests coming to a barbeque and multiplying by 2 to determine how many hot dogs to buy.

Algorithms are guaranteed to find a solution as long as one exists, but they are generally practical only for solving relatively simple problems. Imagine solving for the square root of 16,129 by methodically squaring 1, then 2, then 3, and so forth, each time checking to see if the answer is 16,129. (You would eventually arrive at the right answer, but only on your 127th try.)

One of the most important problem-solving strategies is **mental simulation**— *imagining the steps involved in solving a problem mentally before actually undertaking them*. People conduct mental simulations of this sort every day, such as imagining precisely how they will tell their boss about the vacation they want to take during the busy season, or picturing alternative routes to get to three different stores after work before the stores close.

Although many self-help books encourage people to visualize desired outcomes (the"power of positive thinking"), mentally simulating the steps to *achieving* those outcomes is usually more beneficial (Taylor et al., 1998). One study demonstrated this superiority with introductory psychology students facing a midterm examination. Students in one condition were told to visualize in detail the things they needed to do to get a good grade—for example, picturing themselves on their beds reviewing lecture notes. Students in the "positive-thinking" condition were instructed, instead, to visualize themselves receiving the grade they wanted and how good they would feel. Students who imagined the steps to achieving a good grade studied more hours and scored better on the exam than students in the positive-thinking group, who actually did worse than students in a control condition who did not visualize anything (Figure 7.7).

Problem Solving Gone Awry Most of us muddle through our lives solving problems relatively well. However, human problem solving is far from perfect. One common problem is **functional fixedness**, *the tendency for people to ignore other possible functions of an object when they have a fixed function in mind*. In a classic experiment, participants were asked to mount a candle on a wall so that, when it was lit, no wax would drip on the floor (Duncker, 1946). On a table lay a few small candles, some tacks, and a box of matches (Figure 7.8*a*). The tendency, of course, was to see a matchbox only as a receptacle for the matches. If the matches were *out* of the box, however, subjects solved the problem more easily (Figure 7.8*b*).

Another common error in problem solving is **confirmation bias**, *the tendency for people to search for confirmation of what they already believe* (see Klayman & Ha, 1989; Nickerson, 1998). In one study, the experimenters presented participants with three numbers (2, 4, and 6) and asked them to discover the rule used to construct this sequence of numbers by generating their own sets of numbers (Wason, 1960). Each time the subject generated a set of numbers, the experimenters responded as to whether the subject's numbers correctly illustrated the rule.

In fact, the rule was quite simple: any three numbers, arranged from smallest to largest. However, the way most people tried to solve the problem kept them from finding the rule. Instead of testing a variety of sequences—such as *3, 12, 428 or 7, -4, 46*— until only one rule remained plausible, most participants did just the opposite. Early on, they formed a hypothesis such as"add 2 to each number to form the next number" and repeatedly generated one sequence after another that confirmed this rule until

Outcome	Mental simulation	Positive thinking	Control
Number of hours studying	16.1	11.6	14.5
Grade (% of questions correct)	80.6	72.6	77.7

FIGURE 7.7 Effects of mental simulation on exam performance. Students who mentally simulated the steps involved in solving the problem of getting a good grade studied harder and were more successful than students who either visualized success ("positive thinking") without the steps or did not imagine anything.

Making Connections

A common problem-solving strategy is hypothesis testing—making an educated guess about what might solve the problem and then testing it. Hypothesis testing is not only common in everyday life but is also the basis of scientific method (Chapter 2).

FIGURE 7.8 (*a*) The candle problem. Use the objects on the table to mount a candle on the wall so that when it is lit, no wax drips on the floor. (Solution is on next page.)

FIGURE 7.8 (*b*) Solution to the candle problem. *Source:* Duncker, 1946.

Big Picture φ Question 3

To what extent is human psychology continuous with the psychology of other animals?

they were satisfied they were right. Confirmation bias can be a particular problem for experts in a field; for example, scientists studying a topic may test only those hypotheses and use only those methods that fit with current thinking (Sternberg, 1996).

Solving Problems with Numbers In literate societies, people are constantly called upon to think in numbers. Consider the following examples from two very different sources—a box of brownie mix and an income tax form (McCloskey & Macaruso, 1995):

- Grease bottom of 13 × 9-inch pan. Mix brownie mix, water, oil, and egg in large bowl. Beat 50 strokes by hand.... Bake at 350° F for 35 to 37 minutes.
- If line 32 is $81,350 or less, multiply $2,350 by the total number of exemptions claimed on line 6e. If line 32 is over $81,350, see the worksheet on page 25.

Solving mathematical problems, like most problem solving, involves both working memory and long-term memory and both declarative and procedural knowledge (Chapter 6) (Anderson, 1996). Consider the tax form. Deciding whether the amount on one line is greater than another involves bringing stored declarative information into working memory. The next step is to multiply the two numbers (procedural knowledge). Because these are large numbers (we hope), they place a heavy load on working memory: You have to multiply a digit from two columns, momentarily store the product, add one digit from this to the product of the next set of digits while retaining the other digit in memory, and repeat the process until arriving at a solution. (One of the best ways to increase working memory capacity in this case is to supplement it with a sheet of paper.)

Although cats and monkeys do not typically have tax forms to fill out, humans are not alone in the need to solve numerical problems. When a lion responds to the presence of other lions about to intrude into her territory, she is more cautious if she hears *three* approaching lions roar than she is hearing one, and she is more likely to mount an aggressive response if more of her kin and companions are present (McComb et al., 1994). From an evolutionary perspective, being able to "count" friends and enemies in such situations is essential to survival. Do lions actually have a concept of number? And how does a rat that is rewarded in a learning experiment for pressing a bar every 20th time know when the 20th time is approaching?

Although psychologists are still unraveling the mechanisms by which animals "count" (e.g., Roberts, 1995), research suggests that those of us who have trouble balancing our checkbooks might learn a few things from even the lowly rat (Davis, 1996; Davis & Perusse, 1988). For example, in one study, rats were punished if they ate more than a certain number of food pellets out of 20 pellets in front of them. Showing not only a talent for math but also some impressive self-restraint, the rats learned to eat the right number of pellets and leave the rest. In other studies, rats have even demonstrated an "understanding" that if A<B<C, then A<C (Davis, 1996)!

INTERIM SUMMARY

Problem solving means transforming an initial state into a more satisfying goal state using operators. People frequently rely on **problem-solving strategies** that serve as guides for solving problems, such as **algorithms** (systematic procedures that inevitably produce a solution), and **mental simulations** (imagining the steps involved in solving a problem before actually trying them out). In literate societies, people solve many problems with numbers, although even rats have considerable "mathematical" abilities.

Decision Making

Just as life is a series of problems to solve, it is also a series of decisions to make, from the mundane ("Should I buy the cheaper brand or the one that tastes better?") to the consequential ("What career should I choose?"). **Decision making** is *the process by*

Table 7.2 ■ ■ Calculating Weighted Utility Value

| | | Alternative Apartments | | | | | |
| | | 216 Green St. | | 16 Cedar St. | | 1010 California St. | |
Attributes (in order of importance)	Importance (numerical weight)	Utility Value	Weighted Utility Value	Utility Value	Weighted Utility Value	Utility Value	Weighted Utility Value
Rent	5	+10	×5 = 50	+ 8	×5 = 40	+ 5	×5 = 25
Location	4	0	×4 = 0	+ 3	×4 = 12	+10	×4 = 40
Livability	3	+ 8	×3 = 24	+ 3	×3 = 9	+ 1	×3 = 3
Parking	2	+10	×2 = 20	+10	×2 = 20	− 2	×2 = −4
Pets	1	+10	×1 = 10	−10	×1 = −10	+10	×1 = 10
			104		**71**		**74**

Source: Adapted from Edwards, 1977. Copyright © 1977 IEEE.

Note: Multiplying the utility value of each of several attributes by their importance yields weighted utility values for three apartments on five dimensions. Adding together the weighted utilities leads to a preference for the apartment at 216 Green Street.

which an individual weighs the pros and cons of different alternatives in order to make a choice.

According to one information-processing model, when people make decisions, they consider two things: the *utility* (value to them) of the outcomes of different options, and the *probability* (estimated likelihood) of each outcome (Edwards, 1977; Edwards & Newman, 1986). Suppose, for example, that you have found three apartments and must choose one. According to this model, you begin by deciding on criteria and assigning each a weight according to its importance (Table 7.2). Then you would assign a *utility value* for each key attribute of each option, which indicates how well the potential choice (the apartment) meets each criterion (such as affordable rent). The next step is to multiply the weight of the attribute by its utility value to determine its **weighted utility value**, *a combined measure of the importance of an attribute and the extent to which a given option satisfies it.* Finally, you add up the totals to determine which option has the highest overall weighted utility value.

In reality, of course, we don't always get what we want, and shooting for an unattainable goal may carry heavy costs. For example, the Green Street apartment may be so desirable that you have only a slight chance of getting it. Therefore, to make a rational decision, you must determine each option's **expected utility**, *a combined judgment of the weighted utility and the expected probability of obtaining that outcome.* An expected utility rating is obtained by multiplying the weighted utility by the expected probability of that outcome (Table 7.3).

Table 7.3 ■ ■ Calculating Expected Utility: Alternative Apartments

	216 Green St.	16 Cedar St.	1010 California St.
Weighted utility value	104	71	74
Probability of getting apartment	×.10	×.50	×.90
Expected utility	10.4	35.5	66.6

Source: Adapted from Edwards, 1977. Copyright © 1977 IEEE.

Note: Although the apartment on Green Street has the highest weighted utility value, its improbability makes it the worst choice among the three options.

INTERIM SUMMARY

Decision making is the process by which an individual weighs the pros and cons of different alternatives in order to make a choice. According to one information-processing model, when people make decisions, they consider both the utility of outcomes of different options and their probability. A **weighted utility value** is a combined judgment of the importance of an attribute and the extent to which a given option satisfies it. **Expected utility** is a combined judgment of the weighted utility and the expected probability of obtaining an outcome.

Implicit and Everyday Thinking

The models of problem solving and decision making we have just described largely follow a classical model of rationality that guided Western philosophers for centuries. It is the same model assumed by economists who view people as maximizing the utility of the goods they buy and by political scientists who view voters as rationally choosing the leaders who best reflect their interests. In this view, rationality means considering relevant data for making a judgment and then consciously manipulating this information to come to the most reasonable conclusion.

These models are both *de*scriptive and *pre*scriptive: They attempt to describe the way people think but also to prescribe the way rational people *should* think. The models emerged in the 1960s, when cognitive scientists compared the human mind to a computer and assumed that cognition, like memory, involves explicit, step-by-step activation of information.

As we saw in Chapter 6, however, the models and metaphors used by cognitive psychologists have shifted dramatically in the last decade, and this shift is changing our understanding not only of memory but also of thinking. Some hints about what was missing from these earlier models of **explicit cognition**—*cognition that involves conscious manipulation of representations*—actually came from behaviorist and psychodynamic models. As we saw in Chapter 6, aspects of these approaches are becoming increasingly compatible with contemporary cognitive models. From a behaviorist perspective, the pros and cons of different courses of action—their environmental consequences—determine the decisions people make, whether or not they think about these consequences. People learn, generalize, and discriminate stimuli all the time without conscious thought (Reber, 1992).

From a psychodynamic perspective, most problem solving and decision making involve motivation and emotion. A child with a learning disability who suffers repeated setbacks in school might "solve" this problem by convincing himself that he does not care about success or failure and hence stop making any effort. Further, some of the motives that underlie decisions are unconscious or implicit, a hypothesis that has now received considerable empirical support (Chapter 10).

How Rational Are We?

In recent years, cognitive psychologists have begun to wonder just how rational we humans really are. Some have pointed to the cognitive shortcuts people use that can lead them to make less than optimal decisions, whereas others have suggested that the concept of rationality itself may be limited (Mellers et al., 1998).

Heuristics   The assault on human rationality in psychology began when researchers noticed the extent to which people rely on **heuristics**, *cognitive shortcuts for selecting among alternatives without carefully considering each one*. Heuristics allow people to make rapid, efficient, but sometimes irrational judgments

of the brain invo
cally without cor
judgments (Liebe

Implicit Probl
"aha" experience:
hours or days lat
answer!"). Implic
associational net
active outside aw

For example,
uncommon word

■ Large brigl
with red o

If participants cc
words (in this ca
words, such as *de*
quickly decide w
initially been una
fects, responding
solved problem b
been unable to lc

Information
periods. Over tin
day are likely to s
reaches a potenti
ness (Yaniv & M
wake up from a c
also spread activa

Emotion, Mot

Alongside the re
gists' views of th
tial role played b
ments, inference:

Reason and E
bemoaned the w
10). Numerous st
processes can pr
are much more li
ticket by one dig
missed it" (Kahn
one digit has exa
digit (except, of
misses).

On the othe
sound judgment
posters and rated
al., 1993). The ir
mental group to
poster before rat
Afterward, partic

(Dawes, 1997; Nisbett & Ross, 1980). One example is the **representativeness heuristic**, in which *people categorize by matching the similarity of an object or incident to a prototype but ignore information about its probability of occurring*. Consider the following personality description (Tversky & Kahneman, 1974, p. 1124):

> Steve is very shy and withdrawn, invariably helpful, but with little interest in people or in the world of reality. A meek and tidy soul, he has a need for order and structure and a passion for detail.

Is Steve most likely a farmer, a salesman, an airline pilot, a librarian, or a physician? Most people think he is probably a librarian, even if they are told that librarians are much less common in the population from which Steve has been drawn than the other occupations. Although Steve's attributes seem typical or *representative* of a librarian, if the population has 50 salesmen for every librarian, the chances are high that Steve is a salesman.

Another example is the **availability heuristic**, in which *people infer the frequency of something on the basis of how readily it comes to mind* (Tversky & Kahneman, 1973). That is, people essentially assume that events or occurrences they can recall easily are common and typical. For example, in one study, participants were presented with a list of 26 names, half male and half female (McKelvie, 1997). Some of the names were famous, whereas others were not. When asked how many of the names were male or female, participants overestimated the gender that had more famous names, because famous names were more salient and hence available to consciousness.

The availability heuristic is generally adaptive because things that "stick in our minds" tend to be important; familiar or vivid occurrences come to mind more readily than less familiar or less striking events. Availability can, however, lead to biased judgments when striking or memorable events are in fact infrequent.

A dangerous real-life consequence of this heuristic occurs when parents choose not to have their children vaccinated because of fear of vaccine-induced death. Although news stories about children who die from adverse reactions to vaccines are far more common and memorable than stories about the number of children who no longer die of smallpox or polio, in fact, the likelihood of death from vaccines for childhood illnesses is many times smaller than the likelihood of death without these vaccines (Ritov & Baron, 1990).

Bounded Rationality   Researchers studying heuristics challenged the rational models described earlier by suggesting that human thought is highly susceptible to error. An emerging perspective takes this critique of pure reason one step further, arguing that because people rarely have complete information and limitless time, they are often *better off* using strategies for making inferences and decisions that might seem less than optimal to a philosopher (Gigerenzer & Goldstein, 1996). This view essentially places thought in its ecological context: People tend to do the best they can given the demands of the task and the cognitive resources they have available (H. Simon, 1990).

Underlying this view is the notion of **bounded rationality**, that *people are rational within the bounds imposed by their environment, goals, and abilities*. Thus, instead of making *optimal* judgments, people typically make *good-enough* judgments. Herbert Simon (1978) called this *satisficing*, a combination of *satisfying* and *sufficing*. When we choose a place to have dinner, we do not go through every restaurant in the phone book; rather, we go through a list of the restaurants that come to our minds and choose the one that seems most satisfying at the moment.

According to one theory, when people are called upon to make rapid inferences or decisions, they often use the strategy "take the best, ignore the rest" (Gigerenzer & Goldstein, 1996). Thus, instead of weighing all the information possible, they begin with a quick yes/no judgment; if that works, they stop and assume their inference is

---

Apply & Discuss

Most people believe that driving to a family holiday gathering a few hours away is safer than flying to India or Pakistan, with its history of terrorist activity. Statistically, however, the chances of fatality are much greater driving on a holiday.

■ What might lead to this example of the availability heuristic?

*A conclusion is the pla
thinking.*

—Author Unk

A few weeks later, the experimenters contacted them and asked how satisfied they were with their choice. Participants who had analyzed the reasons for their preferences were significantly less satisfied with their choice of poster than subjects who had chosen without reflection. Conscious thinking appears to have overridden automatic, unconscious reactions, which proved to be a better guide.

Assessing Risk   Many of the decisions people make in everyday life stem from their emotional reactions and their *expected* emotional reactions. This relationship is often apparent in the way people assess risks (Kahneman & Tversky, 1979; Mellers et al., 1997, 1998). Judging risk is a highly subjective enterprise, which leads to some intriguing questions about precisely what constitutes "rational" behavior. For example, in gambling situations, losses tend to influence people's behavior more than gains, even where paying equal attention to the two would yield the highest average payoff (Coombs & Lehner, 1984). Is this irrational?

Consider the following scenario. A person is offered the opportunity to bet on a coin flip. If the coin comes up heads, she wins a $100; if tails, she loses $99. From the standpoint of expected utility theory, the person should take the bet, because on average, this coin flip would yield a gain of $1. However, common sense suggests otherwise. In fact, for most people, the prospect of losing $99 is more negative than winning $100 is positive. Any given loss of X dollars has greater emotional impact than the equivalent gain.

Prospect theory suggests that the value of future gains and losses to most people is in fact asymmetrical, with losses having a greater emotional impact than gains (Kahneman & Tversky, 1979). Unlike expected utility theory, prospect theory describes the way people *actually* value different outcomes, rather than how they *should* value outcomes if they are behaving like the rational actors of economic theory. Prospect theory also predicts that people should be more willing to take a risk to avoid a loss than to obtain a gain.

Of course, how averse people are to risk depends in part on their circumstances. People tend to be more likely to take risks when the chips are down than when they are up (Tversky & Kahneman, 1981). For example, in a simulated tax collection experiment, participants who expected to receive a tax refund were less likely to write off questionable expenses than those who thought their deductions would not cover their taxes. These findings have practical implications for policy makers: If the government deducted more from people's paychecks during the year and gave it back to them in refunds, taxpayers would write off fewer questionable expenses (Robben et al., 1990).

Given the ambiguity of risk, it is not surprising that motivational and emotional factors play an important role in the way people assess it. Scientists who work in corporate research laboratories tend to find the risk of potential cancer-causing agents much smaller than do scientists who work at universities (Kraus et al., 1992). The difference depends upon who pays their salaries and hence what they are motivated to find.

Although prospect theory and other approaches to risk assessment describe the *average* person, people actually differ substantially in their willingness to take risks— and, in fact, in their enjoyment of risky behavior (Zuckerman, 1994). Some people are motivated more by fear, whereas others are motivated more by pleasure. These differences appear in part to reflect differences in whether their nervous systems are more responsive to norepinephrine, which regulates many fear responses, or dopamine, which is involved in pleasure seeking (Chapter 10).

Apply & Discuss

When choosing a mate, people often have criteria in mind, but their choices are guided as much by their "heart" and "gut" as by their head.

▪ When is this rational and when is it irrational?

Big Picture φ Q

To what extent can we i
through reasoning or th
that is, rationalism vers

INTERIM SUMMARY

Implicit cognition refers to cognition outside awareness. Much of learning is implicit, as people implicitly recognize patterns in the environment even though they may not be able to articulate these patterns explicitly. Problem solving can also occur implicitly, as in "aha" experiences. Motivation and emotion play a substantial role in everyday cognition.

Although emotion can disrupt cognition, it can also sometimes be a better guide for be-havior. Motives and emotions substantially influence the way people assess risks. Given the ambiguity involved in risk assessment, there may be no single "rational" assessment that is free of emotional influences.

Connectionism

As we discussed in Chapter 6, psychology is in the midst of a "second cognitive revo-lution," which has challenged the notion of the mind as a conscious, one-step-at-a-time information processor that functions like a computer. One of the major contrib-utors to this revolution is an approach to perception, learning, memory, thought, and language called **connectionism**, or **parallel distributed processing (PDP)**, which *asserts that most cognitive processes occur simultaneously through the action of multiple activated networks* (Holyoak & Simon, 1999; Rumelhart et al., 1986; Smolensky, 1988). Like traditional cognitive psychologists, connectionists use com-puter models to test their theories, but their explicit metaphor for cognitive process-ing is the mind as a set of neurons that activate and inhibit one another, rather than the mind as a computer with memory stores.

Parallel Distributed Processing   The easiest way to get a grasp of PDP models is to understand what is meant by the terms *parallel* and *distributed*. First and fore-most, PDP models emphasize parallel rather than serial processing. Human informa-tion processing is simply too fast and the requirements of the environment too in-stantaneous for serial processing (bringing information into working memory a piece at a time) to be our primary mode of information processing.

For example, in typing the word *vacuum*, the right hand does nothing until the first u, yet high-speed videotapes of skilled typists find that the right hand has moved into position to hit the *u* by the time the left hand is typing the *v*. This movement hap-pens so quickly that the typist cannot possibly be aware of it. Thus, even while the typist is focusing on the action of the left hand, recognition of the word "vacuum" has activated parallel systems that prepare the right hand for action (Rumelhart et al., 1986).

Second, according to PDP models, the meaning of a representation is not con-tained in some specific locus in the brain. Rather, it is spread out, or distributed, throughout an entire network of processing units (*nodes* in the network) that have be-come activated together through experience. Each node attends to some small aspect of the representation, and none alone "stands for" the entire concept. For instance, when a person comes across a barking dog, her visual system will simultaneously ac-tivate networks of neurons that have previously been activated by animals with two ears, four legs, and a tail. At the same time, auditory circuits previously "turned on" by barking will become active. The simultaneous activation of all these neural circuits identifies the animal with high probability as a dog. The person is not aware of any of this. All she consciously thinks is that she has come upon a dog.

These examples indicate how connectionist models explain categorization based on similarity. Current perceptions activate neural networks. A concept stored in memory is nothing but a series of nodes that become activated together and hence constitute a network; thus, if current perceptual experience (such as seeing the shape of a dog and hearing barking) activates a large enough number of those nodes, the stimulus will be classified as an instance of that concept.

However, several concepts may be activated simultaneously because many ani-mals have four legs and a tail. According to connectionist models, the concept that "wins out" is the one that best matches current perceptions, that is, the one with the most nodes in common with current perceptual input. Connectionist models offer a deceptively simple and compelling explanation of memory as well: Remembering a

Apply & Discuss

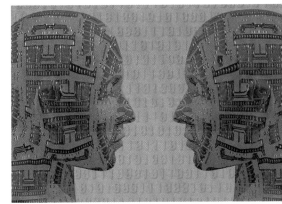

Artificial intelligence refers to the use of comput-ers to mimic human thinking and "intelligence." Movies, such as Steven Spielberg's *A. I.*, and con-ferences devoted to the study of artificial intelli-gence, have been on the rise. What role do you see artificial intelligence playing in the next decade? Do you think that ultimately computers will com-pletely mimic the human brain and be able to do all things humans could do?

FIGURE 7.9 Parallel distributed processing. People are able to decipher ambiguous or distorted messages by simultaneously processing parts (such as letters) and wholes (words and phrases). Source: Rumelhart, 1984, p. 8.

visual scene, such as a sunset, entails activation of a substantial part of the visual network that was active when the sunset was initially perceived.

The Brain Metaphor   According to the connectionist view, then, the brain represents knowledge through the interaction of hundreds, thousands, or millions of neurons, which constitute nodes in a neural network. Perception, memory, categorization, and inference lie in the *connections* among these nodes. Hence the term connectionism.

When neurons interact, they may either excite or inhibit other neurons, through the action of excitatory and inhibitory neurotransmitters (Chapter 3). Connectionist models postulate similar cognitive mechanisms. Consider the simple perceptual problem posed in Figure 7.9. Although the letters are ambiguous, either because they are slanted or because pieces are blotted out, you were probably unaware that your brain was performing some complex "computations" to determine what the letters and words were. Instead, the meaning of the words just seemed obvious.

The incomplete letters shown in Figure 7.9 are actually the norm in handwriting, where letters are never perfectly drawn. People can read handwriting rapidly because they simultaneously process information about the letters and the words. For example, in the top line of Figure 7.9, the second letter of each word could be either an *a* or an *h*. Both letters are thus activated by information-processing units whose job is letter recognition. At the same time, however, a word recognition processing unit recognizes that an *a* would render the first word a nonword and an *h* would do the same for the second word. The two processing modules interact, so that extra activation spreads to the *h* option in *the*, and the impossibility of *tae* as a word leads to inhibition of *a* as an option in that word.

On an even broader level, the phrase *the cat* is also being processed, and because no other phrase is possible using that configuration of letters, the brain is even more likely to come to the "decision" that the first word is *the* (because what else would precede cat and has three letters?), further spreading activation to the *h* in *the*. Similar processes account for the fact that we decode the second word in the figure as *RED*, even though substantial pieces of the letters are covered.

Parallel Constraint Satisfaction   As Figure 7.9 suggests, categorizing, making inferences, reading, and other cognitive processes actually require substantial "decision making" at an implicit level. The brain has to decide whether a letter is an *a* or an *h* or whether a four-legged animal with a tail is a dog or a cat. According to connectionist models, implicit decision making of this sort happens rapidly, automatically, and without awareness through a process of parallel constraint satisfaction.

Constraint satisfaction refers to *the tendency to settle on a cognitive solution that satisfies as many constraints as possible in order to achieve the best fit to the data*. A four-legged creature with a tail could be a dog or a cat, but if it starts barking, barking will further activate the *dog* concept and inhibit the *cat* concept, because the neurons representing barking spread activation to networks associated with dogs and spread inhibition to networks associated with cats.

Similarly, in reading the words in Figure 7.9, the brain has to satisfy constraints imposed by the structure of the word *t_e* as well as by the structure of the phrase *t_e c_t*, which will increase the activation of some possibilities and decrease the activation of others. To put it slightly differently, the nodes in a PDP network are like *hypotheses* about the presence or absence of a given feature, such as whether a letter is an *a* or an *h* (Read et al., 1997). Parallel distributed processing is an implicit everyday form of hypothesis testing, in which the brain weeds out hypotheses that data do not support and converges on hypotheses that best fit the data in light of multiple constraints processed in parallel.

The connections between nodes in a connectionist network are weighted according to the strength of the association between them and whether they excite or inhibit one another. The presence of barking is strong negative evidence for the "cat" hypothesis and strong positive evidence that the animal is a dog. Thus, the weight between *barks* and *cats* is strongly negative, whereas the weight that connects barking with dogs is strongly positive. These weights simply reflect the extent to which the two nodes have been activated together in the past, and they increase and decrease with experience, which accounts for learning. Thus, if a person bought an unusual species of cat that made a barking sound, the weight between *bark* and *cat* would become more positive, at least for this particular type of cat.

We can also use connectionist models to explain complex phenomena such as analogies and inferences (Golden & Rumelhart, 1993; Holyoak & Thagard, 1995). Consider the vignette that began this chapter, in which a woman was beginning to infer that her boyfriend wanted to end their relationship. Figure 7.10 presents a simplified connectionist model of how she might have come to that judgment. She observed two things: He says he loves her, but he seems to be avoiding her. Direct observations carry a lot of weight when making inferences and hence receive high activation values (as indicated by the heavy blue lines, which represent strong positive weights) (Kunda & Thagard, 1996). His saying "I love you," however, could have two interpretations: Either he wants to stay with her, or he is trying to let her down easy. "I love you" has a positive connection to both hypotheses. Wanting to "let her down easy" is associated with wanting to split up, which is also strongly associated with his avoiding her. The *wants to split up* node is doubly activated—directly by the *avoiding me* node and indirectly by the "*I love you*" node—through its connection to the *wants to let me down easy* node. The *wants to stay together* node is relatively weakly activated in comparison because its only positive input is from the "*I love you*" node. Thus, the system is likely to settle on the solution with the highest activation: He wants to leave.

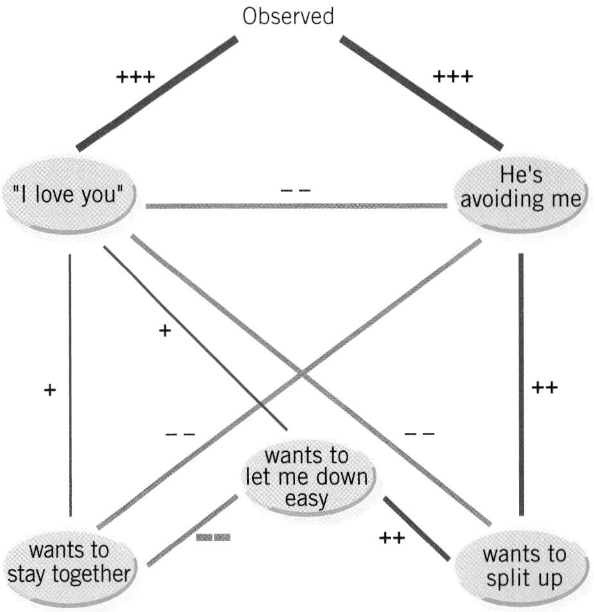

FIGURE 7.10 A connectionist model of inference. Positive weights are indicated in blue, whereas negative weights (inhibitory associations) are indicated in red. Strength of the associative connection (either positive or negative) is indicated by the width of the lines. The woman has observed two behaviors by her boyfriend that are mutually incompatible (indicated by the thick red line connecting them): He says he loves her, and he is avoiding her. Each of these nodes is connected to multiple other nodes. Simultaneous processing of all of these connections leads to the conclusion that he wants to split up, since it has higher activation than the wants to stay together node.

INTERIM SUMMARY

According to **connectionist** or **parallel distributed processing (PDP)** models, most cognitive processes occur simultaneously (in parallel) through the action of multiple activated networks. The meaning of a representation is distributed throughout a network of processing units (nodes) that are activated together through experience. Knowledge thus lies in the connections between these nodes—in the extent to which they are positively or negatively associated with one another. When perceiving, remembering, categorizing, or performing other cognitive tasks, the brain settles on a cognitive solution that satisfies as many constraints as possible in order to achieve the best fit to the data through a process of parallel constraint satisfaction.

The Neuropsychology of Thinking   From Brain to Behavior

Connectionist models treat the brain as a powerful metaphor. Other cognitive scientists are studying the brain itself to try to uncover the mysteries of thought.

Like other psychological functions, thought processes are both distributed—spread out through large networks of neurons—and localized—carried out through specialized processing units in particular regions of the brain. For explicit reasoning, problem solving, and decision making, these regions largely lie in the frontal lobes.

Unlike the other lobes, the frontal lobes receive no direct sensory input. Instead, they receive their input from other parts of the brain. Just as the other lobes combine sensations into perceptions, the frontal lobes combine perceptions into complex ideas. Researchers distinguish two broad regions of the prefrontal cortex that perform differ-

Big Picture φ Question 1

To what extent can mental processes be reduced to the brain or body?

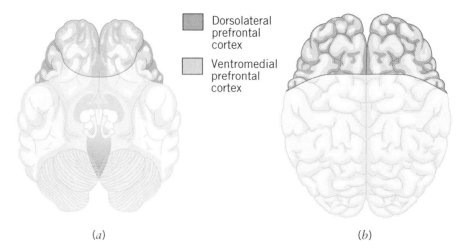

FIGURE 7.11   Prefrontal cortex and thinking. The drawings show two major regions in the frontal lobes involved in thinking, the dorsolateral and ventromedial prefrontal cortex, (*a*) from underneath the brain, and (*b*) from the top of the brain.

ent cognitive functions: the dorsolateral and ventromedial prefrontal cortex (Figure 7.11) (Damasio, 1994; Frith & Dolan, 1996; Fuster, 1989; Robin & Holyoak, 1995).

Dorsolateral Prefrontal Cortex

The **dorsolateral prefrontal cortex** *plays a central role in working memory and explicit manipulation of representations* (conscious thought). (Recall that *dorsal* means toward the top of the brain and *lateral* means to the sides; thus, this region encompasses the upper and side regions of the prefrontal cortex.) This area of the brain has many connections to other regions of the cortex (occipital, temporal, and parietal) as well as to the basal ganglia. The connections to posterior cortical regions (regions toward the back of the brain) allow people to integrate information from multiple senses and to hold multiple kinds of information in mind while solving problems.

Links to the basal ganglia allow people to form and carry out complex sequences of behavior and to develop skills (Ashby & Waldron, 2000). Skill acquisition (such as learning to type, read, or drive a car) at first requires considerable conscious attention and prefrontal activity. However, once a skill is well learned and becomes automatic, the mental work shifts to neurons in the motor cortex of the frontal lobes and in subcortical circuits in the basal ganglia (Frith & Dolan, 1996).

Dorsolateral prefrontal circuits appear to be involved in associating complex ideas, allocating attention, making plans, and forming and executing intentions. Damage to this region is associated with impaired planning, distractibility, and deficits in working memory (Fuster, 1989). We can realize the effect of dorsolateral prefrontal damage in the way patients with damage to this area respond to tasks such as the Tower of London problem (Figure 7.12).

Ventromedial Prefrontal Cortex

Another part of the cortex crucial to judgment and decision making is the ventromedial prefrontal cortex (*ventral* meaning toward the bottom of the brain and *medial* meaning toward the middle). The **ventromedial prefrontal cortex** *serves many functions, including helping people use their emotional reactions to guide decision making and behavior.* Not surprisingly, this region has dense connections with parts of the limbic system involved in emotion (Chapter 10). People with damage to this region show difficulty inhibiting thoughts and actions, loss of social skills, deficits in moral behavior, and disturbances in personality functioning. Phineas Gage, the railroad foreman whose brain was pierced by an iron rod in 1848 (Chapter 1), suffered damage to this region of the brain.

Neurologist Antonio Damasio (1994) has studied many patients with damage to this region. Like Gage, these patients often seem cognitively intact: They can solve problems, manipulate information in working memory, and recall events from the re-

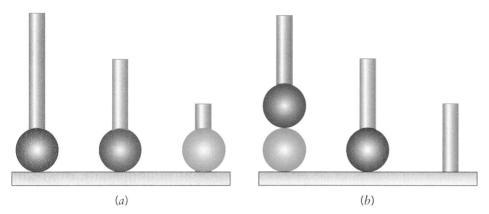

(a)　(b)

FIGURE 7.12 The Tower of London problem. Participants are presented with pegs holding one, two, or three balls (*a*). They have to manipulate the placement of the balls in their minds so that they can produce the desired solution (*b*) because they are only allowed to move one ball at a time. While mentally performing these manipulations, subjects show activation of dorsolateral prefrontal circuits in the same region involved in "central executive" working memory tasks, such as managing multiple simultaneous tasks. This dual activation makes sense because the task requires the person to hold visual information in memory while mentally arranging a sequence of behaviors. *Source:* Frith & Dolan, 1996.

cent and distant past. Nevertheless, something is terribly wrong. Damage to this region demonstrates the importance of *feeling*—and of the ability to connect feelings with thoughts—in making sound decisions (Damasio, 1994).

In one study, Damasio and his colleagues showed patients with ventromedial prefrontal lesions a set of neutral images interspersed with disturbing pictures. Individuals with no brain damage or damage to other parts of the brain showed emotional arousal on viewing the upsetting images, as assessed by measuring skin conductance (sweating). In contrast, patients with lesions to the ventromedial prefrontal cortex showed no emotional reaction at all (see Figure 7.13). One patient acknowledged that the pictures *looked* distressing but did not make him *feel* distressed.

Damasio relates another incident with one of these patients that suggests that reason may not be independent of emotion or motivation. The patient came in for testing on a winter day when icy roads were causing many accidents. Damasio asked him if he had had any trouble driving in. The patient responded, casually, that it was no different from usual, except that he had had to take proper procedures to avoid skidding. The patient mentioned that on one especially icy patch, the car ahead of him had spun around and skidded off the road. Unperturbed, the patient simply drove through the same patch with no particular concern.

The next day, Damasio and the patient were scheduling their next appointment, and the patient had the choice of two days. For the next *30 minutes* the patient performed a careful cost–benefit analysis of every possible reason for choosing one day over the other, ranging from possible other engagements to potential weather conditions. He seemed unable to *satisfice*. Without the emotional input that would have told him that this decision was not worth 30 minutes, he behaved like a "rational problem solver" trying to optimize weighted utility. In this sense, emotion may be the "on–off switch" for explicit thought, letting us know when we can simply settle on a good-enough decision.

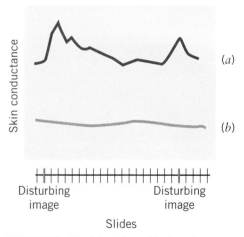

FIGURE 7.13 Physiological reactivity in patients with ventromedial prefrontal damage. The experimenters presented a series of slides to patients with and without ventromedial prefrontal damage. Interspersed among the neutral slides were occasional disturbing scenes of death or destruction. In (*a*), a patient without damage to this region shows spikes in skin conductance immediately after presentation of the disturbing slides, indicating autonomic arousal. In (*b*), a patient with damage to this region of the prefrontal cortex shows no difference in emotional response to neutral and disturbing slides. *Source:* Damasio, 1994.

The frontal cortex plays a substantial role in explicit thought. Circuits in the **dorsolateral prefrontal cortex** are involved in associating complex ideas, allocating attention, making plans, and forming and executing intentions. The **ventromedial prefrontal cortex** is involved in emotional control over decision making and many aspects of social functioning.

Language

We humans do so much thinking with words that understanding thought is impossible without understanding language. Try, for instance, to solve an arithmetic problem without thinking with words or symbols, to think about the concept of *justice* without relying on words, or to do something so seemingly simple as to order from a menu without knowing how to read words.

In the remainder of this chapter we will discuss **language**, *the system of symbols, sounds, meanings, and rules for their combination that constitutes the primary mode of communication among humans*. We begin by considering the ways language and thought shape each other. We then examine the elements of language and how people use language in everyday life. We conclude by considering whether we are alone among species in the capacity to use symbols to think.

Language and Thought

The Hanunoo people of the Philippines have 92 names for rice (Anderson, 1985). Do the Hanunoo think about rice in more complex ways than North Americans, who are hard pressed to do much better than "white rice" and "brown rice"? This line of reasoning led Benjamin Whorf (1956) and others to formulate what came to be called the **Whorfian hypothesis of linguistic relativity**, *the idea that language shapes thought* (Gumperz & Levinson, 1996; Hunt & Agnoli, 1991).

According to the Whorfian hypothesis, people whose language provides numerous terms for distinguishing subtypes within a category actually *perceive* the world differently from people with a more limited linguistic repertoire. In its most extreme version, this hypothesis asserts that even what people can think is constrained by the words and grammatical constructions in their language.

Although Whorf's hypothesis has some substantial grains of truth, subsequent research has not supported its more extreme forms. For example, color is universal in all cultures, but the number of words for colors is not constant. The Dani people of New Guinea, for example, have only two basic color words: *mola* for bright, warm shades and *mili* for dark, cold hues (Anderson, 1985). To what extent, then, does the presence or absence of linguistic labels affect the way people perceive colors?

A series of experiments with Dani and English-speaking subjects explored this question (Rosch, 1973). In one experiment, researchers briefly showed participants a color chip and then asked them 30 seconds later to select a chip of the same color from an array of 160 chips (Figure 7.14). The hypothesis was that English-speaking subjects would perform better if the chip were one of the basic colors for which their language provides a primary name (for instance, a clear, bright red) than if it were an in-between shade, such as magenta or taupe—and indeed they did. Contrary to the Whorfian hypothesis, however, the Dani subjects, too, correctly selected basic colors more often than less distinctive shades, even though their language had no names for them.

Other research suggests that the way people in different cultures think about visual scenes does mirror aspects of the language—such as whether they use phrases such as "it's on my right" versus "it's to the east" (Danziger, 1999; Ozgen & Davies, 2002). Further, with complex concepts language does appear to play a role in shaping thought. Having certain concepts, such as *freedom* or *capitalism*, would be impossible without language. Reasoning deductively would certainly be difficult if people could not construct propositions verbally and draw conclusions based on verbally represented premises.

Different languages also call attention to different information. For example, the English language draws attention to a person's gender. English speakers cannot avoid specifying gender when using possessive pronouns; if someone asks, "Whose car is

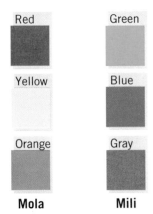

FIGURE 7.14   Language and color. Although the Dani can remember the hue of different-colored chips, they will call the three chips on the left mola and the three on the right mili.

that?" the answer is either "his" or "hers." Many languages have different words for *you* that indicate the relative status of the person being addressed. The more polite, formal form is *usted* in Spanish, *vous* in French, and *Sie* in German. The Japanese have many more gradations of respect, and Japanese professionals often exchange business cards immediately upon meeting so they will know which term to use (Triandis, 1994).

People with political agendas certainly believe language can influence thinking. In the 1960s and 1970s, feminists attempted to raise consciousness about condescending attitudes toward women by objecting to the use of the word *girl* to describe an adult female. Groups for and against abortion rights try to take the moral high ground by referring to themselves as *pro-choice* and *pro-life*.

Although language is an important medium for thought and can sometimes influence it, thought can certainly occur independent of language. Consider the common experience of starting to say something and then correcting it because it did not accurately convey the intended thought, or remembering the "gist" of what was said in a conversation without remembering the exact words (Pinker, 1994). Patients with strokes that damage left-hemisphere language centers can become very frustrated trying to get ideas and intentions across without words, as can young toddlers.

Furthermore, people often mentally visualize activities or behaviors without putting thoughts about those activities into language. For example, professional athletes often mentally rehearse the steps involved in swinging a golf club or serving a tennis ball. Many professional musicians similarly mentally practice playing a piece of music before a performance, for example (Garfield, 1986). In all these cases, the thought appears to be independent of any particular words.

The converse of Whorf's hypothesis—that thought shapes language—is, however, at least as valid. Because rice is critically important to the Hanunoo, it is no accident that their language provides words to describe distinctions in its appearance, texture, and use. We can see the "evolution" of vocabulary in the West, where terms such as *road rage* and *cyberspace* have emerged to describe what previously did not exist. Conversely, words describing phenomena that are no longer part of everyday life (such as *speakeasy* and *hippie*) fall into disuse.

INTERIM SUMMARY

Language is the system of symbols, sounds, meanings, and rules for their combination that constitutes the primary mode of communication among humans. According to the **Whorfian hypothesis of linguistic relativity**, language shapes thought. Subsequent research has not generally supported the hypothesis, although language is central to many abstract concepts and many forms of reasoning. Thought also shapes language, and language evolves to express new concepts.

Transforming Sounds and Symbols into Meaning

One of the defining features of language is that its symbols are arbitrary. The English language could just as easily have called cats *dogs* and vice versa. In this next section, we examine how sounds and symbols are transformed into meaningful sentences, beginning with the basic elements of language. We then explore the grammatical rules people implicitly follow as they manipulate these elements to produce meaningful utterances.

Elements of Language Language is processed hierarchically, from the small units of sound people produce through their mouths and noses to the complex combinations of words and sentences they produce to convey meaning (Table 7.4). *The smallest units of sound that constitute speech*, called **phonemes**, are strung together to create meaningful utterances. In the English language, phonemes include

Apply & Discuss

▪ If language influences thought, do people who are fluent in more than one language think differently when they are speaking different languages? Research by Ross, et al. (2002) suggests that people who are multilingual, in fact, do generate different thoughts depending on the language they are speaking.

Table 7.4 ▪ ▪ **Elements of Language**		
Element	*Definition*	*Examples*
Phonemes	Smallest units of sound that constitute speech	th, s, ā, ă
Morphemes	Smallest units of meaning	anti-, house, the, -ing
Phrases	Groups of words that act as a unit and convey a meaning	in the den, the rain in Spain, ate the candy
Sentences	Organized sequences of words that express a thought or intention	The house is old. Did you get milk?

not only vowels and consonants but also the different ways of pronouncing them (such as the two pronunciations of the letter **a** in **at** and **ate**).

A string of randomly connected phonemes, however, does not convey any message. To be meaningful, strings of phonemes must be combined into **morphemes**, *the smallest units of meaning in language*. Words, suffixes, and prefixes are all morphemes, such as *pillow, horse, the, pre-,* and *-ing*. The word *cognition*, for example, consists of two morphemes: *cognit-*, from the Latin *cogito* (part of the verb "to know"), and *-ion*, meaning "the act of."

Morphemes are combined into **phrases**, *groups of words that act as a unit and convey a meaning*. In the sentence *When people speak, they make many sounds*, the words *when people speak* and *many sounds* are phrases. Words and phrases are combined into **sentences**, *organized sequences of words that express a thought or intention*. Some sentences are intended as statements of fact or propositions; others ask questions or make requests (e.g., "Bill, come here!").

Syntax: The Rules for Organizing Words and Phrases   Speakers of a language intuitively know that they cannot place words or phrases wherever they want in a sentence. (As you can see from Table 7.5, the consequences of misplacing words can, at times, be humorous.) A native English speaker would never ask, "Why you did come here today?" because it violates implicit rules of word placement. Consider, in contrast, the pseudosentence *The sten befted down the flotway*. Although the individual words have no meaning, readers will intuitively recognize it as essentially grammatical: *Sten* is clearly a noun and the subject of the sentence; *befted* is a verb in the past tense (as indicated by the morpheme *-ed*), and *flotway* is the direct object. This pseudosentence

Table 7.5 ▪ ▪ **The Hazards of Misplaced Words: Syntactical Errors Found in Church Bulletins**

- This afternoon there will be a meeting in the South and North ends of the church. Children will be baptized at both ends.

- Tuesday at 4:00 p.m. there will be an ice cream social. All ladies giving milk will please come early.

- Thursday night—Potluck supper. Prayer and medication to follow.

- Weight Watchers will meet at 7 p.m. Please use large double door at the side entrance.

- Low Self-Esteem Support Group will meet Thursday from 7 to 8 p.m. Please use back door.

- The eighth graders will be presenting Shakespeare's "Hamlet" in the church basement on Friday at 7 p.m. The congregation is invited to attend this tragedy.

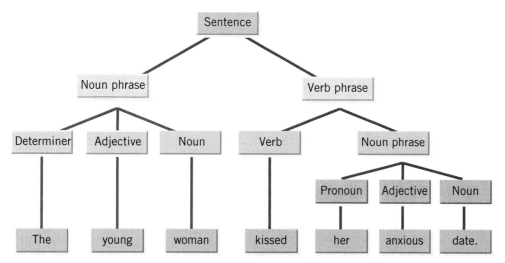

FIGURE 7.15 A syntactic analysis of sentence and phrase structure. Sentences can be broken down through treelike diagrams, indicating noun phrases and verb phrases and their component parts. One of the regularities in language that makes learning syntax easier is that the same principles apply to phrase structures anywhere in the sentence. Thus, the same syntactical rules apply to noun phrases whether they describe the subject (the young woman) or the direct object (her anxious date).

"feels" grammatical to an English speaker because it conforms to the **syntax** of the language, *the rules that govern the placement of words and phrases in a sentence*.

Linguists (people who study the way languages operate) and *psycholinguists* (psychologists who study the way people use and acquire language) map the structure of sentences using diagrams such as the one presented in Figure 7.15 to analyze *The young woman kissed her anxious date.* Two aspects of this mapping are worth noting. The first is the extent to which rules of syntax determine the way people create and comprehend linguistic utterances. Much of the way psychologists think about syntax in sentences like this one reflects the pioneering work of the linguist Noam Chomsky (1957, 1965). Chomsky views **grammar** (which includes syntax) as *a system for generating acceptable language utterances and identifying unacceptable ones.* According to Chomsky, the remarkable thing about language is that by acquiring the grammar of their linguistic community, people can generate an infinite number of sentences they have never heard before; that is, grammar is *generative.*

People can also readily transform one sentence into another with the same *underlying meaning* despite a very different apparent syntactic construction, or *surface structure*, of the sentence. For example, instead of stating "The young woman kissed her anxious date," a speaker could just as easily say "The anxious date was kissed by the young woman."

A second feature of this mapping that is worth noting is the interaction of syntax and **semantics**—*the rules that govern the meanings* (rather than the order) *of morphemes, words, phrases, and sentences*—in understanding what people say. For example, the word *date* has multiple meanings. Perhaps the woman who kissed the date could really love fruit. The presence of *anxious* as a modifier, however, constrains the possible interpretations of *date* and thus makes the fruity interpretation unlikely. But to recognize this semantic constraint, the reader or listener has to recognize a syntactic rule—namely, that an adjective preceding a noun typically modifies the noun.

The interaction between syntax and semantics (which roughly maps onto Broca's area in the prefrontal cortex and Wernicke's area of the temporal lobes, respectively; Chapter 3) is particularly useful in resolving the meaning of ambiguous sentences. Consider, for example, this sentence from the *TV Guide:* "On tonight's show Dr. Ruth will discuss sex with Dick Cavett" (Pinker, 1994). Each morpheme in this sentence is clear and unambiguous, yet the sentence can be construed to mean either that Dr.

Ruth will discuss sex *in general* as she talks with a talk show host or that she will discuss her experience of having sex *with him*.

The remarkable thing about this interaction of semantic and syntactical knowledge is how quickly and unconsciously it takes place. People do not consciously break sentences down into their syntactic structures and then scan memory for the meanings of each word. Rather, both syntactic and semantic analyses proceed simultaneously, in parallel, and create a set of constraints that lead the reader or listener to settle on the most likely meaning of the sentence.

Even this last sentence understates the role of parallel constraint satisfaction in language comprehension, since the person is simultaneously breaking the stream of sound down into phonemes, morphemes, words, phrases, and sentences; processing each level of meaning; and using information at one hierarchical level to inform decisions at other levels. We tend to become aware of one level or another only if we have trouble coming to an implicit solution (e.g., if a word does not seem to fit or a phrase has multiple potential meanings that cannot be resolved without conscious attention). As with induction, understanding language probably relies on a combination of formal rules (in this case, of syntax) and general knowledge (semantics, or the meanings of words).

INTERIM SUMMARY

The smallest units of sound that constitute speech are **phonemes**, which are combined into **morphemes**, the smallest units of meaning. Morphemes, in turn, are combined into **phrases**, groups of words that act as a unit and convey a meaning. Words and phrases are combined into **sentences**, organized sequences of words that express a thought or intention. The rules that govern the placement of words and phrases within a language are called its **syntax**. Syntax is an aspect of **grammar**, the system for generating acceptable language utterances and identifying unacceptable ones. To understand what people are saying, people often use information about both syntax and **semantics**—the rules that govern the meanings of morphemes, words, phrases, and sentences.

The Use of Language in Everyday Life

Two people catch each others' eyes at a party. Eventually, one casually walks over to the other and asks, "Enjoying the party?" A linguist could easily map the syntax of the question: It is a variant of the proposition *You are enjoying the party*, constructed by using a syntactic rule that specifies how to switch words around to make a question (and dropping the *you*, which is the understood subject).

But that assumption would completely miss the point. The sentence is not a question at all, and its meaning has nothing to do with the party. The real message is, "We've caught each other's eyes several times and I'd like to meet you." Psychologists interested in the **pragmatics** of language—*the way language is used and understood in everyday life*—are interested in how people decode linguistic messages of this sort (Blasko, 1999; Fussel & Krauss, 1992; Gibbs, 1981).

For years, Chomsky was such a towering figure in linguistics that his research, much of it on grammar and syntax, set the agenda for psychologists studying language. More recently, some researchers have begun to focus on levels of linguistic processing broader than the isolated sentence. Rather than studying the elements of language from the bottom up, they have turned to the analysis of **discourse**—*the way people ordinarily speak, hear, read, and write in interconnected sentences* (Carpenter et al., 1995; Graesser et al., 1997; McKoon & Ratcliff, 1998; Rubin, 1995).

Much of our time is spent telling and hearing stories—events in our lives, gossip, news stories. Discourse analysts point out that the meaning (and even the syntactic structure) of every sentence reflects the larger discourse in which it is embedded. The question "Enjoying the party?" made sense to both people involved in the conversation because it came in the context of a party and some significant nonverbal communication.

Multiple Levels of Discourse   According to many discourse analysts, people mentally represent discourse at multiple levels (Graesser et al., 1997; Kintsch & Van Dijk, 1983). At the lowest level is the exact wording of the phrases and sentences written or spoken, which is retained in memory only briefly while the rest of the sentence is processed.

When later called upon to remember a sentence (such as *Bill took the car into the shop*), however, people generally remember the *gist*, or general meaning (e.g., Bill took the car to be fixed). They also make inferences, which are largely automatic and implicit (e.g., that the "shop" was an auto shop). These inferences influence both what people "hear" and what they remember (Bransford et al., 1972). Consider the inferences involved when a person reads the familiar instructions, "Wet hair, apply shampoo, lather, rinse, repeat" (Pinker, 1994). If the person did not think beyond the words on the bottle—did not make inferences—she would wet her hair again after each rinse cycle and repeat endlessly (since the instructions never say to stop!).

At the next level, the speaker or narrator asks the audience to enter a certain situation. Consider the vignette that opened this chapter, which began with the words "You are sitting in a café with your closest friend." The aim is to paint an evocative picture that allows readers to suspend reality and enter into a different time and place.

One step higher is the *communication* level, which reflects what the communicator is trying to do, such as impart ideas in a textbook or tell a story. Finally, at the broadest level is the general *type* of discourse, such as a story, a news report, a textbook, a joke, or a comment at a party intended to start a conversation.

Principles of Communication   When people talk or write, their communications are guided not only by syntactic rules that shape the way they put words together but also by a set of shared rules of conversation that are implicit in the minds of both participants (Grice, 1975). For example, people keep track of what their listener knows, and when they introduce a new term or idea, they typically signal it with a change in syntax and embellish it with examples or evocative language.

People also use various cues to signal important information. In writing, they usually put the topic sentence of a paragraph first so that readers know what the main point is. In public speaking, people often use *intonation* (tone of voice) to make particular points forcefully or use phrases such as "the point to remember here is...."

These literary devices of everyday life may seem obvious, but what is remarkable is how effortlessly people use and understand them. Consider again the opening line of the vignette with which this chapter began: "You are sitting in a café with your closest friend, and she tells you tearfully, 'I think my relationship with Brett has hit a dead end.'" By switching to a narrative mode more characteristic of fiction, I was signaling to the reader that something different was happening—that we were "setting the stage" for a chapter and a new set of ideas. I also introduced a second-person construction ("You are..."), which I seldom use in this book, which also served as a syntactic cue that this material was somehow different and required special attention. I suspect, however, that most readers were no more aware of the "rules" I was using to direct their attention than I was in using them.

Nonverbal Communication   People communicate verbally through language, but they also communicate nonverbally, and aspects of speech other than nouns and verbs often speak louder than words. When a parent calls a child by her whole name, it may be to chastise or to praise, depending on the inflection and intonation ("Jennifer Marie Lar*son* [rising tone on last syllable]? *Stop teasing your brother*," versus "*Jennifer Marie Larson* [lowering tone on last syllable of last word]. You are *so cute*.") Even when no words are spoken, clenched fists and a tense look convey a clear message.

Nonverbal communication *includes a variety of signals: body language, gestures, touch, physical distance, facial expressions, and nonverbal vocalizations* (such as sighs or throat clearings) (DePaulo & Friedman, 1998; Dil, 1984). Being conver-

Apply & Discuss

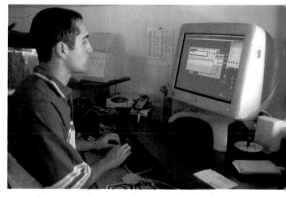

■ To what extent does e-mail communication lose aspects of language that express emotions, intentions, or subtle messages? In what ways can e-mail lead to misunderstandings?

■ How have people learned to communicate some of these aspects of language by e-mail?

■ What do people do to communicate emotion or emphasis? What is it about e-mail communications, however, that leads some people to develop rapid, intimate relationships by e-mail?

HERMAN®

© 1976 Jim Unger/dist. by LaughingStock Licensing Inc.   5-19

"That's just his way of saying he wants you to stay!"

sant in the grammars of nonverbal communication can be just as important in interpersonal relations as understanding the grammar of verbal language. When a person sits too close on a bus or stands too close when talking, the effect can be very unsettling. Like other grammars, this one is largely unconscious.

Just how important is nonverbal communication? In one study participants were shown 30-second video clips of graduate-student teaching assistants (TAs) at the beginning of a term. Participants rated the TAs using a number of adjectives, such as *accepting, active, competent,* and *confident.* The investigators wanted to know whether these brief ratings from a single lecture would predict student evaluations of the TA at the end of the term. The investigators added one extra difficulty: They turned off the sound on the videotapes, so that participants could rely only on nonverbal behavior (Ambady & Rosenthal, 1993).

The findings were extraordinary. Many of the correlations between initial nonverbal ratings and eventual student evaluations were as near perfect as one finds in psychology, in the range of .75 to .85. Teaching assistants who initially appeared confident, active, optimistic, likable, and enthusiastic in their nonverbal behavior were rated much better teachers months later. Correlations remained substantial (though somewhat lower) when judges were asked to rate *two-second* film clips! Nonverbal communication also contributes to language learning. How, for example, does a child of 12 to 18 months figure out which of the hundreds of objects in sight is connected with a new word, as when a parent just says, "Birdie!" Research suggests that children spontaneously recognize very early that they need to follow the gaze of the speaker to figure out the object to which the speaker is referring. This does not appear to be the case for autistic children, who in many ways are isolated in their own mental worlds and often use their own private languages to refer to objects (Baron-Cohen et al., 1997). Autistic children seem unable to recognize that the speaker's gaze is an index of the speaker's *intention* to refer to something. Instead, these children often associate the word with the object in their *own* gaze.

INTERIM SUMMARY

Psychologists interested in the **pragmatics** of language study the way language is used and understood in everyday life. Rather than studying the elements of language from the bottom up, many researchers have turned to the analysis of **discourse**, the way people ordinarily speak, hear, read, and write in interconnected sentences. People mentally represent and discourse simultaneously at multiple levels, from the exact sentences and phrases of a text all the way up to the type of discourse (e.g., news story or joke). When people converse or write, they are guided not only by syntactic rules that shape the way they put their words together but also by implicit rules of conversation. People also use **nonverbal communication**, such as body language, touch, gestures, physical distance, facial expressions, and nonverbal vocalizations.

One Step Further

Big Picture φ Question 3

To what extent is human psychology continuous with the psychology of other animals?

Is Language Distinctly Human?

Tim: Lana want apple?
Lana: Yes. (Thereupon Tim went to the kitchen and got one.) You give this to Lana.
Tim: Give what to Lana.
Lana: You give this which is red.
Tim: This. (Tim held up a red piece of plastic as he responded.)
Lana: You give this apple to Lana.
Tim: Yes. (And gave her the apple.)

(Rumbaugh & Gill, 1977, p. 182)

This conversation is not between two humans but between a human and a chimpanzee named Lana. Apes lack the physiological equipment to speak as humans do, but psychologists have trained several chimpanzees and other primates (such as bonobos, another close relative of humans) to use nonverbal symbols to communicate with humans. Lana learned a computer language called "Yerkish" (named for the Yerkes Regional Primate Research Center in Atlanta where the research took place). Yerkish uses geometric symbols, or *lexigrams*, to represent concepts and relationships. Other apes have learned to use signs from American Sign Language or other systems using lexigrams.

Teaching Language to Apes

Some simian linguists are quite accomplished. A chimpanzee named Sarah learned a vocabulary of about 130 plastic symbols, which she used with 75 to 80 percent accuracy (Figure 7.16) (Premack & Premack, 1972). Chimpanzees have also used symbols taught to them by their trainers to communicate with *each other* (Figure 7.17) (Savage-Rumbaugh et al., 1978, 1983). A chimpanzee named Nim Chimpsky reportedly expressed feelings through signs, saying "angry" or "bite" instead of actually committing angry acts (Terrace, 1979).

Do such findings mean that the chimpanzee is, as one researcher put it, "a creature with considerable innate linguistic competence who has, by accident of nature, been trapped inside a body that lacks the proper [structure for] vocal output" (Savage-Rumbaugh et al., 1983)? Several investigators have questioned whether language is really monkey business. After five years, Nim Chimpsky's utterances ranged from only 1.1 to 1.6 signs, compared with children's progressively longer word combinations (Terrace, 1979). Furthermore, chimpanzees tend to use symbols for purely pragmatic purposes (to request an object) or to imitate their trainers' communications, whereas children use language for many purposes (Seidenberg & Petitto, 1987). Some researchers have compared the linguistic abilities of chimpanzees and other apes to human children at the stage of telegraphic speech (Gardner & Gardner, 1975).

Other psychologists are more convinced by the accomplishments of our primate brethren. Researchers from the Yerkes Center describe a bonobo named Kanzi who spontaneously began to use symbols to communicate (Rumbaugh, 1992; Savage-Rumbaugh et al., 1986). Kanzi was an infant when his mother became the subject of language training. While researchers taught her to communi-

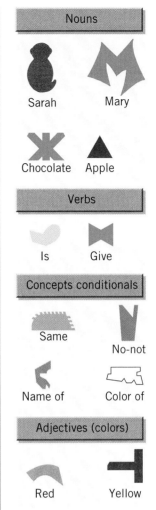

FIGURE 7.16 Sarah's plastic symbols. Researchers provided Sarah, a chimpanzee, with plastic symbols that varied in color, shape, and size. The symbols were backed with metal so that Sarah could arrange them on a magnetic board. Each symbol stood for a single word or concept. (Sarah preferred to write her sentences vertically from top to bottom.) *Source:* Premack & Premack, 1972.

(a)

(b)

(c)

FIGURE 7.17 Two chimpanzees communicating. Sherman and Austin learned to communicate with each other using symbols taught to them by their trainers. In this sequence, (*a*) Sherman requests M&Ms using his symbol board, while Austin watches (*b*). Austin then hands the M&Ms to Sherman (*c*).

cate by pushing geometric symbols on a keyboard, Kanzi played nearby or got into mischief, leaping on the keyboard or snatching food treats.

Two years later, when the mother was away, Kanzi spontaneously began using the keyboard to ask for specific fruits. When presented with apples, bananas, and oranges, he chose the fruit he had requested, demonstrating that he did indeed know what he was asking. In comparing Kanzi to Nim Chimpsky, the researchers suggested that Nim may have been a bit dim, so that his limited accomplishments did not adequately reflect the language capacities of apes. Unlike Nim, over 80 percent of Kanzi's communications occurred spontaneously. Kanzi also used language to point out objects to the researchers and to announce his intentions (e.g., pushing "ball" on the keyboard and then going to search for his ball).

Swinging on the Evolutionary Tree

Psychologists who study language in nonhuman primates continue to disagree as to whether apes are capable of human language (although no one has definitively shown that humans can be taught to use chimpanzee communication systems, either). Chimps apparently have the capacity to use symbolic thought under the right conditions, and lowland gorillas use some forms of symbolic gestures to communicate as well (Tanner & Byrne, 1996).

Perhaps the most distinctive feature of human language, however, is not the capacity to use symbols to stand for objects but the creation of a *system* of symbols whose meaning lies primarily in their relation to *one another*, not to any concrete realities (Deacon, 1996). This is what allows people to imagine what *could* be and to create objects in their minds that they then create in the world. And in this, we are alone.

Linguist Steven Pinker (1994) suggests that the question of whether other primates possess language has actually been badly framed, based on the misconception that humans are the highest and latest rung on an evolutionary ladder that runs from orangutans to gorillas to chimpanzees to *Homo sapiens*. Rather than a ladder, the proper analogy is a bush, with a common trunk but multiple branches (Figure 7.18). Gorillas, chimps, humans, and other living primates shared a com-

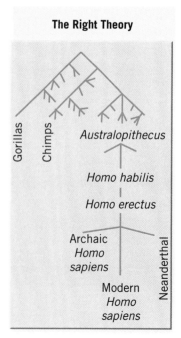

FIGURE 7.18 Two models of the evolution of language. *Source:* Adapted from Pinker, 1994.

mon ancestor 5 to 10 million years ago, at which point their evolutionary paths began to diverge like branches on a bush. Somewhere after that point, language began to evolve in the now-extinct ancestors of *H. sapiens*, such as *H. erectus*. Natural selection has pruned the bush dramatically—roughly 99 percent of all species become extinct. That the bush is now quite sparse has led to the misconception that the species left on the bush are close relatives rather than distant cousins. Pinker (1994) draws a simple conclusion from the debate about language in other primates: "Other species undoubtedly have language. Unfortunately, they're all dead."

Summary

Units of Thought

1. **Thinking** means representing mental representations for a purpose. Much of the time people think using words, **mental images** (visual representations), and **mental models** (representations that describe, explain, or predict the way things work).

2. A **concept** is a mental representation of a category, that is, an internal portrait of a class of objects, ideas, or events that share common properties. The process of identifying an object as an instance of a category—recognizing its similarity to some objects and dissimilarity to others—is called **categorization**. Concepts that have properties clearly setting them apart from other concepts are relatively **well defined**; many concepts, however, are not easily defined by a precise set of features.

3. People typically classify objects rapidly by judging their similarity to concepts stored in memory. They often do this by comparing the observed object they are trying to classify with a **prototype**, an abstraction across many instances of a category, or a good example, called an exemplar. When people rapidly categorize, they probably rely heavily on prototype matching. Complex, deliberate classification tasks often require more explicit evaluation of the data, such as consulting lists of **defining features**.

4. In categorizing objects, people naturally tend to use the **basic level**, the broadest, most inclusive level at which objects share common attributes that are distinctive of the concept. The way people categorize is partially dependent on culture, expertise, and their goals.

Reasoning, Problem Solving, and Decision Making

5. **Reasoning** refers to the process by which people generate and evaluate arguments and beliefs. **Inductive reasoning** means reasoning from specific observations to more general propositions that seem likely to be true. **Deductive reasoning** is logical reasoning that draws conclusions from premises and leads to certainty if the premises are correct. **Analogical reasoning** is the process by which people understand a novel situation in terms of a familiar one.

6. **Problem solving** is the process of transforming one situation into another to meet a goal, by identifying discrepancies between the initial state and the goal state and using various operators to try to eliminate the discrepancies. **Problem-solving strategies** are techniques that serve as guides for solving a problem. One of the most important problem-solving strategies is **mental simulation**—imagining the steps involved in solving a problem mentally before actually undertaking them.

7. **Decision making** is the process by which people weigh the pros and cons of different alternatives in order to make a choice. According to one information-processing model, a rational decision involves a combined assessment of the *value* and *probability* of different options, which provides an estimate of its **expected utility**.

Implicit and Everyday Thinking

8. Psychologists have recently begun to question whether the kind of rationality seen in **explicit cognition** (cognition that involves conscious manipulation of representations) models is always optimal. In everyday life, people make use of cognitive shortcuts, or **heuristics**, that allow them to make rapid judgments. Because people rarely have complete information and limitless time, they often practice **bounded rationality**, or rationality within limits imposed by the environment, their goals, and so forth.

9. Much of human behavior reflects **implicit cognition**, or cognition outside of awareness, including implicit learning and implicit problem solving. Researchers are increasingly recognizing the role of motivation and emotion in everyday judgments, inferences, and decisions.

10. **Connectionist**, or **parallel distributed processing (PDP)**, models propose that many cognitive processes occur simultaneously (in parallel) and are spread (distributed) throughout a network of interacting neural processing units. Connectionist models differ from traditional information-processing models by limiting the importance of serial processing and shifting from the metaphor of mind as computer to mind as brain. These models suggest that perception, memory, and thought occur through processes of **constraint satisfaction**, in which the brain settles on a solution that satisfies as many constraints as possible in order to achieve the best fit to the data.

11. The frontal lobes play a particularly important role in thinking. Two regions of the frontal lobes involved in thinking are the **dorsolateral prefrontal cortex**, which is involved in associating complex ideas, allocating attention, making plans, and forming and executing intentions; and the **ventromedial prefrontal cortex**, which is involved in emotional control over decision making, inhibiting actions that lead to negative consequences, and many aspects of social functioning.

Language

12. Language is the system of symbols, sounds, meanings, and rules for their combination that constitutes the primary mode of communication among humans. Thought and language shape one another, but thought and language are to some extent separable.

13. The smallest units of sound that constitute speech are **phonemes**. Phonemes are combined into **morphemes**, the smallest units of meaning. Morphemes are combined into **phrases**, groups of words that act as a unit and convey a meaning. Words and phrases are combined into **sentences**, organized sequences of words that express a thought or intention. The rules of **syntax** govern the placement of words and phrases within a language.

14. Psychologists interested in the **pragmatics** of language are interested in the way language is used and understood in everyday life. **Discourse**—the way people ordinarily speak, hear, read, and write in interconnected sentences—occurs at multiple levels, such as the exact wording of sentences and the gist of the sentence. **Nonverbal communication** relies on tone of voice, body language, gestures, physical distance, facial expressions, and so forth.

Key Terms

algorithms   241

analogical reasoning   239

availability heuristic   245

basic level   234

bounded rationality   245

categories   231

categorization   231

concept   231

confirmation bias   241

connectionism   249

constraint satisfaction   250

decision making   242

deductive reasoning   237

defining features   232

discourse   258

dorsolateral prefrontal
　　cortex   252

expected utility   243

explicit cognition   244

functional fixedness   241

grammar   257

heuristics   244

ill-defined problems   240

implicit cognition   246

inductive reasoning   237

language   254

mental images   230

mental models   231

mental simulation   241

morphemes   256

nonverbal communication   259

parallel distributed processing
　　(PDP)   249

phonemes   255

phrases   256

pragmatics   258

problem solving   240

problem-solving strategies   241

prototype   232

reasoning   237

representativeness heuristic   245

semantics   257

sentences   256

subgoals   240

subordinate level   234

superordinate level   234

syllogism   237

syntax   257

thinking   230

ventromedial prefrontal
　　cortex   252

weighted utility value   243

well-defined concepts   232

well-defined problems   240

Whorfian hypothesis of linguistic
　　relativity   254

Intelligence

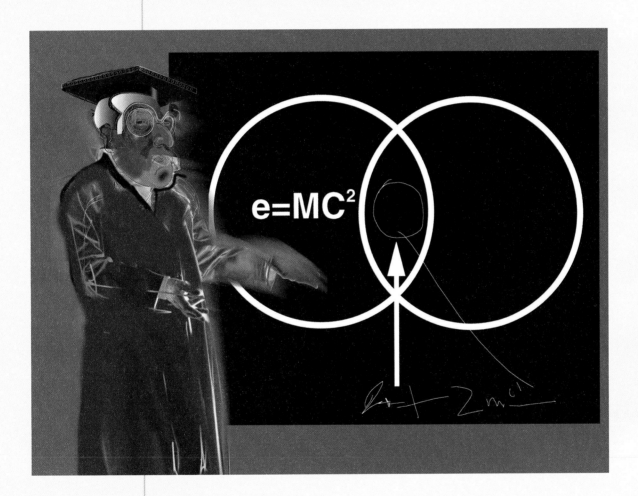

$$e=MC^2$$

eter Franklin, a historian by training, had spent many years of his academic career as the dean of a prestigious liberal arts college. He was also a talented amateur musician and athlete who enjoyed good food and lively conversation. In 1971, while vacationing in Maine, he suffered a stroke. He had been at dinner with a longtime friend, Natalie Hope, and had gone to bed early with a slight headache. He next recalled waking up on the floor with clothing strewn around him, dragging himself outside, and being discovered by Mrs. Hope. He was drooling, disheveled, and confused.

When psychologist Howard Gardner met Mr. Franklin two years later at the hospital where he was being treated, Gardner asked what brought him there. Mr. Franklin replied (Gardner, 1975, pp. 6–7):

> "Now, listen here. Now listen here. Well, I'll tell you. I said, sit down, strewn with clothes, sit, sit down, thank you, thank you. Oh goodness gracious, goodness gracious. Mrs. Hope, thank God, Mrs. Hope, going to bed. Sleeping. All right, all right....I said and, by the way. Dead. All right and two days. Sick....And doctors, doctors. Boys, boys, tip fifty dollars, tip, tip boys."

Recognizing this to be a version of what had happened around the time of Mr. Franklin's stroke, Gardner asked, "Could you tell me what's bothering you now?" Mr. Franklin lashed out, shaking his fist,

> "Now listen here. Irritate. Irritate. Irritate, irritate, irritate, irritate, irritate, irritate! Questions, questions. Stupid doctors. No good, no good. Irritate. Irritate. Dean, dean, yes sir, yes sir....That's all, that's all, forget it, forget it."

Mr. Franklin's abilities were impaired in many ways. He could not converse in a straightforward manner, express himself in writing, or follow complex commands. Standard measures of intelligence showed that he had lost much of his mental capacity, yet many of his abilities remained intact. He could easily hum familiar tunes and startled Gardner with his renditions of show tunes on the piano. He even maintained a sense of humor, kidding Gardner about doctors and their Saturday golf games when Gardner once stopped by on a Saturday.

Mr. Franklin's case points to a number of questions that are central to understanding intelligence. First, what is intelligence? Can a man who cannot speak coherently but can play show tunes flawlessly be described as intelligent? Second, how can we measure intelligence, and how accurate are commonly used measures? Mr. Franklin scored very poorly on IQ tests, yet he maintained a sense of humor as well as other capacities reflecting intelligent thinking. Third, is intelligence a broad trait that cuts across most areas of a person's life, or do people possess different kinds of intelligence, such as one that facilitates verbal conversation and another that allows a person's fingers to dance deftly across the ivories?

This chapter explores each of these questions in turn. We begin by discussing the nature of intelligence and the methods psychologists have devised to measure it. Next, we examine theoretical approaches to intelligence, from those that center on the kinds of abilities that best predict school success to those that include aptitudes in domains such as music and sports. We then address the controversial question of the heritability of intelligence—the extent to which differences between people reflect differences in their genetic endowment.

The Nature of Intelligence

The concept of intelligence successfully eluded definition for so many years that one psychologist long ago defined intelligence somewhat sarcastically as "what intelligence tests measure" (Boring, 1923). When asked what intelligence means, most people emphasize problem-solving abilities and knowledge about the world; they also sometimes distinguish between academic intelligence ("book smarts") and social intelligence or interpersonal skill (Sternberg & Wagner, 1993). In recent years, psychologists have come to recognize that intelligence is many-faceted, functional, and culturally defined.

Intelligence Is Multifaceted and Functional

Intelligence is *multifaceted*; that is, aspects of it can be expressed in many domains. Most readers are familiar with people who excel in academic and social tasks and are equally adept at changing spark plugs and concocting an exquisite meal (without a cookbook, of course). Yet other people excel in one realm while amazing those around them with their utter incompetence in other domains, such as their apparent lack of practical intelligence (see Sternberg et al., 2000). One psychologist with a national reputation in his field was equally well known among his friends and students as the prototypical absent-minded professor. He once drove to a conference out of town, forgot he had driven, and accepted a ride home with a colleague. As we will see, speaking of "intelligence" may be less useful than speaking of "intelligences."

Intelligence is also functional. Intelligent behavior is always directed toward accomplishing a task or solving a problem. According to one definition, intelligence is "the capacity for goal-directed adaptive behavior" (Sternberg & Salter, 1982, p. 3). From an evolutionary perspective, intelligent behavior solves problems of adaptation and hence facilitates survival and reproduction. From a cognitive perspective, intelligence is *applied cognition*, that is, the use of cognitive skills to solve problems or obtain desired ends.

The Cultural Context of Intelligence | A Global Vista

If the function of intelligence is to help people manage the tasks they confront in their lives, then intelligent behavior is likely to vary cross-culturally, because the circumstances that confront people differ from one society to the next. In fact, the kinds of thinking and behavior recognized as intelligent vary considerably (Sternberg, 2000a).

Among the Kipsigi of Kenya, for example, the word *ng'om* is the closest approximation to the English word *intelligent*. The concept of *ng'om*, however, carries a number

Big Picture φ Question 4

To what extent is human nature particular versus universal?

Navigational skills are essential for survival and hence highly developed among the Truk Islanders in Micronesia.

Apply & Discuss

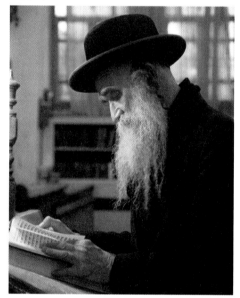

▪ What, if any, is the relationship between intelligence and wisdom?

▪ Are people who are wiser more intelligent?

▪ Are wisdom and intelligence just two words for the same construct?

of connotations that Westerners do not generally associate with intelligence, including obedience and responsibility (Super & Harkness, 1980). The Cree Indians of northern Ontario consider someone a "good thinker" if she is wise and respectful, pays attention, thinks carefully, and has a good sense of direction (Berry & Bennet, 1992).

The attributes a culture considers intelligent are not arbitrary. The personal qualities, skills, and cognitive styles that cultures value and foster tend to be related to their ecology and social structure (see Mistry & Rogoff, 1985). Cultural practices teach people efficient ways of solving everyday problems, and these strategies become part of the way individuals think (J. Miller, 1997; Vygotsky, 1978; Wertsch & Kanner, 1992). Western views of intelligence emphasize verbal ability (such as the ability to comprehend a written passage) and the kinds of mathematical and spatial abilities that are useful in engineering or manufacturing. This view of intelligence (which, perhaps not incidentally, defines the kinds of questions on intelligence tests developed in the West) makes sense in a literate, technologically developed capitalist society.

In contrast, most African cultures define intelligence in terms of practical abilities (Serpell, 1989). Western observers have noted that many members of the !Kung tribe of Africa's Kalahari Desert have an almost encyclopedic knowledge of animal behavior, which is adaptive for a people who must hunt and avoid dangerous animals (Blurton-Jones & Konner, 1976). Cultural groups who depend on the sea for their livelihood often show an extraordinary ability to remember relevant landmarks or calculate locations in navigating the ocean (Gladwin, 1970). Sir Francis Galton, a pioneer in research on intelligence, described one Eskimo (Werner, 1948, p. 147, in Berry & Irvine, 1986):

> With no aid except his memory…[the Eskimo] drew a map of a territory whose shores he had but once explored in his kayak. The strip of country was 1100 miles long as the crow flies, but the coastline was at least six times this distance. A comparison of the Eskimo's rude map with an Admiralty chart printed in 1870 revealed a most unexpected agreement.

Is intelligence, then, a property of individuals, or is it simply a social construction or value judgment? To put it another way, is intelligence solely in the eye of the beholder? Probably not. Some attributes, such as mental quickness or the ability to generate solutions when confronted with novel problems, are valued in any culture; and among cultures at a similar level of technological development, concepts of intelligence tend to share many elements because demands on individuals are similar. An intelligent Belgian is not very different from an intelligent American, although the Belgian is likely to know more languages—itself an aspect of intelligence in a small country surrounded by countries with many languages. As the United States increasingly depends on trading partners around the world, particularly to its south, the lack of fluency in other languages characteristic of most Americans will probably be increasingly defined as unintelligent.

We can thus provisionally define **intelligence** as *the application of cognitive skills and knowledge to learn, solve problems, and obtain ends that are valued by an individual or culture* (see Gardner, 1983). As we will see in the section that follows, intelligence was not always so broadly defined. Only in recent years has the concept been expanded to include much more than what intelligence tests measure.

INTERIM SUMMARY

Intelligence refers to the application of cognitive skills and knowledge to learn, solve problems, and obtain ends that are valued by an individual or culture. Intelligence is multifaceted and functional, directed at problems of adaptation. It is also to some extent culturally shaped and culturally defined, since cultural practices support and recognize intellectual qualities that are useful in the social and ecological context.

Intelligence Testing

Measuring psychological qualities such as intelligence is not as straightforward as stepping on a bathroom scale. Psychologists use **psychometric instruments**—*tests that quantify psychological attributes such as personality traits or intellectual abilities*—to see how people differ from and compare to each other on psychological "scales." Although scientists usually design measures to fit the construct they are trying to quantify (e.g., scales to measure weight or mass), almost the opposite has occurred with the Western concept of intelligence, in which the measures came first and the construct largely evolved to fit the measures. **Intelligence tests** are *measures designed to assess the level of cognitive capabilities of an individual compared to other people in a population*.

Historians credit Sir Francis Galton (1822–1911) of England with the first systematic effort to measure intelligence. A relative of Charles Darwin and a member of his society's aristocracy, Galton set out to evaluate the implications of the theory of evolution for human intelligence (Berg, 1992; Fancher, 2004). He was convinced that intelligence and social preeminence were products of the evolutionary process of "survival of the fittest" and that intelligence runs in families. Galton believed that the building blocks of intelligence are simple perceptual, sensory, and motor abilities. Like his German contemporary Wilhelm Wundt (Chapter 1), Galton argued that by studying the "atoms" of thought one could make inferences about the way they combine into larger intellectual "molecules."

To test his theory, Galton set up a laboratory at London's 1884 International Exposition, where, for threepence, some 10,000 people underwent tests of reaction time, memory, sensory ability, and other intellectual tasks. (Today psychologists pay subjects, not vice versa!) To his surprise, performance on these elementary tasks did not correlate with much of anything, including social class. Galton is remembered not only as the first person who methodically tested mental abilities but also as a pioneering statistician who discovered how to express the relationship between two variables (such as the intelligence of one member of a twin pair with that of the other) using the correlation coefficient (Chapter 2).

Binet's Scale

The most direct ancestor of today's intelligence tests was developed in 1905 in France by Alfred Binet (1857–1911). Unlike Galton, Binet believed that a true measure of intelligence is an individual's performance on *complex* tasks of memory, judgment, and comprehension (Kail & Pellegrino, 1985; Mackintosh, 1998). Binet was also less interested in comparing intellectual functioning in adults than in measuring intellectual potential in children.

Binet's purpose was in fact quite practical. In 1904, an education commission in France recommended the establishment of special schools for retarded children. This project required some objective way of distinguishing these children from their intellectually normal peers (Tuddenham, 1962). Binet and his associate, Theodore Simon, noted that problem-solving abilities increase with age, so they constructed a series of tasks ranging in difficulty from simple to complex to capture the ability of children at different ages. A seven-year-old could explain the difference between paper and cardboard, for instance, whereas a typical five-year-old could not.

To express a child's level of intellectual development, Binet and Simon (1908) introduced the concept of mental age. **Mental age (MA)** is *the average age at which children achieve a particular score*. A child with a chronological (or actual) age of 5 who can answer questions at a seven-year-old level has a mental age of 7. A five year-old who can answer the questions expected for his own age but not for higher ages

Apply & Discuss

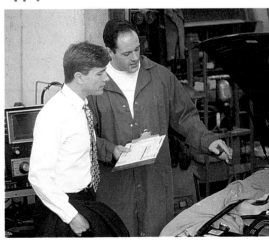

■ Can the same psychological yardstick be used to measure the intelligence that underlies the abilities of a skilled mechanic and a lawyer or engineer?

has a mental age of 5. Thus, for the average child, mental age and chronological age coincide. From this standpoint, a mentally retarded child is just what the term implies: retarded, or slowed, in cognitive development. A mentally retarded seven-year-old might miss questions at the seven- and six-year-old levels and be able to answer only some of the five-year-old items.

Intelligence Testing Crosses the Atlantic

Binet's intelligence test was translated and extensively revised by Lewis Terman of Stanford University, whose revision was known as the *Stanford-Binet scale* (1916). Perhaps the most important modification was the **intelligence quotient**, or **IQ**, *a score meant to quantify intellectual functioning to allow comparison among individuals.* To arrive at an IQ score, Terman relied on a formula for expressing the relation between an individual's mental age and chronological age developed a few years earlier in Germany. The formula derives a child's IQ by dividing mental age by chronological age (CA) and multiplying by 100:

$$IQ = (MA/CA) \times 100.$$

"You did very well on your I.Q. test. You're a man of 49 with the intelligence of a man of 53."

Drawing by Sidney Harris

Thus, if an eight-year-old performs at the level of a 12-year-old (i.e., displays a mental age of 12), the child's IQ is (12/8) × 100, or 150. Similarly, a 12-year-old-child whose test score is equivalent to that expected of an eight-year-old has an IQ of 66; and a 12-year-old who performs at the expected level of a 12-year-old has an IQ of 100. By definition, then, a person of average intelligence has an IQ of 100.

When intelligence testing crossed the Atlantic, another modification occurred that, though seemingly subtle, was profound in its implications. Binet had developed intelligence testing for a purpose—to predict school success—and for that purpose intelligence testing was, and is, highly successful. But in North America, particularly in the United States, IQ became synonymous with "smarts" rather than "school smarts." People became preoccupied with IQ as a measure of general intellectual ability that could predict their children's success in life, like a deck of psychological tarot cards.

Group Tests   Terman's adaptation of Binet's scale gained rapid use, for the intelligence test filled a number of pressing social needs. One of the most important was military (Weinberg, 1989). At the time of Terman's revision (1916), the United States was involved in World War I, and the army needed to recruit hundreds of thousands of soldiers from among millions of men, many of them recent immigrants. IQ testing promised a way of determining quickly which men were mentally fit for military service and, of those, which were likely to make good officers.

The army appointed a committee that included Terman to adapt mental testing to these needs. The result was two tests, the Army Alpha for literate adults and the Army Beta for men who were either illiterate or did not speak English (Figure 8.1). Unlike the Stanford-Binet, which required one-on-one administration by trained personnel, the army tests were *group tests*, paper-and-pencil measures of intelligence that can be administered to a roomful of people at a time. Between September 1917 and January 1919, over 1.7 million men took the Army Alpha test.

Today, group tests are widely used to assess IQ and other psychological attributes. A modern group test familiar to most North American students is the Scholastic Aptitude Test, or SAT, which was designed to predict college performance. Like many other standardized tests, the SAT has been criticized as encouraging schools to "teach

FIGURE 8.1   Selected items from the Army Beta test for nonliterate adults. In this task, subjects are asked to name the part of each picture that is missing.

to the test"; that is, students learn how to do well on the SAT, perhaps at a sacrifice of other types of learning, such as creative problem solving.

Wechsler Intelligence Scales   Although the Army Beta tried to circumvent the problem of language, the intelligence tests used early in this century were linguistically and culturally biased toward native-born English speakers. David Wechsler attempted to minimize these biases by creating a new instrument, the Wechsler-Bellevue tests (Wechsler, 1939; see also Boake, 2002). The latest renditions of these tests are the **Wechsler Adult Intelligence Scale, Third Edition**, or **WAIS-III** (Wechsler, 1997), and the child version (appropriate through age 16), the **Wechsler Intelligence Scale for Children**, or **WISC-III**. *As measured by the WAIS-III and WISC-III, IQ is derived from a number of subtests, which largely attempt to measure verbal and nonverbal intellectual abilities.*

The verbal subtests require facility with symbolic thought and language, such as knowledge of general information, arithmetic skills, ability to hold and manipulate numbers in working memory, and vocabulary. The nonverbal subtests present tasks such as picture arrangement (rearranging a series of randomly ordered cartoon frames to make a story) and picture completion (finding missing elements in a picture) that do not depend as heavily on verbal thinking (Table 8.1).

In addition to a single, overall IQ score, the WAIS-III yields separate scores for each of the 14 subtests, and overall scores for verbal and performance (nonverbal) IQ. In its most recent revision, which was influenced by research in cognitive neuroscience, it also yields more specific subscales of verbal comprehension (how well the person thinks, using language—a predominantly left-hemisphere function), perceptual organization (how well the person thinks, using visual images—a predominantly right-hemisphere function), working memory (which relies substantially on the prefrontal cortex; Chapter 6), and processing speed.

Testing several aspects of intelligence this way allows psychologists to identify specific problem areas or strengths. Peter Franklin, the historian described in the opening vignette, would probably not receive an abnormally low score on the picture arrangement subtest, since his visual processing appeared to be intact and his understanding of social scenarios did not seem impaired except when language problems interfered. On the similarities subtest, however, which requires abstract verbal reasoning (e.g., how is a cup similar to a saucer?), the effects of the stroke would be more be apparent.

Frequency Distribution of IQ Scores   Wechsler was responsible for another important innovation in IQ testing. The original formula for deriving IQ [(MA/CA) × 100] was useful in assessing children's test performance, but it was logically inconsistent when applied to adult test scores. As people grew older, the denominator (chronological age) in the formula grew larger, while the numerator (mental age) remained relatively constant. Thus, subjects seemed to become less intelligent with age. Although this pattern supports the intuitive theories held by many teenagers about their parents, as we will see in Chapter 13, it is not really true.

Wechsler remedied this problem by abandoning the concept of mental age and calculating IQ as an individual's position relative to peers of the same age on a frequency distribution. A fre-

Table 8.1 ▪▪▪ Sample Items Similiar to Those on Selected WAIS-III Verbal and Performance Subtests

Verbal Subtests

Comprehension:
"What does this saying mean: 'A rolling stone gathers no moss'?"

Arithmetic:
"A boy ran 50 yards in 10 seconds. How many yards did he run per second?"

Similarities:
"How are fast and slow alike?"

Digit span:
"Repeat the following numbers backward: 8–4–2–1–9."

Performance Subtests

Picture completion:
Tests speed and accuracy of finding missing parts of picture, e.g., the laces on a boot.

Block design:
Tests speed and accuracy in matching a design with red and white blocks.

Picture arrangement:
Tests speed and accuracy in putting cartoon frames in the right order to tell a story; e.g., frames depicting (1) a robber running from a bank, (2) a robber at a teller's window, and (3) a robber in handcuffs, should be ordered by the subject 2–1–3.

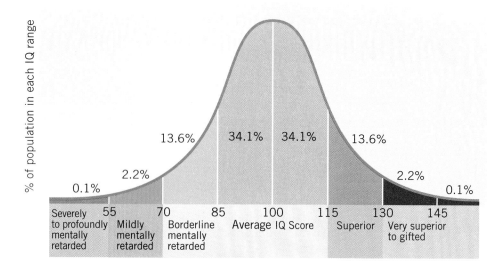

FIGURE 8.2 Frequency distribution of IQ scores. The frequency distribution for IQ takes the form of a bell-shaped curve. Source: Anastasi & Urbina, 1997.

Apply & Discuss

By definition, half the people on the average jury are likely to have below-average IQ.

■ To what extent is high IQ useful or necessary for making competent legal judgments?

quency distribution (Chapter 2) describes the frequency of various scores in the population. Like the distributions for weight, height, and many other human traits, the distribution for IQ takes the form of a normal, bell-shaped curve (Figure 8.2). When a frequency distribution approximates a *normal curve*, the vast majority of subjects receive scores close to the mean, while a progressively smaller percentage fall within ranges that deviate farther from the norm, producing the familiar bell shape. In the case of IQ, extremely high scores, such as 150, are relatively rare, as are extremely low scores, such as 50. Most people's scores fall within the average range, between about 85 and 115.

INTERIM SUMMARY

Intelligence tests are **psychometric instruments** designed to assess an individual's cognitive capabilities relative to others in a population. Binet developed the ancestor of modern intelligence tests for the purpose of identifying retarded children. His scale assigned an individual child a **mental age (MA)**, which refers to the average age at which children can be expected to achieve a particular score. Terman brought intelligence testing to North America, adapted the concept of the **intelligence quotient (IQ)**, and expanded the meaning of IQ from a predictor of school success to a broader index of intellectual ability. IQ was initially calculated by dividing mental age by chronological age and multiplying by 100, but Wechsler abandoned the concept of mental age. Instead, he used a frequency distribution to describe an individual's IQ relative to the scores of peers of equivalent age. The Wechsler scales (the **WAIS-III** and the **WISC-III** for children) yield an overall full-scale IQ score as well as specific scores, such as verbal and nonverbal (performance) IQ.

One Step Further | The Extremes of Intelligence

If individual differences in intelligence can be located on a frequency distribution, what about those whose intelligence is on one extreme or the other of the distribution? Researchers have paid particular attention to the extremes of intelligence—mental retardation and giftedness—as well as the related phenomenon of creativity.

Mental Retardation

On the extreme left-hand side of the normal distribution of intelligence is mental retardation. **Mental retardation** refers to *significantly below average general in-*

tellectual functioning (IQ less than 70), with deficits in adaptive functioning that are first evident in childhood and appear in more than one realm, such as communicating with others, living autonomously, interacting socially, functioning in school or work, and maintaining safety and health. Although low IQ is a component of the definition, IQ is not enough to diagnose retardation (Baroff & Gregory, 1999; Wechsler, 1997).

Roughly 2 percent of the population is mentally handicapped. By far the largest number of people classified as retarded (about 75 to 90 percent) fall in the mild to moderate range (IQ between 50 and 70). Children with mild retardation are frequently not diagnosed until they reach school age, when their difficulties become more apparent (Richardson & Koller, 1996). People with mild to moderate retardation can, however, usually learn to read and write at an elementary school level, and as adults they are capable of self-supporting activities, although often in supervised environments.

Only about 10 percent of mentally handicapped individuals are classified as severely to profoundly retarded (IQ below 50). Many are diagnosed early because of obvious neurological or medical symptoms. Wide-set eyes, flattened facial features, and stunted body shape characterize individuals with Down syndrome, a genetic disorder most frequently caused by an extra chromosome 21 (Cody & Kamphaus, 1999). However, many individuals with Down syndrome fall above the severely mentally handicapped range.

Children with Down syndrome have characteristic facial features as well as mental retardation.

Most cases of severe mental retardation reflect biological causes (Simonoff et al., 1998). One such cause, *phenylketonuria* (PKU), is a genetic disorder that illustrates how a highly heritable condition may be neither immutable (unchangeable) nor free of environmental influence. In PKU, the body does not produce sufficient quantities of an enzyme that converts the amino acid phenylalanine into another amino acid. Left in its original form, the phenylalanine is toxic and damages the infant's developing central nervous system. If detected early, however, PKU is treatable by minimizing phenylalanine in the child's diet. Thus, in the case of PKU, a highly heritable condition leads to retardation only in the presence of certain environmental (dietary) conditions.

Not all causes of mental retardation are genetic. Some environmental causes are biological, such as brain damage to the fetus early in pregnancy because of exposure to alcohol and other drugs, such as cocaine (Jacobson et al., 1993; Lewis & Bendersky, 1995). Other environmental causes are psychosocial. Children in the mild to moderately retarded range often have parents and siblings with low IQs, and they come disproportionately from families who live in poverty (Richardson & Koller, 1996; Stromme & Magnus, 2000). In the development of mild retardation, environmental circumstances appear to be more influential than genetic variables.

Giftedness

On the other end of the bell-shaped distribution of intelligence are people classified as **gifted**, or *exceptionally talented*. Like definitions of intelligence, definitions of giftedness depend on whatever skills or talents a society labels as gifts (Gardner, 2000; Mistry & Rogoff, 1985). In the West, with its emphasis on academic aptitude as measured by psychometric tests, giftedness is often equated with an IQ exceeding 130, although common definitions often extend to other forms of talent, such as social, musical, or athletic ability (Porath, 2000; Winner, 2000).

A common notion—at least since the days of the Roman Empire—is that extreme intelligence is associated with maladjustment. Is this simply wishful thinking on the part of the rest of us? Apparently so. In 1921, Lewis Terman began a longitudinal study of over 1000 California children with IQs above 140; researchers have followed up this sample for decades (Terman, 1925; Tomlinson-Keasey & Lit-

Giftedness can manifest itself in any of a number of different ways.

Apply & Discuss

Researchers have debated whether creativity is a form of intelligence, whether intelligence and creativity overlap, or whether the two constructs have any relation at all (Sternberg & O'Hara, 2000).

■ Can a person who is not intelligent in a domain (e.g., art or science) be creative in that domain?

■ Can a person be creative in one domain but not in others? If so, how general a trait is creativity?

■ To what extent is creativity "born" or learned?

■ Given that so many writers are depressed, is there any link between creativity and mental illness?

tle, 1990; Vaillant & Vaillant, 1990). The data suggest that gifted people tend to have average or above-average adjustment, slightly better chances of marital success, and far greater likelihood of achieving vocational success than the general population (Terman & Oden, 1947). On the other hand, recent research following up the "Termites" in their eighties finds that being labeled gifted early in life may have later costs: Those who had learned early that they had been labeled intellectually gifted were more likely to feel they had failed to live up to expectations by their forties and report less psychological well-being by their eighties (Holahan & Holahan, 1999).

Creativity and Intelligence

A quality related to giftedness is **creativity**, *the ability to produce valued outcomes in a novel way* (Sternberg, 1998). Creativity is moderately correlated with intelligence (Lubart, 2003; Sternberg & O'Hara, 2000), but not all people who are high in intelligence are high in creativity. In the 40-year follow-up of Terman's study of children with superior levels of intelligence, none had produced highly creative works (Terman & Oden, 1959). The skills and personality traits that predispose people toward creativity may not be common among even intellectually gifted children (Winner, 2000).

Because people do not express creativity in any uniform way (otherwise, they would not be creative), creativity can be extremely difficult to measure. Thus, researchers have tried to study creativity in many ways. Some researchers have turned to the study of eminent people, such as Einstein and Darwin, to learn about the nature and origins of creativity (Simonton, 1994, 1997). According to one theory, creativity is not simply a property of individuals but of the match between fertile minds and ripe times.

Other researchers have attempted to devise laboratory measures of creativity. One strategy is to measure **divergent thinking**, *the ability to generate multiple possibilities in a given situation*, such as describing all the possible uses of a paper clip. Whether Mozart or Einstein would have distinguished themselves in finding uses for a paper clip, however, will never be known.

Other tests of creativity focus on creativity as a personality or cognitive trait (Eysenck, 1983a, 1993). Research has linked creativity to such personality traits as high energy, intuitiveness, independence, self-acceptance, a willingness to take risks, and an intensely passionate way of engaging in certain tasks for the sheer pleasure of it (Amabile, 1996; Barron & Harrington, 1981).

From Brain to Behavior Is Bigger Better?

The field of phrenology advanced the perspective that the size of people's heads correlated with their intelligence, leading to the idea that the bigger one's head the better. Is bigger, in fact, better? If we look at the size of the human brain along the course of evolution, we observe a positive correlation between brain size and intelligence. There is, however, an exception: the Cro-Magnon. These humanoids, who inhabited parts of what are now Spain and France, represent an evolutionary dead end. Their skulls were larger than the more successful Neanderthal.

Similarly, if we look at modern humans, brain size does not correlate with intelligence. Einstein donated his brain to science. Scientists found Einstein's brain to be of merely average size with the only detectable difference compared to other "average" brains being a slight increase in the size of the temporal lobe. Indeed, what is critical to intelligence is the quality of the connections between the nerves, rather than the existence of more neurons. During early development, the brain makes many more neurons than we will have as adults. What happens is a selective "pruning" of neurons, in which only the best and the strongest survive.

Paul Erdos, a famous mathematician, had only half of his brain: the right side, or the so-called nonlogical side. How did he come to have only half a brain? He had hydrocephalus—that is, the cerebrospinal fluid in one of the ventricles of his brain had became trapped and, therefore, could not drain. As the brain continued to make cerebrospinal fluid, some of the brain tissue gave way. Nevertheless, even with half a brain, this man became a famous mathematician.

Idiot (autistic) savants provide additional support for the idea that bigger is not necessarily better. Autistic savants have low overall intelligence but have an extraordinary talent in one particular realm of ability. Perhaps the most well-known autistic savant portrayed in the media was Rainman. These abilities are often thought of as right-brain strengths, such as music and art. Down, who coined the term idiot savant in 1887, observed that there was no familial pattern to this phenomenon, and that it occurred more frequently in males than females. The fact that other family members did not have the disorder argues against a sole genetic cause. The fact that it is more common in males than females suggests that the disorder is linked to the Y chromosome.

More recently, researchers have suggested that idiot savants may have experienced an insult to their brain during development. The right cortex of the brain matures earlier than the left cortex. The left cortex houses the areas of the brain specialized for language. Thus, if brain growth is inhibited, the left brain may not mature fully. Males are more vulnerable than females because testosterone slows cortical neurogenesis (new neurons). Thus, if there is an insult to the brain and a person is male, the combination of insult and testosterone may lead to the idiot savant syndrome.

Validity and Reliability of IQ Tests

As we have seen (Chapter 2), two key attributes of a psychological test are its validity and reliability. The *validity* of a psychological test refers to its ability to assess the construct it was designed to measure. If by "intelligence" one means the kind of mental ability that allows people to succeed in school, then intelligence tests have considerable validity.

To assess the validity of a measure, psychologists usually correlate its results with a relevant external measure or criterion. IQ, measured from intelligence tests, is strongly related to school grades, showing a correlation coefficient between .60 and .70 (where 1.0 is a perfect correlation and 0 is no correlation at all) (Brody, 1992; Wilkinson, 1993). In psychological research, this is as strong a correlation as one usually finds and is equivalent to the correlation between height and weight!

Reliability refers to a measure's ability to produce consistent results. Thus, an individual should receive approximately the same score on a test given at two different times, assuming that the individual's level of ability has not changed in the interim. As with validity, tests of intelligence such as the WAIS-III have very high reliability. Even over three-year periods in childhood during which children make significant developmental advances, scores on the WISC-III tend to be very stable (Canivez & Watkins, 1998). Nevertheless, IQ testing has drawn criticism and controversy for many years, largely for two reasons: the lack of a theoretical basis and the potential for culture bias.

Lack of a Theoretical Basis   In many respects, IQ tests have been tests in search of a construct. As one psychologist noted, years ago, "social needs have seemed to lead, and theoretical developments to follow, the changes in mental tests over the last half century" (Tuddenham, 1962, p. 515). Most IQ tests only partially address memory, reasoning, problem solving, and decision making—the domains studied by cognitive scientists. Only in its most recent version has the Wechsler scale, for example, begun to reflect developments in the scientific study of cognition, such as the recognition of the importance of working memory. What, then, do intelligence tests measure? In other words, what is the theoretical meaning of intelligence?

One question raised by this lack of theoretical clarity is whether the kinds of abilities required for academic performance, which IQ assesses with considerable validity, can be equated with general intellectual ability. Critics argue that intelligence tests (and tests such as the SAT) provide little insight into the kind of practical intelligence involved in achieving goals in everyday life (Scribner, 1986; Sternberg, 2000b). Nor do IQ tests assess creativity, interpersonal skill, or, as in Mr. Franklin's case, the ability to play a tune (Gardner, 1983, 1999). Binet himself actually never considered his test a measure of native ability but only a means of diagnosing performance deficits in school (Fass, 1980).

Are IQ Tests Culturally Biased?   A second concern frequently raised about IQ tests is that they are prone to racial, ethnic, or cultural biases (see Blanton, 2000; Jencks, 1998). Indeed, some critics argue that they are *designed* to favor the white middle class in order to justify social inequality (Garcia, 1979; Weinberg, 1989). Not only do whites tend to outperform most other ethnic groups, but IQ is associated with social class (see Williams & Ceci, 1997).Thus, critics charge, using IQ and similar tests for placing school-age children into classes based on ability or for admissions decisions at universities leads to biases that perpetuate current inequalities.

According to critics, linguistic differences within a culture can also bias IQ tests. For example, the Black English spoken in many African-American homes differs substantially from the language assessed in standardized intelligence tests (see Stewart, 1969)—a point driven home almost three decades ago by African-American psychologist Robert L. Williams (1974). At age 15, after receiving an IQ score of 82, Williams had been advised to become a bricklayer. He declined the advice and later illustrated the potential role of linguistic bias in IQ tests—after receiving his Ph.D.—by developing the Black Intelligence Test of Cultural Homogeneity. The test drew from a vocabulary more familiar to African-Americans than to whites (e.g., asking the meaning of terms such as *running a game*). Not surprisingly, blacks tended to outperform whites on the test (Williams, 1974).

Are IQ Tests Valid?   Given the controversies, are IQ tests invalid, useless, and dangerous? The answer is not yes or no. IQ tests are some of the most valid, highly predictive tests psychologists have ever devised, and they can be useful in targeting children on both ends of the bell curve who require special attention. Comparing members of markedly different cultures or subcultures can be problematic, but IQ tests *do* tend to be

Apply & Discuss

In one minute's time, name as many brilliant men as you can think of, historically speaking. Now do the same exercise but this time name brilliant women.

◼ Was there a difference in the number of intelligent male and female historical figures that came to mind?

◼ Given research evidence showing that IQ tests have frequently been biased, is it also possible that there is a gender bias in IQ tests?

◼ Alternatively, is there no gender bias in intelligence testing, but rather a gender difference in intelligence?

valid when comparing two people with similar backgrounds. IQ and SAT scores are just as predictive of school success within African-American samples as within white samples; that is, an African-American student with a high IQ will likely fare better in school than an African-American student with a low IQ (Anastasi & Urbina, 1997). Controlling for dialect (such as translating questions into Black English) does not generally eliminate black–white differences (Quay, 1974). In fact, items on standard IQ tests that show the strongest ethnic differences are not the questions of general knowledge that seem most obviously culturally biased (Jensen, 1998; Nyborg & Jensen, 2000).

Further, despite their biases, IQ tests do evaluate areas of intelligence that are important in a literate industrial society, such as the ability to think abstractly, to reason with words, and to perceive spatial relations quickly and accurately. Whereas for years psychologists accepted the conclusion that intelligence tests predicted very little outside the classroom, more recent evaluations of the evidence suggest, in contrast, that intelligence tests can be powerful predictors of job performance and occupational achievement (Barrett & Depinet, 1991). An evaluation of 85 years of research in industrial/organizational psychology on personnel selection found that tests of general mental ability were essential for prediction of job performance and were particularly useful when used in combination with work samples, tests of integrity, or interviews (Schmidt & Hunter, 1998). Academic controversies aside, few critics of IQ testing would choose a doctor with a low IQ if their child needed treatment for leukemia.

Asking whether IQ tests are valid is in some ways the wrong question. Validity has meaning only in relation to a goal, and it is always enhanced by matching the test to the goal and adding additional measures that can enhance prediction. If the aim is to predict school success, IQ tests, SATs, and the like are highly valid. Nevertheless, all tests include a substantial component of error, so that they overpredict performance in some cases (e.g., predicting that a particular student with high IQ scores will do much better in school than he actually does) and underpredict in others. Thus, admissions committees should never rely exclusively on standardized test scores. If the goal is to predict a complex outcome such as occupational performance, the best strategy is often to combine a measure of intelligence with other measures that more closely mirror the requirements of the job, such as measures of competence at the particular task, motivation, and social skills if the job involves getting along with people.

"WE REALIZE YOU DO BETTER ON YOUR IQ TESTS THAN YOU DO IN ANYTHING ELSE, BUT YOU JUST CANNOT MAJOR IN IQ."

Drawing by Sidney Harris

INTERIM SUMMARY

Critics charge that IQ tests lack a theoretical basis, fail to capture other kinds of intelligence such as practical intelligence and creativity, and have cultural biases. Intelligence tests and similar instruments are highly predictive of school performance and, to a lesser degree, occupational success. Their validity depends on the purpose to which they are put, and they should always be supplemented by other measures.

Making Connections

All tests include some component of error. That is why baseball playoffs rely on best-of-seven series (seven "tests" instead of one) and admissions committees usually rely not only on standardized scores but on other predictors of future performance, such as past grades (Chapter 2).

Approaches to Intelligence

IQ tests place individuals on a continuum of intelligence but do not explain what intelligence is. Three approaches whose aim is to define intelligence are the psychometric approach, the information-processing approach, and the theory of multiple intelligences.

The Psychometric Approach

The **psychometric approach** *tries to identify groups of items in a test that correlate highly with one another in order to discover underlying skills or abilities*. If subjects perform multiple tasks, strong performance on some tasks is likely to predict strong performance on others. For example, people with good vocabularies tend to have strong verbal reasoning skills (e.g., figuring out the meaning of unfamiliar proverbs). Because vocabulary and verbal reasoning are highly correlated, a person's score on one will usually predict his score on the other.

The primary tool of the psychometric approach is **factor analysis**, *a statistical procedure for identifying common elements*, or **factors**, *that underlie performance across a set of tasks*. Using factor analysis, researchers set up a table, or matrix, that shows how scores on tests of different abilities correlate with one another. The aim is to reduce 10, 50, or 100 scores to a few combined "mega-variables" (factors). Once psychologists identify a factor empirically, they examine the various items that comprise it to try to discover the underlying attribute it is measuring, such as verbal intelligence or arithmetical ability.

For example, if researchers tested a diverse sample of people on four kinds of athletic ability and correlated the scores for each measure, the result might look something like the matrix presented in Table 8.2. The correlations between each pair are moderate to strong: People who are good sprinters tend to be good at weight lifting (a correlation of +.35), and so forth. A *common factor* shared by all these variables that accounts for the positive correlations may be physical conditioning or athletic ability. The extremely high correlation between weight lifting ability and number of pullups probably reflects a more *specific factor*, muscle strength.

Table 8.2 ■ ■ Identifying a Common Factor				
	Sprint	*Weights*	*Pullups*	*Situps*
Sprint	—	.35	.45	.41
Weights	—	—	.70	.52
Pullups	—	—	—	.57
Situps	—	—	—	—

Spearman's Two-Factor Theory   The English psychologist Charles Spearman (1863–1945) was the first to apply factor analysis to intelligence tests. Spearman (1904, 1927) set up a matrix of correlations to see how children's test scores on various measures were related to their academic ranking at a village school in England. He proposed a **two-factor theory of intelligence**, *which distinguished two types of factors—general and specific*.

Spearman called the first factor the **g-factor**, or **general intelligence**. That children with the highest academic ranking tended to score well on arithmetic ability, general knowledge, and vocabulary suggested a general intelligence factor. Spearman believed the g-factor explained why almost any two sets of items assessing intellectual functioning tend to correlate with one another.

Yet Spearman also noted that subjects who performed well or poorly on math tests did not *necessarily* score equally well or poorly on other measures. The correlations among different subtests on a correlation matrix were far from uniform, just as the correlation between weight lifting and number of pullups was far higher than the correlation between weight lifting and sprinting speed in Table 8.2. Spearman, therefore, proposed another type of factor, called an *s*-factor ("s" for *specific*), to explain the differences in correlations between different pairs of measures. According to Spearman, **s-factors** reveal *specific abilities unique to certain tests or shared only by a subset of tests*. Individuals vary in overall intellectual ability (the g-factor), but some people are better at mathematical tasks, and others are better at verbal tasks (s-factors).

Recent positron emission tomography (PET) research supports Spearman's hypothesis of a g-factor that cuts across at least verbal and visual tasks (Duncan et al., 2000). The researchers presented participants with tasks that either correlated highly with tests of general intelligence or did not, using both verbal and visual stimuli (Figure 8.3). They then watched to see what areas of the brain "lit up" during "g" tasks. The

Which figure does not belong with the others?

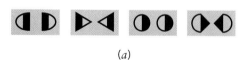

(a)

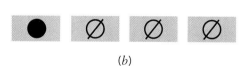

(b)

FIGURE 8.3 Low-*g* and high-*g* visual tasks. The task shown in (*a*) is highly correlated with general intelligence; it requires careful conscious effort to discover that the third pair, unlike the others, is asymmetrical, with the dark part of the geometric forms on the same rather than opposite sides. The task in (*b*) is much simpler and "jumps out" with minimal conscious effort. Tasks requiring focused problem solving, which correlated strongly with *g*, activated areas of the frontal lobes, particularly the dorsolateral prefrontal cortex. *Source:* Duncan et al., 2000, p. 458.

results were striking: Tasks associated with general intelligence consistently led to activation of areas of the frontal lobes (particularly the dorsolateral prefrontal cortex) previously shown to be involved in working memory and problem solving (Chapters 6 and 7). This was true whether the tasks were visual or verbal, suggesting that differences in *g* may reflect differences in frontal networks.

Other Factor Theories Factor analysis has proven useful in identifying common factors in the mountains of statistical data produced by intelligence tests. However, both the number of factors and the types of mental abilities revealed through factor analysis can vary depending on who is doing the analysis. For example, in Table 8.2, we noted a somewhat stronger correlation between weight lifting and pullups and suggested that the factor common to the two might be muscle strength. A factor analyst, however, might conclude that *upper body strength* is the *s*-factor—since we did not directly assess strength of lower body muscles, except in sprinting—or perhaps even motivation to develop strong upper body muscles, which we did not assess, either.

Differing Interpretations Factor analysis can thus yield many varying interpretations of the same findings, and it cannot rule out the possibility that different factors might have emerged if other tasks had been included. The results of factor analysis depend on the categories used by the analyst. For example, consider the words: orange, lemon, banana, grapefruit, pear, apple, and lime. How would you categorize these words? You could define citrus fruits (orange, grapefruit, lime, and lemon) versus noncitrus fruits (apple, banana, and pear). Alternatively, you could define yellow fruit (lemon, grapefruit, banana, and pear) versus nonyellow fruits (orange, lime, and apple). Or you could use some other categories.

In fact, when other psychologists applied Spearman's factor-analytic technique, they arrived at different interpretations. For example, L. L. Thurstone (1938) argued against the existence of an overriding *g*-factor, finding instead seven primary factors in intelligence: word fluency, comprehension, numerical computation, spatial skills, associative memory, reasoning, and perceptual speed.

The most comprehensive reanalysis of over 400 data sets collected from 1927 to 1987 produced a hierarchical, three-level solution that in some ways resembles a compromise between Spearman's and Thurstone's models (Carroll, 1993). At the highest level is a *g*-factor shared by all lower level abilities. At the middle level are more specific factors similar to those Thurstone discovered. At the bottom level of the hierarchy are simple processes, such as speed of recognizing objects, that are ultimately necessary for producing any intelligent action.

Gf–Gc Theory Another major approach, called Gf–Gc theory, also proposes a hierarchical model, with specific factors embedded within more general ones (Cattell, 1957; Horn, 1968; Horn & Noll, 1997). However, instead of a *single g*-factor, **Gf–Gc theory** *distinguishes two general intelligence factors—fluid intelligence and crystallized intelligence*—and seven more specific factors.

Fluid intelligence refers to *intellectual capacities that have no specific content but are used in processing information and approaching novel problems*, such as the ability to draw inferences, find analogies, or recognize patterns. **Crystallized intelligence** refers to *people's store of knowledge*, such as vocabulary and general world knowledge (described by memory researchers as generic memory; Chapter 6). At a lower hierarchical level are seven more specific factors: short-term memory, long-term memory, visual processing, auditory processing, processing speed on simple tasks, decision speed (processing speed on more difficult tasks, such as solving problems), and quantitative knowledge (mathematical reasoning).

Although considerable controversy remains about whether the data support one *g*-factor or two, Gf–Gc theory has two advantages. First, it makes theoretical sense in light of research in cognitive science on the components of information processing, such as

Apply & Discuss

Emotional intelligence refers to a person's ability to perceive and accurately interpret emotions (Salovey et al., 2002).

■ Is there any relationship between intelligence as measured by an intelligence scale and emotional intelligence?

■ What kind of relationship do you think might exist?

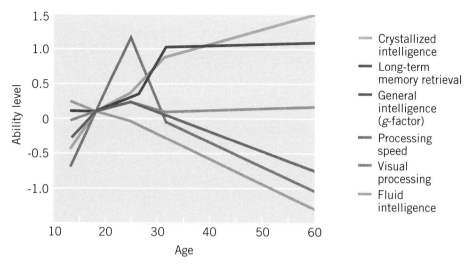

FIGURE 8.4   General and specific intelligence factors over the life span. Whereas *g* remains stable over time, crystallized intelligence tends to increase through at least age 60, whereas fluid intelligence decreases. The capacity to consolidate and retrieve long-term memories increases until age 30 and then levels off. Processing speed and visual processing ability decline steadily after about age 25. *Source:* Adapted from Horn & Noll, 1997, *Intellectual Assessment*, p. 72.

the distinction between long-term and working memory. Second, as we will see in Chapter 13, it distinguishes components of intelligence that change independently over the life span (Figure 8.4). Whereas "*g*" holds constant over many years, crystallized intelligence rises, fluid intelligence falls, and specific factors rise, fall, or remain stable, depending on the factor. Proponents of Gf–Gc theory therefore suggest that relying solely on "*g*" considerably understates the complexity of cognitive changes through the life span.

INTERIM SUMMARY

The **psychometric approach** examines which intellectual abilities tend to correlate statistically with one another. The primary tool of the psychometric approach is **factor analysis**, a statistical technique for identifying common factors that underlie performance across a variety of tasks. Spearman's **two-factor theory** distinguishes a ***g*-factor**, or general intelligence, from ***s*-factors**, or specific abilities. **Gf–Gc theory** is another hierarchical model of intelligence that argues for the presence of two overarching types of intelligence—**fluid intelligence** (intellectual capacities that have no specific content but are used in processing information) and **crystallized intelligence** (people's store of knowledge)—as well as more specific intellectual skills, such as short-term (working) memory.

The Information-Processing Approach

The psychometric approach tries to quantify basic abilities and to compare individuals with respect to these abilities. In contrast, the information-processing or cognitive approach tries to understand the *processes* that underlie intelligent behavior (Sternberg, 1999, 2000b, 2002). In other words, the information-processing approach looks at the "how" of intelligence and not just the "how much." It defines intelligence as a process rather than a measurable quantity and suggests that individual differences in intelligence reflect differences in the cognitive operations people use in thinking (Brody, 1992; Ceci, 1990).

A cognitive psychologist interested in intelligence might test subjects on various information-processing abilities, such as working memory or speed of processing. The aim is to see which of the many "bell curves" of ability—such as ability to encode memories visually, ability to hold information in working memory, and ability to

Big Picture φ Question 8

To what extent can we inform our knowledge through reason or through observation—that is, rationalism versus empiricism?

retrieve declarative information from long-term memory—best predicts some criterion of achievement, such as academic performance or success at engineering, and whether some combination of these abilities is necessary for success in particular endeavors.

Researchers from this perspective have focused on three variables of particular importance in explaining the individual differences seen on intelligence tests: speed of processing, knowledge base, and ability to acquire and apply mental strategies.

Speed of Processing   We commonly use the adjective *slow* to describe people who perform poorly in school or on similar tasks and describe more skilled performers as *quick*. In fact, processing speed is an important aspect of intelligence and a strong correlate of IQ (Ryan et al., 2000; Vernon & Weese, 1993).

One ingenious way of measuring processing speed presents participants with pairs of letters and measures the amount of time they take to decide whether the letters are identical physically (e.g., *AA*) or identical in name (e.g., *Aa*). To judge whether two letters have the same name even though they do not look alike (*Aa*), the subject must first judge whether they look the same (which they do not) but must then perform an additional step: Search long-term memory for the name of each letter form. The difference in response time between *AA* and *Aa* provides an index of the speed of memory search (Posner et al., 1969).

Supporting the view of "mental quickness" as a component of intelligence, response time in tasks such as this correlates with measures of academic achievement. Children and college students with above-average scholastic abilities perform this kind of task more rapidly than their peers (Campione et al., 1982; Lindley & Smith, 1992). Conversely, individuals who are mentally retarded respond much more slowly on a variety of tasks (Nettelbeck & Wilson, 1997). Studies using geometric figures (Figure 8.5) document a similar correlation between achievement and visual processing speed (Mumaw & Pellegrino, 1984).

Knowledge Base   Variation among individuals in intellectual functioning also reflects variation in their **knowledge base**—*the information stored in long-term memory*. Differences in knowledge base include the amount of knowledge, the way it is organized, and its accessibility for retrieval (Schauble & Glaser, 1990).

People who have expertise in a particular knowledge domain have well-developed schemas that facilitate encoding, retrieval, and mental manipulation of relevant information (Chi et al., 1982). People with a broad knowledge base are likely to appear intelligent when talking about their area of expertise because they have a ready way of categorizing and retrieving information, such as the jazz aficionado who can hear the first bar of a tune and know who played it, even if he has never heard the particular piece or version of it before.

Ability to Acquire and Apply Cognitive Strategies   A third variable that correlates with many measures of intelligence is the ability to acquire mental strategies (ways of solving problems) and apply them to new situations. Cognitive strategies are essential for many everyday tasks, from remembering grocery lists to calculating a server's tip (e.g., taking 10 percent and then adding half that amount again to total 15 percent).

Efficient use of cognitive strategies distinguishes children from adults and individuals with differing IQ levels from their peers. For example, children are less likely than adults to apply mnemonic strategies (Chapter 6) spontaneously, such as rehearsal in memorizing information (Flavell & Wellman, 1977). Their performance improves considerably, however, if they are taught and encouraged to use them (Best, 1993).

FIGURE 8.5 Spatial transformation problems. Can the figure on the left be constructed from the pieces on the right? *Source:* Mumaw and Pellegrino, 1984. Answers: 1—yes; 2—no; 3—yes; 4—yes; 5—no.

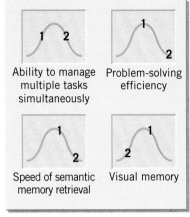

Making Connections

Ability to manage multiple tasks simultaneously

Problem-solving efficiency

Speed of semantic memory retrieval

Visual memory

Memory and problem-solving abilities

People have different degrees of ability and hence fall on different points of multiple bell-shaped curves on various components of information processing (Chapter 6). Subject 2 is superior to subject 1 in problem-solving ability, the central executive functions of working memory, and semantic memory, as indicated by scores that fall further out on the bell curve. Subject 1, however, is superior in visual memory.

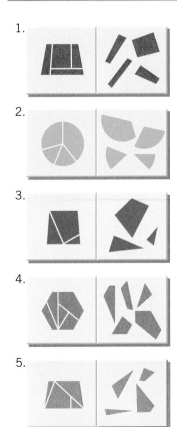

Apply & Discuss

According to some components of the information processing approach to intelligence, such as knowledge base, we might expect a direct relationship between age and intelligence. On the other hand, other components, such as speed of processing, might lead us to hypothesize an inverse relationship between intelligence and aging.

▪ What do you think the relationship between intelligence and aging is?

▪ Do people get more intelligent as they age, or is age a static characteristic of the person?

Apply & Discuss

To recognize the existence of multiple forms of intelligence, Gardner recommends a simple exercise: Instead of asking "How smart are you?" try asking "How are you smart?" (Chen & Gardner, 1997). Map your answers on Gardner's domains and see how well his intelligences cover yours.

▪ Musical
▪ Bodily/kinesthetic
▪ Spatial
▪ Linguistic or verbal
▪ Logical/mathematical
▪ Intrapersonal
▪ Interpersonal

INTERIM SUMMARY

Information-processing approaches to intelligence attempt to describe and measure the specific cognitive *processes* that underlie intelligent behavior. They tend to be more interested in "how" than "how much" in studying intelligence. Three variables on which people differ, and which correlate with IQ and achievement, are speed of processing, **knowledge base**, and the ability to learn and apply mental strategies.

A Theory of Multiple Intelligences

In recent years, a very different approach has expanded the scope of thinking about intelligence. Intelligence tests may measure the kinds of intellectual abilities that foster success in school, but what about practical intelligence (the ability to put plans into action in real life) or emotional intelligence (the ability to read people's emotions and use one's own emotional responses adaptively) (Mayer & Salovey, 1997; Sternberg, 1985)?

A third view of intelligence that addresses questions such as these is Howard Gardner's theory of multiple intelligences (Gardner, 1983, 1999). Gardner views intelligence as "an ability or set of abilities that is used to solve problems or fashion products that are of consequence in a particular cultural setting" (Walters & Gardner, 1986, p. 165). The **theory of multiple intelligences** *identifies seven intelligences: musical, bodily/kinesthetic (such as the control over the body and movement that distinguishes great athletes and dancers), spatial (the use of mental maps), linguistic or verbal, logical/mathematical, intrapersonal (self-understanding), and interpersonal (social skills)*. To put it another way, Gardner's theory suggests that intelligence lies on not one but seven bell curves, one for each type of intelligence. Someone could be a brilliant mathematician but inhabit the lowest percentiles of interpersonal intelligence.

Some of the intelligences on Gardner's list may surprise readers accustomed to equating intelligence with the logical and linguistic abilities assessed by IQ tests. Gardner argues, however, that traditional IQ tests are limited in their assessment of intelligence. A person with high interpersonal intelligence may become a superb salesperson despite having only average logical/mathematical abilities, or a brilliant composer may have poor linguistic skills. Furthermore, the emphasis on verbal and logical/mathematical intelligence in IQ measures reflects a bias toward skills valued in technologically advanced societies; over the broad sweep of human history, musical, spatial, and bodily intelligences have tended to be more highly valued.

Selecting Intelligences Gardner acknowledges that one can never develop "a single irrefutable universally acceptable list of human intelligences" (1983, p. 60). On what basis, then, did he choose each of his seven intelligences?

One criterion was whether an intelligence could be isolated neuropsychologically. According to Gardner's view, people have multiple intelligences because they have multiple neural modules (Chapter 3). Each module has its own modes of representation, its own rules or procedures, and its own memory systems. As in the case of Peter Franklin in the opening vignette, brain damage may impair one system without necessarily damaging others. An intellectual skill that can be specifically affected or spared by brain damage qualifies as an independent intelligence. The modularity of intelligences also means that a person's ability in one area does not predict ability in another (Gardner, 1983, 1999).

Another criterion was the existence of savants or prodigies with talents in specific domains. *Savants* are individuals with extraordinary ability in one area but low ability in others. For example, a young man with an IQ in the mentally retarded range could memorize lengthy and complex piano pieces in only a few hearings (Sloboda et al., 1985). *Prodigies* are individuals with extraordinary and generally early-developing genius in one area but normal abilities in others. The presence of extraordinary intelligence in one area suggests a distinct form of intelligence.

Musician Melissa Etheridge and golf sensation Tiger Woods display forms of intelligence not measured on standard tests.

A third criterion for selecting an intelligence is its distinctive developmental course from childhood to adulthood. The fact that one domain may develop more quickly or slowly than others supports the notion of multiple intelligences. Children learn language and mathematics at very different paces. The existence of prodigies is again instructive. If Mozart could write music before he could even read, then the neural systems involved in musical intelligence must be separate from those involved in processing language.

INTERIM SUMMARY

Gardner's **theory of multiple intelligences** proposes that intelligence is not one capacity but many. The theory distinguishes seven kinds of intelligence: musical, bodily/kinesthetic, spatial, linguistic or verbal, logical/mathematical, intrapersonal, and interpersonal. Gardner argues that intelligences can be isolated based on a number of criteria, including their neurological independence, the presence of savants (who are severely deficient in major intellectual respects but have pockets of giftedness), and their different developmental courses.

Heredity and Intelligence

Having some concept of what intelligence is and how to measure it, we are now prepared to address the most controversial issue surrounding the concept of intelligence: its origins. To what degree is intelligence inherited or learned?

Apply & Discuss

▪ Is the ability to paint or draw an intelligence?
▪ To what extent can intelligence be taught or learned?

Individual Differences in IQ From Brain to Behavior

The influence of both nature and nurture on individual differences in intelligence is well established (see Sternberg, 1997b, 2000a). With respect to environmental effects, as we saw in Chapter 3, early enrichment of the environments of rats not only makes them better learners but actually increases their brain mass (see Bors & Forrin, 1996). In humans, some of the best predictors of a child's performance on tests of IQ and

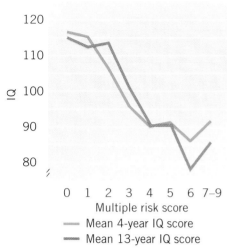

FIGURE 8.6 The impact of the environment on IQ. The figure shows the correlation between number of risk factors and child IQ at ages 4 and 13. By and large, each of several risk factors was highly predictive of IQ on its own, but the combination predicted IQ with a correlation near −.70 at both ages 4 and 13. *Source:* Sameroff et al., 1993, p. 89.

Big Picture φ Question 6

What is the relation between nature and nurture in shaping psychological processes?

language in the toddler and preschool years include an enriched home environment, positive mother–child interactions that foster interest and exploration, and maternal knowledge about child rearing and child development (Bee, 1982; Benasich & Brooks-Gunn, 1996; Hart & Risley, 1992; Landau & Weissler, 1993).

In one *longitudinal study* (a study following individuals over time), the investigators examined the relation between the number of risk factors to which the child was exposed in early childhood and the child's IQ at ages 4 and 13 (Sameroff et al., 1993). Among these risk factors were maternal lack of education, maternal mental illness, minority status (associated with, among other things, low standard of living and inferior schools), and family size. As Figure 8.6 shows, the more risk factors, the lower the child's IQ.

Twin, Family, and Adoption Studies

Although results such as these are striking, they cannot definitively tease apart the relative contributions of heredity and environment. For example, maternal IQ, which is a strong predictor of a child's IQ, could exert an influence genetically or environmentally, and it could indirectly influence some environmental risk factors, such as low maternal education level. Twin, family, and adoption studies can more clearly distinguish some of the influences of nature and nurture. The logic of these studies is to examine subjects whose genetic relatedness is known and to see whether degree of relatedness predicts the size of the correlation between their IQs. If the size of the correlation varies with the degree of relatedness, the effect is likely genetic.

As described in Chapter 3, siblings, dizygotic (DZ) twins, and parents and their children are all genetically related by .50. Monozygotic (MZ) twins are genetically identical (degree of relatedness 1.0), whereas adoptive relatives are unrelated (degree of relatedness 0). Thus, if genetic factors are important in IQ, MZ twins should be more alike than DZ twins, siblings, and parents and their offspring. Biological relatives should also be more alike than adopted children and their adoptive parents or siblings. The data across dozens of studies suggest that IQ, like nearly every psychological trait on which individuals differ, reflects a combination of heredity and environment (Table 8.3). On the one hand, the data clearly suggest an environmental impact: Being born at the same time (and presumably being treated more alike than siblings who are not twins) produces a higher correlation between DZ twins (.62) than between siblings (.41), even though both are related by .50.

On the other hand, the data on MZ twins suggest an even stronger genetic effect. The higher correlation between MZ than DZ twins reared together does not in itself prove a genetic effect; parents tend to treat identical twins more similarly than fraternal twins, which could also influence the size of the correlations between their IQs (Beckwith et al., 1991; Kamin, 1974). However, most data suggest that the genetic effect is more powerful (Kendler et al., 1993; Plomin et al., 1976). For example, identical twins reared apart show an average IQ correlation of about .75, which is even larger than DZ twins reared together (Bouchard et al., 1990; Newman et al., 1937; Plomin & DeFries, 1980; Shields, 1962).

Plomin (1997, 1999) examined the relationship between genes and intelligence. He (1998) compared 37 markers on chromosome 6 in two groups of children: average IQ of 103 and average IQ of 136. He found significant differences in the gene at one of the sites on chromosome 6. The gene is that for a hormone receptor that may be involved in learning and memory. In 1999, he reported on three genes on chromosome 4 that are correlated with differences in intelligence. However, each of these genes predicts only 1 to 3 percent of the variance in IQ. Thus, even Plomin acknowledges that parental IQ will be a better predictor of IQ than genetic identification, at least for the foreseeable future. The potential value of genetics studies of intelligence lies more in understanding the neural development that enhances IQ, and thus the potential for a better understanding of how environmental effects modify the outcome.

Table 8.3 ▇ ▇ Correlations in Intelligence between Pairs of People with Varying Degrees of Relatedness Reared Together or Apart

Relationship	Rearing	Degree of Relatedness	Correlation	Number of Pairs
Same individual		1.0	.87	456
Monozygotic twins	Together	1.0	.86	1417
Dizygotic twins	Together	.50	.62	1329
Siblings	Together	.50	.41	5350
Siblings	Apart	.50	.24	203
Parent–child	Together	.50	.35	3973
Parent–child	Apart	.50	.31	345
Adoptive parent–child	Together	0	.16	1594
Unrelated children	Together	0	.25	601
Spouses	Apart	0	.29	5318

The IQ of adoptive parents has little association with the IQ of their adopted children.

Identical twins score as similarly as the same person taking the test on two occasions.

The environment appears to have a substantial impact, as dizygotic twins and siblings have the same degree of relatedness but different IQ correlations.

Source: Adapted from Henderson, 1982.

Note. The table summarizes the results from family studies comparing IQs among multiple pairs of individuals, contrasting the degree of relatedness with correlation of intelligence scores. For "same individual," the correlation refers to the same person taking the test at two different times.

Adoption studies are particularly important in assessing the relative impact of heredity and environment. Most of these studies compare the IQ of adopted children with other members of their adoptive family, their biological family, and a control group matched for the child's age, sex, socioeconomic status, and ethnic background.

From the earliest adoption studies conducted in the first half of the twentieth century, researchers have found genetic influences to be the primary determinant of differences between individuals on IQ, with environmental circumstances serving to limit or amplify inborn tendencies (Burks, 1928, 1938; Loehlin et al., 1989; Scarr & Carter-Saltzman, 1982; Skodak & Skeels, 1949; Turkheimer, 1991; Weiss, 1992). In one classic study, researchers tested the IQ of each biological mother in the sample at the time of delivery with the Stanford-Binet test and found an average IQ of 86 (Skodak & Skeels, 1949). Thirteen years later, they tested the children, who were reared by adoptive parents (often of higher socioeconomic status), using the same test.

The children scored an average of 107, over 20 points higher than their biological mothers, providing strong evidence for environmental influences on intelligence. However, in this study as in others (e.g., Dudley, 1991; Dumaret, 1985; Schiff et al., 1982), the correlation between the IQ of adopted children and their biological parents

Making Connections

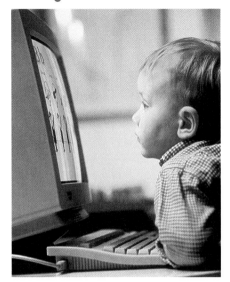

An enriched environment not only makes young rats better learners but actually increases the mass of their brains, suggesting that environmental events influence intellectual development (Chapter 3). The same is likely true in humans, who require certain kinds of stimulation to turn on certain "natural" capacities.

Making Connections

The term "virtual twins" has been used to describe unrelated siblings of the same age who are reared together from infancy (Segal, 2000). Thus, virtual twins have no genetic relationship but share a common rearing environment. In a study of 90 such sibling pairs, the IQ correlation was only 0.26. Although statistically significant (Chapter 2), this relationship is far below the reported correlations for MZ twins (0.86), DZ twins (0.62), and full siblings (0.41). It suggests that, while the environment influences IQ, genetic influences are strong.

was considerably larger than the correlation with their adoptive parents' IQ. Similarly, researchers have found that the correlation between the IQs of adopted (biologically unrelated) *siblings* reared together is below .20, compared with .50 for biological siblings reared together (Segal, 1997). Thus, blood runs thicker than adoption papers in predicting IQ.

In another landmark study, the Texas Adoption Project, psychologists tested 1230 members of 300 Texas families that adopted one or more children from a home for unwed mothers (Horn et al., 1979, 1982; Loehlin et al., 1997). Many of the birth mothers had taken IQ tests while at the home during their pregnancy, and the researchers had access to these scores as well. At the time the project began, the adopted children were between 3 and 14 years old. At this initial assessment, the correlations between the IQ of the adoptive parents and their adopted children were similar to the correlations between the IQ of the adoptive parents and their biological children, suggesting relatively equal contributions of heredity and environment. When the researchers located and retested many of the participants 10 years later, however, the data presented a very different picture: The only correlations that remained above .20 were those between biological relatives (Loehlin et al., 1989).

The results of the Texas Adoption Project, like the findings of several other studies (Loehlin et al., 1997; Scarr & Weinberg, 1976; Segal, 1997), suggest that although genes and environment both influence IQ in childhood, the impact of the family environment decreases with age as the impact of genetics increases. Similarities among the IQs of family members appear to reflect their shared genes more than their shared environment (Brody, 1992).

Are Differences between Individuals Largely Genetic? Two Caveats

Before leaving this discussion, we should consider two important caveats (cautions). First, the formulas used to assess heritability were developed 60 years ago, in the field of "agricultural eugenics," for the purpose of breeding high-quality cattle. Built into them are some assumptions that do not hold in any of the data sets discussed here (Hirsch, 1997). One important assumption is that cows do not choose their environments or their mates.

Humans, however, are very different from cows! If people choose mates whose IQs and cultural experience are similar to their own, and if they choose environments that fit their talents and interests, heritability coefficients will be inflated. In the West, where these studies have largely been conducted, people do both. Indeed, some researchers who have been carefully examining the assumptions of heritability studies argue that shared environment plays a much larger role than heritability statistics suggest (Stoolmiller, 1999).

Second, heritability coefficients apply only to a particular population, and they cannot be generalized outside that population (Chapter 3). The most decisive studies of the heritability of IQ—twin studies—have nearly all used middle-class samples (Neisser et al., 1998a). Their results are thus generalizable only to individuals from middle-class homes. If these studies were to include people from an urban ghetto—or from Liberia or Guatemala—heritability estimates would probably drop substantially because the environments would be so much more varied.

We know, for example, that schooling plays a crucial role in shaping intellectual skills, such as the ability to think abstractly (Chapter 7). Because twin studies have only included literate people, they have eliminated a substantial environmental effect—presence or absence of schooling—before calculating heritability. Recent research suggests, in fact, that genetic influences are substantially smaller (and effects of shared environment between siblings larger) in shaping IQ among children of less educated parents, for whom lack of environmental enrichment and decreased opportunities may limit the expression of innate potential (Rowe et al., 1999).

These comments are not intended to suggest that we should dismiss the findings of these studies. The point is simply that nature and nurture interact in complex ways, and psychological findings must always be understood in the context of the methods that produce them.

Group Differences: Race and Intelligence

Nowhere has controversy loomed larger in psychology than in the attempt to understand group differences in intelligence (see Jencks & Phillips, 1998). Researchers have consistently found a 15-point difference between the average IQ scores of white Americans and African-Americans. Arthur Jensen (1973) created a storm of controversy over 25 years ago when he argued, based on the available data, that "between one-half and three-fourths of the average IQ difference between American Negroes and whites is attributable to genetic factors" (p. 363; see also Jensen, 1969). Many denounced Jensen's interpretation of the data as blatantly racist, questioning both his science and his politics.

Although the data at this point are inconclusive, several lines of evidence argue against a primarily genetic explanation for group difference in IQ (Scarr & Carter-Saltzman, 1982, p. 864). One study examined the IQ of children of various races adopted by white middle-class families (Scarr & Weinberg, 1976, 1983). Black children who had been adopted in the first year of life scored an average IQ of 110, at least 20 points higher than that of comparable children raised in the black community, where economic deprivation was much more common. When the researchers retested as many of the adoptees as they could locate 10 years later, the IQ scores of black adoptees remained above the average IQ of blacks raised in the black community, although their mean IQ was somewhat below the mean IQ for whites in the sample (Weinberg et al., 1992).

Another study capitalized on the fact that many African-Americans have mixed ancestry (Scarr et al., 1977). If a substantial portion of racial IQ differences is attributable to genetics, then IQ levels should rise and fall in direct proportion to the degrees of African and European ancestry. In fact, the researchers found no correlation between ancestry and IQ.

Perhaps most important are data on changes in IQ scores over time (Neisser et al., 1998b). An early study found that black children whose families had moved north to Philadelphia between World Wars I and II gained between 0.5 and 0.7 IQ points for each year they were enrolled in Philadelphia schools (Lee, 1951). More recent research suggests that the average difference in standardized achievement test scores between blacks and whites in the United States has diminished in recent decades as educational opportunities have expanded and African-Americans have climbed up the socioeconomic ladder (Williams & Ceci, 1997).

Further, across all the industrialized countries, IQ appears to be rising about three points a decade, so that a person who is of only average IQ today would have been above average in comparison to other people 50 years ago (Flynn, 1987, 1999). Although the reasons for this increase are unclear, it probably reflects the greater complexity of the occupational and technical tasks required of people today than in their grandparents' day (Neisser et al., 1998). These data suggest that social and environmental conditions can lead to changes in IQ as large as the average difference between blacks and whites.

How can genetic factors be so important in accounting for individual differences in intelligence while environmental factors play such an important role in group differences (see Gould, 1981, 1984)? The answer becomes clear through an analogy. Anyone who has ever visited a war museum notices immediately how small the uniforms were even a century ago. If researchers were to measure skeletal remains, they might find that most men who fought in the American Civil War ranged from 5 feet 2 inches to 5 feet 6 inches, with an average of 5 feet 4 inches. Then, as now, tall fathers

Studies of monozygotic (identical) and dizygotic (fraternal) twins provide a way of studying the impact of genetics on intelligence.

tended to beget tall sons, although "tall" in the 1860s would be short or average today. Were the same researchers to assess men who fought in the Vietnam War 100 years later, they would similarly find high heritability, but the average height would be several inches taller. In both samples—from the same country, a mere century apart—heritability is high, but the difference between the average height in 1865 and 1965 is entirely environmental, largely resulting from nutritional differences. Similarly, genetic differences could account for many of the observed differences between individuals in IQ, while environmental effects could account for observed differences between groups.

Commentary

The Science and Politics of Intelligence

It is tempting to conclude, then, that group differences in intelligence can be explained in terms of environmental differences, such as social disadvantage, nutrition, and quality of education. Although the studies described here seem to refute genetic explanations for racial differences in intelligence, a few words of caution are in order.

The question of genetic versus environmental components of intelligence is a highly emotional issue, particularly with respect to racial differences. The notion that a mental attribute as highly valued in the West as intelligence could be genetically influenced goes against the grain of many of our most fundamental beliefs and values, including the view that we are all created equal. Furthermore, claims of racial superiority have a long and sordid history in human affairs, certainly in the last century. Hence, any psychologist who argues for a genetic basis to any racial differences is immediately suspect, and the psychological community has, by and large, been much less critical of studies that claim to refute genetic or racial differences.

A case in point concerns published reports of an intervention program that took place in the late 1960s and early 1970s. This program, known as the Milwaukee Project, provided an intellectually enriched environment for children at high risk for mental retardation. The program's results seemed impressive. The investigators reported an average difference of 24 IQ points between the program's children and a control group. The findings were described in every introductory psychology textbook for nearly two decades to illustrate the decisive impact of environment, as opposed to heredity, on IQ. Unfortunately, the study had never been published by a journal; thus, it had never been subjected to normal peer review processes and examined for its scientific merit (Sommer & Sommer, 1983). Nor has it ever been replicated. We have no idea whether or not the study had any validity.

Recently, the American Psychological Association (APA) commissioned a distinguished task force to prepare a report on the state of the evidence with respect to intelligence and intelligence testing, including the question of group differences (Neisser et al., 1998). Some of the major conclusions are as follows.

First, intelligence tests are highly predictive of school success, with the average correlation about .50. Other variables contribute to academic success as well, such as persistence, interest in school, and supportive attitudes of parents or peers. Intelligence tests are not, however, biased against particular groups, since these tests predict outcomes such as school performance within as well as between groups.

Second, the heritability of IQ in children is about .45 but reaches about .75 in adulthood; thus, a substantial percentage of the difference in IQ between most individuals is genetic. Heritability does not, however, imply, immutability. Every genetic effect acts within an environmental circumstance, and changing the environment, such as placing a poor child in a middle-class home, can have a substantial impact on IQ.

Third, whites and Asian-Americans tend to have higher IQs than Hispanics, whose IQs are higher, on average, than African-Americans. The lower average IQ of African-Americans could potentially reflect some combination of causes, including poverty and related environmental risk factors, test-taking attitudes and motivational patterns shaped by generations of discrimination, or aspects of African-American culture and genetics. There is no empirical support for genetic explanations, but the evidence for environmental explanations is also weak; thus, at present, no one knows what causes the difference in black and white IQ scores. A definitive study will probably have to wait until psychologists can assess African Americans whose families have been middle or upper class for four or five generations and who have attended schools comparable to those of whites of similar socioeconomic status. Such a study is many years away.

INTERIM SUMMARY

IQ reflects a complex interplay of nature and nurture. Twin, family, and adoption studies suggest that genetic factors are more important in explaining differences among individuals. Studies of the influence of home environment and socioeconomic status suggest that racial differences are likely primarily environmental, although at this point no firm conclusions can be drawn.

Although intelligence is probably best viewed as multifaceted, we still do not know precisely what its facets are, how many "general intelligences" humans really have (whether one, two, seven, or more), or how to measure many of them (such as musical intelligence). Indeed, some facets of intelligence, such as general problem-solving ability, may be universal, whereas others depend on cultural and historical developments. Who would have known 20 years ago that the ability to write computer programs would not only spur one of the greatest periods of technological development in world history but that this "intelligence" would suddenly be so amply rewarded? Would Bill Gates have excelled as an Eskimo navigator, or even as an industrialist at the turn of the nineteenth century, when Henry Ford and others learned to harness labor using assembly lines? Would the same talents that made Gates the richest man in the world have served him as well a century earlier? Perhaps intelligence is as much the match between a person and a time as a quality of a single individual.

Summary

The Nature of Intelligence

1. Intelligence is the application of cognitive skills and knowledge to learn, solve problems, and obtain ends that are valued by an individual or culture. Intelligence is multifaceted, functional, and culturally defined. Some aspects of intelligence are universal, whereas others depend on the tasks of adaptation in a particular society.

Intelligence Testing

2. **Intelligence tests** are **psychometric instruments** designed to assess an individual's cognitive capabilities compared to others in a population. The ancestor of modern IQ tests was invented by Binet for the specific purpose of identifying retarded children. Binet developed the concept of **mental age (MA)**, the average age at which children can be expected to achieve a particular score.

3. The **intelligence quotient**, or **IQ**, is a score meant to represent an individual's intellectual ability, which permits comparison with other individuals. It was initially calculated by dividing mental age by chronological age and multiplying by 100.

4. Wechsler abandoned the concept of mental age and calculated IQ as an individual's position relative to peers of the same age by using a frequency distribution. The Wechsler scales (the **WAIS-III**

and the **WISC-III** for children) include verbal and nonverbal (performance) tests.

5. Intelligence tests are highly predictive of scholastic success, and they also predict occupational success. Critics argue that they lack a theoretical basis, are culturally biased, and fail to capture other kinds of intelligence.

Approaches to Intelligence

6. The **psychometric approach** derives the components and structure of intelligence empirically from statistical analysis of psychometric test findings. The primary tool of the psychometric approach is **factor analysis**, a statistical technique for identifying common **factors** that underlie performance on a wide variety of measures. Spearman's **two-factor theory** distinguishes the **g-factor**, or general intelligence, from **s-factors**, or specific abilities. Other models derived from factor analysis have provided different lists of factors, such as **Gf–Gc theory**, which distinguishes between content-free fluid intelligence and knowledge-based crystallized intelligence.

7. The information-processing approach tries to understand the specific cognitive processes that underlie intelligent behavior. Three of the most important variables on which people differ are speed of processing, **knowledge base**, and ability to learn and apply mental strategies. Unlike the psychometric approach, the information-processing approach is theory driven, drawing on research in cognitive science.

8. Gardner's **theory of multiple intelligences** distinguishes seven kinds of intelligence that are relatively independent, neurologically distinct, and show different courses of development. These include musical, bodily/kinesthetic, spatial, linguistic or verbal, logical/mathematical, intrapersonal, and interpersonal intelligences.

Heredity and Intelligence

9. A central question in the study of intelligence is the extent to which environment and heredity shape intelligence. To examine the heritability of IQ, studies have correlated the IQ scores of subjects with differing degrees of genetic relatedness and of biological and adoptive family members. Twin, family, and adoption studies suggest that heredity, environment, and their interaction all contribute to IQ but that individual differences in IQ are highly heritable.

10. Research does not support the hypothesis that differences among racial or ethnic groups are primarily genetic; at this point, the data are inconclusive. A definitive study will likely require several generations of individuals from multiple ethnic groups who have experienced similar levels of socioeconomic status and opportunity—a study likely to be decades away.

Key Terms

Consciousness

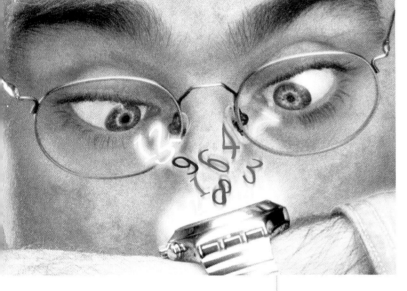

woman named Katherine sees in vivid colors letters and numbers printed in black and white. Not only are the colors vivid, but the relationship of letter to color is consistent: *n's* are always brown, *q's* are always pink, and *a's* are always red. As far as she knew, everyone had this facility. This condition is called *synesthesia*: stimulation of one sensory modality leading to perceptual experience in another sensory modality. Whereas anesthesia refers to the absence of sensation, synesthesia refers to a combination, or synthesis of sensations. This rare phenomenon (less than 1 percent of the population and more common in women) has been reported since the 1700s. Other forms of synesthesia include hearing colors, feeling sounds, or tasting shapes. Famous synesthetes include the poet Baudelaire, the painters Kandinsky and Klee, and the composer Liszt. The novelist and synesthete Vladimir Nabokov wrote that he associated the letter "a" with weathered wood whereas the letter "r" produced a sensation of "a sooty rag being ripped."

In attempting to understand the source of this additional sensory dimension, researchers have looked at both basic visual ability and at more sophisticated central nervous system processing. Synesthetes have normal vision and color vision, and PET scans have revealed that the initial pathways for sensory information arrive at the correct areas of the brain (i.e., visual information goes to the visual cortex and not to the auditory cortex; Paulesu et al., 1996). However, when the information is relayed to the somatosensory cortex and association areas, there appears to be cross-communication in synesthetes that does not occur in nonsynesthetes. Thus, the synesthete receives the same sensory information as you or I, but, after initial processing, a different use of the information results in altered perception and, thus, an "altered" state of consciousness.

We begin this chapter by discussing the nature and functions of consciousness, examining the way attention focuses consciousness at any given time on a narrow subset of the thoughts and feelings of which a person could be aware. We then examine multiple perspectives on consciousness and explore the neural basis of consciousness. The remainder of the chapter is devoted to **states of consciousness—** *qualitatively different patterns of subjective experience*, including ways of experiencing both internal and external events. We start with the most basic distinction, between waking and sleeping, exploring the stages of sleep and the nature of dreaming. We conclude by examining several altered states of consciousness—deviations from the normal waking state—including hypnosis, and drug-induced states.

The Nature of Consciousness

Consciousness, *the subjective awareness of mental events*, is easier to describe than to define. William James (1890) viewed consciousness as a constantly moving stream of thoughts, feelings, and perceptions. Following in the footsteps of the French philosopher René Descartes, who offered the famous proposition *cogito ergo sum* ("I think, therefore I am"), James also emphasized a second aspect of consciousness, the consciousness of self. James argued that part of being conscious of any particular thought is a simultaneous awareness of oneself as the author or owner of it.

Functions of Consciousness

Why do we have consciousness at all? Two of the functions of consciousness are readily apparent: Consciousness monitors the self and the environment, and it regulates thought and behavior (Kihlstrom, 1987). Consciousness as a *monitor* is analogous to a continuously moving video camera, surveying potentially significant perceptions, thoughts, emotions, goals, and problem-solving strategies. The regulatory or *control function* of consciousness allows people to initiate and terminate thought and behavior in order to attain goals. People often rehearse scenarios in their minds, such as asking for a raise or confronting a disloyal friend. Consciousness is often engaged when people choose between competing strategies for solving a problem (Taylor, 2002; Wegner & Bargh, 1998).

Red	Yellow	Green
Blue	Red	Yellow
Green	Blue	Red

FIGURE 9.1 The Stroop color-naming test. The task is to name the color of the ink in which each word is printed as quickly as possible while ignoring the words themselves. Try it yourself—the task is very difficult because the word interferes with color naming when the word is printed in a different color (e.g., when "green" is written in red).

These two functions of consciousness—monitor and control—are intertwined, because consciousness monitors inner and outer experience to prevent and solve problems. For example, consciousness often "steps in" when automatized processes (procedural knowledge, Chapter 6) are not successful. In this sense, consciousness is like the inspector in a garment factory: It does not make the product, but it checks to make sure the product is made correctly. If it finds an imperfection, it institutes a remedy (Gilbert, 1989).

Recent neuroimaging evidence suggests that the dorsolateral prefrontal cortex, which is involved in working memory and conscious decision making (Chapter 6), is activated when people exercise conscious control (Stuss et al., 2001). Researchers in one study (MacDonald et al., 2000) demonstrated this using the *Stroop test*, in which subjects are presented a word (e.g., the name of a color) printed in color and then have to name the color of the ink, as quickly as possible, while ignoring the word (Figure 9.1). This task can be very difficult because the subject has to name the color of the ink and ignore the competing color name—a task that requires considerable conscious attention. This condition markedly slows the response time compared to one in which the words are all printed in black ink or in which the color words are each printed in the appropriate color of ink.

The researchers found that the Stroop test leads to activation of the dorsolateral prefrontal cortex, as subjects "put their mind to" the job of ignoring the words while naming the color (Figure 9.2). A different part of the cortex, the anterior cingulate, becomes active only when the color of the ink and the word conflict but not when the color of the ink is identical with the word (e.g., "red" printed in red ink). This dichotomy suggests that the anterior cingulate is involved in consciously regulating conflicting cues and perhaps in inhibiting responses that are incorrect.

From an evolutionary standpoint, consciousness probably evolved as a mechanism for directing behavior in adaptive ways that was superimposed on more primitive psy-

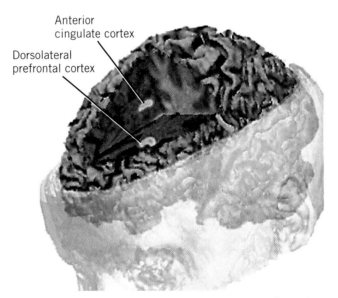

Anterior cingulate cortex

Dorsolateral prefrontal cortex

FIGURE 9.2 Neural pathways in controlling and monitoring tasks. Participants showed more activation in the dorsolateral prefrontal cortex when preparing to exert conscious control but showed more activation in the anterior cingulate when monitoring for conflicts. *Source:* MacDonald et al., 2000.

Big Picture φ Question 6

What is the relation between nature and nurture in shaping psychological processes?

Apply & Discuss

We began this chapter with a discussion of synesthesia.

■ How do you think a synesthete who consistently sees each letter of the alphabet in a different color would respond to the Stroop test?

chological processes such as conditioning (Reber, 1992). Indeed, William James, who was heavily influenced by Darwin, explained consciousness in terms of its function: fostering adaptation. Consciousness is often "grabbed" by things that are unexpected, unusual, contradictory (as in the Stroop test), or contrary to expectations—precisely the things that could affect well-being or survival. Much of the time people respond automatically to the environment, learning and processing information without much attention. Many choices, however, require more careful conscious consideration.

INTERIM SUMMARY

Consciousness refers to the subjective awareness of mental events. **States of consciousness** are qualitatively different patterns of subjective experience, including ways of experiencing both internal and external events. Consciousness plays at least two functions: monitoring the self and the environment and controlling thought and behavior. Consciousness probably evolved as a mechanism for directing behavior in adaptive ways which was superimposed on more primitive psychological processes that continue to function without conscious awareness.

Consciousness and Attention

At any given time, people are dimly aware of much more than what is conscious. For example, while reading the newspaper a person may have some vague awareness of the radiator clanking, voices in the next room, and the smell of breakfast cooking, but none of these is at the center of awareness or consciousness.

Attention **Attention** refers to *the process of focusing conscious awareness*, providing heightened sensitivity to a limited range of experience requiring more extensive information processing. *Selection*—of a particular object, a train of thought, or a location in space where something important might be happening—is the essence of attention (Posner & DiGirolamo, 2000). Attention is generally guided by some combination of external stimulation, which naturally leads us to focus on relevant sensory information, and activated goals, which lead us to attend to thoughts, feelings, or stimuli relevant to obtaining these goals.

Some psychologists have likened attention to a filtering process through which only important information passes (Broadbent, 1958). For example, people frequently become so engrossed in conversation with one person that they tune out all other conversations in the room—an important skill at a loud party. However, if they hear someone mention their name across the room, they may suddenly look up and focus attention on the person who has just spoken the magic word. This phenomenon, called the *cocktail party phenomenon* (Cherry, 1953), suggests that we implicitly process much more information than reaches consciousness.

On the other hand, *people also sometimes divert attention from information that may be relevant but emotionally upsetting*, a process called **selective inattention**. This can be highly adaptive, as when students divert their attention from the anxiety of taking a test to the task itself. It can also be maladaptive, as when people ignore a darkening birthmark on their arm that could be malignant cancer.

Components of Attention and Consciousness Attention and consciousness consist of at least three functions: maintaining alertness, orienting (selecting a restricted sample of all of the available information, internal and external); and controlling behavior and the contents of consciousness (Engle & Singer, 2001). Different neural networks, relying on different neurotransmitter systems, appear to be involved in these functions (Robbins, 1997).

The first function (alertness) is crucial in tasks ranging from focusing on test items in the face of anxiety, to staying alert for hours while watching a radar screen to detect small but potentially meaningful changes. A whole network of neurons from the reticular activating system (RAS, Chapter 3) through the frontal lobes appear to be involved in alertness (Posner, 1995).

Orienting, the second function, involves focusing sensory organs such as the eyes and ears toward a stimulus (Roberts & Rafal, 2000). It also involves spreading extra activation (i.e., increased neural activity) to the parts of the cortex that are processing information about the stimulus and probably inhibiting activation of others. When we attend to a stimulus, such as a mosquito buzzing around the room, the brain uses the same circuits it normally uses to process information that is not the focus of attention. For example, watching the mosquito activates the "what" and "where" visual pathways in the occipital, temporal, and parietal lobes (Chapter 4). What attention does is to enhance processing at those cortical locations (Rees et al., 1997). Orienting to stimuli activates neural circuits in the midbrain (such as the superior colliculi, which help control eye movements), thalamus (which directs attention to particular sensory systems), and parietal lobes (which, among other functions, direct attention to particular locations).

A third function involves controlling the contents of consciousness, such as deciding how much to listen as someone is talking. This takes place in the anatomically elusive working memory (Chapter 6). Despite our subjective experience of consciously controlling what we attend to, the situation is more the other way around: To notice something consciously, unconscious attentional mechanisms have to alert us to its potential significance. Thus, paradoxically, consciousness is, to a large degree, regulated *outside* of consciousness, by unconscious attentional mechanisms that focus conscious awareness. Control of the contents of consciousness and control of voluntary behavior involve areas of the frontal lobes and basal ganglia known to be involved in thought, movement, and self-control.

Divided Attention Everyone has had the experience of being on the telephone and having someone in the room begin talking at the same time. Trying to follow two such conversations is an example of **divided attention**, *splitting attention between two complex tasks* (see Craik et al., 1996).

One way researchers study divided attention is through **dichotic listening** tasks, in which *subjects are fitted with earphones, and different information is simultaneously presented to the left and right ears* (Figure 9.3). Subjects can be instructed to attend only to the information from one ear by repeating aloud what they hear in that ear, a procedure called *shadowing*.

Subjects can become so adept at shadowing that they are completely unable to recognize information in the unattended channel. Nevertheless, the information does appear to be processed to some degree, as demonstrated in research on priming, in which exposure to a stimulus (such as a word) increases performance on tasks involving related stimuli (Chapter 6). For example, subjects who hear "England" (the prime) in the unattended channel in a dichotic listening study may have no recollection of having heard the name of any country. When compared to control subjects who have not been similarly primed, however, they are more likely to say "London" if asked to name a capital city and will more quickly fill in the missing letters when asked for the name of a city when presented with LO—.

Divided attention can be seen in such everyday but remarkably complex events as listening to a lecture while simultaneously taking notes. Psychologists have even trained subjects to take dictation while reading (Spelke et al., 1976). Sometimes people accomplish such feats by rapidly shifting attention back and forth between the two tasks. Much of the time, however, they solve attentional dilemmas by automatizing one task or the other. Automatization develops through practice, as actions previously performed with deliberate conscious effort are eventually processed automatically. When students listen to a lecture, their primary focus of consciousness is on the lecturer's current words, while a largely automatic process, perhaps drawing on some subset of attentional processes, allows note taking.

Apply and Discuss

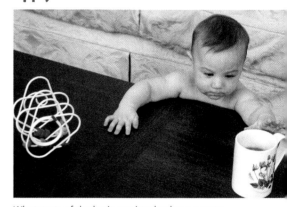

What parts of the brain are involved as a person notices that her baby is playing with something, categorizes the object as dangerous, and moves the object away from the baby?

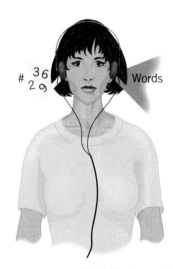

FIGURE 9.3 A dichotic listening task. Subjects are fitted with earphones, and different information is transmitted into each ear simultaneously. Subjects often show effects of information presented in the unattended channel, even when they have no conscious recognition of it.

Apply & Discuss

Daydreaming involves turning attention away from external stimuli to internal thoughts and imagined scenarios, and it is considered to be a major component of the normal flow of consciousness.

▪ What percentage of time do you think college students spend daydreaming? What are they daydreaming about? How much time do *you* spend daydreaming?

▪ How do you think researchers go about studying the normal flow of consciousness?

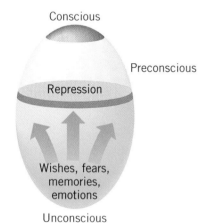

FIGURE 9.4 Freud's model of consciousness. Conscious mental processes are those of which a person is subjectively aware. Preconscious mental processes are not presently conscious but could readily be brought to consciousness. Unconscious mental processes are inaccessible to consciousness because they have been repressed.

Attention refers to the process of focusing conscious awareness, providing heightened sensitivity to a limited range of experience requiring more extensive information processing. **Selective inattention** refers to selectively diverting attention from information that may be emotionally upsetting. Attention and consciousness consist of at least three functions: alerting arousal; orienting attention; and controlling behavior and the contents of consciousness. **Divided attention**, which often involves automatizing one or more tasks or rapidly shifting attention between them, refers to the capacity to split attention or cognitive resources between two or more tasks.

Perspectives on Consciousness

Consciousness occupied a central role in the first textbook on psychology, written by William James in 1890, and figured prominently in Freud's work. When behaviorism (Watson, 1925) came into ascendance, however, consciousness as a focus of investigation became less popular in the scientific community and remained that way until the 1980s. Behavioral psychologists rejected the idea of a conscious mind as an agent that chooses, intends, or makes decisions (Skinner, 1974, p. 169). Organisms as primitive as snails respond to environmental stimuli, but one would not propose that snails, therefore, have consciousness.

Until about 15 years ago, cognitive psychologists also paid little attention to consciousness. As we saw in Chapter 6, however, that all changed with the surge of research on implicit memory and cognition. Spurred by developments in neuroscience and neuroimaging that provide a new window on consciousness, cognitive psychologists—as well as philosophers, neurologists, biologists, and even physicists—have begun rethinking consciousness (e.g., Cohen & Schooler, 1997; Edelman, 1989). In this next section we examine psychodynamic and cognitive perspectives on consciousness and explore some emerging common ground.

The Psychodynamic Unconscious

Freud (1900) defined consciousness as one of three mental systems called the conscious, preconscious, and unconscious (Figure 9.4). **Conscious mental processes *involve subjective awareness of stimuli, feelings, or ideas*** (e.g., consciousness of the sentence you just read—if you were paying attention). **Preconscious mental processes *are not presently conscious but could be readily brought to consciousness*** if the need arose, such as the smell of bacon cooking in the background or the name of a city that is not currently in mind but could easily be retrieved. **Unconscious mental processes *are inaccessible to consciousness because they would be too anxiety provoking and thus have been repressed***(Chapter 12).

Freud likened repression to a censor: Just as a repressive government censors ideas or wishes that it considers threatening, so, too, does the mind censor threatening thoughts from consciousness. Thus, a person may remember an abusive father with love and admiration and have little access to unhappy memories because admitting the truth would be painful. Unconscious processes of this sort are *dynamically unconscious*—that is, kept unconscious for a reason. According to Freud, keeping mental contents out of awareness requires continuing psychological effort or energy, a postulate that has received empirical support in recent years (Wegner & Wheatley, 1999). Freud (1915) recognized that many other psychological processes are *descriptively unconscious*, that is, not conscious even though they are not threatening, such as the processes by which readers are converting symbols on this page into words with psychological meaning.

Unconscious Motivation   The proposition that unconscious cognitive and perceptual processes can influence behavior is no longer controversial. Historically, however, the most distinctively psychodynamic hypothesis is that motivational and emotional processes can be unconscious as well. This proposition has now also gained experimental support (see Bargh & Barndollar, 1996; Epstein, 1994; Westen, 1998).

With respect to motivation, research suggests a distinction between conscious and unconscious motivational systems similar to the distinction between implicit and explicit memory in cognitive science. Numerous studies have shown that when people are not attending to their conscious goals and values, they tend to act on implicit motives (McClelland et al., 1989). As described below, other studies show that priming people with words associated with their motives (e.g., priming people with *success*, which is associated with the need for achievement) makes them more likely to act on these motives, even though they may be completely unaware that they have been primed (Bargh & Barndollar, 1996).

The Cognitive Unconscious

The **cognitive unconscious** of cognitive research refers to *information-processing mechanisms that operate outside awareness* (such as implicit memory) rather than information the person is *motivated* to keep from awareness. In other words, the cognitive unconscious includes what Freud called *descriptively* but not *dynamically* unconscious processes.

Information-processing models often use the terms *consciousness* and *working memory* interchangeably, viewing consciousness as an "on-line" workspace for focusing attention on perceptions, memories, and skills relevant for solving current problems. As we saw in Chapters 6 and 8, most models now distinguish explicit (conscious) and implicit (unconscious) memory and cognition, such as conscious problem-solving strategies versus automatic, unconscious heuristics. Connectionist models further propose that information processing occurs simultaneously in multiple, relatively separate neural networks, most of which are unconscious. The brain synthesizes a unitary conscious experience from the various activated unconscious networks, "highlighting" those that best fit the data (Baars, 1988, 1997; Mandler, 1997; Searle, 2000).

Distinguishing Unconscious Cognitive Processes   From a cognitive perspective, John Kihlstrom (1987, 1996) distinguishes unconscious from preconscious cognitive processes, both of which occur outside of awareness. *Unconscious cognitive processes* are skills or procedures that operate without awareness and are not accessible to consciousness under any circumstance. *Preconscious cognitive processes* refer to associations and schemas (declarative knowledge) activated below the threshold of consciousness that influence conscious thought and behavior. The activity of preconscious processes can be seen in everyday life, as when a person cannot get a song "out of his head" that keeps returning because it continues to be preconsciously activated.

Kihlstrom adds a third aspect of consciousness—consciousness of self—to account for two unusual phenomena. The first is that people given hypnotic suggestions to perform certain actions may do them without any sense of having chosen to do so. The second involves *dissociative disorders*, in which memories or feelings are literally disassociated from consciousness, such as cases of multiple personality (Chapter 15). According to Kihlstrom, these phenomena suggest, as William James asserted, that part of normal consciousness involves consciousness of self. In other words, consciousness includes an activated representation of self linked with the thought or action, so that the person sees her thoughts or actions as *hers*.

The Functions of Conscious and Unconscious Processes   Some cognitive theorists have examined the complementary functions, strengths, and weaknesses of conscious and unconscious processes in everyday behavior. Unconscious processes,

Big Picture φ Question 7

To what extent are psychological processes conscious or unconscious—that is, explicit versus implicit?

Making Connections

When people are consciously focusing on their motives or goals, these goals tend to direct their behavior. When they are not, however, their unconscious or implicit motives control their behavior. That is probably why New Years' resolutions are usually short-lived (Chapter 10).

notably skills and associative processes such as priming and classical conditioning, are extremely fast and efficient (Baars & McGovern, 1996; Mandler, 1997). Since they are usually based on considerable learning, they tend to lead to adaptive responses that make sense in light of observed regularities in the environment (such as avoiding stimuli that would lead to pain).

Another strength of unconscious processes is that they can operate simultaneously. When solving a problem, for example, multiple networks can "collect data" at the same time and come up with independent and "well-researched" potential solutions. Consciousness, in contrast, has limited capacity: We can form only one "scene" at a time in our conscious minds; we cannot, for example, see the classic ambiguous Gestalt figure as both two faces and a vase simultaneously (Chapter 4). We can switch rapidly back and forth between two views of a scene or among tasks that require attention, but ultimately, each will draw conscious cognitive resources from the other. Conscious processes are more flexible, however, than unconscious processes, and because consciousness is not limited to quasi-independent networks operating in parallel in their own small domains, consciousness can survey the landscape and consider the "big picture."

One theory suggests that unconscious processes operating in parallel are like independent teams of "experts," each offering its own advice on how to solve a problem or make a decision (Baars, 1988, 1997). Consciousness is thus like a blackboard on which each team of experts fights to present its solution or several teams brainstorm "at the board" to develop novel answers that none alone could produce. If a "team" manages to get its message on the blackboard, its "solution" is advertised throughout the system and leads other experts to begin trying to find solutions along those lines.

In more technical terms, a central role of consciousness is to redistribute activation among the tens, hundreds, or thousands of networks ("team of experts") active at any given time (Mandler, 1997). When conscious goals are active, they spread extra activation to networks associated with goal attainment. If a person is trying to make a decision or solve a problem, all the networks activated below consciousness vie for conscious access. Those that seem to provide the best potential solutions become represented in consciousness. Becoming conscious in turn spreads further activation to them and inhibits activation of less compelling alternatives.

INTERIM SUMMARY

Freud distinguished types of mental activities: **conscious** processes, of which the person is currently subjectively aware; **preconscious** processes, which are not presently conscious but could be readily brought to consciousness; and **unconscious** processes, which are dynamically kept from consciousness because they are threatening. Recent research also supports the psychodynamic hypothesis that motivational processes can occur outside of awareness. Researchers from a cognitive perspective have been studying the **cognitive unconscious**, which focuses on information-processing mechanisms that operate outside awareness, such as procedural knowledge and implicit memory. Implicit processes tend to be rapid and to operate simultaneously. Conscious processes are slower and less efficient for tasks that require instant responses but are useful for "shining a spotlight" on problems that require more careful consideration.

Commentary　|　# An Integrated View of Consciousness

Fifteen years ago, summarizing psychologists' views of conscious and unconscious processes was easy: Psychoanalysts believed in them, behaviorists did not, cognitive scientists were not particularly interested, and evolutionary psychology was just getting off the ground and had not yet weighed in on the subject. Today, we are beginning to see a rare convergence of views. The state of the art might be summarized as follows.

In humans, as in other animals, most behavior is controlled through implicit processes. Conscious processing is too limited in capacity to regulate and monitor the range of stimuli and goals confronting a person at any given time. Associative learning mechanisms, such as those studied by behaviorists, are generally rapid and efficient, and they served our prehuman ancestors well, long before consciousness arrived on the scene (Reber, 1992). The vast majority of perceptual, cognitive, emotional, and motivational processes are implicit and are thus not available to introspection. We can see the impact of our own implicit processes and form conscious representations of them (e.g., recognizing the kinds of people or situations that "push our buttons"), but our brains are not constructed to give us direct access to them.

Some processes to which we could have access, such as thoughts, fantasies, or motives of which we are ashamed, can also become inaccessible to consciousness if we learn that keeping them from consciousness reduces our discomfort. The mechanisms for keeping uncomfortable material outside of awareness or transforming it into conscious representations that are not threatening (e.g., "I'm not a competitive person; I'm only competitive with myself") are themselves a form of procedural knowledge or skill. These procedures are learned like any other: Those that reduce uncomfortable feelings are reinforced (Chapter 5).

Consciousness is a specialized function that monitors our current state in relation to the environment for the purpose of maximizing adaptation. Consciousness is particularly "grabbed" by news; that is, it is most likely to shine its spotlight on information that is novel or unexpected or on procedures that are not working optimally (Baars & McGovern, 1996). Its control function involves overriding procedures that are ineffective or bringing together quasi-independent "experts" to help provide flexible solutions that cannot be obtained while running on automatic pilot.

Although multiple processes operate in parallel to solve problems outside of awareness, attentional mechanisms also operate outside awareness to "prioritize" cognitive resources, spreading extra activation to those resources that might be adaptively significant or help solve current goals. Once a perception, thought, goal, or motive enters consciousness, it further spreads activation to those neural networks that are relevant to it. Much of the time this increases the likelihood that aspects of those neural networks will become conscious. However, activated networks can influence behavior outside of awareness, and threatening information can be inhibited from consciousness even while it is maximally active.

Neuropsychology of Consciousness From Brain to Behavior

Subjectively, consciousness is the seat of who we are; to lose consciousness permanently is to lose existence as a psychological being. What neural structures produce conscious awareness and regulate states of consciousness?

Insights from Neurological Disorders

One way to learn about the neural pathways involved in consciousness is to examine neurological conditions that disrupt it. People with *split brains*, whose two hemispheres function independently following severing of the corpus callosum, provide one window to the neuropsychology of consciousness. An instructive case, described in Chapter 3, concerned a 10-year-old boy who could only answer written questions orally when inquiries were made to the left hemisphere. The case suggests that information presented to his right hemisphere lacked access to consciousness—although

Big Picture φ Question 1

To what extent can mental processes be reduced to the brain or body?

Making Connections

If a person is unfortunate enough to receive a blow to the base of the skull, and the hindbrain and spinal cord are disconnected from the rest of the brain, they will be in a permanent coma (Chapter 3; Barret et al., 1967). In this case, the forebrain is still functional, but without access to the RAS the forebrain cannot remain alert and thus is in a permanent state of unconsciousness. While there may be moments of opening the eyes and brief twitches, true consciousness does not return.

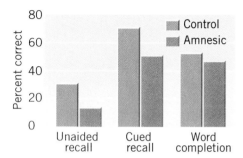

FIGURE 9.5 Priming effects in amnesia. Participants were shown word lists including words like *absent, income,* and *motel* and were asked to recall the words. Amnesic patients were impaired on both un-aided recall and cued recall. However, amnesic patients exhibited normal priming effects when they completed three-letter fragments (e.g., ABS) with the first word that came to mind. *Source:* Squire, 1986.

Big Picture φ Question 1

To what extent can mental processes be reduced to the brain or body?

he could spell answers using his left hand when questions were addressed to his right hemisphere (LeDoux et al., 1977). That the feelings spelled by his nonverbal right hemisphere were consistently more negative than those of his left hemisphere raised questions about the unity of consciousness across the hemispheres.

Studies with *amnesiacs* have shown that people can remember things implicitly even while lacking any consciousness of having seen them. In one series of studies (Squire, 1986), researchers showed amnesic and normal subjects a word list and asked them to recall the words with and without cues. When later tested for explicit memory, amnesic subjects were considerably impaired on both free-recall (recall without cues) and cued-recall tasks (in which participants were given the first three letters of the word) (Figure 9.5). However, amnesiacs were as likely as neurologically intact subjects to use words from the list when shown the first three letters of the word and simply asked to complete them with the first words that came to mind. Implicit memory can show up in some unusual ways in amnesic patients. In one study a psychologist told a joke to a Korsakoff's patient whose ability to remember new experiences was virtually nonexistent (Jacoby & Kelley, 1987). Predictably, the man laughed, but the next time he heard the joke, he thought the joke was "dumb." The patient had apparently anticipated the punch line unconsciously, even though he had no conscious recollection of it.

Where Is Consciousness Located?

Where is consciousness located in the brain? Research over the past two decades has made increasingly clear that this is probably not the right question to ask about any psychological phenomenon. Consciousness, like most psychological functions, involves a distributed network of neurons rather than a single "center." The better question, then, is, "What neural structures are involved in the experience of consciousness?"

The answer to this question, too, has a twist: It depends on which meaning of consciousness we have in mind. If we simply mean the state of being conscious (as opposed to being unconscious or asleep), then hindbrain and midbrain structures, especially the RAS, are particularly important (Bogen, 1995; Franklin et al., 1988; Szymusiak et al., 1989). For example, neuroimaging of surgical patients undergoing anesthesia finds reduced activity in the midbrain (as well as the thalamus, which plays an important role in conscious awareness) (Fiset et al., 1999). Similarly, damage to the RAS through head injury in humans or lesioning in animals can lead to loss of consciousness or coma. The pons and medulla are also involved in regulating states of conscious arousal (Figure 9.6); in contrast, we can lose an entire cerebral hemisphere and remain conscious.

But consciousness has another meaning, which has been our focus thus far in this chapter: consciousness as the center of subjective awareness. In this sense, consciousness is distributed across a number of neural pathways, most of them found in the cortex as well as the RAS (reticular activating system, Chapter 3) and the thalamus (Newman, 1995). The axons of the RAS synapse with nuclei in the thalamus, which in turn synapse with parts of the cortex. A region of particular importance is the prefrontal cortex (Goldman-Rakic, 1995), which is involved in momentarily storing, manipulating, or calling up information from various senses into working memory and hence making them conscious (Chapter 6).

Recent positron emission tomography (PET) data have in fact confirmed that when subjects are consciously attending to stimuli, a pathway from the RAS through the region of the thalamus to which it projects becomes activated (Kinomura et al., 1996). Once the cortex is activated and the person attends to a stimulus, it sends messages back down to another region of the thalamus that signals the first region to limit its activation to the most relevant details of the stimulus, "shining a spotlight" on information that needs to be highlighted and inhibiting attention to irrelevant details (see Crick & Koch, 1998). Thus, the thalamus and cortex appear to have a feedback loop, in which the thalamus and reticular formation "illuminate" a large terrain, the cortex sends messages back to narrow the focus, and the thalamus in turn helps the cortex focus its conscious spotlight on a more specific target (Newman, 1995).

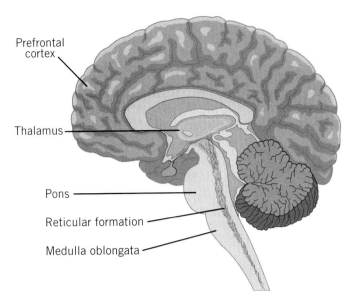

Prefrontal cortex

Thalamus

Pons

Reticular formation

Medulla oblongata

FIGURE 9.6   Neuropsychological basis of consciousness. The reticular activating system, located in the hind and midbrain, the thalamus, and the prefrontal cortex play a particular role in shining a conscious "spotlight" on thoughts, feelings, or perceptions.

Not all areas of the cortex have direct access to consciousness. Some researchers have suggested that early sensory processing areas like area V1 in the visual cortex (one of the first sensory "stops" along the road to visual perception; Chapter 4) do not have connections to the prefrontal cortex and hence cannot directly influence conscious experience (Crick & Koch, 1998). A series of creative neuroimaging studies support this theory. The Necker cube (Figure 9.7), the outline of a see-through cube, produces two distinct conscious percepts that subjectively seem to alternate every few seconds. Because the Necker cube casts a constant image on the retina, and hence a constant "image" on the primary visual cortex, the subjective experience of alternating percepts or images is independent of sensory activation V1. However, changes in conscious attention—even without moving the eyes—can alter activation levels in V1. This suggests that consciousness can focus the spotlight on the sensory building blocks of perception and hence alter perception of what is ultimately seen (Lumer & Rees, 1999; Watanabe et al., 1998).

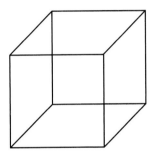

FIGURE 9.7   The Necker cube.

INTERIM SUMMARY

An integrated view suggests that consciousness is a specialized processing function that monitors and controls current states for the purpose of maximizing adaptation. Consciousness thus highlights or inhibits information based on its relevance to adaptation and its emotional consequences. Consciousness involves a network of neurons distributed throughout the brain. Damage to hindbrain structures, particularly the RAS, can lead to a complete loss of consciousness. The neural networks that "shine a spotlight" on perceptions, thoughts, emotions, or goals at any moment appear to involve the prefrontal cortex, the thalamus, and midbrain regions of the RAS.

Apply & Discuss

Recent research (Delfour & Marten, 2001; Marino, 2002) suggests that dolphins and chimpanzees can recognize themselves in a mirror. This was tested by familiarizing the animals with a mirror, then applying a dab of paint to their foreheads. Both attempted to remove the paint from their own face, not from the mirror image. What does this suggest about the level of self-awareness for the dolphin and the chimpanzee? Is their consciousness comparable to ours?

Sleep and Dreaming

We have focused thus far on waking consciousness. We now turn to the major series of changes that occur in consciousness every 24 hours: the sleep–wake cycle. Those who lament that life is too short would be horrified to realize that they will sleep away roughly a third of their time on the earth, about 25 years. Infants sleep two-thirds of each day, and elderly people, about one-fourth.

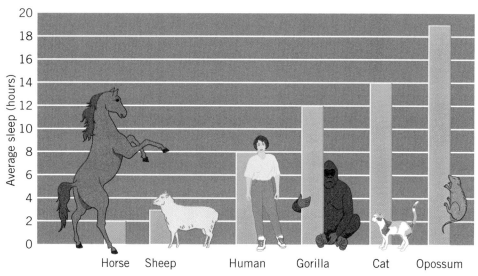

FIGURE 9.8 Average hours of sleep per night. Animals vary according to the amount of sleep they need; humans lie somewhere in the middle.

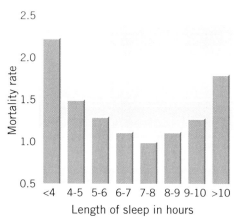

FIGURE 9.9 Sleep duration and mortality. Mortality rates are highest among those at the extremes, who report sleeping less than 5 or more than 10 hours per night. (Mortality rate is scaled against the group with the lowest mortality rate, those who sleep 8 hours.) *Source:* Adapted from Kripke et al., 1979.

The Nature and Evolution of Sleep

Sleep evolved over three billion years ago in some organisms, and the mechanisms that govern the biological clock in humans are apparently over 500 million years old (Lavie, 1996). Although not all animals show the characteristic EEG (electroencephalogram) signs of sleep (described below), nearly all animals show behavioral signs of sleeping: minimal movement, a stereotyped posture, and a high degree of stimulation needed to arouse them. They differ, however, in how much they sleep (Figure 9.8).

Individuals differ widely in the amount of sleep they both need and get, with most people sleeping between 6.5 and 8.5 hours a night (Lavie, 1996). As people get older, they tend to require less sleep. The number of hours people sleep is related to mortality rates, although the reasons for this relationship are unclear. People who report sleeping for unusually long *or* unusually short durations are prone to die earlier than people whose reported sleep is closer to average (Kripke et al., 1979; Figure 9.9).

Researchers have documented rare cases of people who require minimal sleep with no adverse consequences, such as a 70-year-old English nurse who was observed to sleep only one hour every night (Borbély, 1986). Legend has it that Leonardo DaVinci had the unusual habit of sleeping 15 minutes every four hours. From the late 1960s to the early 1990s, college students reported sleeping about an hour less on the average per night (Hicks & Pelligrini, 1991).

Circadian Rhythms The cycle of sleep and waking in humans and other animals, like the ebb and flow of body temperature, hormones, and other life-support processes, is a circadian rhythm. A **circadian rhythm** (from the Latin, *circa*, meaning "about," and *diem*, meaning "day") is *a cyclical biological process that evolved around the daily cycles of light and dark*. Expectant mothers can attest to the fact that circadian rhythms begin before birth: Fetuses begin showing rhythms of sleep and activity by the sixth month in utero.

Rhythms akin to sleep–wake cycles may exist in daytime as well as in sleep. Research supports the distinction between "day people" and "night people," finding that people peak in their alertness and arousal at different times of the day (Wallace, 1993). Researchers studying mice have tracked down the genes responsible for controlling their internal "clock" by examining mutant mice whose clocks do not tick correctly (Antoch et al., 1997; Shearman et al., 2000).

Human circadian rhythms are controlled largely by the hypothalamus but are influenced by light and dark. A special neural tract that projects from the retina to the hypothalamus responds only to relatively intense light, such as sunlight. During periods of darkness, the pineal gland, in the middle of the brain, produces a hormone called *melatonin*. Melatonin levels gradually diminish during daylight hours. Some people have found relief for "jetlag" by using melatonin pills to "reset" their biological clock (Arendt et al., 1997; Claustrat et al., 1992).

Nurses, medical residents on call, police, pilots, and flight attendants, whose shifts change from day to day or week to week, suffer greater incidence of health problems, in part because of disrupted circadian rhythms (Monk, 1997; Tan, 1991). Although some people seem to function well despite these frequent disruptions in their sleep cycle, others become irritable and inefficient—not particularly comforting traits to see in pilots or doctors in training.

Seasonal affective disorder (SAD) is now recognized in the *Diagnostic and Statistical Manual Fourth Edition* (*DSM-IV*, Chapter 15) as a form of depression. In this disorder, afflicted individuals are depressed, but only in the short days of winter (a small percentage experience depression only in the long days of summer) A common treatment is "light therapy" in which individuals supplement their daily light exposure with a bank of lights. Of course, a more pleasant but more expensive solution is to retreat to a tropical climate, where the days are always long!

Sleep Deprivation No one knows precisely what functions sleep serves. Some researchers emphasize its role in conserving energy, since sleep turns down the body's "thermostat" at night and less energy is expended in activities (Berger & Phillips, 1995). Others emphasize restorative functions. In particular, dream sleep may play a role in consolidating memories learned during the day as well as helping to resolve emotional conflicts (see Stickgold, 1998; Walsh & Lindblom, 1997). In contrast, nondream or deep sleep may allow a restorative function for our bodies.

People have known of the ill effects of extreme sleep deprivation for at least 2000 years. In Roman times and during the Middle Ages, sleep deprivation was used as a form of torture. Long-term sleep deprivation reduces the functioning of the immune system and makes the body more vulnerable to diseases ranging from common colds to cancer (Everson, 1997). Rats deprived of sleep die after two or three weeks (Rechtscaffen et al., 1989).

As anyone knows who has ever had a bad night's sleep, the time required to fall asleep drops substantially after even a single sleepless night (Carskadon & Dement, 1982). Researchers have recently discovered that concentration of *adenosine*, a modulatory neurotransmitter, in the thalamus and in structures deep within the cerebrum increases with each additional hour an animal is awake (Porkka-Heiskanen et al., 1997). Adenosine plays an inhibitory role in the brain, shutting down the systems that normally lead to arousal and hence fostering sleep when an animal has been awake too long. Thus, the hormone melatonin is affected by day length and the neurotransmitter adenosine is affected by sleep deprivation, findings that suggest a role for both substances in sleep regulation.

Insomnia Insomnia, or *inability to sleep*, affects virtually everyone at some point, but for some people it is a chronic problem. Although "sleeping pills" are sometimes appropriate and may offer temporary relief, they should always be taken with caution. Sleeping pills can lead to more, rather than fewer difficulties, as the person becomes dependent on them or the brain develops a tolerance requiring higher doses to achieve the same effect (Lavie, 1996). Furthermore, taking many sleeping pills suppresses dream sleep. Many people experience "waking dreams" as their brain attempts to catch up on dreaming. Table 9.1 lists some suggestions by a major sleep researcher for reducing or avoiding insomnia.

Table 9.1 ▮▮ ▪ Suggestions for Avoiding or Reducing Insomnia

1. Avoid spending too much time in bed. If you are awake, get out. Do not let the bed become a conditioned stimulus associated with insomnia and anxiety.

2. Do not try to force sleep. Go to bed when you are ready, and get out if you are not.

3. Do not keep a brightly lit, ticking clock near the bed.

4. Avoid physical activity late at night. It activates the autonomic nervous system, which is incompatible with sleep.

5. Avoid coffee, chocolate, or alcohol before bedtime. Caffeine will keep you up, even if you do not think it affects you, and alcohol often causes people to wake up in the middle of the night.

6. Keep a regular sleep schedule. If you have insomnia, you need more of a routine than most people.

7. Do not eat a large meal before bedtime. If you wake up, do not visit the refrigerator.

8. Avoid sleeping during the day if you have insomnia.

Source: Adapted from P. Lavie, *The Enchanted World of Sleep* (A. Berris, Trans.), Yale University Press, New Haven, CT, 1996, pp. 176–177.

Making Connections

Sleep deprivation has been compared to alcohol in its effects on the body's ability to react, particularly when one is driving. A survey conducted by the National Sleep Foundation found that over 100,000 automobile accidents occurred each year because the driver had not had enough sleep. The reaction times of sleep-deprived drivers are considered to be at least as bad as those of a person with a blood alcohol level of .08, on the edge of the legal limit in most states (Chapter 11).

In some cases, insomnia is caused by other disorders. Most interesting is the relationship with depression. Many individuals are diagnosed with depression when they seek treatment for sleep disorders including difficulty falling asleep, difficulty staying asleep, or excessive sleeping. As indicated in the *DSM IV*, disordered sleeping is one of the criteria for a diagnosis of depression. These individuals are comfortable about seeking help for sleeping disorders, but not for depression. Other people, particularly men, may suffer from *sleep apnea* (a cessation of breathing during sleep). This results in the person's waking repeatedly, but briefly, throughout the night. Apnea leads to an altered and less restorative night's sleep and to daytime sleepiness. One of the symptoms, often noticed by the roommate or spouse, is snoring.

INTERIM SUMMARY

People spend roughly one-third of their lives asleep. The sleep cycle is governed by **circadian rhythms**, cyclical biological "clocks" that evolved around the daily cycles of light and dark. The functions of sleep are not yet known, although sleep appears to be involved in restoration and maintenance of bodily processes such as homeostasis, immune functioning, and consolidation of memory. **Insomnia** is the inability to sleep. Insomnia may mask other problems such as sleep apnea or depression.

Stages of Sleep

Sleep proceeds through a series of stages in an orderly and repetitive pattern (Figure 9.10). To study these stages, researchers measure EEG activity, by attaching electrodes to subjects' heads to assess electrical activity in the brain. They also attach electrodes at the corners of the eyes to track eye movements and electrodes to a major muscle in the arm to assess muscle tone. These three measurements help to identify the various sleep stages. The EEG waves are characterized by two features: (1) frequency (the number of peaks per second) and (2) amplitude (the height of the peaks). In general, as people move from a waking state through deeper stages of sleep, their brain waves become less frequent with a higher amplitude.

From Wakefulness to Sleep   As Figure 9.10 shows, normal waking brain activity has an irregular pattern with high frequency and low amplitude, known as *beta*

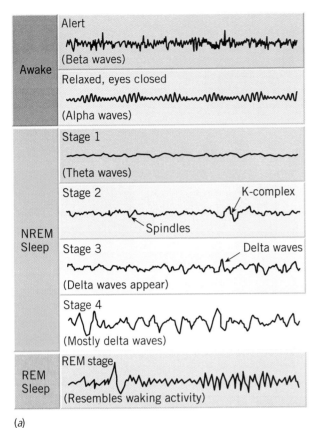

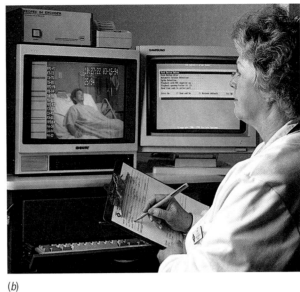

(b)

FIGURE 9.10 Stages of sleep. (*a*) As people move from a waking state through deeper stages of sleep, their brain waves become slower and more rhythmic, decreasing from over 14 cycles per second in the waking state to as little as one-half cycle per second in deep sleep. (*b*) A subject in a sleep laboratory is outfitted with electrodes on the forehead and scalp to measure brain waves using EEG. Electrodes are applied next to the eyes for a similar instrument, an electro-oculogram, to measure eye movements.

(a)

waves. As a person closes her eyes and relaxes, slower frequency, higher amplitude *alpha waves* emerge. Alpha waves are also characteristic of states of meditation.

Stage 1 sleep is typically brief (only a few minutes), marked by the appearance of even slower frequency *theta waves*. During this and subsequent stages of sleep, muscle tone is maintained, although eye movements are absent. From Stage 2 to 4, the EEG pattern becomes successively slower in frequency and higher in amplitude. Stage 2 is also characterized by *sleep spindles* and the occasional high amplitude *K-complexes* (Halasz, 1993). During Stage 2, sleep deepens, as alpha activity disappears.

Stage 3 sleep is marked by large, slow, rhythmic *delta waves*. When delta waves comprise more than 50 percent of recorded brain activity, the person has entered Stage 4 sleep. Together, States 3 and 4 constitute what is called *delta sleep*, a deep sleep characterized by relaxed muscles, decreased rate of respiration, and slightly lower body temperature. People aroused from delta sleep are often groggy and disoriented. During delta sleep, muscles apparently rest and rejuvenate, because people deprived of it frequently complain of muscle aches and tension. After a time in Stage 4 sleep, the sequence reverses itself, but rather than awakening, the person enters a dream state.

Rapid Eye Movement Sleep   When the sleeping person has reascended to Stage 1 sleep, a sudden change occurs: The EEG resembles the awake state, the eyes begin to dart around as if the sleeper were watching a play, and the major muscles become limp. This stage of sleep is called *paradoxical* (because the EEG resembles the awake state) or, more commonly, **rapid eye movement (REM) sleep***, a qualitatively different stage of sleep that is named for the darting eye movements that characterize it*. Because REM sleep is so different from other stages, *Stages 1 to 4 are often collectively called simply* **non-REM** (or **NREM) sleep**.

In REM sleep, autonomic activity increases: Pulse and blood pressure quicken, respiration becomes faster and irregular, and both males and females evidence signs

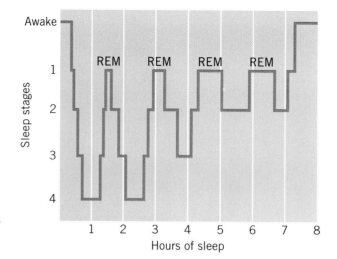

FIGURE 9.11   REM sleep. The stages of sleep follow a cyclical pattern that repeats about every 90 minutes, from Stage 1 through delta sleep and back again. As the night progresses, the person spends less time in deeper sleep and more time in REM sleep. *Source:* Cartwright, 1978.

of sexual arousal that may last for several minutes. At the same time, muscle movement is largely "turned off" (which is a good thing, or we would act out our dreams). The EEG during REM sleep resembles the irregular, faster pattern of waking life, suggesting that, although the body is not moving, the brain is quite active. The function of REM sleep is not clear, but if a person is repeatedly awakened from it, the brain will return to it with increasing persistence.

The mental activity that occurs during REM sleep is dreaming. Roughly 80 percent of the time when people are awakened from REM sleep, they report dream activity. Although many people believe they do not dream, evidence suggests that everyone dreams several times a night, even though they may not remember dreaming. Dreaming also occurs during NREM sleep, but less frequently and the dreams often consist of a simple experience, such as "I dreamed that I went shopping" (Antrobus, 1991; Foulkes, 1995).

Recent PET studies find that a network of neurons, beginning at the pons and extending through the thalamus and amygdala, is active during REM sleep (Maquet et al., 1996). Visual association areas in the occipital and temporal lobes, which are stimulated when people form mental images and identify objects, are also activated during REM sleep, but the primary visual cortex is not (Braun et al., 1998). At the same time, areas of the prefrontal cortex involved in consciousness and attention are inactive or inhibited.

These findings are particularly interesting in light of the fact that watching an event in normal waking consciousness (as opposed to "watching" a dream) involves both primary visual cortex and prefrontal attentional mechanisms. Together, these findings suggest that dreaming involves a neurologically distinct kind of consciousness that does not rely on normal waking attentional mechanisms.

After a period of REM sleep, the person descends again to Stage 4 and repeats itself over the night. A complete cycle of REM and NREM sleep occurs about every 90 minutes, with the proportion of time per cycle spent in REM sleep increasing over the night (Figure 9.11). Rapid eye movement sleep accounts for about 25 percent of all time asleep (on the average, two hours per night). Thus, over the course of a lifetime, the average person spends an estimated 50,000 hours—2000 days, or six full years—dreaming (Hobson, 1988).

INTERIM SUMMARY

Sleep proceeds through a series of stages that can be assessed by EEG. The major distinction is between **rapid eye movement (REM)** and **non-REM (NREM) sleep**. Most dreaming occurs in REM sleep, in which the eyes dart around and the EEG takes on an active pattern resembling waking consciousness.

Three Views of Dreaming

For thousands of years, humans have speculated about the nature and significance of dreams. Some cultures view dreams as indices of the dreamer's deepest desires, revelations from the spiritual world, or sources of supernatural power (Bourguignon, 1979). Here we address three contemporary psychological views of dreaming: psychodynamic, cognitive, and biological.

A Psychodynamic View   Freud (1900) believed that dreams, like all mental events, have meaning but must be deciphered by someone skilled in dream interpretation. Dreams are often vague, illogical, or bizarre and thus require translation into the language of rational waking consciousness. For example, in dreams two people are often condensed into one, or thoughts about one person are displaced onto someone else (i.e., attributed to the wrong person).

According to Freud, unconscious processes are associative processes. During sleep, because a person is not using conscious, rational processes to create or monitor the story, one thought or image can easily be activated in place of another. Because associative thinking replaces logical thought, Freud saw dreams as "the insanity of the night." For example, a man who was angry at his father had a dream of murdering his father's best friend, presumably because anger and murder were associatively linked, as were his father and his father's friend.

Freud distinguished between the **manifest content**, *the story line of the dream*, and the **latent content**, *the dream's underlying meaning*. To uncover the latent content of a dream, the dreamer free-associates to each part of the dream (i.e., simply says aloud whatever thoughts come to mind about it), while the dream analyst tries to trace the networks of association. Freud proposed that the underlying meaning of every dream is an unconscious wish, typically a forbidden sexual or aggressive desire. He suggested that people often rapidly forget their dreams upon awakening because dreams contain anxiety-provoking thoughts that are repressed during normal waking consciousness.

Most contemporary psychodynamic psychologists believe that the latent content of a dream can be a wish, a fear, or anything else that is emotionally pressing. Probably the most central aspect of the psychodynamic approach today is its view of dreaming as *associative thought* laden with *emotional concerns*. This form of thought requires interpretation because the story line has not been constructed using the logical thought processes characteristic of conscious mental activity.

A Cognitive View   A cognitive perspective suggests that dreams are cognitive constructions that reflect the concerns and metaphors people express in their waking thought (Antrobus, 1991; Domhoff, 1996). In other words, dreams are simply a form of thought. At times, they may even serve a problem-solving function, presenting dreamers with potential solutions to problems they are facing during the day (Cartwright, 1996).

Dreams rely on the same metaphors people use in everyday thinking. However, because conscious monitoring is deactivated during dreaming, metaphoric thinking is relatively unconstrained and leads to images or events that may seem bizarre to the conscious mind (Lakoff, 1997).

A Grammar of Dreams   One cognitive view that shares many points with Freud's theory was proposed by dream researcher David Foulkes (1993). Like many contemporary psychodynamic psychologists, Foulkes disagrees that the latent meaning of every dream is an unconscious wish. He proposes instead that dreams simply express current concerns of one sort or another, in a language with its own peculiar grammar. The manifest content is constructed from the latent content through rules of transformation, that is, rules for putting a thought or concern into the "language" of dream-

Apply & Discuss

- Is dreaming a form of the unconscious?
- Do our dreams reveal suppressed thoughts?

Apply & Discuss

If dreaming is a kind of thought, theories of thinking ought to be useful in understanding even an unusual form of cognition (Chapter 7).

■ How might events of the day before prime implicit "thinking" during sleep? What could lead the content of a dream to bear a relation to the content of thoughts shortly before going to bed—or what Freud called the "day residue" of the dream?

■ How might activation of networks during the day result in "problem solving" in dreams? Could dream activity be "productive" even if the person is not consciously trying to solve the problem at night? If so, how might this occur?

ing. In dream language, the thought "I am worried about my upcoming exam" can be translated into a dream about falling off a cliff.

Gender and cross-cultural differences also support the view that dreams express concerns similar to those that people experience in their waking consciousness (Domhoff, 1996). Just as males tend to be more aggressive than females by day, their dreams show a greater ratio of aggressive to friendly interactions than women's dreams. Similarly, the Netherlands and Switzerland are two of the least violent technologically developed societies, whereas the United States is the most violent. Incidents involving physical aggression are about 20 percent more prevalent in the dreams of U.S. males and females than among their Dutch and Swiss counterparts.

A Biological View   Some dream researchers argue that dreams are biological phenomena with no meaning at all (Crick & Mitchison, 1983). According to one such theory (Hobson, 1988; Hobson & McCarley, 1977), dreams reflect cortical interpretations of random neural signals initiated in the midbrain during REM sleep. These signals are relayed through the thalamus to the association cortexes, which try to understand this information in the usual way, namely, by using existing knowledge structures (schemas) to process the information. Because the initial signals are essentially random, however, the interpretations proposed by the cortex rarely make logical sense.

Other biologically oriented researchers have offered another view that emphasizes the role of sleep and dreaming in learning and memory. If they are right, the next time you are tempted to stay up all night to prepare for a big exam, think again: Sleep appears to be involved in the consolidation of memory. Memories for newly learned material are stronger after eight hours of sleep than after eight hours of wakefulness (Smith, 1985; Titone, 2002).

Researchers are in the early stages of tracking down the mechanisms, but the data suggest that during sleep the cortex and hippocampus work together to consolidate newly learned material, that is, to solidify it so it "sticks" (Chapter 6). According to this view, during NREM sleep, the hippocampus "replays" what it has "learned" during the day and activates relevant parts of the cortex to consolidate the memory (Chrobak & Buzsaki, 1994; Wilson & McNaughton, 1994). During REM sleep, activity appears to flow in the other direction—from the cortex to the hippocampus—erasing old memories from the hippocampus that are now fully consolidated in the cortex (Holscher et al., 1997; Stickgold, 1998).

Integrating the Alternative Models   Are these three models of dreaming really incompatible? The psychodynamic and cognitive views converge on the notion that dreams express current ideas and concerns in a highly symbolic language that requires decoding. They differ over the extent to which those concerns involve motives and emotions, although dreams probably express motives (wishes and fears) as well as ideas. Many motives have cognitive components, such as representations of wished-for or feared states. Thus, a fear of failing an examination includes a representation of the feared scenario and its possible consequences. What applies to cognition, then, probably applies to many aspects of motivation as well; thus, dreams are as likely to express motives as beliefs.

Even the biological view of dreams as cortical interpretations of random midbrain events is not necessarily incompatible with either the psychodynamic or the cognitive view. The interpretive processes that occur at the cortical level involve the same structures of meaning—schemas, associational networks, and emotional processes—posited by Freud. Hence, even random activation of these structures would produce dreams that reveal something about the organization of thoughts and feelings in the person's mind, particularly those that have received chronic or recent activation. Further, neurons activated during the day should be more readily triggered at night, with likely similarities of content in daytime and nighttime thoughts. The memory consolidation theory is even more congruent with psychodynamic and cognitive theories, because what matters during the day is what is likely to be replayed and consolidated by night.

INTERIM SUMMARY

Freud viewed dreams as a window to the language of unconscious associative thoughts, feelings, and wishes. He distinguished the **latent content**, or underlying meaning, from the **manifest content**, or story line. Although Freud believed that the latent content of every dream is an unconscious sexual or aggressive wish that has been repressed, empirical data do not support this view. Most psychodynamic theorists instead believe that the latent content can be a wish, a fear, or anything else that is emotionally pressing. The cognitive perspective suggests that dreams are the outcome of cognitive processes and that their content reflects the concerns and metaphors people express in their waking cognition. One biological view of dreaming proposes that dreams reflect cortical interpretations of random neural signals arising from the midbrain during REM sleep. Another points to the role of sleep and dreaming in memory consolidation, as the hippocampus and cortex work together to consolidate memories and then "wipe the slate clean" in the hippocampus. These three perspectives are probably not incompatible.

You would wish to be responsible for everything except your dreams! What miserable weakness, what lack of logical courage! Nothing contains more of your own work than your dreams! Nothing belongs to you so much! Substance, form, duration, actor, spectator—in these comedies you act as your complete selves!

NIETZSCHE,
Thus Spake Zarathustra

Altered States of Consciousness

Sleep is the most common example of a psychological state in which normal waking consciousness is suspended, but it is not the only one. In **altered states of consciousness**, *the usual conscious ways of perceiving, thinking, and feeling are modified or disrupted*. Altered states are often culturally patterned and occur through meditation, hypnosis, ingestion of drugs, and religious experiences.

Meditation

In **meditation**, *the meditator develops a deep state of tranquility by altering the normal flow of conscious thoughts*. Many religions, such as Buddhism, believe that meditation leads to a deepened understanding of reality (Ornstein, 1986). By focusing attention on a simple stimulus or by concentrating on stimuli that are usually in the background of awareness (such as one's breathing), meditation shuts down the normal flow of self-conscious inner dialogue (J. Weinberger, personal communication, 1992). With the usual goal-directed flow of consciousness disrupted, the procedures that normally direct conscious attention are "de-automatized" or disrupted.

Meditation can produce a state of serenity that is reflected in altered brain wave activity. Some forms of meditation facilitate the alpha waves characteristic of the relaxed state of falling into sleep. Others produce beta activity, and still others even produce theta waves, which are rarely observed except in subjects who are fully asleep (Jangid et al., 1988; Matsuoka, 1990). As a result, some experienced meditators in the East can perform remarkable feats, such as meditating for hours in the bitter cold.

Hypnosis

Another type of altered state, hypnosis, was named after Hypnos, the Greek god of sleep, because of the superficial resemblance between the hypnotic state and sleep. **Hypnosis** is *characterized by deep relaxation and suggestibility* (proneness to follow the suggestions of the hypnotist). The subject is likely to experience a number of changes in consciousness, including an altered sense of time, self, volition (voluntary

Making Connections

Some approaches to psychotherapy use altered states such as meditation to reduce stress and approach irrational fears in a more relaxed state, allowing the person to overcome them (Chapter 16).

A hypnotist places a subject in a hypnotic trance.

Big Picture φ Question 7

To what extent are psychological processes conscious or unconscious—that is, explicit versus implicit?

control over actions), and perception of the external world. For instance, a subject directed to raise her arm may have no sense of initiating the action but feel instead as if the arm has a mind of its own (Bowers, 1976).

Not everyone can be hypnotized. People differ in **hypnotic susceptibility**, *the capacity to enter into deep hypnotic states* (Hilgard, 1986). People who are highly hypnotizable tend to be able to form vivid visual images and to become readily absorbed in fantasy, daydreams, movies, and the like (see Kunzendorf et al., 1996).

Hypnotic Effects Under hypnosis, people can experience amnesia (e.g., for events that occurred while under hypnosis) or its opposite, *hyperamnesia*, the recall of forgotten memories. A hypnotist can induce *age regression*, in which hypnotic subjects feel as if they are reliving an earlier experience. Under hypnosis, one subject spoke a language he did not consciously remember but was spoken in his home when he was a very young child (Nash, 1988).

Hypnosis has clear and well-documented therapeutic effects (Kirsch et al., 1995). Hypnotized subjects often demonstrate *hypnotic analgesia*, an apparent lack of pain despite pain-inducing stimulation. Some hypnotic subjects have undergone surgery without anesthesia and shown no signs of conscious pain. Hypnosis can, in fact, be useful in minimizing the experience of pain in many situations, ranging from the dentist's chair to the treatment of burn injuries (Mulligan, 1996; Patterson & Ptacek, 1997).

Hypnosis and Memory Some advocates of hypnosis have claimed that hypnosis can restore forgotten memories. In the late 1970s, a busload of children and their driver were kidnapped at gunpoint. Later, under hypnosis, the driver relived the experience from beginning to end and was able to recall the kidnappers' license plate number with enough clarity to lead to their apprehension.

One researcher found that subjects under hypnosis could even recall events that occurred under anesthesia (Levinson, 1965). While a surgeon was removing a small lump from the lower lip of a patient, the doctor made the comment, "Good gracious…it may be a cancer!" For the next three weeks, the patient was inexplicably depressed. The investigator then hypnotized the woman and induced hypnotic regression to the day of the operation. She remembered the exclamation "Good gracious" and then, crying profusely, recalled, "He is saying this may be malignant" (p. 201). The researcher subsequently demonstrated the capacity for recall of similar events experimentally with a sample of dental patients. Since then, a number of memory researchers have demonstrated both implicit and explicit memory for events occurring during anesthesia, such as later recognition of word lists presented while surgery patients were completely unconscious (Bonebakker et al., 1996; Cork, 1996).

Despite such examples, many psychologists have expressed concern about the use of hypnosis to retrieve memories of crime scenes or experiences from childhood such as sexual abuse. Others have questioned the scientific validity of hypnosis as an aid to memory enhancement for legal purposes (Lynn et al., 1997). In fact, the limits of hypnosis are substantial enough that many states outlaw the use of hypnotically-induced memories in court testimony. One of the major problems is that people under hypnosis are highly suggestible, and a subtle inflection or leading question can lead hypnotized eyewitnesses to report more than they actually know (Wagstaff, 1984).

Hypnosis may also lower the threshold for feeling confident enough to report a memory. This discomfort can increase the capacity to recall actual memories, such as the license plate of the school bus kidnappers described above, but it can also increase the tendency to mistake beliefs, hypotheses, fantasies, or suggestions for true memories (Malpass & Devine, 1980). Controversy over the conditions under which hypnosis leads to genuine or distorted memories is likely to continue for some time (Appelbaum et al., 1997; McConkey, 1995).

Is Hypnosis Real?   **One Step Further**

Hypnosis has drawn considerable skepticism since it first received scientific attention in the nineteenth century, in part because of a history of charlatans using stage hypnosis mixed with liberal doses of deception (such as planting subjects). As we will see in Chapter 17, research over many decades has demonstrated that social pressure can lead people to perform peculiar, deviant, or destructive behavior, even in a normal state of consciousness (see Kirsch & Lynn, 1998). Several researchers have produced evidence to suggest that hypnotic subjects are simply playing the role they believe they are expected to play (Murrey et al., 1992; Spanos et al., 1996).

Other critics contend that aspects of hypnotic suggestion that are not unique to hypnosis, such as heavy reliance on imagery, actually account for hypnotic effects. For example, people instructed to use vivid visual images can often accomplish the same feats as hypnotized subjects, such as eliminating warts (Spanos et al., 1988).

Data supporting the validity of hypnosis, however, come from studies in which subjects are given posthypnotic suggestions—commands to perform a behavior on demand once they are out of the hypnotic trance. In a study designed to test the hypothesis that hypnotized subjects are simply playing roles (and that they are not really in an altered state), the investigators compared the behavior of subjects instructed to act as if they were hypnotized with the behavior of true hypnotized subjects (Orne et al., 1968). When both groups of subjects were distracted from assigned tasks and thus diverted from thinking about what they were supposed to do, hypnotized subjects were three times as likely to carry out the posthypnotic suggestion as simulators.

Neuroscientific data also provide evidence for the validity of hypnosis as an altered state. Not only do studies find distinct EEG patterns in hypnotized subjects (De Pascalis & Perrone, 1996), but recent neuroimaging studies support the distinctness of hypnotic states as well. In one study, researchers suggested to hypnotized subjects that they should see color images in black and white (Kosslyn et al., 2000). Remarkably, their brain scans showed decreased activation in a part of the cortex that processes color (at the borders of the occipital and temporal lobes; Chapter 3), compared with activation while viewing color images without the suggestion. When the researchers made the same suggestion to the same individuals without hypnosis, they showed no reduction in the color area of the cortex. These findings suggest that hypnosis can, in fact, dramatically influence basic components of perceptual experience that psychologists have generally assumed to be independent of people's intentions.

Other strong evidence comes from studies in which hypnotic subjects have endured painful medical procedures, including surgery, without anesthesia. Although some skeptics argue that these patients may be "faking it," it is difficult to imagine undergoing an operation without anesthesia simply to please an experimenter (Bowers, 1976).

At this juncture, the most appropriate conclusion is probably that hypnosis is, in fact, an altered state of consciousness, at least in highly hypnotizable subjects. However, some or many of its effects can be produced under other conditions, such as use of imagery, relaxation, or social pressure.

INTERIM SUMMARY

Altered states of consciousness, in which the usual conscious ways of perceiving, thinking, and feeling are modified or disrupted, are often brought about through meditation, hypnosis, ingestion of drugs, and religious experiences. **Meditation** creates a deep state of tranquility by altering the normal flow of conscious thoughts. **Hypnosis** is an altered state characterized by deep relaxation and suggestibility.

Making Connections

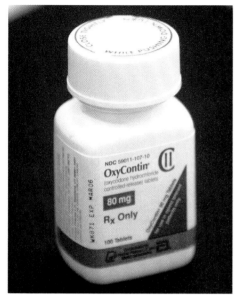

When people think of drug abuse, they often think of the abuse of illegal drugs such as cocaine or heroin. However, people frequently abuse drugs that are designed to be used for legitimate medical purposes. One prime example is oxycontin, a powerful painkiller often prescribed by physicians to people suffering from chronic pain. Oxycontin is prescribed in pill form, with a time-release dosage releasing the drug into the body typically over a 12-hour period. Many adolescents and young adults, however, have figured out that if the pills are ground into powder and then either swallowed or snorted, the time-release function can be circumvented and an immediate high similar to that experienced with heroin can be achieved. The results, particularly if oxycontin is taken while under the influence of other drugs, such as alcohol, can be fatal (Chapter 11).

Drug-Induced States of Consciousness

The most common way people alter their state of consciousness (other than by going to sleep, of course) is by ingesting **psychoactive substances**—*drugs that operate on the nervous system to alter mental activity*. In the West, people use many psychoactive substances, ranging from caffeine in coffee and nicotine in tobacco, to medications that relieve depression or anxiety (Chapter 16), to recreational drugs such as crack cocaine and Ecstasy that seriously alter one's state of consciousness and impair normal functioning. Some psychoactive drugs resemble the molecular structure of naturally occurring neurotransmitters and thus have similar effects at synapses. Others alter the normal processes of synthesis, release, reuptake, or breakdown of neurotransmitters (Chapter 3) and consequently affect the rate of neural firing in various regions of the brain.

The action of psychoactive substances cannot, however, be reduced entirely to their chemical properties. Their impact also depends on cultural beliefs and expectations. Native Americans who use peyote (a potent consciousness-altering drug, mescaline) in religious rituals typically experience visions congruent with their religious beliefs, as well as feelings of reverence or religious awe and relief from physical ailments. In contrast, when peyote is taken out of the context of the ritual religious protocol, the person often experiences frightening visions, extreme mood states, and a breakdown in normal social inhibitions (Wallace, 1959).

The major types of psychoactive substances in widespread use include alcohol and other depressants, stimulants, hallucinogens, and marijuana. Let us briefly examine each in turn.

Alcohol and Other Depressants   **Depressants** are *substances that depress, or slow down, the nervous system*. In fact, at very high doses, depressants reduce the activity of the brain stem neurons (Chapter 3) that stimulate our breathing and heart rate to such an extent that we can die. Common depressants are barbiturates and benzodiazepines. *Barbiturates* ("downers") provide a sedative or calming effect and in higher doses can be used as sleeping pills. *Benzodiazepines*, or anti-anxiety agents, serve as tranquilizers; common examples are Valium and Xanax (Chapter 16). Depressants, like most psychotropic drugs, can produce both psychological and physical dependence.

Alcohol produces a *biphasic* effect on mood: at low doses it is a stimulant, but at higher doses it is a depressant. Researchers are still tracking down the precise neural mechanisms by which alcohol slows down central nervous system activity, but like other sedatives, alcohol appears to enhance the activity of the neurotransmitter GABA (gamma-aminobutyric acid; Buck, 1986). Because GABA inhibits norepinephrine, which is involved in anxiety reactions, alcohol can reduce anxiety. Alcohol also enhances the activity of dopamine and endorphins, which provide pleasurable feelings that reinforce behavior (De Witte, 1996; Di Chiara et al., 1996).

Cross-culturally, alcohol is the most widely used psychoactive substance. In moderate doses—wine with dinner or a drink after work—alcohol can enhance experience and even have positive health consequences, but the social costs of abuse of alcohol and other substances are staggering. In the United States, approximately 1 in 7 people abuse alcohol, and another 1 in 20 misuse other psychoactive substances. The number of people killed in alcohol-related accidents in the United States every year surpasses the total number killed in the entire Vietnam War [Group for the Advancement of Psychiatry (GAP), 1991]. A Swedish study found that reported alcohol consumption in 1973 predicted mortality rates in a large sample followed up over the next 20 years (Andreasson & Brandt, 1997).

Alcohol and Expectations   As with psychoactive substances in general, expectations about alcohol's effects, shaped by culture and personal experience, can sometimes have as much impact on behavior as the drug's direct effects on the nervous system (see Collins et al., 1990; Hittner, 1997). This finding appears to be true cross-culturally (Velez-Blasini, 1997).

Several studies have sought to distinguish the causal roles of two independent variables: whether subjects are drinking alcohol and whether they *think* they are drinking alcohol. The researchers place participants in one of four groups. In one, participants drink an alcoholic beverage and are told they are drinking alcohol; in another, they drink alcohol but are told they are not. (The flavor of the drink makes alcohol detection impossible.) In the other two groups, participants drink a nonalcoholic beverage and are either informed or misinformed about what they are drinking.

The results of these investigations can help "distill" the relative contributions of biology and beliefs to the effects of alcoholic consumption. For example, male subjects who think they are drinking alcohol report greater sexual arousal and less guilt when exposed to sexually arousing stimuli, whether or not they have actually been drinking alcohol. This is even more likely to occur if they have strong beliefs about the impact of alcohol on arousal (see Abrams & Wilson, 1983; Hull & Bond, 1986). In general, people are more likely to behave in ways that are deviant, dangerous, or antisocial if they can attribute their behavior to alcohol.

Consequences of Alcohol Use and Abuse   Alcohol abuse is involved in many violent crimes, including assault, rape, spouse abuse, and murder, but precisely how alcohol contributes to aggression is not entirely clear (see Bushman, 1997; Bushman & Cooper, 1990). One theory suggests that it disengages normal inhibitions; that is, alcohol contributes to aggression "not by stepping on the gas but rather by paralyzing the brakes"(Muehlberger, 1956, cited in Bushman & Cooper, 1990, p. 342). A related theory suggests that alcohol facilitates aggression by derailing other psychological processes that normally decrease the likelihood of aggression, such as the ability to assess risks accurately. A third theory suggests that violence-prone individuals drink so that they can have an excuse for aggression, particularly since they tend to believe that alcohol makes them aggressive. All three processes can operate together: An angry, violent person may drink in part to dull his or her conscience and to provide himself an excuse for his actions.

Long-term ingestion of alcohol produces physical changes in the brain that can seriously affect cognitive functioning, sometimes to the point of dementia (confusion and disorientation) or Korsakoff's syndrome. Imaging techniques such as CT scans reveal that roughly half of alcoholics show cerebral atrophy, and many show subcortical damage as well. Some of the behavioral changes associated with these physiological changes appear to be reversible, however, if the person stops drinking (Bowden, 1990).

Stimulants   **Stimulants** are *drugs that increase alertness, energy, and autonomic reactivity* (such as heart rate and blood pressure). These drugs range from commonly used substances like nicotine and caffeine to more potent ones such as amphetamines and cocaine.

Nicotine increases heart rate and blood pressure while often decreasing emotional reactivity. Thus, cigarette smokers often report that smoking increases their arousal and alertness while also providing a soothing effect. The reason is that nicotine has receptors in both branches of the autonomic nervous system—sympathetic (which increases arousal) and parasympathetic (which reduces it). When one of these branches is active, nicotine tends to produce stronger effects in the other—thus both arousing the slothful and soothing the stressed. Over the long term, however, smoking can cause cancer, heart disease, and other life-threatening conditions (Chapter 11).

Ironically, some of the soothing effect of nicotine is due to the act of smoking, not to the nicotine. Thus, many smokers find it helpful to chew gum or suck on hard candy when attempting to quit. The nicotine patch is a very successful way to reduce

O God, that men should put an enemy in their mouths to steal away their brains; that we should with joy, pleasance, revel and applause, transform ourselves into beasts!
Othello (II, iii)

Making Connections

For children (and some adults!) with attention deficit disorder (ADD) or attention-deficit hyperactivity disorder (ADHD) the drug Ritalin is prescribed (Chapter 16). Ritalin is a stimulant, which would seem to be counterintuitive. However, the current hypothesis is that these children have a deficient production of adrenalin. So, they "self-medicate" by increasing external stimulation to increase internal adrenalin release. By supplementing the deficient adrenalin production, the child is able to remain alert without the maladaptive disruptive activity.

the nicotine craving, but many still miss the habitual behavior of lighting up, holding the cigarette, and sucking it. This is an example of Pavlovian conditioning (Chapter 5), as the ritual of smoking becomes associated with the comfort of the effects of the nicotine.

Caffeine and related compounds are found in coffee, tea, chocolate, soft drinks, and some nonprescription drugs (such as aspirin products, decongestants, and sleep suppressants). Whereas moderate amounts of caffeine can help a person stay awake, high doses can produce symptoms indistinguishable from anxiety disorders, such as "the jitters" or even panic attacks.

Amphetamines lead to hyperarousal and a feeling of "speeding," where everything seems to move quickly. The molecular structure of amphetamines is similar to that of adrenalin, the hormone involved in the fight-or-flight reaction of the sympathetic nervous system (Chapter 3). High doses of amphetamines can induce psychosis in vulnerable individuals; ill health in chronic users, who essentially circumvent the normal signals sent by the brain to protect the body from fatigue and overuse; and even death (usually a heart attack due to excessive stimulation of the heart).

Cocaine has held an attraction for people at least since A.D. 500, when the Inca in Peru learned about the powers of the coca leaf, from which cocaine is derived. The Inca used the coca leaf in religious ceremonies and even treated it as money to compensate laborers. In the late 1800s, physicians discovered cocaine's anesthetic properties; soon many medicines and elixirs were laced with cocaine, as was Coca-Cola (this practice was stopped in 1929).

Cocaine causes hyperarousal, leading to a "rush" that can last a few minutes to several hours. Cocaine is one of the most potent pleasure-inducing substances, as well as one of the most addictive. Experimental animals will press a lever thousands of times to receive a single dose (Siegel, 1990). Like other stimulants, it appears to increase the activity of norepinephrine and dopamine. Chronic use depletes these neurotransmitters and can cause chronic depression similar to the crash that occurs when the initial high is over (GAP, 1991).

Cocaine produces diminished judgment and an inflated sense of one's own abilities. Regular use can also produce paranoia. One study found that 68 percent of cocaine-dependent men in a rehabilitation program reported paranoid experiences on cocaine that lasted several hours, long after the cocaine high was over (Satel et al., 1991). Moreover, 38 percent of the patients who reported paranoia actually responded by arming themselves with guns or knives. A more recent study found that two-thirds of the assailants in domestic violence cases had consumed both cocaine and alcohol on the day they beat their spouse or children (Brookoff et al., 1997).

Hallucinogens   Hallucinogens derive their name from **hallucinations—*sensations and perceptions that occur in the absence of external stimulation*. Hallucinogens *alter the interpretation of sensory information to produce bizarre or unusual perceptions.*** While under the influence of hallucinogens, people may experience time as speeding up or slowing down, or sense colors bursting from the sky, walls moving, or ants crawling under their skin.

Humans have used hallucinogens for thousands of years, but their impact and cultural meaning differ dramatically. In many cultures, people use hallucinogens largely during cultural rituals, as when Australian aboriginal boys ingest hallucinogenic plants during ceremonies initiating them into manhood (Grob & Dobkin de Rios, 1992). In these settings, the meaning of hallucinations is established by the elders, who consider the drugs essential for bringing the young into the community of adults.

In the contemporary West, individuals ingest these substances for recreation and with minimal social control, so the effects are more variable, and vulnerability to addiction is high. Hallucinogenic drug use in Europe and North America dramatically increased in the 1960s with the synthesis of the hallucinogen *lysergic acid diethylamide (LSD)*. The military, not completely understanding the psychological effects of LSD, attempted to use it as a "truth serum." Unfortunately, the "truths" told under the influence of LSD were merely hallucinations. By the late 1970s, concern over the abuse of LSD and other drugs, such as PCP ("angel dust") and hallucinogenic mushrooms ("shrooms"), intensified, and with good scientific reason: Chronic use of LSD is associated with psychotic symptoms, depression, paranoia, lack of motivation, and changes in brain physiology (Kaminer & Hrecznyj, 1991; Smith & Seymour, 1994). Some chronic users repeatedly experience strange visual phenomena, such as seeing trails of light or images as they move their hands. Even when they are not experiencing these symptoms, their EEGs show a pattern of abnormal firing in the visual pathways of the brain (Abraham & Duffy, 1996). The long-term effects of even occasional use of LSD are not entirely clear, although tragic events have occurred with LSD use, such as people leaping from windows, thinking they could fly, and falling to their death.

Marijuana   The use of *marijuana* has been a subject of controversy for decades. Marijuana use among young people peaked in 1979 in the United States, with 60.4 percent of high school seniors reporting having tried the drug at least once. That number dropped to 35.3 percent in 1993, with the percentages fluctuating slightly throughout the 1990s and into the current century (see Hansen & O'Malley, 1996).

Marijuana produces a state of being high, or "stoned," during which the individual may feel euphoric, giddy, unself-conscious, or contemplative. During a marijuana high, judgment is moderately impaired, problem-solving becomes less focused and efficient, and attention is more difficult to direct; some people report paranoia or panic symptoms.

For decades, people have speculated about the detrimental effects of marijuana, but few credible scientific studies have documented negative effects from occasional recreational use (Castle & Ames, 1996). In fact, the most definitive study in this area, a longitudinal follow-up of young adults observed since early childhood, actually found occasional marijuana users and experimenters to be healthier psychologically than either abusers *or* abstainers (Shedler & Block, 1990). Other research finds that marijuana abuse, but not occasional use, is a risk factor for use of harder drugs (Kouri et al., 1995).

Nevertheless, marijuana, like harder drugs, artificially manipulates dopamine reward circuits in the brain (Wickelgren, 1997) and can produce unwanted consequences. For example, residual effects on attention, working memory, and motor abilities can make users unaware of subtle impairment at work, at school, or at the wheel (Pope et al., 1995). Chronic or heavy use, particularly beyond adolescence, is a symptom of psychological disturbance (Chapter 15) and can contribute to deficits in social and occupational functioning. As with other drugs, smoking during pregnancy may have risks for the developing fetus (see Chandler et al., 1996; Fried, 1995). In sum, like alcohol, the extent to which marijuana has negative psychological consequences probably depends on whether or not it is abused.

Recent Trends   As humans, we are ever curious and as such we are always trying new ways to stimulate our intellect. For example, since it is illegal to purchase most psychoactive drugs (including alcohol if you are under 21 and live in the United States), other legally purchased substances are bought to "get high." Aerosol spray cans provide a convenient way for teenagers (and younger) to get high. Unfortunately, the inhaled gases are also toxic to nerve cells and thus can result in the death of brain cells.

When "clubbing," many young people take drugs such as "roofies " (rohypnol), which lower inhibitions and resistance. Others take Ecstasy (a form of adrenalin) to achieve a loving attitude. Unfortunately, because these drugs are not approved by the Federal Drug Administration, there is no quality control. Adverse side effects are not well known, although several young people have died from the combination of alcohol and club drugs.

INTERIM SUMMARY

The most common way people alter their state of consciousness is by ingesting **psychoactive substances**, drugs that operate on the nervous system to alter mental activity. Drugs have their effects not only physiologically but also through cultural beliefs and expectations. **Depressants** such as alcohol slow down, or depress, the nervous system. **Stimulants**, such as amphetamines and cocaine, increase alertness, energy, and autonomic reactivity. **Hallucinogens** such as LSD produce **hallucinations**, sensations and perceptions that occur without external sensory stimulation. Marijuana is a controversial drug that produces a "high" that may include a mixture of pleasurable feelings and a sense of calm or panic and paranoia. Increasingly, people, particularly adolescents and young adults, are achieving altered states of consciousness through "legal" drugs such as Ecstasy.

A Global Vista   Religious Experiences in Cross-Cultural Perspective

Religious experiences are *subjective experiences of being in contact with the divine or spiritual*. They range from relatively ordinary experiences, such as listening passively to a sermon, to altered states of consciousness in which a person feels at one with nature or the supernatural. In his classic work, *The Varieties of Religious Experience*, William James (1902) describes the more dramatic forms of religious experience. In this state, the person experiences a sense of peace and inner harmony, perceives the world and self as having changed dramatically in some way, and has "the sense of perceiving truths not known before" (p. 199). James quotes the manuscript of a clergyman (1902, p. 67):

> I remember the night, and almost the very spot on the hilltop where my soul opened out, as it were, into the Infinite, and there was a rushing together of the two worlds, the inner and the outer.… The ordinary sense of things around me faded. It was like the effect of some great orchestra when all the separate notes have melted into one swelling harmony.

Experiences people consider spiritual occur in a wide variety of settings and may or may not involve organized religion (Wolman, 2001). In most societies, however, dramatic religious experiences occur in the context of ritualized religious practices. For example, in a *possession trance*, the person who is "possessed" believes another person or a supernatural being enters his soul. The altered state typically occurs through drumming, singing, dancing, and crowd participation (Bourguignon, 1979). Many born-again Christian churches include possession trances as part of their regular religious practices (see, e.g., Griffith et al., 1984).

The use of ritualized altered states dates back at least to the time of the Neanderthals. Graves of prehistoric human remains in northern Iraq contained medicinal substances that are still used today to induce trancelike states. The "vision quest" of some Native American tribes frequently included religious trance states. During these states, a young person being initiated into adulthood would come in contact with ancestors or a personal guardian and emerge as a full member of adult society (Bourguignon, 1979). John Lame Deer, a Sioux medicine man, describes an experience that in certain respects resembles that of the Western clergyman quoted by James (Lame Deer & Erdoes, 1972, pp. 14–15):

> I was still lightheaded and dizzy from my first sweatbath in which I had purified myself before going up the hill. Even now, an hour later, my skin still tingled. But it seemed to have made my brain empty.… Blackness was wrapped around me like a velvet cloth. It seemed to cut me off from the outside world, even from my own body. It made me listen to voices within me. I thought of my forefathers,

Humans seem predisposed to be moved by collective experiences. Top, a Balinese ritual; bottom, a spontaneous "ritual" at a rock festival in North America.

who had crouched on this hill before me.... I thought I could sense their presence.... I trembled and my bones turned to ice.

Like James's clergyman, Lame Deer describes a breakdown in the normal boundaries of the inner and outer worlds. Both men also describe a sense of being touched by a presence beyond themselves and an altered experience of reality, perception, and consciousness.

Ritualized religious experiences are simultaneously cultural and psychological phenomena. For individuals, they offer a sense of security, enlightenment, and oneness with something greater than themselves. For the group, they provide a sense of solidarity, cohesiveness, and certainty in shared values and beliefs. The individual is typically swept away in the experience, losing the self-reflective component of consciousness and experiencing a dissolution of the boundaries between self and nonself.

The French sociologist Emile Durkheim (1915) described this phenomenon as "collective effervescence," in which the individual's consciousness seems dominated by the "collective consciousness." Most readers have probably experienced collective effervescence, either during religious ceremonies or in less profound circumstances, such as rock concerts and sporting events. Collective events of this sort, many of which involve chanting or rhythmic movement and speech, seem to tap into a basic human capacity for this kind of altered state.

Summary

The Nature of Consciousness

1. **Consciousness** refers to the subjective awareness of percepts, thoughts, feelings, and behavior. It performs two functions: monitoring the self and environment and controlling thought and behavior. **Attention** is the process of focusing awareness, providing heightened sensitivity to a limited range of experience requiring more extensive information processing. **Divided attention** means splitting attention between two or more stimuli or tasks.

Perspectives on Consciousness

2. Freud distinguished among conscious, preconscious, and unconscious processes. **Conscious mental processes** are at the center of subjective awareness. **Preconscious mental processes** are not presently conscious but could be readily brought to consciousness. Dynamically unconscious processes—or the system of mental processes Freud called the **unconscious**—are thoughts, feelings, and memories that are inaccessible to consciousness because they have been kept from awareness because they are threatening thoughts or behaviors. Motivational processes can also be unconscious or implicit.

3. The **cognitive unconscious** refers to information-processing mechanisms that occur outside of awareness, notably unconscious procedures or skills and preconscious associational processes such as those that occur in priming experiments. Cognitive theorists have argued that consciousness is a mechanism for flexibly bringing together quasi-independent processing modules that normally operate in relative isolation and for solving problems that automatic processes cannot optimally solve.

4. Hindbrain and midbrain structures, notably the RAS, play a key role in regulating states of wakefulness and arousal. Like most psychological functions, consciousness appears to be distributed across a number of neural pathways, involving a circuit running from the RAS through the thalamus, from the thalamus to the cortex (particularly the prefrontal cortex), and back down to the thalamus and midbrain regions of the RAS.

Sleep and Dreaming

5. The sleep–wake cycle is a **circadian rhythm**, a cyclical biological process that evolved around the daily cycles of light and dark. Sleep proceeds through a series of stages that cycle throughout the night. Most dreaming occurs during REM sleep, named for the bursts of darting eye movements.

6. Freud distinguished between the **manifest content**, or story line, and the **latent content**, or underlying meaning, of dreams. Freud believed the latent content is always an unconscious wish, although most contemporary psychodynamic psychologists believe that wishes, fears, and current concerns can underlie dreams. Cognitive theorists suggest that dreams express thoughts and current concerns in a distinct language with its own rules of transformation. Some biological theorists contend that dreams

have no meaning; in this view, dreams are cortical interpretations of random neural impulses generated in the midbrain. Others focus on the role of sleep and dreaming in memory consolidation. These three approaches to dreaming are not necessarily incompatible.

Altered States of Consciousness

7. In **altered states of consciousness**, the usual conscious ways of perceiving, thinking, and feeling are changed. **Meditation** is an altered state in which the person narrows consciousness to a single thought or expands consciousness to focus on stimuli that are usually at the periphery of awareness. **Hypnosis**, characterized by deep relaxation and suggestibility, appears to be an altered

state, but many hypnotic phenomena can be produced under other conditions.

8. **Psychoactive substances** are drugs that operate on the nervous system to alter patterns of perception, thought, feeling, and behavior. **Depressants**, the most widely used of which is alcohol, slow down the nervous system. **Stimulants** (such as nicotine, caffeine, amphetamines, and cocaine) increase alertness, energy, and autonomic reactivity. **Hallucinogens** create **hallucinations**, in which sensations and perceptions occur in the absence of any external stimulation. Marijuana leads to a state of being high—euphoric, giddy, unself-conscious, or contemplative. **Psychoactive substances** alter consciousness biologically, by facilitating or inhibiting neural transmission at the synapse, and psychologically, through expectations shaped by cultural beliefs.

Key Terms

altered states of consciousness   309
attention   294
circadian rhythm   302
cognitive unconscious   297
conscious mental processes   296
consciousness   293
depressants   312

dichotic listening   295
divided attention   295
hallucinations   314
hallucinogens   314
hypnosis   309
hypnotic susceptibility   310
insomnia   303
latent content   307

manifest content   307
meditation   309
non-REM (NREM) sleep   305
preconscious mental processes   296
psychoactive substances   312
rapid eye movement (REM)   305

religious experiences   316
selective inattention   294
states of consciousness   292
stimulants   313
unconscious mental processes   296

Motivation and Emotion

red is overweight. Why is Fred overweight? Is it lack of willpower—he just can't say no to another slice of pie? Or is it the "fault" of his genes? Certainly some individuals are capable of maintaining a lower body weight than they would if they ate all that they wanted to. Look at models and anorexics. And certainly some people do have a physiological disorder, such as diabetes or hypothyroidism, each of which is genetically based and which leads to obesity. But neither of these is the underlying cause of Fred's weight problem.

Fred lacks motivation. Fred is depressed. He doesn't have any friends, his parents are dead, his wife has left him, and he lost his job six months ago. His unemployment checks are about to end. Initially, Fred was frustrated, then discouraged, and now…, well, now he just doesn't care. He lacks the motivation to do anything.

He is so unmotivated that he cannot even summon the energy to commit suicide. What is his solace? Food. Some people find their solace in alcohol or drugs; others, in indiscriminate sex—whatever makes them feel good in the immediate. However, these are bandages on the wound, which is still festering. And these particular bandages only increase the festering. Now, in addition to all of Fred's other woes, he is fat and he is endangering his physical health.

How can Fred regain his motivation? If he does so, will he lose weight? How can he achieve emotional stability and enjoy a good quality of life? The answers to these and other questions are not simple and are not global. That is to say, for each person there is a cause of depression and, for each person, a way of treating the lack of motivation that is a hallmark of depression. When the lack of motivation is effectively treated, the secondary problem, overeating for short-term emotional satisfaction, will no longer be a problem.

This chapter focuses on **motivation**, *the driving force behind behavior which leads us to pursue some things and avoid others*; and on **emotion** (or **affect**), *which is a positive or negative feeling (or response) that typically includes some combination of physiological arousal, subjective experience, and behavioral expression*. In fact, the words "motivation" and "emotion" share the same Latin root, *movere*, which means to move. We first examine the major perspectives on motivation and then consider some of the most important motives that guide human behavior across cultures. Finally, we explore the physiological, subjective, and neural basis of emotion.

Throughout this chapter, several basic issues repeatedly emerge. The first is the extent to which people are driven by internal needs or pulled by external goals or stimuli. Does the arrival of a savory pizza increase the likelihood of feeling hungry, or is one only hungry when in absolute need of calories? A second and related issue is the extent to which human motivation is rooted in biology or influenced by culture and environment. Do the motives of a Western corporate executive and those of a tribal chief in the Sudan differ dramatically, or do both individuals rise to their position out of similar needs for power or achievement?

A third issue is the relative importance of thoughts, emotions, and arousal in motivation. Can a person be motivated simply by a thought or goal, or must goals be connected with emotion or arousal to be motivating? In other words, what transforms a thought or daydream into an intention that directs behavior? A final issue is the function of emotion. What role does emotion really play in people's everyday life?

INTERIM SUMMARY

Motivation refers to the driving force behind behavior that leads us to pursue some things and avoid others. Motives can be divided into biological needs and psychosocial needs (such as needs for dominance, power, achievement, and relatedness to others), although few motives are strictly biological or learned. **Emotion**, or **affect**, is an evaluative response that typically includes physiological arousal, subjective experience, and behavioral or emotional expression.

Perspectives on Motivation

Motivation has two components: *what* people want to do (the goals they pursue), and *how strongly* they want to do it. A number of perspectives, presented in their chronological order here, offer insight into both of these components.

Psychodynamic Perspective

The psychodynamic perspective emphasizes the biological basis of motivation. Humans are animals, and their motives reflect their animal heritage. According to Freud, humans, like other animals, are motivated by **drives**, *internal tension states that build up until they are satisfied*. He proposed two basic drives: sex and aggression. The sexual drive includes desires for love, lust, and intimacy, whereas the aggressive drive includes not only blatantly aggressive or sadistic impulses but desires to control or master other people and the environment. These drives may express themselves in subtle ways. Aggression, for example, can underlie sarcastic comments or enjoyment of violent movies.

Changing Views of Motivation: What Are Our Basic Motives? Initially Freud had proposed self-preservation and sex as the two basic drives, much like the evolutionary concept of reproductive success, which includes survival and reproduction. His decision to change from self-preservation to aggression stemmed in part from living through World War I and witnessing the beginning of World War II in Europe. If aggression on such a massive scale kept breaking through in the most "civilized" societies, he reasoned, it must be a basic motivational force.

Psychodynamic views of motivation have advanced considerably since Freud's death in 1939. In addition to sexual and aggressive desires, psychodynamic theorists now emphasize two other motives in particular: the need for relatedness to others (independent of sexual desires) and the need for self-esteem (feeling good about oneself) (Aron, 1996; Bowlby, 1969, 1973; Kohut, 1977; Mitchell, 1988).

Just as psychodynamic theorists have moved away from Freud's dual-instinct theory (sex and aggression), many have also moved away from his abstract notion of

Making Connections

Few psychologists (or even psychoanalysts) now accept Freud's theory of aggression as an instinct that builds up until discharged. However, the ethnic warfare in Eastern Europe, the Middle East, and Africa in our own times may lead us to think carefully before discarding the idea that a readiness for aggression is an innate human characteristic (Chapter 18).

"drives" to two concepts that seem closer to the data of clinical observation: wishes and fears (Brenner, 1982; Holt, 1976). A *wish* is a representation of a desired state that is associated with emotion or arousal. Wishes range from the obvious and commonplace, such as desires to be promoted at work, to the less obvious and unconscious, such as competitive desires that the individual would feel guilty to acknowledge. Once a wish is achieved, it may become temporarily deactivated or less intense. A *fear* is a representation of an undesired state that is associated with unpleasant feelings. Fears, too, range from the obvious, such as a child's fear of being punished, to the less obvious, the child's fear that if she misbehaves her mother will not love her anymore.

Unconscious Motivation Perhaps the most distinctive aspect of the psychodynamic theory of motivation is the view that motives can be unconscious. An individual may be tremendously competitive in school or sports but vehemently assert that "I'm only competitive with myself." The child of an abusive alcoholic parent may desperately want to avoid an alcoholic mate but just keeps "finding" herself in relationships with abusive alcoholic men. Until recently, the evidence for unconscious motivation was largely clinical and anecdotal. However, laboratory evidence now supports the distinction between unconscious motives and the conscious motives people can self-report (Bargh & Chartrand, 1999; McClelland et al., 1989; Westen, 1998).

To study unconscious motives, researchers often use the Thematic Apperception Test (Morgan & Murray, 1935). The **Thematic Apperception Test (TAT)** consists of *a series of ambiguous pictures about which subjects make up a story*. Researchers then code the stories for motivational themes: Do the stories describe people seeking success or achievement? Power? Affiliation with other people? Intimacy in a close relationship? The motives researchers code from people's TAT stories are in fact highly predictive of their behavior over time. For example, in samples from both the United States and India, the number of times an individual's stories express themes of achievement predicts success in business over many years (McClelland et al., 1989). Similarly, the number of intimacy themes expressed in stories at age 30 predicts the quality of marital adjustment almost 20 years later (McAdams & Vaillant, 1982).

Another way to measure motives is simply to ask people: "Is achievement important to you? Is power? Is intimacy?" The correlation between conscious, self-reported motives and the inferred motives expressed in TAT stories is typically zero. People who demonstrate high achievement motivation in their stories, for example, do not necessarily report high motivation to achieve.

Although the discrepancy could simply mean that one of the two assessment methods is invalid, in fact, each type of measure predicts different kinds of behavior. For instance, achievement motivation assessed by the TAT is far more predictive of long-term entrepreneurial success than the same motive assessed by self-report. However, if subjects in the laboratory are told they must do well on a task they are about to undertake, self-reported achievement motivation is far more predictive of effort and success than TAT-expressed motivation. How can both types of measure predict achievement behavior but not predict each other?

David McClelland and his colleagues (1989) found a solution to this paradox, making a distinction similar to that between implicit and explicit memory (Chapter 6). The TAT taps implicit (unconscious) motives, whereas self-reports reflect explicit (conscious) motives. Implicit or unconscious motivation is expressed over time without conscious effort or awareness, whereas explicit or self-reported motivation becomes activated when people focus conscious attention on tasks and goals. Conscious motives, which are more flexible and controllable, can override unconscious motives but often only temporarily, as anyone knows who has ever made—and broken—a New Year's resolution.

Further research suggests that the two kinds of motives, implicit and explicit, reflect different kinds of child-rearing experiences. For example, parental demands for control, mastery, and autonomy in early life (e.g., early and rigid feeding schedules or

Big Picture φ Question 7

To what extent are psychological processes conscious or unconscious—that is, explicit versus implicit?

A person taking the Thematic Apperception Test (TAT).

toilet training) predict implicit need for achievement decades later. In contrast, parents' *explicit* teaching about values (such as the importance of doing well) predicts later explicit motives (Koestner et al., 1991b; McClelland & Pilon, 1983).

INTERIM SUMMARY

Freud argued that humans are motivated by two **drives**—internal tension states that build up until they are satisfied—sex and aggression. Contemporary psychodynamic theorists emphasize other needs as well, notably self-esteem and relatedness, and conceptualize motives in terms of wishes and fears. The most distinctive aspect of the psychodynamic approach is its distinction between conscious (explicit) and unconscious (implicit) motives, which is receiving increasing empirical support.

Behaviorist Perspective

Although behaviorists usually prefer to avoid terms such as *motivation* that suggest a causal role for internal states, the theory of operant conditioning offers (if only "implicitly") one of the clearest and most empirically supported views of motivation: Humans, like other animals, are motivated to produce behaviors rewarded by the environment and to avoid behaviors that are punished.

Learning theorists recognized many years ago, however, that the internal state of the organism influences reinforcement. A pellet of food will reinforce a hungry rat but not a sated one. Clark Hull (1943, 1952) and other behaviorists addressed this issue through their own concept of *drive*. All biological organisms have needs, such as those for food, drink, and sex. Unfulfilled needs lead to drives, defined by these theorists as states of arousal that motivate behavior. **Drive-reduction theorists** *propose that motivation stems from a combination of drive and reinforcement*.

According to this view, deprivation of basic needs creates an unpleasant state of tension; as a result, the animal begins emitting behaviors. If the animal in this state happens to perform an action that reduces the tension (as when a hungry dog finds food on the dinner table), it will associate this behavior with drive reduction. Hence, the behavior will be reinforced (and the family may have to set another plate). In this example, the drive is a **primary drive**—that is, *an innate drive such as hunger, thirst, and sex*. Most human behaviors, however, are not directed toward fulfilling primary drives. Especially in wealthier societies, people spend much of their waking time in activities such as earning a living, playing, or studying. The motives for these behaviors are secondary, or acquired, drives. A **secondary drive** is *a drive learned through conditioning and other learning mechanisms such as modeling*. An originally neutral stimulus comes to be associated with drive reduction and thus itself becomes a motivator.

For example, in many cultures the desire for money is a secondary drive that ultimately permits the satisfaction of many other primary and secondary drives. Although drive-reduction theories explain a wide range of behaviors, they leave others unexplained. Why, for instance, do people sometimes stay up until 3:00 A.M. to finish a riveting novel, even though they are exhausted? And why are some people, such as Fred, unable to refuse dessert, even after a filling meal? Such behaviors seem motivated more by the presence of *an external stimulus or reward*—called an **incentive**—than by an internal need state.

Incentives control much of human behavior, as when a person not previously hungry is enticed by the smells of a bakery or an individual not previously sexually aroused becomes excited by an attractive, scantily clad body on a beach. In these cases, stimuli *activate* drive states rather than eliminate them. Drive-reduction theories also have difficulty explaining motives to create stimulation, encounter novelty, or avoid boredom, which are present to varying degrees in different individuals (Zuckerman, 1994) and even in other animal species (Premack, 1962).

Big Picture φ Question 6

What is the relation between nature and nurture in shaping psychological processes?

INTERIM SUMMARY

Implicit in the theory of operant conditioning is that humans and other animals are motivated to repeat behaviors that lead to reinforcement and to avoid behaviors associated with punishment. Some behavioral theorists have proposed **drive-reduction theories**, which assert that deprivation of basic needs creates an unpleasant state of tension; if the animal produces a behavior that reduces that tension, the behavior is reinforced. Some drives, called **primary drives**, are innate, whereas others, called **secondary drives**, are learned through their association with primary drives.

Cognitive Perspective

Cognitive theories provide an alternative approach to motivation. One such theory we have considered is *expectancy–value theory* (Chapter 7). Expectancy–value theories view motivation as a joint function of the value people place on an outcome and the extent to which they believe they can attain it. That is, we are driven to attain goals that matter a lot to us but that we also believe we can accomplish.

A considerable body of research has demonstrated the extent to which children's beliefs about their abilities influence their motivation (and subsequent achievement) in school (Wigfield & Eccles, 2000). Students of similar *actual* ability levels often differ tremendously in their success depending on their *perceived* ability. Similarly, research finds that unemployed workers' expectancies about their likelihood of success in job seeking, together with the value they place on work, predict the probability that they will hold a job a year later (Lynd-Stevenson, 1999).

Goal-Setting Theories Cognitive approaches to motivation often focus on **goals**—*desired outcomes established through social learning*—such as getting good grades or making a good impression at a party (Bandura, 1999; Cantor, 1990). A cognitive theory widely used by organizational psychologists interested in worker motivation is goal-setting theory (Locke, 1996; Locke & Latham, 1990). The core proposition of **goal-setting theory** is that *conscious goals regulate much of human behavior*, especially performance on work tasks (Locke, 1991, p. 18). Goals represent desired outcomes that differ in some way from a person's current situation. A salesperson may set a goal of selling 100 computers next month, which is 15 more than she sold last month. Goals activate old solutions that have worked in the past and encourage efforts to create new solutions if the old ones fail.

Research using this theory suggests that maximum job performance occurs only under certain conditions (Locke, 1991; Smith et al., 1996). The person must (a) experience a discrepancy between what she has and wants; (b) define specific goals (e.g., "I've got to improve my serve") rather than general ones (e.g., "I have to play better"); (c) receive continuing feedback that allows her to gauge her progress toward the goal; (d) believe she has the ability to attain the goal; (e) set a high enough goal to remain motivated (so that the goal is not met too early or too easily); and (f) have a high degree of commitment to the goal.

Students can readily apply this theory to improve their classroom performance. Suppose, for example, they want to learn the material in this textbook. If so, they should set specific goals, such as finishing a section of a chapter before a certain time. To give themselves feedback, they should then glance at the words in bold in the interim summary and see if they can define them all before reading the definitions. If they do not understand a term, they should go back to that section of the text and re-read it. If they have momentary failures along the way, they should remind themselves of prior successes rather than jumping to global conclusions about their incompetence. If they find their motivation flagging, they might set themselves more challenging goals, such as responding to the features in the margins that require them to apply the material.

Big Picture φ Question 8

To what extent can we inform our knowledge through reason or through observation—that is, rationalism versus empiricism?

Making Connections

Expectancies—expectations about the things we value and the behaviors necessary to produce them—are central to cognitive accounts of learning, motivation, and personality. For children in ethnic minority groups with a history of discrimination, role models shape expectancies about what is possible or impossible and about what they imagine they can and cannot accomplish (Chapters 5 and 12).

Self-Determination Theory and Intrinsic Motivation   Thirty years ago, Edward Deci began exploring a paradox that has captured psychologists' attention ever since. Thousands of studies from a behaviorist point of view had shown that rewarding people for performing behaviors increases their likelihood to perform them in the future. But does reward increase people's **intrinsic motivation**—their *enjoyment of and interest in an activity for its own sake*—or does it simply make them more likely to perform the behavior when they can expect an external (or "extrinsic") reward (Deci et al., 1999)? This question has profound implications for school, work, and parenting. Do we increase a child's interest in mathematics by rewarding her for good grades or does rewarding her inadvertently extinguish her intrinsic interest in the subject?

Deci offered a controversial and counterintuitive prediction—that reward can actually stifle intrinsic pleasure in learning—a prediction largely supported by available data (Deci et al., 1999; Rawsthorne & Elliot, 1999). The most recent version of the theory, called **self-determination theory**, suggests that *people have three innate needs— competence, autonomy, and relatedness to others*—and that intrinsic motivation flourishes when these needs are fulfilled rather than compromised (Ryan & Deci, 2000).

Rewards (as well as threats, such as strict deadlines accompanied with stiff consequences) tend to compromise people's sense of autonomy. As a result, even though they may develop competence in a domain (such as math or science), they are likely to see the motivation as forced on them and hence to lose intrinsic interest. Thus, the effects of a reward on motivation depend on how the individual perceives the situation. If the person views the reward as compromising her self-determination, intrinsic motivation will decline. If she perceives a reward (such as praise) as an indicator of her competence and not as a bribe or threat, the reward is likely to *increase* intrinsic motivation.

In many respects, this theory places motives in a social context. A supportive social environment that encourages autonomy and independence is likely to be fertile ground for the development of intrinsic motivation. Thus, when possible, parents who want to foster intrinsic motivation in school would do well to praise and support their children's interests and successes. If they do reward success (e.g., with cash for a good report card), they should emphasize the child's *competence* rather than her *compliance*.

Implicit Motives: A Cognitive Perspective on Unconscious Motivation

Although self-determination theory is a cognitive theory, it has drawn heavily from other perspectives. For example, Deci derived his theory that children have innate needs for challenge and mastery from the psychoanalyst Robert White (1959), and the theory is certainly compatible with many humanistic approaches to personality that focus on innate needs for growth or self-development (Chapter 12).

Another cognitive approach to motivation that "crosses theoretical lines" is the work of Jonathan Bargh on **implicit motives**, *motives that can be activated and expressed outside of awareness*. According to Bargh, just as well-learned cognitive procedures can become automatic and occur without conscious awareness (see Chapter 7), so, too, can well-learned goals. Drawing upon principles of association, they argue that if an individual frequently chooses the same goal in a certain situation (e.g., trying to look smart in school), that goal will become associated with the situation. As a result, whenever that situation arises (as when a teacher or professor asks a question in class), the goal state will be activated and guide behavior, whether or not the person has any conscious awareness of the intention (Bargh & Barndollar, 1996, p. 8).

In a series of studies, Bargh and his colleagues tested this hypothesis using priming techniques usually used to assess implicit memory (see Bargh, 1997). They primed subjects by having them make words out of scrambled letters, under one of two conditions. In one condition, the words were related to achievement (e.g., "strive"); in the other, the words were related to affiliation (e.g., "friend"). Next, they informed participants that the study was over but asked if they could help an experimenter down the hall who was allegedly conducting an entirely separate experiment.

Big Picture φ Question 7

To what extent are psychological processes conscious or unconscious—that is, explicit versus implicit?

In this "second experiment," subjects found themselves in a situation of motivational conflict: Each was assigned an incompetent partner (a confederate of the experimenters) and given a puzzle task on which they would receive a joint score reflecting their work as a team. Thus, subjects could succeed—by essentially ignoring what the partner had to say and likely making their partner feel humiliated and stupid—or they could be more interpersonally sensitive but receive a lower score.

As predicted, subjects who had been primed with achievement words outperformed subjects primed with affiliation words (as well as control subjects who had been exposed to neutral primes). When debriefed at the end of the study, none of the subjects had any idea of the connection between the two "experiments." Thus, similar to the conclusions reached by David McClelland and his colleagues (1989), Bargh suggests that motives, like other psychological processes, can be activated either implicitly or explicitly and can guide our behavior even when we have no idea how (or whether) they became active.

INTERIM SUMMARY

According to expectancy—value theories, people are motivated to perform a behavior to the extent that they value the potential outcome and believe they can attain it. **Goal-setting theory** argues that conscious goals regulate much of human action. **Intrinsic motivation** refers to enjoyment of and interest in an activity for its own sake. According to **self-determination theory**, people have innate needs for competence, autonomy, and relatedness, and intrinsic motivation flourishes when these needs are fulfilled. **Implicit motives** are motives that can be activated and expressed outside of conscious awareness.

A Hierarchy of Needs An alternative approach to motivation was advanced by Abraham Maslow (1962, 1970). According to Maslow's **hierarchy of needs**, *lower level needs, beginning with basic survival, must be fulfilled before higher level needs guide a person's behavior* (Figure 10.1). At the most basic level are *physiological needs*, such as those for water and food. Next are *safety needs*, for security and protection. Having satisfied physiological and safety needs to some extent, people are motivated to pursue closeness and affiliation with other people, or what Maslow calls *belongingness needs*. Next in the hierarchy are *esteem needs*, including both self-esteem and the esteem of others.

At the highest level are **self-actualization needs**, *motives to express oneself and grow*, or to actualize one's potential. Self-actualization needs differ from all the previous levels in that they are not *deficiency needs*; that is, they are not generated by a *lack* of something (food, shelter, closeness, the esteem of others). Rather, they are *growth needs*—motives to expand and develop one's skills and abilities.

Many behaviors reflect multiple needs. Going to work, for example, can "bring home the bacon" as well as satisfy needs for esteem, affiliation, and self-actualization. According to Maslow, however, people can spend their lives focused on motives primarily at one level and not develop beyond it. People who are starving are unlikely to think much about art, and motives for self-expression may take a back seat in people who desperately need the esteem of others. In contrast, self-actualized individuals are no longer preoccupied with where they will get their dinner or who will hold them in esteem and are thus free to pursue moral, cultural, or aesthetic concerns. Maslow offered prominent examples of self-actualizers—Gandhi, Martin Luther King, Jr., and Eleanor Roosevelt—but he believed that few people reach this level.

Maslow's theory of self-actualization has proven difficult to test (Neher, 1991). However, one organizational psychologist, Clayton Alderfer, refined and applied aspects of Maslow's model to motivation in the workplace (Alderfer, 1972, 1989). Alderfer was a consultant to a small manufacturing company that was having trouble motivating its workers. In interviewing the employ-

FIGURE 10.1 Maslow's hierarchy of needs. Except for self-actualization, all of Maslow's needs are generated by a lack of something, such as food or shelter.

ees, he noticed that their concerns seemed to fall into three categories: material concerns such as pay, fringe benefits, and physical conditions in the plant; relationships with peers and supervisors; and opportunities to learn and use their skills on the job. His observations led to **ERG theory**, which essentially *condenses Maslow's hierarchy to three levels of need: existence, relatedness, and growth (hence ERG)*.

According to ERG theory, worker satisfaction and motivation vary with the extent to which a job matches a given worker's needs. Workers whose primary concern is pay are unlikely to appreciate attempts to give them more training to expand their skills. In general, however, the best job provides good pay and working conditions, a chance to interact with other people, and opportunities to develop one's skills, thus satisfying the major needs. This theory offers testable hypotheses, although the empirical evidence for it remains sketchy.

INTERIM SUMMARY

Maslow proposed a **hierarchy of needs**—from needs that are basic to survival to needs that guide behavior only once the person has fulfilled needs lower down the hierarchy. The hierarchy includes physiological needs, safety needs, belongingness needs, esteem needs, and **self-actualization needs** (needs to express oneself and grow). **ERG theory**, which applied Maslow's model to the workplace, proposes that workers are motivated by three kinds of needs: existence, relatedness, and growth.

Evolutionary Perspective

In the early part of the twentieth century, psychologists assumed that most motivated behavior in humans, as in other animals, was a result of **instincts**, *relatively fixed patterns of behavior produced without learning* (Tinbergen, 1951). An example is the mating ritual of the ring dove, which must perform an elaborate, stereotyped sequence of behaviors in exactly the right manner to attract a mate. If the male does not bow and coo at the proper point in the ritual, the female will not be receptive (Lehrman, 1956).

Most psychologists eventually abandoned instinct theory, for a number of reasons. First, human behavior varies so substantially across cultures that the motives that seemed "instinctive" in one culture (such as motives for wealth in the West) did not seem so powerful in others. Perhaps more importantly, one of the most distinctive features of human behavior is its *flexibility*—seen in our ability to find novel ways to solve problems or to bow and coo when it suits us. Thus, many psychologists came to argue that learning, not instinct, motivates behavior in humans.

Maximizing Inclusive Fitness　Contemporary evolutionary psychologists contend that motivational systems, like other psychological attributes, have been selected by nature for their ability to maximize reproductive success—that is, survival and reproduction (see Buss, 1999). For some motives, this claim is unremarkable. Organisms that do not replenish their energy by eating do not survive and reproduce. Nature has thus designed humans and other animals with intricate systems for maintaining basic life-support processes.

Some evolutionary explanations, however, are much more controversial. As we saw in Chapter 1, evolutionary theorists have argued that evolution selects animals that maximize their inclusive fitness, which refers to their own reproductive success in addition to their influence on the reproductive success of genetically related individuals (Hamilton, 1964). This theory makes mathematical sense. The probability that any given gene of an individual who protects his child will be available in the gene pool in the next generation is 50 percent because his child shares half his genes. The probability jumps to 75 percent for someone who protects his child *plus* his niece (one-half from his child and one-fourth from his niece). Over many generations, this difference becomes substantial.

Apply & Discuss

▪ To what extent does factory work on this production line satisfy the motives described by Maslow and ERG theory?

▪ What could employers do to increase employee satisfaction in jobs such as this?

Big Picture φ Question 6

What is the relation between nature and nurture in shaping psychological processes?

Apply & Discuss

Many animals have elaborate courting rituals that precede mating.

- To what extent do human "rituals" and those of other animals reflect common evolutionary roots?

- Are the similarities just accidental (and amusing) or do they reflect similar evolutionary histories?

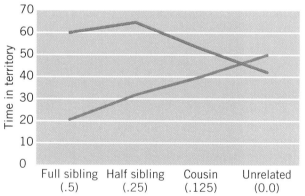

FIGURE 10.2 Pheromonal communication. Pheromones activate sexual and other responses much as hormones do, except that they are secreted by other animals instead of by the animal's own endocrine system.

FIGURE 10.3 Pheromonal mechanisms for kin recognition in crickets. In normal females (blue line), the smaller the degree of relatedness, the more time spent in the territory of a male cricket. Females whose pheromone receptors were covered with wax (red line) did not show the same inverse relationship between degree of relatedness and amount of time in the territory. *Source:* Adapted from Simmons, 1990, p. 194.

Evolutionary psychologists are generally careful to distinguish the theory that evolution *favors* organisms that maximize their inclusive fitness from the assumption that organisms deliberately *seek* to maximize their inclusive fitness, as if they carry inclusive fitness calculators in their pockets. Nevertheless, some basic motivational mechanisms presumably evolved to help organisms select courses of action that foster survival, reproduction, and the care and protection of kin. These mechanisms should guide their behavior so that their degree of investment is roughly proportional to their degree of relatedness.

How then do organisms—whether bees or humans—know who their sons, brothers, or cousins are? Recent research suggests that some species are actually endowed with chemical mechanisms (pheromones) for kin recognition. Pheromones are similar to hormones, except that they allow cell-to-cell communication *between* rather than *within* organisms (Figure 10.2). They are typically detected by specialized neural circuits in the olfactory system (Chapter 4) and may have the same or similar effects as hormones (Sorenson, 1996).

Whether pheromonal communication leads to increased investment in close relatives is unknown, but it does help members of some species avoid mating with members of other species (which wastes precious mating time) and avoid incest, which can produce genetically defective offspring and hence reduce reproductive success (Blaustein & Waldman, 1992; Wilson & Bossert, 1996). In one study, the experimenter allowed female crickets to choose where they would spend their time in an area divided into four territories (Simmons, 1990). Potential male mates were not present, but the experimenter marked each territory with the scent (from droppings) of a male who was a full sibling, a half sibling, a cousin, or an unrelated cricket. Thus, the females could spend time in the territory of male crickets related to them by .5, .25, .125, or 0, respectively.

The results were striking: The amount of time females spent in each territory was inversely proportional to degree of relatedness; that is, the more distant the relation, the more time spent "in the neighborhood" (Figure 10.3). The mechanism for kin recognition proved to be chemical, since female crickets whose pheromone receptors were covered with wax showed no preference for unrelated males.

Humans probably do not rely on pheromones for kin recognition; however, as suggested in Chapter 1, they probably make use of other mechanisms, such as degree of familiarity, particularly from childhood. Throughout the course of much of human evolution, people who grew up together were more than likely family members, so longtime familiarity, particularly from childhood, would be a rough index of degree of kinship, if an imperfect one. In fact, just as crickets avoid sexual contact with other crickets with the scent of family, marriage among children who grow up together in Israeli communal living arrangements, or *kibbutzim*, is almost nonexistent (Shepher, 1978).

Multiple Motivational Systems   From an evolutionary point of view, humans and other animals are likely to have multiple motivational systems—innate response tendencies, many with their own distinct neural circuitry—that evolved to solve particular problems of adaptation. From an evolutionary point of view, the motives we pursue, like the ways we think and behave, evolved over the millions of years of evolution in response to evolutionary pressures.

Central to evolutionary accounts is the notion that organisms evolve through natural selection in directions that maximize survival and reproduction, and this should be no less true of motives than any other psychological functions. The primary motives that emerge in cross-cultural research are power and love, which is not surprising from an evolutionary perspective (Buss, 1991). Power allows animals to dominate potential rivals, establish status (which females tend to find attractive in males), and protect their "turf." Indeed, competition for status is nearly universal among animals, and certainly among primates, where baboon males can be seen to jockey for power in the bush much as human executives jockey in the boardroom. That "love" is a basic motive across cultures also makes evolutionary sense. Love is involved in caring for offspring, mates, kin, and friends who can be counted on "like a brother" or "like a sister." The fact that we use phrases like these to describe close friends may not be accidental.

Not all motives for intimacy, of course, are brotherly or sisterly. The amount of time we spend on activities related to mating or making ourselves attractive to potential mates—and the number of poems, novels, and movies with a central theme of "boy meets girl," "meeting Mr. Right," unfaithful lovers, and so forth—is a testimony to the power of natural selection. Motives related to mating include sexual motivation, competition for desirable partners, making sure our mates are faithful (Chapter 18), and a host of others. Other motives related to reproduction involve motives for parental care, which exist in nearly every animal species. That parents awakened in the middle of the night by a crying baby generally respond with affection rather than aggression is a true testimony to the power of natural selection!

A key evolutionary assumption is that psychological systems—whether motivational, cognitive, or otherwise—serve functions that may have evolved independently in response to particular evolutionary pressures (Buss, 1991, 2000; Cosmides & Tooby, 1995). Just as specialized neural circuits in the cortex and amygdala allow us to recognize the meaning of facial expressions (warning us, for example, that someone is angry and potentially threatening), specific circuits also regulate sexual desire or probably our attunement (and response) to the auditory frequency of a baby's cry.

INTERIM SUMMARY

Early on, psychologists assumed that humans and other animals had **instincts**. Fixed patterns of behavior produced without learning. According to contemporary evolutionary theory, evolution selects animals that maximize their inclusive fitness (their own reproductive success plus their influence on the reproductive success of genetically related individuals). Maximizing inclusive fitness entails a range of motives, such as selecting and competing for mates, taking care of offspring, caring about other genetically related individuals, forming useful alliances, and maintaining one's own survival through eating, drinking, keeping the body warm, and so forth.

Applying the Perspectives on Motivation

How might the different theoretical approaches to motivation explain the puzzling scenario of the apparent lack of motivation for protection against HIV infection many people demonstrate in sexual situations?

From an evolutionary perspective, one answer lies in the discrepancy between the current environment and the circumstances in which our ancestors evolved. Hu-

Apply & Discuss

▪ How might the different theoretical approaches explain the self-inflicted pain people endure in order to sport a tattoo or pierced body parts?

▪ How would Maslow account for such behavior?

mans have neural programs for sexual arousal that were engineered over millennia; AIDS, like other deadly venereal diseases (notably syphilis), is a new disease (in evolutionary time). Thus, these neural programs do not include momentary breaks for condoms. Distaste for condoms should be particularly high among males, who can lose erections while searching for or wearing condoms, whose reproductive success may be compromised by their application, who face less risk of AIDS transmission than do females from heterosexual intercourse, and who in many cultures attract females through apparent bravery ("Nothing scares me, babe").

From a psychodynamic perspective, sex is a basic human motivation, and people are prone to self-deception and wishful thinking; the fact that people frequently deny the risk to themselves of unprotected sex should thus come as no surprise. Furthermore, any sexual encounter reflects multiple motives, and the balance of these motives can sometimes override good judgment. For example, people have casual sex for many reasons beyond biological drive. These include self-esteem motives (to feel desirable), wishes to feel physically or emotionally close to someone, and motives for dominance (the feeling of conquest). Casual, unprotected sex may also reflect blatantly self-destructive motives, as was the case with a suicidal young gay man who regularly attended bathhouses at the height of media attention to the epidemic.

From a behaviorist perspective, sexual behavior, like all behavior, is under environmental control. If condom use is punishing (because it "breaks the mood," decreases genital sensations, or leads to whining by male partners), it will diminish over time. Partners who consent to unsafe sex may also be negatively reinforced for doing so by the cessation of complaining or cajoling and positively reinforced by praise or enjoyable sex.

From a cognitive perspective, people's expectancies about the probable outcomes of high-risk behavior can simply be wrong because of misinformation or inattention to media messages. Moreover, because HIV may not lead to symptoms of AIDS for many years, unprotected sexual contact produces no immediate feedback to deter its continued practice. In fact, the absence of immediate consequences probably bolsters erroneously optimistic expectancies.

From Maslow's perspective, sexual behavior can satisfy both physiological and belongingness needs, so it is likely a powerful source of motivation. When the behavior is life threatening, safety needs should be activated; however, the absence of any obvious negative impact of high-risk behavior for several years could provide a false sense of safety and allow other motives to be expressed in behavior.

A Global Vista   Cultural Influences on Motivation

Although the major approaches to motivation take the individual as their starting point, cross-cultural work suggests that culture plays a substantial role in shaping motivation (Benedict, 1934). For example, some societies, such as the United States, view the personal accumulation of material wealth as a worthy end of individual endeavor and even celebrate wealthy people (achievers of the American Dream). In contrast, other cultures disapprove of accumulating material goods for oneself or one's family, considering it a crime against the community or a mark of poor character. The Kapauka Papuans of New Guinea strictly punish individual wealth (Pospisil, 1963). Disapproval or sanctions against individual consumption are common in agricultural or peasant societies, where resources tend to be limited and people tend to be oriented more to the good of the community (Foster, 1965).

Psychologist Erich Fromm (1955) argued that a culture's socioeconomic system shapes people's motivations so that they *want* to act in ways that the system *needs* them to act. In other words, for an economic system to work, it must create individuals whose personal needs match the needs of the system. A capitalist economy such

Big Picture φ Question 4

To what extent is human nature particular versus universal?

as our own depends on workers and consumers to be materialistic. If advertisements for digital cameras or rewriteable CD drives did not motivate people, entrepreneurs would not create them, and ultimately the economy would stagnate.

The impact of culture can be seen in the conditions that foster intrinsic motivation in children. Contemporary Western cultures are highly individualistic and hence place a high premium on autonomy and self-direction. In contrast, most non-Western cultures are much more group centered. In these cultures, getting along with others, honoring one's family and parents, and participating in the life of the community tend to be more highly valued (Chapter 18).

Recent research suggests that these differences may translate into differences in the kinds of experiences that produce intrinsic motivation (Iyengar & Lepper, 1999). In one study, Anglo-American and Asian-American children (who spoke their parents' native language in the home and hence were not fully assimilated into U.S. culture) were asked to solve a set of anagrams (scrambled words). In one condition, the children were given choices to maximize their sense of self-determination. For example, the anagrams were taken from one of several categories (e.g., words related to animals, food, or San Francisco), and children in this condition were allowed to pick the category. They were also allowed to choose the color of the marker they would use to record their answers.

In another condition, children were given no choices. In fact, they were told that their mother had chosen the category of words and the color of the marker for them. Afterward the children were allowed to play in the room for a few minutes and were told that they could do some more word puzzles if they wanted or that they could play some other games, such as solving crossword puzzles. The investigators then recorded how much time the children continued to solve the anagrams, as a measure of their intrinsic motivation (i.e., whether they found the task intrinsically interesting enough to continue with it even though the experiment had presumably ended).

As predicted, Anglo-American children were more likely to show intrinsic motivation for solving anagrams in the first condition, in which they chose the categories and colors themselves (Figure 10.4). In contrast, the Asian-American children demonstrated the *opposite* pattern: They showed more intrinsic motivation to solve anagrams when they believed that the relevant choices had been made by their mothers. These results suggest that principles of motivation may not be culturally invariant and that the extent to which a culture emphasizes autonomy and individualism may influence the extent to which threats to autonomy influence what people find interesting and worth pursuing.

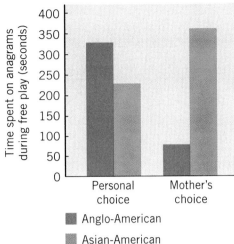

FIGURE 10.4 Culture and intrinsic motivation. Anglo-American children who were given choices spent more time continuing to solve anagrams after they were no longer required to do so. Asian-American children, in contrast, showed more intrinsic motivation to solve anagrams when their mothers made the choices for them. *Source:* Adapted from Iyengar & Lepper, 1999, p. 354.

INTERIM SUMMARY

Social and cultural practices play a substantial role in shaping motives. Influences on what children come to find intrinsically motivating may be very different depending on whether they come from a culture that emphasizes individualism and personal control over choices or one that emphasizes collectivism and group identity.

Eating

Having explored the major perspectives in motivation, we now turn to specific motives, beginning with eating. At its most basic level, the motivation to eat is biologically based, but the story is not that simple. We often eat in advance of severe caloric depletion. We eat because it smells good; we eat because a friend says "How about lunch?"; we eat in response to a vast variety of signals, many of which are not related to need.

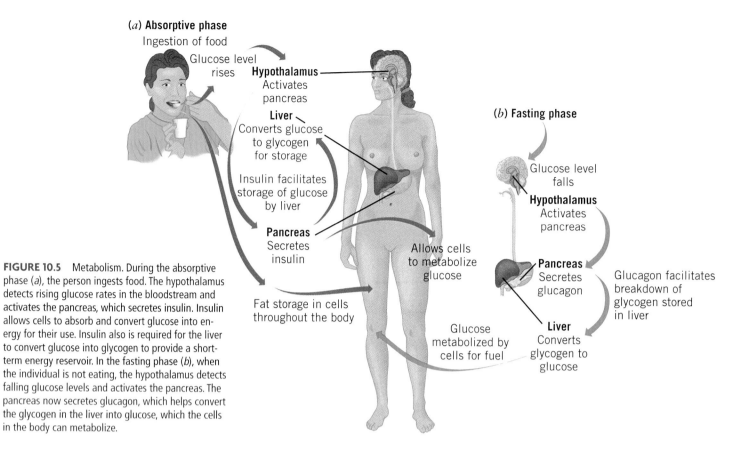

FIGURE 10.5 Metabolism. During the absorptive phase (*a*), the person ingests food. The hypothalamus detects rising glucose rates in the bloodstream and activates the pancreas, which secretes insulin. Insulin allows cells to absorb and convert glucose into energy for their use. Insulin also is required for the liver to convert glucose into glycogen to provide a short-term energy reservoir. In the fasting phase (*b*), when the individual is not eating, the hypothalamus detects falling glucose levels and activates the pancreas. The pancreas now secretes glucagon, which helps convert the glycogen in the liver into glucose, which the cells in the body can metabolize.

However, in general the function of eating is not to relieve anxiety, frustration, or boredom but to convert what were once the cells of other living organisms into energy.

Metabolism refers to *the processes by which the body transforms food into energy* for moving muscles, maintaining body heat, operating the nervous system, and building and maintaining organ tissue. Much of that energy comes from *glucose*, a simple sugar. What makes metabolism a complex process is that the body has to maintain energy at all times, even though we cannot be eating at all times.

Metabolism thus has two phases (Figure 10.5): absorptive and fasting. In the **absorptive phase**, *the person is ingesting food*. During this phase, the body "runs" on some of the food it is absorbing but puts additional reserves into short- and long-term stores. The short-term "fuel tanks" store carbohydrates, by converting glucose to a more complex sugar (*glycogen*), which is stored throughout the body but particularly in the liver. The long-term energy tanks, located under the skin and in the abdomen, contain primarily fats (lipids). Fat cells are capable of expanding enormously when reserves are high. From an evolutionary perspective, the ability to store fat served our ancestors well. When winter came and food was scarce, they had both extra reserves of body fuel and an extra layer of warmth.

The second phase of metabolism, the **fasting phase**, *occurs when a person is not eating*, as the body converts its short- and long-term reserves into energy. In starvation, both these sources of fuel become depleted, and the body starts converting proteins into fuel, often breaking down muscle.

Homeostasis

Biological functions such as eating, drinking, and sleeping are regulated by a process called **homeostasis**, which refers to *the body's tendency to maintain a relatively constant state that permits cells to live and function*. Homeostasis literally means "standing still" (or, more accurately, "standing similarly"). Homeostasis requires mechanisms for both *detecting* the state of the system (e.g., determining whether the body has enough nutrients) and *correcting* the situation to restore the system to the desired state (e.g., searching for food).

Cells in the body can live only within a fairly narrow range of conditions (e.g., at the right temperature and bathed in the right amount of water). Thus, humans, like other animals, evolved systems for regulating these conditions. These systems work much like a thermostat in a house. If the thermostat ("the detector") is set at 70 degrees, the furnace remains off if the temperature inside meets or exceeds 70 degrees. When the temperature drops below that point, a circuit running from the system's thermometer switches on the furnace long enough to restore the temperature to 70 degrees (the correcting mechanism). Once feedback from the thermostat signals that the goal is attained, the furnace is again deactivated.

Eating is part of a complex homeostatic process: Energy reserves become depleted, and the person becomes hungry and eats. As the fuel tanks become full, ingestion stops, until reserves again become depleted. Like other homeostatic systems, the system that regulates food intake includes several features. First, the system has mechanisms that act like a **set point** (or set points), a *biologically optimal level the system strives to maintain* (in this case, nutrients that provide fuel for cells to do their work). Second, the system must have **feedback mechanisms** that *provide information regarding the state of the system with respect to the variables being regulated*. Thus, the body contains receptors that monitor, for example, how much sugar is in the bloodstream and provide feedback to the brain. Finally, the system must have **corrective mechanisms** that *restore the system to its set point when needed* (in this case, finding and ingesting food).

Two features of this description of homeostatic process are worth noting. First, although homeostatic processes most obviously apply to biological needs (e.g., for food, water, and air), similar mechanisms are involved in regulating many motives, such as maintaining closeness to people to whom we are deeply attached (Bowlby, 1969). Similar processes occur with regulation of emotional states as well. For example, an unemployed person who feels stressed after two unsuccessful months on the job market may work even harder to find a job or may start drinking to kill the emotional pain. Both are mechanisms aimed at turning off a painful "feedback" signal (distress), although one is more likely to restore financial security and self-esteem.

Second, in many motivational systems, particularly physiological ones such as hunger and thirst, there may be a substantial lag between the time corrective mechanisms have kicked in to restore the system to homeostasis and the time the system registers their effects. For example, by the time a hungry person has eaten enough to restore his energy reserves, only a small part of this food has actually been digested—the receptors designed to detect nutrient levels do not yet have all the "data" necessary to turn off eating. Thus, the body has evolved two separate systems: hunger, for "turning on" eating; and **satiety mechanisms**, *for turning off ingestive behavior*. The satiety mechanisms are designed to make us feel *sated* so we will close our mouths long enough to let the food "sink in."

INTERIM SUMMARY

Metabolism, the processes by which the body transforms food into energy, has two phases: the **absorptive phase**, in which the person is ingesting food, and the **fasting phase**, during which the body converts its short- and long-term stores into energy. **Homeostasis** refers to the body's tendency to maintain a relatively constant state that permits cells to live and function. Homeostatic processes, including those involved in eating, have several common features. These include a **set point**, or optimal level the system strives to maintain; **feedback mechanisms** that provide the system with information regarding the state of the system with respect to the set point; and **corrective mechanisms** that restore the system to its set point when needed. **Satiety mechanisms** turn off ingestive behavior.

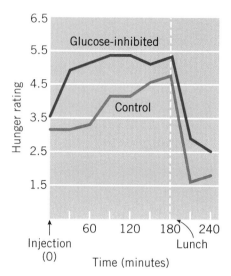

FIGURE 10.6   Hunger and glucose levels. The blue line depicts data from the experimental group, who received injections of a drug that suppresses blood-sugar levels. The red line illustrates data from the control group, who received a saline-solution injection. As the figure illustrates, subjects whose blood-sugar level had been artificially lowered (the glucose-inhibited group) felt considerably more hungry than the control group, even after a meal. *Source:* Thompson & Campbell, 1977.

What Turns Hunger On?

Feelings of hunger caused by physiological need ultimately derive from dropping levels of glucose and lipids in the bloodstream as the body draws increasingly on its long-term stores. Because the nervous system can use glucose (and cannot, like the rest of the body, metabolize fats), it has its own glucose detectors (located on the "brain" side of the blood–brain barrier) that detect falling blood-sugar levels (Carlson, 1999). The body has additional detectors that monitor both glucose and fats, located in the liver, which send specific signals to the brain (Woods et al., 2000). Signals from both liver and brain receptors appear to converge in the brain stem and together play a significant role in feelings of hunger.

Although most people think they become hungry because their stomachs feel empty, glucose levels probably play the most important role in producing feelings of hunger. Even people whose stomachs have been removed because of cancer nonetheless report feeling hunger (Janowitz & Grossman, 1949).

Although we cannot ask rats how hungry they are, injecting small amounts of glucose into their bloodstream when glucose levels begin to drop delays feeding behavior (Campfield et al., 1985). In humans, subjective sensations of hunger increase as glucose levels decrease. Figure 10.6 compares the reported sensations of hunger in two groups of well-fed subjects, one of whom received an injection of a drug that suppresses blood glucose levels. The experimental group felt hungrier, even after a meal (Thompson & Campbell, 1977). In another study, the investigators continuously recorded participants' glucose levels, subjective ratings of hunger, and requests for food (Campfield et al., 1996). Just after momentary decreases in glucose levels, subjects tended to feel hungry and ask for food.

The Role of the Hypothalamus   Above the brain stem, the hypothalamus (Figure 10.7) plays a key role in hunger and eating, as it does in virtually all homeostatic processes (Lawrence et al., 1999). Researchers once believed that one section of the hypothalamus—the lateral hypothalamus—was the "on" switch for eating, whereas another region—the ventromedial hypothalamus—was the "off" switch (Anand & Brobeck, 1951; Teitelbaum, 1961). They based this theory in part on the fact that lesions to the lateral hypothalamus led rats to stop eating, and lesions to the ventromedial hypothalamus led them to eat ravenously.

The theory turned out to have several problems. For example, rats with damage to the lateral hypothalamus show deficits in other motivated behaviors, such as thirst and sex. More recent research suggests that eating, like virtually all psychological functions, reflects the action of neural circuits that run throughout the brain, and that, although the hypothalamus plays a central role, it is not the brain's "eating center" (Sakurai et al., 1998; Winn, 1995).

The lateral hypothalamus does, in fact, play a central role in initiating eating. A neurotransmitter found in this region, called *neuropeptide Y*, is particularly important in turning on eating, and the ventromedial hypothalamus is particularly important in producing off signals. Both regions of the hypothalamus, however, contain chemicals that can turn eating off *and* on, and both require substantial input from brain stem circuits that integrate information about blood glucose levels, taste, and smell. The hypothalamus also feeds information to the cortex, particularly the frontal cortex, which regulates the motor behaviors involved in finding and ingesting food.

The Role of External Cues in Eating   Hunger is the prime motivator for eating, but external factors also influence the inclination to eat. In fact, desire for a food can be motivated either by hunger or simply by its palatability, or taste. Moreover, these two sources of eating motivation are mediated by different neural pathways and neurotransmitters (Berridge, 1996). Palatability plays an important role even in animals not known for their gourmet tastes (Capaldi & VandenBos, 1991; Warwick et al., 1993).

Lateral hypothalamus

Ventromedial hypothalamus

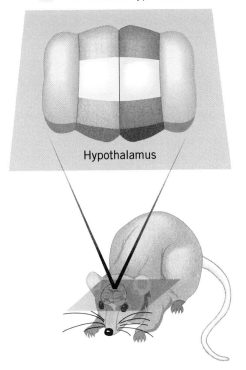

Hypothalamus

(a)

(b)

FIGURE 10.7   The hypothalamus and eating. (a) Decades ago, researchers began studying the roles of the ventromedial hypothalamus (*ventral* meaning toward the bottom of the brain, and *medial* meaning toward the middle) and lateral hypothalamus (*lateral* meaning on the sides) in eating. (b) Destruction of the ventromedial hypothalamus can lead to obesity in rats.

Rats, like humans, like variety in their diets, and as pet owners can attest, dogs and cats may grow tired of a brand of food and walk away from a delightful and nutritious bowl of horse meat or tuna innards even if they are hungry. Some taste preferences are inborn, such as the preference of human infants and baby rats for sweet tastes, while others depend on exposure and learning.

Some researchers argue that learned factors of this sort play a larger role in arousal of hunger than do homeostatic processes (Woods et al., 2000). For example, rats fed consistently at particular times of day will develop classically conditioned hormonal and other chemical responses that prepare the body for food and "turn on" eating behavior. Much of eating is also regulated by learning and habit, as people learn to eat at particular times of day or in particular situations.

Another external factor that influences the motive to eat is the presence of other people. One study gave subjects pocket-sized cards on which they were to record both their food intake and dining companions for seven consecutive days (de Castro & Brewer, 1992). The more people present, the more subjects ate. Meals eaten with a large group of people were 75 percent larger than meals eaten alone.

What Turns Hunger Off?

Although hunger and satiety signals certainly interact, the mechanisms that stop eating are not the same ones that start it. The signals that stop eating begin with tastes and smells, some learned and some innate, that signal that certain food is better left alone. And noticing that our plate is empty or that other people are no longer eating can certainly signal that dinnertime is over.

Feelings of satiety (fullness, or satiation), however, usually begin in the stomach and intestines. Not only does the stomach wall have stretch receptors that send mes-

Big Picture φ Question 6

What is the relation between nature and nurture in shaping psychological processes?

Apply & Discuss

■ Do people differ in the extent to which their eating behavior reflects feelings (e.g., taste and mood), cognitions (e.g., knowledge about calories and body image), and arousal (hunger)?

■ How might these differences develop?

Apply & Discuss

■ Given that virtually all women in the West are exposed to the same skinny models, why do some women develop eating disorders while others do not?

■ How firm is the line between eating disorders and the preoccupation with issues of food and weight shown by many girls and women in the West (Chapter 15)?

sages to the brain signaling that enough is enough, but even more important are receptors in the stomach and intestines that detect levels of nutrients. For example, rats will eat more when their stomachs are full of saline solution than of a high-calorie liquid, a suggestion that glucose receptors are involved in feelings of satiety as well as hunger (Angel et al., 1992; Deutsch & Gonzalez, 1980). Over the long run, knowing when to stop is also regulated by a protein, called leptin, which is secreted by well-stocked fat cells (Chapter 11).

INTERIM SUMMARY

Feelings of hunger derive from dropping levels of glucose and lipids in the bloodstream, which are detected by receptors in the liver and brain stem. This information is transmitted to regions of the hypothalamus involved in both hunger and satiety. Eating is also influenced by external cues, such as palatability, time of day, and presence of other people. Satiety occurs through a number of mechanisms, including tastes and smells but primarily through detection of nutrients in the stomach and intestines.

Obesity

Obesity is one of the easiest to recognize, and most difficult to treat, physical or medical conditions (Devlin et al., 2000). **Obesity** is defined as *body weight 15 percent or more above the ideal for one's height and age*. By this criterion, about one-third of the adult population of the United States is obese, and the percentage is growing.

In industrialized countries, fatness tends to be inversely correlated with socioeconomic status; that is, people in lower social classes tend to be more obese. In developing nations, the direction of this correlation is reversed: the richer, the fatter (at least for women) (Sobal & Stunkard, 1989). The situation in the developing world probably approximates the state of affairs through most of human evolution. Particularly for women, whose pregnancies could extend into times of scarcity, larger *internal* food reserves were adaptive in the face of variable *external* reserves. In fact, societies in which food is scarce tend to associate beauty with bulk, since women who are healthy and have more resources tend to be heavier (Triandis, 1994). From an evolutionary point of view, human eating behavior evolved in conditions of scarcity and unpredictability, leading to evolved mechanisms that likely influence us to eat at our physiological limits when food is available (Pinel et al., 2000). These mechanisms may not be so adaptive when people have to hunt for food on menus instead of in forests.

Obesity places people at increased risk for a number of medical problems, such as heart disease, high blood pressure, and diabetes (Brownell & Rodin, 1994; Pinel et al., 2000). The mortality rates of overweight people are up to four times higher than in people of normal weight (Foreyt, 1987; Woo et al., 1998). On the other hand, the ways people try to lose weight—such as overreliance on "diet pills," semistarvation diets, and self-induced vomiting—can also lead to health risks (Berg, 1999).

Culture, Gender, and Conceptions of Weight and Obesity   Although obesity can be defined objectively, the subjective experience of being overweight varies considerably by individual, gender, and culture. North American culture is preoccupied with thinness, particularly for women. At any given moment, two-thirds of high school girls report that they are trying to lose weight (Rosen & Gross, 1987). From age 9 to 14, girls (unlike boys) show steady increases in concerns about their weight as well as tendencies to binge at least once a month, probably reflecting their efforts to keep their weight down by overly restricting food intake (Field et al., 1999). In Western culture, stereotypes about the obese are extremely negative (Crandall, 1994) and begin as early as kindergarten (Hsu, 1989; Rothblum, 1992). Children who are overweight are teased and often develop both lowered self-esteem and negative expectations about the way others will treat them (Miller & Downey, 1999).

Whereas most white women complain about their weight even when their weight is biologically in the "ideal" range, African-American culture has different norms (Rand & Kuldau, 1990). In one study, African-American women were heavier than their white counterparts, but they were more satisfied with their weight and less likely to find weight on other people (particularly women) unattractive (Harris et al., 1991). Overall, men were more concerned about the weight of their dates than women were, but African-American men were less likely than white men to refuse to date a woman because of her weight. Other research finds that white women rate heavier women (especially other white women) negatively on multiple dimensions (such as attractiveness, intelligence, and popularity), whereas African-American women do not (Hebl & Heatherton, 1998).

Views of beauty and obesity vary not only across and within cultures but also historically. Compared to the "Rubenesque" view of beauty of just a few centuries ago (expressed in the art and culture of the period, in which the artist Rubens was painting nudes that might today be used in advertisements for weight-loss programs!), the prototypes of feminine beauty portrayed in the mass media today look emaciated. The standards have even changed considerably since the 1950s, when the ideal was the voluptuous beauty of Marilyn Monroe, replete with large breasts and slightly protruding abdomen.

The way others behave toward obese people in our culture may actually lead them to *behave* less attractively. In one study, obese and nonobese women conversed on the phone with other subjects who did not know them and could not see them (Miller et al., 1990). College student raters, unaware of the subjects' weights (or even of what the study was about), then listened to the recorded conversations and rated the women on their social skills, likeability, and probable physical attractiveness. Not only did the raters view the obese women more negatively on all dimensions, but correlations between pounds overweight and every other variable suggested that coders could judge physical appearance from purely auditory cues: The heavier the subject, the less socially skilled, likable, and physically attractive she was perceived to be.

We will discuss other aspects of obesity in detail in Chapter 11.

INTERIM SUMMARY

Obesity—having a body weight more than 15 percent above the ideal for one's height and age—is highly prevalent in some countries, particularly the United States. Attitudes about weight vary considerably by culture, class, ethnic group, and level of affluence of a society. The causes of obesity lie in both nature and nurture.

Cultures set standards for body types that are considered attractive and unattractive. In Renoir's time, beautiful meant bountiful. Even in the 1950s and 1960s, the standard of beauty was considerably plumper than it is now. Marilyn Monroe, for example, would probably be considered chubby today—and might well have difficulty making it on television. A study of Playboy's centerfolds and Miss America Pageant contestants found a 10 percent decrease in the ratio of weight to height in both groups from the late 1950s to the late 1970s. This trend was paralleled by a dramatic increase in the number of articles on dieting in popular women's magazines (Garner et al., 1980, cited in Hsu, 1989).

Sexual Motivation

Like hunger, sex is a universal drive based in biology, but its expression varies considerably from culture to culture and from person to person. In fact, sexual motivation is even more variable than hunger. Most people eat two or three meals a day, whereas sexual appetites defy generalizations. Sexual behavior is driven as much by fantasies as by hormones; indeed, the primary sexual organ in humans is arguably not the genitals but the brain.

Although psychoanalysis broke down many of the Victorian taboos against discussing sexuality, sex did not become a respectable area of scientific research until Alfred Kinsey and his colleagues published two massive volumes on the sexual behavior of the human male and female (Kinsey et al., 1948, 1953). Many of Kinsey's findings, based on interviews with thousands of adults, provoked shock and outrage. For instance, some 37 percent of males and 13 percent of females reported having engaged in homosexual activity at some time in their lives. More recent research finds slightly lower rates of male homosexual activity but otherwise paints a similar picture (Seidman & Rieder, 1994). The average sexually active person reports having intercourse between one and three times a week and becomes sexually active between ages 17 and 19 (although many start earlier or later).

Since the time of the Kinsey report, and especially since the sexual revolution of the 1960s and 1970s, sexual attitudes and practices have become much more liberal. For example, in a study that used the original Kinsey data for comparison, both white and black women reported earlier age at first intercourse, a wider range of sexual practices, a larger number of sexual partners, and reduced likelihood of marrying their first lover (Wyatt et al., 1988a, 1988b).

The Sexual Response Cycle

A major step forward in the scientific study of sex was William Masters and Virginia Johnson's (1966) path-breaking book, *Human Sexual Response*. By observing several hundred women and men in the laboratory, Masters and Johnson discovered that *similar physiological changes take place during sex in both women and men*, a pattern they termed the **sexual response cycle** (Figure 10.8).

The sexual response cycle begins with a phase of *excitement*, characterized by increased muscle tension, engorgement of blood vessels in the genitals causing erection

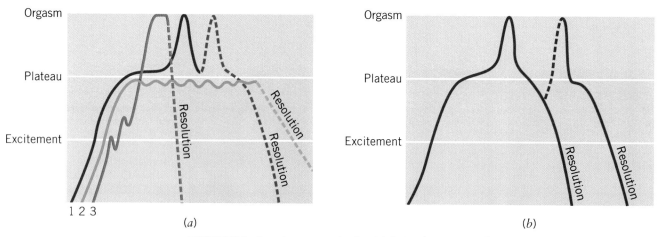

FIGURE 10.8   Sexual response cycles. Part (*a*) depicts the variations of sensation in women's sexual response. Part (*b*) illustrates the typical male sexual response cycle. The two are practically indistinguishable, except for the greater variability in women's experience. *Source:* Masters & Johnson, 1966, p. 5.

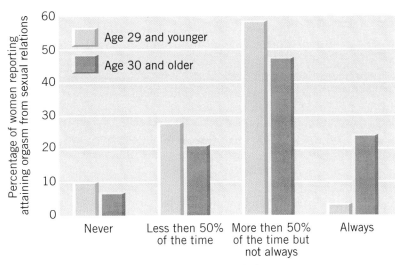

FIGURE 10.9   Female orgasm. Most women achieve orgasm most of the time during sex with male partners, but women over 30 have learned to do so more often. *Source:* Butler, 1976.

of the penis and lubrication of the vagina, and often a skin flush. Maximum arousal occurs during the second, or *plateau*, phase. During this stage, heart rate, respiration, muscle tension, and blood pressure reach their peak. The third phase, *orgasm*, is characterized by vaginal contractions in females and expulsion of semen in males. During the fourth phase, *resolution*, physiological and psychological functioning gradually return to normal.

The subjective experience of orgasm is very similar in men and women. When given written descriptions of orgasms, psychologists, medical students, and gynecologists are unable to distinguish men's from women's if not told the writer's gender (Vance & Wagner, 1976). This finding makes some sense, given that women and men experience similar rhythmic muscular contractions during orgasm.

However, the female sexual response cycle does seem to be more variable. Women describe a few different types of orgasm, from mild pulsations to a sharp climax to repeated sensations of orgasm (Bardwick, 1971). In addition, many women do not reach orgasm with every sexual encounter (Figure 10.9), but they do report a sense of sexual release even without experiencing orgasm (Butler, 1976).

In many animal species, females and males are genetically programmed to follow very specific, stereotyped mating rituals, with attraction and mating behavior often controlled by pheromones. In the American cockroach, pheromone detection leads the male to touch its antennae to the female's antennae, spread its wings, and turn 180 degrees in a courtship dance (Seelinger & Schuderer, 1985). Even in species less reliant on pheromonal communication, mating behavior is often rigidly instinctive.

Humans do not have the same kinds of genetically based mating rituals or mating seasons as other animals. However, biological influences on human dating and mating are obvious, from the "plumage" displayed by both sexes at a fraternity mixer, to scents with names like "Passion" and "Musk," to the simple fact that most humans choose to mate only with members of their own species.

Biology and Sexual Motivation   Many key aspects of sexual behavior in humans and other animals are under hormonal control. Hormones have two effects on the nervous system and behavior: organizational and activational.

Organizational Effects   Hormones exert **organizational effects** *on the circuitry, or "organization," of the brain* and thereby influence sexual behavior. In humans, these effects occur prenatally. Fetuses will develop into females unless something very particular happens. This "something particular" is the presence of two kinds of

Human sexuality differs substantially from sexuality in other animal species—or does it?

Big Picture φ Question 3

To what extent is human psychology continuous with the psychology of other animals?

Apply & Discuss

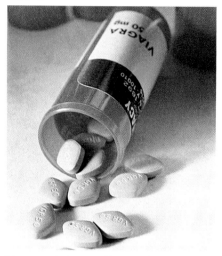

Many people have problems with sexual functioning at some point in their lives. These include trouble getting and keeping an erection, premature ejaculation, inhibited desire, and sexual inhibitions of other sorts that lead to reduced sexual satisfaction or to marital distress.

■ How freely should doctors dispense Viagra without thoroughly examining a patient and his or her partner psychologically as well as physically?

Big Picture φ Question 4

To what extent is human nature particular versus universal?

hormones secreted in the third month of pregnancy. One hormone "turns off" female development. The other set of hormones, called *androgens* (of which the most important is *testosterone*), "turns on" male development. Doctors can often tell the sex of a fetus by the fourth month using ultrasound. Other hormones, such as estrogen, appear to have organizational effects that lead to nonreproductive differences between males and females, such as cognitive differences (McEwen et al., 1998; Chapter 3).

The fact that some hormones turn male development on while others turn female development off explains some otherwise perplexing syndromes (Money, 1987; Money & Ehrhardt, 1972). In **androgen insensitivity syndrome**, *a genetic male develops female genitalia*. The testes secrete androgens, but a genetic defect leads to an absence of androgen receptors. Thus, the body responds as if no androgen were present. The child is reared as a girl, usually leading a perfectly normal life, except that she does not develop internal female organs (and hence is sterile) because the hormone secreted by the testes that *turns off* female development continues to function. People with this disorder, who are by all outward appearances female, are rarely attracted to other females, even though they have testes instead of ovaries. (Their testicles are not externally visible.)

A very different course of development occurs in **congenital adrenal hyperplasia**, *a condition in which the adrenal glands secrete too much androgen, leading to masculinization of the genitals in females*. The result is an enlarged clitoris and labia that may resemble a penis and scrotum. (In utero, the tissue that becomes the scrotum in males will become labia if the testes do not secrete androgens.) Among a sample of women with this very rare disorder who would discuss their sexual orientation, roughly half reported that they were homosexual or bisexual (Money et al., 1984).

In rodents, the organizational effects of hormones continue postnatally. As a result, psychologists can study these effects experimentally (rather than by studying "experiments of nature," such as androgen insensitivity syndrome) by surgically removing the testes in males (castration) or the ovaries in females (ovarectomy). Male rats castrated at birth become sexually receptive to males if given female hormones in adulthood, manifesting the characteristic female mating behavior of hunching over and exposing the hindquarters (Edwards & Einhorn, 1986; Olster & Blaustein, 1989).

Activational Effects   Once the brain circuitry is in place, hormones exert **activational effects**, *activating brain circuits that produce psychobiological changes*, such as the development of secondary sex characteristics (e.g., breasts in adolescent females and facial hair in males). When puberty begins, for example, the hypothalamus sends signals to the pituitary to secrete hormones that in turn activate the testes and ovaries.

In males, hormones produce fluctuations in sexual arousal. Studies show a direct association between levels of testosterone in the bloodstream and sexual activity, desire, and arousal in men (Schiavi et al., 1991; Udry et al., 1985). One study demonstrated the relationship experimentally by administering doses of testosterone to adult males (Alexander et al., 1997). During the time in which their testosterone levels were chemically inflated, the men reported more sexual desire and enjoyment when presented with erotic auditory stimulation. They also showed increased attention to sexual words presented in the unattended channel in a dichotic listening task. The data are less clear for women (see Hedricks, 1994; Regan, 1996).

Culture and Sexual Behavior   Although biology plays an important role in sexual motivation, anthropological studies show enormous cultural diversity in both the ways people carry out sexual acts and the types of behaviors they consider acceptable (Davis & Whitten, 1987). Among the Basongye people of the Congo, for instance, the conventional position for intercourse is for partners to lie facing each other with the woman on her left side and the man on his right; the woman lifts her right leg to allow the man to enter (Merriam, 1971). In many parts of Australia,

Melanesia, and India, the woman typically lies on her back as the man squats between her legs (Gebhard, 1971), whereas in Western culture the male lying prone on top of the female is more typical.

Cultures also differ in their conceptions of male and female sexuality. Western cultures view men as having greater sexual needs. Other cultures believe just the opposite (Gordon & Shankweiler, 1971; Griffitt, 1987).

INTERIM SUMMARY

Sexual motivation and behavior are highly variable across cultures and individuals. Masters and Johnson discovered a common pattern of physiological changes that takes place in both women and men during sex called the **sexual response cycle**. Hormones influence sexual behavior through both **organizational effects**, which influence the developing circuitry of the brain, and **activational effects**, in which hormones activate those circuits.

Sexual Orientation

Sexual orientation refers to *the direction of a person's enduring sexual attraction: to members of the same sex, the opposite sex, or both*. Determining a person's sexual orientation is not as easy as it may seem. Many people report having occasional homosexual fantasies or encounters even though they are not homosexual. Stigma, discrimination, religious values, and violence directed against homosexuals lead some people whose sexual motives and fantasies are primarily homosexual to behave heterosexually or to abstain from sex, to deny their homosexuality, or to take on the trappings of a heterosexual lifestyle, such as marriage to a member of the opposite sex.

Prevalence of Homosexuality An exclusive homosexual orientation is rare among animals, but homosexual behaviors occur frequently among many species, from lizards to chimpanzees (Money, 1987; Srivastava et al., 1991). The incidence of homosexuality has varied substantially historically and cross-culturally (Adams, 1985; Herdt, 1997). In a large part of the world, stretching from Sumatra throughout Melanesia, males almost universally participate in homosexual activities several years before they reach marriageable age (Herdt, 1984, 1997; Money & Ehrhardt, 1972). Yet even in some of these cultures, in which homosexual activity is normative during a particular time in life, the concept of homosexuality as a permanent state does not exist (Herdt, 1997).

In contemporary Western societies, approximately 2 to 7 percent of men and 1 percent of women consider themselves homosexual, although the numbers vary depending on how researchers phrase the questions (see Ellis & Ames, 1987; Pillard et al., 1981). Until relatively recently, both laypeople and the psychiatric community considered homosexuality a disorder; in fact, the official diagnostic manual of the American Psychiatric Association classified it as a disorder until 1973. People harbor many misperceptions about homosexuality, but one of the most pervasive is that homosexuality is a sexual *preference*. Psychologist John Money (1987), who has conducted some of the best-known research on homosexuality (and on sexuality in general), argues that people no more choose their sexual orientation than they select their native language or decide to be right handed.

Early Markers of Homosexual Orientation An accumulating body of research demonstrates that children who prefer to dress or act in ways typically associated with the opposite sex are more likely to become homosexual than other children; this is especially true in males (Bailey & Zucker, 1995). In fact, the best predictor of male homosexuality in adulthood is the presence in childhood of marked behavioral characteristics of the opposite sex, sometimes called "sissy" behavior (Bell et al., 1981; Green, 1987). Although this pattern applies only to a subset of homosexual men, and

Apply & Discuss

▪ Are most males innately wired to find the female form appealing, or is this attraction primarily learned behavior?

cross-gender behavior is present in some boys who do not become homosexual, it is a strong predictor nonetheless.

Consider an example described in an interview with the mother of an eight-year-old boy (Green, 1987, pp. 2–3):

> *Mother:* He acts like a sissy. He has expressed the wish to be a girl. He doesn't play with boys. He's afraid of boys, because he's afraid to play boys' games. He used to like to dress in girls' clothing. He would still like to, only we have absolutely put our foot down. And he talks like a girl, sometimes walks like a girl, acts like a girl.
>
> *Interviewer:* What was the very earliest thing that you noticed?
>
> *Mother:* Wanting to put on a blouse of mine, a pink and white blouse which if he'd put it on it would fit him like a dress. And he was very excited about the whole thing, and leaped around and danced around the room. I didn't like it and I just told him to take it off and I put it away. He kept asking for it.
>
> *Interviewer:* You mentioned that he's expressed the wish to be a girl. Has he ever said, "I am a girl"?
>
> *Mother:* Playing in front of the mirror, he'll undress for bed, and he's standing in front of the mirror and he took his penis and he folded it under, and he said, "Look, Mommy, I'm a girl."

A cross-cultural study reported the same finding in females: A major characteristic distinguishing homosexual and heterosexual females in Brazil, Peru, the Philippines, and the United States was cross-gendered childhood behavior (Whitam & Mathy, 1991). Lesbians in all four cultures were more interested in boys' toys and clothes and less interested in "girl things" as defined by their cultures than were their heterosexual peers.

From Brain to Behavior   The Biology of Homosexuality

Big Picture φ Question 6

What is the relation between nature and nurture in shaping psychological processes?

Apply & Discuss

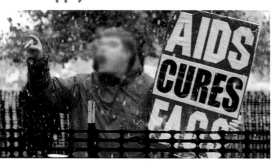

■ If homosexuality is substantially influenced by genetics, is there any difference between intolerance toward homosexuality and persecution of people with blue eyes or diabetes (both of which also show considerable heritability)?

If sexual orientation is not a matter of conscious choice, what are its causes? Homosexuality is probably the end result of many causes, some environmental and some biological. However, most environmental hypotheses (such as absent or weak fathers and dominant mothers) have received little empirical support.

Researchers who emphasize the nature side of the nature–nurture question have had more success, particularly in explaining male homosexuality (Figure 10.10). One study found differences in the neuroanatomy of homosexual and heterosexual men (LeVay, 1991). The investigator compared the brains of homosexual men (who died of AIDS complications) with men and women presumed to be heterosexual. He found that one specific set of nuclei in the hypothalamus was twice as large in heterosexual men as in women and homosexual men.

A more recent study compared the EEG patterns of heterosexual and homosexual men and women while performing a mental rotation task (at which men usually excel) and a verbal task (at which women usually outperform men). Heterosexual and lesbian women did not differ substantially from each other on either task. However, gay men's EEG patterns looked more like those of heterosexual women than heterosexual men on the mental rotation task (Wegesin, 1998). Across a number of studies, a clear finding has also emerged that homosexual men and women are more likely than heterosexuals to be left handed. This suggests early differences between heterosexuals and homosexuals (or, more likely, a subset of homosexual men and women) in the organization of the brain (Lalumiere et al., 2000).

The Behavioral Genetics of Homosexuality

What causes these differences? An increasing body of evidence from behavioral genetics suggests that homosexuality in both men and women is highly heritable (Bailey et al., 1999). Several studies have found a higher incidence of homosexuality among male relatives of male homosexuals than in the general population (Buhrich et al., 1991). Whereas rates of homosexuality in the general population are estimated at 2 to 7 percent, nearly 25 percent of brothers of male homosexuals in one study were reportedly homosexual (Pillard et al., 1981, 1982).

The most definitive study to date found concordance rates for homosexuality much higher among identical than fraternal twins and adoptive brothers (Bailey & Pillard, 1991). Concordance for homosexuality was 52 percent for monozygotic twins, 22 percent for dizygotic twins, and 11 percent for adoptive brothers, with heritability estimated somewhere between .31 and .74.

The same research group conducted one of the only studies of heritability of homosexuality in women and found a similar pattern: 48 percent concordance for monozygotic twins, 16 percent for dizygotic, and 6 percent for adoptive sisters, with heritability estimates ranging from .27 to .76 (Bailey et al., 1993). Other research similarly finds increased rates of lesbianism among the biological relatives of homosexual women (Pattatucci & Hamer, 1995).

Recently, researchers have begun to investigate the genetics of homosexuality experimentally. One team of investigators *created* male homosexuality in fruit flies by inserting genetic material to produce mutations (Yamamoto et al., 1996). These "gay" fruit flies all showed mutations at precisely the same chromosomal locus that has been shown to distinguish heterosexual fruit flies from a bisexual breed. Although generalizations from fruit flies to humans obviously require caution, the fact that genetic alteration in any organism can predictably alter sexual orientation is clearly of importance.

The data thus suggest that homosexuality is substantially, but certainly not entirely (and probably not in all cases), influenced by genetics. If, as appears to be the case, sexual orientation is in part a preference exercised by our genes instead of our souls, this has substantial implications for public policy and attitudes.

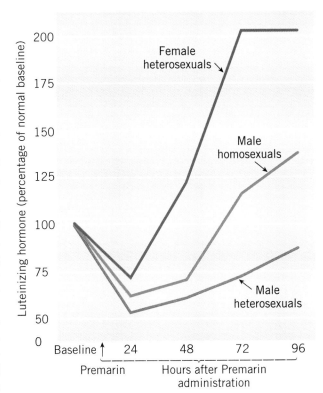

FIGURE 10.10 Hormonal response in male homosexuals. The graph shows the changes in the amount of luteinizing hormone (LH) as a response to injections of the drug Premarin. Premarin increases LH in women and increases testosterone in men. Heterosexual men and women showed the expected hormonal responses to Premarin injection. The response of homosexual males, however, was intermediate between heterosexual men and women. *Source:* Gladue et al., 1984, p. 1496.

INTERIM SUMMARY

Sexual orientation refers to the direction of a person's enduring sexual attraction, to members of the same or opposite sex. Attitudes toward homosexuality differ substantially across cultures. The causes of homosexuality are likely numerous, but particularly for males, mounting evidence suggests that homosexuality is highly heritable and does not likely reflect a "choice."

Psychosocial Motives

Unlike sex, **psychosocial needs** (*personal and interpersonal motives for achievement, power, self-esteem, affiliation, intimacy, and the like*) are less obviously biological; however, many of these needs are strongly influenced by evolved tendencies rooted in our biology. Human infants, like the young of other species, have an inborn tendency to form intense social bonds with their primary caretakers, and toddlers spontaneously exhibit joy at their achievements and frustration at their failures. Once again, nature and nurture jointly weave even the most socially constructed fabrics.

Two major clusters of goals people pursue everywhere are **relatedness** (sometimes called "communion," referring to *motives for connectedness with others*), and

agency (*motives for achievement, autonomy, mastery, power, and other self-oriented goals*) (Bakan, 1966; McAdams, 1999; Woike et al., 1999).

Needs for Relatedness

Human beings have a number of interpersonal needs (Baumeister & Leary, 1995; Weiss, 1986). The earliest to arise in children are related to attachment (Chapter 14). **Attachment motivation** refers to *the desire for physical and psychological proximity (closeness) to another person*, so that the individual experiences comfort and pleasure in the other person's presence. Attachment motives form the basis for many aspects of adult love (Cassidy & Shaver, 1999; Main et al., 1985).

A related need common among adults and older children in some cultures is **intimacy**, *a special kind of closeness characterized by self-disclosure, warmth, and mutual caring* (McAdams et al., 1996; Reis & Shaver, 1988). Intimacy needs are often satisfied in adult attachment relationships and deep friendships.

Another social motive is the need for **affiliation**, or *interaction with friends or acquaintances*. Most people need to be with and communicate with other people, whether that means obtaining support after an upsetting experience, sharing good news, or playing sports together. Individuals differ in the extent to which they seek intimate versus affiliative relationships. Some people have many friends and acquaintances but have little need for intimacy. Others desire one or two intimate friends and have little need for a broad social network (Reis & Shaver, 1988; Weiss, 1986).

Social relationships, particularly with people in whom one can confide, are important for both physical and mental health (Chapter 11). For example, women who report having at least one confidante are 10 times less likely to suffer depression following a stressful event than women who do not have someone in whom they can confide (Brown et al., 1975). Lack of supportive relationships is a risk factor for mortality as well (Farmer et al., 1996; House et al., 1988a).

INTERIM SUMMARY

Two clusters of **psychosocial needs** pursued cross-culturally are **relatedness** and **agency** (achievement, autonomy, mastery, power, and other self-oriented goals). Needs for relatedness include attachment, intimacy, and affiliation. Although relatedness needs are psychosocial, the failure to fulfill them can have powerful biological effects, such as sickness or mortality.

Achievement and Other Agency Motives

Motives for power, competence, achievement, autonomy, and self-esteem form a second cluster of motives common to humans throughout the world. As early as the second year of life, infants seem to have a desire to be competent and effective, even when they are not rewarded by their parents (Kagan et al., 1978). This can be clearly seen in the persistence and pride shown by young children as they learn to walk.

According to some theorists (e.g., Epstein, 1998; White, 1959), humans have an innate need to know and understand the world around them and to feel competent in the exercise of their knowledge. Pleasure in knowing and displeasure in feeling uncertain may have evolved as mechanisms that foster exploration of the environment.

Another self-oriented motive is self-esteem. Theorists of many theoretical persuasions—psychodynamic (Kohut, 1971), humanistic (Rogers, 1959), and cognitive–social (Moretti & Higgins, 1999), among others—view self-esteem motivation, the need to view oneself in a positive light, as a fundamental motivator of behavior (Chapter 17).

Need for Achievement   The **need for achievement**—*to do well, to succeed, and to avoid failure*—is the best researched psychosocial motive. That is not surprising in view of our culture's emphasis on personal achievement in school, sports, careers, and practically every domain in which our actions can be described in terms of success and failure.

People high in achievement motivation tend to choose moderately difficult tasks (those with about a 50/50 chance of success) over very easy or very difficult tasks (Atkinson, 1977; Slade & Rush, 1991). They enjoy being challenged and take pleasure in accomplishing a difficult task but are often motivated to avoid failure. In one classic study, subjects played a ringtoss game and were free to choose their own distance from the target (Atkinson & Litwin, 1960). Those who scored high in achievement motivation selected distances that were challenging but not impossible. In contrast, subjects who scored low in achievement motivation and had a high fear of failure stood either very close to the target or impossibly far, positions that guaranteed either success or a good excuse for failing.

How do experimental findings such as these translate into everyday behaviors? People with a high need for achievement tend to work more persistently than others to achieve a goal, and they take more pride in their accomplishments when they succeed (Atkinson, 1977). Not surprisingly, they are consequently more likely to succeed. They also tend to attribute their past successes to their abilities and their past failures to forces beyond their control, which increases confidence and persistence in the face of adverse feedback (Dweck, 1975; Weiner, 1974). Students with high achievement motivation are likely to select a major that suits their abilities, commit to a study schedule that is rigorous but not impossible, and work hard to succeed within those limits. The consequences of achievement motivation extend far beyond the classroom.

In an economically depressed area of India, where government programs had been ineffective in raising the standard of living, psychologist David McClelland undertook an experiment with far-reaching consequences. He taught local businessmen to fantasize about high achievement and to problem solve ways to succeed (McClelland, 1978; McClelland & Winter, 1969). Over time, they began new businesses and employed new workers at a much higher rate than businessmen in a comparable town in the same region. In Western cultures, achievement motivation predicts not only occupational success but even people's earnings as much as 25 years later (Dunifon & Duncan, 1998).

Pride at mastery appears to emerge spontaneously in the second year of life.

Components of Achievement Motivation   As with other motives, people do not express achievement motivation in every domain. For example, an achievement-oriented premedical student may place little value in succeeding in literature courses and may be undisturbed by her failure to bake a fluffy soufflé. From a cognitive perspective, motives may be expressed selectively because they are hierarchically organized, with some sections of the hierarchy carrying more motivational weight than others (Figure 10.11).

Achievement goals themselves appear to reflect a blend of at least three motives: performance-approach, performance-avoidance, and mastery goals (Elliot & Harackiewicz, 1996; Rawsthorne & Elliot, 1999). **Performance goals** are *motives to achieve at a particular level, usually a socially defined standard*, such as getting an A in a class (Dweck, 1986). The emphasis of performance goals is on the *outcome*—on success or failure in meeting a standard.

Some people are more *motivated to attain a goal* (**performance-approach goals**), whereas others are more *motivated by the fear of not attaining it* (**performance-avoidance goals**). Thus, if I am skiing, I may be motivated by the desire to know (and tell people) I skied a black-diamond slope—a slope of considerable difficulty. Skiing a tough slope is a performance-approach goal. Alternatively, I may stay on the baby slopes to avoid skiing down the hill on my buttocks, a performance-avoidance goal.

Performance goals, whether for approach or avoidance, are about achieving a concrete outcome—obtaining success or avoiding failure. In contrast, **mastery goals**

FIGURE 10.11   Cognitive structure of achievement motivation. A premedical student attaches different motivational weights to different sections of the hierarchy. Red lines indicate strong motivation; blue lines indicate weaker motivation.

are *motives to increase one's competence, mastery, or skill*. If I am motivated by mastery goals, my interest is in developing my skill or technique—enjoying the sheer pleasure of skiing more quickly or competently—not in being able to brag about my exploits or to avoid the snickers of little children passing me by.

The three types of goals underlying achievement actually predict different outcomes. For example, children with high performance-approach goals tend to get good grades, but they may or may not develop intrinsic interest in the material (Elliot & Church, 1997). Students with high performance-avoidance goals tend to get both low grades and less intrinsic pleasure from what they are doing, presumably because of their preoccupation with fears of failure. Children motivated by mastery goals often get good grades as well as develop intrinsic interest in the material.

In the future, researchers are likely to tease apart fine-grained distinctions such as these in most motivational systems. In fact, multiple motives probably underlie most behavior. Asking someone out for dinner may reflect needs for affiliation, attachment, food, sex, altruism, and self-esteem—and a central task of the person being asked out may involve figuring out which motives are primary.

Parenting, Culture, and Achievement   The need for achievement is primarily a learned motive, which numerous studies have linked to patterns of child rearing. Children with high achievement motivation tend to have parents who encourage them to attempt new tasks slightly beyond their reach, praise success when it occurs, encourage independent thinking, discourage complaining, and prompt their children to try new solutions when they fail (McClelland, 1985; Weiss & Schwarz, 1996; Winterbottom, 1953).

Parenting always occurs within a cultural context, and motivation for achievement varies considerably across cultures and historical periods. David McClelland and his colleagues spent years exploring the links among culture, child rearing, and achievement. One hypothesis, based on the theory that cultures teach motives through the stories they tell, is that a culture's myths, folktales, and children's stories should be related to its child-rearing practices and level of economic development. A prominent children's story in our own achievement-oriented society is *The Little Engine That Could*. From a psychological standpoint, the moral of this story is simple: Those who expect success and strive for it despite adversity will succeed ("I think I can, I think I can….").

In one study, McClelland and his colleagues (1953) rated the folktales of eight Native American cultures for the extent to which they expressed achievement themes. Another set of coders independently rated the cultures for independence training, noting the age at which training began and the strength and frequency of punishment for failure to behave autonomously. The results were striking: The more achievement themes in folktales, the more focus on autonomy and independence in child rearing (Table 10.1).

Big Picture φ Question 4

To what extent is human nature particular versus universal?

Table 10.1 ■■ ■ Ranking of Cultures on Need for Achievement and Independence Training

Culture	Rank	
	Need for Achievement Measured from Folktales	Independence Training (Age and Severity)
Navajo	1	1
Central Apache	2	2
Hopi	3	4
Comanche	4	3
Sanpoil	5	5.5
Western Apache	6	5.5
Paiute	7	7
Flatheads	8	8

Source: Adapted from McClelland et al., 1953, p. 294.

INTERIM SUMMARY

Agency needs include motives such as power, competence, achievement, autonomy, and self-esteem. The **need for achievement**—to succeed and to avoid failure—affects the goals people pursue in everyday life, the tasks they choose to tackle, and the extent to which they persist in the face of difficulty. Achievement goals themselves reflect a blend of at least three motives: **performance-approach goals** (the desire to meet a socially defined standard), **performance-avoidance goals** (the desire to avoid failure, particularly when it is publicly observable), and **mastery goals** (the desire to master the skill). Parenting practices, which themselves reflect cultural values, substantially affect achievement motivation.

The Nature and Causes of Human Motives

Having explored a variety of motives from multiple perspectives, we return to the basic questions with which we began. First, to what extent are people pulled by internal needs or pushed by external stimuli? Examination of the most biological of needs—hunger and sex—makes clear that even where a motive is undeniably rooted in biology, its strength depends in part on whether an appropriate stimulus presents itself, whether the stimulus is a hot fudge sundae or a hot date. A stimulus by itself, however, never motivates behavior unless the person has acquired some motivational tendency toward it. A hot fudge sundae that calls one person's name will have no effect on another who is indifferent to ice cream or chocolate.

A second and related question concerns the extent to which human motivation is rooted in biology or in culture and experience. As in nearly every other discussion of nature and nurture in this book, the answer is an intellectually unsatisfying "yes." Much as doing so might make us more comfortable, we cannot neatly parse motives into biological and psychosocial, because the most biological needs are shaped by culture and experience, and the most psychosocial motives draw on innate tendencies.

The third question pertains to the roles of thought, feeling, and arousal in motivation: Do people act on the basis of cognition? Emotion? Generalized arousal? The most likely answer is that motivation typically requires both cognition and some form of emotional energy or arousal. To put it another way, cognitive representations or thoughts provide the direction or goals of a motive, and feelings provide the strength or force behind it, but neither alone is likely to move anyone anywhere. In neuropsychological terms, the cortex provides the map for life's journeys, but the hypothalamus and limbic system largely provide the fuel. In the next section, we continue to examine the fuel as we explore emotion.

Emotion

In this section we explore the nature of emotion. Everyone has an intuitive sense of what an emotion is, but emotion can be exceedingly difficult to define. Imagine explaining the concept of emotion to someone who has never experienced one. **Emotion**, or **affect** (a synonym for emotion, pronounced with the accent on the first syllable, as in *apple*), is an *evaluative response (a positive or negative feeling) that typically includes some combination of physiological arousal, subjective experience, and behavioral or emotional expression*. We examine each component of emotion in turn

Physiological Components

Over a century ago, William James (1884) argued that emotion is rooted in bodily experience. According to James, an emotion-inducing stimulus elicits visceral, or gut, reactions and voluntary behaviors such as running or gesturing. The physical experience in turn leads the person to feel aroused, and the arousal stimulates the subjective experience of, for example, fear. In this view, confronting a bear on a camping trip causes a person to run, and running produces fear.

Making Connections

Performance-approach goals and performance-avoidance goals are related to both operant conditioning (Chapter 5) and emotion.

■ Performance-approach goals are linked to positive reinforcement and positive (pleasurable) emotions, such as pride and excitement.

■ Performance-avoidance goals are linked to punishment, negative reinforcement (avoidance of aversive consequences), and negative (unpleasant) emotions such as anxiety, guilt, shame, and sadness.

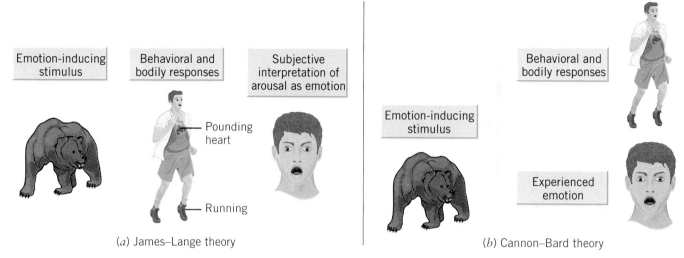

(a) James–Lange theory

(b) Cannon–Bard theory

FIGURE 10.12   The James–Lange and Cannon–Bard theories of emotion. In the James–Lange theory (a), a stimulus leads to a peripheral nervous system response, which in turn is interpreted as an emotion. In the Cannon-Bard theory (b), the stimulus produces simultaneous peripheral responses and subjective experience.

James thus offered a counterintuitive proposition: We do not run because we are afraid; rather, we become afraid because we run (Figure 10.12a). James's theory is sometimes called the *peripheral theory of emotion* because it sees the origins of emotion in the peripheral nervous system. Recall that the peripheral nervous system controls both muscle movements and autonomic responses such as racing heart and shortness of breath in the face of fear-eliciting stimuli (see Chapter 2). At about the same time that James developed his theory, the Danish physiologist Carl Lange (1885) proposed a similar view. Thus, the **James–Lange theory** states that *emotions originate in peripheral nervous system responses that the central nervous system then interprets* (see Lang, 1994).

As the James–Lange theory would predict, some emotional experiences—particularly sexual arousal, fear, and anger—do appear to be blunted in individuals with spinal cord lesions that prevent them from moving or experiencing gut feelings (Hohmann, 1966; Jasmos & Hakmiller, 1975). One man with a cervical spinal cord lesion (a lesion near the neck, which cuts off almost all autonomic signals) compared his feelings of sexual arousal before and after the accident (Hohmann, 1966, p. 148):

> Before I got hurt…I would get a hot, tense feeling all over my body. I've got out and necked a few times since I was hurt, but it doesn't do anything for me. I daydream once in a while about it, and when I'm around a bunch of guys I talk big, but I just don't get worked up anymore.

Other cases of spinal cord injury do not, however, support the James–Lange theory (Bermond et al., 1991), and the theory was challenged on other grounds over a half century ago by Walter Cannon (1927) and Philip Bard (1934). Cannon and Bard noted that autonomic responses are typically slow, occurring about one to two seconds after presentation of a stimulus. In contrast, emotional responses are immediate and often precede both autonomic reactions and behaviors such as running. Further, many different emotional states are linked to the same visceral responses, so that arousal is too generalized to translate directly into discrete emotional experiences. For instance, muscle tension and quickened heart rate accompany sexual arousal, fear, and rage, which people experience as very different emotional states. Thus, the alternative view, known as the **Cannon–Bard theory**, states that *emotion-inducing stimuli simultaneously elicit both an emotional experience, such as fear, and bodily responses, such as sweaty palms* (Figure 10.12b).

Cannon and Bard's first criticism (about the relative speed of autonomic and emotional responses) continues to be valid. However, their second criticism, that visceral arousal is general, has been challenged by more recent research. In fact, although some forms of arousal are probably general, different emotions are in fact associated with distinct patterns of autonomic activity, such as heart rate acceleration, finger temperature, and skin conductance (a measure of sweat on the palms related to arousal or anxiety, also known as *galvanic skin response*, or *GSR*) (Ekman, 1992; Levenson, 1992; Levenson et al., 1990). Anger and fear, for example, produce greater heart rate acceleration than does happiness. This finding makes evolutionary sense, because anger and fear are related to fight-or-flight responses, which require the heart to pump more blood to the muscles.

Anger and fear are also distinguishable from each other autonomically. The language we use to describe anger ("hot under the collar") appears to be physiologically accurate: People who are angry get "heated" in their surface skin temperatures. Data from non-Western cultures such as Indonesia suggest that these links between emotional experience and physiology are similar cross-culturally and appear to be wired into the brain (Levenson et al., 1992).

INTERIM SUMMARY

Emotion, or **affect**, is an evaluative response that typically includes physiological arousal, subjective experience, and behavioral or emotional expression. The **James–Lange theory** asserts that emotions originate in peripheral nervous system responses, which the central nervous system then interprets. The **Cannon–Bard theory** argues that emotion-inducing stimuli simultaneously elicit both an emotional experience and bodily responses. Although people likely experience some forms of general arousal that require interpretation, different emotions are associated with distinct patterns of emotional activation.

Subjective Experience

The most familiar component of emotion is *subjective experience*, or what it feels like to be happy, sad, angry, or elated. Individuals differ tremendously in the intensity of their emotional states (Bryant et al., 1996; Larsen et al., 1996), and these differences are already apparent in preschool children (Cole et al., 1997). At the extreme high end of the bell curve of emotional intensity in adults are people with severe personality disorders (Chapter 15), whose emotions spiral out of control (M. Linehan, 1987a; Wagner & Linehan, 1999).

At the other end of the bell curve are people with a psychological disorder called *Alexithymia*, the inability to recognize one's own feelings (Sifneos, 1973; Taylor & Taylor, 1997). (*A-lexi-thymia* literally means *without language for emotion*) People with alexithymia often report what seem to be meaningful, painful, or traumatic experiences with bland indifference. One alexithymic patient told his doctor about a "strange event" that had occurred the previous day. He had found himself shaking and felt his eyes tearing and wondered if he had been crying. The patient showed no recognition that his tears could have been related to frightening news he had received that morning about the results of a biopsy (D. Hulihan, personal communication, 1992).

Emotional Disclosure   Just as being unaware of one's feelings can lead to illness, knowing and attending to them can have a positive impact on health (Chapter 2). In one study, Holocaust survivors spoke for one to two hours about their experiences during World War II. The investigators then measured the extent to which they had talked emotionally about traumatic events (Pennebaker et al., 1989). The more emotion they expressed as they recounted the events, the better their health for over a year later. In another study, patients with painful arthritis spoke into a tape recorder for 15 minutes a day about either stressful or trivial events (Kelley et al., 1997). Those who spoke about stressful events were in better emotional and physical shape three

Big Picture φ Question 4

To what extent is human nature particular versus universal?

Apply & Discuss

How do you explain that, sometimes, when you are extremely happy, you cry?

months later, and, the more unpleasant emotion they experienced while discussing stressful events, the less painful their joints were three months later. The moral of the story? No pain, no gain.

Researchers have been tracking down some of the precise mechanisms through which emotional disclosure affects health (Pennebaker, 1997a, 1997b; Pennebaker & Seagal, 1999). Writing about stressful or unpleasant events has been shown to increase the functioning of specific cells in the immune system (the system of cells in the body that fight off disease). Disclosure also decreases autonomic reactivity that keeps the body on red alert and takes its toll over time.

Perhaps most importantly, disclosure permits a change in cognitive functioning that allows the person to rework the traumatic experience in thought and memory. People who benefit from disclosure tend to begin with disorganized, disjointed narratives about the event, suggesting emotional disruption of their thinking. After writing, their narratives become more coherent. The more complex and coherent people's narratives after disclosing traumatic events, the more their health improves (Suedfeld & Pennebaker, 1997).

Feeling Happy   Although psychologists tend to focus on unpleasant emotions such as anxiety and depression, increasingly researchers have begun studying the subjective experience of happiness (Diener, 2000; Myers, 2000). Men and women tend to be equally happy, as do older and younger people (contrary to many people's emotional forecasts about their own sense of well-being as they age; see Chapter 14). Rates of reported happiness do, however, differ across cultures. The percentage of people who describe themselves as "very happy" ranges from a low of 10 percent in Portugal to a high of 40 percent in the Netherlands.

One predictor of happiness is the extent to which a culture is more individualistic or collectivistic: People in individualistic cultures, which focus on the needs and desires of individuals, tend to be happier than people in collectivist cultures, which emphasize the needs of the group. Another predictor is political: The correlation between life satisfaction and the number of uninterrupted years of democracy in a country is .85, which is one of the largest observed correlations ever produced in psychology between two seemingly dissimilar variables (Inglehart, 1991).

Big Picture φ Question 4

To what extent is human nature particular versus universal?

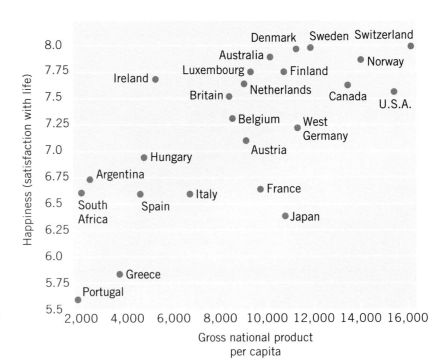

FIGURE 10.13   Happiness in 24 nations. Happiness is strongly correlated with gross national product (GNP), a measure of economic prosperity. *Source:* Adapted from Myers & Diener, 1995, p. 13.

Does money buy happiness? Yes and no. Across cultures, the correlation between self-reported happiness and economic prosperity is substantial (Figure 10.13). Within cultures, however, happiness and income are not highly correlated. Apparently, a decent income is necessary but not sufficient for happiness. Other variables that predict happiness are a large network of close friends and strong religious faith (Myers, 2000).

INTERIM SUMMARY

The subjective experience of emotion refers to what the emotion feels like to the individual. People differ tremendously in emotional intensity. The extent to which people experience happiness is relatively stable across age and gender but differs substantially across cultures.

Emotional Expression

A third component of emotion is **emotional expression**, *the overt behavioral signs of emotion*. People express feelings in various ways, including facial expressions, posture, gestures, and tone of voice.

Facial Expression and Emotion In a twist on William James's peripheral hypothesis of emotion, some theorists argue that the face is the primary center of emotion (Tomkins, 1962, 1980). Whereas James asserted that we feel afraid because we run, these theorists argue that we feel afraid because our face shows fear. In this view, emotion consists of muscular responses located primarily in the face (and, secondarily, muscular and glandular responses throughout the body).

Different facial expressions are, in fact, associated with different emotions (Ekman, 1992; Izard, 1971, 1997). The relationship between emotion and facial muscle movements is uniform enough across individuals and cultures that electrodes attached to the face to detect muscle movements allow psychologists to assess directly both the *valence* (positive or negative tone) and intensity of emotion (Tassinary & Cacioppo, 1992). Some similarity across cultures exists even in the colors people use to describe emotions, such as the association of anger with seeing red—perhaps because anger is associated with facial flushing and an increase in temperature (see Hupka et al., 1997).

Facial expressions not only *indicate* a person's emotional state, they also *influence* the physiological and subjective components of the emotion. In a classic study, researchers gave participants specific directions to contract their facial muscles in particular ways, for instance, as in Figure 10.14 (Ekman et al., 1983). Though the participants (actors) had not been instructed to show a particular emotion, they created expressions characteristic of fear, anger, sadness, happiness, surprise, and disgust. Participants held each expression for 10 seconds, while the experimenters measured their heart rate and finger temperature.

Making Connections

In *Girl Interrupted*, Angelina Jolie plays a young woman with borderline personality disorder, a psychological disorder characterized by intense emotions, particularly anger and depression, that spiral out of control (Chapter 15).

Then imitate the action of the tiger: Stiffen the sinews, summon up the blood, Disguise fair nature with hard-favored rage; Then lend the eye a terrible aspect; Let it pry through the portage of the head Like the brass cannon... Now set the teeth and stretch the nostril wide, Hold hard the breath and bend up every spirit To his full height!

SHAKESPEARE,
Henry V, III i

(a) (b) (c)

FIGURE 10.14 Creating fear in the face. Participants instructed to (*a*) raise their eyebrows and pull them together, (*b*) then raise their upper eyelids, and (*c*) stretch their lips back toward their ears showed physiological changes consistent with fear.

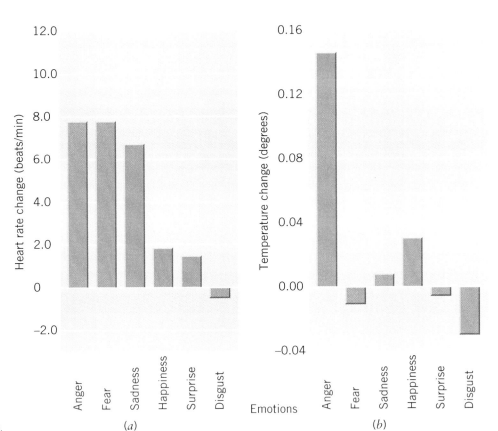

FIGURE 10.15 Facial expression and physiological response. The graph shows changes in heart rate and finger temperature associated with certain emotional expressions. Anger, fear, and sadness elevate heart rate, but of these three emotions, only anger also increases temperature. People presumably learn to distinguish these affects based on subtle physiological cues such as these. *Source:* Ekman et al., 1983, p. 1209.

Big Picture φ Question 4

To what extent is human nature particular versus universal?

The researchers found a striking causal relation between the simple act of changing facial expression and patterns of autonomic response (Figure 10.15). More recent research has found that when people imitate positive and negative expressions in photographs, their own emotions tend to change accordingly (Kleike et al., 1998). Still other studies document distinct EEG activity associated with the different posed emotions and changes in subjective experience that accompany them (Ekman & Davidson, 1993; Izard, 1990; Lanzetta et al., 1976). Similar effects appear to occur with other nonverbal expressions of emotion: People who receive positive feedback about their appearance experience more pride when they receive the feedback while standing upright rather than hunching over (Stepper & Strack, 1993)!

Not only do emotions differ from one another physiologically, but so do genuine and false emotional displays. True and fake smiles appear to be physiologically different and rely on different sets of muscles (Ekman, 1992; Ekman & Keltner, 1997). True smiles use eye muscles not used in fake smiles. Children actually have some capacity to detect these differences as early as the preschool years (Banerjee, 1997).

Culture and Emotional Display Rules Before research documented the physiological and anatomical differences among emotions, psychologists and sociologists hotly debated whether people across cultures ascribe the same meaning to a smile or a frown. In fact, some facial expressions are universally recognized (see Ekman & Oster, 1979; Scherer & Wallbott, 1994). Participants in one classic study viewed photographs showing the faces of North American actors expressing fear, anger, happiness, and other emotions. Participants from diverse cultural groups, ranging from Swedes and Kenyans to members of a preliterate tribe in New Guinea with minimal Western contact, all recognized certain emotions (Ekman, 1971).

Cross-cultural studies have identified six facial expressions recognized by people of every culture that was examined (Figure 10.16): surprise, fear, anger, disgust, hap-

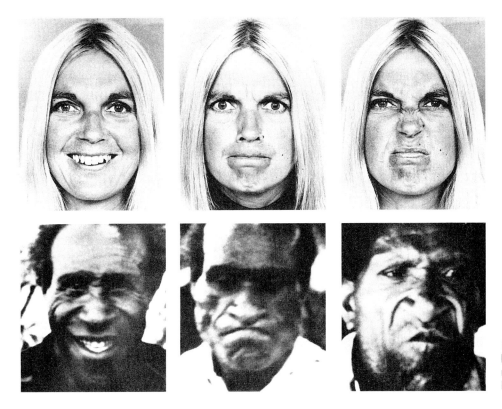

FIGURE 10.16 Universal facial expressions. Members of the remote Fore tribe of New Guinea recognize Western facial expressions, just as Western college students recognize the expressions on Fore faces.

piness, and sadness (Ekman & Oster, 1979). Shame and interest also may have universal facial expressions (Izard, 1977). These findings suggest that some emotions are biologically linked not only to distinct autonomic states but also to certain facial movements, which people in all cultures can decode.

Not all facial expressions, however, are the same from culture to culture. People learn to control the way they express many emotions, using *patterns of emotional expression considered appropriate within their culture or subculture*, called **display rules** (Ekman & Friesen, 1975). Some of these differences appear to reflect such simple variables as geography: A study of a large sample of participants from 26 countries found, as many observers and travelers had long believed, that both within and across countries, southerners tend to be more emotionally expressive than northerners (Pennebaker et al., 1997).

In another study, Japanese and North American participants viewed a film depicting a painful adolescent initiation ceremony involving ritual circumcision. When they were unaware that they were being observed, participants from the two cultures showed the same facial responses. When participants believed they might be observed, however, their reactions were quite different. The North Americans still showed revulsion, but the Japanese, socialized to show far less emotion, masked their expressions (Ekman, 1977). When looking at facial displays of emotion, the Japanese tend to rate facial displays as less intense than Westerners but view the internal experience as *more* intense, a suggestion that when they see a facial display, they expect it to be somewhat masked (Matsumoto et al., 1999).

Gender and Emotional Expression   Do display rules differ by gender as well as culture? The best evidence available suggests that women probably experience emotion more intensely, are better able to read emotions from other people's faces and nonverbal cues, and express emotion more intensely and openly than men (Brody, 1999; Brody & Hall, 2000). For example, a recent study found that women and men differed in both emotional expression and autonomic arousal while watching

Big Picture φ Question 6

What is the relation between nature and nurture in shaping psychological processes?

Big Picture φ Question 5

To what extent are psychological processes the same in men and women?

Apply & Discuss

Research suggests that moving muscles in the face can lead to changes in emotion. Whoever wrote the lyric about letting a smile be your umbrella on a rainy day may have been a savvy psychologist.

▪ When is "putting on a happy face" adaptive? When is it maladaptive?

▪ In what ways can keeping a stiff upper lip influence the way other people respond, which, in turn, may affect health and happiness?

emotional films, suggesting that men and women differ in their experience of emotion (Kring & Gordon, 1998).

These distinctions apply to children as well. While watching videotapes of emotional interactions, girls show facial expressions that more closely match those of the people on the videos, suggesting greater emotional empathy; they are also better at verbally describing the emotions of the people they view (Strayer & Roberts, 1997). Interestingly, even children as young as three years old recognize that females are more likely to express fear, sadness, and happiness and that males are more likely to express anger (Birnbaum, 1983).

The reasons for gender differences in emotion are a matter of debate (Brody, 1999). On the one hand, they likely reflect adaptation to the roles that men and women have historically tended to occupy. Women are generally more comfortable with emotions such as love, happiness, warmth, shame, guilt, and sympathy, which foster affiliation and caretaking. Men, on the other hand, are socialized to compete and to fight; hence, they avoid "soft" emotions that display their vulnerabilities to competitors and enemies or discourage them from asserting their dominance when the need arises (Brody & Hall, 2000).

Parents talk to their children differently about emotion from at least the time they are toddlers. They talk more about feelings with girls, implicitly teaching them how—and how much—to think about and express their emotions (Cervantes & Callahan, 1998; Dunn et al., 1987). Little boys, in contrast, often learn that only "sissies" cry and that feeling scared and showing signs of emotional vulnerability are unmanly. Importantly, however, ethnicity moderates some of these observed gender differences.

Gender differences also make sense from an evolutionary perspective. Nurturing children, for example, requires attention to feelings—which can be dysfunctional for males when they are fighting, defending territory, or competing with other males for mates. This is not, of course, absolute: Men who understand others well, which means being able to read their emotions, are likely to be more socially successful and to compete more successfully for females. Thus, males may have pressures both to feel and not to feel.

INTERIM SUMMARY

Emotional expression refers to the overt behavioral signs of emotion. Different facial muscles are associated with different emotions. Facial expressions not only indicate but can influence the subjective experience of emotion. **Display rules** are patterns of emotional expression considered appropriate within a culture or subculture. Display rules differ not only by culture but also by gender. Women appear to experience emotions more intensely and to read people's emotions more accurately.

A Taxonomy of Emotions

Some aspects of emotion, then, are universal, whereas others vary by culture and gender. How many emotions do humans experience, and how many of these are innate?

Basic Emotions   Psychologists have attempted to produce a list of **basic emotions**, *emotions common to the human species, with characteristic physiological, subjective, and expressive components* (Ekman, 1999; Izard & Buechler, 1980). Basic emotions are similar to primary colors in perception: All other emotions and emotional blends are derived from them.

Although theorists generate slightly different lists, and some even argue against the existence of basic emotions (Ortony & Turner, 1990), most classifications include five to nine emotions (J. Russell, 1991). All theorists list anger, fear, happiness, sadness, and disgust. Surprise, contempt, interest, shame, guilt, joy, trust, and anticipation sometimes make the roster (Plutchik, 1980; Shaver et al., 1987; Tomkins, 1980).

Similar lists of basic emotions were compiled years ago in India (Lynch, 1990) and in China, where an encyclopedia from the first century B.C. included the following entry (*The Li Chi*, cited in Russell, 1991, p. 426):

> What are the feelings of men? They are joy, anger, sadness, fear, love, disliking, and liking. These seven feelings belong to men without their learning them.

Beyond the basic emotions, cultures vary in the extent to which they elaborate and distinguish emotional states (Kitayama & Markus, 1994; Mesquita et al., 1997; J. Russell, 1991). The Tahitian language has 46 different words for anger (much as English has several terms, such as annoyance, frustration, and rage) but no word for sadness. The Tahitians do not even have a word for *emotion*. In some African languages, the same word denotes both anger and sadness; members of these cultures seldom seem to distinguish between the two.

Positive and Negative Affect   A distinction that is perhaps even more basic than the basic emotions is that between **positive affect** (*pleasant emotions*) and **negative affect** (*unpleasant emotions*). Researchers discovered the distinction between positive and negative affect through factor analysis, a statistical procedure that combines variables that are highly correlated with each other into superordinate variables, called factors (Chapter 8). Factor analyses of people's ratings of their tendency to experience a variety of emotions suggest that these two factors, positive and negative affect, underlie people's self-reported emotions across cultures (see Watson, 2000; Watson & Clark, 1992; Watson & Tellegen, 1985). Within these two factors, emotions are substantially intercorrelated. In other words, people who frequently experience one negative emotion, such as guilt, also tend to experience others, such as anxiety and sadness.

Brain imaging studies suggest that positive and negative affect are largely neurologically distinct, although they share *some* neural pathways. In other words, some emotional pathways lead to a general sense of emotional arousal, whereas others add a specific valence (positive or negative) (Lane et al., 1997).

Approach and Avoidance   Positive and negative affect appear to motivate different kinds of behavior and to involve different regions of the cerebral cortex. Positive affect drives pleasure-seeking, approach-oriented behavior, whereas negative affect leads to avoidance (Chapter 5; see also Davidson, 1992; Gray, 1994; Lang, 1995). Approach-oriented feelings and motives are processed to a greater extent in the left frontal lobe, whereas avoidance-oriented feelings and motives are associated with right frontal activation. These circuits appear to be in place by early childhood. For example, four-year-olds who show greater left than right activation by EEG tend to be more socially competent and less interpersonally isolated than four-year-olds who show little difference between the hemispheres or greater right frontal activation (Fox et al., 1995).

Positive and negative affect are regulated by different neurotransmitter systems, leading some researchers to suggest that an individual's tendency to experience one more than the other is related to differences in neurotransmitter functioning (Cloninger, 1998). According to one hypothesis, people who are fear driven have an abundance of or greater reaction to norepinephrine. People who are reward or pleasure driven, in contrast, are slaves to dopamine.

Part of the tendency to experience positive and negative emotions is heritable. For positive affect, estimated heritability (based on studies of twins reared together and apart) is .40. For negative affect, heritability is even higher, at .55 (Gabbay, 1992; Watson & Tellegen, 1985).

Anger   An emotion that does not neatly fit into this distinction between positive and negative affect is anger. Subjectively, anger can feel unpleasant, but anger and

Big Picture φ Question 4

To what extent is human nature particular versus universal?

Apply & Discuss

■ Can complex emotions be read from the face?

■ What other cues may be necessary to "read" emotional blends?

aggression can also have pleasurable components, as anyone knows who has ever fantasized about revenge. Anger can sometimes lead to withdrawal, as when people "swallow it" and say nothing. More often, however, anger is an approach-oriented emotion, because it leads people to approach and attack the object of their anger.

EEG research finds that people who tend to be angry show greater relative activity in the left versus the right frontal lobe, the standard pattern for positive affect (Harmon-Jones & Allen, 1998). This suggests either that anger is more akin to positive affect or that the asymmetry between left and right frontal functioning has less to do with the emotion itself than with the tendency to approach or avoid.

An Emotion Hierarchy   How can the various theories of emotion be reconciled, with their competing claims about the number of emotions and the relative importance of biology and culture? One solution (Figure 10.17) is to organize emotions hierarchically (Fischer et al., 1990). The most universal categories are positive and negative affect. All cultures make this distinction, and it is the first drawn by young children, who use words such as *nice, mean, good, bad, like,* and *don't like.* Physiological data (such as EEG responses) suggest that these factors are already distinct in infancy (Belsky et al., 1996).

The basic emotions at the next level of the hierarchy also apply across cultures. Below this level, however, most emotion concepts are culturally constructed. Western culture, for example, distinguishes different forms of love, such as infatuation, fondness, sexual love, nonsexual love, and puppy love. Indian culture, in contrast, distinguishes only two forms of love: *vatsalya bhava,* a mother's love for her child, and *madhurya bhava,* erotic love (Lynch, 1990). Children recognize these culture-specific distinctions much later than they do the basic emotions.

Apply & Discuss

Anger is an emotion that gets many people in trouble.

▪ Why might the tendency to become angry have evolved in humans and other animals?

▪ Under what circumstances is anger adaptive or maladaptive?

▪ When we "talk ourselves out of" being angry, does the emotion really go away?

INTERIM SUMMARY

Basic emotions—such as anger, fear, happiness, sadness, and disgust—are common to the human species and include characteristic physiological, subjective, and expressive components. Beyond the basic emotions, different cultures distinguish different emotional states. Probably the most fundamental distinction is between **positive affect** (pleasant emotions) and **negative affect** (unpleasant emotions), with positive affect associated with approach-oriented motives and negative affect associated with avoidance-oriented

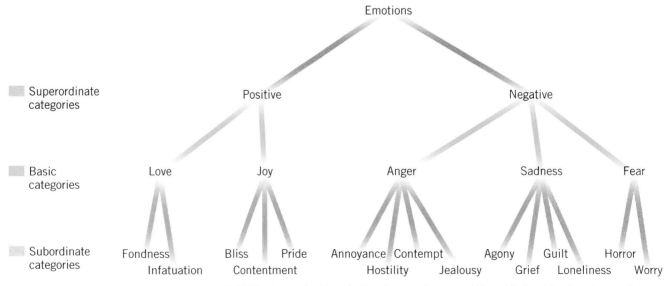

FIGURE 10.17   An emotion hierarchy. Emotions may be arranged hierarchically, with universal categories at the superordinate and basic levels and categories that vary by culture at the subordinate level. Source: Fischer et al., 1990, p. 90.

emotions. These emotional systems are to a substantial degree neurologically distinct. Emotions appear to be organized hierarchically, with positive and negative affect at the superordinate level, followed by basic emotions and then more culture-specific emotions.

The Neuropsychology of Emotion — From Brain to Behavior

Poets often locate emotion in the heart, whereas theorists with a less romantic bent of mind locate it in the face or the peripheral nervous system. Still other researchers have searched for the neural circuits underlying emotion in the central nervous system. They have found that affect, like cognition, is distributed throughout the nervous system and not located in any particular region. Three areas of the brain, however, are particularly important: the hypothalamus, limbic system, and cortex.

The Hypothalamus
Psychologists have known about the role of the hypothalamus in emotion since the 1930s (Papez, 1937). The hypothalamus is a central link in a neural circuit that converts emotional signals generated at higher levels of the brain into autonomic and endocrine responses. (Recall from Chapter 3 that the hypothalamus links the brain to the pituitary gland, which in turn activates other glands in the endocrine system.) In some species, motivation is largely controlled by the hypothalamus and hence by instinctive responses and the emotions linked to them. Thus, electrical stimulation of regions of the hypothalamus can produce attack, defense, or flight reactions, with corresponding emotions of rage or terror.

The Limbic System
In other animals, such as humans, behavior is controlled less by instinct than by learning, which is guided by emotional responses to stimuli. Central to emotional reactions are structures in the limbic system, particularly the amygdala (LeDoux, 1989, 1995). Decades ago, researchers discovered that lesioning a large temporal region (which later turned out primarily to involve the amygdala) produced a peculiar syndrome in monkeys (Kluver & Bucy, 1939). The monkeys no longer seemed to understand the emotional significance of objects in their environment, even though they had no trouble recognizing or identifying them. The animals showed no fear of previously feared stimuli and were generally unable to use their emotions to guide behavior. They would, for example, eat feces or other inedible objects that normally elicited disgust or indifference.

Researchers have subsequently found that lesioning the neurons connecting the amygdala with a specific sense, such as vision or hearing, makes monkeys unable to register the emotional significance of objects perceived by that sense (LeDoux, 1989). The amygdala, with its dense connections to the hippocampus (which is involved in memory), plays a crucial role in associating sensory and other information with pleasant and unpleasant feelings. This allows humans and other animals to adjust their behavior based on positive and negative emotional reactions to objects or situations they encounter. For example, in rats, neurons in a region of the amygdala that receives auditory information respond differently to a tone following classical conditioning of an emotional response (fear) to that tone (Rogan et al., 1997). In humans, neuroimaging data suggest that the amygdala plays a crucial role in detecting *other* people's emotions as well, particularly from observing their facial expressions (Scott et al., 1997).

Two Systems for Processing Emotion
Recent data from a variety of species point to two distinct circuits involving the amygdala which produce emotional responses, particularly fear (Armony & LeDoux, 2000;

Big Picture φ Question 1
To what extent can mental processes be reduced to the brain or body?

Big Picture φ Question 3
To what extent is human psychology continuous with the psychology of other animals?

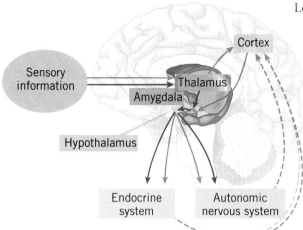

FIGURE 10.18 Two circuits for emotion processing. Emotionally relevant information is relayed from the thalamus simultaneously to the amygdala and the cortex. The first (blue arrows) leads to immediate responses. The second pathway (red solid arrows) allows the person to evaluate the stimulus on the basis of stored knowledge and goals. Both pathways activate the hypothalamus, which produces autonomic and endocrine changes that the cortex must interpret (dashed red arrows, indicating feedback to the cortex). Source: Adapted from LeDoux, 1995.

LeDoux, 1995). The first circuit is evolutionarily primitive and requires no cortical involvement. The thalamus, which processes and routes sensory information to various parts of the brain, sends some relatively simple sensory information directly to the amygdala. This information can elicit an immediate emotional response (such as fear in response to an approaching snake).

Conditioning can occur through this thalamo-limbic circuit, even when links between the amygdala and the cortex have been severed, as long as the neural connections between the amygdala and the hippocampus are intact. (The hippocampus is involved in forming associations between stimuli and emotional reactions.) Thus, an animal can have a rapid response to a stimulus previously associated with fear or pain even before the cortex "knows" anything about what is happening. For primitive vertebrates, this simple circuit was probably the sole basis of emotional reaction.

In humans and many other animals, however, the amygdala is also connected to higher processing centers in the cortex. Thus, when the thalamus sends sensory information to the amygdala, it simultaneously routes information to the cortex for more thorough examination. The cortex then transmits signals down to the amygdala. Based on this more complex information processing, a second emotional response may then occur.

Thus, the emotional reaction to a stimulus may occur in two stages, reflecting the semi-independent action of these two pathways (Figure 10.18). One is a quick response based on a cursory reaction to gross stimulus features, involving a circuit running from the thalamus to the amygdala. (A dark shadow in the water frightens a swimmer.) The second process is slower, based on a more thorough cognitive appraisal, involving a thalamus-to-cortex-to-amygdala circuit. (The bather realizes that the dark shadow is a buoy.) The initial thalamus-to-amygdala response typically occurs faster because it involves fewer synaptic connections; that is, the circuit is shorter and hence faster.

The existence of two circuits for emotional processing raises fascinating questions about what happens when the affective reactions generated by these two circuits are in conflict. For example, a cancer patient may have an immediate aversive conditioned response to the room in which she receives chemotherapy (Chapter 5). At the same time, she recognizes that what happens in this room may be key to her survival. As a result of this second reaction, involving higher level cortical processing, she overrides the avoidance behavior that would ordinarily be elicited by the conditioned emotional response and keeps appearing for her treatments.

The Cortex

The cortex plays several roles with respect to emotion. As noted above, it allows people to consider whether a stimulus is safe or harmful. People with damage to the regions of the frontal cortex that receive input from the amygdala have difficulty making choices guided by their emotions (Chapter 7) (Damasio, 1994). The cortex has a number of other emotional functions as well. One is its role in interpreting the meaning of peripheral responses, as when a person's shaky knees and dry throat while speaking in front of a group clue her in that she is anxious (Pribram, 1980). The frontal cortex plays a central role, as well, in regulating facial displays of emotion for social purposes, such as amplifying, minimizing, or feigning an emotion (Borod, 1992; Rinn, 1984).

The right and left hemispheres of the cortex appear to be specialized, with the right hemisphere dominant in processing emotional cues from others and producing facial displays of emotion (Borod, 1992). In addition, as discussed earlier, approach-related emotions are associated with activation of the left frontal cortex, whereas avoidance-related emotions are linked to activation of the right frontal lobe (Davidson, 1992; Sutton & Davidson, 1997). People who tend toward more left- than right-hemisphere activation generally experience more positive then negative affect, whereas people who show the opposite pattern of hemispheric activation tend to have more negative mood states (Figure 10.19).

Emotion Regulation

Because emotions feel good or bad and can draw positive or negative responses from other people, from early in life people learn to regulate their emotions. **Emotion regulation** (or **affect regulation**) refers to *efforts to control emotional states* (Westen et al., 1997; Gross, 1999; Kopp, 1989).

People can regulate emotions before or after they occur. Whether they try to regulate an emotion before or after the fact, however, has important psychological and physiological consequences. For example, people often *reframe* the meaning of an event before it occurs, trying to put it in a perspective that will make them less upset. In contrast, they may try to *suppress* the emotion after the fact, that is, try not to feel it or show it to others. Although reframing events before they occur often leads to diminished negative feelings, suppression does not. In fact, suppression leads to more sympathetic nervous system activity—that is, arousal—including increased heart rate (Gross, 1998). Suppression also interferes with the ability to engage in other tasks, because it essentially keeps the person "working overtime" to keep the feeling at bay (Richards & Gross, 2000).

Just as people regulate emotions, they similarly regulate **moods**, which are *relatively extended emotional states*. Whereas emotions often grab attention and disrupt ongoing activities, moods provide a background sense of positive or negative well-being (Oatley & Jenkins, 1992). Because moods, like emotions, include subjective feelings of pleasure and pain, they also become targets for emotion regulation strategies.

Emotion regulation strategies can be viewed as a form of procedural knowledge (Chapter 6); that is, they are procedures people use to try to alter their emotional states (Westen, 1994). Many of these strategies are conscious, as when people exercise to "blow off steam" or to take their mind off something that is bothering them. Much of the time, however, people learn what regulates their emotions in everyday life, as they learn many procedures—implicitly. Some people, for example, regularly handle distress by avoiding awareness of unpleasant emotions (Weinberger, 1990). Stable styles of emotion regulation are already observable by the time children enter preschool (Cole et al., 1996; Eisenberg et al., 2000).

Men and women tend to regulate different emotions. Men more often inhibit expressions of fear and sadness, whereas women are more likely to inhibit anger (Brody & Hall, 2000; Brody et al., 1995). This makes sense in light of gender differences in motivation for power versus motivation to maintain relationships (Fischer, 2000). How much gender differences in regulation of anger are really differences in *display* of anger is not entirely clear, however. Recent research finds, for example, that women express as much anger as men—but only if the target of the anger is not present. Furthermore, gender differences in emotional expression may reflect simple differences in what is deemed socially acceptable for men and women.

INTERIM SUMMARY

Emotional processes are distributed throughout the nervous system. The amygdala is involved in evaluating the emotional significance of a stimulus. It is also involved in detecting other people's emotions from their facial expression and vocal tone. The emotional reaction to a stimulus appears to occur through two distinct neural pathways: a quick response based on a circuit running from the thalamus to the amygdala, and a slower re-

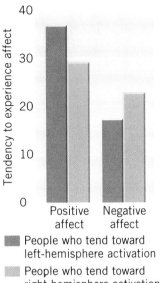

FIGURE 10.19 Emotional experience and hemisphere activation. The figure shows mean positive and negative affect scores for participants with a strong tendency toward left- versus right-midfrontal activation. Participants with a bias toward left-relative to right-hemisphere activation reported more positive and less negative affect. *Source:* Adapted from Tomarken et al., 1992, p. 681.

Big Picture φ Question 2

What is the relationship between reason and desire or, more precisely, between cognition and affect?

Big Picture φ Question 5

To what extent are psychological processes the same in men and women?

sponse based on a more thorough cognitive appraisal, based on a thalamus-to-cortex-to-amygdala circuit. In both cases, the amygdala then passes information on to the hypothalamus, which is involved in regulating autonomic responses. The cortex plays multiple roles with respect to emotion, such as interpreting the meaning of events and translating emotional reactions into socially desirable behaviors. **Emotion regulation** (or **affect regulation**) refers to efforts to control emotional states.

Perspectives on Emotion

Having examined the components of emotion and its basis in the nervous system, we now turn to *perspectives* on emotion. We already explored the behavioral perspective on emotion in some detail in Chapter 5, which emphasizes conditioned emotional responses, such as fear upon seeing a doctor approaching with a hypodermic needle. Each of the other perspectives offers insight into emotion as well.

Psychodynamic Perspective   A growing body of evidence supports a central, and somewhat counterintuitive, contention of psychodynamic theory: that people can be unconscious of their own emotional experience, and that unconscious emotional processes can influence thought, behavior, and even health (Singer, 1990). Researchers from multiple perspectives are increasingly converging on the same view (Westen, 1985, 1998).

Psychodynamic theory also suggests that we regularly delude ourselves about our own abilities and attributes to avoid the unpleasant emotional consequences of seeing ourselves more objectively. A growing body of research supports this hypothesis as well (e.g., Pratkanis et al., 1994; G. Vaillant, 1992a). One set of studies tested the hypothesis that people who disavow negative thoughts and feelings about themselves will pay a price physiologically (Shedler et al., 1993). In the first part of the experiment, participants filled out a questionnaire about their mental health and then described in detail their earliest memories. Participants who self-reported themselves as happy and healthy on the questionnaire but whose early memories were filled with unpleasant emotion (which is empirically associated with psychological disturbance) were categorized as having "illusory mental health."

Next, the experimenters presented subjects with a potentially anxiety-provoking task, such as making up TAT stories or answering items from an IQ test. Subjects with illusory mental health exhibited numerous signs of psychological distress, including elevated heart rate and blood pressure, which are related to heart disease. These subjects also consistently scored highest on indirect measures of anxiety, such as sighing and stammering. All the while, however, they consciously reported the *least* anxiety, suggesting the presence of unacknowledged anxiety (Figure 10.20). Several other researchers have presented similar data on people who tend to keep themselves unaware of their emotions (e.g., Asendorpf & Scherer, 1983; Bell & Cook, 1998; Brosschot & Janssen, 1998; D. Weinberger, 1990).

Cognitive Perspectives   As far back as the fifth century B.C., Western thinkers viewed emotion as a disruptive force in human affairs. Plato, for example, believed that reason must rein in the passions, which otherwise distort rational thinking. Psychologists now study the impact of feelings on cognitive processes such as memory and judgment empirically, as well as studying the reverse—the influence of cognition on emotion (Dalgleish & Power, 1999; Dalgleish & Power, 1999).

Interpretation and Emotion   You have just climbed four flights of stairs to your apartment on a hot, humid day to be confronted by a roommate complaining about dirty dishes in the sink. Your heart is racing, and your face feels flushed. Are you angry? Or is your body simply registering the impact of four flights of stairs in the

Making Connections

Infants and young children learn to regulate their emotions in the context of their primary relationships. Children who feel secure in their relationships with their parents learn that they can find comfort through closeness. Others, particularly those whose parents are themselves uncomfortable with intimacy and physical affection, may learn to "go it alone" and try to shut off feelings of dependence (Chapter 14).

Big Picture φ Question 2

What is the relationship between reason and desire or, more precisely, between cognition and affect?

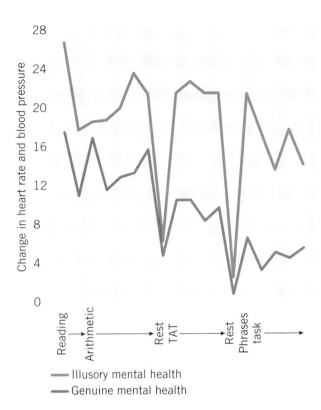

——— Illusory mental health
▬▬▬ Genuine mental health

FIGURE 10.20 Illusory mental health. Participants who were judged high but who self-reported themselves to be low in distress showed substantially larger heart rate and blood pressure increases while performing such mildly stressful tasks as solving arithmetic questions and making up stories in response to TAT cards. Note, however, that during resting periods participants who deluded themselves showed as little reactivity as genuinely healthy participants, suggesting that their unconscious anxiety is activated only when performing a potentially threatening task. *Source:* Shedler et al., 1993.

heat? The way you react may well depend on the **attributions** (*inferences about causes*) you make about these bodily sensations (Chapter 17).

In a classic paper, Stanley Schachter and Jerome Singer (1962) argued that a cognitive judgment or attribution is crucial to emotional experience. That is, when people experience a state of nonspecific physiological arousal, which could be anger, happiness, or any other feeling, they try to figure out what the arousal means. If situational cues suggest that they should be afraid, they interpret the arousal as fear; if the cues suggest excitement, they interpret their arousal as excitement. Thus, according to the **Schachter–Singer theory**, *emotion involves two factors: physiological arousal and cognitive interpretation* (Figure 10.21).

To test their hypothesis, Schachter and Singer injected subjects with either adrenalin (a hormone involved in emotional arousal) or an inert placebo and correctly informed, misinformed, or told them nothing about the possible effects of the injection. Participants then went to a waiting room, where they were joined by a confederate of the experimenter posing as another participant. The confederate either behaved an-

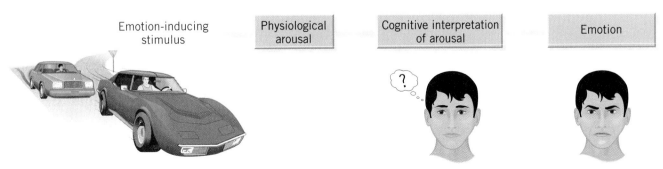

FIGURE 10.21 The Schachter–Singer theory of emotion. According to Schachter and Singer, people must interpret their arousal (e.g., when cut off by a speeding car) in order to experience a specific emotion.

grily and stormed out of the room (designed to elicit anger) or playfully threw paper wads into the wastebasket, flew paper airplanes, and generally enjoyed himself (designed to elicit euphoria).

Schachter and Singer predicted that participants who knew they had been injected with an arousing drug would attribute their arousal to the drug, whereas those who became aroused but did not know why would think they were either angry or euphoric, depending on the condition. The results were as predicted, suggesting that emotional experience is not simply the subjective awareness of arousal. Rather, it is a complex cognitive–affective state that includes inferences about the meaning of the arousal.

Schachter and Singer's conclusions have drawn criticism on a number of grounds (see Leventhal & Tomarken, 1986). First, the findings have not been easy to replicate (Maslach, 1979; Mezzacappa et al., 1999). Second, research shows that people can feel anxious or angry even after taking medication that blocks physiological arousal (Cleghorn et al., 1970; Erdmann & Van-Lindern, 1980). These data suggest that arousal may intensify emotional experience but may not be necessary for an emotion to occur (Reisenzein, 1983). Perhaps most importantly, as the research reviewed earlier suggests, different emotions have distinct physiological correlates; thus, emotion is not simply the interpretation of general arousal.

Nevertheless, numerous studies support the view that *some* degree of interpretation is involved in the experience of many emotional states. For instance, distinguishing between being tired (or fatigued) and being depressed requires interpretation, because the two physiological states share many common features. Excessive caffeine intake can also lead to arousal, which can be misattributed as anxiety and even contribute to the development of panic attacks (Chapter 15).

Cognition and Appraisal   In Schachter and Singer's study, participants initially became aroused by a shot of adrenalin. In normal life, however, people typically become aroused by their experiences rather than by injection. According to many cognitive theorists, people's emotions reflect their judgments and appraisals of the situations or stimuli that confront them (Lazarus, 1999b; Scherer, 1999; Smith & Ellsworth, 1985). For example, an event that affects a person's well-being in the present can lead to joy or distress, whereas an event that influences the person's potential well-being in the future can generate hope or fear (Ortony et al., 1988).

Many of these cognitive principles operate cross-culturally (Mauro et al., 1992; Scherer, 1997). Others, however, depend on cultural conceptions of causality. For example, some preliterate societies believe that prolonged illness is the result of sorcery (Whiting & Child, 1953). Hence, the ill person or his loved ones may direct anger about the illness toward an accused sorcerer. The increased incidence in the United States of malpractice suits against physicians may reflect a similar process, as people look for someone to blame for tragedies.

Cognitive processes also play a central role in interpreting *other* people's emotions. For example, although facial expressions are a major source of information about people's emotions, knowledge about the situation can influence or sometimes override information from the face. In one study, the researchers showed participants the face of a woman that had been unambiguously interpreted in prior studies as expressing fear (Carroll & Russell, 1996). Along with the photograph, however, they told participants that the woman had made a reservation at a fancy restaurant and was kept waiting for over an hour as celebrities and others walked in and were seated immediately. When she reminded the maitre d' of her reservation, he told her that the tables were now full and the wait would likely be over an hour. With this information about the circumstances, the vast majority of participants interpreted the expression as anger, not fear.

These findings suggest that not only emotions but also interpretations of emotion reflect cognitive appraisals. From a connectionist point of view (Chapter 7), facial expressions provide a powerful, "hardwired" set of constraints that influence the inter-

Apply and Discuss

■ How does the Schachter–Singer theory compare to the James–Lange theory?

■ How does it compare to the Cannon–Bard theory?

Big Picture φ Question 4

To what extent is human nature particular versus universal?

Big Picture φ Question 2

TWhat is the relationship between reason and desire or, more precisely, between cognition and affect?

pretation of another person's emotion. However, they are not the only constraints. In everyday life, knowledge about the situation also constrains inferences and may color the way a person interprets another's facial expression.

Cognitive appraisals often underlie emotions, but they do not always do so. Indeed, emotional responses can sometimes precede complex cognitive evaluations of a stimulus—or, as psychologist Robert Zajonc (1980) put it, "preferences need no inferences." Zajonc demonstrated this hypothesis by using a phenomenon called the *mere exposure effect*, whereby people become more positive about stimuli the more times they are exposed to them. The experimenters briefly exposed participants several times to Japanese ideographs (written characters). When later asked about their preferences for particular characters, as expected from the mere exposure effect, participants preferred characters they had previously seen, even when they did not consciously recognize having seen them (Zajonc, 1980). Zajonc thus concluded that the subjective sense of liking or disliking a stimulus may occur independent of cognitions about that stimulus. At the very least, affect may precede the *conscious* cognitive appraisals proposed by many theorists.

Influence of Emotion and Mood on Cognition Just as cognition can influence emotion, so, too, can emotion and mood influence ongoing thought and memory. For example, anxiety can reduce working memory capacity and explicit problem solving by distracting the person from the task at hand (Eysenck, 1982; Richardson, 1996a). Mood can also influence the way people make judgments, inferences, and predictions (Forgas, 1995; Mayer et al., 1992; Ochsner & Schacter, 2000). People who are depressed, for example, tend to underestimate the probability of their own success and overestimate the probability of bad events occurring in the future (Beck, 1976, 1991). Once again, anger does not appear to be a classically negative affect: Whereas fear generally leads to pessimistic judgments of the future, anger can actually lead to optimistic judgments (Lerner & Keltner, 2000).

Emotional states influence both the encoding and retrieval of information in long-term memory (Bower, 1989; Kenealy, 1997; Mathews & Macleod, 1994). Individuals in a positive mood tend both to store and to retrieve more positive information (Isen, 1984, 1993). Positive mood also tends to facilitate memory more generally, independent of its emotional quality (Levine & Burgess, 1997). Negative moods also affect encoding and retrieval, but the mechanisms are more complex. Negative mood at retrieval facilitates recall of negative words, because they are associatively linked in memory by the feeling common to both of them (Ochsner, 2000). However, people actively fight negative moods because they are aversive, so they try to retrieve more positive information (Josephson et al., 1996; Boden & Baumeister, 1997). Thus, a motivational process (regulating a negative mood) may counteract an automatic cognitive process (recall of information congruent with current thought and mood).

Emotional processes can also have a direct physiological effect on memory: Stressful emotional experiences can alter the structure of the brain (Gould et al., 1998). In one study, monkeys in one condition were exposed to an emotionally threatening encounter—being placed in another monkey's cage, who attacked until the "intruder" cowered in the corner. Compared to monkeys in a control condition, the traumatized monkeys showed a reduction in neural cells in the hippocampus, a neural structure that plays a crucial role in memory (Chapter 6).

Evolutionary Perspectives

The evolutionary perspective on emotion derives from Charles Darwin's (1872) view that emotions serve an adaptive purpose. Darwin stressed their communicative function: Animals, including humans, signal their readiness to fight, run, or attend to each other's needs through a variety of postural, facial, and other nonverbal communications (see Buck, 1986). A baby's cry sends a signal to its parents, just as bared teeth display anger. These communications regulate social behavior and increase the individual's chances of survival.

The similarities of facial expressions of emotions such as anger show their common evolutionary roots.

Darwin's theory explains why basic emotional expressions are wired into the organism and recognized cross-culturally. In fact, brain-imaging studies demonstrate the existence of hardwired neural circuits that function to recognize emotion in other people. As we have seen, the amygdala includes specific regions that allow people to recognize emotions such as fear and anger from other people's faces.

Emotion and Motivation Evolutionary theorists also view emotion as a powerful source of motivation—an *internal* communication that something must be done (Izard, 1977; Lang, 1995; Plutchik, 1980, 1997; Tomkins, 1962). For example, when people are threatened, they feel fear, which in turn leads them to deal with the threatening situation through either fight or flight. Emotions and drives may also operate in tandem to motivate action, as when excitement accompanies sexual arousal (Tomkins, 1986). Table 10.2 shows how emotional reactions motivate behaviors that promote survival and reproduction (Plutchik, 1980).

Jealousy: An Evolutionary View An emotion that is less well understood is jealousy. Why do people become jealous in intimate sexual relationships? One series of studies tested evolutionary hypotheses about men's and women's concerns about their partners' fidelity (Buss et al., 1992). From an evolutionary perspective, females can have only a limited number of children during their lifetimes. Thus, to maximize their reproductive success, they should seek relationships with males who have resources to contribute to the care of their offspring. In fact, cross-cultural evidence demonstrates that one of the main mate selection criteria used by females is male resources, whether cattle or Corvettes (Chapter 18). From a female's point of view, then, infidelity by a mate accompanied by emotional commitment to the other woman is a major threat to resources because the male is likely to divert resources or even switch mates.

For males, the situation is different. If a male commits himself to an exclusive relationship with a female, he must be certain that the offspring in whom he is investing are his own. Because a man can never be entirely certain of paternity, the best he can do is prevent his mate from copulating with any other males. In males, then, jealousy should focus less on the female's emotional commitment or resources than on her tendency to give other males sexual access.

Indeed, in species ranging from insects to humans, males take extreme measures to prevent other males from inseminating their mates (Hasselquist & Bensch, 1991). Male birds in some species refuse to let a female out of their sight for days after insemination. In humans, male sexual jealousy is the leading cause of homicides and of spouse battering cross-culturally (Daly & Wilson, 1988).

Table 10.2 ■ ■ Evolutionary Links between Emotion and Behavior in Humans and Other Animals

Stimulus Event	Emotion	Behavior
Threat	Fear, terror, anxiety	Fight, flight
Obstacle	Anger, rage	Biting, hitting
Potential mate	Joy, ecstasy, excitement	Courtship, mating
Loss of valued person	Sadness, grief	Crying for help
Group member	Acceptance, trust	Grooming, sharing
New territory	Anticipation	Examining, mapping
Sudden novel object	Surprise	Stopping, attending

Source: Adapted from Plutchik, 1980, p. 16.

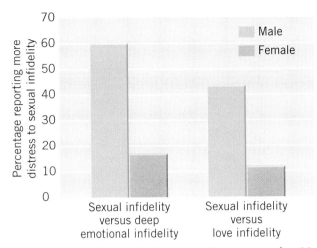

FIGURE 10.22 Jealousy in males and females. The figure shows the percentage of participants reporting more distress to the sexual infidelity scenario than to imagining their lover either becoming deeply attached to someone else (left) or falling in love with someone else (right). Men are more concerned than women with sexual infidelity, and this is particularly true of those who have actually been in a committed sexual relationship. *Source:* Buss et al., 1992.

To test the evolutionary hypothesis that males and females differ in their reasons for jealousy, college students were asked to "imagine that you discover that the person with whom you've been seriously involved became interested in someone else" (Buss et al., 1992). Participants were to choose which of two scenarios would upset them more: "imagining your partner forming a deep emotional attachment to that person" or "imagining your partner enjoying passionate sexual intercourse with that person." They were then asked a second question involving similar scenarios contrasting love and sex: "imagining your partner falling in love with that other person" or "imagining your partner trying different sexual positions with that other person."

As Figure 10.22 shows, 60 percent of males reported greater distress at the thought of sexual infidelity in response to the first question, compared to only 17 percent of the females, who were more concerned about emotional attachment. The second question yielded similar results, as did a third study in which the investigators measured distress *physiologically* rather than by self-report, using indicators such as pulse and subtle facial movements (such as a furrowed brow, which is associated with negative affect).

The evolutionary interpretation of these findings has not gone unchallenged (DeSteno & Salovey, 1996; Harris & Christenfeld, 1996). For example, the findings could be equally attributed to culture, because these studies were conducted in a single culture. More recently, however, cross-cultural researchers have found similar sex differences in countries as diverse as Germany and China, although these differences were slightly less pronounced than in the United States, suggesting both cultural and evolutionary influences on feelings of jealousy (Buunk et al., 1996; Geary et al., 1995).

Big Picture φ Question 4

To what extent is human nature particular versus universal?

INTERIM SUMMARY

According to psychodynamic theory, people can be unconscious of their emotional experience and can act on affects even when they lack subjective awareness of them. According to the **Schachter–Singer theory**, a cognitive approach to emotion, emotion occurs as people interpret their physiological arousal. Subsequent research suggests that cognitive appraisals influence emotion and that mood and emotion can affect thought and memory. From an evolutionary perspective, emotion serves an important role in communication between members of a species. It is also a powerful source of motivation.

Summary

Perspectives on Motivation

1. **Motivation** refers to the moving force that energizes behavior. It includes two components: what people want to do (the direction in which activity is motivated) and how strongly they want to do it (the strength of the motivation). Although some motives (e.g., eating and sex) are more clearly biologically based and others (e.g., relatedness to others and achievement) are more psychogenic or psychosocial, both types of motives have roots in biology and are shaped by culture and experience.

2. Evolutionary psychologists argue that basic human motives derive from the tasks of survival and reproduction. They have expanded the concept of reproductive success to include inclusive fitness, which means that natural selection favors organisms that survive, reproduce, and foster the survival and reproduction of their kin. Natural selection has endowed humans and other animals with motivational mechanisms that lead them to maximize their inclusive fitness.

3. Freud believed that humans, like other animals, are motivated by internal tension states, or **drives**, for sex and aggression. Contemporary psychodynamic theorists focus less on drives than on wishes and fears. They emphasize motives for relatedness and self-esteem, as well as sex and aggression, and contend that many human motives are unconscious.

4. Behavioral theorists use the term *drive* to refer to motivation activated by a need state (such as hunger). According to **drive-reduction theories**, deprivation of basic needs creates an unpleasant state of tension that leads the animal to act. If an action happens to reduce the tension, the behavior is reinforced. Innate drives such as hunger, thirst, and sex are **primary drives**; with **secondary drives**, an originally neutral stimulus comes to be associated with drive reduction and hence itself becomes a motivator.

5. Cognitive theorists often speak of **goals**, valued outcomes established through social learning. **Expectancy–value theories** assert that motivation is a joint function of the value people place on an outcome and the extent to which they believe they can attain it. **Goal-setting theory** proposes that conscious goals regulate much of human action, particularly in work tasks. **Self-determination theory** suggests that people are most likely to develop **intrinsic motivation** (i.e., a genuine interest in the activity for its own sake) in a task or domain when learning is accompanied by feelings of competence, autonomy (i.e., control over their own actions, rather than control by others), and relatedness to others (i.e., a supportive, noncontrolling interpersonal environment). Recently, cognitive researchers have begun to apply experimental methods to study **implicit motives**, which occur outside awareness.

6. According to Maslow's **hierarchy of needs**, basic needs must be met before higher level needs become active. Maslow's hierarchy includes physiological, safety, belongingness, esteem, and self-actualization needs.

Eating

7. Many motives, particularly biological motives related to survival, involve **homeostasis**, the body's tendency to maintain a relatively constant state, or internal equilibrium, that permits cells to live and function. Homeostatic systems such as hunger and thirst share a number of common features, including a **set point** (a biologically optimal level the system strives to maintain); **feedback mechanisms** (which provide the system with information regarding the state of the system with respect to the variables being regulated) and **corrective mechanisms** (mechanisms that restore the system to its set point when needed).

8. **Metabolism** refers to the processes by which the body transforms food into energy. It includes an **absorptive phase**, in which the body is absorbing nutrients; and a **fasting phase**, in which the body is converting short- and long-term fuel stores into energy useful for the brain and body.

9. Eating is regulated both by hunger and by **satiety mechanisms** (mechanisms for turning off eating). Hunger increases as glucose (and, to some extent, lipid) levels fall in the bloodstream. These falling levels signal the brain that short- and long-term fuels stores are diminishing. Hunger also reflects external cues, such as the palatability of food, learned meal times, and the presence of other people. The body relies on multiple mechanisms to signal satiety (fullness), although the most important are receptors in the intestines that let the body know that the "fuel tanks" will soon be full.

10. **Obesity** is a condition characterized by a body weight over 15 percent above the ideal for one's height and age. Genetic factors and dietary fat intake are strong predictors of body fat.

Sexual Motivation

11. Sexual motivation is driven by both fantasies and hormones and is shaped by culture. Hormones control sexual behavior in humans and other animals through **organizational effects** (influencing the structure of neural circuitry) and **activational effects** (activating physiological changes that depend on this circuitry).

12. **Sexual orientation** refers to the direction of a person's enduring sexual attraction—to members of the same sex, the opposite sex, or both. Accumulating evidence on homosexuality suggests a substantial biological influence in both men and women.

Psychosocial Motives

13. **Psychosocial needs** are personal and interpersonal motives for such ends as mastery, achievement, power, self-esteem, affiliation, and intimacy. Across cultures, the two major clusters of motives are **agency** (self-oriented goals, such as mastery or power) and **relatedness** (interpersonal motives for connection, or communion, with others).

14. The **need for achievement** refers to a motive to succeed and to avoid failure, which is heavily influenced by cultural and economic conditions. Underlying achievement motivation are **performance goals** (to approach or achieve a socially visible standard) or **mastery goals** (to master the skill).

15. Even for needs undeniably rooted in biology, such as hunger and sex, the strength of a motive depends in part on whether appropriate stimuli impinge on the organism. Motives also often reflect

a subtle blend of innate factors (nature) and learning and culture (nurture). Motivation usually requires both cognition (representations that provide the direction of motivation) and emotional energy or arousal (providing the "fuel," or strength, of motivation).

Emotion

16. **Emotion**, or **affect**, is an evaluative response (a positive or negative feeling state) that typically includes subjective experience, physiological arousal, and behavioral expression.

17. The **James–Lange theory** asserts that the subjective experience of emotion results from bodily experience induced by an emotion-eliciting stimulus. According to this theory, we do not run because we are afraid; we become afraid because we run (and our hearts pound). In contrast, the **Cannon–Bard** theory proposes that emotion-inducing stimuli simultaneously elicit both emotional experience and bodily responses. Although both theories have their strengths and limitations, recent research suggests that different emotions are, as James believed, associated with distinct, innate patterns of autonomic nervous system arousal.

18. **Emotional expression** refers to facial and other outward indications of emotion, such as body language and tone of voice. Many aspects of emotional expression, particularly facial expression, are innate and cross-culturally universal. Culturally variable patterns of regulating and displaying emotion are called **display rules**.

19. Psychologists have attempted to produce a list of basic emotions, emotions common to the human species from which all other

emotions and emotional blends can be derived. Anger, fear, happiness, sadness, and disgust are listed by all theorists as basic. An even more fundamental distinction is that between **positive affect** and **negative affect**.

20. Emotions are controlled by neural pathways distributed throughout the nervous system. The hypothalamus activates sympathetic and endocrine responses related to emotion. The limbic system, and particularly the amygdala, is part of an emotional circuit that includes the hypothalamus. The cortex plays several roles with respect to emotion, particularly in the appraisal of events.

21. The behaviorist perspective on emotion points to approach and avoidance systems associated with positive and negative affect, respectively. According to the psychodynamic perspective, people can be unconscious of their own emotional reactions, which can nonetheless influence thought, behavior, and health.

22. From a cognitive perspective, the way people respond emotionally depends on the **attributions** they make—that is, their inferences about causes of the emotion and their own bodily sensations. According to the **Schachter–Singer theory**, emotion involves two factors: physiological arousal and cognitive interpretation of the arousal. Emotion and **mood** (relatively extended emotional states that, unlike emotions, typically do not disrupt ongoing activities) have an impact on encoding, retrieval, judgment, and decision making.

23. The evolutionary perspective on emotion derives from Charles Darwin's view that emotions serve an adaptive purpose. Emotion has both communicative and motivational functions.

Key Terms

Health, Stress, and Coping

*J*im Fixx is perhaps best known for his book *The Complete Book of Running* and for playing a major role in the physical fitness movement. He is also well known for dying of a heart attack in 1984 at the age of 52 while running. At the time of his death, sedentary members of the population hailed Fixx as evidence that exercise is a bad thing or at least not necessarily a good thing. Had he not run so much, and had he not been running that particular day, they said, he would not have died. Perhaps. But that's not telling the entire story.

Prior to becoming an avid runner, Jim Fixx was one of those sedentary members of the population. He smoked two packs of cigarettes a day, was 50 pounds overweight, and rarely exercised, except for an occasional game of tennis. Suffering a leg injury, he took up jogging as a means of rehabilitation. Little did he know he would become hooked or that he would become famous because of his running. What the sedentary people are also not telling you is that Fixx would have probably died much sooner had he not exercised. His father had died of a heart attack at the age of 43, and his mother had also died young. In all likelihood, then, Jim Fixx added years to his life because of his avid running.

In spite of that fact, however, questions can be asked about Fixx's approach to health. Did he exercise too much? Estimates are that he ran over 37,000 miles in his life, averaging about 60 miles a week. Was that excessive? He was, after all, a marathon runner. Don't most runners who train for marathons run at least that much every week? Following the death of his father at such a young age, did Fixx receive regular checkups to evaluate the condition of his own heart? Apparently not. At the time of his death, three of his arteries were at least 70 percent blocked, with one of those 99 percent blocked. Results of the autopsy showed extensive scar tissue indicating that he had had three heart attacks in the weeks preceding his death.

Why would someone with a family history of heart trouble not receive regular cardiovascular screenings? Why, for that matter, would someone with his family history have been obese and a smoker to begin with? Why would someone ignore clear warning signs that danger was imminent? Did Jim Fixx believe himself to be invulnerable? Did he believe that his exercise would help protect his heart and save him from the fate that took the life of his father? What could have been done or said to convince Fixx to seek regular medical care? What could have been done to help him moderate his running, given his family history? Why did Jim Fixx, with his healthy lifestyle, die at 52, whereas some others, such as Winston Churchill, who smoke, drink, and are obese, die in their 90s?

Understanding situations and questions such as these is the work of health psychologists. "Health psychology is the aggregate of the specific educational, scientific, and professional contributions of the discipline of psychology to the promotion and maintenance of health, the prevention and treatment of illness, the identification of etiologic and diagnostic correlates of health, illness and related dysfunction, and the analysis and improvement of the health care system and health policy formation" (Matarazzo, 1980, p. 815). Because of changing patterns of illness, global epidemics such as SARS and AIDS, and an increasing emphasis on the role of behavior in health, health psychology is emerging as one of the leading areas within the field of psychology. After considering a brief history of the field of health psychology, we will examine specific health-compromising behaviors that are related to the major causes of death and chronic disease in the world today. We will also discuss barriers to health promotion and prevention. We will then turn our attention to two health-related topics that arguably have received the greatest amount of attention: stress and coping.

Health Psychology

Although people have experienced illness throughout history, until recently psychology played little role in understanding health and illness behavior. Over the last couple of decades, however, the field of psychology, specifically health psychology, has played an increasingly important role in understanding health and illness. "**Health psychology** is devoted to *understanding psychological influences on how people stay healthy, why they become ill, and how they respond when they do get ill*" (Taylor, 2003, p. 3). A health psychologist might be interested in why people fail to exercise even though they know the health benefits of doing so. The health psychologist works to understand the reasons why people do not exercise and then designs interventions to increase the likelihood that they will exercise in the future. The health psychologist also tries to answer why some people get sick and others don't, all other factors being equal. She might examine why one person's stressor (e.g., roller coaster rides) is another person's thrill. The health psychologist might also get involved with local, state, and federal governments to establish health policies and agendas. And, the health psychologist might work to examine the psychological and social factors that determine whether or not people seek medical care when they believe they are sick, the factors that influence this willingness, and how people react when they find out they are sick, particularly with a chronic or terminal illness (Baum & Posluszny, 1999). To understand the importance of health psychology to the study and treatment of health and illness, it is important to see the etiology of the field itself.

History of Health Psychology

The earliest theorists believed that disease arose when evil spirits entered the body. To rid the body of these spirits, a crude type of what today is called neurosurgery was performed using Stone Age tools. This surgery, called **trephination**, involved *drilling holes in the skulls of the diseased individual to allow the evil spirits to escape*. Those individuals who managed to survive the procedure were thought to be cured of their illness. (Scar tissue observed in trephinated skulls suggests that, in fact, many people did survive these procedures.)

Some time later, the Greeks abandoned the idea that disease is caused by evil spirits and ascribed illness instead to poor bodily functioning. Hippocrates

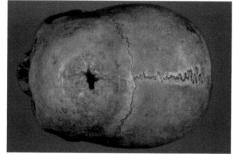

Believing that illness was a function of evil spirits that could be released through holes drilled into the skull, early in history, people used primitive tools to practice trephination.

(460 B.C.–377 B.C.), known to many as the father of modern medicine, proposed the **humoral theory of illness**, which asserts that *disease is caused by an imbalance in the four fluids or humors of the body—blood, phlegm, black bile, and yellow bile*. Fluid imbalance produced both psychological (e.g., personality) and physical (e.g., illness) changes (Lyons & Petrucelli, 1978; Straub, 2002). Balance in the fluids was maintained by health-enhancing behaviors such as appropriate exercise and a balanced diet, a very progressive idea for the day.

Hippocrates' original theory was expanded by Galen (A.D. 129–199) who suggested that four personality types or temperaments were determined by the relative proportions of the four fluids. For example, too much black bile produced a melancholic person who was sad and depressed. Physiologically, an excess of black bile produced ulcers and hepatitis (Straub, 2002). Too much yellow bile produced a person who was quick to anger. Treatments were tailored to the particular fluid that was out of balance. In the case of an excess of black bile, the patient was placed on a special diet and exposed to hot baths. The diets consisted of foods that had characteristics opposite to those of the fluid that was out of balance. For example, black bile was cold and dry, so a person would be prescribed foods that were warm and moist (Clader, 2002). Although the humoral theory has been rejected over time, many of the principles put forth by Hippocrates are suggestive of health enhancement today.

The Middle Ages (c. 476–c. 1450) saw a return to conceptions of disease as a result of mystical forces, reflecting the dominance of religion at the time. Disease was considered to be God's punishment for wrongdoing. Treatments, generally controlled by the Church, focused on torturing the body to atone for wrongdoing. At this time, humans were viewed as beyond the realm of scientific investigation. Thus, for example, human dissection was forbidden (Straub, 2002; Taylor, 2003). To put these views in perspective, the Middle Ages witnessed a barrage of new and pervasive diseases, including leprosy and the Black Death or bubonic plague. The Black Death is believed to have taken the lives of almost a fourth of the European population (Lyons & Petrucelli, 1978). In just five years after the initial outbreak of the disease, 25 million people died! Thus, it is hardly surprising that such horrific and unexplainable illnesses might have been ascribed to God's punishment for wrongdoing.

As implied by the name for the era, the Renaissance, beginning in the fifteenth century, witnessed great strides in medical knowledge and treatment. During this period of time, major contributions were made by Leeuwenhock with microscopy and by Morgagni in the area of autopsy (Taylor, 2003). Furthermore, Vesalius resurrected the practice of dissection, and he published a multivolume series on human anatomy. Together, these scientists spelled the death knell for the humoral theory of illness. Rather than viewing disease as the result of an imbalance of bodily fluids (i.e., hu-

Big Picture φ Question 1

To what extent can mental processes be reduced to the brain or body?

Victims of the Black Death "ate lunch with their friends and dinner with their ancestors in paradise"

(BOCCACCIO)

Making Connections

In the Middle Ages, the Black Death (also known as the bubonic plague) wiped out a large portion of the European population, over 25 million people in just the first five years of its spread. But, these statistics are misleading, because it was over 250 years before the plague was completely over. Today society continues to have illnesses of epidemic proportions, most notably AIDS. The Centers for Disease Control report that there are 42 million people living with HIV or AIDS. In 2002, 5 million new cases of HIV infection were diagnosed, and 3.1 million people died from AIDS and AIDS-related complications.

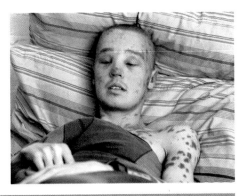

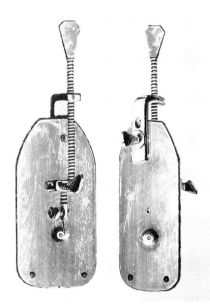

Leeuwenhock's microscope

Big Picture φ Question 1

To what extent can mental processes be reduced to the brain or body?

Big Picture φ Question 7

To what extent are psychological processes conscious or unconscious—that is, explicit versus implicit?

moral theory), they could now identify biological and anatomical causes of disease (i.e., anatomical theory; Straub, 2002). In addition, Descartes (1596–1650) proposed his theory of **Cartesian dualism**, *which contends that the mind and the body are completely separate entities.* To understand the body and illness, one must focus on the body alone. At this time, psychology was a long way from being involved in the treatment and prevention of illness.

With technological advances such as those just mentioned, the role of the body (rather than the mind) in disease took precedence. The development of microscopy led to observations of individual cells within the human body, which laid the foundation for the **cellular theory of illness**, *the idea that illness and disease result from abnormalities within individual cells.* Not surprisingly, then, physicians took over the care of the body and philosophers took over the care of the mind.

This dualistic view of the mind and the body persisted for hundreds of years and became conceptualized as the biomedical model of health. The **biomedical model** takes *a reductionistic view of illness, reducing disease to biological causes at the level of individual cells.* Psychological and social factors that affect health and illness are virtually ignored in the biomedical model. The biomedical model also adopts an illness-based focus, viewing health as simply the absence of illness rather than as an independent state of well-being to be achieved. Although the biomedical model is still the primary model within medicine today, it began to lose some of its punch during the middle of the twentieth century, in large part because of the work of Sigmund Freud.

Freud, who was trained as a physician, realized that some illnesses could not be traced to an underlying biological cause. Based on his work with clients, Freud came to believe that these "unexplained" physical problems stemmed from unconscious conflicts. He labeled these physical manifestations of psychological issues *conversion reactions.* This perspective reunited the mind and the body as contributors to illness.

Building on the work of Freud, other individuals extended Freud's link between unconscious conflicts and disease by saying that unconscious conflicts produce physiological changes within the body. These physiological changes tax the body's resources and ultimately lead to the onset of illness. *The idea that changes in physiology mediate the relationship between unconscious conflicts and illness* constitutes the field of **psychosomatic medicine**. Although some people continue to this day to endorse psychosomatic medicine, the field has not been without its critics. More modern theorists and researchers argue that the link between unconscious conflicts and illness is a complex one, requiring the presence of any of a number of different factors, such as genetic predispositions to illness or environmental stressors (Taylor, 2003). The origin of psychosomatic medicine within Freudian theory also portended poorly for the field as psychodynamic theory itself began to be criticized. Nevertheless, both Freudian theory and psychosomatic medicine laid the groundwork for reuniting the mind and body.

This recognition that psychology and physiology mutually influence one another set the stage for the rise of health psychology and the development of the **biopsychosocial model** of health, *the idea that health and illness stem from a combination of biological, psychological, and social factors.* There were other indicators, however, that the time was ripe for the field of health psychology to emerge. One of the most prominent of these indicators was the changing illness patterns over the last century. Early in the twentieth century, most people died from acute disorders, such as pneumonia and tuberculosis (Grob, 1983). Over the last few decades, however, illness patterns have changed so that many of the leading causes of death today are largely preventable (see Figure 11.1). Mortality rates from heart disease, stroke, and cancer would be largely reduced if people changed one health behavior, smoking. In fact, statistics indicate that mortality rates from the leading causes of death could be reduced by half if people altered their health behavior (Centers for Disease Control, 1980).

Thus, lifestyle choices and health-compromising behaviors are major contributors to the leading causes of death today. In addition, an individual with a chronic

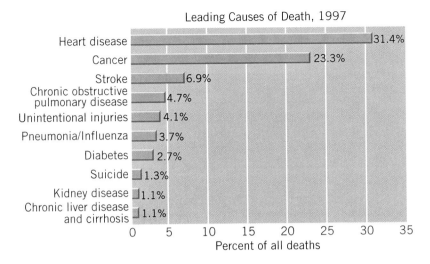

Leading Causes of Death, 1997

Heart disease 31.4%
Cancer 23.3%
Stroke 6.9%
Chronic obstructive pulmonary disease 4.7%
Unintentional injuries 4.1%
Pneumonia/Influenza 3.7%
Diabetes 2.7%
Suicide 1.3%
Kidney disease 1.1%
Chronic liver disease and cirrhosis 1.1%

Percent of all deaths

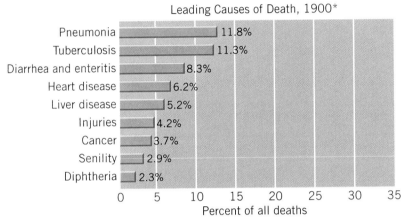

Leading Causes of Death, 1900*

Pneumonia 11.8%
Tuberculosis 11.3%
Diarrhea and enteritis 8.3%
Heart disease 6.2%
Liver disease 5.2%
Injuries 4.2%
Cancer 3.7%
Senility 2.9%
Diphtheria 2.3%

Percent of all deaths

*Not all states are represented

Source: Centers for Disease Control and Prevention, National Center for Health Statistics, National Vital Statistics System, and unpublished data, 1997.

FIGURE 11.1 Changing patterns of illness over the last century. Most of the leading causes of death today are, at least in part, preventable if people would alter their negative health habits.

condition such as cancer may live with that illness for years, with all of the accompanying changes in occupational choices, lifestyle choices, and family adjustments. Clearly, health psychologists are needed both to help eliminate health-compromising behaviors and to facilitate health-promoting behaviors, and to help ill people and their families deal with debilitating health conditions when they arise. People within both the medical profession and public policy are quickly realizing the benefits of health psychology to the treatment of illness and the promotion of health, so much so that many primary care facilities now have a full-time health psychologist on board.

"For the last dozen or so years, health psychology has flourished as one of the most vibrant specialties within the larger discipline of psychology" (Marks et al., 2003). Research within the area of health psychology has burgeoned in the last two decades (Figure 11.2). Health psychologists are involved in examining behavioral and psychological factors that place individuals at risk for illness (e.g., smoking, unsafe sexual practices, alcohol abuse). Because they focus not just on illness, but also on health, health psychologists are also involved in factors that facilitate the development of behaviors that promote health and prevent illness (e.g., exercise, dental hygiene, breast and testicular self-examinations). Finally, health psychologists are increasingly involved in public health policy. What was once a field devoted almost

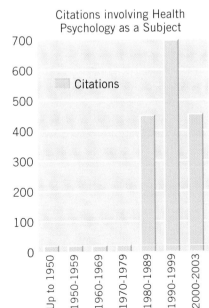

Citations involving Health Psychology as a Subject

Citations

FIGURE 11.2 Citations involving health psychology as a subject. The data presented here are based on a search of citations in PsychINF that included health psychology as a subject term. As the figure indicates, research in the area of health psychology has burgeoned in the last 20 years.

exclusively to research has now become a "health delivery service" (Marks et al., 2003), with the greatest number of placements of health psychologists in recent years being in medical settings (American Psychological Association, 2003).

INTERIM SUMMARY

Health psychology is devoted to understanding psychological influences on how people stay healthy, why they become ill, and how they respond when they do get ill. Understanding the etiology of health psychology requires one to go back in history to the earliest theories of illness and its cure. Early theorists, believing that illness was caused by evil spirits, engaged in the practice of **trephination**, drilling holes in the skull to allow the evil spirits to escape. The role of physiology in illness was identified in the **humoral theory of illness**, which suggested that physical and psychological problems result from an imbalance of the four fluids: blood, black bile, yellow bile, and phlegm. This unity of the mind and body was fractured during the period of the Renaissance by Descartes' theory of **Cartesian dualism**, the contention that the mind and body are completely separate entities. An increased focus on the body as the source of illness led to the **cellular theory of illness**, and, subsequently, the **biomedical model**, the theory that disease can be traced to the level of individual cells. Although still the dominant model of illness within the field of medicine, the biomedical model began to be challenged by Freud and those theorists who endorsed **psychosomatic medicine**. The recognition that social and psychological variables in addition to biological underpinnings laid the foundation for health and illness set the stage for the **biopsychosocial model** of health that guides the field of health psychology today.

Theories of Health Behavior

A number of theories have been proposed to explain why people engage in health-promoting or health-compromising behaviors. These are all social–cognitive theories that focus on the beliefs that individuals hold regarding health threats and their perceived susceptibility to those threats.

Health Belief Model One of the earliest theories of health behavior was the **health belief model** (Hochbaum, 1958; Rosenstock, 1966), which suggests that *health behaviors are predicted by four factors: the perceived susceptibility to the health threat, the perceived seriousness of the health threat, the benefits and barriers of undertaking particular health behaviors, and cues to action* (Figure 11.3*a*). **Perceived susceptibility** to a health threat refers to *a person's perception that he is likely to contract a particular illness*. Sandy had an uncle who recently died from lung cancer after years of smoking cigarettes. Sandy is also a smoker and, since his uncle's death, he believes that if he continues to smoke he, too, is likely to develop lung cancer or some other smoking-related illness. Unfortunately, many people experience an **optimistic bias** (i.e., unrealistic optimism) *by which they believe that they are far less likely than other people to contract particular illnesses* (Klein & Helweg-Larsen, 2002; Weinstein, 1980; Weinstein & Klein, 1996). Thus, they rate their own level of susceptibility lower than they rate that of others. Sandy, for example, may believe that, even though his uncle died of lung cancer, his own chances of succumbing to the same fate are remote.

Perceived seriousness or **severity** of the health threat refers to *an individual's perception of the impact a particular illness would have on her life*. For example, the more pain and discomfort associated with a health threat, the more severe it is perceived to be. Similarly, the more disruptive a medical condition is to one's family or current lifestyle, the more severe the illness is rated as being. Having experienced first hand the death of a close relative due to smoking-induced lung cancer, Sandy has no doubt as to the seriousness of lung cancer.

In deciding whether or not to adopt a health behavior (e.g., quitting smoking), people evaluate whether the **benefits** to be gained from stopping the behavior (e.g., *offsetting a health threat such as lung cancer*) outweigh the costs or **barriers** asso-

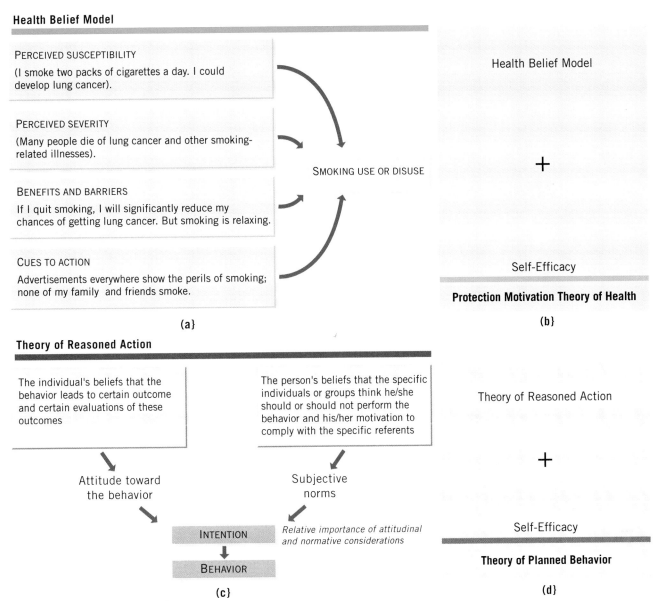

Health Belief Model

PERCEIVED SUSCEPTIBILITY
(I smoke two packs of cigarettes a day. I could develop lung cancer).

PERCEIVED SEVERITY
(Many people die of lung cancer and other smoking-related illnesses).

BENEFITS AND BARRIERS
If I quit smoking, I will significantly reduce my chances of getting lung cancer. But smoking is relaxing.

CUES TO ACTION
Advertisements everywhere show the perils of smoking; none of my family and friends smoke.

SMOKING USE OR DISUSE

(a)

Theory of Reasoned Action

The individual's beliefs that the behavior leads to certain outcome and certain evaluations of these outcomes

The person's beliefs that the specific individuals or groups think he/she should or should not perform the behavior and his/her motivation to comply with the specific referents

Attitude toward the behavior

Subjective norms

INTENTION   *Relative importance of attitudinal and normative considerations*

BEHAVIOR

(c)

Health Belief Model

+

Self-Efficacy

Protection Motivation Theory of Health

(b)

Theory of Reasoned Action

+

Self-Efficacy

Theory of Planned Behavior

(d)

FIGURE 11.3   Theories of health behavior.

ciated with the termination of the behavior (e.g., *side effects of withdrawal associated with quitting smoking, weight gain, alienating peers)*. Sandy can think of a number of benefits associated with quitting smoking, the most notable of which is significantly reducing his chances of contracting lung cancer. On the other hand, not smoking has several negative associations, not the least of which is the discomfort he feels every time he has tried to quit.

Cues to action refer to *ancillary factors that influence whether or not a person is willing to begin a healthy behavior or terminate an unhealthy one*. These cues include advice from friends and family, age, gender, socioeconomic status, and exposure to media campaigns related to health behavior, to name a few.

Will Sandy quit smoking? The answer is not a definitive yes or no. According to the health belief model, if Sandy perceives himself to be susceptible to lung cancer, evaluates lung cancer as severe, believes that the health benefits of terminating smoking outweigh any short-term costs, and believes that his decision to quit is supported by his family and friends, then he will be likely at least to attempt to quit. However, the overall effectiveness of the health belief model in predicting health be-

Big Picture φ Question 2

What is the relationship between reason and desire or, more precisely, between cognition and affect?

Apply and Discuss

All of the primary models of health behavior examine people's attitudes toward positive and negative health behaviors. One of the problems, however, is that people's attitudes are often ambivalent; that is, people hold both positive and negative beliefs about the behavior in question. Take exercise, for example. Most people believe that exercise will improve health and control weight. However, they also believe that exercise takes too much time, can be done to excess, and can result in injury.

▪ What role do you think attitudinal ambivalence (holding both positive and negative attitudes toward a health behavior) has on a person's decision to adopt particular health behaviors?

▪ How would the feelings of a person with ambivalent attitudes compare to those of a person who holds neither positive nor negative attitudes toward exercise or some other health behavior?

haviors is mixed—it depends largely on the particular behavior being examined. The model has done an accurate job predicting preventive dental care (Ronis, 1992), sexual risk-taking behaviors (Aspinwall et al., 1991), and breast self-examination (Champion, 1990, 1994). Of the four components of the health belief model, barriers and costs appear to be the best predictor of health-related behaviors.

Protection Motivation Theory of Health   One of the problems with the health belief model is that even those individuals who believe they are susceptible to a health threat, who evaluate the health threat as severe, for whom the benefits of a positive health behavior outweigh the costs, and for whom the cues to action lead toward health-promoting behaviors may still not alter their behavior. The reason: they may not believe that they *can* successfully alter their current health behaviors. For example, if Sandy perceives himself to be susceptible to lung cancer, views lung cancer as severe, and sees great benefit in quitting smoking, he will not quit if he does not believe that he can actually quit smoking. Given this, during the 1980s, the health belief model was modified to include the component of **self-efficacy**, *a person's belief in her ability to successfully undertake a particular action or behavior* (Bandura, 1977a).*With the addition of self-efficacy, the health belief model assumed a new name:* the **protection motivation theory of health** (see Figure 11.3*b*).

Theory of Reasoned Action   The **theory of reasoned action**, like the health belief model, takes a social-cognitive view toward health behaviors, *broadly stating that behaviors stem from behavioral intentions* (Ajzen & Fishbein, 1980). Although no one would question that intentions do not always translate into behavior, certainly intentions to perform a particular behavior are a necessary first step toward actually performing the behavior. I intend to do a lot of things that I never really do, but rarely do I do something that I did not have an initial intention to do. Behavioral intentions are a function of two components: attitudes toward the behavior and the subjective norms surrounding the behavior (Figure 11.3*c*).

Attitudes represent *the beliefs one has that a particular behavior will produce a particular outcome and one's evaluation of those outcomes*—for example, the belief that practicing safe sex will reduce the likelihood of pregnancy and contracting a sexually transmitted disease; and one's belief that these are favorable outcomes. **Subjective norms** reflect *someone's perception of how significant other individuals will view the behavior and the motivation to comply with the desires of those others*. For example, if Jeff perceives that his parents are opposed to smoking and he wishes to comply with his parents' wishes (and he has favorable beliefs about quitting smoking), then Jeff will be more likely to quit smoking. Like the health belief model, the theory of reasoned action has successfully predicted several health behaviors, including participation in mammography screenings (Montano et al., 1997), smoking cessation (Sutton, 1989), and a willingness to be an organ donor (Kowalski & Bodenlos, 2003).

Theory of Planned Behavior   Like the health belief model, the theory of reasoned action fails to account for those instances in which behavior modification does not occur because an individual does not feel he can successfully modify his behavior. Thus, Ajzen introduced the theory of planned behavior (Figure 11.3*d*). The **theory of planned behavior** *includes all of the components of the theory of reasoned action plus self-efficacy, sometimes referred to as perceived behavioral control* (Ajzen, 1991; Hardeman et al., 2002). The theory of planned behavior has met with considerable success in predicting health behaviors, including sunscreen use (Hillhouse et al., 1996), hand hygiene practice among medical personnel (Jenner et al., 2002), breast (Lierman et al., 1990) and testicular (Brubaker & Wickersham, 1990) self-examinations, intentions to eat healthy foods (Astrom & Rise, 2001), children's intentions to engage in physical activity (Hagger et al., 2001), and intentions to have mammograms and clinical breast examinations (Godin et al., 2001).

INTERIM SUMMARY

Four models of health behavior have been discussed. The **health belief model** theorizes that health behaviors are predicted by an individual's perception of his **perceived susceptibility** to a health threat (a factor that is undermined by the **optimistic bias**), the **perceived seriousness** of the health threat, the **benefits** and **barriers** associated with terminating a compromising health behavior, and **cues to action**. The addition of **self-efficacy**, or an individual's confidence that she can actually engage in the health behavior, to the health belief model creates the **protection motivation theory of health**. The **theory of reasoned action** and the **theory of planned behavior** both suggest that behavior is a function of behavioral intentions. Behavioral intentions are a function of a person's **attitudes** toward the health behavior (i.e., their beliefs that particular outcomes follow from a behavior and their evaluation of those beliefs), and **subjective norms** (i.e., the individual's perception of how significant others feel about the behavior and the person's motivation to comply with those feelings or desires). These two models differ in the inclusion of self-efficacy into the theory of planned behavior.

Health-Compromising Behaviors

Most people can easily list behaviors that are disadvantageous to their health: smoking, excessive alcohol consumption, obesity, lack of sleep, and lack of exercise, to name a few. These same people can even tell you many of the negative consequences that follow from engaging in these health-compromising behaviors, including reduced life expectancy, chronic illnesses, and poor social relationships. Fewer people, however, can claim that they do not engage in any of these behaviors. And, in all likelihood, people engage in more than one and perhaps several of the health-compromising behaviors.

In one of the first empirical attempts to examine not only the practice of health-compromising behaviors, but also the relationship that these behaviors have to morbidity and mortality, researchers conducted a study beginning in the 1960s which examined the practice of seven health behaviors among 7000 residents in Alameda County, California: sleeping 7 to 8 hours each night, not smoking, eating breakfast every morning, not snacking between meals, being no more than 10 percent overweight, getting regular exercise, and having no more than two alcoholic beverages a day (Belloc & Breslow, 1972). Participants in the study were asked about their practice of these seven behaviors, how many illnesses they had experienced, what kind of illnesses, and how much energy they had. Not surprisingly, the more health habits the people practiced, the fewer illnesses they had had and the more energy they had. In short, good health habits and wellness were strongly positively correlated. Perhaps even more interesting, a follow-up study of these same people 9.5 years later revealed significant relationships between the practice of health habits and mortality. Males who practiced the health behaviors had a mortality rate 28 percent that of men who practiced few, if any, of the health behaviors. For women, the rate of mortality was 43 percent that of women who did not reliably practice health behaviors (Breslow & Enstrom, 1980).

Clearly, people's choices about whether or not to smoke, drink, eat to excess, and get enough sleep have serious implications for health. In the sections that follow, we examine in more detail some of the health-compromising behaviors in which people engage on an all too regular basis, namely overeating, smoking, alcohol abuse, and high risk sexual behaviors.

Obesity

Prevalence A June 5, 2003, report by the Centers for Disease Control (CDC) was titled "Obesity Fastest-Growing Health Threat." The World Health Organization has referred to obesity as a global epidemic (WHO, 1998). Researchers at the CDC

Making Connections

The importance of people's attitudes toward health behaviors has been a major focus of advertising campaigns designed to alter health-compromising behaviors. Thus, it is not surprising that these attitudes are reflected in all four of the theories of health behavior (Chapter 17).

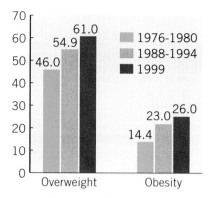

Source: CDC National Center for Health Statistics, Health Health E.Stats.

FIGURE 11.4 Changes in prevalence of obesity. The prevalence of obesity is increasing by epidemic proportions, making it a leading health threat worldwide today. The figure highlights not only the increase in the prevalence of overweight and obese individuals, but also the shocking percentage of people who are, in fact, overweight or obese. *Source:* American Obesity Association, 2003.

recently recalculated causes of death and found that, although tobacco is still the primary health threat, obesity ranks a very close second. Over half of all adult Americans are overweight or obese (Mokdad et al., 1999; U.S. Department of Health and Human Services, 2000), with more women than men being classified as both overweight and obese. Members of some minority populations (e.g., African-Americans) are particularly at risk for excess weight (Kopelman, 2000); over a third of African-American and Mexican-American women are classified as obese (Wadden et al., 2002). Although the prevalence of overweight individuals has increased in the last two decades, the incidence of obesity has doubled (see Figure 11.4)!

The increase in prevalence rates of overweight and obese individuals is not limited to adults. Statistics released by the National Center for Health Statistics (1999-2000) showed that 15 percent of children between the ages of 12-19 are overweight and 15 percent between the ages of 6-11 are overweight (CDC, 2003). A recent study found that weight is even a problem among preschoolers. Three hundred eighty five children between the ages of 2 and 6 who had been referred by a physician because they were overweight participated. In spite of counseling given to the parents of the children, 86 percent of 177 children tested at follow-up were obese by the time they were 6 (Sass, 2003).

Determining whether a person is overweight or obese is typically done by calculating the individual's **body mass index (BMI)**: *the "weight in kilograms divided by the height in meters squared: kg/m²"* (Wadden et al., 2002a; Table 11.1). In pounds and inches, the formula is [weight (pounds) × 703/(height in inches squared)]. **Obesity** refers to *an excessive accumulation of body fat, in excess of 30 percent in women and 20 percent in men* (Lohman, 2002). People are identified as being **overweight** if they have *a body mass index (BMI) between 25 percent and 30 percent*, depending on their gender and age.

Consequences   Obesity is not only a pervasive problem in the United States and other industrialized countries today, but it is also one of the leading contributors to preventable deaths (Pi-Sunyer, 1999). Estimates are that about 280,000 people die in the United States each year because of problems stemming from obesity itself and from complications that obesity creates for other medical illnesses (Allison et al., 1999). Obesity contributes to the development of diabetes, gallstones, heart disease, pregnancy complications, high blood pressure, sleep apnea, and some cancers (e.g., endometrial, breast, and colon) (Corsica & Perri, 2003). People with a BMI of 30 increase their risk of mortality 30 percent. Those with a BMI of 40 or more increase their risk of mortality by 100 percent (Wadden et al., 2002a)! As noted by Kopelman (2000, p. 635), "Obesity should no longer be regarded simply as a cosmetic problem affecting certain individuals, but an epidemic that threatens global well-being."

Problems stemming from obesity are not just physical in nature. People who are obese often experience psychological difficulties as well, stemming in large part from the stigma attached to obesity and the subsequent discrimination experienced by obese individuals. As noted by Corsica and Perri (2003, p. 125), "Obesity may well be the last socially acceptable object of prejudice and discrimination in our country." People who are obese are considered by many to be lazy and out of control (Crandall, 1994, 1995). Relative to people who are not obese, obese individuals are less likely to marry, get desired jobs, be treated respectfully by physicians and other medical personnel, and get into prestigious colleges (Figure 11.5; Corsica & Perri, 2003; Gortmaker et al., 1993; Pingitore et al., 1994; Wadden et

	OBSERVED VALUE	
	OVERWEIGHT (n = 195)	NONOVERWEIGHT (n = 4943)
Married (%) (n = 4922)	28	56
Household income ($) (n = 4286)	18,372	30,586
Income below poverty level (%) (n = 4286)	32	13
Education (yr) (n = 4881)	12.1	13.1
Completed college (%) (n = 4881)	9	21
Self-esteem in 1987 (n = 5138)	32.4	33.6

FIGURE 11.5 Stigma of obesity. People who are obese are clearly discriminated against. As the figure shows, people who are obese are less likely than those who are not obese to be married and to complete college. They also make less money, in all likelihood because they are barred from higher-paying jobs. *Source:* Gortmaker et al., 1993.

Table 11.1 ▉▉ Body Mass Index Table

	Normal						Overweight					Obese										Extreme Obesity														
BMI	19	20	21	22	23	24	25	26	27	28	29	30	31	32	33	34	35	36	37	38	39	40	41	42	43	44	45	46	47	48	49	50	51	52	53	54
Height (inches)																		Body Weight (pounds)																		
58	91	96	100	105	110	115	119	124	129	134	138	143	148	153	158	162	167	172	177	181	186	191	196	201	205	210	215	220	224	229	234	239	244	248	253	258
59	94	99	104	109	114	119	124	128	133	138	143	148	153	18	163	168	173	178	183	188	193	198	203	108	212	217	222	227	232	237	242	247	252	257	262	267
60	97	102	107	112	118	123	128	133	138	143	148	153	158	163	168	174	179	184	189	194	199	203	209	215	220	225	230	235	240	245	250	255	261	266	271	276
61	100	106	111	116	122	127	132	137	143	148	153	158	164	169	174	180	185	1890	195	201	206	211	217	222	227	232	238	243	248	254	259	264	269	275	280	285
62	104	109	115	120	126	131	136	142	147	153	158	164	169	175	180	186	191	196	1202	207	213	218	224	229	235	240	246	251	256	262	267	273	278	284	289	295
63	107	113	118	124	130	135	141	146	152	158	163	169	175	180	186	191	197	203	208	214	220	225	231	237	242	248	254	259	265	270	278	282	287	293	299	304
64	110	116	122	128	134	140	145	151	157	163	169	174	180	186	192	197	204	209	215	221	227	232	238	244	250	256	262	267	273	279	285	291	296	302	308	314
65	114	120	126	132	128	144	150	156	162	168	174	180	186	192	198	204	210	216	222	228	234	240	246	252	258	264	270	276	282	288	294	300	306	312	318	324
66	118	124	130	136	142	148	155	161	167	173	179	186	192	198	204	210	216	223	229	235	241	247	253	260	266	272	278	284	291	297	303	309	315	322	328	334
67	121	127	134	140	146	153	159	166	172	178	185	191	198	204	211	217	223	230	236	242	249	255	261	268	274	280	287	293	299	306	312	319	325	331	338	344
68	125	131	138	144	151	158	164	171	177	184	190	197	203	210	216	223	230	236	243	249	256	262	269	276	282	289	295	302	308	315	322	328	335	341	348	354
69	128	135	142	149	155	162	169	176	182	189	196	203	209	216	223	230	236	243	250	257	263	270	277	284	291	297	304	311	318	324	331	338	345	351	258	265
70	132	139	146	153	160	167	174	181	188	195	202	209	216	222	229	236	242	250	257	264	271	278	285	292	299	306	313	320	327	334	341	348	355	362	369	376
71	136	143	150	157	165	172	179	186	193	200	208	215	222	229	236	243	250	257	265	272	279	286	293	301	308	315	322	329	338	343	351	358	365	372	379	386
72	140	147	154	162	169	177	184	191	199	206	213	221	228	235	242	250	258	265	272	279	287	294	302	309	316	324	331	338	346	353	361	368	375	383	390	397
73	144	151	159	166	174	182	189	197	204	212	219	227	235	242	250	257	265	272	280	288	295	302	310	318	325	333	340	348	355	363	371	378	386	393	401	408
74	148	155	163	171	179	186	194	202	2210	218	225	233	241	249	256	264	272	280	287	295	303	311	319	326	334	342	350	358	365	373	381	389	396	404	412	420
75	152	160	168	176	184	192	200	208	216	224	232	240	248	256	264	272	279	287	295	303	311	319	327	335	343	351	359	367	375	383	391	399	407	415	423	431
76	156	164	172	180	189	197	205	213	221	230	238	246	254	263	271	279	287	295	304	312	320	328	336	344	353	361	369	377	385	394	402	410	418	426	435	443

Source: Adapted from *Clinical Guidelines on the Identification, Evaluation, and Treatment of Overweight and Obesity in Adults: The Evidence Report.*

al., 2002b). They also have lower household incomes, fewer years of education, and personal incomes that are more likely to place them at or below the poverty level (Gortmaker et al., 1993). Those who affiliate with or are even in proximity to the obese are also at increased risk of being stigmatized. In a study illustrating this, researchers found that male job applicants were rated more negatively when they were seen seated next to an overweight (as opposed to an average weight) woman (Hebl & Mannix, 2003). (See Figure 11.6). Specifically, raters indicated that they would be less likely to hire the job applicant affiliated with an obese individual, and they rated his professional qualities and interpersonal skills more negatively.

The personal rejection and social discrimination experienced by obese individuals can have detrimental effects on their personal well-being. A large-scale study involving over 40,000 participants examined the relationship between BMI and depression, suicidal ideation, and suicide attempts. Among women, higher BMIs were

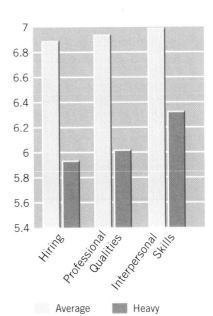

FIGURE 11.6 Discrimination as a result of mere exposure to an obese individual. People rated male job applicants as lower in professional qualities and interpersonal skills and indicated that they would be less likely to hire this individual when he was seated next to an obese as opposed to an average-weight individual. Ratings were based on 12-point scales. *Source:* Hebl & Mannix, 2003.

Apply & Discuss

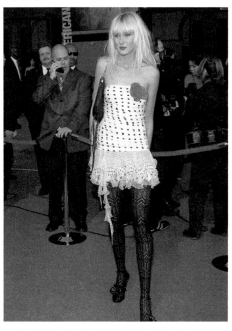

At least within Western culture, women are held to different standards of weight than men. Society tells women that thin is in.

■ Given the differential treatment of men and women in terms of weight, do you think weight-related discrimination affects men and women differently?

■ Why do you think, given societal pressures put on women to be thin, that more women than men are both overweight and obese?

Genes load the gun, the environment pulls the trigger.

BRAY, 1998.

associated with a higher frequency of major depressive episodes and more suicidal ideation. Among men, however, lower BMIs were associated with depression and suicidal ideation (Carpenter et al., 2000), a clear testament to the different standards of attractiveness to which men and women are held in society.

Perhaps nowhere is the stigma attached to obesity more painful than for children who are obese. As we noted earlier, approximately 15 percent of children and 15 percent of adolescents are obese. Children can be cruel under the best of circumstances,

Making Connections

BMI (body mass index) is the most commonly used means of classifying someone as overweight or obese. It is based on a weight-to-height ratio. However, weight comes from more than just fat. Someone with a large amount of lean muscle mass will weigh more than someone of similar height without the muscle. Thus, they will be classified as being overweight but they do not have more fat.

but children and adolescents who are overweight are very ready targets for teasing and bullying (Dietz, 1998). Just as discrimination of obese adults can have negative effects on the self-esteem of those obese individuals, so too can the persistent ridicule to which obese children are frequently exposed. In 1996, Samuel Graham ("Sammy"), tired of the constant teasing he received at school about his weight (Sammy was 5'4" and weighed 174), climbed out of his bedroom window, went into his backyard, and hung himself. He was found by his brothers. In 1994, Brian Head, aged 16, was taunted yet again by peers at school. He pulled out a gun and shot himself in the head in front of his classmates (NAAFA, 2003). At other times, the aggression may be directed outward to others, as a way of expressing pent-up anger at the people who are ridiculing them.

Beyond such incredible personal tolls, obesity also exacts significant economic costs. Treatment for obesity and related illnesses consumes between 2 percent and 7 percent of total health care costs. On top of this are costs associated with lost work hours due to illness and death associated with obesity. Collectively, then, economic costs associated with obesity exceed $100 billion annually (Wolf & Colditz, 1998). Over 39 million workdays are lost each year because of factors related to obesity.

Sammy Graham committed suicide to escape persistent ridiculing about his weight.

Contributors to Obesity The multitude of contributors to obesity include both physiological and environmental sources (Figure 11.7). Physiologically, both hormones and genes have been implicated in obesity. Genetic influences are estimated to account for up to 40 percent of the etiology of obesity (Stunkard et al., 1990; Wadden et al., 2002a). Twin studies reveal that both body weight and the amount of fat in a person's body are highly heritable. Body weight of adoptees correlates with the weight of their biological parents but not with their adoptive parents (Allison et al., 1994; Bouchard, 1989). Heritability for obesity is estimated to range from 30 to 70 percent, which is extremely high (Devlin et al., 2000). Even the amount a person eats is highly heritable, although family environment during childhood also influences food intake years later (de Castro, 1993; Faith et al., 1999).

Tracking down the genes that contribute to obesity is difficult because so many processes influenced by genetics can contribute—such as those regulating hunger, satiety, metabolic rate, fat storage, or activity levels. In fact, researchers have already isolated at least 200 genes likely to contribute to normal and abnormal weight (Yager, 2000). Two physiological factors have received attention for many years, both of which show substantial heritability. The first is the number and size of fat cells in the body. Obese people have many more fat cells than average weight individuals, and the cells

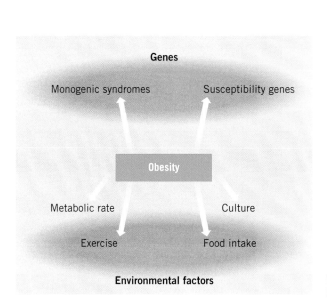

FIGURE 11.7 Factors that influence the development of obesity. *Source:* Reprinted from Kopelman, 2000.

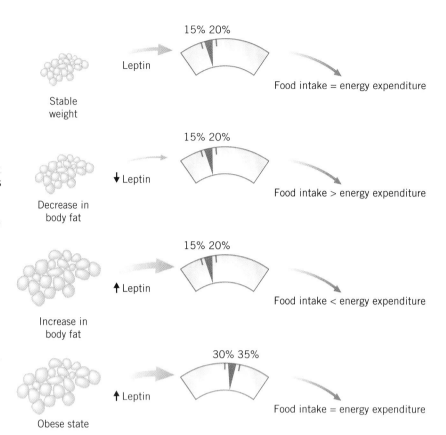

FIGURE 11.8 Leptin and the regulation of adipose tissue mass. The cloning of the *ob* gene and the characterization of leptin has indicated that body fat content is under homeostatic control. The available data suggest that leptin is the afferent signal in a feedback loop regulating adipose tissue mass. At an individual's stable weight (shown as 15–20% body fat in this figure, which is the typical fat content of a nonobese subject) the amount of circulating leptin elicits a state in which food intake equals energy expenditure. Increasing leptin levels result in negative energy balance (energy expenditure < food intake), whereas decreasing levels lead to positive energy balance (food intake > energy expenditure). These effects maintain constancy of fat cell mass within a relatively narrow range. Evidence further suggests that the intrinsic sensitivity to leptin is reduced among the obese and that the set point for body fat content is thus increased (designated as 30–35% in the bottom panel). Most obese individuals have high leptin levels and thus enter a state of negative energy balance when weight is reduced and leptin levels fall. Reprinted from the role of leptin in obesity. *Source:* Reprinted from Friedman, 2000.

Big Picture φ Question 6

What is the relation between nature and nurture in shaping psychological processes?

they do have tend to be larger (Hirsch & Knittle, 1970). Unfortunately, fat cells that develop early in life do not disappear when a person later attempts to lose weight; they only shrink.

One theory suggests that the amount of body fat one has is regulated by the hormone leptin (shown as a monogenic syndrome in Figure 11.7). People with higher levels of leptin generally have higher BMIs (Friedman, 2000). Leptin is produced by fat tissue and operates on the hypothalamus to regulate body weight. In order to maintain homeostasis, decreases in body fat produce decreases in leptin, which triggers the body's desire to take in more food (Figure 11.8). Conversely, an increase in body fat increases the level of leptin, which triggers reduced food consumption. It is through this process that many people's weight hovers around a **set point**, *an ideal body weight for each individual*. Given this regulator, why does everyone's weight not stay around their set point? The answer again is physiological. Some people, those who become obese, appear to be leptin-resistant (Friedman, 2000). Thus, they are unable to effectively control their weight around their set point. Other individuals do not produce enough leptin and have reduced levels of body fat, almost regardless of what food they might consume. A number of genetic, social, and environmental variables can determine how sensitive a particular individual is to leptin. For example, a diet high in fat can lead an individual to become leptin-resistant and thereby increase the likelihood that they will become obese.

Another theory, the **susceptible gene hypothesis**, suggests *that certain genes increase but do not guarantee the development of a particular trait or characteristics (e.g., obesity).* Animal models, usually mice, have also provided useful information in helping researchers map particular genes that are associated with obesity (Straub, 2002; Figure 11.7). In spite of the strong evidence for genetic underpinnings of obesity, it is impossible to rule out environmental contributions to obesity. A case in point is the Pima Indians (see Devlin et al., 2000). In Mexico, where they have to search for food actively every day to survive, individuals weigh on average almost 60 pounds less than their more sedentary Arizona relatives, who share their genetics. Whereas starvation was once a major cause of mortality, in technologically developed societies the opposite, obesity, may be the greater threat.

As the last several decades have witnessed an explosion in the incidence of obesity, genes have remained largely the same—clearly genes are not the only factor or even the primary factor involved. Forty-four percent of dogs of obese people are also obese. For nonobese individuals, only 25 percent of the dogs are obese (Mason, 1970). Obesity rates are higher in industrialized as opposed to nonindustrialized countries. People living in industrialized countries are confronted with a plethora of high-calorie foods that are readily available (e.g., fast-food restaurants). In addition, as jobs have become increasingly sedentary, energy expenditure has decreased. Complicating matters even further, because of the stigma attached to obesity, many obese individuals feel too embarrassed to be seen exercising in public. The lack of physical activity makes it difficult for many people to maintain their weight at an acceptable level.

Women of higher socioeconomic status in technologically developed countries are substantially less obese than women of lower socioeconomic status. The difference between the two groups appears to reflect environmental factors: diet, efforts to restrain eating, and trips to the gym (Garner & Wooley, 1991). Thus, as with IQ, genetics plays a central role in accounting for individual differences in body mass, but group differences may be under greater environmental control.

Other environmental factors substantially affect body weight and obesity. For example, Europeans are often astonished by the size of food portions in U.S. restaurants, and with good reason: One of the best ways to cut obesity is simply to limit portions and to change expectations about how much food should be on the plate (Hill & Peters, 1998). A recent experimental study of children's eating patterns found that cutting back on time watching television and playing video games resulted in decreased fatness (Robinson, 1999). Thus, although DNA plays a key role in obesity, so, too, do Nintendo and McNuggets.

The psychological factors involved in obesity are not entirely clear, in part because different people become obese for different reasons (Friedman & Brownell,1995; Rodin et al., 1989). One frequent psychological correlate of obesity is low self-esteem (Bruch, 1970; Miller & Downey, 1999). Whether self-esteem problems cause or reflect obesity, however, is unclear; the relationship probably runs in both directions, with people sometimes eating to assuage their pain and others feeling bad about themselves *because of* their weight. Anxiety appears to be another psychological variable relevant to obesity (Greeno & Wing, 1994; Palme & Palme, 1999). Both clinical and experimental data suggest that some people overeat to control anxiety (Ganley, 1989; Slochower, 1987). Further, people who are morbidly obese (at least 100 pounds or 100 percent over ideal body weight) are more likely to suffer from depressive, anxiety, and personality disorders (Black et al., 1992).

Another important variable is the motivation to diet or exercise. Exercising is strongly predictive of weight control, but only 15 percent of dieters continue their exercise regimens after reaching their weight goal (Katahn & McMinn, 1990). Health psychologists are attempting to understand the reasons people smoke, eat too much, fail to see the doctor when they are becoming sick, and fail to exercise, and are beginning to zero in on some of the reasons for this seemingly "irrational" behavior (Chapter 10).

Society is also to blame. Society does little to combat obesity in children or adults. The time that children once spent playing outdoors, they now spend playing video games or watching television (Sallis et al., 1999). State budget cuts throughout the United States have resulted in the elimination of many physical education programs in elementary through high school. Thus, caloric intake increases, energy expenditure decreases, and those who are overweight do not exercise for fear of ridicule by others. That increases in sedentary lifestyles, coupled with drive-up food services and remote

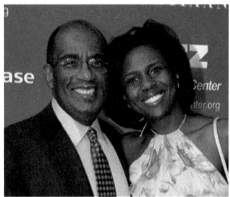

Following surgical intervention (combined with a regular exercise program), Al Roker has experienced noticeable weight loss.

controls, parallels increases in obesity is probably no coincidence (Foreyt & Goodrick, 1995; Wadden et al., 2002a).

Treatment "More people are treated for obesity in the United States than for all other health habits or conditions combined. More than 400,000 people attend weight-loss clinics alone. Amazon.com currently lists 15,401 titles that refer to diet or dieting"(Taylor, 2003, p. 122). People seek treatment for obesity for a number of different reasons. Some individuals need to lose weight because of the health-complicating factors associated with obesity. Others want to lose weight to escape the rejection and ridicule experienced at the hands of others because of their weight. Perhaps because of rejection, others seek help losing weight in order to improve their self-esteem and reduce depression.

Dieting has been and still is the most common step in treating obesity. Many people want a relatively quick fix to their weight problem. Patients who are obese are taught how to restrict their caloric intake and, in addition, how to increase their energy expenditure through physical exercise. However, dietary restrictions are rarely successful in the long term. Estimates are that around 90 percent of people who lose weight via dieting subsequently gain the weight back. As one diet after another is tried (yo-yo dieting), changes in metabolism may actually contribute to the person's gaining back even more weight than she started with. This downside does not even include the decreased self-esteem and increased depression resulting from the failure to successfully maintain long-term weight loss that may then lead the person to consume even more"comfort"food.

Appetite-suppressing drugs may be used to help obese individuals limit their caloric consumption (Bray & Tartaglia, 2000). Two primary problems surround the use of these drugs. First, a few years ago, some of these drugs were removed from the market because of health complications resulting from them. Second, even if the drugs are successful in helping someone lose weight, if the person attributes his success to the drugs, his confidence and self-efficacy about his ability to maintain weight loss are compromised (Rodin et al., 1988). Furthermore, the use of diets or appetite-suppressing drugs can complicate health problems that already exist as a result of the obesity or that were worsened as excess body fat accumulated.

For individuals who are at least 100 percent overweight, more extreme measures of treatment are available, including gastroplasty and gastric bypass. Gastroplasty or stomach stapling involves stapling the stomach so that only a small portion of it remains available for processing food. People who have had gastroplasty and consume too much food experience stomach upset and vomiting. Besides obvious complications associated with any type of surgery, two additional issues accompany the use of gastroplasty. First, although the ingestion of anything more than small amounts of food at any one setting can be aversive, liquids, including high-calorie liquids such as milk shakes, can be more easily accommodated. Second, over time and with the repeated consumption of excess food, the pouch can stretch (Corsica & Perri, 2003).

Gastric bypass is similar to gastroplasty except that, instead of allowing food to move through the remainder of the stomach into the small intestine, a portion of the small intestine is attached directly to the pouch created from the stapling of the stomach. In this way, most of the stomach is "bypassed."Very little food is actually absorbed into the body, stimulating weight loss. The ingestion of sweet or high-calorie foods (including high-calorie liquids) produces nausea and vomiting.

None of these methods of controlling obesity will be completely effective unless they are also accompanied by therapeutic interventions to help obese individuals understand the origins of their obesity, their patterns of disordered eating, and the consequences of obesity for their health. In recognition of the physical, psychological, and social contributions to the accumulation of body fat, some researchers have designed

Vertical Banded Gastroplasty   Roux-en-Y Gastric Bypass

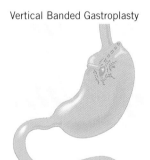

Surgical treatment for obesity

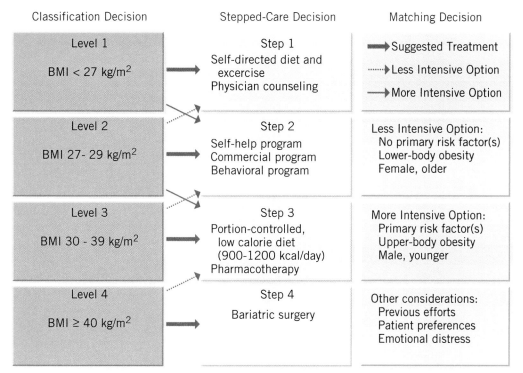

Classification Decision

Level 1	
BMI < 27 kg/m²	

| Level 2 |
| BMI 27- 29 kg/m² |

| Level 3 |
| BMI 30 - 39 kg/m² |

| Level 4 |
| BMI ≥ 40 kg/m² |

Stepped-Care Decision

Step 1
Self-directed diet and
excercise
Physician counseling

Step 2
Self-help program
Commercial program
Behavioral program

Step 3
Portion-controlled,
low calorie diet
(900-1200 kcal/day)
Pharmacotherapy

Step 4
Bariatric surgery

Matching Decision

➡ Suggested Treatment
┈▶ Less Intensive Option
⟶ More Intensive Option

Less Intensive Option:
No primary risk factor(s)
Lower-body obesity
Female, older

More Intensive Option:
Primary risk factor(s)
Upper-body obesity
Male, younger

Other considerations:
Previous efforts
Patient preferences
Emotional distress

FIGURE 11.9 A conceptual scheme showing a three-stage process for selecting treatment. The first step, the classification decision, divides people into four levels based on body mass index (BMI). This level indicates which of four classes of interventions are likely to be most appropriate in the second stage, the stepped-care decision. All individuals are encouraged to control their weight by increasing their physical activity and consuming an appropriate diet. When this approach is not successful, more intensive intervention may be warranted, with the most conservative treatment (i.e., lowest cost and risks of side-effects) tried next. The thick solid arrow between two boxes shows the class of treatments that is usually most appropriate for an individual when less intensive interventions have not been suc- cessful. The third stage, the matching decision, is used to make a final treatment selection, based on the individual's prior weight loss efforts, treatment preferences, and need for weight reduction (as judged by the presence of comorbid conditions or other risk factors). The dashed lines point to treatment options for persons with a reduced need for weight reduction because of a reduced risk of health complications. The thin solid arrows show the more intensive treatment options for persons, who despite relatively low BMI levels, have increased risks of health complications. Adjunct nutritional or psychological counseling is recommended for patients who report marked problems with meal planning, depression, body image, or similar difficulties. *Source*: Reprinted from Wadden et al. (2002, p.514).

more systematic programs for weight loss that are based on an individual's BMI and current health status (Wadden et al., 2002a; see Figure 11.9 for an example of one such program). The advantages of such programs are twofold. First, they are tailored to the individual's own needs and physiological states. Second, they recognize the multiple origins of obesity and target most or all of these.

Cigarette Smoking

Prevalence   Estimates are that, each day, 3000 adolescents begin to smoke. Half of these adolescents who continue to smoke throughout their lives will die from a smoking-related illness (U.S. Department of Health and Human Services, 2000). Approximately 28 percent of high-school aged adolescents smoke regularly, down from 36 percent in 1997 (U.S. Department of Health and Human Services, 2000). Among adults over the age of 18, approximately 23 percent smoked regularly in 2001, down only slightly from the 25 percent who reported regular smoking in 1997. Although more men than women report being regular smokers, more women than men are taking up smoking (Figure 11.10).

"There's no shooting—we just make you keep smoking."

© The New Yorker Collection 2001 Michael Shaw from the cartoonbank.com

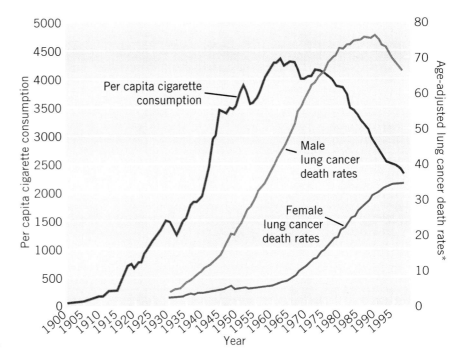

FIGURE 11.10   Tobacco use in the United States, 1900–1998. *Source*: Reprinted from Cancer Prevention and Early Detection Facts and Figures, 2002, p. 4.

Consequences   "Cigarette smoking is the single most preventable cause of illness, disability, and premature death in this country and in much of the world. In the United States alone, it is estimated that 435,000 people a year die from smoking-related illnesses—much more than the combined number of deaths from murders, suicides, AIDS, automobile accidents, alcohol and other drug abuses, and fires." (Straub, 2002, p. 344) (Figure 11.11). Estimates are that, by the end of this century, up to a billion deaths worldwide will be attributable to smoking ("Science historian predicts," 2002). Medical costs associated with smoking exceed $50 billion a year, with an additional $25 billion spent in lost productivity due to absenteeism. Worldwide, 250 million packs of cigarettes are consumed per day (Myers, 2001). Estimates are that each

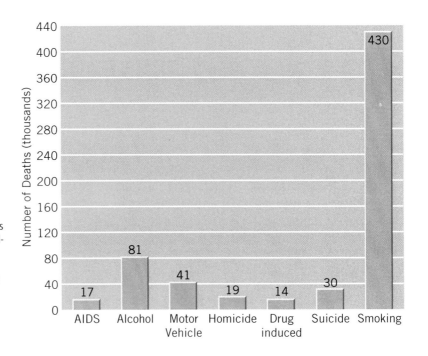

FIGURE 11.11   Comparative causes of annual deaths in the United States. *Sources:* (AIDS) HIV/AIDS Surveillance Report, 1998; (Alcohol) M.J. McGinnis & W. H. Foege. Review: Actual Causes of Death in the United States. *JAMA* 1993; 270: 2207–2212; (Motor vehicle) National Highway Transportation Safety Administration, 1998; (Homicide, Suicide) NCHS, vital statistics, 1997; (Drug Induced) NCHS, vital statistics, 1996; (Smoking) SAMMEC, 1995.

pack costs the United States $7.18 in medical expenses and lost job productivity (Centers for Disease Control, 2002). Not counting deaths associated with secondhand smoke, estimates are that males lost an average of 13 years and females 14.5 years because of smoking. Each cigarette smoked costs the smoker 12 minutes of his life ("A fistful of," 1996). Each time a cigarette is lit, 4000 chemicals are released (Swan et al., 2003).

Not surprisingly, then, smoking is a risk factor for heart disease, lung cancer, emphysema, bronchitis and other respiratory problems, and cancers of the mouth, bladder, esophagus, and pancreas (Newcomb & Carbone, 1992). Smoking during pregnancy results in 1000 infant deaths each year (Centers for Disease Control, 2002). In addition, children whose mothers smoked during pregnancy are at heightened risk for respiratory problems, lower IQs, and attention-deficit hyperactivity disorder (ADHD) (Milberger et al., 1996). And, the risks of smoking are not limited to the smokers themselves. People who are around smokers are exposed to secondhand smoke. Referred to as passive smokers, these individuals are also at increased risk for lung cancer and heart disease. Indeed, some refer to passive smoking as the third leading cause of preventable death (Glantz & Parmley, 1991) (Figure 11.12).

Contributors to Smoking   Contributors to smoking, as with most other health-related issues, are both genetic and environmental, although the origin of smoking has largely social origins, as will be discussed. Addiction to nicotine is, in part, genetically based. Studies of identical twins indicate that heritability of smoking approaches 60 percent (Heath & Madden, 1995). Furthermore, some individuals metabolize nicotine more rapidly than others. Fast metabolizers are less likely than slow metabolizers to experience the negative effects of smoking or to experience smoking as aversive. Thus, fast metabolizers are likely to smoke more than slow metabolizers. The rate at which one metabolizes nicotine is genetically determined (Idle, 1990; Swan et al., 2003). Smokers and nonsmokers also appear to differ in a gene related to dopamine. People with the 9-repeat allele gene are less likely to become smokers than people with another form of the gene (Lerman et al., 1999).

In spite of the clear role that dispositional factors play in the onset of cigarette smoking, environmental and social variables play key roles. Most people begin to smoke (or at least try their first cigarette) during adolescence. The main reason: peer pressure and self-presentational concerns (see One Step Further: Self-Presentation and Health). When asked why he first began to smoke, one young man said "It's peer pressure. Nobody starts smoking because it feels good or it's the right thing to do" ("Movie stars who," 2003). Many adolescents believe that smoking conveys an image of toughness and rebelliousness, perhaps stemming from the image conveyed by Joe Camel. And, in fact, it may. Smokers are twice as likely as nonsmokers to have had sex, three times more likely to have consumed alcohol, and seventeen times more likely to have used marijuana (U.S. Department of Health and Human Services, 1994).

These same social variables contribute to why people continue to smoke. The desire to be accepted by a particular peer group and to maintain desired identity images, such as being rebellious, leads many adolescents to become hooked. Contributing to this social addiction is the physiological addiction. At a physiological level, smoking also has rewarding properties. Nicotine increases levels of epinephrine and norepinephrine, producing improved mental acuity, reduced pain sensitivity, reduced feelings of anxiety, and feelings of relaxation (Heishman, 1999). Nicotine also increases the release of dopamine in the reward centers of the brain (Nowak, 1994). Foregoing these rewards by quitting smoking is difficult for many people.

Treatment   How do smokers quit? Not easily. Because smoking is so difficult to quit and because the health consequences of smoking are so negative, health psychologists direct much of their attention to programs designed to prevent people from

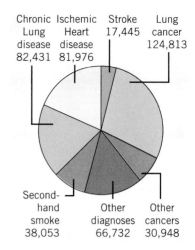

FIGURE 11.12   Annual deaths attributable to smoking in the United States: 1995–1999. *Source:* Centers for Disease Control, 2002.

Big Picture φ Question 6

What is the relation between nature and nurture in shaping psychological processes?

Joe Camel ads may have contributed to the belief of many adolescents that smoking conveys an image of toughness and rebelliousness.

Apply and Discuss

A recent article in the medical journal *The Lancet* stated that teens who watch movies in which the actors smoke are three times more likely to smoke than those who don't watch those same movies.

■ Do you agree with the journal's finding?

■ What other factors might be involved that could possibly distort the findings obtained in this study? How many people do you know who started smoking because of someone they had seen smoking in the movies?

smoking in the first place. Taxes on cigarettes have increased with the idea of making smoking prohibitively expensive for many, particularly adolescents whose funds are already limited. Educational programs intended to inform young people of the hazards of smoking are prevalent in schools. Advertising campaigns have been launched heralding the benefits of a smoke-free lifestyle and highlighting positive peer influence by showing young people who do not smoke and still enjoy satisfactory interactions with others.

In Broward County, Florida, underage smokers are made to appear in court with their parent or legal guardian. While in court, the teenagers watch a video on the negative effects of smoking and are forced to pay a $25 fine or engage in a full day of community service that involves picking up cigarette butts. Failure to comply with the judge's orders can result in the teen's driver's license being revoked. The program seems to be effective. Surveys of teens who had appeared in court revealed that almost 30 percent had reduced their intake of nicotine, and just over 15 percent had stopped smoking altogether (Chamberlain, 2001).

For adults who have been smoking for years and who appear to be immune to media and informational campaigns designed to get them to quit smoking, other methods are available to help with smoking cessation. To curb the physiological urge to smoke, pharmacological treatments, such as the nicotine patch, gum, and inhaler, are available. These pharmacological interventions have met with considerable success, particularly if they are paired with some form of behavioral therapy (Swan et al., 2003). Hypnosis is successful for some individuals who desire to quit smoking, as are other types of individual and group therapy. For both pharmacological and nonpharmacological methods of smoking cessation, social support is a critical variable influencing success. One study found that social support increased success in smoking cessation by 50 percent (Fiore et al., 2000). In reality, though, more smokers than not are unsuccessful in permanently putting out the cigarette. Estimates are that only about 25 percent of people who attempt to quit smoking remain smoke free.

One Step Further | Self-Presentation and Health

Self-presentation (also known as **impression management**; Leary, 1995; Leary & Kowalski, 1990) refers to *people's attempts to control the impressions that others form of them*. Much of what people do and don't do, they do and don't do because of concerns with the impressions other people are forming of them. Although self-presentational concerns as they relate to health can be adaptive, as when people exercise to be physically fit and convey positive impressions to others, self-presentational concerns can also be maladaptive for health and lead individuals to engage in health-compromising behaviors or not to engage in health-promoting behaviors because they want to project a particular image of themselves to others (Leary et al., 1994; Martin et al., 2001). In one study, first year college students were asked, at the end of their first semester at college, the frequency with which they had engaged in a number of health risk behaviors for self-presentational reasons. As Figure 11.13 shows, 75 percent of the college students reported having performed a risky health behavior at least once during their first semester of college. The most frequently reported behaviors were smoking, drinking, and reckless driving. The most frequently cited reasons for doing so: to appear cool. A comprehensive review of the maladaptive aspects of self-presentation for health has been written by Leary et al. (1994). Here, we will simply review a few of these.

	Drink Alcohol	Dangerous Driving	Smoke	Use Drugs	DUI	Unprotected Sex	Fight	Stunts	Ride with a DUI	Over lift
MEN										
Never	45	71	75	92	98	92	90	67	92	73
Once	6	16	8	4	0	8	8	16	4	16
Occasionally	39	10	16	4	2	0	2	16	4	10
Often	10	4	2	0	0	0	0	2	0	2
Cool/laid back	67	40	85	25	100	25	20	18	25	14
Fun/social	90	33	77	50	–	–	–	41	50	–
Brave/risktaker	23	73	7	–	–	50	80	82	50	86
Attractive	7	–	7	–	–	–	–	–	–	43
Mature	7	–	23	–	–	25	20	–	–	–
WOMEN										
Never	48	75	78	85	100	93	98	97	88	97
Once	23	13	9	10	0	5	0	3	9	3
Occasionally	23	8	10	3	0	2	2	0	3	0
Often	3	2	3	0	0	0	0	0	0	0
Cool/laid back	73	43	77	88	–	25	–	33	71	–
Fun/social	93	21	39	50	–	50	–	67	29	–
Brave/risktaker	30	64	39	63	–	25	100	–	14	50
Attractive	7	–	8	–	–	50	–	–	–	100
Mature	7	–	23	–	–	25	–	–	–	–

Note: All values are percentages. Impression values represent the percentage of respondents who engaged in the health risk behavior at least once and who mentioned that impression. Due to rounding, some columns do not add to 100 percent.

FIGURE 11.13   Frequency of students engaging in risky health-related behaviors for self-presentational reasons. *Source:* Reprinted from Martin & Leary, 2001.

Condom Use

Educators and health practitioners have long advocated the use of condoms to prevent pregnancy and the spread of sexually transmitted diseases (STDs). Beginning in 1999, some television networks allowed condom advertisements to be aired to get information out to teens in particular (Wilke, 2001). In spite of the fact that most people are aware of the effectiveness of condoms, many people still fail to use condoms regularly. Even people who have had an STD before are no more likely to use condoms than those who have never been diagnosed with an STD ("Even after having," 2003). One reason: self-presentational concerns. People are concerned with what others will think of them if they purchase condoms or what their partners might think of them if they suggest using them.

Embarrassment about purchasing condoms is a key factor inhibiting condom use among adolescents and young adults (Hanna, 1989; Herold, 1981), so much so that an estimated 25 percent of sexually active adolescents do not use an effective method of birth control (Sauerwein, 1992). What might people think if they saw them buying condoms? (Probably they would think they were going to have sex—the reason, in fact, why they were buying them, right?)

Even if condoms are bought, they will not necessarily be used. Sexually active adolescents and young adults report being concerned that their partner will think they worked to seduce them if they suggest using condoms they have with them

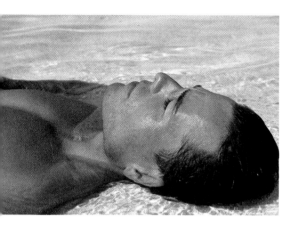

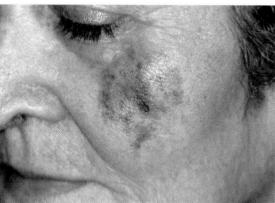

As relaxing as suntanning can be, the hazards of doing so can be serious.

(Kisker, 1985). Alternatively, many people worry that, if they suggest using condoms, their partner will assume that they must have a sexually transmitted disease themselves. Gay males have reported that they are afraid their partner will view them as a wimp if they suggest using condoms (Leary et al., 1994). Clearly, then, people's concerns with the impressions they might create on others can operate as a deterrent to safe-sex behaviors.

Suntanning and Skin Cancer

Few people can say that they have not sunbathed or been to a tanning bed with the purpose of improving their appearance (at least in the short term). Although certainly having a tan can make people "look" healthy, in the long run excessive tanning can have detrimental health consequences—most notably, skin cancer. The incidence of skin cancer has increased significantly in recent years. The prevalence of malignant melanoma (the most serious form of skin cancer) has quadrupled in the last 40 years (Fears & Scotto, 1982; Leary et al., 1994), with the incidence of basal cell carcinoma (the least serious form) increasing at a similar although slightly smaller rate. The primary cause of skin cancer: too much exposure to ultraviolet radiation. Some people, such as construction workers, are frequently exposed to too much ultraviolet radiation by the nature of their jobs; however, others voluntarily expose themselves to too much sun, either natural or artificial.

Although other factors may influence one's desire to engage in excessive tanning, research has shown impression management concerns to be the best predictor for excessive tanning (Leary & Jones, 1993). People who are concerned with how they appear to others are more likely than those who are less concerned with self-presentation to engage in excessive exposure to ultraviolet radiation. Furthermore, when researchers varied the outcome of tanning, making it clear to participants in the research study, that tanning can ultimately lead to less attractiveness, wrinkled skin, and, overall, more negative impressions, people endorsed more safe-sun attitudes (Jones & Leary, 1994).

Smoking, Alcohol, and Illegal Drugs

People's concerns with how they are perceived and evaluated by others play a key role in their initial and continued experiences with smoking, alcohol, and other illegal drugs. How many people do you know had their first cigarette or consumed their first alcoholic beverage alone? The number is very small (Friedman et al., 1985). Rather, peers have a substantial influence on people's initial experiences with nicotine, alcohol, or other drugs. Adolescents who smoke, for example, are perceived as tough and rebellious, an image valued by many adolescents trying to establish some independence from their parents. Adolescents begin and continue to drink or use drugs because they perceive those behaviors as valued by their peer group. They want to fit in and be accepted by their peers, so they go along with what they perceive to be normative behaviors (Clayton, 1991).

Furthermore, the use of alcohol and other drugs can allow an individual to control his image not only directly, but also indirectly. Take Frank, for example. Frank began using alcohol when he was 14 to fit in with his buddies. He quickly discovered that alcohol had secondary effects that also helped him create desired impressions on others. Frank thought of himself as shy, awkward, and socially unskilled. With a little alcohol in his system, however, he became gregarious and, in his mind, much more socially adept. Thus, not only did he fulfill the rebellious image he admired in his buddies, but alcohol allowed his social interactions to proceed much more smoothly, allowing him to make a more favorable impression on others when under the influence.

Self-presentational concerns may also be responsible for the difficulty that people have stopping their use of alcohol, nicotine, or other drugs. Frank may find it very difficult to stop using alcohol because of his feeling that, without alcohol, he will be unable to carry on pleasant interactions with others. Susan, who has smoked for 10 years, may be unwilling to quit smoking for fear that she will gain weight, perhaps compromising the impressions that she makes on others (Klesges & Klesges, 1988).

Exercise

As noted earlier, the desire to make favorable impressions on others can encourage people to exercise. We admire those who are dedicated to exercise, and we think that people who are physically fit look better than those who are not. However, these same self-presentational concerns can actually deter people from engaging in exercise, usually the people who are in most need of exercise. People who are overweight, for example, often fail to exercise because of embarrassment over how they will look when they exercise (Culos-Reed et al., 2002; Hart et al., 1989). One study examining women's experiences with exercise found that "Although factors such as safety, comfort, and quality of instruction affected the women's exercise behavior, the most powerful influences seemed to be the social circumstances of the exercise setting, especially concerns about visibility, embarrassment, and judgment by others (Bain et al., 1989, p. 139).

Accidents and Injuries

Although certainly people can have accidents and develop injuries that have little if anything to do with self-presentation, a fair number of accidents and injuries stem from self-presentational concerns. People, particularly adolescents, often engage in behaviors that they (a) don't want to do and (b) do not have the skills to do, solely to control the impressions that others form of them. So, people play "chicken" (the game where two cars race toward one another to see who swerves first) or Russian roulette to avoid being called chicken. People don't wear seatbelts or they drive too fast on the highway to avoid appearing too cautious. From elementary school up, children often rebel against wearing helmets and safety gear when they ride skateboards or bikes because it looks wimpy, not cool. Athletes who have been injured often continue to play a game in spite of their injury so that they don't appear weak or unskilled.

Clearly, then, self-presentational processes play a role in inhibiting health-promoting behaviors and in facilitating health-compromising behaviors. Of course, self-presentational factors are not the only factor involved, but such concerns are clearly a major source of influence.

Alcohol Abuse   Consider the following statistics:

"Approximately 14 million Americans —7.4 percent of the population—meet the diagnostic criteria for alcohol abuse or alcoholism" ("Health risks," 2000).

"More than one-half of American adults have a close family member who has or has had alcoholism" ("Health risks," 2000).

"Alcohol-related crashes account for one person killed every 33 minutes and one person injured every two minutes every day of the year" (NHTSA, 2002).

"Over one and a half million people are arrested each year for driving under the influence of alcohol or drugs" (NHTSA, 2002).

"The annual economic costs to the United States from alcohol abuse were estimated to be $167 billion in 1995" (U.S. Department of Health and Human Services, 2000).

"It is estimated that one in every two Americans will be in an alcohol-related accident during his or her lifetime" (Taylor, 2003, p. 144).

Prevalence   Clearly alcohol can be a problem, but identifying who is an alcoholic, who is a problem drinker, and who is a responsible drinker can be difficult at times. A person is identified as having **alcoholism** *when he or she is physiologically dependent on alcohol, and, therefore, shows withdrawal symptoms when no alcohol has been consumed.* **Problem drinkers** *are not physiologically addicted to alcohol, but still have a number of problems stemming from alcohol consumption, including problems with work and family, and health-related complications.* Although there are individual variations in these definitions, problem drinkers appear to have more control over their alcohol consumption than alcoholics.

Following close behind smoking and obesity, alcohol is the third leading cause of death. The National Household Survey on Drug Abuse (NHSDA) found that over 48 percent of Americans or 109 million people age 12 and over drink alcohol (SAMHSA, 2001). Just over 20 percent of the same respondents reported binge drinking at least once in the month prior to the survey. Just under 13 million people reported engaging in heavy drinking. More males than females report using alcohol, although the difference is not large. Almost 13 percent of pregnant women who responded indicated that they had consumed alcohol during their pregnancy. In 2001, over 25 million people indicated that they had driven under the influence of alcohol at least once.

Contributors to Alcoholism   Where does an addiction to alcohol come from? Genetics clearly play a role in alcoholism and problem drinking (Vaillant & Hiller-Sturmhofel, 1996). In some alcoholics, a gene has been identified that alters dopamine receptors. Alcoholics may also inherit a tolerance for the negative effects of alcohol and a sensitivity to the positive effects of alcohol (Straub, 2002). Twin studies show a strong concordance rate for alcoholism. In one study of identical twins, in 76 percent of the cases in which one twin was an alcoholic the other was also (Kendler et al., 1997). Children of alcoholics, particularly male children, are at increased risk for abusing alcohol themselves (Plomin et al., 2001). For both males and females, heritability of alcoholism is estimated to be about 30 percent.

Thus, although genetics is clearly involved, it is not the sole contributor to alcohol abuse. In regards to alcohol, biology is not destiny. Social–cognitive factors also play a contributing role in alcohol abuse. Some people drink to mentally "escape" from whatever stressors they are currently facing. Because alcohol alters the thought processes of the consumer, they think differently about issues they are facing. Alcohol provides a mechanism for people to escape self-awareness or escape current thoughts and preoccupations, such as that they are a loser or that no one cares about them (Baumeister, 1991; Hull, 1987). Social support can provide a buffer between stressors and alcohol abuse as a way of dealing with those stressors.

Relatedly, people may drink to provide themselves with an excuse for failure in the event that it occurs. In other words, alcohol serves a self-handicapping function. **Self-handicapping** is *the process by which people set themselves up to fail.* If, for example, Jay gets drunk the night before a big test, he can blame failure on the test on the alcohol. On the other hand, if he passes the test in spite of being hung over, then, in his own mind, he must really be a smart guy (Berglas & Baumeister, 1993).

The social environment in which people find themselves also helps to determine the degree to which they abuse alcohol. Children whose parents or peers consume alcohol and who do so during pleasurable social occasions, learn to associate alcohol with pleasure and reward (Taylor, 2003). Thus, they are more likely than people not exposed to "social" drinking to begin drinking earlier and to have a more favorable association with alcohol. Alcohol consumption among college students is significantly higher while they are enrolled in school than when they leave school. Students who

Big Picture φ Question 6

What is the relation between nature and nurture in shaping psychological processes?

Big Picture φ Question 4

To what extent is human nature particular versus universal?

are members of fraternities and sororities tend to consume more alcohol than students who are not part of the Greek system (Sher et al., 2001).

Personality can also influence whether or not one abuses alcohol, reinforcing once again the age-old nature–nurture debate. Personality is determined in part by genetics. People are generally prewired to respond to particular situations in particular ways. However, the situation and environment determine whether or not those genetic underpinnings are realized. For example, people who are high in negative affectivity—that is, people who are chronically in a bad mood—are more likely to consume alcohol than people who are low in negative affectivity or who are high in positive affectivity.

Consequences of Alcoholism The physical and psychological effects of alcohol abuse are many. Because most alcohol that is consumed is metabolized through the liver, damage to the liver is one of the most obvious physiological effects of excessive alcohol consumption over time. In fact, excess alcohol consumption over time is the leading cause of liver damage and death (Van Thiel, 1996). People who rarely drink experience little, if any damage to their liver. For people who drink excessively and over time, however, the damage can be fatal, as in the case of cirrhosis of the liver. Women appear to be more likely than men to experience liver damage with alcohol abuse (Becker et al., 1996). Alcohol is also a risk factor for certain types of cancer including cancer of the mouth, larynx, stomach, colon, and breast, and for hypertension, stroke, and fetal alcohol syndrome ("Health risks," 2000). Severe cognitive deficits and neurological problems can also result from alcoholism, some of these permanent (Arria & Van Thiel, 1992). Short-term cognitive impairments lead to poor judgment and decision making that can affect non-alcohol-related decisions. For example, because of the disinhibiting effects of alcohol, people, particularly adolescents, engage in high-risk sexual behavior while under its influence (Weinhardt et al., 2001).

The risk of injury or death is higher for alcoholics than nonalcoholics not only from health-related complications, such as liver disease, associated with alcohol abuse, but also from falls and car accidents (Hingson & Howland, 1993). Estimates are that half of the car accidents that occur annually involve alcohol (McGuire, 1982). Although many of the effects of alcohol follow large consumptions, injury risk increases with even very small amounts of alcohol.

Social consequences of alcohol abuse are many. Relationships with family, friends, and co-workers are clearly affected by the individual who abuses alcohol, in part because the incidence of intimate and domestic violence, homicide, and suicide increases with the use of alcohol (Norton & Morgan, 1989). As noted earlier in the chapter, the economic costs associated with alcoholism are staggering, taking the form of medical costs and lost productivity at work. Approximately 15 percent of the national health bill is devoted to alcohol-related costs. Overall, the United States spends close to $200 billion annually on health care costs associated with alcohol and lost worker productivity due to alcohol impairment.

Psychologically, people who abuse alcohol have a higher rate of mental problems than people who do not abuse alcohol. "In fact, alcohol dependence elevates the risk for all types of affective and anxiety disorders" ("Health risks," 2000).

Treatment Some people ***quit drinking or greatly reduce their alcohol intake on their own, without any formal method of intervention***, a process called **spontaneous remission**. Estimates are, however, that only 19 percent of alcoholics and problem drinkers fall within this category (Miller & Hester, 1980). Many of these include college students who engage in

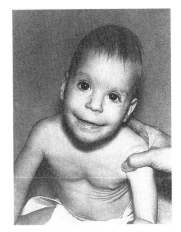

Child with fetal alcohol syndrome.

"Maybe zero tolerance is setting the bar too high."

© *The New Yorker Collection 2000 Lee Lorenz from the cartoonbank.com* binge drinking during college when the alcohol is readily available and when the social situation encourages them to do so, but who markedly reduce their alcohol intake once they leave college and the accompanying social scene. Furthermore, people with support from families and friends are more likely to engage in spontaneous remission than people who lack such social support networks.

The remaining 81 percent of alcoholics and problem drinkers require some type of formalized treatment, although the form that the treatment takes is highly variable. Some alcoholics enter rehabilitation centers. The first stage of rehabilitation is **detoxification** or *the process of drying out*. The inpatient setting allows the alcoholic to go through the withdrawal symptoms associated with abstinence from alcohol in a controlled setting and often with the use of medication to alleviate some of the negative side effects of withdrawal (Ciraulo & Renner, 1991). Detoxification is then followed by a several-week period of intensive inpatient individual and group therapy.

Most alcoholics and problem drinkers do not enter rehabilitation centers, however, instead receiving treatment on an outpatient basis (United States Bureau of the Census, 1999). The purpose of therapy is to allow the individual to see the origins of their drinking behavior, the effects of that behavior on other people, and the consequences of their problem to themselves and others. Some outpatient treatments use **aversion therapy**, or *the introduction of something aversive as a means of discouraging the negative health habit*. A drug, typically Antabuse, is taken daily by the alcoholic or problem drinker. In the absence of alcohol, the drug has few effects, but if the person consumes alcohol while he is taking the medication, severe nausea and vomiting result. One of the biggest problems associated with the use of Antabuse is that people who really want to continue to drink will simply stop taking the drug. To circumvent this problem, some alcoholics, particularly those in an inpatient treatment setting, go through a series of half-hour sessions during each of which they are administered a drug like Antabuse via injection followed by the consumption of alcohol. Over repeated trials, during each of which the person becomes nauseous and vomits, the appeal of alcohol typically diminishes as the patient quickly forms very negative associations to alcohol (Sarafino, 2002).

Particularly for problem drinkers, cognitive–behavioral types of therapy can be effective. Many problem drinkers begin drinking and continue to drink as a means of coping with stressors at work or home. The goal of therapy, then, is to teach stress management techniques so that the impetus for consuming alcohol is gone.

Perhaps the most well-known treatment is the self-help group known as Alcoholics Anonymous (AA). AA was founded in 1935 by a group of problem drinkers. Now, estimates are that membership exceeds two million. The only requirement to be a member of AA is that the individual have a desire to quit drinking. Each member of AA is assigned a sponsor to whom he or she can turn in times of distress. The group meetings provide an open forum in which people can discuss their issues and problems with alcohol. Individual therapy-type meetings are also provided if needed. In addition to providing a forum in which alcoholics can vent their feelings, perhaps the most useful outcome of AA (or related groups such as Al-Anon, for family members of alcoholics, or Alateen, for adolescent children of alcoholics) is the social support that members provide to one another. The overall effectiveness of AA is unknown because the membership is anonymous, but members of the organization itself claim to have a success rate around 75 percent (Miller & Hester, 1980).

Sexually Transmitted Diseases   A discussion of sexually transmitted diseases (STDs) takes a little different form from a discussion of the other types of health compromising behaviors we have examined. The reason is that the term STDs is a catchphrase for over 20 diseases that are transmitted through intimate or sexual contact (see Table 11.2 for a partial listing), the most notable of which is infection with the human immunodeficiency virus (HIV). Well over 50 percent of STDs are contracted by people under the age of 25 (National Institute of Allergy and Infectious Diseases,

Apply & Discuss

Proponents of Alcoholics Anonymous believe that once you are an alcoholic you are always an alcoholic and that even moderate drinking is not possible. Other approaches to treatment, such as some of the cognitive–behavioral approaches, believe that teaching alcoholics and problem drinkers to consume alcohol in moderation is actually a more realistic and successful approach to treatment.

▪ Which viewpoint do you agree with? Why or why not?

Table 11.2 ■ ■ Sexually Transmitted Diseases		
Disease	*New cases annually*	*Primary symptoms*
Genital Herpes	500,000	Blisters in the genital region
Chlamydia	4–8 million	Generally asymptomatic
Gonorrhea	400,000	Discharge from the vagina or penis and painful urination
Genital warts	1 million	Bumps in the vaginal or penile area
Syphilis	11,000	Begins as a sore, but, left unchecked can affect the central nervous system and the heart
HIV/AIDS	> 26,000	Originally appears as something resembling a bad case of the flu. Progresses as the virus attacks the immune system, leaving the person vulnerable to opportunistic infections

1999). Not only is this statistic staggering, but some of these STDs are incurable, so that many individuals spend the majority of their lives with an STD. The annual economic costs in the United States attributable to STDs is over $10 billion. Women are at higher risk than men for contracting a sexually transmitted disease, and the consequences for women tend to be more serious in large part because women are often asymptomatic until the disease has progressed and caused permanent damage, such as sterility (National Institute for Allergy and Infectious Diseases, 1999). In addition, women who are pregnant are at risk of transmitting many of the STDs to their unborn child either during pregnancy or during delivery.

Unlike other health-compromising behaviors, such as obesity or alcoholism, there is no genetic predisposition for STDs beyond perhaps personality factors, such as impulsivity, that might lead someone to engage in high-risk sexual behaviors. The role of health psychologists is clear: stopping people from engaging in sexual behaviors that put them at risk. The role of the health psychologist goes one step further, however: helping those who have contracted STDs cope with the illness and helping to develop treatments for STDs.

Because of the high mortality rate associated with it, we will focus on HIV/AIDS. "When AIDS was first detected in 1980, fewer than 100 Americans had died of the disease. Less than 20 years later, more than 580,000 Americans had been diagnosed with AIDS, more than 360,000 had died from it, and AIDS had become the second leading killer of Americans between 22 and 45 years of age, second only to accidents.... According to the World Health Organization (WHO), by the very beginning of 2001 the number of people living with HIV had grown to 26.1 million, 10 percent more than just 1 year earlier" (Straub, 2002, p. 467). Particularly in African nations, the AIDS epidemic is dramatically lowering life expectancy. In some countries, life expectancy is expected to drop by half because of the number of people dying from AIDS (Carey & Vanable, 2003).

Close to 70 percent of new cases of HIV infection are among men. More than half of new cases involve African Americans (54 percent), followed by Caucasians (26 percent), Hispanics (19 percent), and others (1 percent) (Centers for Disease Control, CDC, 2003). A recent report by the CDC highlighted the fact that, although African-Americans represent a disproportionate share of new cases of HIV infection, race itself is not a risk factor. Rather, compared to other racial and ethnic groups, African Americans are disproportionately exposed to other factors that put them at heightened risk for infection with HIV including poverty, risky partners, substance abuse, and the prevalence of other STDs (CDC, 2003).

HIV is transmitted primarily through sexual behavior or the sharing of intravenous drug needles, with heterosexual intercourse presently considered to be the main mode of transmission (Carey & Vanable, 2003). The use of condoms is considered an effective method of preventing transmission of the virus that causes AIDS. However, only 20 percent of sexually active individuals reported using a condom the last time they had intercourse. Among those most likely to use condoms were those at greatest risk of being infected with HIV. However, only 36 percent of these people used condoms regularly (Anderson, 2003).

Once infected, the disease follows a very predictable course in terms of stages, if not time. A few weeks after being infected, a person will experience symptoms that resemble mononucleosis—fever, fatigue, and sore throat. Following this, infected individuals enter an asymptomatic state during which they are symptom free but very capable of infecting others. A number of years can pass before the infected individual develops AIDS. By this time, the person's immune system is so compromised that he or she is open to opportunistic diseases. In fact, people do not die from AIDS itself, but rather from cancers and infections to which the person is now vulnerable. Furthermore, infection with HIV places people at increased risk for contracting other STDs that, in conjunction with HIV, may result in an even shorter life expectancy.

Health psychologists have played an increasingly active role as the AIDS epidemic continues to spread. Of course, their first plan of action is to prevent people from engaging in high-risk sexual behaviors. In some cases, this involves targeting those who are already engaging in such behaviors and working to get them to stop. In other instances, the health psychologist's goal is to reach young people who are not yet sexually active to prevent them from engaging in risky sexual behaviors to begin with. Their efforts on both of these levels involve working at both the individual and the community level. Individuals are offered instruction on ways in which they can protect themselves, for example, through the consistent use of condoms. They may be given a personal risk assessment to make them aware of behaviors that are placing them at risk (Carey & Vanable, 2003). Communities, including schools, are encouraged to implement programs and informational campaigns designed to change social norms regarding sexual behavior. One community-based behavioral skills program created by Kelly (1995), a leading researcher in the area of AIDS prevention, has met with considerable success. The program involves providing participants with a personalized risk assessment—strategies for reducing their risk including using condoms, reducing alcohol consumption before a sexual encounter, assertiveness training, and the development of social support (Carey & Vanable, 2003). Another intervention involved a teacher-delivered educational program with high school students in New York. Students in the intervention group received formalized instruction on AIDS prevention that included educating students about AIDS, assessing their attitudes toward AIDS and their likelihood of getting it, and teaching them the skills needed to prevent HIV infection (Walter & Vaughan, 1993). Students in the comparison group received no formalized instruction. Three months after the termination of the curriculum, students in the intervention group were more likely than those in the comparison group to have changed their sexual behaviors, including abstinence, regular use of condoms, and avoiding high-risk partners.

INTERIM SUMMARY

In spite of knowledge of the negative health consequences that may befall them, people continue to engage in a number of health-compromising behaviors, including obesity, smoking, alcohol abuse, and high-risk sexual behaviors. Obesity is typically measured in terms of **body mass index (BMI)**. People with a BMI in excess of 30 percent are said to be obese. The prevalence of obesity is even more surprising when examined within the context of **set point**, the ideal body weight for each individual. However, genetic, social, and psychological factors join together to influence someone's ability to regulate his behavior around the set point. Although genetic influences are strong, the degree to which they manifest themselves is determined in part by the environment, an idea germane to the **susceptible gene hypothesis**.

As with obesity, the onset, course, and termination of smoking behavior is also determined by biological, social, and psychological variables. Smoking, along with other health-compromising behaviors, may also be influenced by **self-presentation**, or people's attempt to control the images that other people form of them.

The primary distinction between **alcoholics** and **problem drinkers** is the physiological addiction to alcohol that alcoholics have. Some alcoholics and problem drinkers learn to control their own problem through **spontaneous remission**. Most, however, require some kind of formal treatment, in some cases even inpatient rehabilitation. The first step in inpatient therapy is **detoxification**. **Aversion therapy** is a method for treating alcoholism that may be used on an inpatient or an outpatient basis.

Many individuals also place themselves at risk for acquiring sexually transmitted diseases. Although over 20 STDs have been identified, the most publicized is HIV/AIDS, which, on an international level, has reached epidemic proportions. Health psychologists have played an active role in encouraging people to alter their high-risk behaviors or to avoid engaging in risky behavior to begin with.

Barriers to Health Promotion

Why, given the harmful and even fatal consequences associated with the health-compromising behaviors just described, would someone decide to continue to consume excess fat and calories, smoke, or drink? Why, given that many cancers can be effectively treated if detected early enough, would people fail to get regular preventive health screenings, such as for cervical cancer, breast cancer, and prostate cancer? The answer to these questions is more complex than it may at first appear, but at least four factors or barriers to health promotion are involved (Straub, 2002).

Individual Barriers   People do a lot of things they know they shouldn't do (e.g., smoke) and they don't do a lot of things that they know they should (e.g., receive regular Pap tests). Lack of knowledge is rarely an explanation for people engaging in health-compromising behaviors and failing to engage in preventive health behaviors or health-promoting behaviors. Most people do, in fact, know their negative health behaviors are detrimental to their health. Armed with that knowledge, why would people choose to continue to compromise their health either by engaging in negative health behaviors or by failing to engage in positive health behaviors? One reason is that negative behaviors are rewarding, particularly in the short term. Smoking can reduce anxiety and produce relaxation. Alcohol can allow one to escape intrusive and disturbing thoughts and worries, and can, to a point, increase the ease with which one interacts with others. Eating is enjoyable. Who doesn't occasionally want to consume too much pizza, milk shakes, or chocolate cake? Health promoting-behaviors, such as exercise and eating a healthy diet, however, are generally less enjoyable and take considerably more discipline.

In addition, the negative effects of health compromising behaviors do not occur immediately and are almost always preceded by the positive consequences. Even the negative effects of consuming too much alcohol, including nausea, vomiting, dehydration, and headache, follow positive effects of drinking. Most people begin negative health habits such as smoking during adolescence. It's difficult to convince most adolescents of anything commonsensical—certainly convincing them that smoking, alcohol, unsafe sex, and excessive tanning, for example, will ultimately be detrimental to their health is going to fall on deaf ears. In their own minds, why should they worry about something that might happen 20 or 30 years down the road?

In terms of preventive health care, many people adopt the idea that "what they don't know won't hurt them." In fact, it won't just hurt them, it may kill them! One

Big Picture φ Question 5

To what extent are psychological processes the same in men and women?

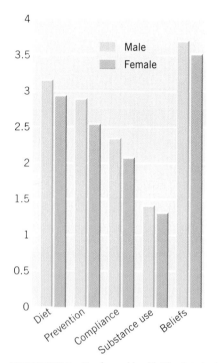

FIGURE 11.14 Gender and health. The data in this table show that men's health habits are worse than women's. Men have riskier dieting behaviors, fewer preventive health behaviors, lower rates of compliance with medical regimens, higher substance use, and riskier health-related beliefs. Adapted from Courtenay et al. (2002).

study found that women who believe that they could effectively deal with cancer should they get it are more likely than women who do not share such a belief to receive regular screenings for cancer (Perlman et al., 1999). Relatedly, people who have a realistic sense of their likelihood of contracting cancer or another chronic condition are more likely to receive preventive health screenings than those individuals who are unrealistically optimistic about their health, believing they are less likely than the average other person to contract a chronic condition. People who are the least likely to receive regular preventive health screenings are those who are uneducated, of lower socioeconomic status, who have no access to heath care or no money to pay for it, and who have not had preventive screenings recommended by their doctor ("Cancer prevention," 2002). People who are self-conscious about their bodies or very attuned to the impressions that other people form of them (see "One Step Further: Self-Presentation and Health") are also less likely to receive preventive health screenings (Kowalski & Brown, 1994).

One important individual barrier is gender. Women are more likely than men to engage in preventive health behaviors and health-promoting behaviors. According to one group of researchers "Being a woman may, in fact, be the strongest predictor of preventive and health-promoting behavior" (Courtenay et al., 2002, p. 220). Men are more likely to engage in risky health behaviors, such as smoking and driving while intoxicated. Men are less likely than women to take care of themselves when they are sick, and they are less likely to seek a physician's care for illness. Women more than men take a realistic view of their risk for illness and disease, which may account, in part, for men's greater risk-taking behaviors. In short, men are more likely than women to view themselves as invincible and to be overly optimistic about their health outcomes. Ironic, isn't it, given that men have a shorter life expectancy than women?

In one study, college-aged men and women completed a survey examining their health behaviors and attitudes. Six domains of health behaviors were assessed: diet, anger and stress, prevention, medical compliance, substance use, and beliefs about masculinity. The results of the study revealed differences between men and women on five of the six dimensions. Only anger and stress showed no effects of gender. Across the other five health domains, men scored worse than women. As shown in Figure 11.14, men engaged in riskier dieting behaviors (e.g., were more likely than women to eat red meat, sugar, salt, and high-fat foods), displayed fewer preventive health behaviors (e.g., doing regular self-examinations for testicular cancer or breast cancer, getting blood pressure screenings, receiving regular physical and dental exams), displayed more substance use (e.g., smoking cigarettes, chewing tobacco, drinking alcohol), had lower rates of medical compliance (e.g., taking medication as prescribed, getting prescriptions filled), and endorsed riskier health-related attitudes (e.g., a person should always try to control his or her emotions, a person should be physically strong).

Family Barriers   Health habits are acquired early, and one of the primary models of health behavior are parents or caregivers. Children frequently model the health behaviors they see their parents or siblings perform. Thus, parents who smoke or abuse alcohol are more likely to have children who smoke and become problem drinkers. Parents who rarely exercise have a higher likelihood of having children who do not exercise. Parents who are obese tend to have children (and even pets) who are obese. Parents who do not engage in preventive health behaviors have children who also do not engage in preventive behaviors. Indeed, those same parents may be the ones who do not take their young children to their yearly well-baby checks or have their children properly immunized. Although genetics could, and do, account for part of this intergenerational transmission of health habits, they do not account for the entire picture. Children emulate what their parents and older siblings model. Because they see their parents experience immediate rewards from negative health habits, they assume they will as well. Positive health habits, such as regular brushing and flossing, are unlikely to be implemented as adults if the behavior was not practiced regularly as a child.

Children model the health behaviors that their parents display.

Health System Barriers   As we discussed early in the chapter, the biomedical model has dominated the field of medicine for some time. Doctors are trained to focus on illness, not health. Thus, even when they do ask patients about circumstances leading up to their illness, their primary focus is on treating the illness itself, not the negative health habits that might have contributed to the development of the illness. The situation is compounded by the fact that people often do not go to the doctor when they are well. This practice is unfortunate, both because conditions that could be prevented or treated if caught early go unnoticed and because it is often during these preventive visits to a physician that time is spent discussing health-compromising and health-promoting behaviors. Table 11.3 presents the percentages of people who receive certain types of preventive health screening. Although the

Table 11.3 ▪ ▪ Percentages of People Who Receive Preventative Health Screening			
Characteristic	*Mammography*	*Pap Test*	*Fecal Occult Blood Test*
Race/Ethnicity			
White (non-Hispanic)	68	80	36
Black (non-Hispanic)	66	83	30
Hispanic	61	74	23
American Indian/Alaska Native	45	72	24
Asian/ Pacific Islander	61	67	31
Education (years)			
11 or fewer	53	69	29
12	66	78	36
13 or more	73	85	44
Total	67	79	37

Source: National Health Interview Survey, 1998, National Center for Health Statistics, Centers for Disease Control and Prevention. Adapted from Cancer Prevention & Early Detection Facts and Figures, 2002, American Cancer Society. Mammography refers to women over 40 in the United States who, in 1998, reported that they had received a mammogram within the last 2 years. Pap test data were based on reports by women 18 years of age or older who had received a Pap test within the last 3 years. Colorectal cancer screening is conducted using a fecal occult blood test. The data here are based on people's reports of having received a fecal occult blood test within the last 2 years.

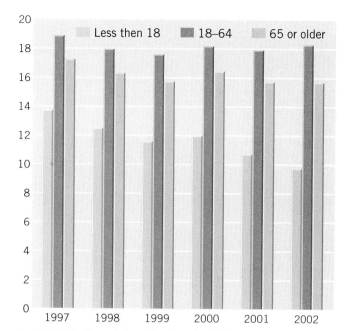

FIGURE 11.15 Percent of people without health insurance from 1997 to 2002. *Source:* National Center for Health Statistics.

percentages listed in the table may be higher than you might have expected and, indeed, they are higher than national averages for a particular year, note the span of time during which the screenings were allowed. For example, statistics for the percentage of women who had received a Pap test asked whether or not they had received one in the last three years, not in that particular year ("Cancer Prevention," 2002).

One factor inhibiting people from taking preventive health measures is the lack of health insurance. In 2001, almost 15 percent of the population of the United States did not have health insurance. That amounts to more than 41 million people (U.S. Census Bureau, 2002; Figure 11.15). The people most likely to be uninsured (e.g., African- and Hispanic-Americans) are among those most susceptible to health threats that could be averted with preventive care. Sadly, one major illness can wipe out an entire family's finances in the absence of health insurance. Even among those who do have health insurance, the coverage often is either inadequate or does not apply to preventive health services. Thus, people who want to receive regular or yearly preventive health screenings must do so at their own expense.

Yet another health system variable concerns the relationships between patients and practitioners. One night during my 7th month of pregnancy, I (RMK) became very sick and was hospitalized. The next day, my least favorite obstetrician came in and asked me "What do you call a deer who is blind?" In response to my "I don't know," he said "no-eyed deer, and that's what you have—no idea." I failed to see the humor in the joke and prayed at that moment that he would not be the doctor that delivered my twins. Fortunately, he was not. And, indeed, the difference between the doctor who treated me when I was sick and the one who delivered my twins highlights exactly the point I'm making here: the ways in which physicians treat and respond to their patients is a major factor influencing the degree to which those patients will hear what the physician is saying and then comply with the advice that was offered.

Certainly my experiences are not unique. Patients who feel that their physician is unresponsive are unlikely to be completely forthcoming about symptoms they are experiencing. Given that up to 80 percent of treatment is based on information provided by patients during consultations with their physicians, this mismatch between patient and provider can be extremely harmful (Straub, 2002). Patients who are uncomfortable with or who feel demeaned by their doctor are also significantly less likely to follow through with treatment regimens recommended by their doctor. Noncompliance is high even among patients who trust and like their physician. Thus, you can imagine the rates of noncompliance among people who do not trust or who dislike their health care provider. Sadly, people who have one bad experience with a physician may generalize their negative feelings to other health care providers, increasing the likelihood that they will engage in delay behavior when future symptoms arise, and decreasing the likelihood that they will go to a physician for preventive health screenings.

What do doctors do that is so off-putting to their patients? The use of medical jargon or, at the other extreme, baby talk, is one way of putting distance between the patient and the physician. In the case of too much jargon, patients cannot understand the recommendations made by their doctor and are often unwilling to state that. In the case of baby talk, patients feel demeaned and talked down to. Many doctors also give clear indications that they are in a hurry and do not have sufficient time to spend with any particular patient. The patient, on the other hand, has waited perhaps weeks for an appointment, no doubt waited in the waiting room, and thought through a list of symptoms to report to the doctor and questions to ask—only to get into the examining room and be quickly dismissed. Research has shown that, on average, doctors interrupt patients after the patient has been talking only 18 seconds (Beckman & Frankel, 1984)!

Communication problems between a physician and patient are compounded even further when they literally do not speak the same language. Trying to understand a patient's complaints in a short period of time is not easy. Add language difficulties and the situation is often futile. Similar outcomes often follow when physicians are met by patients whom they really don't want to treat, perhaps because of negative experiences with this patient in the past, because of the particular illness the patient has, or because of physical features of the person, such as their gender, race, or age. To improve the ways in which physicians interact with their patients, the U.S. Medical Licensing Examination Board is now requiring medical students to take a clinical-skills exam (Sobol, 2003). The test is designed to examine the doctor's communication skills (e.g., beside manner) and his or her skills at acquiring information during physical exams.

Importantly, however, physicians are not entirely to blame. With problems in the health care system itself, doctors today are often inundated by paperwork and encouraged to treat as many people as possible. The doctors, too, are overwhelmed with malpractice insurance costs and the ever present threat of a lawsuit. Furthermore, patients themselves are often at least partly to blame for faulty patient–practitioner interactions. The anxiety they currently feel over the meaning of their symptoms, the fact that they may have been using home remedies to treat their symptoms, and feelings of inferiority relative to the physician can all create anxiety that makes it difficult for patients to adequately relate their symptoms. Because of the physiological effects of anxiety, it may magnify a patient's symptoms or the anxiety may, in fact, be the reason the patient is seeing the doctor (Graugaard & Finset, 2000). Research has shown that up to two-thirds of visits to physicians are for psychological rather than physical problems (Coyne et al., 2002; Taylor, 2003), problems that many physicians are unable either to detect or to treat properly if detected. Given this deficiency, it is hardly surprising that many primary care facilities either have or would like to have a health psychologist on staff full-time.

Patient expectations for physicians may also be too high. Beyond the practical expectations, such as that a physician will see them immediately, patients often expect their physician to provide them with an immediate solution to whatever ails them, clearly, in most cases, an unrealistic expectation. Nevertheless, unmet expectations may lead patients to be dissatisfied with their physician and the quality of care provided, which may then affect the degree to which they are willing to comply with the physician's recommendations (Jackson & Kroenke, 2001). Unrealistic expectations are one of the things that physicians find most frustrating in their interactions with patients (Stein & Kwan, 1999).

Given that children learn from their parents and other caretakers, the role of pediatricians in health promotion is critical. Pediatricians who spend only brief periods of time with their little patients and who fail to relay important information about health promotion to parents of those patients do little to endear themselves to the children whose health they are supposed to be promoting. Fortunately, however, there are exceptions. In a recent visit to the pediatrician with one of my sons (both of whom are terrified of going to the doctor), I was happily surprised at the behavior of the physician. She walked into the room, picked up a children's book on her way in, sat down, and began reading to my son. As you can imagine, she made a great impression on me, but, more importantly, on my son. When I recently asked him which doctor he wanted to see for his three-year checkup, you can guess which one he said. (Good thing, because I had already made the appointment with her!)

Community, Cultural, and Ethnic Barriers   People's willingness to engage in preventive health behaviors, to avoid negative health habits, and to terminate those

Big Picture φ Question 4

To what extent is human nature particular versus universal?

Table 11.4 ▬ ▪ Healthy People 2010 Focus Areas
1. Access to Quality Health Services
2. Arthritis, Osteoporosis, and Chronic Back Conditions
3. Cancer
4. Chronic Kidney Disease
5. Diabetes
6. Disability and Secondary Conditions
7. Educational and Community-Based Programs
8. Environmental Health
9. Family Planning
10. Food Safety
11. Health Communication
12. Heart Disease and Stroke
13. HIV
14. Immunization and Infectious Diseases
15. Injury and Violence Prevention
16. Maternal, Infant, and Child Health
17. Medical Product Safety
18. Mental Health and Mental Disorders
19. Nutrition and Overweight
20. Occupational Safety and Health
21. Oral Health
22. Physical Activity and Fitness
23. Public Health Infrastructure
24. Respiratory Diseases
25. Sexually Transmitted Diseases
26. Substance Abuse
27. Tobacco Use
28. Vision and Hearing

negative health habits once they begin is, to a great extent, influenced by the norms of the community in which they live, work, and play. People who live and work in environments that encourage the use of alcohol as a means of fitting in will likely initiate or continue alcohol use. As work settings have increasingly become smoke free, the percentage of people who smoke at work where they have to go outside to do so, has decreased. The rise of fitness centers within companies has helped to establish new norms and expectations regarding fitness. Needless to say, more fit workers are a financial boon to the company, manifested in reduced absenteeism and turnover.

But the story goes much further than that. In 1979, the first "Healthy People" initiative was launched and titled *Healthy People: The Surgeon General's Report on Health Promotion and Disease Prevention*. This report was followed in 1990 by the *Healthy People 2000* initiative, which outlined 319 health objectives to be achieved. Of these objectives, 60 percent were achieved (National Center for Health Statistics, 2000). In 2000, *Healthy People 2010* was released, outlining 467 health objectives in 28 different focus areas that revolve around two primary goals (see Table 11.4). "The first goal, which addresses the fact that we are growing older as a Nation, is to increase the quality and years of healthy life. The second goal, which addresses the diversity of the population, is to eliminate health disparities" (U.S. Department of Health and Human Services, 2000).

Health disparities in terms of both the incidence of disease and treatment for disease are most evident when comparing Caucasians to members of other ethnic groups. As a first step toward minimizing some of these health disparities, the Office for Research on Minority Health was established in 1990 with the intent of focusing increased attention on issues of health specific to minority populations. In 1998, then President Clinton "committed the United States to the elimination of health disparities in racial and ethnic groups by the year 2010" (Whitfield et al., 2003, p. 545). This push then became integrated as one of the primary goals of *Healthy People 2010*.

In order to understand why this goal is so important, we must first understand the nature of health disparities that exist across racial and ethnic groups. To illustrate this, we will focus on health disparities between Caucasians and African-Americans. "On virtually every major index of health status, African Americans look worse than whites, and these differences in health occur across the lifespan" (Taylor et al., 1997, p. 6). Mortality rates from all causes are 60 percent higher among African-Americans than among Caucasians. Of particular interest are discrepancies in the incidence of cardiovascular disease and stroke, both of which are substantially higher among African-Americans than among Caucasians (Whitfield et al., 2003). The mortality rate from heart disease is more than 40 percent higher in African-Americans than in Caucasians, and the death rate from all types of cancer 30% higher (U.S. Department of Health and Human Services, 2000).

These disparities are of particular interest to health psychologists because their origin lies, in large part, in behaviors that place people within particular minority groups at heightened risk. For example, more African-Americans than Caucasians or than members of other minority groups smoke (Escobedo & Peddicord, 1996). Compared to Caucasians, significantly more African-Americans are overweight. Twenty percent more African-American women are overweight compared to Caucasian women (National Center for Health Statistics, 2000). Part of this difference may stem from divergent social pressures placed on African-American and Caucasian women. Caucasian women are socialized to believe that "thin is in," a message perpetrated throughout the advertising industry. African-American women, on the other hand, are socialized to believe that heavier bodies are more attractive. This is compounded by the fact that African-Americans on average exercise less than Caucasians (Young et al., 1998), making them more susceptible to weight gain and other health-related complications.

Complicating matters even further, African-Americans rank higher than other racial and ethnic groups in cardiovascular reactivity to stress (Whitfield et al., 2003). Communities in which they live and socioeconomic status (SES) levels are correlated with cardiovascular reactivity, such that poorer communities and lower personal SES levels are associated with higher cardiovascular reactivity. Relative to Caucasians, of whom about 11 percent live in poverty, more African Americans (33 percent) live in poor communities and at lower SES levels, exposing them to more stressors and putting them at risk for cardiovascular reactivity and, thus, cardiovascular disease and stroke. People at lower SES levels have higher rates of cancer, respiratory problems, and heart disease (Taylor et al., 1997). They live in overcrowded housing and more violence-prone neighborhoods. Although some of these stressors are psychological, others are environmental in the form of toxins that set the stage for the development of certain types of cancer in African-Americans to which members of other ethnic groups are less susceptible (Taylor et al., 1997).

Comparisons of the health outcomes of people from different racial and ethnic backgrounds and the behavioral, social, and environmental factors that place these individuals at risk highlight the role of social and psychological factors in health. Environmental factors include not only physical environmental variables, such as toxins, but also the groups and communities to which people belong, including communities, work, family, and peer groups (Taylor et al., 1997; Figure 11.16). Patterns of interaction within these groups and communities, social norms that characterize them, and the "social impoverishment" characteristic of them can create risk factors for health-related problems (Taylor et al., 1997, p. 412).

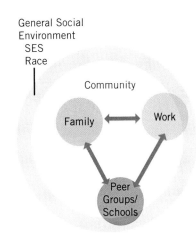

FIGURE 11.16 Environmental factors influencing health. Family, work, and peer influences on health are included within community influences which are included within a general social environment that reflects variables such as SES and race. *Source:* Reprinted from Taylor et al., 1997, *Annual Review of Psychology, 48,* 412.

INTERIM SUMMARY

A myriad of reasons exist to account for why people continue to engage in negative health behaviors and why they fail to engage in positive health behaviors. A useful way of compartmentalizing these reasons is to group them into four barriers to health promotion: individual barriers, family barriers, health system barriers, and community barriers. However, as with most things in life, barriers can be overcome, and the barriers to heath promotion presented here are no exception.

Stress

One of the most frequently researched topics within health psychology is stress (Hobfoll et al., 1998). **Stress** refers to *a challenge to a person's capacity to adapt to inner and outer demands*. Stressful experiences typically produce physiological and emotional arousal and elicit cognitive and behavioral efforts to cope with the stress.

Stress as a Psychobiological Process

Stress is a psychobiological process, with both physiological and psychological components and consequences. An early contribution to the understanding of stress was Walter Cannon's (1932) description of the fight-or-flight response (Chapter 3), in which an organism prepares for danger with endocrine and sympathetic nervous system activation. If the danger does not abate, however, the organism remains perpetually aroused. This can lead to deteriorating health as the body continues to divert its resources away from everyday maintenance and toward emergency readiness.

Another major contribution to the understanding of stress occurred when a young Canadian scientist, Hans Selye, accidentally uncovered some of the physiological mechanisms of stress. Selye (1936, 1976) was experimenting with what he thought was a new sex hormone, which he injected into rats to test its effects. What he ultimately discovered was that a wide range of stressful events, from injections of various substances (including his "sex hormone") to fatigue to extreme cold, led the

Big Picture ϕ Question 1

To what extent can mental processes be reduced to the brain or body?

Big Picture φ Question 2

What is the relationship between reason and desire or, more precisely, between cognition and affect?

Only a few years of exceptional stress can take a toll on the body. President George W. Bush seemed to have aged tremendously during his first three years in the White House, as have other presidents before him.

body to respond with a **general adaptation syndrome** *consisting of three stages: alarm, resistance, and exhaustion.*

The first stage, *alarm*, involves the release of adrenalin and other hormones such as cortisol as well as activation of the sympathetic nervous system. This is what occurs biologically in fight-or-flight responses: Blood pressure, heart rate, respiration, and blood sugar rise as blood is diverted from the gastrointestinal tract to muscles and other parts of the body that may be called upon for an emergency response.

The alarm stage cannot last indefinitely, however, and the body may eventually enter the second stage, *resistance.* The parasympathetic nervous system returns respiration and heart rates to normal. However, blood glucose levels remain high (for energy), and some stress-related hormones (including adrenalin and cortisol) continue to circulate at elevated levels. Essentially, the organism remains on red alert, with heightened energy and arousal, but it has begun to adapt to a higher level of stress.

Remaining on red alert takes its toll, making the organism especially vulnerable to illness. Overworked college students in the resistance stage, for example, are susceptible to influenza, mononucleosis, and whatever garden-variety colds happen to be making the rounds. The situation is analogous to a country that deploys all its military troops to one border to protect against an invasion, leaving its other borders unprotected.

If the resistance phase lasts long enough, the body eventually wears down, and the organism enters a third stage, *exhaustion.* Physiological defenses break down, resulting in greatly increased vulnerability to serious or even life-threatening disease. Organs such as the heart that are vulnerable genetically or environmentally (from smoking, too much lifelong cholesterol intake, etc.) are the first to go during this stage.

Stress as a Transactional Process

A major step forward in the study of stress came when Richard Lazarus developed his *transactional model* of stress. According to this view, stress is typically a *transaction* between the individual and the environment, rather than a property of either the person or the environment alone (Lazarus, 1981, 1993). Just as the amount of stress on a rope is jointly determined by the quality of the rope and the amount of weight pulling on it, so, too, is the amount of stress people experience a joint function of their internal resources and the external situations "tugging" at them.

Stress entails an individual's perception that demands of the environment tax or exceed her available psychosocial resources. That is, stress depends on the *meaning* of an event to the individual. An event that fills one person with excitement, such as a new business opportunity, can make another feel overwhelmed and anxious. The extent to which an event is experienced as stressful, therefore, depends on the person's appraisal of both the situation and her ability to cope with it.

Lazarus's model identifies two stages in the process of stress and coping (neither of which is necessarily conscious). In a **primary appraisal** of the situation, *the person decides whether the situation is benign, stressful, or irrelevant.* If she appraises the situation as stressful (e.g., the professor who fails to make tenure), she must determine what to do about it. In the second stage, **secondary appraisal**, *the person evaluates the options and decides how to respond* (e.g., deciding that she is better off leaving the university to work for an Internet firm and make a better living). Both stages involve **emotional forecasting**, *predicting what feelings the situation will produce* (primary appraisal) and predicting the likely emotional impact of each potential response (secondary appraisal).

Lazarus distinguishes three types of stress. The first is *harm* or *loss*, as when a person loses a loved one or something greatly valued, such as a job. The second is *threat*, or anticipation of harm or loss. The third form of stress is *challenge*, opportunities for growth that may nonetheless be fraught with disruption and uncertainty. Examples of challenges include getting married or entering college. These events can be exceedingly stressful—that is, psychologically and physiologically taxing—because of all the changes and adjustments they entail, even though they are also accompanied by positive affect. Thus, not all stress comes from negative events.

INTERIM SUMMARY

Stress refers to a challenge to a person's capacity to adapt to inner and outer demands. Stress is a psychobiological process, with both physiological and psychological components and consequences. The **general adaptation syndrome** consists of three stages: alarm, resistance, and exhaustion. Stress is also a *transactional* process—a transaction between the individual and the environment, in which the individual perceives that demands of the environment tax or exceed her psychosocial resources. In a **primary appraisal** of the situation, the person decides whether the situation is benign, stressful, or irrelevant. Part of this process involves **emotional** forecasting in which a person evaluates what feelings particular situations will produce. During **secondary appraisal**, the person evaluates the options and decides how to respond.

Sources of Stress

Stress is an unavoidable part of life. *Events that often lead to stress* are called **stressors**. Stressors range from the infrequent, such as the death of a parent, to the commonplace, such as a demanding job or a noisy neighbor. Research on stressors has focused on life events, catastrophes, and daily hassles.

Life Events One of the most significant sources of stress is change. Virtually any event that requires someone to make a readjustment can be a stressor. The Holmes–Rahe scale, a portion of which is reproduced in Table 11.5, measures stress related to 43 common *life events* that require change and adaptation (Holmes & Rahe, 1967). An important feature of the Holmes–Rahe scale is that it includes both negative items (e.g., death of a spouse) and positive items (e.g., marriage) that can be stressful.

Although the Holmes–Rahe scale offers a good rough estimate of the amount of stress a person is encountering (by summing all the life change units experienced over the past 12 months), it does not take into account the meanings of various experiences for different individuals. Consequently, some researchers have turned, instead, to measures of *perceived stress*—that is, the extent to which people *consider* the experiences they have undergone stressful (Blascovich & Mendes, 2000).

Major Stressors One of the most stressful events any individual can experience is the death of a spouse or child—a stress that can take its toll for many years afterward. For example, a study of people who lost a spouse or child in a car accident indicated that, for many bereaved persons, distress lasts as long as four to seven years after a sudden loss. Symptoms of prolonged distress included depression, sleep disturbances, fatigue, panic attacks, loneliness, and increased mortality rate. Additionally, parents who had unexpectedly lost a child were at substantially higher risk for divorce (Lehman et al., 1987).

Striking findings on the relation between loss and mortality emerged in a study of over one million people from Finland (Martikainen & Valkonen, 1996). The investigators charted the mortality rates of individuals who had lost a spouse over a five-year period. Those who lost a spouse were at substantially elevated risk for death by accident, violence, and al-

Table 11.5 ■ ■ Top 15 Stressors on the Holmes–Rahe Life Events Rating Scale		
Rank	Life Event	Mean Value
1	Death of spouse	100
2	Divorce	73
3	Marital separation	65
4	Jail term	63
5	Death of a close family member	63
6	Personal injury or illness	53
7	Marriage	50
8	Fired at work	47
9	Marital reconciliation	45
10	Retirement	45
11	Change in health in family member	44
12	Pregnancy	40
13	Sex difficulties	39
14	Gain of new family member	39
15	Business readjustment	39

Source: Holmes & Rahe, 1967.

Stress often reflects broader social and economic forces. Stress levels rise as unemployment levels rise, as do rates of child abuse, violence against spouses, alcoholism, suicide, and disease.

Table 11.6	■ Relative Risk of Death Following Death of a Spouse						

				Cause of Death			
	Cancer	*Chronic Heart Disease*	*Alcohol-Related Illness*	*Motor Vehicle Accidents*	*Other Accidents and Violence*	*Suicide*	*All Causes*
Men	1.31	2.08	3.98	1.52	3.05	3.02	1.66
Women	1.04	1.71	2.91	1.52	2.45	2.30	1.25

Source: Adapted from P. Martikainen & T. Valkonen (1996). Mortality after the death of a spouse: Rates and causes of death in a large Finnish cohort. *American Journal of Public Health, 86,* 1090.

cohol. Deaths from heart disease doubled—perhaps a confirmation of the popular view that people can "die of a broken heart." The relative risk of dying was particularly high within six months of the death of a spouse and was highest in younger people (Table 11.6). Other research finds that bereaved spouses displaying a higher proportion of "fake" smiles to "real" smiles are at greater risk for depression in the following years (Keltner & Bonanno, 1997; Keltner et al., 1999). Suppressing genuine feelings does not appear to be a particularly healthy strategy, at least for dealing with loss.

Another major stressor, unemployment, can also impair physical and mental health, although the effects are generally not as dramatic as the death of a spouse (Jahoda, 1988; Kessler et al., 1987a). For example, another large Finnish study followed workers for several months after a plant layoff (Viinamaeki et al., 1996). Those who remained unemployed were at increasing risk for depression, subjective distress, and stress-related illnesses as the months wore on.

Major stressors, such as loss of a loved one or unemployment, actually include many specific sources of stress. The effect on a given person depends on the individual's vulnerabilities to these specific stressors (Monroe & Simons, 1991). For example, unemployment can be devastating because of the financial strain on an individual or family. It can also lead to marital strain, forced relocation, and loss of social contact with friends from work (Bolton & Oatley, 1987; Kessler et al., 1989). Thus, even a person who has other sources of income, such as unemployment compensation or savings, may experience lowered self-esteem, loneliness, or anxiety following unemployment.

Making Connections

Catastrophes, such as the war in Bosnia, sometimes lead to post-traumatic stress disorder (PTSD). PTSD includes symptoms such as nightmares, flashbacks to the traumatic event, depression, and anxiety. Most severe life events, such as losses, actually do not elicit PTSD. The major exception is rape, which leads to PTSD 80 percent of the time (Chapter 15).

Acculturative Stress A severe stressor that is increasingly confronting people throughout the world is acculturative stress (Berry, 1989; Berry et al., 1997; Rogler et al., 1991). Acculturation means coming into contact with a new, typically dominant culture. Thus, **acculturative stress** refers to *the stress people experience in trying to adapt to a new culture.* Acculturative stress can occur whether people willingly emigrate for better opportunities or flee as refugees. Symptoms may include anxiety, depression, uncertainty and conflict about ethnic identity, and alcohol abuse.

Like other major life stresses, acculturative stress includes many specific stressors. People entering new cultures frequently encounter language difficulties, racial or ethnic prejudice, lower socioeconomic status (such as Russian doctors working in North America as paramedics because of licensing requirements), and separation from family. Immigrants also face conflicts over preserving their old values and beliefs and adapting to the mores of their new culture—conflicts often played out across the generations, as children shun their parents' Old World attitudes. Finally, many refugees must also come to terms with torture or with the torture or murder of loved ones back home.

Catastrophes

Catastrophes are *stressors of massive proportions.* Catastrophes may be caused by nature, such as the earthquakes that have struck Turkey and India in recent years, or by humans, such as the recent civil wars in Somalia, Rwanda, and

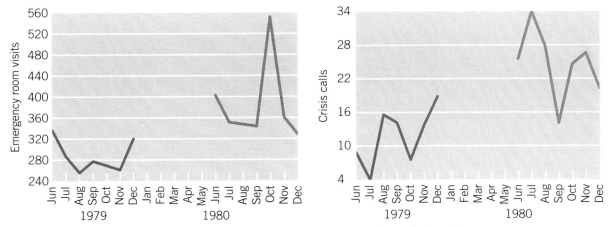

FIGURE 11.17 Impact of catastrophic stress. The number of emergency room visits and crisis calls jumped dramatically after the Mount St. Helens eruption, demonstrating the powerful effects of catastrophic stress. *Source:* Adams & Adams, 1984, p. 257.

the Balkans. One natural catastrophe studied by psychologists was the 1980 eruption of the Mount St. Helens volcano, which spewed a heavy covering of ash over a large area of Washington State (Adams & Adams, 1984). Because the Mount St. Helens ash fall was predictable, researchers could compare people's predisaster and postdisaster functioning. In the small agricultural town of Othello, for example, emergency room visits, court cases, crisis hotline calls, and mental health appointments significantly increased for months after the eruption (Figure 11.17).

One stress of catastrophic proportions, practiced by dozens of countries, is torture (Basoglu, 1997). In any given year, over 150 countries in the world practice torture, and between 5 and 35 percent of the world's 14 million refugees have been subjected to at least one episode of torture. The most common psychological effects include anxiety and depression, social withdrawal, problems with memory and attention, sexual dysfunction, nightmares, insomnia, and personality changes. A study of torture victims in Turkey found that years later nearly half the survivors continued to suffer from nightmares and other symptoms of post-traumatic stress (Basoglu et al., 1994). The average subject was tortured 291 times over four years in captivity, with forms of torture including beating, electric shock, prevention of urination or defecation, rape, and twisting of the testicles.

Daily Hassles   Although the concept of stressors tends to bring to mind major events such as death, unemployment, and catastrophes, more mundane events can be important as well and are often central to the subjective experience of stress (Hahn & Smith, 1999). **Daily hassles** are *"the irritating, frustrating, distressing demands that to some degree characterize everyday transactions with the environment"* (Kanner et al., 1981, p. 3). Daily hassles range from interpersonal conflicts to commuting during rush hour. The most common daily hassles include concerns about weight, ill health of a family member, rising prices of common goods, home maintenance, too many things to do, and misplacing or losing things (Kanner et al., 1981).

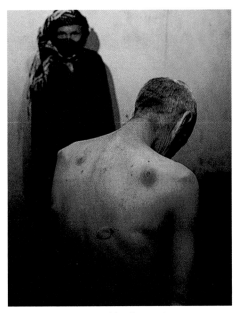

A Kurdish man tortured by the Iraqis.

*It's not the large things that send a man to the madhouse....
no, it's the continuing series of small tragedies that send a man to the madhouse...
not the death of his love but a shoelace that snaps with no time left....*

C. BUKOWSKI
"The Shoelace," 1980

INTERIM SUMMARY

Events that often lead to stress are called **stressors**. Life events are stressors that require change and adaptation. Perceived stress refers to the extent to which people consider the experiences they have undergone stressful. **Acculturative stress** refers to the stress people experience in trying to adapt to a new culture. **Catastrophes** are stressors of massive proportions, including both natural and human-made disasters. **Daily hassles** are minor annoyances of everyday life that contribute to stress.

Big Picture φ Question 1

To what extent can mental processes be reduced to the brain or body?

Apply & Discuss

Research has shown men and women to be susceptible to different types of stressors. Specifically, women report more stress following interpersonal rejection whereas men report more stress in achievement situations (Stroud et al., 2002). What role, if any, might women's susceptibility to interpersonal stressors play in the higher incidence of affective or mood disorders among women?

People living close to the Three-Mile Island nuclear plant experienced greater reductions in immunological functioning following the nuclear meltdown than people who lived some distance away from the nuclear reactor (Davidson & Baum, 1986).

Stress and Health

Stressful events obviously can have a substantial impact on psychological well-being. They can also affect other psychological functions, such as memory. Anyone who has ever been in a frightening car accident, suddenly lost a loved one, or even "pulled an all-nighter" studying for a final exam knows that stress can impair the ability to focus and commit information to memory. Researchers are now beginning to unravel the reasons stressful events can affect memory.

As we discussed in Chapter 6, the prefrontal cortex plays a particularly important role in working memory (e.g., momentarily holding in mind a phone number), and the hippocampus is involved in long-term memory (e.g., remembering the number over several weeks or years). Stress interferes with the functioning of both of these structures (Arnsten, 1998; McEwan, 1999). In fact, chronic stress leads to permanent cell death and a reduction in the size of the hippocampus (Bremner, 1999).

Thus, stress can alter the structure and function of the brain. It can also have a substantial effect on *physical* health and mortality (Kemeny & Laudenslager, 1999; O'Leary et al., 1997; Watkins & Maier, 2000). People under stress often suffer from headaches, depression, and other health problems such as influenza, sore throat, and backache (Cohen et al., 1991; DeLongis et al., 1988). Several studies have linked stress to vulnerability to cancer and have found that psychotherapy aimed at realistically but optimistically facing the cancer and maximizing social support may increase life expectancy in some cancer patients (Jacobs & Charles, 1980; Levenson & Bemis, 1991; Spiegel, 1999; Spiegel & Kato, 1996).

How does stress affect health? Stress can have a *direct* effect by decreasing the body's capacity to fight illness. It can also affect health *indirectly* by instigating behaviors that weaken the body's defenses or lead to exposure to *pathogens* and toxic agents that can produce physical illness (Figure 11.18). People under stress tend to drink more alcohol, smoke more, sleep less, and exercise less than their peers (Cohen & Williamson, 1991; O'Leary, 1992).

Other variables can increase or decrease the impact of stress on health. Stress is more likely to affect people's health, for example, if they do not have adequate social support (Baron et al., 1990; Cohen & Williamson, 1991). Exercise can also reduce the impact of stress on health. One study compared the number of visits to the health clinic of college students who were either high or low in physical fitness (Brown, 1991). Physically

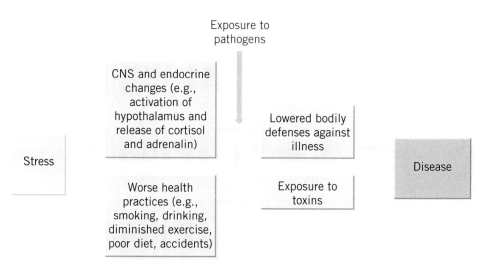

FIGURE 11.18 Pathways linking stress to infectious diseases. Stress can influence the onset of infectious disease in a number of ways. It can lead to CNS (central nervous system) and endocrine responses that diminish immune system functioning, leaving the person vulnerable to infection and illness from random exposure to pathogens such as airborne viruses. Alternatively, stress can lead to nonrandom exposure to toxins through poor health practices such as smoking. *Source:* Adapted from Cohen & Williamson, 1991, p. 8.

fit participants made fewer visits even when reporting many negative life events. Participants who were less physically fit tended to become ill when stressed (Figure 11.19).

Stress and the Immune System   **Psychoneuroimmunology** examines *the influence of psychosocial factors on the functioning of the immune system* (Kiecolt-Glaser et al., 2002; Stowell et al., 2003). The **immune system** is *the body's "surveillance and security" system, which detects and eliminates disease-causing agents in the body such as bacteria and viruses*. Three important types of cells in the immune system are *B cells, T cells,* and *natural killer cells.*

B cells produce **antibodies,** *protein molecules that attach themselves to foreign invaders and mark them for destruction.* Some T cells search out and directly destroy invaders, while others (T-helper cells) stimulate immune functioning. T-helper cells are the primary target of HIV, the virus that causes AIDS. Natural killer cells fight viruses and tumors (Weisse, 1992). Both acute (i.e., short-term) and chronic (i.e., long-term) stress can affect the efficiency and availability of cells in the immune system and hence the body's capacity to fight off disease (O'Leary et al., 1997).

When a group of people are exposed to an infectious disease, such as respiratory illness, only some of them actually become sick. Consequently, one way to explore the effects of stress on the immune system is to see whether people under stress are more likely to suffer from infectious diseases. The evidence suggests that they are. For example, one study (Jemmott et al., 1983) investigated the relationship between academic pressure and immunological functioning (specifically, the secretion of an antibody called immunoglobulin A, or IgA). During periods of the academic calendar rated by both the researchers and participants as most stressful, the secretion rate of IgA was lower; that is, the immune response was reduced. Similarly, studies of caregivers of patients with Alzheimer's disease show reduced immunological responses over time (Kiecolt-Glaser et al., 1987).

Perhaps the most conclusive study yet of the influence of stress on both immune functioning and illness assessed 394 healthy participants for degree of life stress and then administered nasal drops containing one of five different viruses (Cohen et al., 1991). Participants reporting higher stress showed greater rates of infection for all five viruses (Figure 11.20).

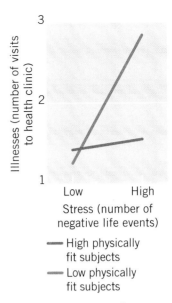

FIGURE 11.19 Interaction between stress and physical fitness. Students who were physically fit did not become sick when confronted with stress. Less fit participants, however, became ill when confronted with negative life events. *Source:* Brown, 1991, p. 559.

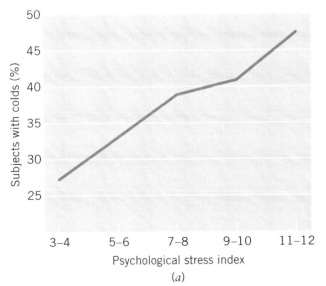

(a)

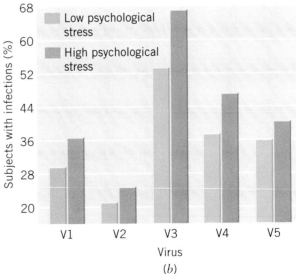

(b)

FIGURE 11.20 The relation between stress and illness following viral exposure. Part (a) shows the relation between the amount of self-reported psychological stress and the percentage of participants judged by a physician to have a clinical cold after exposure to a virus. As can be seen, the more stress, the more colds.

Part (b) presents data from a biological test of participants' blood for presence of infection. For each of five viruses, participants reporting higher stress showed higher rates of infection. *Source:* Cohen et al., 1991, pp. 609–610.

Stress and Health-Seeking Behavior   Stress can influence health in a more subtle way by influencing the way the person interprets bodily symptoms (Cameron et al., 1998; Leventhal & Leventhal, 1993). When symptoms are unambiguous and ominous, such as severe stomach pain accompanied by bloody stools, people tend to seek help immediately. Many symptoms, however, are ambiguous, and this ambiguity can lead to several alternative responses.

For example, a middle-aged man might ignore chest pains or take a "wait-and-see attitude" if they go away. This strategy may represent an effort to cope with the emotion he would likely feel (fear) if he took the symptom seriously. By deciding that "it's probably nothing," he may be trading short-term reassurance for long-term danger. People's appraisals of health risk also reflect their judgments about the context of the symptom, as when a person who experiences chest pain in the weeks following a job loss decides that "it's just stress."

At other times, and for other people, stress can have precisely the opposite effect, leading them to seek medical care for one minor complaint after another, fearing that each new symptom could be a sign of serious disease. In fact, people who are depressed, anxious, or recently stressed by experiences such as job loss tend not only to *have* more physical illnesses but also to *interpret* their illnesses more seriously and to experience the pain as greater (Leventhal & Leventhal, 1993). Thus, stress can lead people either to take their health too seriously or to not take it seriously enough.

Stress, Health, and Personality   Whether a person under stress remains healthy or becomes ill also depends on the person's enduring personality traits (O'Brien & De-Longis, 1996; Suls et al., 1996). Personality can influence stress and health through the motives people pursue, the way they tend to appraise circumstances (e.g., easily becoming angry or sad), or the way they tend to cope with stress (such as through drinking, cigarette smoking, avoiding doctors, or suppressing emotions).

For example, in one study, participants kept a daily diary of their moods and the events of the day (Suls et al., 1998). The higher participants were in neuroticism—the tendency to experience negative emotions such as depression or anxiety (Chapter 12)—the more daily problems they reported, the more reactive they were to stressors, and the more they were distressed by bad things that happened to them.

A more recent study powerfully demonstrates the impact of personality on both stress and health (Caspi, 2000). A team of investigators has been following a sample of about a thousand people born in Dunedin, New Zealand, during one year in the early 1970s. They have assessed the group repeatedly, beginning at age 3. At age 18, they assessed aspects of their personality. Then, three years later, they assessed four high-risk behaviors associated with stress and health: alcohol dependence, violent crime, unprotected sex with multiple partners, and dangerous driving habits.

Personality at age 18 was a powerful predictor of high-risk behaviors three years later: Those who tended to engage in all four behaviors were lower on traditionalism, concern about avoiding danger, ability to regulate impulses, and social closeness. They were also higher on aggression. Perhaps more striking, risk behaviors at age 21 were predictable from the initial assessment of participants at age 3. Those who were classified in preschool as undercontrolled—that is, impulsive, poorly behaved, and aggressive—were more likely to engage in all four high-risk behaviors than their better controlled (and particularly overcontrolled) peers.

Genetic factors affect stress as well, in two ways: by influencing the probability a person will place herself in stressful situations and by influencing her vulnerability to the stressors she encounters (Kendler, 1995). For example, studies comparing monozygotic and dizygotic twins have found that the likelihood of being robbed, assaulted, or confronted with financial difficulties is moderately heritable, with heritability estimated between 30 and 40 percent! The correlation between monozygotic (identical) twins' reports of financial difficulties is .44, whereas for dizygotic (fraternal) twins the correlation is only .12. As we will see (Chapter 12), the tendency to take risks is itself heritable, in large part because people who are fearful take fewer risks and those who are more pleasure-driven take more. Once a person experiences a stressful event, the tendency to experience negative affect, which is also heritable, can then amplify the individual's distress.

Type A Behavior Pattern and Hostility   One of the most thoroughly researched links between personality and health, which was first observed by two cardiologists and later corroborated by psychological research, is between heart disease and the **Type A behavior pattern***, a personality style characterized by impatience, ambition, competitiveness, hostility, and a "hard-driving" approach to life* (Friedman & Rosenman, 1959). Type B individuals, on the other hand, are more relaxed, easy-going, and less easily angered.

One psychologist illustrated the differences between Type A and Type B behavior in describing a fishing trip he took with a colleague (Schwartz, 1987, p. 136):

> I baited the hook and dropped the line over in a relaxed fashion, watched the gulls, and swayed with the swells. But what really struck [my colleague] was my talking to the fish when they bit the hook: "That's nice" or "Take your time, I'm in no rush."

In contrast to his own Type B pattern, a man fishing in a boat nearby exhibited Type A behavior (Schwartz, 1987, p. 136):

> He was fishing with two poles, racing back and forth between them, and tangling his lines while cursing the fish that happened to be on the line beyond his reach. If the fish eluded him while others caught them, he would pull up the anchor in frustration, start the engine with a roar, and race to another part of the bay.

A comparison of bus drivers in North America and India suggests that these behavioral patterns occur cross-culturally, at least in some form (Evans et al., 1987). In both samples, Type A bus drivers reported greater job stress and had more accidents and absences per month than Type B drivers. In addition, in India, Type A bus drivers braked, blew their horns, and passed more frequently than Type B drivers.

More recent research suggests that subcomponents of the Type A pattern may be differentially related to heart disease (Dembroski & Costa, 1987; Siegman, 1994). In particular, hostility—or the combination of defensiveness, negative affect, and suppressed hostility—has been implicated in narrowing of the arteries leading to the heart. Angry people also tend to die slightly younger (Miller et al., 1996).

Type A and Type B behavior on the tennis court.

Optimism/Pessimism   Another personality dimension related to immune functioning and health is optimism/pessimism (Carver, 1998; Peterson, 1995). One study found that coronary artery bypass patients who reported higher levels of optimism on a questionnaire recovered more quickly and returned to normal life more easily than pessimistic participants (Scheier et al., 1989). Another found that college students with a pessimistic explanatory style (a tendency to explain bad events in negative, self-blaming ways; see Chapter 5) experienced more days of illness and visited physicians more frequently than other students (Peterson, 1988).

Even more striking results emerged in a 35-year study of 99 graduates of Harvard University. Participants with a pessimistic explanatory style at age 25 were more likely to be in poor health or dead at ages 45 to 50—even after controlling statistically for physical and mental health at age 25 (Peterson et al., 1988). People who are pessimistic do not take as good care of themselves, do not cope as well, and have poorer immune functioning, all of which lead to greater illness (Kamen & Seligman, 1987; Lin & Peterson, 1990).

INTERIM SUMMARY

Psychoneuroimmunology examines the influence of psychosocial factors on the functioning of the immune system. Stress can affect physical health in two ways: directly, by weakening the **immune system** (the system of cells that detects and destroys disease-causing agents), and indirectly, by leading to behaviors that weaken the body's defenses or lead to exposure to pathogens (toxic agents). Personality factors also affect stress levels and health, such as the tendency to experience negative affect (neuroticism), hostility and suppressed hostility, and pessimism.

Coping

That people get sick or experience unpleasant emotions in response to stress should come as no surprise. What may seem more surprising is that most people who experience life crises remain healthy (Hobfoll et al., 1998; Moos & Schaefer, 1986). This resiliency in the face of stress reflects *the ways people deal with stressful situations*, called ways of **coping** (or **coping mechanisms**).

Coping Mechanisms

Researchers often distinguish two or three basic types of coping strategies (Folkman & Lazarus, 1980; Folkman & Moskowitz, 2000; Moos & Billings, 1982). Strategies aimed at changing the situation producing the stress are called *problem focused*, because they try to deal with the stressor itself. Two other types of strategy—efforts to alter thoughts *about* the situation, and efforts to alter the unpleasant emotional consequences of stress—are called *emotion focused*. Their aim is to regulate the emotions generated by a stressful experience. Thus, if a person cannot change a stressful situation directly, she can try to change her perception of it or the emotions it produces. Alcohol and drug use are common mechanisms for escaping emotional distress (Kushner et al., 2000).

Efforts to cope by changing the situation typically involve problem solving (Chapter 7). The individual may try to remove the stressor, plan ways of resolving the situation, seek advice or assistance from others to change the situation, or try to avoid the stressor altogether by planning ahead (Aspinwall & Taylor, 1997; Carver et al., 1989). Children whose mothers have a problem-focused coping style tend to be better adjusted and more socially skilled than their peers (Eisenberg et al., 1996).

A number of studies suggest that religious faith often helps people cope with stressful events, such as contracting a terminal disease or losing a child. Their beliefs allow them to ascribe meaning to the event or strengthen their sense of closeness to the divine (Pargament & Park, 1995). For example, one study found that people who used their religion to cope with a major life stress—a kidney transplant—tended to have better outcomes 3 and 12 months later, as did their significant others if they relied on their faith (Tix & Frazier, 1998).

Apply & Discuss

■ Why do people engage in behaviors such as smoking and excessive drinking that increase the negative impact of stress on their health?

■ Why do people often fail to act in ways that promote health, such as exercising and getting prompt medical attention?

Big Picture φ Question 4

To what extent is human nature particular versus universal?

A Global Vista | **The Impact of Culture on Coping Styles**

The way people respond to stress, as well as the situations they consider stressful, are in part culturally patterned. Relative to children in less technologically developed societies, such as Mexico, children in countries such as the United States and Canada tend to take a more active coping approach, directed at removing obstacles toward their goals (e.g., Diaz-Guerrero, 1979). This is not surprising in light of data showing that the emphasis on mastering the environment, characteristic of highly technologically developed societies, is relatively new in human history. Most cultures in human history have believed that humans should adjust to nature, not the other way around (Kluckhorn & Strodtbeck, 1961).

These findings suggest possible limits to Western theories and research linking an active coping style (characterized by a sense of mastery, self-efficacy, and control) to mental and physical health. In capitalist societies, which are based on entrepreneurship and personal initiative, an active coping style and a strong belief in one's own ability are highly adaptive traits. In societies organized around family, community, or tribal ties, such traits may be unrelated to mental and physical health. Coping is always relative to its cultural context, and coping strategies considered useful in one society (such as wailing at a funeral) may engender disapproval, and hence additional stress, in another.

Low-Effort Syndrome

Understanding patterns of culture and coping may also lead to a better understanding of dilemmas facing African-American and other minority adolescents in multicultural societies. For years, educators, social scientists, and policy makers have wrestled with the large gap between the educational performance of whites and some minority groups in the United States, such as African- and Latino-Americans, and the absence of such a gap for other immigrant groups, such as Arabs, Chinese, and West Indians.

John Ogbu (1991) argues that, throughout the world, minority groups who experience a ceiling on their economic prospects over several generations because of job discrimination develop a low-effort syndrome not seen in new immigrants who voluntarily move to a culture in search of a better life. **Low-effort syndrome**—*the tendency to exert minimal effort to escape stressful social and economic circumstances*—is an adaptive coping strategy when social barriers make effort and achievement fruitless and when hard work and academic success would only increase frustration and anger. The school performance of Koreans in Japan, who have been an underclass there for many years, is very poor, whereas Korean immigrants to North America tend to excel.

Low-effort syndrome is an example of a coping strategy that solves one problem (minimizing frustration in the face of racism and barriers to success) but creates another, particularly if opportunities and social attitudes toward race change faster than coping styles developed over several generations. Because African-Americans for years faced impassable barriers to upward mobility, scholastic achievement became defined in many black communities as "white" behavior. Thus, for many black adolescents today the fear of being ridiculed for "acting white," together with a subcultural ambivalence toward achievement, inhibits scholastic achievement.

John Henryism

Low-effort syndrome among people who historically faced external limits on what they could hope to achieve can be understood as an adaptation to a social and political system that eliminated rewards for effort. Recent research suggests another way in which, paradoxically, low effort among African Americans for years made adaptive sense: Those who tried harder died earlier.

A legend is told (and a song sung) of a "steel-drivin' man" named John Henry, a black man known among railroad workers in the late-nineteenth century for his tremendous strength and endurance. As the legend goes, in a famous steel-driving contest, after an extraordinary battle of man versus machine, Henry beat a mechanical steam drill with mighty blows from his nine-pound hammer. Moments later, however, he died from exhaustion (Sherman, 1994).

This may not have been an isolated incident. Physicians have been puzzled for years by the increased rate of high blood pressure in African-Americans, which is associated with greater rates of stroke. Genetics and food preferences may explain some

Making Connections

Efforts at achievement can sometimes lead to anxiety in even the most accomplished African-American students because of associations they, like their white peers, have formed over years between skin color and success. Simply filling out information on race or ethnicity before taking a standardized test like the SAT can prime negative associations, translating directly into lower test scores (Chapter 17).

Big Picture φ Question 3

To what extent is human psychology continuous with the psychology of other animals?

of the difference between blacks and whites, but researchers have recently identified a coping style among some African-Americans that may also play a role, which researchers have called John Henryism (Sherman, 1994; Wright et al., 1996).

John Henryism is *the tendency among members of minority groups to work hard and cope actively despite difficult circumstances*. Individuals with this coping style show a single-minded determination to succeed despite the odds. Several studies show that individuals high in John Henryism are vulnerable to high blood pressure, particularly when they are black, and particularly when they are of low socioeconomic status. In some sense, low-effort syndrome may actually have been an adaptive solution to a system that psychologically put a noose around the neck of those who tried to better themselves. To what extent the physiological consequences of John Henryism will change as opportunities continue to expand for African-Americans is as yet unknown.

INTERIM SUMMARY

Coping mechanisms are the ways people deal with stressful events. *Problem-focused coping* involves changing the situation. *Emotion-focused coping* aims to regulate the emotion generated by a stressful situation. The ways people respond to stress, as well as the situations they consider stressful, are in part culturally patterned. Members of minority groups who, for generations, experience a ceiling on their economic prospects because of discrimination sometimes develop a **low-effort syndrome** in which they seemingly stop making the kinds of active efforts that might alleviate some of their hardships. In African-Americans, **John Henryism**—the tendency to work hard and cope actively despite difficult circumstances—is associated with high blood pressure.

Social Support

An important resource for coping with stress is **social support**, *the presence of others in whom one can confide and from whom one can expect help and concern*. Social support is as important for maintaining physical health as it is mental health (Berkman, 1995; Salovey et al., 1998). A high level of social support is associated with protection against a range of illnesses, from hypertension and herpes to cancer and heart disease (Cohen & Herbert, 1996; Manne, 2003; Sarason et al., 1997; Spiegel & Kato, 1996). The presence of social support enhances the functioning of the immune system whereas the absence of social support compromises the immune system (Stowell et al., 2003).

The benefits of social support are apparent in humans as well as other social animals. In rhesus monkeys, immune functioning is suppressed when adult monkeys are separated from their social group but alleviated if they are given a companion (Gust et al., 1994; Laudenslager & Boccia, 1996). In humans, the number of social relationships a person has, and the extent to which the individual feels close to other people, is a powerful predictor of mortality (House et al., 1988a; J. Johnson et al., 1996). In fact, the evidence supporting the link between social relationships and health is as strong as the data linking smoking and ill health.

Two hypotheses have been advanced to explain the beneficial effects of social support, both of which have received empirical support (Cohen & Wills, 1985; Taylor, 1991). The *buffering hypothesis* proposes that social support is a buffer or protective factor against the harmful effects of stress during high-stress periods. In a classic study, urban women who experienced significant life stress were much less likely to become depressed if they had an intimate, confiding relationship with a boyfriend or husband (Brown & Harris, 1978). Among the elderly, social support provides a buffer between the experience of stressful events, such as the loss of a spouse, and the development of depression (Kraaij & Garnefski, 2002). The magnitude of this effect can be seen in light of the fact that depression is the leading psychological cause of suicide in the elderly.

An alternative hypothesis views social support as a continuously positive force that makes the person less susceptible to stress in the first place. In this view, people with supportive relationships are less likely to make a primary appraisal of situations as stressful, and they are more likely to perceive themselves as able to cope. For example, taking a new job is much more threatening to a person who has no one in whom to confide and no one to tell her,"Don't worry, you'll do well at it."Another important aspect of social support is the opportunity for emotional disclosure, which, as we have seen, strengthens the immune system.

Although researchers often associate social support with the actual receipt of aid (i.e., received social support), for some individuals merely the perception that social support would be available if needed (i.e., perceived social support) is sufficient to cope with stressful life events (Cobb, 1976). And, in fact, sometimes the actual provision of aid can interfere with an individual's ability to cope. When Larry's father died, for example, a multitude of people descended on the family home bringing food and words of support and consolation. Although Larry knew these people meant well, and that this was just the way things were done, he wanted this time alone to grieve. Later on, of course, when the funeral was over and Larry really needed a listening ear, all of the people had returned to their own homes and were unavailable.

The flipside of social support—loneliness—is a major source of stress in humans. Loneliness takes a physiological as well as a psychological toll, leading both to increased autonomic arousal during stressful situations and slower recovery from negative emotional states (Cacioppo et al., 2000).

The relationship between social support and stress is not, however, simple or uniform. For example, stress can erode social support, leading to a vicious cycle, particularly if the person under stress responds with anger or helplessness (Lane & Hobfoll, 1992). Severely stressful life events, such as getting cancer, can also overwhelm significant others, who may withdraw because they, too, feel helpless and distressed (Bolger et al., 1996). Further high-conflict or unsupportive relationships can actually have detrimental effects on health and psychological well-being (e.g., Major et al., 1997).

Social support protects against stress and illness in humans and other animals.

INTERIM SUMMARY

Social support refers to the presence of others in whom a person can confide and from whom the individual can expect help and concern. In humans and other primates, lack of social support predicts disease and mortality. The *buffering hypothesis* proposes that social support protects people against the harmful effects of acute stress. An alternative hypothesis suggests that social support is a continuously positive force that makes the person less susceptible to stress. Social support is not, however, uniformly beneficial. Bad relationships do not promote health, and significant others often have difficulty themselves being supportive at times of crisis.

Disclosure and Health

One Step Further

The physical and psychological benefits of having other people on whom we can rely are well known. Other people provide a listening ear and a sounding board against which we can bounce ideas and"hear"ourselves think. People who lack social support and have no one to whom they can express their thoughts and feelings show reduced psychological and physiological functioning (Stowell et al., 2003). They frequently ruminate about stressors they are experiencing, and they

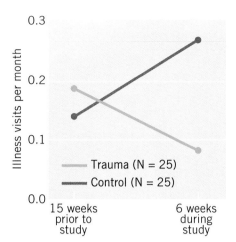

FIGURE 11.21 Mean health center illness visits for the periods before and during the experiment. (Note that the standard deviation for visits per month ranged from .12 to .40, averaging .26 over the four observations.) *Source:* Reprinted from Pennebaker et al., 1988, p. 243.

experience heightened bouts of anxiety and depression relative to people who are able to discuss their stressors with others.

One of the leading researchers in this area of emotional disclosure and health, Jamie Pennebaker, has conducted numerous fascinating studies examining the mediating role of emotional expression between experiences of stress and illness (Chapter 3). For example, in one study, college students were randomly assigned to one of two conditions. Participants in the trauma group wrote for 20 minutes a day for four consecutive days about the most traumatic event of their life. Participants in the control condition wrote for the same amount of time about different topics assigned by the researcher including their plans for the rest of the day and describing what kind of shoes they were wearing (Pennebaker et al., 1988). As shown in Figure 11.21, participants who wrote about traumatic events showed better immune functioning than participants in the trauma group as attested to by the fact that those in the trauma condition had significantly fewer visits to the university health center in the six weeks following the experiment. These effects were most pronounced for participants who had never disclosed the information prior to the experiment.

In a related study, half of the participants were assigned to an experimental group where they wrote about the facts and emotions surrounding a recent romantic breakup (Lepore & Greenberg, 2002). The other half of the participants were assigned to a control group and wrote about innocuous aspects of relationships. Post-experimental comparisons of participants in the two groups revealed that those in the control group experienced significantly more upper respiratory problems, greater levels of fatigue, and more intrusive thoughts than those in the control group. In addition, the data suggested that those participants in the experimental group were more likely to reunite with their former partner than those in the control group!

In yet another study, Pennebaker interviewed over 60 survivors of the Holocaust who had never talked with anyone about their experiences in the concentration camps. One of the things that emerged from these interviews was the painful memories and intrusive thoughts that these victims had lived with for over 40 years (Chapter 15)). Many reported remembering numerous times a day horrendous images they had witnessed during that time. In his book *Opening Up*, Pennebaker (1990) recounts one woman's intrusive memory, a memory she sees in her mind several times a day: "They were throwing babies from the second floor window of the orphanage. I can still see the pools of blood, the screams, and the thuds of their bodies. I just stood there afraid to move. The Nazi soldiers faced us with their guns." As in his other studies, Pennebaker found both psychological and physical benefits of disclosure among the Holocaust survivors. Over time, those who were labeled high disclosers reported improved affect and fewer illnesses than those who were labeled low disclosers (Pennebaker et al. 1989).

Collectively, these studies highlight the role that emotional disclosure has on physical and psychological health, although the precise mechanism though which emotional expression improves health remains unclear. One possibility is that talking or writing about traumatic or troubling events allows people to cognitively process the event, and, thereby, give some meaning to the event (Graybeal et al., 2002; Pennebaker, 1990). Others have suggested that talking about troubling events that have produced negative affect and intrusive thoughts reduces the negativity associated with the cognitive intrusions (Lepore, 1997). Alternatively, inhibiting disclosure of traumatic events compromises immune functioning, thereby increasing an individual's susceptibility to illness. It is also possible that people may be motivated to escape the intrusive thoughts associated with inhibition, and may use alcohol or another mind-altering chemical to provide such an escape.

The Future of Health Psychology

When you stop and think about how far the field of health psychology has come in the last 20–30 years, the thought is staggering, and there is no reason to think that the same level of progress won't continue in years to come. In spite of media and informational campaigns designed to alter people's negative health behaviors, people will continue to engage in behaviors that put them at risk. As the proportion of the population that constitutes the older generation continues to grow, new issues will arise that are ripe for psychological research and intervention (Siegler et al., 2002).

Increasingly, the focus of health psychologists will turn to the environment as an influence on people's health behaviors, where the environment includes not only the physical environment in which people live, but also their communities, families, and work and peer groups (Keefe et al., 2002). Part of this focus will examine the effects of "westernization" on the health of immigrant people. Research has consistently shown that, once groups of people live in Western culture, and assume Westernized diets and habits, their health and health habits deteriorate (Daniel et al., 1999; deGonzague et al., 1999; Eaton & Konner, 1985; Price et al., 1993).

Health psychologists who work in clinical settings as therapists will likely increase their attention to the involvement of family members and even peer group members in treatment of people suffering from obesity or drug addiction, for example. This emphasis will also allow psychologists to examine the co-dependent role that family members and friends may play in perpetuating health-related illness and negative health behaviors. In addition, epidemics such as SARS and the possibility of a smallpox outbreak have taken health concerns to an international level. Thus, health psychologists will increasingly be asked to become involved on an international level (Oldenburg, 2002).

As reflected in the goals of *Healthy People 2010*, reducing health disparities both within cultures and between cultures is a major priority. In spite of the fact that patterns of illness have changed markedly over the last several decades, major health problems in developing countries still center around acute and infectious diseases (Oldenburg, 2002; WHO, 1999). "Among children, diarrhea, acute respiratory infections, malaria, measles, and perinatal conditions account for 21% of all deaths in developing countries, compared to 1% in developed countries" (Oldenburg, 2002, p. 4). Many of the health disparities throughout the world could be eliminated if one factor were eliminated: poverty. As stated in a report issued by the World Health Organization in 1995:

> The world's biggest killer and the greatest cause of ill health and suffering across the globe is listed almost at the end of the International Classification of Diseases. It is given the code Z59.5—Extreme Poverty. Poverty is the main reason why babies are not vaccinated, why clean water and sanitation are not provided, why curative drugs and other treatments are unavailable and why mothers die in childbirth. It is the underlying cause of reduced life expectancy, handicap, disability, and starvation. Poverty is a major contributor to mental illness, stress, suicide, family disintegration and substance abuse. (Executive Summary, p. 1).

Technology will also help to advance the use of services provided by health psychologists and the efficiency of those services (Keefe et al., 2002). The computer is increasingly being used as a means of allowing clients to receive information about health services (e.g., pain management information) without having to visit a health clinic (Naylor et al., 2002). Similarly, health psychologists are increasingly using the Internet as a provider of information about health prevention and health promotion (Humphreys & Klaw, 2001; Woodruff et al., 2001). Instructing people how to tease apart the medically sound advice from the myths found on the Internet is another area in which health psychologists will find themselves.

The Internet may also be useful as a way of reducing people's self-presentational concerns regarding health behaviors such as condom use. The ability to order condoms on-line as opposed to having to purchase them face-to-face may facilitate their use. Advances in virtual reality therapy are allowing patients experiencing post-traumatic stress disorder, for example, to confront fear-producing situations in a simulated real world. Virtual reality has also been used as a distraction tool for children who are undergoing painful medical procedures (Hoffman et al., 2000). In a variation of virtual reality therapy, know as augmented reality, the patient experiences a virtual stressor while in a real-world setting. "In augmented reality, a mobile patient can learn to confront the virtual world while continuing to interact with people in the real word" (Keefe et al., 2002).

As knowledge continues to advance in all areas of psychology, increasing cross-fertilization between health psychologists and researchers in other areas of psychology can be expected to increase. For example, health psychologists are trained by receiving a degree in clinical psychology with a health track. Many social psychologists (author RMK included) who study topics such as attitudes, self-presentation, self-efficacy, self-handicapping, and attributions find themselves immersed in applying social psychological theories to health psychology. Health psychologists are increasingly drawing on the work of cognitive psychologists to understand the ways in which people think about events that happen to them (e.g., the development of a chronic illness). Personality psychologists and physiological psychologists have much to offer the area of health psychology, given that virtually all of the health-compromising behaviors are facilitated by particular personality traits and genetic predispositions. And the list goes on and on.

Recent changes in societal threats and epidemic illness threats will also necessitate increasing interventions by health psychologists. The terrorist attacks of September 11, 2001, created fears and stress among many Americans, fears that, for many, continue to this day. Helping people, particularly victims and their families, deal with the stress of those attacks and, for many, the post-traumatic stress disorder they experienced as a result, is the job of health psychologists. Similar fears arise from strange new illnesses that are arising and, in some cases, reaching epidemic proportions. "Some 30 new diseases have cropped up since the mid-1970s—causing tens of millions of deaths—and forgotten scourges have resurfaced with alarming regularity" (Cowley, 2003). In Africa, Ebola fever is spreading. In the Netherlands, a variation of the avian flu has spread from birds to humans. And, recently seen in the news is the epidemic of SARS. As more and more of these epidemics loom on the horizon, health psychologists will find themselves increasingly involved not only in trying to uncover the etiology of these diseases, but also in helping people deal with their fears of the illnesses and cope with the consequences should they contract one of these illnesses.

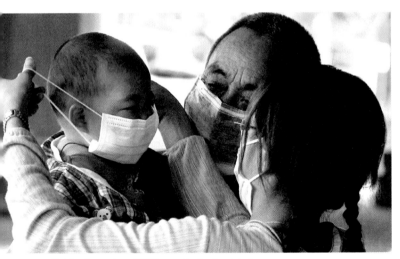

Epidemics such as SARS provide focal points for health psychologists to do their work.

Summary

Health

1. **Health psychology** examines the biological, psychological, and social influences on how people stay healthy, why they become ill, and how they respond when they do get ill.

2. Although the field has taken off only in the last two decades, it has a rich heritage in the fields of medicine and philosophy. This history began with the early theorists and the practice of **trephination**, continued through the **humoral theory of illness**, and the Renaissance, and received one of its major boosts from Freud and the field of **psychosomatic medicine**.

3. A number of theories have been created to explain why people

engage in positive or negative health habits. Among the most prominent of these are the **health belief model**, the **protection motivation theory of health**, the **theory of reasoned action**, and the **theory of planned behavior**.

4. **Obesity** is second only to nicotine as the primary health threat. Assessments using body mass index indicate that over half of Americans are overweight or obese. Obesity extracts a sizable physical and psychological toll, and it does not have a quick fix. The origins of obesity lie in both genetic and environmental influences.

5. Cigarette smoking is the most preventable cause of illness today. As with obesity, underlying causes are both genetic (e.g., personality variables) and environmental, although the emphasis is on environmental facilitators of smoking.

6. People do and don't do a lot of health-related behaviors because of concerns with the impressions other people are forming of them, a process termed **self-presentation**. Most people who do not wear condoms, who tan excessively, and who use alcohol or other drugs, do so, in part, for self-presentational reasons.

7. **Alcoholism** and **problem drinking** are major problems in society today. A number of genetic and environmental variables contribute to the development of alcohol abuse. Some alcoholics enter **spontaneous remission** whereas others require more formalized methods of treatment, such as **aversion therapy**.

8. Over 20 sexually transmitted diseases have been identified, most notably HIV/AIDS. Given that behavior is clearly involved in the transmission of STDs, they are a frequent focus area for health psychologists.

9. Four broad barriers to health promotion have been identified: individual barriers, family barriers, health system barriers, and community barriers.

Stress

10. **Stress** refers to a challenge to a person's capacity to adapt to inner and outer demands, which may be physiologically arousing and emotionally taxing and call for cognitive and behavioral responses. Stress is a psychobiological process that entails a transaction between a person and her environment. Selye proposed that the body responds to stressful conditions with a **general adaptation syndrome** consisting of three stages: alarm, resistance, and exhaustion.

11. From a psychological standpoint, stress entails a person's perception that demands of the environment tax or exceed his available psychosocial resources. Stress, in this view, depends on the meaning of an event to the individual. Lazarus's model identifies two stages in the process of stress and coping: **primary appraisal**, in which the person decides whether the situation is benign, stressful, or irrelevant, and **secondary appraisal**, in which the person evaluates the options and decides how to respond.

12. Events that often lead to stress are called **stressors**. Stressors include life events, catastrophes, and daily hassles.

13. Stress has a considerable impact on health and mortality, particularly through its effects on the **immune system**. Whether a person under stress remains healthy or becomes ill also depends in part on the person's enduring personality dispositions. **Type A behavior pattern**, and particularly its hostility component, has been linked to heart disease. Neuroticism (the tendency to experience negative affective states) and optimism/pessimism are other personality traits linked to stress and health.

Coping

14. The ways people deal with stressful situations are known as strategies for **coping**; these **coping mechanisms** are in part culturally patterned. People cope by trying to change the situation directly, changing their perception of it, or changing the emotions it elicits.

15. A major resource for coping with stress is **social support**, which is related to health and mortality.

Key Terms

Personality

O skar and Jack were identical twins who shared dozens of idio-syncrasies. They dressed alike (both wore wire-rimmed glasses and two-pocket shirts), read magazines from back to front, and wrapped rubber bands around their wrists. Their personalities were similar, from their basic "tempo," or speed of activity, to the way they responded to stress, their sense of well-being, and their style of interacting socially. None of this may seem un-usual; they were, after all, identical twins. What makes this remarkable, however, is that Oskar Stohr was raised as a Catholic and a Nazi by his mother in Germany, while his twin brother Jack Yufe was raised as a Jew by his father and lived part of his life on an Israeli kibbutz. Separated shortly after birth, the men did not meet again until they were adults, when they participated in a study of twins (Holden, 1980).

The term *personality* is a part of everyday speech. When people make statements such as "Jim isn't the best-looking, but he has a nice personal-ity," they typically use the term to denote the manner in which a person acts across a variety of situations. Psychologists use the term to describe not only an individual's *reputation*—the way the person acts and is known socially—but also the *inter-nal processes* that create that reputation (Hogan, 1983, 1987). **Personality** refers to *the enduring patterns of thought, feel-ing, motivation, and behavior that are expressed in different circumstances*.

Personality psychologists have two aims. The first is to construct theories that describe the **structure of personality**; that is, *the organization of enduring patterns of thought, feeling, motivation, and behavior*. The second task is to study **individual differences** in personality—*the way people differ from one another*. Thus, personality psychologists study both how people resemble one another and how they differ. The two are intimately related: Theories of personality structure specify the central elements of personality, and these are the characteristics on which people differ.

The approach psychologists use to carry out this dual mis-sion depends, once again, on their theoretical perspective. We begin by exploring Freud's models of the mind and the evolu-tion of psychodynamic thinking about personality since Freud's time. We then consider cognitive–social approaches, derived from theories of learning and cognition, which we have already examined in some detail. Next, we explore trait theories, which use everyday language to describe personality, and ex-amine the extent to which personality traits are inherited, as suggested by the case of Jack and Oskar. We then turn to humanistic theories, which focus on the way people wrestle with fundamental human concerns, such as mortality and meaning in life. We conclude by considering the extent to which personality differs across cultures.

Each of these theories differs in what its proponents believe to be the basic elements of personality: motives, thoughts, feelings, traits, behavior. As you will see, no single answer has emerged to that question; in fact, it is one of the most hotly debated issues in the field of personality psychology. What psychologists do agree about is that personality lies at the intersection of virtually all psychological processes—cognition, emotion, behavior—and occurs through the interplay of those processes. Our personality is not just our motives; nor is it just the way we solve problems or the ways we interact with other people. Personality is the way our motives, emotions, and ways of thinking about ourselves, others, and the world interact in particular situations to produce ways of responding that are characteristically "ours."

Throughout, we address two main questions. First, what are the basic elements of personality? In other words, what are the components of personality that endure over time and give each of us our own distinct psychological "fingerprint"? Second, how stable is personality? To what extent is an individual "the same person" over time and across situations? And how much of this stability, as in the case of Oskar and Jack, reflects genetic influences?

INTERIM SUMMARY

Personality refers to the enduring patterns of thought, feeling, motivation, and behavior that are expressed in different circumstances. Personality psychologists construct general theories of the **structure of personality** (the way personality processes are organized) and **individual differences** (the way people vary in their personality characteristics).

Psychodynamic Theories

Sigmund Freud developed the first comprehensive theory of personality. As a neurologist practicing in the 1880s before the advent of psychiatry and clinical psychology, Freud encountered patients with a wide range of psychological disturbances. A particularly perplexing disorder was *hysteria*, in which a number of patients, most of them women, suffered from paralysis, numbness, and fainting spells, with no apparent biological origin.

In seeking a treatment for the disorder, Freud was particularly influenced by the work of Jean Martin Charcot. Charcot, a French neurologist, demonstrated that hysterical symptoms could be produced—and alleviated, at least temporarily—through hypnosis. Paralyzed patients could walk again under the influence of a hypnotic suggestion, but the symptoms usually returned before long. These patients *wanted* to walk, but something seemed to override their conscious determination or will, much as many individuals today with bulimia cannot stop binging and purging.

Freud reasoned that if a symptom is not of physiological origin and the patient is consciously trying to stop it but cannot, then opposing the conscious will must be an unconscious counter-will of equal or greater magnitude. This basic assumption was the centerpiece of Freud's theory of **psychodynamics**, *psychological dynamics analogous to dynamics among physical forces*. According to Freud, psychological forces such as wishes, fears, and intentions have a direction and an intensity. When several such motives collide and conflict, the balance of these forces determines the person's behavior, as in the case of a patient suffering from a hysterical paralysis, whose will to move her leg is unconsciously overridden.

Big Picture φ Question 7

To what extent are psychological processes conscious or unconscious—that is, explicit versus implicit?

Freud's Models

Why would a counter-will be unconscious? And what balance of unconscious forces could lead to paralysis or to a need to starve or drink oneself to death? Freud tried to answer these questions throughout his career by developing a series of models. Before turning to Freud's models and those of later psychodynamic theorists, a brief comment about method is in order. Many of the data presented in the next several pages are different from the laboratory data to which the reader is by now accustomed. Although we will emphasize laboratory evidence for psychodynamic theories, the basis for these theories has largely been observations during clinical sessions with patients.

Many critics have rightfully pointed to the problems with case study data of this sort: They cannot easily be observed by other scientists, they are filtered through the biases of the investigator, and they do not easily permit generalization from one subject to another. Nevertheless, clinical observation has led to the discovery of many important phenomena, such as unconscious processes, that for up to a century were ignored or rejected by advocates of other perspectives for want of reliable methods to study them. As we have seen, psychological science cannot survive on a steady diet of case studies, but such studies can be extremely useful in formulating hypotheses (Chapter 2).

Topographic Model   Freud's (1900) first model, the **topographic model**, *used a spatial metaphor (the mind as split into sectors) that divided mental processes into three types: conscious, preconscious, and unconscious* (Chapter 9). **Conscious mental processes** are *rational, goal-directed thoughts at the center of awareness*. **Preconscious mental processes** are *not conscious but could become conscious at any point*, such as knowledge of the color of robins. Finally, **unconscious mental processes** are *irrational, organized along associative lines rather than by logic*. They are inaccessible to consciousness because they have been repressed, that is, kept from consciousness to avoid emotional distress.

Unconscious processes, while barred from consciousness, are not inert. Because they are not consciously acknowledged, they may leak into consciousness and affect behavior in unexpected and often unwelcome ways, as in slips of the tongue. For example, a woman in her late thirties who was dating a man several years her junior was asked about the age difference. She replied, "Oh, I don't think it really mothers." Apparently, a part of her was not so sure. Freud also used the topographic model to understand dreams, distinguishing between their story line—the manifest content—and their underlying message—the latent content (Chapter 9).

Conflict and Ambivalence   A central feature of Freud's theory of psychodynamics was its emphasis on **ambivalence**—*conflicting feelings or motives*. From childhood on, we constantly interact with people who are important to us, but those interactions include both pleasant and unpleasant experiences. The same people who teach us how to love invariably teach us about frustration and rage.

For example, a patient named Bill was terrified that he would someday marry a woman who would treat him in the same harsh and belittling way that he felt his mother had treated his father. Unfortunately, Bill's most ingrained unconscious models of femininity and marital interaction were profoundly shaped by observing his parents as a child.

Years later, Bill and his friend Pete were in a bar, where they noticed two women. Pete thought they looked somewhat severe, that their gestures and facial expressions seemed harsh or angry, and that they were sending clear signals that they had no interest in being disturbed. Bill laughingly disagreed and insisted that he and Pete introduce themselves. Within 10 minutes, both men felt, in Bill's words, like "bananas in a blender"; the women spoke to them with sarcasm and barely veiled hostility for

Big Picture φ Question 2

What is the relationship between reason and desire or, more precisely, between cognition and affect?

Making Connections

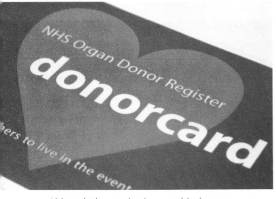

Although the emphasis on ambivalence was once unique to psychodynamic approaches, today researchers studying attitudes recognize the ambivalence characteristic of many attitudes, such as mixed feelings about donating blood or donating their organs (Chapter 17).

Apply and Discuss

- If, as Freud suggests, people's behavior is motivated by unconscious forces, to what degree are people actually responsible or accountable for their actions?

- If the unconscious is behind the behavior, can it be fair to say that the person "intended" to act in a particular way?

- Were Hitler or Saddam Hussein responsible for their actions or was their behavior simply dictated by unconscious motives and drives?

about 5 minutes and then simply turned back to each other and ignored them. Shortly afterward, Bill asked his friend, "How could you tell they'd treat us that way?" Pete replied, "The more interesting question is, how could you *not* tell?"

Bill's behavior reflects a classic psychodynamic **conflict**, *a tension or battle between opposing motives*. On the one hand, he is consciously determined to avoid women like his mother; on the other, he is unconsciously compelled to provoke hostility or to pursue hostile women, which he did on many occasions. Bill may not recall incidents from his childhood in which he came to associate excitement, love, sensuality, and sexuality with a woman's scorn, but his behavior nonetheless reflects those unconscious associations. In contemporary cognitive language, Bill's explicit, declarative beliefs and desires do not match the implicit, procedural tendencies expressed in his behavior.

Research on ambivalence suggests that excessive conflict among competing motives can, in fact, exact a toll—in psychological symptoms, negative emotions, and even ill health. For example, one study asked students to list 15 of their "personal strivings" or goals, defined as objectives "that you are typically trying to accomplish" (Emmons & King, 1988). To generate a measure of motivational conflict, the investigators then asked participants to rate the extent to which each striving conflicted with every other striving. Participants also reported how *unhappy* they would be if they were successful at each striving (a direct measure of ambivalence).

To see whether motivational conflict and ambivalence are associated with negative outcomes, the researchers then measured participants' mood twice a day over 21 consecutive days. They also had participants report any bodily ailments such as headaches, coughing, and acne as well as number of visits to the health service. The results were striking: The more conflict and ambivalence, the more anxiety, depression, physical complaints, and trips to the doctor.

Compromise Formations   According to Freud, a single behavior or a complex pattern of thought and action, as in Bill's case, typically reflects compromises among multiple and often conflicting forces. *The solutions people develop to maximize fulfillment of conflicting motives simultaneously* are called **compromise formations** (Brenner, 1982).

Compromise formations occur in normal as well as abnormal functioning. For example, people are constantly faced with the conflicting motives of seeing themselves accurately and maintaining their self-esteem (Bosson & Swann, 1999; Morling & Epstein, 1997; Swann, 1997). Understanding ourselves has obvious adaptive value, since it allows us to know what we can and cannot accomplish, what strategies we can use that will likely succeed, and so forth. On the other hand, few of us can withstand too close a look in the mirror.

Thus, a psychodynamic theorist would predict that, when faced with a conflict between accuracy and self-enhancement, people compromise, creating a distorted self-portrait that allows them a balance of satisfaction of both motives. Empirical research supports this view (see Chapter 17). For example, when extroverted people are induced to believe that introversion is a predictor of academic success, they come to view themselves as less extroverted, but they will not completely deny their extroversion (see Kunda, 1990).

INTERIM SUMMARY

Freud's **topographic model** divided mental processes into **conscious** (rational, goal-directed thoughts at the center of awareness), **preconscious** (not conscious but could become conscious at any point), and **unconscious** (irrational, organized along associative lines, and repressed). In this view, **ambivalence** (conflicting feelings or motives) and **conflict** (a tension or battle between opposing forces) are the rule in mental life. People resolve conflicts through **compromise formations**, which try to maximize fulfillment of conflicting motives simultaneously.

Drive Model   Freud's topographic model addressed conflict between conscious and unconscious motives. His second model, the **drive**, or **instinct model**, was *Freud's model of what drives or motivates people.* Influenced by the work of Charles Darwin, Freud stressed the continuity of human and nonhuman behavior. He hypothesized that humans are motivated by drives, or instincts, like other animals.

Freud (1933) proposed two basic drives: sex and aggression. He defined *the sexual drive*, or **libido**, more broadly than its colloquial usage. Libido refers as much to pleasure seeking, sensuality, and love as it does to desires for sexual intercourse. Expressions of libido may be as varied as daydreaming about sex or romance, enjoying a close friendship, or selecting a career likely to attract a potential spouse because of its status or income potential. People also express aggression in various ways, some socially acceptable and others not. We see aggression on the sports field, in the corporate boardroom, and in just about every video game on the market. Freud would not have been surprised by the two criteria used to determine whether television shows and movies are acceptable for general viewing—the amount of sex and the amount of aggression—because these are the same things that individuals regulate and censor in themselves.

Developmental Model   Freud (1933) considered the development of the libidinal drive the key to personality development and hence proposed a theory of **psychosexual stages**—*stages in the development of personality, sexuality, and motivation* (Table 12.1). The psychosexual stages define Freud's **developmental model**, *his model of how children develop.* These stages reflect the child's evolving quest for pleasure and growing realization of the social limitations on this quest. At each stage, libido is focused on a particular part of the body, or *erogenous zone* (region of the body that can generate sexual pleasure).

To understand these stages, we must view them both narrowly and broadly. That is, the stages describe specific bodily experiences, but they also represent broader psychological and psychosocial conflicts and concerns (Erikson, 1963). Freud's psychosexual stages may sound preposterous at first, but if you try to imagine yourself a child at each stage—sucking your mother's breast for nourishment, fighting with your parents about toilet training (a fight that can go on for a year), or sobbing and shrieking as your parents leave you alone in your room at night—the broader issues may seem less absurd than at first glance.

Oral Stage   During the **oral stage (roughly the first 18 months of life), children explore the world through their mouths**. Many parents are aghast to observe that their infants literally put anything that is not nailed down into their mouths. During the oral stage, sucking the breast or bottle is the means by which infants gain nourishment, but it is also a prime avenue for *social* nourishment, that is, warmth and closeness.

From a broader standpoint, in the oral stage children develop wishes and expectations about *dependence* because they are totally dependent on their caretakers. Diffi-

Big Picture φ Question 3

To what extent is human psychology continuous with the psychology of other animals?

Table 12.1 ■■ ■ Freud's Psychosexual Stages

Stage	Age	Conflicts and Concerns
Oral	0–18 months	Dependency
Anal	2–3 years	Orderliness, cleanliness, control, compliance
Phallic	4–6 years	Identification with parents (especially same sex) and others, Oedipus complex, establishment of conscience
Latency	7–11 years	Sublimation of sexual and aggressive impulses
Genital	12+ years	Mature sexuality and relationships

Apply & Discuss

Many people doubt Freud's depiction of the anal region as an erogenous zone.

- Are buttocks an object of desire in Western culture? If so, why?
- What other theories might account for how desires for pleasure involving the buttocks are learned?

culties (such as chronic dissatisfaction or discomfort) during the oral stage—or any of the stages—can lead to **fixations**, *conflicts or concerns that persist beyond the developmental period in which they arise*. According to Freud, people with fixations at the oral stage may be extremely clingy and dependent, with an exaggerated need for approval, nurturance, and love. More concretely, the soothing and pleasure associated with mouthing and sucking during this stage may lead to fixated behavior such as thumb sucking and nail biting.

Anal Stage   The **anal stage (roughly ages 2 to 3) is characterized by conflicts with parents about compliance and defiance, which Freud linked to conflicts over toilet training.**

Freud argued that these conflicts form the basis of attitudes toward order and disorder, giving and withholding, and messiness and cleanliness. Imagine a toddler, having scarcely been told "no" to anything, who finds himself barraged by rules during his second year, with the ultimate insult of being told to control his own body! This is the age during which the child learns to do unto others what they are now constantly doing unto him: saying *no*.

More concretely, Freud proposed that in the anal stage the child discovers that the anus can be a source of pleasurable excitation. If this seems preposterous, ask any child care worker or parent about the way young children seem to enjoy this part of the body and its warm, squishy contents. Within a few short years the anal region is experienced as so disgusting that we cannot even touch it without the intervention of a piece of paper. Paradoxically, however, anal elements often enter into adult sexual interest and arousal ("Nice buns!"), foreplay (looking at or touching the buttocks or anus), and intercourse. Freud would suggest that apparent contradictions of this sort—is it disgusting or erotically arousing?—point to the presence of conflict, between impulses for pleasure and prohibitions against them.

People with anal fixations exhibit a variety of behavioral tendencies. On the one hand, they may be overly orderly, neat, and punctual or, on the other, extremely messy, stubborn, or constantly late. They may have conflicts about giving and receiving or about compliance versus noncompliance with other people's demands. Research finds that people with these character traits tend to find anal humor particularly compelling (O'Neill et al., 1992)! Children can also *regress* to anal issues, particularly in times of stress. **Regression** means *reverting to conflicts or modes of managing emotion characteristic of an earlier stage*, as when young children whose parents are undergoing a divorce suddenly start soiling themselves again (an anal regression) or sucking their thumbs (regression to the oral stage).

Phallic Stage   During the **phallic stage (roughly ages 4 to 6), children enjoy the pleasure they can obtain from touching their genitals and even from masturbating**. Preschool teachers can attest that children commonly masturbate while rocking themselves to sleep at naptime, and during bathroom visits little boys can be seen comparing the size of their penises. During this stage children also become very aware of differences between boys and girls and mommies and daddies.

More broadly, during the phallic stage the child identifies with significant others, especially the same-sex parent. **Identification** means *making another person part of oneself*: imitating the person's behavior, changing the self-concept to see oneself as like the person, and trying to become more like the person by adopting his or her values and attitudes. According to Freud, much of adult personality is built through identification, as the child internalizes motives, behaviors, beliefs, and ideals.

A longitudinal study of children's attitudes toward themselves provides some empirical support for Freud's theory of identification (Koestner et al., 1991b). The extent to which girls were self-critical at age 12 correlated with observer ratings of their mothers as restrictive and rejecting at age 5. For boys, self-criticism correlated with these same behaviors manifested by their fathers, not their mothers. This suggests that boys' and girls' attitudes toward themselves may be strongly influenced by identification with the same-sex parent, although, of course, children identify with both parents.

Identification has many roots. Freud emphasized its link to the Oedipus complex, named after the character in Greek tragedy who unknowingly slept with his mother. The **Oedipus complex** refers to *Freud's hypothesis that little boys want an exclusive relationship with their mothers, and little girls want an exclusive relationship with their fathers.* From a young boy's perspective, "Why should Mommy spend the night alone with Daddy? Why can't I go in there instead?" (Many children manage a compromise by finding ways to spend the night in the middle.) Children sometimes make astoundingly Oedipal comments. One four-year-old matter-of-factly declared to his mother, "Mommy, Daddy has to leave. I don't like him anymore." When the child's mother asked why, the boy baldly acknowledged, "He has a bigger penis than I do!"

Thus, according to Freud, children learn about love and sensual gratification from their parents, and they desire an exclusive sexual relationship with the parent of the opposite sex (bearing in mind the broad meaning of "sexual" in Freud's theory). At the same time, these wishes are so threatening that they are quickly repressed or renounced (consciously given up). *Boys unconsciously fear that their father, their ultimate rival, will castrate them because of their desires for their mother* (the **castration complex**). The fear is so threatening that they repress their Oedipal wishes and identify with their father. In other words, they internalize a moral prohibition against incest as a way of preventing themselves from acting on their wishes, which would be dangerous, and they instead become like their father in the hopes of someday obtaining someone like their mother. Girls, too, renounce their secret wishes toward their fathers and identify with their mothers because they fear losing her love.

According to Freud, during the phallic stage, girls develop **penis envy**, *the belief that because they lack a penis they are inferior to boys.* Taken on a metaphorical level, penis envy refers to the envy a girl develops in a society in which men's activities seem more interesting and valued (Horney, 1926). Given the concreteness of childhood cognition, that a five-year-old might symbolize this in terms of having or not having a penis would not be surprising. Parents often report that their daughters cry when bathing with brothers, who have "one of those things."

Latency Stage During the **latency stage (roughly ages 7 to 11), children repress their sexual impulses and continue to identify with their same-sex parent.** They also learn to channel their sexual and aggressive drives into socially acceptable activities such as school, sports, and art. Whereas people fixated at the phallic stage may be preoccupied with attracting mates or take on stereotypical characteristics of their own or the opposite gender, individuals fixated at the latency stage may seem totally asexual.

Genital Stage During the **genital stage (approximately age 12 and beyond), conscious sexuality resurfaces after years of repression, and genital sex becomes the primary goal of sexual activity.** At this stage, people become capable of relating to and loving others on a mature level and carrying out adult responsibilities such as work and parenting.

Prior elements of sexuality do not disappear—most people's foreplay continues to have oral and anal components—but these "pre-genital" elements become integrated into patterns of sexual activity involving genital satisfaction. This stage was probably least elaborated by Freud, who believed that the major aspects of personality become firmly established in childhood and may require considerable effort to change thereafter.

Experimental data provide surprising support for some aspects of Freud's psychosexual theories, such as his theory of the Oedipus complex (see Fisher & Greenberg, 1985, 1996). For example, in one study researchers asked parents of children age

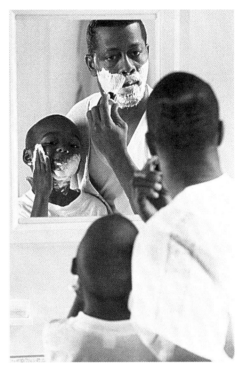
Identification is a powerful force in the life of a child.

Big Picture φ Question 5

To what extent are psychological processes the same in men and women?

*So be sweet and kind to mother,
now and then have a chat
Buy her candy and some
flowers or a brand new hat
But maybe you had better let it go at that.*

TOM LEHRER, *"Oedipus Rex"*

Some people appear to take the Oedipus complex literally.

Apply & Discuss

If you run down a list of obscenities—verbally taboo words—you will find that most reflect one or another of Freud's stages. Indeed, perhaps the most vulgar thing someone can call another person in our society has a distinctly Oedipal ring (you can figure this one out on your own), and its originators were surely not psychoanalysts.

▪ How might Freud have explained this?

▪ What other explanations could make sense of this phenomenon?

Big Picture φ Question 2

What is the relationship between reason and desire or, more precisely, between cognition and affect?

3 to 6 to record the number of affectionate and aggressive acts the children displayed toward their same- and opposite-sex parents over a seven-day period (Watson & Getz, 1990). As predicted by Freud, affection toward the opposite-sex parent and aggression toward the same-sex parent were significantly more common than the reverse pattern.

Even the notion of castration anxiety, perhaps Freud's most seemingly outlandish concept, may account for certain observations. In the men's dressing room of a department store, two boys around age 5 were struggling with a curtain that would not quite close—pulling the curtain one way only seemed to open up the other side—when one of them was overheard saying, "You've got to make sure it closes so no one can come in and steal your ding." Surely no one had warned the child to protect his "ding" at the department store.

INTERIM SUMMARY

According to Freud's **drive** or **instinct model**, people have two instincts, sex and aggression. His **developmental model** proposes a series of **psychosexual stages**. During the **oral stage**, pleasure is focused on the mouth, and children wrestle with dependence. During the **anal stage**, children derive pleasure from the anus and wrestle with issues of compliance, orderliness, and cleanliness. During the **phallic stage**, children's personalities develop through **identification** with others. They also experience the Oedipus complex, in which they want an exclusive relationship with their opposite-sex parent. In the **latency stage** children repress their sexual impulses. In the **genital stage** they develop mature sexuality and a capacity for emotional intimacy.

Structural Model   The final model Freud developed was his **structural model**, which *described conflict in terms of desires on the one hand and the dictates of conscience or the constraints of reality on the other* (Freud, 1923, 1933). Previously, Freud had seen conflict in terms of conscious versus unconscious forces, but he came to believe that conflicts between what we want and what we believe is moral lead to most psychological distress.

Id, Ego, and Superego   The structural model posits three sets of mental forces, or structures: id, ego, and superego. The **id** is *the reservoir of sexual and aggressive energy*. It is driven by impulses and, like the unconscious of the topographic model, is characterized by **primary process thinking**: *wishful, illogical, and associative thought*.

To counterbalance the "untamed passions" of the id (Freud, 1933, p. 76), the **superego** *acts as a conscience and source of ideals*. The superego is the parental voice within the person, established through identification.

The **ego** is *the structure that must somehow balance desire, reality, and morality*. Freud described the ego as serving three masters: the id, the external world, and the superego. Unlike the id, the ego is capable of **secondary process thinking**, which is *rational, logical, and goal directed*. The ego is thus responsible for cognition and problem solving (Hartmann, 1939). It is also responsible for managing emotions (Chapter 10) and finding compromises among competing demands.

To demonstrate how conflict among these forces plays out, consider an example taken from the psychotherapy of an angry, somewhat insecure junior partner at a law firm who felt threatened by a promising young associate. The partner decided to give the associate a poor job performance evaluation, even though the associate was one of the best the firm ever had. The partner convinced himself that he was justified because the associate could be working harder, and he wanted to send a message that laziness would get the young barrister nowhere—an admirable goal indeed!

From the perspective of the structural model (Figure 12.1), the perceived threat activated aggressive wishes (id) to hurt the associate (give him a poor evaluation). The partner's conscience (superego), on the other hand, would not permit such a blatant display of aggression and unfairness. Hence, he unconsciously forged a compromise (ego): He satisfied his aggression by giving the poor evaluation, but he cloaked his action in the language of the superego, claiming to be helping the young associate by discouraging his laziness, and hence satisfying his own conscience.

Defense Mechanisms   When people confront problems in their lives, they typically draw on problem-solving strategies that have worked for them in the past, rather than inventing new solutions to every problem (Chapter 7). The same is true of emotional problem solving. According to psychodynamic theory, people regulate their emotions and deal with their conflicts by employing **defense-mechanisms—** *unconscious mental processes aimed at protecting the person from unpleasant emotions (particularly anxiety) or bolstering pleasurable emotions.* Psychodynamic psychologists have identified a number of defense mechanisms, many of which have been studied empirically (Cramer, 1996; A. Freud, 1936; Vaillant, 1992a, 1992b, 1977; Vaillant & Vaillant, 1998).

One defense we have encountered before is **repression**, in which *a person keeps thoughts or memories that would be too threatening to acknowledge from awareness* (Chapter 6). A similar mechanism is **denial** in which *a person refuses to acknowledge external realities or emotions* (such as anxiety). Denial is at work when an individual notices a peculiar skin growth but concludes that "it's nothing." Much of the time it *is* nothing, but this defense can lead to failure to seek treatment for a potentially life-threatening cancer (see Strauss et al., 1990; Zervas et al., 1993).

Projection is *a defense mechanism by which a person attributes his own unacknowledged feelings or impulses to others.* The hard-driving businessman who thinks his competitors, suppliers, and customers are always trying to cheat him may in fact be the one with questionable ethics. To recognize his own greed and lack of concern for others would conflict with his conscience, so instead he sees these traits in others.

Recent research suggests a cognitive mechanism through which projection may occur (Newman et al., 1997). Paradoxically, keeping a thought out of awareness keeps it chronically activated at an implicit level. To stop a thought from attaining consciousness, the mind essentially sets up an automatic mechanism to "keep a lookout" for the thought; this process has the unintended by-product of keeping the thought active (Wegner, 1992). Thus, when a person is trying not to see himself as dishonest, the concept of *dishonesty* remains active implicitly. When someone else then behaves in a way that could be interpreted as either accidental or dishonest, the concept *dishonesty* is already activated and is thus more likely to be used to interpret the person's behavior.

Reaction formation is *a defense mechanism whereby a person turns unacceptable feelings or impulses into their opposites.* For example, at the same time that televangelist Jimmy Swaggart was preaching the evils of sex to millions, he was regularly seeing a prostitute. His conscious repulsion toward sexuality, and particularly illicit sexuality, apparently masked a tremendous need for it.

Sublimation is *a defense that involves converting sexual or aggressive impulses into socially acceptable activities.* A young boy may turn his feelings of competition with his father or brother into a desire to excel in competitive sports or to succeed in business when he is older.

Rationalization is *a defense in which the person explains away actions in a seemingly logical way to avoid uncomfortable feelings, especially guilt or shame.* A student who plagiarizes her term paper and justifies her actions by saying that passing the course will help her earn her public policy degree and serve the community is using rationalization to justify her dishonesty.

Another defense mechanism, **passive aggression**, is *the indirect expression of anger toward others.* One administrator frustrated everyone around him by "sitting

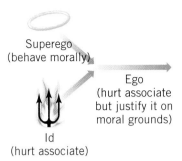

Superego
(behave morally)

Ego
(hurt associate but justify it on moral grounds)

Id
(hurt associate)

FIGURE 12.1   Freud's structural model. Conflict among various forces leads to a compromise forged by the ego.

Apply and Discuss

Even people who are vehemently opposed to Freud's theorizing find themselves using his terminology in their everyday speech and his defense mechanisms in their everyday behavior.

▪ Which of these defense mechanisms that we discussed have you engaged in? Why?

▪ What circumstances or feelings prompted you to use a defense mechanism? Do you tend to favor one mechanism over another?

▪ Is it easier to identify the use of a defense mechanism in yourself or in other people? Why or why not?

Making Connections

The psychoanalyst Erik Erikson proposed a psychosocial model of development, which stresses the interpersonal nature of human development, to complement Freud's psychosexual model. For example, alongside Freud's oral stage, Erikson proposed a more interpersonal stage, in which the child wrestles with how much she can trust people. Similarly, adolescence is a time of discovering a sense of self, or identity, and not just maturing sexually (Chapter 14).

on" important documents that required a fast turnaround. To be actively aggressive would run afoul of his moral standards and potentially lead to reprimand from his boss, so he accomplished the same goal—frustrating co-workers and thus satisfying his aggressive impulses—in a way that allowed him to disavow any intention or responsibility.

Using defenses is neither abnormal nor unhealthy. In fact, some degree of defensive distortion may be useful, such as the tendency for people to see themselves more positively than is warranted by reality (Taylor & Armor, 1996; Taylor & Brown, 1988). A bit of denial can also be essential to surmounting seemingly insurmountable odds, as when an aspiring novelist persists despite repeated rejection and suddenly gets a break.

Defense mechanisms are generally considered properties of individuals, but some defenses are patterned at a cultural level (Spiro, 1965). In the Kerala province of India, where cows are considered sacred and cannot be killed, an anthropologist observed that the mortality rate for male cows was twice as high as for females (Harris, 1979). Although all the farmers espoused the Hindu prohibition against slaughtering cattle, they were essentially starving the males to death because males cannot give milk and were a drain on scarce economic resources.

INTERIM SUMMARY

Freud's **structural model** focuses on conflict among the **id** (the reservoir of instincts or desires), **superego** (conscience), and **ego** (the structure that tries to balance desire, reality, and morality). People regulate their emotions and deal with their conflicts by employing **defense mechanisms**, unconscious mental processes aimed at protecting the person from unpleasant emotions (particularly anxiety) or bolstering pleasurable emotions.

Object Relations Theories

During Freud's lifetime, psychodynamic theory evolved from an "id psychology" to an "ego psychology." Freud began with a focus on motivation and instinct (his drive theory, which formed the basis of his theory of the id). Later, he and other psychoanalysts turned their attention to the ways people cope with their feelings (defenses) and adapt to reality while trying to fulfill their needs (ego functions).

Perhaps the most important theoretical development in psychoanalysis since Freud's death has been the emergence of object relations theories. When once asked what the healthy person should be able to do, Freud responded, "to love and to work." Object relations theories attempt to account for the difficulties of people with high impairment in both domains (love and work), who may show an extreme inability to maintain commitment or trust in relationships, a disavowal of any wish for intimate human contact at all, or an inability to sustain employment because of chronic interpersonal conflicts with co-workers and employers. **Object relations** refers to *enduring patterns of behavior in intimate relationships and to the motivational, cognitive, and affective processes that produce those patterns*. (The term comes from Freud's view that an instinct has an aim, which is some kind of gratification, and an object, which is usually a person. Thus, object relations theories are about people's relationships with others.)

Of particular importance are people's representations of self, significant others, and relationships (Bowlby, 1982; Jacobson, 1964; Sandler & Rosenblatt, 1962). Empirically, people who have difficulty maintaining relationships tend to view themselves and others in more negative ways, frequently expecting abuse or malevolence in relationships (Nigg et al., 1992). They also have trouble maintaining *constancy* of their representations; that is, they have difficulty holding in mind positive representations of people they love during the inevitable interpersonal conflicts that friends, family members, and lovers experience (Baker et al., 1992; Kernberg, 1984). As a result, they may break off or irreparably damage their relationships while angry.

Instead of explaining such behavior in terms of neurotic compromise solutions to unconscious conflicts, object relations theorists explain severe interpersonal problems in terms of maladaptive interpersonal patterns laid down in the first few years of life. Whereas Freud described development as a sequence of psychosexual stages, object relations theorists describe it as a progressive movement toward more mature relatedness to others. Like defensive processes, many aspects of object relations theory have been studied empirically (Ackerman et al., 2000; Blatt et al., 1997; Masling & Bornstein, 1994; Stricker & Healey, 1990; Westen, 1991, 1992).

A recent outgrowth of object relations theories, called relational theories, extends this line of thinking to people who are less troubled, arguing that for all individuals adaptation is primarily adaptation to other people (Aron, 1996; Mitchell, 1988; Mitchell & Aron, 1999;). According to **relational theories**, *the need for relatedness is a central motive in humans, and people will distort their personalities to maintain ties to important people in their lives*. Like object relations theorists, relational theorists also argue that many of the ways adults interact with one another, particularly in intimate relationships, reflect patterns of relatedness learned in childhood.

INTERIM SUMMARY

Object relations theories focus on interpersonal disturbances and the mental processes that underlie the capacity for relatedness to others. **Relational theories** argue that for all individuals adaptation is primarily adaptation to other people.

Assessing Unconscious Patterns

The core assumption of all psychodynamic approaches, that many personality processes are unconscious, raises a difficult question: How can one assess what one cannot directly *access*? This dilemma led to a number of methods of personality assessment, including indirect methods called projective tests.

Life History Methods
Life history methods *aim to understand the whole person in the context of his life experience and environment* (see Alexander, 1990; McAdams & de St. Aubin, 1998; McAdams & West, 1997; Runyan, 1984). They are the bread and butter of psychodynamic investigation, typically involving case studies in which the psychologist studies an individual in depth over an extended time. Information may be gathered through psychotherapy, historical or biographical sources, or research interviews.

In one creative study, researchers turned this method on none other than B. F. Skinner! On the assumption that enduring personality dynamics influence an individual's personal and professional lives, the researchers took the opening paragraph from Skinner's first major work and from his autobiography and mapped out the underlying themes in each (Demorest & Siegel, 1996). They then randomly interspersed these two "maps" of Skinner's dynamics with similar thematic maps taken from other people and asked undergraduate coders to rate the resemblance between the various pairs of thematic maps to test for a resemblance between Skinner's underlying themes expressed in such different contexts. Despite the fact that one passage described the way rats entered a chamber and the other described the geography of Skinner's hometown, coders rated his two productions as substantially more similar to each other than to any of the other thematic maps included in the sample.

One Step Further

Big Picture φ Question 7

To what extent are psychological processes conscious or unconscious—that is, explicit versus implicit?

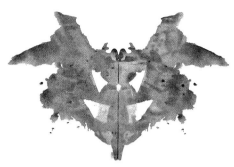

FIGURE 12.2 The Rorschach inkblot test. Subjects' responses provide insight into their subconscious perceptual, cognitive, and emotional processes. (Reproduced with permission. This inkblot is not part of the Rorschach test.)

FIGURE 12.3 Thematic Apperception Test (TAT). This is an artist's rendering of a TAT-like image. The actual card is not reproduced to protect the valid use of the test.

Projective Tests

Projective tests *present subjects with an ambiguous stimulus and ask them to give some kind of definition to it, to "project" a meaning into it.* The assumption is that in providing definition where none exists in reality, people will fill in the gaps in a way that expresses some of their characteristic ways of thinking, feeling, and regulating emotions—that is, aspects of their personalities.

Developed by Swiss psychiatrist Hermann Rorschach in 1921, the **Rorschach inkblot test** *asks a subject to view a set of inkblots and tell the tester what each one resembles.* For example, a teenager whose parents were divorcing and battling for custody of her was shown an inkblot similar to the one reproduced in Figure 12.2. The subject saw a girl being torn apart down the middle, "with feelings on each side," just as she felt torn by her parents' conflict.

In another projective test, the Thematic Apperception Test, or TAT (Chapter 10), the subject is asked to make up a story about each of a series of ambiguous drawings, most of which depict people interacting. The assumption is that in eliminating the ambiguity, the individual will create a story that reflects her own recurring wishes, fears, and ways of experiencing relationships.

Consider the TAT story of a subject with a borderline personality disorder, which typically manifests itself in unstable relationships, repeated suicide attempts, and difficulty controlling rage, anxiety, and sadness (Chapter 15). When shown a TAT card depicting a man and woman similar to the one in Figure 12.3, the subject responded (Westen et al., 1991):

> This guy looks a lot like my father—my father going off the handle, ready to beat one of us kids. My mother was trying to control him; she'd get beaten along with the rest of us. Did you choose these pictures by what I told you? The woman in the picture is feeling fear for her kids, thinking of ways to stop him—thinking and feeling fear for herself. What this man is thinking or feeling is beyond me. I don't like this picture—as you can tell—it bothers me bad. (She flips the card over.) The resemblance between this and pictures of my father and me when I was younger is uncanny.

The subject brings in themes of abuse, which is typical of the stories of borderline patients, many of whom were abused as children (Herman et al., 1989; Ogata et al., 1989; Zanarini, 1997). Further, while most people generate stories that are independent of themselves, this subject cannot keep herself out of the cards, a sign of egocentrism or self-preoccupation characteristic of the TAT responses of patients with this disorder (Westen et al., 1990). After another card also reminded her of herself, the subject later wondered whether these cards were chosen just for her, demonstrating a degree of paranoia consistent with her personality disorder.

Psychologists have criticized projective tests for years, citing various inadequacies (Mischel, 1968; Wood et al., 2000). Projective tests are often less useful in predicting behavior than simple demographic data such as the subject's age, sex, and social class (Garb, 1984); they are frequently used idiosyncratically by clinicians, who may offer very different interpretations of the same response; and they have sometimes been misused to make predictions about behaviors for which the tests are not valid, such as potential job performance.

Other evidence suggests, however, that projective tests can be used with high reliability and validity for *particular purposes*, such as for assessing disturbances in thinking and in object relations and distinguishing patients with particular kinds of disorders (and even their biological relatives) (e.g., Coleman et al., 1996; Loevinger, 1976, 1985). For example, one study asked four- and five-year-olds to complete 10 story stems (stories that the investigators started and asked children

"MR. KILGORE, I HAVE REASON TO BELIEVE YOUR LACTOSE INTOLERENCE IS PSYCHOLOGICAL."

to finish) (Oppenheim et al., 1997). The more a child's stories included themes of positive interaction and nonabusive discipline, the less depressed, misbehaving, and aggressive the child's mother reported him to be. Conversely, the presence of themes such as physical or verbal abuse strongly predicted troubles with aggression and misbehavior. From a cognitive perspective, projective tests essentially tap implicit processes (Chapter 6), such as implicit associational networks, particularly those in which emotional elements are prominent (Westen et al., 1991).

Contributions and Limitations of Psychodynamic Theories

Although many of Freud's original formulations are, as we might expect, somewhat dated a century after he began his work, the tradition he initiated emphasizes five aspects of personality that have now received widespread empirical support. These include the importance of (1) unconscious cognitive, emotional, and motivational processes; (2) ambivalence, conflict, and compromise; (3) childhood experiences in shaping adult interpersonal patterns; (4) mental representations of the self, others, and relationships; and (5) the development of the capacity to regulate impulses and to shift from an immature dependent state in infancy to a mutually caring, interdependent interpersonal stance in adulthood (Westen, 1998). Perhaps most importantly, psychodynamic approaches emphasize that human thought and action are laden with meaning, and that interpreting the multiple meanings of a person's behavior requires "listening with a third ear" for ideas, fears, and wishes of which the person himself may not be aware.

A major limitation of psychodynamic theory is its inadequate basis in scientifically sound observation (see Crews, 1998; Grunbaum, 1984; Mischel, 1973; Wallerstein, 1988b). Some aspects of the theory seem particularly problematic, such as Freud's theory of female development. Freud's theory of drives has also not stood the test of time (Holt, 1985). Aggression does not appear to be a bodily need in the same way as sex or hunger, and the theory generally overemphasizes sexual motivation. Still other critics charge that psychodynamic theory pays too much attention to childhood experiences and not enough to adult learning.

In evaluating psychodynamic theory, the reader should keep in mind what it is *not*. Psychodynamic theory is no longer a single theory forged by a single thinker, Sigmund Freud. Most contemporary psychodynamic psychologists think about motivation in terms of wishes and fears, not sexual and aggressive drives, although they

Apply and Discuss

What are the basic components of personality from a psychodynamic perspective? Apply this model to yourself or someone you know well.

■ How would you describe your own wishes, fears, conflicts, compromises, desires or thoughts you would rather not admit, fixations or regressions, ego functions (including defenses), and object relations?

■ To what extent are these elements of personality stable over time? Could a person change them, and if so, how?

agree with Freud that many motives, such as sex and love, are biologically rooted and fundamentally shaped in childhood. Contemporary psychodynamic psychologists also tend to rely on concepts like conflict, compromise, mental representation, and self-esteem, rather than id, ego, and superego.

Although Freud developed psychoanalysis as a method of exploring and interpreting meaning, and not of predicting behavior, there can be little doubt that psychodynamic theories would be much farther along today if psychoanalysts had taken more interest in testing and refining their ideas empirically. However, many other theories offer little help in interpreting meaning. Prediction and interpretation should both be central aims of any approach to personality.

Cognitive–Social Theories

Cognitive–social theories offered the first comprehensive alternative to psychodynamic theories of personality. First developed in the 1960s, these theories go by several names, including social learning theory, cognitive–social learning theory, and social–cognitive theory. Cognitive–social theories developed from behaviorist and cognitive roots; we have already examined several aspects of these theories in some detail (Chapter 5).

From a behaviorist perspective, personality consists of learned behaviors and emotional reactions that are relatively specific and tied to particular environmental stimuli or events. Many of these behaviors are selected through operant conditioning on the basis of their rewarding or aversive consequences. Cognitive–social theories share the behaviorist belief that learning (rather than instinct, conflict, or defense) is the basis of personality and that personality dispositions tend to be relatively specific and shaped by their consequences. However, they also focus on beliefs, expectations, and information processing.

According to this approach, personality reflects a constant interplay between environmental demands and the way the individual processes information about the self and the world. Thus, people's actions reflect an interaction between the requirements of the situation (e.g., in school people are expected to work hard, come to class on time, and follow the directives of teachers) and the person's learned tendencies to behave in particular ways under particular circumstances. These tendencies reflect their knowledge and beliefs.

For example, Albert Bandura (1986, 1999) argues that people are not driven by inner forces, as proposed by many psychodynamic theories, nor are they automatically shaped and controlled by external stimuli, as asserted by behaviorists such as B. F. Skinner. Rather, people's actions reflect the schemas they use in understanding the world, their expectations of what will happen if they act in particular ways, and the degree to which they believe they can attain their goals. Whereas psychodynamic theory centers on the irrational, cognitive–social theories tend to be eminently rational. Whereas behaviorists downplay the role of thought in producing behavior, cognitive–social theorists emphasize it.

According to cognitive–social theories, several conditions must be met for a behavior to occur (Figure 12.4) (Bandura 1977b, 1986, 1999; Mischel & Shoda, 1998). The person must encode the current situation as relevant to her goals or current concerns, and the situation must have enough personal meaning or value to initiate goal-driven behavior. The individual must believe that performing the behavior will lead to the desired outcome and that she has the ability to perform it. The person must also actually have the ability to carry out the behavior. Finally, the person must be able to regulate ongoing activity in a way that leads to goal fulfillment—perhaps by monitoring behavior at each step of the way until she fulfills the goal, as in decision-making theories, or changing the goal if she cannot fully achieve it. If any of these conditions is not met, the behavior will not occur.

Big Picture φ Question 6

What is the relation between nature and nurture in shaping psychological processes?

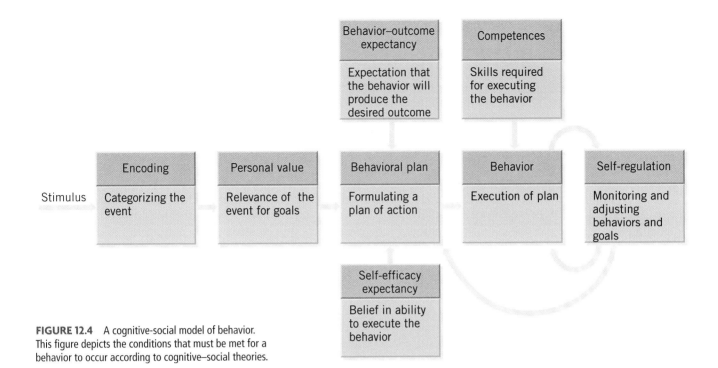

FIGURE 12.4 A cognitive-social model of behavior. This figure depicts the conditions that must be met for a behavior to occur according to cognitive–social theories.

To illustrate, imagine you have just been stood up for a date (the stimulus). When you realize what has happened (encoding as personally relevant), your self-esteem plummets, you see that your plans for the evening are ruined, and you would like to make the person feel bad and think twice before doing that again (personal value). You therefore decide to confront your date (behavioral plan).

In formulating a behavioral plan, however, you must decide whether any action you take will actually achieve the desired result (expectation of link between behavior and outcome). Will your date simply ignore you and make up an excuse? On top of that, your expectations and beliefs must be accurate: You must actually be able to respond quickly (competence) or you will emit the wrong behavior, such as saying, "Oh, that's OK. I found something else to do. Do you want to get together some other time?" Finally, as you begin to execute the action, you will need to monitor progress toward your goal—is your date squirming enough yet?—as you go along.

We now examine each of these components in more detail.

INTERIM SUMMARY

Cognitive–social theories developed from behaviorist and cognitive roots and consider learning, beliefs, expectations, and information processing central to personality. For a behavior to occur, several conditions must be met: The person must encode the current situation as relevant, endow the situation with personal meaning or value, believe performing the behavior will lead to the desired outcome, believe she has the ability to perform it, have the ability to carry out the behavior, and regulate ongoing activity in a way that leads toward fulfilling the goal.

Encoding and Personal Relevance

For people to respond to a situation, they must first encode its meaning and determine its relevance to them. Responding to a situation is difficult if we cannot categorize it, and responding is unnecessary if it is not demanded by the situation or relevant to our goals.

Big Picture φ Question 8

To what extent can we inform our knowledge through reason or through observation—that is, rationalism versus empiricism?

Encoding   George Kelly (1955) developed an early cognitive approach to personality that focused on **personal constructs**—*mental representations of the people, places, things, and events that are significant to a person*. According to Kelly, people can understand and interpret the world in many different ways, which defines their personality. Kelly looked for the roots of behavior not in motivation, as in psychodynamic theory, but in cognition. For example, if a delinquent or maladjusted boy is accidentally bumped by a peer, he may punch his unwitting assailant because he encoded the bump as deliberate (Crick & Dodge, 1994).

People are not always able to articulate their personal constructs when asked. Thus, Kelly and his colleagues developed a technique for assessing them indirectly, called the *repertory grid technique* (Blowers & O'Connor, 1996). Subjects are asked to describe the dimensions on which important people in their lives resemble and differ from one another (e.g.,"How is your father like your sister? In what ways are they unlike your mother?"). By eliciting enough comparisons, the psychologist can discover the constructs that the subject implicitly uses in thinking about people.

Nancy Cantor and John Kihlstrom (1987; Kihlstrom & Cantor, 2000) combined Kelly's emphasis on personal constructs with information-processing theory to create a cognitive theory of personality. They argue that the way people conceive of themselves and others and encode, interpret, and remember social information is central to who they are. In this view, individuals who have more accurate and well-organized schemas about people and relationships have greater social intelligence and should be more effective in accomplishing their interpersonal goals, such as making friends and getting desirable jobs.

Personal Value and Goals   Individuals have elaborate schemas about people and situations that have relevance or personal value to them. **Personal value** refers to *the importance individuals attach to various outcomes or potential outcomes* (Mischel, 1979). Whether a situation or anticipated action has a positive or negative value for an individual often depends on the person's goals.

Cantor and Kihlstrom (1987) define motivation in terms of **life tasks**, *the conscious, self-defined problems people attempt to solve*. For a college student, salient life tasks may involve establishing independence from parents, getting good grades, or making and keeping friends (Cantor, 1990; Cantor & Blanton, 1996).

INTERIM SUMMARY

For people to respond to a situation, they must first encode it as relevant. George Kelly proposed that **personal constructs**—mental representations of the people, places, things, and events that are significant to a person—substantially influence their behavior. People tend to focus on and select behaviors and situations that have **personal value** to them, which are relevant to their goals or **life tasks** (conscious, self-defined problems people try to solve).

Expectancies and Competences

Whether people carry out various actions depends substantially on both their **expectancies**, or *expectations relevant to desired outcomes* (Chapter 5), and their competence to perform the behaviors that would solve their problems or achieve their goals.

Expectancies   Of particular importance are behavior–outcome expectancies and self-efficacy expectancies. A **behavior-outcome expectancy** is *a belief that a certain behavior will lead to a particular outcome*. A **self-efficacy expectancy** is *a person's conviction that she can perform the actions necessary to produce the desired outcome*. For example, a person will not start a new business unless she believes both that starting the business is likely to lead to desired results (such as wealth or satisfaction) *and* that she has the ability to get a new business off the ground. Similarly, a person will not quit smoking unless he believes that quitting will decrease his likelihood of developing lung cancer and that he can actually quit smoking successfully (Chapter 11).

Bandura (1977a, 1982, 1995) argues that self-efficacy expectancies are generally the most important determinant of successful task performance. Research in a number of areas documents that people who are confident in their abilities are more likely to act, and ultimately succeed, than those plagued by self-doubts. James Joyce weathered 22 rejections when trying to publish *Dubliners*, and a prominent psychologist was once told that "one is no more likely to find the phenomenon [that he eventually discovered and documented] than bird droppings in a cuckoo clock" (Bandura, 1989, p. 1176).

Competences   Believing in one's abilities is one thing, but truly having them is another. Thus, another crucial variable that impacts behavior is **competences**, that is, *skills and abilities used for solving problems*. Social intelligence includes a variety of competences that help people navigate interpersonal waters, such as social skills that allow them to talk comfortably with strangers at a cocktail party, or the ability to end an argument to maintain a friendship (see Cantor & Harlow, 1994; Cantor & Kihlstrom, 1987). Individuals develop highly specific skills for handling particular tasks through operant conditioning, observational learning, practice, and deliberate conscious effort.

Self-Regulation

The final variable required to execute a behavior successfully is self-regulation. **Self-regulation** refers to *setting goals, evaluating one's performance, and adjusting one's behavior to achieve these goals in the context of ongoing feedback* (Bandura, 1986, 1999; Mischel & Shoda, 1998).

Cognitive–social theorists take a problem-solving or decision-making approach to personality, much like information-processing approaches to cognition (Chapter 7) and goal-setting and expectancy–value theories of motivation (Chapter 10). In other words, people are constantly setting goals, applying their skills to achieve them, and monitoring their thoughts and actions until their goals are reached or have to be modified.

In this view, personality is nothing more or less than the problem-solving efforts of people trying to fulfill their life tasks (Harlow & Cantor, 1994). Successful problem solving requires constant feedback, which people use to self-regulate. Feedback on performance can help people solve problems if it focuses their attention on the problem and ways to achieve a solution. However, feedback can *diminish* performance if it leads people to focus on themselves with self-doubt or anxiety (Kluger & DeNisi, 1996).

One study applied a cognitive–social approach to organizational decision making (Wood & Bandura, 1989). Graduate business students were asked to allocate workers and resources using a computer simulation. The simulation involved 18 decision-making trials, with each trial followed by performance feedback useful for the next. Half the participants (the acquirable-skill group) were told that in "acquiring a new skill, people do not begin with faultless performance. However, the more they practice, the more capable they become." Essentially, these participants were encouraged to use the task to develop their skills rather than to evaluate their ability. The other half (the fixed-ability group) were led to believe that the simulation would test their underlying ability as a manager, a basic competence they either did or did not have.

The researchers wanted to know how this manipulation would affect participants' perceived self-efficacy, goal setting, efficiency in problem solving, and managerial success in running the simulated company. Self-efficacy was assessed by regularly asking participants how confident they were of achieving production goals following feedback on their performance. Performance goals were assessed by asking them after each trial what they were striving for on the next trial. The researchers also mea-

Making Connections

Our expectancies about what we can accomplish and how well things will turn out influence virtually everything we do, such as how much we are willing to take risks. Our specific expectancies (such as whether now is the time to invest in technology stocks) reflect not only our personalities but also our knowledge and experience (Chapter 5).

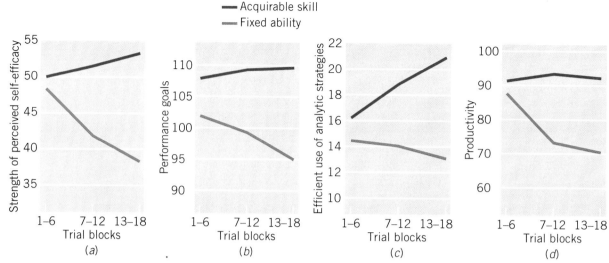

FIGURE 12.5   An experimental study in self-regulation. Participants who believed they could learn from the task showed consistent increases in perceived self-efficacy, unlike participants who believed their ability to be fixed (*a*). The latter showed a steady decline in performance goals (*b*), efficiency of problem solving (*c*), and actual performance (*d*). *Source:* Wood & Bandura, 1989, pp. 411–413.

sured the efficiency of participants' problem-solving strategies as well as their actual level of performance on the task (Figure 12.5).

Participants who believed they could learn from the task showed consistent increases in perceived self-efficacy, unlike those who believed their ability was fixed. The fixed-ability group showed a steady decline in self-efficacy performance goals, efficiency of problem solving, and actual performance. Essentially, in confronting a difficult task, the group that believed their skills were fixed steadily lowered their estimates of their efficacy and their level of aspiration, and their performance steadily declined. In other words, managers are much more likely to be successful if they *believe* they can be successful.

INTERIM SUMMARY

People's **expectancies**, or expectations relevant to desired outcomes, influence the actions they take. A **behavior–outcome expectancy** is a belief that a certain behavior will lead to a particular outcome. A **self-efficacy expectancy** is a person's conviction that she can perform the actions necessary to produce a desired outcome. A **competence** is a skill used for solving problems. **Self-regulation** refers to setting goals, evaluating one's performance, and adjusting one's behavior to achieve these goals in the context of ongoing feedback.

Contributions and Limitations of Cognitive–Social Theories

Cognitive–social theories have contributed substantially to the study of personality, bringing into focus the role of thought and memory in personality. The way people behave clearly reflects the expectations and skills they have developed, which are encoded in memory and activated by particular situations. Furthermore, unlike psychodynamic theory, which can be difficult to test, cognitive–social theory is readily testable through experimentation.

Cognitive–social approaches are limited, however, in two respects. First, they tend to emphasize the rational side of life and underemphasize the emotional, motivational, and irrational. If personality is really reducible to cognitive processes (Cantor, 1990), one would have difficulty accounting for the psychological abnormalities of a man like Adolph Hitler. Because Hitler was tremendously adept at getting people to follow him and had an extraordinary sense of self-efficacy, one would have to rate him high on several dimensions of social intelligence. Yet his social motives and his ways of dealing with his emotions were clearly disturbed.

A related problem is the tendency to assume that people consciously know what they think, feel, and want and hence can report it. Would most of us accept Hitler's self-report of his life task of bettering the world by creating a master race? Or would we suspect that his dreams of world domination and his program of genocide reflected thoughts, feelings, and motivations that he could not easily have described?

In some ways, psychodynamic and cognitive–social approaches each offer what the other lacks. Psychodynamic theory is weak in its understanding of cognition and conscious problem solving; cognitive–social theory is weak in its understanding of emotion, motivation, and personality processes that occur outside awareness.

Researchers are, however, beginning to see some important areas of convergence, as they have become interested in developments in cognitive science (e.g., Bucci, 1997; Horowitz, 1988; Shevrin et al., 1996) and cognitive–social researchers have become interested in implicit processes and interactions of emotion and cognition (Mischel & Shoda, 1995). Further, integrative approaches have begun to emerge, such as those that focus on the construct of *emotional intelligence*, the ability to adapt to the environment, particularly the social environment, in flexible ways that allow goal fulfillment and satisfying social relationships (e.g., Block & Kremen, 1996; Goleman, 1995; Mayer et al., 2000).

Apply and Discuss

A young lawyer receives feedback from her boss that her work is of high caliber but that she is not producing enough because she is working too slowly. In fact, she is a perfectionist who refuses to turn in a brief until she is absolutely certain she has it "right."

■ What are the basic elements of personality from a cognitive–social perspective?

■ How might each element—from the way the young lawyer encodes the situation to the way she self-regulates—be involved in her work performance?

■ What would need to change for her to turn the situation around and get a better review the next time?

Driving Mr. Albert   From Brain to Behavior

Cognitive–social theories suggest that the way people encode, process, and think about information determines their personality. A question that, as yet, remains unanswered is whether individual differences in cognitive processing can be related to differences in the structure or function of people's brains. Answering this question is the role of cognitive neuroscientists.

But it is not scientists alone who are interested in such questions. A recent book by Paterniti entitled *Driving Mr. Albert: A Trip Across America with Einstein's Brain* reveals the interest of the lay public in the relationship between brain functioning and personality. The author recounts his cross-country travels with the pathologist Dr. Thomas Harvey, who in 1955 had examined Einstein's brain. Accompanying the two men in the car is a container containing parts of Einstein's brain, hence the title of the book. The question with which the pathologist is confronted is whether Einstein's genius could be located in his brain. Some evidence seemed to suggest that this was the case. An article published in 1999 indicated that the part of Einstein's cerebral cortex associated with mathematical ability was larger than that of normal individuals (Witelson et al., 1999), suggesting that a personality trait could be linked to a specific brain structure.

Evidence from functional magnetic resonance imaging (fMRI) shows different patterns of brain activation associated with different types of cognitive activity. However, as discussed

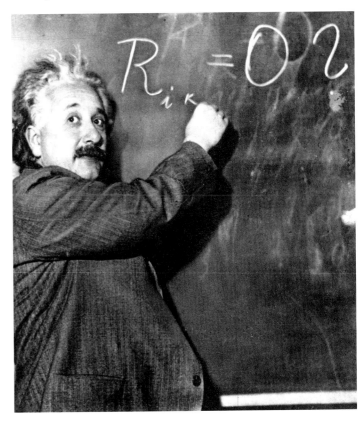

Albert Einstein

Big Picture φ **Question 1**

To what extent can mental processes be reduced to the brain or body?

by Pervin (2003), two factors are worth noting. First, even though specific areas of the brain are activated with particular cognitive tasks, most cognitive activity involves activation of multiple areas of the brain, so that any particular type of cognitive activity is unlikely to be localized solely in a single area of the brain. Second, even though there are genetic influences on brain structure that could account for differences in cognitive functioning, brain structure and function can also be influenced by cognitive activity.

Trait Theories

When people talk about traits, they are referring to the words people use to describe themselves and others in their everyday lives, beginning with adjectives like *shy, devious, manipulative, open,* or *friendly*. **Traits** are *emotional, cognitive, and behavioral tendencies that constitute underlying personality dimensions on which individuals vary*.

According to Gordon Allport (1937; Allport & Odbert, 1936), who developed the trait approach to personality, the concept of trait has two separate but complementary meanings. On the one hand, a trait is an observed tendency to behave in a particular way. On the other, a trait is an inferred, or hypothesized, underlying personality disposition that generates this behavioral tendency. Presumably, a tendency to be cheerful (an observed trait) stems from an enduring pattern of internal processes, such as a tendency to experience positive affect, to think positive thoughts, or to wish to be perceived as happy (inferred dispositions).

How do psychiatrists measure traits? The most straightforward way is the same way people intuitively assess other people's personalities: Observe their behavior over time and in different situations. Because extensive observation of this sort can be very cumbersome and time consuming, however, psychologists often use two other methods. One is to ask people who know the subject well to fill out questionnaires about the person's personality. The second, more commonly used method is to ask subjects themselves to answer self-report questionnaires.

To describe personality from a trait perspective, one must know not only how to measure traits but also which ones to measure. The case of Oskar and Jack, which opened this chapter, described twins who dressed alike and were similar in their sense of well-being. Are these central personality traits?

With literally thousands of different ways to classify people, choosing a set of traits that definitively describe personality seems like a Herculean task. Allport and Odbert (1936) compiled a list of some 18,000 words from *Webster's* unabridged dictionary that could be used to distinguish one person from another. Many of these words denote similar characteristics, however, so over the years trait psychologists have collapsed the list into fewer and fewer traits.

Raymond Cattell (1957, 1990) reduced the list to just 16 traits, such as warm, emotionally stable, intelligent, cheerful, suspicious, imaginative, sensitive, and tense. To select these key traits, Cattell relied on factor analysis (Chapter 8) to group together those adjectives on Allport's and Odbert's list that were highly correlated with each other. Factor analysis allows researchers to find underlying traits by grouping together adjectives that assess similar qualities (e.g., *angry* and *hostile*) into overarching factors.

In addition to reducing the vast number of traits identified by Allport to a much more manageable number, Cattell is also known for his investigations into how much heredity and the environment contributed to the development of specific traits. Cattell and his colleagues (Hundleby et al., 1965) concluded that two-thirds of the development of traits was determined by the environment with the remaining third being

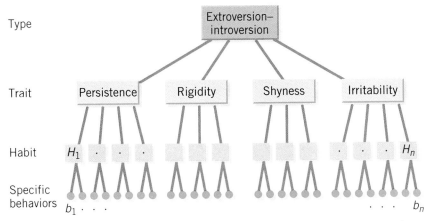

Type

Trait

Habit

Specific
behaviors

FIGURE 12.6 Eysenck's model of personality. Extroversion–introversion is a type, a group of traits that correlate highly with one another. Persistence, rigidity, and so forth are traits—groups of correlated behavioral tendencies (habits). Habits are abstractions derived from observations of specific instances of behavior. *Source*: Adapted from Eysenck, 1953, p. 13.

determined by heredity. Cattell's research in this area laid the groundwork for the field of behavioral genetics.

Eysenck's Theory

One of the best-researched trait theories was developed by Hans Eysenck (1953, 1990). By distinguishing traits and types, with *types* representing a higher order organization of personality, Eysenck differed from Cattell in the number of traits he believed described personality (Figure 12.6). In his view, individuals produce specific behaviors, some of which are frequent or habitual (i.e., they are habits). A trait is a group of correlated habits—a person who has one of these habits tends to have the other habits that constitute the trait. For example, avoiding attention in a group, not initiating conversation, and avoiding large social gatherings are habitual behaviors of people with the trait of shyness. A type is a group of correlated traits. People who are shy, rigid, and inward-looking are introverts.

On the basis of thousands of studies conducted over a half century, Eysenck identified three overarching psychological types: extroversion–introversion, neuroticism–emotional stability, and psychoticism–impulse control. **Extroversion** refers to *a tendency to be sociable, active, and willing to take risks*. Introverts, who score at the low end of the extroversion scale, are characterized by social inhibition, seriousness, and caution. **Neuroticism** defines *a continuum from emotional stability to instability*. It is closely related to the construct of negative affect (Chapter 10). People high on neuroticism report feeling anxious, guilty, tense, and moody, and they tend to have low self-esteem.

Psychoticism describes *people who are aggressive, egocentric, impulsive, and antisocial*. People low on psychoticism are empathic and able to control their impulses. Like Cattell, Eysenck was also interested in the respective contributions of nature and nurture to the development of traits, but his primary focus was on the biological underpinnings of traits and the evolutionary significance of particular traits.

The Five Factor Model

Most theorists who have used factor analysis to arrive at a taxonomy of traits have found that their long lists boil down to *five superordinate personality traits, known as the Big Five factors*, or the **Five Factor Model (FFM)** (Goldberg, 1993;

Apply & Discuss

Most early personality theories began with in-depth interviewing, usually of patients seeking help. In contrast, trait theories arose from the study of words in the English language that describe personality and relied, at least initially, on normal samples.

■ What are the advantages of deriving hypotheses about personality from in-depth interviews, case studies, and patient samples? What are the disadvantages?

■ What are the advantages and disadvantages of relying on everyday language and people's self-reports for trait descriptions?

Table 12.2 ▪ ▪ The Five Factor Model and Its Facets

Neuroticism	Extroversion	Agreeableness	Conscientiousness	Openness
Anxiety	Warmth	Trust	Competence	Fantasy (active fantasy life)
Angry hostility	Gregariousness	Straightforwardness	Order	Aesthetics (artistic interests)
Depression	Assertiveness	Altruism	Dutifulness	Feelings (emotionally open)
Self-consciousness	Activity	Compliance	Achievement striving	Actions (flexible)
Impulsivity	Excitement seeking	Modesty	Self-discipline	Ideas (intellectual)
Vulnerability	Positive emotion	Tenderness	Deliberation	Values (unconventional)

Source: Adapted from McCrae and Costa, 1997, p. 513.

Note: These are the higher-order and lower-order traits ("facets") that constitute the Five Factor Model. Within each factor, traits are highly correlated; across factors, they are not.

Big Picture φ Question 4

To what extent is human nature particular versus universal?

Apply & Discuss

The FFM provides a comprehensive assessment of the personality traits that most people perceive in themselves and others.

▪ Rate yourself or someone you know well on each of the factors in Table 12.2, including the lower order traits (facets).

▪ How well does the model account for your own or someone else's personality?

McCrae & Costa, 1997; Norman, 1963). Different studies yield slightly different factors, and theorists label them in different ways, but the lists are strikingly consistent. Costa and McCrae (1990, 1997) use the labels *openness to experience, conscientiousness, extroversion, agreeableness*, and *neuroticism*. (A good acronym to remember them is OCEAN.) Each of the five factors represents an amalgam of several more specific traits. For example, as Table 12.2 shows, people high on neuroticism tend to be anxious, depressed, impulsive, and so forth. These lower order traits are called "facets" of the FFM.

The delineation of basic factors in personality initially arose from the assumption that important individual differences are likely to show up in language, so that classifying hundreds of adjectives into a small group of higher order trait descriptions would generate an adequate taxonomy of traits (Goldberg, 1981). Interestingly, the same five factors seem to appear almost regardless of the specific data used, including adjectives, antonym pairs, or statements such as "I often feel…" (Goldberg, 1993; John, 1990). The five factors even emerged in a cross-cultural study using a *nonverbal* personality test (Paunonen et al., 1992). Subjects in Canada, Finland, Poland, and Germany viewed drawings of people engaged in behaviors related to various traits and rated how often they engage in similar behaviors. Once again, five traits seemed to encompass the spectrum of personality dispositions they ascribed to themselves.

Is the FFM cross-culturally universal? Research in multiple countries has produced remarkably similar results (see Church, 2000, 2001; John & Srivastava, 1999; McCrae & Costa, 1997; McCrae et al., 1998a; Somer & Goldberg, 1999; Stumpf, 1993). This is particularly impressive because of the wide array of languages from different linguistic families that have reproduced the FFM, from English and German to Turkish and Korean (Saucier & Goldberg, 2001). *Los Cinco Grandes* also emerge in Hispanic-American samples (Benet-Martinez & John, 1998).

The strongest cross-cultural confirmations of the FFM occur when researchers translate Western instruments into other languages. Findings are not quite as clear when researchers draw adjectives from the native language, as in a study of university students in Taiwan (Kuo-shu & Bond, 1990). In this study, participants described people they knew well using two sets of adjectives: adjectives included in Cattell's inventory (reflecting Western concepts), and adjectives culled from Chinese newspapers (to represent native conceptions of personality). Factor analysis of the Western words produced the FFM. In contrast, factor analysis of the Chinese-derived words produced only three factors with some similarity to the FFM.

A study that factor-analyzed personality descriptions taken from interviews and open-ended questionnaires in the Philippines similarly produced a factor structure that only partially mapped onto the FFM (Katigbak et al., 1996). Factors resembling

Kinship	Correlation	Number of Pairings
MZ twins reared together	.86	4,672
MZ twins reared apart	.72	66
DZ twins reared together	.60	5,546
Siblings reared together	.47	26,473
Siblings reared apart	.24	203
Single parent-child reared together	.42	8,433
Single parent-child reared apart	.22	814
Half-siblings	.31	200
Cousins	.15	1,176
Adopted/natural siblings	.29	369
Adopted/adopted siblings	.34	369
Adoptive parent-adopted child	.19	1,397
Spouses	.33	3,817

Source: Reprinted from T. J. Bouchard & M. McGue (1981). Familial studies of intelligence: A review, *Science, 212*, 1055-1059.

FIGURE 12.7   Kinship Correlations for IQ

conscientiousness, agreeableness, and openness emerged, but the other factors could not be mapped onto neuroticism and extroversion. Thus, whether the same five factors emerge cross-culturally depends in part on the culture from which the list of objectives or statements originally came.

INTERIM SUMMARY

Traits are emotional, cognitive, and behavioral tendencies that constitute underlying personality dimensions on which individuals vary. Eysenck identified three overarching psychological types, or constellations of traits: **extroversion** (tendency to be sociable, active, and willing to take risks), **neuroticism** (emotional stability or negative affect), and **psychoticism** (tendency to be aggressive, egocentric, impulsive, and antisocial). According to the **Five Factor Model (FFM)**, personality can be reduced to five factors—openness to experience, conscientiousness, extroversion, agreeableness, and neuroticism—each of which includes several lower order factors or *facets*. Many of these factors appear to be cross-culturally universal.

Is Personality Consistent?

The concept of personality traits described thus far implies that personality has some degree of consistency. If John is an honest person, we can assume he is likely to behave honestly in various situations and to be honest two years from now. No one is honest all the time, however, and people do change. Furthermore, a particular personality trait can manifest itself in different types of behavior. Thus, two questions arise: Is personality consistent from one situation to another, and is personality consistent over time?

Consistency across Situations   In 1968, Walter Mischel touched off a 30-year debate by arguing that **situational variables**—*the circumstances in which people find themselves*—largely determine their behavior. In other words, what people do largely reflects where they find themselves, not who they are. In an influential book,

Making Connections

A hotly debated issue among personality theorists centers around the heritability of intelligence. Although research has clearly demonstrated that the IQ scores of biologically related individuals are more strongly related than those of unrelated individuals or those of more distantly related biological relatives (see Figure 12.7), the question remains regarding the extent to which intelligence is inherited versus due to the environment. Although clearly aspects of intelligence are inherited, the most heritable aspect of intelligence appears to be vocabulary (Rowe et al., 1999; Rowe & Rodgers, 2002). In case this strikes you as odd, given that people can simply sit down and memorize vocabulary words, the ability to do so is dependent upon brain structures and memory abilities (Chapter 3).

Walter Mischel

he marshaled considerable evidence of the inconsistency of people's behavior across situations and showed that most personality tests had only modest correlations with behaviors in the real world. For example, trait measures tended to be far less predictive of whether a psychiatric patient would require future hospitalization than the weight of the patient's psychiatric chart!

Mischel almost single-handedly slew the mighty field of personality. If personality is not consistent, psychologists have nothing to measure, so they might as well pack up their questionnaires and go home. Indeed, the field of personality languished for years after Mischel's critique.

Several psychologists, however, challenged Mischel's arguments. Seymour Epstein (1979, 1986, 1997) pointed out that any single behavior has multiple causes, so that trying to predict a single behavior from a personality trait is virtually impossible. No measure of "honesty," for example, can predict whether a child will cheat on an examination on a *particular* occasion. However, averaging across multiple occasions, measures of honesty do predict whether or not a child will cheat. Using the **principle of aggregation**, researchers such as Epstein concluded that "*a trait does not refer to a specific behavior in a specific situation but rather to a class of behaviors over a range of situations*" (Pervin, 2003, p. 60).

Other psychologists argued that psychologists cannot predict all of the people all of the time, but they *can predict some of the people some of the time* (Bem & Allen, 1974; Biesanz et al., 1998; Kenrick & Stringfield, 1980). The key is to figure out which people tend to be consistent on which traits, and which traits are relevant for which people. For example, people's self-descriptions tend to be highly predictive of the way others see them on traits they view as central to their personality (Zuckerman et al., 1988). Further, some people are more open and easy to "read"; their behavior is thus easier for people who know them well to predict (Colvin, 1993).

Consistency over Time Researchers have now also documented considerable consistency in many aspects of personality over long periods of time, a factor referred to as the stability of personality (Caspi, 1998, 2000; Mischel & Shoda, 1995). When we use phrases such as "He's a dishonest person" or when psychologists describe a person as "low in conscientiousness," we are making statements about what we can expect from the person over time and across situations. One example is *inhibition to the unfamiliar*, a cluster of attributes in children that includes shyness and anxiety in the face of novelty (Gest, 1997; Kagan, 1989). Inhibition to the unfamiliar appears to be an aspect of **temperament**, that is, *a basic personality disposition heavily influenced by genes* (Chess & Thomas, 1987). Infants who are inhibited (roughly 10 percent of the population) show a distinct pattern of crying and motor behavior as early as four months of age when confronted with unfamiliar stimuli. These infants continue to show more fear responses than uninhibited children at 9, 14, and 21 months when confronted with novel stimuli (such as an unfamiliar room, application of painless electrodes to the skin, or application of liquid through a dropper to the mouth or eye). At seven and a half years of age, inhibited children also have significantly more fears outside the laboratory about attending summer camp, public speaking, remaining alone at home, and so forth.

Psychologists have documented consistency from childhood through early adulthood on various traits as well. One group of investigators reanalyzed data from a longitudinal project that assessed every third child born during the years 1928 and 1929 in Berkeley, California (Caspi et al., 1990). The most striking finding was that 8-, 9-, and 10-year-old boys characterized as ill-tempered, who had repeated temper tantrums, were characterized at age 30 by maladaptive personality traits, poor occupational performance, and disrupted marriages. As adults they were also rated as undercontrolled, irritable, moody, unethical, and undependable.

In another study, children described as inhibited at age 3 were more likely than others to be depressed at age 21, whereas children described at age 3 as impulsive were more likely to be diagnosed as antisocial (aggressive, lacking guilt, and so forth)

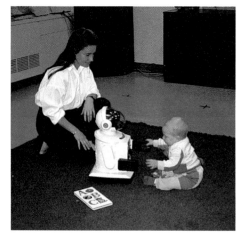

An infant in Kagan's laboratory shows little inhibition to the unfamiliar.

at age 21 (Moffit et al., 1996). A Swedish study similarly found that children (particularly boys) rated as aggressive at ages 10 and 13 by their teachers were disproportionately represented among criminals (especially perpetrators of violent crime) at age 26 (Stattin & Magnusson, 1989).

One of the most important studies to document consistency over time examined the childhood personality antecedents of depressive tendencies in 18-year-olds (J. H. Block et al., 1991). Several preschool teachers rated aspects of the children's behavior and personality at ages 3 and 4. The same subjects were then observed in depth at ages 7, 11, 14, and 18 by various teachers and psychologists.

The investigators offered a more complex hypothesis than simply that depression in childhood would predict depression in adulthood. Their previous research suggested that an important variable that could influence the results was gender: Based on their knowledge of research on the way boys and girls are socialized (boys to be autonomous and girls to be more attuned to social demands), they hypothesized that the personality antecedents of depression in males and females might be quite different.

The results supported their hypothesis. Boys who later showed depressive tendencies were characterized when young as aggressive, self-aggrandizing, and unable to control their impulses. Girls who later became depressed, in contrast, showed almost the opposite attributes in childhood: They were shy, obedient, conscientious, and unassuming. Boys who were less bright were also more prone to depression at age 18, whereas girls who were *more* intelligent were more likely to report depression at age 18. Table 12.3 shows some of the correlations between personality at age 7 and depression at age 18.

Personality also shows considerable stability *throughout* adulthood. A study of the FFM in a sample of adults ages 30 to 96 found that personality stabilizes by age 30 and remains consistent thereafter (Costa & McCrae, 1988, 1990).

A More Complex View of Personality and Consistency   If personality shows substantial consistency across situations and over time, was Mischel wrong? The answer is not a simple yes or no. On the one hand, Mischel clearly overstated the case for the role of situations in behavior and understated the case for personality variables. A 21-year-old man who was impulsive and undercontrolled at age 3 is more likely to be aggressive when someone accidentally bumps into him on the street and to steal from a store than a man who was better adjusted in preschool. That is quite remarkable.

Making Connections

Social psychologists study how the presence of others can alter people's behavior, often focusing on the situational causes of behavior (rather than causes residing in the individual) (Chapter 18). In groups, for example, people often behave in ways that are violent, antisocial, or very different from the way they usually respond alone.

■ What happens to people's personality in a group? Can personality be "overridden" by a group?

■ Does personality just "disappear" in group situations, or do people's actions still reflect something about who they are—that is, about their personality?

Big Picture φ Question 6

What is the relation between nature and nurture in shaping psychological processes?

Table 12.3 ■ ■ Gender Differences in Selected Personality Traits at Age 7 That Correlate with Depressive Symptoms at Age 18

Trait at Age 7	Correlation with depression at age 18	
	For Males	For Females
Characteristically stretches limits	.37	−.22
Teases other children	.25	−.32
Tries to be center of attention	.30	.29
Is empathic	−.30	.29
Can be trusted; is dependable	−.37	.20
Is obedient and compliant	−.22	.30

Many of the same traits at age 7 correlate with depression in *opposite directions* at age 18 in males and females

Source: Adapted from J. Block et al., 1991.

Note: The table reports the correlations between personality dimensions assessed at age 7 with degree of depression reported at age 18. As can be seen, on many dimensions, predictors of depression in males and females differed considerably.

Apply & Discuss

One of the issues with which trait psychologists have struggled regards how many traits are needed to describe the core of people's personalities. Eysenck believed there were three basic personality traits (introversion/extraversion, neuroticism, and psychoticism). Cattell identified 16 personality traits measured in his personality test, the Sixteen Personality Factors or 16PF. Proponents of the Five Factor Model obviously endorse the perspective that five traits are central to describing people's personalities.

■ How many traits do you think are necessary to describe personality?

■ Can you think of traits that the Five Factor Model may have omitted?

■ How many traits can you think of to describe yourself?

On the other hand, Mischel forced personality psychologists to move beyond simple statements such as "John is an aggressive person" to more complex statements about the *circumstances* under which John will be aggressive. In other words, Mischel's critique of traits led to a recognition of **person-by-situation interactions**—that is, *people express particular traits in particular situations*.

In fact, in his most recent statements of his approach, Mischel argues that personality lies in *if–then* patterns—stable ways in which particular situations trigger specific patterns of thought, feeling, and behavior (Mischel & Shoda, 1995, 1998). For example, one man may become aggressive when another man appears to be threatening or humiliating him; another may become aggressive when he feels vulnerable with his wife, which leads him to feel unmasculine. Both men may be equally aggressive when their behavior is averaged across situations, but the difference between them lies in the circumstances (the "if") that elicit the response (the "then"). One of the exciting aspects of this approach is that Mischel explicitly attempts to integrate his own cognitive–social theory with both trait theory (arguing for enduring personality dispositions) and psychodynamic theory (focusing on personality dynamics that get activated under particular conditions, often outside of awareness).

Mischel's recent research, like that of other psychologists who have been tracking down the nature of person-by-situation interactions (e.g., Funder & Colvin, 1991), supports a contention of early trait theorists that seemed to get lost for many years: Consistency is most likely to emerge in similar situations (Allport, 1937; Rotter, 1990). A person who is generally quite low on neuroticism may nevertheless tend to become extremely distressed when criticized. Her difficulty coping with criticism is just as much a part of her personality as her generally placid nature; the only difference is that the circumstances that activate neurotic behavior are much more specific than those that activate its opposite.

INTERIM SUMMARY

Data from studies of behavioral genetics suggest that most personality variables are 15 to 50 percent heritable. Personality demonstrates many consistencies across time and situations. The debate over the extent to which personality is consistent led to a recognition of the importance of **person-by-situation interactions**—ways in which people express personality dispositions only under specific circumstances. According to Mischel, personality lies in *if–then* patterns—stable ways in which particular situations trigger specific patterns of thought, feeling, and behavior.

Contributions and Limitations of Trait Theories

The trait approach to personality has several advantages. Traits lend themselves to measurement and hence to empirical investigation through questionnaires. Without the trait approach, we would not have been able to assess the heritability or consistency of personality. Further, trait theories are not committed to theoretical assumptions that may be valid for some people but not for others. Psychodynamic and cognitive–social theories offer universal answers to questions such as "Are humans basically aggressive?" or "Are people basically rational?" Trait theories, in contrast, offer a very different answer: "Some people are, some aren't, and some are in between" (McCrae & Costa, 1990). Perhaps for these reasons the trait approach, and the FFM in particular, has breathed new life into personality as an important and scientifically sound area of psychological research.

Like all approaches, however, trait approaches have limitations (see Block, 1995; McAdams, 1992a; Westen, 1995). First, they rely heavily on self-reports, and people often cannot or do not give an accurate assessment of themselves. For example, people who consider themselves psychologically healthy may deny statements about themselves that are true but threaten their self-concept (Shedler et al., 1993).

Second, trait theories can be no more sophisticated than the theories of personality held by lay people, because the basic terms of trait theory come from everyday language (see Block, 1995). Trait theory may be as much a theory of the way *everyday people* think about personality as it is a theory of personality. Where do concepts developed by experts such as expectancies, unconscious processes, or emotion regulation strategies fit?

Third, as in factor-analytic studies of intelligence, the factor structure that emerges depends in part on the items that are included and a number of highly subjective decisions made by the factor analyst. Although most personality researchers have converged on the FFM, others have repeatedly found three or four factors (e.g., Di Blas & Forzi, 1999; Eysenck, 1990; Stallings et al., 1996), and some have found seven (e.g., Benet-Martinez & Waller, 1997).

Fourth, trait psychology does not examine the dynamic nature of personality. It focuses on the descriptors that people use to label other people (or themselves) and their behavior, but it does nothing to explain the underpinnings of that behavior—why the person behaves the way he does.

Fifth, although there does appear to be cross-cultural consistency in the five factors used to describe personality, these factors may not mean precisely the same thing in different cultures, and their role in affecting behavior may also vary across cultures. Specifically, people in collectivist cultures, such as Japan, where the emphasis is more on the collective or the community rather than the individual, may place less emphasis on traits than do people from more individualistic Western cultures (Church, 2000).

Finally, trait theories often provide more insight into the *how much* of personality than the *how* or the *why* (Block, 1995). A person may rank high in aggressiveness, but this ranking says little about the internal processes that occur when the person is behaving aggressively or why he behaves aggressively in some circumstances but not in others. Trait approaches that attempt to provide causal mechanisms—for example, by linking traits to underlying biology and genetics—tend to be more powerful.

Making Connections

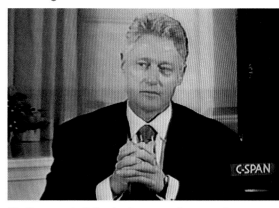

Like Spearman's distinction between s-factors and g-factors in intelligence (Chapter 8), some personality traits are specific to particular situations, whereas others are probably more general, or global.

■ Is "character" a specific or a general trait?

■ How might a personality psychologist make sense of former President Clinton's dedication to equal opportunity for African-Americans, which was not always helpful to him politically but seemed to reflect deeply held values, and his sexual indiscretions?

■ Can a person be extremely honorable in one domain and dishonorable in another?

Humanistic Theories

During the 1950s and especially the 1960s, an approach to personality emerged as an alternative to psychoanalysis and behaviorism. Unlike these approaches, **humanistic approaches** to personality *focus on aspects of personality that are distinctly human, not shared by other animals*. How do people find meaning in life, and how can they remain true to themselves in the midst of pressures they experience from the first days of life to accommodate other peoples' wishes and preconceptions? Many humanistic psychologists argue that scientific methods borrowed from the natural sciences are inappropriate for studying people, whose actions, unlike those of fish or asteroids, reflect the way they understand and experience themselves and the world.

Although humanistic psychology has its roots in European philosophical thinking of the late nineteenth century, the humanistic approach to personality emerged during the 1960s, a decade that challenged traditional values. People were tired of fitting into roles others set for them and instead sought ways to be true to themselves and their personal beliefs (see M. B. Smith, 1978, 1988, 1994). Here we examine representative humanistic theories: the person-centered approach of Carl Rogers and existential theories of personality.

Rogers's Person-Centered Approach

The most widely used humanistic theory of personality is Carl Rogers's **person-centered approach** (1951, 1959). Philosophically, Rogers descended from the French philosopher Jean-Jacques Rousseau, who two centuries earlier wrote that "man is born free but everywhere he is in chains." Rousseau meant that people are innately free and compassionate to their fellows but somehow in the course of growing up, they become mean-spirited, selfish, and trapped by convention.

Rogers similarly believed that human beings are basically good but their personalities become distorted by interpersonal experiences, especially in childhood. In his view, psychology should try to understand individuals' **phenomenal experience**—that is, *the way they conceive of reality and experience themselves and their world*. According to Rogers and other humanistic psychologists, psychologists should not be studying people as *objects* of their investigations but as *subjects* who construct meaning. Thus, the fundamental tool of the psychologist is not a projective test, an experiment, or a questionnaire but **empathy**, *the capacity to understand another person's experience cognitively and emotionally*.

Rogers, like other humanistic theorists, postulated that individuals have a **true self**—*a core aspect of being, untainted by the demands of those around them*—but that they often distort this into a **false self**—*a mask they wear and ultimately mistake to be their true psychological "face."* According to Rogers, the false self emerges because of people's natural desire to gain the positive regard of other people. *As children develop, they learn that to be loved they must meet certain standards*; in the process of internalizing these **conditions of worth**, they distort themselves into being what significant others want them to be.

According to Rogers, the self, or **self-concept**, is *an organized pattern of thought and perception about oneself*. When the self-concept diverges too much from the **ideal self** (*the person's view of what she should be like*), the individual may distort her behavior or the way she sees herself to avoid this painful state. Thus, people's internalized expectations of what others want them to be may lead them to abandon their own talents or inclinations and ignore their own needs and feelings. The artistic student who becomes an accountant because that is what his father always wanted him to be is, in Rogers's view, sacrificing his true self to meet internalized conditions of worth.

Rogers proposed that the primary motivation in humans is an **actualizing tendency**, *a desire to fulfill the full range of needs that humans experience*, from the basic needs for food and drink to the needs to be open to experience and to express one's true self. These needs were similarly described by Maslow, another humanistic psychologist (Chapter 10). Opposing the actualizing tendency, however, are the needs for positive regard from others and for positive self-regard, which often require distorting the self to meet imposed standards.

INTERIM SUMMARY

Humanistic approaches focus on distinctively human aspects of personality, such as how to find meaning in life or be true to oneself. According to Carl Rogers's **person-centered approach**, psychology should try to understand individuals' **phenomenal experience**—the way they conceive of reality and experience themselves and their world—through **empathy**. Rogers defines the self, or **self-concept**, as an organized pattern of thought and perception about oneself, which can diverge from the **ideal self**, leading to distortions in personality.

Existential Approaches to Personality

Existentialism is *a school of twentieth-century philosophy that similarly focused on subjective existence*. According to many existentialist philosophers, the individual is alone throughout life and must confront what it means to be human and what values to embrace. According to the existential philosopher Jean-Paul Sartre (1971), unlike other animals and physical objects, people have no fixed nature and must essentially *create themselves*.

Existential Questions Sartre argued that the meaning we find in life is essentially our own invention and dies along with us. The paradox inherent in the human condition is that we must find meaning in our lives by committing ourselves to values, ideals, people, and courses of action while simultaneously recognizing that these things are finite and have no intrinsic meaning, that we have simply endowed them with meaning in order to make our lives seem worthwhile.

Sartre would object to the idea that we have a personality at all, if personality implies a static or unchanging set of traits. What distinguishes humans, he asserted, is that we are ever-changing and free to alter our course of action at any time. Thus, we *have* no essence, no personality, except if we choose to delude ourselves into believing that we have no choice.

According to existential psychologists, the dilemmas at the heart of existential philosophy are central to personality. Although many different theoretical perspectives have developed within existential psychology (Frankl, 1959; May, 1953; May et al., 1958), they converge on several key issues:

* the importance of subjective experience;
* the centrality of the human quest for meaning in life;
* the dangers of losing touch with what one really feels; and
* the hazards of conceiving of oneself as thing-like, rather than as a changing, ever-forming, creative source of will and action.

Chief among the problems humans face is **existential dread**, *the recognition that life has no absolute value or meaning and that, ultimately, we all face death*. People spend their lives denying their mortality and the nothingness hidden behind their values and pursuits (Becker, 1973; Brown, 1959).

Experimental Investigations of Death Anxiety Many existential and humanistic psychologists have avoided testing their hypotheses or developing methods of personality assessment because of their concern about methods that turn people into objects to be studied rather than subjects to be understood. Nevertheless, a team of creative researchers has been systematically testing an existential theory developed by Ernest Becker (1973) that proposes that cultural beliefs and values serve to protect people from facing the reality of their mortality.

According to Becker's theory, an unfortunate by-product of the evolution of human intelligence is that people can imagine their own death and the death of those they love. To avoid the anxiety that would result from facing this tragic reality, we create and embrace cultural beliefs and values that symbolically deny death and allow hope in the face of mortality and meaninglessness (Solomon et al., 1991, p. 96).

The researchers testing Becker's theory have demonstrated across a series of studies that, when confronted with experimental procedures designed to stimulate death anxiety (such as a questionnaire asking participants to think about their own death), people cling more tenaciously to their cultural values (Greenberg et al., 1994; Greenberg et al., 1995; Solomon et al., 1991). For example, in one study, municipal court judges served as subjects (Rosenblatt et al., 1989). Half the judges received the mortality salience manipulation (the death questionnaire), whereas the other half (the control group) did not. The experimenters then asked the judges to set bond for a prostitute in a hypothetical case. Prostitution was chosen as the crime because of its culturally defined moral overtones. As predicted, judges who filled out the mortality questionnaire were significantly more punitive, setting bond substantially higher than judges in the control group, whose death anxiety had not been activated.

Not only does mortality salience heighten attraction to cultural norms, but these cultural norms can subsequently affect behavior. People who adhere to valued cultural norms gain social approval, increased self-esteem, and, according to existential

No one of us can help the things life has done to us. They're done before you realize it, and once they're done, they make you do other things until at last everything comes between you and what you'd like to be, and you've lost your true self forever.

—EUGENE O'NEILL
Long Day's Journey into Night

	Death Salience		Control	
	M	SD	M	SD
How beneficial is this charity to society?	17.31	2.96	14.73	3.91
How much does society need this charity?	17.37	2.70	15.80	3.62
How desirable is this charity to you personally?	16.06	3.29	13.40	4.12
Favorability composite	50.75	7.60	43.93	10.68

FIGURE 12.8   Means and standard deviations for participants' ratings of the charities. Participants for whom mortality was made salient gave more favorable ratings to valued charities than those participants for whom death was not salient. Adherence to cultural norms that dictate prosocial behavior and concern for the needs of others serve as a buffer against the anxiety that arises when mortality is made salient. *Source:* Jones et al., 2002, p. 1345.

theorists, a buffer against death anxiety. In a test of this idea, researchers interviewed pedestrians either in front of a funeral home (high mortality salience) or several blocks away from the funeral home (low mortality salience) (Jonas, Schimel et al, 2002). They then asked the participants their feelings about two different charities that the participants had deemed to be moderately important. Participants for whom mortality was salient expressed more favorable attitudes toward the charities than those for whom death was not made salient (Figure 12.8). These results were interpreted in terms of mortality salience heightening attraction to cultural norms of helping those in need, which affected participants' attitudes toward the charitable organizations.

Recently, research has turned to the development of close relationships as a means of buffering people against mortality salience (Mikulincer et al., 2003). People for whom death is salient appear to seek out close relationships with others more readily than those for whom death is not immediately salient. Furthermore, being in close relationships with others seems to buffer people from the salience of reminders of death.

INTERIM SUMMARY

According to **existential** approaches to psychology, people have no fixed nature and must essentially create themselves. Sartre argued that people must find meaning in their lives by making commitments while recognizing that these commitments have no intrinsic meaning. **Existential dread** is the recognition that life has no absolute value or meaning and that we all face death. Research supports Becker's theory that people deny death by committing to cultural worldviews that give them a sense of meaning and immortality.

Contributions and Limitations of Humanistic Theories

Humanistic psychology has made a number of contributions to the study of personality. Perhaps the most important is its unique focus on the way humans strive to find meaning in life, a dimension other approaches have failed to address. In day-to-day life this need may not be readily observable because culture confers meaning on activities, relationships, and values. The salience of this aspect of personality emerges, however, in times of personal crisis or loss (Janoff-Bulman, 1992), when life may seem meaningless. The search for meaning also becomes apparent in times of rapid cultural change (Wallace, 1956), when a culture's values and worldview are breaking down and no longer fulfill their function of making life predictable and meaningful (see also Baumeister, 1991).

Big Picture φ Question 4

To what extent is human nature particular versus universal?

The humanistic approach has two major limitations. First, it does not offer a comprehensive theory of personality in the same way that psychodynamic and cognitive–social theories do. It does not, for example, offer a general theory of cognition, emotion, behavior, and psychological disorder, although different theorists at times address many of these. Second, with some notable exceptions (e.g., Rogers, 1959), humanistic psychology has not produced a substantial body of testable hypotheses and research, in part because of its rejection of empiricism as a philosophy of science (Chapter 2).

Genetics and Personality

Why is one person extroverted and another introverted? Few would doubt the influence of learning and environment on personality. However, a considerable body of evidence supports an idea first proposed by the Greek physician Galen 2000 years ago, that a substantial part of personality is inherited (Krueger, 2000; Plomin & Caspi, 1999). The case of Oskar and Jack that opened this chapter is not unusual in finding strong similarities among people with shared genes (Jang et al., 1998; Lykken et al., 1993; McGue et al., 1993; Tellegen et al., 1988; Vierikko et al., 2003). Despite the fact that adopted children may have lived with their adoptive family from birth, biological relatives tend to be more similar than adoptive relatives, even if they have had no contact with one another (Loehlin et al., 1988; Plomin & Caspi, 1999). Some heritable personality traits emerge quite early in development. Extroversion, task orientation, and activity level already show high heritability in one- and two-year-olds (Braungart et al., 1992; Rowe, 1999). **Heritability** refers to *the proportion of variance in a particular trait that is due to genetic influences* (Pervin, 2003; see Figure 12.9).

The most definitive studies in this area compare twins reared together and twins reared apart, a procedure that can distinguish cleanly between genetic and environ-

Apply and Discuss

Earlier in this chapter, we discussed projective measures that are used particularly by psychoanalytic theorists to assess personality. Trait theorists, on the other hand, rely on more objective means, such as self-report measures, to determine personality.

■ How might psychoanalytic theorists use projective tests to measure traits as opposed to unconscious motivations.

■ How might trait theorists, for example, use self-report personality inventories to measure underlying motives and urges?

Big Picture φ Question 6

What is the relation between nature and nurture in shaping psychological processes?

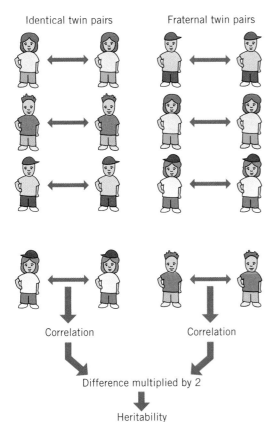

Identical twin pairs   Fraternal twin pairs

Correlation   Correlation

Difference multiplied by 2

Heritability

FIGURE 12.9 The twin study method examines pairs of identical and same-sex fraternal twins. The members of each pair are compared on the variable of interest, and a separate correlation is computed for each type of twin. One of these correlations is then subtracted from the other. Multiplying this difference by 2 gives an index of the heritability of the characteristic, an estimate of the variance in it that is accounted for by inheritance. Reprinted from Carver & Scheier (2000, p.129).

Table 12.4 ■ ■ Correlations between Minnesota Twins Reared Together and Apart on a Multidimensional Personality Measure

	Reared Apart		Reared Together		
	MZ	DZ	MZ	DZ	
Well-being	.48	.18	.58	.23	Substantial differences between MZ and DZ twins suggest a genetic effect.
Achievement	.36	.07	.51	.13	
Social closeness	.29	.30	.57	.24	
Stress reaction	.61	.27	.52	.24	
Alienation	.48	.18	.55	.38	Substantial differences between MZ twins reared apart and together suggest an environmental effect.
Aggression	.46	.06	.43	.14	
Traditionalism	.53	.39	.50	.47	
Positive emotionality	.34	−.07	.63	.18	
Negative emotionality	.61	.29	.54	.41	
Constraint	.57	.04	.58	.25	

Source: Tellegen et al., 1988, p. 1035.

mental influences (Chapter 8). A Minnesota study (Tellegen et al., 1988) examined 217 monozygotic (MZ) and 114 dizygotic (DZ) adult twin pairs who had been reared together and 44 MZ and 27 DZ adult twin pairs who had been reared apart (average age 22). Table 12.4 displays the correlations between MZ and DZ twins reared together and apart on a personality test measuring such traits as well-being, achievement, aggression, and traditionalism. The MZ twins showed substantially higher correlations (averaging .51) than DZ twins (averaging .23) on almost every trait, even when they were reared apart.

A series of studies of Swedish adoptees with a much larger sample but a higher mean age of subjects (in their fifties rather than their twenties) also found considerable evidence for genetic influences but yielded lower heritability estimates, averaging about .27 (see Plomin et al., 1990). The correlations for MZ twins reared together were considerably larger than those reared apart, demonstrating substantial environmental influences on personality. In this study, two factors from the FFM, agreeableness and conscientiousness, showed minimal heritability (low correlations for MZ twins reared apart) but substantial environmental influence (contrastingly high correlations for MZ twins reared together). Openness was largely heritable, while extroversion and neuroticism showed substantial genetic *and* environmental impact (see also McCrae, 1996; Viken et al., 1994). More recent research suggests that some of the specific *facets* of the FFM are moderately heritable, such as self-discipline and self-consciousness (Jang et al., 1998).

The evidence thus points to heritability estimates in the range of 15 to 50 percent for most personality traits, with the balance attributable to the environment. Despite this strong environmental influence, the same family does not necessarily produce children with similar personalities. Adoptive siblings, for example, tend to share few personality traits, and even natural siblings show great variations. While this may be surprising in one sense, in another, it may simply attest to the flexibility with which human beings can respond to similar circumstances. In a family with erratic alcoholic parents, one sibling may cope by turning inward, becoming introverted and studious, while another may cope by becoming wild, poorly controlled, and eventually alcoholic. In both cases, their personalities have been shaped by a similar environment, even though they took very different roads. Each sibling in a family also has different experiences within that family and outside of it, and these unshared experiences can be important in shaping personality.

Behavioral geneticists are increasingly examining the complexities of genetic transmission of psychological characteristics. For example, some inherited traits may only find behavioral expression if each sibling has *several* genes that interact to produce it or if both siblings have the same dominant gene (see Saudino, 1997). Some genes that control personality may, for example, be dominant, like genes for brown eyes. Thus, identical twins with the gene will be highly similar, whereas nonidentical twins or other siblings will be entirely different if they do not both inherit the dominant gene or if they do not inherit the constellation of genes required to produce the trait.

Genetic tendencies may also trigger a cascade of events that include *environmental* responses that lead to highly heritable traits. For example, in a longitudinal study from Finland, aggression at age 8 predicted chronic unemployment 30 years later (Kokko & Pulkkinen, 1997). Although aggression in childhood can reflect in part genetic influences, the data suggested that aggressive children developed problems at school and problems with substance abuse by adolescence. These difficulties, in turn, began to shape their lives and foreclose employment options as they moved into adulthood.

INTERIM SUMMARY

Genetic views on personality suggest that many personality traits are inherited. Heritability refers to the proportion of variance in a particular trait that is due to genetic influences. Evident in support of a genetic basis of personality has relied primarily on twin studies comparing monozygotic (MZ) and dizygotic (DZ) twins.

Personality and Culture

Two things are notable about the relationship between personality and culture. First, although there is an incredible amount of variability in personality among individuals, there is also a remarkable degree of consistency in many of the traits and behaviors that characterize people across cultures (Leary, 1999). People in all cultures experience anxiety, embarrassment, and threats to their self-esteem. Everyone, regardless of their cultural background, fears particular things, whether they be an upcoming speech or death. Most normal individuals have a yearning for unconditional positive regard as recommended by Rogers, and for inclusion in individual or group relationships with others. Thus, in spite of the wide range of individual differences that can be observed, there are some universals to personality that extend across cultures and across people (Barkow et al., 1992).

Second, the theories we have explored in this chapter represent our own culture's most sophisticated attempts to understand personality. Other cultures, however, have alternative views. Thus, although there are universals in personality, the explanations offered by particular cultures to account for personality vary. In fact, every culture has some implicit, commonsense conception of personality.

The Cheyenne of North America, for example, distinguish several aspects of personhood (Straus, 1977). The individual's basic nature and identity reside in the heart. The person's power, called *omotome*, is distinguished from spirit, which is the storehouse of learning, experience, and memory. To some degree, the Cheyenne believe in behavioral genetics, holding that certain behaviors run in families and that children are born predisposed to behave in particular ways. Theirs is also a somewhat psychodynamic view of childhood as an extremely important period of life, crucial for learning and spiritual development.

Unlike contemporary Western theories, however, the Cheyenne do not believe personality resides entirely or even primarily in individuals. Rather, they believe, like

Big Picture φ Question 4

To what extent is human nature particular versus universal?

many preliterate societies, that the innermost parts of the soul or personality are in part communal, shared by kin and community (see Cross & Markus, 1999; Geertz, 1963; Shweder & Bourne, 1982; Westen, 1985). East–West differences in the extent to which individuals are seen as "free agents" appear to lie behind some subtle differences noted in journalism across the world: Newspaper accounts of corporate scandals in the West focus on particular executives, whereas those in Japan and Hong Kong focus on particular organizations (Menon et al., 1999).

Linking Personality and Culture

Although most Western theories of personality have been constructed with Western subjects in mind, the complex interactions of personality and culture have intrigued psychologists and anthropologists since the early part of the twentieth century (see Church & Lonner, 1998; LeVine, 1982). Do cultures with harsh child-rearing practices create hostile or paranoid personalities? And how do cultural practices help individuals satisfy psychological needs, such as escaping from death anxiety? We briefly consider three approaches to culture and personality: Freud's, the culture pattern approach, and interactionist approaches.

Freud's Approach   Freud viewed cultural phenomena as reflections of individual psychodynamics. The Freudian method of analyzing cultures is the same method applied to dreams, neurotic symptoms, and conscious beliefs in individuals: Look beneath manifest content to find latent content (see Spain, 1992).

Freud thought cultural phenomena such as myths, moral and religious beliefs, and games to be expressions of the needs and conflicts of individuals. For example, my friends are all aghast to find that I am a devotee of boxing. Because I do not appear to be a very aggressive person, they cannot understand how I can enjoy watching two grown men dancing around on a piece of canvas, trying to destroy each other's cerebellum with flurries of punches. The function of boxing for me, no doubt, is to express aggressive impulses that I would not permit myself in my daily life.

Freud (1928) similarly argued that institutions such as religion can be understood in terms of their functions for individuals. Should one be surprised to find representations in Western culture of a Holy Father and a Sacred Mother? The monotheistic concept of God in many religions is remarkably similar to a young child's conception of his father: a strong, masculine, frightening figure who can be both loving and vengeful. (Interestingly, empirical research suggests that people's concepts of God actually tend to resemble their descriptions of their *mothers*, particularly when they are closer to their mother than to their father; see Wulff, 1997.) A Freudian might also note that the virgin mother of Christian theology is a perfect resolution of Oedipal conflict: No child wants to think that his parents have sex, and the best way of keeping mother pure is to imagine that she could have had a virgin birth.

The Culture Pattern Approach   A second approach asserts that individual psychology reflects cultural practices, not the other way around. The **culture pattern approach** sees *culture as an organized set of beliefs, rituals, and institutions that shape individuals to fit its patterns*. Some cultures stress community and pursuit of the common good, and their members generally internalize these values. Others foster a paranoid attitude, which individuals express in their relations with neighbors or outsiders, such as the Nuer of the Sudan (Evans-Pritchard, 1956) or the Aymaya of South America (LaBarre, 1966). As the American anthropologist Ruth Benedict (1934) put it, "The life history of the individual is first and foremost an accommodation to the patterns and standards traditionally handed down in the community" (p. 2).

From the standpoint of the culture pattern approach, culture is a great sculptor that chisels the raw biological material of an individual from infancy on until it conforms to the sculptor's aesthetic ideal. Some slabs of humanity, however, are very dif-

A Holy Mother is a motif that recurs in religious imagery throughout the world.

ficult to chisel and are labeled deviant or thrown back into the quarry after being deformed by the hand of the frustrated artist. Those whose temperament and personality patterns do not readily conform to culture patterns may thus find themselves ostracized or incarcerated, viewed in various societies as sinners, criminals, dissidents, or mentally ill.

Interactionist Approaches to Personality and Culture | A Global Vista

The approaches described thus far essentially reduce one broad set of variables to another: personality to economics, culture to personality, or personality to culture. More complex approaches, however, combine the virtues of each. These **interactionist approaches** *to personality view causality as multidirectional* (LeVine, 1982; Whiting & Whiting, 1975). Personality must certainly accommodate to economic and cultural demands, but cultural and economic processes themselves are in part created to fulfill psychological needs. These in turn are shaped by cultural and economic practices, so that causality runs in more than one direction.

For example, societies that treat children more abusively tend to have more aggressive myths and religious beliefs (Rohner, 1975a). From an interactionist perspective, this should not be surprising. On the one hand, the schemas or representations that children develop about relationships in childhood color their understanding of supernatural relationships. Thus, children with hostile or abusive parents are likely to respond emotionally to images of evil or sadistic gods when they grow older. Indeed, one could argue that in the West, as child-rearing practices have become less harsh since the Middle Ages, the image of God has shifted from a vengeful, angry father to a loving, nurturant one.

On the other hand, causality runs in the opposite direction as well, from aggressive myths to abusive child-rearing practices. Societies use myths and religious beliefs to train people to behave in ways valued by the culture. People reared on a steady diet of myths depicting aggressive interactions are likely to treat their children more aggressively, which in turn produces children who resonate with the aggression in the myths they will teach their own children.

The Western conception of God was once much more frightening and judgmental, as in Michelangelo's depiction of God creating the world (from the Sistine Chapel).

Other interactionist approaches consider historical as well as cultural factors. The psychoanalyst Erik Erikson (1969) examined the lives of powerful leaders like Gandhi and Hitler and explored the intersection of their personality dynamics, the needs of their followers, and cultural and historical circumstances. Erikson argued, for example, that Hitler's strong need for power and his grandiosity, sensitivity to humiliation, and disgust for anyone he saw as weak contributed to the development of Nazi ideology, which stressed the greatness of Germany (with which Hitler identified) and the need to destroy groups Hitler perceived as either powerful (and hence threatening) or powerless. This ideology appealed to a nation that had been humiliated in World War I and forced to pay reparations to its adversaries, and it appealed to members of a culture whose child-rearing patterns left them vulnerable to feeling humiliated and unable to express their rage (Chapter 17).

INTERIM SUMMARY

Freud reduced culture to personality, seeing cultural phenomena as reflections of individual psychodynamics. The **culture pattern approach** sees culture as an organized set of beliefs, rituals, and institutions that shape individuals to fit its patterns. **Interactionist approaches** view causality as multidirectional, with personality, economics, and culture mutually influencing one another.

Summary

1. **Personality** refers to the enduring patterns of thought, feeling, and behavior that are expressed in different circumstances. Personality psychologists study both the **structure of personality** (the organization or patterning of thoughts, feelings, and behaviors) and **individual differences** in dimensions of personality.

Psychodynamic Theories

2. Freud's theory of **psychodynamics** holds that psychological forces such as wishes, fears, and intentions determine behavior. His **topographic model** distinguished among **conscious, preconscious**, and **unconscious mental processes**. Freud argued that mental conflict is ubiquitous and that ambivalence—conflicting feelings or intentions—is the rule rather than the exception in human experience. The solutions people develop in an effort to maximize fulfillment of conflicting motives simultaneously are called **compromise formations**.

3. Freud's **drive**, or **instinct, model** views sex **(libido)** and aggression as the basic human motives. His **developmental model** proposed a series of **psychosexual stages**—stages in the development of personality and sexuality. These include the **oral, anal, phallic, latency**, and **genital stages**. Problematic experiences during a stage can lead to **fixations**—prominent conflicts and concerns that are focused on wishes from a particular period—or **regressions**, in which issues from a past stage resurface. During the phallic stage, the child must resolve the **Oedipus complex**, the desire for an exclusive, sensual/sexual relationship with the opposite-sex parent.

4. Freud's **structural model** distinguished among **id** (the reservoir of sexual and aggressive energy), **superego** (conscience), and **ego** (the rational part of the mind that must somehow balance desire, reality, and morality). Unconscious strategies aimed at minimizing unpleasant emotions or maximizing pleasant emotions are called **defense mechanisms**. Common defense mechanisms include **repression, denial, projection, reaction formation, sublimation, rationalization**, and **passive aggression**.

5. Object relations theories stress the role of representations of self and others in interpersonal functioning and the role of early experience in shaping the capacity for intimacy.

6. Psychodynamic approaches usually assess personality using **life history** and **projective methods**, such as the **Rorschach inkblot test** and Thematic Apperception Test (TAT), though they also use experimental procedures to test hypotheses.

Cognitive–Social Theories

7. Cognitive–social theories argue for the importance of encoding, personal value, expectancies, competencies, and self-regulation in personality. The schemas people use to encode and retrieve social information play an important role in personality.

8. **Personal value** refers to the importance individuals attach to various outcomes or potential outcomes. **Expectancies** are expectations relevant to desired outcomes. A **behavior–outcome expectancy** is a belief that a certain behavior will lead to a particular outcome. **Self-efficacy expectancies** are people's beliefs about their ability to perform actions necessary to produce a desired outcome. **Competences** are skills and abilities used to solve problems.

9. **Self-regulation** means setting goals, evaluating one's own performance, and adjusting one's behaviors to achieve goals in the context of ongoing feedback. Cognitive–social theories view personality as problem solving to attain goals.

Trait Theories

10. Trait theories are based on the concept of **traits**, emotional, cognitive, and behavioral tendencies that constitute underlying dimensions of personality on which individuals vary. Using factor analysis, different theorists have proposed different theories of the major factors that constitute personality.

11. Eysenck considers the major factors (which he calls *types*) to be **extroversion, neuroticism**, and **psychoticism**. The current consensus among trait psychologists is that personality consists of five traits, known as the *Big Five factors* or **Five Factor Model (FFM)** (openness to experience, conscientiousness, extroversion, agreeableness, and neuroticism).

12. The heritability of personality traits varies considerably; most are influenced by nature and nurture, but some are highly heritable, with heritability estimates often in the range of 15 to 50 percent.

13. A debate about the consistency of personality has raged for the past 30 years, sparked by Mischel's arguments against consistency. Mischel's work sensitized researchers to the complexities of **person-by-situation interactions**, in which personality processes become activated only in particular situations.

Humanistic Theories

14. **Humanistic** theories focus on aspects of personality that are distinctly human, not shared by other animals, such as how to find meaning in life and how to be true to oneself.

15. Rogers's **person-centered approach** aims at understanding individuals' **phenomenal experience**, that is, how they conceive of reality and experience themselves and their world. According to Rogers, individuals have a **true self** (a core aspect of being, untainted by the demands of those around them), which is often distorted into a **false self** by the desire to conform to social demands. When the **self-concept** diverges too much from the individual's **ideal self** (the person's view of what she should be like), she may distort the way she behaves or the way she sees herself to avoid this painful state of affairs. Psychological understanding requires **empathy**.

16. **Existential** personality theories stress the importance of subjective experience and the individual's quest for meaning in life. Chief among the problems human beings face is **existential dread**, the recognition that life has no absolute value or meaning and that death is inevitable. The ways people handle issues of meaning, mortality, and existential dread are central aspects of personality.

17. Substantial evidence supports the idea that much of personality is inherited. Studies of monozygotic and dyzygotic twins reared together and reared apart show evidence for the **heritability** of certain traits.

Personality and Culture

18. Some aspects of personality are probably universal, whereas others are culturally specific. The **culture pattern approach** sees personality primarily as an accommodation to culture. According to **interactionist approaches**, personality is shaped by economic and cultural demands, but cultural and economic processes themselves are in part created to fulfill psychological needs.

Key Terms

actualizing tendency   448
ambivalence   423
anal stage   426
behavior–outcome
    expectancy   436
castration complex   427
competences   437
compromise formations   424
conditions of worth   448
conflict   424
conscious mental processes   423
culture pattern approach   454
defense mechanisms   429
denial   429
developmental model   425
drive model   425
ego   428
empathy   448
existential dread   449
existentialism   448
expectancies   436

extroversion   441
false self   448
Five Factor Model (FFM)   441
fixations   426
genital stage   427
heritability   451
humanistic approaches   447
id   428
ideal self   448
identification   426
individual differences   421
instinct model   425
interactionist approaches   455
latency stage   427
libido   425
life history methods   431
life tasks   436
neuroticism   441
object relations   430
Oedipus complex   427
oral stage   425

passive aggression   429
penis envy   427
personal constructs   436
personality   421
personal value   436
person-by-situation
    interactions   446
person-centered approach   447
phallic stage   426
phenomenal experience   448
preconscious mental
    processes   423
primary process thinking   428
principle of aggregation   444
projection   429
projective tests   432
psychodynamics   422
psychosexual stages   425
psychoticism   441
rationalization   429

reaction formation   429
regression   426
relational theories   431
repression   429
Rorschach inkblot test   432
secondary process thinking   428
self-concept   448
self-efficacy expectancy   436
self-regulation   437
situational variables   443
structural model   428
structure of personality   421
sublimation   429
superego   428
temperament   444
topographic model   423
traits   440
true self   448
unconscious mental
    processes   423

Physical and Cognitive Development

 ear God,
I saw Saint Patrick's Church last week when we went to New York. You live in a nice house.

        Frank

Frank is a young child whose letter was part of a research project studying children's developing ideas about God (Heller, 1986, p. 16). As Frank's letter suggests, young children translate cultural concepts like God into their own "language." Frank converted the idea of the church as God's home into his own concrete notion of what constitutes a "nice house." Children's drawings similarly reveal the way they translate adult spiritual beliefs into "childese" (Figure 13.1).

In religious belief as in other areas, children frequently wrestle with concepts beyond their grasp, and their efforts reveal much about childish thought. Consider the mighty task faced by a six-year-old trying to make sense of the relation between Jesus and God in Christian theology: "Well, I know Jesus was a president and God is not...sort of like David was a king and God is not" (Heller, 1986, p. 40).

Whether children are reared Jewish, Baptist, Catholic, Muslim, or Hindu, their views of God, like their understanding of most objects of thought, are initially concrete. By the time they move into adolescence, they are likely to offer abstract conceptions, such as "God is a force within us all." If cultural conditions permit, they may also express considerable skepticism about religious notions, since they are able to imagine and reflect on a variety of possible realities.

Changes in the way children understand reality and cultural beliefs are a central focus of **developmental psychology**, *which studies the way humans develop and change over time*. For years, psychologists focused largely on childhood and adolescence and tended to consider development complete by the teenage years. More recently, however, psychologists have adopted a *life-span developmental perspective* that considers both constancy and change, and gains and losses in functioning, that occur at different points over the entire human life cycle (Baltes, 1998).

In this chapter, we first consider three issues that reverberate throughout all of developmental psychology: the roles of nature and nurture, the importance of early experience, and the extent to which development occurs in "stages." After addressing the question of how to study development, we focus on the central topics of this chapter: physical development and

FIGURE 13.1 Children's concepts of God. Children translate cultural beliefs into their own "language." In this picture, God is a man with a halo wearing a white smock. Another child, a preschooler, attributed the origins of the universe to "God, Mother Nature, and Mother Goose."

its impact on psychological functioning (e.g., how does an individual adapt to a changing body during puberty, menopause, or old age?), cognitive development (e.g., what can an infant remember?), and cognitive changes in adulthood (e.g., is "senility" the inevitable endpoint of development?). The acquisition of language and successively more complex thinking are also discussed.

Issues in Developmental Psychology

Nature and Nurture

Big Picture φ Question 6

What is the relation between nature and nurture in shaping psychological processes?

For almost as many years as psychologists have been interested in development, they have wrestled with the extent to which changes in individuals over time reflect the influence of genetically programmed maturation (nature) or of learning and experience (nurture). **Maturation** refers to *biologically based changes that follow an orderly sequence*, each step setting the stage for the next step according to an age-related timetable (Wesley & Sullivan, 1986). Infants crawl before they walk, and they utter single syllables and words before they talk in complete sentences. Unless reared in a profoundly deprived environment or physically impaired, virtually all human infants follow these developmental patterns in the same sequence and at roughly the same age, give or take a few months.

Most psychologists believe that development, like intelligence or personality, reflects the action and mutual influence of genes and environment (Loehlin et al., 1997; Plomin et al., 1994). Nature provides a fertile field for development, but this field requires cultivation. Thus, the question is not *which* is more important, nature or nurture, or even *how much* each contributes, but rather *how* nature and nurture contribute interactively to development (Anastasi, 1958).

In fact, in many respects the contrast of nature *versus* nurture is misplaced, because genetic blueprints do not express themselves without environmental input (Bors & Forrin, 1996; Gottlieb, 1991). Environmental events turn genes on and off. Thus, sensory stimulation is necessary for some genes to become activated, such as genes that shape the functioning of neurons in the occipital lobes involved in vision (Gottlieb et al., 1998).

Psychologists now distinguish between the *action* of genetic and environmental influences (i.e., the way they independently affect development) and two more complex nature–nurture linkages: their interaction and correlation (or *correlated* action). The *interaction* of heredity and environment occurs when the effect of having both genetic *and* environmental vulnerabilities is different from that which would be predicted by simply adding up their independent effects. For example, mounting evidence suggests that both genetic and environmental factors predict later development of anxiety disorders, but that the presence of *both* multiplies the likelihood of disorders (Chapter 15). Gene–environment *correlations* occur when genes influence the environments people choose or the experiences to which they are exposed. For example, a genetic propensity toward antisocial behavior can lead a teenager to choose "bad company," which in turn encourages further antisocial behavior.

The Importance of Early Experience

Before dawn on January 9, 1800, a remarkable creature came out of the woods near the village of Saint-Sernin in southern France.... He was human in bodily form and walked erect. Everything else about him suggested an animal. He was naked except for the tatters of a shirt and showed...no awareness of himself as a human person.... He could not speak and made only weird, meaningless cries. Though very short, he appeared to be a boy of about eleven or twelve, with a round face under dark matted hair. [From Shattuck, 1980, p. 5.]

The Wild Boy of Aveyron created an immediate sensation in Europe. To scientists, the child was a unique subject for exploring the question of **critical periods** in human development, *periods of special sensitivity to specific types of learning and sensory stimulation that shape the capacity for future development*. Would a boy who was raised, at best, by wolves be able to develop language, interact with other people, and develop a conscience? A young doctor named Jean-Marie Itard became the boy's tutor. Itard's efforts met with limited but nonetheless substantial success: The boy became affectionate and learned to respond to some verbal instructions, but he never learned to talk.

Evidence for Critical Periods The concept of critical periods initially came from embryology, as researchers discovered that toxic substances could affect the developing fetus but only if the fetus were exposed at very specific points in development. Critical periods in *psychological* development have been demonstrated in many animal species. The first few hours after hatching are a critical period for goslings. They are biologically prepared to follow whatever moving object they see, usually their mother (Lorenz, 1935).

The concept of critical periods in humans is more controversial. Can a child who does not experience nurturant caretaking in the first five years of life ever develop the capacity to love? Human development is more flexible than development in other animals, but the brain is in fact particularly sensitive to certain kinds of environmental input at certain times (see Bornstein, 1989). During some periods, the nervous system is most sensitive to forming new synapses between neurons, given the right environmental stimulus. Equally important is the pruning of neurons: Infants are born with an abundance of neural connections, and those that are not used or activated by the environment are gradually lost (Greenough, 1991).

Research on nonhuman animals has documented the importance of early environmental experience on the developing brain. In one study, researchers surgically closed the eyelids of newborn monkeys, depriving them of visual experience for their first 12 months (Carlson et al., 1987). Then, over the following 12 months, they tested the monkeys on visual tasks. Although the monkeys could perform some tasks, such as following a large object with their eyes, they had difficulty using vision as a guide in exploring their environment, as shown in Figure 13.2.

Big Picture φ Question 3

To what extent is human psychology continuous with the psychology of other animals?

Big Picture φ Question 7

To what extent are psychological processes conscious or unconscious—that is, explicit versus implicit?

  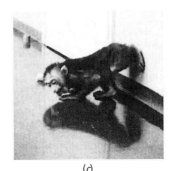 

(a) (b) (c) (d)

FIGURE 13.2 The importance of early environmental experience. Visually deprived monkeys showed a number of peculiarities in the way they explored their environments in the year following deprivation. Photo (*a*) shows a monkey carefully moving about the floor, in a "spider walk"; (*b*) shows a monkey anchoring itself to a chair while exploring with one hand; (*c*) shows similar anchoring to the wall; and (*d*) shows a monkey exploring the wall with its hands. Lacking early perceptual experience, these monkeys could not navigate their world visually.

Making Connections

Language acquisition is much easier in childhood than in adulthood, supporting the view that early experience is central in shaping some aspects of later psychological functioning. When people try to learn new languages as adults, they use different neural circuits than if they had learned the language at age 5 or 6, and they almost always speak with an accent (Chapter 7).

The Impact of Early Abuse or Deprivation   As we discussed in Chapter 3, the human brain, like that of other mammals, appears to have evolved with many innate potentials that require environmental input to activate. Given appropriate stimulation, most children will learn to speak, think, solve problems, and love in ways accepted and encouraged by their culture. In this view, the brain has essentially been "programmed" by natural selection to expect a range of input. That range is wide, but it is not infinite.

What happens to children whose experience is outside that range? As we will see later in this chapter, one famous case concerned a girl named Genie, who received almost no exposure to language from early in life until she was discovered at age 13 (Fromkin et al., 1974; Rymer, 1993). Like the Wild Boy of Aveyron, Genie learned some aspects of language, but her use of syntax never reached normal levels (Fromkin et al., 1974).

Other psychologists, however, have questioned whether the impact of early deprivation is so indelible (Kagan, 1984; Kagan & Zentner, 1996; Lerner, 1991). In one study, children who spent their first 19 months in an overcrowded and understaffed orphanage experienced average IQ gains of 28.5 points after being moved to an environment that provided individual care (Skeels, 1966). Even the case of Genie can be used to counter the notion of critical periods, since she demonstrated remarkable progress in social and intellectual skills in just a few short years (Kagan, 1984). On the other hand, after her initial gains, Genie's functioning stabilized and never approached the levels of a normal adolescent or adult, and she always remained socially awkward.

A similar pattern is emerging from data on severely deprived children from Romanian orphanages who were adopted before age 2 into homes in the United Kingdom: Although all children showed substantial improvement once they left the orphanage, the longer they experienced severe deprivation (e.g., for two years rather than just the first six months of life), the more severe their cognitive impairments remained four to six years later (O'Connor et al., 2000).

Does the evidence, then, support the notion of critical periods in humans? Probably the most appropriate conclusion to be reached at present is that humans have **sensitive periods**—*times that are more important to subsequent development than others*. In some domains, such as language, these sensitive periods may actually be critical; appropriate environmental input at certain points may be required or further development is permanently impaired. In most domains, however, sensitive periods are simply sensitive—particularly important but not decisive.

From Brain to Behavior The Gendered Brain

Our genetic sex is determined by whether we have two X chromosomes (female) or one X and one Y chromosome (male). The sexual phenotype (the interaction of genetics and the environment) can be influenced during the early stages of development. One example of this was the masculinization of a genetic female's brain if her mother took the drug diethylstibesterol (DES) to help reduce the negative symptoms of pregnancy. What does it mean to masculinize the brain? All of us, genetic males and genetic females, will develop a female brain if the brain is not organized to be masculine—that is, the organization of the brain for gender (sex) in terms of whether at puberty the brain releases sex hormones in a cyclical pattern (the menstrual cycle for females) or noncyclical pattern (the male condition) depends on exposure to sex hormones early in development.

If a mistake occurs, due to one of many different events during development, the brain may remain feminine in a genetic male, or masculine in a genetic female. The female children of mothers who took DES had their brain masculinized: when they reached the age of puberty, they did not start their menstrual periods, because the brain had been masculinized and did not release the sex hormones in a cyclical pattern. Unfortunately, the brain is organized at a critical period, and once that critical period is over the brain is set in its ways. It cannot be changed, at least with the current stage of medical understanding.

Simon LeVay has published some highly controversial data in which he measured the size of the lateral preoptic (LPO) area of the hypothalamus in gay men. Males in general have a smaller LPO than females. The LPOs of the gay men were similar in size to a female's LPO. Does this mean that the LPO determines our sexual identity? Perhaps, or perhaps not. Because the LPO was measured in postmortem tissue, researchers cannot determine whether the LPO was smaller from birth, or if a gay lifestyle altered the size of the LPO. In other words, they cannot untangle which is cause and which is effect.

Do such changes mean that the individual's sexual identity is affected? Perhaps. As with all individuals, however, sexual identity depends in part on how many X chromosomes you have, the organization of the brain that occurs during early development, and the rearing conditions (i.e., if little boys are dressed as girls, etc.). Further, other genes may influence sexual preference: Genes that are not located on the X or Y chromosome, but influence our behavior in ways similar to shyness, intelligence, and aggressiveness. Thus, one's choice of partner is not determined by any one factor, but by multiple factors, from genetic to environmental.

Stages or Continuous Change?

The third basic issue in development concerns the nature of developmental change. According to one view, development occurs in **stages**, *relatively discrete steps through which everyone progresses in the same sequence*. Behavior in one stage is not just *quantitatively* different from the next, involving a little less or more of something, but *qualitatively* different. As we will see, a stage theorist might suggest that the ability to engage in abstract thinking is a novel development in adolescence—not just a gradual refinement of the way younger children think—and that this qualitative difference may reflect maturation of the frontal cortex.

An alternative perspective sees development as *continuous*, characterized less by major transformations than by steady and gradual change. From this point of view, what may look like a massive change, such as becoming literate between the ages of 5 and 8 or rebellious at 13, may actually reflect a slow and steady process of learning at school or increased reinforcement for independent behavior. Although the behavioral change may appear to be a new stage, in fact, it may have been practiced, and be making an appearance only when "practice has made perfect."

Many theorists suggest that development involves both stages and continuous processes (Bidell & Fischer, 1992, 2000; Piaget, 1972). Stagelike phenomena are much more obvious in childhood, when the nervous system is maturing. As individuals move into adulthood, they are likely to develop in a number of alternative directions, many of which vary substantially by culture (e.g., whether a culture has a concept of "retirement").

INTERIM SUMMARY

Developmental psychology studies the way humans develop and change over time. Nature and nurture both contribute to development, and their roles are not easily separated because environmental events often turn genes on and off. Human development is characterized by **critical periods** (periods central to specific types of learning that modify future development) or **sensitive periods** (times that are particularly important but not definitive for subsequent development), and whether development occurs in **stages** (relatively discrete steps through which everyone progresses in the same sequence) or is continuous (involving steady and gradual change) is still a matter under discussion.

Studying Development

At first glance, studying development might seem relatively straightforward: To see if 5- and 10-year-olds differ in working memory capacity or in the way they form relationships with peers, simply collect a sample at each age and see how differently they respond. In fact, however, matters are more complex. Psychologists primarily use three types of research designs to study development: cross-sectional, longitudinal, and sequential.

Cross-Sectional Studies

Cross-sectional studies *compare groups of subjects of different ages at a single time to see whether differences exist among them*. For example, a research group in Georgia is studying centenarians—people who have reached 100 years of age—to compare them on a number of dimensions with people in their 60s and 80s (Poon et al., 1992). Cross-sectional studies are useful for providing a snapshot of *age differences*, or variations among people of different ages.

The major limitation of cross-sectional studies is that they do not directly assess *age changes*, that is, changes within the same individuals that occur with age. As a result, they are vulnerable to confounding variables (Chapter 2), such as cultural change. For example, the Georgian centenarian researchers recognized that one of their groups of subjects grew up in the South shortly after the Civil War, another during World War I, and the third during the Great Depression and World War II. These different historical experiences could profoundly influence differences among the three *cohorts* (groups of people born around the same time) (Elder, 1998). Cultural changes in education, mass communication, and nutrition could also have a profound impact on people's later ways of thinking and acting. Cross-sectional studies are most useful when **cohort effects**—*differences among age groups associated with differences in the culture*—are minimal, as when assessing differences in the self-concepts of four- and six-year-olds.

Longitudinal Studies

Longitudinal studies *assess the same individuals over time*, providing the opportunity to assess age changes rather than age differences. The advantage of longitudinal studies is their ability to reveal differences *among* individuals as well as changes *within* individuals over time. Thus, longitudinal research can examine whether the same person becomes more or less conservative or experiences changes in memory, over time.

Like cross-sectional designs, longitudinal designs are vulnerable to cohort effects. Because they investigate only one cohort, they cannot rule out the possibility that people born at a different time might show different developmental paths or trajectories. For example, the data from four longitudinal studies of gifted women at midlife showed that gifted women born after 1940 scored higher on all measures of psychological well-being than gifted women born before that time (Schuster, 1990). The impact of giftedness on women's well-being appears to depend in part on cultural attitudes toward women's intelligence and opportunities for achievement.

Sequential Studies

Sequential studies *minimize cohort effects by studying multiple cohorts longitudinally*. In an ideal sequential design, researchers study a group of people at one age and follow them up over time. As the study progresses, a new, younger cohort is added

Apply & Discuss

A team of researchers interested in the development of children's comfort with computers conducts the following study. They ask 30 third graders, 30 ninth graders, and 30 60-year-olds to solve a set of crossword puzzles on a PC. Then they ask them to rate how comfortable they felt solving the problems and how comfortable they would have felt solving them on paper. They find that all three groups show relatively similar levels of comfort solving the problems on the PC, but the 60-year-olds report a slight preference for doing crossword puzzles on paper.

▪ What kind of design is this: cross-sectional, longitudinal, or sequential?

▪ What can the investigators conclude?

▪ What can they not conclude, and why?

Table 13.1 ■ ■	Example of a Sequential Study, Controlling for Age and Calendar Year				
Cohort 1	Age 3	Age 6	Age 9		
	Cohort 2	Age 3	Age 6	Age 9	
		Cohort 3	Age 3	Age 6	Age 9
Year	2000	2003	2006	2009	2012

to the study, beginning at the same age at which the first cohort began. Essentially, a sequential design combines cross-sectional and longitudinal comparisons, allowing researchers to distinguish between age effects (differences associated with age) and cohort effects. The design in Table 13.1 shows how the effects of 9/11 on children's development could be controlled for by staggering the study of the changes between age 3 and 9 across three cohorts, one beginning before 9/11, the other two beginning after 9/11. Only those changes that occurred in all three cohorts, independent of current events such as 9/11, would be considered to be consistent markers of development.

Sequential designs solve most of the problems of both cross-sectional and longitudinal designs, but they have one catch: They take years or decades to complete. The moral of the story is that, ideally, psychologists should live a long time; conduct sequential studies, preferably in several cultures; and find successors to carry on their research after they are dead. Short of that, researchers should (and do) try to use the best methods at their disposal and remain aware of the methodological limitations on the generalizability of their results.

INTERIM SUMMARY

Cross-sectional studies compare groups of subjects of different ages at a single time to provide a picture of age *differences*. **Longitudinal studies** assess the same individuals over time, providing the opportunity to assess age *changes*. **Sequential studies** minimize **cohort effects** by studying multiple cohorts longitudinally.

Physical Development and Its Psychological Consequences

Having examined some of the basic issues and methods of developmental psychology, we turn now to physical development and its impact on psychological functioning. Many of those changes are obvious even to the untrained eye. Children develop rapidly during the early years, outgrowing clothes before wearing them out. Some of the most dramatic aspects of physical development, however, cannot be observed directly, because they take place before birth.

Prenatal Development

One of the most remarkable aspects of development is that a single cell, forged by the union of a sperm and an egg, contains the blueprint for an organism that will emerge—complete with billions of specialized cells—nine months later. The *prenatal period* (before birth, also called the *gestation period*) is divided into three stages (Figure 13.3). During the *germinal period* (approximately the first two weeks after conception),

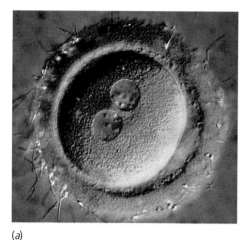

(a)

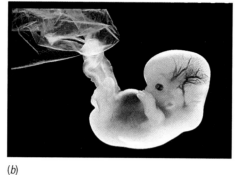

(b)

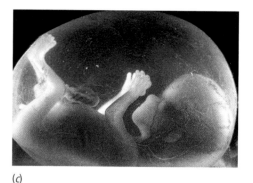

(c)

FIGURE 13.3 Prenatal development. The photo in (a) shows a fertilized egg surrounded by sperm. Photo (b) shows a six-week-old embryo. Only eight weeks later (c), the fetus is recognizably human.

Big Picture φ Question 3

To what extent is human psychology continuous with the psychology of other animals?

the fertilized egg becomes implanted in the uterus. The *embryonic period* (from the beginning of the third week to about the eighth week of gestation) is the most important period in the development of the central nervous system and of the organs. By the end of this stage, the features of the embryo become recognizably human, the rudiments of most organs have formed, and the heart has begun to beat. During the *fetal period* (from about nine weeks to birth), muscular development is rapid. By about 28 weeks, the fetus is capable of sustaining life on its own. (The term *fetus* is often used more broadly to refer to the organism between conception and birth.)

Mothers often sense that their child is "willful" or has a "personality" before birth. In part, this undoubtedly reflects vivid maternal imagination. Recent research suggests, however, that fetuses of many species can behave and even learn *in utero* (prenatally) (Smotherman & Robinson, 1996). Inserting a nipple into the mouth of a rat fetus produces the same sucking responses seen in newborns. Rat fetuses (in utero) can also learn to associate one stimulus with another through classical conditioning as shown by the acquisition of a learned taste aversion to apple juice injected into the amniotic fluid, when paired with a chemical (LiCl) that causes nausea. Similarly, given the appropriate environment the fetus can learn to press a miniature paddle to get milk delivered into its mouth.

In a sense, these findings should not surprise us. When a child of any species is born, it has to be ready to respond to features of its environment—that it can eat, for example. The ways human children "behave" in utero are also highly predictive of the ways they will behave once they are born (DiPietro et al., 1996a). For example, fetuses that are more active in the womb tend to be more active and difficult babies at six months.

Environmental Influences on Prenatal Development   Understanding the stages of prenatal development is important to every expectant parent, because at different stages the developing fetus is susceptible to different dangers at different points. **Teratogens *are environmental agents that harm the embryo or fetus*.** They include drugs, radiation, viruses that cause maternal illness such as rubella (German measles), and toxic chemicals. Cigarette smoking during pregnancy, for example, has been linked to a wide range of negative outcomes, ranging from cognitive deficits in childhood to criminality in adulthood (Brennan et al., 1999; Day et al., 2000).

One of the most widespread teratogens is alcohol. In the 1970s, researchers identified fetal alcohol syndrome (FAS), a serious condition affecting up to half the babies born to alcoholic mothers (Jones et al., 1973). Babies with FAS are born with numerous physical deformities and a wide range of mental abnormalities, including learning disabilities, behavior problems, and attention difficulties (Steinhausen et al., 1993; Streissguth et al., 1985, 1989).

Whether any amount of maternal alcohol ingestion is dangerous or whether alcohol use must cross some threshold is a matter of controversy (see Knupfer, 1991; Passaro & Little, 1997). Research with rhesus monkeys finds that even moderate exposure to alcohol (the monkey equivalent of one to two drinks a day) during pregnancy produces subtle deficits in attention and motor abilities in infant monkeys (Schneider et al., 1997). The most recent research suggests that women who are trying to conceive or who know they are pregnant would do well to abstain from alcohol (Braun, 1996). The teratogenic effect appears to be highest in the early weeks of pregnancy, often before the woman knows she is pregnant, and increases with greater consumption (Barr et al., 1990).

Another increasingly prevalent teratogen is crack cocaine (Inciardi et al., 1997). Prenatal cocaine exposure carries risk of premature birth, malformed internal organs, withdrawal symptoms, respiratory problems, delayed motor development, and death (Arendt et al., 1996; Bendersky & Lewis, 1998). "Crack babies" tend to be triply exposed: to the teratogenic effect of cocaine prenatally, to neglectful parenting postnatally, and to poverty and environmental hazards throughout childhood.

One last teratogen is worth noting: maternal stress. Researchers have known for some time that children whose mothers were under significant stress during pregnancy tend to have more problems with attention and motor development. Recent research with rhesus monkeys, who are genetically similar to humans (although I still wouldn't marry one), suggests that the first trimester is a sensitive period during which maternal stress affects the developing nervous system, with decreasing effects through the second trimester (Schneider et al., 1999).

INTERIM SUMMARY

The *prenatal*, or *gestational*, period is a time of rapid physical and neurological growth that can be disrupted by exposure to **teratogens**, harmful environmental agents that damage the embryo or fetus. One of the most prevalent teratogens is alcohol. Maternal alcohol abuse can lead to *fetal alcohol syndrome (FAS)*, but increasing evidence suggests that even moderate levels of drinking can impair the developing child. During gestation, neurons develop at the rate of hundreds of thousands per minute. Development continues for years thereafter and also involves considerable pruning of potential neural connections that are not strengthened by environmental input.

Infancy

When asked about their babies, parents almost uniformly begin with motor milestones, such as "Jennifer can sit up now by herself" or "Now that Brandon is crawling, I have to babyproof everything in the house" (Thelen, 1995). How infants move from flailing bundles of flesh to willful little creatures with radar for breakable objects reflects a complex mixture of nature and nurture (Bertenthal & Clifton, 1998; Thelen, 1995; Thelen & Smith, 1994).

At birth, an infant possesses many adaptive reflexes. For example, the *rooting reflex* helps ensure that the infant will get nourishment: When touched on the cheek, an infant will turn her head and open her mouth, ready to suck. The *sucking reflex* is similarly adaptive: Infants suck rhythmically in response to stimulation 3 or 4 centimeters inside their mouths. Many early reflexes disappear within the first six or seven months, as infants gain more control over their movements. In general, motor skills progress from head to toe: Infants first master movements of the head, then the trunk and arms, and finally the legs (Rallison, 1986).

Motor development in infancy follows a universal sequence, from smiling, turning the head, and rolling over, to creeping, walking with support, and ultimately standing alone and walking unaided (Figure 13.4). Nevertheless, cross-cultural evidence suggests that environmental stimulation can affect the *pace* of development.

Big Picture φ Question 6

What is the relation between nature and nurture in shaping psychological processes?

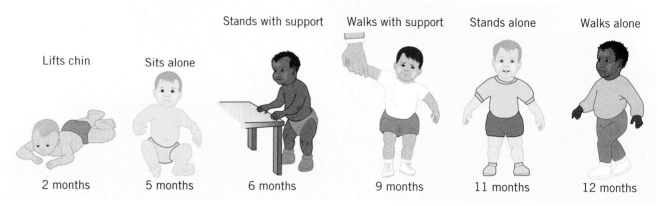

Stands with support Walks with support Stands alone Walks alone

Lifts chin Sits alone

2 months 5 months 6 months 9 months 11 months 12 months

FIGURE 13.4 Milestones in infant motor development. The maturational sequence of motor development is universal, although the age at which skills are acquired varies. This figure shows average ages at which children reach these milestones. *Source:* Adapted from Frankenburg and Dodds, 1967.

The Kipsigis of Kenya teach their infants to sit, stand, and walk at an early age. At five or six months, infants are placed in a specially constructed hole in the ground that supports them while they sit upright, and at seven or eight months, their mothers hold them either under the arms or by the hands to help them practice walking. As a result, Kipsigi infants walk at a considerably earlier age than North American infants (Super, 1981).

In North America and the rest of the West, pediatricians are finding that infants are now walking even later than they did 25 years ago. To help prevent death from Sudden Infant Death Syndrome (SIDS), a disease in which the immature brain stem fails to "jump start" and the infant stops breathing, parents are instructed to put infants to bed on their backs (rather than stomachs) to sleep. An unintended consequence is that infants accustomed to lying on their backs develop crawling skills (and leg muscles) more slowly—and hence walk later.

Childhood and Adolescence

Some of the most important maturational changes that influence psychological development involve changes in the size and shape of the body. A remarkable aspect of human development is the extent to which children can maintain the sense that they are the same person over time despite massive changes in the sheer size of their bodies and the shape of their faces.

Growth rates for girls and boys are roughly equal until about age 10. At that point, girls begin a growth spurt that usually peaks at age 12, and boys typically follow suit about two or three years later. Individuals of both sexes vary, however, in the age at which they enter **puberty**, *the time at which they become capable of reproduction*. Girls usually experience the onset of menstruation (known as *menarche*) at about age 11 to 13. For boys mature sperm production is somewhat later, about 14.5 years (Rallison, 1986).

Unusually early or late maturation tends to affect boys and girls differently. Boys whose growth spurt comes early are more likely to excel at athletics and be more popular, relaxed, and high in status than late-maturing boys. For girls, early onset of puberty tends to be associated with greater distress and delinquency than later maturation (Caspi et al., 1993; Dick et al., 2000; Ge et al., 1996). Parents report more conflict with early-maturing than late-maturing daughters but less conflict with early-maturing than late-maturing sons (Ge et al., 1996; Savin-Williams & Small, 1986).

Early maturation in girls may not only be a cause of stress in their families but also a consequence of it: Stressful homes tend to trigger the physiological mecha-

Big Picture φ Question 4

To what extent is human nature particular versus universal?

Big Picture φ Question 5

To what extent are psychological processes the same in men and women?

nisms that initiate puberty; so, too, does the presence of a male living in the home other than the girl's biological father, such as a stepfather (Ellis & Garber, 2000).

INTERIM SUMMARY

At birth, infants possess many adaptive reflexes, such as rooting and sucking, which help ensure that the infant will get nourishment. Individuals vary in the age at which they enter **puberty**, the stage during which they become capable of reproduction. Early pubertal development tends to be associated with positive outcomes for boys but negative outcomes for girls.

Adulthood and Aging

By the end of adolescence, physical growth is virtually complete, and the changes that occur thereafter tend to be gradual and less dramatic. People often gain a few centimeters in height and several more centimeters in fat between ages 18 and 28—and many more centimeters in fat with middle age. By their 30s, people are already deteriorating physically, with muscular strength and sensory abilities showing subtle but clear signs of decline (see Spence, 1989; Spirduso & MacRae, 1990).

Individuals differ tremendously, however, in the extent and pace of these changes, as some 80-year-olds run marathons in seniors' track meets. Whether the variable is muscle strength or intellectual ability, the rule of thumb is *use it or lose it*: Both mental and physical capacities atrophy with disuse.

Menopause　For women perhaps the most dramatic physical change of middle adulthood is *menopause,* the cessation of the menstrual cycle. Menopause usually begins in the 40s or 50s and may last several years; in Western cultures, the average age is 51 (Riley, 1991). The clinical definition of menopause is 5 consecutive years without a menstrual period. Since most women now live into their 70s or 80s, the postmenopausal period encompasses roughly a third of their lives.

Some women consider menopause to be traumatic because of the loss of the capacity for childbearing and symptoms such as "hot flashes," "night sweats," aching joints, and irritability. However, research now suggests that only the minority of women experience menopause as traumatic (Matthews, 1992). Many women enjoy the increased freedom from monthly periods and birth control. Moreover, most of the uncomfortable symptoms can be alleviated medically with hormone replacement therapy (HRT), which compensates for the ovaries' reduced estrogen production (Freedman, 2002; Rymer et al., 2003; Sherwin, 1993; Stewart & Robinson, 1997). Although controversial, because the HRT can lead to certain cancers, it also helps to prevent or reduce the symptoms of osteoporosis and Alzheimer's.

Making Connections

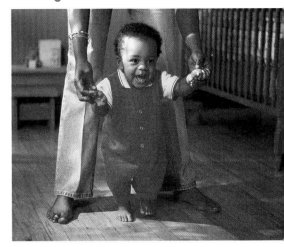

Similar to connectionist models in cognitive science, contemporary models suggest that movement involves the simultaneous coordination of multiple processes outside awareness, as the brain settles on solutions that solve problems (such as how to sip from a cup) by adapting and combining preexisting skills (Chapter 7).

Whereas psychologists once believed that the development of motor control was mostly a matter of maturation of physical "equipment," today they recognize that "simple" feats such as walking uphill and downhill require very different muscles, and infants have to learn how to adjust their gait continuously as they move across a surface that is not absolutely level (Thelen, 1995).

Menopause in a Mayan Village　A Global Vista

Big Picture φ Question 4

To what extent is human nature particular versus universal?

Because menopause is both a physiological and a psychological event, its impact on a woman reflects an interplay of biological processes and personal expectations (Robinson, 1996). Women who expect menopause to be very distressing tend to have more symptoms (Matthews, 1992), and many of these expectations depend on culture. Indeed, the experience of menopause differs substantially across cultures.

One researcher studied 100 pre-, peri- (i.e., during), and postmenopausal women in a rural Mayan Indian village in Yucatan, Mexico (Beyene, 1986). Mayan women marry and begin having children in their teens. They are frequently grandmothers in their 30s, and the onset of menopause typically occurs in the 30s or early 40s. As in many traditional societies, old age is a period of power and respect, particularly for women, who become the head of the extended family households of their married sons.

The Mayans believe that menstruating women carry danger. Women, therefore, stay home during their menstrual periods to avoid contaminating other people, particularly newborn babies. Not surprisingly, Mayan women are glad when menopause lifts the restrictions and taboos. Premenopausal women reported looking forward to menopause and did not expect any adverse physical or psychological effects. Peri- and postmenopausal women, like others in the community, were unfamiliar with the concept of hot flashes, and local physicians, midwives, and healers reported that they had never treated any women of the village for menopause-related symptoms.

The absence of a common physical symptom of menopause, hot flashes, could be attributed to many causes, from the psychological to the physical (such as bearing a large number of babies and early onset of menopause). Cross-cultural research suggests that the presence of hot flashes varies tremendously from culture to culture. Fifty to 80 percent of European and North American women report hot flashes, whereas these experiences are unusual in Japan and India (Hulka & Meirik, 1996; Robinson, 1996). The experience of menopause among the Mayans underscores the role of culture in shaping what may at first seem strictly a matter of biological maturation.

A profile of middle age?

Midlife Changes in Men   The term male menopause is part of the American vernacular, although male reproductive ability does not undergo any specific or dramatic period of physical change. Healthy men can produce sperm and engage in sexual activity as long as they live, although male sexuality does change gradually with age. Sexual desire from the 40s to the 70s shows substantial declines as testosterone levels drop (Schiavi et al., 1990; see also Chapter 10). The ability to sense touch and vibration in the penis also diminishes with age and is correlated with reduced sexual activity (see Johnson & Murray, 1992). As with women, however, individual differences are substantial, and men can enjoy sexuality through their 90s if they live that long and have an available partner. (In fact, men in retirement communities often report very active sex lives because the ratio of women to men in old age is so high!) Contrary to youthful stereotypes, masturbation is also a lifelong affair for many men and women (Gibson, 1996).

Later Life   As in childhood, some of the most apparent signs of aging are in physical appearance, such as wrinkled skin and gray hair. Sensory changes are also substantial. Older adults have reduced sensitivity to visual contrasts—for example, climbing stairs can be difficult because they have trouble seeing where one step ends and another begins (Fozard, 1990). Older adults also take a longer time adapting to the dark, which can cause problems driving at night, as oncoming headlights may create temporary flashes of brightness (*AARP News Bulletin*, 1989). Hearing loss is also common. Many older people experience **presbycusis**, *the inability to hear high-frequency sounds* (Fozard, 1990; Spence, 1989), which can make hearing the telephone ring or understanding high-pitched voices more difficult.

The inability to understand what others are saying can have disturbing psychological consequences. We often lose patience with older adults who constantly ask others to repeat what they have said. Younger people may also inadvertently treat older individuals with hearing loss condescendingly, simplifying their communications instead of speaking more loudly or distinctly.

Deterioration in certain areas of functioning is an inevitable part of aging, but development throughout the life span is characterized by gains as well as losses (Baltes, 1997). Many Western images of the elderly stem from negative cultural myths and stereotypes, such as the idea that sexuality ends in the 40s or 50s or that senility is inevitable. *Gerontologists*—scientists who study the elderly—refer to such stereotypes as examples of **ageism**, or *prejudice against old people* (Butler, 1969; Schaie, 1988). Although not all negative attitudes toward aging represent prejudice (older people do, for example, tend to have less physical and mental speed than younger people), ageism can lead not only to condescending treatment of the elderly ("How are *we* today, Mrs. Jones?") but also to employment discrimination.

Experimental evidence suggests that people in the West process information about the aged in a negative way automatically, without conscious awareness (Perdue & Gurtman, 1990). Using a priming procedure (Chapter 6), investigators in one study presented college students with 18 positive adjectives (such as *skillful* and *helpful*) and 18 negative adjectives (such as *clumsy* and *impolite*) on a computer screen. Immediately prior to presenting each adjective, the computer screen randomly flashed the word *old* or *young* briefly enough to register but too briefly to be recognized consciously. The investigators measured participants' reaction time (in milliseconds) in identifying whether each word was positive or negative.

If people differentially associate old and young with positive and negative traits, then flashing "young" should facilitate responding about positive words, while "old" should reduce reaction time in identifying negative words. In fact, participants were quicker to identify negative traits when presented with "old" and substantially faster in identifying positive traits when presented with "young" (Figure 13.5).

INTERIM SUMMARY

With aging comes a gradual decline in physical abilities, including muscular strength, sensory functioning, and reaction time. People differ tremendously, however, in their physical competence throughout life. The rule-of-thumb is *use it or lose it*. For women, the most dramatic physical change of middle adulthood is menopause; for men, sexuality changes more gradually. Deterioration in certain areas of functioning is an inevitable part of aging, but the extent of deterioration in part reflects internalization of **ageist** stereotypes.

Big Picture φ Question 7

To what extent are psychological processes conscious or unconscious—that is, explicit versus implicit?

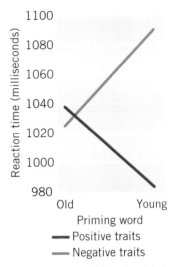

FIGURE 13.5 Implicit ageism. Priming subjects with "old" led to slightly decreased reaction time in identifying negative words. In contrast, priming with "young" markedly facilitated identification of positive traits in comparison to negative ones. *Source:* Perdue & Gurtman, 1990, p. 21.

Cognitive Development in Infancy, Childhood, and Adolescence

In a study performed three decades ago, three- and six-year-old children petted a good-natured cat named Maynard (DeVries, 1969). When asked what kind of animal Maynard was, every child responded correctly. In plain sight of the children, the researcher then put a dog mask on Maynard and again asked whether Maynard was a dog or a cat. Unlike the older children, the three-year old children were confused: Most of them said Maynard was now a dog!

How do children learn that physical entities, such as their pets, parents, or teddy bears, remain constant over time? This is the kind of question explored by psychologists who study cognitive development. We begin by describing perceptual and cognitive development in infancy and then examine the ways psychologists have conceptualized cognitive development through adolescence.

Perceptual and Cognitive Development in Infancy

For many years, psychologists underestimated the cognitive capacities of infants (Bower, 1982). With neither motor control nor the ability to describe what they are thinking, newborn infants do not appear to be a particularly impressive lot. Infants also have notoriously short attention spans, falling asleep so frequently that a researcher must schedule two hours of laboratory time for every five minutes of useful experimental time (Butterworth, 1978)!

New Methods, New Discoveries A very different picture of infancy has emerged, however, as methods to study it have become more sophisticated. Three decades ago, psychologists discovered that they could learn about infant perception and cognition by taking advantage of the *orienting reflex*, the tendency of humans, even from birth, to pay more attention to novel stimuli than to stimuli to which they have become *habituated*, or grown accustomed (Fantz et al., 1975). Thus, even though a picture of a face might hold an infant's attention at first, after repeated exposures, the infant will show much less interest.

By recording the amount of time an infant looks at visual stimuli (i.e., the infant's *fixation time*), researchers can tell when an infant is discriminating between two objects, such as the face of its mother and the face of another woman. For example, if researchers present infants with pictures of cats and horses and then show them novel examples of these categories (e.g., a kind of cat they have not seen before), 10-month-olds will consistently discriminate the two kinds of animals, but 7-month-olds will not (Younger & Fearing, 1999). Thus, we know that by 10 months infants are already forming basic-level categories for animals (Chapter 7).

Researchers have subsequently found other ways of assessing infants' knowledge, such as measuring brain wave activity: Certain waveforms assessed by EEG (Chapter 2) indicate when an infant differentiates between an old stimulus and a new one. Also, because infants prefer novelty, with the use of a simple conditioning procedure they can be conditioned to suck in response to novel stimuli. Sucking rate decreases as the infant habituates to a stimulus (i.e., gets used to it and stops responding; Chapter 5) and increases with the presentation of a new one. Thus, researchers can answer some very subtle questions about infant perception, memory, and cognition. For example, can infants form abstractions of concepts such as *ball*? Will they habituate quickly to a red ball they have never seen if they have previously habituated to blue and yellow balls—a response implying that they "get" the general concept of a ball?

Apply & Discuss

The attention infants pay to various objects in their environment is not arbitrary. Infants pay particular attention to human faces and objects with qualities similar to faces—objects that move, are complex, are skin colored, and produce sounds (Siegler, 1991).

▪ From an evolutionary perspective, how might the tendency to focus on faces have evolved?

▪ What advantages would this tendency have conferred on infants over the course of human evolution?

▪ What kinds of information do faces convey?

What Can Infants Sense and Perceive? Infants are born with many sensory capabilities, some better developed than others, such as the sense of hearing. Even before birth, fetal heart rate and movements increase in response to loud sounds, and habituation studies in newborns show that infants hear and recognize their mother's voices before they are born, despite a wall of flesh and an earful of amniotic fluid.

By contrast, vision is not well developed at birth. The visual cortex, retina, and some other structures are still immature (Candy et al., 1998). At birth, visual acuity is estimated to be approximately 20/500 (i.e., an object 20 feet away looks as clear as an object 500 feet away would look to an adult), but it improves to about 20/100 by six months (Dobson & Teller, 1978). Infants focus best on objects between 7 and 8 inches away—approximately the distance between a nursing infant and its mother's face.

Intermodal Understanding Sensory processing occurs in anatomically discrete neural modules (Chapter 4). Thus, when infants hear their mothers talking and see their mouths moving, different circuits in the brain become active. How and when do infants connect these sights and sounds? Do infants associate the voice with the visual image, or is the world like a dubbed movie, with lips moving and people talking out of sync? And do infants *learn* to make these connections across sensory modes, or are these capacities innate?

Research over the last 25 years suggests that infants are far more capable of **intermodal processing**—*the ability to associate sensations of an object from different senses or to match their own actions to behaviors they have observed visually*—than anyone would have expected. Infants show some recognition of the relation between sights and sounds even minutes after birth, turning their eyes toward the direction of a sound (Bower, 1982; Wertheimer, 1961). By three months infants pay more attention to a person if speech sounds are synchronized with lip movements (Dodd, 1979; Kuhl & Meltzoff, 1988). By four to five months, they follow a conversation by shifting visual attention between two speakers (Horner & Chethik, 1986). Thus, they recognize not only *features* of objects from different senses but also the temporal order of those features—that is, that events across different senses unfold over time, such as lips moving and sounds of particular sorts coming out of them (Bahrick & Lickliter, 2000; Lewkowicz, 2000).

In one study, infants appeared to know by sight something they had explored by touch (Meltzoff, 1990). One-month-old infants sucked on one of two kinds of pacifiers—smooth, or with nubs—exploring them with their lips and tongues (Figure 13.6). The experimenters then visually presented similar objects constructed from orange Styrofoam, reasoning that the infants would fixate on the stimulus they had sucked. In fact, of 32 infants tested, 24 stared longer at the shape they had sucked, demonstrating that they knew with their eyes what they had felt with their mouths. In another study, newborns between 12 and 21 days old were able to imitate the facial gestures of an adult (Figure 13.7) (Meltzoff & Moore, 1977).

How does an infant—who has no idea what a tongue is—recognize that she can move her own as an adult model does? Although such capacities are probably in large measure innate, since they have been demonstrated in children as young as *42 minutes* old and in many other species (Lewkowicz, 2000), research with other animals suggests that they may also depend in part on experience in utero (Lickliter & Bahrick, 2000).

Perceiving Meaning   Infants may perceive more than psychologists once imagined, but do they attribute meaning to the objects they perceive? According to *ecological* theorists, who understand perception in its environmental, adaptive context, they do

FIGURE 13.6   Stimuli used for tactile exploration. One-month-old infants sucked on one of two pacifiers like those depicted here. Later, they explored similar objects with their eyes. Most stared longer at the shape they had sucked, demonstrating that they knew with their eyes what they had felt with their mouths. *Source:* From Meltzoff & Borton (1979).

Big Picture φ Question 6

What is the relation between nature and nurture in shaping psychological processes?

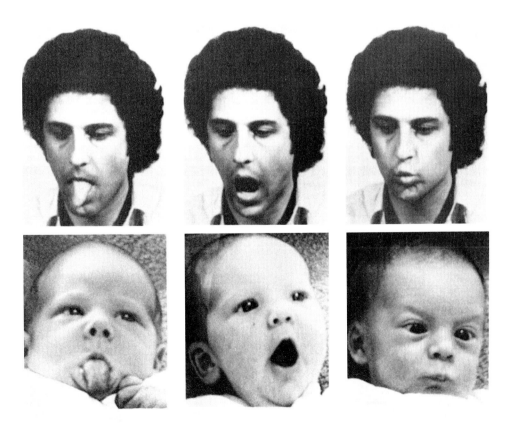

FIGURE 13.7   Imitation in infants. These photographs, published in 1977, show two- to three-week-old infants imitating the facial gestures of an adult. Infants who observed an adult sticking out his tongue were more likely to stick out their own tongues, while those who observed other facial movements, such as opening the mouth, were more likely to perform those behaviors.

FIGURE 13.8 Looming objects. Infants show distress and defensive responses to looming objects as early as two weeks of age. Because they would not yet have had the opportunity to associate a looming object with the risk of being hit, many psychologists consider their response evidence of innate knowledge. *Source:* Adapted from Bower, 1971.

Big Picture φ Question 7

To what extent are psychological processes conscious or unconscious—that is, explicit versus implicit?

(Gibson, 1984; 1964). Ecological theorists argue that the nervous system is wired to recognize certain dangers, and to recognize the potential "value" of some stimuli, without prior learning (Chapter 4).

Ecological researchers have used looming-object studies to demonstrate their point (Figure 13.8). As an alert infant sits in a seat, an object suddenly begins moving directly toward the infant at a constant rate. The object may be real, such as the box shown in the figure, or it may be an expanding shadow. As early as two weeks after birth, infants show a defensive response to the looming object, drawing their heads back, jerking their hands in front of their faces, and showing distress (Bower, 1971).

What Can Infants Remember? *Most people completely lack explicit memory for events before age 3 or 4*, a phenomenon known as **infantile amnesia**. This does not imply, however, that experience is lost on infants and young children. What infants remember varies considerably depending on the task and reflects in large part the maturation of neural circuits involved in different kinds of memory (Meltzoff, 1995; Nelson, 1995; Newcombe et al., 1995).

For example, various forms of implicit memory are present from birth. In one study, six-month-olds exposed once to a stimulus responded faster to it *two years later* than peers not previously exposed to it (Perris et al., 1990). Infants as young as three months old who have been conditioned to kick their legs to make a mobile move will begin kicking their legs sooner than other infants several weeks later, demonstrating implicit memory about the relation between the behavior and its consequence (Rovee-Collier, 1990). Some intriguing recent research finds few differences at all between implicit learning in children as young as age 4 and adults, suggesting that the machinery of implicit learning and memory may be "up and running" very early (Vinter & Perruchet, 2000).

The rudiments of *explicit* memory are also present from birth, but more complete development of explicit memory depends on maturation of the hippocampi and the temporal lobes sometime between 8 and 18 months (Nelson, 1995). In the earliest days of life, infants prefer novel words to those to which they habituated a day before, suggesting recognition memory that lasts at least a day (Swain et al., 1993). EEG recordings suggest that five-month-olds can even tell the difference between tones of two different pitches—preferring the novel one—a day later (Thomas & Lykins, 1995).

The rudiments of working memory can be seen by six months of age, as infants appear to be able to hold spatial information in mind for 3 to 5 seconds (Gilmore & Johnson, 1995). However, working memory appears to be the slowest developing memory system, relying on the maturation of the prefrontal cortex (Chapter 6).

INTERIM SUMMARY

Although infants have various sensory deficits compared to adults, they are able to perceive subtle differences, such as the sound of their mother's and another woman's voice, from birth. They can also associate sensations of an object from different senses and match their own actions to behaviors they have observed visually, a phenomenon called **intermodal processing**. Research from an ecological viewpoint suggests that infants innately appreciate the meaning of some experiences important to adaptation. Whereas various forms of implicit memory are present at birth and rudiments of explicit memory also exist in early infancy, explicit memory requires maturation of the hippocampus over at least the first 18 months of life. Working memory is the slowest developing memory system.

Piaget's Theory of Cognitive Development

The first psychologist to trace cognitive development systematically was Jean Piaget (1896–1980). The philosopher of science Thomas Kuhn (1970) observed that major innovations often come from outsiders who have not yet been indoctrinated into the discipline, and this was the case with Piaget. Although Piaget waited until age 21 to complete his doctorate in biology, he published his first paper at the ripe old age of 11 and was offered the curatorship of a Geneva museum's mollusk collection while still in high school. (The offer was rescinded when the museum realized he was a child.) How did this precocious biologist become a world-famous psychologist by age 30?

A Philosophical Question and a Psychological Answer   Piaget had a keen interest in *epistemology*, the branch of philosophy concerned with the nature of knowledge. The British empiricist philosophers, such as John Locke, argued that all knowledge comes from experience. To know what a dog is like, a person has to examine a number of dogs, experience them with the senses, and come to some conclusions about their common properties.

In contrast, the German philosopher Immanuel Kant argued that some forms of knowledge do *not* come from observation but are innate. People impose certain categories of thought—such as space, time, and causality—on the data of their senses, but these categories are not derived from experience. Similarly, the rules of logic and mathematics seem to work in the world, yet they are not mere summaries of sensory information. No one has ever seen the square root of 2 or π, but these concepts have real-world applications, as any engineer or architect can attest. Kant argued that the human propensity for mathematical thinking, like the tendency to use certain categories of thought, is innate.

Kant's ideas were the starting point for Piaget's life work. His hunch was that Kant was both right and wrong. Kant was right that people's understanding of time, space, and logic is not simply derived from experience but wrong that people are born with this knowledge. Piaget therefore decided to spend a year or two looking into the way children develop an understanding of time, space, and so forth—a "temporary" diversion from philosophy that occupied the next 60 years of his life.

Piaget (1970) proposed that children develop knowledge by inventing, or *constructing*, reality out of their own experience, mixing what they observe with their own ideas about how the world works. Thus, the preschooler who sees a dog's mask placed on Maynard the cat applies her own rules of logic—"When things look different, they are different"—to conclude that Maynard is a dog. Similarly, a toddler who notices that a shadow is attached to his feet no matter where he is on a sunny playground may use his own logic to conclude that the shadow is following him. These cognitive constructions are creative, but they are not arbitrary, since they are constrained by both physical realities (such as the fact that cats and dogs usually do not change into one another) and brain development (Brainerd, 1996).

Making Connections

Cognitive psychologists distinguish several kinds of memory, regulated by different neural circuits (Chapter 6). Explicit memory refers to memories that can be consciously recalled. Implicit memory is memory expressed in behavior that may not be represented consciously. Working memory involves information held briefly in consciousness.

■ What would be an example of explicit memory in infants?

■ What would be an example of implicit memory in infants?

■ How could a psychologist measure working memory capacity in infants?

Big Picture φ Question 6

What is the relation between nature and nurture in shaping psychological processes?

Making Connections

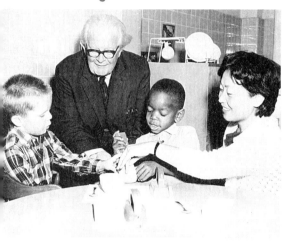

Piaget began his career working in Alfred Binet's intelligence-testing laboratory (Chapter 8). Whereas Binet was primarily interested in *how well* children answered questions, Piaget was interested in *how* they arrived at their answers. He noticed that children of the same age tended to make the same types of mistakes. They not only gave the same kinds of wrong answers, but when questioned about their reasoning, they provided similar explanations. He concluded that children think in qualitatively different ways at different ages, leading him to a stage theory of cognitive development.

Assimilation and Accommodation   Piaget viewed intelligence as the individual's way of adapting to new information about the world. He argued that children cognitively adapt to their environment through two interrelated processes, assimilation and accommodation (Piaget & Inhelder, 1969). **Assimilation** involves *interpreting actions or events in terms of one's present schemas*—that is, fitting reality into one's existing ways of understanding. According to Piaget, a **schema** is *an organized, repeatedly exercised pattern of thought or behavior* (Flavell, 1992), such as an infant's tendency to suck anything that will fit into its mouth (a nipple, a finger, a pacifier, etc.). All of these objects can be assimilated—taken in without modifying an existing schema—by sucking. Similarly, a person with a cognitive schema about police can drive into a crowded intersection and immediately understand the role of the person directing traffic.

If humans only assimilated information into existing schemas, no cognitive development would take place. The second process, **accommodation**, is *the modification of schemas to fit reality*. At the behavioral level, accommodation takes place when an infant with a sucking schema is presented with a cup: She must modify her existing schema to drink from this new device. At the thought level, accommodation is likely to occur if the reader looks carefully at the spelling of *accommodation*—it has two *c*'s and two *m*'s, which is highly unusual in English. The word "accommodation" requires revision of the implicit schema most people hold that would lead them to double only one consonant or the other.

For Piaget, the driving force behind cognitive development is **equilibration**—that is, *balancing assimilation and accommodation* to adapt to the world. When a child comes across something she does not understand, she finds herself in a state of cognitive disequilibrium that motivates her to try to make sense of what she has encountered. She may attempt to fit it into existing schemas (assimilation) or she may combine schemas or construct an entirely new schema to fit the new reality (accommodation). Thus, an infant whose father is holding her in front of a large mirror may not realize that *she* is the baby at whom she is smiling so broadly, but she has to make sense of the fact that there seem to be two identical daddies in the room, one holding her and one smiling at her in the mirror! Eventually she constructs the understanding that a mirror is a special kind of surface that reflects images.

INTERIM SUMMARY

Piaget argued that children develop knowledge by *constructing* reality out of their own experience, mixing what they observe with their own ideas about how the world works. They do this through a process of **equilibration**, which means balancing **assimilation** (fitting reality into their existing knowledge) and **accommodation** (modifying schemas to fit reality).

Stages of Cognitive Development   According to Piaget, people assimilate and accommodate when confronted with new information throughout their lives. *At each stage of development, however, children use a distinct underlying logic*, or **structure of thought**, *to guide their thinking*. The same four stages—sensorimotor, preoperational, concrete operational, and formal operational—occur in the same sequence for everyone, although the age for each individual may vary somewhat (Table 13.2). A fundamental principle of Piaget's developmental theory is that every stage builds on the next, as children wrestle with problems their old structures will not resolve and work their way toward new solutions by trying out and adjusting schemas currently in their repertoire (Siegler & Ellis, 1996).

Sensorimotor Stage   The **sensorimotor stage**, *in which infants think with their hands, mouths, and senses, lasts from birth to about two years of age.* Sensorimotor thought primarily takes the form of action, as infants learn about the world by mouthing, grasping, watching, and manipulating objects. According to Piaget, the

Table 13.2 ▪▪▪ Piaget's Stages of Cognitive Development

Stage	Approximate Ages (Years)	Characteristics
Sensorimotor	0–2	Thought and action are virtually identical, as the infant explores the world with its senses and behaviors; object permanence develops; the child is completely egocentric.
Preoperational	2–7	Symbolic thought develops; object permanence is firmly established; the child cannot coordinate different physical attributes of an object or different perspectives.
Concrete operational	7–12	The child is able to perform reversible mental operations on representations of objects; understanding of conservation develops; the child can apply logic to concrete situations.
Formal operational	12 +	The adolescent (or adult) can apply logic more abstractly; hypothetical thinking develops.

practical knowledge infants develop during this period forms the basis for their later ability to represent things mentally.

The label "sensorimotor" emphasizes that infants are bound by their sensations and actions and are capable of little explicit reasoning beyond what they are sensing and doing. They know about an object, such as a toy duck, only in terms of the sensations and actions associated with it, not as an objective reality.

A major achievement of the sensorimotor stage is the development of **object permanence**, *the recognition that objects exist in time and space independent of the child's actions on, or observation of, them*. According to Piaget, before the age of about 8 to 12 months, an object such as a ball exists for an infant only when it is in sight. If it is hidden from view, it no longer exists. When a child acquires object permanence, he will look for the ball, even when it is hidden from view, and will be delighted to find it. Piaget suggested that the attainment of object permanence lies behind infants' endless fascination with games such as peek-a-boo, which affirm their newfound understanding. Subsequent research suggests that children acquire *aspects* of object permanence much earlier than Piaget supposed (Baillargeon & DeVos, 1991), even by four or five months, but a comprehensive understanding of the permanence of objects does appear to evolve gradually during infancy (Halford, 1989).

During the sensorimotor stage children are extremely **egocentric**, *thoroughly embedded in their own point of view*. When an infant closes her eyes, the whole world becomes dark; when a ball is no longer in view, it ceases to exist. For Piaget, development entails a gradual movement away from egocentrism toward a recognition of alternative points of view (see Flavell, 1996; Selman, 1980).

During the sensorimotor stage, children learn with their hands and mouths.

Preoperational Stage The **preoperational stage** *begins roughly around age 2 and lasts until ages 5 to 7. It is characterized by the emergence of symbolic thought*—the ability to use arbitrary symbols, such as words, to represent concepts. Once children learn to manipulate symbols and mental images, thought becomes detachable from action. To put it another way, when children can play with the world in their minds, they no longer have to think exclusively with their hands or mouths. Symbolic thought allows preschool children to converse with other people and imagine solutions to problems before actually doing anything.

FIGURE 13.9   The three-mountain task. Preoperational children typically do not recognize that the stuffed animal "sees" the mountain from a perspective different from their own, although they can do so if the stimulus is very simple.

Preoperational thought continues, however, to be limited by egocentrism. A classic demonstration of egocentrism at this stage occurs in the *three-mountain task*. A child is seated at a table displaying three model mountains (Figure 13.9), with a teddy bear or doll seated at another chair at the same table. The child is shown a number of pictures of the table from different perspectives and is asked which view the teddy bear is seeing.

Preschool children often answer that the bear sees their own view of the table (Piaget & Inhelder, 1956). They are not egocentric in every situation and can even solve simplified versions of the three-mountain task (Burke, 1975; Ford, 1979; Lempers et al., 1977). Nevertheless, preschoolers are much more likely to make egocentric cognitive errors than older children, like the three-year-old who covers her eyes and declares, "You can't see me!"

A related limitation of preoperational thought is *centration*, the tendency to focus, or *center*, on one perceptually striking feature of an object without considering other features that might be relevant. When asked which of two candy bars is bigger, a long, thin one or a short, thick one, the preschooler is likely to pick the longer one and ignore thickness, even though the amount of chocolate is identical.

Preoperational thinking also tends to be fairly literal. The mother of a three-year-old tried to teach her son the meaning of "compromise" when he wanted her to read him three bedtime stories instead of the usual one. She suggested they compromise on two. A few days later, they were debating whether he should go to bed at eight or nine o'clock, and the mother asked, "Billy, do you remember what 'compromise' means?" "Yes," he replied earnestly, "*two*."

Perhaps the major limitation of preoperational thought is the feature that gave this stage its name. For Piaget, to *know* an object is to operate or act on it. **Operations** are *internalized (i.e., mental) actions the individual can use to manipulate, transform, and then return an object to its original state* (Piaget, 1972). Alphabetizing a list of names is an operation, because a person can put names in alphabetical order and then scramble their order again. Similarly, imagining what one could have said to someone who behaved rudely is an operation. Operations are like actions a person "tries out" in her head. According to Piaget, the capacity to carry out mental operations of this sort is the defining feature of the next stage of development.

INTERIM SUMMARY

Piaget argued that cognitive development occurs through a series of stages. During the **sensorimotor stage**, infants think with their hands and eyes. A major achievement of the sensorimotor stage is **object permanence**, when infants recognize that objects exist in time and space. During the sensorimotor stage children are extremely **egocentric**. The **preoperational stage** is characterized by the emergence of *symbolic* thought, which allows preschool-age children to imagine solutions to problems mentally rather than through action. Children at this stage remain egocentric; they have difficulty imagining reality from other viewpoints, and they have a tendency to center on one perceptually striking feature of an object.

Concrete Operational Stage   Piaget called the third stage of cognitive development the **concrete operational stage**, *roughly ages 7 to 12. At this point, children are capable of operating on, or mentally manipulating, internal representations of concrete objects in ways that are reversible*. In other words, children can imagine performing mental manipulations (operations) on a set of objects and then mentally put them back the way they found them (Piaget, 1972). For example, school-age children are able to imagine different ways of explaining why they came home late from playing with their friends, picture the likely consequences of each, and pick the one with

Big Picture φ Question 8

To what extent can we inform our knowledge through reason or through observation—that is, rationalism versus empiricism?

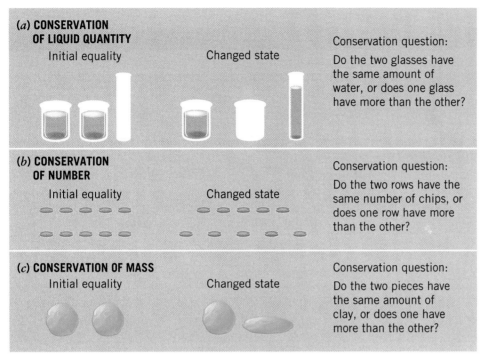

FIGURE 13.10 Conservation. (*a*) Conservation of liquid quantity: Unlike preoperational children, concrete operational children understand that the amount of liquid remains unchanged even though it has been poured into a beaker of a different shape. (*b*) Conservation of number: Preoperational children believe that altering the physical configuration changes the number of objects present. (*c*) Conservation of mass: Preoperational children fail to realize that mass is conserved despite changing the shape of a ball of clay.

the best odds. Younger children, in contrast, are more likely to blurt out an obvious lie or the truth, neither of which may satisfy their cognitively more developed parents.

The major achievement of the concrete operational stage is demonstrated in Piaget's classic experiments with conservation problems. According to Piaget, once children reach this third stage, they are able to understand the concept of **conservation**—that *basic properties of an object or situation remain stable (are conserved) even though superficial properties may be changed*.

For example, if preoperational children are shown the three beakers in part (*a*) of Figure 13.10, they easily recognize that the two same-sized beakers contain the same amount of liquid. They will not realize, however, that the tall and short beakers contain the same amount of liquid even if they watch the experimenter pour the liquid from the short to the tall beaker. In contrast, concrete operational children understand that the amount of liquid remains unchanged even though it has been poured into a beaker of a different shape. If asked to justify their answers, they usually say something like, "You just poured it from one container to another!" Whereas preoperational thought is characterized by *centration* on one dimension, concrete operational thinkers are able to *decenter*, that is, to hold in mind multiple dimensions at once.

Two other types of conservation problems, conservation of number and conservation of mass, are shown in parts (*b*) and (*c*), respectively, of Figure 13.10. Children typically master different kinds of conservation at slightly different ages. Many children understand conservation of number by age 6 but do not understand conservation of mass until about age 8 (Elkind, 1981; Katz & Beilin, 1976).

At the concrete operational stage children also understand *transitivity*—that if $a < b$ and $b < c$, then $a < c$. Although preoperational children can be trained to make some transitive inferences, they have difficulty keeping enough information in mind to solve transitive thinking problems (Bryant & Trabasso, 1971). One transitivity problem asks, "If Henry is taller than Jack, and Jack is taller than Claude, which boy is the

Apply & Discuss

Piaget proposed that children's thinking develops in stages.

▪ If cognition develops in stages, should children show the same level of thinking in all domains, such as math, science, and interpersonal understanding?

▪ What drives cognitive development? What maturational and social factors might lead a child to move out of sensorimotor into preoperational intelligence, or from the sensorimotor to the preoperational stage?

▪ When adults learn a new field, such as psychology, does their thinking develop in stages, or do they just gradually build up their knowledge?

shortest?" Preschoolers are equally likely to pick Jack or Claude because each one is shorter than someone else. They fail to put together the two pieces of information about relative height into a single transitive proposition. In general, before age 7 or 8, children have difficulty recognizing logical inconsistencies (e.g., that a person cannot be both tall and short, except in relation to different people) (Ruffman, 1999).

Formal Operational Stage   Piaget's fourth stage, formal operations, begins about ages 12 to 15, when children start to think more abstractly. The **formal operational stage** *is characterized by the ability to manipulate abstract as well as concrete objects, events, and ideas mentally*. That is, teenagers can reason about "formal" propositions (e.g., whether democracy is the best form of government) rather than concrete events. Teenagers are less likely to argue that the two beakers in the conservation task contain the same amount of liquid because they saw the liquid being poured back and forth. They may instead discuss the law of conservation or argue that surface appearances do not always reflect the underlying reality. Another hallmark of formal operational reasoning is the ability to frame hypotheses and figure out how to test them systematically (Inhelder & Piaget, 1958).

Putting Piaget in Perspective   Piaget's theory literally defined cognitive development for several decades, and it continues to have a profound influence. Nevertheless, researchers now criticize a number of aspects of his theory.

First, Piaget focused too heavily on the kind of rational thinking typical of scientific or philosophical pursuits and underplayed the extent to which people's thinking is biased, irrational, and influenced by motives or emotions. For example, despite their ability to think abstractly, teenagers show the same kinds of biases as adult scientists in weighing arguments against their pet theories (see Klaczynski, 1997, 2000).

Another criticism concerns Piaget's assumption that a child's thinking tends to be "at" one stage or another. Cognitive development often progresses unevenly, as the same child shows higher level reasoning in one domain than another (e.g., the ability to think abstractly in science but a lack of complexity in thinking about social relationships) (Case, 1992; Flavell, 1982). Children also exhibit a range of responses on any task and when "thinking aloud" while solving a problem often provide responses that range from quite mature to quite immature (Siegler & Ellis, 1996).

Piaget also underestimated the capacities of infants and preschool children (Gelman & Baillargeon, 1983). For example, research suggests that at 20 *days* infants are aware, at least for a few seconds, that a hidden object still exists, and by two months they can distinguish between an object moved out of sight and one that ceases to exist (Breuer, 1985). Preoperational children can sometimes accomplish conservation tasks as well. By age 5, children recognize that a substance can dissolve and no longer be seen but still preserve certain qualities, such as sweet taste (Rosen & Rozin, 1993). Children most often fail when conservation tasks are unfamiliar and the answer is quantitative (Siegler & Ellis, 1996).

In some respects, a difference between Piaget and his critics is that he generally required his subjects to demonstrate *explicit* knowledge before he would describe them as "getting" a concept or task. Explicit knowledge also tends to produce generalizability to other domains, because if a child can reason explicitly about conservation of liquids, she can probably do the same for solids. Subsequent researchers, in contrast, have documented a multitude of ways in which children *implicitly* show that they grasp certain concepts, as expressed in their behavior, even though they may be able to do so only under certain circumstances.

Other critics charge that Piaget failed to pay enough attention to the role of culture in development. Numerous cross-cultural studies have found that children progress through stages similar to those described by Piaget but that the age at which children attain particular stages often varies greatly and depends on the task (Mishra, 1997; Price-Williams, 1981). By and large, cognitive development proceeds more

Big Picture φ Question 2

What is the relationship between reason and desire or, more precisely, between cognition and affect?

Apply & Discuss

In planning their curricula, school systems pay attention to what children are capable of thinking at different ages. At what stage should children begin to learn the alphabet? At what stage are children likely ready to learn algebra? Chemistry? Do these stages correspond with the ages at which schools generally teach children their ABCs, x's and y's, and H_2O?

slowly in preliterate societies, although children's abilities tend to reflect their cultural and environmental circumstances. Mexican children of potters show delayed development on the conservation task using beakers, but they demonstrate a relatively early understanding of conservation when asked if a ball of clay has the same volume when it is stretched into an oblong shape (Price-Williams et al., 1969). Similarly, children in nomadic societies, which travel from location to location for their survival, tend to outperform other children on spatial tasks (Dasen, 1975; Dasen & Heron, 1981).

In sum, Piaget was correct in many of the broad strokes he used to describe cognitive development: Children become less egocentric, increasingly able to think symbolically, and increasingly able to reason abstractly as they develop (Halford, 1989). At the same time, many of the specific strokes, hues, and textures of his portrait require revision. Development is less uniform and unitary than his model suggests, and infants and young children appear to be more competent—and adults less competent—than Piaget believed (Flavell, 1992).

INTERIM SUMMARY

During the **concrete operational stage**, children can mentally manipulate representations of concrete objects in ways that are reversible, as can be seen in their understanding of **conservation** (that basic properties of an object or situation remain stable even though superficial properties change). The **formal operational stage** is characterized by the ability to manipulate abstract as well as concrete representations, to reason about formal propositions rather than concrete events. Many of Piaget's broad principles have withstood the test of time, but many specifics of the theory no longer appear accurate.

Information-Processing Approach to Cognitive Development

The information-processing approach is well suited to sketching some of the finer details of cognitive development. Information-processing researchers have tried to track down the specific processes that account for cognitive development and have focused on continuous, quantitative changes more than the broad, qualitative stages studied by Piaget.

Processing Speed   One of the variables that appears to account most for cognitive development is surprisingly simple: processing speed (Kail, 2000; Miller & Vernon, 1997). As we saw in Chapter 8, mental quickness is a central aspect of intelligence. As children get older, they are able to do faster a range of cognitive tasks from categorizing objects to making decisions (Figure 13.11). This increase in speed allows

Big Picture φ Question 7

To what extent are psychological processes conscious or unconscious—that is, explicit versus implicit?

Big Picture φ Question 4

To what extent is human nature particular versus universal?

Making Connections

Piaget began his work studying intelligence, and his theory is fundamentally about the way intelligence develops in children. Researchers studying intelligence have many different theories, ranging from theories that emphasize general intelligence—a "g-factor" that cuts across all domains—and specific intelligences, such as verbal and mathematical (Chapter 8).

■ Does Piaget's theory presuppose a theory of general intelligence?

■ Can Piaget's theory be reconciled with Howard Gardner's theory of multiple intelligences, which proposes that people have many different kinds of intelligence, such as mathematical, musical, and interpersonal intelligence?

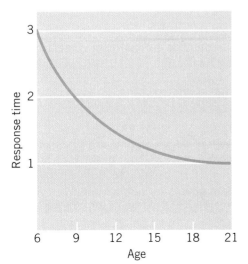

FIGURE 13.11   Processing speed and age. Here, processing speed (scaled as the ratio of children's speed relative to adult speed) follows an exponential function—and can in fact be predicted with mathematical precision (Kail, 1991). In other words, speed increases rapidly from about ages 6 to 12 and starts to level off by age 15.
Source: Adapted from Fry & Hale, 1996.

Children can remember the names and personalities of dozens of cartoon characters that all look alike to their parents.

Big Picture φ Question 8

To what extent can we inform our knowledge through reason or through observation—that is, rationalism versus empiricism?

them, among other things, to hold more information in working memory at any given moment and hence to solve problems more effectively. Speed of processing across a wide array of simple and complex tasks increases throughout childhood and levels off around age 15 (Kail, 1991a,b).

Automatic Processing A second factor that influences children's cognitive skill is their increasing ability to perform cognitive tasks automatically (Chaiken et al., 2000; Sternberg, 1984). **Automatization** refers to *the process of executing mental processes with increasing efficiency so that they require less and less attention*. In many tasks, from performing addition problems to driving a car, increased competence involves shifting from conscious, controlled processing to automatic, or implicit, processing. In reading, for example, children begin by sounding out words bit by bit. As they get more proficient, they immediately recognize common words and only have to sound out new, more complicated words.

Knowledge Base Another factor that influences children's cognitive efficiency is their **knowledge base**, or *accumulated knowledge*. Compared to adults, children's knowledge bases are obviously limited because of their comparative inexperience with life. To what extent, then, does the limited size of children's knowledge base, rather than some other factor, account for their cognitive inefficiency compared with adults?

One study explored this question by reversing the usual state of affairs, selecting children who were *more* knowledgeable than their adult counterparts (Chi, 1978). The cognitive task was to remember arrangements of pieces on a chessboard. Child participants (averaging age 10) were recruited from a local chess tournament; adult participants had no particular skill at chess. That the children easily outperformed the adults demonstrates that knowledge base was more important than age-related factors in this cognitive task. Other studies have corroborated this finding using stimuli such as cartoon characters with which children are more familiar than adults (Lindberg, 1980).

Cognitive Strategies Use of *cognitive strategies* also develops throughout childhood and adolescence (Siegler, 1996). In memory tasks, young children tend to rely on simple strategies such as rote repetition. As they get older, children use increasingly sophisticated rehearsal strategies (Chapter 6), such as arranging lists into categories before trying to remember the items (see Alexander & Schwanenflugel, 1994; Brown et al., 1983). In many respects, cognitive development reflects a process akin to evolution: Children try out new "mutations" (different problem-solving strategies), weed out those that do not work as well, and gradually evolve new strategies depending on changes in the situation (Siegler, 1996).

Metacognition A final variable involved in cognitive development is **metacognition**—*thinking about thinking* (Bogdan, 2000; Flavell, 1977; Metcalfe & Shimamura, 1994). To solve problems, people often need to understand how their mind works—how they perform cognitive tasks such as remembering, learning, and solving problems. For example, when asked if they understand something, young children often have trouble discriminating whether they understand something or not, so they simply nod in assent or fail to ask questions (Brown et al., 1983). Similarly, preschoolers do not recognize the importance of "inner speech"—using words inside one's head—while performing tasks such as mental arithmetic (Flavell et al., 1997).

An important aspect of metacognition is *metamemory*—knowledge about one's own memory and about strategies that can be used to help remember (Flavell & Wellman, 1977; Metcalfe, 2000). Metamemory is impaired in many patients with frontal lobe damage (Shimamura, 1995). Not surprisingly, it is also less developed in children, whose frontal lobes remain immature for many years. In one classic study, researchers asked younger and older children to view some pictures and predict how many they could remember. The younger children often predicted total recall (Flavell et al., 1970)! Although metamemory, like metacognition in general, frequently involves explicit processes, many metamemory processes are implicit, such as knowing how, where, and how long to search memory (Reder & Schunn, 1996).

INTERIM SUMMARY

Many aspects of information processing change with age. Among the most important are processing speed, children's **knowledge base** (store of accumulated knowledge), **automatization** (executing mental processes automatically and relatively effortlessly, with increasing efficiency and decreased attention), more efficient use of cognitive strategies, and **metacognition** (knowledge about how one's mind works—or cognition about cognition).

Integrative Theories of Cognitive Development

Piaget viewed cognitive development as a progression through qualitatively different stages, whereas the information-processing approach focuses on small-scale, quantitative refinements in children's ability to think and remember. As different as these viewpoints are, they are not mutually exclusive. Cognitive development may be characterized by both qualitative and quantitative changes and general and specific processes (Fischer, 1980; Fischer & Bidell, 1997).

Neo-Piagetian theorists *attempt to integrate Piagetian and information-processing theories.* With Piaget, they argue that children actively structure their understanding, that knowledge progresses from a preconcrete to a concrete and then to an abstract stage, and that all of these aspects occur in roughly the order reported by Piaget (Bidell & Fischer, 1992; Case, 1998; Fischer, 1980). Like information-processing theorists, however, the neo-Piagetians pay more attention to discrete components of cognitive processing and emphasize domain-specific development—that is, the way cognition can develop in one domain without simultaneously developing in others.

One such theory was proposed by Robbie Case (1992, 1998). Case argues for a general stage theory similar to Piaget's, from a sensorimotor stage to an abstract, complex, formal operational stage. Each stage differs qualitatively from the others in the way children represent problems and strategies for solving them (Case, 1984).

Case's theory differs from Piaget's, however, in some key respects. Case argues that cognitive progress *within* each stage is possible because humans are innately motivated to solve problems, explore, imitate others, and engage in social interaction. Development occurs within each stage as children set goals, formulate problem-solving strategies, and evaluate the results of those strategies. They then integrate existing problem-solving strategies to create more elaborate strategies as new situations arise, and they practice those new strategies until they become automatic.

According to Case, development *across* stages also depends on cultural input, but the most important factor in qualitative changes in development (i.e., movement across stages) is an increasing capacity for working memory. Attending to both length and width in a conservation task is much easier if a child has large enough working memory capacity to hold both dimensions in mind simultaneously while imagining how, for example, a ball of clay might look if those dimensions changed. Research suggests that the central executive function of working memory, which is involved in allocating attention, coordinating different kinds of information held in short-term storage, and handling multiple tasks at once, continues to develop throughout childhood, at least through age 10 (Hale et al., 1997).

Figure 13.12 illustrates the way expanded working memory allows for more complex cognition. Ten- to eighteen-year-olds were asked to draw a picture of a mother looking out the window to see her son in the park across the street playing peek-a-

Big Picture φ Question 7

To what extent are psychological processes conscious or unconscious—that is, explicit versus implicit?

Big Picture φ Question 8

To what extent can we inform our knowledge through reason or through observation—that is, rationalism versus empiricism?

Making Connections

Working memory refers to the capacity to hold information in consciousness long enough to use, consider, or manipulate it (Chapter 6). Working memory capacity expands as children automatize more and more processes that once required conscious attention and become more efficient in their use of cognitive strategies. According to Case, these developments allow children to keep progressively more things in mind simultaneously and to coordinate previously separate actions and ideas.

FIGURE 13.12   Artistic skill and working memory. Subjects ages 10 to 18 were asked to draw a picture of a mother looking out the window to see her son playing peek-a-boo with her in the park. The 10-year-old who drew this picture accurately depicted both parts of the scene but failed to integrate them, drawing the mother and son both facing the artist instead of each other.

boo with her (Dennis, 1992, cited in Case, 1992). The youngest subjects could keep in mind the image of the mother in the house and the image of the boy in the park, but they could not integrate the two images. This study illustrates the advantages of a neo-Piagetian model over classical Piagetian theory. Certain broad processes, particularly limitations in working memory, *constrain* the thinking of young children, putting an upper limit on what a child within a given age range can achieve. This leads to qualitative differences in thought at different stages that appear across a variety of domains (such as art, language, and mathematics), just as Piaget postulated.

At the same time, neo-Piagetian models recognize that development occurs in specific domains and is influenced by culture and experience (Bidell & Fischer, 2000). By ages 8 to 10, children in Western cultures incorporate artistic conventions developed over the past several centuries for depicting perspective (Chapter 4), such as representing closer objects as larger. However, a four-year-old with a crayon is unlikely to outperform an adult regardless of culture or experience.

INTERIM SUMMARY

Neo-Piagetian theorists attempt to integrate an understanding of the broad stages of Piaget's theory with an information processing approach. According to Case's theory, the main variable responsible for cognitive development *across* stages is expansion of working memory capacity.

Apply & Discuss

Unlike most periods in human history, in times of rapid technological change the knowledge and strategies used by one generation may be irrelevant or unproductive 20 or 30 years later. Thus, to younger individuals, an older person's reliance on "accumulated wisdom" may look like a sign of cognitive rigidity.

■ Under what circumstances does the knowledge and experience of a 50-, 60-, or 70-year-old lead to better performance in the workplace?

■ Under what circumstances is age an impediment to good performance?

Cognitive Development and Change in Adulthood

All cultures consider adolescents and adults better decision makers than children, but they differ dramatically in their beliefs about cognition and aging. Many cultures associate age with wisdom. In contrast, Western cultures associate age with decline. Although real changes in speed of processing and capacity for learning and memory occur cross-culturally (Crook et al., 1992), as we will see, cognitive decline varies not only across cultures but also across individuals within a single culture.

Cognitive Changes Associated with Aging

A number of cognitive changes occur with aging, ranging from changes in psychomotor speed to changes in memory (Craik & Salthouse, 2000; Park & Schwarz, 2000).

Psychomotor Speed   One of the clearest changes that accompanies aging is **psychomotor slowing,** *an increase in the time required for processing and acting on information* (Park et al., 1996; Salthouse, 1996, 2000). This deceleration actually begins early, around the mid-20s. Psychomotor slowing can be observed on both relatively simple tests, such as pushing a button when a light flashes, and on tests that require more complex thinking (Era et al., 1986; Spirduso & MacRae, 1990). In practical terms, psychomotor slowing can be seen in the difficulty older people have relative to younger people when first learning to use a mouse at the computer—particularly double-clicking (Smith et al., 1999)!

For most people, psychomotor slowing is so gradual that it goes unnoticed until the 50s or 60s. For professional athletes, however, increased reaction time means a re-

In the United States, people can vote at 18, but the minimum age to run for the presidency is 35. Apparently, the framers of the Constitution held some implicit theory of cognitive development in adulthood. John Kennedy and Bill Clinton were "youngsters" when they assumed the U.S. presidency—in their forties.

tirement age in the early 30s. Middle-aged athletes, such as George Foreman, who shocked the world in 1994 by winning back the heavyweight championship in his late 40s, know their days are numbered. Even so, they can stage temporary comebacks through extra practice, increased skill, and compensatory strategies.

Does reaction time matter much for the rest of us, whose livelihood does not depend on ducking blows or anticipating the direction of a ball heading toward us at 90 miles an hour? Actually, it does, because it has indirect effects on all kinds of reasoning and problem-solving abilities (Parkin & Java, 1999). Researchers are just beginning to tease apart the reasons why processing speed appears to matter so much, but two explanations may help explain the link between speed and intellectual functioning (Salthouse, 1996).

The first is limited time. If complex mental operations rely on the execution and coordination of many simpler mechanisms, in the brief period of time people have to make most decisions, including implicit decisions, the person will simply have less time to process multiple pieces of information and combine them in complex ways. From a connectionist perspective (Chapter 7), if people categorize, perceive, and remember through processes of parallel constraint satisfaction (finding the solution that best fits all the constraints active at the moment), people who think quickly can weigh a greater number of constraints and hence come to a more informed conclusion.

A second way decreased processing speed can affect cognitive performance is its influence on working memory. If cognitive processes take longer to execute, less information is available simultaneously in working memory, and relevant information may no longer be available by the time the person needs to think about it.

Memory   A common stereotype is that older people are constantly forgetting things—names of people they have just met, what they did yesterday, or where they put their house keys. This stereotype has grains of truth but is far too sweeping. Understanding declines in memory requires distinguishing different types of memory (Chapter 6).

Working Memory   Older people do well on simple short-term storage tasks, such as remembering a string of digits (Hultsch & Dixon, 1990; Labouvie-Vief & Schell, 1982). However, they show substantial deficits in complex working memory tasks, such as repeating a list of digits *backward*, dealing with multiple tasks at once, or dividing their attention between tasks (Einstein et al., 1997; Ponds et al., 1988). These deficits translate into very practical problems, such as how to keep track of multiple cars at an intersection with a four-way stop. If neo-Piagetian theorists such as Robbie

Making Connections

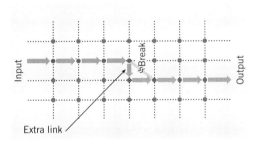

Connectionist models propose that when we perceive, think, and remember, we activate networks of neurons that have been activated together in the past (Chapter 7). Thus, connectionist models suggest one possible reason for slowed reaction time with age: If a mental process or representation is distributed across a number of neurons that form a circuit, any small break that occurs with aging will require additional steps to recomplete the circuit. Because every synaptic connection adds processing time, the more broken connections that amass over the years, the more time required to find alternative routes to carry out psychological processes (from Cerella, 1990, p. 203).

Apply & Discuss

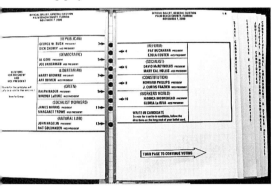

In the 2000 U.S. presidential election, nearly 20,000 voters in West Palm Beach, Florida, a city with a high percentage of elderly residents, appeared to have cast their votes accidentally for right-wing candidate Pat Buchanan while intending to vote for Democratic candidate Al Gore. Several voters brought suit, unsuccessfully, to have a re-vote, arguing that they were confused by the "butterfly ballot" and by instructions that mistakenly told them always to punch the hole to the right of the candidate's names.

▪ No psychological testimony was ever offered or solicited in the legal case brought by the West Palm Beach voters. Should it have been?

▪ West Palm Beach also imposed a time limit of 5 minutes in the polling booth, to prevent voters, who were voting on many candidates other than those running for president, from taking too long. Could the combination of a time limit and the challenges posed by the butterfly ballot for working memory have inadvertently disenfranchised elderly voters?

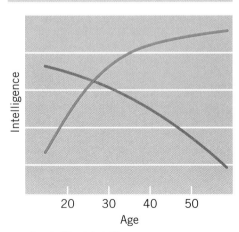

— Crystallized intelligence
— Fluid intelligence

FIGURE 13.13 Fluid and crystallized intelligence throughout the life span. Unlike fluid intelligence, crystallized intelligence increases through at least the 40s and 50s and then levels off. *Source:* Horn & Hofer, 1992, p. 79.

Case are right that the key to cognitive development in childhood is increased working memory capacity, then advanced aging means development in reverse.

Indeed, neuroimaging studies find not only decreased activation of areas of the prefrontal cortex known to be involved in working memory in people in their 60s and older but also less *efficient* activation (Reuter-Lorenz & Stanczak, 2000; Rypma & D'Esposito, 2000). For example, older people show activation of both right and left hemispheres in verbal working memory tasks, which are lateralized to the left hemisphere in younger people (Chapter 6).

Long-Term Memory   As for long-term memory, some aspects remain intact throughout the life span, whereas others decline. Although older people take more time to learn new information than younger people, given ample encoding time, their performance approaches that of younger subjects (Perlmutter, 1983). Furthermore, if they are healthy, people continue to add to their knowledge base until the day they die; in this sense, people can add to their supply of "wisdom" until their last breath (Horn & Hofer, 1992; Salthouse, 1992, 2000). Nor is implicit memory impaired with age, as assessed by tasks such as the tendency to complete a word stem (e.g., *per-*) with a previously primed word (e.g., perfume) (Gaudreau & Peretz, 1999; Russo & Parkin, 1993; Schacter et al., 1992).

The problems older people have with long-term memory lie more in retrieving explicit memories than in either encoding new information or in learning or expressing knowledge implicitly. Although some studies find small declines in recognition memory (e.g., "Did you see the word *dove* on the list presented a few minutes ago?"), older people have particular trouble in recall tasks (e.g., "What words did you see on that list?").

If older people have trouble retrieving new information, do they "live in the past"? Interestingly, the years between 10 and 30 seem to be peak years for storing significant episodic (autobiographical) memories (Rubin et al., 1998). When older adults are asked to recall significant episodic memories (memories of events they have experienced), they tend to remember memories from that period more than other memories, and the memories they produce are more vivid. They also show greater semantic knowledge for facts such as current events and who won an Oscar or the World Series during that period.

Everyday Memory   Many researchers interested in *everyday memory*—memory as applied in everyday life (Chapter 6)—have wondered whether the somewhat gloomy picture painted by some laboratory studies of memory in older people reflects the realities of their daily lives (see Blanchard-Fields & Chen, 1996).

In everyday tasks, changes in cognition appear to involve both gains and losses (Baltes, 1987, 1998). For example, when asked to remember the events of a story, middle-aged and older participants in one study remembered slightly fewer details of the story but were more likely than late adolescents (age 16 to 19) to get the "gist" of it—that is, to encode and remember its *meaning* (Adams, 1991). This can be seen in people's work lives: An analysis of nearly 100 studies with a combined total of more than 38,000 subjects found that the correlation between worker productivity and age is essentially zero (McEvoy & Cascio, 1989). Older workers apparently compensate for declines in processing power with a larger knowledge base and alternative strategies for carrying out tasks (Baltes, 1987; Perlmutter et al., 1990).

Intelligence has many facets, and different aspects of intelligence change in different ways as people age. As we saw in Chapter 8, *fluid intelligence* refers to intellectual capacities used in many forms of information processing (assessed by measures of speed of processing, ability to solve analogies, etc.), whereas *crystallized intelligence* refers to people's store of knowledge (Horn & Cattell, 1967; Horn & Hofer, 1992).

Fluid intelligence peaks in young adulthood and then levels off and begins declining by mid-adulthood, largely because of a decline in speed of processing. In contrast, crystallized intelligence increases throughout most of life, showing declines only in very old age (Figure 13.13) (Horn, 1998; Horn & Hofer, 1992). In sum, intelligence is multifaceted and cumulative, and most of us would do well to be half as productive or creative at 20 or 30 as Picasso was at 90.

Individual Differences in Aging and Cognition   Many of the studies showing declines with aging have been cross-sectional. A major limitation of these studies is that they can show, on *average*, how people fare at different ages, but they cannot show the *proportion* of people whose cognitive capacities decline. Statistically, if a sizable *minority* of older people show substantial cognitive deterioration, mean scores for their age group will be lower than for younger groups, leading to an apparent conclusion that intelligence declines with age. But longitudinal studies can ask a different question: Of people in different age groups, how many actually deteriorate?

A major longitudinal project, called the Seattle Longitudinal Study (Schaie, 1990, 1994), provides an important corrective to a view of inevitable cognitive decline. The investigators followed a large sample ranging in age from 25 to 81 over several years, administering a battery of cognitive tests. The results were striking: Most people do not show significant mental declines. Even on the average, intellectual functioning does not decline until the 60s and 70s (Figure 13.14). In fact, cognitive decline can be an indicator of impending death: Older people who begin to show signs of substantial psychomotor slowing and declines in crystallized intelligence are more likely to die in the next several years than those whose cognitive functioning remains relatively intact (Bosworth & Schaie, 1999).

The Seattle study, like other longitudinal studies, shows that people differ tremendously in the way they age. People who are healthy and mentally active experience fewer mental declines than those who are not (Diamond, 1978; Horn & Meer, 1987). The "use it or lose it" theory applies to mental functioning as much as to physical. B. F. Skinner, Pablo Picasso, Sigmund Freud, Eleanor Roosevelt, Jean Piaget, and a host of other septagenarians and octogenarians have shown remarkable cognitive longevity in diverse fields. Data from a recent 11-year longitudinal study of a large community sample found that "using it" early in life may also be important for "keeping it" later: People who had less than 8 years of formal education showed substantially greater cognitive declines than those who had 9 or more (Lyketsos et al., 1999). Having a certain amount of intellectual training early in life may reduce future deterioration.

Although most people function well for most or all of their lives, cognitive decline generally escalates in the mid-80s as the brain's hardware begins to wear out

Apply & Discuss

Increasing numbers of older people are returning to universities to get or complete their education after retirement.

- Which tasks involved in obtaining a college education would be most difficult for older people?
- At which tasks would they more likely excel?

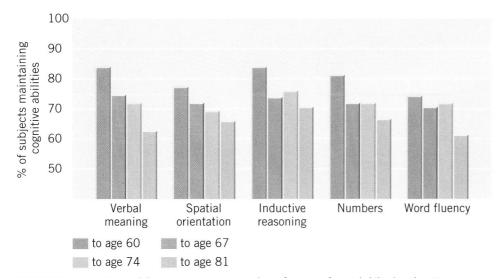

FIGURE 13.14   Cognitive stability over seven-year intervals. On five tests of mental ability, less than 25 percent of subjects tested every seven years showed any decline prior to age 60. Even by age 81, over 60 percent of all subjects showed stable cognitive functioning rather than decline. *Source:* Adapted from Schaie, 1990, p. 297.

(Korten et al., 1997). A prime culprit appears to lie in the frontal lobes (Parkin & Java, 1999; Souchay et al., 2000). Most cognitive tasks that involve bringing material to consciousness and manipulating it—from remembering a phone number to figuring out how to solve a novel problem to having that "feeling of knowing" when asked whether this is the street to turn on—rely on an intact prefrontal cortex. As the frontal lobes begin to function less effectively, not only does working memory become impaired, as we have seen, but explicit memory and decision making decline or at best hold steady if the person finds alternative ways to compensate (see Parkin et al., 1995; West, 1996). Neuroscientists have long suggested a simple maxim that applies to developmental gains in childhood and losses in late life: last in, first out. The frontal lobes are the last to mature in childhood and adolescence, and they seem to be among the first (and most) affected by normal aging.

Aging and "Senility"

One of the most pervasive myths about aging is that old people lose their memory and their ability to think and reason—that is, they become "senile" (Butler, 1975). In fact, only about 5 percent of the population suffers progressive and incurable **dementia**, *a disorder marked by global disturbance of higher mental functions* (Morris & Baddeley, 1988). Another 10 to 15 percent experience mild to moderate memory loss. The majority of people—around 80 percent—retain sharp mental functioning even through old age (Butler, 1984; Schaie, 1990).

Organic brain disease, or what people often call senility, is far more prevalent among people in their 80s and 90s than among those in their 60s and 70s. Rates of dementia vary slightly across cultures but are everywhere linked to advancing age (van Duijn, 1996). Even among people in their 80s, however, only about 20 percent are affected by senile dementia (Roth, 1978).

Senile dementia has a variety of causes, including reduced blood supplies to the brain and exposure to toxins such as alcohol. Roughly 10 to 20 percent of dementias are curable by diagnosing and eliminating an environmental toxin (Elias et al., 1990). Well over half the cases, however, are caused by **Alzheimer's disease**, *a progressive and incurable illness that destroys neurons in the brain, severely impairing memory, reasoning, perception, language, and behavior* (see Ashford et al., 1996; Gilleard, 2000). Although early warning signs (particularly decreased ability to think abstractly and to retain new information) may not be apparent to the naked eye, a recent longitudinal study of a community sample of over a thousand people found that those who developed Alzheimer's showed subtle declines on neuropsychological tests a decade before developing overt symptoms (Elias et al., 2000).

The characteristic changes in brain tissue in Alzheimer's include tangled neurons and protein deposits that disrupt the functioning of cells in the cortex. Alzheimer's patients also have abnormally low levels of several neurotransmitters, most importantly acetylcholine, which plays a central role in memory functioning (Coull & Sahakian, 2000). Recent neuroimaging research has found a direct correlation between the extent of damage in the temporal lobes, particularly the hippocampus and axons connecting it to the cortex, and the degree of cognitive impairment in Alzheimer's patients, which makes sense in light of the pervasive effects of the disease on explicit memory (Bierer et al., 1995; Schroder et al., 1997). The result of lesions to this area may be difficulty in remembering what happened moments earlier—or remembering which story the affected individual just told.

Alzheimer's disease may have several different causes, but at least one major form of the disorder is genetic (Coyle, 1991; Nussbaum & Ellis, 2003; Rosenberg, 2003; Williams, 2003). Researchers have isolated genes on at least three chromosomes implicated in the genetic transmission of Alzheimer's. One form of the disease has been linked to a defect on chromosome 21 (Holland & Oliver, 1995), the chromosome implicated in Down syndrome, a form of mental retardation (Chapter 8). Down syndrome patients who live into late middle age often develop symptoms and neurological changes similar to Alzheimer's disease.

INTERIM SUMMARY

Cognitive declines in later life tend to be selective rather than global. Processing speed decreases; working memory capacity declines; explicit memory retrieval becomes more difficult; problem-solving strategies become less efficient; and fluid intelligence declines. Other functions show little or no noticeable decline, including many encoding processes, implicit memory, aspects of everyday memory, and crystallized intelligence. People also show tremendous variability in the way their minds change with aging. About 5 percent of the population suffers progressive and incurable **dementia**, a disorder marked by global disturbance of higher mental functions. The most common cause of dementia is **Alzheimer's disease**.

Language Development

For most people who have ever studied a foreign language and then visited a country where that language is the native tongue, watching five-year-olds speak is a humbling experience. Without benefit of years of coursework and hours of rote memorization, these tiny creatures with their half-baked cortexes typically run linguistic circles around their fumbling foreign elders. How do they do it?

In this section we consider the mystery of how children acquire language so quickly and effortlessly. We begin by exploring the roles of nature and nurture in language development and then examine stages of language acquisition.

A Critical Period for Language Development?

The interplay of nature and nurture in language development has led to another hotly debated question among psychologists and linguists: Does a *critical period* exist for language learning; that is, is the brain maximally sensitive to language acquisition at a certain point in development (Lenneberg, 1967)?

Readers who have tried to learn a foreign language as teenagers or young adults have probably found that language acquisition is not so easy at later stages of life. As we have seen (Chapter 3), the development of the brain depends on certain kinds of environmental enrichment, and neurons and neuronal connections not used at age-appropriate times may die or disappear. Exposure to language may be necessary for normal lateralization of linguistic processes to the left hemisphere, which is typically completed between ages 2 and 5 (Kinsbourne & Smith, 1974; Marcotte & Morere, 1990).

Similarly, exposure to particular phonemes in the first three years may be required in order to attain native fluency in a second language, particularly if that language is very different from one's own (such as Chinese and English). Learning a second language becomes steadily more difficult after age 3, up until at least age 12. After that point, people are seldom able to attain even near-native fluency, and the brain appears to recruit different neural circuits to carry out linguistic tasks than it uses to process first languages (McDonald, 1997).

Perhaps the most convincing evidence of critical periods comes from the study of deaf children whose parents did not know sign language and who did not become exposed to sign language until enrolled in schools for the deaf as late as adolescence (Mayberry & Eichen, 1991; McDonald, 1997). Late learners generally do not catch up to early learners in their ability to use sign language, particularly if they begin in adolescence. They have more trouble learning to comprehend the language fluently and

Big Picture φ Question 6

What is the relation between nature and nurture in shaping psychological processes?

Making Connections

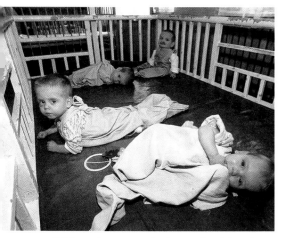

Children who grow up in abnormal social environments in their first few years, such as orphanages, may have lifelong difficulties forming and maintaining relationships. This has raised questions about whether humans have a critical period for the capacity for forming intimate relationships (Chapter 14).

to produce signs as rapidly and effortlessly, suggesting that they "speak with an accent," much like adults who try to learn a second language. Even after 30 years of using sign language, native signers outperform people who learned to sign later in childhood, who in turn outperform later learners (Newport, 1990).

Researchers have also examined a handful of cases of children who were not exposed early to language because they were raised in extreme isolation. The most famous case was a child known as Genie. Authorities found Genie at age 13; she had been living in a tiny room tied to a chair from the time she was 20 months. Her abusive father rarely spoke to her except for occasional screaming. After Genie was discovered, linguists and psychologists worked with her intensively. She acquired a reasonable vocabulary and learned to combine words into meaningful phrases, but she never progressed beyond sentences like "Genie go" (Curtiss, 1977, 1989). She also did not appear to have the normal left-hemisphere lateralization for language.

INTERIM SUMMARY

For many years psychologists have debated the existence of a critical period for language learning. The first three years of life seem to be the optimal time to attain native fluency. After age 12, even near-native fluency is difficult to achieve, and language appears to be processed using different neural circuits than in native speakers.

What Infants Know about Language

Although psychologists disagree about the relative roles of nature and nurture in language development, no one doubts that children learn language with extraordinary speed. First, however, they must learn to *segment* the continuous streams of speech they hear into units so they can distinguish one phoneme, morpheme, word, or phrase from another. As anyone knows who has ever traveled to a country with an unfamiliar language, this is no easy task, because native speakers talk rapidly and do not typically "brake" for learners.

Infants use a number of cues to segment speech, such as pauses, pitch, and duration. By the time they are nine months old, they already show a preference for speech interrupted at the boundaries of phrases (Jusczyk et al., 1999; McDonald, 1997). They can also recognize recurring patterns in a string of uninterrupted syllables (such as *badigo* in *badigotabitabadigo*) (Saffran et al., 1996).

Although infants must learn to segment speech, they appear to have an innate sensitivity to distinctions among the phonemes that make up human languages long before they even start speaking (L. B. Cohen et al., 1992a; Miller & Eimas, 1995). Researchers have documented this ability by measuring the rate at which one- and four-month-old infants suck on a pacifier as they listen to various sounds (Eimas et al., 1971, 1985). Infants have a preference for novel stimuli, and over time, they will suck faster on a specially wired pacifier when presented with a new stimulus when they realize that their sucking controls what they see. This allows psychologists to learn how infants think and perceive.

One classic study found that a change in phonemes that could signal a different meaning if used in a word (e.g., from a *b* to a *p*) produced a much greater increase in sucking rate than a similar change that carried no potential linguistic meaning (Eimas, 1985). Interestingly, though, humans are not alone in their capacity to distinguish linguistic sounds. Newborn human infants can distinguish Dutch from Japanese—but so can cotton-top tamarin monkeys (Ramus et al., 2000)! Human language seems to take advantage of sound processing mechanisms present in other animals (Bonvillian, personal communication, 2000).

Once infants learn to segment speech, one of the next tasks is to classify words into syntactic categories, such as nouns, verbs, and noun phrases (McDonald, 1997). That young children implicitly classify words into parts of speech by noticing regularities in their use can be seen in the tendency of preschoolers to overgeneralize (to generalize rules that normally apply to irregular instances). For example, just as they create words such as *hisself*, they also create sentences such as *She hitted me*.

From Babbling to Bantering

Babies' first recognizable speech sounds are called **babbling**. These utterances, such as "lalala" or "baba," begin sometime between six months and one year. However, by the end of this period, even before they speak their first words, their language development bears the imprint of their culture. Babies' innate attention to phonemic distinctions becomes markedly limited to phonemes in the language they habitually hear, so that their babbling sounds resemble their parents' language sounds (Eimas, 1985; Miller & Eimas, 1995). One study showed that at six months, infants of English-speaking families could discern phonemic distinctions typical of both the Hindi language and a Native American language called Salish. By 12 months, however, their ability to discriminate phonemes from these foreign languages had declined substantially (Werker & Tees, 1984).

Using Words Sometime between about one and one and a half years, babbling gives way to a stage in which children utter one word at a time. Children's first words refer to concrete things or action, such as "mama," "ball," or "go." So, too, do the non-linguistic symbolic gestures children often develop even before they have words, such as a knob-turning motion that means "I want to go out" (Goodwyn & Acredolo, 1998).

At about 18 to 20 months, toddlers begin to form two-word phrases. From that point, the number of morphemes they combine in their utterances steadily increases. The use of grammatical niceties such as articles, prepositions, and auxiliary verbs expands as well.

Young children characteristically use **telegraphic speech**, *utterances composed of only the most essential words for meaning* (as in a telegram). Thus, "Dog out" might stand for "The dog is outside." The words they tend to omit are words like *if*, *the*, and *under*. Although they tend not to use these words in speech, children as young as 2 actually *comprehend* some of these words, responding more accurately to sentences that include them (Gerken & McIntosh, 1993). By age 4, the vast majority of children's sentences are fully grammatical (Stromswold, 1995). Table 13.3 illustrates the progression from telegraphic to grammatical speech in five children whose language was studied intensively.

Table 13.3 ■ ■ Progression from Telegraphic Speech to Complete Sentences in Children Ages 25 1/2 to 35 1/2 Months

Model Sentence	Imitations of Spoken Sentences				
	Eve, 25½	Adam, 28½	Helen, 30	Ian, 31½	June, 35½
1. It goes in a big box.	Big box.	Big box.	In big box.	It goes in the box.	C
2. Read the book.	Read book.	Read book.	—	Read a book.	C
3. I will not do that again.	Do again.	I will that again.	I do that.	I again.	C
4. I do not want an apple.	I do apple.	I do a apple.	—	I do not want apple.	I don't want apple.
5. Is it a car?	't car?	Is it car?	Car?	That a car?	C
6. Where does it go?	Where go?	Go?	Does it go?	Where do it go?	C

Source: Brown & Fraser, 1963.

Note:—indicates no intelligible imitation was obtained; C indicates imitation was correct

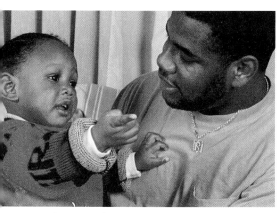

Sometime after the first year of life, children utter a single word at a time, often pointing to things.

Children's vocabulary increases exponentially after they achieve their first 50 to 100 words. Their repertoire of words blossoms to several thousand by the time they are six years old (Bloom, 1993; MacWhinney, 1998).

Influences on Language Development   Although the stages of language development are virtually universal, children acquire language at widely different rates (Goldfield & Snow, 1989; Richards, 1990). These differences in part stem from genetic predispositions, but they also reflect environmental influences. Probably the most important environmental factor is the day-to-day input and feedback that children get from their caregivers.

One way caregivers facilitate infants' language development is by speaking "Motherese." Everyone is familiar with this dialect, as it is virtually irresistible when talking to a baby. Motherese is characterized by exaggerated intonation, a slow rate of speech, and high pitch (Fernald & Kuhl, 1987). Among other things, the exaggerated style of Motherese may help infants recognize where phrases and sentences begin and end (Gleitman et al., 1988; Morgan, 1986). With young babies, people often speak "multimodal motherese," which combines motion or touch with words (Gogate et al., 2000).

The content of the primary caregiver's speech is also important in language acquisition. When parents repeat themselves ("Shall we go to the store? Let's go to the store") and expand on their children's telegraphic utterances (e.g., responding to "dog out" with "Is the dog out?"), their children tend to develop earlier in their ability to use verbs correctly. In contrast, merely acknowledging what the child has said without adding any new information ("That's right") is associated with delayed syntax development (Hoff-Ginsberg, 1990; Newport et al., 1977).

Deafness and Early Language Acquisition   In addition, at least one study suggests that simple sign language can facilitate the development of language (Goodwyn et al., 2000). Participants were 40 babies who began signing their needs, starting at 11 months of age. By age 3, their verbal ability was 4 months ahead of nonsigning babies. An added bonus was that both baby and parent were less frustrated by not knowing what was the cause of distress: hunger or a wet diaper. By communicating with signs, before language develops, the infants strengthened the connections that were critical for communication.

INTERIM SUMMARY

Language development progresses through a series of stages. Before infants can start to acquire vocabulary or syntax, they have to learn to *segment* the continuous streams of speech they hear into units. They then have to learn to classify words into syntactic categories. Babies' first recognizable speech sounds occur as **babbling** in the first year. Sometime in the second year they begin to speak in one-word utterances. Young children use **telegraphic speech**, leaving out all but the essential words. By age 4, most of the sentences children produce are grammatical. Although the stages of language development are virtually universal, children acquire language at widely different rates depending on environmental input.

The Nature of Development

This chapter began with three questions about development: What are the relative contributions of nature and nurture? To what extent is development characterized by critical or sensitive periods? And to what extent is development stagelike or continuous? All three questions address the way maturational, cultural, and environmental forces interact over time to create an organism capable of responding adaptively to its social and physical environment.

Maturational factors provide both the possibilities and limits of physical and cognitive development. Young children cannot think in the abstract ways that adolescents can about justice, God, or conservation of matter. Maturation of the frontal lobes permits a new kind of thinking that may well be described as a new "stage." Old people cannot think as quickly as their younger counterparts, and in their ninth or tenth decades, they may become much less efficient in their thinking. In both young and old, the nervous system determines the range within which people can function. Except in cases of mental retardation or severe neural degeneration, however, that range is extraordinarily large. Experience, genetics, and physical health all play a substantial part in determining where in that range people find themselves.

Even this conclusion—that neural hardware constrains the kind of "software" that can be run on it—does not tell the whole story because, as we have seen, the hardware changes in response to the environment. Although the nervous system establishes certain constraints on and possibilities for cognitive functioning, the nervous system is itself partially a product of its environment. Experience can enrich the developing brain, increasing the connections among neurons that underlie the capacity for complex thought, just as impoverished experience, particularly during sensitive periods of development, can constrain psychological functioning by limiting the processing power of the brain. The human brain evolved to "assume" certain basic experiences, such as caregivers who speak. Without these experiences, the brain will compensate as best it can, but it is unlikely to do so with the efficiency of a nervous system that got the right environmental input at the right time.

Understanding development thus means living with ambiguities. Perhaps that is a developmental achievement in itself.

Summary

1. **Developmental psychology** studies the way humans develop and change over time. A *life-span developmental perspective* examines both constancy and change, and gains and losses in functioning, that occur at different points over the human life cycle.

2. Three basic issues confront developmental psychologists. The first concerns the relative roles of nature (particularly genetically programmed **maturation**) and nurture. The second is the relative importance of early experience and whether human development is characterized by **critical** or **sensitive periods**. The third issue is the extent to which development occurs in **stages**—relatively discrete steps through which everyone progresses in the same sequence—or whether it is continuous or gradual.

Studying Development

3. Developmental psychologists rely on three types of research designs. **Cross-sectional studies** compare groups of different aged subjects at a single time to see if differences exist among them. **Longitudinal studies** follow the same individuals over time and thus can directly assess age changes rather than age differences. **Sequential studies** minimize the confounding variable of cohort by studying multiple cohorts longitudinally.

Physical Development and Its Psychological Consequences

4. Prenatal (before birth) development is divided into three stages: the germinal, embryonic, and fetal periods. Prenatal development can be disrupted by harmful environmental agents known as **teratogens**, such as alcohol.

5. Neural development, both prenatally and throughout childhood, proceeds through myelination, trimming back of neurons, and increasing dendritic connections.

6. Physical development and psychological development are intertwined. At birth, an infant possesses many adaptive reflexes. Motor development follows a universal maturational sequence, although cross-cultural research indicates that the environment can affect the pace of development. By the end of adolescence, physical growth is virtually complete. With aging comes a gradual decline in physical and sensory abilities with which people must cope psychologically.

Cognitive Development in Infancy, Childhood, and Adolescence

7. For many years psychologists underestimated the substantial abilities of infants. Researchers now know, for example, that ba-

bies are capable of **intermodal** understanding—the ability to associate sensations about an object from different senses and to match their own actions to behaviors they observe visually—in the earliest days of life.

8. Piaget proposed that children develop knowledge by inventing, or *constructing*, a reality out of their own experience. According to Piaget, people cognitively adapt to their environment through two interrelated processes. **Assimilation** means interpreting actions or events in terms of one's present schemas, that is, fitting reality into one's previous ways of thinking. **Accommodation** involves modifying schemas to fit reality.

9. Piaget proposed a stage theory of cognitive development. During the **sensorimotor stage**, thought primarily takes the form of perception and action. Gradually, children acquire **object permanence**, recognizing that objects exist in time and space independent of their actions on or observation of them. Sensorimotor children are extremely **egocentric**, or thoroughly embedded in their own point of view. The **preoperational stage** is characterized by the emergence of symbolic thought. Operations are mental actions the individual can use to manipulate, transform, and return an object of knowledge to its original state. Piaget called the third stage the **concrete operational stage** because at this point children can operate on, or mentally manipulate, internal representations of concrete objects in ways that are reversible. The concrete operational child understands **conservation**—the idea that basic properties of an object or situation remain stable even though superficial properties may change. The **formal operational stage** is characterized by the ability to reason about formal propositions rather than concrete events.

10. In its broadest outlines, such as the movement from concrete, egocentric thought to abstract thought, Piaget's theory appears to be accurate. Psychologists have, however, criticized Piaget for underestimating the capacities of younger children, assuming too much consistency across domains, and downplaying the influence of culture.

11. The information-processing approach to cognitive development focuses on the development of different aspects of cognition. Several variables that develop over time are children's **knowledge base**, their **automatization** of processing, their ability to use cog-

nitive strategies, and their metacognitive abilities (understanding their own thinking processes).

12. Integrative, or **neo-Piagetian**, theories attempt to wed stage conceptions with research on information processing and domain-specific knowledge.

Cognitive Development and Change in Adulthood

13. As with muscle strength, the rule-of-thumb with intellectual ability is *use it or lose it*: Mental capacities atrophy with disuse.

14. Although many cognitive functions decline in later life, substantial intellectual decline occurs in only a minority of people. The most common declines with age are **psychomotor slowing**; difficulty with explicit memory retrieval; and decreased speed and efficiency of problem solving. Whereas fluid intelligence (intellectual capacities used in processing many kinds of information) begins to decline gradually in midlife, crystallized intelligence (the person's store of knowledge) continues to expand over the life span.

15. Senile **dementia** is a disorder marked by global disturbance of higher mental functions. Well over half the cases of senile dementia result from **Alzheimer's disease**, a progressive and incurable illness that destroys neurons in the brain, severely impairing memory, reasoning, perception, language, and behavior.

Language Development

16. For years researchers have debated the existence of a critical period for language learning. The first three years of life seem to be the optimal time to attain native fluency. After age 12, even near-native fluency is difficult to achieve.

17. Cross-culturally, children go through similar stages of language development. They begin by **babbling** in the first year and produce one-word utterances toward the beginning of the second year. Young children's speech is **telegraphic speech**, omitting all but the essential words. By age 4, children's sentences largely conform to the grammar of their language. The stages of language development are virtually universal; however, the precise timing and course of individual language development depend on both nature and nurture.

Key Terms

Social Development

nfancy and early childhood were a series of seeming mishaps for Ben. Ben's birth mother was an alcoholic and a drug addict, chemicals to which he was born addicted. Although Ben's mother wanted to raise Ben herself, she was unable to provide the care that he needed. Frequently, she neglected Ben and failed to feed him when he cried; she ultimately put Ben up for adoption when he was 13 months old. A difficult baby, Ben was moved from one foster home to another. By the time he was 3, he had lived with six different foster families.

During his early years of life, Ben's behavior became increasingly erratic. He seemed mistrustful and unable to form any kind of bond or attachment with others. Foster families in which other children were present were unable to keep Ben for long because he was aggressive and frequently acted out toward the other children.

Finally, at the age of 3, Ben was diagnosed as suffering from reactive attachment disorder, also known simply as attachment disorder (Sheperis et al., 2003; Wilson, 2001). Even at this young age, Ben showed little evidence of a conscience, seldom displaying concern for the thoughts and feelings of others.

Ben could be a poster child for reactive attachment disorder. His prenatal exposure to drugs, neglect by his mother, and multiple foster care situations set the stage for the development of a child with little trust in or feelings for others. The critical period for the development of reactive attachment disorder is believed to be the first two years of life. Although separations from parents or parental neglect can be harmful to children at any age, children react to separations very differently at different ages. At age 2, separation can be devastating for a child; by age 6, a few weeks away may only result in occasional homesickness. The difference reflects **social development**, *changes in interpersonal thought, feeling, and behavior throughout the life span*.

We begin by discussing the earliest relationships—between an infant and her caregivers—and consider how, and how much, these relationships lay the groundwork for later relationships. Next, we examine how children learn the ways of their culture. For example, how and when do children take on the attributes expected of their gender? Then we explore children's relationships with friends and siblings, their changing conceptions of themselves and others, and their developing capacity for moral judgment and action. We conclude by expanding the focus to the entire life span. Although the range of topics may seem enormous, what unites them is a focus on the types of relationships people form throughout life, from intimate attachments in infancy through adulthood to sibling and peer relationships; the development of beliefs and feelings about themselves and others; and the way these beliefs and feelings are expressed in different social contexts.

Throughout, we will address two issues. The first, raised in Chapter 13, has provided a consistent thread across psychological research for over a century: the question of nature and nurture. What are the relative contributions of innate characteristics, culture, and experience to social development? How do evolutionary, biological, and social pressures converge to create a social person? The second issue is, what is the relation between social development and cognitive development? To what extent does the development of children's experience of friendship, morality, or gender depend on their cognitive development?

Attachment

In the middle of the twentieth century, psychoanalysts observed that children reared in large institutional homes, with minimal stimulation and no consistent contact with a loving caretaker, often became emotionally unstable, lacking in conscience, or mentally retarded. Now, many of these children would be classified as suffering from reactive attachment disorder much like Ben. These observations led to recognition of the importance of **attachment**, *the enduring affectional ties that children form with their primary caregivers* (Ainsworth & Bell, 1970; Bowlby, 1969). Attachment includes a desire for proximity to an attachment figure, a sense of security derived from the person's presence, and feelings of distress when the person is absent. Attachment is not unilateral; rather, it involves an interaction between two people who react to each other's signals.

Attachment in Infancy

For many years, psychoanalysts and behaviorists were in rare agreement on the origins of attachment behavior, both linking it to feeding. Psychoanalysts assumed that the gratification of oral needs led infants to become attached to people who satisfy those needs. According to behaviorists, mothers became secondary reinforcers through their association with food, which is a primary (innate) reinforcer (Chapter 5). Unfortunately, the two theories were similar in one other respect: They were both wrong. Definitive evidence came from a series of classic experiments performed by Harry Harlow (Harlow & Zimmerman, 1959).

Harlow reared infant rhesus monkeys in isolation from their mothers for several months and then placed them in a cage with two inanimate surrogate "mothers" (Chapter 2). One, a wire monkey that provided no warmth or softness, held a bottle from which the infant could nurse. The other was covered with terrycloth to provide softness, but it had no bottle, so it could not provide food. Baby monkeys spent much of their time clinging to the softer mother. They would also run to the softer surrogate when they were frightened, but they virtually ignored the wire surrogate except when hungry. Harlow's findings established that perceived security, not food, is the crucial element in forming attachment relationships in primates; he referred to the ties that bind an infant to its caregivers as *contact comfort*. As shown in Figure 14.1, some infants and children are raised with little or no human contact. These children, called feral children, basically raise themselves in the wild, and show predictable deficits in physical, social, and language development.

Bowlby's Theory of Attachment   John Bowlby (1969, 1973, 1982), who developed attachment theory, linked Harlow's findings to the psychodynamic literature on

FIGURE 14.1   Feral children are children who are raised with little or no human contact. They derive their name from the suggestion that some of these children are "adopted" by wolves and raised with them. Their development in the areas of language, sociability, and physical development are greatly affected. One of the most famous instances of feral children is Victor of Aveyron (Wild Boy of Aveyron).

FIGURE 14.2 Imprinting. Normally, imprinting leads young animals to follow an adult member of their species. At times, however, Mother Nature may lead her children astray. Here, geese follow Konrad Lorenz, on whom they imprinted when young.

Big Picture φ Question 3

To what extent is human psychology continuous with the psychology of other animals?

Making Connections

Bowlby's model of attachment relies on the concept of *homeostasis*—the tendency of biological organisms to monitor variables relevant to survival, detect deviations from these goals (feedback), and respond with corrective mechanisms (Chapter 10). The child's goal is to remain physically close to the attachment figure. When this goal is threatened, as when a toddler's mother leaves the room, the child experiences a feedback signal: distress. Distress motivates the child to cry or search for his mother. If either behavior is successful, the child receives a sense of security that temporarily deactivates the attachment system. A similar system operates in adults. For example, social anxiety is viewed as an interrupt mechanism, alerting individuals that they are behaving in ways that may jeopardize the degree to which they are included (i.e., attached) to others.

children reared in institutional settings. Bowlby was both a psychoanalyst and an ethologist (a scientist interested in comparative animal behavior), and he proposed an evolutionary theory of attachment. He argued that attachment behavior is prewired in humans, as is similar behavior in other animal species, to keep immature animals close to their parents.

Bowlby noted the relation between human attachment behavior and a phenomenon studied by the ethologist Konrad Lorenz (1935) called imprinting. **Imprinting** is *the tendency of young animals of certain species to follow an animal to which they were exposed during a sensitive period early in their lives* (Figure 14.2). According to Lorenz (1937), imprinting confers an evolutionary advantage: A gosling that stays close to its mother or father is more likely to be fed, protected from predators, and taught skills useful for survival and reproduction than a gosling that strays from its parents. Bowlby argued that attachment behavior in human infants, such as staying close to parents and crying loudly in their absence, evolved for the same reasons.

Thus, when a child feels threatened, the attachment system "turns on," leading the child to cry or search for its attachment figure. Once the child feels safe again, she is free to play or explore the environment. The attachment figure thus becomes a safe base from which the child can explore (Ainsworth, 1979) and to whom he can periodically return for "emotional refueling" (Mahler et al., 1975). Toddlers who are playing happily often suddenly look around to establish the whereabouts of their attachment figures. Once they locate their caregiver or even run to a comforting lap, they return to play, refueled for the next period of time. Later in life, a college student's phone calls home may serve a similar function.

The Origins of Attachment   Attachment behavior emerges gradually over the first several months of life, peaking some time during the second year and then diminishing in intensity as children become more confident in their independence (Ainsworth, 1967). Among the first precursors of attachment is a general preference for social stimuli (such as faces) over other objects in the environment (Carver et al., 2003). Visual recognition of the mother (the primary caregiver studied in most research) occurs at about three months (Olson, 1981); by five or six months, infants recognize and greet their mothers and other attachment figures from across the room.

At six to seven months, infants begin to show **separation anxiety**, *distress at separation from their attachment figures*. Separation anxiety emerges about the same time in children of different cultures (Figure 14.3), despite widely different child-rearing practices (Kagan, 1976). Similarly, blind children show a comparable pattern (although the onset is a few months later), becoming anxious when they no longer hear the familiar sounds of their mother's voice or movements (Fraiberg, 1975). These data suggest a maturational basis for separation anxiety. In fact, separation anxiety emerges about the same time infants begin to crawl, which makes sense from an evolutionary perspective.

INTERIM SUMMARY

Social development involves changes in interpersonal thought, feeling, and behavior throughout the life span. **Attachment** refers to the enduring ties children form with their primary caregivers; it includes a desire for proximity to an attachment figure, a sense of security derived from the person's presence, and feelings of distress when the person is absent. John Bowlby, who developed attachment theory, argued that attachment, like **imprinting** (the tendency of young animals to follow another animal to which they were exposed during a sensitive period), evolved as a mechanism for keeping infants close to their parents while they are immature and vulnerable.

Individual Differences in Attachment Patterns

Bowlby observed that young children typically exhibit a sequence of behaviors in response to separations from their attachment figures. They initially *protest* by crying or throwing tantrums. However, like Ben, they may ultimately become *detached* and indifferent to the attachment figure if she is gone too long.

Attachment Patterns   Bowlby's colleague Mary Ainsworth recognized that children vary in their responses to separation: While some seem secure in their relationship with their attachment figure, others seem perpetually stuck in protest or detachment. Ainsworth demonstrated these differences among infants using an experimental procedure called the *Strange Situation*. In the Strange Situation, the mother leaves her young child (aged 12 to 18 months) alone in a room of toys. Next, the child is joined for a brief time by a friendly stranger. The mother then returns and greets the child (Ainsworth, 1973, 1979, 1991).

Ainsworth found that children tend to respond to their mothers' absence and return in one of three ways, one of which she called *secure*, and the others, *insecure*. *Infants who welcome the mother's return and seek closeness to her* have a **secure attachment style**. *Infants who ignore the mother when she returns* display an **avoidant attachment style**, whereas *infants who are angry and rejecting while simultaneously indicating a clear desire to be close to the mother* have an **ambivalent attachment style** (also sometimes called *anxious-ambivalent* or *resistant*). Avoidant children often seem relatively unfazed by their mother's departure, whereas ambivalent children become very upset.

More recent research with infants in high-risk samples, such as those who have been maltreated, has uncovered another variant of insecure attachment, called disorganized, or disorganized-disoriented (Lyons-Ruth et al., 1997; Main & Solomon, 1986). Children with a **disorganized attachment style** *behave in contradictory ways, indicating helpless efforts to elicit soothing responses from the attachment figure*. Disorganized infants often approach the mother while simultaneously gazing away, or appear disoriented, as manifested in stereotyped rocking and dazed facial expressions. Whereas the other attachment patterns seem organized and predictable, the disorganized child's behavior is difficult to understand and typically comes in the context of parenting that is *itself* unpredictable, and hence difficult to understand from the infant's point of view (see Carlson, 1998).

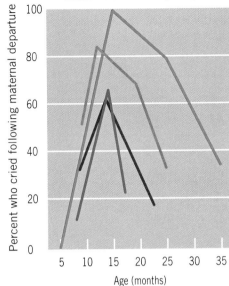

FIGURE 14.3 legend:
— Botswana Bushmen
— Antigua, Guatemala (urban)
— Israeli kibbutz
— Guatemalan Indian (rural)

Y-axis: Percent who cried following maternal departure
X-axis: Age (months)

FIGURE 14.3 Separation anxiety across cultures. Separation anxiety, as measured by the percentage of children who cry when separated from their mother, peaks at approximately the same time across various cultures. *Source:* Kagan, 1983, p. 198.

Big Picture φ Question 4

To what extent is human nature particular versus universal?

Apply & Discuss

Separation anxiety appears to rely on evolved mechanisms.

■ Under what environmental conditions might separation anxiety not emerge? Would children in orphanages whose caregivers are inconsistent or who do not provide comfort develop separation anxiety?

■ If the normal appearance of separation distress requires the presence of an attachment figure, can we call separation anxiety "innate"? Do innate capacities sometimes—or most of the time—require environmental input to develop?

Big Picture φ Question 2

What is the relationship between reason and desire or, more precisely, between cognition and affect?

Making Connections

The concept of internal working models of relationships dovetails with other constructs psychologists have used to describe mental representations. Mental models are representations of how things work (Chapter 7). Schemas are enduring ways of processing information about an object of thought, such as the self and relationships (Chapters 6 and 17). Object representations are representations of self, others, and relationships, such as the malevolent representations of relationships that characterize individuals with borderline personality disorder, whose emotions tend to spiral out of control (Chapters 12 and 15).

Secure attachment is the most commonly observed attachment pattern around the world (see Main, 1990; van Ijzendoorn & Kroonenberg, 1988). Nevertheless, the frequency of different styles of attachment differs substantially across cultures. For example, infants reared on Israeli kibbutzim (collective living arrangements) are much more likely to have ambivalent attachments to their mothers than infants in the West. Further, unlike European and North American children, the quality of an infant's attachment to its daytime mother surrogate on the kibbutz, not to its parents, predicts later social adjustment in childhood (Sagi, 1990; Sagi et al., 1994).

Internal Working Models of Relationships   Attachment does not just refer to a pattern of behavior. Bowlby proposed that infants develop **internal working models**, or *mental representations of attachment relationships that form the basis for expectations in close relationships* (Bowlby, 1969, 1982; Bretherton, 1990; Main, 1995; Stevenson-Hinde & Verschueren, 2002). For example, a child whose early attachment to her mother is marked by extreme anxiety resulting from inconsistent or abusive caretaking may form a working model of herself as unlovable or unworthy. She may also see significant others as hostile or unpredictable. Her behavior will appear disorganized or disoriented because she cannot form a coherent working model or representation of her relationship with her mother that both makes sense and provides a feeling of security.

The concept of internal working models may help explain why infants and toddlers who are secure with one caretaker may not be secure with another (Howes & Hamilton, 1992; Verschueren & Marcoen, 1999). A child's experience with one person, such as the mother, may feel secure, while another relationship (such as with a father or preschool teacher) may feel less comfortable or predictable because the child has different internal working models of the relationships. The concept of internal working models may also help explain why attachment classification in infancy predicts not only social but cognitive variables years later, such as the ability to sustain attention: Infants who feel safe and secure will have more freedom to explore their environment than insecure infants, whose time and attention are more likely to be consumed by attachment-related thoughts, feelings, and motivations.

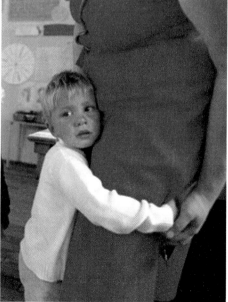

Basic attachment mechanisms appear very similar in human and other primates, such as the rhesus macaque.

Temperament, Experience, and Their Interaction in the Development of Attachment Styles

From Brain to Behavior

Why do infants differ in their patterns of attachment? Some researchers emphasize temperament; others emphasize the way caregivers respond to the infant. Both appear to influence attachment security, along with an important interaction between the two: the fit between the child and parent (Belsky & Isabella, 1988; Rosen & Rothbaum, 1993; Seifer et al., 1996).

Like all psychological processes, attachment can be understood in part at a psychobiological level. Attachment-related behavior such as protest at separation probably does not occur in the first six months of life because myelination of neurons has not sufficiently progressed in limbic structures that regulate emotional distress, particularly fear and anxiety (Konner, 1991). Protest, distress, and despair at separation after that time appear to be mediated by several neurotransmitter systems, notably dopamine, norepinephrine, and serotonin, which are involved in arousal, anxiety, and depression (Kraemer, 1992). For example, monkeys separated from their mothers show elevated norepinephrine levels, which are consistent with behavioral responses indicating distress. (Attachment is a two-way affair: Rhesus monkey *mothers* separated from their newborn infants similarly show elevated stress hormones for days; Champoux & Suomi, 1994.)

These normal neurotransmitter responses to separation can be altered in monkeys either pharmacologically, using chemicals that disrupt neural transmission, or through abnormal rearing, in which the infant is removed from the mother at birth and reared in isolation or with peers. Abnormal rearing conditions alter neuronal development in the cortex, cerebellum, and limbic system in monkeys, a suggestion that *environmental* events can produce lasting *biological* changes in the systems that mediate attachment behavior. These monkeys are particularly vulnerable to despair responses upon later separations (see Suomi, 1999).

The relation between attachment style and temperament is a matter of controversy. In humans, researchers have identified three infant temperaments—easy, difficult, and slow to warm up—which correspond in certain respects to secure, ambivalent, and avoidant attachment styles (Chess & Thomas, 1986). Some researchers have argued that attachment security largely reflects temperament (see Kagan, 1984; Mangelsdorf et al., 1990). An inborn tendency to be timid or fearful, for example, could produce anxious behavior in the Strange Situation (Goldsmith & Alansky, 1987). The temperamental variable most highly predictive of attachment status across several studies is negative affect (Chapter 10)—that is, the tendency to experience emotions such as anxiety and depression. The correlation, however, is only .30 (Vaughn et al., 1992), which suggests that temperament is only one determinant of attachment style.

Temperament does not, however, operate in a vacuum. An environmental variable that appears to have a tremendous impact on security of attachment is the mother's sensitivity to her baby's signals (Ainsworth, 1979; Sroufe & Waters, 1977). Mothers who are sensitive to their infants enjoy interacting with them, behave in ways that express warmth and encouragement, and stimulate their curiosity (De Wolff & van Ijzendoorn, 1997). These interactions tend to be mutually rewarding and to produce secure babies. In contrast, infants whose mothers do not respond to their needs form less secure attachment bonds and display more anger, fear, and avoidance (De Wolff & van Ijzendoorn, 1997; Pederson et al., 1990; Waters et al., 2000a). The role of the father in attachment is an area of continued debate (see van IJzendoorn & De Wolff, 1997), although paternal sensitivity is an important predictor of the parent–child relationship as well.

Both biology and experience thus affect individual differences in attachment. However, the interaction of the two—such as the match between children and their

Big Picture φ Question 1

To what extent can mental processes be reduced to the brain or body?

caregivers—may be just as important. For example, infants who are temperamentally prone to distress may be more likely to become insecurely attached if their caretakers are rigid and emotionally controlled (Mangelsdorf et al., 1990). Similarly, infants with an easy temperament may be more likely to become securely attached despite an unresponsive caregiver than would infants with a more difficult temperament.

Implications of Attachment for Later Development

Attachment patterns that begin in infancy can persist and find expression in a wide range of social behaviors throughout the life span (Waters et al., 2000a, 2000b). Children rated avoidant in infancy tend to be described by their teachers as insecure and detached in nursery school and to have difficulty discussing feelings about separation at age 6. In contrast, preschoolers who were securely attached as infants tend to have higher self-esteem, are more socially competent, show greater sensitivity to the needs of their peers, and are more popular (see DeMulder et al., 2000; LaFreniere & Sroufe, 1985; Waters et al., 1979).

Security of attachment in infancy predicts a range of behaviors as children grow older, from self-control and peer acceptance to competent behavior in the classroom (Bretherton, 1990; Howes et al., 1998). Children with a disorganized style in infancy tend to be rated by their teachers in early elementary school as impulsive, disruptive, and aggressive, particularly if they are also below average intellectually (Lyons-Ruth et al., 1997).

Individual differences in attachment style are also related to different patterns of response in everyday social interactions. Using a diary methodology by which people describe their social interactions each day for a period of weeks, researchers found that securely attached individuals reported more satisfying daily interactions with others and felt that others were more responsive to them than insecurely attached individuals (Kafetsios & Nezlek, 2002). Based on the results of this study, attachment styles affect not only long-term patterns of relating, but also daily satisfaction with those social interactions.

The theory of internal working models helps make sense of why attachment security with parents predicts the quality of peer relationships years later, particularly close peers, as well as with later attachment figures, notably mates (Cassidy et al., 1996; Lieberman et al., 1999). Children who are secure with their parents have more positive expectations about what they can expect from relationships. This security leads them to be more trusting and engaging with peers and lovers, who are then more likely to respond to them positively. As a result, they then form more positive representations of peer and love relationships—creating a self-reinforcing cycle, in which positive initial working models foster good relationships, which maintain those models.

Apply & Discuss

Research on attachment in infancy and early childhood has largely focused on patterns of attachment that children develop through interactions with their parents or other primary caregivers. What role do you think close relationships with pets or the creation of imaginary friends might play in facilitating attachment behavior in infants and young children? Could children get needs for companionship and connectedness met from these alternative types of relationships? In other words, could pets and/or imaginary friends serve as surrogate attachment figures?

INTERIM SUMMARY

Researchers have discovered four patterns of infant attachment: **secure, avoidant, ambivalent**, and **disorganized**. Whereas secure infants are readily comforted by their attachment figures, insecure infants tend to shut off their needs for attachment (avoidant), have difficulty being soothed (ambivalent), or behave in contradictory ways that reflect their difficulty predicting or understanding the way their attachment figures will behave (disorganized). Infant attachment patterns reflect a combination of temperament, parental responsiveness, and the interaction of the two. Attachment security in infancy predicts social competence as well as school grades from preschool through adolescence.

Adult Attachment   Some of the infants first assessed in longitudinal studies using the Strange Situation are just reaching adulthood, and evidence suggests that early attachment patterns remain influential in adult life (Waters et al., 2000b). **Adult**

attachment refers to *ways of experiencing attachment relationships in adulthood*. Researchers study adult attachment by interviewing subjects and coding the way they describe and recall their relationships with their parents (Main, 1995; Main et al., 1985) or by measuring the ways they describe their experiences with attachment figures such as spouses on self-report questionnaires (Brennan et al., 1998).

Patterns of Adult Attachment   Adults with secure adult attachment styles speak freely and openly about their relationships with their parents. People with ambivalent styles appear preoccupied with and ambivalent about their parents. Avoidant adults dismiss the importance of attachment relationships or offer idealized generalizations about their parents but are unable to back them up with specific examples. When asked about times when they felt rejected or mistreated or were separated from their parents in childhood, adults with an avoidant style tend to deny having such experiences—all the while spiking on measures of physiological reactivity indicating emotional distress (Dozier & Kobak, 1992).

Individuals with an attachment style characterized as *unresolved* (similar to the disorganized style seen in infancy) have difficulty speaking coherently about attachment figures from their past and have generally been unable to cope with losses or other traumatic experiences from their past. As a result, their narratives are often confused and confusing, and they send conflicting signals to their own children, particularly when their own unmet attachment needs get activated under stress.

How common are these attachment patterns? Data from multiple sources find similar rates of each type of attachment pattern in adults as in infants. A large stratified random sample of over 8000 individuals in the United States, using a self-report measure of the first three adult attachment patterns, found that roughly 60 percent of people reported a secure attachment pattern, whereas 25 percent were classified as avoidant and about 10 percent anxiously attached (Mickelson et al., 1997). Interview studies across several cultures similarly classify roughly 60 percent of people as securely attached in relation to their own parents, with varying numbers in the other three categories (van Ijzendoorn & Bakermans-Kranenburg, 1996).

Predicting Behavior from Adult Attachment Patterns   Attachment patterns in adults predict a range of phenomena, from whether people want to have children (Rholes et al., 1997), to how they balance the needs of those children with the needs of work (Vasquez et al., 2002), to how they cope with stressful life events (Mikulincer & Florian, 1997; Myers & Vetere, 2002), to how upset they get at airports when separating from their romantic partner (Fraley & Shaver, 1998), and to how troublesome they find the increasing independence of their adolescent children to be (Hock et al., 2001). Perhaps most importantly, adults' attachment patterns in relation to their own parents, as assessed by interview, predict their own children's attachment styles with remarkable accuracy (Main, 1995; Steele et al., 1996; van Ijzendoorn, 1995). For example, mothers who are uncomfortable or avoidant in describing their own attachment to their mothers tend to have avoidant infants and children (Fonagy et al., 1991; Main et al., 1985).

Considerable evidence suggests that mothers whose early attachment experiences were disrupted—through death of a parent, divorce, abuse or neglect, or long-term separation from their parents—are more likely to have difficulty forming close attachment relationships with their own infants and to have infants with a disorganized attachment pattern (Lyons-Ruth et al., 1997; Ricks, 1985; Rutter et al., 1983; Zeanah & Zeanah, 1989). Mothers who have insecure attachment relationships with their own mothers are less responsive and have more difficulty maintaining physical proximity to their infants and young children (Crowell & Feldman, 1991).

Stability of Early Attachment Patterns   Is history destiny? Can a person ever overcome a bad start in childhood or infancy? Problematic early attachments substantially increase vulnerability to subsequent difficulties. Disturbances in childhood at-

Apply & Discuss

Some people, like writer Dave Pelzer, author of *A Child Called "It,"* are resilient in the face of even highly traumatic childhood experiences.

▪ What factors are likely to make some people resilient in the face of abuse, neglect, or other experiences in childhood that increase people's risk for later social and emotional problems?

▪ Can anyone be truly "unscarred" by physical or sexual abuse in childhood? How could researchers design studies to find out? What kind of subtle measures would they need to include?

tachment relationships predict later difficulties in childhood and adolescence (Bowlby, 1969; Ricks, 1985; Spitz, 1945). Disrupted attachments are associated with severe personality disturbances (Ludolph et al., 1990; Zanarini et al., 1989), depression (Brown et al., 1986), antisocial behavior and adjustment problems (Tizard & Hodges, 1978), and difficulty behaving appropriately as a parent (Ricks, 1985). Childhood experiences such as parental neglect or mistreatment or even parental divorce make people more vulnerable to insecure attachment in adulthood (Mickelson et al., 1997).

All generalizations such as these, however, are *probabilisitic* statements—that is, statements about probabilities, or increased risk. Early attachment experiences are not the only determinant of later functioning. Some children are remarkably resilient in the face of neglectful or abusive life experiences (Anthony & Cohler, 1987; Luthar et al., 2000). Furthermore, as circumstances change, so do patterns of attachment (Lewis et al., 2000). Indeed, some of Harlow's monkeys who had been raised in isolation and were extremely socially maladapted showed marked improvement in social interactions after developing a close relationship with a normal monkey who served as a simian "therapist" (Chamove, 1978; Novak & Harlow, 1975). Internal working models, like the schemas described in previous chapters, are inherently conservative, but they are not immutable (Lamb, 1987). Longitudinal research suggests that childhood risk factors such as parental loss or divorce, life-threatening illness of parent or child, and child abuse can turn securely attached infants into insecurely attached adults (Waters et al., 2000b; Weinfield et al., 2000).

One study provides dramatic evidence of the possibilities for altering problematic patterns of attachment in the opposite direction. The investigators provided a group of high-risk infants and mothers with a weekly home visitor. The mothers were poor, often depressed, and exhibited enough signs of inadequate caretaking to warrant referrals from health, educational, or social service professionals (Lyons-Ruth et al., 1990). The home visitor offered support and advice, modeled positive and active interactions with the infant, and provided a trusting relationship for the mother. The results were compelling: Compared to an untreated control group, infants in the intervention group scored 10 points higher on an infant IQ measure and were twice as likely (roughly 60 versus 30 percent) to be classified as securely attached at 18 months.

INTERIM SUMMARY

Researchers studying **adult attachment** find that roughly 60 percent of people appear to have a secure attachment style. Parents tend to produce children with an attachment style similar to their own. Attachment patterns have considerable stability because internal working models tend to change slowly, but as life circumstances change, so can attachment styles.

Socialization

Attachment relationships provide the child's first social experiences and serve as a model for many future relationships, but they are only one avenue for initiating the child into the social world. ***To function as adults, children must learn the rules, beliefs, values, skills, attitudes, and behavior patterns of their society, a process called* socialization**. Children learn from a variety of *socialization agents*, individuals and groups that transmit social knowledge and values to the child.

Before we consider research on socialization, several caveats are in order. First, socialization is not a one-way process in which adults fill children's minds with values and beliefs. Rather, it is a two-way street, or *transactional*. Children are active participants in their own socialization, who must construct an understanding of social rules and gradually come to experience cultural beliefs and values as their own (Bell, 1968; Kochanska, 1997a; Maccoby, 1992; Sapir, 1949). Although we tend to think of socialization as a process through which parents and other adults "leave their mark" on children, from an evolutionary perspective, children are also *biologically prepared* to be socialized (Bugental & Goodnow, 1998). Children come prepared to experience emotions such as shame and guilt that render them readily shaped by parents into the kinds of people who will one day be accepted in their society.

Children also have innate temperaments that influence attempts to shape them. Inherited tendencies tend to increase in their expression throughout adolescence. Thus, the quality of parent–child relationships continues to be shaped not just by infant temperament but by genetic predispositions that may become most apparent many years afterward (Elkins et al., 1997). Indeed, the way children behave shapes the way their parents respond. Children who are impulsive and poorly controlled elicit ineffective parenting, just as ineffective parents can create troubled children (Stice & Barrera, 1995).

A second point to remember in thinking about socialization is that socialization is a lifelong process. Individuals learn throughout their lives to play different roles, such as student, parent, friend, wage-earner, or retiree, and roles change from one phase of life to the next.

Finally, socialization always occurs within a broader social and economic context (Bronfenbrenner, 1998; McLoyd, 1989; Parke & Buriel, 1998). The way parents behave with their children depends on cultural values and practices (Harkness & Super, 1996; Harwood et al., 1996). Although deliberate teaching is important, much of socialization is implicit, as when children learn about the importance of being on time by the regular sounding of school bells between classes (see Strauss & Quinn, 1998). Economic stresses and marital satisfaction also affect the way parents parent and the extent to which their children function well socially and academically (Brooks-Gunn et al., 1997; Conger et al., 1993; Fincham, 1998).

The Role of Parents

The question of how important parents are to development is now hotly debated (Collins et al., 2000; Harris, 1998, 2000). For years psychologists assumed that parenting is the most important determinant of personality and social development. In the last decade, this point of view has been challenged by a steady stream of behavioral genetic studies. These studies suggest that the family environment shared by siblings has little impact on personality, social, or cognitive traits, particularly when compared with genetic influences and environmental influences not shared by siblings, such as experiences with peers (Chapters 8 and 12). Recently, Judy Harris (1998) created a storm of controversy when she published a book challenging the idea that parents matter much at all. The available data suggest, she argued, that genetic and peer influences primarily determine who we are.

Can it be true that our parents, who socialize us from the beginning and whose homes we inhabit and whose rules and attitudes govern our behavior for the first 18 years of our lives (and in many cultures, long after), have little influence on our subsequent development? The data clearly do not support the old view that parenting is the central determinant of individual differences in personality and social development, but neither do they support the swing of the pendulum in the other direction.

The problems with the "parenting doesn't matter" hypothesis are complex, but many hinge on the way researchers interpret data on heritability (see Collins et al., 2000). As we have seen (Chapters 1 and 8), the size of heritability coefficients is highly dependent on the samples researchers use in their studies. A sample that consists primarily of white middle-class people in the United States has already eliminated many of the most important parenting effects—such as the differences between parental behavior in Uganda and Dallas, which are likely to be far greater than any differences

Big Picture φ Question 7

To what extent are psychological processes conscious or unconscious—that is, explicit versus implicit?

Big Picture φ Question 6

What is the relation between nature and nurture in shaping psychological processes?

among white middle-class parents in Dallas. The tendency of human children to use language is clearly rooted in our genes, but no one would similarly argue that parents have little influence on the language their children speak. Further, two children in the same family will elicit different patterns of parenting. Although these are often interpreted as genetic effects, they actually reflect transactions between the child's genes and the ways parents respond.

What about the argument that peers are more important than parents? As we will see, peers play a substantial role in development, and their influence can be seen in problems such as delinquency or substance abuse in adolescence. However, adolescents *choose* their peers, and both the peers they choose and their susceptibility to "bad company" depend heavily on the social skills, expectations, and capacities for intimacy they developed at home in their attachment relationships (Collins et al., 2000; Ladd, 1999). Children with histories of maltreatment by their parents, for example, tend to have poor peer relationships (Bolger et al., 1998).

Perhaps most importantly, when researchers carefully *measure* parenting, they typically find substantial effects on personality and social development (Bates et al., 2003; Kremen & Block, 1998; Westen, 1998). These effects are most apparent when parents behave in unusual or damaging ways, such as abusing their children, but they also appear with more subtle differences in parenting styles.

Over 30 years ago, Diana Baumrind (1967, 1971, 1991) discovered three styles of parenting, distinguished by the extent to which parents control their children's actions and respond to their feelings. **Authoritarian** *parents place high value on obedience and respect for authority.* They do not encourage discussion of why particular behaviors are important or listen to the child's point of view. Rather, they impose a set of standards to which they expect their children to adhere, and they are likely to punish their children frequently and physically. In contrast, **permissive** *parents impose virtually no controls on their children*, allowing them to make their own decisions whenever possible. Permissive parents tend to accept their children's impulsive behaviors, including angry or aggressive ones, and rarely dole out punishments. **Authoritative** *parents set standards for their children and firmly enforce them, but they also encourage give and take and explain their views while showing respect for their children's opinions.*

A fourth style of parenting that has been proposed more recently is **uninvolved** *parents who consistently place their own needs above the needs of their child.* (See Figure 14.4 for a comparison of how the four parenting styles differ along the dimensions of nurturing and control.) Although children's genetic endowments clearly influence parenting styles, the data also suggest that different parenting styles tend to produce different kinds of children. The most self-controlled, independent, curious, academically competent, and sociable children tend to have authoritative parents (Baumrind, 1987; Steinberg et al., 1994; Weiss & Schwarz, 1996). Authoritarian parenting has been linked, however, to low independence, vulnerability to stress, low self-esteem, and an external locus of control (a sense that one has little control over what happens in life) (Buri et al., 1988; Loeb et al., 1980; Steinberg et al., 1994). Children with permissive parents tend to be low in self-reliance and impulse control (Martin et al., 1981; Olweus, 1980) and to have more trouble with substance abuse in adolescence (Baumrind, 1991). Children of uninvolved parents typically display low self-esteem and aggressive behavior (Bukatko & Daehler, 2004; Hatfield et al., 1967; Loeb et al., 1980). The match between a child's temperament and parenting styles is also important: Difficult, hard-to-manage children tend to have fewer behavior problems later on if their parents are firm with rules (Bates et al., 1998).

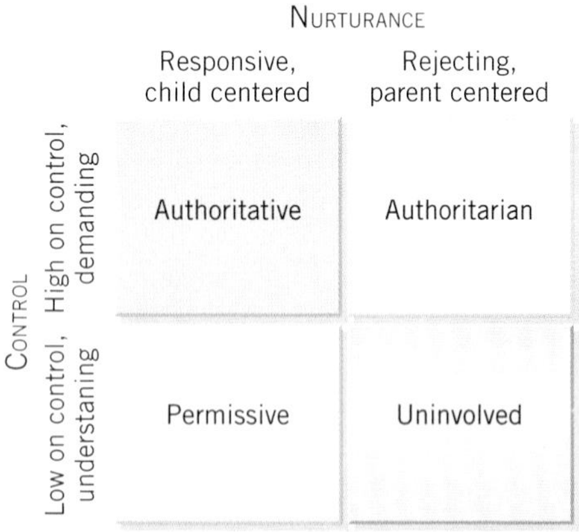

FIGURE 14.4 Variations in nurturing and control as a function of parenting style. As this figure illustrates, each style of parenting represents its own unique combination of nurturance and control. Not surprisingly, these different combinations are expected to influence the kind of children that subsequently develop. Reprinted from Bukatko & Daehler (2004).

INTERIM SUMMARY

Socialization is the process by which children learn the rules, beliefs, values, skills, attitudes, and behavior patterns of their society. Socialization is a transactional and lifelong process. Socialization also always occurs in a broader social context. **Authoritarian** parents place high value on obedience and respect for authority. **Permissive** parents impose minimal controls on their children. **Authoritative** parents enforce standards but explain their views and encourage verbal give-and-take. **Uninvolved** parents consistently place their own needs above the needs of their child.

The Role of Culture

Although authoritative parenting tends to produce outcomes most people in the West would consider "better," two qualifications are worth noting. First, good parenting is *flexible* parenting and changes as children mature. For example, preschoolers and their siblings tend to get along much better if their parents intervene before their squabbles turn into brawls. In contrast, school-age children tend to develop better sibling relationships if their parents let them resolve their own disputes (Kramer et al., 1999).

Second, an authoritative parenting style is rare or nonexistent in many cultures and is probably not the most adaptive pattern everywhere (Whiting & Edwards, 1988; Whiting & Whiting, 1973, 1975). Agricultural societies usually value obedience far more than autonomy or independence. Among the Mayan Zinacanteco Indians of Mexico, for example, an entire family shares a single-room 200-square-foot hut, and every member contributes to the family's survival by farming (Brazelton, 1972). In this culture, where people have no real choice in the roles they will fill, socialization for independence and free choice would often prove frustrating or counterproductive.

Training for independence versus embeddedness in kin or clan begins in the first days of life, through implicit forms of learning that predict adult personality and social characteristics (Harwood et al., 1999; Whiting, 1964). For example, infants in most cultures sleep in the same beds, or at least the same rooms, as their mothers. In contrast, North American pediatricians often discourage parents from bringing the child into their bed, and most middle-class parents give infants their own rooms by three to six months. Thus, North American children learn early that they are, and can be, on their own.

In a study comparing the sleeping patterns of Mayan and North American infants, Mayan infants tended simply to fall asleep when they were tired, whereas American families had elaborate bedtime rituals that might begin with a bath and toothbrushing and include reading bedtime stories, singing lullabies, and providing the baby with a special object (Morelli et al., 1992). One North American mother jokingly reported, "When my friends hear that it is time for my son to go to bed, they teasingly say, 'See you in an hour.'"

Mayan parents were generally aghast to hear that parents could separate infants from their mothers at night and seemed to consider it tantamount to child neglect. One horrified Mayan mother asked, "But there's someone else with them there, isn't there?" The Mayan children typically slept with their mothers until another child was born, at which time they joined their fathers or siblings.

Parental Acceptance and Rejection in Cross-Cultural Perspective · A Global Vista

One of the most important ways parents vary across and within cultures is the extent to which they are accepting or rejecting of their children (Rohner, 1975a, 1986; Veneziano & Rohner, 1998). Parents can express acceptance verbally through praise, compliments, and support, or nonverbally through hugging, approving glances, and smiling. Like acceptance, parents can express rejection verbally (bullying or harsh criticism) or nonverbally (hitting, beating, shaking, or simply neglecting).

Parental acceptance and rejection were once considered polar opposites of a single dimension, and they are clearly related. However, like positive and negative affect

Big Picture φ Question 4
To what extent is human nature particular versus universal?

Big Picture φ Question 4
To what extent is human nature particular versus universal?

Table 14.1 ■ Correlations between Parental Acceptance and Personality Characteristics

Personality Characteristic	Degree of Parental Acceptance	
	Children	Adults
Hostility	-.48	-.31
Dependence	-.30	-.39
Self-esteem	.72	.38
Emotional stability	—	.62
Generosity	—	.41
Nurturance	—	.39

Source: Adapted from Rohner, 1975a, p. 260.
Note: Dashes indicate missing data.

(Chapter 10), they can be measured independently and have somewhat independent effects. A parent who is often loving can also sometimes be harsh or even abusive (Pettit, 1997).

Whether a specific behavior is accepting or rejecting depends in part on shared cultural meanings. For example, in European-American samples, the more parents use harsh physical discipline, the more their children (particularly boys) are likely to be impulsive, aggressive, and poorly controlled. The same correlation does not hold for African-American children: Up to a point, the more discipline, the fewer behavior problems children tend to have (Deater-Deckard et al., 1996). Severe parenting that is clearly abusive, however, appears to have the same meaning regardless of cultural circumstances and predicts poorer outcomes in children cross-culturally (Khaleque & Rohner, 2002; Rohner & Britner, 2002).

In general, findings both within the West and across cultures show that parental acceptance is quite consistently associated with high self-esteem, independence, and emotional stability, whereas the opposite is true of parental rejection (MacKinnon-Lewis et al., 1997; Rohner & Britner, 2002). One longitudinal study with a Western sample found that individuals who had a warm or affectionate parent are more likely, 35 years later, to have a long and happy marriage, children, and close friendships in middle age (Franz et al., 1991).

A converging body of data suggests that parents (particularly mothers) who interact with their infants and preschoolers in ways that show mutual responsiveness and "connectedness" tend to have children with better peer relationships, greater empathy for others, and accelerated moral development (Clark & Ladd, 2000; Kochanska et al., 2000). Conversely, multiple studies find that abused children and adults with childhood histories of abuse are more likely than their nonabused peers to view the world as a dangerous place, have poor self-esteem, and have difficulty maintaining close relationships (see Bolger et al., 1998; Finkelhor, 1994; Gelinas, 1983).

A large cross-cultural study correlating parental acceptance–rejection with personality traits in children and adults demonstrated that these patterns are indeed universal (Rohner, 1975a). Cultures in which parents were more rejecting (as rated from anthropological reports) produced children who were more hostile and dependent and adults who were less emotionally stable than cultures with more benign parenting practices (Table 14.1).

The Alorese, who inhabit a Pacific island off Java, exemplify a culture with highly rejecting parenting practices (see DuBois, 1944; Rohner, 1975b). Alorese women return to the fields within two weeks of childbirth—if they have not had an abortion, which is common because they tend to find children burdensome. After a brief initial period of benign and playful caretaking, Alorese infants receive very inconsistent care, such as sporadic feeding. Alorese children are constantly teased, ridiculed, and frightened for sport by older children and adults. Mothers may tease young children they are weaning by nursing the neighbor's baby. Parents threaten children with abandonment and send them to live with relatives if they are too difficult. As young children, the Alorese are left for the day without food unless they can get some by begging or screaming at their elders.

Generalizations about an entire people are, of course, always overgeneralizations, because individual differences exist in all cultures. Nevertheless, anthropologists describe Alorese adults as hostile, aggressive, and distrustful, characteristics that make sense in the context of Alorese child rearing. The Alorese are intensely sensitive to insults and humiliation, and adult relationships are fraught with discord. Males strive to amass as much wealth as they can, always expecting others to cheat and deceive them. Marital affairs are common in both sexes, divorce is rampant, and men often

Alorese children are fed at their parents' convenience and frequently have temper tantrums when they are frustrated.

beat their wives in jealousy or anger. Direct aggression between males is strongly discouraged, although women at times may openly brawl. Even the supernatural world of the Alorese is hostile and unstable, with the Good Beings under constant attack in their myths. In Alor, as elsewhere, patterns of child rearing reflect cultural beliefs and values, and parents tend to harvest what they sow.

Socialization of Gender

Among the most powerful roles into which people are socialized are **gender roles**, which *specify the range of behaviors considered appropriate for males and females* (see Martin, Ruble & Szkrybalo, 2002). The distinction between sex and gender is not always clear, but in general, sex refers to a biological categorization based on genetic and anatomical differences. **Gender**, in contrast, refers to the *psychological meaning of being male or female*, which is influenced by learning.

When a new baby is born, people greet its arrival with one of two announcements: "It's a girl!" or "It's a boy!" This response rests on a relatively small anatomical feature, but it has important consequences for the way the person will come to think, feel, and behave (Archer & Lloyd, 1985). *The process by which children acquire personality traits, emotional responses, skills, behaviors, and preferences that are culturally considered appropriate to their sex* is called **sex typing** (Perry & Bussey, 1979).

Differential treatment of boys and girls begins at the very beginning. In one study, first-time mothers of young infants were asked to play with a six-month-old baby (not their own) for 10 minutes (Smith & Lloyd, 1978). Several toys were available. Some, like a squeaky hammer and a stuffed rabbit wearing a bow tie and trousers, were typical masculine toys; others, like a doll and a squeaky Bambi, were more feminine. The mothers did not know the babies were cross-dressed—that the six-month-old in the little boy's outfit was actually a little girl and the baby in the pink dress was a boy. The mothers tended to offer the infants "gender-appropriate" toys and to encourage more physical activity in the "boys." Similar results emerge from experimental studies with older children: Adults tend to compliment and encourage girls more, particularly in nurturance play, such as taking care of dolls. They hold higher expectations for boys and provide them with more reinforcements for meeting goals (Day, cited in Block, 1978).

Naturalistic investigations of parents' behavior with their children indicate that, throughout childhood, parents (especially fathers) tend to encourage traditional sex-typed behavior, discouraging play with toys that are typical of the opposite gender (Langlois & Downs, 1980). The extent to which fathers are more traditional in their attitudes toward gender plays a particularly important role in shaping children's sex-typed attitudes and behaviors (McHale et al., 1999). Boys in Europe and North America receive more encouragement to compete, more punishment, and more pressure not to cry or express feelings from both parents. Girls receive more warmth, affection, and trust, although they are kept under closer surveillance than boys (Block, 1978). Mothers tend to talk more and speak in more supportive ways with their daughters than their sons (Leaper et al., 1998).

Gender-role socialization is not limited to parents, however. Teachers also contribute to the socialization of males and females to engage in gender-appropriate behaviors. Although the tide is turning, traditionally males have been encouraged to pursue careers (and course work) in science, math, and engineering. Girls, on the other hand, are socialized to pursue careers (if they pursue them at all) in disciplines such as the humanities. Educators, even unwittingly, create a "chilly classroom climate" for girls, whereby they are given less verbal feedback, praise, and encouragement than their male peers (Whitt et al., 1999), with subsequent effects on the self-esteem, cognitive outcomes, and career strivings of male and female students.

Big Picture φ Question 5

To what extent are psychological processes the same in men and women?

Children are also socialized toward stereotypical gender roles by their peers, beginning as early as preschool. Boys and girls are rewarded and punished, respectively, by their peers for engaging in gender-appropriate and gender-inappropriate behavior. Thus, boys who play with dolls or girls who play with trucks are likely to be teased and ridiculed by members of their peer group for playing with toys "of the other sex" (Fagot & Patterson, 1969; Lamb & Roopnarine, 1979; Lamb et al., 1980).

INTERIM SUMMARY

Cultural practices affect virtually every aspect of socialization, such as the relative importance placed on independence and autonomy. Parental acceptance and rejection also differ substantially across cultures. Rejection and abuse have negative effects on children everywhere. Among the most powerful roles into which people are socialized are **gender roles**, which specify the range of behaviors considered appropriate for males and females.

Peer Relationships

We have focused thus far primarily on children's relationships with their parents and other adults. Equally important, however, are peer relationships. The need for peer relationships appears so strong that children who do not have natural peers—first-born and only children—are more likely to invent "imaginary companions" to accompany them (Gleason, 2002; Gleason et al., 2000). The presence of friends can protect children from some of the negative effects of child abuse (Schwartz et al., 2000), just as social support can steel adults against the effects of major stressors such as loss (Chapter 11). Here we focus on two important kinds of peers: friends and siblings.

Friendships

Children's friendships are almost exclusively same-sex friendships. Children simply like same-sex peers better (Bukowski et al., 1994). Cross-sex relationships account for only about 5 percent of friends in childhood (Hartup, 1989). In fact, in one large study, only 0.3 percent of children had a best friend of the opposite sex (Kovacs et al., 1996). Part of the preference for peers of the same sex results from the gender segregation of activities in childhood. Boys are encouraged to play with boys and engage in "boy" activities, and girls are encouraged to play with girls and engage in "girl" activities. In this way, appropriate gender-role socialization can more easily be assured.

A qualifier is in order, however. Although children do show a preference for friends of the same sex, this stated preference depends on the context in which the friends will play together. In one study, preadolescent and adolescent boys and girls were asked whether they would prefer a same-sex or an other-sex partner for a project at school and whether or not they would prefer a same-sex or an other-sex friend to play with at home. Preadolescent children showed the strongest preferences, although not always for the same sex. These children indicated that they would prefer to work on the project with a same-sex friend at school, but would prefer other-sex friends when playing at home (Strough & Marie-Covatto, 2002).

The Development of Friendship Friendships marked by commitment and reciprocity (sharing and give and take) begin to emerge around age 3 (see Hartup, 1989). Even these preschool friendships have remarkable stability, with friendships typically enduring unless one member of the pair moves away (see Collins & Gunnar, 1990). (One of my closest friends to this day, present at the hospital even for the birth

Apply and Discuss

Given the importance of parents, teachers, and peers to a child's social development, how might these respective influences change as a child matures?

▪️ Does the role of parents diminish and the role of peers increase?

▪️ What about the continuity of the role of other authority figures, such as teachers, across the life span?

of my children, I met when I was two and a half years old. Although we have both experienced multiple moves over the years, the friendship has endured.)

The meaning of friendship, however, changes throughout childhood (Damon, 1977; Selman, 1980). Young children describe friends as people who give them things or let them play with their toys. By middle childhood, children recognize some of the longer term payoffs of specific friendships. When asked why one girl was her friend, an eight-year-old responded, "Because…she cheers me up when I'm sad, and she shares…. I share so she'll share" (Damon, 1977, pp. 159–160). Adolescents express more concern with *intimacy* in friendships (mutual self-disclosure and empathy) (Buhrmester, 1990). Girls tend to self-disclose more than boys, and when boys self-disclose, they generally do so with girls (Youniss & Haynie, 1992).

The role of friends, siblings, and parents changes over the course of social development. Between the fifth and twelfth grades (roughly ages 10 to 18), the amount of time North American children spend with their families drops by more than half, from 35 to 14 percent (Larson et al., 1996). The experience of relationships as sources of conflict and support also changes during this period (Blos, 1967; Sullivan, 1953). One large cross-sectional study asked children, adolescents, and college students to rate the degree of support and conflict they experienced in several relationships (Furman & Buhrmester, 1992). Mothers and fathers are the primary sources of support for fourth graders, but this wanes during the adolescent years, when conflict with parents is at a peak. Friends loom much larger as sources of support in seventh grade but are gradually replaced by romantic partners by college age. Romantic relationships, like relationships with parents, are emotionally intense. They are experienced as most supportive at the same time as they are most conflictual.

These patterns are not, however, the same everywhere (see Arnett, 1999; Ladd, 1999). In much of the West, where individualism is strong, parents socialize their children for independence, and they often get more than they asked for in adolescence. In more collectivist cultures, where autonomy from parents is not such a strong value, the shift from parents to friends and lovers is much less apparent (DeRosier & Kupersmidt, 1991). In Japan, for example, children are socialized from birth to accommodate to others, not to separate from them (F. Rothbaum et al., 2000). Japanese mothers tend to spend more time with their infants than do U.S. mothers, and when they talk to their infants, they spend less time pointing to objects (things in the outside world) than in making sweet vocalizations that keep the baby's focus on their relationship. Japanese parents also spend more time in skin-to-skin contact with their infants, often bathing with them, and they are more likely to have their infants and young children sleep in their bed. By adolescence, Japanese children have learned that closeness to parents is an important value and do not show the same kind of "radical separatism" seen in many Western societies.

Peer Status　Most primates are hierarchical animals, and humans are no exception. From preschool onward, children assume positions in status hierarchies. Most readers can probably remember and pinpoint their peers' relative positions in status hierarchies in high school with remarkable accuracy. In fact, researchers rely on peer reports of "who is in" and "who is out" to study peer status in children.

Children differ substantially in the way they form relationships and the way other children respond to them (Ladd, 1999; Rubin et al., 1998). ***Children who are disliked by their peers*** are called **rejected children**. Some rejected children are teased and ostracized by their peers; others are bullies. Still other children, called **neglected children**, *are ignored by their peers*. Researchers study peer acceptance using peer nomination methods: They ask students in a class, for example, to write down the names of children they really like and dislike. Rejected children are those whose names frequently show up on the "disliked" list; neglected children receive no mention at all.

Children develop reputations among their peers by the time they are in preschool, and these reputations affect the way other children behave toward them (Denham &

Particularly during early childhood, children show a marked preference for interactions with same-sex playmates.

Big Picture φ Question 4

To what extent is human nature particular versus universal?

Holt, 1993). Personality characteristics and peer responses can produce a vicious cycle, in which children who are unhappy, aggressive, or socially unskilled elicit peer rejection, which in turn intensifies their low self-esteem and awkward social behavior, leading to further rejection (Hodges & Perry, 1999). Not all children who develop early negative reputations maintain this status throughout the rest of their school careers. But children who are actively disliked by peers (rejected) tend to have low self-esteem and other difficulties later in life, such as higher incidence of school dropout and delinquency in adolescence and more troubles at work and in relationships in adulthood (Dunn & McGuire, 1992; Parker & Asher, 1987; Richards et al., 1998). Neglected children, however, often perform better academically than more popular peers, as they immerse themselves into their school work. Rejected children tend to do poorly in school, but only if they are also aggressive (Wentzel & Asher, 1995).

Quality of Friendship   Children's friendships differ not only in the quantity—in how many friends a child has and how readily other children "take" to him—but also in their quality (Hartup, 1996). Whereas having friends is typically a good thing, research supports the commonsense notion that having the wrong kinds of friends—alienated, angry, and delinquent—can be detrimental to development, particularly for children who are already at risk (Vitaro et al., 1997).

Beyond the company they keep, another important dimension of children's friendship is the *way* they interact with one another (Bukowski et al., 1993; Hartup, 1996). Some children tend to have relatively negative, hostile, angry interactions with their friends. Others have more mutually pleasurable, supportive interactions. As in the study of emotion, these aspects of children's friendships are surprisingly independent: As in adult relationships, people can have passionate friendships that are high on both positive and negative affect.

Sibling Relationships

Until the 1980s, relationships with siblings received almost no attention from researchers. This is surprising, given that children often spend as much time with siblings as with parents.

Sibling relationships involve rivalry and conflict as well as warmth and companionship (Collins & Gunnar, 1990). From an evolutionary perspective, we would expect both conflict and love between siblings. On the one hand, siblings are genetically related by half, so the welfare of each influences the inclusive fitness of the other (Chapter 10). Thus, natural selection should have selected mechanisms encouraging humans and other animals to care for their siblings.

On the other hand, particularly in childhood, siblings compete for precious parental resources, which can mean the difference between life and death when conditions are scarce (see Trivers, 1972). As they mature, they may compete for familial resources that attract mates. Squabbling over an estate is, in fact, a major source of conflict among adult siblings cross-culturally. For example, among the Gabbra of Kenya, a nomadic people, the number of camels in a household predicts reproductive success for males but not females (Mace, 1996). Not surprisingly, sibling competition for resources is much higher in Gabbra society among males, for whom resources are a central component of status.

The birth of a sibling can be a difficult event for children. Parents report a wide range of responses, such as increased dependency, anxiety, bed-wetting, toilet "accidents," and aggressiveness (Dunn & McGuire, 1992). The younger the child's age at the birth, the more difficulty the child has with being displaced (Kramer & Gottman, 1992). Not knowing whether to express hostility or nurturance, young children often alternate between the two. Consider, for example, this description of a toddler coping with the birth of his little sister (from an e-mail from a friend): "My son is heroic in his efforts to be the 'big man' and big brother, who offered to buy his new sister a birthday truck, though on a few occasions, he has broken down and uttered the most heart-

Identical twins, who share 100 percent of their genetic makeup, should, from the perspective of evolutionary theory, be even more inclined than fraternal twins or nontwin siblings to look after the welfare of one another.

rending sobs imaginable, pleading that we put her back in my belly, take her back to the hospital, or at least put her away somewhere. Mostly, he pats her gently, though sometimes gets a good jab in."

INTERIM SUMMARY

Friendship patterns develop substantially in childhood and adolescence, from largely same-sex experiences involving mutual play to more intimate interactions in adolescence. **Rejected children** are teased, ostracized, or disliked by their peers. **Neglected children** are ignored. Children develop reputations among their peers by preschool. Children also differ in both the company they keep and the extent to which their friendships are characterized by positive and negative interactions. Sibling relationships involve rivalry and conflict as well as warmth, both of which make sense from an evolutionary standpoint.

Development of Social Cognition

The changing nature of children's friendships results in part from children's emotional and motivational development, such as an increasing concern with intimacy and an expanding capacity to commit to relationships despite momentary ups and downs. Children's friendships also change as their *understanding of themselves, others, and relationships*—that is, their **social cognition**—develops.

The Evolving Self-Concept

One of the initial tasks of social–cognitive development is acquiring a sense of self as a distinct entity with its own physical qualities and psychological processes (Stern, 1985). As adults, we tend to assume that we have always had a **self-concept**, *an organized view of ourselves or way of representing information about the self*. However, children are not born knowing that other people have thoughts and feelings or that their own experience is not the center of the universe. How do we evolve from fetuses—who are capable of sensation and learning but have no idea that their "world" is in someone else's body or that the voice they can recognize in the womb belongs to someone else, their mother—to beings who understand that their own thoughts and feelings are theirs?

Self-Concept in Infants and Young Children   Because infants cannot talk about themselves, researchers have had to devise indirect methods to learn how the self-concept develops in the first few years. One of the most reliable methods, first developed to assess the self-concept of chimpanzees (Gallup, 1972), is to put rouge on the child's nose and observe the way the child responds to its image in a mirror (Amsterdam, 1972; Asendorpf & Baudonniere, 1993; Lewis & Brooks-Gunn, 1979). Infants of different ages respond very differently to the image they see. Children younger than 15 months rarely touch their noses, unlike the vast majority of two-year-olds, who recognize a discrepancy between the way they look and the way they should look. Thus, infants appear to develop a visual self-concept between 15 and 24 months.

Development of the visual self-concept is, however, not complete by two years. When investigators secretly place a sticker on the forehead of three-year-olds and then show them a videotape of themselves from a week or a few minutes earlier, they do not touch their foreheads. Four- and five-year-olds, in contrast, only touch their foreheads after watching the tape of themselves from a few minutes earlier, a suggestion that that they know what they *generally* do and do not look like (Povinelli & Simon, 1998).

During the toddler years, children begin to categorize themselves on various dimensions, especially age and gender (Damon & Hart, 1988). Throughout early childhood, the categories they use are largely concrete. When asked to describe themselves, they refer to their membership in groups ("I live with my mommy and my daddy"), material possessions ("I have a pretty room"), things they can do ("I can tie my shoes"), and appearance.

These global categories do not imply, however, that the self-concept of young children is entirely devoid of subtlety. Even preschoolers can sometimes observe consistencies in their own behaviors that resemble adult categories of personality, such as extroversion ("I usually play with my friends" versus "I usually play by myself"). However, they have difficulty making generalizations about their enduring feelings, such as "I don't usually get mad" or "I don't like myself" (Eder, 1990; Harter, 1998, 1999).

Self-Concept in Childhood and Adolescence   Around age 8, children begin to define themselves based on internal, psychological attributes as much as on the obviously perceptible qualities or appearances that dominate all cognition in early childhood (Broughton, 1978; Damon & Hart, 1988; Harter, 1999). In other words, they start to think about their abilities, their likes and dislikes, and the ways they tend to feel and think—namely, their personality. Conceiving the self at this point often involves comparisons with other children ("I'm good at math" or "I'm the best skateboarder in my school"). Children at this age also begin to describe themselves more relationally, saying things such as "I'm smarter than anyone else in my class," or "I'm more helpful around the house than my brother" (Harter, 1999).

In adolescence, representations of the self become much more subtle (Figure 14.5) (Harter, 1998; Harter & Monsour, 1992). For example, a 17-year-old interviewed for a research project on the development of children's representations of self and others described herself as follows, "I seem really shy on the outside, but *inside* I'm really involved when I'm with people, thinking a lot about what they are saying and doing. And with people I'm comfortable with, I probably don't seem shy at all" (Westen et al., 1991).

Although we have focused here on developmental trends that apply to most children, an important influence on *individual differences* in self-concept (and self-esteem) that increases as children age is genetics (McGuire et al., 1999). As with other attributes such as intelligence (Chapter 8), heritability coefficients for self-concept and self-esteem tend to increase during adolescence, as genetic influences that were less apparent in childhood express themselves in behavior.

In addition, gender plays a role not only in the attributes that children and adolescents use to describe themselves, but also in the evaluations that they assign to

Big Picture φ Question 8

To what extent can we inform our knowledge through reason or through observation—that is, rationalism versus empiricism?

Big Picture φ Question 1

To what extent can mental processes be reduced to the brain or body?

Big Picture φ Question 5

To what extent are psychological processes the same in men and women?

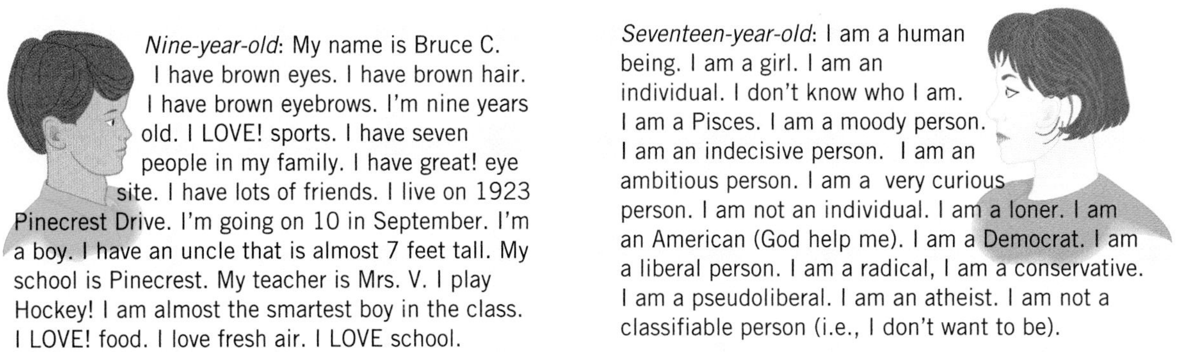

Nine-year-old: My name is Bruce C. I have brown eyes. I have brown hair. I have brown eyebrows. I'm nine years old. I LOVE! sports. I have seven people in my family. I have great! eye site. I have lots of friends. I live on 1923 Pinecrest Drive. I'm going on 10 in September. I'm a boy. I have an uncle that is almost 7 feet tall. My school is Pinecrest. My teacher is Mrs. V. I play Hockey! I am almost the smartest boy in the class. I LOVE! food. I love fresh air. I LOVE school.

Seventeen-year-old: I am a human being. I am a girl. I am an individual. I don't know who I am. I am a Pisces. I am a moody person. I am an indecisive person. I am an ambitious person. I am a very curious person. I am not an individual. I am a loner. I am an American (God help me). I am a Democrat. I am a liberal person. I am a radical, I am a conservative. I am a pseudoliberal. I am an atheist. I am not a classifiable person (i.e., I don't want to be).

FIGURE 14.5 Self-concept in childhood and adolescence. School-age children most frequently mention activities, significant others, and attitudes when describing themselves, as in this excerpt from an interview with a nine-year-old boy. With age, the self-concept becomes more abstract and complex, as in the response by a 17-year-old girl. *Source:* Montemayor & Eisen, 1977, pp. 317–318.

these attributes. As shown in Figure 14.6, females evaluate themselves as weaker on appearance and athletics than males (Harter, 1999). And, this gender difference has been observed across a range of different cultures.

Concepts of Others

Coming to understand other people, like coming to understand the self, is a lengthy developmental process (Flavell & Miller, 1998). In infancy, a central accomplishment is the recognition that social interactions are reciprocal—that other people's actions depend on one's own. By the third or fourth month infants learn that smiling brings playful responses from caregivers, whereas crying usually means being picked up and held.

Infants also learn to read emotions in people's faces. As early as 12 months, an infant "consults" the mother by looking to her for reassurance when introduced to a new toy. If the mother's face shows concern, the infant approaches the mother rather than the toy (Klinnert et al., 1983; Saarni, 1998). If the infant receives a smile from one parent but a fearful look from the other, the child becomes confused and distressed (Hirshberg, 1990).

From early childhood until about age 8, children tend to focus on relatively simple, concrete attributes of other people, such as the way they look or the roles they perform (Shantz, 1983). For instance, a typical seven-year-old described a neighbor she liked as follows: "She is very nice because she gives my friends and me toffee. She lives by the main road" (Livesley & Bromley, 1973, p. 214). Around age 8, however, children's representations of others begin to change, and they become more complex through adolescence.

Perspective-Taking and Theory of Mind

An important social–cognitive ability that develops throughout childhood and adolescence, and probably beyond, is **perspective-taking**, *the ability to understand other people's viewpoints or perspectives* (Chapter 13). Taking other people's perspectives—from visualizing what they see, as in Piaget's three-mountains task, to understanding in the midst of an argument why the other person is angry—involves moving out of egocentrism and representing the other person's mind in one's own.

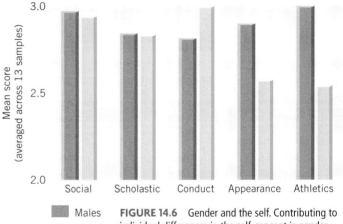

FIGURE 14.6 Gender and the self. Contributing to individual differences in the self-concept is gender. Males and females do not always evaluate themselves equally along different dimensions. As shown in this figure, females rate themselves lower on the categories of appearance and athletics than males. Ratings for each dimension were made along a 4-point scale. *Source:* Reprinted from Bukatko & Daehler (2004).

A prerequisite to perspective-taking is the development of a **theory of mind**—*an implicit set of ideas about the existence of mental states, such as beliefs and feelings, in oneself and others* (Flavell, 1999; Gopnik, 1993). Researchers have argued about precisely when children develop a coherent theory of mind, but it appears to arise somewhere in the toddler years, between ages 2 and 4. Before that time, children have trouble understanding that people can hold false beliefs, because they have trouble recognizing that thought and reality can differ.

Precursors to a theory of mind can be seen, however, in infancy. For example, as early as the middle to end of the first year, infants appear to understand that people's actions reflect their goals, such as grabbing a particular object (Woodward & Sommerville, 2000). Infants also engage in joint visual attention, when their parents look at something and point to it—recognizing that they should look at the object and not the parent (Deak et al., 2000; Flavell, 1999). By the middle of the second year, children can infer from the face an experimenter makes after eating a food that the experimenter does not want it—even if the child likes that food (Repacholi & Gopnik, 1997).

Theory of mind and perspective-taking also develop considerably beyond the preschool years. Early school-age children, for example, do not clearly understand that certain activities, such as listening, pretending, or deliberately performing mental or physical actions, require consciousness and cannot occur while people are asleep (Flavell et al., 1999). One ingenious technique researchers have devised for assessing perspective-taking involves observing the way children play games of strategy (Flavell et al., 1968; Selman, 1980). In a game called "Decoy and Defender" (Selman, 1980), which is played on a checkerboard, each player has two "flag carriers" as well as several less valuable tokens. The object is to move one's flag carriers to the opponent's side of the board. Because, from the opposite side of the table, all the pieces look alike, players must figure out which pieces to block by observing their opponents' moves.

Apply & Discuss

These are excerpts from interviews with a ninth and a twelfth grader who were asked to describe their relationship with their mothers (*Source:* Westen et al., 1991).

■ In what ways do the two accounts differ?

■ Consider the complexity of each girl's representation of herself and her mother, as well as the coherence of the narrative—that is, the extent to which it makes sense and people's actions are well explained. What differs between the two vignettes?

■ How do the two girls differ in their capacity for taking the perspective of their mother?

Ninth grader: In the fifth grade I was getting really bad grades and my mom yelled at me all the time and we got in big fights all the time, and before that we were real close— The whole year and summer my mom and I were always fighting, and then in the sixth grade my mother—well, I made the honor roll and we became close again—and I was on the Student Council. And then in the eighth grade I got Ds and Cs and we were fighting a lot but after graduation from middle school we were close again, and this year I was on the honor roll first quarter, and then last quarter I got 3 Cs and 3 Bs and she's yelling at me again, and we're not as close as before.

Twelfth grader: As I'm getting older we argue more, disagree on more—disagree on a lot more things. But I think we're getting closer now, more on the same level than when I was a little girl. Like, one time I was getting ready for a competition—we had a lot of misunderstanding, beforehand—I didn't feel she understood. She'd been in so many of these competitions and won, and I didn't feel she really cared about this one I was in. She hadn't felt I was serious about it. I didn't think she cared, and she didn't think I was serious. So finally we talked about it—realized it was a misunderstanding. I think we're closer now—I realized we do have to talk about things when we have misunderstandings.

The strategies used by children of different ages illustrate the stagelike development of perspective-taking ability. Children aged 3 to 6 have an egocentric perspective, totally failing to take their opponent's perspective into account. Typical of this age is the "rush for glory" strategy: The child simply moves her flag carrier as quickly as possible across the board. By ages 6 to 8, children become craftier but in a transparent fashion: They often announce, "I'm moving my flag carrier now" while moving an unimportant token. (They may even clear their throat first for effect.) They are beginning to recognize that to win they must influence the *beliefs* of their opponents. Other research similarly indicates that by age 5 children start to recognize the value of trying to influence other people's mental states in order to alter their behavior (Peskin, 1992).

By ages 8 to 10, children show more sophistication. For example, in the "double-take" strategy, they might advance their flag carrier with considerable fanfare, expecting that the other player would not think they would be so stupid. Behind this strategy is a more complex perspective-taking process: "He's thinking that I'm thinking...." The subtlety and complexity of this kind of back-and-forth thinking expand throughout adolescence.

"How would you feel if the mouse did that to you?"

© *The New Yorker Collection 1997 William Steig from the cartoonbank.com.*

INTERIM SUMMARY

Children develop in their **social cognition**, their understanding of themselves, others, and relationships. Researchers studying children's **self-concept** have found that children are not born with self-knowledge; even learning to represent their physical appearance is an achievement of the toddler years. Throughout early childhood, children tend to think of themselves and others in relatively concrete ways, such as their age, gender, group membership, and possessions. Around age 8, they begin to think more about enduring personality attributes. By adolescence, social cognition, like all cognition, is much more subtle and abstract. **Perspective-taking** also increases steadily throughout childhood and adolescence, beginning with children's development of a **theory of mind**—an implicit set of ideas about the existence of mental states in the self and others.

Children's Understanding of Gender

Children's social cognition thus develops in complexity and abstractness, much as cognition does in nonsocial domains (Chapter 13). The same is true of children's understanding of what gender is and how it applies to them, which changes dramatically over the first several years of life and continues to evolve throughout the life span.

One cognitive–developmental theory proposes that children progress through three stages in understanding gender (Kohlberg, 1966). In the first stage, usually attained by age 2, children acquire **gender identity**, *the ability to categorize themselves (and others) as either male or female* (Slaby & Frey, 1976). Precursors to gender knowledge of this sort can be seen as early as six to nine months of age, when habituation studies show that infants can discriminate males and females (see Martin & Ruble, 1997).

The second stage, **gender stability**, occurs when *children understand that their gender remains constant over time*. Girls learn that they will never grow up to be Batman, Superman, or even a garden-variety father, and boys learn that they will not become Wonder Woman, Madonna, or a mommy. Even after they recognize that they will never change their sex, however, children are not absolutely certain that this is also true of other people. Before age 6 or 7, some children believe that boys who wear dresses may eventually become girls and girls may metamorphose into boys if they do enough boyish things (Marcus & Overton, 1978; McConaghy, 1979). For example,

Big Picture φ Question 8

To what extent can we inform our knowledge through reason or through observation—that is, rationalism versus empiricism?

Making Connections

With gender constancy, children understand that gender does not change with changes in appearance. The development of gender constancy is related to a major cognitive achievement that occurs around the same time: understanding conservation of physical properties such as mass (Chapter 13). In both social and nonsocial cognition, children around age 7 or 8 develop the capacity to distinguish between the "essence" of a person or thing and its momentary appearance.

Big Picture φ Question 4

To what extent is human nature particular versus universal?

Big Picture φ Question 5

To what extent are psychological processes the same in men and women?

when a four-year-old saw his father dressed as a woman for Halloween, he exclaimed, "Two mommies!" In general, children know things about their own gender earlier than they can generalize this knowledge to others.

The third stage, **gender constancy**, occurs when *children learn that a person's gender cannot be altered by changes in appearance or activities* (except, of course, in exceptional circumstances). Gender constancy may seem a simple achievement to us, but it does not necessarily come easily. One psychologist tells the story of a four-year-old boy who wore a barrette to nursery school. When another little boy called him a girl, the first child pulled down his pants to demonstrate that he was indeed still a boy. The other child, however, found this unconvincing. In a "you can't fool me" tone of voice, he responded, "Everyone has a penis; only girls wear barrettes" (Bem, 1983, p. 607).

Gender Schemas   While some researchers have focused on the *structure* (e.g., the level of complexity) of children's thinking about gender, others have turned their attention to the *content* of children's knowledge. Cross-culturally, children begin to show an awareness of their culture's beliefs about gender by the age of 5; by middle childhood they share many of the stereotypes common in their society (Best et al., 1977; Huston, 1983). They encode and organize information about their culture's definitions of maleness and femaleness in **gender schemas**, *mental representations that associate psychological characteristics with each sex* (Bem, 1985).

Gender schemas can be quite persistent across the life span. Consider the following scenario, familiar to any female doctor, reported by a colleague, a psychologist:

"Is Dr. Williams in?"

"Yes, speaking."

"I'm calling regarding one of the doctor's patients. May I speak with the doctor please?"

"This is the doctor."

"No, I need to speak with the doctor, Dr. Williams."

"This is Dr. Williams."

Because the caller's gender schema associates doctors with masculinity, the person has difficulty recognizing that the doctor is, indeed, on the phone. Interestingly, the caller was female.

Gender schemas across the globe show considerable similarities as well as differences. One team of researchers gave an adjective checklist with 300 items (e.g., aggressive, arrogant, artistic, bossy) to university students in 25 countries and asked them to rate whether the words were more characteristic of men, women, or neither (Best & Williams, 1998; Williams & Best, 1982). Although many adjectives were categorized differently in different countries, a number were almost universally associated with men or with women. Broadly speaking, people everywhere consider men more active, aggressive, and dominant, and perceive women as more affectionate, emotional, and sensitive (Table 14.2).

The consistency of these findings is striking, although two qualifications are in order. First, technological change is reducing the distinctions between the sexes. Using a similar method, in a follow-up to their initial investigation the researchers examined **sex-role ideology**, *beliefs about appropriate behaviors of the sexes*, in 14 countries (Williams & Best, 1990). Technologically developed, urban, individualistic societies tended to have more egalitarian sex roles, with less divergent views of appropriate behaviors for men and women. Protestant countries were also more likely to be egalitarian, while people in predominantly Muslim countries tended to believe men should be dominant and women, submissive.

A second qualification is that gender differences are *average* differences (Maccoby & Jacklin, 1974; Williams, 1983). For most traits, such as aggressiveness or sensitivity, the bell-shaped curves for males and females overlap substantially. Thus, within a culture, some women score higher than some men even on "masculine" traits, and vice versa, although the *typical* member of each sex is higher on gendered traits than the average member of the opposite sex (Figure 14.7). For example, women and men differ on the importance they attach to a vast number of criteria when selecting jobs, but the differences tend to be relatively small (Konrad et al., 2000).

Cross-Cultural Gender Stereotypes   Why are gender stereotypes so similar cross-culturally? As early as age 2, Western boys prefer blocks and transportation toys such as trucks and cars, and girls prefer dolls and soft toys. Boys play more actively at manipulating objects and are more likely to engage in forbidden activities (Fagot, 1985; Smith & Daglish, 1977), whereas girls are more likely to play dress-up and dance. Girls also tend to talk earlier than boys (Schachter et al., 1978). Cross-cultural research with a large sample of preindustrial societies shows that the vast majority socialize boys from early childhood to be brave and self-reliant and girls to be responsible, self-restrained, obedient, and sexually restrained (Low, 1989).

Why do so many cultures socialize children in similar ways? As we saw in exploring the links between gender differences and brain structures in Chapter 3, where nature lays a foundation, culture tends to adorn, embellish, and reshape it. This is likely to be the case with the most well-documented difference between the sexes, that males are more aggressive and females more nurturant (see Clinchy & Norem, 1998; Jacklin, 1989; Maccoby & Jacklin, 1974). These differences occur across cultures and species and are evident well before children begin school. Boys display higher rates of aggression in virtually every society and are far more likely to engage in rough-and-tumble play (Edwards & Whiting, 1983). Girls have never been found to be more prone to initiate aggressive encounters in any society (Maccoby & Jacklin, 1980).

Biology and Evolution   The male hormone testosterone appears to be related to aggression in both males and females (Chapter 18). Highly suggestive data come from studies of girls with *adrenogenital syndrome*, a malfunction of the adrenal glands that exposes the female fetus to unusually high levels of male hormones (Chapter 10). The result is not only an increase in aggressiveness but also a general increase in "tomboy" behavior during childhood (Erhardt & Baker, 1974; Money & Erhardt, 1972). From an evolutionary perspective, sex differences in aggression and nurturance are products of natural selection. In many species, including most primates, males compete for sexual access to females, often physically establishing dominance over other males by fighting. Hence, males' tendency to exhibit aggressive behavior and to practice such behavior in childhood would optimize reproductive success. Behavioral

Table 14.2 ■ ■ **Adjectives Associated with Males and Females across Cultures**	
Male	*Female*
Active	Affectionate
Adventurous	Attractive
Aggressive	Dependent
Clear thinking	Emotional
Coarse	Fearful
Courageous	Gentle
Cruel	Sensitive
Dominant	Sentimental
Egotistical	Sexy
Forceful	Submissive
Hardhearted	Weak
Lazy	
Self-confident	
Unemotional	
Wise	

Source: Williams & Best, 1982, p. 77.

Note: For these adjectives, over 20 of 25 countries share the gender stereotype.

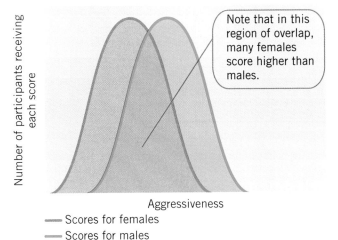

FIGURE 14.7   Aggressiveness in men and women. In this hypothetical distribution of scores on a measure of aggressiveness, one for men and one for women, the male curve is shifted to the right, signifying that most men are more aggressive than most women. Note the significant region of overlap, however, in which many women score higher than many men.

Apply & Discuss

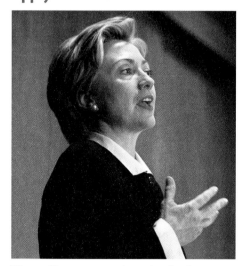

Women, like men, respond emotionally when people violate gender stereotypes. Many women, for example, find Senator and former First Lady Hillary Clinton's no-nonsense, take-charge style off-putting.

▪ To what extent do men's and women's reactions to Senator Clinton reflect the discrepancy between her public behavior and cultural views of the way "ladies" (especially First Ladies) should behave?

▪ Women in the United States still earn less than three-quarters of what men earn for equivalent work, and when women begin to predominate in a formerly male occupation (such as teaching, which became feminized in the twentieth century), salaries decline. How much does this depend on explicit discrimination versus implicit expression of gender stereotypes?

Big Picture φ Question 1

To what extent can mental processes be reduced to the brain or body?

Big Picture φ Question 6

What is the relation between nature and nurture in shaping psychological processes?

differences would likely have been selected alongside physical differences such as the greater body mass in males of most species, including humans. Females, in contrast, carry infants in their uterus for nine months and hence have already made substantial investments in their offspring by birth. In the context of these sex differences, a division of labor may have evolved in which males tend to fight for status and protect the group and females tend to care for infants and young children.

Culture and Social Learning   A strictly biological version of this hypothesis about sex differences would be difficult to sustain because research finds that males are quite capable of nurturant behavior (Fogel et al., 1986). In fact, changing gender roles now allow fathers to care for infants and young children in ways that would have been considered "unnatural" decades ago, and children whose fathers are more involved and nurturant with them tend to benefit psychologically in multiple ways (e.g., Black et al., 1999).

A social learning interpretation of sex differences holds that most behavioral differences observed between women and men result not primarily from innate differences but from expectancies, which in turn reflect the way society is organized (Eagly, 1983; Eagly & Wood, 1999). Women and men frequently find themselves in hierarchical relationships in which men are in positions of power and status and women are subordinate (e.g., doctor/nurse, executive/administrative assistant). Because these occur so often, people see them as natural and generalize to other situations, even where status is presumably equal, such as dinner-table discussions of politics. That they also adapt themselves to the roles in which they are likely to find themselves leads to substantial gender differences in behavior.

Nature and Nurture: An Integrative View   Although the social learning hypothesis is compelling, it does not account for the fact that such similar social structures have emerged across cultures. Nor does it account for the finding that boys are more active in utero than girls, even before their parents have begun to push them toward more rough-and-tumble play (DiPietro et al., 1996a).

A more integrated account considers the interaction among biological evolution, cultural evolution, and learned expectations. (In fact, advocates of both evolutionary and social learning approaches tend to acknowledge the importance of both evolution and learning but focus on one side or the other; e.g., Eagly & Wood, 1999.) From an integrative standpoint, biological evolution produced motivational "pulls" that diverge in various ways for the two sexes, such as a tendency toward aggressive behavior in males and nurturant behavior in females, along with physical differences such as body size and strength. Based on these biological differences, nearly all cultures create a division of labor between the sexes and amplify innate tendencies. Simply noting the differences in size and strength between the average man and woman, for example, most cultures would be expected to enlist men and not women in warfare.

As ecological conditions shift (such as the disappearance of hand-to-hand combat or the ability of women to compete on an equal footing in the workplace), cultural ideology changes, and so do socialization practices. In fact, cross-cultural data document that where women have more power (where they control resources such as property), girls are taught to be less submissive and more aggressive, although they still remain less aggressive than males (Low, 1989). It is important to note, as well, that evolutionary pressures would not likely select men and women to have completely divergent behavioral tendencies. Women in all cultures need aggression in their behavioral repertoire, just as men need nurturance to maximize their reproductive success. Evolution has undoubtedly selected for flexibility in human behavior.

The Politics and Science of Gender   One of the great difficulties of drawing conclusions about gender differences is the extent of passion and politics involved (Eagly, 1995). The systematic study of gender differences emerged in the 1970s with the rise of the feminist movement, which attempted to use psychological findings to discredit pervasive stereotypes that devalued women. Yet more recent research challenges the view that gender differences tend to be small. Men and women differ substantially in a number of ways, particularly in their relative attraction to and ability for verbal versus mathematical tasks and their tendency to be nurturant or aggressive (e.g., Feingold, 1994). Whereas the first wave of feminist influence on the understanding of gender attempted to show that gender differences are actually small, more recent thinking suggests that men and women do differ in some important respects, but that the problem lies less in those differences than in our tendency to devalue the things at which women excel.

INTERIM SUMMARY

Children's understanding of their own and other people's gender begins in the toddler years, when they start to classify themselves and others according to gender. Over time, they develop **gender constancy**, the knowledge that gender cannot be altered by changes in appearance or activities. Children encode and organize information about their culture's definitions of maleness and femaleness in **gender schemas**. People everywhere share certain stereotypes about men and women, which appear to be rooted in both evolved differences between the sexes and social and cultural practices and beliefs.

Moral Development

INTERVIEWER:	Should boys get more? Why should they get more?
FOUR-YEAR-OLD BOY:	Because they always need more.
INTERVIEWER:	Why do they need more?
BOY:	Because that's how I want it.

[Damon, 1977, p. 121]

Fortunately, children's thinking about what is fair (and why) changes dramatically over the years, so that older children and adults do not operate at the same level of morality as the four-year-old above (or they do it with more subtlety and conviction borne of biased reasoning). Researchers who study the development of *morality*—the set of rules people use to balance the conflicting interests of themselves and others—have focused on the roles of cognition and emotion in children's evolving sense of right and wrong (see Rest, 1983; Turiel, 1998).

The Role of Cognition

Several theories focus on cognition in moral development. These include cognitive–developmental, cognitive–social, and information-processing theories.

Cognitive–Developmental Theories   The cognitive–developmental models of Jean Piaget and Lawrence Kohlberg focus on moral *reasoning*. These models propose that moral development proceeds through a series of stages that reflect cognitive development.

Piaget's Theory   Piaget observed a simple type of event—games of marbles among children—and noted important differences in the way younger and older children thought about the rules (Piaget, 1932/1965). The youngest children, who were essentially pre-moral, arbitrarily altered the rules to enhance their enjoyment of the game and their chances of winning. Once children accepted the notion of rules, however,

Big Picture φ Question 5

To what extent are psychological processes the same in men and women?

Big Picture φ Question 8

To what extent can we inform our knowledge through reason or through observation—that is, rationalism versus empiricism?

they would stick staunchly to them. If asked where the rules for playing marbles came from, they would reply with answers like, "They just are," "From Daddy," or "From God!"

Piaget called this first stage of moral judgment, in which *children believe that morals are absolute*, the **morality of constraint**. This form of moral reasoning is typical of children before the age of 9 or 10. Piaget described this morality as one "of duty pure and simple," in which children conform to societal rules that are viewed as unchanging and unchangeable (1932/1965, p. 335). When judging the actions of others, children in this stage tend to center on the most salient characteristic of the act— its severity—and have difficulty simultaneously keeping in mind other aspects of the act, such as the intention behind it.

Consider what happens when a child is asked to decide who is more blameworthy, a boy who went to steal a cookie from the kitchen and broke a glass while reaching into the cookie jar or another boy who accidentally slipped and broke five glasses. In line with the tendency of preoperational children to focus on only one salient attribute at a time (Chapter 13), a five-year-old is likely to reason that the boy who broke more glasses has committed the worse offense, even though his "crime" was accidental.

Older children and adults focus more on their inferences about others' intentions. They also tend to view rules as means to ends, as strategies for keeping social interactions safe, fair, and comfortable. In this **morality of cooperation**, *moral rules can be changed if they are not appropriate to the occasion, as long as the people involved agree to do so*. Older children playing marbles may thus change the rules by mutual consent without believing they are violating something sacred.

Kohlberg's Theory Lawrence Kohlberg shared two of Piaget's central convictions about moral development. The first is that changes in moral reasoning result from basic changes in cognitive structures—that is, changes in ways of thinking. For example, as children's thinking becomes more abstract, so, too, does their moral reasoning. Second, Kohlberg conceptualized children as active constructors of their own moral reality, not passive recipients of social rules.

Kohlberg (1976; Kohlberg & Kramer, 1969) proposed a sequence of three levels of moral development, each comprised of two stages. He assessed moral development by presenting subjects with hypothetical dilemmas and asking them how these dilemmas should be resolved and why. Each dilemma forces a person to choose between violating the law and helping another person in need. An example is the dilemma of Heinz and the druggist (Kohlberg, 1963, p. 19).

In Europe a woman was near death from a special kind of cancer. There was one drug that the doctors thought might save her. It was a form of radium that a druggist in the same town had recently discovered. The drug was expensive to make, but the druggist was charging ten times what the drug cost him to make. He paid $200 for the radium and charged $2,000 for a small dose of the drug. The sick woman's husband, Heinz, went to everyone he knew to borrow the money, but he could only get together about $1,000, which is half of what it cost. He told the druggist that his wife was dying and asked him to sell it cheaper or let him pay later. But the druggist said, "No, I discovered the drug, and I'm going to make money from it." So Heinz got desperate and broke into the man's store to steal the drug for his wife. Should the husband have done that?

Kohlberg's example of Heinz and the druggist turned out years later to be a real-life moral dilemma that found its way into the courtroom, when the South African government tried to compel the Western pharmaceutical industry to sell medications for life-threatening illnesses such as AIDS to people who could not otherwise afford them.

The level of moral development a person shows in answering this question depends not on the particular answer (to steal or not to steal) but on the reasoning be-

Apply & Discuss

During the 1980s, Carol Gilligan suggested that males and females differ in the types of moral reasoning or "voices" they are most likely to use. She suggested that men advocate a voice of justice ("Who is right?"), whereas women operate according to a voice of care ("Is anyone likely to be hurt by this moral dilemma?"). Since Gilligan's research first appeared, however, little support for gender differences in moral reasoning have been obtained.

■ Do you think that men and women differ in their levels of moral reasoning? Why or why not?

■ What levels of moral reasoning do you think men and women are most likely to use?

Big Picture φ Question 8

To what extent can we inform our knowledge through reason or through observation—that is, rationalism versus empiricism?

Table 14.3 ◼ ◼ Kohlberg's Levels of Moral Development

Level	Reasons to Steal the Drug	Reasons Not to Steal the Drug
Preconventional: Morality centers on avoiding punishment and obtaining reward.	He should steal it if he likes her a lot; if he gets caught, he won't get much of a jail term, so he'll get to see her when he gets out.	He'll get caught; he shouldn't have to pay with jail time for his wife's problem.
Conventional: Morality centers on meeting moral standards learned from others, avoiding their disapproval, and maintaining law and order.	If he doesn't steal it, everyone will think he's a terrible person; it's his duty to care for his wife.	If he steals it, everyone will think he's a criminal; he can't just go stealing things whenever he wants to—it isn't right.
Postconventional: Morality centers on abstract, carefully considered principles.	If he has to run from the police, at least he'll know he did the right thing; sometimes people have to break the law if the law is unjust.	If he steals it, he'll lose all respect for himself; other people might say it was okay, but he'll have to live with his conscience, knowing he's stolen from the druggist.

hind the response (Table 14.3). At the first level, **preconventional morality**, *children follow moral rules either to avoid punishment* (Stage 1) *or to obtain reward* (Stage 2). A preconventional child might conclude that Heinz should steal the drug "if he likes having his wife around." At the second level, **conventional morality**, *children (and adults whose moral reasoning remains conventional) define what is right and wrong by the standards they have learned from other people, particularly respected authorities such as their parents.* People with conventional morality justify their choice of moral actions on the basis of their desire to gain the approval or avoid the disapproval of others (Stage 3) or on the need to maintain law and order (e.g., "if everyone stole whenever he wanted to, what would this world come to?") (Stage 4).

The third level, **postconventional morality**, is *a morality of abstract, self-defined principles* that may or may not match the dominant morals of the times. A postconventional adult, like a preconventional child, might condone stealing the drug, but for a very different reason, such as "the value of a human life far exceeds any rights of ownership or property." (Distinctions between two postconventional stages originally outlined by Kohlberg have not proven empirically useful and will thus not be described here.) Only about 5 percent of people actually reach the postconventional level (Colby & Kohlberg, 1984).

The basic logic of Kohlberg's theory is that at the *pre*conventional level, the person accepts moral standards only if doing so is personally advantageous; this is an ethic of hedonism or self-interest. The child is *pre*conventional in the sense that he has not yet come to accept society's conventions in their own right as rules that good people should follow. At the conventional level, the individual believes in the moral rules he has learned. The person with postconventional morality, in contrast, views the values of the time as conventions—rules established by social contract rather than by any absolute or divine power—and hence as both potentially fallible and changeable. Virtually all normal children progress to Stage 3 by the age of 13. Beyond Stages 3 and 4, however, the development of moral reasoning is not related to age and is more a matter of individual differences and culture.

Kohlberg developed his theory during the 1960s, a time of social turbulence in which people questioned the norms and values of their parents and the larger society. In particular, the Vietnam War led many to question the wisdom of authorities and the moral legitimacy of conventional beliefs about war, patriotism, and duty. Kohlberg argued that people who never question their parents' moral beliefs are less mature in their moral reasoning than people who consider alternative ways of thinking about morality.

Cognitive–Social Theories Cognitive–social theories (Chapters 5 and 12) focus less on moral reasoning than on moral *behavior*. According to behaviorist and cognitive–social theories, moral behaviors, like other behaviors, are learned through processes such as conditioning and modeling (Bandura, 1977b; Mischel & Mischel, 1976). Cognitive–social researchers measure moral development in terms of **prosocial behavior**—*behavior that benefits other individuals or groups* (Holmgren et al., 1998; Mischel & Mischel, 1976). Anyone who has ever watched (or been) a child knows how powerful the words "good boy!" or "good girl!" can be in shaping prosocial behavior.

From this point of view, morality develops as children come to discover through trial and error and deliberate instruction that certain actions will be reinforced or punished. Thus, children learn that stealing is wrong because they are punished for it, see someone else punished (vicarious conditioning), or are told they will be punished (direct tutelage). They acquire expectancies about the outcome of their behaviors under different circumstances (whether they will or will not be punished), and they develop conditioned emotional responses (such as anxiety or guilt) to behaviors that are regularly punished. They also generalize from one situation to the next, recognizing, for example, that talking in one library is no more acceptable than talking in another.

Clear cultural differences in how altruistically children behave toward others have been observed (Whiting & Edwards, 1988). Children raised in more individualistic cultures, such as the United States, behave more selfishly and with less concern for the needs and well-being of others. In more collectivist cultures, however, where the needs of the group are emphasized and children are required to contribute to the family income, empathy and concern for others is much more apparent.

Information-Processing Theories　An alternative cognitive view of moral development is an information-processing approach (Darley & Schultz, 1990; Grusec & Goodnow, 1994; Nelson & Crick, 1999). Information-processing theories do not postulate broad stages of moral development. Rather, they break moral thinking down into component processes and examine the way each of these processes changes during childhood.

According to one such view (Schultz & Schliefer, 1983), when adults make decisions about whether an act is immoral and whether it deserves punishment, as in jury deliberations, they make a series of sequential judgments. As Figure 14.8 shows, the first question concerns cause: Did the person cause or contribute to the damage? If so, the next question is one of moral responsibility, which rests on intentions (did he mean to?) and judgment (could he have foreseen the results?).

Big Picture φ Question 4

To what extent is human nature particular versus universal?

Big Picture φ Question 8

To what extent can we inform our knowledge through reason or through observation—that is, rationalism versus empiricism?

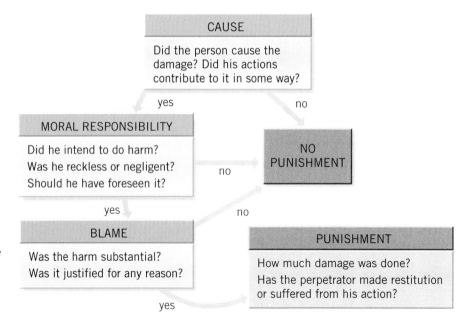

FIGURE 14.8　An information-processing model of moral decision making. According to this model, when people make decisions about whether an act is immoral and whether it deserves punishment, they make a series of sequential judgments, such as whether the person caused the event, was morally responsible, is blameworthy, and deserves punishment. *Source:* Adapted from Darley & Schultz, 1990, p. 532.

If the individual is morally responsible, the next question is whether he is blame-worthy—that is, did he do significant harm, and were his actions justified in some way? For example, jurors often make very different judgments about blameworthi-ness of defendants who attacked someone who molested their child. Finally, if the person caused unjustified harm, what should be his punishment? People in the West tend to determine appropriate punishment, whether in a jury trial or in the discipline of their children, according to three criteria: the extent of the damage, whether the perpetrator has already made appropriate restitution (e.g., by apologizing), and whether the perpetrator has suffered as a result of his actions.

From an information-processing view, then, understanding moral development means understanding changes in the way children answer these multiple questions. For example, when do children come to understand the difference between directly causing someone to suffer (e.g., taking something from them) as opposed to taking an action that, combined with someone else's action, produces suffering (e.g., forget-ting to lock a door, which contributed to a theft)? According to this view, global stage theories cannot capture developmental changes in the multiple components of moral reasoning, which often occur at different times.

INTERIM SUMMARY

Cognitive theories stress the role of thought and learning in moral development. Accord-ing to Piaget, children at first believe moral rules are immutable but ultimately come to understand that they are the product of convention. Young children also tend to center on consequences rather than intentions in making moral judgments. Kohlberg distinguished three levels of moral development: **preconventional morality** (people follow moral rules either to avoid punishment or to obtain rewards); **conventional** (individuals define what is right by the standards they have learned from other people, particularly respected au-thorities), and **postconventional** (people reason using abstract, self-defined moral prin-ciples that may not match conventional moral beliefs). Cognitive–social approaches mea-sure moral development in terms of **prosocial behavior**. Information-processing approaches examine changes in the component processes involved in moral thinking.

The Role of Emotion

The theories discussed thus far emphasize the role of cognition—judgment and deci-sion making—in moral development. Other approaches, however, focus on the emo-tional side (see Eisenberg, 2000), particularly on guilt and empathy as motivators of moral action.

Psychodynamic Theories   The psychodynamic view of moral development pro-poses that children start out relatively *narcissistic* (self-centered and interested in gratifying their own needs), as when a young child who wants an extra piece of cake simply grabs it. This orientation begins to change with the development of a con-science between ages 2 and 5 (Chapter 12) but can be seen in individuals with *narcis-sistic* and *antisocial personality disorders*, who remain self-centered and focused on their own needs as adults (Chapter 15).

From a psychodynamic perspective, moral development occurs through identifi-cation or *internalization*: Children take in the values of their parents, which are at first external, and gradually adopt them as their own. Empirically, parents and their chil-dren do tend to think similarly about moral questions (Speicher, 1994), and four-year-olds, unlike older children (whose conscience is more internalized), do not associate lying with self-disapproval, or truth-telling with positive feelings about themselves (Bussey, 1999).

From a psychodynamic perspective, guilt is the primary emotion that motivates people to obey their conscience. A substantial body of research supports the role of guilt in moral development and behavior (Eisenberg, 2000). Guilt arises from discrepancies between what people feel they should do and what they contemplate or observe themselves doing. When toddlers are learning about morals, they may feel anxious or ashamed at being caught. Yet they do not experience genuine guilt until they actually internalize their parents' values as their own—that is, until they not only *know* these values but also believe in them.

Young children's moral beliefs are very concrete and specific and are often tied directly to a mental image of a parent. Toddlers may thus be observed telling themselves "No!" even as they follow a forbidden impulse, or repeating their parents' admonitions as a way of stopping themselves from doing something they have been told is wrong ("Don't make a mess!"). Research suggests that as children get older, they rely less on an internalized parent "sitting on their shoulder" and more on abstract moral demands integrated from their parents and the wider culture (see Williams & Bybee, 1994).

Empathy   Unpleasant emotions such as guilt, anxiety, and shame are not the only emotions involved in moral behavior. Some theorists emphasize the motivational role of **empathy**, or *feeling for another person who is hurting* (see Holmgren et al., 1998). Empathy has both a cognitive component (understanding what the person is experiencing) and an emotional component (experiencing a similar feeling). Research supports the view that empathy contributes to prosocial behavior, although empathizing *too* much emotionally can actually make people self-focused and hence *less* helpful (Strayer, 1993).

According to one theory (Hoffman, 1978, 1998), the ability to respond empathically changes considerably over the course of development. During the first year, infants experience global empathy; that is, they feel the same distress as the other person but cannot separate whose distress is whose. An 11-month-old who witnesses another child fall and cry may put her thumb in her mouth and bury her head in her mother's lap as if she were hurt herself.

As children become better able to distinguish their own thoughts and feelings from those of others, they begin to experience genuine **empathic distress**—*feeling upset for another person*—which motivates moral or prosocial behavior. As early as the second year of life, children can recognize when someone is hurting, feel bad for that person, and try to take action to make the person feel better (Zahn-Waxler et al., 1992a). The response may nonetheless be egocentric: A 13-month-old may give a sad-looking adult his own favorite stuffed animal or bring his own mother over to comfort a crying playmate, reflecting the immature perspective-taking ability of the young child.

As children get older, they respond more accurately to cues about what other people are feeling. By adolescence, a more mature form of empathy emerges, as individuals begin to think about suffering that exists beyond the immediate moment and hence become concerned about broader issues such as poverty or moral responsibility.

If empathy leads to prosocial actions, what type of actions does an individual who lacks empathy display? Do they try to hurt others or are they simply unaware of the needs and feelings of others? The answer appears to favor the former. For example, children with conduct disorder display violent and aggressive behavior directed toward other people and/or animals. They may also destroy property and lie. In short, they display behaviors that clearly run counter to the social norms of society. Although a number of explanations have been offered to explain the origins of conduct disorder, one recent hypothesis suggests that people with conduct disorder lack empathy. To test this idea, levels of empathy among individuals with conduct disorder and normal individuals were compared. The adolescents viewed videotaped vignettes portraying people in distress. They then completed a series of questionnaires assessing their reactions to the vignettes. Indeed, the individuals with conduct disorder showed significantly less empathy than did the normal controls to whom they were compared (Cohen & Strayer, 1996).

Apply & Discuss

Moral values tend to be highly similar in fathers and sons. A prime example: President George W. Bush and his father, former President George Bush.

▪ Explain this similarity from a psychodynamic perspective.

▪ Explain this similarity from a behaviorist perspective.

▪ Explain this similarity from a cognitive perspective.

▪ To what extent do phenomena such as this require a behavioral genetic point of view, which focuses on the genetic transmission of individual differences in personality traits such as conservatism (Chapters 3 and 12)?

Making Sense of Moral Development

Cognitive and emotional approaches to moral development each present part of the picture, but none alone covers the entire landscape.

Cognitive Approaches

The strength of the cognitive–social approach is its emphasis on precisely what is missing from most other approaches, namely, moral or prosocial *behavior*. Thinking about morality is irrelevant if it does not affect action. Research does not, in fact, show particularly strong correlations between moral reasoning and prosocial behavior in older children and adults; correlations between empathy and prosocial behavior tend to be relatively small as well (see, e.g., Eisenberg et al., 1991; Miller et al., 1996).

The cognitive–social approach, however, tends to *assume* that certain behaviors are prosocial and generally does not address situations that require choices between imperfect moral options. For example, during the Vietnam War, people agonized over the question of what was moral or "prosocial." Was it moral to answer the draft, even though many considered the war immoral or nonsensical? Evade the draft and let other people die instead? Protest the war? These kinds of questions are the essence of moral decision making.

Cognitive–developmental models have advantages and disadvantages as well. Kohlberg's theory highlights a phenomenon that no other theory addresses—that moral development may go beyond the internalization of society's rules. This has been the principle of many moral leaders, from Jesus to Gandhi to Martin Luther King.

At the same time, Kohlberg's theory has drawn considerable criticism. People at the higher stages of moral reasoning do not necessarily behave any differently from people who are conventional in their moral reasoning. The philosopher Martin Heidegger, who reflected deeply and abstractly on a range of human experiences, found ways to rationalize cooperation with the Nazi regime, which many more "ordinary" Europeans did not (Chapter 18).

Relatedly, moral reasoning does not always translate into moral behavior. Indeed, as noted earlier, Kohlberg was less concerned with the ultimate decision a person makes and more with the reasoning processes by which they arrive at that decision. Thus, according to the model, morality is clearly determined by the level of reasoning rather than the behavior itself.

Other critics argue that Kohlberg's model overlooks the role of educational level in influencing moral reasoning. People with higher educational levels display higher levels of moral reasoning than people with less education, but this characteristic does not necessarily mean that they are more moral. Rather, they are more articulate in their reasoning abilities (Eckensberger, 1994). Furthermore, people do not always display the same level of moral reasoning in different situations (Fishkin et al., 1973). In other words, in the face of one moral dilemma, a person's reasoning may be at the conventional level; when confronted with another moral dilemma, the person may reason at the postconventional level of morality.

Yet other critics, notably Carol Gilligan (1982, 1996), contend that Kohlberg's theory is gender biased. In Kohlberg's early studies, women rarely transcended Stage 3 morality, which equates goodness with pleasing or helping others. Men more often reached Stage 4, which focuses on maintaining social order. Does this mean women are morally inferior? Gilligan thinks not—and a glance around the globe at most of the perpetrators of violence supports her view. According to Gilligan, women and men follow divergent developmental paths, with one no less mature than the other. Women's moral concerns, she argues, more likely center on care and responsibility

Big Picture φ Question 4

To what extent is human nature particular versus universal?

for specific individuals, whereas men tend to favor the justice orientation emphasized by Kohlberg. A *meta-analysis* (a review that summarizes the data across dozens or hundreds of studies quantitatively, by averaging their findings; Chapter 16) found that women and men do tend toward care and justice orientations, respectively, but that the differences are relatively small (Jaffee & Hyde, 2000).

Both Gilligan's and Kohlberg's theories may require some modification when applied to cultures in which concepts of duty and caring are different and less gender based than in the West—that is, where both men and women show a greater orientation toward relationships and community than in the West (Miller, 1994). For example, when six-year-olds in the United States and China tell stories in response to pictures or describe emotional memories, Chinese children show a greater concern with social engagement and obedience to authority, whereas Western children's stories show more themes related to autonomy (Wang & Leichtman, 2000).

The information-processing approach to moral development fills in and clarifies many of the broad strokes painted by stage theories. Nevertheless, it leaves many questions unanswered, particularly about the way motivation influences moral reasoning and behavior. Why do children accept values in the first place, when doing so produces guilt? Why are they willing to control their impulses at all? How do their judgments about their own guilt or responsibility differ from their judgments about others'? Asking people to make judgments about what other people have done is very different from understanding their own struggles to remain faithful to their lovers, to report their income honestly to the Internal Revenue Service, or to resist saying something unkind behind a friend's back.

Emotional Approaches

Perspectives that focus on the emotional side of morality fare better in answering these questions. Because morality so often requires self-sacrifice and self-restraint, an emotional counterweight such as anxiety or guilt seems essential to balance out the net losses in gratification. Empathy adds a further source of motivation for moral behavior: Helping other people leads to a sense of satisfaction and reduces the empathic distress that comes from observing someone else's suffering (Chapter 18).

Emotional approaches, however, also have their pitfalls. Why children internalize moral values is unclear. Freud linked identification with the father to the fear of castration in boys (Chapter 12). This seems a rather unlikely impetus for the development of morality and cannot account for moral development in females. Moreover, research indicates that mothers are more responsible for moral training in most Western families (Hoffman & Saltzstein, 1967) and that internalization of values is associated with the extent to which mothers engage in an emotionally responsive, reciprocal relationship with their children (Kochanska et al., 2000). Identification with the father is probably not as central as Freud supposed, although research on moral reasoning does show particularly strong links between fathers' level of moral reasoning and the moral reasoning of both their sons and daughters (Speicher, 1994).

Empathy theories do not provide insight into specifically *moral* questions, which arise when people's needs are in conflict. Prosocial responses are common by 18 to 20 months when infants witness other people's distress but *not* when they cause the distress themselves (Zahn-Waxler et al., 1992b). Infants as young as 12 to 18 months often share toys with other children or with their parents, but by age 2 they are less likely to share if it means giving up their toys (Hay et al., 1991). Perhaps not incidentally, by this age most children have mastered the word "mine." Prosocial responses aimed at making up for a transgression emerge around two years, precisely when theorists have argued for the beginnings of moral conscience fueled by guilt.

Research suggests that the roots of conscience may lie in both the fear emphasized by Freud and the empathy emphasized by recent researchers (Kochanska,

1997). For children who have a fearful temperament, gentle discipline by mothers predicts conscience at age 4. For children who have a fearless temperament and are less responsive to discipline, *positive* mother–child interactions appear to predict conscience development. These data make sense in light of research suggesting that some people are more driven by fear, whereas others are more pulled by rewards (Chapter 10). What is interesting is the possibility that these basic temperamental variables may affect the way children internalize moral values as well.

An Integrated View

An integrated account of moral development would spell out the interactions of cognition, affect, and motivation that are involved when children and adults wrestle with moral questions. Infants and toddlers have many selfish impulses, but they also have prosocial impulses based on an innate capacity for empathy. When self-centered and other-centered motives clash, young children tend to opt for the most gratifying course of action.

This behavior probably changes over time for a number of reasons. Children mature in their capacity to love and care about other people and to understand the perspective of others. They also become more able to regulate their impulses as neural circuits in the frontal lobes mature and as expanding cognitive abilities allow them to transform situations in their minds.

Furthermore, through social learning, children come to associate actions such as sharing with positive reinforcement and hitting and lying with punishment. By identifying with people they fear and admire, children's fear of punishment gradually becomes transformed into fear of their own internal monitor of right and wrong—and hence into guilt. Eventually, they reflect more abstractly about moral questions and try to integrate the moral feelings and beliefs they have accrued over the course of their development.

INTERIM SUMMARY

Emotion, like cognition, is central to moral development. Psychodynamic theories emphasize the role of guilt in moral development and argue that conscience arises through identification with parents. Other theories emphasize **empathy**, or feeling for another person who is hurting. Moral development probably reflects an interaction of cognitive and affective changes that allow children to understand and feel for other people as well as to inhibit their own wishes and impulses.

Social Development across the Life Span

In discussing social development, we have thus far focused on the first quarter of the life span. Like physical and cognitive development, however, social development continues throughout life. In this section, we begin by examining the most widely known theory of life-span development, formulated by Erik Erikson (1963). We then examine central aspects of life-span development from adolescence through old age.

Erikson's Theory of Psychosocial Development

Erikson's is not the only model of adult development, but it has three important features. First, it is culturally sensitive, reflecting Erikson's experience living in and study-

Table 14.4   ■ ■ Erikson's Psychosocial Stage Model of Development

Psychosocial Stage (Approximate Age)	Developmental Task
0–12 to 18 months	Trust versus mistrust
1 to 2 years	Autonomy versus shame and doubt
3 to 6 years	Initiative versus guilt
7 to 11 years	Industry versus inferiority
Teenage years (adolescence)	Identity versus identity confusion
20s and 30s (Young adulthood)	Intimacy versus isolation
40s to 60s (Midlife)	Generativity versus stagnation
60s on	Integrity versus despair

ing several cultures, from Denmark and Germany to a Sioux reservation. Research since Erikson's time suggests that when and where people develop is crucial to the way they grow and change throughout their lives, even within a single culture (Elder, 1998). For example, people who were young children during the Great Depression never forgot the lessons of poverty, even when they were financially secure years later.

Second, Erikson's theory integrates biology, psychological experience, and culture by grounding development simultaneously in biological maturation and changing social demands (Chapter 1). For example, like his mentor, the psychoanalyst Anna Freud (1958), Erikson observed that adolescents wrestle with questions about who they are and what they believe during puberty, a time in which teenagers have a surge of new feelings and impulses. Reconstituting a self-concept that now includes the self as a sexual being is a major task spurred by biological maturation. The extent to which adolescents find this conflictual, however, depends on the beliefs, values, rituals, and sexual practices of their culture (Mead, 1928).

Third, although Erikson's theory offers a very broad framework, many aspects of his developmental model have received empirical support in cross-sectional, longitudinal, and sequential studies (e.g., Bradley & Marcia, 1998; Marcia, 1987, 1999; McAdams et al., 1998; Whitbourne et al., 1992).

Erikson intended his model of **psychosocial stages**—*stages in the development of the person as a social being*—to supplement Freud's psychosexual stages (see Table 14.4). Thus, the toddler years are not only a time of toilet training but also, more generally, a time of learning what it means to submit to authority, to control impulses, and to assert one's own autonomy. At each of eight stages, the individual faces a **developmental task**, *a challenge that is normative for that period of life*. Each successive task provokes a *crisis*—an opportunity for steaming ahead or a danger point for psychological derailment. These alternative "tracks" at each juncture are not, of course, absolute. No infant, for example, ever feels *totally* trusting or mistrusting, and people have many opportunities over the course of development to backtrack or take a new route.

Childhood   During the first stage, **basic trust versus mistrust**, *infants come to trust others or to perceive the social world as hostile or unreliable*. This stage comprises roughly the first 18 months of life, when infants are developing their earliest internal working models of relationship.

By age 2, children have learned to walk and talk—a result of biological maturation that has profound psychological consequences. Now they can say what they want and move where they want. This is the time of the "terrible twos," in which toddlers regularly assert their will. Erikson calls the period from around ages 2 to 3 **autonomy versus shame and doubt**, because *toddlers at this stage learn to feel se-*

cure in their independence or to experience doubt in their newfound skills and shame at their failures.

Empirically, some of the feelings of excitement and shame children experience at this age are self-generated, whereas others can be traced to the ways their parents respond to their successes, failures, and efforts at mastery. During the second year, children spontaneously set standards for themselves and experience pride in their accomplishments (Kagan, 1984). Yet research also finds that two-year-olds whose mothers are critical and controlling as they attempt to teach their toddlers achievement-related tasks in the laboratory tend to demonstrate more shame and less persistence at similar tasks a year later (Kelley et al., 2000).

The third stage, roughly between ages 3 and 6, is called **initiative versus guilt.** *The poles of this stage are a sense of goal-directness and responsibility versus a rigid, tyrannical conscience.* Initiative enables a child to follow through with ideas and goals. Children who have difficulty with this stage, in contrast, may be highly self-critical, or may become rigid and constricted to avoid acting on feelings and impulses they have learned to think of as "bad."

The next stage, which occurs roughly between ages 7 and 11, is **industry versus inferiority**. In this stage, *children develop a sense of competence (industriousness) or of inadequacy*, as they begin to develop and practice skills they will use for a lifetime in productive work. In literate cultures, children enter school during this stage, and their experiences of academic and social success or failure shape both their self-concepts and the strategies they use to protect their self-esteem. Some children become caught in a vicious cycle, in which a sense of inferiority leads them to give up quickly on tasks, which in turn increases the probability of further failure.

Adolescence   According to Erikson, the *developmental crisis of adolescence* is **identity versus identity confusion. Identity** refers to *a stable sense of who one is and what one's values and ideals are* (Erikson, 1968). **Identity confusion** occurs when *the individual fails to develop a coherent and enduring sense of self and has difficulty committing to roles, values, people, or occupational choices*. Empirically, individuals differ in the extent to which they explore and maintain commitments to ideologies, occupational choices, and interpersonal values (Marcia, 1987). Some establish an identity after a period of soul searching, while others commit early without exploration, foreclosing identity development. Still others remain perpetually confused or put off identity consolidation for many years while trying on various roles throughout their 20s.

These different paths to identity depend heavily on culture (Erikson, 1968; Schlegel & Barry, 1991). Many traditional cultures have **initiation rites**, *ceremonies during adolescence that initiate the child into adulthood and impose a socially bestowed identity*. A period of identity confusion occurs primarily in technologically more advanced societies or in cultures that are undergoing rapid change, as in much of the contemporary world.

Sometimes adolescents have trouble establishing a positive identity; they may be doing poorly in school or lack models of successful adulthood with whom to identify. As a result, they may develop a **negative identity**, *defining themselves as **not** something or someone (such as a parent) or taking on a role society defines as bad*. This is a path often taken by gang members and chronic delinquents, who seemingly revel in their "badness."

Failure to form a cohesive identity beyond adolescence can signify problems later on. Girls who have difficulty forming an identity in late adolescence are more likely than their peers to experience marital disruption at midlife. Boys with late-adolescent identity problems are more likely to remain single and be unsatisfied with their lives in middle age (Kahn et al., 1985). Identity disturbances are common in certain forms of personality disorder in adulthood (Chapter 15), such as borderline personality disorder (Wilkinson-Ryan & Westen, 2000).

Apply & Discuss

■ How might an infant's innate temperament and early experiences together shape its sense of trust or mistrust—or, in the language of attachment theory, its attachment security?

■ How might an insecure or mistrustful infant or young child behave in ways that actually reinforce its view of relationships?

Adulthood   Erikson was one of the first theorists to take seriously the notion of development after adolescence. He describes the developmental task confronting young adults as **intimacy versus isolation**, *establishing enduring, committed relationships or withdrawing and avoiding commitment*. The task applies to friendships as well as romantic relationships.

Erikson describes the crisis of midlife as **generativity versus stagnation**, in which *people begin to leave some kind of lasting legacy or feel alienated from relationships and community*. **Generativity** means *concern for the next generation as well as an interest in producing (generating) something of lasting value to society*. People express their generative impulses through rearing children, participating in culturally meaningful institutions such as churches or civic organizations, mentoring younger workers, or creating something that will last beyond them, such as a work of art. Empirically, people in midlife express more generative themes than younger adults when describing their lives, and they report more generative activities (de St. Aubin et al., 2004; McAdams et al., 1993; McAdams et al., 1998). As Erikson hypothesized, individuals also differ in the extent to which they maintain an active, generative stance during middle age (Bradley & Marcia, 1998). People who have difficulty with generativity experience **stagnation**, *a feeling that the promise of youth has gone unfulfilled*. Stagnation may be expressed as dissatisfaction with a marital partner, alienation from one's children, or chronic feelings of boredom or unhappiness.

Erikson's final stage is **integrity versus despair**, *a time in which individuals look back on their lives with a sense of having lived it well or with despair and regret*. In many respects, the balance between integrity and despair is fluid, as individuals must inevitably cope with losing people who have made their lives meaningful. For example, whereas roughly two-thirds of people in the United States are married in middle age, by age 65, that number has dropped to half for women, and by age 75, it has dropped below half for men and to about one-fourth for women (U.S. Bureau of the Census, 1998a). Thus, members of both sexes, but particularly women, face the death of a spouse (because women tend to live longer and to marry older men) while dealing with the gradual health declines of aging themselves.

INTERIM SUMMARY

Erikson proposed a life-span model of **psychosocial stages**—stages in the development of the person as a social being. In **basic trust versus mistrust**, infants come to trust others or perceive the social world as hostile or unreliable. In **autonomy versus shame and doubt**, toddlers come to experience themselves as independent sources of will and power or feel insecure in their newfound skills. In **initiative versus guilt**, young children develop the capacity to form and carry out plans, but their emerging conscience can render them vulnerable to guilt. In **industry versus inferiority**, school-age children develop a sense of competence but may suffer from feelings of inadequacy. Erikson described adolescence as a period of **identity versus identity confusion**, in which the task is to establish a stable sense of who one is and what one values. The crisis of young adulthood is **intimacy** (establishing enduring, committed relationships) **versus isolation**. In **generativity versus stagnation**, middle-aged individuals attempt to pass something on to the next generation. In **integrity versus despair**, people look back on their lives with a sense of satisfaction or sadness and regret.

Development from Adolescence through Old Age

Erikson's theory provides a backdrop for empirical research on social development throughout the life span. Here we focus on some of the central issues in the study of development from adolescence through old age.

Adolescence   Psychologists have offered two conflicting views of adolescent social and personality development (Arnett, 1999; Westen & Chang, 2000). One ap-

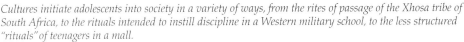

Cultures initiate adolescents into society in a variety of ways, from the rites of passage of the Xhosa tribe of South Africa, to the rituals intended to instill discipline in a Western military school, to the less structured "rituals" of teenagers in a mall.

proach emphasizes that as adolescents grow less dependent on their parents and try out new values and roles, they often become rebellious and moody, shifting from compliance one moment to defiance the next. According to this **conflict model**, put forth at the turn of the twentieth century (Hall, 1904) and later elaborated by psychodynamic theorists (Blos, 1962; A. Freud, 1958), *conflict and crisis are normal in adolescence*. Conflict theorists argue that adolescents need to go through a period of crisis to separate themselves psychologically from their parents and to carve out their own identity. Beeper studies (which page or "beep" participants at random intervals over the course of a day to measure what they are thinking or feeling at the moment; Chapter 9) show that adolescents do, in fact, experience a wider range of moods over a shorter period of time than adults (Csikszentmihalyi & Larson, 1984). Longitudinal studies find decreases in hostility and negative emotionality and increases in diligence, self-control, and congeniality as teenagers move into early adulthood (see McGue et al., 1993).

Other theorists argue, however, that the stormy, moody, conflict-ridden adolescent is the exception rather than the rule (Compas et al., 1995; Douvan & Adelson, 1966; Offer et al., 1990). According to the **continuity model**, *adolescence is not a turbulent period but is essentially continuous with childhood and adulthood*. Research supporting this view finds that roughly 80 percent of adolescents show no signs of severe storm and stress (Offer & Offer, 1975).

How do we reconcile these two views of adolescence? Adolescence is a time of enormous individual differences, with many alternative paths that vary according to the individual, culture, and historical period (see Hauser & Safyer, 1994). As we will see, researchers have increasingly moved away from models of life-span development that propose a single pathway to "normal" or "successful" development, particularly in adolescence and adulthood, when biological maturation is not the driving force it is in childhood and cultural differences make generalizations much more difficult. Thus, adolescence may not *inherently* be a stormy era, but "storm and stress" is *more likely* in adolescence than in either childhood or adulthood, as suggested by data on adolescents' conflicts with parents, mood disruptions, and high-risk behavior (Arnett, 1999).

Aside from *individual* differences, children show some increasing *gender* differences in adolescence. For example, across a number of domains, boys tend to become more confident and less dissatisfied with themselves over time, whereas the opposite occurs for girls. Already by third or fourth grade, and increasingly through at least early adolescence, boys tend to overestimate their scholastic ability, and girls underestimate it (Cole et al., 1999). Similarly, at age 13, boys and girls show similar levels of body dissatisfaction (Figure 14.9), but after that point their paths diverge, at least in Western cultures (Rosenblum & Lewis, 1999).

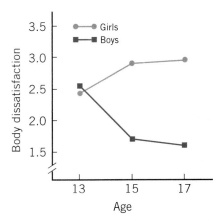

FIGURE 14.9 Body dissatisfaction in boys and girls. At age 13, girls and boys show similar levels of satisfaction with their bodies. By age 15, however, gender differences are substantial. *Source:* Rosenblum & Lewis, 1999, p. 54.

Big Picture φ Question 5

To what extent are psychological processes the same in men and women?

Apply & Discuss

■ Does personality develop over the course of adulthood, as it does through childhood, or does it simply change, as the person encounters different situations and developmental tasks?

■ What does it mean to say that personality, morality, or cognition develops?

■ Can any theory of adult change or development apply to the range of circumstances cross-culturally? Do some universal principles exist, as they do in memory and cognition? If so, what might account for them?

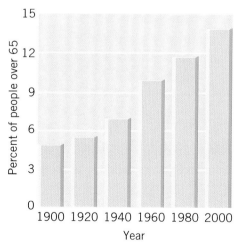

FIGURE 14.10   The aging population. In much of the world, advances in medicine and public health have led to increasing numbers of people who live long lives, and hence to a redefining of the life cycle and concepts of "old age." *Source:* Adapted from U.S. Bureau of the Census, 1998b.

Early Adulthood and Middle Age   Erikson described the central task of young adulthood as the development of intimacy—establishing lifelong friendships and settling down and beginning to have a family of one's own. Empirically, Erikson was probably right to name a stage of adult development "intimacy" and to tie it to finding a long-term mate. In the United States, for example, over 95 percent of people have married at least once by the age of 55, and many of the remaining 5 percent have lived with a partner outside matrimony (U.S. Bureau of the Census, 1998a).

Marital intimacy does not, however, come easily: In Western cultures, marital distress actually increases over the first three years of marriage, and maintaining intimate relationships in the face of conflict and disillusionment is a challenge that requires continuous negotiation and compromise (Gottman, 1998). Over half of divorces occur in the first three years of marriage (Whitbourne, 2001). Marital conflict is at its peak when children are young, when housework doubles, financial pressures mount, and intimate time alone is difficult to find (Belsky & Hsieh, 1998; Belsky & Pensky, 1988; Berman & Pedersen, 1987).

Women's satisfaction with marriage appears to suffer more than men's after the birth of a child (Cowan & Cowan, 1992). Motherhood usually involves a redefinition of roles and reallocation of time. The household division of labor tends to become more traditional, and women who are used to autonomy and invested in their work suddenly find themselves taking on more and more responsibility at home (Hoffman & Levy-Shiff, 1994). For men, fatherhood means that they are no longer the primary recipients of their wives' attention and love; at the same time, they incur new financial and household and child-care responsibilities (Lamb, 1987).

Precisely when young adulthood ends and middle age begins is difficult to pinpoint. Some observers have described this period as a time of *midlife crisis* (Jacques, 1965; Levinson et al., 1978; Sheehy, 1976). One researcher found that roughly 80 percent of the men he interviewed were in a state of crisis around age 40, as they began to think of themselves as middle-aged instead of young and to question the basic structure of their lives (Levinson, 1978). In Western culture, people are frequently at the height of their careers in their 40s and 50s, enjoying leadership positions at work or in the community. At the same time, however, the death of parents, the occasional jarring death of siblings or contemporaries, and an aging body inevitably lead people to confront their mortality and to consider how they will live their remaining years.

As with adolescence, however, many psychologists have challenged the view of midlife as a time of crisis and suggest that midlife crisis may be a phenomenon that occurs primarily in upper middle class men (see Rosenberg et al., 1999). Empirically, only a minority of people report experiencing a midlife crisis, and in these cases, the crisis usually occurs along with a specific interruption in the normal rhythm of life, such as loss of a job or divorce (Costa & McCrae, 1988; Neugarten, 1977).

Old Age   The meaning of old age changed dramatically over the course of the twentieth century. The average life span increased by almost 30 years, and the proportion of people over age 65 in North America grew from 1 in 30 in 1900 to a projected 1 in 5 by the year 2040 (see Figure 14.10) (U.S. Bureau of the Census, 1998b). This demographic shift has produced substantial changes in perceptions of old age. Even three decades ago, people were considered "old" in their 60s. Today, no one is surprised to see 70-year-olds on the tennis court.

Technologically developed and Western cultures tend to devalue the elderly more than most cultures and to emphasize the despairing end of the continuum. William Shakespeare's characterization of old age, from *As You Like It* (Act II, Scene vii), presents a grim picture that is not far from the contemporary Western conception of life's final phase:

Last scene of all,
That ends this strange eventful history,

Is second childishness and mere oblivion,
Sans teeth, sans eyes, sans taste, sans every thing.

Although genuine declines do make life much more difficult as people grow old, fortunately Shakespeare took some poetic license, as reality is nowhere near this bleak. For example, contrary to stereotypes, only about 5 percent of the population over 65 have physical or mental impairments serious enough to require continuous nursing care (Tolliver, 1983). In fact, most people report having more positive and less negative affect as they move toward the end of middle age, and most people cross-culturally report being happy in old age (Diener & Suh, 1998; Helson & Klohnen, 1998; Mroczek & Kolarz, 1998). Why, then, are our stereotypes so negative?

One explanation is that many stereotypes of aging are built on our emotional forecasts of how we imagine we would feel if we gained weight, lost some hair, grayed, and suffered many of the more serious indignities of old age. The reality is that humans have a remarkable capacity for dealing with life's blows with equanimity—for gradually adjusting to realities we cannot change and regaining our emotional equilibrium. As the writer Dostoevsky once said, humans are capable of adjusting to nearly anything.

A prime culprit in our negative views of old age may also be technological development (Cowgirl & Holmes, 1972). Ironically, the same factor that has prolonged life by decades has undermined the status of the aged by making their jobs obsolete, limiting the applicability of their beliefs and values in a radically changed social and cultural milieu, and eroding the concept of the extended family. The geographical mobility associated with economic development also means that children may live hundreds if not thousands of miles from their aging parents. In contrast, in more traditional societies, the aged are by definition the most knowledgeable because they have lived the longest and accumulated the most information, and mutual ties of affection between the generations are reinforced by daily interaction.

In the face of physical decline, negative stereotypes, and the loss of spouse, friends, and social roles, what allows an individual to find satisfaction, or what Erikson describes as integrity, in the final years of life? In one study of around 1000 people aged 65 to 72, several variables predicted life satisfaction: close relationships, an active social and community life, continuing recreation, good health, and sufficient income (Flanagan, 1978). In general, research suggests that people who find satisfaction in later life tend to be characterized by three factors: lack of significant disease, high cognitive and physical functioning, and an active engagement in productive activity and community with others (Rowe & Kahn, 1997).

Longitudinal studies suggest that earlier factors also predict happiness and physical and mental health in later life (Sears, 1977; Valliant & Valliant, 1990). These include marital and career fulfillment as a younger adult, sustained family relationships, and long-lived ancestors. Risk factors from young and middle adulthood include defense mechanisms that grossly distort reality (such as projection; see Chapter 12), alcoholism, and depression before age 50. The quality of old age thus appears to depend to a substantial degree on the quality of youth.

Shakespeare would be surprised by the way senior citizens have responded to changing views of "appropriate" behavior in old age.

INTERIM SUMMARY

Some researchers adopt a **conflict model** of adolescence, arguing that conflict and struggle are normal in adolescence; others propose a **continuity model**, viewing adolescence as essentially continuous with childhood and adulthood. Each model probably applies to a subset of adolescents. Similarly, researchers disagree on the extent to which midlife crisis is common in middle age. In all likelihood, "crises" in both adolescence and at midlife depend on individual differences and cultural and historical circumstances. Although old age inevitably involves many losses, the realities appear far better than the negative stereotypes of aging seen in many technologically developed societies.

Apply & Discuss

At least in the West, parents tend to value their relationship with their adult children more than their adult children value their relationship with their parents (Christensen, 1992).

■ Explain this from an evolutionary perspective. Why would parents' investment in their children be greater than their adult children's investment in their aging parents?

Summary

1. **Social development** refers to predictable changes in interpersonal thought, feeling, and behavior over the life span.

Attachment

2. **Attachment** refers to the enduring emotional ties children form with their primary caregivers. **Separation anxiety**—distress at separation from attachment figures—occurs around the same time in all human cultures and peaks in the second year of life. Harlow's experiments with monkeys showed that security, not food, is the basis for attachment. Integrating psychodynamic and evolutionary theory, Bowlby proposed that attachment is a mechanism to keep immature animals close to their parents.

3. Using a procedure called the Strange Situation, researchers have identified four styles of attachment: **secure, avoidant, ambivalent**, and **disorganized**. Early attachment patterns have a powerful impact on later social functioning and form the basis of **adult attachment** styles. Infants develop **internal working models**, or mental representations of attachment relationships, which form the basis for their expectations in later close relationships.

Socialization

4. **Socialization** refers to the processes through which individuals come to learn the rules, beliefs, values, skills, attitudes, and behavior patterns of their society. Socialization is transactional (involving mutual influence of "teachers" and "learners"), lifelong, and multifaceted. Like all psychological processes, it also occurs within constraints imposed by biology and the broader economic and cultural context.

5. Parents are particularly important socialization agents. Research distinguishes **authoritarian, permissive, authoritative**, and **uninvolved** parenting styles. Each parenting style tends to produce children with different characteristics. Parents vary across and within cultures in the extent to which they are accepting and rejecting of their children. Parental warmth and sensitivity are associated with self-esteem, independence, and emotional stability.

6. Among the most powerful roles into which people are socialized are **gender roles**, the range of behaviors considered appropriate for males and females. Unlike sex (a biologically based categorization), **gender** (the psychological meaning of being male or female) is influenced by learning, although evolutionary pressures have probably contributed to gender differences that cultures embellish and magnify. Gender socialization begins in the first days of life.

Peer Relationships

7. Children differ in the extent to which they are accepted by their peers. **Rejected children** are often teased and ostracized, although they may also elicit dislike if they are bullies. **Neglected children** are less likely to draw a positive or negative response from their peers and are more likely to be friendless or ignored. Sibling relationships have many dimensions, including both rivalry and closeness.

Development of Social Cognition

8. As with cognitive development in nonsocial domains, children develop in their **social cognition**—the way they conceptualize themselves, others, and relationships. The **self-concept** refers to a person's organized way of representing information about the self. Initially, children lack a distinct concept of self. Their views of themselves, like their views of others, begin concrete and gradually become more abstract. By adolescence, they are much more likely to think about their own and others' internal psychological processes such as feelings and personality traits. An important cognitive–social skill that develops gradually is **perspective-taking**, the ability to understand other people's viewpoints.

9. Children's understanding of what gender is and how it applies to them develops substantially throughout the first several years of life. Children develop **gender schemas**—mental representations that associate psychological characteristics with one sex or the other—by integrating cultural beliefs with their personal experiences. Gender schemas share striking similarities across cultures, which appear to reflect an interaction between biology and social learning.

Moral Development

10. Moral development refers to the acquisition of values and rules for balancing the potentially conflicting interests of the self and others. Behaviorist and cognitive–social theories assert that **prosocial behavior** (behavior that benefits others), like other behaviors, is learned through processes such as operant conditioning and modeling. Cognitive–developmental models focus less on moral behaviors than on moral reasoning. Kohlberg's stage theory distinguishes three levels of moral reasoning: **preconventional** (following moral rules to avoid punishment or obtain reward), **conventional** (defining right and wrong according to learned cultural standards), and **postconventional** (applying abstract, self-defined principles). Information-processing approaches break moral development down into component processes and examine the way each changes during childhood.

11. Psychodynamic and other theories suggest that children internalize their parents' values, and that guilt motivates people to obey their conscience. Other research emphasizes the role of **empathy** (feeling for someone who is hurting) in motivating prosocial behavior. Recent research suggests that the paths to internalization of conscience in children depend on an interaction of temperament and parenting styles. Moral development reflects an interaction of cognitive and emotional development.

Social Development across the Life Span

12. The most widely known theory of life-span development is Erik Erikson's theory of **psychosocial stages: basic trust versus mistrust, autonomy versus shame and doubt, initiative versus guilt**, and **industry versus inferiority** in childhood; **identity versus identity confusion** in adolescence; and **intimacy versus isolation, generativity versus stagnation**, and **integrity versus despair** during adulthood.

13. Psychologists disagree on the extent to which people experience "crises" in adolescence and midlife, but in general, there does not appear to be any single path to "successful aging." Nor do the data support a stereotypically bleak view of aging. People who have high life satisfaction in later life tend to have had fulfilled lives earlier and to be characterized by physical and cognitive health and active engagement with productive activities and other people.

Key Terms

adult attachment 503
ambivalent attachment style 499
attachment 497
authoritarian 506
authoritative 506
autonomy versus shame and doubt 530
avoidant attachment style 499
basic trust versus mistrust 530
conflict model 533
continuity model 533
conventional morality 523
developmental task 530
disorganized attachment style 499

empathic distress 526
empathy 526
gender 509
gender constancy 518
gender identity 517
gender roles 509
gender schemas 518
gender stability 517
generativity 532
generativity versus stagnation 532
identity 531
identity confusion 531
identity versus identity confusion 531

imprinting 498
industry versus inferiority 531
initiation rites 531
initiative versus guilt 531
integrity versus despair 532
internal working models 500
intimacy versus isolation 532
morality of constraint 522
morality of cooperation 522
negative identity 531
neglected children 511
permissive 506
perspective-taking 515
postconventional morality 523
preconventional morality 523

prosocial behavior 524
psychosocial stages 530
rejected children 511
secure attachment style 499
self-concept 513
separation anxiety 499
sex-role ideology 518
sex typing 509
social cognition 513
social development 496
socialization 504
stagnation 532
theory of mind 516
uninvolved 506

Psychological Disorders

*T*wenty years after his tour in Vietnam, Joseph found that he was still suffering the ill effects of the war. He regularly experienced nightmares and night sweats. He was constantly sick with one type of illness after another, not the least of which were panic attacks triggered by the sound of backfiring cars, sudden noises, or kids firing toy guns. His third marriage was beginning to unravel, and his relationships with his children were damaged because of his short temper, something he rarely experienced prior to the war. While in Vietnam, Joseph had seen some of his fellow battalion members killed right before his eyes. He himself had killed three enemy soldiers. He saw villages burned, and women exposed to atrocities he still was unable to talk about. Ten years ago, he was diagnosed with post-traumatic stress disorder (PTSD), a psychological and physical reaction to extreme trauma and stress.

What is interesting about Joseph's case is that not every Vietnam veteran experienced the same symptoms. Some of them returned home seemingly unscathed.

Was there something about Joseph that made him more vulnerable to the stresses experienced by many soldiers in Vietnam. Was he predisposed to psychological problems because of his genetic history? Or, was he simply exposed to more trauma in Vietnam than veterans who did not develop PTSD? Could it be both? Could the stresses of Vietnam have activated some underlying genetic predisposition for psychological problems?

In this chapter, we examine **psychopathology** (literally, sickness, or *pathology*, of the mind), or ***problematic patterns of thought, feeling, or behavior that disrupt an individual's sense of well-being or social or occupational functioning***. We begin by discussing the cultural context of psychopathology, considering how people like Joseph become classified as normal or disordered. Next we examine the differing theoretical viewpoints on psychopathology. Then, in the bulk of the chapter, we turn to a description of the nature and causes of the major forms of psychopathology. Throughout, two key questions surface: Why do people fall ill psychologically? And what are the relative roles of nature and nurture in generating psychological disturbances?

The Cultural Context of Psychopathology

Every society has its concept of "madness," and what a society considers normal or abnormal is constantly changing. The kind of competitive, every-person-for-himself stance taken for granted in many large cities would have been a sign of bad character—or in today's language, personality pathology—by the rural grandparents of many contemporary city-dwellers (and by the vast majority of cultures in human history). Some of the psychopathological syndromes clinicians encounter today were identified and classified as early as 2500 B.C. by the ancient Sumerians and Egyptians. Over the centuries Western culture has attributed mental illness to a variety of causes, such as demon possession, supernatural forces, witches, and Satan. To what extent does culture shape and define mental illness? And are diagnoses anything but labels a culture uses to brand its deviants?

Culture and Psychopathology

Cultures differ in both the disorders they spawn and the ways they categorize mental illness (Guarnaccia & Rogler, 1999; Kleinman, 1988, Mezzich et al., 1996; Miranda & Fraser, 2002). *Prevalence* rates (i.e., the percentage of a population with a disorder) vary considerably both across and within cultures (Table 15.1). So, too, do the ways people express symptoms of the same disorder (Fabrega, 1994). In rural Ireland, which is almost uniformly Catholic, people with schizophrenia are more likely than North Americans with the same disorder to have religious delusions, such as the conviction that their body has become inhabited by the Virgin Mary (Scheper-Hughes, 1979).

Cultures also differ on what they consider pathological and how they classify it. For example, one Alaskan Eskimo group's conception of "crazy" includes elements similar to our own, such as talking to oneself or screaming at people who do not exist. However, their definition of severe mental illness also includes some symptoms unusual in the rest of North America, such as believing that a loved one was murdered by witchcraft when no one else thought so, drinking urine, and killing dogs (Murphy, 1976).

Is Mental Illness Nothing but a Cultural Construction?

If definitions of abnormality vary across cultures, can we really speak of mental illness at all? Or, as argued by some prominent researchers and social critics in the 1960s and 1970s, is mental illness simply a construct used by a society to brand and punish those who fail to respect its norms? For example, psychiatrist Thomas Szasz, who wrote a popular book called *The Myth of Mental Illness* (1974), proposed that mental illness is a myth used to make people conform to society's standards of normality. In his view, which was highly influential in changing laws for commitment to mental institutions, people should be treated for mental illness only if *they* consider their symptoms a problem.

A variation of this view, called **labeling theory**, similarly argued that *diagnosis is a way of stigmatizing individuals a society considers deviant* (Scheff, 1970). Labeling can be dangerous because it turns people into "patients," whose subsequent

Big Picture φ Question 4

To what extent is human nature particular versus universal?

Table 15.1 ▪ ▪ Culture and Mental Illness

	Percentage of Sample with the Disorder		
Community	Alcoholism	Schizophrenia	Major Depression
Metropolitan Taipei	5.17	0.34	0.94
Small Taiwan towns	9.96	0.23	1.61
Urban North Carolina	8.97	1.36	5.13
Rural North Carolina	9.60	1.21	2.44
West Los Angeles	14.37	0.46	7.03

Source: Adapted from Compton et al., 1991, pp. 1700–1701.

actions are interpreted as part of their "craziness" and who may face discrimination based on their diagnoses. Labeled individuals may also take on the role of a sick or crazy person and hence actually begin to play the part into which they have been cast—a phenomenon known as a self-fulfilling prophecy (Chapter 17).

In one study, contacts were made with 180 people who had advertised rooms for rent. When they were asked if the room was still available, the answer was almost always yes. However, when the individual calling mentioned that she needed the accommodations because she was about to be released from a mental hospital, the answer as to availability was "no" 75 percent of the time (Page, 1977). Follow-up calls to see whether the room had actually been rented to someone else or whether the landlords were discriminating against the individual because of mental illness revealed that the majority of the rooms were actually still available (see also, Page, 1977).

A Case of Misdiagnosis?   A classic study raised some of these issues in a dramatic way. David Rosenhan (1973) had himself and seven other normal people around the United States admitted to psychiatric hospitals by faking symptoms of schizophrenia, complaining of hearing voices that said "empty," "hollow," or "thud." All but one of these "pseudopatients" were subsequently diagnosed with schizophrenia. Once on the psychiatric wards, however, the pseudopatients behaved as they normally would and told staff they no longer heard voices. Psychiatric staff nonetheless interpreted their behavior as evidence of disturbance. For example, when the pseudopatients took copious notes while on the unit, hospital personnel commented in their psychiatric records about their "peculiar note-taking behavior." When they were finally discharged, which took an average of 19 days, almost all were given the label "schizophrenia, in remission." Rosenhan's study set off a wave of controversy, for it appeared to demonstrate that psychiatric illness is in the eye of the beholder and that even trained eyes are not very acute.

Critics argued, however, that the study led to some very dramatic but largely incorrect conclusions (see Spitzer, 1985). Behavior is meaningful only when it is understood in context. Singing is normal in a chorus but would be very peculiar during a lecture. Similarly, taking notes *does* appear abnormal for a patient in a psychiatric hospital who has complained of hallucinations. Had the pseudopatients not lied about their initial symptoms, this would have been an appropriate inference. Furthermore, in medical terminology "in remission" means simply that a patient has previously reported symptoms that are no longer present. One critic concluded that the study did little more than illustrate that people can fool a clinician if they try hard enough (Spitzer, 1985), just as they can trick a neurologist by complaining of all the symptoms of stroke, or a potential employer by creating a false resume.

The Myth of the Myth of Mental Illness   Although labeling theory clearly has grains of truth, its claims have not held up well over time. First, many disorders (such as depression and schizophrenia) are recognized cross-culturally—a suggestion of some universality to their occurrence (Draguns, 1990; Mezzich et al., 1999). Second, although the negative consequences of labeling can indeed be profound, psychologists could neither treat nor research a problem without trying to distinguish those who have it from those who do not. Classification has its pitfalls, particularly when a category is socially undesirable (such as a mental illness) (Chapters 7 and 17), but that does not free us from the need to categorize. Third, as described below, an accumulating body of evidence suggests that schizophrenia is an illness of the brain, much like Alzheimer's disease, which no one would similarly describe as an "alternative way of seeing the world." Finally, the notion of the noble schizophrenic being branded as crazy by a conformist society tends to romanticize mental illness. No one in his "right mind" would really want to take on the problems that accompany schizophrenia, such as the inability to trust one's own thoughts and the profound sense of isolation that arises from chronically misunderstanding others and feeling misunderstood.

Apply & Discuss

Cuban-Americans who practice a religion called *Santería* believe that people can be possessed by spirits and communicate with deceased ancestors.

■ Can clinicians treat or diagnose patients without understanding—or sharing—their cultural backgrounds?

■ If a practitioner of Santería claimed to be possessed, how could a psychologist distinguish this mental state from a genuine mental disorder?

INTERIM SUMMARY

Psychopathology refers to problematic patterns of thought, feeling, or behavior that disrupt an individual's sense of well-being or social or occupational functioning. Many forms of psychopathology are found across cultures; however, cultures differ in the disorders to which their members are vulnerable and the ways they categorize mental illness. One view sees mental illness as a myth used to make people conform to society's standards of normality; **labeling theory** similarly argues that diagnosis is a way of stigmatizing deviants. Both approaches have some validity but understate the realities of mental illness.

Contemporary Approaches to Psychopathology

Although few contemporary psychologists view mental illness as a myth (or ascribe its causes to demon possession), they differ considerably in the way they conceptualize the nature and causes of psychological disorders. Consider the case of Charlie, a 24-year-old business school student with an intense fear of being in groups. Whenever Charlie is at a party, he feels tremendously anxious and usually ends up leaving shortly after he arrives. In class and in social engagements, he worries that people will laugh at and ostracize him. His mouth becomes dry, his hands become clammy, and his stomach knots. Charlie reports that his problem has intensified since he began business school. Paradoxically, he feels most anxious when he should feel most confident, as when he has expertise in the topic being discussed. He notes that his father, who never attended college, ridiculed him for his decision to enter graduate school ("Why don't you get a job?").

The way different psychologists would understand Charlie's anxiety depends on their theoretical orientation. We first examine psychodynamic and cognitive–behavioral perspectives. Next we consider two very different approaches—biological and systems theories—and then consider what evolutionary theory has to offer to the understanding of psychopathology.

Psychodynamic Perspective

Psychodynamic theorists distinguish three broad classes of psychopathology that form a continuum of functioning, from the least to the most disturbed: neuroses, personality disorders, and psychoses (Figure 15.1). **Neuroses** are *problems in living*, such as phobias, constant self-doubt, and repetitive interpersonal problems such as trouble with authority figures. Neurotic problems occur in most, if not all, people at different points in their lives and usually do not stop them from functioning reasonably well. **Personality disorders** are characterized by *enduring maladaptive patterns of thought, feeling, and behavior that lead to chronic disturbances in interpersonal and occupational functioning*.

People with personality disorders often have difficulty maintaining meaningful relationships and employment, interpret interpersonal events in highly distorted ways, and may be chronically vulnerable to depression and anxiety. **Psychoses** are *gross disturbances involving a loss of touch with reality*. A person who is psychotic may hear voices telling him to kill himself or believe (without good reason) that the CIA is trying to assassinate him. People tend to function at one level or another; however, neurotic symptoms (such as phobias) also occur in more severely disturbed individuals, and psychotic states can occur episodically (i.e., periodically, in discrete episodes) in people who are otherwise relatively healthy. Many people with bipolar disorder (manic-depression), for example, are largely unimpaired between episodes.

According to psychodynamic theorists (e.g., Kernberg, 1984), these three levels of pathology also lie on a continuum with respect to **etiology** (*origins of psychological disturbance*). Psychoses result primarily from biological abnormalities, with some environmental input. Neuroses and personality disorders stem more from environ-

Level of Disturbance	Capacities		
	Love	**Work**	**Relation to Reality**
Normal to neurotic	Able to maintain relationships	Able to maintain employment	Able to see reality clearly
	May have minor difficulties such as conflicts with significant others or a tendency to be competitive	May have difficulties such as rigidity, defensiveness, underconfidence, workaholism, overambition, or underachievement	May have minor defensive distortions, such as seeing the self and significant others as better or worse than they really are
Personality disordered	Unable to maintain relationships consistently	Difficulty maintaining employment	Prone to gross misinterpretations in interpersonal affairs
	May avoid relationships, jump into them too quickly, or end them abruptly	May be grossly underemployed, unable to get along with bosses, or likely to terminate employment abruptly	May have chronically idiosyncratic thinking that does not reach psychotic levels
Psychotic	Tremendous difficulty maintaining relationships	Unable to maintain employment anywhere near intellectual level	Unable to distinguish clearly between what is real and what is not
	May be socially peculiar	Large percentage are chronically unemployed	Has delusions, hallucinations, or other psychotic thought processes

FIGURE 15.1   Continuum of psychopathology. Psychodynamic theorists place disorders on a continuum of functioning, reflecting the maturity and strength of the person's underlying personality structure.

mental (particularly childhood) experiences, often interacting with biological vulnerabilities (Figure 15.2).

To assess psychopathology, a psychodynamic psychologist gathers information about the patient's current level of functioning and life stress, the origins and course of the symptom, and salient events in the person's developmental history. The clinician uses all of this information to make a **psychodynamic formulation**, *a set of hypotheses about the patient's personality structure and the meaning of the symptom*. This formulation attempts to answer three questions: What does the patient wish for and fear? What psychological resources does the person have at his disposal? And how does he experience himself and others (Westen, 1998)?

The first question focuses on the person's dominant *motives and conflicts*. Psychodynamic clinicians view many neurotic symptoms as expressions of, or compromises among, various motives. In this view, symptoms reflect unconscious conflicts among wishes and fears and efforts to resolve them. Symptoms may also result from beliefs, often forged in childhood (such as the belief that anger is "wrong"), which lead to conflicts and defenses (such as efforts to avoid feeling or acknowledging anger). For example, a psychodynamic clinician might hypothesize that Charlie's symptoms reflect a conflict over success, because his anxiety is strongest when he is in a position to shine and increases as he gets closer to achieving his goals. Charlie wants to be successful and display his abilities, but this desire evokes ridicule by his father (and, we might suspect, an internalized critic who may beat his father to the punch). Charlie might also unconsciously equate success with outdoing his father, who had minimal education, leading to anxiety or guilt.

The second question is about *ego functioning*—the person's ability to function autonomously, make sound decisions, think clearly, and regulate impulses and emotions (see Bellack et al., 1973). A psychodynamic psychologist would want to assess whether Charlie's ability to function and adapt to the environment is impaired in other ways or whether his social phobia is a relatively isolated symptom. For example, is he generally

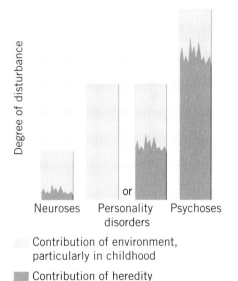

FIGURE 15.2   Heredity and experience in psychopathology. From a psychodynamic point of view, neuroses are often primarily environmental in origin, although they may reflect genetic vulnerabilities. Personality disorders stem either from extreme childhood experiences or from an interaction of genetic and environmental vulnerabilities. Psychoses are primarily genetic in origin, although childhood and adult experiences shape their expression.

fearful and inhibited? Does he turn to dysfunctional behaviors such as drinking to alleviate his anxiety? Is he able to reflect on his fears and recognize them as irrational?

The third question addresses *object relations* (Chapter 12), that is, the person's ability to form meaningful relationships with others and to maintain self-esteem. Are Charlie's interpersonal problems specific to groups or are they part of a more serious underlying difficulty in forming and maintaining relationships (attachment and object relations)? For example, is he able to develop enduring friendships and love relationships, or are his interpersonal fears so pervasive that he has been unable to form meaningful relationships by his mid-twenties?

INTERIM SUMMARY

Psychodynamic theorists distinguish among three broad classes of psychopathology that form a continuum of functioning: **neuroses** (enduring problems in living that cause distress or dysfunction), **personality disorders** (chronic, severe disturbances that substantially inhibit the capacity to love and to work), and **psychoses** (gross disturbances involving a loss of touch with reality). A **psychodynamic formulation** is a set of hypotheses about the patient's personality structure and the meaning of the symptom. It focuses on the person's motives and conflicts, adaptive functioning, and ability to form meaningful relationships and maintain self-esteem.

Cognitive–Behavioral Perspective

In clinical psychology, many practitioners consider themselves **cognitive–behavioral**, *integrating an understanding of classical and operant conditioning with a cognitive–social perspective* (S. M. Turner et al., 1992). They focus not on a hypothesized underlying personality structure but on discrete processes, such as thoughts that precede an anxiety reaction or physiological symptoms (e.g., racing heart) that accompany it. From a more behavioral perspective, many of the problems that require treatment involve conditioned emotional responses (Chapter 5), in which a previously neutral stimulus has become associated with an emotionally arousing stimulus. For example, a person like Charlie might have had bad experiences in school when he would speak and thus came to associate speaking in groups with anxiety. This anxiety might then have generalized to other group situations. Making matters worse, his fear of groups would then likely lead to his avoiding them, resulting not only in continued social anxiety but also in poor social skills.

A behaviorally oriented clinician carefully assesses the conditions under which symptoms such as depression and anxiety arise and tries to discover the stimuli that elicit them. What stimuli have become associated with depressed or anxious feelings through classical conditioning? What behaviors is the person engaging in that increase negative emotions, such as negative interactions with a spouse (see Gottman, 1998)? Under what circumstances does the individual become so distressed that she becomes suicidal or tries to hurt herself as a way of controlling the feeling (Linehan, 1993)?

From a more cognitive perspective, psychopathology reflects dysfunctional cognitions, such as low self-efficacy expectancies (Chapter 5 and 12), a tendency to believe that situations are hopeless, and negative views of the self (Abramson et al., 1989; Alloy et al., 2000; Beck, 1976; Clark et al., 1999; Ellis, 2002a, 2002b). The clinician thus focuses on irrational beliefs and maladaptive cognitive processes that maintain dysfunctional behaviors and emotions.

For example, a number of studies show that patients with different kinds of disorders show attentional biases that may perpetuate their psychopathology (Gilboa & Gotlib, 1997; Lundh et al., 1999). Depressed people tend to be "on the lookout" for negative information about themselves. When asked to report the color in which a set of words is printed (and to ignore the words), they are slowed down by words like "sad," "weak," and "loser," which automatically grab their attention. Patients with anxiety disorders tend to notice potentially threatening stimuli that would not catch other people's attention and to interpret ambiguous information in a threatening way (such as a random comment by a friend that could be interpreted as subtle rejection). People with personality disorders tend to be particularly attuned to threatening interpersonal events, such as ridicule or abandonment (see Korfine & Hooley, 2000).

From a behavioral point of view, Charlie's phobia is a conditioned emotional response (classical conditioning). In addition, the more he avoids the phobic situation, the more his avoidance behavior is negatively reinforced; in other words, avoidance reduces anxiety, which reinforces avoidance (operant conditioning). Further, Charlie's anxiety may actually *make* him less socially competent. As a result, others respond less positively to him, which in turn makes him more anxious and avoidant. To try to unravel the conditions eliciting his anxiety, the behaviorally oriented clinician would ask precisely where and when Charlie becomes anxious. Are there group situations in which he does not become anxious? Does he only become anxious when he is expected to talk, or does he become anxious even when he can remain silent?

Working more cognitively, the cognitive–behavioral clinician assesses the thoughts that run through Charlie's mind as his anxiety mounts. For instance, Charlie may erroneously believe that if people laugh at him, he will "die" of embarrassment or some other calamity will befall him. The clinician examines the way such irrational ideas maintain the phobia. Charlie might feel anxious in any situation that requires him to speak articulately because he does not believe he can do so. Alternatively, he may hold the irrational belief that he must excel in all situations if people are to respect him and consequently become terrified at the possibility of failure.

INTERIM SUMMARY

Cognitive–behavioral clinicians integrate an understanding of classical and operant conditioning with a cognitive–social perspective. From a behavioral perspective, many psychological problems involve conditioned emotional responses, in which a previously neutral stimulus has become associated with unpleasant emotions. Irrational fears in turn elicit avoidance, which perpetuates them and may lead to secondary problems, such as poor social skills. From a cognitive perspective, many psychological problems reflect dysfunctional attitudes, beliefs, and other cognitive processes, such as a tendency to interpret events negatively.

Biological Approach

To understand psychopathology, mental health professionals often move from a mental to a physiological level. Practitioners from all theoretical perspectives evaluate patients for potential biological contributions to their symptoms, as when they take a family history to assess possible genetic vulnerabilities or inquire about head injuries in childhood to assess possible influences on the developing brain. Some researchers and clinicians, however, believe that biology holds the key to most forms of psychopathology.

Neural Circuits   The biological approach looks for the roots of mental disorders in the brain's circuitry. For example, normal anxiety occurs through activation of neural circuits involving, among other structures, the amygdala and frontal lobes (Chapter 10). Thus, one might expect pathological anxiety to involve heightened or easily triggered activation of those circuits—a hypothesis supported by neuroimaging studies of many anxiety disorders (Reiman, 1997). Although, as we will see, abnormal neural firing can have genetic *or* environmental roots (e.g., people with severe childhood abuse histories may show damage to the hippocampus; Bremner, 1998), a central focus of biological approaches is on the heritability of psychopathology. Thus, like all competent clinicians, biologically oriented clinicians are likely to assess carefully for family history of disorders.

Aside from genetics, biological researchers have searched for the roots of psychopathology primarily in two areas. First, they have examined specific regions of the

brain that differ between people with a particular disorder and those without it (Wright et al., 2000). For example, as we will see, a large body of research shows differences in the frontal and temporal lobes between the brains of patients with schizophrenia and the brains of people without the disorder (see Bertolino et al., 2000). This finding makes sense given that the frontal lobes regulate consciousness and thought and the temporal lobes are involved in language—domains of particular difficulty for patients with schizophrenia.

Second, researchers have looked for evidence of neurotransmitter dysfunction in particular disorders, on the assumption that too much or too little neurotransmitter activity could disrupt normal patterns of neural firing. For example, if normal anxiety reactions involve the neurotransmitter norepinephrine (Chapter 3), then individuals whose genes predispose them to produce too much of this neurotransmitter or whose receptors are overly sensitive in circuits involving the amygdala are likely to experience pathological anxiety.

Although these efforts will surely continue, recent thinking reflects a view of brain functioning that we have encountered in several other chapters (e.g., Chapters 1, 3, 4, and 7). This viewpoint emphasizes that mental processes and behavior typically emerge from the coordination of circuits of neurons distributed throughout the brain, rather than from a single region (Lewis, 2000). Any "break" in a circuit—such as a circuit regulating thought, attention, and consciousness that runs from the frontal lobes through the thalamus and cerebellum—could produce similar symptoms by derailing the functioning of the whole operation (Andreasen, 1999). Thus, many diagnoses, such as schizophrenia, may be heterogeneous categories that apply to people with similar symptoms but whose problems have very different causes. For example, a gene that causes dysfunction of the thalamus could prevent the frontal lobes from working properly if it affects a circuit from the thalamus to the frontal lobes and could thus produce similar symptoms to a gene that directly affects the frontal lobes.

Big Picture φ Question 6

What is the relation between nature and nurture in shaping psychological processes?

Integrating Nature and Nurture: The Diathesis–Stress Model The biological approach is not incompatible with the perspectives described thus far. Charlie's anxiety may indeed be associated with his conflicts about achieving success or he may be caught in a spiral of negatively reinforced avoidance of social situations. Nevertheless, his tendency to become anxious in the first place could reflect a biological predisposition.

Theorists of various persuasions often adopt a **diathesis–stress model**, which proposes that *people with an underlying vulnerability (called a diathesis) may exhibit symptoms under stressful circumstances*. The diathesis may be biological, such as a genetic propensity for anxiety symptoms caused by overactivity of norepinephrine; or environmental, stemming from events such as a history of neglect, excessive parental criticism, or uncontrollable painful events in childhood (see Barlow, 2002). Upsetting events in adulthood, such as the loss of a lover or a failure at work, might then activate the vulnerability.

INTERIM SUMMARY

The biological approach looks for the roots of mental disorders in the brain's circuitry, such as neurotransmitter dysfunction, abnormalities of specific brain structures, or dysfunction anywhere along a pathway that regulates behavior or mental processes. Theorists of various persuasions often adopt a **diathesis–stress model**, which proposes that people with an underlying vulnerability (called a diathesis) may exhibit symptoms under stressful circumstances.

Systems Approach

A social systems approach looks for the roots of psychopathology in the broader social context. A **systems approach** *explains an individual's behavior in the context of a social group, such as a couple, family, or larger group.* An individual is part of a **system,** *a group with interdependent parts,* and what happens in one part of the system influences what happens in others. From this standpoint, diagnosing a problem in an individual without considering the systems in which he operates is like trying to figure out why a car is getting poor gas mileage without considering traffic conditions or the quality of the gasoline the car is burning. For example, a recent study found that roughly one-third of mothers who brought their child in for treatment of depression had a current psychiatric disorder themselves, and that 43 percent had nondiagnosable but clinically recognizable psychopathology (i.e., problems that did not quite meet the "official" threshold for diagnosis) (Ferro et al., 2000). A child caught in stressful maternal "traffic" could easily lose some psychological "horsepower."

Like the biological approach, a systems approach is not incompatible with other perspectives because it operates at another level of analysis. For example, a child who has problems with aggressive behavior at school may be part of a broader family system in which violence is a way of life. Nevertheless, in clinical practice, practitioners who take a systems approach frequently consider it their primary theoretical orientation, much as some psychiatrists (medical doctors trained in the treatment of mental illness) view most psychopathology biologically.

Family Systems   Most systems clinicians adopt a **family systems model**, which *views an individual's symptoms as symptoms of dysfunction in the family* (Hoffman, 1981, 1991). In other words, the *identified patient* (the person identified as the one who needs help) is the *symptom bearer* (the person displaying the family's difficulties), but the real problem lies in the family, not primarily in the individual. For example, one couple brought their child to see a psychotherapist because he was disruptive at school and punishment had been ineffective. The psychologist inquired about the parents' marriage and found that it had been very shaky until the child began having difficulties at school. Once the child became symptomatic, the parents worked together to help him, and their marital problems subsided. Thus, the problem was not so much a disruptive child as a disruptive marriage. The child not only *expressed* his parents' marital problems through his symptom but also helped *preserve* their marriage by becoming symptomatic. Empirically, marital problems appear to exacerbate a range of psychological and physical conditions, from depression to chronic pain and cancer (Fincham & Beach, 1999).

Systems theorists refer to the *methods family members use to preserve equilibrium in a family* (such as keeping tension levels down or preserving a marriage) as **family homeostatic mechanisms**. These mechanisms operate much like the homeostatic mechanisms discussed in Chapter 10 on motivation. In the case above, marital tension evoked a set of behaviors in the child, which in turn reduced the marital tension, much as a furnace turns on until the temperature in a room reaches the temperature set on the thermostat. From this viewpoint, psychological symptoms are actually dysfunctional efforts to cope with a disturbance in the family.

Family systems theorists also focus on the ways families are organized, including family roles, boundaries, and alliances (see Boszormenyi-Nagy & Spark, 1973; Haley, 1976; Minuchin, 1974). **Family roles** are *the parts individuals play in repetitive family "dramas"—typical interaction patterns among family members*. Playing roles is not in itself pathological; it occurs in every social group (Chapter 18). For example, one child may take on the role of mediator between two siblings who are often in conflict. In some families, a child and parent may switch roles, a phenomenon known as *role reversal*, in which the child takes care of the parent, attends to the parent's needs, and takes on the parent's responsibilities. Empirically, role reversal is more common among people with a history of physical or sexual abuse, and is already apparent in the preschool years (Macfie et al., 1999).

Assessing the Family System   In assessing a family, a psychologist with a systems orientation examines the *marital subsystem* (the relationship between the parents) and the roles different family members play. The clinician may want to explore **family**

boundaries, or *physical and psychological limits of the family system and its subsystems* (see Goldstein, 1988). Some families are *enmeshed*—that is, too involved with each other's business—and privacy and autonomy are impossible. Others are *disengaged*, with minimal contact among family members (see Olson, 1985, 2000). Some families have rigid boundaries with the outside world, punishing their members if they disclose too many family secrets or spend too much time away from home. Others seem to lack *internal* boundaries, as when a parent refuses to allow a child any privacy.

The systems-oriented psychologist assesses other interaction patterns as well, such as **family alliances**, or *who sides with whom in family conflicts*. A child who begins abusing drugs, for example, may be expressing frustration at feeling excluded from or consistently attacked by an alliance between a parent and a sibling who is seen as the "good" child. The clinician also looks for problematic *communication patterns*, as when a couple communicates primarily by fighting.

A psychologist working from a systems approach might evaluate Charlie first in one session by himself and then in another with his father or family. Although systems theorists differ considerably in their specific approaches, the clinician might assess the extent to which Charlie is bringing issues from his family of origin into his new relationships (Bowen, 1978, 1991). The systems clinician would likely observe the way Charlie and his father communicate, looking for mutually unsatisfying patterns in their interactions. The clinician might also try to understand these patterns in the context of the family's subculture, which may have particular ways of regulating emotional expression and communication between the generations. For example, Charlie's conflicts about success may be heightened by the fact that his father is an immigrant who does not approve of Charlie's occupational choice and believes that a son should follow his father's directives.

INTERIM SUMMARY

A **systems approach** explains an individual's behavior in the context of a social group, such as a couple, family, or larger group. Most systems clinicians adopt a **family systems model**, which views an individual's symptoms as symptoms of family dysfunction. The methods family members use to preserve equilibrium in a family are called **family homeostatic mechanisms**. Family systems theorists focus on the ways families are organized, including **family roles** (the parts individuals play in the family), **boundaries** (physical and psychological limits of the family and its subsystems), and **alliances** (patterns in which family members side with one another). They also focus on problematic communication patterns.

Evolutionary Perspective

Although the evolutionary perspective does not offer the kind of comprehensive system for understanding (and treating) psychopathology, as we see in the approaches described above, evolutionary psychologists are likely to provide insight into psychopathology in the years ahead (see Cosmides & Tooby, 1999). In one sense, psychopathology is a paradox from an evolutionary perspective, since psychopathology is *mal*adaptation, and evolution is about natural selection of adaptive traits. Nevertheless, an evolutionary perspective explains psychopathology in at least three ways.

First, nothing in the nature of evolution requires that every organism is well adapted to its environment. In fact, natural selection acts on random variation in genotypes by weeding out those that lead to less adaptive phenotypes. As in all evolutionary analyses, evolutionary pressures are always relative to a specific environment. In some circumstances, a tendency to be anxious could confer an evolutionary advantage by making individuals vigilant to potential dangers; in others, a tendency to be anxious could be socially stigmatizing and hence reduce reproductive success.

A challenging question for evolutionary psychologists is how to explain the presence, over several generations, of a stable percentage of the population that has a de-

Making Connections

Social psychologists emphasize the powerful impact of social situations on behavior (Chapter 18).

■ How might family dynamics contribute to a teenager's tendency to abuse drugs or alcohol?

■ Can peer influence create problems such as alcoholism in teenagers, or do such problems require a prior vulnerability?

bilitating mental disorder. How, for example, can an evolutionary theorist explain the worldwide presence of schizophrenia, a disease that clearly diminishes an individual's capacity for both survival and reproduction?

A second evolutionary explanation, though still speculative at this point, uses the analogy of sickle cell anemia. Sickle cell anemia is common only in people whose ancestors came from parts of the world where malaria was prevalent. The reason is that people who inherit the sickle cell gene from one parent are protected from malaria. If they inherit the gene from both parents, however, they will die from sickle cell anemia. Over time a population will evolve a stable percentage of sickle cell genes: If the presence of the gene gets too high in the population, more people die of sickle cell, which reduces its prevalence; if the percentage gets too low, more people die of malaria, and those who survive are more likely to carry the gene.

A similar phenomenon could explain genes for mental disorders such as anxiety disorders or schizophrenia. The mechanisms in some cases may be obvious and intuitive, whereas in others they may be completely unexpected. An obvious example might occur in anxiety disorders, which are to some degree heritable. As we will see, having too little anxiety can contribute to antisocial personality traits and reckless behavior that lead to premature death. In contrast, having too much anxiety can lead to anxiety disorders. The levels of anxiety in the population attributable to genes could thus reflect a relatively simple mechanism of natural selection that, across the *population*, maximizes survival and reproduction, but produces dysfunction in *individuals* whose genetic inheritance places them at one extreme or another.

The evolutionary "trade-offs" that produce a stable percentage of disordered individuals might actually be much less obvious because a single gene or set of genes could also act on two very different traits. For example, the genes that predispose individuals to schizophrenia could also render nondisordered bearers of the gene less vulnerable to some kind of deadly viral infection such as smallpox. The result would be a stable percentage of the population with schizophrenia, just as is the case for sickle cell. Recent research finding a negative association between schizophrenia and rheumatoid arthritis provides a suggestive example (Narita et al., 2000).

A third evolutionary explanation for psychopathology centers on the interplay of genes and environments. Psychopathology could reflect normal processes gone awry because of abnormal circumstances. Fear is a highly adaptive, inborn mechanism that keeps people away from circumstances associated with danger. However, if those circumstances cannot be avoided or if the person is traumatized by them, he may become preoccupied with fear and less able to function adaptively.

Making Connections

Research suggests that males tend to emphasize youth and physical attractiveness in selecting mates, and females tend to emphasize males' status and resources—a difference evolutionary psychologists attribute to natural selection (Chapter 18).

▪ How might this emphasis influence the disorders females tend to develop? In other words, what kinds of vulnerabilities to specific forms of psychopathology might this produce?

▪ How might this influence the disorders men tend to develop? To what kinds of problems might competition for status or wealth predispose males?

INTERIM SUMMARY

Evolutionary psychologists could explain psychopathology in at least three ways: as random variation likely to be weeded out by natural selection; as the result of broader population pressures that select rates of genes in the population that can be either functional or dysfunctional depending on the other genes an individual inherits; and as the maladaptive environmental "tuning" of psychological mechanisms that are normally adaptive.

Descriptive Diagnosis:
DSM-IV and Psychopathological Syndromes

The approaches discussed thus far all assume a particular point of view about the nature and origins of psychopathology. A *descriptive* approach, in contrast, attempts to be *atheoretical*, that is, not wedded to any theoretical perspective on etiology. In **descrip-**

tive diagnosis, *mental disorders are classified in terms of* **clinical syndromes**, *or constellations of symptoms that tend to occur together*. For example, in a depressive syndrome, depressed mood is often accompanied by loss of interest in pleasurable activities, insomnia, loss of appetite, poor concentration, and decreased self-esteem.

DSM-IV

Until the early 1950s, psychologists and psychiatrists lacked a standard set of diagnoses. Psychologists from each school of thought used their own preferred terms, and systematic empirical investigation of most psychiatric disorders was impossible (see Nathan, 1998). This lack of a guiding framework changed when the American Psychiatric Association (1994) published the first edition of the *manual of clinical syndromes that researchers and clinicians use to make diagnoses*, called the *Diagnostic and Statistical Manual of Mental Disorders* **(DSM)**, now in its fourth edition **(DSM-IV)**. The major diagnostic categories of DSM-IV are listed in Table 15.2.

Descriptive diagnosis allows researchers and clinicians in many different settings to diagnose patients in a similar manner, regardless of their theoretical orientation (see Spitzer et al., 1992). In reality, however, not even a descriptive approach can be entirely atheoretical, and psychologists continue to search for alternatives to the DSM approach (see Barron, 1998; Beutler & Malik, 2002). The descriptive approach embodied in DSM-IV tends to be most compatible with a *disease model* of psychopathology, which presumes that psychological disorders fall into discrete categories, much like

Table 15.2 ■■■ Selected Diagnostic Categories of DSM-IV

Category	Description
Disorders usually first diagnosed in infancy, childhood, or adolescence	Disorders involving deviations from normal development, such as attention-deficit/hyperactivity disorder and conduct disorder
Substance-related disorders	Disorders associated with drug abuse (including alcohol) as well as side effects of medication and exposure to toxins
Schizophrenia and other psychotic disorders	Disorders characterized by loss of contact with reality, marked disturbances of thought and perception, and bizarre behavior
Mood disorders	Disorders characterized by disturbances of normal mood, notably depression, mania, or alternating periods of each
Anxiety disorders	Disorders in which anxiety is the main symptom (such as generalized anxiety, panic, phobic, post-traumatic stress, and obsessive–compulsive disorders)
Somatoform disorders	Disorders involving physical symptoms that lack a physical basis, such as hypochondriasis (excessive preoccupation with health and fear of disease without a realistic basis for concern)
Dissociative disorders	Disorders characterized by alterations or disruptions in consciousness, memory, identity, or perception, such as psychologically induced amnesia
Sexual and gender identity disorders	Disorders of sexuality and gender identity, including sexual dysfunctions, paraphilias (sexual urges, fantasies, or behaviors involving unusual objects, nonconsenting partners, or pain or humiliation, which cause significant distress or dysfunction), and gender identity disorders (such as cross-dressing), that lead to considerable distress or impairment in functioning.
Eating disorders	Disorders characterized by severe disturbance in eating behavior, such as anorexia nervosa and bulimia nervosa
Adjustment disorders	Disorders that are usually relatively mild and transient, in which clinically significant emotional or behavioral symptoms develop as a consequence of some identifiable stressor
Personality disorders	Disorders characterized by long-standing patterns of maladaptive behavior that deviate from cultural expectations and are pervasive and inflexible, such as borderline and antisocial personality disorders

Source: Adapted from *Diagnostic and Statistical Manual of Mental Disorders*, 4th ed., American Psychiatric Association, Washington, D.C., 1994.

medical disorders such as tuberculosis or melanoma. Not surprisingly, then, psychiatrists tend to emphasize descriptive diagnoses more than psychologists, although nearly all mental health professionals use descriptive diagnoses when initially evaluating a patient. A common language is essential, however, if researchers are to study disorders and clinicians are to communicate with one another, and DSM-IV constitutes the best current approximation of a comprehensive diagnostic system.

DSM-IV uses a **multiaxial system of diagnosis**, which *places symptoms in their biological and social context by evaluating patients along five axes* (Table 15.3). *These axes cover not only symptoms and personality disturbances but also relevant information such as medical conditions and environmental stressors.* Axis I lists the clinical syndromes for which a patient seeks treatment, such as depression or schizophrenia. Axis II lists personality disorders and mental retardation. The assumption behind the distinction between the two axes is that Axis I describes *state* disorders—the patient's current condition, or state—whereas Axis II describes *trait* disorders—enduring problems with the person's functioning. Thus, a person who is severely depressed (a state disorder, coded on Axis I) may have an enduring personality disorder that renders him vulnerable to depression, or he may simply have had difficulty coping with the death of a spouse (and hence receive no Axis II diagnosis). (Although Axis II also includes mental retardation, as a shorthand most researchers treat "Axis II" and "personality disorders" as synonyms, since personality disorders are much more prevalent in psychiatric populations.)

Axis III lists any general medical conditions that may be relevant to understanding the person's psychopathology (such as diabetes or hypothyroidism, which can affect mood). Axis IV is reserved for psychosocial and environmental stressors (life events such as the death of a family member that could be contributing to emotional problems). Axis V rates the patient's current level of functioning (on a scale of 0 to 100) and the highest level of functioning the patient has attained during the past year. Table 15.4 shows how Charlie might be diagnosed using this multiaxial system.

In the sections that follow, we examine some of the major clinical syndromes, starting with disorders that usually become evident in childhood. Before doing so, however, a word of warning is in order. You may have experienced some of these symptoms at one time or another and may start to worry that you have one (or all) of the disorders. This reaction is similar to the "first-year medical student syndrome" experienced by many doctors in training, who imagine they have whichever disease they are currently studying. Thus, you may recognize yourself or someone you know in many of the symptoms or syndromes described, in part because these disorders are in fact highly prevalent in the population and in part because we all experience anxiety, sadness, and interpersonal difficulties at various points in our lives (often appropriately, as at the death of a loved one). Bear in mind that only when symptoms disrupt a person's functioning or sense of well-being would a trained mental health professional actually diagnose a disorder, and that most forms of psychopathology can be treated (Chapter 16).

Table 15.3 ■ ■ Axes of DSM-IV

Axis	Description
I	Symptoms that cause distress or significantly impair social or occupational functioning
II	Personality disorders and mental retardation—chronic and enduring problems that impair interpersonal or occupational functioning
III	Medical conditions that may be relevant to understanding or treating a psychological disorder
IV	Psychosocial and environmental problems (such as negative life events and interpersonal stressors) that may affect the diagnosis, treatment, and prognosis of psychological disorders
V	Global assessment of functioning—the individual's overall level of functioning in social, occupational, and leisure activities

Source: Adapted from *Diagnostic and Statistical Manual of Mental Disorders*, 4th ed., American Psychiatric Association, Washington, D.C., 1994.

Table 15.4 ■ ■ Multiaxial Diagnosis of Charlie

Axis	Description
I	Social phobia (disorder marked by fear that occurs when the person is in a social situation)
II	Rule out (possible) avoidant personality disorder (disorder marked by avoidance of interpersonal situations, fear of being disliked or rejected, and view of self as inadequate or inferior)
III	None (no medical conditions)
IV	Business school, father's criticism (current stressors)
V	Global assessment of functioning: 55 (*moderate symptoms*, on a scale from 0 to 100)

INTERIM SUMMARY

In **descriptive diagnosis**, mental disorders are classified into **clinical syndromes**, constellations of symptoms that tend to occur together. The descriptive approach embodied in DSM-IV tends to be most compatible with a disease model that presumes psychological disorders fall into discrete categories. DSM-IV uses a **multiaxial system**, placing symptoms in their biological and social context by evaluating patients along five axes: clinical syndromes, personality disorders (and mental retardation), medical conditions, environmental stressors, and global level of functioning.

Disorders Usually First Diagnosed in Infancy, Childhood, or Adolescence

Several mental disorders typically arise during infancy, childhood, or adolescence; these range from disturbances of eating and feeding (such as eating rocks and other inedible objects) to severe separation distress upon leaving home for school. Two of the most common are attention-deficit hyperactivity disorder and conduct disorder.

Attention-Deficit Hyperactivity Disorder   Many children and adolescents are brought to mental health professionals because of behavioral difficulties at school or at home. Consider the case of Jimmy, a six-year-old whose teacher reports that he cannot sit still, does not pay attention, and is constantly disturbing his classmates. Jimmy fidgets in his chair, and when his teacher directs him to work, he can only concentrate for a few seconds before becoming disruptive, making noises or throwing paper wads across the room. Jimmy's teacher suspects he has **attention-deficit hyperactivity disorder (ADHD)**, *a disorder characterized by inattention, impulsiveness, and hyperactivity inappropriate for the child's age*.

Although children with ADHD may exhibit symptoms by age 4, the disorder often goes unrecognized until they enter school, since children are not usually required to comply with stringent social demands before that time (Campbell, 1985). Setting a standard for hyperactive behavior in preschoolers is difficult; in fact, as many as 50 percent of mothers of four-year-old boys believe their son is hyperactive (Varley, 1984)! The prevalence of ADHD is estimated at 5 percent of school-aged children (Rhee et al., 1999). The disorder is four to nine times more prevalent in males than females.

Attention-deficit hyperactivity disorder runs in families (Faraone et al., 2000). Moreover, families of children with ADHD have a higher incidence of alcoholism and personality disorders in both parents, especially fathers (Samudra & Cantwell, 1999; Pihl et al., 1990). Although many cases probably stem from central nervous system dysfunction, the more *risk factors* a child experiences (such as severe marital discord between parents, low social class, maternal psychopathology, and paternal criminality), the more likely he is to develop the disorder (Biederman et al., 1995).

Data on the extent to which children "grow out of" this disorder are conflicting (Mannuzza et al., 1998; Weiss et al., 1985), in part because some of the symptoms, such as hyperactivity, may decline, whereas others, such as inattention, may not (Biederman et al., 2000). However, children with ADHD are clearly at increased risk for other psychiatric and social problems in adolescence and adulthood, particularly antisocial behavior and substance abuse (Biederman et al., 1996; Mannuzza et al., 1998).

Conduct Disorder   Another relatively common disturbance of childhood is **conduct disorder**, characterized by *persistent violation of societal norms and the rights of others*. Symptoms include physical aggression toward people or animals, chronic fighting, vandalism, persistent lying, and stealing. Such children are obstinate, resent taking direction, lack empathy and compassion, and seldom express remorse for their destructive behavior. Roughly 6 to 16 percent of boys and 2 to 9 percent of girls have this disorder.

Both genetic and environmental factors contribute to the etiology of conduct disorder, and delinquent behavior more generally (Biederman et al., 1995; O'Connor et al., 1998), highlighting again the joint contribution of nature and nurture to behavior. Some children with conduct disorders appear to be relatively unresponsive to conditioning, because they are physiologically less responsive to rewards and especially punishments (Kruesi et al., 1992; Raine & Venables, 1984). Because their autonomic nervous systems are less reactive, they lack the anxiety that motivates other children to adjust their behavior to avoid threatening consequences. Ineffectively lax or excessively punitive parenting can also lead to delinquent behavior (see Eysenck, 1982; Patterson & Bank, 1986), although recent research suggests that poor parenting may itself be partly genetic, reflecting the same genes in parents that predispose their children to develop conduct disorders (Slutske et al., 1997).

One study illustrates the complex interplay of nature and nurture in the etiology of conduct disorders. Researchers compared adopted children who either had or did not have a biological parent with a history of criminality (Cadoret et al., 1995). Genetic and environmental variables each contributed to the likelihood of the child to have conduct and other disorders, but so did their interaction. In other words, an unstable home environment was particularly dangerous to children who were genetically vulnerable.

INTERIM SUMMARY

Attention-deficit hyperactivity disorder (ADHD) is characterized by inattention, impulsiveness, and hyperactivity inappropriate for the child's age. It is more prevalent in boys and runs in families, apparently for both genetic and environmental reasons. The same is true of **conduct disorder**, in which a child persistently violates societal norms and the rights of others.

Substance-Related Disorders

The disorders discussed thus far begin in childhood and often continue in one form or another into adulthood. Both ADHD and conduct disorders predispose individuals to one set of adult disorders, **substance-related disorders**, which are *characterized by continued use of a substance (such as alcohol or cocaine) that negatively affects psychological and social functioning*.

The most common substance-related disorder is **alcoholism** (*abuse of alcohol*). In the United States, for example, an estimated 13 million people are alcoholics (Chapter 11). Alcoholism appears in every social class. A longitudinal study of Harvard undergraduates over 50 years found that 21 percent met criteria for alcohol abuse at some point in their lives, and nearly 60 percent of those were still abusing alcohol in their 60s (Vaillant, 1996). As in other Western countries, alcoholism is the third largest health problem in the United States, following heart disease and cancer, and the most common psychiatric problem in males (Kessler et al., 1994). Alcoholism also appears to be steadily rising in the United States since World War II, typically beginning in adolescence (Nelson et al., 1998).

Nature and Nurture in the Etiology of Substance-Related Disorders

Why would someone abuse alcohol or other substances when the effects are clearly destructive to relationships, professional ambitions, and physical health? As in much research on psychopathology, the major controversy concerns the relative contributions of genetics and environment. Perhaps the best predictor of whether someone will become alcoholic is a family history of alcoholism (Cadoret et al., 1985; Marlatt & Baer, 1988). Children of alcoholics are four times as likely to develop alcoholism as children of nonalcoholics (Peele, 1986). Family history, however, could support both genetic and environmental hypotheses.

Big Picture φ Question 6

What is the relation between nature and nurture in shaping psychological processes?

Big Picture φ Question 6

What is the relation between nature and nurture in shaping psychological processes?

The best data on the etiology of addictions support two primary conclusions. First, both genes and environment are involved in the development of substance abuse, with genes playing the major part in use and abuse of some drugs but environmental variables contributing more in others (Figure 15.3) (Kendler et al., 2000a). Second, most of the genetic and environmental sources of vulnerability to substance abuse are common to all or most drugs. In other words, people who abuse one drug are at risk for abusing several—a suggestion that genes and experience conspire to create a general risk for substance abuse.

On top of this general vulnerability to addiction, however, are some specific vulnerabilities to particular classes of drugs (Bierut et al., 1998; Merikangas et al., 1998). For example, a large study of male twins found that men whose twins abused heroin had a particularly high likelihood of abusing heroin as well, above and beyond their general vulnerability to substance abuse, and that the majority of this vulnerability was genetic (Tsuang et al., 1998). Similarly, men whose twin abused marijuana were particularly likely to do so, with most of the vulnerability coming from genetics.

The influence of heredity on alcoholism is well established (Finn et al., 2000; Prescott & Kendler, 1999). Children whose biological parents are alcoholic may respond differently to alcohol physiologically than children of nonalcoholic parents (Gordis, 1996; Schuckit, 1984, 1994). They may, for example, be predisposed to like the taste, to find alcohol rewarding, or to find alcohol emotionally soothing. Alternatively, children could inherit a predisposition to other emotional disorders that indirectly lead to alcoholism, such as anxiety or depression.

Other research suggests multiple routes to alcoholism that involve differing degrees of genetic and environmental influence (Cadoret et al., 1985; Kendler et al., 1994). According to one model, severe, early-onset alcoholism associated with delinquency, antisocial personality disorder, and other forms of substance abuse is highly heritable in males; if it is heritable in females, its heritability is low (Kendler et al., 1994; McGue et al., 1992). The more common form of alcoholism, which is less severe and not associated with such significant psychopathology, stems largely from environmental factors shared by family members, such as parents who model alcoholic behavior or whose parenting leads to poor self-esteem in their children, who are then vulnerable to alcohol as self-medication for depression (Babor et al., 1992; Cloninger et al., 1981; Pickens et al., 1991).

Big Picture φ Question 1

To what extent can mental processes be reduced to the brain or body?

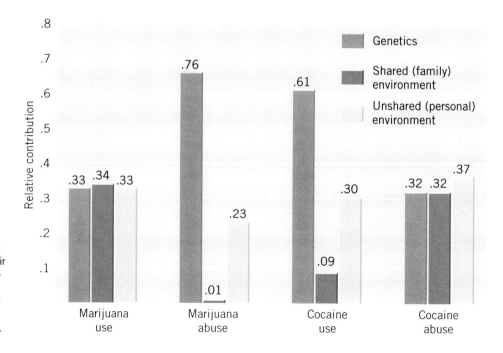

FIGURE 15.3 Relative roles of heredity, shared environment, and unshared environment in substance use and abuse. This figure shows data from a sample of 1198 male twins who were interviewed about their patterns of substance use and abuse. The relative impact of genetic factors, shared (family) environment, or unshared (personal or individual) environment appears to depend on both the drug and whether the drug is used or abused. *Source:* Kendler et al., 2000a.

Another model, which applies to other forms of drug abuse as well, is based on studies of children adopted away from their biological parents. This model distinguishes *two* heritable paths to substance abuse, in addition to the environmental pathway described above (Cadoret et al., 1985, 1995). In the first genetic route, a tendency to alcoholism in the biological parent leads directly to the same genetic vulnerability in the child. A second pathway is less direct: A parent with a history of criminality transmits his genes to the child, who is more likely to develop conduct disorder and antisocial traits. Later, the delinquent child becomes involved in substance abuse. This model suggests that some people may be genetically vulnerable to the drug itself, whereas others are vulnerable to becoming antisocial and aggressive—traits leading *socially* to substance-related disorders, since drug abuse can be a form of antisocial behavior.

When Substance Use Is Pathological   A large national sample of individuals age 12 and older found that 15.9 million Americans (7.1 percent of the population) currently (i.e., within the last month) used illegal drugs (U.S. Department of Health and Human Services, 2001; Figure 15.4). This percentage does not include statistics related to the use of alcohol and tobacco, given that these products are legal to some individuals included in the sample.

A similar larger national sample of individuals aged 15 to 54 in the United States found that slightly over half had used illegal drugs at some point in their lives, and 7.5 percent had been drug dependent at some point in their lives (Warner et al., 1995). Substance abuse can be a crippling psychological disorder, but the relation between substance use and abuse is not always clear. Most people drink alcohol, but this does not mean that most people are alcoholics. Similarly, is minor, occasional, or experimental use of drugs such as marijuana a sign of mental disorder?

Contrary to popular wisdom, the most definitive study in the area found that late teenagers (age 18) who experimented with marijuana in moderate amounts actually tended to be healthier psychologically than those who either used marijuana frequently or abstained completely (Shedler & Block, 1990). Abstainers were more anxious, emotionally inhibited, and lacking in social skills than "experimenters" (defined as individuals who used marijuana no more than once a month and had tried no

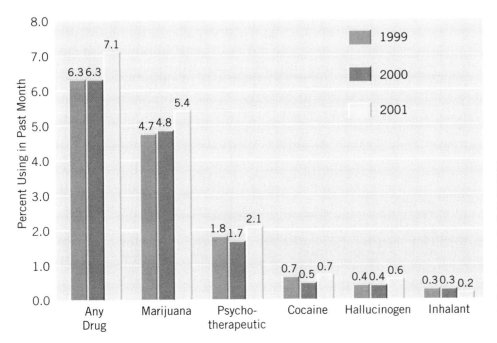

FIGURE 15.4   Past month illicit drug use among persons aged 12 or older by drug. Marijuana is the most commonly used illicit drug. In 2001, it was used by 76 percent of current illicit drug users. Approximately 56 percent of current illicit drug users consumed only marijuana, 20 percent used marijuana and another illicit drug, and the remaining 24 percent used an illicit drug but not marijuana in the past month. Therefore, about 44 percent of current illicit drug users in 2001 (7.0 million Americans) used illicit drugs other than marijuana and hashish, with or without using marijuana as well. *Source:* Reprinted from 2001 National Household Survey on Drug Abuse, U.S. Department of Health and Human Services.

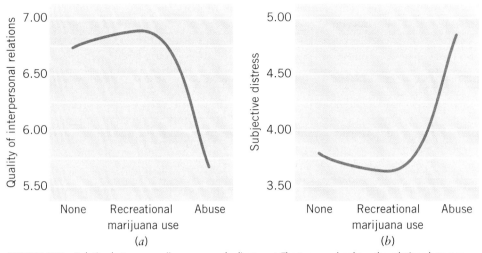

FIGURE 15.5 Relation between marijuana use and adjustment. The two graphs show the relations between level of marijuana use and two measures of psychological adjustment: quality of interpersonal relations (*a*) and subjective distress (*b*). The relation between marijuana use and these variables is clearly not linear; that is, more marijuana use does not uniformly predict worse mental health. No use, mild use, and frequent use are qualitatively different, not on a continuum of abuse. *Source:* Shedler & Block, 1990, p. 624.

Making Connections

Alcohol's effects are both biological and psychological. Alcohol can weaken people's inhibitions and embolden them to take risks through its effects on neurotransmitters, particularly GABA (gamma-aminobutyric acid) and dopamine. Simply believing they have been drinking can have similar effects because of expectancies about alcohol's effects (Chapter 9).

more than one other illicit drug). Conversely, frequent users were more impulsive and alienated than experimenters (see Figure 15.5). The study suggests that experimentation may be a relatively normal expression of adolescent rebellion and the desire to try new experiences.

The researchers were also able to predict future substance use patterns by watching interactions between subjects and their mothers when subjects were five years old. The most positive, mutually pleasurable mother–child interactions occurred in the group who later experimented with marijuana but did not abuse it. The mother-child interactions of both abstainers and frequent users at age 5 were rated as more hostile, more critical, less spontaneous, less relaxed, and less enjoyable to the child than the mother–child interactions of those who later experimented with marijuana. Note that the findings of this study did not apply to use of hard drugs such as cocaine or heroin. Marijuana use and hard drug use in this sample appeared to mean very different things (Block et al., 1988). In girls, for example, marijuana use was not correlated with depression, but hard drug use was. Hard drug use also correlated with mood swings and identity confusion.

What is the take-home message of this and other research on alcoholism and drug abuse? First, for marijuana and alcohol, substance *use* and *abuse* are not synonymous. Neither drug is uniformly toxic to people who are not at risk. Second, people with family histories of substance abuse should avoid even casual use or experimentation with any drug. The risks far outweigh the benefits, and the odds that they will follow in their parents' footsteps despite their best intentions are extremely high.

INTERIM SUMMARY

Substance-related disorders are characterized by continued use of a substance (such as alcohol or cocaine) that negatively affects psychological and social functioning. The most common substance-related disorder is **alcoholism**. Research has clearly demonstrated both environmental and genetic contributions to alcoholism, although researchers are still trying to track down precisely how genetic transmission occurs in different individuals. With marijuana, as with alcohol, substance *use* and *abuse* are not synonymous, although for vulnerable individuals, use tends to lead to abuse.

Schizophrenia

Of all the mental disorders that can afflict a human being, schizophrenia is probably the most tragic. **Schizophrenia** is *an umbrella term for a number of psychotic disorders that involve disturbances in nearly every dimension of human psychology, including thought, perception, behavior, language, communication, and emotion.* Most forms of schizophrenia begin in the late teens and early twenties. In the United States, between 1.2 and 6 million people suffer from schizophrenia, or roughly 0.5 to 2.5 percent of the population. Many studies find the rate of schizophrenia higher among economically impoverished groups, which may reflect the effect of poverty on people vulnerable to the illness or the fact that individuals with schizophrenia have difficulty holding employment and tend to be downwardly mobile.

Although estimates vary, only 10 to 20 percent of individuals with schizophrenia ever fully recover, less than half show even moderate improvement after falling ill, and of those who do improve, almost half fall ill again within a year of leaving the hospital (Carone et al., 1991; Hegarty et al., 1994; Herz et al., 2000). Most people with schizophrenia periodically experience acute phases of the illness and otherwise suffer *residual* (continuing) impairment in social and occupational functioning throughout life. This pattern appears to hold true cross-culturally (Marengo et al., 1991). However, *relapse* rates (percent of patients who become ill again) and severity of the illness tend to be higher in the industrialized West (Jenkins & Karno, 1992). People with good *premorbid* social functioning (i.e., social functioning prior to falling ill) are least likely to relapse over time (Robinson et al., 1999).

Symptoms Perhaps the most distinctive feature of schizophrenia is a disturbance of thought, perception, and language. Individuals with schizophrenia often suffer from **delusions**—*false beliefs firmly held despite evidence to the contrary.* The person may believe the CIA is trying to kidnap him or that his thoughts are being broadcast on the radio. **Hallucinations**—*perceptual experiences that distort or occur without external stimulation*—are also common. Auditory hallucinations (hearing voices) are the most frequent kind of hallucinations in schizophrenia.

Schizophrenic thinking is also frequently characterized by a **loosening of associations**, *the tendency of conscious thought to move along associative lines rather than to be controlled, logical, and purposeful.* One patient with schizophrenia was talking about her sister April: "She came in last night from Denver, in like a lion, she's the king of beasts." Whereas a poet might use a similar metaphor deliberately to express the sentiment that a person is angry or hostile, the individual with schizophrenia often has minimal control over associative thinking and intersperses it with rational thought. In this case, the patient's associations apparently ran from April to March, to a proverb about March coming in like a lion, and then to another network of associations linked to lions. People with schizophrenia may thus speak what sounds like gibberish, as they substitute one word for another associatively connected to it or simply follow a train of associations wherever it takes them.

Schizophrenic symptoms can be categorized into positive and negative symptoms (Crow, 1980; Strauss et al., 1974). **Positive symptoms**, such as *delusions, hallucinations, and loose associations*, are most apparent in acute phases of the illness and are often treatable by antipsychotic medications. They are called positive symptoms because they reflect the *presence* of something not usually or previously there, such as delusions. Recent research suggests a further distinction between two kinds of positive symptoms: *disorganized* (inappropriate emotions, disordered thought, and bizarre behavior) and *psychotic* (delusions and hallucinations) (Andreasen et al., 1995).

Negative symptoms (so named because they signal something *missing*, such as normal emotions), are *relatively chronic symptoms of schizophrenia such as flat affect (blunted emotional response), lack of motivation, socially inappropriate behavior and withdrawal from relationships, and intellectual impairments such*

Making Connections

In many respects, schizophrenia is a disorder of consciousness, in which the normal monitor and control functions of consciousness are suspended (Chapter 9). People with schizophrenia have trouble keeping irrelevant associations out of consciousness and controlling the contents of their consciousness to solve problems. In fact, multiple studies have found deficits in focusing and maintaining attention and in using working memory effectively in patients with schizophrenia (Cornblatt & Kelip, 1994; Gold et al., 1997).

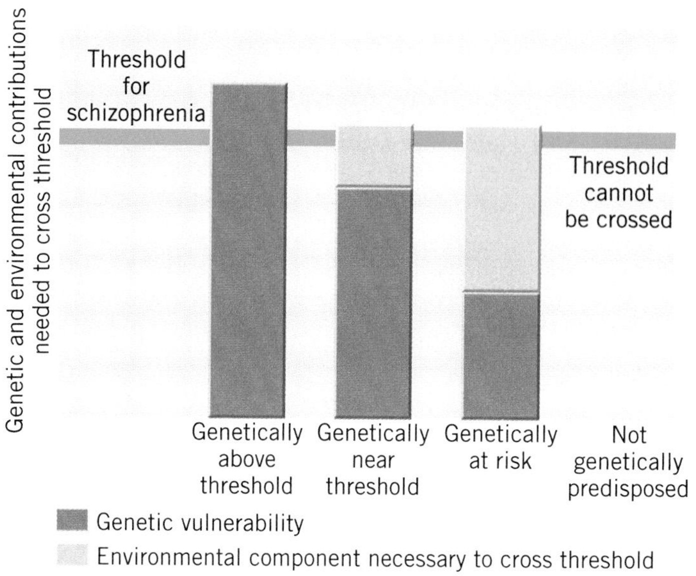

FIGURE 15.6 Diathesis–stress model of schizophrenia. Some individuals probably have a genetic makeup that puts them above threshold for schizophrenia. For others, differing degrees of environmental stress activate the vulnerability or diathesis. People who are not biologically at risk will generally not develop the disorder, regardless of environmental circumstances.

as impoverished thought (lack of complex thought in response to environmental events). Positive and negative symptoms appear to involve different neural circuits and to respond to different kinds of medications (Chapter 16).

INTERIM SUMMARY

Schizophrenia is an umbrella term for a number of psychotic disorders that involve disturbances in thought, perception, behavior, language, communication, and emotion. **Positive symptoms** include disorganized (e.g., disordered thought and bizarre behavior) and psychotic (e.g., **delusions** and **hallucinations**) symptoms. **Negative symptoms** are relatively chronic and include flat affect, lack of motivation, peculiar or withdrawn interpersonal behavior, and intellectual impairments.

Big Picture φ Question 6

What is the relation between nature and nurture in shaping psychological processes?

Theories of Schizophrenia Over the last century, researchers have advanced several theories to explain the causes of schizophrenia. Most contemporary theorists adopt a diathesis–stress model, hypothesizing that people with an underlying biological vulnerability develop the disorder or fall into an episode under stress (Rosenthal, 1970; Walker & Diforio, 1997). Most of the time this diathesis is genetic, but other cases of schizophrenia probably reflect early damage to the brain (Garver, 1997). Some individuals are probably genetically above threshold for the illness—that is, they will develop schizophrenia regardless of environmental circumstances (Figure 15.6). Others are near threshold, requiring only a small environmental contribution. Still others, simply at risk, will not develop the disorder without exposure to substantial pathogenic (disease-causing) experiences (Fowles, 1992).

From Brain to Behavior The Biology of Schizophrenia

Big Picture φ Question 1

To what extent can mental processes be reduced to the brain or body?

Genes undoubtedly play a primary role in the etiology of schizophrenia (Gottesman, 1991; Kendler et al., 2000b). A recent study of all twins born in Finland between 1940 and 1957 estimated heritability at 83 percent (Cannon et al., 1998)—an estimate virtually identical to a study of twins in England in which at least one twin had a history of psychiatric disorder (Cardno et al., 1999a).

Table 15.5 shows the risk of developing schizophrenia in people with differing degrees of relatedness to a person with schizophrenia. The table is based on data pooled across over 40 studies conducted over nearly 60 years (Gottesman, 1991). As we would expect for a disorder with a genetic basis, concordance rates between individuals with schizophrenia and their relatives increase with the degree of relatedness; that is, people who share more genes are more likely to share the diagnosis. Also supporting the role of genetics is the fact that the offspring of the healthy twin in a *discordant* pair of monozygotic twins (i.e., in which one twin has the disorder and the other does not) are just as likely as the offspring of the twin with schizophrenia to develop the disorder (Gottesman & Bertelsen, 1989).

Dopamine and Glutamate

Precisely how a genetic defect produces schizophrenia is not entirely clear. The **dopamine hypothesis** *implicates the neurotransmitter dopamine in schizophrenia*. Several lines of evidence suggest that the brains of individuals with schizophrenia produce too much dopamine. First, amphetamines increase dopamine activity, and high doses of amphetamines induce psychotic-like symptoms such as paranoia and hallucinations in normal people (Kleven & Seiden, 1991). An amphetamine-induced psychosis is even more likely to occur in individuals with a predisposition to schizophrenia.

A second line of evidence supporting the dopamine hypothesis is the response of psychotic patients to antipsychotic medications (Chapter 16) that decrease dopamine activity in the brain (Kapur et al., 2000). These medications block dopamine from binding with postsynaptic receptors, thus preventing neural transmission. The result is a reduction or elimination of positive symptoms such as hallucinations.

An excess of dopamine cannot, however, account for several important pieces of data. Not all patients respond to medicines that block dopamine activity, and different types of dopamine receptors control different psychological processes. Other neurotransmitters, particularly serotonin, also appear to be involved, in ways that are not yet well understood (perhaps in modulating the effects of dopamine).

Another formulation of the dopamine hypothesis suggests that different neural circuits underlie the positive and negative symptoms of schizophrenia (Duval et al., 2003; Kahn et al., 1996; Tamminga et al., 1992). Subcortical circuits projecting from the midbrain to the limbic system and basal ganglia have *excess* dopamine and seem to be responsible for positive symptoms. In contrast, a circuit that projects from the midbrain to the prefrontal cortex seems to be characterized by too *little* dopamine. This circuit is thought to be responsible for negative symptoms and many of the cognitive deficits seen in schizophrenia, since frontal activation is necessary for emotion, attention, and social judgment. This multicircuited view of schizophrenia may explain why most antipsychotic medications, which reduce positive symptoms by diminishing the action of dopamine, do not alleviate negative symptoms and may even exacerbate them.

Although dopamine plays an important role in schizophrenia, another neurotransmitter, glutamate, may be important as well (Farber et al., 1999; Li et al., 2003). As we have seen, one of the primary pieces of evidence for the dopamine hypothesis is amphetamine-induced psychosis, in which amphetamines produce positive symptoms of schizophrenia by increasing dopamine activity. Researchers have now discovered, however, that phencyclidine hydrochloride (PCP, or "angel dust") can produce both positive *and* negative symptoms of schizophrenia. PCP reduces the responsivity of a particular kind of glutamate receptor (see Chapter 9).

Precisely how dopamine and glutamate may both be involved is not yet clear. Dopamine can inhibit glutamate, so that too much dopamine could lead to too little glutamate activity. Another possibility is that some cases of schizophrenia reflect a primary dopamine dysfunction, whereas others reflect decreased glutamate activity, which can lead to similar symptoms.

Table 15.5 ▪ ▪ Risk of Schizophrenia and Degree of Genetic Relatedness

Relationship	Degree of Relatedness	Risk (%)
Identical twin	1.0	48
Fraternal twin	.5	17
Sibling	.5	9
Parent	.5	6
Child	.5	13
Second-degree relatives	.25	4

Source: Adapted from Gottesman, 1991, p. 96.

Each of these identical quadruplets later developed schizophrenia.

Apply and Discuss

Although it is, as yet, unclear as to precisely why many people with schizophrenia show corresponding changes in brain anatomy, one suggestion has been that prenatal trauma may be responsible.

■ Could exposure to malnutrition, maternal infection during pregnancy, and birth trauma account for some cases of schizophrenia?

■ Would being born during the winter when cases of flu and disease are more common make one more susceptible to schizophrenia?

Neural Atrophy and Dysfunction

Other data point to more global abnormalities in the brains of individuals with schizophrenia. One such abnormality is brain atrophy or neuronal loss, reflected in enlargement of the *fluid-filled cavities in the brain* called **ventricles**, indicating that the neural regions surrounding them have degenerated (Figure 15.7). The brain appears to deteriorate over the course of the illness, with larger ventricles seen in patients with chronic schizophrenia (Zipursky et al., 1998), although neuronal loss is already seen in first-episode schizophrenic patients (Gur et al., 1999). Ventricular enlargement and other forms of neuronal loss do not appear to be exclusive to schizophrenia, however, as they have been observed in patients with other psychotic disorders (Andreasen et al., 1990; Weiner, 1985) and even in patients with recurring depression and anxiety disorders (Elkis et al., 1995; Szeszko et al., 1999).

Atrophy is most apparent in the temporal and frontal lobes and in neural tissue connecting the frontal lobes to emotion-processing circuits in the limbic system (Goldstein et al., 1999; Sanfilipo et al., 2000). One study found that severity of symptoms (particularly auditory hallucinations) correlated strongly with the degree of atrophy in a region of the left temporal cortex specialized for auditory processing of language (Barta et al., 1990). Analysis of dopamine receptors and EEG recordings in the same region have detected abnormalities in patients with schizophrenia (Bruder et al., 1999; Goldsmith et al., 1997). Atrophy and other cellular abnormalities have also been repeatedly confirmed in the prefrontal cortex (i.e., the most anterior regions of the cortex) of patients with schizophrenia (Gur et al., 2000; Kim et al., 2000; Park & Holzman, 1993). The prefrontal cortex is a particularly likely site for pathology in schizophrenia because one section is involved in working memory (Chapter 6) and another in social and emotional functioning (Chapter 7).

Relatives of Patients with Schizophrenia

Several studies have shown a variety of subtle impairments in the perceptual and cognitive functioning of relatives of patients with schizophrenia who do not themselves have the disorder. These impairments resemble the more blatant disturbances in individuals with schizophrenia, such as deficits in working memory and attention, but they are usually much less severe (e.g., Conklin et al., 2000; Faraone et al., 1995; Farmer et al., 2000). One study examined the presence of disordered thinking in adoptive and biological relatives of people with schizophrenia by recording speech samples and later coding them for idiosyncrasies of thinking (Kinney et al., 1997). Biological relatives of patients diagnosed with schizophrenia, particularly their siblings and half-siblings, showed elevated rates of thought disorder compared to relatives of control subjects.

Recent research has even found enlarged ventricles in siblings of schizophrenic patients who do not themselves have the disorder (Staal et al., 2000). Relatives of pa-

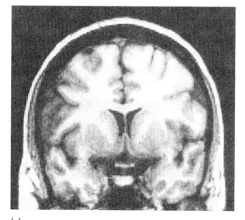
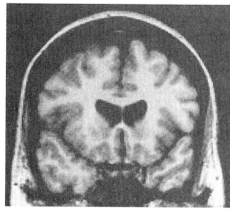

FIGURE 15.7 Ventricular enlargement in patients with schizophrenia. Magnetic resonance imaging (MRI) shows a biological basis for schizophrenia: (*a*) shows the brain of a 30-year-old woman with normal ventricles; (*b*) shows the enlarged ventricles of a 36-year-old woman with schizophrenia.

(*a*)   (*b*)

tients with schizophrenia, like the patients themselves, also show minor physical abnormalities, most often of the head, face, hands, or feet, although again these abnormalities are less pronounced than in the affected sibling (Ismail et al., 1998). Data such as these point to processes in utero that derail both physical and neural development in patients with schizophrenia, which may or may not produce "soft signs" of disorder in their relatives.

Environmental Contributions Although a biological vulnerability appears to be essential for most or all cases of schizophrenia, environmental variables play an important role in both the onset and course of the disorder. A large body of research focuses on patterns of communication and expression of emotion within the families of schizophrenic patients (Doane et al., 1981; Hooley & Hiller, 1998; Wynne & Singer, 1963). Adoption studies show that biological children of individuals with schizophrenia are likely to develop the disorder if their adoptive families have hostile or confusing communication patterns, but not if the adoptive family functions normally (Kety et al., 1975; Tienari, 1991).

A particularly important environmental variable is **expressed emotion**, *the tendency of family interactions to be characterized by criticism, hostile interchanges, and emotional overinvolvement or intrusiveness by family members*. Researchers study expressed emotion by asking family members to talk about the patient and then coding their responses for comments that indicate criticism, hostility, and so forth. Roughly 65 to 75 percent of patients with schizophrenia who return to homes high in expressed emotion relapse relatively quickly, compared to 25 to 35 percent of those whose homes have less intense and less negative emotional climates (Brown, 1972, 1985; Butzlaff & Hooley, 1998; Jenkins et al., 1986).

Culture and the Course of Schizophrenia These findings on expressed emotion have been replicated cross-culturally, particularly the link between criticism and relapse. High expressed emotion, however, is much less common in families of people with schizophrenia outside the West (Jenkins & Karno, 1992). Although the incidence of schizophrenia is similar across cultures (Jablensky, 1989), the relapse rate tends to be lower, and the course of the illness more benign, in cultures low in expressed emotion, such as India.

One explanation is that the cultures of developing countries are less individualistic and committed to concepts of personal responsibility than are Western cultures. Thus, they are less likely to assign blame to people with schizophrenia for their actions. Western family members high in expressed emotion tend to have an internal locus of control; that is, they believe they control their own destiny. They also tend to believe their schizophrenic relatives could fight their symptoms if they just exercised more willpower (Hooley, 1998). Theorists in Western cultures generally consider an internal locus of control a sign of positive adjustment, but this view is not universal and probably understates the negative side effects of an individualistic worldview. Believing that people can control their destiny may be destructive when it is not true.

Environmental Causes of Biological Dysfunction Although the term *environmental* typically connotes something nonbiological, researchers have considered other possible environmental causes of schizophrenia such as birth complications, viruses, and malnutrition (Mirsky & Duncan, 1986). Events that affect the developing nervous system in utero can later lead to a vulnerability to schizophrenia (Venables, 1996; Wyatt, 1996). For example, people exposed during the first trimester of pregnancy to rubella (German measles) during an epidemic in 1964 were more likely to develop psychotic disorders than were people unexposed to the disease (Brown et al., 2000a). Similarly, a Dutch study found that people exposed to famine in utero (particularly during the second trimester of pregnancy) during World War II showed a twofold in-

Big Picture φ Question 4

To what extent is human nature particular versus universal?

crease in rates of schizophrenia decades later compared to unexposed subjects born at the same time (Susser et al., 1996). Exposure to famine in the second and third trimesters of pregnancy confers a risk for mood disorders as well (Brown et al., 2000b).

Birth complications are also more common among individuals who develop schizophrenia, particularly if they result in temporary deprivation of oxygen to the newborn (Rosso et al., 2000; Zornberg et al., 2000). Recent research comparing monozygotic twins discordant for schizophrenia finds that the affected twin tends to have larger ventricles and a smaller hippocampus. Complications during delivery—particularly prolonged labor—tend to predict whether twin pairs will show these differences in brain structure (McNeil et al., 2000).

INTERIM SUMMARY

Most theorists adopt a diathesis–stress model of schizophrenia. Heritability of schizophrenia is at least 50 percent. According to the **dopamine hypothesis**, positive symptoms of schizophrenia reflect too much dopamine activity in subcortical circuits involving the basal ganglia and limbic system, whereas negative symptoms reflect too little dopamine activity in the prefrontal cortex. Glutamate may also play a role, at least in some individuals with schizophrenia. Other data implicate abnormalities in the structure and function of the brain, such as enlarged **ventricles** and corresponding atrophy (degeneration) in the frontal and temporal lobes. Environmental variables, notably **expressed emotion** (criticism, hostile interchanges, and emotional overinvolvement by family members), play an important role in the onset and course of the disorder. Prenatal and perinatal events that affect the developing nervous system may also be involved in some cases of schizophrenia.

Mood Disorders

Whereas the most striking feature of schizophrenic disorders is disordered thinking, **mood disorders** are characterized by *disturbances in emotion and mood*. In most cases the mood disturbance is negative, marked by persistent or severe feelings of sadness and hopelessness, but a mood disturbance can also be dangerously positive, as in manic states. During **manic** episodes, *people feel excessively happy or euphoric and believe they can do anything*. As a consequence, they may undertake unrealistic ventures such as starting a new business on a grandiose scale.

Depression and mania have been the subject not only of scientific writing but also of many forms of art and poetry. The author William Styron wrote a book about his experience with severe depression. Billy Corrigan of Smashing Pumpkins has described his struggles with depression in his lyrics, and in "Lithium," Kurt Cobain wrote about the manic and depressive episodes that apparently contributed to his suicide. As we have seen (Chapter 8), depression and mania are not uncommon among creative artists, and depression is an experience to which most people can relate.

Types of Mood Disorders   Depression was reported as far back as ancient Egypt, when the condition was called melancholia and treated by priests. Occasional blue periods are a common response to life events such as loss of a job, end of a relationship, or death of a loved one. In a depressive disorder, however, the sadness may emerge without a clear trigger, (or *precipitant*), continue long after one would reasonably expect, or be far more intense than normal sadness, including intense feelings of worthlessness or even delusions.

Major Depressive Disorder   The most severe form of depression is **major depressive disorder**, *characterized by depressed mood and loss of interest in pleasurable activities (anhedonia)*. Major depression also includes disturbances in appetite, sleep, energy level, and concentration. People in a major depressive episode may be so fatigued that they sleep day and night or cannot go to work or do household chores. They often feel worthless, shoulder excessive guilt, and are preoccupied with thoughts of suicide. Major depressive episodes typically last about five months (Solomon et al., 1997).

At any given moment, 2 to 3 percent of males and 5 to 9 percent of females suffer from major depression. The lifetime risk for major depressive disorder is 5 to 12 percent in men and 10 to 26 percent in women (American Psychiatric Association, 1994). The vast majority of patients who experience a major depressive episode will have one or more recurrences within 5 to 15 years (Figure 15.8) (Mueller et al., 1999; Solomon et al., 2000).

Dysthymic Disorder   A less severe type of depression is dysthymic disorder. **Dysthymic disorder** (or **dysthymia**) refers to *a chronic low-level depression lasting more than two years*, with intervals of normal moods that never last more than a few weeks or months. The effects of dysthymic disorder on functioning may be more subtle, as when people who are chronically depressed choose professions that underutilize their talents because of a lack of confidence, self-esteem, or motivation. Dysthymic disorder is a chronic disorder characterized by continuous depression punctuated by bouts of major depression: When followed up over five years, roughly three-quarters of dysthymic patients with no prior history of major depression have their first major depressive episode (Klein et al., 2000).

Bipolar Disorder   A manic episode, or **mania**, is characterized by *a period of abnormally elevated or expansive mood*. While manic, a person usually has an inflated sense of self that reaches grandiose proportions. During a manic episode people generally require less sleep, experience their thoughts as racing, and feel a constant need to talk. *Individuals with* **bipolar disorder** *have manic episodes but often experience both emotional "poles," depression and mania.* (These symptoms are in contrast to those of **unipolar depression**, in which *the person experiences major depression but not mania*.) About 15 to 20 percent of patients who have manic episodes also develop psychotic delusions and hallucinations (Lehmann, 1985).

The lifetime risk for bipolar disorder in the general population is low—somewhere between 0.5 and 1.6 percent—but it can be one of the most debilitating and lethal psychiatric disorders, with a suicide rate between 10 and 20 percent (Goodwin & Ghaemi, 1998; MacKinnon et al., 1997). Disorders on the bipolar "spectrum" are much more common, however, if less severe variants of the disorder are included, in which the individual experiences *hypomanic* episodes, which have features similar to mania but are less intense.

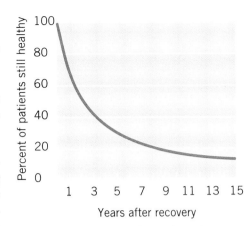

FIGURE 15.8   Recurrence of major depression over 15 years after initial recovery. The data show the percent of patients who remained well for 15 years following an initial major depressive episode. Only 15 percent avoided recurrence. *Source:* Mueller et al., 1999, p. 1002.

INTERIM SUMMARY

Mood disorders are characterized by disturbances in emotion and mood, including both depressed and **manic** states (characterized by symptoms such as abnormally elevated mood, grandiosity, and racing thoughts). The most severe form of depression is **major depressive disorder**, characterized by depressed mood and loss of interest in pleasurable activities. **Dysthymic disorder** refers to a chronic low-level depression lasting more than two years, with intervals of normal moods that never last more than a few weeks or months. In **bipolar disorder**, individuals have manic episodes and may also experience intense depression.

Theories of Depression   Depression can arise for many different reasons. As in schizophrenia, biological and psychological processes often interact, with environmental events frequently "igniting" a biological vulnerability. However, unlike schizophrenia, depression is common even among people without a genetic vulnerability.

Genetics   Although heritability is considerably lower than in schizophrenia, genes clearly play a major role in many cases of depression (see Kendler et al., 1999a; Lyons

Big Picture φ Question 1

To what extent can mental processes be reduced to the brain or body?

Big Picture φ Question 6

What is the relation between nature and nurture in shaping psychological processes?

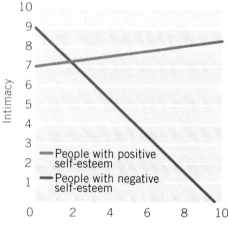

FIGURE 15.9 Intimacy as a function of positivity of spouse's appraisal. The graph shows self-reported intimacy with spouse (intimacy defined in terms of both feelings of closeness and spending time together) for people with positive and negative views of themselves. Unlike people with positive views of themselves, people who view themselves negatively, who are vulnerable to depression, report the most intimacy with partners who view them negatively. *Source:* De La Ronde & Swann, 1998, p. 378.

Big Picture φ Question 2

What is the relation between reason and desire, or, more precisely, between cognition and affect?

et al., 1998). Most heritability estimates for major depression are in the range of 30 to 40 percent; to put it another way, a family history of depression doubles or triples an individual's risk of a mood disorder.

Bipolar disorder, like schizophrenia, probably requires a biological predisposition. Roughly 80 to 90 percent of individuals with bipolar disorder have a family history of some mood disorder (Andreasen et al., 1987; Winokur & Tanna, 1969). First-degree relatives of bipolar patients have an 11.5 percent risk of developing the disease, which is 15 to 20 times higher than in the general population (Schlesser & Altshuler, 1983). Twin studies provide strong support for the role of genetic factors in the development of the disorder as well, with heritability estimated to be as high as 84 percent (Cardno et al., 1999a).

Neural Transmission   Serotonin and norepinephrine have been implicated in both major depression and bipolar disorders (e.g., Bellivier et al., 1998; Mann et al., 2000). This finding makes neurobiological sense because these same neurotransmitters are involved in the capacity to be aroused or energized and in the control of other functions affected by depression, such as sleep cycles and hunger. Drugs that increase the activity of these neurotransmitters decrease the symptoms of depression (and hence are called antidepressants; Chapter 16).

Environmental Factors   Environmental factors are important as well, both in creating underlying diatheses for depression such as rejection-sensitivity or depressive ways of viewing the self and the world, and in triggering episodes of major depression (Lewinsohn et al., 1999). Early childhood and familial experiences play an important role in the etiology of depression (Kendler et al., 1993). Depressed adults are more likely than other people to have been raised in disruptive, hostile, and negative home environments (Brown & Harris, 1989). Depressed children report a greater incidence of negative life events (such as family deaths and divorce) than their nondepressed peers (Nolen-Hoeksema et al., 1992).

Adult experiences also play a significant role. Severe stressors (such as loss of a significant other or a job) tend to occur within six to nine months prior to the onset of depression in roughly 90 percent of people who become depressed (Brown & Harris, 1978; Brown et al., 1994; Frank et al., 1994). High levels of expressed emotion (especially criticism) in the families of patients with major depression predict relapse, much as in schizophrenia—a finding that has been replicated cross-culturally (Hooley & Teasdale, 1989; Okasha et al., 1994). Lack of an intimate relationship is also a risk factor for depression, particularly in women (Brown & Harris, 1989).

Adult experiences influence the course of bipolar illness as well. In one study, bipolar patients with high life stress were over four times more likely to relapse than those with few significant stressors (Ellicott et al., 1990). In another study, bipolar patients who experienced severe negative life events took three times as long to recover from an episode than patients with less severe stressors (Johnson & Miller, 1997).

The negative environments of depressed people are not always independent of their actions, however (Joiner, 2000). Behavioral–genetic analyses suggest that about one-third of the stressors that precipitate depression—such as accidents, or alcohol-related injuries—themselves reflect genetic tendencies toward high-risk behavior (Kendler et al., 1999b). Experimental research also finds that depressed people seek out partners who view them negatively, and they prefer negative to positive feedback (Giesler et al., 1996; Swann et al., 1992a, 1992b). Like other people, depressed individuals seek others who see them as they see themselves (Chapter 17)—even when this means being surrounded by people who view them negatively. This characteristic extends to romantic partners as well: People who view themselves negatively report greater intimacy with partners who view them similarly (Figure 15.9) (De La Ronde & Swann, 1998).

Cognitive Theories   Cognitive theories look for the roots of depression in dysfunctional patterns of thinking. Learned helplessness theory ties depression to expectancies of helplessness in the face of unpleasant events (Chapter 5). According to help-lessness theory, the way people feel depends on the way they explain events or out-comes to themselves, particularly aversive events (Abramson et al., 1978; Peterson & Seligman, 1984). People with a pessimistic explanatory style, who interpret the causes of bad occurrences as internal (their own fault), stable (unchanging), and global (far-reaching), are more likely to become depressed. Upon being jilted by a lover, for ex-ample, a person vulnerable to depression may conclude that he is unlovable.

Depressed people differ both in the *content* of their thinking—how negative their ideas about themselves and the world are—and in their cognitive *processes*—the ways they manipulate and use information (Hollon, 1988). Aaron Beck (1976, 1991), who developed the major cognitive theory of depression, argues that depressed people in-terpret events unfavorably, do not like themselves, and regard the future pessimisti-cally. Beck calls this ***negative outlook on the world, the self, and the future*** the **neg-ative triad** (Figure 15.10).

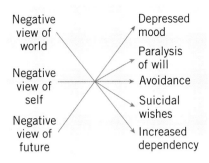

FIGURE 15.10   Beck's negative triad. A negative outlook on the world, the self, and the future—the negative triad—affects mood, motivation, and behavior. *Source:* Beck, 1976, p. 256.

Research suggests that depressed individuals process information about them-selves in a negative way automatically and implicitly, perceiving even neutral or posi-tive information negatively (Bargh & Tota, 1988; Mineka & Sutton, 1992). An out-growth of learned helplessness theory, called *hopelessness theory,* draws on Beck's observation that depressed people view the future negatively (Abramson et al., 1989; Alloy et al., 2000). According to this view, depression in some people reflects the loss of hope that things will improve in the future.

Beck (1976) calls ***the cognitive mechanisms by which a depressed person nega-tively transforms neutral or positive information* cognitive distortions**. Consider the following interaction between a therapist and a highly intelligent patient who was afraid to go back to school to pursue a career in law (Beck, 1976):

PATIENT: I can't go back to school. I'm just not smart enough.
THERAPIST: How did you do the last time you were in school?
PATIENT: Um…I got mostly As. But that was a long time ago. And what have I ever done career-wise that suggests I could handle being a lawyer?
THERAPIST: That's not really a fair question is it? Don't you think your low image of yourself has something to do with why you haven't done anything "spectacular" career-wise?
PATIENT: I guess you're right. I'm as smart as my sister, and she's a lawyer.
THERAPIST: Right.
PATIENT: But what have I ever done career-wise that says I could handle being a lawyer?

The patient repeatedly doubts herself, ignores her past successes, and generalizes in ways that do not fit the "data." At the end, she simply repeats a self-doubting question that she has just admitted is based on a faulty premise.

Beck (1976, 1985) has identified a number of cognitive errors typical of depressed patients. In *arbitrary inference,* the person draws a conclusion in the absence of sup-porting evidence or in the presence of contradictory evidence. The patient above used arbitrary inference when she concluded with little reason that she could not succeed at school despite prior success. Similarly, when faced with contradictory evidence (her prior grades), she arbitrarily dismissed that as "a long time ago."

Magnification and *minimization* are biases in evaluating the relative importance of events. For example, a man reacted to storm damage to his house by thinking, "The side of the house is wrecked…. It will cost a fortune to fix it." In fact, the damage was minor and cost only about $50 to repair (Beck, 1976). *Personalization* occurs when de-pressed people relate external events to themselves without good reason, as when a student with the highest grades in a class assumed the teacher had a low opinion of him whenever she complimented another student. *Overgeneralization* occurs when a person draws a general conclusion on the basis of a single incident. For example, one depressed patient, after a disagreement with his parents, concluded, "I can't get along with anybody" (Beck, 1985).

Psychodynamic Theories   Psychodynamic theorists argue that depression may have a number of roots, such as identification with a depressed or belittling parent or an attachment history that predisposes the person to fear of rejection or abandonment (Blatt & Homann, 1992). Unlike cognitive theories, which focus on faulty cognition, psychodynamic explanations focus on motivation. For example, the patient described above by Beck who was afraid to go back to law school and denied her prior successes might have been afraid to get her hopes up and thus defended against them with pessimism. If we do not wish, we cannot be disappointed.

From a psychodynamic perspective, depression cannot be isolated from the personality structure of the individual experiencing it (see Kernberg, 1984). A person who has poor object relations (difficulty investing in relationships and maintaining a constant view of the self) may experience depression because he is prone to feeling abandoned, empty, and alone. Such patients frequently report feeling that they are totally evil and not just helpless or incompetent. Similarly, a person who is so self-centered and narcissistic that he cannot form deep attachments to other people is likely to become depressed in middle age, when he becomes more aware of his mortality and realizes that the grandiose dreams of his youth are not likely to be actualized.

In contrast, a depressed person with a greater capacity for relationships may feel that he is a failure at meeting standards and consequently be vulnerable to feeling guilty or inadequate (Blatt & Zuroff, 1992; Wixom et al., 1993). Psychodynamic and cognitive theorists have recently converged on a distinction between two kinds of vulnerability to depression, one related to interpersonal distress and the other to failure to meet standards. People whose depression focuses on interpersonal issues tend to develop depression in the face of rejection or loss, whereas people whose depression focuses on autonomy and achievement issues tend to become depressed by failures (Bieling et al., 2000).

Gender and Mood Disorders

Women are more likely to suffer from mood disorders than men. Statistics indicate that women are about twice as likely to suffer from depression as men (DSM-IV, 1994; Franks, 1986). Men are more likely than women to experience problems with alcohol, antisocial personality disorder, and attention-deficit hyperactivity disorder. Part of this difference may reflect biological differences between men and women. However, history and culture seem to discount this explanation. Only in the last few decades have women seemed to surpass men in the frequency with which they are diagnosed with mood disorders, particularly depression (Unger, 1979). Furthermore, men in developing countries, such as India, are more likely than women to report symptoms associated with depression (Rothblum, 1983). Even within the United States, ethnic differences in prevalence rates of depression as related to gender have been observed. Asian-American men and women show few differences in the incidence of depression, for example (Crawford & Unger, 2000).

If biology is not the most viable explanation, perhaps differences in the prevalence rates of different disorders among men and women reflect differences in learning and socialization. As women internalize things more than men, the frequency of depression and other mood disorders would be expected to be higher among women. As men are socialized to be more active, it is not surprising that psychological disorders in men manifest themselves in more active ways, such as conduct disorder. In support of this explanation, more traditional women report higher prevalence rates of depression and other mood disorders than less traditional women (Huselid & Cooper, 1994).

Yet again, gender differences in psychological problems may reflect differences in the willingness of men and women to disclose problems they are having and differences in their willingness to seek psychological help. Women are more likely than men both to talk about problems they are having and to seek professional help for

Big Picture φ Question 7

To what extent are psychological processes conscious or unconscious—that is, explicit versus implicit?

Big Picture φ Question 5

To what extent are psychological processes the same in men and women?

those problems. In short, women are more likely to come to the attention of psychologists and psychiatrists than men.

Depression on a Hopi Reservation A Global Vista

Depression, like most mental disorders, has equivalents in every culture, but the way people view and experience depression varies considerably. Depressed Nigerians complain that "ants keep creeping in parts of my brain," whereas Chinese complain that they feel "exhaustion of their nerves" and that their hearts are being "squeezed and weighed down" (Good & Kleinman, 1985, p. 4). While people in Western society tend to view depression as originating within themselves, the Maori believe that distressing emotional states such as sadness are inflicted from the outside, often by angry spirits (Smith, 1981).

Do these differences imply that the actual subjective experience of depression differs cross-culturally? The answer appears to be yes. Members of less individualistic societies tend to focus more on the behavioral dimensions of depression (such as lethargy, fatigue, loss of appetite, and slowness of movement) than on the subjective experience. In contrast, contemporary Westerners are far more attuned to their internal psychological states than people in most cultures in human history. When they suffer from depression, they typically focus on their inner sense of helplessness, hopelessness, guilt, and low self-esteem.

Guilt is a common component of depression in the contemporary West, yet this is not the case in most developing countries (Good & Kleinman, 1985) or the West of previous epochs. When the Greek physician Hippocrates described depression 2500 years ago, he listed symptoms such as irritability, sleeplessness, and despondency. Not until the sixteenth to seventeenth centuries did physicians note a relationship between depression and guilt (Jackson, 1986). That this occurred at the same time as the beginning of the Industrial Revolution is probably no accident, since technological development brings with it social changes that lead to increased individualism and that put a premium on personal responsibility (Chapter 18). The shift to urban living may also have played a role in heightening vulnerability to guilt. As people moved to cities and lost the constant interpersonal surveillance of smaller groups, parents began to social-

Big Picture φ Question 4
To what extent is human nature particular versus universal?

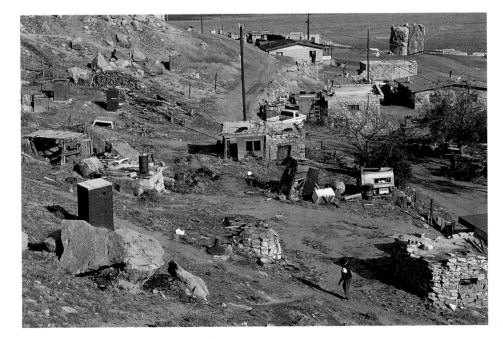

A Hopi reservation, where depression, alcoholism, and suicide are common emotional problems.

ize their children to monitor themselves more closely, to bring significant others *inside* themselves psychologically to watch over their behavior (Piers & Singer, 1953).

Spero Manson and his colleagues (1985) studied the Hopi of northeastern Arizona, whose culture was disrupted by the conquest by white settlers in the nineteenth century. Like many contemporary Native American peoples who live on reservations, the Hopi suffer from disproportionate rates of depression, alcoholism, suicide, and antisocial behavior. Instead of assuming that Western categories apply to the Hopi, the investigators began by asking their Hopi informants, "What are the sicknesses or things that can be wrong with people's minds or spirits?"

The researchers identified several categories of illness recognized by their subjects: worry sickness, unhappiness, heartbrokenness, drunken-like craziness with or without alcohol, and disappointment or "turning one's face to the wall" (pouting). When the participants were asked if they knew of any Hopi word or phrase that corresponds to the English term "depression," 93 percent indicated that they did not. The nearest equivalent seems to be "heartbrokenness," the illness ascribed to most Hopi people diagnosed in Western terms with major depression. Thus, the Western concept of depression can be translated into Hopi culture, but some of the nuances of experience that depressed Hopi verbalize often get lost.

INTERIM SUMMARY

Genetic factors increase the vulnerability to depressive disorders, particularly major depression, and play a central role in the etiology of bipolar disorder. Serotonin and norepinephrine have been implicated in both major depression and bipolar disorder. Both childhood and adult experiences also play a significant role in the etiology and course of mood disorders. According to cognitive theories, dysfunctional thought patterns play a crucial role in depression. Depressed people transform neutral or positive information into depressive cognitions through **cognitive distortions**. According to psychodynamic theory, depressive symptoms, like other psychological symptoms, can be understood only in the context of the individual's personality structure. Depression has equivalents in all cultures, but the way people view and experience it varies considerably.

Anxiety Disorders

Anxiety, like sadness, is a normal feeling. Anxiety typically functions as an internal alarm bell that warns of potential danger. In **anxiety disorders**, however, *the individual is subject to anxiety states that may be intense, frequent, or even continuous*. These "false alarms" may lead to dysfunctional avoidance behavior, as when a person refuses to leave the house for fear of a panic attack. Anxiety disorders are the most frequently occurring category of mental disorders in the general population, affecting around 9 percent of the population at any given time (see Mendlowicz & Stein, 2000). Women are twice as likely as men to be afflicted; this gender difference already exists by age 6 (Lewinsohn et al., 1998). Although many anxiety disorders are triggered under particular circumstances, some people (about 2 percent of the population) have a **generalized anxiety disorder**, characterized by *persistent anxiety at a moderate but disturbing level* and excessive and unrealistic worry about life circumstances (Rapee, 1991).

Types of Anxiety Disorders   In this section we review the symptoms of some other common anxiety disorders. Although we discuss them separately, people with one anxiety disorder often have others (Barlow et al., 1998; Kendler et al., 1992).

Phobia   At any given time, about 5 percent of the population has at least one *irrational fear*, or **phobia**, and more than twice that percent have a phobia at some point in their lifetimes (Magee et al., 1996; Ohman & Mineka, 2001). For most people, mild phobic responses to spiders or snakes have minimal effect on their lives. For others with diagnosable phobias, irrational fears can be extremely uncomfortable, such as fear of riding in airplanes.

A common type of phobia is **social phobia**, *a marked fear that occurs when the person is in a specific social or performance situation*, such as intense public speaking anxiety (see Hofmann & DiBartolo, 2001). The lifetime prevalence for this disorder is almost 15 percent (Magee et al., 1996). Recent research suggests the potential importance of distinguishing two kinds of social phobias: public speaking phobias, which often occur in people without any other psychiatric problems, and other social phobias, such as intense anxiety at interacting with other people, which typically suggest greater disturbance (Kessler et al., 1998).

Panic Disorder   **Panic disorder** is characterized by *attacks of intense fear and feelings of doom or terror not justified by the situation*. The attacks typically include physiological symptoms such as shortness of breath, dizziness, heart palpitations, trembling, and chest pains (Barlow, 2002). Psychological symptoms include fear of dying or going crazy. Lifetime prevalence for panic disorder is in the range of 1.4 to 2.9 percent cross-culturally, in countries as diverse as Canada, New Zealand, and Lebanon (Weissman et al., 1997).

Agoraphobia   A related disorder is **agoraphobia**, *a fear of being in places or situations from which escape might be difficult*, such as crowded grocery stores or elevators. Between 6 and 7 percent of the population suffer from agoraphobia at some point in their lives (Magee et al., 1996). Agoraphobia can be extremely debilitating. The person may not leave the house because of intense fears of being outside alone, in a crowd, on a bridge, or traveling in a train, car, or bus. Agoraphobia is often instigated by a fear of having a panic attack; ultimately the individual suffering from this disorder may avoid leaving home for fear of having a panic attack in a public place.

Obsessive–Compulsive Disorder

Mrs. C is a 47-year-old mother of six children who are named in alphabetical order. For 10 years she had been suffering with a compulsion to wash excessively, sometimes 25 to 30 times a day for five- to ten-minute intervals. Her daily morning shower lasts two hours, with rituals involving each part of her body.... If she loses track of her ritual, she must start at the beginning. Mrs. C's compulsions affect her family as well. She does not let family members wear a pair of underwear more than once and prohibits washing them. The family spends large sums of money buying new underwear for daily use. Mrs. C has hoarded various items such as towels, sheets, earrings, and her own clothes for the past two decades. (From Prochaska, 1980)

Obsessive–compulsive disorder is marked by *recurrent obsessions and compulsions that cause severe distress and significantly interfere with an individual's life*. **Obsessions** are *persistent irrational thoughts or ideas*, such as the notion that a terrible accident is about to occur to a loved one or that underwear is filled with germs. **Compulsions** are *intentional behaviors or mental acts performed in response to an obsession and in a stereotyped fashion*, often as a magical way of warding off the obsessive thought (e.g., washing every part of the body over and over in the shower in a prescribed order). People with obsessive–compulsive disorder experience their compulsions as irresistible acts that must be performed, even though they generally recognize them as irrational.

Common compulsions include counting, hand washing, and touching; common obsessions are repetitive thoughts of contamination, violence, or doubt (Jenike, 1983). Typically, obsessive–compulsive people experience intense anxiety or even panic if they are prevented from performing their rituals. Obsessive–compulsive disorders typically begin during childhood, adolescence, or early adulthood. A longitudinal

Making Connections

Although plane crashes kill far fewer people than cigarettes, phobias of flying are far more common than cigarette phobias. Learning theorists have proposed that we are biologically prepared to fear certain stimuli, such as extreme heights, darkness, and snakes, which posed dangers to our ancestors (Chapter 5).

study found that roughly half of people with the disorder continued to have it over 40 years later (Skoog & Skoog, 1999).

Post-traumatic Stress Disorder   An anxiety disorder that began receiving wide attention following the Vietnam War is **post-traumatic stress disorder (PTSD)**, as evidenced in the story about Joseph that began this chapter. This disorder is marked by *flashbacks and recurrent thoughts of a psychologically distressing event outside the range of usual human experience*. Often the traumatic event is of horrific proportions, such as seeing someone murdered, being raped, or losing one's home in an earthquake or other natural disaster. One study examined Cambodian refugees who escaped massive genocide during the 1980s but experienced multiple losses, uprooting from their homes, torture, rape, as well as immigration to a new country with a new language. Over 80 percent had PTSD (Carlson & Rosser-Hogan, 1991). High rates of PTSD symptoms were similarly found in a large study of ethnic Kosovars, the majority of whom reported having been victims of starvation, violence, or rape at the hands of Serbian troops who forced them from their homes in 1998 (Cardozo et al., 2000).

Even in countries such as the United States that have not had war on their soil for over a century, lifetime prevalence of PTSD is near 8 percent, with men most commonly traumatized by combat exposure and women by rape or childhood sexual molestation (Kessler et al., 1995). PTSD is not, however, an automatic consequence of trauma. Only about 10 percent of people develop PTSD following a traumatic event; violent assaults are most likely to trigger the disorder (Breslau et al., 1999).

Post-traumatic stress disorder has a number of symptoms: nightmares, flashbacks, deliberate efforts to avoid thoughts or feelings about the traumatic event, diminished responsiveness to the external world, and psychological numbness. Other symptoms include hypervigilance (constant scanning of the environment), an exaggerated startle response (such as jumping when tapped on the shoulder), and autonomic activation when exposed to stimuli associated with the traumatic event. The disorder frequently emerges only some time after the trauma. A longitudinal study of Gulf War veterans found, for example, that rates of PTSD more than doubled between five days and two years after veterans returned home from the war (Wolfe et al., 1999). The disorder can last a lifetime, as demonstrated in research on combat veterans, prisoners of war, torture victims, and Holocaust survivors (see Basoglu et al., 1994; Sutker et al., 1991; Chapter 11).

INTERIM SUMMARY

In **anxiety disorders**, people experience frequent, intense, and irrational anxiety. **Generalized anxiety disorder** is characterized by persistent anxiety and excessive worry about life circumstances. A common type of **phobia** (irrational fear) is **social phobia**, which occurs when the person is in a specific social or performance situation. **Panic disorder** is characterized by attacks of intense fear and feelings of doom or terror not justified by the situation. **Agoraphobia** involves a fear of being in places or situations from which escape might be difficult. **Obsessive–compulsive disorder** is marked by recurrent **obsessions** (persistent thoughts or ideas) and **compulsions** (stereotyped acts performed in response to an obsession). **Post-traumatic stress disorder** is marked by flashbacks and recurrent thoughts of a psychologically distressing event outside the range of usual human experience.

Etiology of Anxiety Disorders   As in depression, genetic vulnerability often contributes but is not essential to the development of most anxiety disorders (Carey, 1990; Gorman et al., 2000; Kendler et al., 1992). Twin and family studies show genetic contributions to many anxiety syndromes, such as panic and simple phobia (Fyer et al., 1995; Goldstein et al., 1997). Obsessive–compulsive disorder shows particularly high heritability, with concordance rates in the range of 85 percent for identical twins and 50 percent for fraternal twins (see Nestadt et al., 2000).

Stressful life events play an important role in most anxiety disorders as well. Roughly 80 percent of patients suffering from panic attacks report a negative life event that coincided with their first attack, and panic patients report a higher incidence of stressful life events in the months preceding the onset of their symptoms than comparison subjects (Finlay-Jones & Brown, 1981). Stressful events occurring in childhood, such as loss of a parent or childhood sexual abuse, also predispose people to anxiety disorders in adulthood (Barlow, 2002; Brewin et al., 2000). For example, separation from a parent in childhood makes people more likely to develop PTSD after exposure to a traumatic event in adulthood, as does exposure to previous traumas, particularly in childhood (Breslau et al., 1997, 1999). High expressed emotion in family members is also related to anxiety symptoms (Chambless & Steketee, 1999).

Personality, coping styles, and intellectual functioning can predispose people to anxiety disorders as well. For example, one study examined Gulf War veterans at two points after the war (Benotsch et al., 2000). The best predictor of PTSD symptoms at the second assessment (roughly a year after the first) was the use of avoidant coping strategies—that is, efforts to avoid thinking about painful events. These data make considerable sense in light of research on emotional suppression (Chapter 10), which finds that suppression of thoughts or feelings keeps them at a high state of implicit activation. This implicit activation renders people who have experienced traumatic events likely to remain vigilant toward them and to experience unintended "breakthroughs" of memories or intrusive thoughts.

Another study found that Vietnam veterans with lower IQ (assessed prior to service in the military) were more likely to develop PTSD than veterans with higher IQ when exposed to similar experiences (Macklin et al., 1998). Although the reasons are not entirely clear, a likely explanation is that greater intelligence allows more flexible coping, and greater verbal ability allows people to put traumatic events into words more easily and hence focus on and remember rather than suppress them.

David Barlow (2002), a leading cognitive–behavioral theorist and researcher, has offered a comprehensive model of the development of anxiety disorders, focusing in particular on panic (Figure 15.11). In Barlow's view, a combination of heritable negative affect and stressful early experiences can generate a vulnerability to anxiety and depression, which provides fertile ground for the development of an initial panic at-

Many Vietnam veterans with untreated post-traumatic stress disorder cannot escape the past.

Big Picture φ Question 6

What is the relation between nature and nurture in shaping psychological processes?

Apply and Discuss

People who suffer from panic attacks are ever vigilant of any signs of arousal, attributing that arousal to the onset of a panic attack.

■ Is it possible that these individuals might misattribute the source of their arousal?

■ What factors or substances might produce physiological arousal in the body that may be interpreted as a panic attack by individuals who experience them?

■ Would chemicals such as caffeine or nicotine produce such arousal?

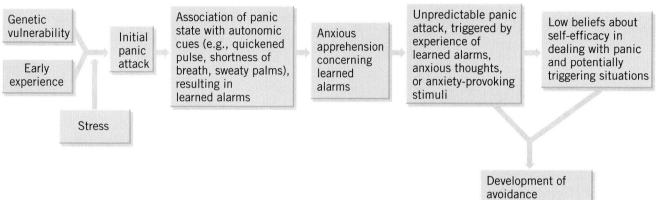

FIGURE 15.11 Barlow's model of the development of panic symptoms. Biological vulnerabilities, environmental stresses, or their interaction lead to an initial panic attack. The attack includes autonomic responses that become associated through classical conditioning with the panic state, so whenever the person starts to experience them, she becomes frightened that a panic attack will occur. *Source:* Adapted from Barlow, 2002.

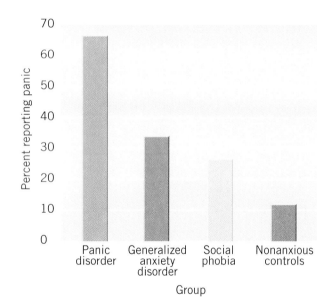

FIGURE 15.12 Precipitation of panic episodes by exposure to carbon dioxide-enriched air. Subjects with various anxiety disorders were exposed to air with a slightly elevated carbon dioxide content (5.5 percent elevation), which makes the air feel harder to breathe. Anxiety disordered patients were more likely to panic than normal subjects; panic patients were particularly prone to experience panic symptoms. *Source:* Rapee et al., 1992, p. 545.

tack. The attack includes autonomic responses such as quickened pulse, pounding heart, difficulty breathing, dry mouth, and sweaty palms—responses that then become associated with the panic state through classical conditioning. Thus, whenever the person starts to experience these feelings, she becomes frightened that a panic attack will occur. To put it another way, the individual develops a *fear of fear* (Goldstein & Chambless, 1978; Kenardy et al., 1992).

People with panic disorders thus become especially aware of their autonomic activity and are constantly on the lookout for signals of arousal. Panic patients show heightened awareness of cardiac changes such as rapid heartbeat and palpitations (Ehlers & Breuer, 1992; Schmidt et al., 1997a, 1997b). They are also more likely to panic when exposed to air that contains slightly more carbon dioxide than normal (Figure 15.12), presumably because they start to feel short of breath (Rapee et al., 1992). In panic-prone individuals, fear of their own autonomic responses magnifies anxiety and may trigger future attacks (Barlow, 2002). Repeated experiences of this sort may lead them to avoid situations associated with panic attacks or physiological arousal. Thus, people with panic disorders may give up jogging because it produces autonomic responses such as racing pulse and sweating that they associate with panic attacks. Such avoidance behavior may ultimately lead to agoraphobia.

INTERIM SUMMARY

As in other disorders, heredity and environment both contribute to the etiology of anxiety disorders as do adult and childhood stressors. Behaviorist theories implicate classical conditioning and negative reinforcement of avoidance behavior in the etiology and maintenance of anxiety disorders. Cognitive theorists emphasize negative biases in thinking, such as attention to threatening stimuli. A comprehensive cognitive–behavioral model suggests that patients develop classically conditioned fear of their own autonomic responses, which, combined with fearful thoughts, perpetuates anxiety and can trigger panic episodes.

Eating Disorders

Some of the most common disorders that afflict women are eating disorders. The two most prevalent are anorexia nervosa and bulimia nervosa.

Anorexia Nervosa and Bulimia Nervosa   **Anorexia nervosa** is *an eating disorder in which the individual starves herself, exercises excessively, or eliminates food in other ways (such as vomiting) until she is at least 15 percent below her ideal body weight)*. Anorexia is a life-threatening illness that can lead to permanent physiological changes (such as brittle bones) and death, usually through heart attack. Patients with anorexia have a distorted body image, often seeing themselves as fat even as they are wasting away (Siegfried et al., 2003). The disorder is about 10 times more prevalent in women than in men, and it typically begins in adolescence or the early adult years.

Some variant of anorexia appears to have existed for at least seven centuries— mostly in the form of "holy fasting" to escape the flesh in the name of God—and clear cases were described in the medical literature in the nineteenth century; however, the incidence appears to have skyrocketed in the late twentieth century (Bell, 1985; Bynum, 1987). The disorder only emerges in cultures and historical periods of relative affluence; people who are starving never develop anorexia (Bemporad, 1996).

Bulimia is characterized by *a binge-and-purge syndrome*. The person gorges on food (typically massive amounts of carbohydrates such as bags of Oreos or potato chips) and then induces vomiting, uses laxatives, or engages in some other form of behavior to purge herself of calories. The typical result is a feeling of relief, but it is often accompanied by depression and a sense of being out of control.

Like anorexia, bulimia is almost exclusively a female disorder; some 90 percent of reported cases are female. About 3 to 5 percent of the female population has bulimia (Hoek, 1993; Kendler et al., 1991). Also like anorexia, bulimia is more common among white women than black women (Striegel-Moore et al., 2003). Longitudinal follow-up studies find that the long-term prognosis for bulimia is substantially better than for anorexia but that somewhere between 30 and 50 percent of women with the disorder continue to have eating problems, if not eating disorders, 5 to 10 years after initially seeking treatment (e.g., Collings & King, 1994; Herzog et al., 1999).

Etiology of Eating Disorders   Researchers are still tracking down the etiology of eating disorders, although these disorders clearly run in families, with the presence of anorexia or bulimia in a patient substantially increasing the likelihood that relatives will have one or the other disorder (Strober et al., 2000). On the biological side, a number of studies have documented genetic links between bulimia on the one hand and mood and anxiety disorders on the other, and have suggested that all three types of disorder share a common problem with serotonin regulation (Brewerton, 1995; Halmi, 1999; Kaye et al., 1998).

Many researchers have also emphasized the environmental influence of mass media and cultural norms that equate beauty and thinness. Dieters in the United States spend as much per year on weight-loss programs and products as the entire federal budget for education, training, employment, and social services combined (Garner & Wooley, 1991). For some women, obsession with thinness may put them at risk for the development of an eating disorder (Mumford, 1993; Wakeling, 1996). In this view, culture itself may be a diathesis for the development of a disorder that can be activated by particular stressors.

This cultural approach dovetails with an evolutionary view, which suggests that cultural norms that influence a person's capacity to attract high-status mates should create culture-specific vulnerabilities to psychopathology. Because physical appearance is a criterion males use in selecting mates (Chapter 18), cultures that emphasize thinness as a criterion for beauty should generate a preoccupation among females about their weight (see Hamida et al., 1998).

Other researchers have examined personality as a diathesis for the development of anorexia and bulimia. Researchers and clinicians have long noted that women with anorexia are often bright, talented perfectionists who are preoccupied with feeling in control (Bruch, 1973; Casper et al., 1992; Fairburn et al., 1999) and that controlling food intake seems to be a way of maintaining control in general, particularly over im-

Big Picture φ Question 6

What is the relation between nature and nurture in shaping psychological processes?

Big Picture φ Question 4

To what extent is human nature particular versus universal?

pulses (Strauss & Ryan, 1987). Research also supports an observation first made by clinicians working with anorexic patients, namely that they often have a wish to avoid becoming a physically mature woman (Garner & Garfinkel, 1979; Hick & Katzman, 1999). They are often successful in this aim: Severely restricted food intake can stop the development of secondary sex characteristics such as breasts, halt menstruation, and make the body look like a prepubescent girl's.

Unlike anorexics, bulimics are not characterized by any particular or consistent set of personality traits (Keel & Mitchell, 1997; Striegel-Moore et al., 1986), probably because patients who binge and purge are not a homogeneous group. Recent research suggests, in fact, that patients with eating disorders tend to fall into one of three groups based on their personality profiles (Goldner et al., 1999; Sohlberg & Strober, 1994; Westen & Harnden-Fischer, 2001). One group is high functioning, perfectionistic, and self-critical. These patients may have symptoms of either disorder. Patients in the second group, who are more likely to have anorexia than bulimia, are overly controlled, inhibited, avoidant of relationships, depressed, and emotionally "shut down." Patients who match the profile of the third group, who tend to be bulimic, are *under*controlled—impulsive, sexually promiscuous, frequently suicidal, and prone to emotions that spiral out of control.

INTERIM SUMMARY

Two eating disorders are **anorexia nervosa**, in which the individual drops below 85 percent of ideal body weight because of refusal to eat, and **bulimia**, in which the person binges and then purges. Research on etiology points to vulnerabilities caused by genetics, cultural norms for thinness, and personality.

Dissociative Disorders

A central feature of a class of disorders akin to PTSD is **dissociation**, whereby *significant aspects of experience are kept separate and distinct* (i.e., *disassociated*) *in memory and consciousness*. In **dissociative disorders**, *the individual experiences disruptions in consciousness, memory, sense of identity, or perception*. The patient may have significant periods of amnesia, find herself in a new city with no recollection of her old life, or feel separated from her emotions and experience, as if her mind and body were in two different places. Dissociation is usually a response to overwhelming psychic pain, as when victims of severe physical abuse or rape mentally separate themselves from the situation by experiencing themselves and their feelings as outside of their bodies.

The most severe dissociative disorder is **dissociative identity disorder** (popularly known as *multiple personality disorder*), in which *at least two separate and distinct personalities exist within the same person*. One patient with this disorder had two lives, including two addresses, two sets of doctors, and two lovers who did not understand why she was so often unavailable.

The prevalence of dissociative identity disorder is a matter of controversy. The disorder appears to be quite rare (see Modestin, 1992; Ross et al., 1991), despite the attention it has drawn by gripping accounts such as *Sybil* (Schreiber, 1973) and *The Three Faces of Eve* (Thigpen & Cleckley, 1954). Although poorly trained clinicians may overdiagnose the disorder or "create" it in highly suggestible patients whose sense of identity is already tenuous, some intriguing data suggest that the different personalities in genuine cases may be both psychologically and physiologically distinct. For example, not only do they have access to different memories and look strikingly different on personality tests, but they may also differ in physiological qualities such as muscle tension, heart rate, and even allergies (Putnam, 1991). Two different personalities may also differ in handedness (Henninger, 1992).

Individuals with dissociative disorders typically come from chaotic home environments and have suffered physical and sexual abuse in childhood. In fact, a history of extreme trauma, usually sexual abuse, is found in nearly all cases of dissociative disorder (Lewis et al., 1997a; Scroppo et al., 1998), leading some to view dissociative disorders much like post-traumatic stress disorder (Putnam, 1995). Unlike most psychological disorders, a recent twin study suggests that environmental variables account for the disorder with little or no genetic influence (Waller & Ross, 1997). The vast majority of cases are female, probably because of the greater incidence of sexual abuse in females.

Personality Disorders

As we have seen, *personality disorders* are chronic and severe disturbances that substantially inhibit the capacity to love and to work. For example, people with *narcissistic personality disorder* have severe trouble in relationships because of a tendency to use people, to be hypersensitive to criticism, to feel entitled to special privileges, and to become rageful when others do not respond to them in ways they find satisfying or appropriate to their status. Individuals with this disorder show little empathy for other people. One patient who was asked about the feelings of a woman he had just rejected callously remarked, "What do I care? What can she do for me anymore? Hey, that's the breaks of the game–sometimes you dump, sometimes you get dumped. Nobody would be crying if this had happened to me."

Table 15.6 shows the personality disorders in DSM-IV. The prevalence of personality disorders in the general population is unknown, but the best estimates are in the range of 10 percent (Lenzenweger et al., 1997). We examine two of them here, borderline personality disorder, which is more prevalent in women, and antisocial personality disorder, which is more prevalent in men.

Borderline Personality Disorder   The movie *Fatal Attraction* portrayed a disturbed woman (played by Glenn Close) who took revenge on a married man with whom she had had an affair. This character, with her dramatic suicidal gestures and extreme mood swings, would likely be diagnosed with a severe borderline personality disorder.

Borderline personality disorder is *marked by extremely unstable interpersonal relationships, dramatic mood swings, an unstable sense of identity, intense fears of separation and abandonment, manipulativeness, and impulsive behavior*. Also characteristic of this disorder is self-mutilating behavior, such as wrist-slashing, carving words on the arm, or burning the skin with cigarettes. Patients

Making Connections

Personality refers to enduring patterns of thought, feeling, motivation, and behavior that are activated in particular circumstances (e.g., when interacting with peers, authority figures, and women) (Chapter 12). A key feature of personality disorders is that these patterns are often not only socially peculiar or inappropriate but also relatively inflexible, so that the person cannot tailor the way he or she responds to the circumstance.

Table 15.6   DSM-IV Personality Disorders

Personality Disorder	Description
Paranoid	Distrust and suspiciousness
Schizoid	Detachment from social relationships; restricted range of emotional expression
Schizotypal	Acute discomfort in close relationships; cognitive or perceptual distortions; and eccentricity
Antisocial	Disregard for and violation of the rights of others
Borderline	Impulsivity and instability in interpersonal relationships, self-concept, and emotion
Histrionic	Excessive emotionality and attention seeking
Narcissistic	Grandiosity, need for admiration, and lack of empathy
Avoidant	Social inhibition and avoidance; feelings of inadequacy; and hypersensitivity to negative evaluation
Dependent	Submissive and clinging behavior and excessive need to be taken care of
Obsessive–compulsive	Preoccupation with orderliness, perfectionism, and control

Source: Adapted from *Diagnostic and Statistical Manual of Mental Disorders*, 4th ed., American Psychiatric Association, Washington, D.C., 1994, p. 629.

Apply & Discuss

▪ Could a man who deliberately ordered the murder of hundreds of his own people, such as former Iraqi leader Saddam Hussein, be psychologically sound?

▪ What is the difference between being "bad" and being "ill"? How do we draw the line between sin and sickness?

Big Picture φ Question 6

What is the relation between nature and nurture in shaping psychological processes?

with borderline personality disorder tend not only to be highly distressed but to act on it: Close to 10 percent of patients with the disorder commit suicide, and between 10 and 30 percent of people who commit suicide carry the diagnosis (Linehan, 2000).

Although people with borderline personality disorder may seem superficially normal, the volatility and insecurity of their attachments become clear in intimate relationships. In part, these reflect the ways they form mental representations of people and relationships. Their representations are often simplistic and one-sided, strongly influenced by their moods and needs (Kernberg, 1975; Kernberg et al., 1989; Westen et al., 1990). Borderline patients are particularly noted for *splitting* their representations into all good or all bad—seeing people as either on their side or bent on hurting or leaving them—and rapidly changing from one view of the person to another (Baker et al., 1992; Kernberg et al., 1989).

For example, one woman with a borderline personality disorder had been involved with a man for only three weeks before deciding he was "the only man in the world who could love me." She began calling him constantly and suggested they live together. He became concerned about the intensity of her feelings and suggested they see each other only on weekends so they could get to know each other a little more slowly. She was furious and accused him of leading her on and using her. This example illustrates another feature of the disorder documented in a number of studies, the proneness to attribute negative or malevolent intentions to other people and to expect abuse and rejection (Bell et al., 1988; Nigg et al., 1992).

Antisocial Personality Disorder **Antisocial personality disorder** is *marked by irresponsible and socially disruptive behavior in a variety of areas* (see Stoff et al., 1997). Symptoms include stealing and destroying property and a lack of empathy and remorse for misdeeds. Individuals with antisocial personality disorder are often unable to maintain jobs because of unexplained absences and harassment of co-workers, lying, stealing, vandalism, impulsive behavior, and recklessness. People with the disorder can be exceedingly charming and are often described as "con artists."

Typically, an antisocial personality disorder is evident by age 15. The characteristic behaviors are similar to those of childhood conduct disorder. In fact, nearly all adult antisocial personality disorders were conduct disordered as children, although only 40 to 50 percent of conduct-disordered children become antisocial adults (Lytton, 1990). The syndrome is more prevalent in men (3 percent of adult males) than women (less than 1 percent). It is also more commonly found in poor urban areas.

Antisocial individuals rarely take the initiative to seek treatment. Rather, they most commonly wind up in courts, prisons, and welfare departments (Vaillant & Perry, 1985). When they do seek psychiatric treatment, it is usually to avoid some legal repercussion. For example, Mr. C was a tall, muscular man with a scruffy beard and steely blue eyes. He came to a clinic complaining of depression and lack of direction in life. He presented a very moving description of a childhood filled with abuse at the hands of his father and neglect by his severely mentally ill mother, which may well have been accurate. He talked about wanting to come to understand why his life was not going well and wanting to work hard to change. He also described chronic depression and feelings of boredom and worthlessness that are common in antisocial personalities.

By the end of the first session, however, Mr. C disclosed a troubling history of violence, in which he had escalated several bar brawls by hitting people in the face with empty bottles or pool cues. His casual response when asked about whether they were seriously hurt was, "You think I stuck around to pick their face up off the floor?" He also had a history of carrying weapons and spoke of a time in his life during which he had his finger on the trigger "if anybody even looked at me wrong." When asked why he had finally come in for help now, he admitted that he had been "falsely accused" of breaking someone's nose at a bar and that his lawyer thought "seeing a shrink" would help his case—but that this, of course, had nothing to do with his genuine desire to turn his life around.

Theories of Personality Disorders   Once again, both genetic and environmental factors play a role in the genesis of many personality disorders (Nigg & Goldsmith, 1994; Siever & Davis, 1991). For many years psychodynamic theorists suggested that borderline personality disorder originates in highly troubled attachment relationships in early childhood, which render the person vulnerable to difficulties in intimate relationships later in life (Adler & Buie, 1979; Kernberg, 1975; Masterson & Rinsley, 1975). Empirical research supported this view (Ludolph et al., 1990). Several studies also implicate sexual abuse in the etiology of this disorder, which may account for its prevalence in females (Herman et al., 1989; Zanarini, 1997). The best available evidence suggests that a chaotic home life (Golomb et al., 1994), a mother with a troubled attachment history, a male relative who is sexually abusive, and a genetic tendency toward impulsivity and negative affect (Chapter 10) provide fertile ground for the development of this syndrome.

In many respects, the etiology of antisocial personality disorder resembles that of borderline personality disorder, except that physical abuse is more common than sexual abuse and biological contributions to the disorder are better established (see Pollock et al., 1990). Both cognitive–behavioral and psychodynamic approaches implicate physical abuse, neglect, and absent or criminal male role models. Young adult experiences can also contribute to the development of the disorder: The extent of combat exposure in Vietnam predicts the extent to which veterans have antisocial symptoms (Barrett et al., 1996a), perhaps because men tend to respond to violent traumas with violence.

Adoption studies demonstrate the role of both biological and environmental variables in the etiology of antisocial personality disorder (Cadoret et al., 1995). An adult adoptee whose *biological* parent had an arrest record for antisocial behavior is three times more likely to have problems with aggressive behavior than a person without a biological vulnerability (Figure 15.13). A person whose *adoptive* parent had antisocial personality disorder is also more than three times more likely to develop the disorder, regardless of biological history. Twin studies suggest that environmental factors are more important in predicting antisocial behavior in adolescence, whereas genetic factors are more important as individuals get older (Lyons et al., 1995). This finding makes sense in light of other data from behavioral genetics that show that heritability of personality and IQ increase with age—that is, that similarities between biological relatives tend to be stronger as they get older (Chapters 8 and 12).

Aggressive adoptee

		No	Yes
Biological parent with antisocial personality disorder	No	84	16
	Yes	52	48

FIGURE 15.13   Genetic contribution to aggressive behavior problems. Among individuals without an antisocial biological parent, aggressive behavior problems were unusual. In contrast, almost half of the biological offspring of antisocial parents had problems with aggression. *Source:* Adapted from Cadoret et al., 1995, p. 48.

INTERIM SUMMARY

Dissociative disorders are characterized by disruptions in consciousness, memory, sense of identity, or perception. In **dissociative identity disorder**, at least two distinct personalities exist within the person. Dissociative disorders generally reflect a history of severe trauma. **Personality disorders** are characterized by enduring maladaptive patterns of thought, feeling, and behavior that lead to chronic disturbances in interpersonal and occupational functioning. **Borderline personality disorder** is marked by extremely unstable interpersonal relationships, dramatic mood swings, an unstable sense of identity, intense fears of separation and abandonment, manipulativeness, impulsive behavior, and self-mutilating behavior. **Antisocial personality disorder** is marked by irresponsible and socially disruptive behavior.

Are Mental Disorders Really Distinct?   One Step Further

Although we have followed DSM-IV in describing specific syndromes, most practicing clinicians and many researchers question whether psychopathology can be so neatly categorized (Baron, 1998; Beutler & Malik, 2002). One question is whether disorders really fall into discrete *categories* or whether syndromes such as depression fall along *continua* of severity (e.g., Kendler & Gardner, 1998; Lewinsohn et al., 2000; Widiger & Sankis, 2000). A major challenge to the categorical approach to diagnosis is the fact that *subclinical* cases—that is, cases that are clinically significant but are not severe enough to warrant a diagnosis—are as common, if not more common, than the diagnosable cases of mental disorders (Zinbarg et al., 1994).

Further, that many people who have one disorder have several raises questions about whether they really suffer from several disorders or from one or two underlying vulnerabilities that can express themselves in multiple ways. For example, depression tends to occur simultaneously with numerous other syndromes, including anxiety, eating, and substance-related disorders (Coryell et al., 1992; Mineka et al., 1998). Genetic studies show that if one twin has one of these disorders, the other twin is likely to have one or more of the others (Kendler et al., 1995).

Cross-cultural evidence suggests that most nonpsychotic disorders involve some mixture of anxiety and depression (Kleinman, 1988), a finding consistent with data on negative affect, which show that people who tend to experience one unpleasant emotion tend to experience others (Chapter 10). Indeed, many researchers are coming to the view that anxiety and depression are both expressions of an underlying vulnerability to negative affect (Brown et al., 1998; Zinbarg & Barlow, 1996). Negative affect, in turn, can lead to other disorders, such as substance abuse, as people who are depressed or anxious turn to alcohol or other substances to help regulate their moods (see Dixit & Crum, 2000).

A particularly problematic diagnostic category is *schizoaffective disorder*, used to describe individuals who seem to have attributes of both schizophrenia and psychotic depression and may not easily fit the criteria for just one or the other. The disorder appears genetically related to both schizophrenia and major depression (Erlenmeyer et al., 1997) and is too common to be explained as the accidental co-occurrence of the two disorders in the same individual.

Perhaps the most complex questions pertain to the relationship between Axis I disorders and personality disorders (Axis II). Most patients with severe Axis I disorders of all sorts—anxiety, mood, eating, substance use—have concurrent personality pathology, if not diagnosable personality disorders (e.g., Shea et al., 1987). Trying to distinguish enduring aspects of personality from specific episodes of illness may be problematic when the personality itself is the wellspring of diverse symptoms. We may also misattribute consequences to disorders such as depression that result from personality pathology such as dysfunction at work or poor parenting skills (see Daley et al., 1999; Ilardi & Craighead, 1999). Furthermore, with all of the disorders, the question of etiology arises. Is the disorder(s) due to genetic influences or to the environment, to nature or to nurture? As we have seen, the answer is not that simple.

Environmental events can activate biological vulnerabilities, so that neither heredity nor environment alone bears the blame. Something as seemingly innocuous as the amount of sunlight to which people are exposed can influence people with the "right" biological vulnerability. Most people show mild seasonal mood changes; however, for some, lack of sunlight in the winter months can trigger *seasonal affective disorder (SAD)*—a depressive syndrome that occurs during a particular season that can be treated by exposing patients to high-intensity fluorescent lights (see Terman et al., 1998).

Although SAD has a clear environmental trigger, the tendency to experience it is partly heritable (Madden et al., 1996). Thus, the vulnerability to an environmental event is itself inherited! This is likely true of virtually all environmental circumstances that contribute to psychopathology. Sexual abuse, for example, can proba-

Big Picture φ Question 6

What is the relation between nature and nurture in shaping psychological processes?

bly have the damaging effects it can have only because humans have evolved mechanisms that make incest repugnant and traumatizing—mechanisms that normally prevent inbreeding.

Psychologically damaging life events can also create changes in the brain that become part of an individual's "nature" (Kandel, 1999). Monkeys separated from their mothers for prolonged periods show neuropsychological changes—permanent alterations in the number and sensitivity of receptors for neurotransmitters in the postsynaptic membrane (Gabbard, 1992; Suomi, 1999). Similarly, people who experience traumatic events often develop abnormalities in hypothalamic, pituitary, and hippocampal functioning (Bremner, 1998). To speak of the causes as completely environmental, however, is not entirely accurate either. Repeated separation from attachment figures only produces biological abnormalities because the brain has evolved to be innately sensitive to attachment-related stimulation. Environmental causes presuppose a nervous system that makes them relevant.

INTERIM SUMMARY

Using classification systems to diagnose mental illness has been challenged by researchers and theorists in recent years. One reason for this is that people often experience multiple problems simultaneously making it difficult to apply a single diagnosis. Furthermore, distinguishing the roles of nature and nurture in the etiology of psychological disturbances is more difficult than may first appear. Inherited characteristics typically determine which environmental events are psychologically toxic, and environmental events can translate into changes in the brain.

Summary

1. **Psychopathology** refers to patterns of thought, feeling, or behavior that disrupt a person's sense of well-being or social or occupational functioning.

The Cultural Context of Psychopathology

2. The concept of mental illness varies historically and cross-culturally. Cultures differ in the ways they describe and pattern psychopathology, but "mentally ill" is not simply an arbitrary label applied to deviants.

Contemporary Approaches to Psychopathology

3. Psychodynamic theorists make a general distinction among **neuroses, personality disorders**, and **psychoses**, which form a continuum of disturbance. A **psychodynamic formulation** involves assessing the person's wishes and fears, cognitive and emotional resources, and experience of the self and others.

4. The **cognitive–behavioral** perspective integrates principles of classical and operant conditioning with a cognitive perspective. Psychopathology results from environmental contingencies and dysfunctional cognitions.

5. Understanding psychopathology often requires shifting to a biological level of analysis. The biological approach proposes that psychopathology stems from faulty wiring in the brain, particularly in the abundance, overreactivity, or underreactivity of specific neurotransmitters.

6. **Diathesis–stress models** of psychopathology propose that people with an underlying vulnerability may become symptomatic under stressful circumstances.

7. A **systems approach** attempts to explain an individual's behavior in the context of a social group, such as a couple, family, or larger social system. A **family systems model** suggests that the symptoms of any individual are really symptoms of dysfunction in a family.

8. From an evolutionary perspective, psychopathology can reflect random variation, broader population pressures that can produce stable rates of psychopathology if they confer an offsetting advantage, and normally adaptive mechanisms gone awry.

Descriptive Diagnosis: DSM-IV and Psychopathological Syndromes

9. The *Diagnostic and Statistical Manual of Mental Disorders-IV*, or **DSM-IV**, is the official manual of mental illnesses pub-

lished by the American Psychiatric Association. It is the basis for **descriptive diagnosis**.

10. One disorder usually first diagnosed in childhood or adolescence is **attention-deficit hyperactivity disorder**, characterized by inattention, impulsiveness, and hyperactivity. Another is **conduct disorder**, a disturbance in which a child persistently violates the rights of others as well as societal norms.

11. **Substance-related disorders** refer to continued use of substances that negatively affect psychological and social functioning. Worldwide, **alcoholism** is the most common substance use disorder. As with most psychological disorders, the roots of alcoholism lie in genetics, environment, and their interaction.

12. **Schizophrenia** is a disorder or set of disorders in which people lose touch with reality, experiencing both **positive symptoms** (such as **hallucinations, delusions**, and **loosening of associations**) and **negative symptoms** (such as flat affect and poor social skills). Schizophrenia is a highly heritable disease of the brain, although environmental circumstances such as a critical family environment can trigger or worsen it.

13. **Mood disorders** are characterized by disturbances in emotion and mood. In **manic** states, people feel excessively happy and believe they can do anything. The most severe form of depression is **major depressive disorder**. **Dysthymic disorder** refers to a long-standing, less acute depression of more than two years duration. **Bipolar disorder** is a mood disturbance marked by mania, often alternating with major depressive episodes. Genetics contribute to the etiology of many mood disorders and play a particularly powerful role in bipolar disorders. Environmental and cognitive processes also contribute to the development of depression.

14. **Anxiety disorders** are characterized by intense, frequent, or continuous anxiety. **Panic disorders** are distinguished by attacks of intense fear and feelings of doom or terror not justified by the sit-uation. **Agoraphobia** refers to a fear of being in places or situations from which escape might be difficult. **Obsessive–compulsive disorder** is marked by recurrent **obsessions** (persistent thoughts or ideas) and **compulsions** (intentional behaviors performed in response to an obsession and in a stereotyped fashion). **Post-traumatic stress disorder** is marked by flashbacks and recurrent thoughts of a psychologically distressing event outside the range of usual human experience. Anxiety disorders, like depression, show substantial heritability but do not require a genetic predisposition. Cognitive–behavioral theories link them to conditioned emotional responses and dysfunctional cognitions.

15. The most prevalent eating disorders are anorexia nervosa and bulimia nervosa. **Anorexia nervosa** is characterized by a distorted body image and efforts to lose weight that lead to dangerously low body weight. **Bulimia** is characterized by a binge-purge syndrome.

16. **Dissociative disorders** are characterized by disruptions in consciousness, memory, sense of identity, or perception of the environment. The primary feature is **dissociation**, whereby significant aspects of experience are kept separate and distinct in consciousness. The most severe type is **dissociative identity disorder**, popularly known as *multiple personality disorder.*

17. **Personality disorders** are characterized by maladaptive personality patterns that lead to chronic disturbances in interpersonal and occupational functioning. **Borderline personality disorder** is marked by extremely unstable interpersonal relationships, dramatic mood swings, an unstable sense of identity, intense fears of separation and abandonment, manipulativeness, impulsive behavior, and self-mutilating behavior. **Antisocial personality disorder** is marked by a pattern of irresponsible and socially disruptive behavior in a variety of areas. Genetics plays a role in some personality disorders, as do childhood experiences such as abuse and neglect.

Key Terms

Treatment of Psychological Disorders

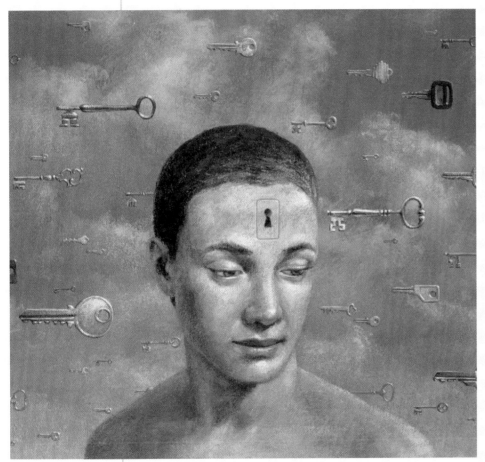

Jenny was a frail, bright, strong-willed 19-year-old from Boston. Had her parents not brought her kicking and screaming to the hospital, she would likely have been dead two weeks later. Jenny was 5 feet 3 inches tall and weighed 72 pounds—she suffered from anorexia nervosa.

During her 10 weeks in the hospital, Jenny was not the easiest of patients. Like many patients hospitalized for anorexia, she regularly played cat-and-mouse games with her nurses. When weigh-in time came each morning, she had to wear a hospital gown because otherwise she would fill her pockets with coins to fool the scales. Jenny also required a watchful eye at mealtime to make certain she did not skillfully dispose of her food.

In the hospital, Jenny received several forms of treatment. She met with a psychotherapist twice a week to try to understand why she was starving herself. The therapist also set up a behavior plan to reward Jenny for weight gain, with increased privileges (beginning with walks on the hospital grounds and eventually trips to the movies), and to punish weight loss with increased restrictions. Jenny and her family met twice a week with a family therapist, who explored the role of family dynamics in her disorder. Her mother, a very anxious woman with a severe personality disorder, was dependent on Jenny in many ways. Jenny was her mother's caretaker, sometimes even missing school to stay home with her when her mother was anxious. Jenny's mother was especially anxious about Jenny's sexuality and regularly left Jenny long letters about AIDS, rape, serial killers, and so forth. Jenny herself considered sex disgusting and was pleased when she lost so much weight that she stopped menstruating and lost her feminine shape. Jenny's father was preoccupied with her severely mentally retarded sister, whom Jenny always resented for consuming his attention. By becoming so frail herself, Jenny finally caught her father's eye.

In addition to individual and family therapy, Jenny participated in a therapy group for patients with eating disorders. In the group her peers confronted her rationalizations about her eating behavior; Jenny could also see in the other group members some of the patterns she could not see in herself.

Once Jenny left the hospital, with her weight stabilized, she spent the next four years in psychotherapy. The therapy focused primarily on her need for control over everything (including her body), her discomfort with having any kind of impulses, her fear of her sexuality, her use of starving to regulate feelings of sadness and aloneness, her anger at her sister, and her desperate wish for her father to notice her. At one point during her treatment, when she moved out of her family's home for the first time, she became so anxious at being away from her mother that her therapist also recommended medication for a short time.

By the end of her treatment, Jenny's life-threatening disorder had not returned, and she was no longer preoccupied with food. She was now able to deal more appropriately with her mother, was openly able to acknowledge her mixed feelings toward her sister, had a much more satisfying relationship with her father, and was happily involved in a romantic relationship (something she could not even imagine at the beginning of treatment).

Jenny's case is unusual because people rarely receive so many different (and such extensive) forms of treatment. In fact, the variety of psychotherapies is astounding—at least 400 different types (see Bergin & Garfield, 1994)—and the treatment people receive generally depends less on the nature of the disorder than on the theoretical perspective of the therapist. In this chapter, we focus on the most widely practiced treatments for psychological disorders: psychodynamic, cognitive–behavioral, humanistic, group, family, and biological (Table 16.1). We will discuss the psychodynamic perspective first not to emphasize its importance over the other approaches but rather because of its historical chronology. Throughout, we address two key issues. First, what kinds of treatment work and for what kinds of patients? Second, how can we use scientific methods to develop effective psychotherapies?

Table 16.1 ■ ■ Varieties of Psychological Treatment

Therapy	Description
Psychodynamic	Attempts to change personality patterns through insight (using free association and interpretation) and the therapist–patient relationship (analysis of transference)
Psychoanalysis	Intensive therapy, three to five times per week, in which the patient lies on a couch and talks about whatever comes to mind, using free association
Psychodynamic psychotherapy	Moderately intensive therapy, one to three times per week, in which the patient discusses issues that come to mind while sitting face to face with the therapist
Cognitive–behavioral	Attempts to change problematic behaviors and cognitive processes
Systematic desensitization	Classical conditioning technique in which the therapist induces relaxation and encourages the patient to approach a phobic stimulus gradually in imagination
Exposure techniques	Classical conditioning techniques in which the therapist exposes the patient to the feared object in real life, either all at once (flooding) or gradually (graded exposure)
Operant techniques	Therapeutic approach in which the therapist induces change by altering patterns of reinforcement and punishment
Participatory modeling	Cognitive–social technique in which the therapist models behavior and encourages the patient to participate in it
Skills training	Cognitive–social technique in which the therapist teaches behaviors necessary to accomplish goals, as in social skills or assertiveness training
Cognitive therapy	Therapeutic approach aimed at altering problematic thought patterns that underlie dysfunctional feelings and behavior
Humanistic	Attempts to restore a sense of genuineness and attunement with inner feelings
Gestalt	Focuses on the "here and now" and brings out disavowed feelings
Client-centered	Uses empathy and unconditional positive regard to help patients experience themselves as they really are
Family and marital	Attempts to change problematic family or marital patterns, such as communication patterns, boundaries, and alliances
Group	Attempts to use the group process and group interaction to help people change problematic patterns, either with the help of a therapist or through self-help
Biological	Attempts to change problematic brain physiology responsible for psychological symptoms

Psychodynamic Therapies

Big Picture φ Question 1

To what extent can mental processes be reduced to the brain or body?

Modern psychotherapy developed in the late nineteenth century out of the work of Sigmund Freud. The psychodynamic approach to therapeutic change rests on two principles: the role of insight and the role of the therapist–patient relationship.

Insight refers to *the understanding of one's own psychological processes*. According to psychodynamic theory, symptoms result primarily from three sources: maladaptive ways of viewing the self and relationships, unconscious conflicts and compromises among competing wishes and fears, and maladaptive ways of dealing with unpleasant emotions. Therapeutic change requires that patients come to understand the internal workings of their mind and, hence, as one adolescent patient put it, to become "the captain of my own ship."

Becoming the captain of one's own ship means acquiring the capacity to make conscious, rational choices as an adult about behavior patterns, wishes, fears, and ways of regulating emotions that may have been forged in childhood. Insight is not, however, a cold cognitive act. Psychodynamic clinicians often speak of "emotional insight," stressing that knowing intellectually about one's problems is not the same as really confronting intense feelings and fears (such as Jenny's fear that if she did not take care of her mother something terrible might happen).

A second principle of psychodynamic treatment is that the relationship between the patient and therapist is crucial for therapeutic change for three reasons. First, *a patient has to feel comfortable with the therapist in order to speak about emotionally significant experiences*, a phenomenon called the **therapeutic alliance** (Luborsky, 1985). Across all forms of psychotherapy, quality of the therapeutic alliance is in fact predictive of positive outcome (Martin et al., 2000). Second, many psychodynamic (and humanistic) therapists argue that being with someone who listens empathically rather than critically is inherently therapeutic. Third, as we explore below, psychodynamic therapists assume that patients often bring enduring and troubling interpersonal patterns into the relationship with the therapist, which can then be more readily explored and changed.

Therapeutic Techniques

To bring about therapeutic change, psychodynamic psychotherapies rely on three techniques: free association, interpretation, and analysis of transference.

Free Association   If a person becomes anxious without knowing why, or starves herself despite a thorough knowledge of the dangers of malnutrition, an important goal is to understand the unconscious events guiding behavior—or, as Freud put it, "to make the unconscious conscious." The patient and his therapist must find a way to map his unconscious networks of association to see what fears or wishes are linked to his symptoms. **Free association** is *a technique for exploring associational networks and unconscious processes involved in symptom formation*. The therapist instructs the patient to say whatever comes to mind—thoughts, feelings, images, fantasies, memories, dreams from the night before, or wishes—and to try to censor nothing. The patient and therapist then collaborate to solve the mystery of the symptom, piecing together the connections in what has been said and noting what has not been said (i.e., what the patient may be defending against). As in any good detective story, the most important clues are often those that are concealed, and only by examining gaps in the suspect's ac-

"I UTILIZE THE BEST FROM FREUD, THE BEST FROM JUNG AND THE BEST FROM MY UNCLE MARTY, A VERY SMART FELLOW."

count does one find hidden motives and concealed data. The difference, however, is that in psychotherapy the patient is both the co-detective and the prime suspect.

Interpretation   Although the patient may work hard to understand her associations, the therapist has two advantages in solving the mystery: The therapist is trained in making psychological inferences and is not personally embroiled in the patient's conflicts and ways of seeing reality. For example, Jenny's aversion to sexuality seemed natural to her until she discovered how she had learned to associate sex and danger from her mother. Thus, a central element of psychodynamic technique is the **interpretation** of conflicts, defenses, compromise-formations (Chapter 12), and repetitive interpersonal patterns, whereby *the therapist helps the person understand her experiences in a new light*.

One patient, for example, repeatedly had affairs with married men. As she talked about sneaking around the wife of one man in order to see him, her associations led to her parents' divorce. At one point, her mother had refused to allow her to see her father, so the patient had arranged secret meetings with him. The therapist interpreted the connection between the patient's pattern of seeking out married men and sneaking around her mother's back to see her father. The therapist wondered if the rage she felt toward her mother for not letting her see her father was now being directed toward the wives of the men with whom she had affairs, about whom she spoke callously, and which allowed her to rationalize sleeping with their husbands.

An important kind of interpretation addresses **resistance**, *barriers to free association or to the treatment more generally, which the patient creates*. As both sleuth and suspect, the patient is consciously on the trail of mental processes she is unconsciously covering up. Resistance emerges because the patient originally developed her symptoms to reduce anxiety; the closer she comes to its source, the more she is motivated to run from it. Jenny, for example, insisted for two years that her attitudes toward sexuality were totally realistic and refused to discuss the matter further.

Analysis of Transference   The relationship between the patient and the therapist provides a particularly useful source of information in psychotherapy (Freud, 1912; Gill, 1982; Luborsky & Crits-Christoph, 1990). Freud observed that patients tend to play out with their therapists many of the same interpersonal scenarios that give them trouble in their lives. For example, a man who came to therapy complaining of problems getting along with people in positions of authority immediately added, "By the way, I don't believe in this psychotherapy crap." In so doing, he had already replicated his symptom with a new authority figure—the therapist—in the first moments of the treatment!

The therapy relationship is a very intimate relationship in which the patient communicates personal experiences to someone commonly perceived as an authority or attachment figure. As research documents, this relationship consequently tends to become a magnet for experiences from prior relationships involving intimacy and authority, particularly parental relationships (Luborsky et al., 1990). In fact, the quality of a patient's relationships with his parents is a good predictor of his capacity to form a strong therapeutic alliance with a therapist—which in turn predicts the likely success of the treatment (Hilliard et al., 2000).

Transference refers to *the process whereby people experience similar thoughts, feelings, fears, wishes, and conflicts in new relationships as they did in past relationships*. Freud thought of this as the transferring of feelings from childhood relationships onto adult relationships, particularly with the therapist. For example, one patient had experienced his father as extremely critical and impossible to please. In therapy, the patient tended to interpret even neutral comments from the therapist as severe criticism and would then respond by doing things (like missing appointments without calling) that would elicit criticism and hostility in most relationships. By examining such transferential processes, the patient and therapist can learn about the pa-

Apply and Discuss

In an effort to probe for information that a patient may have left unsaid, a psychodynamic therapist might ask questions suggestive of events that may have happened or feelings that the patient may be experiencing but has not yet disclosed.

■ Is it possible that such probing may actually plant ideas of events and feelings that did not exist to begin with?

■ For example, is it possible that suggestions by the therapist might "create" memories of childhood sexual abuse when, in fact, no such abuse occurred?

Making Connections

Research on memory suggests that much of what we know is stored in networks of association—ideas connected to each other—and that these networks are *implicit*, or unconscious (Chapter 6). In this sense, free association is a technique for learning about patients' implicit networks, much like word association tasks used by memory researchers. The difference is that cognitive scientists study associations shared by most people who speak the same language (e.g., between bird and robin), whereas psychodynamic clinicians try to explore the *idiosyncratic* associations that can produce psychological problems.

MACBETH: *Canst thou not minister
    to a mind diseas'd,
Pluck from the memory a rooted sorrow,
Raze out the written troubles of the brain,
And with some sweet oblivious antidote
Cleanse the stuff'd bosom of that perilous stuff
Which weighs upon the heart?*
DOCTOR: *Therein the patient must minister to
    himself.*

SHAKESPEARE
Macbeth, V.iii

Contemporary psychologist's office.

tient's dynamics directly. Freud wrote that the relationship between the patient and therapist creates "new editions of the old conflicts" (1917, p. 454). The aim of working with transference is to rewrite the new edition in light of new information.

Experimental research from a cognitive-social perspective has documented transference processes in everyday relationships. In one study, the investigators asked participants to describe significant others and then embedded pieces of those descriptions in descriptions of fictional characters (Andersen & Cole, 1991). Thus, if a participant described his mother as intelligent, feminine, gentle, and courageous, the investigators would create a fictional character who was described, among other things, as gentle. The investigators then presented participants with descriptions of these fictional characters and later asked them to remember them. Upon recall, participants attributed qualities of the significant other (such as courage) to the character, even though these qualities had not been part of the character's initial description. Essentially, participants transferred aspects of one representation to another.

More recently, researchers have shown that people similarly transfer feelings from significant others onto descriptions of a person who is allegedly in the room next door and that these feelings lead them to either want to meet or avoid the person (Andersen et al., 1996). The same effects occur when descriptions of significant others are embedded in descriptions of hypothetical people and presented subliminally (Glassman & Andersen, 1997). Thus, this research documents that transference can influence thought, feeling, and memory and that it can do so outside of awareness.

Varieties of Psychodynamic Therapy

The main contemporary forms of psychodynamic treatment are psychoanalysis and psychodynamic psychotherapy.

Psychoanalysis   *The first kind of psychotherapy developed was* **psychoanalysis,** *in which the patient lies on a couch and the analyst sits behind him.* The purpose of the couch is to create an environment in which people can simply let associations come to mind. This arrangement can also make disclosing sensitive material easier because the person does not have to look the therapist in the eye. Patients usually undergo psychoanalysis three to five times a week for several years, making it a very intensive, extensive, and expensive form of treatment.

Psychodynamic Psychotherapy   In **psychodynamic psychotherapy**, *the patient and therapist conduct the treatment sitting face-to-face*, with the patient in a chair rather than on the couch. The therapy is more conversational than psychoanalysis, although the aim is still exploration of unconscious processes. The techniques are similar to psychoanalysis, but the therapist and patient are usually more goal directed because time is much more limited.

Psychodynamic psychotherapy is particularly appropriate for addressing repetitive interpersonal patterns or difficulties in relationships, such as consistently choosing the wrong kind of lover or fearing vulnerability in close relationships. This kind of treatment proved crucial for Jenny, who initially had trouble maintaining an appropriate weight after she left the hospital. It allowed her to confront her feelings about herself, her retarded sister, her parents, and her sexuality that appeared to have contributed to a life-threatening symptom.

Psychodynamic therapy takes place one to three times a week and, like psychoanalysis, can last several years. (A common misperception about psychodynamic psychotherapy is that the more times a week a person attends a session, the "sicker" he is. In fact, the purpose of multiple sessions per week is simply to allow more time to explore associational networks, not to "hold the person together.") Recent research suggests that patients who meet twice weekly in long-term psychotherapy get considerably more benefit than those who come once weekly (Freedman et al., 1999).

Making Connections

Research on adult attachment finds that adults characterized as preoccupied with attachment are afraid of being rejected or abandoned in close relationships and are vulnerable to anxiety (Chapter 14).

■ How would a psychodynamic therapist try to help a person with this attachment style become less anxious? To what extent would the therapist focus on anxiety symptoms versus the person's way of forming relationships?

■ What aspects of psychodynamic psychotherapy could be used to alter an attachment style a person has had for 25 years?

■ If attachment styles can change with psychotherapy, how quickly or slowly is this likely to occur? Under what conditions is therapy likely to change attachment styles?

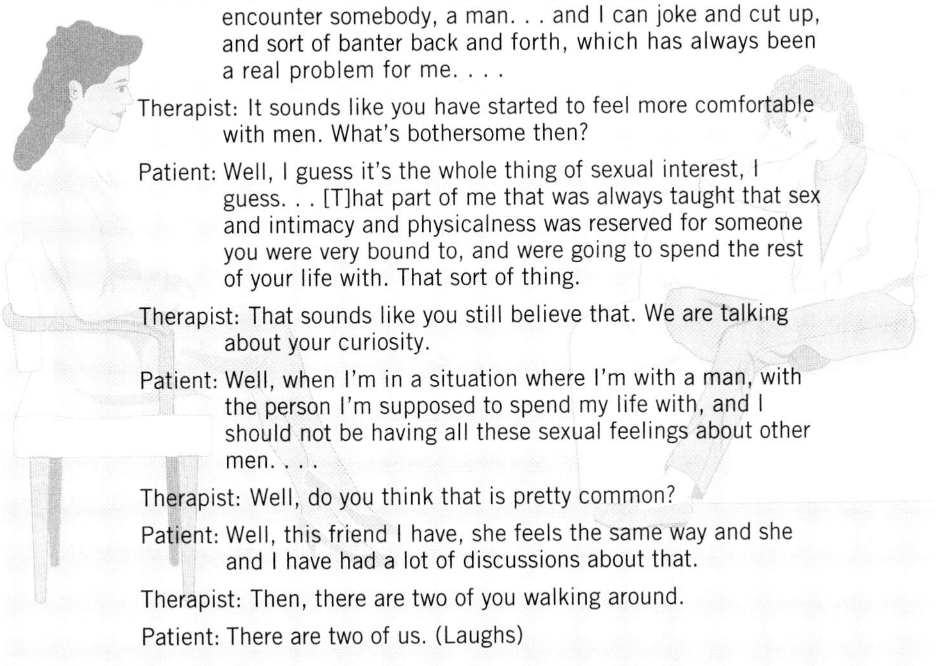

Loretta was a woman in her late 30s who sought treatment for long-standing anxiety and depression and an unsatisfying sexual relationship with her husband. Loretta came from a very conservative religious family and described her father as aloof and her mother as extremely critical. In the excerpt below, she describes feeling more relaxed with men, an exciting but still unsettling feeling:

Therapist: How would you experience men before you started feeling this way?

Patient: Sort of avoidance. I didn't—difficulty relating to them. . . .

Therapist: Is that different now?

Patient: It's a little different now. In fact, I've noticed it. I can even encounter somebody, a man. . . and I can joke and cut up, and sort of banter back and forth, which has always been a real problem for me. . . .

Therapist: It sounds like you have started to feel more comfortable with men. What's bothersome then?

Patient: Well, I guess it's the whole thing of sexual interest, I guess. . . [T]hat part of me that was always taught that sex and intimacy and physicalness was reserved for someone you were very bound to, and were going to spend the rest of your life with. That sort of thing.

Therapist: That sounds like you still believe that. We are talking about your curiosity.

Patient: Well, when I'm in a situation where I'm with a man, with the person I'm supposed to spend my life with, and I should not be having all these sexual feelings about other men. . . .

Therapist: Well, do you think that is pretty common?

Patient: Well, this friend I have, she feels the same way and she and I have had a lot of discussions about that.

Therapist: Then, there are two of you walking around.

Patient: There are two of us. (Laughs)

FIGURE 16.1 Transcript from a short-term psychodynamic psychotherapy. In this excerpt, the therapist helps the patient distinguish between fantasies, for which one need not feel guilty, and actions. The therapist is nonjudgmental and helps Loretta understand that her feelings are normal, through the joke about "two of you walking around." *Source:* Strupp & Binder, 1984.

Since Freud's time, some psychodynamic therapists and researchers have developed short-term therapies (Binder et al., 1995; Crits-Christoph, 1992; Davanloo, 1985; Mann, 1982; Sifneos, 1987). Short-term dynamic psychotherapies rely on the same principles as other forms of psychodynamic therapy, but they generally last a year or less (Luborsky et al., 1993). Unlike more intensive psychodynamic treatments, short-term therapies usually have a specific focus, which is formulated in the first few sessions. Formulating the focus entails linking the patient's initial complaint with a hypothesized conflict or dynamic issue, such as unresolved grief, repressed anger, or authority conflicts. A brief transcript from a short-term psychodynamic therapy is reproduced in Figure 16.1.

INTERIM SUMMARY

Psychodynamic therapy rests on two principles: **insight** (coming to an understanding of the way one's mind works) and the relationship between the patient and therapist. To bring about change, therapists rely on three techniques: **free association** (exploring associational networks by having the patient say whatever comes to mind); **interpretation** (efforts to help the patient come to understand her experiences in a new light); and examination of **transference** (whereby people transfer thoughts, feelings, fears, wishes, and conflicts from past relationships onto the therapist, reenacting repetitive interpersonal interaction patterns). The main contemporary forms of psychodynamic treatment are **psychoanalysis** (in which the patient lies on the couch and meets with the therapist three or more times a week) and **psychodynamic psychotherapy** (in which the patient and therapist sit face-to-face and usually meet once or twice a week).

Cognitive–Behavioral Therapies

Psychodynamic approaches were the first approaches to psychotherapy, and they emerged from clinical practice. In the late 1950s and early 1960s an alternative approach emerged from the laboratory. This approach viewed symptoms as maladaptive learned behavior patterns that could be changed by applying behaviorist principles of learning (Eysenck, 1952, 1964; Wolpe, 1964). Although many therapists continue to practice behavior therapy (treatment based primarily on behaviorist learning principles), most who make use of learning principles today are **cognitive–behavioral** in their orientation, *using methods derived from behaviorist and cognitive approaches to learning*.

Basic Principles

Cognitive–behavioral therapies are typically short term. Unlike psychodynamic therapies, they are not concerned with exploring and altering underlying personality patterns or unconscious processes (see Eysenck, 1987b; Goldfried & Davison, 1994). The focus is on the individual's present behavior and cognitions, not on childhood experiences or inferred motives. Cognitive–behavioral therapists are much more directive than their psychodynamic counterparts. They suggest specific ways patients should change their thinking and behavior, assign homework, and structure sessions with questions and strategies.

Cognitive–behavioral therapists begin with a careful behavioral analysis, examining the stimuli or thoughts that precede or are associated with a symptom. *They then tailor procedures to address problematic behaviors, cognitions, and emotional responses. The effectiveness of this type of therapy lies in its ability to target highly specific psychological processes (Overholser, 2002).*

Panic attacks, for example, include physiological arousal, a subjective experience of terror, anxious thoughts, and a tendency to avoid stimuli associated with anxiety. Panic patients come to associate autonomic reactions such as a racing heart and a feeling of suffocation with an impending panic attack; they also frequently develop expectancies of helplessness in the face of impending panic and may have catastrophic thoughts such as "Everyone will be able to see that I am helpless and incompetent" or "I am about to die" (Chapter 15). The therapist addresses different components of the problem with different techniques. These may include paced breathing exercises to deal with feelings of breathlessness (Salkovskis et al., 1986), repeated exposure to the experience of a racing heart (e.g., through climbing up and down stairs) to extinguish the emotional response, and rational analysis of the accuracy of catastrophic beliefs (Barlow, 2002; Clark, 1994). The success of these treatments in extinguishing fear of autonomic arousal is impressive: Exposing panic patients to air heavy in carbon dioxide (which leads to the feeling of breathlessness) leads roughly 75 percent to experience a panic attack prior to treatment but only 20 percent to do so after treatment (Schmidt et al., 1997a, 1997b).

Classical Conditioning Techniques

The earliest, and some of the most powerful, cognitive–behavioral techniques emerged from research on classical conditioning. Prominent among these are desensitization and exposure.

Systematic Desensitization   One of the most widely used cognitive–behavioral techniques is **systematic desensitization**, in which *the patient gradually confronts a phobic stimulus mentally while in a state that inhibits anxiety* (Wolpe, 1958). In classical conditioning of emotional responses (Chapter 5), a previously neutral stimulus comes to elicit an emotion when paired with a stimulus that already elicits the emotion. The assumption behind desensitization is that through classical conditioning phobics have learned to fear what should be a neutral stimulus.

For example, a person who has an automobile accident feels afraid to drive afterward because being behind the wheel of a car (conditioned stimulus) is associated with a terrifying experience (unconditioned stimulus). Normally, future encounters with the conditioned stimulus (driving) in the absence of the stimulus that elicited the fear (the accident) will extinguish the response (fear). However, if the person starts walking instead of driving, this short-circuits an adaptive learning process: He avoids the fear by not driving, but because this prevents extinction from occurring, the fear will remain. Thus, phobic responses, like all avoidance responses, become particularly resistant to extinction.

To extinguish irrational fear responses, then, the patient must confront the feared stimulus. This is the aim of systematic desensitization, which takes place in four steps. First, the therapist teaches the patient relaxation techniques, such as tensing and then relaxing muscle groups throughout the body or breathing from the diaphragm. Then the therapist questions the patient about his fears and uses this information to construct a hierarchy of feared imagined stimuli from scenes that provoke mild anxiety to those that induce intense fear. For the patient who is afraid of driving, the scenes might range from sitting behind the wheel of a nonmoving car to driving on a crowded expressway on a rainy night (Figure 16.2). The third step, which usually begins in the third or fourth session, is desensitization proper. The patient relaxes, using the techniques he has learned, and is then instructed to imagine vividly the first (i.e., least threatening) scene in the hierarchy. When the patient can imagine this scene comfortably, perhaps with additional relaxation instructions, he then imagines the next scene, and so on up the hierarchy. In the fourth step, the therapist encourages the patient to confront his fears in real life and monitors his progress as he does so, desensitizing additional scenes as needed to eliminate anxiety and avoidance.

In a variant of systematic desensitization, researchers in one study compared the role of humor desensitization to systematic desensitization (Ventis et al., 2001). Participants who were afraid of spiders were randomly assigned to a humor desensitization condition, a systematic desensitization condition, or a control condition. Participants in both of the desensitization groups were asked to rate the fearfulness of different hierarchy scenes depicting spiders. For those participants in the systematic desensitization group, these scenes were presented in order from least to most fearful and the participants were taught relaxation techniques to help them cope with the scenes presented. Participants in the humor sensitization group followed the same procedure except their hierarchy scenes were accompanied by humor. Participants in the control condition were not exposed to relaxation techniques or the hierarchy scenes. As shown in Figure 16.3, both desensitization groups were equally effective and both were more effective than was the control group.

FIGURE 16.2 Systematic desensitization. The patient exposes himself to progressively more threatening imagined approximations of the phobic stimulus. Exposure techniques confront the patient with the feared stimulus directly.

Least 1

Sitting behind the wheel of a nonmoving car in the driveway.

2

Driving along an empty, quiet street on a sunny day.

3

Driving along a busy street on a sunny day.

4

Driving on the same street at night.

5

Driving on a busy expressway in daylight, in the rain.

6

Most

Driving on a busy expressway on a rainy night.

Amount of anxiety

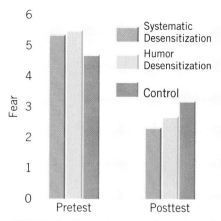

FIGURE 16.3 Humor desensitization. Ratings of fears of spiders before and after treatment. Ratings were based on 10-point scales. Both desensitization groups were equally effective at reducing fears of spiders, and more effective than no treatment. *Source:* Ventis et al. (2001).

Apply & Discuss

A patient comes to a cognitive–behavioral therapist with symptoms of post-traumatic stress disorder after watching television coverage of the terrorist attacks on the World Trade Center towers (Duggal et al., 2002). The individual is so distressed that he contemplates suicide.

▪ How might the therapist help him with his fear of future terrorist attacks?

▪ How might the therapist use exposure techniques to help him with his nightmares regarding the events of September 11, 2001?

▪ Given that exposure to television triggered the post-traumatic stress reaction to begin with, how effective do you think therapeutic exposure techniques might be?

Desensitization has been used to treat a long list of anxiety-related disorders, including phobias, impotence, nightmares, obsessive–compulsive disorders, social anxiety, and even fears of death (Lindemann, 1996; McGlynn et al., 1981). In one striking case, desensitization was used to help a 20-year-old woman overcome a fear of babies (Free & Beekhuis, 1985). Initially the patient was unable even to look at photographs of babies long enough to establish a hierarchy. By the end of treatment and at a one-year follow-up, she could approach babies without discomfort. This form of therapy is markedly different from a psychodynamic therapy, which would have explored what babies meant to her: Was she feeling guilty about an abortion she had had? Was she a victim of incest who unconsciously associated babies with her childhood fear that she was pregnant? In contrast, the cognitive–behavioral therapist aims to extinguish the fear response, not to search for insight into its origins.

Exposure Techniques　A related cognitive–behavioral strategy based on classical conditioning is exposure. **Exposure techniques** *present patients with the actual phobic stimulus in real life*, rather than having them merely imagine it. Exposure techniques for simple phobias are some of the most successful treatments devised for any disorder (Carter et al., 2003; Hahlweg et al., 2001; Roth et al., 1996; Rothbaum & Schwartz, 2002). For example, fear of flying affects 10 to 25 percent of the population and can be treated with about 90 percent success with either exposure to airplanes or "virtual exposure" in a virtual reality flight simulator (B. O. Rothbaum et al., 2000).

In **flooding**, *the patient confronts the phobic stimulus all at once*. The theory behind flooding is that inescapable exposure to the conditioned stimulus eventually desensitizes the patient through extinction or related mechanisms. Flooding, like desensitization, prevents the person from escaping the onset of the conditioned stimulus (such as sitting in the driver's seat of a running car). From a more cognitive perspective, when faced with inescapable exposure, patients eventually recognize that the situation is not really catastrophic and that they have the self-efficacy to confront it. One case report described the use of flooding to treat a young woman with an intense fear of escalators (Nesbitt, 1973). With considerable coaxing from the therapist, the patient rode the escalators in a large department store for hours, first with the therapist and then alone, until the symptom subsided. In another case, a patient who was terrified of driving over speed bumps spent hours driving, with her therapist, over speed bumps on a college campus. As you well know, given the number of speed bumps on a college campus, she received more than her share of exposure.

From the patient's point of view, flooding can be a frightening procedure. A modification of the technique that is less difficult to endure is **graded exposure**, *a procedure in which the patient is gradually exposed to the phobic stimulus*. Like flooding, graded exposure uses real stimuli, but like desensitization, the stimuli are graduated in intensity. One psychologist used graded exposure with a 70-year-old woman who had developed a fear of dogs after having been savagely bitten by one (Thyer, 1980). During the first two sessions, she was exposed to a small dog, first at the other end of the room and then gradually closer until she let it lick her hand. During the third session, she made an hour-long visit to the humane society, where she was exposed to the barking of dozens of dogs. During the fourth and fifth sessions, she repeated the earlier treatments but with large dogs. After five sessions, her symptom disappeared.

Recent technological advances have altered the ways in which some therapists use graded exposure. Now, therapists can use **virtual reality exposure therapy** to treat phobias. Patients are exposed to *virtual images of the feared stimulus as opposed to the actual stimulus*. The first study detailing the use of virtual reality therapy was published in 1995 (Rothbaum et al., 1995) and describes the use of virtual reality to treat acrophobia or the fear of heights. Subsequent studies using virtual reality exposure therapy have included Vietnam veterans with post-traumatic stress disorder (Rothbaum et al., 2001), people with a fear of flying (Maltby et al., 2002), and children with spider phobias (Dewis et al., 2001). The advantages of virtual reality therapy are that it allows therapists to treat phobias that otherwise would be costly or time-consuming to treat. For example, someone who was agoraphobic would have to be accompanied on excursions outside the confines of their house as they worked to overcome their fear of open spaces. In addition, virtual reality therapy goes beyond simply asking participants to visualize the phobic stimulus. Instead, clients are exposed to virtual images of the feared object or situation (Mahoney, 1997).

One therapist who was treating a survivor who had post-traumatic stress disorder from the September 11, 2001, terrorist attacks used virtual reality therapy. The client was systematically exposed to "virtual planes flying over the WTC, jets crashing into the WTC with animated explosions and sound effects, virtual people jumping to their deaths from the burning buildings, towers collapsing, and dust clouds" (Difede & Hoffman, 2002, p. 529). Virtual reality exposure therapy represents one of the newest ways to treat phobias. Rather than being exposed to the actual feared stimulus or simply asked to visualize the stimulus in their minds, clients are presented with the stimulus in virtual reality. These treatments have met with considerable success in the treatment of phobias.

Understanding exposure sheds light on not only the treatment but also the nature of many anxiety disorders. For example, people who have post-traumatic stress disorder (PTSD) often alternate between numbness and lack of memory for the incident on the one hand and intruding thoughts of it on the other. As we have seen (Chapters 2 and 10), disclosure of painful events tends to improve health and psychological functioning, and the reason is probably that disclosure involves exposure. People who have experienced traumatic events and expose themselves to memories of them are more likely to overcome them.

Virtual realiity exposure therapy.

The role of exposure in PTSD was demonstrated graphically in a study following up several hundred soldiers who, during World War II, found themselves unwitting participants in a U.S. military experiment. The military was testing the efficacy of various methods of protecting against mustard gas, a toxic chemical used in the war and banned internationally thereafter (Schnurr et al., 2000). Over one-third still had PTSD 50 years later, and one of the best predictors of whether they developed the disorder was whether they had been threatened with prosecution if they ever told anyone about what had happened to them. For these men, not only did the military expose them to trauma, but it prevented them from talking about, and hence resolving it.

A key component of all exposure techniques is **response prevention**—*preventing the patient from producing responses that allow avoidance of the feared stimulus*. Avoidance can be quite subtle. For example, a person with a social phobia can get himself to go to a party by telling himself that at any moment he can excuse himself to the bathroom or leave. Although this approach seems intuitively sensible, in fact, it is not: For exposure to be successful, the therapist needs to help the patient nail shut all "escape hatches" that prevent the person from fully confronting the fear. Response prevention is central to the treatment of obsessive–compulsive disorders, for example, because the patient typically uses various rituals to prevent anxiety (see Martin et al., 2000).

Operant Conditioning Techniques

In operant conditioning, behavior is controlled by its consequences (Chapter 5). Therapies based on operant conditioning therefore use reinforcement and punishment to modify unwanted behavior, as when Jenny, whose case opened this chapter, was rewarded for gaining weight with increased privileges. Operant procedures are used in virtually all psychiatric hospitals and are used unsystematically by all therapists, whether or not they are aware of it, as they reward certain kinds of behavior and discourage others. Researchers using operant procedures more systematically have found that offering rewards to patients in treatment for alcoholism quadruples the likelihood that they will stay in treatment, which in turn substantially improves outcome (Petry et al., 2000).

Operant techniques can be particularly effective in working with children and their parents because parents often intuitively apply rewards and punishments in ineffective or counterproductive ways (see Kendall, 1993). Skillfully managing contingencies of reinforcement can bring unwanted behaviors under control, as in the treatment of a 12-year-old girl who repeatedly scratched herself raw and then picked at the scabs. The behavior gradually decreased as she was rewarded with "points" that she could exchange for privileges when she did not pick at herself (Latimer, 1979). Of course, a possible downside of this is that the child or patient comes to depend on the reward, so that adaptive behaviors cease to be performed in the absence of the reward.

Modeling and Skills Training

As learning theory began to broaden its scope in the 1960s to include cognition and social learning (Chapter 5), so, too, did behavior therapists. Two early additions to the therapeutic repertoire of cognitive–behavioral therapists were modeling and skills training.

Modeling   The recognition that people learn not only through their own experiences but also by observing the behavior of others led psychologists to develop modeling procedures in psychotherapy. In **participatory modeling**, *the therapist models the desired behavior and gradually induces the patient to participate in it*. Bandura and his colleagues (1969) demonstrated the effectiveness of this technique in treating patients with snake phobias. The therapist first handles snakes without showing anxiety and without being harmed. Then the therapist coaxes the patient to handle the snakes.

Watching the therapist handle snakes, the patient begins to recognize that doing so is safe (vicarious conditioning; Chapter 5). This then allows the patient to approach the snake (exposure). Participatory modeling also alters self-efficacy expectancies, because observing the model safely approach a snake suggests to the patient that he can, too. Participating with the therapist in snake handling then leads to continued revisions of his expectancies.

Skills Training   Another cognitive-behavioral technique, **skills training**, involves *teaching the behaviors necessary to accomplish relevant goals*. Skills are a form of procedural knowledge and are typically carried out automatically (Chapter 6). Acquiring new skills, however, usually requires that the individual focus conscious awareness on and practice a set of procedures until they gradually become routine (Meichenbaum, 1977, 1990).

Skills training draws on theories of problem solving and self-regulation (Chapters 7 and 12). For example, skills training with impulsive and hyperactive children teaches them to decide what the problem is, divide it into components, develop ways to solve each part, and use feedback to determine whether each part (and eventually the entire problem) has been successfully handled (Antshel & Remer, 2003; Meichenbaum, 1977). In one procedure, the therapist teaches impulsive children to ask themselves a series of questions: "What is my problem?"; "What can I do about it?"; "Am I using my plan?"; "How did I do?" (Figure 16.4).

FIGURE 16.4   Skills training for children. This approach was designed to treat impulsive children. It teaches them how to solve a problem, from framing the problem to self-monitoring and attending to feedback. *Source:* Camp & Bash, 1981.

1   What is my problem?

2   What can I do about it?

3   Am I using my plan?

4   How did I do?

Social skills training involves *teaching new skills to people with specific interpersonal deficits, such as social awkwardness or lack of assertiveness* (see Hersen & Bellack, 1999). Following assessment, treatment usually begins with direct teaching of skills or modeling of behavior on film, on videotape, or in person. The next stage is rehearsal of the new skills—practicing gestures, imagining responses, role playing various scenarios, and so forth—which is followed by feedback and renewed practice (Ladd & Mize, 1983).

INTERIM SUMMARY

Cognitive–behavioral therapists use methods derived from behaviorist and cognitive approaches to learning. Treatment begins with a **behavioral analysis** of the symptom and the stimuli or thoughts associated with it, which define the targets of treatment. Behavioral techniques relying on classical conditioning include **systematic desensitization**, in which the patient mentally confronts a phobic stimulus gradually while in a state that inhibits anxiety, and **exposure techniques** that present the patient with the actual phobic stimulus, including **virtual reality exposure therapy**. Operant techniques attempt to control maladaptive behavior by altering its consequences. Social learning techniques include **participatory modeling**, in which the therapist models the desired behavior and gradually induces the patient to participate in it, and **skills training**, which involves teaching the behaviors necessary to accomplish relevant goals.

Cognitive Therapy

Whereas most cognitive–behavioral techniques try to alter behavior, **cognitive therapy** focuses on *changing dysfunctional cognitions presumed to underlie psychological disorders*. Cognitive therapies target what Aaron T. Beck (1976, 1993) calls **automatic thoughts**, *the things individuals spontaneously say to themselves and the assumptions they make* (see also Ellis, 1962). By questioning the patient's assumptions and beliefs and asking her to identify the data underlying them, the therapist engages the patient in hypothesis testing (Hollon & Beck, 1994). Cognitive therapies also rely on behavioral techniques but largely to induce patients to implement therapeutic suggestions (see Ellis, 1984). Two approaches to combating cognitive distortions are Ellis's rational–emotive behavior therapy and Beck's cognitive therapy.

Ellis's Rational–Emotive Behavior Therapy   Albert Ellis began as a psychoanalyst but came to believe that psychodynamic treatments take too long and are too often ineffective (Ellis, 1962, 1989). According to Ellis, what people think and say to themselves about a situation affects the way they respond to it. He proposed the **ABC theory of psychopathology**, where *A refers to activating conditions, B to belief systems, and C to emotional consequences* (Ellis, 1977, 1999). Activating conditions such as loss of a job (A) do not lead directly to consequences such as depression (C). The process that turns unpleasant events into depressive symptoms involves dysfunctional belief systems, often expressed in a person's self-talk, such as, "I am not a worthy person unless I am very successful" (B).

Ellis thus developed **rational–emotive behavior therapy** (also called *rational–emotive therapy*), which proposes that *patients can rid themselves of most psychological problems by maximizing their rational and minimizing their irrational thinking* (Ellis, 1962, p. 36). The therapist continually brings the patient's illogical or self-defeating thoughts to his attention, shows him how they are causing problems, demonstrates their illogic, and teaches alternative ways of thinking (Ellis, 1962, 1977, 1987). If the source of psychological distress is irrational thinking, then the path to eliminating symptoms is increased rationality.

Beck's Cognitive Therapy   Like Ellis, Aaron T. Beck was a disenchanted psychoanalyst. Also like Ellis, he views cognitive therapy as a process of "collaborative empiricism,"

Making Connections

Even if self-efficacy expectancies are high, people cannot emit a behavior they lack the competence to perform (Chapter 12). Bandura (cited in Goldfried & Davison, 1994) warns that desensitizing people who are socially phobic but who actually do lack the ability to interact in socially competent ways produces little more than "relaxed incompetents." Thus, cognitive–behavioral therapists use various techniques to teach people skills that can help them cope with stressful events and handle interpersonal problems more effectively.

Big Picture φ Question 2

What is the relationship between reason and desire or, more precisely, between cognition and affect?

Big Picture φ Question 2

What is the relationship between reason and desire or, more precisely, between cognition and affect?

Big Picture φ Question 8

To what extent can we inform our knowledge through reason or through observation—that is, rationalism versus empiricism?

in which the patient and therapist work together like scientists testing hypotheses (Beck, 1989). Cognitive therapy began as a treatment for depression, but clinicians now apply cognitive techniques to disorders ranging from anxiety to eating disorders (e.g., Beck, 1992; Borkovec & Costello, 1993; Chambless & Gillis, 1993; Peterson & Mitchell, 1999).

In therapy sessions, which typically number only 12 to 20, the therapist and patient work on changing maladaptive patterns of thought and behavior. Often the patient keeps a log, recording thoughts and moods so she can observe the relation between them and track her progress in therapy. The sessions are highly structured; they begin with setting an agenda. The therapist teaches the patient the theory behind the treatment, often assigning books or articles to read, and trains the patient to fill in the cognitive link between the stimulus that leads to depressed or anxious feelings and the feelings generated in the situation. For example, a patient who felt sad whenever he made a mistake was instructed to focus on his thoughts the next time he made a mistake. At his next session, he reported that he would think, "I'm a dope" or "I never do anything right" (Beck, 1976).

The core of Beck's therapy, like Ellis's, is challenging cognitive distortions. The therapist questions the data on which the patient's assumptions are based and identifies errors in thinking. A woman who was suicidal believed she had nothing to look forward to because her husband was unfaithful. Underlying her suicidal feelings were the beliefs that she was nothing without her husband and that she could not save her marriage. The dialogue between the therapist and this patient included the following exchange (Beck, 1976):

THERAPIST: You say that you can't be happy without Raymond.... Have you found yourself happy when you are with Raymond?

PATIENT: No, we fight all the time and I feel worse.

THERAPIST: You say you are nothing without Raymond. Before you met Raymond, did you feel you were nothing?

PATIENT: No, I felt I was somebody.

THERAPIST: If you were somebody before you knew Raymond, why do you need him to be somebody now?

PATIENT: [Puzzled] Hmmm....

Eventually, this patient concluded that her happiness did not, in fact, depend on her husband and, divorcing him, was able to enjoy a more stable life.

INTERIM SUMMARY

Cognitive therapy focuses on changing dysfunctional cognitions that underlie psychological disorders. Ellis's **rational–emotive behavior therapy** attempts to address the belief systems that mediate between activating conditions and maladaptive emotional reactions. Beck's **cognitive therapy** targets cognitive distortions.

Humanistic, Group, and Family Therapies

Although psychodynamic and cognitive–behavioral are the most widely practiced psychotherapies, clinicians have many other alternatives. The most common are humanistic, group, and family therapies.

Humanistic Therapies

In the 1960s, a number of therapists took issue with what they perceived as mechanistic and dehumanizing aspects of both psychoanalysis and behaviorism. Humanistic therapies, like humanistic personality theories (Chapter 12), focus on the phenomenology of the patient—on the way each person consciously experiences the self, relationships, and the world. The aim of **humanistic therapies** is to *help people get in touch with their feelings, with their "true selves," and with a sense of meaning in life*. The two most widely practiced humanistic therapies are Gestalt therapy and Carl Rogers's client-centered therapy.

Gestalt Therapy   **Gestalt therapy** is *an approach to treatment that emphasizes awareness of feelings*. Gestalt therapy developed in response to the belief that people had become too socialized—that they controlled their thoughts, behaviors, and even their feelings to conform to social expectations. According to Gestalt therapists, losing touch with one's emotions and one's authentic inner "voice" leads to psychological problems such as depression and anxiety.

In some respects Gestalt therapy resembles psychodynamic psychotherapy, although Gestalt therapists try to avoid focusing on explanations of current difficulties, believing that doing so leads people further away from their emotions, not toward them (Perls, 1969, 1989). In this view, understanding why one feels a certain way is far less important than recognizing that one feels that way. Gestalt therapy thus focuses on the "here and now" rather than the "then and there."

A technique commonly used by Gestalt therapists is the **empty-chair technique**: *The therapist places an empty chair near the client and asks him to imagine that the person to whom he would like to express his feelings (such as a dead parent) is in the chair*. The client can then safely express his feelings by "talking" with the person without consequences. A variant of this technique is the *two-chair technique*, in which the patient "places" two sides of a dilemma in two different chairs and expresses each side while sitting in the appropriate chair.

For example, one woman was torn between staying with her husband, with whom she felt "dead inside," and leaving him. She desperately wanted to leave but had trouble admitting this to herself because she felt so guilty. In one chair, she described why she wanted to stay with him; in the other, she voiced all her frustrations and disappointments with her husband and their marriage. By the end of the session, what was most striking to her was how passionately she voiced her desires to leave and how weakly she really felt about staying in the marriage.

Les Greenberg using the two-chair technique, which encourages clients to address "unresolved business" with a person imagined to be in the other chair, or to express conflicting sides of themselves while taking the perspective of the other chair.

Client-Centered Therapy Carl Rogers was among the first therapists to refer to people who seek treatment as clients rather than patients. He rejected the disease model implied by "patients" and suggested that people come to therapy seeking help in solving problems, not cures for disorders. **Client-centered therapy** is *based on Rogers's view that people experience psychological difficulties when their concept of self is incongruent with their actual experience* (Chapter 12). For example, a man who thought of himself as someone who loved his father came to realize through therapy that he also felt a great deal of rage toward him. He had denied his negative feelings because he learned as a child that he should always be loving and obedient and that feeling otherwise was "bad." The aim of client-centered therapy is to help clients experience themselves as they actually are—in this case, for the man to accept himself as a person who can feel both love and rage toward his father and thus to alleviate tension and anxiety (Rogers, 1961; Rogers & Sanford, 1985).

Rogerian therapy assumes that the basic nature of human beings is to grow and mature. Hence, the goal is to provide a supportive environment in which clients can start again where they left off years ago when they denied their true feelings in order to feel worthy and esteemed by significant others. The therapist creates a supportive environment by demonstrating **unconditional positive regard** for the client—that is, *expressing an attitude of fundamental acceptance toward the client*, without any requirements or conditions (Rogers, 1961, 1980)—and by listening empathically. Rogers stressed the curative value of empathy, the process of becoming emotionally in tune with and understanding the patient's experience without judging it. Therapeutic change occurs as the client hears his own thoughts and feelings reflected by a caring, empathic, nonjudgmental listener. The Rogerian therapist, often called a counselor, evaluates clients' thoughts and feelings only for their authenticity, not for their unconscious meanings or their rationality.

INTERIM SUMMARY

Humanistic therapies focus on the way each person consciously experiences the self, relationships, and the world. They aim to help people get in touch with their feelings, their "true selves," and a sense of meaning in life. **Gestalt therapy** tries to help people acknowledge their feelings so they can act in accordance with them. Rogers's **client-centered therapy** assumes that problems in living result when people's concept of self is incongruent with their actual experience. Therapeutic change occurs as the therapist empathizes with the client's experience, demonstrating **unconditional positive regard** (an attitude of fundamental acceptance).

Group Therapies

The therapies described thus far all start with the individual. In contrast, group and family therapies treat multiple individuals simultaneously, although they often apply psychodynamic, cognitive–behavioral, or humanistic principles.

In **group therapy**, *multiple people meet together to work toward therapeutic goals*. Typically 5 to 10 people meet with a therapist on a regular basis, usually once a week for two hours (Vinogravdov & Yalom, 1989; Yalom, 1995). As in individual therapy, members of the group talk about problems in their own lives, but they also gain from exploring a **group process**, or *the way members of the group interact with each other*. Some cognitive-behavioral therapy also takes place in groups, particularly where the aim is to teach skills that do not require individual instruction, such as stress management, or where group interaction is itself a form of exposure, as in the treatment of social phobia.

Group therapy is designed to produce benefits that may not arise from individual therapy (Dies, 1992; Yalom et al., 1975). For example, for newcomers to a group, the presence of other members who have made demonstrable progress can instill a therapeutic sense of hope. Discovering that others have problems similar to their own may also relieve shame, anxiety, and guilt. In addition, the group provides opportunities for members to repeat, examine, and alter the types of relationships they experienced with their own families, which they may bring with them to many social situations.

Groups assembled for therapy may be more or less heterogeneous. Heterogeneous therapy groups work on the kinds of problems each person would address in individual therapy, such as anxiety, depression, or trouble finding and maintaining satisfying intimate relationships. Group members typically vary not only in symptoms but also in age, socioeconomic status, and gender. In contrast, homogeneous groups usually focus on a common issue or disorder, such as incest, bulimia, or borderline personality disorder (Koerner & Linehan, 2000; Linehan, 1993). Group therapy can be quite helpful in part because members can see and confront in other members what they cannot acknowledge in themselves, as when Jenny observed other obviously emaciated anorexics complain that they were fat.

A variation on group therapy is the **self-help group**, *which is not guided by a professional* and often has many more than the 5 to 10 participants in therapist-guided groups. Millions of people every year turn to self-help groups in the United States alone; self-help groups tend to flourish when a disease or disorder is stigmatizing, such as alcoholism or AIDS (Davison et al., 2000). One of the oldest and best known self-help groups is Alcoholics Anonymous (AA; Chapter 11). Others include Adult Children of Alcoholics, Weight Watchers, Gamblers Anonymous, and groups for cancer patients or parents who have lost a child.

Psychotherapists frequently refer patients to self-help groups to supplement individual therapy, particularly if the patient has a problem such as overeating or alcoholism. Self-help groups can be effective for many people suffering from alcoholism (Tonigan et al., 2000) and other psychological and medical problems (Davison et al., 2000). Their main limitation can be a tendency to oversimplify the problem and its causes, leading some members to conclude that all their difficulties can be reduced to being "co-dependent," an "adult child of an alcoholic," and so forth.

An Alcoholics Anonymous meeting.

Family Therapies

The aim of **family therapy** *is to change maladaptive family interaction patterns*. As in group and psychodynamic therapy, the focus of family therapy is often on process as well as content. In other words, the process that unfolds in the therapy hour—a transference reaction to a therapist, a sibling-like competitive relationship in a group, or a round of accusations and counteraccusations between a husband and wife—is as important as the content of what the patient says. In family therapy the therapist takes a relatively active role and often assigns the family tasks to carry out between sessions.

Approaches to Family Therapy Family therapy has many schools of thought. Some approaches (called *structural* and *strategic*) focus on the organization (structure) of the family system and use active interventions (strategies) to disrupt dysfunctional patterns. Therapists who operate from this standpoint attend to boundaries between generations, alliances and schisms between family members, the hierarchy of power in the family, and family homeostatic mechanisms (Aponte & VanDeusen, 1981; Laroi, 2003; Minuchin, 1974). For example, in one family with an anorexic daughter, the therapist discovered that the father forbade his children to close the doors to their rooms and felt more intimate with his daughter than his wife. Hypothesizing that the father–daughter relationship might have contributed to the girl's refusal to eat (particularly since the symptom postponed physical maturation and puberty), the therapist prescribed as a first step that the daughter be allowed to keep her door closed for two hours a day and that the parents spend an hour each evening together in their room with the door closed (Hoffman, 1981).

Apply & Discuss

Family therapies are predicated on the view that a family is a system of interdependent parts. In this view, the problem lies in the structure of the system itself rather than in the family member who is merely expressing the symptom (Haley, 1971; Wynne, 1961).

▪ Can a therapist work successfully with a child without thoroughly evaluating the family? What about an adolescent?

▪ Adults are often in couples and families, too, but most clinicians never meet adult patients' spouses, parents, siblings, or children. When can a clinician assume it is "safe" to treat a patient as an individual? What are the trade-offs involved in treating an adult—or adolescent—in individual versus family therapy?

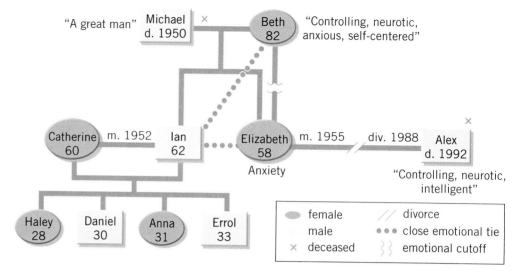

FIGURE 16.5 A genogram. The patient, Elizabeth, sought treatment for anxiety. From the genogram, the therapist could see that she was cut off from her mother, who remained close to her brother, which made Elizabeth feel left out. She also appeared to have married a man somewhat like her mother and to be anxious like her mother.

One assessment technique used widely by family therapists to map family dynamics and to try to understand their origins is a **genogram**, *a map of a family over three or four generations* (Figure 16.5). The clinician supplements this barebones picture of the family by adding the patient's comments about each person or relationship depicted in the genogram, looking for possible similarities between current difficulties and the family's past (Foster et al., 2002; Milewski-Hertlein, 2001).

Couples Therapy   *A variant of family therapy, called* **marital** *or* **couples therapy***, focuses on a smaller system, the marital unit or couple.* The therapist may see the members of the couple individually and/or together.

Many therapists take a family systems approach to couples work, looking for problematic communication or interaction patterns. For example, one couple was trapped in a cycle in which the husband did something, the wife criticized it, and the husband felt angry and helpless and tried to defend himself (Haley, 1971, pp. 275–276). When the therapist pointed out the pattern, the wife responded, "I have to criticize, because he never does what he should," to which the husband replied, "Well, I try"—which was precisely the pattern repeating itself again.

Marital therapists may also adopt psychodynamic or cognitive–behavioral perspectives. The goal of psychodynamic marital therapy is to help members of the couple recognize and alter patterns of interacting that reflect patterns from the past. A man who complained that his wife was unsupportive repeatedly changed the subject or criticized his wife during therapy sessions every time she was about to do or say something supportive. The therapist hypothesized that he was replaying his experience of his parents' highly critical relationship, which guided his expectations of his wife and their interactions and formed an unconscious internal working model (Chapter 14) of relationships.

Behavioral couples therapy rests on the assumption that people stay in relationships when they receive more reinforcement than punishment (Christensen & Heavey, 1999; Chapter 18). Thus, behavior therapists address the ways spouses often control each other's behavior in ineffective and punishing ways. Empirically, a strong predictor of marital dissatisfaction and divorce is **negative reciprocity**, *the tendency of members of a couple to respond to negative comments or actions by their partner with negative behaviors in return* (Gottman, 1998). As a result, arguments spiral out of control without resolution. Thus, the marital therapist aims to help couples break these negative spirals.

Researchers have recently begun to study, as well, the role of positive interactions in maintaining marital satisfaction, particularly the extent to which couples engage in behavior that is accepting or validating (Jacobson et al., 2000). As in research on positive and negative affect (Chapter 10) and on parental rejection and acceptance (Chapter 14), the data suggest that negative and positive marital interactions are not simply opposite sides of the same coin. Some couples are high on both accepting and rejecting behavior toward one another; some are low on both; and others are high on one and low on the other. A couple can be unhappy even if they do not argue much, just as a couple can be happy even if they argue regularly, depending on how much they are also warm and accepting toward one another (Johnson & Jacob, 2000).

INTERIM SUMMARY

In **group therapy**, multiple people meet together to work toward therapeutic goals. A variation on group therapy is the **self-help group**, which is not guided by a professional. The aim of **family therapy** is to change maladaptive family interaction patterns. Family therapists often construct a **genogram** (a map of a family over three or four generations) to pinpoint recurring family patterns over generations. **Marital** or **couples** therapy focuses on the relationship between members of a couple and can rely on psychodynamic, systemic, cognitive, or behavioral principles.

Culture and Psychotherapy | A Global Vista

Cross-culturally, as well as within multicultural societies, methods of treatment depend on cultural value systems and beliefs about personality and psychopathology (Kaplan & Sue, 1997; Kleinman, 1988). Psychoanalysis is predicated on the notion that exploring one's own mind is the key to therapeutic change—a view that would not likely have emerged outside the individualistic, industrialized West. Similarly, the role played by the cognitive–behavioral therapist—who acts in many respects like a behavioral engineer repairing malfunctioning psychological machinery—is readily understood and embraced by people in a technologically developed society.

Although psychotherapy is an invention of the twentieth-century West, all known cultures have attempted to understand and treat psychopathology. Many cultures treat psychological disturbances by bringing the community together in healing rituals (Boesch, 1982; Turner, 1969). These rituals give the ill person a sense of social support and solidarity, similar to the healing properties of empathic relationships in many Western therapies. At the same time, by uniting families or extended kin whose conflict may be contributing to the individual's symptoms, community healing rituals perform functions similar to family systems therapy.

Among the Ndembu of northwestern Zambia, a ritual doctor thoroughly "researches" the social situation of a person afflicted with illness, mental or physical (Turner, 1967). He listens to gossip and to the patient's dreams and persuades community members to confess any grudges. In one case, the patient held a position of power in the community but was greatly disliked. During the curing ritual, the patient was required to shed some blood, and members of the community were required to confess their hostilities. In this way, the ritual appeased all parties: The patient paid for his character defects with his blood, and the confession repaired social relationships. At the end of the ritual, the mood was jubilant, and people who had been estranged for years joined hands warmly.

To the extent that successful treatment requires faith in the possibility of help, all psychotherapy—if not all medicine—is to some degree "faith healing." The factors that confer faith, however, differ dramatically from culture to culture (Torrey, 1986). Western cultures value academic achievement, and patients tend to respect therapists whose walls are filled with advanced degrees. In non-Western cultures, such as Nige-

Big Picture φ Question 4

To what extent is human nature particular versus universal?

Ndembu doctor.

ria, where shamans have practiced medicine for generations, family lineage and claims to supernatural powers are more likely to enhance a "therapist's" prestige.

One Step Further | Psychotherapy Integration

Although theory and research have focused largely on the "brand-name" psychotherapies described here, in everyday practice about twice as many psychologists report crossing over "party lines" in their work with patients as those who report staying within one of the two most prevalent orientations, psychodynamic and cognitive-behavioral (Norcross et al., 1997). **Psychotherapy integration—*the use of theory or technique from multiple therapeutic perspectives*—**comes in two forms (Arkowitz, 1997; Stricker, 1996; Westen, 2000).

The first is *eclectic* psychotherapy, in which clinicians combine techniques from different approaches, often to fit the particular case. One recent study, for example, examined the efficacy of an intensive, comprehensive treatment for schizophrenia that combined education about the disorder, medication, weekly group therapy, family therapy, and close monitoring of symptoms to allow active intervention at the first signs of relapse (Herz et al., 2000; see also Louw & Straker, 2002). Compared with treatment as normally practiced in the community, the treatment cut relapse rates 18 months later from roughly 40 to 20 percent (Figure 16.6).

The second form of psychotherapy integration is less about picking and choosing among strategies from different approaches than about developing an approach to treating patients based on *theories* that cut across theoretical lines. This approach to treatment, usually called *integrative* psychotherapy, is intuitively appealing but difficult in practice, because the assumptions, methods, and techniques of the various approaches are so different (Arkowitz & Messer, 1984; Messer & Winokur, 1980). How can a clinician integrate principles of therapy based on theories of unconscious conflict and compromise with others that focus on classical and operant conditioning or cognitive distortions?

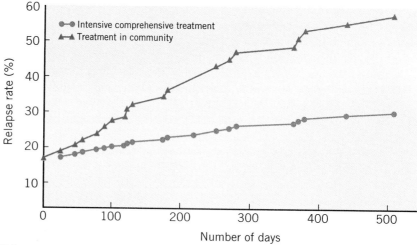

FIGURE 16.6   Schizophrenia relapse rates in an eclectic treatment program. Patients in an intensive, comprehensive relapse prevention program showed substantially lower rates of relapse than patients in "treatment as usual" in the community. *Source:* Herz et al., 2000, p. 280.

The best example of an integrative approach is the work of Paul Wachtel (1977, 1993, 1997). One of his most important contributions is the concept of *cyclical psychodynamics*, in which people's fears and expectations create self-reinforcing behaviors that often lead them to get precisely what they fear. A considerable body of evidence has documented just such processes experimentally (e.g., Swann et al., 1992a, 1992b). For example, one team of researchers studied couples in which one or both partners were high in rejection-sensitivity, that is, who fear rejection and are chronically "on the lookout" for signs of it (Downey et al., 1998). Not only were the relationships of rejection-sensitive people more likely to dissolve—confirming their fear of rejection—but in laboratory sessions with their partners they tended to elicit more rejecting behavior from their partners by behaving more negatively in discussing conflicts in the relationship.

How might a clinician practicing from an integrative perspective treat complex patterns of this sort, in which people unwittingly elicit what they fear? According to Wachtel, insight into the problem is an important first step, but behavioral techniques can be invaluable in encouraging the patient to confront the problem and develop the skills to master it. For example, consider a patient who reports never feeling angry but who "somehow" finds himself embroiled in one conflict after another with everyone around him, after which everyone else is furious and he feels misunderstood. Empirically, patients like this are relatively common in clinical practice (Westen & Shedler, 1999). Suppose the patient has begun to recognize that he is afraid to acknowledge his anger and has begun to realize how he evokes anger in other people. He may still be unable to confront people, because the anxiety associated with doing so is a conditioned emotional response that motivates avoidance. The therapist may thus need to take a more active stance, encouraging the patient, applying operant techniques (such as rewarding confrontive behavior with praise), and examining instances in which the patient avoids becoming angry at the therapist (e.g., for "pushing" him to be more open with his anger).

Wachtel has also proposed ways of integrating psychodynamic and family systems therapy based on the notion that maladaptive interpersonal strategies are maintained through both internal processes and the behavior of significant others, who serve as "accomplices" (Wachtel, 1984). A patient who is depressed and self-hating is often part of a larger family or marital system, and other people in the system may have vested interests in the symptom. The husband of a patient who sought treatment for low self-esteem seemed to keep sabotaging all of his wife's efforts to get better until the therapist brought him into the treatment. Examination of his behaviors and history suggested that he was trying to control and humiliate his wife much as his father had done with his mother—something he had vowed as a child never to do. Thus, a single mode of treatment (e.g., addressing the wife's self-esteem with cognitive or psychodynamic therapy) may fail if it leaves untouched other important factors that maintain the problem.

The treatment of Jenny, whose case began this chapter, provides a good example of both eclectic and integrative therapy. The treatment she received in the hospital was eclectic, bringing together behavioral, psychodynamic, systems, and group approaches to try to address multiple aspects of a life-threatening disorder. Her individual psychotherapy as an outpatient was integrative, combining behavioral and psychodynamic principles. For example, after she left the hospital, Jenny's weight was at first precarious, so her therapist required her to weigh in at her doctor's office each week and bring a slip to therapy reporting her weight. Because Jenny found this acutely embarrassing, her therapist made a behavioral contract with her: If she maintained her weight for several weeks, he would stop asking to see her weight unless she obviously appeared to be losing again. Aside from promoting a healthy weight through negative reinforcement (removal of an aversive consequence), this arrangement led to exploration of Jenny's need to be in control (and her anger at feeling controlled by her therapist). It also led to examination of her feelings about her body as she kept her weight at a normal level and once again began to look like a woman instead of a child.

Biological Treatments

Big Picture φ Question 1

To what extent can mental processes be reduced to the brain or body?

The approaches we have examined thus far all use psychological and interpersonal interventions to address psychological problems. A very different type of treatment emerges from the view that psychological disorders reflect pathology of the brain.

Biological treatments use medication to restore the brain to as normal functioning as possible (pharmacotherapy). If medications are ineffective, clinicians may turn to electroconvulsive (shock) therapy (ECT) or, in extreme cases, psychosurgery. (Unlike psychotherapy, which can be administered by psychologists and other mental health practitioners, biological treatments can be administered only by physicians, most commonly psychiatrists.)

From Brain to Behavior | Psychotropic Medications

For many years, patients with severe mental illness were sent to state mental hospitals, which provided little more than custodial care in overcrowded wards. But the discovery of **psychotropic medications—*drugs that act on the brain to affect mental processes*** (Table 16.2)—changed the care of psychiatric patients dramatically. In 1956, chlorpromazine (trade name Thorazine) was introduced to treat schizophrenia, and the population of state mental institutions dropped rapidly (Figure 16.7). New and better medications have been developed over the ensuing decades. The recent discovery of novel chemical agents, such as clozapine and olanzapine, has led to substantial improvement in a large percentage of psychotic patients who did not respond to chlorpromazine or other medications (Wahlbeck et al., 1999). The benefits of these

Table 16.2 ▪▪ Psychotropic Medications

Symptom	Type of Medication	Examples
Psychosis	Antipsychotics	Chlorpromazine (Thorazine), Clozapine (Clozaril)
Depression	Tricyclic antidepressants	Trazodone (Desyrel), Amitriptyline (Elavil), Desipramine (Norpamin)
	MAO inhibitors	Phenelzine (Nardil)
	Selective serotonin reuptake inhibitors	Fluoxetine (Prozac), Paroxetine (Paxil), Sertraline (Zoloft)
Mania	Mood stabilizers	Lithium (Lithonate)
Anxiety	Anxiolitics	Benzodiazepines (Valium, Xanax)
	Antidepressants	Fluoxetine (Prozac)

medications can be so substantial that some researchers are beginning to use them as the treatment of choice for first-episode psychosis (Sanger et al., 1999).

Many of the first drugs for treating mental illness were discovered accidentally, when physicians and researchers using them to treat one medical condition noticed that they altered another. For example, when J. F. Cade, an Australian researcher, gave animals a lithium salt as part of his research into animal metabolism and behavior, he noticed that the animals became calm and quiet. Further investigation showed that lithium was an effective treatment for bipolar disorder.

Most psychotropic medications act at neurotransmitter sites (Figure 16.8). Some inhibit overactive neurotransmitters or receptors that are overly sensitive and hence lead neurons to fire too frequently. One way they can do this is by "locking up" the postsynaptic membrane, binding with receptors that would naturally bind with the neurotransmitter (Figure 16.8a). This process renders the postsynaptic neuron unlikely to fire as frequently or at all.

Other medications have the opposite effect, increasing the action of neurotransmitters that are underactive or in short supply. They may do this in various ways. Some medications prevent the neurotransmitter from being taken back into the presynaptic membrane, causing the neurotransmitter to remain in the synapse and hence to facilitate further firing (Figure 16.8b). Others prevent the neurotransmitter from being broken down once it has returned to the presynaptic neuron, leading to continued availability of the neurotransmitter at the synapse (Figure 16.8c).

Recent theories suggest that some psychotropic medications, particularly for depression, may act at the *intracellular* level, rather than at the synapse (Duman et al., 1997). They do this by altering the way neurons process information inside the cell. Once a neurotransmitter binds with a receptor, a series of events occurs within the postsynaptic neuron that affects its rate of firing, as chemicals within the cell carry messages from the receptors to the cell's nucleus and activate the cell's DNA (Chapter 3). Much of thought and memory appears to reflect changes in the way neurons respond to chronic activation from other neurons (Chapter 6; Chapter 7). Intracellular mechanisms may help explain why some medications, particularly medications for

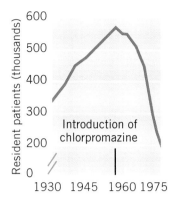

FIGURE 16.7 Impact of chlorpromazine on institutionalization. The populations of state and county psychiatric hospitals declined rapidly after the introduction of the antipsychotic medication chlorpromazine. *Source:* Adapted from Davis, 1985.

(*a*) Decreases neural transmission by "locking up" receptor sites

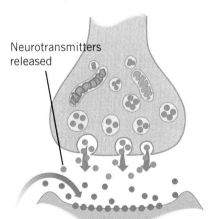

Drug binds with receptors to prevent them from being activated by the neurotransmitters in the synapse.

(*b*) Increases neural transmission by blocking reuptake

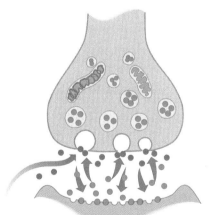

Drug blocks neurotransmitters from being taken back into the presynaptic membrane, leaving the neurotransmitters in the synapse longer.

(*c*) Increases neural transmission by blocking breakdown of neurotransmitters in synaptic vesicles

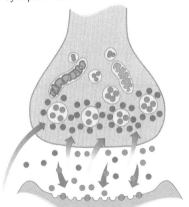

Drug prevents the neurotransmitter returning from the synapse from being broken down for storage, which keeps it available at the synapse.

FIGURE 16.8 The therapeutic action of psychotropic medications. This figure depicts three neural mechanisms by which psychotropic medications can reduce symptoms. Psychotropics can decrease neural transmission of overactive neurotransmitters (*a*), or increase neural transmission where neurotransmitters are depleted (*b*, *c*).

depression, only begin to have an effect weeks after the person starts to take them: Long-term cellular changes take time to occur.

Not all the beneficial effects of psychotropic medications stem from their molecular structure. Because a patient's expectation of cure is influenced by personal and cultural beliefs about the causes and treatment of psychological problems, even drugs or herbal remedies that have no known physiological action can promote health simply because the person has faith that they will work (Torrey, 1986). In the same way, placebo effects (Chapter 2) can boost the power of medications that are biologically efficacious. Thus, chemical agents can affect the mind via the brain or they can affect the brain via the mind.

Although psychotropic medications are clearly beneficial and life-saving in many instances, they are not without their downside. Some psychotropic medications lead to both physical and psychological dependence (Julien, 1998). Barbiturates, for example, which were a key treatment for anxiety disorders for years, can lead to physical addictions, such that termination of the medication can lead to hallucinations and problems with sleeping. Furthermore, because barbiturates reduce anxiety and, thus, more pleasant feelings, they can lead to psychological dependence and, in the extreme, abuse of the drug. Drugs such as lithium can produce other side effects, including gastrointestinal problems such as nausea and vomiting (Julien, 1998). Lithium is also associated, in some patients, with memory impairments and weight gain. Indeed, "up to 30 percent of patients [on lithium] become frankly obese, a prevalence of obesity three times greater than in the general population" (Silverstone & Romans, 1996, cited in Julien, 1998). Not surprisingly, the experience of such side effects leads many people simply to stop taking the medication.

INTERIM SUMMARY

Psychotropic medications act on the brain to affect mental processes. Most psychotropic medications act at neurotransmitter sites. Some bind with postsynaptic receptors, hence preventing neural transmission. Others increase the action of underactive or depleted neurotransmitters, often by preventing them from being taken back into the presynaptic membrane or preventing them from being stored once they do return. Others act at the intracellular level.

Antipsychotic Medications

Medications used to treat schizophrenia and other acute psychotic states are called **antipsychotic medications**. They are also sometimes called major tranquilizers because many are highly sedating, but their efficacy is not reducible to their tranquilizing effect. Antipsychotic medications generally inhibit dopamine, which has been implicated in positive symptoms such as hallucinations. They are typically much less effective for negative symptoms such as flattened affect and interpersonal difficulties (e.g., Goff et al., 1999).

Antipsychotic medications are essential in treating schizophrenia and other psychotic states (such as psychosis that often accompanies mania). However, most of them have significant side effects. Many of these side effects reflect the fact that dopamine exists in multiple regions of the brain and serves many functions. Thus, blocking its overactivity in one region may inhibit its normal functions in another. The most serious side effect is a movement disorder called **tardive dyskinesia** (*tardive*, meaning late or tardy in onset, and *dyskinesia*, meaning disorder of movement), in which the patient develops ***involuntary twitching, typically involving the tongue, face, and neck***. According to one theory, lowering the amounts of dopamine in the brain leads receptors in motor circuits that require dopamine for normal functioning to become supersensitive. As a result, the neurons in those regions fire too readily.

Tardive dyskinesia does not occur in all patients, and it is more likely to arise in people who have taken antipsychotic medications for many years (Sweet et al., 1995), but it is unpredictable and largely irreversible. Between 30 and 40 percent of patients in a long-term ward of a Montreal hospital who had received antipsychotics on the average for 20 years showed symptoms of tardive dyskinesia (Yassa et al., 1990). Because the side effects of prolonged administration can be so severe, and because antipsychotics are often ineffective for treating the more chronic negative symptoms, they are usually prescribed in high doses during acute phases and lower doses between episodes (Gilbert et al., 1995). The discovery of multiple types of dopamine receptors in different parts of the brain, however, is leading to the development of drugs that target specific dopamine receptors and avoid tampering with others, which will likely lead to breakthroughs in the treatment of schizophrenia (e.g., Gurevich et al., 1997).

Antidepressant and Mood-Stabilizing Medications

Particularly for patients with severe depressions that include physiological symptoms such as sleep disturbance or loss of appetite, antidepressants can also be very effective (Maj et al., 1992; Montgomery, 1994a, 1994b). **Antidepressant medications** *increase the amount of norepinephrine, serotonin, or both in synapses and appear to reduce depression by correcting for depletion of these neurotransmitters*.

Types of Antidepressants   Several different types of medication have proven effective in treating depression. The **tricyclic antidepressants**, named for their molecular structure, *block reuptake of serotonin and norepinephrine into the presynaptic membrane*. In other words, they force the neurotransmitter to stay in the synapse longer, compensating for depleted neurotransmitters.

Double-blind studies, in which neither the patient nor the physician knows whether the patient is taking a tricyclic drug or a placebo (Chapter 2), have found improvement rates of 70 to 80 percent compared to 20 to 40 percent for the placebo (Maj et al., 1992). Frequently prescribed tricyclics include trazadone (trade name Desyrel), amitriptyline (Elavil), and desipramine (Norpramin).

Some patients who do not respond well to tricyclics respond to monoamine oxidase (MAO) inhibitors. **MAO inhibitors** *keep the chemical MAO from breaking down neurotransmitter substances in the presynaptic neuron, and thus make more neurotransmitter available for release into the synapse*. MAO inhibitors are more effective than tricyclics in treating many depressed patients with personality disorders, particularly borderline personality disorders, but physicians rarely prescribe them before trying other antidepressants because they require substantial food restrictions (e.g., no red wine or cheese) and can be lethal if used in a suicide attempt (Cowdry & Gardner, 1988; Gunderson, 1986).

Selective serotonin reuptake inhibitors (SSRIs) are *antidepressants designed to target serotonin*, so named because they prevent the reuptake of serotonin into the presynaptic neuron and hence keep the neurotransmitter active at the synapse longer. SSRIs have fewer side effects than other antidepressants and are better tolerated over prolonged periods. As a result, they are now the first-line medical treatment against not only depression but a variety of other disorders, with sales over $6 billion per year in the United States alone (Schatzberg, 2000). The best known SSRI is fluoxetine (Prozac), which has vastly expanded the patient population for whom antidepressants are prescribed. Although the side effects for most of the SSRIs are milder than other antidepressants, the one important exception is sexual dysfunction, which often occurs with these medications (e.g., Michelson et al., 2000).

Serotonin reuptake inhibitors (such as Prozac, Paxil, and Zoloft) can help some people with chronic low-grade depression, so that people with severe depression are no longer the only candidates for antidepressants (Julien, 1998; Kramer, 1993; Levkovitz et al., 2002). Furthermore, patients with chronic bouts of depression typically have a smaller hippocampus than patients with intermittent bouts of depression. SSRIs such as Prozac have been shown to protect the brain from the detrimental effects of depression on the hippocampus (Sheline, 2003; Sheline et al., 2002). On the other hand, the routine use of psychotropic medications for people who are not seriously depressed has drawn fire from many critics, particularly when prescribed by primary care physicians, who are not trained in psychiatry or psychology and often prescribe medications without exploring potential psychosocial causes or treatments.

For bipolar disorder, **lithium** *is the treatment of choice,* although antiseizure medications are often effective for manic patients who are not responsive to it (Goodwin & Ghaemi, 1997). Between 30 and 80 percent of bipolar patients respond to lithium, depending on the sample; however, relapse rates range from 50 to 90 percent (Baldessarini et al., 2000; Gershon & Soares, 1997). Lithium acts relatively slowly, often taking three or four weeks before taking effect. In the acute phases of mania psychiatrists therefore usually treat patients simultaneously with antipsychotics to clear their thinking until the lithium "kicks in." Although researchers are still tracking down the mechanisms by which lithium works, research suggests that lithium may operate by altering intracellular mechanisms that carry signals from the receptor to the nucleus of the postsynaptic neuron (Manji et al., 1995).

Perhaps the most serious side effect of medications for both unipolar and bipolar depression is that they can be lethal if used for suicide attempts. Prescribing potentially toxic drugs to depressed people obviously carries risks of overdose although the risk is lower with the SSRIs than with previously developed antidepressants. Antidepressants can also have minor side effects, including weight gain, dry mouth, sweating, blurred vision, or decreased sexual desire. The side effects of lithium are usually mild compared to the potentially disastrous effects of the disorder or the side effects of antipsychotic medications; patients may experience a fine tremor, weight gain, nausea, and lightheadedness. However, lithium levels in the bloodstream have to be monitored carefully, both because the drug is highly toxic and because if levels drop, the patient may be at risk for relapse.

Antianxiety Medications

Antianxiety medications called **benzodiazepines** *can be useful for short-term treatment of anxiety symptoms,* as with Jenny, who experienced a brief period of intense anxiety. The earliest drug of this class that was widely prescribed was diazepam (Valium); it has since been supplanted by other medications such as alprazolam (Xanax) that are more effective in treating panic symptoms.

Psychiatrists are now more likely to prescribe antidepressants (particularly SSRIs) for anxiety, particularly for panic disorder (Broocks et al., 1998; Varia & Rauscher, 2002). Although the impact on depression generally takes three to four weeks, anxiety symptoms usually respond to antidepressants within a week. The notion of prescribing antidepressants to treat anxiety seems counterintuitive; however, many neurotransmitters have multiple functions. Neurotransmitter systems are also interdependent, so that altering one can lead to widespread effects on others.

Antianxiety medications are not without their drawbacks. Patients can become both physiologically and psychologically dependent on them. Many fear that if they get off the medications they will become crippled with panic again. They may in fact be right: The relapse rate after discontinuing antianxiety drugs is very high (see Mavissakalian & Perel, 1992). Nevertheless, some anxiety symptoms such as recurrent panic attacks can be so unpleasant or debilitating that medications are in order, particularly in combination with psychotherapy or until exposure-based therapies have been initiated.

Making Connections

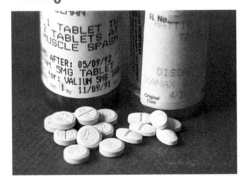

Benzodiazepines, such as Valium and Xanax, can be helpful in short-term relief of anxiety. They work by increasing the activity of GABA, a neurotransmitter that inhibits activation throughout the nervous system. Thus, by increasing the activity of an inhibitory neurotransmitter, they reduce anxiety (Chapter 3).

Electroconvulsive Therapy and Psychosurgery

Two other biological treatments that were more widely used in previous eras and are now generally seen as treatments of last resort are electroconvulsive therapy and psychosurgery.

Electroconvulsive Therapy   **Electroconvulsive therapy (ECT)**, *also known as electroshock therapy, is currently used in the treatment of severe depression.* Patients lie on an insulated cart or bed and are anesthetized. Electrodes are then placed on their heads to administer an electric shock strong enough to induce a seizure. The mechanisms by which ECT works are not known, although its efficacy appears to require strong enough doses of electricity to produce a seizure (Krystal et al., 2000). (Researchers are now exploring another, less traumatic way of altering electrical activity in the brain—the use of powerful magnets—to try to achieve similar effects; see George et al., 1999.)

The horrifying idea of deliberately shocking a person conjures up images of unscrupulous or overworked mental health professionals using technology to control unruly patients. For many years ECT was clearly used irresponsibly, but today it can be the only hope for some patients with crippling depression and can sometimes be extremely effective. Studies have found that ECT is more effective than antidepressant drugs in treating very severe cases of depression, particularly delusional depressions, which have psychotic features (Goodwin & Roy-Byrne, 1987). As with other therapies for depression, however, relapse rates are high, sometimes requiring readministration a few months later (Weiner & Coffey, 1988). ECT can also sometimes be useful in treating mania (Hanin et al., 1993), but it is ineffective for schizophrenia, for which it was once widely used (and abused). The main side effect of ECT is memory loss. This has been lessened, however, by the discovery that applying electrodes to only one hemisphere of the brain is virtually as effective as the bilateral procedures that were once common (Abrams et al., 1989).

Those who consider "shock therapy" a brutal invention of technologically developed Western societies are actually incorrect in another respect. Hieroglyphics on the walls of Egyptian tombs depict the use of electrical fish (such as eels) to numb emotional states, and a number of Greek writers, including Aristotle, refer to the practice. A medieval priest living in Ethiopia observed the use of electrical catfish to drive the devil out of the human body (Torrey, 1986).

Psychosurgery   Another procedure once widely practiced is **psychosurgery**, *brain surgery to reduce psychological symptoms.* Like ECT, psychosurgery is an ancient practice. Fossilized remains from thousands of years ago show holes bored in the skulls, presumably to allow demons to escape from the heads of mentally ill individuals, much the same as in some preliterate cultures studied by anthropologists today.

The most widely practiced Western psychosurgery technique was *lobotomy*, which involved severing tissue in a cerebral lobe, usually the frontal (Valenstein, 1988). Before the development of psychotropic drugs, some clinicians, frustrated in trying to treat the mentally ill patients who jammed the state institutions, embraced psychosurgery as a way of calming patients who were violent or otherwise difficult to manage. One of the leaders of psychosurgery in the middle of the last century, a psychiatrist named Walter Freeman, traveled the United States demonstrating his technique, which involved inserting a cutting tool resembling an ice pick into the socket of each eye and rotating it to cut the fibers at the base of the frontal lobes.

Lobotomy reached its peak between 1949 and 1952, during which time neurosurgeons performed about 5000 a year in the United States alone (Valenstein, 1986, 1988). Unfortunately, the procedure rarely cured psychosis (Robin, 1958) and often had devastating side effects. Patients became apathetic and lost self-control and the ability to think abstractly (Freeman, 1959), as portrayed in the popular book and film,

Making Connections

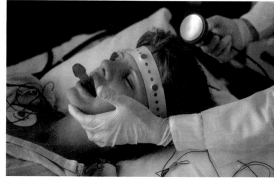

An Italian neurologist named Ugo Cerletti was the first person to use electroconvulsive shock therapy. Experimenting with animals first, Cerletti fine-tuned a device that would allow him to deliver electric shocks to induce convulsions. His first work with humans involved individuals with schizophrenia, who showed marked improvements following the procedure.

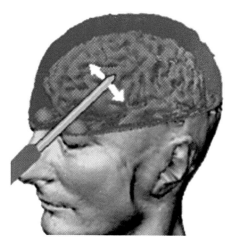

The "ice-pick lobotomy" technique developed by Walter Freeman, although less time-consuming than traditional methods of lobotomy, nevertheless was met with strong criticism by both the lay pubic and medical professionals.

One Flew over the Cuckoo's Nest. Recently, however, psychiatrists have been experimenting with a much more limited surgical procedure to treat severely debilitating cases of obsessive–compulsive disorder that do not respond to other forms of treatment (Baer et al., 1995; Jenike et al., 1991).

INTERIM SUMMARY

Antipsychotic medications treat schizophrenia and other acute psychotic states. **Antidepressant medications** can be useful for treating multiple disorders, particularly depression and anxiety disorders. **Lithium** is the treatment of choice for bipolar disorder. Both **benzodiazepines** and antidepressants can be useful for treating anxiety. **Electroconvulsive therapy (ECT)**, also known as electroshock therapy, is currently used as a last resort in the treatment of severe depression. Another treatment of last resort, now primarily used for severe cases of obsessive–compulsive disorder, is **psychosurgery**.

Evaluating Psychological Treatments

Over the course of any given year, roughly 10 to 15 percent of the population in the United States will have sought help for psychological problems (Kessler et al., 1999). But how well do these treatments work?

Pharmacotherapy

The benefits of pharmacotherapy for many disorders are well established. Antipsychotic medication is essential in the treatment of schizophrenia, although full recovery is unusual. Lithium and other mood-stabilizing drugs are similarly indispensable for bipolar disorder, although some bipolar patients remain chronically unstable and most are vulnerable to relapse. In addition, as we have seen, medication can be useful in treating many anxiety and mood disorders, particularly major depression, panic, and obsessive–compulsive disorder (e.g., Thase & Kupfer, 1996; Quitkin et al., 2000).

A major problem associated with biological treatments is the high relapse rate when pharmacotherapy is terminated. One way to minimize this drawback is to continue the medication for a considerable length of time after the treatment has succeeded, usually at a lower dosage (see Montgomery, 1994a, 1994b). As shown in Figure 16.9, most people who experience a major depressive episode will experience another within five years, but continued preventive use of antidepressants can temper the tendency to relapse (Maj et al., 1992). Another way to minimize relapse is to combine medication with psychotherapy, which can be effective in the treatment of many disorders, such as major depression, bipolar disorder, and schizophrenia (Frank et al., 1999; Rosenheck et al., 1999; Scott, 2001; Thase, 2000).

Psychotherapy

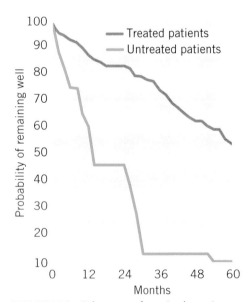

FIGURE 16.9 Relapse rates for major depression with and without medication. The figure shows the effects of the preventive use of antidepressant medication on lithium. Virtually all untreated patients relapsed within three years. Preventive use of medication was clearly helpful, although a substantial number of patients (46 percent) nevertheless relapsed by five years. *Source:* Maj et al., 1992.

People who enter into psychotherapy also fare considerably better than those who try to heal themselves (Parloff et al., 1986; Snyder & Ingram, 2000). Researchers have demonstrated this using a statistical technique called **meta-analysis**, which *aggregates, or combines, the findings of diverse studies*, to yield a quantified estimate of the average effect of psychotherapy on the average patient. Beginning with a pioneering study in the late 1970s (Smith & Glass, 1977), meta-analyses have shown that the average patient who receives psychotherapy is essentially 25 percent better off than the average control subject, as shown in Figure 16.10 (see Landman & Dawes, 1982). In other words, the bell-shaped curve for subjects who have been treated is shifted in the direction of mental health, so that a person in the 50th percentile of mental health in the group receiving treatment would be in the 75th percentile of subjects if now placed in the control group. This is a substantial shift, equivalent to the difference in reading skill between a third-grader who goes to school and one who stays home and gets no instruction for a year (Lambert et al., 1986).

The Efficacy of Specific Therapies How successful are the specific psychotherapies we have examined? The answer is more complicated than it seems because of many possible ways to think about success (see Haaga & Stiles, 2000; Kendall et al., 1999). For example, a researcher could measure average improvement, percentage of patients who improve, or relapse rate. One treatment might lead to 90 percent improvement but in only 50 percent of patients, whereas another could reduce symptoms by only 50 percent but do so in 90 percent of patients. Still another treatment might be very effective for most people but slow and costly. Another issue is the time frame of assessment of outcome. A long-term follow-up study of marital therapy, for example, found no differences initially between outcome of insight-oriented psychodynamic treatment and behavioral marital therapy. At four-year follow-up, however, only 3 percent of couples treated psychodynamically were divorced, compared with 38 percent of those treated with behavioral techniques (Snyder et al., 1991).

The efficacy of cognitive–behavioral therapy is much better established than any other form of psychotherapy, especially for anxiety disorders (Barlow et al., 1998; Chambless & Gillis, 1993; Stanley et al., 2003; Zinbarg et al., 1992). Some of the most impressive data have come from cognitive–behavioral treatments of panic (Barlow, 2002) and PTSD (Foa et al., 1999). These treatments involve exposing patients to feared thoughts, images, and feelings as well as helping them avoid ways of thinking and behaving that perpetuate their anxiety. Considerable research has also demonstrated the efficacy of cognitive therapy in treating depression (Hollon et al., 1993; Thase et al., 1991), eating disorders (Agras et al., 2000), and multiple other conditions (Otto et al., 2003).

With the exception of a few promising studies (Bateman & Fonagy, 1999; Blatt et al., 1994; Freedman et al., 1999; Wallerstein, 1989), empirically sound studies of long-term psychodynamic treatments are rare. Studies of short-term psychodynamic psychotherapies are much more common (Crits-Christoph, 1992; Piper et al., 1999; Shefler et al., 1995). Humanistic and other treatments (such as family therapy) are, like psychodynamic psychotherapies, less empirically grounded than cognitive–behavioral therapies. Rogers, however, conducted a large number of studies of client-centered therapy 40 years ago, and some treatments drawing on his work are showing promising results (e.g., Greenberg & Safran, 1990; Paivio & Greenberg, 1995). For example, motivational interviewing is an approach to helping patients with alcoholism overcome their ambivalence about giving up drinking that combines a supportive, empathic stance with a realistic appraisal of the impact of drinking on the person's life (Yahne & Miller, 1999; Stephens et al., 2000). One of the most distinctive features of motivational interviewing is its brevity: Research suggests that just four sessions can be as effective as treatments that last three times as long (see Babor et al., 1999).

Comparing Psychotherapies Although advocates of different treatments typically argue for the superiority of their own brand, most research finds that, with a few notable exceptions (mostly in the anxiety disorders), different therapies yield comparable effects (Lambert & Bergin, 1994; Litt et al., 2003; Smith & Glass, 1977). This is certainly counterintuitive. For example, how could a treatment based on the view that psychopathology stems from unconscious fears or conflicts have the same effect as one that focuses on behaviors or cognitions?

Common Factors One explanation is that, alongside specific mechanisms (such as altering defenses, exposing patients to threatening stimuli, or inhibiting negative au-

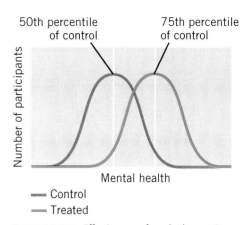

FIGURE 16.10 Effectiveness of psychotherapy. Researchers combined the findings of 375 studies to assess the effectiveness of psychotherapy. Subjects treated with psychotherapy were, on the average, substantially better off than untreated control subjects. *Source:* Adapted from Smith & Glass, 1977.

tomatic thoughts), most approaches share **common factors**—*shared elements that produce positive outcomes* (Arnkoff et al., 1993; Frank, 1978; Weinberger, 1995). Such factors include empathy, a warm relationship between therapist and client, and a client's sense of hope or efficacy in coping with the problem (Grencavage & Norcross, 1990).

Methodological Challenges in Comparing Treatments   Other explanations are methodological (see Kendall, 1999; Kendall et al., 1999). Recruiting subjects and training therapists to deliver treatments in standardized ways are very difficult, so that most studies have relatively small samples, typically around 15 to 20 patients in each experimental condition. Statistically, that is about a quarter of the number required to detect real differences among treatments.

Another complication in comparing treatments is experimenter bias: One of the best predictors of the relative efficacy of one treatment over another in any given study is the strength of the investigator's commitment to that treatment (Smith et al., 1980). A recent study found that experimenter allegiance—that is, the experimenter's preference for one treatment or another prior to conducting the study—accounted for over 60 percent of the differences between experimental conditions in even well-conducted double-blind studies, for reasons that have been difficult to detect (Luborsky et al., 1997).

Making matters more complicated, patients differ in their response to different treatments (Beutler, 1991). Even patients who share a diagnosis, such as depression or alcoholism, vary substantially in other respects. Comparing mean outcome scores across treatment groups may thus obscure the fact that different treatments are successful with different patients (see Litt et al., 1992).

The NIMH Collaborative Study   The most definitive evidence yet collected about the relative efficacy of different treatments comes from a nonpartisan study of depression conducted by the National Institutes of Mental Health (NIMH) (Elkin et al., 1989). The NIMH project studied the treatment of 250 patients, a very large sample compared to most prior studies. It compared three treatments for patients with major depression: cognitive therapy, interpersonal therapy (a short-term offshoot of psychodynamic psychotherapy), and imipramine (an antidepressant) combined with supportive clinical management (regular meetings with a concerned physician). A fourth group (the control group) received a placebo with supportive clinical management. The purpose of giving supportive management to the latter two groups, particularly the placebo group, was to determine whether the effectiveness of psychotherapy is reducible simply to providing regular and kind attention. The study was conducted at several treatment sites, and collaborators from different perspectives administered treatments according to standardized treatment manuals in order to minimize any biases imposed by investigator allegiances.

For all intents and purposes, the three treatments fared equally well. At the end of treatment, none of the treatments worked significantly better than the others. A more sobering picture emerged, however, when patients were followed up two years later. Most patients were less depressed than when they began treatment, but relapse was common across all groups, and only a minority met criteria for full recovery (Shea et al., 1992). In fact, a recent meta-analysis found similar results across studies of depression: Most treatments tested in the laboratory initially work for about half of patients, but at 18-month to two-year follow-up, only half of these patients—or 25 percent of patients who enter treatment—remain well (Westen & Morrison, 2001).

Efficacy versus Effectiveness: The Consumer Reports Study   Recently researchers have distinguished between efficacy and effectiveness studies of psychotherapy (Seligman, 1995). **Efficacy studies** *assess treatment outcome under highly controlled conditions*: random assignment of patients to different treatment or control groups, careful training of therapists to adhere to a manual that prescribes the ways they should address patients' problems, standardized length of treatment, and so forth. **Effectiveness studies** *assess treatment outcome under less controlled circumstances*, as practiced by clinicians in the field. Efficacy studies emphasize internal validity—the validity of the experimental design—and allow researchers to draw strong causal inferences about the effects of receiving one kind of treatment or another (Chapter 2). Effectiveness studies emphasize external validity—that is, applicability of the therapy to patients in everyday clinical practice.

Sparked in part by the development of practice guidelines by other organizations that tended to ignore the data for the efficacy of psychotherapy (giving preference to medical interventions), the Division of Psychotherapy (Division 12) of the American Psychological Association created a task force that aimed to develop a list of treatments for which strong evidence of efficacy exists. These treatments are generally referred to as empirically validated or empirically supported therapies (ESTs) (Kendall, 1998). The goal of the task force was to guide clinical practice based on empirical data rather than on each clinician's own experience and judgment.

The task force report, published in 1995, has stirred considerable controversy, for a number of reasons. On the one hand, it challenged clinicians who practice without any guidance from controlled studies to base their practice on science. On the other, it placed greater emphasis on efficacy than effectiveness studies, because efficacy studies have more rigorous designs and are far more numerous. Indeed, many researchers have called for psychotherapy practice and training to be limited to treatments that have demonstrated efficacy in randomized controlled trials (Calhoun et al., 1998; Chambless & Hollon, 1998).

The same year, Martin Seligman published an equally controversial article on the findings of a large *Consumer Reports* survey on the effectiveness of psychotherapy (1995). Seligman described how this survey, involving 2900 respondents who had undergone psychotherapy, led him to reverse his opinion on the superiority of short-term treatments developed and tested in efficacy studies. Perhaps the most important finding of the *Consumer Reports* study concerned length of treatment: The most successful treatments—those in which respondents reported the greatest decline in symptoms, improvement in overall level of functioning, and general satisfaction—were psychotherapies lasting more than two years. In fact, degree of consumer satisfaction was directly related to length of treatment (Figure 16.11). These findings matched those of other effectiveness studies (Bovasso et al., 1999; Howard et al., 1986, 1994), but they drew fire from many researchers because of methodological problems inherent in naturalistic and correlational studies (Chapter 2).

The current controversy over empirically supported therapies, efficacy versus effectiveness, and the *Consumer Reports* study reflects in some respects a tension that has long existed between clinicians and researchers (Chapter 1). Despite a burgeoning experimental literature on psychotherapy outcome, clinicians tend to practice without empirical guidance (Beutler et al., 1995), dismissing research findings as irrelevant to their practice. Conversely, researchers often view clinicians as undisciplined and unscientific in their thinking, which limits the kind of cross-talk that might foster mutual feedback and learning on both sides.

Nevertheless, there are some very important and suggestive findings: Cognitive–behavioral treatments for anxiety can be highly efficacious for anxiety disorders, particularly simple phobia, social phobia, panic, obsessive–compulsive disorder, and PTSD. Longer-term treatments may be more suitable for multisymptom problems seen by many clinicians in the community, particularly those that involve repetitive interpersonal patterns, which sometimes can take weeks or months to pinpoint, let alone to target for change. These patterns may explain why effectiveness studies support longer treatments. But clinicians are a long way from knowing which patients with PTSD or bulimia—such as those with sexual abuse histories or troubled early attachment relationships—are likely to respond or not respond to different interventions.

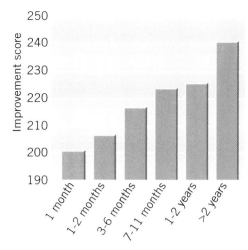

FIGURE 16.11 The *Consumer Reports* study. Like prior research on the relation between length and efficacy of treatment, the *Consumer Reports* study found a strong association between length and effectiveness. Patients treated for one to two months and three to six months reported considerably less help from, and satisfaction with, psychotherapy. Satisfaction was measured on a 300-point scale, including reduction of specific problems, general satisfaction with the therapist and the job he or she did, and global life improvement. *Source:* Seligman, 1995, p. 968.

Empirical questions—such as what works and for whom—require empirical answers (Roth et al., 1996). Researchers and therapists need not abandon scientific methods to assess a complex clinical phenomenon such as response to psychotherapy. The key is to adapt these methods and use multiple research designs to try to converge on the most accurate conclusions (see Borkovec & Castonguay, 1998; Goldfried & Wolfe, 1998). When internal and external validity sharply collide, as they have in psychotherapy research, the best strategy is not to err consistently on one side or the other but to conduct studies that err on each side, with some aiming to assess causality with the rigor of tightly controlled experimentation and others using quasi-experimental and correlational designs (Chapter 2) that sacrifice an ounce of control for a pound of generalizability.

INTERIM SUMMARY

Pharmacotherapy is essential for some disorders (such as schizophrenia and bipolar disorder) and can be extremely helpful for others (such as major depression and anxiety disorders). Relapse rates, however, are high when medication is discontinued, and complete cures are uncommon for most disorders. Research has provided substantial evidence for the utility of psychotherapy for many disorders, with the most successful treatments thus far being cognitive–behavioral treatments for anxiety disorders. An important distinction is between **efficacy studies** that assess treatment outcome under controlled experimental conditions and **effectiveness studies** that assess treatment as practiced by clinicians in the community.

Summary

Psychodynamic Therapies

1. Psychodynamic therapy is predicated on the notion that **insight**—understanding one's own psychological processes—is important for therapeutic change, as are aspects of **therapeutic alliance**.

2. **Free association** is a technique designed to explore associational networks and unconscious processes. Another central element of psychodynamic therapy is the **interpretation** of conflicts, defenses, compromise formations, and transference reactions. **Transference** in psychotherapy refers to the experience of thoughts, feelings, fears, wishes, and conflicts from past relationships, particularly childhood, in the patient's relationship with the therapist.

3. The main contemporary forms of psychodynamic treatment are **psychoanalysis** (which is very intensive and long term) and **psychodynamic psychotherapy** (which relies on the same principles but is more conversational).

Cognitive–Behavioral Therapies

4. **Cognitive–behavioral** therapies are relatively short term and directive, and focus on specific symptoms. They rely on operant and classical conditioning as well as cognitive–social and more strictly cognitive interventions.

5. In **systematic desensitization**, the patient gradually approaches feared stimuli mentally while in a relaxed state. **Exposure techniques**, like desensitization, rely on classical conditioning, but they present the patient with the actual phobic stimulus in real life rather than having the patient merely imagine it. Therapies based on operant conditioning apply rewards and punishments to modify unwanted behavior.

6. In **participatory modeling**, the therapist not only models the desired behavior but also gradually encourages the patient to participate in it. **Skills training** teaches the procedures necessary to accomplish relevant goals; **social skills training** helps people with specific deficits in interpersonal functioning.

7. **Cognitive therapy** attempts to replace dysfunctional cognitions with more useful and accurate ones. Ellis, who developed **rational–emotive behavior therapy**, proposed an **ABC theory of psychopathology**; A refers to activating conditions, B to belief systems, and C to emotional consequences. Beck's cognitive therapy similarly proposes that correcting cognitive distortions is crucial to therapeutic change.

Humanistic, Group, and Family Therapies

8. **Humanistic therapies** focus on the phenomenal (experiential) world of the patient. **Gestalt** therapy emphasizes an awareness of feelings. Rogers's **client-centered therapy** aims at helping individuals experience themselves as they really are, through therapeutic empathy and **unconditional positive regard**.

9. Group, family, and marital therapies treat multiple individuals simultaneously. **Group therapy** focuses on both individual dynamics and group process. A variation on group therapy is the **self-help group**, which is not guided by a professional. **Family therapy** presumes that the roots of symptoms lie in the structure of the family system, so that therapy should target family interaction patterns. A variant of family therapy, **marital** or **couples therapy**, treats the couple as a unit and may employ systems, psychodynamic, behavioral, or cognitive–behavioral techniques.

Biological Treatments

10. The aim of biological treatments is to alter the functioning of the brain. Pharmacotherapy, the use of medications to treat psychological disorders, is the major type of biological treatment.

11. **Psychotropic medications** affect mental processes by acting at neurotransmitter sites or at the intracellular level. **Antipsychotic medications** are useful in treating psychotic symptoms, particularly the positive symptoms of schizophrenia. **Tricyclic antidepressants, MAO inhibitors**, and **selective serotonin reuptake inhibitors (SSRIs)** can be useful in treating depression, while **lithium** is the treatment of choice for bipolar disorder. Both **ben-**zodiazepines (antianxiety medications) and certain kinds of antidepressants can be useful in treating anxiety.

12. **Electroconvulsive therapy (ECT)**, or shock therapy, is currently used as a last resort in the treatment of severe depression. Although **psychosurgery** was once widely practiced and abused, today researchers are experimenting with limited forms of psychosurgery as a last resort for obsessive–compulsive disorder.

Evaluating Psychological Treatments

13. Pharmacotherapy is well established as an effective treatment for schizophrenia, bipolar disorder, and many other forms of psychopathology. The two major problems with pharmacotherapy are relapse rates and side effects.

14. Researchers have found that all psychotherapies are relatively effective, although some treatments are superior for some disorders to others. Cognitive–behavioral treatments have received the most empirical attention and support in **efficacy studies** (carefully controlled experimental studies with relatively homogeneous samples and highly standardized therapeutic procedures). The long-term **effectiveness** (usefulness in clinical settings with a more heterogeneous population) of short-term treatments is more controversial than that for long-term treatments.

Key Terms

ABC theory of psychopathology 593
antidepressant medications 605
antipsychotic medications 604
automatic thoughts 593
behavioral analysis 588
benzodiazepines 606
client-centered therapy 596
cognitive–behavioral 588
cognitive therapy 593
common factors 610
effectiveness studies 611
efficacy studies 610
electroconvulsive therapy (ECT) 607
empty-chair technique 595
exposure techniques 590
family therapy 597
flooding 590
free association 584
genogram 598
Gestalt therapy 595
graded exposure 590
group process 596
group therapy 596
humanistic therapies 595
insight 584
interpretation 585
lithium 606
MAO inhibitors 605
marital or couples therapy 598
meta-analysis 608
negative reciprocity 598
participatory modeling 592
psychoanalysis 586
psychodynamic psychotherapy 586
psychosurgery 607
psychotherapy integration 600
psychotropic medications 602
rational–emotive behavior therapy 593
resistance 585
response prevention 591
selective serotonin reuptake inhibitors (SSRIs) 605
self-help group 597
skills training 592
social skills training 593
systematic desensitization 589
tardive dyskinesia 604
therapeutic alliance 584
transference 585
tricyclic antidepressants 605
unconditional positive regard 596
virtual reality exposure therapy 590

Social Cognition

When people think of prejudice, they often think of apartheid in South Africa or Ku Klux Klan rallies. We think of racial and ethnic stereotypes as beliefs people overtly hold or express about other people based on arbitrary qualities such as the color of their skin. But recent research suggests that negative stereotypes can get *under* the skin in some subtle but powerful ways.

In a remarkable series of studies, Claude Steele (1997; Steele & Aronson, 1995) has demonstrated how racial stereotypes can affect even the people who are the targets of them. In one experiment, Steele and his colleagues presented black and white Stanford undergraduates—an elite group selected for their high achievement, who should have few doubts about their intellectual abilities—difficult verbal items from the Scholastic Assessment Test (SAT) (Steele & Aronson, 1995). Black and white students were matched in SAT scores, so that both groups were of similar intellectual ability. In one condition, students were told that the test did not measure anything significant about them. In the other condition, they were told that it measured their intellect.

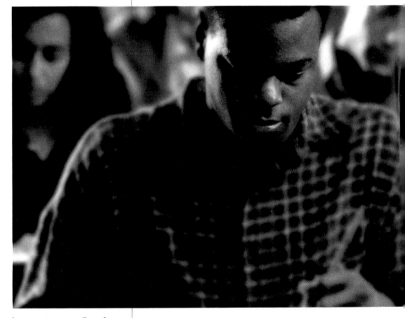

Black and white students in the first condition performed equally well, as one would expect, since they had similar SAT scores before entering college. In the second condition, however, the performance of black students dropped substantially. What happened? In the United States, blacks and whites are both exposed to negative stereotypes about the intellectual abilities of blacks. These stereotypes become part of their associative networks—their implicit understanding of race—even if they do not explicitly believe them. So when an African-American student takes a test he or she believes will be diagnostic of his of her ability, these associations become active. Particularly if scholastic success is important to the student, stereotype activation will generate performance anxiety, which can in turn lead to diminished performance.

Just how much do these processes operate in real life? In a second experiment, Steele and his colleagues once again had black and white Stanford students answer difficult SAT items. The study had two conditions, with a seemingly minor difference between them: In the demographic questionnaire students filled out before taking the test, *race* was included in one condition but not the other. The results are depicted in Figure 17.1: Priming African-American students' racial associations simply by asking them to fill in their race led to a dramatic decline in their performance.

Steele suggests that the impact of processes of this sort are profound and likely extend to groups as diverse as the Maori minority in New Zealand and the West Indian minority in Britain. They are also not limited to race: Steele and his colleagues have documented that activation of negative stereotypes about women's mathematical abilities similarly leads to declines in their performance on math tests (Spencer et al., 2002). Over time, repeatedly feeling anxious or "choking" on tests can cause some students to distance themselves from school and stop trying, leading to further declines in performance. Based

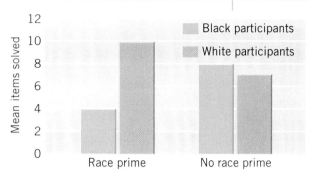

FIGURE 17.1 Performance on a difficult verbal test as a function of whether race was primed. *Source:* Steele, 1997, p. 521.

on his findings, Steele has begun testing a new intervention approach aimed at breaking this downward spiral, and initial results have been very promising.

Steele's research is a classic example of **social psychology**, *which examines the influence of social processes on the way people think, feel, and behave* (Allport, 1968). Because almost everything people do is social, the subject matter is enormous and varied. In this chapter, we focus on social cognition or interpersonal thinking. We begin with a discussion of the processes by which people make sense of each other, from the first impressions they form to enduring beliefs, including stereotypes. Next, we turn to a discussion of attitudes and how they change. This topic is of central concern to advertisers, who try to shape attitudes toward their products, as well as to politicians, who want to shape—and follow—public opinion. We conclude by considering the way people think about one of the major actors in their social worlds and one of the main directors of social cognition: themselves.

Throughout, we address one central question: To what extent do the principles of thought and memory discovered by cognitive scientists apply to *interpersonal* thought and memory? In other words, when we think about ourselves and others, do we use the same mechanisms as when we learn lists of words or theories of how chemicals combine to form molecules? Or, are social thought and memory qualitatively different?

Social Cognition

A friend has just told you she has the "perfect person" for you. She describes the individual as intelligent, witty, engaging, and articulate and thinks the two of you would make a great pair. You immediately form an impression of this person, which probably includes traits such as attractive, kind, outgoing, and generous. Now suppose instead your friend describes a potential date with precisely the same words—intelligent, witty, engaging, and articulate—but first warns that this person is a "real con artist." This time your impression probably includes less favorable traits, such as selfish, cold, and ruthless.

How does a simple phrase ("perfect for you" versus a "real con artist") change the meaning of a series of adjectives and lead to an entirely different impression? The answer lies in **social cognition**, *the processes by which people make sense of themselves, others, social interactions, and relationships; in other words, how people perceive and think about themselves and other people.*

The study of social cognition has closely followed developments in cognitive science, which has provided many of its basic models and metaphors (Macrae & Bodenhausen, 2000). Cognitive psychologists have proposed a number of different models of how information is represented in long-term memory (Chapters 6 and 7), which have guided research on social cognition (see Smith, 1998). Some models emphasize principles of association, arguing that memories are stored as interconnected nodes or *networks of association*. Activation of one node in a network spreads activation to other nodes linked to it through experience.

Other models emphasize *schemas*, organized patterns of thought that direct attention, memory, and interpretation. Activation of a schema (such as a theater schema) makes a person more likely to hear the word "play" as referring to a theater production than as something children do in a school yard. Still other models focus on *concepts*, mental representations of categories, such as birds. In these models, categorizing a novel stimulus involves comparing it to an abstract prototype (a generalized image or idea of a class of stimuli), a set of defining features (such as a list of attributes common to all birds), or a salient example or exemplar (such as a robin).

More recently, supporters of connectionist models have proposed that representations are not so much "things" that are "stored" in the brain but patterns of activation in networks of neurons (Chapter 7). According to these models, when a person sees an object, multiple neural circuits are activated simultaneously (i.e., in parallel). Somehow the system has to weed out less likely hypotheses about what the object is and settle on a solution. It does this by taking into account the multiple constraints imposed by the data.

Thus, the presence of wings on an animal in the garden activates multiple possible bird representations (robin, sparrow, etc.). At first, the brain automatically favors the most common birds, which begin with the highest level of activation because they are the most frequently encountered. However, that the bird's wings are flapping at an extremely rapid pace is inconsistent with the representation of garden-variety birds (at least in most parts of the world), so these representations are inhibited. The representation that is left "standing" at the end of this battle of competing networks is the one that receives the greatest activation: hummingbird.

These various models, or "languages," for speaking about representations all continue to be used in research on social cognition. Researchers are just beginning to sort out the extent to which they are compatible or incompatible and the conditions under which one model may be more accurate than another (Smith, 1998). As we will see, however, social psychologists are increasingly applying connectionist models to phenomena that they have previously understood using other models of representation, such as attitudes (Simon & Holyoak, 2002), the self (Humphreys & Kashima, 2002), attributions (Van-Overwalle & Van-Rooy, 2001), and stereotypes (Kunda & Thagard, 1996).

Because social cognition focuses on how people make sense of themselves, other people, and the world, it is a broad encompassing term for a number of more discrete phenomena within social psychology. Among the specific phenomena we will discuss here are person perception, stereotypes and prejudice, attribution, attitudes, and the self. As you will see, all of these constructs share in common an emphasis on cognition and the relevance of cognitive processes to social phenomena (Fiske & Taylor, 1991).

Apply & Discuss

Social cognition is all about inference in the face of ambiguity. The most important information—what is going on in another person's mind—is never directly accessible.

■ How different is this from our understanding of cars, atoms, or other nonhuman objects?

■ How can we know if we have ever really understood another person? What indicators do we have of other people's thoughts and feelings, and how fallible are these indicators?

INTERIM SUMMARY

Social cognition refers to the processes by which people make sense of themselves, others, social interactions, and relationships. Changing concepts of representation in cognitive science are beginning to lead to similar changes in the study of social cognition, such as the increasing use of connectionist models, which view representations as patterns of activation of networks of neurons operating in parallel.

Perceiving Other People

Social cognition is pervasive in everyday life, from the first impressions people form of other people to their more enduring knowledge about people, situations, and relationships.

First Impressions   Even before the field of social cognition emerged as a distinct discipline, psychologists interested in interpersonal perception studied **first impressions**, *the initial perceptions of another person that affect future beliefs about that person* (Asch, 1946). One early study demonstrated the power of first impressions. Participants read the two passages shown in Figure 17.2, but in different order

Paragraph A

Jim left the house to get some stationery. He walked out into the sun-filled street with two of his friends, basking in the sun as he walked. Jim entered the stationery store, which was full of people. Jim talked with an acquaintance while he waited for the clerk to catch his eye. On his way out, he stopped to chat with a school friend who was just coming into the store. Leaving the store, he walked toward school. On his way out he met the girl to whom he had been introduced the night before. They talked for a short while, and then Jim left for school.

Paragraph B

After school Jim left the classroom alone. Leaving the school, he started on his long walk home. The street was brilliantly filled with sunshine. Jim walked down the street on the shady side. Coming down the street toward him, he saw the pretty girl whom he had met on the previous evening. Jim crossed the street and entered a candy store. The store was crowded with students, and he noticed a few familiar faces. Jim waited quietly until the counterman caught his eye and then gave his order. Taking his drink, he sat down at a side table. When he had finished his drink he went home.

FIGURE 17.2 First impressions. In this classic study, the order of presentation of two paragraphs had a substantial influence on the impression subjects formed of Jim. *Source:* Luchins, 1957, pp. 34–35.

(Luchins, 1957). The order of the material substantially influenced participants' evaluations of the person described: Seventy-eight percent of subjects who read paragraph A first considered Jim friendly, compared to only 18 percent who read paragraph B first.

One of the early, premiere researchers in this area, Soloman Asch (1946), suggested that first impressions create a frame of reference within which everything else that is learned about a person is interpreted. Thus, if you form an initial impression that another person is hostile and cold, you will interpret anything that he subsequently does in light of the initial impression. For example, you would perceive a funny comment by this person as sarcastic rather than humorous (see also, Kelley, 1950).

A particularly salient characteristic of first impressions is physical appearance, especially attractiveness. Individuals who are physically attractive benefit from the **halo effect**, *the tendency to assume that positive qualities cluster together*. This phenomenon, also referred to as the "what is beautiful is good" stereotype, refers to the process by which people who are physically attractive are assumed to possess a number of other favorable qualities as well, such as being warm, friendly, and intelligent (Dion et al., 1972). Researchers have found halo effects for physical attractiveness across a wide array of situations. For example, more attractive people get lighter jury sentences and higher salaries (Hamermesh & Biddle, 1994; Landy & Aronson, 1969)! Researchers have also found that both young and old alike succumb to the halo effect as it relates to physical attractiveness. Rather than "outgrowing" the tendency to assign positive traits to attractive individuals, people over 65 continue to demonstrate the halo effect (Larose & Standing, 1998). Given these findings, it's little wonder that the number of people who get plastic surgery for cosmetic reasons has skyrocketed in recent years.

The positive glow of beauty, of course, has its limits (Eagly et al., 1991; Feingold, 1992; Larose & Standing, 1998). Not surprisingly, it is most powerful when people have minimal information about each other. It also extends to some traits more than to others. For example, people typically attribute greater sociability and social competence to attractive people, but they do not expect them to have more integrity, modesty, or concern for others. This latter finding, however, is culturally specific, applying primarily to individualistic cultures, such as the United States. In more collectivist cultures, such as Korea, where an emphasis is placed on group harmony and connections with others, physical attractiveness is more likely to be associated with traits such as integrity and less likely to be associated with traits such as competency (Wheeler & Kim, 1997).

An even more important variable than actual physical attractiveness, however, may be how attractive people *perceive* themselves to be. Individuals who perceive themselves as physically attractive report being more extroverted, socially comfortable, and mentally healthy than those who are less comfortable with their appearance (Feingold, 1992). Although they may simply be deluded in every realm of their lives, it is equally likely that seeing themselves as attractive produces a self-fulfilling prophecy, in which feeling attractive leads to behaviors perceived by others as attractive. In fact, research consistently finds that when people feel and act attractive, others are more likely to see them that way.

Schemas and Social Cognition   First impressions are essentially the initial schemas people form when they encounter someone for the first time. Schemas—the patterns of thought hypothesized to organize human experience (Chapters 4 and 6)—apply in the social realm as in other areas of life (see Fiske, 1993, 1995; Taylor & Crocker, 1980). We form schemas about specific people or types of people (e.g., extroverts, Hispanics, women); situations (e.g., how to behave in a classroom or restaurant); and roles and relationships (e.g., how a professor, student, parent, or friend is supposed to act) (Baldwin, 1992).

As in other cognitive domains, schemas guide information processing about people and relationships. They direct attention, organize encoding, and influence retrieval. For example, an employer who suspects that a job candidate may be exaggerating his accomplishments is likely to scrutinize his resume with special care and inquire about details that would normally not catch her eye. If later asked about the candidate, the first thing she may remember is that he described a part-time job as a courier at a radio station as a "communications consultant."

People are especially prone to recall *schema-relevant* social information—behaviors or aspects of a situation related to an activated schema (Hannigan & Tippens, 2001; Higgins & Bargh, 1987). For example, participants presented with a vignette about a librarian are likely a week later to remember information congruent with their librarian schema, such as a bun hairstyle and glasses. They are also prone to remember highly discrepant information, such as her tendency to go out dancing every night. If a librarian schema is active during encoding or retrieval, what people are *least* likely to remember are details irrelevant to the schema, such as her brown hair color.

INTERIM SUMMARY

First impressions can have an important influence on subsequent information processing. One of the features that strongly affects the way people perceive others upon first meeting is physical attractiveness. People process information about other people and relationships using schemas, which guide information processing by directing attention, organizing encoding, and influencing retrieval.

Stereotypes and Prejudice

Schemas are essential for social cognition. Without them, people would walk into every new situation without knowing how to behave or how others are likely to act. Thus, schemas can be very functional in allowing us to predict some of what will happen in particular situations. Schematic processing can go awry, however, when schemas are so rigidly or automatically applied that they preclude the processing of new information. This often occurs with **stereotypes**, *characteristics attributed to people based on their membership in specific groups*.

Stereotypes are often overgeneralized, inaccurate, and resistant to new information. Like other schemas, however, they save cognitive "energy." In other words, they simplify experience and allow individuals to categorize others quickly and effortlessly (Allport, 1954; Hamilton & Sherman, 1994; Macrae et al., 1994).

Stereotypes are intimately related to prejudice. **Prejudice**, which literally means *prejudgment*, involves *judging people based on (usually negative) stereotypes*. Prejudice involves one's thoughts or cognitions about another person or group, whereas **discrimination** refers to *behaviors that follow from negative evaluations or attitudes toward members of particular groups* (Fiske, 1998). Racial, ethnic, and religious prejudice has contributed to more bloodshed over the past century than perhaps any other force in human history. Its path of destruction can be traced through the violence and institutionalized discrimination against blacks in the United States and South Africa, to the Holocaust, the Arab–Israeli conflict, the tension between Anglophones and Francophones in Quebec, the carnage in Northern Ireland, the tribal warfare and genocide in Rwanda and other African countries, the civil war and atrocities in Bosnia, other civil wars that erupted after the breakup of the Soviet Union, and terrorist activities in the United States and throughout the world. The list is long and grim.

Since the 1930s, psychologists have proposed a number of explanations for prejudice, based on their answers to two central questions: Do the roots of prejudice lie in individual psychology (such as personality dynamics or cognition) or in social dynamics (the oppression of one group by another)? And are the causes of prejudice found in cognition or motivation—in the way people think or in the way they *want* to think? As we will see, the absence of a single widely accepted theory of prejudice probably reflects the fact that researchers have often tried to choose among these options (see Duckitt, 1992).

"It required years of labor and billions of dollars to uncover the secret of the atom. It will take still a greater investment to gain the secrets of man's irrational nature. It is easier…to smash an atom than a prejudice."

GORDON ALLPORT (1954, P. XI)

Apply & Discuss

Prejudice has a grim history, from cross-burnings and lynchings by the Ku Klux Klan (*a*) to concentration camps in Bosnia (*b*) that seemed eerily similar to the Nazi camps a half-century earlier.

▪ Are some cultures more prone to prejudice than others, or is the belief that they are simply one more example of prejudice?

▪ What social conditions give rise to prejudice, and what protects against it?

▪ Is prejudice a personality trait? Would we all become prejudiced if our brother or sister were killed in a civil war based on ethnic or religious divisions?

(*a*)

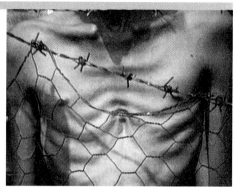

(*b*)

The Authoritarian Personality   Around the time of World War II, psychologists turned to psychodynamic theory to explain the racism that was devouring Europe and eating away at the United States.

A team of researchers who fled Nazi persecution in the middle of the last century suggested that some people are likely to be attracted to racist ideology because of their personality characteristics. Theodore Adorno and his colleagues (1950) identified what they called the **authoritarian personality**, *characterized by a tendency to hate people who are different or downtrodden*. These individuals tended to have a dominant, stern, and sometimes sadistic father and a submissive mother—interestingly, like the family of Adolph Hitler. According to the theory, children in such families fear and hate their fathers, but they would be brutally punished if they expose these feelings, so they repress them. As adults, authoritarian individuals displace or project their rage onto groups such as Jews, blacks, homosexuals, or others who do not conform to social norms.

Adorno and colleagues thought (and hoped) that authoritarian personality dynamics were limited to, or especially common in, Nazi Germany. However, their research in the United States suggested otherwise. Despite criticism of Adorno's methodology, more recent work supports many of the original findings, such as the link between this personality style and harsh parenting requiring strict obedience (Snyder & Ickes, 1985).

Subtle Racism   Recent cognitive approaches to prejudice, specifically racial prejudice, emerged from the observation that racism has changed in the last three decades, particularly in the United States. Today, overt racial discrimination against ethnic minorities is generally met with public disapproval. Gone are the days of old-fashioned racism, characterized by separate buses, drinking fountains, and bathrooms for whites and blacks. But, racism of a seemingly different kind seems to remain alive and well. Several researchers contend that new, more subtle kinds of racism exist in the wake of old-fashioned racism (Devine et al., 1991; Dovidio & Gaertner, 1993; Fiske, 1998). For example, many people claim not to be racist but in fact hold one after another attitude that "just happens" to be unfavorable to minorities, such as attitudes toward welfare or immigration (McConahay & Hough, 1976). Part of this reluctance to admit to racial attitudes in a society that now emphasizes political correctness may simply reflect people's desires not to publicly appear untoward in spite of private beliefs to the contrary.

Paralleling the change from old-fashioned racism to subtle racism is a change from old-fashioned sexism to a more subtle brand of sexism (Swim et al., 1995). Although some people claim that they do not discriminate against women, in reality they continue to do so and to devalue the opinions of women relative to those of men.

Another kind of subtle racism occurs in people who experience a conflict between two attitudes (Katz & Hass, 1988). On the one hand, they believe in what the sociologist Max Weber called the *Protestant work ethic*, the idea that hard work is the key to "making it," with the implication that people who are not successful have simply not applied themselves. On the other hand, they believe in equality of opportunity and recognize that all people in their society do not start out at the same place. This ambivalence can lead to extreme responses, both positive and negative, as they sometimes "land hard" on one side of the ambivalence or the other.

Implicit and Explicit Racism   Another form of conflict is that between explicit and implicit attitudes toward members of minority groups. Like the African-American participants in Steele's studies described at the beginning of the chapter, who found themselves prey to their implicit associations, most white people have absorbed negative attitudes toward people of color over the course of their lives (Dovidio & Gaertner, 1993). They often express nonbigoted explicit attitudes, but when acting or responding without much conscious attention, unconscious stereotypes slip through the cracks (Devine et al., 2002; Greenwald et al., 2002). For example, in ambiguous situations, whites tend to be less helpful to blacks than to other whites, and they are more likely to impose stiffer penalties for black criminals.

In part, this discrepancy between what people say and what they do reflects a simple cognitive process. When people process information without much conscious thought, they are more likely to rely on stereotypes, to treat people as part of a category rather than as a specific individual (see Olson & Zanna, 1993). Negative stereotypes, like other attitudes, may thus be activated without awareness, as when a white man automatically checks his wallet after standing next to a young black man on the subway. Emotional arousal can also render people more susceptible to stereotypic thinking, in part because it draws limited attentional resources away from conscious reflection (Bodenhausen, 1993). The less people make conscious attributions, the more their unreflective, implicit attitudes prevail (Gilbert, 1995).

A growing body of research has begun to demonstrate just how different people's implicit and explicit racial attitudes can be (Devine et al., 2002; Dovidio et al., 2000; Greenwald et al., 1998; Kawakami et al., 2000). These studies have used priming procedures (Chapter 6), activating racial associations and then observing their effects on thought and behavior. In one of the first studies of this kind, the experimenter primed white subjects with words related to stereotypes of blacks, such as watermelon and Harlem (Devine, 1989). Subjects then read information about a fictional character. Simply activating stereotypes related to blacks led participants to rate the character more negatively (e.g., as more aggressive) than participants who were not primed with race-related words. In another study, researches sent 5000 resumes to various companies seeking employees. They varied the names on the resumes such that some were distinctively white-sounding and others black-sounding. Companies showed a significantly higher response rate to resumes with white-sounding as opposed to black-sounding names ("Job search harder," 2003).

Another study found that people's implicit and explicit racial attitudes may be completely unrelated to each other—and may control different kinds of behavior (Fazio et al., 1995). To measure implicit attitudes, the investigators presented participants with a series of black and white faces followed by either a positive or a negative adjective. The participant's task was simply to press a key indicating whether the adjective was positive or negative. The theory behind the study was that negative attitudes are associatively connected to negative words (because they share the same emotional tone). Thus, the extent to which people have negative associations to blacks should be directly related to how quickly they recognize negative words after exposure to black faces. In other words, the speed with which participants respond to negative adjectives following priming with a black face can serve as a measure of their implicit attitudes toward blacks. The experimenters also measured *explicit* racial atti-

Big Picture φ Question 7

To what extent are psychological processes conscious or unconscious—that is, explicit versus implicit?

Making Connections

In 1998, Anthony Greenwald and his colleagues introduced the Implicit Associations Test (IAT) as a means of assessing people's implicit attitudes. Specifically, the test measures automatic associations between particular constructs (e.g., black or white) and descriptive attributes (e.g., pleasant or unpleasant). Researchers regularly use the IAT to demonstrate automatic associations. To assess your own implicit attitudes, you can complete any of a number of different demonstrations of the IAT at http://buster.cs.yale.edu/

tudes using self-report questionnaires asking about participants' beliefs about race-related issues and their attitudes about the Rodney King beating and the riots that followed acquittal of the police officers who beat him.

Implicit attitudes did not predict explicit attitudes. For example, many people who denied conscious, explicit racism showed substantial implicit racism as measured by their response to adjectives following black and white primes. But these implicit attitudes *did* predict something very important: subjects' behavior toward a black confederate of the experimenter who met them at the end of the study and simply rated the extent to which they seemed friendly and interested in what she had to say. Participants who had responded more quickly to negative adjectives after priming with black faces received lower ratings, regardless of what they believed explicitly.

Recent neuroimaging data suggest that implicit attitudes about race "run deep." Recall that the amygdala plays an important role in generating unpleasant emotions, particularly fear, in both rats and humans (Chapter 10). In one study, the higher that subjects scored on implicit racism, the more their brains showed activation of the amygdala as they looked at pictures of black faces (Phelps et al., 2000). Explicit, conscious attitudes, on the other hand, do predict other conscious attitudes and beliefs, such as beliefs about what should happen to people who commit hate crimes. These findings directly parallel the results of studies distinguishing implicit motives, which predict long-term behavioral trends (such as success in business), from explicit motives, which control behavior only when people are consciously thinking about them (Chapter 10).

A Connectionist Model of the Influence of Stereotypes on Judgments   Recently, researchers have applied connectionist models to social–cognitive and attitudinal phenomena such as stereotyping, demonstrating some of the ways implicit processes can affect ongoing thought and behavior (Kunda & Thagard, 1996). Consider what happens when a white person observes a white or black man shoving someone (Figure 17.3). The person could interpret the shove as an aggressive act (a violent push) or a playful, jovial shove. Because the person associates the category "black" with the trait "aggressive," activation spreads from "black" to "aggressive" to "violent push," and simultaneously inhibits interpretation of the action as a jovial shove. In contrast, because "white" is not associated one way or the other with "aggressive" (or may actually be slightly negatively associated

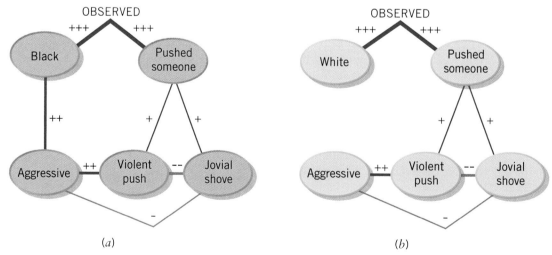

FIGURE 17.3   A connectionist model of the impact of stereotypes on inferences about behavior. The difference between the neural networks that lead to interpretation of an ambiguous shove by (*a*) a black man and (*b*) a white man lies in the weights that connect the nodes of the networks (the circles). Blue lines indicate positive weights, red lines indicate negative weights (inhibitory connections between nodes), and the thickness of the line indicates the strength of the connection (either positive or negative). *Source:* Adapted from Kunda & Thagard, 1996, p. 286.

with it), less activation spreads to the "violent push" interpretation (represented as a node in a network). Thus, in an ambiguous situation, satisfaction of multiple constraints can lead to inferences that are biased by stereotypes.

Suppressing Implicit Racism Implicit racism (or sexism, which shows similar properties; Skowronski & Lawrence, 2001) may interact with motivational factors. No one wants to be a hypocrite. When conscious beliefs and values conflict with deep-seated, automatic negative stereotypes, people may alternate between extreme positions, either laying excessive blame at the feet of members of devalued groups or refusing to hold them accountable for their behavior. Alternatively, they may learn to recognize their unconscious tendencies toward racist thinking and perpetually monitor their reactions to try to prevent racist attitudes from coloring their actions (Devine & Monteith, 1993).

Researchers have begun examining the conditions under which people will express or suppress their stereotypes. In one series of studies, the investigators used a simple manipulation—the presence of a mirror—to heighten participants' focus on themselves while responding to a questionnaire about the acceptability of stereotypes (Macrae et al., 1998). The researchers hypothesized that under conditions of self-focus, people will be more likely to suppress stereotypic attitudes. That is precisely what they found: Participants in the mirror condition considered stereotyping less appropriate than control subjects without the mirror.

Suppressing a stereotype, however, can lead to rebound effects, in which the person later responds even more stereotypically. In another study, the investigators asked participants to evaluate a male hairdresser. After completing the task, the experimenter apologetically told them that some equipment had failed and asked them to do the task again, this time evaluating another male hairdresser. Some participants had the mirror in the room both times, others had the mirror initially but not while evaluating the second hairdresser, and some had no mirror on either occasion.

As predicted, those who had the mirror present initially produced less stereotypical descriptions of the first hairdresser. However, participants who had suppressed the stereotype the first time showed a substantial increase in stereotyping the second time if the mirror was removed (Figure 17.4). Thus, fighting a stereotype does not make it go away; in fact, it can intensify its expression when the person least expects it.

Can we fight stereotypes more effectively? This is the focus of some recent research. One method involves perspective taking: In a study of implicit attitudes toward the elderly (Chapter 14), individuals who were asked to imagine the world from the perspective of older people subsequently expressed fewer stereotypes both implicitly and explicitly (Galinsky & Moskowitz, 2000). Conscious efforts to combat stereotypes can also sometimes be effective in sensitizing people to their pervasive influence (Blair & Banaji, 1996; Kawakami et al., 2000). In fact, simply being aware of the labels one is using can reduce the impact of stereotypes. A recent neuroimaging study found reduced amygdala activation when participants intentionally thought of the stereotype label (e.g., "African-American") while viewing a face than when they saw the face without thinking of the label (Lieberman et al., 2001).

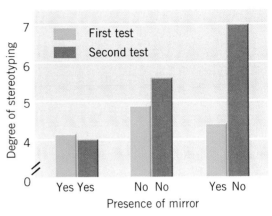

FIGURE 17.4 Stereotype suppression and rebound. Participants who initially suppressed their stereotype because of the presence of a mirror showed a rebound effect if the mirror was not present the second time. *Source:* Adapted from Macrae et al., 1998.

INTERIM SUMMARY

Stereotypes are characteristics attributed to people based upon their membership in groups. **Prejudice** means judging people based on (usually negative) stereotypes. An early approach to prejudice focused on a personality style called the **authoritarian personality**, characterized by a tendency to project blame and rage onto specific groups. Cognitive researchers have focused on subtle forms of racism, many of which involve ambivalent attitudes. Of particular importance is implicit racism, which resides in the structure of people's associations toward members of minority groups rather than their explicit attitudes and often controls everyday behavior.

Prejudice and Social Conditions   In the late 1950s and 1960s, the civil rights movement in the United States was at its peak, and social scientists were optimistic about eradicating social evils such as poverty and racism. This optimism in part reflected research suggesting that the roots of prejudice lay less in personality dynamics than in social dynamics, particularly in socialization that teaches children racist attitudes (Duckitt, 1992; Pettigrew, 1958).

Prejudice is indeed transmitted from one generation to the next, and it takes hold early. In India, which has seen continued violence between Muslims and Hindus, children show signs of prejudice by age 4 or 5 (Saraswathi & Dutta, 1988). In multiethnic societies such as the United States, children from both minority and majority subcultures tend to express preferences toward the majority culture by the preschool years (see Spencer & Markstrom-Adams, 1990). Such culturally patterned associations can later make identity formation difficult for adolescent members of devalued groups, who must somehow integrate a positive view of themselves with negatives stereotypes others hold of them. And as Steele's research described at the opening of the chapter showed, these associations can also lead to self-fulfilling prophecies.

The roots of prejudice may lie in social conditions in yet another way. Many theorists, from Karl Marx to contemporary sociologists, have argued that prejudiced social attitudes serve a function: They preserve the interests of the dominant classes. Promulgating the view that blacks are inferior justifies a social order in which whites hold disproportionate power. Disparities in wealth and property ownership often create the fault lines along which societies crumble with ethnic strife because the haves and have-nots frequently differ in color, religion, or ethnicity.

Ingroups and Outgroups   Prejudice requires a distinction between **ingroups** and **outgroups**—*people who belong to the group and those who do not* (Brewer & Brown, 1998). The impact of ingroups and outgroups was demonstrated in a remarkable classroom experiment. Third-grade teacher Jane Elliott (1977), who taught in a rural, all-white community, one day announced that the brown-eyed children in her class were superior and the blue-eyed children, inferior. Soon the brown-eyed children refused to play with their blue-eyed classmates, and the blue-eyed children began to do poor work because they thought of themselves as stupid and bad. Although this study has been replicated, it has not been without its critics, who state that the results could simply reflect the operation of demand characteristics.

Us and Them   Similar ingroup–outgroup behavior occurs with adults and is particularly powerful in naturally occurring groups such as families, clans, and communities. One process that intensifies stereotyping is that people tend to perceive members of outgroups as much more homogeneous than they really are and to emphasize the individuality of ingroup members (Moreland, 1985; Rothgerber, 1997). Thus, people of other races "all look alike," and members of other fraternities or sororities are seen to share many core traits—which is highly unlikely, given the tremendous differences in personality that exist within any group of people.

Interpretation of other people's behavior also depends on their ingroup–outgroup status. A set of studies with Hindu and Muslim students in Bangladesh showed that both groups attributed helpful behavior of ingroup members to their personal goodness and unhelpful behavior to environmental causes (Islam & Hewstone, 1993). The reverse applied to outgroup members, who did not similarly receive the benefit of the doubt.

Favoring the ingroup and denigrating the outgroup may at first appear to be polar opposites. However, as we have seen elsewhere in this book (Chapters 10, 14, and 15), research on a number of seemingly unrelated phenomena—positive and negative affect, parental acceptance and rejection, positive and negative interactions in couples, and positive and negative components of attitudes—has shown an interesting and counterintuitive phenomenon: What look like opposite ends of a single di-

Big Picture φ Question 4

To what extent is human nature particular versus universal?

Jane Elliott, best know for her blue-eyed/brown-eyed study examining prejudice and discrimination.

mension are often actually separate dimensions. The same is true with positive feelings toward ingroups and negative feelings toward outgroups (Brewer & Brown, 1998). In most situations, ingroup favoritism is actually more common than outgroup derogation or devaluation.

In fact, another form of subtle racism or group antagonism may lie less in the *presence* of hostile feelings than in the *absence* of the positive feelings that normally bind people together and lead them to help each other (Pettigrew & Meertens, 1995). The readiness to create and act on ingroup–outgroup distinctions probably rests on both motivational and cognitive processes. From a motivational point of view, casting ingroup members in a positive light gives oneself a positive glow as a member of the group (Tajfel, 1981). In fact, one study showed that after watching their team win, basketball fans showed an increased belief in their abilities at an unrelated task (Hirt et al., 1992). From a cognitive perspective, ingroup effects reflect our continuous and automatic efforts to categorize and schematize information.

Although everyone, at times, makes ingroup–outgroup distinctions, those who are most likely to do so are those who derive their primary sense of self or identity from their group memberships. **Social identity theory** *suggests that people derive part of their identity from the groups to which they belong* (Abrams & Hogg, 1999; Tajfel, 1982). Thus, individuals whose identities are based largely on the groups to which they belong will have more of a need to maintain positive feelings for their ingroup and negative feelings for the outgroup.

Not surprisingly, situational events can also enhance the degree to which people define themselves in terms of particular groups and, thus, the degree to which they are likely to display ingroup favoritism and outgroup derogation (Kowalski & Wolfe, 1994). One has only to think back to how Americans displayed their patriotic fervor following the terrorist attacks of September 11, 2001. All of a sudden people displayed their national pride and identified themselves as Americans in a way they never had before. Similar displays of national pride can be found in most countries throughout the world. At the same time, discrimination against Arab-Americans rose to new heights as some people assumed—incorrectly, of course—that anyone with Arab ties must be evil.

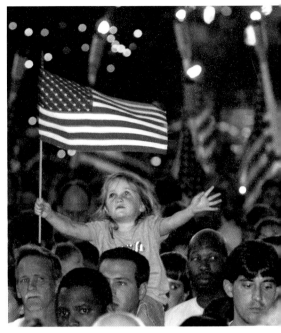

Identification with the groups (e.g., nations) to which people belong may facilitate patriotism.

Reducing Group Antagonisms   Research on ingroups and outgroups inevitably led to interest in techniques for reducing group antagonisms. In a classic experiment, researchers created friction between two groups of 11-year-old boys, dubbed the Rattlers and the Eagles, at a Boy Scout summer camp (Sherif et al., 1961). Then the experimenters fostered strong ingroup sentiments by instructing the children to give their group a name, wear special clothes, and so forth. They also encouraged rivalries through competitive activities. Within a short time, the competition became so heated that it degenerated into overt hostility.

Initial attempts to defuse the hostility, such as bringing the groups together for pleasant activities, failed. Another approach was more successful: The experimenters contrived situations that created **superordinate goals**—*goals requiring the groups to cooperate for the benefit of all*. In one instance, the experimenters arranged for a truck transporting food for an overnight trip to stall. Eventually, both groups cooperated in pulling the truck with a rope. Similarly, when the camp's water supply stopped, both groups worked together to solve the problem.

The researchers concluded that contact alone is not enough to reduce conflict; the contact must also involve *cooperation* (see Sherif & Sherif, 1979). This finding has important implications for social policies such as school desegregation, because it suggests that simply placing children from two different races in the same school may not minimize animosities; it may in fact exacerbate them (Anson, 2000; Stephan, 1987). Compare this to sports teams, where black and white players work together for common goals and do not distinguish at the end of a winning game who they will throw their arms around based on race.

Apply & Discuss

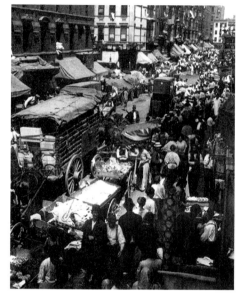

At the beginning of the twentieth century, the United States was seen as a great melting pot, where people of many cultures could come and become "Americans." By the end of the century, a different attitude had emerged, emphasizing the multiethnic nature of the society and encouraging ethnic pride, leading people to define themselves as "hyphenated-Americans" (e.g., African-American, Asian-American).

■ Is fear of "the other"—particularly if the other speaks a different language, looks different, and has different values and beliefs—a tendency that is "built into" the human psyche, or is it entirely learned?

■ Is ethnic pride a threat to the ties that bind a multiethnic nation together? How can we maximize the conditions that allow people of different ethnicities to preserve their heritage without fostering ingroup–outgroup antagonism?

Other factors also influence whether contact leads to increased tolerance or animosity. First, individuals must have the opportunity to get to know one another on a one-to-one basis, as in sports teams and musical groups, and to have relatively equal status (Brewer & Brown, 1998). People from different groups also need to have enough shared values, beliefs, interests, culture, and skills so that their interactions dissolve stereotypes rather than confirm them. Unfortunately, members of cultures and subcultures often differ on precisely these things—a characteristic that increases the need for superordinate goals and shared or complementary skills that deemphasize differences and emphasize commonalities.

INTERIM SUMMARY

Prejudice lies not only in people's minds but also in social institutions and socialization practices that foster it. Prejudice requires a distinction between **ingroups** and **outgroups** (people who belong to the group and those who do not). People often attribute more homogeneity to outgroups than ingroups and make more positive interpretations of the behavior of ingroup members. Ingroup–outgroup distinctions probably reflect both motivational and cognitive factors. Contact between groups can decrease prejudice and hostility if it is accompanied by shared goals, personal acquaintance with members of the outgroup, relatively equal status, and enough shared values and culture to dissolve stereotypes.

Attribution

Whether trying to understand the causes of inner-city violence or a curt response from a boss, people are constantly thinking about the "whys" of social interaction. *The process of inferring the causes of one's own and others' mental states and behaviors* is called **attribution** (Gilbert et al., 1998a). Attribution plays a central role in virtually every social encounter. For example, an attribution about why a friend did not call back when she said she would can affect the friendship, just as the attributions a student makes for a weak performance on a test can affect her self-esteem and motivation in the future.

Intuitive Science People attribute causes by observing the *covariation* of situations, behavior, and specific people. In other words, they assess the extent to which the presence of one variable predicts the presence of another—that is, whether the two variables *co-vary* (Heider, 1958; Kelley, 1973, 1992). An employee who receives a terse response from his boss may have noticed that his boss is often brusque when she is stressed by approaching deadlines. Thus, he attributes her behavior to the situation rather than to her feelings about him.

According to one view, when people make attributions, they are like **intuitive scientists**: *They rely on intuitive theories, frame hypotheses, collect data about themselves and others, and draw conclusions as best they can based on the pattern of data they have observed* (Heider, 1958; Ross, 1977). In the language of connectionism, they are essentially trying to settle on a solution that takes into account as many constraints as possible.

Making Inferences Understanding other people's behavior requires figuring out when their actions reflect demands of the situation, aspects of their personalities (often called personality *dispositions*), or interactions between the two (the ways specific people behave in particular situations). Thus, people sometimes make **external attributions**, or *attributions to the situation*, whereas other times they make **internal attributions**, *attributions to the person* (Chapter 5). Often they combine the two, as when the employee notices an interaction effect: that his boss tends to become tense and brusque (internal, or dispositional, attribution) when she is stressed by deadlines (external, or situational, attribution).

In making attributions, people rely on three types of information: consensus, consistency, and distinctiveness (Kelley, 1973, 1979). **Consensus** refers to *the way most people respond*. If everyone in the organization responds tersely to his questions, the employee might attribute his boss's brusque behavior to something situational (such as the organizational culture, or atmosphere of the company). **Consistency** refers to *the extent to which a person always responds in the same way to the same stimulus*. If the boss is frequently brusque, the employee will likely make an internal attribution about her personality. The **distinctiveness** of a person's action refers to *the individual's likelihood to respond this way to many different stimuli*. If the boss treats other people brusquely, the employee is likely to conclude that brusqueness is an enduring aspect of her personality, rather than a reflection of her attitude toward him. Consistency and distinctiveness are the intuitive scientist's versions of the concepts of consistency across time and consistency over situations debated by personality psychologists (Chapter 12).

Part of the difficulty in making accurate attributions is that most actions have multiple causes, some situational and some dispositional. In deciding how much to credit or blame a person, people generally adjust for the strength of situational demands through two processes, discounting and augmentation (Trope & Liberman, 1996). **Discounting** occurs when *people downplay (discount) the role of one variable (such as personality, intelligence, or skill) because they know that others may be contributing to the behavior in question* (Heider, 1958; McClure, 1998). For example, the employee may discount his boss's bad manners because she is under the strain of an approaching deadline, or because her father recently died. The opposite situation occurs with **augmentation**—that is, *increasing (augmenting) an internal attribution for behavior that has occurred despite situational demands*. The employee may attribute particular coldness to his boss if she continues to respond tersely to his questions when the workload is low.

Making an attribution is typically a three-step process (Gilbert & Malone, 1995). First, people categorize the behavior they have observed (e.g., did the boss sound angry?). Then, based on the way they have interpreted the behavior, they categorize the person's personality (e.g., this is a hostile person). Finally, if the situation seems to have elicited or contributed to the behavior (e.g., the angry comment was provoked), they may discount the attribution of hostility. Experimental research supporting this theory shows that distracting participants while they are making attributions leads them to make automatic attributions to the person, which they would have discounted if they had had time to think about the situation. In other words, people first jump to conclusions about personality implicitly, and they then correct these attributions if they have the time to think about it.

People differ in the types of attributions they are likely to make and in the implications that these attributions have for the individual. *A person's habitual manner of assigning causes to behaviors or events* is referred to as his **attributional style** (Buchanan & Seligman, 1995). For example, some people view the world through rose-colored glasses and typically adopt an optimistic explanatory style. They believe that good events and outcomes are due to internal factors about themselves that are likely to remain stable over time. Conversely, other people take a much darker view of the world and adopt a pessimistic explanatory style. These individuals make attributions for negative events to internal factors that are stable and that will pervade virtually everything that they do. For example, a student with a pessimistic explanatory style will attribute failure on a test to the fact that she is not smart (internal attribution), she will never be smart (stable attribution), and she will likely fail tests in other courses as well (global attribution). Not surprisingly, people who explain events using a pessimistic explanatory style are at greater risk for depression than those who use more optimistic attributional styles (Peterson & Seligman, 1984).

Researchers have also found cultural variations in the attributions people typically make. Specifically, people in collectivist cultures make more external attributions

As the first plane flew into one of the towers of the World Trade Center on the morning of September 11, 2001, many people found themselves wondering about the causes of this horrible event. Was something wrong with the plane? Did something happen to the pilot? These initial attributions were quickly dispelled, however, when a second plane flew into the other tower, followed shortly after by a plane flying into the Pentagon in Washington, D.C. Inferences regarding the causes of these events now changed to focus on terrorism. To this day, however, we must still ask "Why?" What caused these people to do what they did and to sacrifice not only their own lives but the lives of so many other people?

Big Picture ϕ Question 4

To what extent is human nature particular versus universal?

Apply & Discuss

Attributions are central to legal decision making. Suppose, for example, a person is charged with killing another person using a handgun.

▪ What attributions lead to a charge of first degree murder rather than a lesser charge, such as manslaughter?

▪ What attributions affect the severity of the sentence once a person has been convicted?

for others' behavior than do people from individualistic cultures. Data suggest that people in collectivist cultures take more time before assigning causes to people or events. Thus, they are more likely to take into account all relevant factors, including situational ones, that may have influenced behavior (Choi et al., 2003).

INTERIM SUMMARY

Attribution is the process of inferring the causes of one's own and others' mental states and behaviors. People attribute causes by observing the covariation of social stimuli or events. People are like **intuitive scientists**, who use intuitive theories, frame hypotheses, and try to draw inferences from the data they have collected. They sometimes make **external attributions** (attributions to the situation), **internal attributions** (attributions to the person), or attributions that reflect the *interaction* of the two. Although people can make any of these attributions in a particular situation, they tend to develop **attributional styles** or habitual ways of assigning causes to events.

Biases in Social Information Processing

Although individuals in some sense act like intuitive scientists, their "studies" often have substantial methodological shortcomings. Indeed, rigorous application of the scientific method is so important in social psychology precisely because it prevents researchers from making the same kinds of intuitive errors we all make in everyday life.

Social psychologists have identified several biases in social information processing. Here we examine two of the most widely studied and then explore the cognitive and motivational roots of biased social cognition.

Correspondence Bias   One of the most pervasive biases in social cognition, the **correspondence bias**, is *the tendency to assume that other people's behavior corresponds to their internal states rather than external situations*—that is, to attribute behaviors to people's personalities and to ignore possible situational causes (Gilbert & Malone, 1995; Heider, 1958; Ross, 1977). A good illustration occurs while driving—which in the extreme case can turn into "road rage." I may, for example, draw highly sophisticated inferences about a person's character (e.g., "what a jerk!") from the fact that he is holding me up on my way to work by driving slowly—only to recognize when I see his license plate that he is from another state and probably has no idea where he is going.

The correspondence bias (also known as the *fundamental attribution error*; Ross, 1977) occurs primarily when explaining others' behavior. When explaining our own behavior, we are far more likely to look for causes outside ourselves. Thus, we are more likely to make external as opposed to internal attributions for our own behavior. Researchers have found, however, that this effect can be reversed by getting participants to view their own behavior much as an outside observer would. Storms (1973) had participants interact with another individual while both were being watched by an observer. When the participant and the observer were asked about the causes of the participant's behavior, the observer, not surprisingly, made more internal attributions whereas the participant made more external attributions for his own behavior. When the perspectives were reversed, however, and participants watched themselves on video and then made attributional evaluations of their own behavior, they, too, made more internal as opposed to external attributions.

Furthermore, the degree to which the correspondence bias occurs depends on which culture is being observed. East Asians display the correspondence bias less than people in Western culture (Choi et al., 1999). What's interesting about this finding is that it is not that East Asians do not make dispositional attributions for other people's behavior; they simply give more attention to situational influences on the person than do people in Western culture. In other words, they are less likely to discount the role of the situation. In a study by Norenzayan, Choi, and Nisbett (1998, cited in Choi et al., 1999), European-American and Korean participants read vignettes that included two types of information: information implying personality traits that might motivate someone's behavior and information about situational variables that might also lead a person to behave a particular way. Whereas European-American participants relied solely on the dispositional information when making predictions about a person's behavior, Korean individuals used both dispositional and situational information, as long as the situational information was made clear in the vignettes.

Self-Serving Bias   Another pervasive bias in social cognition is the **self-serving bias**, in which *people tend to see themselves in a more positive light than others see them* (Baumeister, 1998; Epstein, 1992; Greenwald, 1980). The self-serving bias takes a number of forms. For example, as we will consider in detail later in this chapter, a majority of people rate themselves as above average on most dimensions. This is, of course, statistically impossible (Taylor & Brown, 1988). People are also more likely to recall positive than negative information about themselves (Kuiper & Derry, 1982; Kuiper et al., 1985) and to see their talents as more striking and unusual than their deficiencies (Campbell, 1986). In addition, they attribute greater responsibility to themselves for a group product than other group members attribute to them (Ross & Sicoly, 1979) and assume that they are less driven by self-interest than those around them (Miller & Ratner, 1998). Finally, people take credit for their successes and attribute failure to external, situational factors (Campbell & Sedikides, 1999).

Self-serving biases are not without their limits. Most people will not totally ignore reality (see Kunda, 1990), but they do differ tremendously in their tendency to let their needs for self-enhancement interfere with their objectivity. One study observed MBA students in simulated corporate decision-making meetings over a weekend (John & Robins, 1994). At the conclusion, participants ranked their own performance and that of their peers. The researchers also observed their behavior and ranked each participant.

Participants were fairly objective in ranking their peers' performance: Peer and psychologist rankings correlated at about .50. However, they were less objective about themselves. The correlation between self-rankings and psychologist rankings was only about .30. Moreover, 60 percent overestimated their own performance, a finding that suggests a self-serving bias. And those who were rated as more narcissistic by the researchers showed the greatest biases of all! The data indicate that most people wear mildly rose-tinted glasses when they look in the mirror, but that people who are narcissistic keep a pair of opaque spectacles on hand in case the spotlight shines too brightly on their flaws (see also Epley & Dunning, 2000; Robins & Beer, 2001).

Like other biases in social cognition, the self-serving bias may depend in part on culture (Kitayama et al., 1997). This bias is pervasive in the West but much less so in Eastern and other collectivist cultures, in which people do not define themselves as much in terms of their individual accomplishments. When people in the United States describe themselves, they tend to list about five times as many positive as negative traits (Holmberg et al., 1995). This pattern is unheard of in cultures such as Japan, where people do not toot their horns so loudly, either in private or in public.

Recent research suggests that as Asians become assimilated into Western culture, their conscious self-descriptions begin to show the Western bias; however, deeper, implicit processes (assessed, for example, by the speed with which they recognize the words *good* and *bad* after priming with the word *me*) may take a generation to change (Pelham et al., 1998, cited in Fiske et al., 1998).

Faulty Cognition   What causes biases in processing social information? The answers appear to lie in both cognition and motivation.

Cognitive Biases   Some of the errors people make reflect the same kinds of cognitive biases people display in nonsocial cognition (Chapter 7). For example, heuristics can lead to biases in social thinking, as when people assume that "all politicians are crooks"

Big Picture φ Question 4

To what extent is human nature particular versus universal?

Most of these people believe they are smarter, more personable, and better looking than the person next to them.

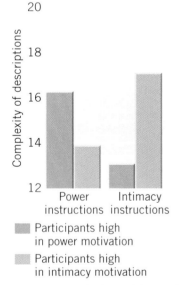

FIGURE 17.5 Motivation and the complexity of social cognition. When the instructions stressed power, participants high in power motivation showed greater cognitive complexity in describing potential research assistants. When the instructions stressed intimacy, participants high in intimacy motivation thought more complexly. *Source:* Woike & Aronoff, 1992, p. 102.

because of some salient examples that come to mind (the *availability heuristic*). In fact, one of the main reasons politicians often appear crooked is that their behavior—including their tax returns, business dealings, and so forth—is so closely scrutinized.

As in nonsocial cognition, heuristics can lead people awry, but they are essential to everyday functioning, because they allow us to make decisions and judgments rapidly and without conscious reflection. People frequently lack the time or information they need to make accurate attributions, so they do the best they can. Often, these rapid, good-enough attributions are just that—good enough. On the other hand, phrases like "I had no idea he would turn out to be that way" or "I can't believe I didn't see that" express the regrets people feel when they discounted or failed to piece together some initial "clues" as they employed heuristics that turned out to be not quite good enough.

Motivational Biases   Other biases reflect motivation (Fiske, 1992; Kunda, 1990; Tagiuri et al., 1953; Westen, 1991, 1998). Schemas and attributions are influenced by wishes, needs, and goals. For example, people who are currently involved in romantic relationships tend to perceive opposite-sex peers as less attractive and sexually desirable than people who are uninvolved (Simpson et al., 1990). This bias is useful because it makes maintaining a monogamous relationship easier.

Motivation can also influence the extent to which people think complexly about themselves and others. For example, one study compared people high in need for intimacy with those high in need for power (Woike & Aronoff, 1992). Participants were asked to evaluate potential research assistants by watching them interact with each other on videotape. In one condition, the investigators emphasized the need to be sensitive and empathic toward the applicant. In the other condition, the investigators stressed the importance of taking control of the situation and exercising decision-making power.

After watching the videotapes, the researchers instructed participants to describe the candidates and then coded the complexity of subjects' responses. The investigators reasoned that participants motivated by power would think more deeply and complexly when their power motives were activated, and those high in intimacy motivation would think more complexly when motivated by instructions emphasizing intimacy. The findings strongly supported the hypothesis (Figure 17.5), suggesting that the extent to which people think deeply about others depends on their motivation to do so. Motivated biases can occur at the societal level as well as the personal, especially when nations are on the verge of war (Winter, 1987, 1993). One researcher studied the motives attributed by Northern and Southern newspapers to Abraham Lincoln and his Confederate counterpart, Jefferson Davis, following a series of speeches in 1861 (Winter, 1987). The Northern media saw Davis as power-hungry; the Southern media saw Lincoln as power-hungry. The Southern newspapers also saw Lincoln as low on the socially desirable motive, affiliation (which was rather ironic, since he was trying to keep the South from "disaffiliating" from the union!).

Interactions of Cognition and Motivation   Although social psychologists have spent many years debating whether particular biases are cognitive *or* motivational in origin, many biases probably reflect both (Tetlock & Levi, 1982). Consider the *confirmation bias*—the tendency to seek out information that confirms one's hypotheses. When presented with the task of finding out whether a target person is extroverted, subjects tend to ask the person questions that elicit extroverted responses and to fail to ask questions like "Do you enjoy spending time alone?" (Snyder & Cantor, 1979). People are more likely to commit the confirmation bias when they are not particularly motivated or when they lack the cognitive resources to do a more thorough assessment—for example, if they are distracted by a second task (Liberman & Trope, 1998).

Even more powerful biases can occur when individuals are motivated to come to a particular conclusion. For example, during the Lewinsky scandal in 1998, many people, psychologists in particular, could predict six months in advance (with a fairly high degree of accuracy) whether people would ultimately believe that President Clinton's actions met the criteria set forth in the Constitution for impeachable offenses ("high crimes and misdemeanors") based on their *feelings* about Clinton, Democrats and Republicans, feminism, and infidelity (Westen & Feit, 1999). These feelings appeared to lead people to listen to television commentators and read magazine articles that provided more data for their point of view and to weigh arguments in ways that would support their emotional prejudices.

Similar findings emerged during the contested 2000 election. People's beliefs about whether hand or machine counting of votes produces more accurate results reflected a mixture of their feelings toward Gore, Bush, Democrats, and Republicans. Providing them with new data that seemed to prove the advantage of one or the other (an experimental manipulation) had little influence on their beliefs (Westen et al., 2001.)

If people are intuitive scientists, research suggests that they could use a basic course in research design. Aside from cognitive errors, social perceivers have many goals besides the scientific objective of seeking truth, and these other agendas often influence their "findings." They are interested in looking good, maintaining positive feelings about themselves, believing good things will happen to them, protecting their idealized views of people they care about, and maintaining negative schemas of people (or groups) they dislike. Because motives play a fundamental role in attention, encoding, retrieval, and problem solving, social cognition is inherently intertwined with social motivation (see Fiske, 1993).

Applications

The information on biases in social information processing just presented clearly shows that people are not always accurate perceivers of their social world. People jump to conclusions about others on the basis of first impressions. These first impressions create a frame of reference within which all subsequent information that is learned about a person is interpreted. People use schemas and rely on stereotypes to cognitively process the myriad of information with which they are confronted on a daily basis. And, people succumb to biases, such as the correspondence bias, as they interpret the behavior of others, and the self-serving bias, as they interpret their own. You might think that, with training, the occurrence of errors in social information processing could (and should) be attenuated. Surely, clinical psychologists, for example, are immune from the same social information processing errors that plague the rest of us. To invoke the correspondence bias in explaining the difficulties being experienced by her client would lead a clinician to ignore any environmental factors (family, work, etc.) that may be contributing to the problem. To let an initial diagnosis influence everything else that is perceived about a client would lead the clinician to ignore other relevant factors and diagnoses that could be more accurate.

Unfortunately, research shows that clinicians, although perhaps better at overcoming social cognitive errors than members of the lay public, are still human. Clinicians succumb (although one hopes to a lesser degree) to the social information processing biases that afflict us all. The Rosenhan (1973) study discussed in Chapter 15 provides a nice exemplar of these shortcomings.

Social and Nonsocial Cognition

Although social psychologists have followed developments in cognitive science closely and have borrowed many of their models from cognitive science, they also recognize a number of ways in which social cognition differs from nonsocial cognition (see Fiske, 1995; Zajonc & Markus, 1985). The differences are not black and white, but social and nonsocial cognition fall on opposite sides of a number of dimensions.

First, a person observing a social interaction is almost always missing the most relevant data: the unspoken intentions, thoughts, and feelings of the people involved. Because observers of a social interaction have access only to behaviors, they must

Making Connections

People often see what they expect to see and fail to test alternative hypotheses, leading to false confirmation of schemas (Chapter 7). When a couple buys a car together, the salesperson often talks primarily to the man, assuming that the man knows more and is more interested in cars—and may not discover, for example, that the woman is more knowledgeable or making the decision. (My husband and I just bought a new car. Because I am a better wheeler and dealer than my husband and far less likely to get taken, I negotiated the price of the car while my husband stood by. Still, people in the business office seemed to want to deal with him more than me.) Gender stereotypes of this sort are widespread and can be highly resistant to change (Chapter 14).

infer what those behaviors mean. Ambiguity is thus the rule in social cognition, leaving substantial opportunities for error, bias, and idiosyncratic interpretation. Second, social cognition is inherently intertwined with emotion. People either like or dislike their roommate; their psychology professor is either interesting or boring; the clerk is either courteous or rude. Thinking about chemical formulas, in contrast, may not engender quite so much feeling.

Third, although culture influences many cognitive processes, such as categorization, it plays a particularly important role in social cognition. An individual who is competitive and driven to accumulate wealth may appear perfectly normal in Western culture, and hence draw little attention. The same person may be classified as antisocial or self-centered in many other cultures. Social cognition is inherently infused with cultural value judgments because categories (such as men, nurses, or doctors) carry with them implications for how people who fit them *should* behave (Shweder, 1980).

Culture also influences the way people interpret interpersonal events by providing intuitive theories of personality and causality. When children and adults in the West explain their successes and failures, they rely on concepts such as skill, effort, and luck (Weiner, 1980). In contrast, Buddhist children from Sri Lanka sometimes attribute achievement and failure to good and bad deeds in past lives. Good deeds from another life lead to good karma, a positive moral force that guides one's fate (Little, 1987). Finally, social cognition is reciprocal. The "object" being perceived in social cognition may respond to the perceiver—and change its actions based on how it believes it is being perceived. Getting annoyed at a textbook for being thick and boring does not change it. Getting annoyed at a professor for the same reasons, however, may well influence the way he lectures.

Understanding basic principles of thought and memory is thus necessary for understanding social thought and memory, but it is not sufficient. Humans are social animals, and this aspect of human nature has shaped the way we think about ourselves and others. (In the next chapter, we will consider the way humans as social animals *behave*.)

Big Picture φ Question 4

To what extent is human nature particular versus universal?

INTERIM SUMMARY

The **correspondence bias** is the tendency to attribute behaviors to people's personalities and to ignore possible situational causes. The **self-serving bias** is the tendency to see oneself in a more positive light than one deserves. Biases in social cognition reflect both cognitive factors (such as the use of heuristics) and motivational factors (the impact of wishes, needs, and goals). These biases are not limited to the lay public, but characterize even the cognitions of people who have been trained to avoid them, such as clinicians.

Attitudes

Perhaps more than any topic that falls within the arena of social cognition, attitudes have received the greatest attention. Indeed, at one time, the study of attitudes essentially constituted social psychology. Although research attention to attitudes has diminished since the 1970s, attitudes are still probably the most fundamental concept in social psychology because they are involved in all social behavior, from political decisions to stereotyping and prejudice (Allport, 1935).

The Nature of Attitudes

An **attitude** is *an association between an act or object and an evaluation* (Ajzen, 2000; Eagly & Chaiken, 1992; Fazio, 1986). To put it another way, an attitude—whether toward Pepsi, Reebok, or Osama Bin Laden—is a tendency to evaluate a person, concept, or group positively or negatively (Eagly & Chaiken, 1998; Petty et al., 1997). To say that alcohol (an attitude object) is a dangerous drug (evaluation) is to express an attitude. Some psychologists distinguish three components of an attitude: a *cognitive component* or belief (alcohol contributes to social problems such as traffic fatalities and child abuse); an emotional or *evaluative component* (alcohol is bad); and a *behavioral disposition* (alcohol should be avoided).

At first glance, attitudes seem relatively straightforward—a person is either for abortion or against it, favorable or unfavorable toward affirmative action, or more positive toward Nike than Reebok or vice versa. Recently, however, researchers have discovered a number of variations in attitudes that make them far more complex (see Ajzen, 2001; Eagly & Chaiken, 1998).

Attitude Strength   One dimension on which attitudes vary is their strength. Whereas some attitudes are enduring over time and very resistant to change (high attitude strength), others are much less resilient and very susceptible to being changed or discarded (Ajzen, 2001; Bizer & Krosnick, 2001). Personally, I like the Miami Dolphins, but as someone who is only minimally interested in professional football, my feelings toward the team are relatively weak. If they lose to the Bills, I do not lose much sleep. Further, my beliefs about the team—the cognitive components of my attitude toward the Dolphins—also tend to sway in the wind. If my colleague tells me they are going to be great next year, I am perfectly happy to believe him and will likely continue believing him until someone else informs me otherwise.

Attitude strength refers to *the durability and impact of an attitude* (Bassili & Krosnick, 2000; Petty & Krosnick, 1995). An attitude is durable if it tends to persist over time and is resistant to change. An attitude has impact if it affects behavior and influences the way the person thinks and feels. Using this definition, my attitude toward the Dolphins is very weak: It is highly unstable and has minimal impact on what I do on a Sunday afternoon or how I feel if the team loses. It also has little effect on whether I think a referee made the right call.

Although research has shown that many different variables can affect an attitude's strength, two particularly relevant, and related, ones are *attitude importance* and *attitude accessibility*. **Attitude importance** refers to *the personal relevance of an attitude and the psychological significance of that attitude for an individual* (Bizer & Krosnick, 2001). The more importance or personal relevance assigned to an attitude the greater its strength.

For an attitude to have an impact on ongoing thought and behavior, it must be cognitively accessible, that is, readily pulled from memory. **Attitude accessibility** refers to *the ease with which an attitude comes to mind* (Bizer & Krosnick, 2001; Fazio, 1990, 1995). Highly accessible attitudes come to mind rapidly and automatically when primed by environmental events. For example, a person with positive attitudes toward women may have an immediate and positive initial reaction when the doctor at the clinic who comes out to examine her is female. The more accessible an attitude, the more likely it is to affect behavior and the stronger the attitude is.

Variation in accessibility makes sense from an adaptive (evolutionary) standpoint: The more frequently we encounter something, and the more its potential impact on our lives, the more quickly we should be able to react to it—and the more accessible our attitude toward it is likely to be. A downside of high accessibility, however, is its potential interference with our ability to detect changes in the attitude object (Fazio et al., 2000). A highly accessible attitude toward a politician may make a voter less likely to notice that the politician no longer votes the way he used to—and hence that the voter should reevaluate her attitude.

The relationship between attitude importance and attitude accessibility is an interesting and not completely understood one. On one hand, the greater the importance one attaches to an attitude, the more accessible that attitude is likely to become, a suggestion that attitude importance precedes attitude accessibility. Thus, if I believe that wearing seatbelts is very important and I have a relative who recently died in a car accident in which he was not belted in, my attitude toward seatbelt use is likely to become more accessible. I will think about seatbelt use more frequently and process information related to seatbelt use more completely than someone whose attitude about seatbelts is less strong.

On the other hand, it is possible that attitude accessibility precedes attitude importance. The more easily an attitude comes to mind, the more importance we may assume that attitude holds for us (Bizer & Krosnick, 2001). Thus, if I can easily extract from memory my feelings toward seatbelt use, I may infer that my attitude toward seatbelts is important.

One of the most controversial issues related to attitudes research concerns the heritability of attitudes, with the belief that heritable attitudes are stronger than attitudes that are not inherited (Tesser, 1993). Evidence for the heritability of attitudes can be found in twin studies comparing the attitudes of monozygotic twins and same-sex dizygotic twins. Stronger relations exist in the attitudes of monozygotic as opposed to dizygotic twins (Olson et al., 2001), and heritable attitudes are more resistant to attitude change than nonheritable attitudes (Tesser et al., 1998). No one would suggest that there are specific genes that influence attitudes and, subsequently, behavior. However, research on the heritability of attitudes looks at biological underpinnings that may account for people's attitudes (Chapters 1 and 12).

Implicit Attitudes   As with emotions, motives, and cognitions, social psychologists are increasingly recognizing the importance of distinguishing between explicit (conscious) attitudes and **implicit attitudes**—*associations between attitude objects and feelings about them that regulate thought and behavior unconsciously and automatically* (Greenwald & Banaji, 1995; Greenwald et al., 1998; Rudman et al., 1999). Someone who has just attended a lecture on alcohol-related fatalities is unlikely to stop at the bar on the way home because a conscious attitude is active. He may well, however, overindulge at a happy hour a few days later when his implicit attitudes toward alcohol—which reflect years of associations between drinking and enjoyment—become active. In fact, implicit attitudes of this sort play a more important role in predicting drug and alcohol use than people's conscious attitudes (Stacy, 1997).

As noted earlier in the discussion of implicit and explicit racism, implicit and explicit attitudes are not necessarily correlated with one another. The attitudes that someone may express publicly to allow him to make a desirable impression on others (explicit attitudes) may differ markedly from those that he holds privately or that are revealed when he fails to devote conscious attention to the attitudes being expressed.

Cognitive Complexity   The cognitive components of an attitude vary on a number of dimensions. For example, they can be relatively specific (a large tax cut right now would produce a budget deficit and hurt the economy) or general (tax cuts provide a strong stimulus for the economy in times of recession). An important dimension on which attitudes differ is their *cognitive complexity* (Bieri, 1966; Suedfeld & Granatstein, 1995). The beliefs of two people with equally positive attitudes toward a tax cut may have very different levels of complexity. One person might simply believe that "big government isn't the answer to our problems" and hence *always* favor tax cuts. Another might believe that large tax cuts foster investment and hence can stimulate a flagging economy. On a simple attitude rating of 1 to 5 (where 1 means the person is very unfavorable to a tax cut and 5 means very favorable), both people might nevertheless rate a 5.

Researchers have used some ingenious methods to assess the complexity of people's attitudes. For example, in one study, researchers read political speeches and coded them for the extent to which the thinking was complex (Tetlock, 1989). They found that people at both political extremes—far right and far left—tended to show less attitudinal complexity than people who were politically more moderate.

Big Picture φ Question 7

To what extent are psychological processes conscious or unconscious—that is, explicit versus implicit?

Cognitive complexity varies with both gender and culture. Responses to self-report measures of cognitive complexity show females to be more cognitively complex than males (Adams-Webber, 2001), although the same research showed that men and women in close relationships display similar levels of cognitive complexity. Thus, although there may be overall gender differences in cognitive complexity, we are drawn to those at our same level of complexity.

Culture as a mediator of cognitive complexity appears to depend on the nature of the situation being examined. Research with Chinese and Western students showed that students of both nationalities display cognitively complex attitudes, but typically with different attitudinal objects (Conway et al., 2001).

Attitudinal Ambivalence Another dimension on which attitudes differ is the extent to which an attitude object is associated with conflicting feelings. For many years researchers measured attitudes by asking respondents to rate the extent to which they were for or against abortion, liked or disliked particular political candidates, and so forth. Periodically, however, attitude researchers have wondered whether this focus really captures the complexity of the *emotional* component of people's attitudes. Think, for example, about how you feel about exercise. More than likely, you have both positive attitudes toward exercise (e.g., exercise can be fun, exercise is good for my health, exercise provides an effective means of controlling weight), and negative attitudes toward exercise (e.g., exercise takes too much time, exercise is boring). If you were asked simply how positively or negatively you felt about exercise, you would likely check the middle score on an attitude scale to reflect the positive and negative feelings you have toward exercise. But this middle score would suggest you have neutral feelings toward exercise, when, in fact, you don't.

Researchers studying **attitudinal ambivalence**—*the extent to which a given attitude object is associated with conflicting evaluative responses*—argue that attitudes include two evaluative dimensions, positive and negative, that are relatively independent (Cacioppo & Gardner, 1999; Jonas et al., 1997; Priester, 2002; Priester & Petty, 1996). Each of these two components can be relatively weak or relatively strong. Low positive/low negative attitudes will have minimal impact on behavior because the person is indifferent (i.e., does not care much either way) about the attitude object.

Weakly held attitudes of this sort are very different from highly ambivalent attitudes—high positive/high negative—but they often yield precisely the same (moderate) scores on bipolar attitude measures that assume that attitudes run from negative to positive.

Determining the degree to which a person holds ambivalent attitudes is important in assessing the relationship between attitudes and behavior. Most researchers suspect that nonambivalent attitudes are more predictive of behavioral intentions and, subsequently, actual behavior, than ambivalent attitudes. If I am completely in favor of organ donation, I am much more likely to become an organ donor, than if I hold very positive attitudes toward organ donation but some negative attitudes as well. More recent research, however, found just the opposite—attitudinal ambivalence predicted behavioral intentions better than did nonambivalence (Jonas et al., 1997; see also Gardner & Cacioppo, 1996; cited in Cacioppo et al., 1997). Participants in one study were provided with consistent versus inconsistent information about fictitious shampoos. Greater consistency between attitudes and behavioral intentions were observed among participants exposed to the evaluative inconsistent information than the evaluatively consistent information (Jonas et al., 1997). Apparently, attitudinal ambivalence produces more cognitive activity and systematic processing than nonambivalence (Ajzen, 2001).

Coherence A final dimension on which attitudes vary is **attitudinal coherence**—*the extent to which an attitude is internally consistent* (Eagly & Chaiken, 1998). Logically, the cognitive and emotional aspects of attitudes should be congruent be-

Big Picture φ Question 5

To what extent are psychological processes the same in men and women?

Big Picture φ Question 4

To what extent is human nature particular versus universal?

Making Connections

Positive and negative affect are somewhat independent and rely on different neural circuits (Chapter 10). Thus, it is not surprising that a person could associate a single attitude object with both positive and negative feelings—such as mixed feelings toward an enticing sundae that could necessitate an extra trip to the gym.

cause an emotional evaluation of an object should reflect a cognitive appraisal of its qualities. That is, we should like things we believe have positive consequences.

In fact, however, the beliefs and feelings comprising an attitude frequently develop separately and can change independently (see Petty & Cacioppo, 1981, 1986a). A classic example occurred in the U.S. presidential election in 2000. Many voters liked the policies of the Clinton administration, represented by Vice President Al Gore, but did not like Gore despite his policies. As political consultants well understand, the emotional component of a political attitude can be decisive in voting behavior and rests as much on implicit assessments of nonverbal gestures, likeability, and apparent sincerity as on the issues (Epstein, 1994).

INTERIM SUMMARY

An **attitude** is an association between an act or object and an evaluation. Attitudes can differ in a number of ways. **Attitude strength** refers to the durability and impact of an attitude on behavior. It is influenced by both **attitude importance** and **attitude accessibility** or the ease with which an attitude comes to mind. Attitudes can also be either explicit or implicit. **Implicit attitudes** regulate thought and behavior unconsciously and automatically. Attitudes vary in their degree of cognitive complexity as well as the extent to which the attitude object is associated with conflicting evaluative responses (**attitudinal ambivalence**). **Attitudinal coherence** refers to the extent to which an attitude (particularly its cognitive and evaluative components) is internally consistent.

Attitudes and Behavior

Logic would suggest that attitudes should predict behavior. For example, people's attitudes toward exercise should be closely related to how much they exercise. Once again, however, the empirical David is mightier than the logical Goliath: Broad attitudes predict behavior, but not very well (Ajzen, 1996; Fishbein & Ajzen, 1974). People's attitudes toward exercise are not good predictors of the probability that they will exercise, any more than religious attitudes predict attendance at religious ceremonies (Wicker, 1969).

Why are attitudes and behaviors so imperfectly correlated, and what factors affect the link between what we think and feel and how we behave? First, people's attitudes *do* predict their actions if the attitude and action are both relatively specific (Ajzen & Fishbein, 1977; Kraus, 1995). Asking people their attitude toward protecting the environment does not predict whether they will recycle, but asking their attitude toward recycling does (Oskamp, 1991).

Second, and perhaps most importantly, people's attitudes are only one of many influences on what they do (Ajzen & Fishbein, 1977). From a behaviorist perspective, behavior is under the control of environmental consequences. An environmentally minded person who buys one small bag of groceries a week might re-use her own canvas shopping bag each week and thus contribute to the longevity of tropical rain forests. An equally environmentally conscious person who totes groceries for her family up six flights of stairs might find the convenience of plastic bags such overwhelming reinforcement that she contributes instead to the longevity of landfills.

Third, consistent with social identity theory discussed earlier in this chapter, the consistency between people's attitudes and their behavior is higher if members of important groups appear to share and endorse similar attitudes (Terry & Hogg, 2001; White et al., 2002). Implicit or explicit attitudinal support from group members provides validation for an individual's own attitudes which, subsequently, are more likely to drive behavior.

Fourth, the recognition that attitudes vary along a number of dimensions points to some previously unrecognized complexities in the way attitudes affect behavior. As noted earlier, much of behavior is controlled by implicit procedures (Chapter 6), or habits, that people develop through experience, rather than by their explicit (con-

Making Connections

Because attitudes are only one of the factors that influence behavior, they may not be useful in predicting who a person will vote for in a particular election; but over the long run they will in fact predict the party the individual tends to endorse at the ballot box. As we saw in Chapter 12, human behavior is so complex that a single variable—whether an attitude or a personality trait—is rarely likely to predict what a person will do in a specific circumstance.

By aggregating (averaging) across behaviors, however, researchers get a clearer picture of a person's behavioral tendencies. Attitudes, like personality traits, predict behavior over the long run.

Big Picture φ Question 7

To what extent are psychological processes conscious or unconscious—that is, explicit versus implicit?

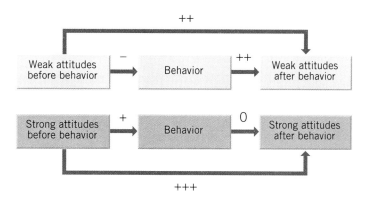

FIGURE 17.6 A model of attitude strength as a predictor of behavior. Positive signs indicate positive relationships between the two variables. Negative signs indicate negative relationships (i.e., as one variable increases, the other decreases; Chapter 2). The number of plus and minus signs for a particular relationship indicates how good a predictor one variable is of another. Thus, for example, strong attitudes before the behavior of donating to Greenpeace, were strongly predictive of strong attitudes after donating money. (Adapted from Holland et al., 2002).

scious) attitudes (Ouellette & Wood, 1998). Explicit attitudes predict some behaviors, particularly when people are consciously reflecting on them. Much of the time, however, implicit attitudes, which tend to be rapid and automatic, regulate people's actions and reactions, as when a white person who thinks she is unprejudiced makes less eye contact with black than white strangers.

Relatedly stronger attitudes are more predictive of behavior than weaker attitudes. In an examination of this, researchers measured participants' attitudes toward Greenpeace and their attitude strength. A week later, participants were asked if they would be willing to donate money to Greenpeace. Participants with more strongly held attitudes showed a greater willingness to donate than people with more weakly held attitudes (Holland et al., 2002) (Figure 17.6).

Finally, the way attitudes are acquired influences their impact on behavior. Attitudes shaped by personal experience are especially likely to influence action (Fazio & Zanna, 1981; Millar & Millar, 1996; Smith & Swinyard, 1983). For example, one study examined students' attitudes toward a campus housing shortage that forced many to sleep on cots in makeshift quarters for weeks (Regan & Fazio, 1977). Both the affected students and their more comfortably housed peers had negative attitudes toward the situation, but those who were personally affected were much more likely to write letters and sign petitions.

INTERIM SUMMARY

The cognitive, evaluative, and behavioral components of an attitude may vary independently of each other. Although attitudes are generally believed to include a behavioral disposition, they often do not predict specific behaviors, for several reasons: The behavior and the attitude are often at different levels of generality; other variables influence behavior; and attitudes vary in different ways that make prediction complex, such as the extent to which they are implicit or explicit.

Persuasion

People often have a vested interest in changing others' attitudes, whether they are selling products, running for political office, or trying to convince a lover to reconcile one more time. **Persuasion** refers to *deliberate efforts to change an attitude*.

Components of Persuasion   Interest in persuasion has a venerable past. Long before modern psychology, Aristotle described *rhetoric*—the art of persuasive speaking—as a combination of *ethos* (characteristics of the speaker), *pathos* (the appeal of the message), and *logos* (the logic of the argument). Psychologists have expanded Aristotle's view to identify several components of persuasion, including the source, message, channel (the medium in which the message is delivered), context, and re-

Apply & Discuss

Surprisingly, these people are not much more likely to recycle their glass and plastic at home than the average person.

■ Identify the basic dimensions on which attitudes toward the environment and recycling might vary?

■ Consider your own attitudes toward the environment and recycling. Where do they fall on each of these dimensions? For example, how complex are your feelings toward environmental protection in general, and recycling in particular?

■ What factors actually influence whether or not you recycle? How much do your attitudes determine your behavior on this issue?

ceiver (Lasswell, 1948; McGuire, 1985; Petty & Wegener, 1998; Petty et al., 1997). Attending to each of these aspects is crucial to the success of a persuasive appeal, whether the goal is to sell a car or get someone to agree to a date.

Source Speakers tend to be more persuasive when they appear credible (expert and trustworthy), attractive, likable, powerful, and similar to the recipient of the message (Chaiken, 1980; Simons et al., 1970). For politicians, particularly in countries such as the United States where presidential candidates must appeal directly to voters, winning votes is often a balancing act in which the successful candidate must seem likable but authoritative, powerful yet able to understand the concerns of everyday citizens.

Message The type of appeal (e.g., presenting one side of the argument or both) and the way it is delivered also affect attitude change. As we have seen, the match between the recipient's willingness and ability to think about the message and the way the message is delivered is crucial for persuasion. A jingle about a low-fat margarine will not convince someone who has compared the fat content of multiple brands and cares about the difference.

Fear appeals—efforts to induce fear to try to change attitudes—can sometimes be effective, but they can backfire if they induce too much fear and lead people to stop attending to the message and instead to focus on managing their anxiety (Insko et al., 1965). For example, messages about AIDS may fall on deaf ears if they are so frightening that people simply deny the realities. Fear can, however, be useful in inducing attitude change if the recipients of the message believe the danger applies to them and that they can do something to avoid it (see Olson & Zanna, 1993).

Channel The channel of persuasion is the means by which a message is sent—in words or images, verbally or nonverbally, in person or through media such as telephone or television. Choosing the right channel can be as important as selecting the right message. Because turning someone down for a date is much more difficult face to face than on the telephone, suitors of reluctant "targets" should make their pitch in person. Emotional appeals to contribute to emergency relief funds are more effective when the target of the communication can see starving children with distended stomachs rather than simply hear about their plight.

Context The context in which a message is presented can also influence attitude change (Petty & Wegener, 1998). Soft music in the background may lead an ambivalent "recipient" to agree to a second date, and a roomful of cheering supporters can make a political message seem much more exciting. An important aspect of the context is the presence of competing messages. Things would be easier for Coke if Pepsi did not advertise, and vice versa.

Psychologists and advertisers have devised many methods to increase resistance to contrary appeals. One is to get there first: Being the first to make a pitch renders a persuasive appeal more effective (Insko, 1964; Miller & Campbell, 1959). Another method, called **attitude inoculation**, involves *building up the receiver's "resistance" to a persuasive appeal by presenting weak arguments for it or forewarning against it* (McGuire, 1961; McGuire & Papageorgis, 1962). Thus, much as a vaccine builds the body's defenses through exposure to small, inert amounts of a virus, weak and easily assailable arguments supporting the other point of view prompt the person to develop counterarguments that serve as attitudinal "antibodies." Salespeople frequently use this technique when they know a customer is about to visit a competitor ("He'll tell you Dell has better customer service, but don't believe him").

Receiver Receiver characteristics—qualities of the person the communicator is trying to persuade—also affect the persuasiveness of a communication. People with strong attitudes on a topic are obviously less likely candidates for attitude change, and some people are simply more difficult to persuade in general (see Haugtvedt & Petty, 1992; Hovland & Janis, 1959). Further, people bias their information processing in order to preserve attitudes they do not want to change (MacCoun, 1998). Coffee drinkers, for example, discount messages about the dangers of caffeine (Liberman & Chaiken, 1992).

Individuals also vary in the extent to which they are likely to attend to and reflect on careful arguments, referred to as the *need for cognition* (Jarvis & Petty, 1996). People who focus on the substance of the arguments, however, do not necessarily form "better" attitudes. People can exercise considerable effort in preserving their biases and carefully attacking arguments that do not support their position.

The Elaboration Likelihood Model of Persuasion   As helpful as it is to understand all of the different components of persuasion, original models of persuasion that theorized about these components failed to address the question of "How?" How and when are people persuaded by a speaker's credibility? How do characteristics of the message alter audience member's attitudes? To address the "How" of persuasion, Richard Petty and John Cacioppo introduced the Elaboration Likelihood Model of Persuasion (ELM; Petty & Cacioppo, 1981; Petty & Wegener, 1998). The ELM suggests that there are two routes through which people can be persuaded (Chen & Chaiken, 1999; Eagly & Chaiken, 1992; Petty & Cacioppo, 1981, 1986a; Petty & Wegener, 1998).

The first, or **central route**, *involves inducing the recipient of a message to think carefully and weigh the arguments*. People who process centrally are highly involved with the issue, tend to be higher in their need for cognition or their need to think about issue-relevant arguments, and are attentive to the quality of the arguments that are presented. The second, or **peripheral route**, *appeals to less rational and thoughtful processes*. The peripheral route bypasses the cortex and often heads straight for points south, such as the limbic system, the heart, or the gut. Most beer commercials, for example, have little to offer in terms of rational persuasion. Were weekends really made for Michelob? When you say "Bud," have you *really* said it all? Thus, people who process persuasive communications peripherally may be influenced not by the quality of the arguments presented but rather by the sheer number of arguments presented or the attractiveness of the communicator.

The **elaboration likelihood model** *of persuasion posits that knowing how to appeal to people requires figuring out the likelihood that they will think much about (or elaborate on) the arguments* (Petty & Cacioppo, 1986b). Rational appeals are more likely to change the attitude of a person who both is motivated to think about a topic and has time to consider the arguments. In other words, when elaboration likelihood is high, appeals to logic are most likely to be persuasive.

Much of the time, however, people do not have the time, interest, or ability to weigh every argument about every possible attitude object that crosses their paths. Do I buy Green Giant string beans or Del Monte? If I am a true green bean devotee, I might spend the extra 30 seconds in the aisle at the grocery store pondering the merits of two brands (or walk over to the fresh produce aisle). However, as we have seen (Chapter 7), in everyday cognition people have to choose how to allocate their cognitive resources, because both working memory and time are limited commodities. People often use simple heuristics (cognitive shortcuts or rules of thumb) to make judgments about attitude objects. For example, they may simply follow the majority opinion (hence, laugh tracks on television shows, which tell people that the jokes are funny, in case they did not notice) or accept appeals to unknown experts (e.g., "nine out of ten dentists prefer …") (Chaiken, 1980; Chaiken et al., 1997).

The distinction between central and peripheral routes to attitude change parallels the distinction between explicit and implicit judgment and decision making (Chapter 7). Whereas explicit attitude change (the central route) requires conscious deliberation, implicit attitude change (the peripheral route) can occur in several ways. One is through classical conditioning of an object with an emotional response. Advertisers populate their commercials with beautiful women and virile men, subtly implying that using their product or drinking their beer will increase consumers' reproductive success (rather than their beer gut).

Another way to influence implicit attitude change is simply to repeat a message enough times that people start to believe it (Arkes et al., 1991). Politicians are well aware of this—a reason why they often repeat inaccurate information if they can get away with it. Repetition has persuasive effects for several reasons: It produces familiarity, which tends to produce liking (Zajonc, 1968, 1998); it strengthens the association between the two pieces of information; and it capitalizes on the fact that, over time, people tend to forget the source of a message and assume that if they have heard it enough, it must have some credibility.

Thus, changing someone's attitude requires attention to several variables. If the attitude really matters to the person, if the recipient of the message is knowledgeable about the subject, if the recipient has time to evaluate the arguments, and if the attitude was initially generated rationally by weighing costs and benefits, then the best appeal is to the head (central processing). In this case, the persuader should avoid distractions (glitzy campaigns, jingles, and hoopla) that impede conscious, rational processing and annoy the receiver. If, however, the attitude is not strongly held and is based on minimal knowledge, the best route is usually to the heart or the gut—or, at any rate, as far from the frontal lobes as possible.

INTERIM SUMMARY

Persuasion refers to deliberate efforts to change an attitude. Characteristics of the source, message, channel, context, and receiver all affect the effectiveness of persuasive appeals. Persuasion can occur through a **central route**, inducing the message recipient to think about the argument, or a **peripheral route**, appealing to less thoughtful processes. According to the **elaboration likelihood model**, the central route to attitude persuasion is more effective when the person is both motivated and able to think about the arguments, whereas the peripheral route is more effective when the likelihood that the person will engage in high-effort cognitive processing is low.

Cognitive Dissonance

Although attitude change often involves deliberate efforts at persuasion, another path to attitude change is cognitive dissonance. According to Leon Festinger (1957, 1962), who developed cognitive dissonance theory, attitude change can occur when various objects of thought, which he called "cognitive elements," are logically inconsistent— that is, when they are *dissonant* with one another. These objects of thought can be attitudes, behaviors, new information—virtually anything a person can think about. **Cognitive dissonance** thus refers to *a perceived discrepancy between an attitude and a behavior or between an attitude and a new piece of information*. For example, if a person holds the belief that smoking is dangerous (element 1) but does not smoke (element 2), she does not experience dissonance; the two cognitive elements are consistent. If, on the other hand, she knows that smoking is dangerous (element 1) but also knows she smokes (element 2), she experiences a discrepancy between her beliefs and behavior.

According to Festinger, this kind of discrepancy leads to a state of psychological tension similar to anxiety. The tension, in turn, motivates the individual to change the attitude, the behavior, or the perception of the inconsistent information to eliminate unpleasant arousal or anxiety. For example, if the person knows that smoking is bad but smokes anyway, she may change the belief component of her attitude toward smoking ("it's not really that dangerous—I don't know anyone who has died of lung

Apply & Discuss

Advertisers are keenly interested in shaping attitudes toward brands, products, and political candidates.

▪ To what extent can we use the same principles to understand attitudes toward cars and toward political figures?

▪ Are advertisers wise to rely on the same principles to guide advertising campaigns for a brand of soda and a political candidate? If not, what should be different in persuading a consumer versus a voter?

cancer from smoking"), or she may quit smoking. Alternatively, she may add some additional cognitive element that resolves the dissonance (e.g.,"I don't plan to smoke that many years, so it won't hurt me").

In a classic experiment testing the utility of cognitive dissonance theory, Festinger and Carlsmith (1959) had participants perform monotonous tasks for an hour. The experimenters told them that the aim of this procedure was to test their performance, but the actual purpose was to create a negative attitude toward the tasks. The investigators then asked some participants to tell the next "participant" (who was really a confederate of the experimenter) that the experiment was enjoyable. They paid the participants either $1 or $20 for their compliance.

We might expect that people who received $20 for hyping a boring task would feel more positive toward the task than those paid only $1. In fact, just the opposite occurred. Those who received only $1 rated the experimental tasks more enjoyable, and they more frequently agreed to participate in a similar experiment again. Although these results seem counterintuitive, they exquisitely matched the predictions of dissonance theory: To say that a boring task is interesting for a meager payment creates considerable dissonance. Participants who received only $1 either had to change their attitude toward the task or face the dissonance associated with knowing that they had sold their souls rather cheaply. In contrast, those who received $20 reduced their dissonance and thus avoided the need to change their attitude because they could readily explain their behavior in terms of the payment, a considerable amount in the late 1950s.

In Festinger's terms, participants in both conditions ($1 and $20 payment) experienced a discrepancy between what they believed (cognitive element 1,"the task is boring") and what they did (cognitive element 2,"I told this poor sucker that the task is interesting"). When participants in the $1 condition tried to explain this to themselves, they had *insufficient justification* for their action and hence had to change their attitude toward the task. In contrast, participants paid $20 could add a third cognitive element ("I told the guy it was interesting because they paid me a lot to do it"); a cognition relieved the logical inconsistency between what they believed and what they said.

Two variables that influence the extent to which dissonance arises and requires resolution are the perception of choice and the size of rewards and punishments (Cooper & Fazio, 1984; Wood, 2000). A person with a gun to his head will not feel much pressure to cling to attitudes he publicly professed at the time. Coerced statements create little dissonance because they are uttered with minimal choice. Similarly, as in Festinger and Carlsmith's study, the smaller the reward or punishment, the greater the attitude change because larger incentives minimize dissonance.

Dissonance Reduction   Cognitive dissonance theory is essentially a drive-reduction theory (Chapter 10). That is, reducing an uncomfortable emotional state (a drive) reinforces an attitude change. Suppose, for example, Linda has been dating Justin for a few weeks. She was really interested in him when they began dating, but he has seemed somewhat unenthusiastic, often preferring to go out with his buddies on weekends. Whether Linda is free to date other people is ambiguous; they are involved enough to suggest otherwise, but Justin's level of commitment hardly seems to imply an exclusive relationship.

The plot thickens when Bob asks her out for Saturday night. Bob seems like a nice enough guy, and Linda has no intention of spending the evening at home while Justin spends another night out with the boys, so she accepts. Then she begins to worry whether she has made the right choice—a phenomenon called *postdecision regret*. The tension she experiences may lead her to convince herself that Bob is more attractive than he is—essentially justifying a choice she has made that is inconsistent with another choice, dating Justin. She may also talk with her friends about the situation in a way that solicits a particular answer—for example, talking only to friends who dislike the way Justin has treated her, or "talking up" Bob's virtues. These are examples of *postdecision dissonance reduction*—or dissonance reduction after the fact.

We can see similar dissonance reduction effects following situations in which people have invested a considerable amount of time and effort only to have their expectations disconfirmed (Aronson & Mills, 1959). Some college men endure a great deal of hazing, harassment, and humiliation as they go about pledging a fraternity. Once they have been admitted to the fraternity, they find that it is not all it was cracked up to be. The result: Dissonance or inconsistency between their original expectations or beliefs and the reality. In order to reduce the dissonance, fraternity members build up the group in which they have invested so much time and energy. Through this *effort justification* process, dissonance is reduced and perceptions of the group are favorably influenced.

To what extent is dissonance reduction a conscious process, whereby people change their attitudes or behaviors based on conscious reflection? Recent research with amnesiacs provides some important clues. If dissonance reduction requires conscious awareness of a discrepancy between present and past attitudes or behavior, then amnesiacs who cannot consciously recall their behavior should show little dissonance reduction when faced with dissonant information. In fact, however, amnesiacs show *more*, not less, dissonance reduction than people with intact memory (Lieberman et al., 2001; see also Shultz & Lepper, 1995). This finding suggests that dissonance reduction occurs automatically, without conscious reflection.

Alternative Explanations　The original formulation of cognitive dissonance theory explained the results of these experiments in terms of the motivation to reduce dissonance. Not all researchers agree, however, that motivation is necessarily involved. An alternative nonmotivational explanation, derived from behaviorism, is self-perception theory. **Self-perception theory** holds that *individuals infer their attitudes, emotions, and other internal states by observing their own behavior* (Bem, 1967, 1972). Thus, if they see themselves telling someone that they like a task and they have received only $1 for doing so, they conclude that they must have liked it or they would not be saying so. According to self-perception theory, the attitudes people report depend on their behavior; as their behavior changes (because of changes in reinforcement contingencies) so again will their attitude. No motivation, tension, or perceived inconsistency is involved.

Recall the study of Greenpeace in which participants with strongly held attitudes were more willing to donate money than those with weakly held attitudes. By the second week of the study, however, something very different happened. The attitudes of participants with weak attitude strength but not strong attitude strength were affected by their donation behavior. In other words, participants with weak attitude strength who donated money changed their attitudes toward Greenpeace more than those who did not donate money or those who already held strong attitudes toward Greenpeace.

Other theories provide alternative motivational explanations of the results of dissonance experiments. For example, a *self-presentation* explanation suggests that what appear to be changes in attitudes in dissonance studies are really changes in *reported* attitudes (Tedeschi et al., 1971). Because people want to present themselves as rational and do not want to look foolish by behaving inconsistently, they report attitudes they do not really hold.

Still another motivational explanation maintains that people feel guilty, ashamed, or lacking in integrity after doing something that conflicts with their values, such as lying about a task. Thus, they change their attitudes to minimize their discomfort and preserve their self-esteem (see Abelson, 1983; Scher & Cooper, 1989; Steele, 1988).

Most likely, each of the explanations offered to explain the results of cognitive dissonance experiments is applicable at various times. When people do things that

Making Connections

Theories of cognitive dissonance that emphasize motivation resemble models of stress and coping and emotion regulation (Chapter 11). The person makes an appraisal of the situation as problematic—whether the problem is logical inconsistency, immorality, or the appearance of foolishness—which in turn leads to a negative or stressful emotional state. She then employs coping strategies (such as changing her attitude, changing her behavior, rationalizing her behavior by adding a third cognitive element, or changing the emotion directly by exercising, drinking, etc.) to reduce the unpleasant feeling.

do not seem "like them" but that do not have unpleasant consequences for other people, simple self-perception processes may explain why they change their attitudes. However, experiments measuring physiological responses demonstrate that dissonant information *can* produce emotional arousal that people experience as uncomfortable and that these feelings can indeed be reduced by changing a belief—or by other emotion-regulation strategies (Chapter 11). For example, watching a funny movie or misattributing the cause of discomfort to something irrelevant like a pill just taken can all reduce the need to change a dissonant belief (Fried & Aronson, 1995; Zanna & Cooper, 1974). Unpleasant feeling states are most likely to lead to attitude change when the person has done something that leads to shame, guilt, or anxiety, such as looking foolish to someone else or breaking a moral standard.

Culture and Dissonance   The extent to which cognitive dissonance is universal has recently come into question (Fiske et al., 1998). Research with Western subjects has shown that giving people positive feedback prior to a dissonance manipulation decreases the motivation to reduce dissonance (because the person is less threatened about his self-worth). In contrast, negative feedback increases attitude change through dissonance reduction because it essentially heightens the person's sense of incompetence, immorality, lack of integrity, or similar feelings (Steele, 1988).

One study compared responses of Japanese and Canadian subjects to see if these findings would hold in a non-Western sample (Heine & Lehman, 1997). Participants were first given a fake "personality test" and told the results would be available shortly. Next, the investigators asked participants to choose 10 CDs from a list of 40 they would most like to own and to indicate how much they would like each CD by making a mark on an unmarked 118-mm line labeled "wouldn't like this CD at all" on the left and "would like this CD very much" on the right.

Immediately afterward, participants received the "results" of the personality test. Some received negative feedback, some positive, and some no feedback at all, after which they had a few minutes to ponder the results. Then the experimenter came back with subjects' fifth- and sixth-choice CDs and gave them a choice between them. After a few more minutes of filling out some irrelevant information (to give time for dissonance-reduction processes to occur), participants again rated each of the 10 CDs using the same 118-mm line.

The results for Canadian participants were just as expected (Figure 17.7). Those who had received no feedback showed a substantial difference between their post-choice ratings of the two CDs; on the average, they preferred the one they had chosen by over 9 mm on a 118-mm line. Those who had been given positive feedback showed a much smaller effect, whereas those who had received negative feedback substantially changed their attitudes in favor of the CD they had chosen. No such effect occurred for the Japanese: They did not show a significant preference for the CD they had chosen under any condition.

Research with other Asian samples has produced similar findings. Why would this be? The authors suggest that the difference lies in the way Asians and North Americans view themselves. North Americans, like other people in the West, are individualistic and independent. To make a bad choice has strong implications for self-esteem, leading to attitude change in dissonance experiments. Asians, on the other hand, tend to be much more collectivist and interdependent in their views of themselves (Fiske et al., 1998; Markus & Kitayama, 1991). Their self-esteem rises and falls more with their ability to meet social expectations and maintain a sense of connection with those around them than it does with individual choices that indicate how smart or savvy they are.

Big Picture φ Question 4

To what extent is human nature particular versus universal?

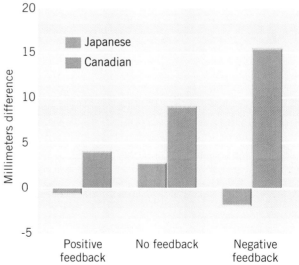

FIGURE 17.7   Dissonance reduction and culture. Canadian participants tended to reduce dissonance by increasing their relative preference for the CD they chose over the one they turned down, as assessed by the difference in the number of millimeters on a line on which they indicated their preference. This was particularly true under conditions of threat to their view of themselves (negative feedback). For Japanese participants, no dissonance reduction occurred under any of the three conditions. *Source:* Heine & Lehman, 1997, p. 396.

INTERIM SUMMARY

> **Cognitive dissonance** occurs when a person experiences a discrepancy between an attitude and a behavior or between an attitude and a new piece of information. This leads to a state of tension that can motivate attitude change. According to **self-perception theory**, attitudes change in dissonance experiments as people observe their own behavior. Other explanations emphasize self-presentation (trying to look good) or efforts to regulate unpleasant emotions such as guilt and shame. To some extent, cognitive dissonance may presume a particular way of thinking about and evaluating the self that is distinctively Western.

The Self

Thus far, we have paid little attention to the social stimulus to which people attend more than any other: the self. The concept of self has a long and rather serpentine history in psychology, slithering in and out of vogue. In some eras, such as the present, psychologists have viewed the self as a central aspect of psychological functioning (Baumeister, 1998; Epstein, 1994; Markus & Cross, 1990). In other eras, particularly during the heyday of behaviorism, psychologists viewed the self as a fuzzy, mushy concept, unobservable and hence scientifically unknowable. Currently, the self is one of the most widely studied topics within social psychology. Many of the most recent studies on the self have focused on "how the self directs social cognition and social behavior" (Banaji & Prentice, 1994, p. 298).

As often as the word "self" is uttered in people's day-to-day conversations (e.g., "I was just talking to myself," "I'm trying to find myself," "I have low self-esteem"), understanding what the self is and how it is best conceptualized would seem to be an easy task. However, one of the greatest challenges in describing the self seems to be defining it. Many behaviorists have justifiably complained that psychologists have used the same word to denote dozens of discrete phenomena and hence have failed to provide a coherent, empirically valid construct of the self. For years, theorists of nearly every persuasion have defined the self as the self-concept—the way people see themselves. The problem with this definition is that it is logically impossible: If the self-concept is a concept of something, it must be a concept of the self.

The only logically sensible definition, then, is that the **self** is *the person, including mental processes, body, and personality characteristics*. From this definition several others logically follow. The **self-concept** is *the person's concept of himself*, a schema about the self that guides the way we think about and remember information relevant to ourselves (Markus, 1977; Markus & Wurf, 1987; Rogers et al., 1977). It is a concept like any other (Chapter 7), such as squirrel, tree, or hairdresser. **Self-esteem** refers to *a person's evaluation of himself, how much he likes and respects the self*. The self-concept could be referred to as the cognitive element of the self (how we think about ourselves), with self-esteem representing the affective element (how we feel about ourselves).

Self-Esteem

Individuals have multiple motives that guide the way they think about themselves, such as the motive to see themselves accurately (Banaji & Prentice, 1994; Baumeister, 1998). Another primary motive regarding the self, which often competes with accuracy motivation, is the motivation to maintain high self-esteem (Chapter 10), sometimes referred to as the motive for self-enhancement. Just as individuals can conjure up a typical or prototypical self-concept, they have a core or global sense of self-esteem (Rosenberg, 1979), a usual way they feel about themselves. They also experience momentary fluctuations in self-esteem, depending on which self-schemas are cur-

Apply & Discuss

▪ In what ways does cognition about ourselves follow similar principles to cognition about others?

▪ To what extent do similar principles of memory apply? In what ways is cognition about ourselves different from cognition about others?

rently active. An athlete who wins a competition sees herself as a winner and enjoys a momentary boost in self-esteem, regardless of whether being a winner is part of her prototypical self-concept.

Research with Western subjects suggests that self-esteem is hierarchically organized, presumably tied to a hierarchically organized view of the self. Thus, nested below a general level of self-esteem, people have feelings about themselves along specific dimensions, such as their morality, physical appearance, and competence (Coopersmith, 1967; Harter et al., 1998). A person with generally low esteem for his athletic prowess may nevertheless recognize himself to be a decent tennis player. People generally maintain positive self-esteem by giving greater emotional weight to areas in which they are more successful.

In this way, people cannot only maintain their self-esteem, but they can also enhance their self-esteem, at least in areas where they are more successful. People appear to have an almost innate need to maintain a positive sense of self. Although there are a number of possible ways in which people can create this positive self view, one way is by evaluating themselves as better than the average other person. For example, Garrison Keillor (known for his radio variety show "A Prairie Home Companion") in his Lake Wobegon books describes a society "where all the women are strong, all the men are good-looking, and all the children are above average." Although the logical impossibility of this world fails to escape anyone's attention, what people fail to notice is the degree to which they engage in the same sort of illogical thinking. Positive illusions such as this were illustrated quite convincingly in a study in which college students rated themselves and the average other college student of the same sex on 20 positive traits and 20 negative traits. On average, participants rated themselves as better than average on 38 of the 40 traits (Alicke et al., 1995).

A *U.S. News & World Report* (March 31, 1997, p. 18) survey several years ago illustrated this same phenomenon. A group of Americans were surveyed regarding how likely they thought it was that 15 famous individuals were to go to Heaven. Sixty-six percent of the respondents thought that Oprah Winfrey was "very likely" or "somewhat likely" to go to Heaven. Mother Teresa received similar ratings by 79 percent of those responding. Only 28 percent perceived that Dennis Rodman was "somewhat likely" to go to Heaven. Although these perceptions are interesting in and of themselves, the most interesting ratings involved people's assessments of their own likelihood of going to Heaven. A whopping 87 percent of the Americans thought that they were likely to go to Heaven, even more than thought Mother Teresa would go to Heaven!

Much research that has been done on the self has examined different mechanisms by which people go about trying to maintain high self-esteem. For example, when people compare themselves with other people on a particular dimension, a process termed *social comparison*, they often use as their comparison group individuals who are worse off than they are (i.e., *downward social comparison*; Wills, 1981; Wood, 1989). By comparison to these "downtrodden" individuals, people can maintain a positive view of their own traits and abilities. In addition, people may engage in **self-handicapping**, *a process by which they set themselves up to fail when success is uncertain in order to preserve their self-esteem* (Higgins et al., 1990; Jones & Berglas, 1978). In this way, people can control the attributions that others make for their performance. In the event of failure, other people will attribute the lack of success to the impediment that "prevented" success. Should success occur in spite of the barrier, then the person must really be talented and worthy of others' praise.

One study tested self-handicapping in an arena in which handicapping is not unfamiliar: golf. Stone (2002) led participants to believe that an athletic test was a measure either of their natural athletic ability or simply of general sports performance. White participants who feared that they would confirm the stereotype of poor white athleticism (i.e., those who thought the test was a measure of their natural ability) self-handicapped by practicing less before the actual test (based on golf) than those who did not process the information in terms of a stereotype threat (i.e., people

Likelihood of Women Living in a Specific Southeastern State as a Function of Their First Name

| | First Name | | | |
State	Florence	Georgia	Louise	Virginia
Florida	**13,145 (9,641)**	1,920	8,820	8,822
Georgia	2,591	**2,202 (1,103)**	5,335	2,985
Louisiana	2,646	926	**4,303 (3,175)**	2,054
Virginia	3,861	1,298	5,671	**8,880 (5,940)**

FIGURE 17.8   People show a preference for living in cities and states that begin with the same letter as their own name. The numbers in parentheses represent the number of individuals with that particular name who, by chance, would be expected to live in cities. As you can see, however, the actual number of people with a name that resembles the state or residence exceeds that chance value. Adapted from Pelham et al., 2002, p. 474.

who believed the test was a measure of general sports performance). Should individuals in the former condition not perform well on the test, they, and others, could attribute their poor performance to the lack of practice. Should they succeed on the golf test in spite of the lack of practice, then they must be athletically talented, indeed. Interestingly, this study was conducted during the era of Tiger Wood's dominance over golf. Had he not been such a presence in the sport, white participants may have felt less of a need to self-handicap.

People may not be aware of just how much their efforts at maintaining self-esteem can determine their life choices, even when they are not aware of it. One study demonstrated what the researchers referred to as *implicit egotism* by showing that people prefer to live in cities and to work in occupations that begin with the letter of either their first or last name (Pelham et al., 2002). They conducted 11 studies in which they showed, for example, that Marys are overrepresented in Maryland as are Philips in Philadelphia and Georges in Georgia (see Figure 17.8). Similarly, women disproportionately chose to live in cities that began with "Saint" followed by their own name. For example, women named Anne were disproportionately represented in cities named St. Anne. The data indicated that the frequency with which this happened was 44 percent greater than chance! In terms of occupations, people whose names started with L were more likely than chance to be lawyers, whereas those whose name began with R were more inclined to be roofing specialists.

One final means (among many) by which a person may maintain or even enhance her self-esteem is *basking in reflected glory* or *BIRGing* (Cialdini et al., 1976). People who BIRG publicly announce their affiliation with another person or group that is successful, even though they had nothing to do with the success of that other person or group. When your college football team wins, who do people say won the game? They say "*We* won!" When the team loses, however, the chant changes to "*They* lost!" Thus, we associate ourselves with success and distance ourselves from failure.

Although self-esteem often feels like something we "have," self-esteem reflects as much a dynamic set of skills for *maintaining* positive feelings about the self as it does the accessibility of positive attitudes toward the self. Individuals with high self-esteem think and behave in ways that lead to positive feelings. When experimentally forced into a bad mood, they tend to problem solve and think positive thoughts, which in turn make them feel better (and better about themselves). In contrast, people with low self-esteem tend to respond to bad moods with negative thoughts (Smith & Petty, 1995). Similarly, people with high, but not low, self-esteem are more likely to help someone out while in a negative mood, which then makes them feel better about themselves (Brown & Smart, 1991).

Although everyone engages in behaviors to maintain or enhance their self-esteem, some are more inclined to do so than others. One question related to this behavior concerns the degree to which men and women differ in their proclivity to work toward self-esteem maintenance. Some studies have found that women have higher self-esteem than men, whereas other studies have found the opposite. A recent meta-analysis examining the collective findings across studies (Chapter 2) found that men have higher global self-esteem than women, but that the overall difference was very small (Kling et al., 1999). It would probably be safer to conclude that there are as many within-group differences (i.e., differences among men or among women) than there are between-group differences (i.e., differences between men and women). This is particularly likely when assessments of self-esteem focus on specific traits or abilities as opposed to more global evaluations.

Big Picture φ Question 5

To what extent are psychological processes the same in men and women?

Self-Consistency

A less obvious motive guiding the self is **self-consistency**, *the motive to interpret information to fit the way one already sees oneself and to prefer people who verify rather than challenge that view* (Lecky, 1945; Pinel & Swann, 2000; Swann, 1990). Most of the time, self-consistency and self-esteem motives do not conflict; because most people hold relatively favorable views of themselves, they prefer positive information because it enhances self-esteem and bolsters their existing self-concept.

For people who do not like themselves, however, these two motives can lead in opposite directions. They want to feel better about themselves, but they also dislike evidence that contradicts their self-concept (Swann et al., 1987).

Depressed people actually prefer to interact with others—including marital partners—who have a negative view of them (Chapter 15). Individuals who perceive themselves negatively appear to avoid people who give them feedback to the contrary for several reasons: They consider the feedback untrue, they feel that the relationship will be smoother and more predictable if the other person understands them, and they believe people who view them positively are less perceptive (Swann et al., 1992a).

Self-Presentation

Yet another strategy that people use to gain self-knowledge and to maintain favorable views of the self is self-presentation. The self does not exist in a vacuum. Although we all have aspects of ourselves that are known only to us, much of the self is determined and influenced by our interactions with others, what William James referred to as the "social self." Indeed, Cooley (1902) coined the term *looking glass self* to refer to the fact that other people are a mirror in which we see ourselves. In other words, much of our self-concept is reflected back to us by other people with whom we interact.

Given the interpersonal side to our "self," few of us are surprised to discover that people attempt to regulate the way that they present their "self" in interactions with others. *The process by which people attempt to control the impressions that others form of them* is called **self-presentation** or *impression management* (Leary, 1995; Leary & Kowalski, 1990; Chapter 11). To get a handle on self-presentation, think about all of the behaviors you perform on a given day at least in part to influence how other people see you. Before leaving for class each day, you probably shower, brush your teeth, and dress in a way that will be approved of by others. You eat with utensils as opposed to your hands, and conduct yourself appropriately and respectfully in class. Although there are multiple reasons why you might perform these behaviors, one of those reasons is self-presentation or your desire to influence how others perceive you.

Although it was once thought that people generally try to make favorable impressions on others, researchers now know that the goal is to create desired impressions, either favorable or unfavorable. Thus, although some people might be motivated to put their best foot forward in their interactions with others, still others want to be perceived as threatening or intimidating. They present themselves in ways that will lead others to perceive them in these desired, albeit negative, ways (Leary, 1995).

Attempts to make impressions, particularly favorable impressions, on others often fail, however. *Instances in which our desires to influence the impressions other people form of us fail* are termed **self-presentational predicaments**, and the emotion most frequently experienced in such situations is embarrassment. For example, when people trip on the stairs, the first thing they do is look around to see if anyone saw them fall. Tripping on the stairs creates a self-presentational predicament whereby one's desire to be seen as a competent, coordinated individual is thwarted. Confronted with such predicaments, people engage in behaviors designed to repair damage to their image. For example, blushing that may follow a fall on the stairs is considered a type of nonverbal apology (Leary et al., 1992). People may also try to distance themselves from their own embarrassing behavior. Participants in one study who were actually in favor of affirmative action were forced to read essays against affirmative action in the presence of an African-American person. These individuals reported significantly more discomfort and engaged in a greater number of distancing behaviors, such as providing excuses for their actions, than participants who read the essays in front of a white person. The purpose of the distancing behaviors was to restore their damaged image before the African-American person (Fleming & Rudman, 1993).

Even though self-presentation is a universal behavior, some people are more likely to impression manage than others. *Individual differences in the degree to which people manage their impressions* are referred to as **self-monitoring** (Gangestad & Snyder, 2000; Snyder, 1974). High self-monitors resemble social chameleons. Who they are and how they present themselves varies with the situation in which they find themselves. Low self-monitors, on the other hand, are much less concerned with the impressions that others form of them.

Gender differences related to self-presentation also exist. Both men and women attempt to regulate the impressions that other people form of them, but they tend to do so in different arenas. In other words, desired identity images for men and women differ. Societal norms dictate that men should present themselves as dominant and assertive (i.e., as masculine individuals). Women, on the other hand, are socialized to present themselves in more feminine ways, such as appearing more nurturing and as more relationship-oriented. Consistent with this, women who desire to make a favorable impression eat "more lightly" than men, because eating lightly is associated with being feminine (Pliner & Chaiken, 1990). One study showed that this effect was particularly salient when the women thought they were interacting with a man who perceived them as being unfeminine (Mori et al., 1987). Eating less was a way of restoring a desired and socially accepted social image of being feminine.

Big Picture φ Question 5

To what extent are psychological processes the same in men and women?

From Brain to Behavior | Physical Health and Views of the Self

People have schemas or mental representations not only about the way they are but also about the way they *wish* they were or *fear* becoming (Markus & Nurius, 1986; Niedenthal et al., 1992). One theory distinguishes three kinds of self-concepts: actual, ideal, and ought (Higgins, 1987, 1999). The **actual self** refers to *people's views of how they actually are*. The **ideal self** refers to *the hopes, aspirations, and wishes that define the way the person would like to be*. The **ought self** includes *the duties, obligations, and responsibilities that define the way the person should be*.

Thus, a person may see himself as a moderately successful businessman (actual self) but hope to become the chief executive officer of a company (ideal self). At the same time, he may volunteer at a soup kitchen on Thanksgiving to satisfy a nagging sense that he is not contributing enough to his community (ought self). People have actual, ideal, and ought selves from a number of points of view, including their own and those of significant others. A person may feel she is meeting her "ought" standards for herself but that she has failed to meet her mother's expectations.

Discrepancies between these various self-schemas are associated with particular types of emotion (Higgins, 1987; Strauman, 1992). When people perceive a discrepancy between their actual self and their ideal self, they tend to feel emotions such as disappointment, dissatisfaction, shame, and embarrassment. These are characteristic feelings of individuals who are depressed, who feel their wishes and hopes are unfulfilled.

People who experience a discrepancy between actual self and ought self feel emotions such as anxiety, fear, resentment, guilt, self-contempt, or uneasiness. These feelings are characteristic of anxious individuals, who believe they have failed to meet their obligations and hence may be punished.

Research suggests that these schemas may influence not only mood but physical health. As we have seen (Chapter 11), emotional distress can depress immune-system functioning, making a person vulnerable to ill health. Enduring ways of perceiving the self may thus lead to chronic feelings that increase vulnerability to illness.

One remarkable study demonstrated this effect by comparing people who were anxious, depressed, or neither (Strauman et al., 1993). The investigators asked participants to describe their actual, ideal, and ought selves, thanked them for their participation, and told them the experiment was over. Six weeks later, their research assistants, allegedly conducting a different experiment, primed discrepancies between actual and ideal self in depressed participants and between actual and ought self in anxious participants. They did this by exposing participants to words they had previously mentioned that were related to these discrepancies. For example, the investigators might ask an anxious subject who described his actual self as shy but his ought self as confident to think about the importance of being confident. (They also included words that were irrelevant to the person so that participants would not figure out what was happening.)

A week later, the experimenters exposed participants to a set of entirely irrelevant words (actually, taken from other participants), which they compared against the results of the previous session. Control subjects were similarly exposed one day to self-referential words (words taken from their first session) and another day to irrelevant words. After each session, the investigators took blood samples to ascertain levels of natural killer cells, a rough index of immune response.

The main findings are reproduced in Figure 17.9. The killer cell activity of control subjects, who were neither depressed nor anxious, went up slightly when they were exposed to self-referential words. Depressed subjects showed a slight decrease in killer cell activity when exposed to words related to their ideal-self discrepancies, although this was not statistically significant. The most striking finding was that for anxious subjects, whose killer cell levels were significantly lower after being exposed to words related to their self-perceived failings (actual/ought discrepancies). Thinking about their unfulfilled obligations or unmet standards made them momentarily more vulnerable to illness. These findings are preliminary, but they suggest that chronic discrepancies between the way one believes one is and the way one ought or ideally should be might have a lasting impact on health.

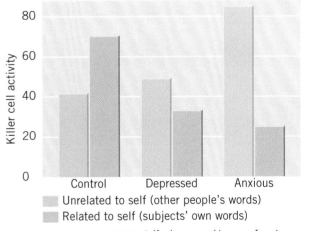

FIGURE 17.9 Self-schemas and immune functioning. Exposing nondepressed, nonanxious control subjects to words related to their ideal and ought selves led to a slight increase in killer cell activity—that is, to heightened immune functioning. For depressed and especially for anxious subjects, in contrast, exposure led to diminished immune functioning. *Source:* Adapted from Strauman et al., 1993, p. 1049.

INTERIM SUMMARY

Considered to be a driving force behind social cognition, the **self** is one of the most researched topics in social psychology today. Particular attention has been devoted to people's attempts to maintain and enhance their **self-esteem** (the need to view oneself positively) through such behaviors as downward social comparison, self-handicapping, implicit egotism, and basking in reflected glory. At times conflicting with the motive to maintain self-esteem is the motive for **self-consistency** (the motive to interpret information to fit existing self-concepts). Another strategy for maintaining favorable views of the self is **self-presentation** or people's attempts to control the impressions that others form of them. Although much of our behavior is motivated by self-presentational concerns, at times, **self-presentational predicaments** occur that threaten the image we would like to portray. The self that people sometimes present in their interactions with others is the **actual self** (how they really are). They may also self-present in ways that reflect their **ideal self** (the self they would like to be) or the **ought self** (the self they feel they should be).

A Global Vista   **Culture and Self**

Big Picture φ Question 4

To what extent is human nature particular versus universal?

The notion that people have a self-concept and some core of selfhood that distinguishes them from others seems intuitively obvious to people living in twenty-first century Western societies. This view would not, however, be commonsensical to people in most cultures in most historical epochs (Geertz, 1974; Markus & Kitayama, 1991; Shweder & Bourne, 1982). That the term "the individual" is synonymous with "the person" in contemporary usage demonstrates how the individualism of our culture is reflected in its language. Not coincidentally, the prefix "self-," as in "self-esteem" or "self-representation," did not evolve in the English language until around the time of the Industrial Revolution.

A Relational View of the Self

The contemporary Western view of "the person" is of a bounded individual, distinct from others, who is defined by more or less idiosyncratic attributes. In contrast, most cultures, particularly the nonliterate tribal societies that existed throughout the vast expanse of human history, view the person in her social and familial context, so that the self-concept is far less distinctly bounded.

When the Wintu Indians of North America described being with another person who was closely related or intimate with them, they would not use a phrase such as "John and I," but rather, "John we." They reserved "and" to signify distance between people with minimal relation. When anthropologist Dorothy Lee (1950) tried to elicit an autobiography from a Wintu woman, she received an extensive account of the lives of the woman's ancestors. Only with considerable prompting did the woman eventually discuss "that which was in my mother's womb." Cheyenne autobiographies similarly tend to begin with "My grandfather…" (Straus, 1982).

This relational view of selfhood is not confined to North American tribes. It is common among African groups (Comaroff, 1980) and has been observed in many Asian and Indo-Chinese cultures. For example, traditional Hindus in India frequently give their caste and village along with their name when they are asked to identify themselves (DeVos et al., 1985).

Why Does the Self Differ Across Cultures?

Two factors seem to explain the differences between contemporary Western and other views of the self. First, some cultures are simply more group centered or collectivist and others more individualistic (Fiske et al., 1998; Markus & Kitayama, 2001; Triandis, 1989). Because Japanese culture emphasizes cooperation rather than the Western ideal of autonomy, the Japanese experience the self less in terms of internal states than in terms of social relationships (Cousins, 1989; De Vos & Suarez-Orozzo, 1986). Thus, for the Japanese, *sincerity* describes behavior that conforms to a person's role expectations (carrying out one's duties), whereas for North Americans it means behaving in accordance with one's inner feelings (De Vos et al., 1985). Sincere behavior in Japan may thus be very insincere to an American. In general, the Western self tends to be conceptualized as more independent, whereas the Asian self tends to be conceptualized as more *inter*dependent (Kitayama et al., 1998).

A second influence on conceptions of selfhood is technological development (Westen, 1985, 1991). Careful examination of historical documents suggests that only a few centuries ago the Western concept of self was much closer to the non-Western, group-centered view (Baumeister, 1998). The values, attitudes, and self-concepts of people in rural Greece, for example, resemble the collectivistic orientation one finds in China more than the individualism of contemporary Athens (see Triandis, 1989).

Ten thousand years ago, before the advent of agriculture, humans lived in bands (small groups). In these band societies, a concept of self distinct from other people and nature was generally absent, and moral values focused on the interests of the clan or band. With the rise of agriculture, which allowed accumulation of personal resources and led to social classes, people became more aware of individuality. At the same time, however, this awareness was countered by cultural proscriptions against it.

Around the time of the Industrial Revolution, something remarkable happened: The concept of the individual, free of attachments and duties, was born. And the individual has been born again wherever technological development has taken hold. Technological development seems to facilitate individualism, and with it a more individuated sense of selfhood, for several reasons. The first is geographical mobility. People who remain in a small community, as their kin have before them, tend to view themselves in a different context than people who may relocate hundreds or thousands of miles away. In addition, changing work conditions, such as wage labor and work that is not performed communally with kin or clan, lead to a sense of individual competence.

Furthermore, in technologically developed societies people earn much of their status through their actions rather than their family affiliations. They also frequently take up occupations different from those of their parents. When a man is no longer a hunter or farmer like his father, his representations of self and father diverge. Literacy and education also personalize skills and competences, which are no longer experienced as collective knowledge because they may be learned through individual study.

In addition, increased life span and higher standard of living make personal pleasures, desires, and interests more important. Factors such as family size and whether children have their own rooms probably have a subtle influence as well. Whether the cultural differences that now divide Japan and the West will remain despite the pressures of industrialization is a profound psychological question that will probably be resolved over the course of this next century.

In the late nineteenth century, Americans thought nothing of lending neighbors a hand for days or weeks to build a barn. Just a century later, this seems inconceivable to many people, with the highly individualized sense of self associated with industrialization.

Summary

1. **Social psychology** examines the influence of social processes on the way people think, feel, and behave.

Social Cognition

2. **Social cognition** refers to the processes by which people make sense of others, themselves, social interactions, and relationships.

3. **First impressions** are the initial representations people form when they encounter someone for the first time. **Schemas**—patterns of thought that organize experience—guide attention, en-

coding, and retrieval of information about people, situations, and relationships.

4. **Stereotypes** are characteristics attributed to people based on their membership in specific groups. **Prejudice** refers to judging an individual based on (usually negative) stereotypes. Racial and ethnic prejudice has roots both in motivation and cognition, and in the person and the broader social system. Stereotypes can be implicit or explicit. Prejudice typically requires the distinction between **ingroups** and **outgroups**.

5. The process of making inferences about the causes of one's own

and others' thoughts, feelings, and behavior is called **attribution**. People can make **external attributions** (attributions to the situation), **internal attributions** (attributions to the person), and attributions about interactions between the person and the situation. In making these attributions, they rely on three types of information: **consensus** (how everyone acts in that situation), **consistency** (how this person typically reacts in that situation), and **distinctiveness** (how this person usually reacts in different situations). **Discounting** occurs when people downplay the role of a variable that could account for a behavior because they know other variables may be contributing to the behavior in question. The opposite situation occurs with **augmentation**, which involves increasing an internal attribution for behavior that has occurred despite situational pressures.

6. Social cognition may be biased in a number of ways, including the tendency to attribute behavior to other people's dispositions even when situational factors could provide an explanation (the **correspondence bias**), and the propensity to see oneself in a more positive light than one deserves (the **self-serving bias**).

Attitudes

7. An **attitude** is an association between an object and an evaluation, which usually includes cognitive, evaluative, and behavioral components. These three components can, however, vary independently. Attitudes vary on a number of dimensions, such as their strength, accessibility, and complexity; whether they are implicit or explicit; and the extent to which they involve ambivalence. They also differ on their coherence (particularly the fit between cognitive and evaluative components). Broad attitudes tend not to be good predictors of behavior.

8. **Persuasion** refers to deliberate efforts to change an attitude. The effectiveness of a persuasive appeal depends on a number of factors related to the source of the communication, the message, the channel (the means by which a message is sent), the context, and the receiver. It can occur through either careful, explicit thought (the **central route**) or less explicit and rational processes (the **peripheral route**). Persuading people to change their behavior can also lead them to change their attitudes.

9. **Cognitive dissonance** occurs when a person experiences a discrepancy between an attitude and a behavior or between an attitude and a new piece of information that does not fit with it. Cognitive dissonance can motivate attitude change, although several distinct processes may underlie dissonance phenomena.

The Self

10. The **self** refers to the person. An individual's concept of the self is the **self-concept**.

11. **Self-esteem** refers to a person's feelings toward the self. People's views of themselves are motivated by self-enhancement motivations but also by the need for **self-consistency**, interpreting information to fit the way they already see themselves.

12. As a means of maintaining desired images of the self, people engage in **self-presentation**, the process by which they try to control the images that other people form of them.

13. The contemporary Western view of the person is of a bounded individual, distinct from significant others, who is defined by more or less idiosyncratic attributes. In contrast, most cultures have understood the person in social and familial context. Technological development has fostered individualism.

Key Terms

actual self   648
attitude   632
attitude accessibility   633
attitude importance   633
attitude inoculation   638
attitude strength   633
attitudinal ambivalence   635
attitudinal coherence   635
attribution   626
attributional style   627
augmentation   627
authoritarian personality   620
central route   639

cognitive dissonance   640
consensus   627
consistency   627
correspondence bias   628
discounting   627
discrimination   619
distinctiveness   627
elaboration likelihood model   639
external attributions   626
first impressions   617
halo effect   618
ideal self   648

implicit attitudes   634
ingroups   624
internal attributions   626
intuitive scientists   626
ought self   648
outgroups   624
peripheral route   639
persuasion   637
prejudice   619
self   644
self-concept   644
self-consistency   647
self-esteem   644

self-handicapping   645
self-monitoring   648
self-perception theory   642
self-presentation   647
self-presentational predicaments   648
self-serving bias   629
social cognition   616
social identity theory   625
social psychology   616
stereotypes   619
superordinate goals   625

Interpersonal Processes

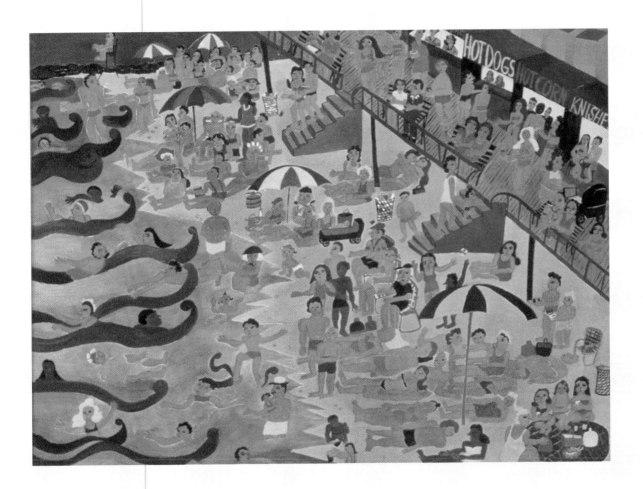

amuel Oliner was 12 years old when the Nazis invaded the Jewish ghetto in Poland where he lived. His entire family was killed, but Samuel managed to escape. After two days of hiding, during which he witnessed a child bayoneted and a baby shot with a pistol, he found his way to the home of a Christian woman with whom his father had done business. She fed him and taught him how to pass for a Christian peasant, and he survived the war. Years later, Oliner wrote a book about the small number of people who risked their lives and the lives of their families to protect Jews during the Holocaust (Oliner & Oliner, 1988; see also, Oliner, 2002). He and his research team interviewed over 400 rescuers and compared them with 72 individuals who neither helped nor hindered the Nazis. They sought to answer a simple question: What made the rescuers perform such extraordinary acts of **altruism**, that is, *helping another person with no apparent gain, and even potential cost, to oneself*?

The altruism of these individuals seems to defy theories of moral development (Chapter 14). For example, according to cognitive–social theories, reward, punishment, and expectancies control behavior. Everyone in Germany and the occupied countries during the war faced the same contingencies of reinforcement—to be caught rescuing Jews meant certain execution—but several thousand people did so nonetheless. According to cognitive–developmental theories, moral heroism should occur only among people with a high level of moral reasoning. Yet only about half of Oliner's rescuers referred to complex or abstract principles. In fact, several offered strikingly conventional reasons for their actions, such as, "I am an obedient Christian; the Lord wanted us to rescue those people and we did" (Oliner & Oliner, 1988, p. 155).

Rescuers differed from nonrescuers on both **situational variables** (*the situations in which people find themselves*) and **dispositional variables** (*their personalities and attitudes*). Perhaps surprisingly, one of the variables that distinguished the two groups was completely situational: Rescuers had more available rooms in their houses and were more likely to have a cellar. On the dispositional side, rescuers reported having come from closer knit families and having had parents who sometimes reasoned with them as a mode of discipline, rather than simply punishing them. Overwhelmingly, they reported being taught to treat people fairly regardless of their race, color, or class.

Understanding why some people risked their lives while others did nothing—and why still others have used ultranationalist ideology as an excuse to steal, rape, and murder—is the work of social psychologists. In the previous chapter we focused on the cognitive processes people use to try to understand themselves and others. In this chapter we will address motives, emotions, and behaviors that emerge in social interaction. We begin by examining interpersonal attraction and relationships, from brief encounters through long-term love relationships. We then turn to two very different forms of social interaction, which Oliner encountered in his childhood odyssey: altruism and aggression. Next we investigate the influence of other people on the way individuals behave and consider what happens when individuals participate in groups. We conclude by placing the psychology of our era in its social and historical context and returning to some of the big picture questions with which we began in the opening chapter.

Throughout, we address a key question: To what extent does our behavior depend on the groups of which we are a part? In other words, do the same psychological principles apply when people are alone as when they are with groups? Can we understand social behavior through principles of individual psychology, or do people function differently when they are together? And how do social and cultural change affect individual psychology?

Relationships

People *affiliate*, or seek out and spend time with others, for many reasons. Sometimes they interact to accomplish instrumental goals, such as raising money for a charity or meeting over dinner to discuss a business deal. Other interactions reflect family ties, shared interests, desires for companionship, or sexual interest (Fiske, 1992; Mills & Clark, 1994). Here we focus on two lines of research, one that examines the factors that attract people to each other and another that explores a particular kind of attraction in enduring relationships: love.

Factors Leading to Interpersonal Attraction

Although everyone likes to be alone at times, most people thrive on their relationships with others. Indeed, social psychologists believe that humans have a great **need to belong**, *to be involved in relationships with others* (Baumeister & Leary, 1995). Much of what people do and don't do they do and don't do to assure that they remain included by important others and that they avoid being excluded. Given this intense need to belong, what determines the individuals with whom we choose to be included? What draws us to some people but not to others? According to social psychologists, several key factors determine **interpersonal attraction**, *the reasons people choose to spend time with other people*.

Proximity   Sometimes the reason people spend time with particular others is as simple as proximity: Numerous studies have documented that people tend to choose their friends and lovers from individuals nearby. Driving home today I heard the Steven Stills' lyrics "If you can't be with the one you love, love the one you're with," suggesting that love and attraction can stem from proximity. One study surveyed 44 Maryland State Police trainees who had been assigned rooms and classroom seats in alphabetical order (Segal, 1974). When the trainees were asked to name their three closest friends on the force, the closer together their surnames, the more likely they were to be friends.

Proximity plays an equally important role in romantic relationships. As one observer wryly commented, "Cherished notions about romantic love notwithstanding, the chances are about 50–50 that the 'one and only' lives within walking distance"

(Eckland, cited in Buss & Schmitt, 1993, p. 205). Social–psychological research has repeatedly shown that situational influences such as proximity (or merely having a spare room in Nazi-occupied Germany) have a remarkably strong impact on behavior.

Of course, people neither become friends nor fall in love *simply* because the other person is within walking distance. Rather, proximity allows people to get to know one another. It also sets the stage for familiarity, and familiarity tends to breed affection (Zajonc, 1968, 1998). From an evolutionary perspective, the link between familiarity and liking may be part of our genetic endowment: People who are familiar are likely to be safe, and they are likely to be relatives or alliance partners.

Increased proximity and familiarity with someone initially disliked, however, can lead to increasing dislike over time if nothing changes to "dislodge" the initial impression (Festinger et al., 1950; Klinger & Greenwald, 1994). At the same time, proximity may lead to negative feelings even for those we initially liked, a phenomenon referred to as *environmental spoiling* (Ebbesen et al., 1976). Being in close proximity to others exposes us to their bad habits and qualities as well as their good ones. If the bad outweigh the good, environmental spoiling occurs.

Although early research showed a strong relationship between proximity and interpersonal attraction, recent research suggests that it is *interaction accessibility* rather than close physical proximity that really determines attraction (Berscheid & Reis, 1998). With the widespread use of the Internet, interaction accessibility takes on a whole new meaning. Defining proximity in terms of the accessibility of others widens the scope of people to whom a person might be attracted.

Interpersonal Rewards A second factor that influences interpersonal attraction is the degree to which interaction with another person is rewarding. From a behaviorist point of view, the more people associate a relationship with reward, the more likely they are to affiliate (Byrne & Murnen, 1988; Clark & Pataki, 1995; Newcomb, 1956).

One ingenious experiment tested a classical conditioning theory of attraction: that children should prefer other children they meet under enjoyable conditions (Lott & Lott, 1974). The investigators placed first and third graders in groups of three. They gave some of the children a chance to succeed on a task, rewarding them for it, and rigged the task so that others would fail. Later, they asked the children to name a classmate they would like to take on a family vacation. One out of four children in the success condition chose a child who had participated in the study with them, compared to only one in *20* children in the failure condition.

Social exchange theories, based on behaviorist principles, ***consider reciprocal reward the foundation of relationships*** (Homans, 1961). In this view, in the social as in the economic "market," people try to maximize the value they can obtain with their resources (Kenrick et al., 1993). Or to put it another way, choosing a relationship is like trying to get the best "bang for the buck." The resources (the "bucks") in social relationships are personal assets: physical attractiveness, wit, charm, intelligence, material goods, and the like. In romantic relationships, people tend to choose others of similar value (as culturally defined) because both partners are trying to maximize the value of their mate.

Similarity A third factor that influences attraction is similarity. People tend to choose casual acquaintances, as well as mates and best friends, on the basis of shared attitudes, values, and interests. One study periodically assessed the attitudes and patterns of affiliation of incoming male college transfer students assigned to the same dormitory (Newcomb, 1961). Over the course of the semester, as the students had a chance to learn one another's attitudes, friendship patterns began to match initial attitude profiles. Surrounding oneself with like-minded others seems to be rewarding, leading to the kind of interpersonal reinforcement described by social exchange theorists.

Folk wisdom that "birds of a feather flock together" thus tends to have more than a grain of truth. Thus, what do we make of the opposite adage, that "opposites attract"?

Although people tend to like others who share their values and attitudes, they often prefer being with people whose resources, needs, or behavioral styles complement their own (Dryer & Horowitz, 1997; Pilkington et al., 1991). For example, dominant people tend to prefer to interact with others who are more submissive, and vice versa.

Physical Attractiveness   A final factor that influences interpersonal attraction is physical attractiveness (Chapter 17). Even in nonsexual relationships, physically attractive people are magnets (Berscheid & Reis, 1998; Eagly et al., 1991). Attractive children tend to be more popular among their peers and are treated more leniently by adults (Clifford & Walster, 1973; Dion & Berscheid, 1974). Attractive adults receive more cooperation and assistance from others (Sigall et al., 1971), better job recommendations (Cash et al., 1977), and higher pay (Hamermesh & Biddle, 1994) than do less attractive people. They also rate their interactions with others on a daily basis as more pleasant than do people who are less attractive (Reis, Nezlek, & Wheeler, 1980).

Not surprisingly, physical attractiveness tends to have a greater impact on romantic than nonromantic relationships (Fletcher et al., 1999; Sprecher & Regan, 2002). Attractiveness is a major, if not *the* major, criterion college students use in judging initial attraction (e.g., Curran & Lippold, 1975; Walster et al., 1966). One study asked students to indicate whether they were attracted to strangers pictured in photographs. The experimenters gave another group the same photographs but stapled them to surveys showing the strangers' attitudes. Information about the strangers' attitudes had virtually no effect (Byrne et al., 1968). At first meeting, attraction appears to be skin deep.

Given that only a small percentage of people can occupy the choice locations on the bell curve of attractiveness, how do the rest of us ever get a date? In reality, people follow the **matching hypothesis**, *choosing partners they perceive to be equally attractive to themselves*, not necessarily the most beautiful or handsome (Berscheid et al., 1971). One set of studies clarified how and why this happens. In one condition, male participants were told that a number of different women would gladly date them; in the other condition, they were offered no such assurance. Men in the second condition chose less attractive partners. By doing so, they were apparently trying to maximize the beauty of their partner while minimizing their risk of rejection (see Huston, 1973).

The matching hypothesis at its best.

Across a number of studies, the average correlation between rated attractiveness of members of a couple is around .50, suggesting that people do indeed tend to find someone of equivalent attractiveness (Feingold, 1988). In economic terms, one of the major "assets" people take on the dating "market" is their appearance, and they tend to exchange "goods" of relatively equal value.

Standards of physical attractiveness vary tremendously from culture to culture (and from individual to individual; Berscheid & Reis, 1998). Nevertheless, views of beauty are not entirely culture specific. People across the world tend to rate facial attractiveness in similar ways (Berscheid & Reis, 1998; Cunningham et al., 1995; Dion, 2002; Wheeler & Kim, 1997), with correlations between raters across cultures generally exceeding .60. Several studies have also found that infants in the West who have not yet been socialized to norms of physical beauty gaze longer at faces rated attractive by adults. This occurs whether the faces are of adults or infants, males or females, or blacks or whites (Langlois et al., 1991).

Why does physical attractiveness play such a role in interpersonal attraction? Research in neuroscience suggests that eye contact with a physically attractive individual activates an area in the brain called the ventral striatum (Kampe et al., 2001). When the eye contact is broken, activity in this area of the brain decreases. This particular area of the brain is associated with reward. Thus, eye contact with an attractive person stimulates activity in a reward center of the brain, whereas loss of eye contact with an attractive other decreases activity and thus reward.

Just How Shallow Are We?   The research on interpersonal attraction described thus far suggests that we humans are a shallow lot indeed. What we most desire is

Big Picture φ Question 4

To what extent is human nature particular versus universal?

someone a few doors down, who brings us a cold drink on a warm afternoon, reminds us of ourselves, and looks like Denzel Washington or Julia Roberts.

We may be shallow creatures, but probably not quite that shallow. An important caveat about this body of research is that most studies were conducted in brief laboratory encounters between college students who did not know each other. Although all the identified factors are probably important, the extent to which each influences interpersonal attraction outside this special circumstance is not clear. People tend to emphasize physical attractiveness more during the late teens and early twenties than in any other life stage. Concerns about identity in late adolescence also probably promote a preference for peers who are similar because they reinforce the individual's sense of identity (Sears, 1986).

College students may not be representative for research on relationships for another reason: Few have had long-term relationships, simply by virtue of their age. The importance of various dimensions of attraction waxes and wanes at different points in a relationship. Studies using broader community samples find that marital satisfaction is typically high initially, lower during child-rearing years (especially when children are toddlers), and higher again once the children leave home, particularly during retirement (Sillars & Zietlow, 1993).

Making Connections

A defining feature of some severe personality disorders is indifference to social contact (Chapter 15).

■ Are humans "born to love"—that is, do we innately need other people?

■ Are people who do not seek relationships genuinely disordered, or is this simply a cultural value judgment?

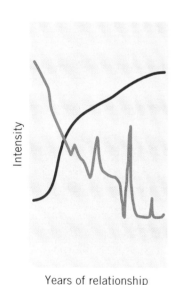

Years of relationship
— Passionate love
— Companionate love

FIGURE 18.1 Passionate and companionate love in a long-term relationship. The figure depicts the intensity of two kinds of love over time. Passionate love is high at the beginning of a relationship but tends to diminish over time, with periodic resurgences, or "peaks." Companionate love usually grows over time.

Love

Researchers aware of these limitations have turned their attention to long-term adult love relationships (Berscheid & Reis, 1998) in an attempt to convert this enigmatic experience from sonnets to statistics, or from poetry to *p*-values.

Classifying Love   At considerable risk to themselves from Cupid's arrows, some researchers have tried to classify love. One important distinction is that between passionate and companionate love (Hatfield, 1988). **Passionate love** is a wildly emotional condition, *marked by intense physiological arousal and absorption in another person*. It is the stuff of Hollywood movies, sleepless nights, and daytime fantasies. In contrast, **companionate love** involves *deep affection, friendship, and emotional intimacy*. It grows over time through shared experiences and increasingly takes the place of passionate love—which, alas, does not last forever. However, the two kinds of love generally coexist (Figure 18.1), and people experience resurgences of passionate love throughout long relationships (Baumeister & Bratslavsky, 1999).

Another classification, the *triangular theory of love*, divides love into three components: *intimacy* (feelings of closeness), *passion* (sensual arousal), and *commitment* (dedication to the other person and to the relationship) (Sternberg, 1988, 1998a). According to this view, relationships can differ in the extent to which they are based on one component or another. Some, for example, are all passion with little intimacy or commitment. Others involve mixtures of all three (see Figure 18.2).

Yet another conceptualization views love as a story that reflects a person's expectations and beliefs about love (Sternberg, 1998b, 2001). At least 25 different love stories exist including the traveling story (e.g., love is a journey that begins when you first meet someone), the gardening story (e.g., relationships must not be left unattended or they will die), and the horror story (e.g., love involves one or both partners' being afraid of one another). No one love story necessarily predicts greater success in a relationship than another. Rather, people who enjoy the greatest satisfaction in their relationships are those whose love stories are similar to one another. Two people who both define love as a journey will be likely to feel more compatible than a couple where one individual views love as a horror story and the other sees love as a gardening story.

An Evolutionary Perspective   From an evolutionary perspective, the feelings and behaviors we associate with the concept of love are evolved mechanisms that tend to lead to reproductive success (Buss & Kenrick, 1998). Caring for offspring (parental love), courtship, sexual intimacy, and concern for family all maximize the likelihood that we, and those related to us, will reproduce (and survive to reproduce in the future). Romantic love, in this view, is an adaptation that fostered the reproductive success of our ancestors by bonding two people likely to become parents of an infant who would need their reliable care (Hazan & Shaver, 1987).

Neither love nor lust, however, inevitably leads to monogamous marriage. In fact, a relatively permanent union of two individuals is just one mating strategy that occurs across species. Even among humans, 80 percent of cultures have practiced polygamy, which permits men multiple wives or mistresses. In Western cultures, premarital sex is virtually ubiquitous, and roughly half of married people at some point have extramarital affairs (Buss & Schmitt, 1993).

Sexual Strategies Evolutionary psychologists have studied the **sexual strategies** (***tactics used in selecting mates***) people use in different kinds of relationships, from brief romantic liaisons to marriages (Buss & Kenrick, 1998; Buss & Schmitt, 1993). Whereas many researchers studying interpersonal attraction and relationships generalize across genders, evolutionary theorists argue that males and females face very different selection pressures and hence have evolved different sexual strategies. Because a man can have a virtually infinite number of offspring if he obtains enough willing partners, he can maximize his reproductive success by spreading his seed widely, inseminating as many fertile females as possible. In contrast, women can bear only a limited number of children, and they make an enormous initial investment in their offspring during nine months of gestation. As a result, women should be choosier about their mating partners and select only those who can and will commit resources to them and their offspring.

From these basic differences ensues a battle of the sexes. Females maximize their reproductive success by forcing males with resources to commit to them in return for sexual access. The short- and long-term mating strategies of females should be relatively similar. (Bear in mind that sexual strategies, like other mechanisms for adaptation, were selected in an environment very different from our own, tens or hundreds of thousands of years ago, long before condoms and birth control pills. Changing conditions are likely to alter their expression but not eliminate them entirely.)

For males, in contrast, short- and long-term sexual strategies may be very different. In the short term, the female with the greatest reproductive value is one who is both fertile (young) and readily available for copulation. In the long run, committed relationships provide exclusive sexual access to a female, which allows the male to contribute resources to offspring without uncertainty about paternity (Chapter 1). Long-term relationships also bring potential alliances and resources from the woman's family. Thus, for long-term relationships, men should prefer less promiscuous partners who are young enough to produce many offspring and attractive enough to elicit arousal over time and increase the man's status. Men should also be choosier in long-term than in short-term encounters because the women chosen for a long-term relationship will provide half the genes of the offspring in whom they invest.

Aspects of this portrait of male and female sexual strategies probably sound familiar to anyone who has ever dated, although, of course, cultural and historical factors have substan-

Taxonomy of Kinds of Love

Kind of Love	Intimacy	Passion	Decision/ Commitment
Non-love	–	–	–
Liking	+	–	–
Infatuated love	–	+	–
Empty love	–	–	+
Romantic love	+	+	–
Compassionate love	+	–	+
Fatuous love	–	+	+
Consummate love	+	+	+

Note: + = component present; – = component absent. These kinds of love represent idealized cases based on the triangular theory. Most loving relationships will fit between categories, because the components of love occur in varying degrees, rather than being simply present or absent. Reprinted from Sternberg (1987).

FIGURE 18.2 The triangular theory of love. + = component present; – = component absent. These kinds of love represent idealized cases based on the triangular theory. Most loving relationships will fit between categories, because the components of love occur in varying degrees, rather than being simply present or absent. *Source:* Reprinted from Sternberg (1987).

Is love unique to humans?

Apply & Discuss

Single white female, 28, 5'4", romantic, non-smoker. Seeking financially secure, college-educated and family-oriented single male for friendship, long-term relationship. Call 623-9864.

Single male, 37, handsome, spontaneous. Likes to do anything and everything. Seeking single female, 18-30, slender, outgoing, attractive, for good times, possibly more. Call 222-8252.

Some researchers have examined the content of advertisements in "the personals" to test the evolutionary view of men as success objects and women as sex objects (Davis, 1990; Mills, 1995).

▪ To what extent do personal ads support or not support evolutionary hypotheses? Would your own personal ad fit evolutionary theory?

▪ How else could gender differences in ads be explained? What other factors affect the qualities potential suitors "advertise" and seek?

tial influences on sexual behavior as well (Chapter 10). Consider the Casanova who professes commitment and then turns out a few months later not to be ready for it; the man who gladly sleeps with a woman on a first date but then does not want to see her again, certainly not for a long-term relationship; or the woman who only dates men of high status and earning potential. From an evolutionary perspective, these are well-known figures because they exemplify common mating strategies.

The Empirical Evidence How well do the data support these evolutionary predictions? Although the differences between the sexes are not always enormous, they tend to be consistent. For example, a study of 37 cultures found that in all but one, males tended to value the physical attractiveness of their mates more than females, whereas females were more concerned than males about the resources a spouse could provide (Buss & Angleitner, 1989). Males also consistently prefer females who are younger and hence have greater reproductive potential. Females prefer males who are older and hence are more likely to possess resources (Buss & Schmitt, 1993; Kenrick & Keefe, 1992; Kenrick et al., 1993). Figure 18.3 shows the results of some tests of evolutionary hypotheses in several cultures.

Studies of North American undergraduates also corroborate many evolutionary predictions about sexual strategies. For example, when males are asked to identify desired characteristics of potential partners, they prefer good-looking, promiscuous women for the short run, but they dislike promiscuity and pay somewhat less attention to physical appearance in the long run. In general, compared to women, men report a desire for a greater number of short-term sexual partners, a greater number of sexual partners in a lifetime, and a willingness to engage in intercourse after less time has elapsed (Buss & Schmitt, 1993).

These evolutionary hypotheses are, of course, controversial. Some critics argue that they could be used to justify a double standard ("Honey, I couldn't help it, it's in my genes") or date rape (i.e., males have an "innate" tendency to see women as sexually more interested in them than they are). Others argue that the social learning of gender roles could produce similar results (see Chapter 14). From this point of view, increasing gender equality in a given culture should erode gender differences in mate preferences, a hypothesis that has received empirical support (Eagly & Wood, 1999).

Further, evolutionary theory does not adequately explain the large numbers of extramarital affairs among females, the choice to limit family size or remain childless among couples with plenty of resources in cultures like our own, or homosexuality

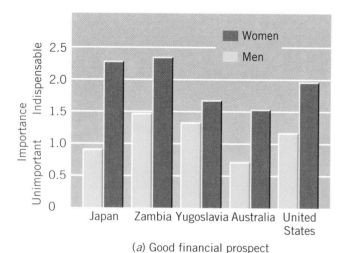

(a) Good financial prospect

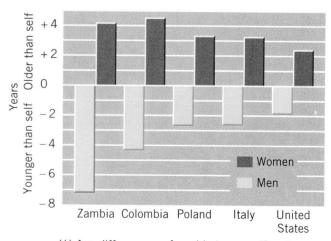

(b) Age difference preferred between self and spouse

FIGURE 18.3 Preferred characteristics of mates across cultures. Across cultures, financial prospects are more important to females than males in choosing a mate (a). Nearly everywhere, males prefer females who are younger, while females prefer males who are older (b). *Source:* Buss & Schmitt, 1993, pp. 204–232.

(although evolutionary theorists have attempted to offer explanations for all these apparently "evolutionarily maladaptive" phenomena). Nevertheless, evolutionary theory offers some very challenging explanations for phenomena that are not otherwise easily explained. When tempered by a recognition of the role of culture in channeling evolved reproductive tendencies, evolutionary theory provides a powerful source of testable hypotheses.

Romantic Love as Attachment   Another theory of love based on evolutionary principles comes from attachment theory. Romantic love relationships share several features with attachment relationships in infancy and childhood (Hazan & Diamond, 2000; Kafetsios & Nezlek, 2002; Shaver et al., 1996). Adults feel security in their lover's arms, desire physical proximity to them, and experience distress when their lover is away for a considerable period or cannot be located (Shaver et al., 1988). Adults respond to wartime and job-related marital separations with much the same pattern of depression, anger, and anxiety as that observed in childhood separations, suggesting that attachment processes continue into adulthood (Vormbrock, 1993). Romantic love also brings security, contentment, and joy, like the satisfaction an infant feels in its mother's arms.

"I dreamt I had a Harem, but they all wanted to talk about the relationship."

The bond between lovers does, of course, differ from infant attachment. Care for offspring and sexuality are components of adult romantic love absent from infant attachment. Nevertheless, the love between infant and mother and between two lovers may have more in common than may first appear.

Attachment styles may be especially evident in adults when they are under stress because the attachment system is activated by threats to security. One study examined coping mechanisms among Israeli college students during the Gulf War, when Iraq was bombarding civilian areas of Israel (Mikulincer et al., 1993). Subjects who lived in areas directly threatened by missile attacks differed from one another in the ways they coped with the danger. Securely attached subjects tended to seek support from others and generally experienced less distress from the bombings. Avoidantly attached people used distancing strategies (such as "I tried to forget about the whole thing"). Their distress was manifested primarily in physical symptoms, as might be expected given their difficulty experiencing emotional distress consciously. Ambivalently attached subjects used coping strategies aimed at calming themselves and quelling their emotions, which makes sense given their high level of conscious distress.

Making Connections

Attachment theorists argue that people pattern their adult love relationships on the mental models they constructed of earlier attachment relationships. Thus, the way individuals love as adults—particularly whether they are secure or insecure in their attachments—tends to reflect the way they loved and were loved as children (Chapter 14).

Love in Cross-Cultural Perspective   A Global Vista

Western theorists were not the first to recognize a link between infant and adult love. The Japanese have a concept of love that combines the experience of attachment and dependence, called *amae*, derived from the word for "sweet" (Doi, 1992). *Amae* is both what infants desire with their mothers and what adults feel in the presence of their beloved.

Although adult romantic love may have its origins in the biological proclivity of infants to form attachments, by the time people have participated in relationships for 15 to 20 years, their manner of loving as adults is highly influenced by their culture (Dion & Dion, 1996). Many societies have arranged marriages, which are as much economic bonds linking families or clans as personal and sexual bonds between lovers. In parts of India where marriages have traditionally been arranged, people may experience passionate love, but they typically hide it (Traiwick, 1990). Public dis-

Big Picture φ Question 4

To what extent is human nature particular versus universal?

plays of affection are avoided, although they are tolerated more between an unmarried than a married couple.

Chinese culture, too, has historically expected couples to consider their obligations to family in choosing a marriage partner: "An American asks, 'How does my heart feel?' A Chinese asks, 'What will other people say?'" (Hsu, 1981, p. 50). Indeed, in Chinese culture, love is so secondary to family obligations that the term *love* does not refer to a legitimate, socially sanctioned relationship between a man and a woman but connotes an illicit, shameful affair (see also Dion & Dion, 1988). In feudal China, passionate love was likely to constitute a reason why a couple should *not* marry. The female protagonist in Chinese love stories was more likely to be a concubine than a woman eligible for marriage. The marriage contract was signed by the fathers of the bride and groom; the engaged couple was not required to endorse the contract (Lang, 1946).

Does the passionate, romantic love seen on movie screens exist everywhere, or is it a Western (or Hollywood) creation? Romantic, passionate love probably does not exist *everywhere*, but it is common across cultures. A study using data from 42 hunter-gatherer societies from around the globe (compiled by anthropologists over the last century) found evidence of romantic love in 26 of them, or about 60 percent (Harris, 1995). Only six cultures allowed pure individual choice of marital partners, however; the other 36 required some degree of parental control, either in the form of veto power or arranged marriages.

Why is the concept of romantic love so central to contemporary Western culture that it fills our fairy tales (e.g., *Cinderella, Sleeping Beauty*) and movie screens? In a paradoxical way, the *individualism* of countries such as the United States or Australia may in part explain our preoccupation with passionate coupling. Contemporary Western culture is unique in its focus on individual satisfaction as a valued end (Chapter 17). This orientation extends into relationships, which are viewed as vehicles for personal gratification. Just 30 years ago, marriage in the West was something people entered and rarely exited. Today, if a marriage is unsatisfying, people often opt to leave and seek passion or satisfaction elsewhere. Romantic love may be a human potential, but cultures shape the ways we love—and leave.

Maintaining Relationships   Maintaining a relationship over time is no easy task. Oscar Wilde once quipped that the chains of matrimony are so heavy that it often takes three to carry them. Relationships pass through many phases (Borden & Levinger, 1991; Huston, 1994), and the majority of marriages in the United States and some other Western countries now end in divorce. The real question may be not what causes relationships to end but what allows some to last for 50 years or more!

In part, people decide whether to stay in a relationship by weighing its relative costs and benefits (Kelley & Thibaut, 1978; Levinger, 1976; Rusbult & Van Lange, 2003; Wieselquist et al., 1999). Whether a person remains committed over time depends on the balance of pleasure and discomfort it brings. Commitment to a relationship also depends on how much the person has invested in it and what the alternatives look like (Rusbult & Van Lange, 2003). People will tend to stay in a relatively unhappy marriage if they feel they have put so much into it that they cannot leave and if they do not think they can do any better.

Researchers interested in long-term relationships have attempted to track down the causes of marital satisfaction, dissatisfaction, and dissolution (Gottman, 1998). For example, people with successful relationships know how to stop spirals of *negative reciprocity*, in which one person's hostile or aversive behavior (e.g., sarcastic criticism) provokes a counterattack, leading to an escalation of conflict (Rusbult et al., 1991; Chapter 16). One of the most characteristic features of marriages that last is the ability to stop such cycles and to avoid the simmering feelings of hatred and disgust they tend to breed.

People in satisfying relationships also tend to make relatively benign attributions of their partners' actions, giving them the benefit of the doubt in difficult situations (Karney & Bradbury, 2000). People in satisfying relationships also frame their thinking about how to change the relationship in terms of how to approach a better relationship ("How can we become closer?") than how to escape a bad one ("How can we stop drifting apart?") (Gable & Reis, 1999). If anything unites these factors, it is probably the tendency both to accept the other person as he or she is, and to avoid repetitive and spiraling aversive encounters.

People whose relationships are stable also tend to overlook or "reframe" each other's faults. Studies of both dating and married couples across cultures find that people report greater satisfaction with—and stay longer in—relationships when they have a somewhat idealized or moderately unrealistically positive perception of their partner (Endo et al., 2000; Murray & Holmes, 1997, 1999). These findings make sense in light of research on "positive illusions," which suggests that people often enhance their sense of well-being by holding mildly positive illusions about who they are and what they can accomplish (Chapter 10).

Most people reap substantial rewards from their partners' slightly idealized views of them. However, people with low self-esteem (Chapter 17) have difficulty taking advantage of their partners' illusions. Despite the fact that their partners tend to hold idealized views of them, people with low self-esteem have difficulty basking in the warm glow of spousal unreality and instead assume that their own negative view of themselves is shared by their partner (Murray et al., 2000). When threatened, people with low self-esteem tend to doubt their partner's regard even more; in contrast, those with high self-esteem respond by inflating their beliefs about their partners' regard for them and hence use the relationship to insulate themselves from negative feelings, particularly about themselves (Murray et al., 1998).

The Dark Side of Relationships

Alas, not everyone is able to hold on to idealized perceptions of their partner or to put a positive spin on repetitive, annoying behaviors. People often meet their greatest criticism and experience their deepest hurts within their close relationships. "On any given day, 44% of us are likely to be annoyed by a close relational partner.... On average, young adults encounter 8.7 aggravating hassles in their romantic relationships *each week*.... Most people (66%) get angry at somebody in any given week..., and every seven days *most* young adults will be distressed by different encounters with a lover's (a) criticism, (b) stubbornness, (c) selfishness, *and* (d) lack of conscientiousness, at least once.... Over time, people are meaner to their intimate partners than to anyone else they know" (Miller, 1997, p. 15). People wouldn't dare criticize the food to the neighbor who prepared it, yet they quickly point out to their spouses the deficits in their cooking.

The types of annoyances that people perpetrate and experience within their close relationships include complaining, teasing, ostracism, guilt-induction, intentional embarrassment, arrogance, gossip, and swearing to name a few (Kowalski, 1997, 2001). On one hand, this behavior makes sense. Close friends and romantic partners are the people with whom we are closest, with whom we spend the majority of our time, and around whom we feel we can be ourselves (including our less appealing selves). On the other hand, many of the pet peeves that people ultimately develop with relationship partners and that, over time, chip away at the relationship are things that initially were appealing or funny (Miller, 1997). A partner's silliness when dating becomes a sign of immaturity five years into the relationship. Furthermore, positive illusions held early in a relationship may become tarnished over time.

In spite of the fact that people can and do list hundreds of annoyances that they have with relationship partners, friends, or family (simply type in pet peeve as a search term on the Internet and you will find ample evidence of this; Kowalski et al., 2002), some of the most intriguing research centers on ostracism. Within the context of close relationships, ostracism can take the form of the silent treatment, in which one partner refuses to interact with the other, treating him as if he doesn't exist. A survey of over 2000 Americans involved in close relationships revealed that 67 percent had intentionally used the silent treatment with another person, and 75 percent reported having the silent treatment used on them (Faulkner et al., 1997, cited in Williams, 2001). The fear of being ostracized or excluded from close relationships motivates much of people's behavior as they work to maintain their inclusionary status in those relationships (Leary, 2001).

Everyone has been ostracized to various degrees at some point in his or her life, but perhaps none so much as Benjamin Davis, Jr., the first black brigadier general in the United States Army. During the four years he was at West Point, Benjamin Davis was completely ostracized because he was black. No one ate with him, spoke to him, or roomed with him during his entire college career (Williams, 2001). In spite of this, he graduated and, in 1998, received an honorary promotion to four star general.

Ostracism can also take place on a much smaller, but still hurtful, scale. In one study, participants sat in a room with two confederates, or accomplices of the experimenter. The three individuals could not talk among themselves. However, while the experimenter left the room looking for a fourth participant, one of the confederates discovered a ball and proceeded to throw it to the other two individuals. In the inclusion condition, all three individuals continued to throw the ball to each other for five minutes. In the ostracism condition, the two confederates initially threw the ball to the participant but then begin throwing the ball only to one another, ostracizing the participant. Not surprisingly, the participants in the ostracism condition experienced distress, bewildered as to why these other two individuals would choose to exclude them. Some of these individuals simply disengaged from what was going on, whereas others undertook different types of activities, such as fiddling with their hair or looking through their wallets (Williams, 2001).

Whether the behavior is ostracism, failing to put the toilet seat down, or leaving lights on throughout the house, annoyances will always characterize close relationships. The challenge to the couple is to find ways in which they can learn to accommodate one another's pet peeves in constructive and accommodating ways as opposed to destructive and belittling ways.

Making Connections

Research across a number of areas consistently finds that negative and positive feelings not only are physiologically distinct but also have independent effects on a variety of outcomes (Chapter 10). Parental warmth and hostility each have an impact on a growing child's self esteem and psychological health, just as the tendency of spouses to display acceptance and warmth toward one another contributes to marital satisfaction independently of the extent to which the couple fights. Some couples with good marriages have "knock-down-drag-out" arguments but are genuinely loving toward each other most of the time. Others with bad marriages are too indifferent to one another to fight.

INTERIM SUMMARY

Several factors lead to interpersonal attraction, including proximity, interpersonal rewards, similarity, and physical attractiveness. One taxonomy of love contrasts **passionate love** (intense physiological arousal and absorption in another person) with **companionate love** (love that involves deep affection and intimacy). Some theorists argue that romantic love is a continuation of attachment mechanisms that first emerge in infancy. Evolutionary theorists emphasize **sexual strategies**, tactics used in selecting mates, which reflect the different evolutionary selection pressures on males and females. Love appears to be rooted in attachment but is shaped by culture and experience. Maintaining relationships over time is a difficult task. People in satisfying long-term relationships tend to avoid negative spirals, give their partners the benefit of the doubt, and hold slightly idealized views of their partners. Nevertheless, all relationships have a dark side characterized by pet peeves and annoyances.

Altruism

One behavior that appears to have few negative associations and brings people together is altruism. A person who donates blood, volunteers in a soup kitchen, or risks death (like the heroes of Oliner's World War II experience that opened this chapter) is displaying altruism. Many forms of altruistic behavior are so common that we take them for granted—holding open a door, giving a stranger directions, or trying to make someone feel comfortable during a conversation. Indeed, charitable contributions in the United States alone exceed $50 billion a year (Batson, 1995).

We begin this section by examining theories of altruism. We then consider experimental research on a particular form of altruism, bystander intervention.

Theories of Altruism

For centuries, philosophers have debated whether any prosocial act—no matter how generous or unselfish it may appear on the surface—is truly altruistic. When people offer money to a homeless person on the subway, is their action motivated by a pure desire to help, or are they primarily alleviating their own discomfort?

Ethical Hedonism   Many philosophers argue for **ethical hedonism**, *the doctrine that all behavior, no matter how apparently altruistic, is—and should be—designed to increase one's own pleasure or reduce one's own pain*. As one observer put it, "Scratch an 'altruist' and watch a hypocrite bleed" (Gheslin; cited in Batson, 1995).

People have many selfish reasons to behave selflessly (Batson, 1991, 1998). People are frequently motivated by their emotions (Chapter 10), and behaving altruistically can produce positive emotions and diminish negative ones. The overwhelming majority of Oliner's subjects who saved Jews from the Nazis reported that their emotions—pity, compassion, concern, or affection—drove them to help (Oliner & Oliner, 1988). Prosocial acts can also lead to material and social rewards (gifts, thanks, and the esteem of others) as well as to positive feelings about oneself that come from meeting ideal-self standards (Wedekind & Milinski, 2000). Helping may also be motivated by efforts to avoid the guilt associated with not helping (Batson et al., 2002).

Some theorists adopt the aversive-arousal reduction model and explain the motivation to act on another's behalf in terms of *empathic distress*: Helping relieves the negative feelings aroused through empathy with a person in distress (Batson et al., 2002; Hoffman, 1982). This mechanism does not appear to be unique to humans. In one study, researchers trained rhesus monkeys to pull a chain to receive food (Masserman et al., 1964). Once the monkeys learned the response, the investigators placed another monkey in an adjacent cage, who received an electric shock every time they pulled the chain. Despite the reward, the monkeys stopped pulling the chain, even starving themselves for days to avoid causing the other monkey to suffer. Research with humans suggests, however, that nonaltruistic motives for helping take precedence over empathy-based motivations, calling into question, again, whether true altruism really exists (Maner et al., 2002).

Empathizing with others apparently does involve actually *feeling* some of the things they feel. In one experiment, participants watched videotaped interactions between spouses and were asked to rate the degree of positive or negative affect one of the spouses was feeling at each instant (Levenson & Ruef, 1992). To assess the accuracy of these ratings, the experimenters correlated participants' ratings with the spouses' own ratings of how they felt at each point. Participants who accurately gauged these feelings showed a pattern of physiology similar to the person with whom they were empathizing, such as a similar level of skin conductance—but only for unpleasant emotions. In other words, when people "feel for" another's pain, they do just that—feel something similar, if less intensely—and use this feeling to gauge the other person's feeling. With positive emotions, people apparently use their head instead of their gut.

To the degree that people are genuinely altruistic, they should help regardless of momentary personal or situational variations, such as mood or modeling others helping. However, these variables do influence helping behavior, lending additional support to the theory of ethical hedonism. Moods, both good and bad, have a significant effect on helping behavior. People who are in a good mood help to maintain the positive feelings they have (Salovey et al., 1991). People in mild to moderately bad moods

Big Picture φ **Question 3**

To what extent is human psychology continuous with the psychology of other animals?

Apply & Discuss

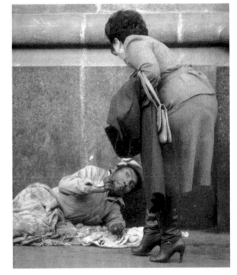

How might each of the following perspectives explain why some people give money to street beggars?

- Behaviorist
- Psychodynamic
- Cognitive
- Evolutionary

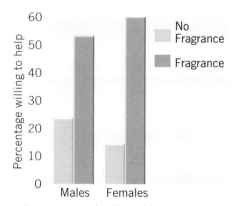

FIGURE 18.4 Both males and females were more likely to help another same-sex individual in a shopping mall when the incident occurred in the presence of a pleasant odor, such as baking cookies or roasting coffee. *Source:* Adapted from Baron (1996).

Big Picture φ Question 3

To what extent is human psychology continuous with the psychology of other animals?

How selfish soever man may be supposed, there are evidently some principles in his nature, which interest him in the fortune of others, and render their happiness necessary to him, though he derives nothing from it except the pleasure of seeing it. Of this kind is pity or compassion, the emotion which we feel for the misery of others, when we either see it, or are made to conceive it in a very lively manner.

ADAM SMITH, 1759
A Theory of Moral Sentiments

help to alleviate their negative mood state (Cialdini & Kenrick, 1976). Even odors have an effect on helping. People provided with the opportunity to help a same-sex individual in a shopping mall by picking up a dropped pen or providing change for a dollar were more likely to help if the incident occurred in the presence of a pleasant fragrance, such as cookies baking or coffee roasting (Baron, 1997) (see Figure 18.4).

Genuine Altruism   An alternative philosophical position is that people can be genuinely altruistic. Jean-Jacques Rousseau, the French romantic philosopher, proposed that humans have a natural compassion for one another and that the only reason they do not always behave compassionately is that society beats it out of them. Adam Smith, an early capitalist economist, argued that people are generally self-interested but have a natural empathy for one another that leads them to behave altruistically at times.

Some experimental evidence suggests that Rousseau and Smith may have been right. People who have the opportunity to escape empathic distress by walking away, or who are offered rewards for doing so, still frequently choose to help someone in distress (Batson, 1991, 2002; Batson & Moran, 1999). People also may behave altruistically for the benefit of a group, usually one with which they identify themselves. Passengers aboard United Airlines Flight 93 that crashed in Somerset County, Pennsylvania, on September 11 fit this latter example of altruism well.

The difficulty in defining an instance of helping as motivated by selfish or selfless motives is in assessing the motives themselves, particularly given that both types of motives may be operative at any one time. My twin sons recently began attending a new daycare center. The older twin (by only 6 minutes), Noah, closely watches out for the younger twin, Jordan, who was having difficulty adjusting to the schedule of the new center, particularly at naptime. Observing his brother's difficulty in getting to sleep, Noah began rubbing Jordan's head to help him get to sleep. When he had checked to make sure that Jordan was finally asleep, Noah lay down and went to sleep himself. Was this behavior an example of genuine altruism, designed solely for the benefit of Jordan? Or, was the behavior also motivated by a desire on Noah's part to alleviate his own distress created by witnessing the difficulty his twin brother was having? The fact that they are only two years old would lead me to believe it is the former; yet, the closeness between the two boys would suggest that Noah's own distress may have also been alleviated by helping his brother. In reality, the actual motive behind Noah's helping in this situation doesn't matter, any more than it does in most helping situations. Whether or not something is "true" altruism is missing the point. Even if other motives are operating, if a person's ultimate goal in helping another is to benefit that other person, then the behavior should be considered altruism (Batson, 2002).

An Evolutionary Perspective   Evolutionary psychologists have taken the debate about altruism a step further by redefining self-interest as reproductive success (McAndrew, 2002). By this definition, protecting oneself and one's offspring is in an organism's evolutionary "interest."

Evidence of this type of altruistic behavior abounds in the animal kingdom. Some mother birds will feign a broken wing to draw a predator away from their nest, at considerable potential cost to themselves (Wilson, 1975). Chimpanzees "adopt" orphaned chimps, particularly if they are close relatives (Batson, 1995). If reproductive success is expanded to encompass inclusive fitness (Chapter 10), we would expect humans and other animals to care preferentially for themselves, their offspring, and their relatives. Organisms that paid little attention to the survival of related others, or animals that indiscriminately invested in kin and nonkin alike, would be less represented in the gene pool with each successive generation. The importance of these evolutionary mechanisms has been documented in humans, who tend to choose to help related others, particularly those who are young (and hence still capable of reproduction), in life-and-death situations (Burnstein et al., 1994).

Why, then, do people sometimes behave altruistically toward others unrelated to them? Was Mother Teresa an evolutionary anomaly? And why does a flock of black jackdaws swarm to attack a potential predator carrying a black object that resembles a jackdaw when it means some may be risking their feathers for a bird to which they are genetically unrelated?

To answer such questions, evolutionary theorists invoke the concept of **reciprocal altruism**, which holds that *natural selection favors animals that behave altruistically if the likely benefit to each individual over time exceeds the likely cost* (Caporael & Baron, 1997; Trivers, 1971). In other words, if the dangers are small but the gains in survival and reproduction are large, altruism is an adaptive strategy. For example, a jackdaw takes a slight risk of injury or death when it screeches or attacks a predator, but its action may save the lives of many other birds in the flock. If most birds in the flock warn one another, they are *all* more likely to survive than if each behaves "selfishly."

The same applies to humans. Social organization for mutual protection, food gathering, and so forth permits far greater reproductive success for each member on the average than a completely individualistic approach that loses the safety of numbers and the advantages of shared knowledge and culture.

INTERIM SUMMARY

Altruism refers to behaviors that help other people with no apparent gain or with potential cost to oneself. Philosophers and psychologists disagree as to whether an act can be purely altruistic or whether all apparent altruism is really intended to make the apparent altruist feel better (**ethical hedonism**). Evolutionary psychologists propose that people act in ways that maximize their inclusive fitness and are more likely to behave altruistically toward relatives than others. Natural selection also favors animals that behave altruistically toward unrelated others if the likely benefit to each individual over time exceeds the likely cost, a phenomenon known as **reciprocal altruism**.

Bystander Intervention

Although philosophers and evolutionists may question the roots of altruism, apparent acts of altruism are so prevalent that their *absence* can be shocking. A case in point was the brutal 1964 murder of Kitty Genovese in Queens, New York. Arriving home from work at 3:00 a.m., Genovese was attacked over a half-hour period by a knife-wielding assailant. Twice he left, only to return again to stab her. Although her screams and cries brought 38 of her neighbors to their windows, not one came to her assistance or even called the police, until some time after she was already dead. These bystanders put on their lights, opened their windows, and watched while Genovese was repeatedly stabbed.

To understand how a group of law-abiding citizens could fail to help someone who was being murdered, social psychologists John Darley and Bibb Latané (1968) designed several experiments to investigate **bystander intervention**, or *helping a stranger in distress*. Darley and Latané were particularly interested in whether being part of a group of onlookers affects an individual's sense of responsibility to take action.

In one experiment, male college students arrived for what they thought would be an interview (Darley & Latané, 1968). While the students waited, either by themselves or in groups of three, the investigators pumped smoke into the room through an air vent. Students who were alone reported the smoke 75 percent of the time. In contrast, only 38 percent of the students in groups of three acted, and only 10 percent acted when in the presence of two confederates who behaved as if they were indifferent to the smoke.

A Model of Bystander Intervention   Based on their experiments, Darley and Latané developed a multistage model of the decision-making process that underlies

This quiet street in New York was the scene of a brutal murder—and the impetus for research attempting to understand why Kitty Genovese's neighbors did nothing to help.

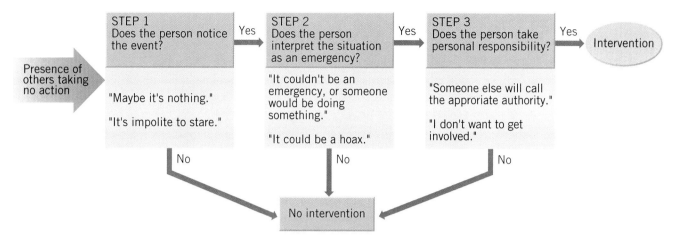

FIGURE 18.5　A decision-making model of bystander intervention. In the first stage, the bystander must notice the emergency. In stage 2, the bystander must interpret the incident as an emergency. In stage 3, the bystander must assume responsibility. Once the bystander accepts responsibility, he must then decide what to do and try to do it. *Source:* Adapted from Darley & Latané, 1968, pp. 70–71.

bystander intervention: Bystanders must *notice* the emergency, *interpret* it as one, *assume personal responsibility* to intervene, *decide how* to intervene, and then *actually intervene* (Figure 18.5). At any point in this process, a bystander may make a decision that leads to inaction.

This model helps explain why the presence of others can foster action or inaction. In the first two stages (noticing the emergency and interpreting it as one), other people serve as both a source of information ("Is there a crisis here or isn't there?") and a source of reassurance if they do not react strongly. At the next stage, the presence of others leads to a **diffusion of responsibility**—*a diminished sense of personal responsibility to act because others are seen as equally responsible*. At this point people also consider the consequences of action and are less willing to intervene (and more likely to justify inaction) if it jeopardizes their own safety or if they fear they might look foolish if they have misinterpreted the situation. Bystanders who are anonymous, like Kitty Genovese's neighbors and most German citizens during the reign of Nazism, are less likely to help.

The findings of these studies actually support a long tradition of sociological theory suggesting that the anonymity of city life reduces individuals' sense of personal responsibility for the welfare of others. Research comparing the responses of urban and rural subjects largely supports this view (see Solomon et al., 1982). Population density—the number of people crammed into a small urban space—also predicts rates of altruism: The more densely populated a city, the less people help (Levine et al., 1994).

How Bleak Is This Picture?　Most of the bystander studies described so far involved simulated emergencies in laboratory settings. Under other experimental conditions, however, the results are sometimes quite different. One study examined whether bystanders are more likely to respond to an emergency in a natural setting where their compatriots are friends rather than strangers. The investigators staged a rape in a campus parking lot (Harari et al., 1985). When unsuspecting male bystanders observed the female victim struggling with her attacker and heard her cries for help, 85 percent of those walking in groups of two or three responded, versus 65 percent of those walking alone. In this study, the presence of several people increased, rather than decreased, bystander intervention—probably because the naturalistic setting, the clarity of the victim's plight, the ability of group members to see and talk to one another, and the reality of strength in numbers made intervention more likely.

Situational variables, such as the presence or absence of other people, aside, some people are simply more likely to help those in need than others. The reason: personality traits. People who are higher in empathy feel more responsible for helping. Those high in self-efficacy or the feeling that they will be able to do something in an emergency, more readily identify ways to help. High self-monitors, who are concerned with the impressions that others are forming of them, help when doing so will make themselves look good to others. Individuals high in emotionality more readily interpret a situation as an emergency than those low in emotionality (Bierhoff et al., 1991).

Evidence regarding the role of gender and helping is somewhat mixed. When the type of help needed involves potentially dangerous situations such as aiding a stranded motorist, men are more likely than women to intervene. However, when little danger is involved, such as helping out with children, women are more likely than men to help (Eagly & Crowley, 1986). What remains unclear are the factors that motivate men and women to help and whether there are differences between the sexes in these motives. On average, women are more likely than men to be motivated by feelings of empathy (George et al., 1998), but there could also be a social desirability bias operating such that men are less willing than women to admit empathic feelings for those in need.

Big Picture φ Question 5

To what extent are psychological processes the same in men and women?

INTERIM SUMMARY

Researchers studying **bystander intervention** have found that individuals often do not help in a crisis in the presence of other people. To intervene, a person must notice the event, define it as an emergency, and assume personal responsibility for intervening. **Diffusion of responsibility**, a diminished sense of personal responsibility to act, is one important reason people do not intervene. Situational determinants of whether or not people will help interact with individual difference variables, such as gender, to determine when helping will occur.

Aggression

Although charitable contributions may exceed $50 billion a year in the United States, that is less than half the military budget. **Aggression**—*verbal or physical behavior aimed at harming another person or living being*—is at least as characteristic of human interaction as altruism (Anderson & Bushman, 2002).

Aggression is often elicited by anger , as when someone lashes out at a perceived injustice, and is referred to as **hostile aggression**. However, aggression can also be carried out for practical purposes without anger, as when a driver leans on the horn to protest reckless lane-changing that could cause an accident.

Calm, pragmatic aggression, called **instrumental aggression**, is often used by institutions such as the judicial system to punish wrongdoers (Anderson & Bushman, 2002; Geen, 1998, 2001). Aggressive acts are also frequently mixed with other motives. The behavior of kamikaze pilots during World War II, terrorists who carry out suicide bombings, and many soldiers in wartime involve blends of aggression and altruism, depending upon one's point of view.

Violence and Culture

The prevalence and forms of aggression vary considerably across cultures. Among technologically developed countries, the United States has the highest rates of aggression. Indeed, violence has overtaken communicable diseases as the leading cause of death among the young. Homicide rates are up to 10 times higher in the United

Big Picture φ Question 4

To what extent is human nature particular versus universal?

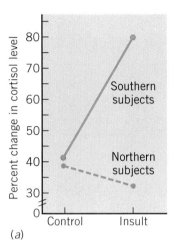

(a)

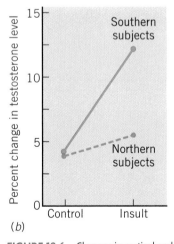

(b)

FIGURE 18.6 Changes in cortisol and testosterone levels for insulted and noninsulted southerners and northerners. In (a), cortisol levels (measured both before and after the experimental manipulation) showed dramatic increases for insulted southerners. In (b), the same was true for testosterone. *Source:* Cohen et al., 1996.

Big Picture φ Question 5

To what extent are psychological processes the same in men and women?

States than in Europe (see Lore & Schultz, 1993), and the murder rate in some major U.S. cities dwarfs the annual number of murders in all of Canada. In Canada, roughly 600 people a year die from homicides, compared with 24,000 in the United States. Taking into account the larger population in the United States, the murder rate is still over five times higher in the United States. Cross-cultural data have demonstrated that much of the difference in murder rates is attributable to the ready availability of firearms in the United States (Archer, 1994).

Across and within societies, cultural differences play an important role in violence and aggression. Psychologists have recently begun studying a cultural difference between men (particularly white men) from the northern and southern United States which is related to a tendency to behave violently (Cohen & Nisbett, 1997). Homicide rates are higher in the South, but not for crimes committed during felonies such as burglaries. The difference lies in the tendency of southern men to resort to violence in the midst of conflicts or arguments.

According to one explanation, the South is characterized by what anthropologists call a *culture of honor*, where small disputes between men can turn violent because they become contests of reputation and status. For reasons rooted in the ancestry, history, and economy of the South, to be dishonored—to show cowardice or a lack of "manliness" in the face of possible insult—is to lose face and status. Thus, southern men are more likely than northerners to respond with violence to insults or ambiguous situations that could suggest an insult.

Researchers demonstrated this difference in a fascinating study at the University of Michigan. In one condition, an associate of the experimenter bumped into northern and southern male students, called them an obscene name, and walked off into another room (Cohen et al., 1996). In the control condition, northern and southern participants received no such insult.

The researchers measured a number of variables, including observers' ratings of how amused versus angry participants appeared after the bump and how they completed a hypothetical scenario in which a woman complained to her boyfriend that a mutual male friend kept making passes at her. They also assessed participants' physiological stress during the incident by analyzing cortisol levels in their saliva (recall from Chapter 11 that cortisol is a hormone secreted during stress) and testosterone levels before and after the incident (testosterone provides, among other things, a physiological index of readiness to fight).

The results were striking. The majority of northern students responded to the insult with more amusement than anger; in contrast, 85 percent of southerners displayed more anger than amusement. Roughly half the northerners who were insulted completed the hypothetical scenario with a violent ending; the percentage who did so was similar in the experimental and control conditions. In contrast, 75 percent of southerners in the experimental condition (who received the insult) wrote a violent ending, compared with 20 percent of "unbumped" southerners. Southern men thus appeared to be gentlemen when they were not insulted but when primed with an insult were ready to act with aggression.

The biological findings led to precisely the same conclusion (Figure 18.6): Whereas northerners showed virtually no physiological reaction to the insult, both cortisol and testosterone levels jumped dramatically in southern men who were insulted. Thus, cultural factors can influence not only how people feel, think, and act when confronted with a situation that could potentially lead to violence, but also how they respond physiologically.

Violence and Gender

Gender differences in aggression are remarkably consistent across cultures. In most societies, males commit the majority of criminal and aggressive acts, over 90 percent. Male adolescents are particularly likely to be the perpetrators; in fact, fluctuations in crime rates in most countries can be predicted simply from the proportion of adolescent males in the population (see Segall, 1988).

Violence perpetrated by men against men has been so universal that until recently it drew little attention from either psychologists or policy makers (Goodman et al., 1993). The number of women battered by their male partners is unknown because many women do not report domestic violence, but the U.S. Department of Justice estimates that over 2 million women are battered each year in the United States alone (Frieze & Browne, 1989; Harway, 2000). Other estimates suggest that as many as 10 percent of marriages in the United States are marred by violent assaults, the most severe typically committed by the man (Dutton, 1996). Most batterers do not begin abusing their partners until the woman has made an emotional commitment to them, and attacks are most likely to occur during pregnancy or upon separation or divorce (Russell, 1991).

Sexual aggression against women is as old as the species. Men have traditionally viewed rape as one of the spoils of war. Some studies suggest that as many as 14 to 25 percent of women have been forced into sex by strangers, acquaintances, boyfriends, or husbands at some point in their lives (Goodman et al., 1993; Koss, 1993). A substantial percentage of women (27 percent) also report histories of childhood sexual abuse (as do 16 percent of men) (Finkelhor et al., 1990).

Gender differences also exist in the types of aggression most likely perpetrated by men and women. Whereas men engage in more direct aggression, women perpetrate aggression more indirectly. For example, adolescent males are more likely to bully their peers through verbal or physical aggression. Adolescent females, on the other hand, are more likely to socially exclude or ostracize the target of their bullying (Eagly & Steffen, 1986; Simmons, 2002).

INTERIM SUMMARY

Aggression refers to verbal or physical behavior aimed at harming another person or living being. Rates of violence vary cross-culturally, but across cultures, males tend to be more aggressive than females. Researchers are increasingly recognizing the prevalence of male violence perpetrated against women, including battering and rape.

The Roots of Violence

The universality of aggression and the individual differences seen in aggressive behavior have led to considerable controversy about its origins. Some theories maintain that the roots of aggression lie in biology and evolution; others look to the environment and social learning. In this section we explore instinctual, evolutionary, cognitive-neoassociation, and cognitive-social approaches (which integrate cognitive and behavioral perspectives). We also examine the biopsychological processes that underlie aggressive behavior, and offer a tentative integration of multiple standpoints.

Instinctual Perspective Some theorists view aggression and aggressive drives as instinctual. For example, Freud viewed aggression as a basic instinct in humans (Chapter 10), related to *thanatos* or the death instinct. Although most psychodynamic psychologists no longer accept this theory, they still view aggression as an inborn behavioral potential that is usually activated by frustration and anger. In fact, in every human society ever observed, socialization to control aggressive impulses is one of the most basic tasks of parenting (see Whiting & Child, 1953). Infants and toddlers bite, scratch, and kick when they do not get what they want; as children get older, they show less overt aggression (Hartup, 1977, 1998). This change in behavior suggests that societies have to teach children to *inhibit* aggression, rather than that aggression is primarily learned. (As we will see, other theories take the opposite perspective.)

Perhaps the most distinctive aspect of the psychodynamic approach to aggression regards the role of consciousness. From a psychodynamic perspective, aggressive mo-

Apply & Discuss

■ Why are we so captivated by horror and violence in films? What psychological functions do scary or violent movies serve?

■ Is pleasure in watching violence in the movies a learned response? Or is fascination with violence part of our genetic heritage?

Big Picture φ Question 7

To what extent are psychological processes conscious or unconscious—that is, explicit versus implicit?

tives may blend with other motives to produce behavior not consciously intended as sadistic, as in "good-humored" teasing among buddies, enjoyment of aggressive movies or sports, "forgetting" to pick up the dry cleaning after an argument with one's spouse (passive aggression), harsh parenting, or playful biting or pinching during sex. Aggressive motives may also blend with other motives, such as achievement or altruism, in choice of occupation, such as a career in the military (or the Internal Revenue Service!).

The *triggers* for aggression can also be unconscious. For example, James Gilligan spent years working with violent prisoners and conducted extensive interviews with a sample of men incarcerated for violent crimes (Gilligan, 1996). Asked to tell the stories of the acts that landed them behind bars, one after another told stories in which they lashed out after feeling "dissed"—treated with perceived disrespect. Gilligan concluded that one of the major triggers for violence is the feeling of shame in individuals prone to feeling inadequate or disrespected.

Recent research points to the importance of *implicit* shame in activating aggression. One study compared the tendency to experience shame in men with histories of sexual abuse who either did or did not go on to perpetrate sexual violence themselves (Conklin, 1999). Those who became abusers reported minimal shame on self-report questionnaires—they were consciously *shameless*. But the stories they told in response to the Thematic Apperception Test (TAT), an instrument used to assess implicit motives and emotions (Chapter 10), told a different story: Their responses were filled with themes of shame. Men who went on to become perpetrators appeared to suffer from *unacknowledged* shame.

Sharing in common only certain features with the psychodynamic approach, Konrad Lorenz also viewed aggression as instinctual. According to Lorenz and other ethologists, aggression gradually builds up over time. Unless this aggression is released by triggers or sign stimuli, the aggression will ultimately spill over, much like water that is not controlled will ultimately spill over a dam. One problem with Lorenz' theory, however, is that it suggests that everyone periodically feels the need to behave aggressively, which most people would discount. Furthermore, it fails to account for individual differences in aggression. To the degree that aggression is instinctive, then all members of a particular species should behave similarly, and we know they don't.

An Evolutionary Perspective Theorists who viewed aggression as instinctual often did not specifically address the evolutionary adaptations of aggression. Aggression, including killing members of one's own species, occurs in all animals. From an evolutionary standpoint, the capacity for aggression evolved because of its value for survival and reproduction (Lore & Schultz, 1993). Males typically attack other males to obtain access to females and to keep or take over territory. In many animal species, including some lions and monkeys, a male who takes over a "harem" from another male kills all the infants so that the females will breed with him and devote their resources only to *his* offspring, maximizing his reproductive success. Females often try to fight back in these circumstances. Across species, overt female aggression is elicited largely by attacks on their young.

Contemporary evolutionary psychologists believe that humans, like other animals, have evolved aggressive mechanisms that can be activated when circumstances threaten their survival, reproduction, the reproductive success of their kin, or the survival of alliance partners. In this view, aggression is like a pilot light that is always on but can burst into flames if conditions threaten reproductive success (Buss & Shackelford, 1997; de Waal, 1989).

Although aggression is common to all animal species, the degree of violence toward members of their own species is remarkable in humans, who slaughter each other on a scale

Wolves have innate mechanisms that can stop a confrontation from becoming lethal.

unimaginable to even the cruelest of beasts (see Lorenz, 1966). Other animals have evolved inhibitory mechanisms that stop them from ravaging their own. A wolf can call off the most vicious fight simply by rolling over and exposing his jugular. This typically leads the attacker to halt his aggression immediately—an innate mechanism especially prevalent in animals with built-in weaponry, such as powerful jaws.

Primates, including humans, have a variety of appeasement gestures to avoid violence, notably facial expressions, vocalizations, and gestures (de Waal, 1989). Unfortunately, humans are unique in their capacity to override evolved mechanisms for inhibiting aggression, particularly when divided by nationality, ethnicity, or ideology. Furthermore, as Konrad Lorenz noted, humans have developed the ability to kill one another from a distance. Not seeing our victims suffer prevents activation of natural inhibitions against killing members of the species, such as empathic distress responses, which are probably involved in both inhibiting aggression and promoting altruism. We are not, sadly, as civilized as wolves.

Biological Foundations of Aggression | From Brain to Behavior

Instinctual and evolutionary psychologists presume that aggression is built into the human behavioral repertoire. If a tendency to behave aggressively is innate, it must be rooted in the nervous system and perhaps in the endocrine system as well. Mounting evidence in animals and humans supports this view.

Neural Systems

The neural systems that control aggression, like those involved in other forms of behavior, are hierarchically organized: Neurons in evolutionary primitive structures such as the hypothalamus are part of circuits regulated by more recent (in evolutionary time) structures, notably the cortex (Figure 18.7). As we have seen (Chapters 3, 10, and 11), the amygdala and hypothalamus are involved in emotional reactions and drive states. When researchers electrically stimulate regions of the lateral hypothalamus of a normally nonpredatory cat or rhesus monkey, the animal immediately attacks (Egger & Flynn, 1963; Robinson et al., 1969). Similar results occur in humans when electrodes are implanted in the amygdala during surgery. With electrical stimulation, a normally submissive, mild-mannered woman became so hostile and aggressive that she tried to strike the experimenter—who was able to control the outburst by switching off the current (King, 1961).

Lesioning parts of the midbrain can also eliminate an animal's ability to respond with species-typical aggressive motor movements (such as hissing and bared teeth in cats), suggesting a substantial role for midbrain structures in aggression (Carlson, 1999). Brain scans of incarcerated murderers with no history of abuse and of individuals with antisocial personality disorder showed that the prefrontal cortex of the incarcerated murderers was 14 percent less active than normal and 15 percent smaller in the antisocial individuals, suggesting, again, that

Big Picture φ Question 1

To what extent can mental processes be reduced to the brain or body?

Big Picture φ Question 3

To what extent is human psychology continuous with the psychology of other animals?

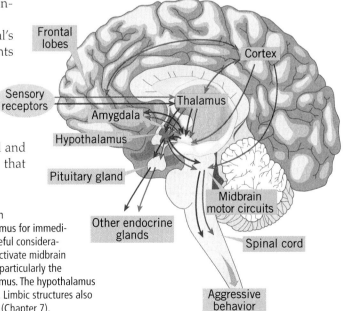

FIGURE 18.7 Areas of the brain involved in aggressive behavior. Stimulus information (e.g., a threatening gesture) is relayed via the thalamus to the amygdala and hypothalamus for immediate action. The information is also relayed from the thalamus to the cortex for more careful consideration. One or both of these pathways can generate an aggressive response, which may activate midbrain motor mechanisms involved in species-specific aggressive responses. Limbic structures, particularly the amygdala, assess the emotional significance of the stimulus and activate the hypothalamus. The hypothalamus then triggers endocrine responses, which in turn affect arousal and readiness for action. Limbic structures also activate the frontal lobes, which integrate cognitive and emotional responses to stimuli (Chapter 7).

neural systems play a critical role in at least some forms of aggression (Raine et al., 1998, 2000).

Although sensory information processed by the thalamus (e.g., a threatening gesture) can probably trigger responses directly, in humans aggression is under substantial cortical control. Sophisticated processing at the cortical level can either inhibit or facilitate aggression. A threatening gesture, for example, can be interpreted as either an attack or a joke, and a person with intact frontal lobes (Chapters 3 and 6) can usually decide to "hold back" before lashing out physically or verbally.

Testosterone and Serotonin

Hormones play a substantial role in the tendency to behave aggressively. In species after species, males are more aggressive than females, and these sex differences appear linked to action of the hormone testosterone both before birth and during development (Archer & Lloyd, 1985). Recall that hormones both *organize* and *activate* neural circuits (Chapter 10). With respect to organizational effects (i.e., influences on the development of the brain), female rats and monkeys that receive testosterone in utero exhibit increased play fighting after birth (Meaney & McEwen, 1986). Similarly, prenatal exposure to synthetic hormones can lead to increased aggression in childhood and adolescence (Reinisch, 1981).

With respect to activational effects (i.e., direct influences of hormones on behavior), studies with rats find that the amount of aggressive behavior displayed by both sexes correlates with circulating blood testosterone levels (with additional hormones involved in females) (Albert et al., 1991). Testosterone does not, however, tend to cause aggression in the absence of environmental triggers, such as competition between males for females, or repeated exposure to unfamiliar members of the same species.

The data in humans are less definitive, but several studies provide suggestive evidence. One examined the relation between physical and verbal aggression and levels of testosterone in adolescent boys (Olweus et al., 1980). Participants with higher levels of testosterone tended to be more impatient and irritable. Men convicted of violent crimes also tend to have higher testosterone levels than nonviolent offenders and nonoffenders (see Archer, 1991). The dramatic increase in male aggression that occurs at sexual maturation (puberty) in many species and cultures is also likely related to a surge in testosterone levels (see Segall, 1988). The problem with drawing conclusions about the relationship between testosterone and aggression is that the two constructs represent something of a chicken–egg problem. Although testosterone may increase aggression, behaving aggressively can also increase testosterone (see, however, Archer et al., 1999).

Testosterone is not the only hormone linked to aggression. A number of studies in humans and other animals implicate low serotonin levels (which are also associated with depression; Chapter 15) (Bernhardt, 1997; Cleare & Bond, 1997; Suomi, 2000). In addition, intentionally lowering serotonin levels of participants in a laboratory decreases their tolerance for frustration and increases their likelihood of aggressing. Serotonin and testosterone appear to regulate different aspects of aggression. Testosterone is linked to social dominance and thus leads to aggression in the service of maintaining status within a social hierarchy (Olweus, 1988). Serotonin is linked instead to impulsivity (acting without thinking) and thus leads to unprovoked and socially inappropriate forms of aggression (Higley et al., 1992).

Thus far, research focused on biochemical influences on aggression has been limited primarily to testosterone, more commonly associated with males. Variations in female hormones, specifically estrogen and progesterone, also show links to more aggressive tendencies. Although the legitimacy of the phenomenon "premenstrual syndrome" is open for debate, women who commit crimes in some countries while experiencing PMS have been given reduced sentences for their crimes (Dalton, 1987; Lewis, 1990). The basis for this defense is that the women's behavior was under the influence of raging hormones, leading to a state of temporary insanity.

Big Picture φ Question 5

To what extent are psychological processes the same in men and women?

Making Connections

Correlational studies show that higher levels of testosterone in men are associated with higher levels of aggression. However, these studies cannot definitively show whether circulating testosterone levels cause violent behavior or whether aggression leads to heightened testosterone levels. The reason is that correlation cannot demonstrate causation: When two variables correlate highly, one could cause the other, or some third variable could explain the link between them (Chapter 2).

Genetics

Genetic factors also contribute to individual differences in aggressive behavior. Successful attempts to breed highly aggressive strains of rats, mice, and rabbits demonstrate that among these animals, individuals can inherit an aggressive temperament (see Cologer-Clifford et al., 1992; Moyer, 1983). Questionnaire studies comparing monozygotic and dizygotic twin pairs find aggressive behavior, like other personality traits, to be heritable in humans (Caspi, 1998; DiLalla, 2002). Researchers have recently focused attention on a gene on chromosome 11 that is involved in regulating serotonin in the brain (Nielsen et al., 1997). Presence of a particular allele at this level of the chromosome is associated with unprovoked aggression as assessed by self-report (Manuck et al., 1999).

INTERIM SUMMARY

Instinctual theorists view aggression as an inborn potential usually activated by frustration or anger. They argue that aggressive motives can blend with other motives and be triggered unconsciously. Evolutionary theorists similarly view aggression as an inborn human potential that gets activated under conditions that affect reproductive success, such as competing for territory or mates and protecting oneself and related others. The neural control of aggression is hierarchically organized, with the amygdala, hypothalamus, and cortex (particularly the frontal lobes) playing prominent roles. Aggression is also partially controlled by hormones, particularly testosterone and serotonin.

Cognitive Neoassociation Theory   People exposed to aversive situations (e.g., frustrations, hot temperatures, annoyances) often experience negative affect and physiological arousal in response to those events. This arousal lays the groundwork for potential aggression by triggering thoughts and behaviors associated with aggression (Anderson & Bushman, 2002). Thoughts and feelings associated with negative affect and aggression become activated in the presence of aversive events.

In 1939, John Dollard, Neal Miller, and their colleagues at Yale University proposed one of the first theories of aggression, the **frustration–aggression hypothesis**, which states that *when people are frustrated in achieving a goal, they may become aggressive*. The child who wants a cookie and is told to wait until after dinner may throw a tantrum or the college student who had his heart set on a particular graduate school and was rejected may become not only sad but furious.

This model is simple and intuitively appealing. It was initially hailed as a significant advance toward a comprehensive theory of aggression because it tied aggression to environmental events rather than solely to instincts. However, researchers soon realized that not all aggression results from frustration and not all frustration leads to aggression. Physical pain may cause aggression, and frustrated goals can lead one person to become aggressive, another to become depressed, and still another to become more determined.

A reformulated frustration–aggression hypothesis suggests that frustration breeds aggression to the extent that a frustrating event elicits an unpleasant emotion (Berkowitz, 1989). I well remember returning to graduate school one Sunday afternoon after a weekend away only to get stuck in a very large (and time-consuming) traffic jam—the kind where people are standing outside their cars talking. I was in a hurry to get back and was very frustrated that the traffic was at a complete standstill. I was even more frustrated by the fact that no alternative routes were available to me to reach my goal. Feelings of irritation welled up inside. However, after sitting there for about an hour, I found out that a traffic accident had occurred and a woman had lost her life. Suddenly, all feelings of frustration and aggression disappeared.

As frustrating as blocked goals can be, innumerable other unpleasant experiences can also produce arousal and frustration. Air pollution, tobacco smoke, and other

Big Picture φ Question 2

What is the relationship between reason and desire or, more precisely, between cognition and affect?

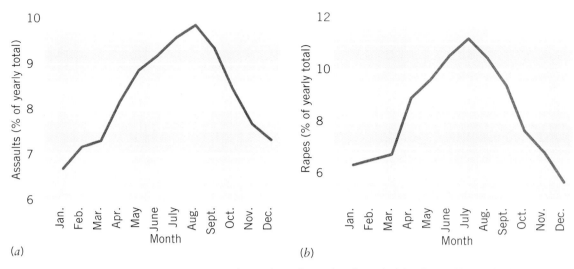

FIGURE 18.8 Aggression and time of year. The number of assaults (a) and rapes (b) varies by the time of year and is highest in the hottest months. Data were averaged across studies from North America and Europe over the last hundred years. *Source:* Anderson, 1989, pp. 85–86.

I pray thee, good Mercutio, let's retire: The day is hot, the Capulets abroad, And, if we meet, we shall not 'scape a brawl; For now, these hot days, is the mad blood stirring.

SHAKESPEARE
Romeo and Juliet (III, i)

noxious odors have all been linked to increases in aggressive behavior (Rotton et al., 1979; Zillman et al., 1981).

The relation between heat and aggression is particularly well documented (Anderson, 1989; Rotton & Cohn, 2000). As temperature rises, so does temper. One study found a strong correlation between temperature and the incidence of riots in U.S. cities between 1967 and 1971 (Carlsmith & Anderson, 1979). Rape, murder, assault, and prison unrest all vary with the time of the year, peaking in the hot summer months (Figure 18.8). Within countries as diverse as Spain, Italy, France, and the United States, the southern regions typically have the highest rates of violent crime (Anderson, 1989). Even the number of batters hit by pitches in professional baseball varies with the temperature (Reifman et al., 1991)! Thus, according to cognitive neoassociation theories, people can become angry and behave aggressively no matter how the underlying emotional state was elicited—whether through an insult, an uncomfortable temperature, or an unpleasant memory. However, aroused, negative emotions will activate similar cognitions stored in memory, one reason getting rid of negative emotions is so difficult.

A Cognitive–Social Perspective   The capacity for aggression appears to be innate, but the activation and inhibition of aggression depends on culture and learning. Harsh parental discipline, for example, produces children who are more aggressive than children whose parents spare the rod (Weiss et al., 1992). According to cognitive–social theories, children and adults learn to behave aggressively through social rewards and punishments. They also learn through observational learning such as modeling (Bandura, 2001). In his classic Bobo doll study, Bandura (1967) demonstrated that children who watch adults abusing dolls are much more likely to do so themselves (Chapter 5). Cognitive processes, especially the attributions people make for the causes of their misfortunes, play a role in eliciting and controlling aggression as well. Individuals are more likely to become aggressive, for example, if they believe someone has willfully and knowingly inflicted harm (see Geen, 1995).

Research from a cognitive–social perspective has contributed to the public debate about the influence of television and other media violence on aggressive behavior (Bushman & Anderson, 2001). Reports from the American Psychological Association suggest that children watch between 20 and 25 violent incidents on a Saturday morning while watching children's cartoons. These reports also discuss evidence indicating that watching violence on television is associated with increased aggression. By watching media violence, children learn aggressive scripts that guide their own behavior at later times (Huesmann, 1998). The more that children are exposed to media violence, the more cognitively accessible their aggressive scripts become (Chapter 17; Bushman, 1998). (It is worth noting, however, that the most important modeling for aggression is closer to home than the television screen: Media violence pales as a predictor of aggressive behavior in comparison with violence witnessed in the family, in the schools, or in the streets; Gunter & McAleer, 1990.)

Estimating the long-term effects of television violence on behavior is very difficult because people who are aggressive tend to seek out aggressive shows, and they do this from the time they are young. Experimental data show that in the short run, children and adolescents are in fact more likely to behave aggressively immediately after viewing violent television shows, particularly if they are provoked (Singer & Singer, 1981; Smith & Donnerstein, 1998; Wood et al., 1991). This could occur because watching television violence increases arousal, decreases inhibition, provides aggressive models, or desensitizes children to violence by making violent acts seem commonplace (Gunter & McAleer, 1990).

The data are less conclusive for long-term effects (see Gadow & Sprafkin, 1993; McGuire, 1986). Rather than having a global effect on every child or adult, televised violence is likely to have a stronger impact on people who are already highly aggressive. In fact, experimental research suggests that people who test high in aggressiveness not only prefer violent films but become more angry and aggressive after watching them (Bushman, 1995; Kiewitz & Weaver, 2001). Thus, the impact of televised aggression on violence likely reflects a *person-by-situation interaction* (Chapter 12)—that is, a tendency of certain people to behave in certain ways under certain conditions—rather than a general phenomenon. Similar results emerge from research assessing the effects of pornography on sexual violence. Viewing pornography does not cause sexual violence, but viewing pornographic *aggression* appears to desensitize men to the brutality of rape and other sexual crimes against women (see Malamuth & Donnerstein, 1982). As with television violence, pornographic aggression may affect a person's emotional response to violence or slightly weaken inhibitions in deviant individuals with poor internal controls. Nonetheless, most people will not kill or rape after watching a violent or pornographic movie.

A recent examination of all of the studies examining the relationship between media violence and aggression published between 1987 and 2000 revealed a strengthening of this relationship over time (Bushman & Anderson, 2001). As shown in Figure 18.9, positive relationships between watching media violence and aggression have increased markedly, particularly in the last decade. Whether this increase is the result of more violence in the media (on television, the Internet, and video games) or whether people are increasingly drawn to media violence or whether rates of aggression are simply on the rise remains to be seen.

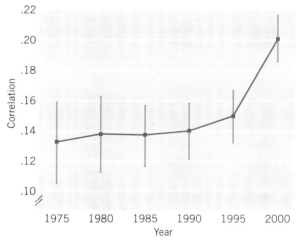

FIGURE 18.9 From 1975 to 2000 stronger and stronger correlations between media violence and aggression were observed. Reprinted from Bushman & Anderson, 2001, p. 484.

The General Aggression Model The General Aggression Model (GAM) was created to give meaning to the myriad of theories that currently exist to explain aggression. Incorporating what researchers viewed as the best of each of the earlier theories of aggression, the GAM examines how person and situation input variables influence aggression through the cognitions, affect, and arousal they generate. In short, person variables, such as personality traits, genetics, attitudes, values, and scripts interact with situational variables, including aggressive cues, provocation, and aversive situations, to produce particular cognitions and feelings. Thus, if a highly aggressive individual is placed in a situation where guns are present, the guns will activate aggressive scripts (that are probably easily accessible because of the individual's underlying aggressive personality) that will subsequently drive aggressive behavior, referred to as the output (Anderson & Bushman, 2002).

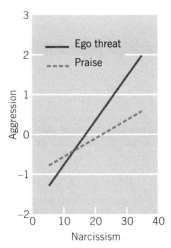

FIGURE 18.10 People with unstable self-esteem, such as narcissists, react to ego threats with higher levels of aggression than people who score lower on narcissism. Reprinted from Bushman & Baumeister (1998, p. 223).

In 1991, the world was shocked by a home video of Los Angeles police officers beating black motorist Rodney King after a high-speed chase. When a jury at first acquitted the officers, the African-American community erupted in anger. Enraged mobs looted stores, pulled people from their vehicles and beat them senseless, set buildings and cars on fire, and attacked anyone whose race placed him in the wrong neighborhood at the wrong time. The riots left 54 people dead, over 2000 injured, and racial tensions burning like the streets of the city. Both the behavior of the officers and the behavior of the rioters raise questions about why people behave the way they do in "mobs."

Recent research on self-esteem and aggression provides support for this model. Most people assume that low self-esteem is more closely allied with aggression than high self-esteem, but this assumption is incorrect. In fact, narcissists and high self-esteem individuals react more aggressively when they receive negative evaluations than low self-esteem individuals (Baumeister et al., 1996; Bushman & Baumeister, 2002; Stucke & Sporer, 2002). Defined as *threatened egotism*, this relationship among self-esteem (a person variable), negative evaluations (situational inputs), and aggression (output) lends support to the General Aggression Model.

Not all high self-esteem people are more likely to behave aggressively. People with stable high self-esteem (i.e., people whose self-esteem is rarely influenced by situational variables) are no more likely to behave aggressively than anyone else. People with unstable high self-esteem, however, do behave more aggressively when their shaky sense of self is threatened with negative evaluations. Participants in one study were either insulted or praised for an essay they had written. They were then given the opportunity to aggress against the evaluator by giving a noxious blast of noise to that person (Bushman & Baumeister, 1988). Narcissistic individuals exhibited the highest levels of aggression as a reaction to the ego threat (see Figure 18.10).

INTERIM SUMMARY

According to cognitive–social theories, the roots of aggressive behavior lie in social rewards and punishments, cognitive processes such as attributions, and observational learning. The general aggression model states that person variables interact with situational inputs to determine aggressive output. The capacity for aggression appears to be innate, but the activation and inhibition of aggression depends on culture and learning.

Social Influence

By the late nineteenth century, sociologists and philosophers had recognized that people behave differently in crowds than they do as individuals and that a crowd is more than the mere sum of its parts. In a classic book published in 1895, called *The Crowd*, Gustave Le Bon argued that people in a crowd may lose their personal identities and ability to judge right and wrong, a phenomenon now referred to as *deindividuation*. They become anonymous and no longer consider themselves accountable for their behavior. Le Bon had in mind events of the eighteenth and nineteenth centuries, such as the frenzied mobs of the French Revolution, but his reflections could equally apply to the behavior of the police officers who beat Rodney King or the rioters who rampaged through Los Angeles after the officers' acquittal.

Since Le Bon's time, social psychologists have examined a number of forms of **social influence**, *effects of the presence of others on the way people think, feel, and behave*. Social influence processes can be remarkably subtle. For example, Robert Rosenthal and his colleagues discovered decades ago that teachers' expectations of students—-their beliefs about their abilities—can have a profound impact on students' performance (Rosenthal & Jacobson, 1966). Teachers who are led to believe that a particular student is smarter than he appears will tend to behave in ways that lead the student to perform better. Similarly, teachers who hold negative implicit attitudes toward particular minority groups (Chapter 17) are likely to respond to student members of those groups in ways that lead them to underachieve.

The influence of implicit and explicit expectations of this sort provides the basis for **self-fulfilling prophecies**, in which *false impressions of a situation evoke behavior that, in turn, makes these impressions become true* (Merton, 1957). Mark Snyder and his colleagues (1977) conducted a classic study of self-fulfilling prophecies, in which pairs of male and female college students conversed from separate rooms through an intercom system. The students had never met, but each male student thought he knew what his partner looked like from a photograph.

Actually, the photo was not of her: Half the participants received a picture of a college-age woman rated by other students as physically very attractive, and the other half received an unattractive mugshot. Not surprisingly, males who believed their partners were attractive were more sociable and sexually warm toward them. The more interesting finding came from studying the responses of the females. Judges who listened to the taped conversation with the male's comments edited out rated the women in the attractive photograph condition more friendly, sociable, witty, and appealing. Conversely, women who were treated as if they were unattractive actually behaved unattractively.

In this section we focus on three forms of social influence that are pervasive in social life: obedience, conformity, and group processes. We then turn to a discussion of social influence processes in everyday life.

Obedience

In 1978, in the small community of Jonestown, located in a Guyana jungle, over 900 members of the People's Temple cult drank cyanide-laced Kool Aid to commit mass suicide. The cult's leader, Jim Jones, told his people that a "revolutionary suicide" would dramatize their dedication. According to the few survivors, some people resisted, but most took their lives willingly, with mothers giving cyanide to their children and then drinking it themselves. An equally grizzly example of misplaced obedience was the mass suicide of California cult members who believed salvation was just around the corner with the arrival of the Hale–Bopp comet.

Psychological research on **obedience**, or *compliance with authority*, increased dramatically following World War II, primarily as an attempt to understand the horrors of the Third Reich. Many American social psychologists were refugees from the Nazis who presumed that the blind obedience they had witnessed was an aberration or anomaly caused by flaws in the German character or by the political, social, and economic upheaval that left Germany in ruin after World War I. Subsequent research on authoritarian personality dynamics in their new land (Chapter 17) led instead to a disquieting conclusion: Many people in the United States were also attracted to ideology glorifying blind obedience (Adorno et al., 1950).

The Milgram Experiments   In the 1960s, Stanley Milgram (1963, 1974) conducted a series of classic studies on obedience at Yale University that took many people, including psychologists, by surprise. The results of his investigations suggested that the philosopher Hannah Arendt may have been right when she said that the horrifying thing about the Nazis was not that they were so deviant but that they were "terrifyingly normal."

The basic design of the studies was as follows. The experimenter told subjects they were participating in an experiment to examine the effect of punishment on learning. Subjects were instructed to punish a "learner" (actually a confederate of the researcher) in the next room whenever the learner made an error, using an instrument they believed to be a shock generator. Panel switches were labeled from 15 volts (slight shock) to 450 volts (danger: severe shock). The experimenter instructed the subjects to begin by administering a slight shock and increase the voltage each time the learner made an error. The learner actually received no shocks, but subjects had no reason to disbelieve what they were told—especially since they heard protests and, later, screaming from the next room as they increased the punishment.

Milgram was not actually studying the impact of punishment on learning. Rather, he wanted to determine how far people would go in obeying orders. Before conducting the study, Milgram had asked various social scientists to estimate how many sub-

Apply & Discuss

In the small South Vietnamese village of My Lai on March 16, 1968, at the height of the Vietnam War, three platoons of American soldiers massacred several hundred unarmed civilians, including children, women, and the elderly. The platoons had arrived in Vietnam only a month before but had sustained heavy casualties, leaving the surviving soldiers scared and vengeful. Any inhibitions the soldiers might have had against killing innocent civilians disappeared when their commander, Lt. William Calley, ordered them to shoot the villagers, whom he suspected of being enemy sympathizers. The issues raised by the My Lai massacre resurfaced recently when former U.S. Senator Bob Kerry publicly described a massacre in which he participated during the Vietnam War, which left at least 13 unarmed women and children dead.

■ Do soldiers relinquish their ability—or duty—to judge right and wrong when receiving orders?

■ Can a military function if soldiers make independent moral judgments? How can the military maximize the likelihood that soldiers will both respect their commanders and respect human rights?

Shock Level	Verbal Designation and Voltage Level	Number of Participants Who Refused to Go Further
Slight Shock		
1	15	
2	30	
3	45	
4	60	
Moderate Shock		
5	75	
6	90	
7	105	
8	120	
Strong Shock		
9	135	
10	150	
11	165	
12	180	
Very Strong Shock		
13	195	
14	210	
15	225	
16	240	
Intense Shock		
17	255	
18	270	
19	285	
20	300	5
Extreme Intensity Shock		
21	315	4
22	330	2
23	345	1
24	360	1
Danger: Severe Shock		
25	375	1
26	390	
27	405	
28	420	
XXX		
29	435	
30	450	26

Mean maximum shock level   27.0

Percentage obedient subjects   65.0 percent

FIGURE 18.11 Data from the original Milgram experiment. The numbers correspond to the number of people who refused to administer shocks beyond that point. So, for example, five individuals administered shocks at an intensity of 300 volts, but refused to go further. *Source:* Reprinted from Milgram (1969).

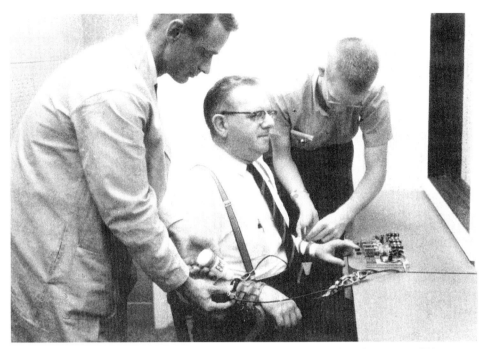

Milgram's research on obedience shocked both psychologists and the lay public, who never would have imagined that participants would have been willing to shock a stranger at the command of an authority who told them that he would take responsibility for their action.

jects would go all the way to 450 volts. The experts estimated that a very deviant subsample—well below 5 percent—might administer the maximum.

They were wrong. As you can see in Figure 18.11, approximately *two-thirds* of subjects administered the full 450 volts, even though the learner had stopped responding (screaming or otherwise) and was apparently either unconscious or dead. Many participants were clearly distressed by the experience, but each time they asked if they should continue to administer the shocks, the experimenter told them that the experiment required that they continue. If they inquired about their responsibility for any ill effects the learner might be experiencing, the experimenter told them that he was responsible, and that the procedure might be painful but it was not dangerous. The experimenter never overtly tried to coerce subjects to continue; all he did was remind them of their obligation.

To Milgram, the implications were painfully clear: People will obey, without limitations of conscience, when they believe an order comes from a legitimate authority (Milgram, 1974).

Apply & Discuss

Milgram's experiments drew storms of controversy from psychologists concerned that he did not safeguard the rights of his subjects, who were often visibly distressed by the experience. In fact, the Milgram studies played an important role in the development of institutional review boards that determine whether a study meets ethical standards (Chapter 2). Today, Milgram's studies could not be conducted.

▪ Milgram debriefed his subjects at the end of the experiment to minimize any impact the experience might have had on them, and none reported regretting their participation. Did the knowledge generated by these experiments outweigh the costs to participants?

▪ Could we possibly know what we now know had Milgram not performed his experiments?

▪ Could a different, less stressful, research design have led to such important results?

Factors That Influence Obedience   By varying the experimental conditions, Milgram discovered several factors that influence obedience. One is the proximity of the victim to the subject. Obedience declined substantially if the victim was in the room with the subject, if a voice replaced pounding on the wall, and if the subject had to force the victim's hand onto a shock plate to administer further punishments (see Figure 18.12). Proximity to the experimenter also affected the decision to obey. The closer the subject was to the experimenter, the more difficult was disobedience; when the experimenter sat in another room, obedience dropped sharply. More recent research implicates personality variables such as authoritarianism and hostility that can influence the likelihood of obedience as well (Blass, 1991, 2000). Conversely, gender had little effect on obedience in Milgram's studies—women were as likely to comply with the experimenter as were men.

The results of the Milgram studies are in sharp contrast to what most of us believe about ourselves—that is, that we would never obey in such a situation. The disjunction between our beliefs about how we would behave and the way most of us would *actually* behave highlights a consistent finding in social psychology—that is, our blindness to the power of situations over our own behavior. The effects of powerful situations tend to be implicit and hence to occur automatically and without conscious awareness (Epley & Gilovich, 1999; Wegner & Bargh, 1998). Thus, when we predict our own behavior, we tend to picture what we would *consciously* think and feel and to underestimate the power of implicit situational "pulls."

One of the issues surrounding Milgram's obedience studies was the ethics of the study. Was it ethical to deceive participants in this way and to cause them visible distress? Although many people immediately denounced the study as inherently unethical, research suggests that perceptions of the ethics of the Milgram obedience study and related experiments rest not so much on the design of the experiment but rather on the study's outcome. Participants asked to judge the ethics of Milgram's obedience study decried its ethics more when they thought obedience was high compared to when they thought obedience was low. If the study itself was unethical, no differences in perceptions of its ethics would exist. If, however, ethical decisions are made on the basis of the outcomes obtained, differences may exist as they did in these studies (Bickman & Zarantonello, 1978; Schlenker & Forsyth, 1977).

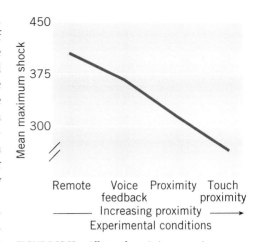

FIGURE 18.12   Effects of proximity on maximum shock delivered. Subjects in the Milgram experiments generally obeyed, but the closer they were to the victim, the less they tended to obey. *Source:* Milgram, 1965, p. 63.

Big Picture φ Question 7

To what extent are psychological processes conscious or unconscious—that is, explicit versus implicit?

Conformity

Whereas obedience refers to compliance with the demands of an authority, **conformity** means *changing attitudes or behavior to accommodate the standards of peers or groups*. The pressure to conform can be immense, even if subtle. Wearing a thin tie when wide is in vogue makes many men uncomfortable, as does wearing the wrong brand of tennis shoes for many teenagers.

The Asch Studies   A series of classic studies by Solomon Asch (1955, 1956) documented the power of conformity, much as Milgram's studies established the power of obedience. Asch assembled groups of seven to nine college students and told them they were participating in an experiment on visual judgment. All but one of the students were actually confederates, so their responses were planned in advance.

The experimenter asked the "subjects" to match the lines on two white cards (Figure 18.13). The first card had one line printed on it; the second had three lines, one of which clearly matched the line on the first card in length. The subject's task was to select the line on the second card that matched the line on the first.

On the first and second trials, everyone—subject and confederates alike—gave the right answer. On subsequent trials, however, the confederates (who went first) unanimously chose a line that was obviously incorrect. Their answers placed the subject in the uncomfortable position of having to choose between publicly opposing the view of the group or answering incorrectly.

 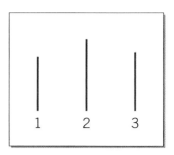

FIGURE 18.13   The Asch conformity experiments. Participants in Asch's experiments on conformity were asked which of the three lines in the box on the right matched the one on the left. Pressure to conform swayed their responses. *Source:* Asch, 1955, p. 193.

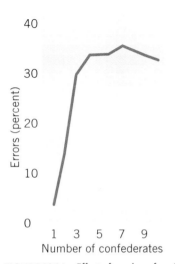

FIGURE 18.14   Effect of number of confederates on performance. Participants in Asch's experiments tended to conform when three or more confederates chose the wrong line. *Source:* Asch, 1955, p. 193.

Without peer pressure to conform, subjects chose the wrong line less than 1 percent of the time. However, when faced with a unanimous (but incorrect) opinion of the confederates, subjects made the same incorrect choice as the confederates 36.8 percent of the time. Up to a point, the more confederates, the greater the tendency to conform (Figure 18.14). Subjects only conformed, however, if the confederates all gave the same answer. If at least one confederate gave a different answer from that of the others, subjects followed their own judgment most of the time. Apparently, bucking the majority is extremely difficult without at least one other dissenter.

The Asch studies powerfully demonstrate the *power of situations* to influence behavior and attitudes. Personality factors, however, also influence the tendency to conform. Individuals with low self-esteem and those who are especially motivated by a need for social approval are more likely to conform (Crowne & Marlowe, 1964; Dittes, 1959; Moeller & Applezweig, 1957; Strang, 1972).

To what extent subjects actually alter their beliefs in the Asch studies rather than simply comply with situational demands to avoid disapproval is a matter of debate. Many of Asch's subjects reported that they believed their (incorrect) answers, perhaps because of cognitive dissonance or a desire not to look foolish. Nevertheless, the main implication of these studies is that many people will change at least the public expression of their beliefs when confronted with a group that disagrees with them.

Conformity and Culture   Conformity varies by culture and appears to be linked to the way people earn their livelihood (Price-Williams, 1985). People in hunter-gatherer societies exercise more independent judgments than people in agricultural societies (Berry, 1979). Agricultural societies depend heavily on communal organization and coordinated action; too much independent judgment can be counterproductive during planting and harvest times, when work needs to be done. Agricultural societies also have much higher population density, whereas hunter-gatherer societies are often highly dispersed across a territory and may thus require less compliance with social norms (see Barry et al., 1957).

In general, conformity is higher in collectivist than in more individualistic cultures (Bond & Smith, 1996). One study with an East Asian sample found that participants preferred to conform rather than to be different even when "independence" had no cost (Kim & Markus, 1999). When given a choice among pens, Americans overwhelmingly chose the one pen that was a different color from the others; East Asians preferred a pen of the same color as all the others (Kim & Markus, 1999).

Conformity also varies *within* cultures in systematic ways. In both North America and Australia, low-income and rural parents tend to emphasize obedience and conformity in their child-rearing practices as compared with urban and middle-class parents (Cashmore & Goodnow, 1986; Peterson & Peters, 1985). This finding, too, makes

Big Picture φ Question 4

To what extent is human nature particular versus universal?

adaptive sense because parents typically prepare their children for work similar to their own (LeVine, 1982), and laborers have less autonomy than professionals.

Conformity and Gender   Gender differences in conformity and susceptibility to social influence are a matter of debate. Much of the early research in social psychology (along with most people's commonsensical notions) suggested that women are more open to influence than men (Asch, 1955). Lay stereotypes suggest that women's desire to maintain harmony in social relationships leads them to go along publicly with the opinions and decisions of others. However, a closer look at the data indicates that these stereotypes are wrong. A meta-analysis looking at the overall effect size of this gender difference showed it to be very small (Eagly & Carli, 1981). In most instances, women are only slightly, if at all, more likely to succumb to social influence than men, with one notable exception. When women are placed in a situation where their responses are public and involve face-to-face interactions, they are more likely to conform than men (Eagly, 1978). Although it is possible that women are simply more gullible than men, it is also possible that men are simply more resistant to social influence tactics in public settings (Cialdini & Trost, 1998).

Big Picture φ Question 5

To what extent are psychological processes the same in men and women?

INTERIM SUMMARY

Social influence refers to the effects of the presence of others on the way people think, feel, and behave. **Obedience** refers to compliance with authority. The Milgram experiments demonstrated that most people will obey, without limitations of conscience, when they believe an order comes from a legitimate authority. **Conformity** means changing attitudes or behavior to accommodate the standards of peers or groups. The Asch experiments demonstrated that people tend to conform rather than be the lone dissenting voice. Conformity varies across and within cultures and tends to reflect economic and ecological demands. In spite of commonsensical notions, few, if any, gender differences in conformity exist.

Group Processes

The Asch conformity experiments illustrate just how powerful group processes can be. A **group** is *a collection of people whose actions affect the other group members*. When a collection of people congregate for even relatively short periods of time, their interactions tend to become patterned in various ways; the same is true of more enduring social institutions such as families and corporations.

Characteristics of Groups   The behavior of people in groups is dictated in large part by the norms operating within particular groups and the roles that individual members of the group play. **Norms**, or *standards for behavior* , guide thought, feeling, and behavior, from the way people dress to their attitudes about sex, Republicans, and lawyers. Sometimes norms are explicit (e.g., a written dress code), but much of the time they are implicit (men do not wear dresses; peers do not issue commands to each other). Different groups have different norms, and particularly in complex societies, people must pick and choose the norms to obey at any given moment because they belong to many groups, which may have conflicting norms. Adolescents, for example, frequently find themselves choosing between the norms of adults and peers.

The way people respond to norms depends on their attitude toward the groups with which the norms are associated. *Groups whose norms matter to an individual, and hence have an impact on the individual's behavior* , are known as **reference groups**. In other words, these are the groups to which a person *refers* when taking action.

A reference group can be positive or negative. A reference group is considered *positive* if the person tries to emulate its members and meet their standards. When a teenage boy gets drunk on weekends because his friends do, his friends are a positive reference group (but not necessarily a positive influence). A reference group is *negative* if a person rejects its members and disavows their standards. If a teenager gets drunk every weekend to establish her independence from her teetotaling parents, her parents are a negative reference group. In both cases, the reference group is influencing the teenager's behavior (which he might be loath to admit).

The norms operating in groups determine, in part, the roles that individual group members play. A **role** is *a position in a group that has norms specifying appropriate behavior for its occupants* (see Merton, 1957; Parsons, 1951). Roles are essentially norms that are specific to particular people or subgroups.

Roles reflect shared expectations about how particular members of a group are supposed to behave. They tend to be flexible, allowing the individual to make decisions about specific actions, much like roles in improvisational theater. A mother can decide how she will care for her child in a given circumstance, but her culture provides general guidelines for acceptable maternal behavior, such as whether she should stay home with her child or what forms of discipline she should employ.

Individuals internalize roles as *role schemas*, which direct their behavior when they are in a particular role and lead them to expect certain responses from people with complementary roles (such as husband and wife, teacher and student). Several roles routinely emerge in groups, even in brief, unstructured ones (see Bales, 1953). When strangers enter into groups in the laboratory and are asked to solve problems, *the group members who take responsibility for seeing that the group completes its tasks* are called **task leaders**, or **instrumental leaders**. Others, called **social–emotional leaders**, *try to keep the group working cohesively and with minimal animosity*.

Because people often define themselves by their roles, roles can have a profound impact on behavior. One of the most dramatic illustrations of the influence of roles on social behavior occurred in a study by Philip Zimbardo (1972, 1975). Twenty-two male college student volunteers played the roles of prisoners and guards in a simulated prison. To make the experiment as realistic as possible, students designated as prisoners were arrested at their homes and searched, handcuffed, fingerprinted, and booked at a police station. They were then blindfolded and driven to the simulated prison where they were stripped, sprayed with a delousing preparation (actually a deodorant spray), and told to stand alone naked in the cell yard. After a short time, they were given a uniform and placed in a cell with two other "prisoners." The guards received minimal instructions and were free to devise their own rules. The only prohibition was against physical punishment.

Soon after the experiment began, Zimbardo noted marked differences between the behavior of the guards and the prisoners. The guards became increasingly aggressive, treating the prisoners as less than human, seldom using their names (instead calling them by number, if referring to them as individuals at all), and subjecting them to roll calls that could last for hours. Many acted with clear sadistic pleasure.

The prisoners, for their part, initiated progressively fewer actions and appeared increasingly depressed. Half the prisoners (five participants) suffered such extreme depression, anxiety, or psychosomatic illness that they had to leave the experiment. The prisoners talked almost exclusively about prison life, maintaining the illusion of their roles. By the fifth day, those who remained were brought before a mock parole board, which would determine whether or not they would be released. Most were willing to forfeit all the money they had earned in the experiment if they could be released. When their requests for parole were denied, they obediently returned to their cells.

The study was originally designed to last two weeks, but the shocking results led Zimbardo to abort it after only six days. The study provides a powerful demonstration of the way roles structure people's behavior and ultimately their emotions, attitudes, and even their identities. Although participants were, in reality, college students randomly assigned to be prisoners or guards, within days they had *become* their roles—in action, thought, and feeling.

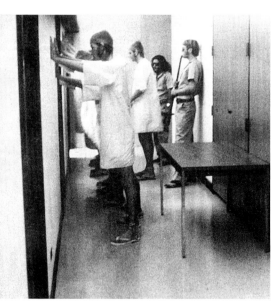

Zimbardo's prison study showed how powerful the demands of roles and situations can be on individual behavior.

Group Social Influence The presence of other people in a group can exert a substantial influence on the behavior of individual group members. Nowhere does this become more apparent than in the performance of group members when in the presence of others. *The presence of other people can either help or hurt individual performance*, a process called **social facilitation** (Triplett, 1898). When people are performing dominant, well-learned behaviors, the presence of other people can facilitate performance. On the other hand, when people are performing nondominant behaviors, or behaviors with which they are unfamiliar, the presence of others can hurt performance (Zajonc, 1965). Driving a car, particularly with a manual transmission, provides a good example of the difference between dominant and nondominant responses. When a person is first learning to drive a car with manual transmission, he turns the radio off, does not want to engage in conversation, and certainly doesn't eat, drink, or smoke while driving. During the learning phase, driving is a nondominant response. Other tasks, such as talking to other people, are distracting. However, once the person practices driving so that driving a manual transmission becomes a well-learned behavior, he can shift, talk, listen to music, eat, and drink all at the same time (although that's definitely not recommended!). Driving with a manual transmission is now a dominant response.

The facilitative effects of other people on performance have their limitations, however, as demonstrated most aptly with the *choking under pressure* phenomenon. In spite of the fact that playing championship games in front of a home audience would seem to be an advantage (i.e., home field advantage), such does not appear to be the case. The pressure to win key games, particularly in front of a home audience, can be so great that team players become increasingly self-conscious and what was once a dominant response (e.g., playing basketball) resembles a nondominant response. Roy Baumeister demonstrated this phenomenon with professional ball players. He found that, in key World Series games and championship basketball tournaments, the team playing at home typically loses (Baumeister, 1984). Not only did visiting teams win 59.2 percent of the time, but the number of errors made by home teams averaged 1.31 errors in key games compared to only .61 in noncritical games.

Furthermore, the facilitative effects of group membership depend on the type of task (Steiner, 1972). Participation in a tug-of-war, for example, is certainly enhanced by the more people present; however, not as much as you would think. If we could determine how much each individual involved in a tug-of-war could pull, the group output would, in fact, be less than the sum of these individual inputs. The more people involved in a task, the harder it is to coordinate efforts—to say nothing of the fact that people in a group frequently rely on others to pick up the slack for them. *This process by which people exert less effort when in a group is referred to as* **social loafing** (Williams et al., 1981).

On yet other tasks, some individuals will perform at least as well alone as part of a group. Tasks in which there is a single answer (e.g., yes/no) are referred to as disjunctive tasks (see Figure 18.15). The individual in a group who can solve the problem would perform just as well alone as she would as part of the group. Although she might benefit from group discussions that lead to the solution of the problem, the presence of other people could also be distracting, such that the time to completion of the task is actually lengthened.

Apply & Discuss

▪ Why do people so readily slip into roles, such as prisoners and guards?

▪ Why are social processes so compelling that they can seemingly override individuals' normal ways of behaving and responding morally?

INTERIM SUMMARY

A **group** is a collection of people whose actions affect the other group members. All groups develop **norms**, or standards for behavior. People also frequently play particular **roles** in groups (positions in the group that have norms specifying appropriate behavior for their occupants). **Task leaders** take responsibility for seeing that the group completes its tasks; **social-emotional leaders** try to keep the group working cohesively and with minimal conflict. Roles can have a dramatic influence on behaviors, as demonstrated in

Disjunctive Puzzles

Disjunctive tasks come in two varieties: Eureka and non-Eureka. When we are told the answer to a Eureka problem, we are very certain that the answer offered is correct. It fits so well, we react with an "Aha!" or "Eureka!" The answers to non-Eureka problems, in contrast, are not so satisfying. Even after arguing about them, we often wonder if the recommended answer is the correct answer. Examples of both types of problems are listed below, and their answers can be found at the end of the chapter.

1. What is the next letter in the following sequence?

   O T T F F S S

2. A man bought a horse for $60 and sold it for $70. Then he bought it back for $80 and again sold it for $90. How much money did he make in the horse-trading business? (*Source*: Maier & Solem, 1952)

3. Three missionaries and three cannibals are on one side of a river. They want to cross to the other side by means of a boat that can only hold two persons at a time. All the missionaries but only one cannibal can row. For obvious reasons, the mis-sionaries must never be outnumbered by the cannibals, under any circumstances or at any time, except where no missionaries are present at all. How many crossings will be necessary to transport the six people across the river? (*Source*: Shaw, 1932)

4. Issac is staying at a motel when he runs short of cash. Checking his finances, he discovers that in 23 days he will have plenty of money, but until then he will be broke. The motel owner refuses to let Issac stay without paying his bill each day, but since Issac owns a heavy gold chain with 23 links, the owner allows Issac to pay for each of the 23 days with one gold link. Then, when Issac receives his money, the motel owner will return the chain. Issac is very anxious to keep the chain as intact as possible, so he doesn't want to cut off any more of the links than absolutely necessary. The motel owner, however, insists on payment each day, and he will accept no advance payment. How many links must Issac cut while still paying the owner one link for each successive day? (*Source*: Marquart, 1955).

Source: Reprinted from Forsyth, 1990, p. 264.

FIGURE 18.15   Disjunctive tasks can take a number of forms. The problems presented here will give you some idea of what is meant by a disjunctive task, and the difficulty inherent in solving some of these tasks.

Zimbardo's prison experiment, which had to be aborted because people became immersed too deeply in their assigned roles. The influence of groups on individuals can be seen readily in studies investigating **social facilitation** and individual performance in groups working on a variety of tasks.

Leadership   As we have seen, groups tend to have formal or informal **leaders**, *people who exercise greater influence than the average member*. A major initial impetus to research on leadership was Adolf Hitler. Social scientists were astonished that an individual so manifestly disturbed could arouse such popular sentiment and create such a well-oiled war machine. Could democratic forms of leadership be as effective or efficient?

Leadership Styles   In a classic study, Kurt Lewin and his colleagues (1939) randomly assigned 10-year-old boys to one of three groups for craft activities after school. Each group was led by an adult who took one of three leadership styles: He made all the decisions (an *autocratic* leadership style); involved himself in the group and encouraged members to come to decisions themselves (a *democratic* style); or simply let things happen, intervening as little as possible (a *laissez-faire* style).

Boys with an autocratic leader produced more crafts, but they were more likely to stray from the task when the leader left the room, and their products were judged inferior to those produced in the democratic condition. Boys in the democratic group expressed greater satisfaction and displayed less aggression than the others. Laissez-faire leadership led to neither satisfaction nor efficiency. Lewin and his colleagues concluded that autocratic leadership breeds discontent but can be efficient, whereas democratic leadership seems to be both efficient and motivating.

Industrial/organizational (I/O) psychologists have conducted much of the research on leadership, trying to translate theory and research on effective leadership into interventions to make organizations more efficient. Contemporary organizational psychologists emphasize two dimensions on which leaders vary: *task orienta-*

tion and *relationship orientation* (see Blake & Mouton, 1964; Hersey & Blanchard, 1982; Misumi & Peterson, 1985; Stogdill & Coons, 1957). In other words, leaders differ in the extent to which they focus on efficiency and on the feelings of their employees. The distinction is similar to the two major clusters of psychosocial motives found cross-culturally, agency and communion (Chapter 10).

Cultural values and norms also guide leadership styles (see Gerstner & Day, 1994). Managers in societies like Greece and India tend to prefer autocratic leadership styles with passive subordinates; by contrast, leaders in societies like Japan, the United States, Canada, and England prefer subordinates who are active and participatory (Barrett & Franke, 1969; Negandhi, 1973). A study of managers in the United States, Hong Kong, and China found American managers more concerned with worker productivity and Chinese managers more concerned with maintaining a harmonious work environment (Ralston et al., 1992). Hong Kong managers expressed moderate concerns about both productivity and harmony, presumably reflecting Hong Kong's economic similarity to the United States and cultural similarity to China.

Leadership style and effectiveness also depend on the leader's personality (Hogan et al., 1994). Research on the Five Factor model and similar dimensions of personality (Chapter 12) finds that successful leaders tend to be high on extroversion (including dominance, energy, and orientation toward status), agreeableness, and conscientiousness. Thus, effective leaders tend to be outgoing, energetic, powerful, kind, hard working, and attentive to the task at hand. Ineffective leaders tend to be perceived as arrogant, untrustworthy, selfish, insensitive, and overambitious—in a word, narcissistic.

These generalizations, however, require the same caveat as all generalizations about personality traits: They are more likely to apply in some situations than in others (Chapter 12). Situational factors that influence the effectiveness of a particular management style include the motivation and ability of employees, the extent to which tasks require autonomy and creativity, the leader's position in the organizational hierarchy, the degree of pressure to produce, the type of organization, and the extent to which the environment is competitive (Dipboye et al., 1997). A good leader is one who can adjust her leadership style to the context in which she leads—and, where appropriate, to adjust the context in the process of leading.

Interactional Models of Leadership   Although much of the theoretical and empirical work on leadership has focused on leadership styles, more recent attention has been devoted to a leader's ability to adapt her leadership style to the particular situation in which she finds herself. Interactional theories suggest that an effective leader is a person who can adapt his leadership style to match the needs of the followers and of the situation. One of the most prominent of these theories is Fiedler's (1978, 1981) Contingency Theory.

Fiedler determined leadership style by having participants complete the Least Preferred Co-Worker (LPC) Scale. Participants think of the individual with whom they found it most difficult to work. They then rate this person on 20 bipolar adjectives (e.g., good–bad, pleasant–unpleasant). A person who found it difficult to work with this individual yet who still accords them high ratings is predominantly relationship-oriented. Those who assign negative ratings are primarily task-oriented.

According to Fielder, whether a task- or a relationship-oriented leader is most effective depends on three situational variables: task structure (i.e., the task is either very structured and clear or very unstructured and unclear); leader–member relationships, which can range on a continuum from very good to very bad; and position power (i.e., the status accorded to the leader by the followers). Under highly favorable conditions (i.e., leader–member relations are good, the task is structured, and the leader has strong power over the followers) or under highly unfavorable conditions (i.e., leader–member relations are poor, the task is unstructured, and the leader has little power over group members), a task-oriented leader is best (see Figure 18.16). Under moderately favorable situational conditions, a relationship-oriented leader is more effective.

Making Connections

Lewin's leadership categories parallel Diana Baumrind's findings on parenting styles (Chapter 14). Baumrind showed that authoritative parenting is more effective than either authoritarian (autocratic) or permissive (laissez faire) parenting. Authoritative parenting is not democratic, because it recognizes the limits of children's judgment, but it is participatory and allows input by "citizens" of the family.

Big Picture φ Question 4

To what extent is human nature particular versus universal?

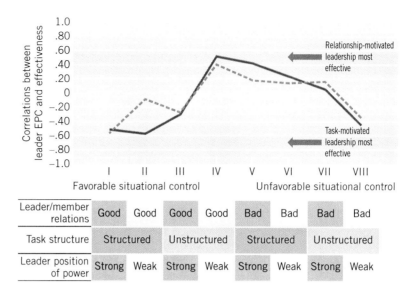

FIGURE 18.16 Fiedler's Contingency Theory of Leadership. *Source:* Adapted from Fielder, 1978.

INTERIM SUMMARY

Leaders are people who exercise greater influence than the average member of a group. Leaders tend to vary in the extent to which they are *task oriented* or *relationship oriented*. Leadership styles that are optimal or considered appropriate in one culture or setting may not be optimal in others. Leadership style (and effectiveness) differs across cultures as well as across individuals. At least in the West, effective leaders tend to be extroverted, agreeable, and conscientious. The most effective leadership style is one that is matched to particular situational demands. Fiedler's Contingency Theory of Leadership outlines three situational variables that together influence what style of leadership will be most effective: task structure, leader–member relations, and position power.

Everyday Social Influence

When we read about social influence processes such as the blind obedience to authority described earlier with the Milgram study, it is easy to distance ourselves from such findings by telling ourselves that we would never shock another person who had stopped responding. In truth, however, we are all victims of social influence on a daily basis. In a compelling book called *Influence*, Robert Cialdini discusses various principles of social influence or ways in which people are taken in by others on a regular basis.

One of the first principles of social influence is the *principle of reciprocity*. Most people have a compelling need to reciprocate that which has been done to them. Indeed, most people are socialized to behave this way. A compelling demonstration of this involved two researchers who sent Christmas cards to a group of randomly selected strangers (Kunz & Woolcott, 1976). The response rate in the form of return Christmas cards was overwhelming. Only six individuals who replied indicated that they did not remember the sender.

Although perhaps not as extreme as the Christmas card example, the number of examples of the principle of reciprocity are limitless, with all of them pointing to the fact that we all find ourselves victims of social influence on a regular basis. No one wants to be perceived as a moocher, so people reciprocate.

The principle of reciprocity is so strong that it lies at the heart of an everyday social influence tactic, the **door-in-the-face technique**, *when we intentionally make a request that we know will be turned down, so that when we back down from our request, the other individual should reciprocate our concession*. In a demonstration of this technique, Cialdini and his research assistants posed as members of the

"County Youth Counseling Program." They approached university students and asked if they would chaperone a group of juvenile delinquents to the zoo for a day. Eighty-three percent of the students refused the request. When they approached a second group of students, the researchers first asked if they would be willing to spend two hours a week for the next two years working as counselors to juvenile delinquents. Not surprisingly, the vast majority of participants refused this large request. Subsequently, researchers asked this group of participants if they would be willing to chaperone a group of juvenile delinquents on a day trip to the zoo. Compared to the first group of students, three times more participants (a total of 50 percent) indicated that they would be willing to comply with this request (Cialdini et al., 1975).

We shouldn't think that our need to reciprocate extends only to positive situations. Indeed, we also feel the need to reciprocate negative things that people do to us. If someone cuts us off in traffic, we feel the need to reciprocate in kind. If someone plays a practical joke on us (that they may find funny, but we don't), we feel it necessary to play a practical joke on them in return. Reciprocity of negative behaviors constitutes the essence of revenge.

A second principle of social influence that allows us to be taken is the *principle of commitment*. Because people are concerned with the impressions that others are forming of them (Chapter 17), they feel the need to behave consistently with prior impressions or commitments they have made. Thus, if someone can get you to make an initial commitment, no matter how small, they've generally got you. The **foot-in-the-door technique** *refers to this process by which people who get us to commit to a small request are much more likely to get us to commit to a larger request.*

In a demonstration of the foot-in-the-door technique, Freedman and Fraser (1966) went door-to-door asking people if they would be willing to have a billboard placed in their yard that said "Drive Carefully." After viewing a picture showing that the billboard would obscure the house, only 17 percent of the participants in one group agreed. Another group of individuals, however, had been previously asked if they would place a three-inch sign in their window that said "Be a Safe Driver." When the people in this group were subsequently asked whether or not they would put the billboard in their front yard, 76 percent complied! The enormous difference in compliance rates of the two groups of individuals can be explained only by the fact that those people in the second group had committed to a small request before they were asked the larger request—they had become victims of the foot-in-the-door technique.

The principle of commitment also underlies a second specific technique of social influence—**low-balling**. People who low-ball others *get a commitment to a request and then they change the conditions of the request*. Car dealers are infamous for low-balling their customers. Recently when I bought a car, the salesperson and I reached an agreement on the price. Just before I signed the paperwork, he reminded me that floor mats were not included in the car and would cost another hundred dollars. Knowing I was being low-balled, I convinced him to throw the floor mats in for nothing.

One final principle of social influence that gets us all is the *principle of liking*. Just last week, I was invited to a children's clothing party. As a mother of twin boys, certainly the party is appealing. However, the clothes that will be offered for sale at this party are expensive, AND, because a relative asked me to the party, I feel obligated to buy clothes that I actually don't even like. All sorts of similar parties abound today, taking the form of Tupperware parties, Discovery Toys parties, or Longerberger basket parties, to name a few. The form the party takes doesn't matter. What matters is the principle of liking that makes us feel obligated to buy costly products we normally would not buy. We do things for people that we like out of a sense of obligation and so that they will continue to like us in return.

As we discussed earlier in the chapter, a number of variables, such as physical attractiveness and similarity, determine those to whom we are attracted. People who use the principle of liking as a social influence tool capitalize on some of these features. For example, car salespersons often want to see the trade-in not only to assess

The twentieth century brought more dramatic social change than any other century in human history, presenting people everywhere with profound psychological challenges.

its value but also to get a profile of the customer. Infant car seats indicate that the customer has children, golf clubs that he likes golf. These observations can then be used as points of similarity whereby the salesperson can talk about her own fondness for golf, a point of similarity that breeds liking and that, in this case, translates into a sale.

Reading about social influence begs the question of why? Why are we so easily influenced by others? Why can't we be more resilient in the face of interpersonal pressure. Although there are many answers to this question, one of the simplest is *mindlessness*. Each day we are inundated with innumerable stimuli vying for our attention. Obviously, no one can process everything with which he is confronted on a daily basis, so some of what we say and do follows from mindless processing. In a clever demonstration of mindlessness, Ellen Langer and her colleagues (1978) asked a favor of people using a copier machine. They established three different conditions in the study. In the first condition, people using the copier were approached with the request "Excuse me, I have five pages. May I use the Xerox machine because I'm in a rush?" Ninety-four people complied with this request. In a second condition, however, compliance rates were lower (only 60 percent). These individuals were simply asked "Excuse me, I have five pages. May I use the Xerox machine?"

Although these results might be expected, the third condition was the most surprising. Participants in the third condition were approached with the request: "Excuse me, I have five pages. May I use the Xerox machine because I have to make some copies?" In the latter case, 93 percent of the people complied! As the researchers expected, simply providing a reason for the request being made was sufficient to induce compliance even if the reason was ridiculous—of course the person had to make copies. Why else would he be using a copier? Hearing the word "because" alerted participants to the fact that a reason was to follow. What that reason was apparently didn't matter and was simply tuned out.

Individuals, Groups, and the Nature of Human Nature

We began this chapter with a key question: To what extent does our behavior depend on the groups of which we are a part? The data from a century of social–psychological research are clear: We are social animals. As we saw in the last chapter, the cultures, groups, and families of which we are a part get "under our skin"—they become part of the way we think, feel, and behave, from the attitudes we hold to the ways we view ourselves. And, as we have seen in this chapter, the tendency to behave in groups in ways that seem "out of character" appears to be very much a part of our character. Much as we might look with horror and astonishment on the subjects in Milgram's studies, the only difference between them and us is that they know the truth about themselves.

In this sense, people's behavior in groups clearly differs qualitatively from their behavior when they are alone. A group is more than a sum of its parts. In another sense, however, we are never actually alone at all. We are always living with mental representations of the people who matter to us—people we love, hate, admire, and interact with every day. We are always in the presence of real or imagined others.

These are very special times to study psychology, because the cultures that get "under our skin" and so powerfully influence everything we do are so rapidly changing. In the twentieth century, we witnessed the most momentous period of social change in human history, as the vast majority of the world's people shifted from agricultural, nomadic, or hunter-gatherer societies to industrial nation-states. Not since the rise of agriculture thousands of years ago has the structure of human society changed so dramatically, and never as rapidly as in the present epoch. A century ago, most people lived with their extended families and believed in the values of their parents and ancestors. Within a few brief generations, traditional values and beliefs have broken down, and technology has advanced beyond anyone's wildest predictions.

People cope with social change in many ways. Some embrace new ideologies, technologies, and values. Others, coping with spiritual unease or feelings of envy, inferiority, and hatred of the dominant cultures that swept away their traditions, search for the future in the past, embracing fundamentalist ideologies that rigidly define good and evil, eliminate ambiguity, and offer a blueprint for how to live (Lifton, 1963). Another route to personal meaning lies in transferring loyalties from family and clan to large nation-states (see Geertz, 1963). Unfortunately, this process can produce the kind of fervent nationalism that left so many dead in the twentieth century, from Nazi Germany to Bosnia. Still another strategy for coping with social change is to synthesize the old and the new, to preserve a continuity with the past while somehow mooring one's identity in the future, as was Gandhi's path.

These psychological responses to the social and political realities of our age lie at the intersection of brain, behavior, and culture. The aggression that fuels conflicts between nations, like the powerful feelings of kinship and solidarity that unite people and give their lives meaning, springs from a brain constructed to make possible the passions that divide and unite. We all share a core of human nature rooted in biology. But the way that nature develops and expresses itself is as diverse as the cultures and individuals who populate the globe.

Big Picture φ Question 1

To what extent can mental processes be reduced to the brain or body?

Summary

Relationships

1. Several factors lead to **interpersonal attraction**, including proximity, similarity, rewards, and physical attractiveness. **Social exchange theory** holds that the foundation of relationships lies in reciprocal rewards.

2. Psychologists studying love distinguish the factors that produce initial attraction from those that maintain or corrode relationships over time. Two kinds of love seen in long-term relationships are **passionate love** (marked by intense physiological arousal and absorption in another person) and **companionate love** (love that involves deep affection, friendship, and emotional intimacy).

3. Evolutionary theorists understand love in terms of contributions to reproductive success. From this point of view, romantic love shares many features of attachment, and may have evolved to bind parents together to take care of their children. **Sexual strategies**, tactics used in selecting mates, vary by gender and reflect the different evolutionary selection pressures on males and females. The capacity for love is rooted in biology, but its specific nature is shaped by culture.

4. As desirable as relationships with others are, they also have a dark side. People experience their greatest criticisms and most painful hurts in the context of close relationships, as anyone who has ever been ostracized by a close other can attest.

Altruism

5. **Altruism** means behaving in a way that helps another person with no apparent gain or with potential cost to oneself. Philosophers and psychologists disagree as to whether any act can be genuinely altruistic or whether all apparent altruism is really aimed at making

the apparent altruist feel better (**ethical hedonism**). Altruistic behavior probably reflects a blend of selfish and unselfish motives.

6. Evolutionary psychologists propose that people act in ways that maximize their inclusive fitness and hence are most likely to behave altruistically toward their relatives. Natural selection favors animals that behave altruistically toward unrelated members of the species if the likely benefit to each individual over time exceeds the likely cost, a phenomenon known as **reciprocal altruism**.

7. Researchers studying **bystander intervention** have found that in the presence of other people who do not take action, people often do not help in a crisis. In part this reflects a **diffusion of responsibility** (a diminished sense of personal responsibility to act).

Aggression

8. **Aggression** refers to verbal or physical behavior aimed at harming another person or living being. Across cultures, males tend to be more aggressive than females. Researchers are increasingly recognizing the prevalence of male violence perpetrated against females, including battering and rape.

9. Instinctual and evolutionary psychologists view aggression as rooted in biology. The neural control of aggression is hierarchically organized, with the amygdala, hypothalamus, and frontal lobes playing prominent roles. Aggression is also partially controlled by hormones, particularly testosterone.

10. Cognitive neoassociation theories suggest that exposure to aversive stimuli trigger thoughts and behaviors associated with aggression. One exemplar of this model is the **frustration-aggression hypothesis**, which suggests that aggressive behavior arises from frustrated needs or desires. A reformulated version of this hypothesis suggests that frustrating or unpleasant circumstances are likely to

evoke aggression if they elicit unpleasant emotion. Cognitive–social approaches explain aggressive behavior as a result of rewards and punishments, cognitive processes (such as attributions about people's intentions), and social learning (such as modeling).

11. The General Aggression Model unifies the multitude of theories created to explain aggression. According to the GAM, person and situational input variables combine to determine the presence or absence of aggressive output.

Social Influence

12. **Social influence** refers to the influence of the presence of other people on thought, feeling, and behavior. **Obedience** is a social influence process whereby individuals follow the dictates of an authority. The Milgram studies demonstrated that most people will obey without limitations of conscience if they believe the authority is legitimate.

13. **Conformity** is the process by which people change their attitudes or behavior to accommodate the standards of peers or groups. Asch's studies demonstrated that a substantial number of people will conform when confronted by a group with a consensus opinion, even if the opinion is manifestly wrong. Conformity is highest in agricultural societies with dense populations, where independence may be less adaptive than in hunter-gatherer or urban, technologically developed societies.

14. A **group** is a collection of people whose actions affect the other group members. Naturally occurring groups routinely have **norms** (standards for the behavior of group members), **roles** (socially patterned positions within a group that define appropriate behavior for the people occupying them), and **leaders** (people who exercise greater influence than the average member).

15. The presence of others in a group substantially influences the behavior of individual group members, as illustrated with **social facilitation**, whereby the presence of others can either facilitate or inhibit individual performance. The degree to which groups influence individual performance is influenced, in part, by the nature of the task. Frequently, people will engage in **social loafing**, where they will exert less effort when in a group as opposed to when alone.

16. In spite of the fact that people like to view themselves as immune to social influence attempts, everyone falls victim to social influence on a regular basis. Common social influence tactics to which people succumb include the **door-in-the-face** technique (asking for a large request that we know will be turned down and then backing down from that request to induce similar behavior in another), the **foot-in-the-door** technique (asking for a small commitment to ensure agreement with a larger commitment at a later time), and **low-balling** (getting a commitment and then changing the conditions).

17. People behave differently in the presence of others, although they also carry "others" with them all the time in the form of mental representations. The massive social changes in the last century, such as rapid technological development and the breakdown of traditional family structures and values, have created profound psychological changes and dilemmas for coping.

Key Terms

aggression 669
altruism 654
bystander intervention 667
companionate love 658
conformity 681
diffusion of responsibility 668
dispositional variables 654
door-in-the-face technique 688
ethical hedonism 665

foot-in-the-door technique 689
frustration–aggression hypothesis 675
group 683
hostile aggression 669
instrumental aggression 669
instrumental leaders 684
interpersonal attraction 655
leaders 686

low-balling 689
matching hypothesis 657
need to belong 655
norms 683
obedience 679
passionate love 658
reciprocal altruism 667
reference groups 683
role 684

self-fulfilling prophecies 678
sexual strategies 659
situational variables 654
social–emotional leaders 684
social exchange theories 656
social facilitation 685
social influence 678
social loafing 685
task leaders 684

Answers to Disjunctive Puzzles (p.686)

1. The answer to this Eureka problem is E. The letters are the first letters of the first eight digits: One, Two, Three, Four, Five, Six, Seven , and Eight

2. This non-Eureka puzzle is known as the Horse-Trading Problem. The answer is $20.

3. The missionary/cannibal problem is a non-Eureka problem. The entire process requires the following 13 crossings of the missionaries (M1, M2, and M3), the two nonrowing cannibals (C1 and C2), and the cannibal who can row (RC).

   1. M1 and C1 cross
   2. M1 returns
   3. RC and C2 cross
   4. RC returns
   5. M1 and M2 cross
   6. M1 and C1 return
   7. RC and M1 cross
   8. M1 and C2 return
   9. M1 and M3 cross
   10. RC returns
   11. RC and C1 cross
   12. RC returns
   13. RC and C2 cross

4. The chain puzzle is a Eureka puzzle. Many groups answer 11, since that would involve cutting only every other link. The correct answer, however, is 2. If the 4th and 11th links are cut, all the values from 1 to 23 can be obtained by getting "change" back from the motel owner. Separate links (the 4th and the 11th) are given on Days 1 and 2, but on Day 3 the 3-link unit is given to the owner, who returns the separate links. These links are then used to pay on Days 4 and 5, but on Day 6 the 6-link unit is used, and the owner returns the others as change. This process can be continued for 23 days.

Source: Reprinted from Forsyth, 1990, pp.266–267

Glossary

A

ABC theory of psychopathology Albert Ellis's theory of psychopathology, in which A refers to activating conditions, B to belief systems, and C to emotional consequences. (p. 593)

absolute threshold The minimum amount of physical energy (stimulation) needed for an observer to notice a stimulus. (p. 106)

absorptive phase The phase of metabolism during which a person is ingesting food.(p. 332)

accommodation In vision, the changes in the shape of the lens that focus light rays; in Piaget's theory, the modification of schemas to fit reality. (pp. 113, 476)

acculturative stress The stress people experience while trying to adapt to a new culture. (p. 406)

acetylcholine (ACh) A neurotransmitter involved in muscle contractions, learning, and memory. (p. 70)

action potential A temporary shift in the polarity of the cell membrane, which leads to the firing of a neuron. (p. 65)

activational effects Effects of hormones activating brain circuitry to produce psychobiological changes. (p. 340)

actualizing tendency The primary motivation in humans, according to Carl Rogers, which includes a range of needs that humans experience, from the basic needs for food and drink to the needs to be open to experience and express one's true self. (p. 448)

actual self People's views of how they actually are. (p. 648)

adaptive traits A term applied to traits that help organisms adjust to their environment. (p. 19)

adrenal glands Endocrine glands located above the kidneys that secrete adrenaline and other hormones during emergency situations. (p. 71)

adrenalin A hormone that triggers physiological arousal, particularly in potential danger situations. (p. 71)

adult attachment Patterns of mental representation, emotion, and proximity-seeking in adults related to childhood attachment patterns. (p. 503)

affect A positive or negative feeling state that typically includes arousal, subjective experience, and behavioral expression; a synonym for emotion. (p. 320)

affect regulation See emotional regulation. (p. 359)

afferent neurons See sensory neurons. (p. 62)

affiliation Interaction with friends or acquaintances. (p. 344)

ageism A form of prejudice against old people comparable to racism and sexism. (p. 471)

agency Motives for achievement, mastery, power, autonomy, and other self-oriented goals. (p. 344)

aggression Verbal or physical behavior aimed at harming another person or living being. (p. 669)

agoraphobia The fear of being in places or situations from which escape might be difficult. (p. 569)

alcoholism The tendency to use or abuse alcohol to a degree that leads to social or occupational dysfunction. (pp. 392, 553)

algorithm A systematic problem-solving procedure that inevitably produces a solution. (p. 241)

alleles Forms of a gene. (p. 90)

altered states of consciousness Deviations in subjective experience from a normal waking state. (p. 309)

altruism Behaving in a way that helps another person with no apparent gain, or with potential cost, to oneself. (p. 654)

Alzheimer's disease A progressive and incurable illness that destroys neurons in the brain, causing severe impairment of memory, reasoning, perception, language, and behavior. (p. 488)

ambivalence Conflicting feelings or intentions. (p. 423)

ambivalent attachment style Response to separation in which infants who are angry and rejecting simultaneously indicate a clear desire to be close to the mother. (p. 499)

amplitude The difference between the minimum and maximum pressure levels in a sound wave, measured in decibels; amplitude corresponds to the psychological property of loudness. (p. 124)

amygdala A brain structure associated with the expression of rage, fear, and calculation of the emotional significance of a stimulus. (p. 81)

analogical reasoning The process by which people understand a novel situation in terms of a familiar one. (p. 239)

anal stage The psychosexual phase occurring roughly around ages 2 to 3, which is characterized by conflicts with parents over compliance and defiance. (p. 426)

androgen insensitivity syndrome A condition in which androgens are secreted in utero, but a genetic defect leads to an absence of androgen receptors, so that a genetic male develops female genitalia. (p. 340)

anorexia nervosa An eating disorder in which a person refuses to eat, starving herself to the point that physical complications and sometimes death may occur. (p. 572)

antibodies Protein molecules that attach themselves to foreign agents in the body, marking them for destruction. (p. 409)

antidepressant medications Biological treatment of depression that increases the amount of norepinephrine and/or serotonin available in synapses. (p. 605)

antipsychotic medications Medications used to treat schizophrenia and other psychotic states, which has sedating effects and reduces positive symptoms such as hallucinations and delusions. (p. 604)

antisocial personality disorder A personality disorder marked by irresponsible and socially disruptive behavior in a variety of areas. (p. 576)

anxiety disorder A disorder characterized by intense, frequent, or continuous anxiety, which may lead to disruptive avoidance behavior. (p. 568)

assimilation The interpretation of actions or events in terms of one's present schemas. (p. 476)

association areas The areas of cortex involved in putting together perceptions, ideas, and plans. (p. 82)

attachment Enduring affectional ties that children form with their primary caregivers and that become the basis for later love relationships. (p. 497)

attachment motivation The desire for physical and psychological proximity to an attachment figure. (p. 344)

attention The process of focusing consciousness on a limited range of experience. (p. 294)

attention-deficit hyperactivity disorder (ADHD) A disorder characterized by age-inappropriate inattention, impulsiveness, and hyperactivity. (p. 552)

attitude An association between an action or object and an evaluation. (pp. 376, 632)

attitude accessibility The ease with which an attitude comes to mind or is activated. (p. 633)

attitude importance The personal relevance of an attitude and the psychological significance of that attitude for an individual. (p. 633)

attitude inoculation Building up a receiver's resistance to an opposing attitude by presenting weak arguments for it or forewarning of a strong opposing persuasive appeal. (p. 638)

attitude strength The durability of an attitude (its persistence and resistance to change) and its impact on behavior. (p. 633)

attitudinal ambivalence A condition in which an attitude object is associated with conflicting evaluative responses. (p. 635)

attitudinal coherence The extent to which an attitude is internally consistent. (p. 635)

attribution The process of making inferences about the causes of one's own and others' thoughts, feelings, and behavior. (pp. 361, 626)

attributional style A person's habitual manner of assigning causes to behaviors or events. (p. 627)

audition Hearing. (p. 123)

auditory nerve The bundle of sensory neurons that transmit auditory information from the ear to the brain. (p. 126)

augmentation Attributional phenomenon in which people emphasize an internal explanation for a behavior because it occurred despite situational pressures. (p. 627)

authoritarian A way of parenting that places high value on obedience and respect for authority. (p. 506)

authoritarian personality A personality type that is prone to hate people who are different or downtrodden. (p. 620)

authoritative A way of parenting that sets standards for children and firmly enforces them but also provides explanations for the parents' actions and encourages verbal give-and-take. (p. 506)

automatic thoughts The things people say spontaneously to themselves, which can lead to irrational feelings and behaviors. (p. 593)

automatization The process of executing mental processes with increasing efficiency, so that they require less and less attention. (p. 482)

autonomic nervous system The part of the peripheral nervous system that serves visceral or internal bodily structures connected with basic life processes, such as the beating of the heart and breathing. It consists of two parts: the sympathetic nervous system and the parasympathetic nervous system. (p. 74)

autonomy versus shame and doubt In Erikson's theory, the stage in which children begin to walk, talk, and get a sense of themselves as independent sources of will and power. (p. 530)

availability heuristic A strategy that leads people to judge the frequency of a class of events or the likelihood of something happening on the basis of how easy it is to retrieve from explicit memory. (p. 245)

aversion therapy The introduction of something aversive as a means of discouraging a negative health habit. (p. 394)

avoidance learning A negative reinforcement procedure in which the behavior of an organism is reinforced by the prevention of an expected aversive event. (p. 171)

avoidant attachment style Response to separation in which infants ignore the mother when she returns. (p. 499)

axon The long extension from the cell body of a neuron through which electrical impulses pass. (p. 63)

B

babbling A child's earliest language utterances that are spontaneous and incomprehensible. (p. 491)

barriers Costs of terminating a health behavior. (p. 374)

basal ganglia A set of structures located near the thalamus and hypothalamus involved in the control of movement and in judgments that require minimal conscious thought. (p. 81)

basic emotions Feeling states common to the human species from which other feeling states are derived. (p. 354)

basic level The level of categorization to which people naturally go; the level at which objects share distinctive common attributes. (p. 234)

basic trust versus mistrust In Erikson's theory, the stage in which infants come to trust others or to perceive the social world as unfriendly or unreliable. (p. 530)

behavioral analysis In cognitive–behavior therapy, the process of assessing the symptom and the stimuli or thoughts associated with it. (p. 588)

behavioral approach system (BAS) The anatomical system that is associated with pleasurable emotional states and is responsible for approach-oriented operant behavior. (p. 181)

behavioral genetics A field that examines the genetic and environmental bases of differences among individuals on psychological traits. (p. 20)

behavioral inhibition system (BIS) The anatomical system that is associated with anxiety and avoidance behavior. (p. 181)

behavioral neuroscience A field of investigation that examines the physical basis of psychological phenomena such as motivation, emotion, and stress; also called biopsychology. (p. 4)

behaviorism See behaviorist perspective. (p. 13)

behaviorist perspective The perspective pioneered by John Watson and B. F. Skinner, which focuses on the relation between observable behaviors and environmental events or stimuli; also called behaviorism. (p. 13)

behavior–outcome expectancy Belief that a certain behavior will lead to a particular outcome. (p. 436)

benefits Beneficial consequences associated with terminating a negative health behavior. (p. 374).

benzodiazepines Antianxiety medications that indirectly affect the action of norepinephrine. (p. 606)

binocular cells Neurons that receive information from both eyes. (p. 141)

binocular cues Visual input integrated from two eyes that provides perception of depth. (p. 141)

biofeedback A procedure for monitoring autonomic physiological processes and learning to alter them at will. (p. 178)

biomedical model A reductionistic view of illness, reducing disease to biological causes at the level of individual cells. (p. 372)

bipolar cells Neurons in the retina that combine information from many receptors and excite ganglion cells. (p. 113)

bipolar disorder A psychological disorder marked by extreme mood swings; also called manic-depression. (p. 563)

biopsychology The field that examines the physical basis of psychological phenomena such as motivation, emotion, and stress; also called behavioral neuroscience. (p. 4)

biopsychosocial model The idea that health and illness stem from a combination of biological, psychological, and social factors. (p. 372)

blindsight A phenomenon in which individuals with cortical lesions have no conscious visual awareness but can make discriminations about objects placed in front of them. (p. 118)

blind spot The point on the retina where the optic nerve leaves the eye and which contains no receptor cells. (p. 114)

blind studies Studies in which subjects are kept unaware of or "blind" to important aspects of the research. (p. 46)

blocking When a stimulus fails to elicit a conditioned response because it is combined with another stimulus that already elicits the response. (p. 165)

body mass index Statistical index that reflects a person's weight in kilograms divided by the height in meters squared. (p. 378)

borderline personality disorder A personality disorder characterized by extremely unstable interpersonal relationships, dramatic mood swings, an unstable sense of identity, intense fears of abandonment, manipulativeness, and impulsive behavior. (p. 575)

bottom-up processing Perceptual processing that starts with raw sensory data that feed "up" to the brain; what is perceived is determined largely by the features of the stimuli reaching the sense organs. (p. 149)

bounded rationality The notion that people are rational within constraints imposed by their environment, goals, and abilities. (p. 245)

Broca's area A brain structure located in the left frontal lobe at the base of the motor cortex, involved in the movements of the mouth and tongue necessary for speech production and in the use of grammar. (p. 85)

bulimia A disorder characterized by a binge-and-purge syndrome in which the person binges on food and then either induces vomiting or uses laxatives to purge. (p. 573)

bystander intervention A form of altruism involving helping a person in need. (p. 667)

C

Cannon-Bard theory A theory of emotion that asserts that emotion-inducing stimuli elicit both emotional experience and bodily response. (p. 348)

Cartesian dualism The doctrine of dual spheres of mind and body. (pp. 13, 372)

case study In-depth observation of one subject or a small group of subjects. (p. 38)

castration complex In Freud's theory, the fear the boy has in the phallic stage that his father will castrate him for his wishes toward his mother. (p. 427)

catastrophes Rare, unexpected disasters such as earthquakes, floods, and other traumatic events that affect a group of people. (p. 406)

categorical variable A variable comprised of groupings, classifications, or categories. (p. 33)

categorization The process of identifying an object as an instance of a category, recognizing its similarity to some objects and dissimilarity to others. (p. 231)

category A grouping based on a common property (p. 231)

cell body The part of the neuron which includes a nucleus containing the genetic material of the cell (the chromosomes), as well as other microstructures vital to cell functioning. (p. 63)

cellular theory of illness The idea that illness and disease result from abnormalities within individual cells. (p. 372)

central nervous system (CNS) The brain and spinal cord. (p. 73)

central route to persuasion A method of persuasion that involves inducing the recipient of a message to think carefully and weigh the arguments. (p. 639)

cerebellum A large bulge in the dorsal or back area of the brain, responsible for the coordination of smooth, well-sequenced movements as well as maintaining equilibrium and regulating postural reflexes. (p. 78)

cerebral cortex The many-layered surface of the cerebrum, which allows complex voluntary movements, permits subtle discriminations among complex sensory patterns, and makes possible symbolic thinking. (p. 82)

cerebral hemispheres The two halves of the cerebrum. (p. 83)

cerebrum The "thinking" center of the brain, which includes the cortex and subcortical structures such as the basal ganglia and limbic system. (p. 96)

chaining A process of learning in which a sequence of already established behaviors is reinforced step by step. (p. 178)

chromosomes Strands of DNA arranged in pairs. (p. 90)

chunking The process of organizing information into small, meaningful bits to aid memory. (p. 203)

circadian rhythm Biological rhythm that evolved around the daily cycles of light and dark. (p. 302)

classical conditioning A procedure by which a previously neutral stimulus comes to elicit a response after it is paired with a stimulus that automatically elicits that response; the first type of learning to be studied systematically. (p. 159)

client-centered therapy A therapeutic approach developed by Carl Rogers, based on the as-sumption that psychological difficulties result from incongruence between one's concept of self and one's actual experience, and that empathy is curative. (p. 596)

clinical syndromes A constellation of symptoms that tend to occur together. (p. 550)

closure A Gestalt rule of perception which states that people tend to perceive incomplete figures as complete. (p. 138)

cochlea The three-chambered tube in the inner ear in which sound is transduced. (p. 126)

cognition Thought and memory. (p. 15)

cognitive–behavioral Approach in clinical psychology in which practitioners integrate an understanding of classical and operant conditioning with a cognitive–social perspective. (pp. 544, 588)

cognitive dissonance A phenomenon in which a person experiences a discrepancy between an attitude and a behavior or between an attitude and a new piece of information incongruent with it, which leads to a state of tension and a subsequent change in attitude, behavior, or perception. (p. 640)

cognitive distortions Cognitive mechanisms by which a depressed person transforms neutral or positive information in a depressive direction. (p. 565)

cognitive maps Mental representations of visual space. (p. 182)

cognitive perspective A psychological perspective that focuses on the way people perceive, process, and retrieve information. (p. 15)

cognitive–social theory A theory of learning that emphasizes the role of thought and social learning in behavior. (p. 182)

cognitive therapy A psychological treatment that focuses on the thought processes that underlie psychological symptoms. (p. 593)

cognitive unconscious Information processing mechanisms that operate outside of awareness, such as procedural memory and implicit associative processes, as opposed to the psychodynamic unconscious, which includes information the person is motivated to keep from awareness. (p. 297)

cohort effects Differences among age groups associated with differences in the culture. (p. 464)

color constancy The tendency to perceive the color of objects as stable despite changing illumination. (p. 144)

common factors Shared elements in psychotherapies that produce positive outcomes. (p. 610)

companionate love Love that involves deep affection, friendship, and emotional intimacy. (p. 658)

competences Skills and abilities used for solving problems. (p. 437)

complexity The extent to which a sound wave is composed of multiple frequencies. (p. 124)

compromise formations A single behavior, or a complex pattern of thought and action, which typically reflects compromises among multiple (and often conflicting) forces. (p. 424)

compulsion An intentional behavior or mental act performed in a stereotyped fashion. (p. 569)

computerized axial tomography (CT scan) A brain-scanning technique used to detect lesions. (p. 53)

concept A mental representation of a category of objects, ideas, or events that share common properties. (p. 231)

concrete operational stage Piaget's third stage of cognitive development, in which children are capable of mentally manipulating internal representations of concrete objects in ways that are reversible. (p. 478)

conditioned response In classical conditioning, a response that has been learned. (p. 159)

conditioned stimulus A stimulus that the organism has learned to associate with the unconditioned stimulus. (p. 159)

conditioning A form of learning. (p. 159)

conditions Values or versions of the independent variable that vary across experimental groups. (p. 44)

conditions of worth In Carl Rogers' theory, standards children internalize that they must meet in order to esteem themselves. (p. 448)

conduct disorder A childhood disorder in which a child persistently violates the rights of others as well as societal norms. (p. 552)

cones One of two types of photoreceptors, which are specialized for color vision and allow perception of fine detail. (p. 113)

confirmation bias The tendency for people to search for information that confirms their expectations. (p. 241)

conflict A battle between opposing motives. (p. 424)

conflict model Theoretical model of adolescence that holds that conflict and crisis are normal in adolescence. (p. 533)

conformity The process of changing attitudes or behavior to accommodate the standards of a group. (p. 681)

confounding variable A variable that produces effects of independent variables. (p. 47)

congenital adrenal hyperplasia A disorder in which the adrenal glands secrete too much androgen, thus masculinizing the genitals in females. (p. 340)

connectionism A model of human cognitive processes in which many cognitive processes occur simultaneously so that a representation is spread out (i.e., distributed) throughout a network of interacting processing units; also called parallel distributed processing (PDP). (p. 249)

conscious mental processes Processes that involve a subjective awareness of stimuli, feelings, or ideas (pp. 296, 423)

consciousness The subjective awareness of mental events. (p. 293)

consensus In attribution theory, a normative response in a social group. (p. 627)

conservation Recognition that basic properties of an object remain stable even though superficial properties may change. (p. 479)

consistency In attribution theory, the extent to which a person always responds in the same way to the same stimulus. (p. 627)

constraint satisfaction The tendency to settle on a cognitive solution that satisfied as many constraints as possible in order to achieve the best fit to the data. (p. 250)

construct validity The degree to which a measure actually assesses what it claims to measure. (p. 37)

continuity model The theoretical model that holds that adolescence for most individuals is essentially continuous with childhood and adulthood and not distinguished by turbulence. (p. 533)

continuous reinforcement schedule When the environmental consequences are the same each time an organism emits a behavior. (p. 174)

continuous variable A variable that can be placed on a continuum, from none or little to much. (p. 33)

control group Subjects in an experiment who receive a relatively neutral condition to serve as a comparison group. (p. 46)

conventional morality The level of morality in which individuals define what is right by the standards they have learned from other people, particularly respected authorities. (p. 523)

coping The ways people deal with stressful situations; also called coping mechanisms. (p. 412)

coping mechanisms The ways people deal with stressful situations. (p. 412)

cornea The tough, transparent tissue covering the front of the eyeball. (p. 113)

corpus callosum A band of fibers that connect the two hemispheres of the brain. (p. 83)

corrective mechanisms Processes that restore a homeostatic system to its set point (p. 333)

correlate In research, to assess the extent to which the measure of one variable predicts the measure of a second variable. (p. 51)

correlational research Research that assesses the degree to which two variables are related, so that knowing the value of one can lead to prediction of the other. (p. 50)

correlation coefficient An index of the extent to which two variables are related. (p. 51)

correlation matrix A table presenting the correlations among several variables. (p. 52)

correspondence bias The tendency to assume that people's behavior corresponds to their internal states rather than external situations. (p. 628)

cortex See cerebral cortex. (p. 96)

couples therapy Psychotherapy that treats a couple; also called marital therapy. (p. 598)

cranial nerves Pairs of specialized nerves in the brain. (p. 76)

creativity The ability to produce valued outcomes in a novel way. (p. 274)

criterion validity The degree to which a measure allows a researcher to distinguish among groups on the basis of certain behaviors or responses. (p. 37)

critical period A period of special sensitivity to specific types of learning that shapes the capacity for future development. (p. 461)

cross-cultural psychology The field that attempts to test psychological hypotheses in different cultures. (p. 6)

cross-sectional studies The type of research that compares groups of different-aged subjects at a single time to see whether differences exist among them. (p. 464)

crystallized intelligence People's store of knowledge. (p. 279)

cues to action Ancillary factors that influence whether or not a person is willing to begin a healthy behavior or terminate an unhealthy one. (p. 375)

cultural models Shared cultural concepts, which organize knowledge and shape the way people think and remember. (p. 219)

culture pattern approach An approach to personality and culture that views culture as an organized set of beliefs, rituals, and institutions that shape individuals to fit its patterns. (p. 454)

cycle A single round of expansion and contraction of the distance between molecules of air in a sound wave. (p. 124)

D

daily hassles The small, but irritating demands that characterize daily life. (p. 407)

decay theory The notion that memories are lost as a result of a fading of the memory trace. (p. 222)

decibel (dB) The unit of measure of amplitude (loudness) of a sound wave. (p. 124)

decision making The process by which people weigh the pros and cons of different alternatives in order to make a choice among two or more options. (p. 242)

declarative memory Knowledge that can be consciously retrieved and "declared." (p. 204)

deductive reasoning The process of reasoning that draws logical conclusions from premises. (p. 237)

defense mechanisms Unconscious mental processes aimed at protecting a person from experiencing unpleasant emotions, especially anxiety. (p. 429)

defining features Qualities that are essential, or necessarily present, in order to classify an object as a member of a category. (p. 232)

degree of relatedness The probability that two people share any particular gene. (p. 91)

delusion A false belief firmly held despite evidence to the contrary. (p. 557)

demand characteristics The influence of subjects' perception of the researchers' goals on subjects' behavior. (p. 46)

dementia A disorder marked by global disturbance of higher mental functions. (p. 488)

dendrites Branchlike extensions of the neuron that receive information from other cells. (p. 63)

denial A defense mechanism in which the person refuses to acknowledge external realities or emotions. (p. 429)

dependent variables Subjects' responses in a study, hypothesized to depend on the influence of the independent variables. (p. 44)

depressant A drug that slows down the nervous system. (p. 312)

depth perception The organization of perception in three dimensions; also called distance perception. (p. 141)

descriptive diagnosis A classification of mental disorders in terms of clinical syndromes. (p. 550)

descriptive research Research methods that cannot unambiguously demonstrate cause and effect, including case studies, naturalistic observation, survey research, and correlational methods. (p. 38)

descriptive statistics Numbers that describe the data from a study in a way that summarizes their essential features. (p. 47)

detoxification The process during which an alcoholic dries out. (p. 394)

developmental model Freud's model of how children develop, defined by his psychosexual stages. (p. 425)

developmental psychology The field that studies the way thought, feeling, and behavior develop through the life span. (p. 459)

developmental task Challenge that is normative for a particular period of life. (p. 530)

Diagnostic and Statistical Manual of Mental Disorders-IV (DSM-IV) The manual of clinical syndromes published by the American Psychiatric Association and used for descriptive diagnosis. (p. 550)

diathesis–stress model The model of psychopathology that proposes that people with an underlying vulnerability (also called a diathesis) may develop a disorder under stressful circumstances. (p. 546)

dichotic listening A procedure in which different information is presented to the left and right ears simultaneously. (p. 295)

difference threshold The smallest difference in intensity between two stimuli that a person can detect. (p. 108)

diffusion of responsibility The phenomenon in which the presence of other people leads to a diminished sense of personal responsibility to act. (p. 668)

direct perception A theory which states that sensory information intrinsically carries meaning. (p. 147)

discounting The attributional phenomenon in which people downplay the role of one variable that might explain a behavior because they know another may be contributing. (p. 627)

discourse The way people ordinarily speak, hear, read, and write in interconnected sentences. (p. 258)

discrimination The behavioral component of prejudiced attitudes. (p. 619)

discriminative stimulus A stimulus that signals that particular contingencies of reinforcement are in effect. (p. 176)

disorganized attachment style Response to separation in which infants behave in contradictory ways, indicating helpless efforts to elicit soothing responses from the attachment figure. (p. 499)

display rules Patterns of emotional expression that are considered acceptable in a given culture. (p. 353)

dispositional variables Personalities and attitudes. (p. 654)

dissociation A disturbance in memory and consciousness in which significant aspects of experience are kept separate and distinct (or dis-associated). (p. 574)

dissociative disorders Disorders characterized by disruptions in consciousness, memory, sense of identity, or perception of the environment. (p. 574)

dissociative identity disorder The most severe dissociative disorder; also known as multiple personality disorder. (p. 574)

distinctiveness In attribution theory, the extent to which an individual responds in a particular way to many different stimuli. (p. 627)

divergent thinking The ability to generate multiple possibilities in a given situation. (p. 274)

divided attention The process by which attention is split between two or more sets of stimuli. (p. 295)

dizygotic (DZ) twins Fraternal twins who, like other siblings, share only about half of their genes, having developed from the union of two sperm with two separate eggs. (p. 91)

door-in-the-face Everyday social influence tactic whereby people intentionally make a request that they know will be turned down, but follow up on that request with a smaller request. Based in the principle of reciprocity. (p. 689)

dopamine A neurotransmitter with wide-ranging effects in the nervous system, involved in thought, feeling, motivation, and behavior. (p. 69)

dopamine hypothesis Hypothesis that implicates an imbalance in the neurotransmitter dopamine in schizophrenia. (p. 559)

dorsolateral prefrontal cortex An area in the brain that plays a central role in working memory and explicit manipulation of representations. (p. 252)

double-blind study A study in which both subjects and researchers are blind to the status of subjects. (p. 47)

drive According to Freud, an internal tension state that builds up until satisfied; according to behaviorist theory, an unpleasant tension state that motivates behavior, classified as either primary or secondary (acquired). (pp. 180, 321)

drive model Freud's theory of motivation, which held that people are motivated by sexual and aggressive instincts or drives. (p. 425)

drive-reduction theories Mid-twentieth century behaviorist theories which proposed that motivation stems from a combination of drive and reinforcement, in which stimuli become reinforcing because they are associated with reduction of a state of biological deficit. (pp. 180, 323)

dysthymia Chronic low-level depression of more than two years' duration, with intervals of normal moods that never last more than a few weeks or months. (p. 563)

E

eardrum The thin, flexible membrane that marks the outer boundary of the middle ear; the eardrum is set in motion by sound waves and in turn sets in motion the ossicles; also called the tympanic membrane. (p. 125)

echoic storage An auditory sensory registration process by which people retain an echo or brief auditory representation of a sound to which they have been exposed. (p. 196)

effectiveness studies Studies that assess the outcome of psychotherapy as it is practiced in the field rather than in the laboratory. (p. 611)

efferent neurons See motor neurons. (p. 62)

efficacy studies Studies that assess psychotherapy outcome under highly controlled conditions, such as random assignment of patients to different treatment or control groups, careful training of therapists to adhere to a manual, and standardized length of treatment. (p. 610)

ego The structure in Freud's model of the mind that must somehow balance desire, reality, and morality. (p. 428)

egocentric Being thoroughly embedded in one's own point of view. (p. 477)

elaboration likelihood model The model of persuasion that proposes that knowing how to appeal to a person requires figuring out the likelihood that he or she will think much about (or elaborate on) the arguments. (p. 639)

elaborative rehearsal An aid to long-term memory storage that involves thinking about the meaning of information in order to process it with more depth; see also depth of processing. (p. 196)

electroconvulsive therapy (ECT) A last-resort treatment for severe depression, in which an electric shock to the brain is used to induce a seizure. (p. 607)

electroencephalogram (EEG) A record of the electrical activity toward the surface of the brain, used especially in sleep research and diagnosis of epilepsy. (p. 53)

emotion A positive or negative feeling state that typically includes arousal, subjective experience, and behavioral expression; also called affect. (pp. 320, 347)

emotion regulation Efforts to control emotional states; also called affect regulation. (p. 359)

emotional expression The variety of models (e.g., facial expression, posture, hand gestures, voice tone) through which people express feelings. (p. 351)

emotional forecasting Predicting emotional reactions to future events (p. 404)

empathic distress Feeling upset for another person. (p. 526)

empathy Feeling for another person who is hurting, which includes a cognitive component (understanding what the person is experiencing) and an emotional component (experiencing a feeling of empathic discomfort; in Rogers' theory of personality, the capacity to understand another person's experience cognitively and emotionally. (pp. 448, 526)

empiricism The belief that the path to scientific knowledge is systematic observation and, ideally, experimental observation. (p. 25)

empty chair technique A technique associated with Gestalt therapy, in which clients practice emotional expression by imagining that the person to whom they would like to speak is seated in the chair. (p. 595)

encoded Refers to information that is cast into a representational form or "code," so that it can be readily accessed from memory. (p. 210)

encoding specificity principle The notion that the match between the way information is encoded and the way it is retrieved is important to remembering. (p. 211)

endocrine system The collection of ductless glands that secrete hormones into the bloodstream and control various bodily and psychological functions. (p. 71)

endorphins Chemicals in the brain similar to morphine that elevate mood and reduce pain (p. 70)

episodic memory Memories of particular episodes or events from personal experience. (p. 204)

equilibration According to Piaget, a balancing of assimilation and accommodation in trying to adapt to the world. (p. 476)

ERG theory A theory of worker motivation distinguishing existence, relatedness, and growth needs. (p. 327)

error That part of a subject's score on a test that is unrelated to the true score. (p. 37)

escape learning A negative reinforcement procedure in which the behavior of an organism is reinforced by the cessation of an aversive event that already exists. (p. 171)

estrogen Hormone produced by the female gonads, the ovaries, which control sex drive as well as the development of secondary sex characteristics. (p. 72)

ethical hedonism The school of philosophical thought that asserts that all behavior, no matter how apparently altruistic, is and should be designed to increase one's own pleasure or reduce one's own pain. (p. 665)

ethology The field that studies animal behavior from a biological and evolutionary perspective. (p. 20)

etiology Causes of a disorder. (p. 542)

everyday memory Memory as it occurs in daily life. (p. 208)

evolution Examines changes in genetic frequencies over several generations. (p. 93)

evolutionary perspective The viewpoint built on Darwin's principle of natural selection that argues that human behavioral proclivities must be understood in the context of their evolutionary and adaptive significance. (p. 18)

evolutionary psychologists Apply evolutionary thinking to a wide range of psychological phenomena. (p. 20)

evolutionary theory See evolutionary perspective. (p. 93)

existential dread The recognition that life has no absolute value or meaning, that any meaning that does exist we create for ourselves, and that ultimately, we all face death. (p. 449)

existentialism A school of modern philosophy that focuses on each individual's subjective existence or phenomenology and on the way the individual comes to terms with basic issues such as meaning in life and mortality. (p. 448)

expectancies Expectations relevant to desired outcomes. (pp. 184, 436)

expected utility A combined assessment of the value and probability of different options. (p. 243)

experimental research A research design in which investigators manipulate some aspect of a situation and examine the impact of this manipulation on the way subjects respond. (p. 43)

experimenter's dilemma The trade-off between internal and external validity. (p. 34)

explanatory style The way people make sense of events or outcomes, particularly aversive ones. (p. 185)

explicit cognition Thinking that involves conscious manipulation of representations. (p. 244)

explicit memory The conscious recollection of facts and events. (p. 205)

exposure techniques Behavior therapy techniques based on classical conditioning in which the patient is confronted with the actual phobic stimulus. (p. 590)

expressed emotion The tendency of family interactions to be characterized by criticism, hostile interchanges, and emotional overinvolvement or intrusiveness by family members, implicated in the etiology and maintenance of schizophrenia and other disorders. (p. 561)

external attributions An explanation of behavior that attributes the behavior to the situation rather than the person. (p. 626)

external locus of control The belief that one's life is determined by forces outside (external to) oneself. (p. 184)

external validity The extent to which the findings of a study can be generalized to situations outside the laboratory. (p. 34)

extinction In classical conditioning, the process by which a conditioned response is weakened by presentation of the conditioned stimulus without the unconditioned stimulus; in operant conditioning, the process by which the connection between an operant and a reinforcer or punishment is similarly broken. (p. 163)

extroversion The tendency to be sociable, active, and willing to take risks. (p. 441)

F

face validity The degree to which a measure appears to measure what it purports to measure. (p. 36)

factor analysis A statistical technique for identifying common factors that underlie performance on a wide variety of measures. (p. 278)

factors Common elements that underlie performance across a set of tasks. (p. 278)

false self A condition in which people mold themselves to other people's expectations and to the demands of the roles they play. (p. 448)

falsifiability criterion The ability of a theory to be proven wrong as a means of advancing science. (p. 12)

family alliances Patterns of taking sides in family conflicts. (p. 548)

family boundaries In family systems theory, the physical and psychological limits of a family or system. (p. 548)

family homeostatic mechanisms Methods members use to preserve equilibrium in a family. (p. 547)

family roles Parts individuals play in repetitive family interaction patterns. (p. 547)

family systems model The model of psy-

chopathology which suggests that an individual's symptoms are really symptoms of dysfunction in a family. (p. 547)

family therapy A psychological treatment that attempts to change maladaptive interaction patterns among members of a family. (p. 597)

fasting phase The second stage of metabolism, when the body converts glucose and fat into energy. (p. 332)

feature detector A neuron that fires only when stimulation in its receptive field matches a particular pattern or orientation. (p. 119)

Fechner's law The law of psychophysics proposed by Gustav Fechner, that the subjective magnitude of a sensation grows as a proportion of the logarithm of the stimulus. (p. 109)

feedback mechanisms Processes that provide information regarding the state of a homeostatic system with regard to its set point or steady state. (p. 333)

fight–flight system Anatomical system associated with unconditioned escape and defensive aggression and the emotions of terror and rage. (p. 181)

figure–ground perception A fundamental rule of perception described by Gestalt psychology which states that people inherently differentiate between figure (the object they are viewing, sound to which they are listening, etc.) and ground (background). (p. 138)

first impressions Initial perceptions of another person that can be powerful in shaping future beliefs about the person. (p. 617)

Five Factor Model (FFM) A trait theory which asserts that personality consists of five traits (openness to experience, conscientiousness, extroversion, agreeableness, and neuroticism). (p. 441)

fixations In psychoanalytic theory, prominent conflicts and concerns focused on wishes from a particular period. (p. 426)

fixed-interval (FI) schedules of reinforcement When the organism receives rewards for its responses only after a fixed amount of time. (p. 175)

fixed-ratio (FR) schedules of reinforcement When the organism receives reinforcement at a fixed rate, according to the number of responses emitted. (p. 174)

flashbulb memories Especially vivid memories of exciting or highly consequential events. (p. 221)

flooding Cognitive–behavioral technique designed to eliminate phobias, in which the patient confronts the real phobic stimulus all at once. (p. 540)

fluid intelligence Intellectual capacities that have no specific content but are used in processing information. (p. 279)

foot-in-the-door technique Persuasive technique often used by salespeople, which involves getting people to comply with a small request in order to induce their compliance with a larger request. (p. 689)

forgetting The inability to retrieve memories. (p. 219)

formal operational stage Piaget's fourth stage of

cognitive development, which begins at about age 12 to 15, and is characterized by the ability to manipulate abstract as well as concrete objects, events, and ideas mentally. (p. 480)

form perception The organization of sensations into meaningful shapes and patterns. (p. 138)

fovea The central region of the retina, where light is most directly focused by the lens. (p. 114)

free association The therapeutic technique for exploring associational networks and unconscious processes involved in symptom formation. (p. 584)

free will versus determinism The philosophical question of whether people act on the basis of their freely chosen intentions, or whether their actions are caused or determined by physical processes in their bodies or in the environment in which they live. (p. 7)

frequency In a sound wave, the number of cycles per second, expressed in hertz and responsible for subjective experience of pitch. (p. 124)

frequency theory The theory of pitch that asserts that perceived pitch reflects the rate of vibration of the basilar membrane. (p. 137)

frontal lobes Brain structures involved in coordination of movement, attention, planning, social skills, conscience, abstract thinking, memory, and aspects of personality. (p. 84)

frustration–aggression hypothesis The hypothesis that when people are frustrated in achieving a goal, they may become aggressive. (p. 675)

functional fixedness The tendency to ignore other possible functions of an object when one already has a function in mind. (p. 241)

functional magnetic resonance imaging (fMRI) A brain-scanning technique used as an individual carries out tasks. (p. 53)

functionalism An early school of thought in psychology influenced by Darwinian theory that looked for explanations of psychological processes in terms of their role, or function, in helping the individual adapt to the environment. (p. 8)

G

GABA Acronym for gamma-aminobutyric acid, one of the most widespread neurotransmitters in the nervous system, which largely plays an inhibitory role in the brain. (p. 69)

galvanic skin response An electrical measure of the amount of sweat on the skin that is produced during states of anxiety or arousal; also called skin conductance or electrodermal activity (EDA). (p. 163)

ganglion cells Nerve cells in the retina that integrate information from multiple bipolar cells, the axons of which bundle together to form the optic nerve. (p. 113)

gender The psychological meaning of being male or female. (p. 509)

gender constancy The recognition that people's gender cannot be altered by changes in appearance or activities. (p. 517)

gender identity The categorization of oneself as either male or female. (p. 517)

gender roles The range of behaviors considered

appropriate by society for males and females. (p. 509)

gender schemas Representations that associate psychological characteristics with one sex or the other. (p. 518)

gender stability The understanding that one's gender remains constant over time. (p. 517)

gene The unit of hereditary transmission. (p. 90)

General Adaptation Syndrome Selye's model of stress that includes the three stages of alarm, resistance, and exhaustion. (p. 404)

generalizability The applicability of a study's finding to the entire population of interest. (p. 34)

generalized anxiety disorder Persistent anxiety at a moderate but disturbing level. (p. 568)

generalized expectancies Expectancies that influence a broad spectrum of behavior. (p. 184)

generativity A concern for the next generation as well as an interest in producing something of lasting value to society. (p. 532)

generativity versus stagnation In Erikson's theory, the stage in which people in mid-adulthood experience concern for the next generation as well as an interest in producing something of lasting value to society. (p. 532)

generic memory General world knowledge or facts; also called semantic memory. (p. 204)

genital stage In Freudian theory, psychosexual stage that occurs at approximately age 12 and beyond, when conscious sexuality resurfaces after years of repression. (p. 427)

genogram A map of a family over three or four generations, drawn by a therapist to explore possible similarities between current difficulties and the family's past. (p. 598)

Gestalt psychology A school of psychology that holds that perception is an active experience of imposing order on an overwhelming panorama of details by seeing them as parts of larger whole (or gestalts). (pp. 23)

Gestalt therapy A psychological treatment based on the assumption that psychological distress results from losing touch with one's emotions and one's authentic inner voice, and that focusing on the "here and now" is curative. (p. 595)

g-**factor** The general intelligence factor that emerges through factor analysis of IQ tests. (p. 278)

Gf–Gc theory A hierarchical model of intelligence that argues for the presence of two overarching types of intelligence—fluid intelligence and crystallized intelligence, as well as more specific intellectual skills, such as short-term memory. (p. 279)

gifted Exceptionally talented. (p. 273)

glial cells Origin of the myelin sheath. (p. 63)

glutamate One of the most widespread neurotransmitters in the nervous system, which largely plays an excitatory role; also called glutamic acid. (p. 69)

goals Desired outcomes established through social learning. (p. 324)

goal-setting theory The theory of motivation that suggests that conscious goals regulate much human action, particularly performance tasks. (p. 324)

gonads Endocrine glands that influence much of sexual development and behavior. (p. 72)

good continuation A Gestalt rule of perception which states that, if possible, the brain organizes stimuli into continuous lines or patterns rather than discontinuous elements. (p. 138)

graded exposure A modified version of the behaviorist flooding technique for treating anxiety, in which stimuli are real but are presented to the patient in a gradual manner. (p. 590)

graded potentials A spreading voltage change that occurs when the neural membrane receives a signal from another cell. (p. 65)

grammar A system of rules for generating understandable and acceptable language utterances. (p. 257)

group A collection of people whose actions affect the other group members. (p. 683)

group process The interactions among members of a group. (p. 596)

group therapy A treatment method in which multiple people meet together to work toward therapeutic goals. (p. 596)

gustation Taste. (p. 131)

H

habituation The decreasing strength of a response after repeated presentations of the stimulus. (p. 157)

hair cells Receptors for sound attached to the basilar membrane. (p. 126)

hallucinations Sensory perceptions that distort, or occur without, an external stimulus. (pp. 314, 557)

hallucinogen A drug that produces hallucinations. (p. 314)

halo effect A tendency to attribute additional positive characteristics to someone who has one salient quality, such as physical attractiveness. (p. 618)

Health Belief Model Theory that states that health behaviors are predicted by the perceived susceptibility to the health threat, the perceived seriousness of the health threat, the benefits and barriers of undertaking particular health behaviors, and cues to action. (p. 374)

health psychology Field of psychology devoted to understanding psychological influences on how people stay healthy, why they become ill, and how they respond when they are ill. (p. 370)

heritability The extent to which individual differences in phenotype are determined by genetic factors or genotype. (pp. 91, 451)

heritability coefficient The statistic that quantifies the degree to which a trait is heritable. (p. 91)

hertz (Hz) The unit of measurement of frequency of sound waves. (p. 124)

heterozygous Both alleles are the same. (p. 90)

heuristics In problem solving, cognitive shortcuts or rules of thumb. (p. 244)

hierarchy of needs. Maslow's theory that needs are arranged hierarchically, from physiological needs, safety needs, belongingness needs, and esteem needs, through self-actualization needs. (p. 326)

hindbrain The part of the brain above the spinal cord that includes the medulla, cerebellum, and parts of the reticular formation. (p. 77)

hippocampus A structure in the limbic system involved in the acquisition and consolidation of new information in memory. (p. 81)

homeostasis The body's tendency to maintain a relatively constant state that permits cells to live and function. (p. 332)

homozygous The two alleles are different. (p. 90)

hormones Chemicals secreted directly into the bloodstream by the endocrine glands. (p. 71)

hostile aggression Aggression that is elicited by anger. (p. 669)

hue The sensory quality people normally consider color. (p. 121)

humanistic approaches Theories that focus on aspects of personality that are distinctly human, not shared by other animals, such as how to find meaning in life and how to be true to oneself. (p. 447)

humanistic therapies Psychological treatments that focus on the patient's conscious or lived experience and on the way each person uniquely experiences relationships and the world. (p. 595)

humoral theory of illness Theory asserting that disease is caused by an imbalance in the four fluids or humors of the body. (p. 371)

hypnosis An altered state of consciousness characterized by deep relaxation and suggestibility which a person voluntarily enters through the efforts of a hypnotist. (p. 309)

hypnotic susceptibility The capacity to enter into deep hypnotic states. (p. 310)

hypothalamus The brain structure situated directly below the thalamus involved in the regulation of eating, sleeping, sexual activity, movement, and emotion. (p. 79)

hypothesis A tentative belief or educated guess that purports to predict or explain the relationship between two or more variables. (p. 32)

I

iconic storage A visual sensory registration process by which people retain an afterimage of a visual stimulus. (p. 195)

id In Freudian theory, the reservoir of sexual and aggressive energy, which is driven by impulses and is characterized by primary process thinking. (p. 428)

ideal self A person's view of what she/he would like to be. (pp. 448, 648)

identification Making another person part of oneself by imitating the person's behavior, changing the self-concept to see oneself as more like that person, and attempting to become more like the person by accepting his or her values and attitudes. (p. 426)

identity A stable sense of knowing who one is and what one's values and ideals are. (p. 531)

identity confusion A condition in which the individual fails to develop a coherent and enduring sense of self, and has difficulty committing to roles, values, people, and occupational choices in his or her life. (p. 531)

identity versus identity confusion In Erikson's

theory, stage in which adolescents develop a stable sense of who they are and a stable set of values and ideals. (p. 531)

ill-defined problem A situation in which both the information needed to solve a problem and the criteria that determine whether the goals are attained are vague. (p. 240)

immune system A system of cells throughout the body that fights disease. (pp. 162, 409)

implicit attitudes Attitudes that regulate thought and behavior unconsciously and automatically. (p. 634)

implicit cognition Thinking that occurs outside awareness. (p. 246)

implicit memory Memory that cannot be brought to mind consciously but can be expressed in behavior. (p. 205)

implicit motives Motives that can be activated and expressed outside of awareness. (p. 325)

impression management See self-presentation. (pp. 388, 647)

imprinting The tendency of young animals of certain species to follow an animal to which they were exposed during a sensitive period early in their lives. (p. 498)

incentive An external motivating stimulus (as opposed to an internal need state). (p. 323)

inclusive fitness The notion that natural selection favors organisms that survive, reproduce, and foster the survival and reproduction of their kin. (p. 21)

incomplete dominance Heterozygous state is intermediate between the recessive and the dominant alleles. (p. 90)

independent variables The variables an experimenter manipulates, or whose effects the experimenter assesses. (p. 44)

individual differences The way people resemble and differ from one another in personality or intelligence. (p. 421)

inductive reasoning The process of reasoning from specific observations to generate propositions. (p. 237)

industry versus inferiority In Erikson's theory, the stage in which children develop a sense of competence as they begin to practice skills they will use in productive work. (p. 531)

infantile amnesia The inability to recall early childhood memories. (p. 474)

inferential statistics Procedures for assessing whether the results obtained with a sample are likely to reflect characteristics of the population as a whole. (p. 47)

information processing The transformation, storage, and retrieval of environmental inputs through thought and memory. (p. 15)

informed consent A subject's ability to agree to participate in a study in an informed manner. (p. 57)

ingroups People perceived as belonging to a valued group. (p. 624)

initiation rites Ceremonies such as the rites found in many cultures in adolescence, which initiate a person into a new social role, such as adulthood. (p. 531)

initiative versus guilt In Erikson's theory, the

stage in which children develop a sense of planfulness and responsibility. (p. 531)

insight In learning theory, the ability to perceive a connection between a problem and its solution; in psychodynamic treatments, the understanding of one's own psychological processes. (pp. 183, 584)

insomnia The inability to sleep. (p. 303)

instinct A relatively fixed pattern of behavior that animals produce without learning. (p. 327)

instinct model Freud's theory of motivation, which held that people are motivated by sexual and aggressive instincts or drives. (p. 425)

instrumental aggression Calm, pragmatic aggression that may or may not be accompanied by anger. (p. 669)

instrumental leaders See task leaders. (p. 684)

integrity versus despair In Erikson's theory, stage in which older people look back on their lives with a sense of satisfaction that they have lived it well, or with despair, regret, and loss for loved ones who have died. (p. 532)

intelligence The application of cognitive skills and knowledge to learn, solve problems, and obtain ends that are valued by an individual or culture. (p. 268)

intelligence quotient (IQ) A score originally derived by dividing mental age and chrono- logical age and multiplying by 100, but now generally established by comparing the individual's performance to norms of people his or her own age. (p. 270)

intelligence test A measure designed to assess an individual's level of cognitive capabilities compared to other people in a population. (p. 269)

interactionist approaches Multidirectional view of personality which asserts that personality is shaped by economic and cultural demands but that cultural and economic processes themselves are in part created to fulfill psychological needs. (p. 455)

interference The intrusion of similar memories on one another. (p. 223)

interitem reliability See internal consistency. (p. 36)

intermittent schedule of reinforcement An operant procedure in which an organism is reinforced only some of the time it emits a behavior; also called partial schedule of reinforcement. (p. 174)

intermodal processing The capacity to associate sensations of an object from different senses, or to match one's own actions to behaviors that are observed visually. (p. 472)

internal attributions An explanation of behavior that attributes it to the person rather than the situation. (p. 626)

internal consistency A type of reliability that assesses whether the items in a test measure the same construct. (p. 36)

internal locus of control The belief that one is the master of one's fate. (p. 184)

internal validity The extent to which a study is methodologically adequate. (p. 34)

internal working model A mental representation of the attachment relationship, which forms the

basis for expectations in close relationships. (p. 500)

interneurons Neurons that connect other neurons to each other, found only in the brain and spinal cord. (p. 62)

interpersonal attraction The factors that lead people to choose to spend time with other people. (p. 655)

interpretation A therapeutic technique whereby the therapist helps the patient understand his or her experiences in a new light. (p. 585)

interrater reliability A measure of the similarity with which different raters apply a measure. (p. 36)

interstimulus interval The duration of time between presentation of the conditioned stimulus and the unconditioned stimulus. (p. 164)

interval schedules of reinforcement Operant conditioning procedures in which rewards are delivered according to intervals of time. (p. 174)

interviews A research tool in which the investigator asks the subject questions. (p. 40)

intimacy A kind of closeness characterized by self-disclosure, warmth, and mutual caring. (p. 344)

intimacy versus isolation In Erikson's theory, the stage in which young adults establish enduring, committed friendships and romantic relationships. (p. 532)

intrinsic motivation The motivation to perform a behavior for its own sake, rather than for some kind of external (or extrinsic) reward. (p. 325)

introspection The method used by Wundt and other structuralists in which trained subjects verbally reported everything that went through their minds when presented with a stimulus or task; more generally, refers to the process of looking inward at one's own mental contents or process. (p. 8)

intuitive scientists The conception of people as lay scientists who use intuitive theories, frame hypotheses, collect data about themselves and others, and examine the impact of various experimental manipulations when trying to understand themselves and others; also called intuitive psychologist. (p. 626)

iris The ring of pigmented tissue that gives the eye its blue, green, or brown color; its muscle fibers cause the pupil to constrict or dilate. (p. 113)

J

James-Lange theory A theory of emotion that asserts that emotion originates with peripheral arousal, which people then label as an emotional state. (p. 348)

John Henryism The tendency among members of minority groups to work hard and cope actively despite difficult circumstances. (p. 414)

just noticeable difference (jnd) The smallest difference in intensity between two stimuli that a person can detect. (p. 108)

K

kinesthesia The sense that provides information about the movement and position of the limbs and other parts of the body; receptors in joints transduce information about the position of the bones, and receptors in the tendons and muscles transmit messages about muscular tension. (p. 136)

knowledge base Accumulated information stored in long-term memory. (pp. 281, 482)

L

labeling theory The theory that psychiatric diagnosis is a way of labeling individuals a society considers deviant. (p. 540)

language The system of symbols, sounds, meanings, and rules for their combination that constitutes the primary mode of communication among humans. (p. 254)

language acquisition device (LAD) The prewired, innate mechanism that allows for the acquisition of language hypothesized by Noam Chomsky. (p. 94)

latency stage The psychosexual phase that occurs roughly around ages 6 to 11, when children repress their sexual impulses. (p. 427)

latent content According to Freud's dream theory, the meaning that underlies the symbolism in a dream. (p. 307)

latent inhibition A phenomenon in classical conditioning in which initial exposure to a neutral stimulus without a UCS slows the process of later learning the CS–UCS association and developing a CR. (p. 165)

latent learning Learning that has occurred but is not currently manifest in behavior. (p. 182)

lateralized Localized on one or the other side of the brain (p. 86)

law of effect Law proposed by Thorndike which states that the tendency of an organism to produce a behavior depends on the effect the behavior has on the environment. (p. 169)

laws of association First proposed by Aristotle, basic principles used to account for learning and memory, which describe the conditions under which one thought becomes connected, or associated, with another. (p. 158)

leader A person who exercises greater influence than the average member of a group. (p. 686)

learned helplessness The expectancy that one cannot escape from aversive events. (p. 185)

learning Any relatively permanent change in the way an organism responds based on its experience. (p. 157)

lens The disk-shaped, elastic structure of the eye that focuses light. (p. 113)

level of processing The degree to which information is elaborated, reflected upon, or processed in a meaningful way during encoding of memory. (p. 210)

libido In Freudian theory, the human sexual drive, which refers as much to pleasure seeking and love as to sexual intercourse. (p. 425)

life history method A method of personality assessment whose aim is to understand the whole person in the context of his or her life experience and environment. (p. 431)

life tasks The conscious, self-defined problems people attempt to solve. (p. 436)

limbic system Subcortical structures responsible for emotional reactions, many motivational

processes, learning, and aspects of memory. (p. 80)

linkage studies Method used to locate particular genes. (p. 90)

lithium The drug treatment of choice for bipolar disorder. (p. 606)

localization of function The extent to which different parts of the brain control different aspects of functioning. (p. 4)

locus of control of reinforcement Generalized expectancies people hold about whether or not their own behavior will bring about the outcomes they seek. (p. 184)

longitudinal study Type of research that follows the same individuals over time. (p. 464)

long-term memory (LTM) Memory for facts, images, thoughts, feelings, skills, and experiences that may last as long as a lifetime. (p. 197)

long-term potentiation The tendency of a group of neurons to fire more readily after consistent stimulation from other neurons. (p. 167)

loosening of associations A tendency common in individuals with schizophrenia, in which conscious thought is directed along associative lines rather than by controlled, logical, purposeful processes. (p. 557)

loudness The psychological property corresponding to a sound wave's amplitude. (p. 124)

low-balling Method of persuasion by which people get a commitment to a request and then change the conditions. (p. 689)

low-effort syndrome The tendency to exert minimal effort to escape stressful social and economic circumstance. (p. 413)

M

magnetic resonance imaging (MRI) Brain-scanning technique. (p. 53)

maintenance rehearsal The process of repeating information over and over to maintain it momentarily in STM. (p. 196)

major depressive disorder A form of psychopathology, characterized by depressed mood, loss of interest in pleasurable activities, and disturbances in appetite, sleep, energy level, and concentration. (p. 562)

mania A period of abnormally euphoric, elevated, or expansive mood. (p. 563)

manic Relating to a mood disturbance in which people feel excessively happy or euphoric and believe they can do anything. (p. 562)

manifest content The obvious storyline of a dream. (p. 307)

MAO inhibitors Antidepressant medication that keeps the chemical MAO from breaking down neurotransmitter substances in the presynaptic neuron, which makes more neurotransmitter available for release into the synapse. (p. 605)

marital therapy Psychotherapy that treats a couple; also called couples therapy. (p. 598)

mastery goals Motives to increase one's competence, mastery, or skill. (p. 345)

matching hypothesis Phenomenon whereby people tend to choose as partners people they perceive to be equally attractive to themselves. (p. 657)

maturation Biologically based development. (p. 460)

mean The statistical average of the scores of all subjects on a measure. (p. 42)

measure A concrete way of assessing a variable. (p. 35)

median The score that falls in the middle of the distribution of scores, with half of subjects scoring below it and half above it. (p. 42)

meditation A relaxation practice, often associated with religion, characterized by a state of tranquility. (p. 309)

medulla An extension of the spinal cord, essential to life, controlling such vital physiological functions as heartbeat, circulation, and respiration. (p. 77)

medulla oblongata See medulla. (p. 77)

mental age (MA) The average age at which children can be expected to achieve a particular score on an intelligence test. (p. 269)

mental image A visual representation of a stimulus. (p. 230)

mental models Representations that describe, explain, or predict the way things work. (p. 231)

mental retardation Significantly subaverage general intellectual functioning, existing concurrently with deficits in adaptive behavior and manifested during childhood. (p. 272)

mental simulation A problem-solving strategy in which people imagine the steps to problem solving mentally before actually undertaking them. (p. 241)

meta-analysis A statistical technique that allows researchers to combine findings from various studies and make comparisons between the effects of treatment and no treatment. (p. 608)

metabolism The processes by which the body transforms food into energy. (p. 332)

metacognition People's understanding of the way they perform cognitive tasks such as remembering, learning, or solving problems. (p. 482)

method of loci A memory aid or mnemonic device in which images are remembered by fitting them into an orderly arrangement of locations. (p. 213)

midbrain The section of the brain above the hindbrain involved in some auditory and visual functions, movement, and conscious arousal and activation. (p. 79)

mind–body problem The question of how mental and physical events interact. (p. 7)

mnemonic devices Systematic strategies for remembering information. (p. 213)

modal score See mode. (p. 42)

mode The most common or most frequent score or value of a variable observed in a sample. (p. 42)

modeling A social learning procedure in which a person learns to reproduce behavior exhibited by a model. (p. 187)

modules Discrete but interdependent processing units responsible for different kinds of remembering. (p. 198)

monocular cues Visual input from a single eye alone that contributes to depth perception. (p. 141)

monozygotic (MZ) twins Twins identical in their genetic makeup, having developed from the union of the same sperm and egg. (p. 91)

moods Relatively extended emotional states that do not shift attention or disrupt ongoing activities. (p. 359)

mood disorder A disorder characterized by disturbances in emotion and mood. (p. 562)

morality of constraint According to Piaget's theory of moral development, the first stage of moral judgment, in which children believe that morals are absolute. (p. 522)

morality of cooperation According to Piaget's theory of moral development, the stage at which moral rules can be changed if they are not appropriate to the occasion as long as the people involved agree to do so. (p. 522)

morpheme In language, a basic unit of meaning. (p. 256)

motion detectors Ganglion cells that are particularly sensitive to movement. (p. 143)

motion parallax A monocular depth cue involving the relative movements of retinal images of objects; nearby objects appear to speed across the field of vision, whereas distant objects barely seem to move. (p. 142)

motion perception The perception of movement in objects. (p. 142)

motivated forgetting Forgetting for a reason, which leads to inhibition of retrieval. (p. 223)

motivation The moving force that energizes behavior. (p. 320)

motor cortex The primary zone of the frontal lobes responsible for control of motor behavior. (p. 84)

motor neuron A neuron that transmits commands from the brain to the glands or musculature of the body, typically through the spinal cord; also called efferent neuron. (p. 62)

Müller–Lyer illusion A perceptual illusion in which two lines of equal length appear different in size. (p. 146)

multiaxial system of diagnosis The system used in DSM-IV that places mental disorders in their social and biological context, assessing the patient on five axes. (p. 551)

myelin sheath A tight coat of cells composed primarily of lipids, which serves to insulate the axon from chemical or physical stimuli that might interfere with the transmission of nerve impulses and speeds neural transmission. (p. 63)

N

natural selection A theory proposed by Darwin which states that natural forces select traits in organisms that help them adapt to their environment. (p. 19)

naturalistic observation The in-depth observation of a phenomenon in its natural setting. (p. 39)

nature–nurture controversy The question of the degree to which inborn biological processes or environmental events determine human behavior. (p. 18)

need for achievement A motive to do well, to succeed, and to avoid failure. (p. 344)

need to belong Strong, possibly innate, need to be involved in relationships with others. (p. 655)

negative affect A general category of emotions related to feeling bad. (p. 355)

negative correlation A relation between two variables in which the higher one is, the lower the other tends to be. (p. 51)

negative identity Taking on a role that society defines as bad but that nevertheless provides one with a sense of being something. (p. 531)

negative reciprocity The tendency of members of a couple to respond to negative comments or actions by their partner with negative behaviors in return. (p. 598)

negative reinforcement The process whereby a behavior is made more likely because it is followed by the removal of an aversive stimulus. (p. 171)

negative reinforcer An aversive or unpleasant stimulus that strengthens a behavior by its removal. (p. 171)

negative symptoms Symptoms of schizophrenia such as flat affect, socially inappropriate behavior, and intellectual impairments that reflect a deficit or a loss of something that was once present or should be present. (p. 557)

negative triad In Beck's cognitive theory of depression, negative outlook on the world, the self, and the future. (p. 565)

neglected children Children who are ignored by their peers. (p. 511)

neo-Piagetian theories Theories that attempt to wed a stage model of cognitive development with research on information processing and domain-specific knowledge. (p. 483)

nervous system The interacting network of nerve cells that underlies all psychological activity. (p. 62)

networks of association Clusters of interconnected information stored in long-term memory. (p. 214)

neuroimaging techniques Methods for studying the brain that use computer programs to convert the data taken from brain-scanning devices into visual images (p. 53)

neurons Cells in the nervous system. (p. 62)

neuroses Problems in living, such as phobias, chronic self-doubts, and repetitive interpersonal problems. (p. 542)

neuroticism A continuum from emotional stability to emotional instability. (p. 441)

neurotransmitter Chemical that transmits information from one neuron to another. (p. 66)

node A cluster or piece of information along a network of association. (p. 214)

non-REM (NREM) sleep States of sleep in which rapid eye movements (REM sleep) are not present. (p. 305)

nonverbal communication Mode of communication that relies on gestures, expressions, intonation, body language, and other unspoken signals. (p. 259)

noradrenalin A hormone that triggers physiological arousal, particularly in potential danger situations. (p. 71)

norms Standards for the behavior of group members. (p. 683)

O

obedience Overt compliance with authority. (p. 679)

obesity A condition characterized by a body weight over 15 percent above the ideal for one's height and age. (pp. 336, 378)

object permanence In Piaget's theory, the recognition that objects exist in time and space independent of one's actions on, or observation of, them. (p. 477)

object relations Behavioral patterns in intimate relationships and the motivational, cognitive, and affective processes that produce them. (p. 430)

observational learning Learning that occurs by observing the behavior of others. (p. 186)

obsessions Persistent unwanted thoughts or ideas. (p. 569)

obsessive–compulsive disorder A disorder characterized by recurrent obsessions and compulsions that cause distress and significantly interfere with an individual's life. (p. 569)

occipital lobes Brain structures located in the rear portion of the cortex, involved in vision. (p. 83)

Oedipus complex In Freudian theory, process that occurs during the phallic stage of development when the child desires an exclusive, sensual/sexual relationship with the opposite sex parent. (p. 427)

olfaction Smell. (p. 129)

olfactory epithelium Thin pair of structures in which transduction of smell occurs. (p. 130)

olfactory nerve The bundle of axons from sensory receptor cells that transmits information from the nose to the brain. (p. 130)

operant A behavior that is emitted by the organism rather than elicited by the environment. (p. 169)

operant conditioning Learning that results when an organism associates a response that occurs spontaneously with a particular environment effect; also called instrumental conditioning. (p. 169)

operation In Piagetian theory, a mental action that the individual can use to manipulate, transform, and return an object of thought to its original state. (p. 478)

operationalizing Turning an abstract concept or variable into a concrete form that can be defined by some set of operations or actions. (p. 45)

opponent-process theory A theory of color vision that proposes the existence of three antagonistic color systems: a blue-yellow system, a red-green system, and a black-white system; according to this theory, the blue-yellow and red-green systems are responsible for hue, while the black-white system contributes to perception of brightness and saturation. (p. 122)

optic nerve The bundle of axons of ganglion cells that carries information from the retina to the brain. (p. 114)

optimistic bias Unrealistic optimism. (p. 374)

oral stage In Freudian theory, the psychosexual phase occurring roughly in the first year of life, when children explore the world through their mouths. (p. 425)

organizational effects Effects of hormones that influence the structure of the brain. (p. 339)

ought self The duties, obligations, and responsibilities that define the way the person should be. (p. 648)

outgroups People perceived as not belonging to a valued group. (p. 624)

overweight A body mass index between 25 percent and 30 percent depending on age and gender. (p. 378)

P

panic disorder A disorder characterized by attacks of intense fear and feelings of doom or terror not justified by the situation. (p. 569)

paradigm A broad system of theoretical assumptions employed by a scientific community to make sense out of a domain of experience. (p. 10)

parallel distributed processing (PDP) A model of human cognitive processes in which many cognitive processes occur simultaneously (i.e., in parallel), so that a representation is spread out (i.e., distributed) throughout a network of interacting processing units; also called connectionism. (p. 249)

parasympathetic nervous system The part of the autonomic nervous system involved in conserving and maintaining the body's energy resources. (p. 75)

parietal lobes Brain structures located in front of the occipital lobes, involved in a number of functions, including sense of touch and the experience of one's own body in space and in movement. (p. 83)

Parkinson's disease A disorder characterized by uncontrollable tremors, repetitive movements, and difficulty in both initiating behavior and stopping movements already in progress. (p. 69)

partial schedule of reinforcement An operant procedure in which an organism is reinforced only some of the time it emits a behavior; also called intermittent schedule of reinforcement. (p. 174)

participants The individuals who participate in a study; also called subjects. (p. 34)

participatory modeling A cognitive–behavioral technique in which the therapist models desired behavior and gradually induces the patient to participate in it. (p. 592)

passionate love A highly emotional form of love marked by intense physiological arousal and absorption in another person. (p. 658)

passive aggression The indirect expression of anger toward others. (p. 429)

penis envy In Freudian theory, feeling of envy that emerges in girls, who feel that because they lack a penis they are inferior to boys. (p. 427)

perceived seriousness (severity) An individual's perception of the impact a particular illness would have on his life. (p. 374)

perceived susceptibility A person's perception that he is likely to contract a particular illness. (p. 374)

perception The process by which the brain selects, organizes, and interprets sensations. (p. 102)

percepts Meaningful perceptual units, such as images of particular objects. (p. 137)

perceptual constancy The organization of changing sensations into percepts that are relatively stable in size, shape, and color. (p. 144)

perceptual illusions Perceptual misinterpretations produced in the course of normal perceptual processes. (p. 140)

perceptual interpretation The process of generating meaning from sensory experience. (p. 147)

perceptual organization The process of integrating sensations into meaningful perceptual units. (p. 137)

performance-approach goals Goals that center on approaching or attaining a standard. (p. 345)

performance-avoidance goals Goals that center on avoiding failure, particularly publicly observable failure. (p. 345)

performance goals Motives to achieve at a particular level, usually one that meets a socially defined standard. (p. 345)

peripheral nervous system (PNS) A component of the nervous system that includes neurons that travel to and from the central nervous system; includes the somatic nervous system and the autonomic nervous system. (p. 73)

peripheral route to persuasion A method of persuasion that appeals less to rational and thoughtful processes than to automatic or emotional ones. (p. 639)

permissive A way of parenting that imposes few controls on children, allowing the children to make their own decisions whenever possible. (p. 506)

personal constructs Mental representations of the people, places, things, and events that are significant in a person's life. (p. 436)

personality The enduring patterns of thought, feeling, and behavior that are expressed by individuals in different circumstances. (p. 421)

personality disorder A chronic and severe disorder that substantially inhibits the capacity to love and to work. (p. 542)

personal value The importance individuals attach to various stimuli and to the outcomes they expect as a result of their behavior. (p. 436)

person-by-situation interaction Process by which some personality dispositions are activated only under certain circumstances. (p. 446)

person-centered approach Carl Rogers' theory of personality, which focuses on understanding the individual's phenomenal world. (p. 447)

perspectives Broad ways of understanding psychological phenomena, including theoretical propositions, shared metaphors, and accepted methods of observation. (p. 10)

perspective taking The ability to understand other people's viewpoints or perspectives. (p. 515)

persuasion Deliberate efforts to induce attitude change. (p. 637)

pessimistic explanatory style A tendency to explain bad events that happen in a self blaming manner, viewing their causes as global and stable. (p. 185)

phallic stage In Freudian theory, the psychosexual phase occurring roughly around ages 4 to 6, when children discover that they can get pleasure from touching their genitals. (p. 426)

phantom limbs Misleading "sensations" from missing limbs. (p. 133)

phenomenal experience The way individuals conceive of reality and experience themselves and their world. (p. 448)

pheromone A chemical secreted by organisms in some species that allow communication between organisms. (p. 129)

phobia An irrational fear of a specific object or situation. (pp. 161, 568)

phoneme The smallest unit of speech that distinguishes one linguistic utterance from another. (p. 255)

phrase A group of words that act as a unit and convey a meaning. (p. 256)

pitch The psychological property corresponding to the frequency of a sound wave; the quality of a tone from low to high. (p. 124)

pituitary gland Often referred to as the "master gland" of the endocrine system because many of the hormones it releases stimulate and thus regulate the hormonal action of other endocrine glands. (p. 71)

placebo effect A phenomenon in which an experimental intervention produces an effect because subjects believe it will produce an effect. (p. 47)

place theory A theory of pitch which proposes that different areas of the basilar membrane are maximally sensitive to different frequencies. (p. 127)

population A group of people or animals of interest to a researcher from which a sample is drawn. (p. 34)

positive affect A general category of emotions related to feeling good. (p. 355)

positive correlation A relation between two variables in which the higher one is, the higher the other tends to be. (p. 51)

positive reinforcement The process by which a behavior is made more likely because of the presentation of a rewarding stimulus. (p. 169)

positive reinforcer A rewarding stimulus that strengthens a behavior when it is presented. (p. 170)

positive symptoms Symptoms of schizophrenia such as delusions and hallucinations that reflect the presence of something that was not there previously and is not normally present. (p. 557)

positron emission tomography (PET) A computerized brain-scanning technique that allows observation of the brain in action. (p. 53)

postconventional morality In Kohlberg's theory, the level of morality in which individuals follow abstract, self-defined principles which may or may not accord with the dominant mores or morals of the times. (p. 523)

post-traumatic stress disorder (PTSD) An anxiety disorder characterized by symptoms such as flashbacks and recurrent thoughts of a psychologically distressing event outside the normal range of experience. (p. 570)

pragmatics The way language is used and understood in everyday life. (p. 258)

preconscious mental processes Thoughts that are not conscious but could become conscious at any point, much like information stored in long-term semantic memory. (pp. 296, 423)

preconventional morality In Kohlberg's theory, the level of morality in which children follow moral rules either to avoid punishment or to obtain reward. (p. 523)

prejudice Judging people based on negative stereotypes. (p. 619)

preoperational stage Piaget's second stage of cognitive development, beginning roughly around age 2 and lasting until age 5 to 7, characterized by the emergence of symbolic thought. (p. 477)

prepared learning Responses to which an organism is predisposed because they were selected through natural selection. (p. 165)

presbycusis The inability to hear high-frequency sounds, which usually occurs with aging. (p. 470)

primary appraisal The first stage in the process of stress and coping in which the person decides whether the situation is benign, stressful, or irrelevant. (p. 404)

primary area The area of the cortex involved in sensory functions and in the direct control of motor movements. (p. 82)

primary drive An innate drive such as hunger, thirst, and sex. (p. 323)

primary process thinking Associative thinking described by Freud, in which ideas connected in people's minds through experience come to mind automatically when they think about related ideas; primary process thought is also wishful and unrealistic. (p. 428)

primary reinforcer A stimulus that is innately rewarding to an organism. (p. 180)

priming effects The processing of specific information is facilitated by prior exposure to the same or similar information. (p. 206)

principle of aggregation Averaging across multiple situations to find evidence of particular personality traits. (p. 444)

proactive interference A phenomenon in which old memories that have already been stored interfere with the retrieval of new information. (p. 223)

probability value The probability that obtained findings were accidental or just a matter of chance; also called *p-value*. (p. 50)

problem drinkers People who are not physiologically addicted to alcohol but who still have a number of problems stemming from alcohol consumption. (p. 392)

problem solving The process of transforming one situation into another that meets a goal. (p. 240)

problem-solving strategy A technique used to solve problems. (p. 241)

procedural memory Knowledge of procedures or skills that emerges when people engage in activities that require them. (p. 204)

projection A defense mechanism in which a person attributes his own unacknowledged feelings or impulses to others. (p. 429)

projective test A personality assessment method in which subjects are confronted with an ambiguous stimulus and asked to define it in some way; the assumption underlying these tests is that when people are faced with an unstructured, undefined stimulus, they will project

their own thoughts, feelings, and wishes into their responses. (p. 432)

proprioceptive senses Senses that provide information about body position and movement; the two proprioceptive senses are kinesthesia and vestibular sense. (p. 136)

prosocial behavior Behavior that benefits either specific individuals or society as a whole. (p. 524)

prospective memory Memory for things that need to be done in the future. (p. 209)

protection motivation theory of health The health belief model plus self-efficacy. (p. 376)

prototype A particularly good example of a category. (p. 232)

proximity A Gestalt rule of perception which states that, other things being equal, the brain groups objects together that are close to each other. (p. 138)

psychoactive substance Any drug that operates on the nervous system to alter patterns of mental activity. (p. 312)

psychoanalysis An intensive therapeutic process in which the patient meets with the therapist three to five times a week, lies on a couch, and uses free association, interpretation, and transference. (p. 586)

psychodynamic formulation A set of hypotheses about the patient's personality structure and the meaning of a symptom. (p. 543)

psychodynamic perspective The perspective initiated by Sigmund Freud that focuses on the dynamic interplay of mental forces. (p. 11)

psychodynamic psychotherapy A form of psychotherapy based on psychodynamic principles, in which the patient meets the therapist somewhat less frequently than in psychoanalysis and sits face to face with the therapist. (p. 586)

psychodynamics A view analogous to dynamics among physical forces in which psychological forces such as wishes, fears, and intentions have a direction and an intensity. (pp. 11, 422)

psychological anthropologists People who study psychological phenomena in other cultures by observing the way the natives behave in their daily lives. (p. 6)

psychology The scientific investigation of mental processes and behavior. (p. 3)

psychometric approach An approach to the study of intelligence, personality, and psychopathology which tries to derive some kind of theoretical meaning empirically from statistical analysis of psychometric test findings. (p. 278)

psychometric instruments Tests that quantify psychological attributes such as personality traits or intellectual abilities (p. 269)

psychomotor slowing An increase in the time required for processing and acting on information that occurs with age. (p. 484)

psychoneuroimmunology The study of the interactions among behavior, the nervous system, the endocrine system, and the immune system. (pp. 72, 409)

psychopathology Problematic patterns of thought, feeling, or behavior that disrupt an individual's sense of well-being or social or occupational functioning. (p. 539)

psychophysics Branch of psychology that studies the relationship between attributes of the physical world and the psychological experience of them. (p. 104)

psychosexual stages Freud's hypothesized stages in the development of personality, sexuality, and motivation. (p. 425)

psychoses Gross disturbances involving a loss of touch with reality. (p. 542)

psychosocial needs Personal and interpersonal motives that lead people to strive for such ends as mastery, achievement, power, self-esteem, affiliation, and intimacy with other people. (p. 343)

psychosocial stages In Erikson's theory, the stages in the development of the person as a social being. (p. 530)

psychosomatic medicine The idea that changes in physiology mediate the relationship between unconscious conflicts and illness. (p. 372)

psychosurgery Brain surgery to reduce psychological symptoms. (p. 607)

psychotherapy integration The use of theory or technique from multiple theoretical perspectives. (p. 600)

psychoticism A dimension whose low end is defined by people who display empathy and impulse control and the high end is defined by people who are aggressive, egocentric, impulsive, and antisocial. (p. 441)

psychotropic medications Drugs that act on the brain to affect mental processes. (p. 602)

puberty The stage at which individuals become capable of reproduction. (p. 468)

punishment A conditioning process that decreases the probability that a behavior will occur. (p. 169)

pupil The opening in the center of the iris that constricts or dilates to regulate the amount of light entering the eye. (p. 113)

Q

quasi-experimental designs Research designs that employ the logic of experimental methods but lacks absolute control over variables. (p. 48)

questionnaires Research tools in which the investigator asks subjects to respond to a written list of questions or items. (p. 40)

R

random sample A sample of subjects selected from the population in a relatively arbitrary manner. (p. 41)

range A measure of variability that represents the difference between the highest and the lowest value on a variable obtained in a sample. (p. 42)

rapid eye movement (REM) sleep The period of sleep during which darting eye movements occur, autonomic activity increases, and patterns of brain activity resemble those observed in waking states. (p. 305)

rational–emotive behavior therapy A psychological treatment in which the therapist helps uncover and alter the illogical thoughts that provoke psychological distress. (p. 593)

rationalist philosophers Emphasize the role of reason in creating knowledge. (p. 16)

rationalization A defense mechanism that involves explaining away actions in a seemingly logical way to avoid uncomfortable feelings. (p. 429)

ratio schedules of reinforcement Operant conditioning procedures in which an organism is reinforced for some proportion of responses. (p. 174)

reaction formation A defense mechanism in which the person turns unacceptable feelings or impulses into their opposites. (p. 429)

reasoning The process by which people generate and evaluate arguments and beliefs. (p. 237)

recall The explicit (conscious) recollection of material from long-term memory. (p. 206)

receptive field A region within which a neuron responds to appropriate stimulation. (p. 115)

receptors In neurons, protein molecules in the postsynaptic membrane that pick up neurotransmitters; in sensation, specialized cells of the sensory systems that respond to the environmental stimuli and typically activate sensory neurons. (p. 68)

reciprocal altruism The theory that natural selection favors animals that behave altruistically if the likely benefit to each individual over time exceeds the likely cost to each individual's reproductive success. (p. 667)

recognition Explicit (conscious) knowledge of whether something currently perceived has been previously encountered. (p. 206)

recognition-by-components The theory that asserts that we perceive and categorize objects in our environment by breaking them down into component parts and then matching the components and the way they are arranged against similar "sketches" stored in memory. (p. 139)

reference group The group to which a person refers when taking a particular action. (p. 683)

reflex A behavior that is elicited automatically by an environmental stimulus. (pp. 95, 157)

regression Reverting to conflicts or modes of managing emotion characteristic of an earlier particular stage. (p. 426)

rehearsal Repeating or studying information to retain it in memory. (p. 196)

reinforcement A conditioning process that increases the probability that a response will occur. (p. 169)

reinforcer An environmental consequence that occurs after an organism has produced a response and makes the response more likely to recur. (p. 169)

rejected children Children who are disliked by their peers. (p. 511)

relatedness Interpersonal motives for connectedness with other people; also called communion motives. (p. 343)

relational theories Theories that propose that the need for relatedness is a central motive in humans and that people will distort their personalities to maintain ties to important people in their lives. (p. 431)

reliability A measure's ability to produce consistent results. (p. 36)

religious experiences Subjective experiences of

being in contact with the divine, which can range from relatively ordinary experiences, such as listening passively to a sermon, to altered states of consciousness in which a person feels at one with nature or the supernatural. (p. 316)

representative A sample that reflects characteristics of the population as a whole. (p. 34)

representativeness heuristic A cognitive shortcut used to assess whether an object or incident belongs in a particular class. (p. 245)

repression A defense mechanism in which thoughts that are too anxiety-provoking to acknowledge are kept from conscious awareness. (p. 429)

reproductive success The capacity to survive and reproduce offspring. (p. 20)

resistance Barriers to psychotherapy created by the patient in an effort to reduce anxiety. (p. 585)

response bias In signal detection theory, the subject's readiness to report detecting a signal when uncertain; also called decision criterion. (p. 107)

response prevention Preventing the patient from producing responses that allow avoidance of the feared stimulus. (p. 591)

resting potential Condition in which the neuron is not firing. (p. 64)

reticular activating system A diffuse network of neurons that extends from the lowest parts of the medulla in the hindbrain to the upper end of the midbrain, serving to maintain consciousness, regulate arousal levels, and modulate the activity of neurons throughout the central nervous system. (p. 78)

retina The light-sensitive layer of tissue at the back of the eye that transduces light into neural impulses. (p. 113)

retrieval Bringing information from long-term memory into short-term, or working, memory. (p. 197)

retrieval cues Stimuli or thoughts that can be used to stimulate retrieval. (p. 211)

retroactive interference Interference of new information with the retrieval of old information. (p. 223)

retrospective memory Memory for events that have already occurred. (p. 209)

rods One of two types of photoreceptors; allow vision in dim light. (p. 113)

role A position within a group that defines appropriate behavior for the person occupying it. (p. 684)

Rorschach inkblot test A projective personality test in which a subject views a set of inkblots and tells the tester what each inkblot resembles. (p. 432)

S

sample A subgroup of a population likely to be representative of the population as a whole. (p. 34)

satiety mechanisms Processes that turn off ingestive behavior. (p. 333)

Schacter-Singer theory The theory that asserts that emotion involves cognitive interpretation of general physiological arousal. (p. 361)

schema Integrated pattern of knowledge stored in

memory that organizes information and guides the acquisition of new information. (pp. 151, 476)

schizophrenia Psychotic disorders characterized by disturbances in thought, perception, behavior, language, communication, and emotion. (p. 557)

secondary appraisal The second stage in the process of stress and coping during which the person evaluates the options and decides how to respond. (p. 404)

secondary drive A motive learned through classical conditioning and other leaning mechanisms such as modeling; also called acquired drive. (p. 323)

secondary process thinking Rational, logical, goal-directed thinking. (p. 428)

secondary reinforcer A stimulus that acquires reinforcement value after an organism learns to associate it with stimuli that are innately reinforcing. (p. 180)

secure attachment style Response to separation in which infants welcome the mother's return and seek closeness to her. (p. 499)

selective inattention The process by which important information is ignored. (p. 294)

selective serotonin reuptake inhibitor (SSRI) A class of antidepressant medications, including Prozac, that blocks the presynaptic membrane from taking back serotonin, and hence leaves it acting longer in the synapse. (p. 605)

self The person, including mental processes, body, and attributes. (p. 644)

self-actualization needs In Maslow's theory, the needs to express oneself, grow, and actualize or attain one's potential. (p. 326)

self-concept A person's view of him/herself. (pp. 448, 513, 644)

self-consistency The motivation to interpret information to fit the self-concept and to prefer people who verify rather than challenge it. (p. 647)

self-determination theory A theory of motivation that proposes that people have three innate needs—competence, autonomy, and relatedness to others—and that intrinsic motivation flourishes when these needs are fulfilled rather than compromised. (p. 325)

self-efficacy A person's conviction that he or she can perform the actions necessary to produce an intended behavior. (p. 376)

self-efficacy expectancy See self-efficacy. (p. 436)

self-esteem The degree to which a person likes, respects, or esteems the self. (p. 644)

self-fulfilling prophecies False impressions of a situation that evoke behavior that, in turn, makes impressions become true. (pp. 184, 678)

self-handicapping A process by which people set themselves up to fail when success is uncertain to preserve their self-esteem. (pp. 392, 645)

self-help groups Groups that are leaderless or guided by a nonprofessional, in which members assist each other in coping with a specific problem, as in Alcoholics Anonymous. (p. 597)

self-monitoring Individual differences in the degree to which people manage their impressions. (p. 648)

self-perception theory Alternative explanation of cognitive dissonance phenomena which holds that individuals become aware of their attitudes, emotions, and other internal states by observing their own behavior. (p. 642)

self-presentation The process by which people attempt to control the impressions that others form of them. (pp. 388, 647)

self-presentational predicaments Instances in which our desires to influence the impressions other people form of us fail. (p. 648)

self-regulation Setting goals, evaluating one's own performance, and adjusting one's behaviors flexibly to achieve these goals in the context of ongoing feedback. (p. 437)

self-serving bias A phenomenon in which people tend to see themselves in a more positive light than they deserve. (p. 629)

semantic memory General world knowledge or facts; also called generic memory. (p. 204)

semantics The rules that govern the meanings, rather than the order, of morphemes, words, phrases, and sentences. (p. 257)

sensation The process by which the sense organs gather information about the environment. (p. 102)

sensitive period Developmental period during which environmental input is especially important, but not absolutely required, for future development in a domain. (p. 462)

sensorimotor stage Piaget's first stage of cognitive development, from birth to about 18 months of age, with thinking primarily characterized by action. (p. 476)

sensory adaptation The tendency of sensory systems to respond less to stimuli that continue without change. (p. 111)

sensory neuron Neuron that transmits information from sensory cells in the body called receptors to the brain. (p. 62)

sensory receptors Specialized cells in the nervous system that transform energy in the environment into neural impulses that can be interpreted by the brain. (p. 105)

sensory registers Memory systems that hold information for a very brief period of time. (p. 195)

sensory representation Information that is represented in one of the sense modalities. (p. 194)

sentence A unit of language that combines a subject and predicate and expresses a thought or meaning. (p. 256)

separation anxiety Distress at separation from attachment figures. (p. 499)

sequential study Type of research in which multiple cohorts are studied over time. (p. 464)

serial position effect The phenomenon that people are more likely to remember information that appears first and last in a list than information in the middle of the list. (p. 197)

serotonin A neurotransmitter involved in the regulation of mood, sleep, eating, arousal, and pain. (p. 70)

set point The value of some variable that the body is trying to maintain, such as temperature. (pp. 333, 382)

sex-role ideology Beliefs about appropriate behaviors of the sexes. (p. 518)

sex typing The process by which children come to acquire personality traits, emotional responses, skills, behaviors, and preferences that are culturally considered to be appropriate to their sex. (p. 509)

sexual orientation The direction of a person's enduring sexual attraction to members of the same sex, the opposite sex, or both. (p. 341)

sexual response cycle The pattern of physiological changes during sexual stimulation, consisting of four phases: excitement, plateau, orgasm, and resolution. (p. 338)

sexual strategies Tactics used in selecting mates. (p. 659)

s-factors Specific cognitive abilities. (p. 278)

shape constancy The perception that an object's shape remains constant despite the changing shape of the retinal image as the object is viewed from varying perspectives. (p. 145)

shaping The process of teaching a new behavior by reinforcing closer and closer approximations of the desired response. (p. 178)

short-term memory (STM) Memory for information that is available to consciousness for roughly 20 to 30 seconds; also called working memory. (p. 196)

similarity A Gestalt rule of perception which states that the brain tends to group similar elements within a perceptual field. (p. 138)

simplicity A Gestalt rule of perception which states that people tend to perceive the simplest pattern possible. (p. 138)

single-blind study A study in which subjects are kept blind to crucial information, notably about the experimental condition in which they have been placed. (p. 47)

situational variables Aspects of the situation that interact with aspects of the person to produce behavior. (pp. 443, 654)

size constancy The perception that the shape of objects remains unchanged in spite of the fact that different impressions are made on the retina each time the object is encountered. (p. 145)

skills training A technique that involves teaching behaviors or procedures for accomplishing specific goals. (p. 592)

social cognition The processes by which people make sense of others, themselves, social interactions, and relationships. (pp. 513, 616)

social development Predictable changes in interpersonal thought, feeling, and behavior. (p. 496)

social–emotional leader A role that may emerge in a group in which that member seeks to maximize group cohesion and minimize hostility. (p. 684)

social exchange theories Theories based on behaviorist principles that suggest the foundation of relationships is reciprocal reward. (p. 656)

social facilitation The phenomenon in which the presence of other people facilitates performance. (p. 685)

social identity theory Theory suggesting that people derive part of their identity from groups to which they belong. (p. 625)

social influence The ways in which the presence of other people influences a person's thought, feeling, or behavior. (p. 678)

socialization The process by which children and adults learn the rules, beliefs, values, skills, attitudes, and patterns of behavior of their society. (p. 504)

social learning Learning in which individuals learn many things from the people around them, with or without reinforcement. (p. 186)

social loafing A reduction in individual effort when in a group. (p. 685)

social phobia A marked fear that occurs when a person is in a specific social or performance situation. (p. 569)

social psychology A subdiscipline that examines the influence of social processes on the way people think, feel, and behave. (p. 616)

social skills training A cognitive–behavioral technique that involves instruction and modeling, and was designed to help people develop interpersonal competence. (p. 593)

social support Relationships with others that provide resources for coping with stress. (p. 414)

sociobiology A field that explores possible evolutionary and biological bases of human social behavior. (p. 20)

somatic nervous system The division of the peripheral nervous system that consists of sensory and motor neurons that transmit sensory information and control intentional actions. (p. 74)

somatosensory cortex The primary area of the parietal lobes, located behind the central tissue, which receives sensory information from different sections of the body. (p. 83)

sound localization Identifying the location of a sound in space. (p. 128)

sound wave A pulsation of acoustic energy. (p. 123)

spacing effect The superior long-term retention of information rehearsed in sessions spread out over longer intervals of time. (p. 212)

speciation Phenomenon in which members of a previously common gene pool have become separated and over time genetic drift has acted to such an extent that the two subpopulations can no longer interbreed. (p. 92)

spinal cord The part of the central nervous system that transmits information from sensory neurons to the brain, and from the brain to motor neurons that initiate movement; it is also capable of reflex actions. (p. 76)

split brain The condition that results when the corpus callosum has been surgically cut, blocking communication between the two cerebral hemispheres. (p. 86)

spontaneous recovery The spontaneous reemergence of a response or an operant that has been extinguished. (p. 163)

spontaneous remission When people quit drinking or greatly reduce their alcohol intake without any formal method of intervention. (p. 393)

spreading activation theory The theory that the presentation of a stimulus triggers activation of closely related nodes. (p. 215)

SQ3R method A mnemonic device designed for helping students remember material from textbooks, which includes five steps: survey, question, read, recite, and review. (p. 213)

SSRIs See selective serotonin reuptake inhibitor (p. 70)

stages Relatively discrete steps through which everyone progresses in the same sequence. (p. 463)

stagnation A feeling that the promise of youth has gone unfulfilled. (p. 532)

standard deviation (SD) The amount that the average subject deviates from the mean of the sample on a measure. (p. 42)

standardized procedures Procedures applied uniformly to subjects to minimize unintended variation. (p. 34)

states of consciousness Different ways of orienting to internal and external events, such as awake states and sleep states. (p. 292)

stereotypes Schemas about characteristics ascribed to a group of people based on qualities such as race, ethnicity, or gender rather than achievements or actions. (p. 619)

Stevens's power law A law of sensation proposed by S. S. Stevens, which states that the subjective intensity of a stimulus grows as a proportion of the actual intensity raised to some power. (p. 110)

stigmatization Process by which people with some discrediting feature are excluded from social interactions. (p. 93)

stimulant A drug that increases alertness, energy, and autonomic reactivity. (p. 313)

stimulus An object or event in the environment that elicits a response in an organism. (p. 157)

stimulus discrimination The tendency for an organism to respond to a very restricted range of stimuli. (p. 163)

stimulus generalization The tendency for learned behavior to occur in response to stimuli that were not present during conditioning but that are similar to the conditioned stimulus. (p. 162)

stratified random sample A sample selected to represent subpopulations proportionately, randomizing only within groups (such as age or race). (p. 41)

stress A challenge to a person's capacity to adapt to inner and outer demands, which may be physiologically arousing, emotionally taxing, and cognitively and behaviorally activating. (p. 403)

stressors Situations that often lead to stress, including life events, catastrophes, and daily hassles. (p. 405)

structuralism An early school of thought in psychology developed by Edward Titchener, which attempted to use introspection as a method for uncovering the basic elements of consciousness and the way they combine with each other into ideas. (p. 8)

structural model Freud's model of conflict between desires and the dictates of conscience or the constraints of reality, which posits three sets of mental forces or structures: id, ego, and superego. (p. 428)

structure of personality The way enduring patterns of thought, feeling, and behavior are organized within an individual. (p. 421)

structure of thought In Piaget's theory, a distinct underlying logic used by a child at a given stage. (p. 476)

subcortical forebrain Structures within the cerebrum, such as the basal ganglia and limbic system, which lie below the cortex. (p. 79)

subgoals Mini-goals on the way to achieving a broader goal. (p. 240)

subjective norms Someone's perception of how significant other individuals will view a particular health behavior, and the motivation to comply with the desires of those others. (p. 376)

subjects The individuals whom a researcher observes in a study; also called participants. (p. 34)

sublimation A defense mechanism that involves converting sexual or aggressive impulses into socially acceptable activities. (p. 429)

subordinate level A level of categorization below the basic level in which more specific attributes are shared by members of a category. (p. 234)

substance-related disorders Disorders involving continued use of a substance (such as alcohol or cocaine) that negatively affects psychological and social functioning. (p. 553)

superego In Freudian theory, the structure that acts as conscience and source of ideals, or the parental voice within the person, established through identification. (p. 428)

superordinate goals Goals requiring groups to cooperate for the benefit of all. (p. 625)

superordinate level The most abstract level of categorization in which members of a category share few common features. (p. 234)

superstitious behavior A phenomenon that occurs when the learner erroneously associates an operant and an environmental event. (p. 170)

survey research Research asking a large sample of subjects questions, often about attitudes or behaviors, using questionnaires or interviews. (p. 40)

susceptible gene hypothesis Certain genes increase but do not guarantee the development of a particular trait or characteristic. (p. 382)

syllogism A formal statement of deductive reasoning, which consists of two premises that lead to a logical conclusion. (p. 237)

sympathetic nervous system A branch of the autonomic nervous system, typically activated in response to threats to the organism, which readies the body for "fight-or-flight" reactions. (p. 75)

synapse The place at which transmission of information between neurons occurs. (p. 64)

syntax Rules that govern the placement of specific words or phrases within a sentence. (p. 257)

system A group with interdependent parts. (p. 547)

systematic desensitization A cognitive–behavioral procedure in which the patient is induced to approach feared stimuli gradually, in a state that inhibits anxiety. (p. 589)

systems approach An approach that explains an individual's behavior in the context of a social group, such as a couple, family, or larger group. (p. 546)

T

tardive dyskinesia A serious, unpredictable, irreversible side effect of prolonged use of antipsychotic medications, in which a patient develops involuntary or semivoluntary twitching, usually of the tongue, face, and neck. (p. 604)

task leader The group member who takes responsibility for seeing that the group completes its tasks. (p. 684)

taste buds Structures that line the walls of the papillae of the tongue (and elsewhere in the mouth) that contain taste receptors. (p. 131)

tectum A midbrain structure involved in vision and hearing. (p. 79)

tegmentum Midbrain structure that includes a variety of neural structures, related mostly to movement and conscious arousal and activation. (p. 79)

telegraphic speech Speech used by young children that leaves out all but the essential words in a sentence. (p. 491)

temperament Basic personality dispositions heavily influenced by genes. (p. 444)

temporal lobes Brain structures located in the lower side portion of the cortex that are important in audition (hearing) and language. (p. 85)

teratogen A harmful environmental agent, such as drugs, irradiation, and viruses that cause maternal illness, which can produce fetal abnormalities or death. (p. 466)

terminal buttons Structures at the end of the neuron that receive nerve impulses from the axon and transmit signals to adjacent cells. (p. 63)

testosterone The hormone produced by the male gonads (testes). (p. 72)

test-retest reliability Tendency of a test to yield relatively similar scores for the same individual over time. (p. 36)

thalamus A structure located deep in the center of the brain that acts as a relay station for sensory information, processing it and transmitting it to higher brain centers. (p. 80)

Thematic Apperception Test (TAT) A projective test consisting of a series of ambiguous pictures about which subjects are asked to make up a story. (p. 322)

theory A systematic way of organizing and explaining observations. (p. 32)

theory of mind An implicit set of ideas about the existence of mental states, such as beliefs and feelings, in oneself and others that children begin to develop in the toddler years. (p. 516)

theory of multiple intelligences Howard Gardner's theory of seven intelligences used to solve problems or produce culturally significant products. (p. 282)

theory of planned behavior The theory of reasoned action plus self-efficacy. (p. 376)

theory of reasoned action Behaviors stem from behavioral intentions, which are a function of a person's attitude toward the behavior, and his perception of the subjective norms surrounding the behavior. (p. 376)

trephination The practice of drilling holes in the skulls of diseased individuals to allow evil spirits to escape. (p. 370)

therapeutic alliance The patient's degree of comfort with the therapist, which allows him or her to speak about emotionally significant experiences. (p. 584)

thinking Manipulating mental representations for a purpose. (p. 230)

thyroid gland Endocrine structure located next to the trachea and larynx in the neck, which releases hormones that control growth and metabolism. (p. 71)

timbre The psychological property corresponding to a sound wave's complexity; the texture of a sound. (p. 124)

tip-of-the-tongue phenomenon The experience in which people attempting but failing to recall information from memory know the information is "in there" but are not quite able to retrieve it (p. 206)

top-down processing Perceptual processing that starts with the observer's expectations and knowledge. (p. 149)

topographic model Freud's model of conscious, preconscious, and unconscious processes. (p. 423)

traits Emotional, cognitive, and behavioral tendencies that constitute underlying dimensions of personality on which individuals vary. (p. 440)

transduction The process of converting physical energy into neural impulses. (p. 105)

transference The phenomenon in which the patient displaces thoughts, feelings, fears, wishes, and conflicts from past relationships, especially childhood relationships, onto the therapist. (p. 585)

trichromatic theory of color A theory of color vision initially proposed by Thomas Young and modified by Herman Von Helmholtz that proposes that the eye contains three types of receptors, each sensitive to wavelengths of light that produce sensations of blue, green, and red; by this theory, the colors that humans see reflect blends of the three colors to which the retina is sensitive; also called the Young–Helmholtz theory. (p. 121)

tricyclic antidepressant A class of medications for depression that compensates for depleted neurotransmitters. (p. 605)

true self A core aspect of being, untainted by the demands of others. (p. 448)

tutelage The teaching of concepts or procedures primarily through verbal explanation or instruction. (p. 188)

two-factor theory of intelligence A theory derived by Charles Spearman that holds that two types of factors or abilities underlie intelligence. (p. 278)

tympanic membrane Eardrum. (p. 125)

Type A behavior pattern A pattern of behavior and emotions that includes ambition, competitiveness, impatience, and hostility. (p. 411)

U

unconditional positive regard An attitude of total acceptance expressed by the therapist toward the client in client-centered therapy. (p. 596)

unconditioned reflex A reflex that occurs naturally, without any prior learning. (p. 159)

unconditioned response (UCR) An organism's unlearned, automatic response to a stimulus. (p. 159)

unconditioned stimulus (UCS) A stimulus that produces a reflexive response without any prior learning. (p. 159)

unconscious mental processes In Freud's theory, mental processes that are inaccessible to consciousness, many of which are repressed. (pp. 296, 423)

uninvolved Parents who consistently place their own needs above the needs of their child. (p. 506)

unipolar depression A mood disorder involving only depression; see also bipolar disorder. (p. 563)

V

valid Said of a study whose procedures are sound. (p. 34)

validity The extent to which a test measures the construct it attempts to assess, or a study adequately addresses the hypothesis it attempts to assess. (p. 36)

variability of scores The extent to which subjects tend to vary from each other in their scores on a measure. (p. 42)

variable A phenomenon that changes across circumstances or varies among individuals. (p. 32)

variable-interval (VI) schedule of reinforcement An operant conditioning procedure in which an organism receives a reward for its responses after an amount of time that is not constant. (p. 175)

variable-ratio (VR) schedule of reinforcement An organism receives a reward for a certain percentage of behaviors that are emitted, but this percentage is not fixed. (p. 175)

ventricles Fluid-filled cavities of the brain that are enlarged in schizophrenics suggesting neuronal atrophy. (p. 560)

ventromedial prefrontal cortex An area in the brain that serves many functions, including helping people use their emotional reactions to guide decision making and behavior. (p. 252)

verbal representations Information represented in words. (p. 194)

vestibular sense The sense that provides information about the position of the body in space by sensing gravity and movement. (p. 136)

vicarious conditioning The process by which an individual learns the consequences of an action by observing its consequences for someone else. (p. 187)

virtual reality exposure therapy A treatment for phobias in which virtual images of the feared stimulus are shown as opposed to the actual stimulus. (p. 590)

visual cliff A clear table with a checkerboard directly beneath it on one side and another checkerboard that appears to drop off like a cliff on the other, used especially with human infants in depth perception studies. (p. 148)

W

wavelength The distance over which a wave of energy completes a full oscillation. (p. 112)

Weber's law The perceptual law described by Ernst Weber that states that for two stimuli to be perceived as differing in intensity, the second must differ from the first by a constant proportion. (p. 109)

Wechsler Adult Intelligence Scale, Third Edition (WAIS-III) An intelligence test for adults that yields scores for both verbal and nonverbal (performance) IQ scores. (p. 271)

Wechsler Intelligence Scale for Children (WISC-III) An intelligence test for children up to age 16 that yields verbal and nonverbal (performance) IQ scores. (p. 271)

weighted utility value In expectancy value theory, a combined measure of the importance of an attribute and how well a given option satisfies it. (p. 243)

well-defined concept A concept that has properties clearly setting it apart from other concepts. (p. 232)

well-defined problems Problems in which there is adequate information to solve the problem and clear criteria by which to determine whether the problem has been solved. (p. 240)

Wernicke's area A brain structure located in the left temporal lobe involved in language comprehension. (p. 85)

what pathway The pathway running from the striate cortex in the occipital lobes through the lower part of the temporal lobes, involved in determining what an object is. (p. 120)

where pathway The pathway running from the striate cortex through the middle and upper regions of the temporal lobes and up into the parietal lobes, involved in locating an object in space, following its movement, and guiding movement toward it. (p. 120)

Whorfian hypothesis of linguistic relativity The notion that language shapes thought. (p. 254)

working memory Conscious "work-space" used for retrieving and manipulating information, maintained through maintenance rehearsal; also called short-term memory. (p. 199)

Y

Young–Helmholtz theory A theory of color vision initially proposed by Young and modified by Helmholtz which proposes that the eye contains three types of receptors, each sensitive to wavelengths of light that produce sensations of blue, green, and red; by this theory, the colors that humans see reflect blends of the three colors to which the retina is sensitive; also called trichromatic theory. (p. 121)

References

AARP News Bulletin. (January 1989). New study finds older drivers "capable, safe." *30*, 14.

Abelson, R. B. (1995). *Statistics as principled argument.* Hillsdale, NJ: Lawrence Erlbaum.

Abelson, R. P. (1983). Whatever became of consistency theory? *Personality and Social Psychology Bulletin, 9*, 37–54.

Abraham, H. D., & Duffy, F. H. (1996). Stable quantitative EEG difference in post-LSD visual disorder by split-half analysis: Evidence for disinhibition. *Psychiatry Research: Neuroimaging, 67*, 173–187.

Abramov, I., & Gordon, J. (1994). Color appearance: On seeing red—or yellow, or green, or blue. *Annual Review of Psychology, 45*, 451–485.

Abrams, D., & Hogg, M. A. (Eds.). (1999). *Social identity and social cognition.* Oxford: Blackwell.

Abrams, D. B., & Wilson, G. T. (1983). Alcohol, sexual arousal, and self-control. *Journal of Personality and Social Psychology, 45*, 188–198.

Abrams, R., Swartz, C. M., & Vedak, C. (1989). Antidepressant effects of right versus left unilateral ECT and the lateralization theory of ECT action. *American Journal of Psychiatry, 146*, 1190–1192.

Abramson, L. Y., Metalsky, G. I., & Alloy, L. B. (1989). Hopelessness depression: A theory-based subtype of depression. *Psychological Review, 96*, 358-372.

Abramson, L. Y., Seligman, M. E. P., & Teasdale, J. D. (1978). Learned helplessness in humans: Critique and reformulation. *Journal of Abnormal Psychology, 87*, 49–74.

Abrous, D. N., Rodriquez, J., le Moal, M., Moser, P. C., & Barneoud, P. (1999). Effects of mild traumatic brain injury on immunoreactivity for the inducible transcription factors c-Fos, c-Jun, JunB, and Krox-24 in cerebral regions associated with conditioned fear responding. *Brain Research, 826*, 181–192.

Ackerman, S. J., Hilsenroth, M. J., Clemence, A. J., Weatherill, R., & Fowler, J. C. (2000). The effects of social cognition and object representation on psychotherapy continuation. *Bulletin of the Menninger Clinic, 64*, 386-408.

Adams, B. D. (1985). Age, structure, and sexuality. *Journal of Homosexuality, 11*, 19–33.

Adams, C. (1991). Qualitative age differences in memory for text: A life-span development perspective. *Psychology and Aging, 6*, 323–336.

Adams, H. E., Wright, L. W., & Lohr, B. A. (1996). Is homophobia associated with homosexual arousal? *Journal of Abnormal Psychology 105*, 440–445.

Adams, P. R., & Adams, G. R. (1984). Mount Saint Helens' ashfall: Evidence for a disaster stress reaction. *American Psychologist, 39*, 252–260.

Adams-Webber, J. R. (2001). Cognitive complexity and role relationships. *Journal of Constructivist Psychology, 14*, 43–50.

Adcock, R. A., Constable, R. T., Gore, J. C., & Goldman-Rakic, P. S. (2000). Functional neuroanatomy of executive processes involved in dual-task performance. *Proceedings of the National Academy of Science, U.S.A., 97*, 3567–3572.

Ader, R., & Cohen, N. (1985). CNS immune system interactions: Conditioning phenomena. *Behavioral and Brain Sciences, 8*, 379–426.

Adler, G., & Buie, D. H. (1979). Aloneness and borderline psychopathology: The possible relevance of child development issues. *International Journal of Psychoanalysis, 60*, 83-96.

Adolphs, R. (1999). Social cognition and the brain. *Trends in Cognitive Sciences, 3*, 469–479.

Adolphs, R., Damasio, H., Tranel, D., & Damasio, A. R. (1996). Cortical systems for the recognition of emotion in facial expressions. *Journal of Neuroscience, 16*, 7678-7687.

Adorno, T. W., Frenkel-Brunswik, E., Levinson, D., & Sanford, R. N. (1950). *The authoritarian personality.* New York: W.W. Norton.

A fistful of risks. (1996). *Discover, 17*, 82–84.

Aggleton, J. P. (Ed). (1992). *The amygdala: Neurobiological aspects of emotion, memory, and mental dysfunction.* New York: Wiley-Liss.

Agras, W. S., Walsh, T., Fairburn, C. G., Wilson, G. T., & Kraemer, H. C. (2000). A multicenter comparison of cognitive-behavioral therapy and interpersonal psychotherapy for bulimia nervosa. *Archives of General Psychiatry, 57*, 459–466.

Ainsworth, M. D. (1991). Attachments and other affectional bonds across the life cycle. In C. M. Parkes, J. Stevenson-Hinde, et al. (Eds.), *Attachment across the life cycle* (pp. 33–51). London: Tavistock/Routledge.

Ainsworth, M. D. S. (1967). *Infancy in Uganda.* Baltimore, MD: Johns Hopkins University.

Ainsworth, M. D. S. (1973). The development of infant–mother attachment. In B. Caldwell & H. Ricciuti (Eds.), *Review of child development research* (Vol. 3). Chicago: University of Chicago Press.

Ainsworth, M. D. S. (1979). Infant–mother attachment. *American Psychologist, 34*, 932–937.

Ainsworth, M. D. S., & Bell, S. M. (1970). Attachment, exploration, and separation: Illustrated by the behavior of one-year-olds in a strange situation. *Child Development, 41*, 49–67.

Ajzen, I. (1991). The theory of planned behavior. *Organizational Behavior and Human Decision Processes, 50*, 179–211.

Ajzen, I. (1996). The directive influence of attitudes on behavior. In P. M. Gollwitzer & J. A. Bargh (Eds.), *The psychology of action: Linking cognition and motivation to behavior.* (pp. 385–403). New York: Guilford Press.

Ajzen, I. (2000). Nature and operation of attitudes. *Annual Review of Psychology, 27*, 27–58.

Ajzen, I., & Fishbein, M. (1977). Attitude-behavior relations: A theoretical analysis and review of empirical research. *Psychological Bulletin, 84*, 888–918.

Ajzen, I., & Fishbein, M. (1980). *Understanding attitudes and predicting social behavior.* Englewood Cliffs, NJ: Prentice-Hall.

al-Absi, M., & Rokke, P. D. (1991). Can anxiety help us tolerate pain? *Pain, 46*, 43–51.

Albert, D. J., Jonik, R. H., & Walsh, M. (1991). Hormone-dependent aggression in the female rat: Testosterone plus estradiol implants prevent the decline in aggression following ovariectomy. *Physiology & Behavior, 49*, 673–677.

Albert, M. K. (1993). Parallelism and the perception of illusory contours. *Perception, 22*, 589–595.

Alberts, A. C. (1989). Ultraviolet visual sensitivity in desert iguanas: Implications for pheromone detection. *Animal Behaviour, 38*, 129–137.

Alderfer, C. (1972). *Existence, relatedness, and growth: Human needs in organizational settings.* New York: Free Press.

Alderfer, C. P. (1989). Theories reflecting my personal experience and life development. *Journal of Applied Behavioral Science, 25*, 351–365.

Alexander, G. M., Swerdloff, R. S., Wang, C. W., & Davidson, T. (1997). Androgen-behavior correlations in hypogonadal men and eugonadal men: I. Mood and response to auditory sexual stimuli. *Hormones & Behavior, 31,* 110–119.

Alexander, I. (1990). *Personology: Method and content in personality assessment and psychobiography.* Durham, NC: Duke University Press.

Alexander, J. M., & Schwanenflugel, P. J. (1994). Strategy regulation: The role of intelligence, metacognitive attributions, and knowledge base. *Developmental Psychology, 30,* 709–723.

Alicke, M. D., Klotz, M. L., Breitenbecher, D. L., Yurak, T. J., & Vredenburg, D. S. (1995). Personal contact, individuation, and the better-than-average effect. *Journal of Personality and Social Psychology, 68,* 804–825.

Allen, S. W., & Brooks, L. R. (1991). Specializing the operation of an explicit rule. *Journal of Experimental Psychology: General, 120,* 3–19.

Allison, D. B., Fontaine, K. R., Manson, J. E., Stevens, J., & VanItallie, T. B. (1999). Annual deaths attributable to obesity in the United States. *Journal of the American Medical Association, 282,* 1530–1538.

Allison, D. B., Heshka, S., Neale, M. C., & Lykken, D. T. (1994). A genetic analysis of relative weight among 4,020 twin pairs, with an emphasis on sex effects. *Health Psychology, 13,* 362–365.

Alloy, L. B., Abramson, L. Y., Hogan, M. E., Whitehouse, W. G., Rose, D. T., Robinson, M. S., Kim, R. S., & Lapkin, J. B. (2000). The Templen-Wisconsin Cognitive Vulnerability to Depression Project: Lifetime history of Axis I psychopathology in individuals at high and low cognitive risk for depression. *Journal of Abnormal Psychology, 109,* 403–418.

Allport, G. (1935). Attitudes. In C. Murchison (Ed.), *Handbook of social psychology* (pp. 798–844). Worcester, MA: Clark University Press.

Allport, G. (1937). *Personality: A psychological interpretation.* New York: Henry Holt.

Allport, G. (1954). *The nature of prejudice.* Cambridge, MA: Addison-Wesley.

Allport, G. (1968). The historical background of modern social psychology. In G. Lindzey & E. Aronson (Eds.), *Handbook of social psychology* (Vol. I). Reading, MA: Addison-Wesley.

Allport, G., & Odbert, H. (1936). *Trait-names: A psycho-lexical study.* Psychological Monographs, Vol. 47, No. 1. Princeton, NJ: Psychological Review.

Altamura, A. C., Pioli, R., Vitto, M., & Mannu, P. (1999). Venlafaxine in social phobia: A study in selective serotonin reuptake inhibitor nonresponders. *International Clinical Psychopharmacology, 14,* 239–245.

Alvarez–Borda, B., Ramirez–Amaya, V., Perez–Montfort, R., & Bermudez– Rattoni, F. (1995). Enhancement of antibody production by a learning paradigm. *Neurobiology of Learning & Memory, 64,* 103–105.

Amabile, T. M. (1996). Creativity in context. *Update to "The Social Psychology of Creativity."* Boulder, CO: Westview.

Ambady, N., & Rosenthal, R. (1993). Half a minute: Predicting teacher evaluations from thin slices of nonverbal behavior and physical attractiveness. *Journal of Personality and Social Psychology, 64,* 431–441.

American Association on Mental Retardation. (1992). *Mental retardation: Definition, classification, and systems of supports* (9th ed.). Washington, DC: American Association on Mental Retardation.

American Cancer Society. (2002). Cancer prevention and early detection facts and figures.

American Obesity Association. (2003). AOA fact sheets.

American Psychiatric Association. (1994). *Diagnostic and statistical manual of mental disorders* (4th ed.). Washington, DC: Author.

American Psychological Association, Committee for the Protection of Human Participants in Research. (1973). *Ethical principles in the conduct of research with human subjects.* Washington, DC.

American Psychological Association. (1997). Report of the ethics committee, 1996. *American Psychologist, 52,* 897–905.

American Psychological Association. (2003). Division 38—Health psychology home page. [Online].

Amsterdam, B. (1972). Mirror self–image reactions before age two. *Developmental Psychology, 5,* 297–305.

Anand, B., & Brobeck, J. (1951). Hypothalamic control of food intake in rats and cats. *Yale Journal of Biological Medicine, 24,* 123–140.

Anastasi, A. (1958). Heredity, environment, and the question "How?" *Psychological Review, 65,* 197–208.

Anastasi, A., & Urbina, S. (1997). *Psychological testing* (7th ed.). Upper Saddle River, NJ: Prentice- Hall.

Andersen, S., & Cole, S. (1991). Do I know you? The role of significant others in general social perception. *Journal of Personality and Social Psychology, 59,* 384–399.

Andersen, S. M., Reznik, L., & Manzella, L. M. (1996). Eliciting facial affect, motivation, and expectancies in transference: Significant-other representations in social relations. *Journal of Personality and Social Psychology, 71,* 1108–1129.

Anderson, C. (1989). Temperature and aggression: Ubiquitous effects of heat on occurrence of human violence. *Psychological Bulletin, 106,* 74–96.

Anderson, C. A., & Bushman, B. J. (2002). Human aggression. *Annual Review of Psychology, 53,* 27–52.

Anderson, J. (1983). *The architecture of cognition.* Cambridge, MA: Harvard University Press.

Anderson, J. E. (2003). Condom use and HIV risk among US adults. *American Journal of Public Health, 93,* 912–914.

Anderson, J. R. (1985). *Cognitive psychology and its implications* (2nd ed.). New York: Freeman.

Anderson, J. R. (1995). *Learning and memory: An integrated approach.* New York: John Wiley.

Anderson, J. R. (1996). ACT: A simple theory of complex cognition. *American Psychologist, 51,* 355–365.

Andreasen, N. C. (1999). A unitary model of schizophrenia: Bleuler's "fragmented phrene" as schizencephaly. *Archives of General Psychiatry, 56,* 781–787.

Andreasen, N. C., Arndt, S., Miller, D., Flaum, M., et al. (1995). Correlational studies of the Scale for the Assessment of Negative Symptoms and the Scale for the Assessment of Positive Symptoms: An overview and update. *Psychopathology, 28,* 7–17.

Andreasen, N. C., Rice, J., Endicott, J., Coryell, W., Grove, W. M., & Reich, T. (1987). Familial rates of affective disorder: A report from the National Institute of Mental Health collaborative study. *Archives of General Psychiatry, 44,* 461–469.

Andreason, N. C., Swayze, V., Flaum, M., Alliger, R., & Cohen, G. (1990). Ventricular abnormalities in affective disorder: Clinical and demographic correlates. *American Journal of Psychiatry, 147,* 893–900.

Andreasson, S., & Brandt, L. (1997). Mortality and morbidity related to alcohol. *Alcohol & Alcoholism, 32,* 173–178.

Andrzejewski, S. J., Moore, C. M., Corvette, M., & Hermann, D. (1991). Prospective memory skill. *Bulletin of the Psychonomic Society, 29,* 304–306.

Angel, I., Hauger, R., Giblin, B., & Paul, S. (1992). Regulation of the anorectic drug recognition site during glucoprovic feeding. *Brain Research Bulletin, 28,* 201–207.

Anthony, E., & Cohler, B. (Eds.). (1987). *The invulnerable child.* New York: Guilford Press.

Antoch, M. P., Song, E. J., Chang, A. M., Vitaterna, M. H., Zhao, Y. L., Wilsbacher, L. D., et al. (1997). Functional identification of the mouse circadian clock gene by transgenic bac rescue. *Cell, 89,* 655–667.

Antrobus, J. (1991). Dreaming: Cognitive processes during cortical activation and high afferent thresholds. *Psychological Review, 98,* 96–121.

Antshel, K. M., & Remer, R. (2003). Social skills training in children with attention deficit hyperactivity disorder: A randomized-controlled clinical trial. *Journal of Clinical Child and Adolescent Psychology, 32,* 153–165.

Aponte, H. J., & VanDeusen, J. M. (1981). Structural family therapy. In A. S. Gurman and D. P. Kniskern (Eds.), *Handbook of family therapy.* New York: Brunner/Mazel.

Applebaum, P. S., Uyehara, L. A., & Elin, M. R. (Eds.). (1997). *Trauma and memory: Clinical and legal controversies.* New York: Oxford University Press.

Archer, D. (1994). American violence: How high and why? *Law Studies, 19,* 12–20.

Archer, J. (1991). The influence of testosterone on human aggression. *British Journal of Psychology, 82,* 1–28.

Archer, J. (2001). Grief from an evolutionary perspective. In M. S. Stroebe & R. O. Hansson (Eds.), *Handbook of bereavement research: Consequences, coping, and care* (pp. 263–283). Washington, DC: American Psychological Association.

Archer, J., Birring, S. S., & Wu, F. C. W. (1998). The association between testosterone and aggression among young men. *Aggressive Behavior, 24,* 411–420.

Archer, J., & Lloyd, B. (1985). *Sex and gender* (2nd ed.). New York: Cambridge University Press.

Arena, J. G., & Blanchard, E. B. (1996). Biofeedback and relaxation therapy for chronic disorders. In R. J. Gatchel, D. C. Turk, et al. (Eds.), *Psychological approaches to pain management: A practitioner's handbook.* (pp. 179–230). New York: Guilford Press.

Arendt, J., Skene, D. J., Middleton, B., Lockley, S. W., & Deacon, S. (1997). Efficacy of melatonin treatment in jet lag, shift work, and blindness. *Journal of Biological Rhythms, 12*(6), 604–617.

Arendt, R. E., Minnes, S., & Singer, L. T. (1996). Fetal cocaine exposure: Neurologic effects and sensory-motor delays. In L. S. Chandler & S. J. Lane (Eds.), *Children with prenatal drug exposure* (pp. 129–144). New York: Haworth Press.

Arkes, H., Boehm, L., & Xu, G. (1991). Determinants of judged validity. *Journal of Experimental Social Psychology, 27,* 576–605.

Arkowitz, H. (1997). Integrative theories of therapy. In P. L. Wachtel, S. B. Messer, et al. (Eds.), *Theories of psychotherapy: Origins and evolution* (pp. 227–288). Washington, DC: American Psychological Association.

Arkowitz, H., & Messer, S. B. (Eds.). (1984). *Psychodynamic therapy and behavior therapy: Is integration possible?* New York: Plenum Press.

Armony, J. L., & LeDoux, J. E. (2000). How danger is encoded: Toward a systems, cellular, and computational understanding of cognitiveemotional interactions in fear. In M. S. Gazzaniga (Ed.), *The new cognitive neurosciences* (2nd ed., pp. 1067–1080). Cambridge, MA: MIT Press.

Arnett, J. J. (1999). Adolescent storm and stress, reconsidered. *American Psychologist, 54,* 317–326.

Arnkoff, D., Victor, B., & Glass, C. (1993). Empirical research on factors in psychotherapeutic change. In G. Stricker & J. Gold (Eds.), *Comprehensive handbook of psychotherapy integration* (pp. 27–42). New York: Plenum Press.

Arnsten, A. F. T. (1998). Catecholamine modulation of prefrontal cortical cognitive function. *Trends in Cognitive Sciences, 2,* 436–447.

Aron, L. (1996). *A meeting of minds: Mutuality in psychoanalysis.* Hillside, NJ: Analytic Press.

Aronson, E. (2000). *Nobody left to hate: Teaching compassion after Columbine.* New York: Freeman.

Aronson, E., & Mills, J. (1959). The effect of severity of initiation on liking for a group. *Journal of Abnormal and Social Psychology, 59,* 177–181.

Arria, A. M., & Van Thiel, D. H. (1992). The epidemiology of alcohol-related chronic disease. *Alcohol Health and Research World, 16,* 209–217.

Arrigo, J. A., & Pezdek, K. (1997). Lessons from the study of psychogenic amnesia. *Current Directions in Psychological Science, 5,* 148–152.

Arvey, R. D., McCall, B., & Bouchard, T. J. (1994). Genetic influence on job satisfaction and work values. *Personality and Individual Differences, 17,* 21–33.

Asch, S. E. (1946). Forming impressions of personality. *Journal of Abnormal and Social Psychology, 41,* 258–290.

Asch, S. E. (1955). Opinions and social pressure. *Scientific American, 193,* 31–35.

Asch, S. E. (1956). Studies of independence and conformity: A minority of one against unanimous majority. *Psychological Monographs: General and Applied, 70,* 1–69.

Asendorpf, J., & Baudonniere, P. (1993). Self-awareness and other-awareness: Mirror self-recognition and synchronic imitation among unfamiliar peers. *Developmental Psychology, 29,* 88–95.

Asendorpf, J., & Scherer, K. (1983). The discrepant repressor: Differentiation between low anxiety, high anxiety, and repression of anxiety by autonomic-facial-verbal patterns of behavior. *Journal of Personality and Social Psychology, 45,* 1334–1346.

Ashby, F. G., & Waldron, E. M. (2000). The neuropsychological bases of category learning. *Current Directions in Psychological Science, 9,* 10–14.

Ashford, J. W., Schmitt, F. A., & Kumar, V. (1996). Diagnosis of Alzheimer's disease. *Psychiatric Annals, 26,* 262–268.

Aspinwall, L. G., Kemeny, M. E., Taylor, S. E., Schneider, S. G., & Dudley, J. P. (1991). Psychsocial predictors of gay men's AIDS risk-reduction behavior. *Health Psychology, 10,* 432–444.

Aspinwall, L. G. & Taylor, S. E. (1997). A Stitch in Time: Self-Regulation and Proactive Coping. *Psychological Bulletin, 121,* 417–436.

Astrom, A. N., & Rise, J. (2001). Young adults' intention to eat healthy food: Extending the theory of planned behavior. *Psychology and Health, 16,* 223–237.

Atkinson, J. W. (1977). Motivation for achievement. In T. Blass (Ed.), *Personality variables in social behavior.* Hillsdale, NJ: Erlbaum.

Atkinson, J. W., & Litwin, G. H. (1960). Achievement motive and test anxiety conceived as motive to approach success and motive to avoid failure. *Journal of Abnormal and Social Psychology, 60,* 52–63.

Atkinson, R. C., & Shiffrin, R. N. (1968). Human memory: A proposed system and its control processes. In K. W. Spence & J. T. Spense (Eds.), *The psychology of learning and motivation,* (Vol. 2). New York: Academic Press.

Aviezer, O. (2003). Bedtime talk of three-year olds: Collaborative repair of miscommunication. *First Language, 23,* 117–139.

Baars, B. (1995). Tutorial commentary: Surprisingly small subcortical structures are needed for the stage of waking consciousness, while cortical projection areas seem to provide perceptual contents of consciousness. *Consciousness and Cognition, 4,* 159–162.

Baars, B. J. (1988). Momentary forgetting as a "resetting" of a conscious global workspace due to competition between incompatible contexts. In M. J. Horowitz (Ed.), *Psychodynamics and cognition* (pp. 269–293). University of California.

Baars, B. J. (1997). *In the theater of consciousness: The workspace of the mind.* New York: Oxford University Press.

Baars, B. J., & McGovern, K. (1996). Cognitive views of consciousness: What are the facts? How can we explain them? In M. Velmans (Ed.), *The science of consciouness: Psychological, neuropsychological and clinical reviews* (pp. 63–95). London.

Babor, T., Hoffman, M., DelBoca, F., Hesselbrock, V., Meyer, R. E., Dolinsky, Z., & Rounsaville, B. (1992). Types of alcoholics, I: Evidence for an empirically derived typology based on indicators of vulnerability and severity. *Archives of General Psychiatry, 49,* 599–608.

Babor, T. F., Miller, W. R., DiClemente, C., & Longabaugh, R. (1999). A study to remember: Response of the project MATCH research group. *Addiction, 94,* 66–69.

Baddeley, A. (1986). *Working memory.* New York: Oxford University Press.

Baddeley, A., Gathercole, S., & Papagno, C. (1998). The phonological loop as a language learning device. *Psychological Review, 105,* 158–173.

Baddeley, A., & Hitch, G. J. (1994). Developments in the concept of working memory. *Neuropsychology, 8,* 485-493.

Baddeley, A. D. (1992). Working memory. *Science, 255,* 556–559.

Baddeley, A. D. (1995). Working memory. In M. Gazzaniga (Ed.), *The cognitive neurosciences* (pp. 754–764). Cambridge, MA: Bradford/MIT Press.

Baddeley, A. D., & Patterson, K. (1971). The relation between long-term and short-term memory. *British Medical Bulletin, 27,* 237–242.

Baer, L., Rauch, S. L., Ballantine, H. T., Martuza, R., Cosgrove, R., Cassem, E., et al. (1995). Cingulotomy for intractable obsessive-compulsive disorder: Prospective long-term follow-up of 18 patients. *Archives of General Psychiatry, 52,* 384–392.

Bahrick, H. P. (1985). Associationism and the Ebbinghaus legacy. *Journal of Experimental Psychology: Learning, Memory, & Cognition, 11,* 439–443.

Bahrick, H. P., Bahrick, L. E., Bahrick, A. S., & Bahrick, P. E. (1993). Maintenance of foreign language vocabulary and the spacing effect. *Psychological Science, 4,* 316–321.

Bahrick, H. P., & Hall, L. K. (1991). Lifetime maintenance of high school mathematics content. *Journal of Experimental Psychology: General, 120,* 20–33.

Bahrick, H. P., Hall, L. K., & Berger, S. A. (1996). Accuracy and distortion in memory for high school grades. *Psychological Science, 7,* 265–271.

Bahrick, L. E., & Lickliter, R. (2000). Intersensory redundancy guides attentional selectivity and perceptual learning in infancy. *Developmental Psychology, 36,* 190–201.

Bailey, C. H., & Kandel, E. R. (1995). Molecular and structural mechanisms underlying long-term memory. In M. S. Gazzaniga, et al. (Eds.),

The cognitive neurosciences (pp. 19–36). Cambridge, MA: MIT Press.

Bailey, J. M., & Pillard, R. (1991). A genetic study of male sexual orientation. *Archives of General Psychiatry, 48,* 1089–1096.

Bailey, J. M., Pillard, R. C., Dawood, K., Miller, M. B., Farrer, L. A., Trivedi, S., & Murphy, R. L. (1999). A family history study of male sexual orientation using three independent samples. *Behavior Genetics, 29,* 79–86.

Bailey, J. M., Pillard, R. C., Neale, M. C., & Agyei, Y. (1993). Heritable factors influence sexual orientation in women. *Archives of General Psychiatry, 50,* 217–223.

Bailey, J. M., & Zucker, K. J. (1995). Childhood sex-typed behavior and sexual orientation: A conceptual analysis and quantitative review. *Developmental Psychology, 31,* 43-55.

Baillargeon, R., & DeVos, J. (1991). Object permanence in young infants: Further evidence. *Child Development, 62,* 1227–1246.

Bain, L. L., Wilson, T., & Chaikind, E. (1989). Participant perceptions of exercise programs for overweight women. *Research Quarterly for Exercise and Sport, 60,* 134–143.

Bakan, D. (1966). The duality of human existence: An essay on psychology and religion. New York: Rand McNally.

Baker, L., Silk, K. R., Westen, D., Nigg, J. T., & Lohr, N. E. (1992). Malevolence, splitting, and parental ratings by borderlines. *Journal of Nervous and Mental Disease, 180,* 258–264.

Baldessarini, R. J., & Tohen, M., & Tondo, L. (2000). Maintenance treatment in bipolar disorder. *Archives of General Psychiatry, 57,* 490–492.

Baldwin, M. (1992). Relational schemas and the processing of social information. *Psychological Bulletin, 112,* 461–484.

Bales, R. F. (1953). The equilibrium problem in small groups. In T. Parsons, R. F. Bales, & E. A. Shils (Eds.), *Working papers in the theory of action.* Glencoe, IL: Free Press.

Baltes, P. (1987). Theoretical propositions of life-span developmental psychology: On the dynamics between growth and decline. *Developmental Psychology, 23,* 611–626.

Baltes, P. B. (1997). On the incomplete architecture of human ontogeny: Selection, optimization, and compensation as foundation of developmental theory. *American Psychologist, 52,* 366–380.

Baltes, P. B. (1998). Theoretical propositions of life-span developmental psychology: On the dynamics between growth and decline. In M. P. Lawton & T. A. Salthouse (Eds.), *Essential papers on the psychology of aging. Essential papers in psychoanalysis.* (pp. 86–123). New York: New York University Press.

Baltes, P. B., & Staudinger, U. M. (2000). Wisdom: A metaheuristic (pragmatic) to orchestrate mind and virtue toward excellence. *American Psychologist, 55,* 122–136.

Banaji, M. R., & Prentice, D. A. (1994). The self in social contexts. *Annual Review of Psychology, 45,* 297–333.

Bandler, R. (1982). Identification of neuronal cell bodies mediating components of biting attack behavior in the cat: Induction of jaw opening following microinjections of glutamate into hypothalamus. *Brain Research, 245,* 192–197.

Bandura, A. (1967). The role of modeling personality development. In C. Lavatelli & F. Stendler (Eds.), *Readings in childhood and development* (pp. 334–343). New York: Harcourt Brace Jovanovich.

Bandura, A. (1977a). Self-efficacy: Toward a unifying theory of behavioral change. *Psychological Review, 84,* 191–215.

Bandura, A. (1977b). *Social learning theory.* Englewood Cliffs, NJ: Prentice-Hall.

Bandura, A. (1982). Self-efficacy mechanisms in human agency. *American Psychologist, 37,* 122–147.

Bandura, A. (1986). *Social foundations of thought and action: A social cognitive theory,* Englewood Cliffs, NJ: Prentice-Hall.

Bandura, A. (1989). Human agency in social cognitive theory. *American Psychologist, 44,* 1175–1184.

Bandura, A. (1995). *Self-efficacy in changing societies.* New York: Cambridge University Press.

Bandura, A. (1999). Social cognitive theory of personality. In L. Pervin & O. John (Eds.), *Handbook of personality: Theory and research* (2nd ed., pp. 154–196). New York: Guilford Press.

Bandura, A. (2001). Social cognitive theory: An agentic perspective. *Annual Review of Psychology, 52,* 1–26.

Bandura, A., Blanchard, E. B., & Ritter, B. (1969). Relative efficacy of desensitization and modeling approaches for inducing behavioral, affective, and attitudinal changes. *Journal of Personality and Social Psychology, 13,* 173–199.

Bandura, A., Ross, D., & Ross, S. (1961). Transmission of aggression through imitation of aggressive models. *Journal of Abnormal and Social Psychology, 66,* 3–11.

Bandura, A., Ross, D., & Ross, S. (1963). Vicarious reinforcement and imitative learning. *Journal of Abnormal and Social Psychology, 67,* 601–607.

Banerjee, M. (1997). Hidden emotions: Preschoolers' knowledge of appearance-reality and emotion display rules. *Social Cognition 15,* 107–132.

Bar, M., & Biederman, I. (1998). Subliminal visual priming. *Psychological Science, 9,* 464–469.

Bard, P. (1934). On emotional expression after desortication with some remarks on certain theoretical views. *Psychological Review, 41,* 309–328.

Bardwick, J. (1971). *Psychology of women.* New York: Harper & Row.

Bargh, J. (1997). The automaticity of everyday life. In J. S. Wyer, Jr. (Ed.), *Advances in social cognition* (Vol. 10). Hillsdale, NJ: Lawrence Erlbaum.

Bargh, J., & Barndollar, K. (1996). Automaticity in action: The unconscious as repository of chronic goals and motives. In P. M. Gollwitzer & J. Bargh (Eds.), *The psychology of action: Linking cognition and motivation to behavior* (pp. 457–481). New York: Guilford.

Bargh, J. A., & Chartrand, T. L. (1999). The unbearable automaticity of being. *American Psychologist, 54*(7), 462–479.

Bargh, J. A., & Tota, M. E. (1988). Context-dependent automatic depression: Accessibility of negative constructs with regard to self but not others. *Journal of Personality and Social Psychology, 54,* 925–939.

Barinaga, M. (1997). New imaging methods provide a better view into the brain. *Science, 276,* 1974–1976.

Barkow, J. H., Cosmides, L., & Tooby, J. (1992). *The adapted mind.* New York: Oxford University Press.

Barlow, D. (2002). *Anxiety and its disorders.* New York: Guilford.

Barlow, D. H., Esler, J. L., & Vitali, A. E. (1998). Psychosocial treatments for panic disorders, phobias, and generalized anxiety disorder. In P. E. Nathan, J. M. Gorman, et al. (Eds.), *A guide to treatments that work* (pp. 288–318). New York: Oxford University Press.

Baroff, G. S., & Gregory, O. J. (1999). *Mental retardation: Nature, cause, and management.* Bristol, PA: Brunner/Mazel.

Baron, C. S. (1998). Modularity in developmental cognitive neuropsychology: Evidence from autism and Gilles de la Tourette syndrome. In J. A. Burack & R. M. Hodapp (Eds.), *Handbook of mental retardation and development* (pp. 334-348). New York: Cambridge University Press.

Baron, R. (1996). The sweet smell of …Helping: Effects of pleasant ambient fragrance on prosocial behavior in shopping malls. *Personality and Social Psychology Bulletin, 23,* 498–503.

Baron, R. S., Cutrona, C. E., Hicklin, D., Russel, D. W., & Lubaroff, D. M. (1990). Social support and immune function among spouses of cancer patients. *Journal of Personality and Social Psychology, 59,* 344–352.

Baron-Cohen, S., Baldwin, D. A., & Crowson, M. (1997). Do children with autism use the speaker's direction of gaze strategy to crack the code of language? *Child Development, 68,* 48–57.

Barr, H., Pytkowicz, Streissguth, Darby, B., & Sampson, P. (1990). Prenatal exposure to alcohol, caffeine, tobacco, and aspirin: Effects on fine and gross motor performance in 4-year-old children. *Developmental Psychology, 26,* 339–348.

Barrett, D. H., Resnick, H. S., Foy, D. W., Dansky, B. S., Flanders, W. D., & Stroup, N. E. (1996). Combat exposure and adult psychosocial adjustment among U.S. Army veterans serving in Vietnam, 1965–1971. *Journal of Abnormal Psychology, 105,* 575–581.

Barrett, G. V., & Depinet, R. L. (1991). A reconsideration of testing for competence rather than for intelligence. *American Psychologist, 46,* 1012–1024.

Barrett, G. V., & Franke, R. H. (1969). Communication preference and performance: A cross-cultural comparison. *Proceedings of the 77th Annual American Psychological Association Convention,* 597–598.

Barron, F., & Harrington, D. M. (1981). Creativity, intelligence, and personality. *Annual Review of Psychology, 32,* 439–476.

Barron, J. W. (1998). *Making diagnosis meaningful: Enhancing evaluation and treatment of psychologi-*

cal disorders. Washington, DC: American Psychological Association.

Barry, H. M., et al. (1957). A cross-cultural survey of some sex differences in socialization. *Journal of Abnormal Social Psychology, 55,* 327–332.

Barta, P., Pearlson, G., Powers, R. E., Richards, S. S., & Tune, L. (1990). Auditory hallucinations and smaller superior temporal gyral volume in schizophrenia. *American Journal of Psychiatry, 147,* 1457–1462.

Bartlett, F. C. (1932). *Remembering: A study in experimental and social psychology.* Cambridge: Cambridge University Press.

Bartoshuk, L. M. (2000). Comparing sensory experiences across individuals: Recent psychophysical advances illuminate genetic variation in taste perception. *Chemical Senses, 25,* 447–460.

Bartoshuk, L. M., & Beauchamp, G. K. (1994). Chemical senses. *Annual Review of Psychology, 45,* 419–449.

Basoglu, M. (1997). Torture as a stressful life event: A review of the current status of knowledge. In T. W. Miller (Ed.), *Clinical disorders and stressful life events* (pp. 45–70). Madison, CT: International Universities Press.

Basoglu, M., Paker, M., Paker, O., Ozmen, E., Marks, I., Sahin, D., & Sarimurat, N. (1994). Psychological effects of torture: A comparison of tortured with nontortured political activists in Turkey. *American Journal of Psychiatry, 151,* 6–81.

Bassili, J. N., & Krosnick, J. A. (2000). Do strength-related attitude properties determine susceptibility to response effects? New evidence from response latency, attitude extremity, and aggregate indices. *Political Psychology, 21,* 107–132.

Bateman, A., & Fonagy, P. (1999). Effectiveness of partial hospitalization in the treatment of borderline personality disorder: A randomized controlled trial. *American Journal of Psychiatry, 156,* 1563–1569.

Bates, J., Pettit, G., Dodge, K., & Ridge, B. (1998). Interaction of temperamental resistance to control and restrictive parenting in the development of externalizing behavior. *Developmental Psychology, 34,* 982–995.

Bates, L., Luster, T., & Vandenbelt, M. (2003). Factors related to social competence in elementary school among children of adolescent mothers. *Social Development, 12,* 107–124.

Bates, M. S. (1987). Ethnicity and pain: A biocultural model. *Social Science and Medicine, 24,* 47–50.

Batson, C. D. (1991). Evidence for altruism: Toward a pluralism of prosocial motives. *Psychological Inquiry, 2,* 107–122.

Batson, C. D. (1995). Altruism. In A. Tesser (Ed.), *Advanced social psychology.* New York: McGraw-Hill.

Batson, C. D. (1998). Altruism and prosocial behavior. In D. T. Gilbert, S. T. Fiske, & G. Lindzey (Eds.), *The handbook of social psychology* (Vol. 2, 4th ed., pp. 282–316). Boston, MA: McGraw-Hill.

Batson, C. D., Ahmad, N., Lishner, D. A., & Tsang, J. (2002). Empathy and altruism. In C. R. Snyder & S. J. Lopez (Eds.), *Handbook of positive psychology* (pp. 485–498). New York: Oxford University Press.

Batson, C. D., & Moran, T. (1999). Empathy-induced altruism in a prisoner's dilemma. *European Journal of Social Psychology, 29,* 909–924.

Battacchi, M. W., Pelamatti, G., Umilta, C., & Michelotti, E. (1981). On the acoustic information stored in echoic memory. *International Journal of Psycholonguistics, 8,* 17–29.

Batteau, D. W. (1967). The role of the pinna in human localization. *Proceedings of the Royal Society of London, Series, B, 168,* 158–180.

Batuev, A. S., & Gafurov, B. G. (1993). The chemical nature of the hypothalamocortical activation underlying drinking behavior. *Neuroscience of Behavioral Psychology, 23,* 35–41.

Baum, A., & Posluszny, D. M. (1999). Health psychology: Mapping biobehavioral contributions to health and illness. *Annual Review of Psychology, 50,* 137–163.

Baumeister, A. A., & Francis, J. L. (2002). Historical development of the dopamine hypothesis of schizophrenia. *Journal of the History of the Neurosciences, 11,* 265–277.

Baumeister, R. (1991). *Meanings of life.* New York: Guilford Press.

Baumeister, R. F. (1991). *Escaping the self.* New York: Basic Books.

Baumeister, R. F. (1998). The self. In D. T. Gilbert & S. T. Fiske (Eds.), *The handbook of social psychology* (Vol. 2, pp. 680-740). New York: McGraw-Hill.

Baumeister, R. F. (1984). Choking under pressure: Self-consciousness and paradoxical effects of incentives on skillful performance. *Journal of Personality and Social Psychology, 46,* 610–620.

Baumeister, R. F., & Bratlavsky, E. (1999). Passion, intimacy, and time: Passionate love as a function of change in intimacy. *Personality and Social Psychology Review, 3,* 49–67.

Baumeister, R. F., & Leary, M. R. (1995). The need to belong: Desire for interpersonal attachments as a fundamental human motive. *Psychological Bulletin, 117,* 497–529.

Baumeister, R. F., Smart, L., & Boden, J. M. (1996). Relation of threatened egotism to violence and aggression: The dark side of high self-esteem. *Psychological Review, 103,* 5–33.

Baumeister, R. F., & Tice, D. M. (1990). Anxiety and social exclusion. *Journal of Social and Clinical Psychology, 9,* 165-195.

Baumeister, R. J. (1998). The self. In D.T. Gilbert, S. T. Fiske, & G. Lindzey (Eds.), *The handbook of social psychology* (Vol. 2, 4th ed., pp. 680–740). Boston, MA: McGraw-Hill.

Baumrind, D. (1967). Child care practices anteceding three patterns of preschool behavior. *Genetic Psychology Monographs, 75,* 43–88.

Baumrind, D. (1971). Current patterns of parental authority. *Developmental Psychology Monograph, 4,* 1–103.

Baumrind, D. (1987). A developmental perspective on adolescent risk taking in contemporary America. *New Directions for Child Development, 37,* 93–125.

Baumrind, D. (1991). The influence of parenting style on adolescent competence and substance use. *Journal of Early Adolescence, 11,* 56–95.

Bechara, A., Tranel, D., Damasio, H., Adolphs, R., Rockland, C., & Damasio, A. (1995). Double dissociation of conditioning and declarative knowledge relative to the amygdala and hippocampus in humans. *Science, 29,* 1115–1118.

Beck, A. (1985). *Anxiety disorders and phobias: A cognitive perspective.* New York: Basic Books.

Beck, A. (1989). *Cognitive therapy in clinical practice: An illustrative casebook.* New York: Routledge.

Beck, A. (1991). Cognitive therapy: A 30-year retrospective. *American Psychologist, 46,* 368–375.

Beck, A. (1992). Cognitive therapy: A 30 year retrospective. In J. Cottraux, P. Legeron, et al. (Eds.), *Which psychotherapies in year 2000? Annual series of European research in behavior therapy.* (Vol. 6, pp. 13–28). Amsterdam, The Netherlands: Swets & Zeitlinger.

Beck, A. T. (1976). *Cognitive therapy and the emotional disorders.* New York: International Universities Press.

Beck, A. T. (1993). Cognitive therapy: Past, present, and future. *Journal of Consulting and Clinical Psychology, 61,* 194–198.

Becker, E. (1973). *The denial of death.* New York: Free Press.

Becker, U., Deis, A., Sorensen, T. I., Gronbaek, M., Borch-Johnsen, K., Muller, C. F., Schnohr, P., & Jensen, G. (1996). Prediction of risk of liver disease by alcohol intake, sex, and age: A prospective population study. *Hepatology, 23,* 1025–1029.

Beckman, H. B., & Frankel, R. M. (1984). The effect of physician behavior on the collection of data. *Annals of Internal Medicine, 101,* 692–696.

Beckwith, J., Geller, L., & Sarkar, S. (1991). Sources of human psychological differences: The Minnesota Study of Twins Reared Apart: Comment. *Science, 252,* 191.

Bee, H. (1982). Prediction of IQ and language skill from perinatal status, child performance, family characteristics, and mother-infant interaction. *Child Development, 53,* 1134–1156.

Bekesy, G. von. (1959). Synchronism of neural discharges and their demultiplication in pitch perception on the skin and in learning. *Journal of the Acoustical Society of America, 31,* 338–349.

Bekesy, G. von. (1960). *Experiments in hearing.* New York: McGraw-Hill.

Bekesy, G. von, & Rosenblith, W. A. (1951). The mechanical properties of the ear. In S. S. Stevens (Ed.), *Handbook of experimental psychology.* New York: John Wiley.

Belar, C. D., McIntyre, T. M., & Matarazzo, J. D. (2003). Health psychology. In D. K. Freedheim (Ed.), *Handbook of psychology: History of psychology* (Vol. 1). Hoboken, NJ: John Wiley & Sons.

Bell, A. J., & Cook, H. (1998). Empirical evidence for a compensatory relationship between dream content and repression. *Psychoanalytic Psychology, 15,* 154–163.

Bell, A. P., Weinberg, M. S., & Hammersmith, S.

(1981). *Sexual preference: Its development in men and women.* Bloomington: University of Indiana Press.

Bell, M., Billington, R., Cicchetti, D., & Gibbons, J. (1998). Do object relations deficits distinguish BPD from other diagnostic groups? *Journal of Clinical Psychology, 44,* 511–516.

Bell, R. M. (1985). *Holy anorexia.* Chicago: University of Chicago Press.

Bell, R. Q. (1968). A reinterpretation of the direction of effects in studies of socialization. *Psychological Review, 75,* 71–85.

Bellack, L., Hurvich, M., & Geldman, H. (1973). *Ego functions in schizophrenics, neurotics, and normals.* New York: John Wiley.

Bellivier, F., Leboyer, M., Courtet, P., Buresi, C., Belloc, N. D., & Breslow, L. (1972). Relationship of physical health status and family practices. *Preventive Medicine, 1,* 409–421.

Belsky, J., Campbell, S. B., Conn, J. F., & Moore, G. (1996). Instability of infant-parent attachment security. *Developmental Psychology, 32,* 921-924.

Belsky, J., & Hsieh, K. (1998). Patterns of marital change during the early childhood years: Parent personality, coparenting, and division-of-labor correlates. *Journal of Family Psychology, 12,* 511–528.

Belsky, J., & Isabella, R. (1988). Maternal, infant, and social-contextual determinants of attachment security. In J. Belsky & T. Nezworsky (Eds.), *Clinical implications of attachment* (pp. 41–94). Hillsdale, NJ: Lawrence Erlbaum.

Belsky, J., & Pensky, E. (1988). Marital change across the transition to parenthood. *Marriage and Family Review, 12,* 133–156.

Bem, D. J. (1967). Self perception: An alternative interpretation of cognitive dissonance phenomena. *Psychological Review, 74,* 183–200.

Bem, D. J. (1972). Self-perception theory. In L. Berkowitz (Ed.), *Advances in experimental social psychology* (Vol. 6). New York: Academic Press.

Bem, D. J., & Allen, A. (1974). On predicting some of the people some of the time: The search for cross-situational consistencies in behavior. *Psychological Review, 81,* 506–520.

Bem, S. L. (1983). Gender schema theory and its implications for child development: Raising gender-aschematic children in a gender-schematic society. *Signs, Journal of Women in Culture and Society, 8,* 354–364.

Bem, S. L. (1985). Androgyny and gender schema theory: A conceptual and empirical integration. In T. B. Sonderegger (Ed.), *Nebraska symposium on motivation: Psychology and gender* (Vol. 32). Lincoln: University of Nebraska Press.

Bemporad, J. R. (1996). Self-starvation through the ages: Reflections on the pre-history of anorexia nervosa. *International Journal of Eating Disorders, 19,* 217–237.

Benasich, A. A., & Brooks-Gunn, J. (1996). Maternal attitudes and knowledge of child-rearing: Associations with family and child outcomes. *Child Development, 67,* 1186–1205.

Benbow, C., & Stanley, J. (1983). Sex differences in mathematical reasoning ability: More facts. *Science, 222,* 1029–1030.

Bendersky, M., & Lewis, M. (1998). Arousal modulation in cocaine-exposed infants. *Developmental Psychology, 34,* 555–564.

Benedict, R. (1934). *Patterns of culture.* New York: Mentor/New American Library.

Benet-Martinez, V., & John, O. P. (1998). Los Cinco Grandes across cultures and ethnic groups: Multitrait-multimethod analyses of the Big Five in Spanish and English. *Journal of Personality & Social Psychology, 75,* 729–750.

Benet-Martinez, V., & Waller, J. G. (1997). Further evidence for the cross-cultural generality of the Big Seven factor model: Indigenous and imported Spanish personality constructs. *Journal of Personality, 65,* 567–598.

Bennett, K. K., & Elliott, M. (2002). Explanatory style and health: Mechanisms linking pessimism to illness. *Journal of Applied Social Pscyhology, 32,* 1508–1526.

Benotsch, E. G., Brailey, K., Vasterling, J. J., Uddo, M., Constans, J. I., & Sutker, P. B. (2000). War zone stress, personal and environmental resources, and PTSD symptoms in Gulf War veterans: A longitudinal perspective. *Journal of Abnormal Psychology, 109,* 205–213.

Berg, C. (1992). Perspectives for viewing intellectual development throughout the life course. In R. J. Sternberg & C. A. Berg (Eds.), *Intellectual development* (pp. 1–15). New York: Cambridge University Press.

Berg, F. M. (1999). Health risks associated with weight loss and obesity treatment programs. *Journal of Social Issues, 55,* 277–297.

Berger, R. J., & Phillips, N. H. (1995). Energy conservation and sleep. *Behavioural Brain Research, 69,* 65–73.

Berglas, S., & Baumeister, R. F. (1993). *Your own worst enemy.* New York: Basic Books.

Berkman, L. F. (1995). The role of social relations in health promotion. *Psychosomatic Medicine, 57,* 245–254.

Berkowitz, L. (1989). Frustration-aggression hypothesis: Examination and reformulation. *Psychological Bulletin, 106,* 59–73.

Berman, P. W., & Pedersen, F. A. (1987). Research on men's transitions to parenthood: An integrative discussion. In P. W. Berman & F. A. Pederson (Eds.), *Men's transitions to parenthood: Longitudinal studies of early family experience.* Hillsdale, NJ: Lawrence Erlbaum.

Bermond, B., Nieuwenhuyse, B., Fasotti, L., & Schuerman, J. (1991). Spinal cord lesions, peripheral feedback, and intensities of emotional feelings. *Cognition & Emotion, 5,* 201–220.

Bernhardt, P. C. (1997). Influences of serotonin and testosterone in aggression and dominance: Convergence with social psychology. *Current Directions in Psychological Science, 6,* 44–48.

Bernstein, I. L. (1991). Aversion conditioning in response to cancer and cancer treatment. *Clinical Psychology Review, 11,* 185–191.

Berridge, K., & Zajonc, R. (1991). Hypothalamic cooling effects elicit eating: Differential effects on motivation and pleasure. *Psychological Science, 2,* 184–189.

Berridge, K. C. (1996). Food reward: Brain sub-

strates of wanting and liking. Special Issue: Society for the Study of Ingestive Behavior, Second Independent Meeting. *Neuroscience & Biobehavioral Reviews, 20,* 1–25.

Berry, J. W. (1979). A cultural ecology of social behavior. In L. Berkowitz (Ed.), *Advances in experimental social psychology* (Vol. 12). New York: Academic Press.

Berry, J. W. (1989). Psychology of acculturation. In J. Berman (Ed.), *Nebraska Symposium on Motivation,* (Vol. 37, pp. 201–234). Lincoln: University of Nebraska Press.

Berry, J. W., & Bennet, J. A. (1992). Cree conceptions of cognitive competence. *International Journal of Psychology, 27,* 73–88.

Berry, J. W., Dasen, P. R., Saraswathi, T. S. (Eds.). (1997). *Handbook of cross-cultural psychology: Vol. 2. Basic processes and human development* (2nd ed.). Boston, MA: Allyn & Bacon.

Berry, J. W., & Irvine, S. H. (1986). Bricolage: Savages do it daily. In R. J. Sternberg & R. K. Wagner (Eds.), *Practical intelligence: Nature and origins of competence in the everyday world* (pp. 271–303). New York: Cambridge University Press.

Berry, J. W., Poortinga, Y. H., Segall, M. H., & Dasen, P. R. (1992). *Cross-cultural psychology: Research and applications.* New York: Cambridge University Press.

Berscheid, E., Dion, K., Walster, E., & Walster, G. (1971). Physical attractiveness and dating choice: A test of the matching hypothesis. *Journal of Experimental Social Psychology, 7,* 173–189.

Berscheid, E., & Reis, H. T. (1998). Attraction and close relationships. In D. T. Gilbert, S. T. Fiske, et al. (Eds.), *The handbook of social psychology* (Vol. 2, 4th ed., pp. 193–281). Boston, MA: McGraw-Hill.

Bersoff, D. N. (Ed.). (1999). *Ethical conflicts in psychology* (2nd ed.). Washington, DC: American Psychological Association.

Bertenthal, B. I. (1996). Origins and early development of perception, action, and representation. *Annual Review of Psychology, 47,* 431–459.

Bertenthal, B. I., & Clifton, R. K. (1998). Perception and action. In W. Damon (Ed. in Chief) and N. Eisenberg (Vol. Ed.), *Handbook of child psychology* (Vol. 2, (pp. 51–102). New York: John Wiley.

Bertolino, A., Esposito, G., Callicott, J. H., Mattay, V. S., Van Horn, J. D., Frank, J. A., Berman, K. F., & Weinberger, D. R. (2000). Specific relationship between prefrontal neuronal N-acetylaspartate and activation of the working memory cortical network in schizophrenia. *American Journal of Psychiatry, 157,* 26–33.

Best, D. L. (1993). Inducing children to generate mnemonic organizational strategies: An examination of long-term retention and materials. *Developmental Psychology, 29,* 324–336.

Best, D. L., & Williams, J. E. (1998). Masculinity and femininity in the self and ideal self descriptions of university students in 14 countries. In G. Hofstede (Ed.), *Masculinity and femininity: The taboo dimension of national cultures. Cross-cultural psychology series* (Vol. 3, pp. 106–116). Thousand Oaks, CA: Sage Publications, Inc.

Best, D. L., Williams, J. E., Cloud, J. M., Davis, S. W., Robertson, L. S., Edwards, J. R., Giles, H., & Fowles, J. (1977). Development of sex trait stereotypes among young children in the United States, England, and Ireland. *Child Development, 48,* 1375–1384.

Bettner, B. L., & Lew, A. (2000). Talking to parents about hitting. *Journal of Individual Psychology, 56,* 110–114.

Beufils, B., Samolyk, D., et al. (1998). Association between the tryptophan hydroxylase gene and manic-depressive illness. *Archives of General Psychiatry, 55,* 33–37.

Beutler, L. E. (1991). Have all won and must all have prizes? Revisiting Luborsky et al's verdict. *Journal of Consulting and Clinical Psychology, 59,* 226–232.

Beutler, L. E., & Malik, M. L. (2002). *Rethinking the DSM: A psychological perspective.* Washington, DC: American Psychological Association.

Beutler, L. E., Williams, R. E., Wakefield, P. J., & Entwistle, S. R. (1995). Bridging scientist and practitioner perspectives in clinical psychology. *American Psychologist, 50,* 984–994.

Beyene, Y. (1986). Cultural significance and physiological manifestations of menopause. A biocultural analysis. *Culture, Medicine, & Psychiatry, 10,* 47–71.

Beyer, C., Caba, M., Banas, C., & Komisaruk, B. R. (1991). Vasoactive intestinal polypeptide (VIP) potentiates the behavior effect of substance P intrathecal administration. *Pharmacology, Biochemistry, and Behavior, 39,* 695–698.

Bickel, W. K., Green, L., & Vuchinich, R. E. (1995). Behavioral economics. Special Issue: Behavioral economics. *Journal of the Experimental Analysis of Behavior, 64,* 257–262.

Bickman, L., & Zarantonello, M. (1978). The effects of deception and level of obedience on subjects' ratings of the Milgram study. *Personality and Social Psychology Bulletin, 4,* 81–85.

Bidell, T. R., & Fischer, K. W. (1992). Beyond the stage debate: Action, structure, and variability in Piagetian theory and research. In R. Sternberg & C. Berg (Eds.), *Intellectual development* (pp. 100–140). Cambridge: Cambridge University Press.

Bidell, T. R., & Fischer, K. W. (1997). Between nature and nurture: The role of human agency in the epigenesist of intelligence. In R. J. Sternberg & E. L. Grigorenko (Eds.), *Intelligence, heredity, and environment* (pp. 193-242). New York: Cambridge University Press.

Bidell, T. R., & Fischer, K. W. (2000). The role of cognitive structure in the development of behavioral control: A dynamic skills approach. In W. J. Perrig & A. Grob (Eds.). *Control of human behavior, mental processes, and consciousness: Essays in honor of the 60th birthday of August Flammer* (pp. 183–201). Mahwah, NJ: Lawrence Erlbaum.

Biederman, I. (1987). Recognition by components: A theory of human image understanding. *Psychological Review, 94,* 115–147.

Biederman, I. (1990). Higher-level vision. In D. N. Osherson, S. M. Kosslyn, et al. (Eds.), *Visual cognition and action: An invitation to cognitive science* (Vol. 2, pp. 41–72). Cambridge, MA: MIT Press.

Biederman, I., Glass, A. L., & Stacy, E. W., Jr. (1973). Searching for objects in real-world scenes. *Journal of Exerimental Psychology, 97,* 22–27.

Biederman, I., Mezzanotte, R. J., & Rabinowitz, J. C. (1982). Scene perception: Detecting and judging objects undergoing relational violations. *Cognitive Psychology, 14,* 143–177.

Biederman, I., Mezzanotte, R. J., Rabinowitz, J. C., Francolini, C. M., & Plude, D. (1981). Detecting the unexpected in photointerpretation. *Human Factors, 23,* 153–164.

Biederman, J., Faraone, S., Milberger, S., Guite, J., Mick, E., Chen, L., et al. (1996). A prospective 4-year follow-up study of attention-deficit hyperactivity and related disorders. *Archives of General Psychiatry, 53,* 437–446.

Biederman, J., Mick, E., & Faraone, S. V. (2000). Age-dependent decline of symptoms of attention deficit hyperactivity disorder: Impact of remission definition and symptom type. *American Journal of Psychiatry, 157,* 816–818.

Biederman, J., Milberger, S., Faraone, S. V., Kiely, K., Guite, J., Mick, E., et al. (1995). Family-environment risk factors for attention-deficit hyperactivity disorder: A test of Rutter's indicators of adversity. *Archives of General Psychiatry, 52,* 464–470.

Bieling, P. J., Beck, A. T., & Brown, G. K. (2000). The Sociotropy-Autonomy Scale: Structure and implications. *Cognitive Therapy and Research, 24,* 763–780.

Bierer, L. M., Hof, P. R., Purohit, D. P., Carlin, L., et al. (1995). Neocortical neurofibrillary tangles correlate with dementia severity in Alzheimer's disease. *Archives of Neurology, 52,* 81–88.

Bierhoff, H. W., Klein, R., & Kramp, P. (1991). Evidence for the altruistic personality from data on accident research. *Journal of Personality, 59,* 263–280.

Bieri, J. (1966). Cognitive complexity and personality development. In O. J. Jarvey (Ed.), *Experience, structure and adaptability.*

Bierut, L. J., Dinwiddie, S. H., Begleiter, H., Crowe, R. R, Hesselbrock, V., Nurnberger, J. I., Jr., Porjesz, B., Schuckit, M. A., & Reich, T. (1998). Familial transmission of substance dependence: Alcohol, marijuana, cocaine, and habitual smoking: A report from the collaborative study on the genetics of alcoholism. *Archives of General Psychiatry, 55,* 982–988.

Biesanz, J., West, S. G., & Graziano, W. (1998). Moderators of self-other agreement: Reconsidering temporal stability in personality. *Journal of Personality and Social Psychology, 75,* 467–477.

Binder, J. L., Strupp, H. H., & Henry, W. P. (1995). Psychodynamic therapies in practice: Time-limited dynamic psychotherapy. In M. B. Bongar and L. E. Beutler (Eds.), *Comprehensive textbook of psychotherapy: Theory and practice. Oxford textbooks in clinical psychology* (Vol. 1, pp. 48–63). New York: Oxford University Press.

Binet, A., & Simon, T. (1908). Le developpement de l'intelligence chez les enfants. *L'Annee Psychologique, 14,* 1–94.

Birnbaum, D. W. (1983). Preschooler's stereotypes about sex differences in emotionality: A reaffirmation. *Journal of Genetic Psychology, 143,* 139–140.

Bishop, J. A., & Cook, L. M. (1975). Moths, melanism and clean air. *Scientific American, 232,* 90–99.

Bizer, G. Y., & Krosnick, J. A. (2001). Exploring the structure of strength-related attitude features: The relation between attitude importance and attitude accessibility. *Journal of Personality and Social Psychology, 81,* 566–586.

Bjork, E. L., & Bjork, R. A. (1996). Continuing influences of to-be-forgotten information. *Consequences & Cognition: An International Journal, 5,* 176–196.

Bjork, E. L., Bjork, R. A., & Anderson, M. C. (1998). Varieties of goal-directed forgetting. In J. M. Golding & C. M. MacLeod (Eds.), *Intentional forgetting: Interdisciplinary approaches* (pp. 103-137). Mahwah, NJ: Lawrence Erlbaum Associates.

Bjorklund, A., & Gage, F. (1985). Neural grafting of neutrodegenerative diseases in animal models. *Annals of the New York Academy of Sciences, 457,* 53–81.

Bjorklund, D. F., & Pellegrini, A. D. (2001). *The origins of human nature: Evolutionary developmental psychology.* Washington, DC: American Psychological Association.

Black, D. W., Goldstein, R. B., & Mason, E. E. (1992). Prevalence of mental disorder in 88 morbidly obese bariatric clinic patients. *American Journal of Psychiatry, 149,* 227–234.

Black, M. M., Dubowitz, H., & Starr, R. H. (1999). African American fathers in low income, urban families: Development, behavior, and home environment of their three-year-old children. *Child Development, 70,* 967–978.

Blair, I. V., & Banaji, M. R. (1996). Automatic and controlled processes in stereotype priming. *Journal of Personality & Social Psychology, 70,* 1142–1163.

Blake, R., & Hirsch, H. V. B. (1975). Deficits in binocular depth perception in cats after alternating monocular deprivation. *Science, 190,* 1114–1116.

Blake, R., & Mouton, J. (1964). *The managerial grid.* Houston, TX: Gulf.

Blakemore, C., & Cooper, G. F. (1970). Development of the brain depends on the visual environment. *Nature, 228,* 477–478.

Blampied, N. M. (1999). A legacy neglected: Restating the case for single-case research in cognitive- behaviour therapy. *Behaviour Change, 16,* 89–104.

Blanchard-Fields, F., & Chen, Y. (1996). Adaptive cognition and aging. *American Behavioral Scientist, 39,* 231–248.

Blandt, C. W. (2002). Towards a psychodynamic understanding of binge drinking in first-semester college freshmen. *Journal of College Student Development, 43,* 775–791.

Blanton, C. K. (2000)."They cannot master abstractions, but they can often be made efficient workers": Race and class in the intelligence testing of Mexican Americans and African Americans in Texas during the 1920s. *Social Science Quarterly, 81,* 1014–1026.

Blascovich, J., & Mendes, W. B. (2000). Feeling and thinking: The role of affect in social cognition. In J. P. Forges, et al. (Eds.), *Challenge and threat appraisals: The role of affective cues.* New York: Cambridge University Press.

Blasko, D. G. (1999). Only the tip of the iceberg: Who understands what about metaphors. *Journal of Pragmatics, 31,* 1675–1683.

Blass, T. (1991). Understanding behavior in the Milgram obedience experiment: The role of personality, situations, and their interactions. *Journal of Personality and Social Psychology, 60,* 398–413.

Blass, T. (2000). *Obedience to authority: Current perspectives on the Milgram paradigm.* Mahwah, NJ: Lawrence Erlbaum.

Blatt, S., Ford, R., Berman, W., Cook, B., Cramer, P., & Robins, C. E. (1994). *Therapeutic change: An object relations perspective.* New York: Plenum Press.

Blatt, S., & Zuroff, D. (1992). Interpersonal relatedness and self-definition: Two prototypes for depression. *Clinical Psychology Review, 12,* 527–562.

Blatt, S. J., Auerbach, J. S., & Levy, K. N. (1997). Mental representations in personality development, psychopathology, and the therapeutic process. *Review of General Psychology, 1,* 351–374.

Blatt, S. J., & Homann, E. (1992). Parent child interaction in the etiology of dependent and self-critical depression. *Clinical Psychology Review, 12,* 47–91.

Blaustein, A. R., & Waldman, B. (1992). Kin recognition in anuran amphibians. *Animal Behavior, 44,* 207–221.

Bliss, T. V., & Lomo, T. (1973). Long-lasting potentiation of synaptic transmission in the dentate area of the anaesthetized rabbit following stimulation of the perforant path. *Journal of Physiology, 232,* 331–356.

Block, J. (1995). A contrarian view of the five-factor approach to personality description. *Psychological Bulletin, 117,* 187–215.

Block, J., Block, J. H., & Keyes, S. (1988). Longitudinally foretelling drug usage in adolescence: Early childhood personality and environmental precursors. *Child Development, 59,* 336–355.

Block, J., & Kremen, A. (1996). IQ and ego-resiliency: Conceptual and empirical connections and separateness. *Journal of Personality and Social Psychology, 70,* 349–361.

Block, J. H. (1976). Issues, problems, and pitfalls in assessing sex differences: A critical review of "The Psychology of Sex Differences." *Merrill Palmer Quarterly, 22,* 283–308.

Block, J. H. (1978). Another look at sex differentiation in the socialization behaviors of mothers and fathers. In J. Sherman & F. L. Denmark (Eds.), *The psychology of women: Future directions of research.* New York: Psychological Dimensions.

Block, J. H., Gjerde, P., & Block, J. H. (1991). Personality antecedents of depressive tendencies in 18-year-olds: A prospective study. *Journal of Personality and Social Psychology, 60,* 726–738.

Blokland, A. (1997). Acetylcholine: A neurotransmitter for learning and memory? *Brain Research Reviews, 21,* 285–300.

Bloom, L. (1993). *The transition from infancy to language: Acquiring the power of expression.* New York: Cambridge University Press.

Blos, P. (1962). *On adolescence: A psychoanalytic interpretation.* New York: Free Press.

Blos, P. (1967). The second individuation process of adolescence. *Psychoanalytic study of the Child, 22,* 162–186.

Blowers, G. H., & O'Connor, K. P. (1996). *Personal construct psychology in the clinical context.* Ottawa, Canada: University of Ottawa Press.

Blum, G. S. (1954). An experimental reunion of psychoanalytic theory with perceptual vigilance and defense. *Journal of Abnormal and Social Psychology, 49,* 94–98.

Blurton-Jones, N., & Konner, M. (1976). !Kung knowledge of animal behavior. In R. B. Lee & I. De Vore (Eds.), *Kalahari hunter-gatherers* (pp. 326–348). Cambridge, MA: Harvard University Press.

Boake, C. (2002). From the Binet-Simon to the Wechsler-Bellevue: Tracing the history of intelligence testing. *Journal of Clinical and Experimental Neuropsychology, 24,* 383–405.

Boccaccio (1349/1903). *Decameron.* Trans. J. M. Rigg. Publisher.

Bock, P. K. (2001). Culture and personality revisited. *American Behavioral Scientist, 44,* 32–40.

Boden, J. M., & Baumeister, R. F. (1997). Repressive coping: Distraction using pleasant thoughts and memories. *Journal of Personality and Social Psychology, 73,* 45–62.

Bodenhausen, G. (1993). Emotions, arousal, and stereotypic judgments: A heuristic model of affect and stereotyping. In D. Mackie & D. Hamilton (Eds.), *Affect, cognition, and stereotyping: Interactive processes in group perception.* New York: Academic Press.

Boesch, E. E. (1982). Ritual und Psychotherapie. *Zeitschrift fuer Klinische Psychologie und Psychotherapie, 30,* 214–234.

Bogdan, R. J. (2000). Minding minds: Evolving a reflexive mind by interpreting others. Cambridge, MA: The MIT Press.

Bogen, J. E. (1995). On the neurophysiology of consciousness: I. An overview. *Consciousness & Cognition: An International Journal, 4,* 52–62.

Bolger, K. E., Patterson, C. J., & Kupersmidt, J. B. (1998). Peer relationships and self-esteem among children who have been maltreated. *Child Development, l69,* 1171–1197.

Bolger, N., Foster, M., Vinokur, A. D., & Ng, R. (1996). Close relationships and adjustment to a life crisis: The case of breast cancer. *Journal of Personality and Social Psychology, 70,* 283–294.

Bolton, W., & Oatley, K. (1987). A longitudinal study of social support and depression in unemployed men. *Psychological Medicine, 17,* 453-460.

Bond, R., & Smith, P. B. (1996). Culture and conformity: A meta-analysis of studies using Asch's (1952b, 1956) line judgment task. *Psychological Bulletin, 119,* 111–137.

Bonebakker, A. E., Bonke, B., Klein, J., & Wolters, G. (1996). Information processing during general anesthesia: Evidence for unconscious memory. *Memory & Cognition, 24,* 766–776.

Bonvillian, J. D. (1999). Sign language development. In M. Barrett (Ed.), *The development of language.* London: UCL Press.

Borbély, A. (1986). *Secrets of sleep.* New York: Basic Books.

Borden, V. M. H., & Levinger, G. (1991). Interpersonal transformations in intimate relationships. In W. H. Jones, D. Perlman, et al. (Eds.), *Advances in personal relationships: A research annual: Vol. 2. Advances in personal relationships* (pp. 35–56). London: Jessica Kingsley Publishers.

Boring, E. G. (1930). A new ambiguous figure. *American Journal of Psychology, 42,* 444–445.

Borkovec, T. D., & Costello, E. (1993). Efficacy of applied relaxation and cognitive-behavioral therapy in the treatment of generalized anxiety disorder. *Journal of Consulting and Clinical Psychology, 61,* 611–619.

Borkovec, T. D., & Castonguay, L. G. (1998). What is the scientific meaning of empirically supported therapy? *Journal of Consulting & Clinical Psychology, 66,* 136–142.

Bornstein, M. H. (1989). Sensitive periods in development: Structural characteristics and causal interpretations. *Psychological Bulletin, 105,* 179–197.

Bornstein, R. F., & Pittman, T. S. (Eds.). (1992). *Perception without awareness: Cognitive, clinical, and social perspectives.* New York: Guilford Press.

Borod, J. (1992). Interhemispheric and intrahemispheric control of emotion: A focus on unilateral brain damage. *Journal of Consulting and Clinical Psychology, 60,* 339–348.

Bors, D. A., & Forrin, B. (1996). The effects of post-weaning environment, biological dam, and nursing dam on feeding neophobia, open field activity, and learning. *Canadian Journal of Experimental Psychology, 50,* 197–204.

Bosson, J. K., & Swann, W. B., Jr. (1999). Self-liking, self-competence, and the quest for self-verification. *Personality and Social Psychology Bulletin, 25,* 1230–1241.

Bosworth, H. B., & Schaie, K. W. (1999). Survival effects in cognitive function, cognitive style and sociodemographic variables in the Seattle longitudinal study. *Experimental Aging Research, 25,* 121–139.

Boszormenyi, N. J., & Spark, G. M. (1973). *Invisible loyalties: Reciprocity in intergenerational family therapy.* New York: Harper & Row.

Bouchard, C. (1989). Genetic factors in obesity. *Medical Clinics of North America, 73,* 67–81.

Bouchard, T. J., Lykken, D. T., McGue, M., &

Segal, N. L. (1990). Sources of human psychological differences: The Minnesota study of twins reared apart. *Science, 250,* 223–228.

Bouchard, T. J., & McGue, M. (1981). Familial studies of intelligence: A review. *Science, 212,* 1055-1059.

Bourguignon, E. (1979). *Psychological anthropology: An introduction to human nature and cultural differences.* New York: Holt, Rinehart & Winston.

Bovasso, G. B., Eaton, W. W., & Armenian, H. K. (1999). The long-term outcomes of mental health treatment in a population-based study. *Journal of Consulting and Clinical Psychology, 67,* 529–538.

Bovbjerg, D., Redd, W. H., Maier, L. A., Holland, J. C., Leske, L. M., Niedzwiecki, D., Rubin, S. C., & Herkes, T. B. (1990). Anticipatory immune suppression and nausea in women receiving cyclic chemotherapy for ovarian cancer. *Journal of Consulting and Clinical Psychology, 58,* 153–157.

Bowd, A. D. (1990). A decade of animal research in psychology: Room for consensus? *Canadian Psychology, 31,* 74–82.

Bowden, S. C. (1990). Separating cognitive impairment in neurologically asymptomatic alcoholism from Wernicke-Korsakoff syndrome: Is the neuropsychological distinction justified? *Psychological Bulletin, 107,* 355–366.

Bowen, M. (1978). *Family therapy in clinical practice.* New York: Jason Aronson.

Bowen, M. (1991). Alcoholism as viewed through family systems theory and family psychotherapy. *Family Dynamics of Addiction Quarterly, 1,* 94–102.

Bower, G. (1975). Cognitive psychology: an introduction. In W. K. Estes (Ed.), *Handbook of learning and cognitive processes: Vol. 1. Introduction to concepts and Issues* (pp. 25–80). Hillsdale, NJ: Lawrence Erlbaum.

Bower, G. H. (1970). Analysis of a mnemonic device. *American Scientist, 58,* 496–510.

Bower, G. H. (1981). Mood and memory. *American Psychologist, 36,* 129–148.

Bower, G. H. (1989). In search of mood-dependent retrieval. *Journal of Social Behavior & Personality, 4,* 121–156.

Bower, T. G. R. (1971). The object in the world of the infant. *Scientific American, 225,* 30–38.

Bower, T. G. R. (1982). *Development in infancy* (2nd ed.). San Francisco: Freeman.

Bowers, J. S., & Schacter, D. L. (1990). Implicit memory and test awareness. *Journal of Experimental Psychology: Learning, Memory, and Cognition, 16,* 404–416.

Bowers, K. (1976). *Hypnosis for the seriously curious.* Monterey, CA: Brooks/Cole Publishing Co.

Bowers, K., Regenr, G., Balthazard, C., & Parker, K. (1990). Intuition in the context of discovery. *Cognitive Psychology, 22,* 72–110.

Bowlby, J. (1969). *Attachment and loss: Vol. I. Attachment.* New York: Basic Books.

Bowlby, J. (1973). *Separation, attachment, and loss* (Vol. 2). New York: Basic Books.

Bowlby, J. (1982). Attachment and loss: Retrospect and prospect. *American Journal of Orthopsychiatry, 52,* 664–678.

Boysen, S. T., & Himes, G. T. (1999). Current issues and emerging theories in animal cognition. *Annual Review of Psychology, 50,* 683–705.

Bradley, C. L., & Marcia, J. E. (1998). Generativity- stagnation: A five-category model. *Journal of Personality, 66,* 39–64.

Brainerd, C. J. (1996). Piaget: A centennial celebration. *Psychological Science, 7,* 191–195.

Brandimonte, M., Einstein, G. O., & McDaniel, M. A. (Eds.). (1996). *Prospective memory: Theory and applications.* Mahwah: Lawrence Erlbaum.

Bransford, J. D., Barclay, J. R., & Franks, J. J. (1972). Sentence memory: A constructive versus interpretive approach. *Cognitive Psychology, 3,* 193-209.

Braun, A. R., Balkin, T. J., Wesensten, N. J., Gwadry, F., Carson, R. E., Varga, M., et al. (1998). Dissociated pattern of activity in visual cortices and their projections during human rapid movement sleep. *Science, 279,* 91–95.

Braun, S. (1996). New experiments underscore warnings on maternal drinking. *Science, 273,* 738–739.

Braungart, J., Plomin, R., DeFries, J., & Fulker, D. (1992). Genetic influence on tester-rated infant temperament as assessed by Bayley's infant behavior record: Nonadoptive and adoptive siblings and twins. *Developmental Psychology, 28,* 40–47.

Bray, G. A. (1998). *Contemporary diagnosis and management of obesity.* Newton, PA: Handbooks in Health Care.

Bray, G. A., & Tartaglia, L. A. (2000). Medicinal strategies in the treatment of obesity. *Nature, 404,* 672–677.

Brazelton, T. B. (1972). Implications of infant development among the Mayan Indians of Mexico. *Human Development, 15,* 90–111.

Breer, H., Wanner, I., & Strogmann, J. (1996). Molecular genetics of mammalian olfaction. *Behavior Genetics, 26,* 209–219.

Breland, K., & Breland, M. (1961). The misbehavior of organisms. *American Psychologist, 16,* 681–684.

Bremner, J. D. (1998). Neuroimaging of posttraumatic stress disorder. *Psychiatric Annals, 28,* 445–450.

Bremner, J. D. (1999). Does stress damage the brain? *Biological Psychiatry, 45,* 797–805.

Brennan, K. A., Clark, C. L., & Shaver, P. R. (1998). Self-report measurement of adult attachment: An integrative overview. In J. A. Simpson & W. S. Rholes (Eds.), *Attachment theory and close relationships* (pp. 46–76). New York: Guilford Press.

Brennan, P. A., Grekin, E. R., & Mednick, S. A. (1999). Maternal smoking during pregnancy and adult male criminal outcomes. *Archives of General Psychiatry, 56,* 215–219.

Brenner, C. (1982). *The mind in conflict.* New York: International Universities Press.

Breslau, N., Chilcoat, H. D., Kessler, R. C., & Davis, G. C. (1999). Previous exposure to trauma and PTSD effects of subsequent trauma: Results from the Detroit Area Survey of Trauma. *American Journal of Psychiatry, 156,* 902–907.

Breslau, N., Davis, G. C., Andreski, P., Peterson, E. L., & Schultz, L. R. (1997). Sex differences in posttraumatic stress disorder. *Archives of General Psychiatry, 54,* 1044–1048.

Breslow, L., & Enstrom, J. E. (1980). Persistence of health habits and their relationship to mortality. *Preventive Medicine, 9,* 469–483.

Bretherton, I. (1990). Communication patterns, internal working models, and the intergenerational transmission of attachment relationships. *Infant Mental Health Journal, 11,* 237–257.

Breuer, K. (1985). Intentionality and perception in early infancy. *Human Development, 28,* 71–83.

Brewer, J. B., Zhao, Z., Desmond, J. E., Glover, G. H., & Gabrieli, J. D. E. (1998). Making memories: Brain activity predicts how well visual experience will be remembered. *Science, 281,* 1185–1187.

Brewer, M. B., & Brown, R. J. (1998). Intergroup relations. In D. T. Gilbert, S. T. Fiske, et al. (Eds.), *The handbook of social psychology* (Vol. 2, 4th ed., pp. 554–594). Boston, MA: McGraw-Hill.

Brewer, W. F., & Treyens, J. C. (1981). Role of schemata in memory for places. *Cognitive Psychology, 13,* 207–230.

Brewerton, T. D. (1995). Toward a unified theory of serotonin dysregulation in eating and related disorders. *Psychoneuroendocrinology, 20,* 561–590.

Brewin, C. R., Andrews, B., & Valentine, J. D. (2000). Meta-analysis of risk factors for posttraumatic stress disorder in trauma-exposed adults. *Journal of Consulting and Clinical Psychology, 68,* 748–766.

Briere, J., & Conte, J. R. (1993). Self-reported amnesia for abuse in adults molested as children. *Journal of Traumatic Stress, 6,* 21–31.

Brislin, R. M. (1986). The culture general assimilator: Preparation for various types of sojourns. Special issue: Theories and methods in cross-cultural orientation. *International Journal of Intercultural Relations, 10,* 215–234.

Brislin, R. W., & Keating, C. F. (1976). Cultural differences in the perception of a three-dimensional Ponzo illusion. *Journal of Cross-Cultural Psychology, 7,* 397–412.

Broadbent, D. E. (1958). The hidden preattentive processes. *American Psychologist, 32,* 109–118.

Brody, L., & Hall, J. (2000). Gender, emotion, and expression. In M. Lewis & J. Haviland-Jones (Eds.), *Handbook of emotions* (2nd ed., pp. 338–349). New York: Guilford Press.

Brody, L. R. (1999). *Gender, emotion, and the family.* Cambridge, MA: Harvard University Press.

Brody, L. R., Lovas, G. S., & Hay, D. H. (1995). Gender differences in anger and fear as a function of situational context. *Sex Roles, 32*(1–2), 47–78.

Brody, N. (1992). *Intelligence* (2nd ed.). San Diego, CA: Academic Press.

Bronfenbrenner, U. (1999). Environments in developmental perspective: Theoretical and operational models. In S. L. Friedman & T. D. Wachs (Eds.), *Measuring environment across the life span: Emerging methods and concepts* (pp. 3-28).

Washington, DC: American Psychological Association.

Broocks, A., Bandelow, A., Pekrun, G., George, A., Meyer, T., Bartmann, U., et al. (1998). Comparison of aerobic exercise, clomipramine, and placebo in the treatment of panic disorder. *American Journal of Psychiatry, 155,* 603–609.

Brookoff, D., O'Brien, K., Cook, C. S., & Thompson, T. D. (1997). Characteristics of participants in domestic violence. *Journal of the American Medical Association, 277,* 1369–1373.

Brooks-Gunn, J., Duncan, G., & Aber, L. (Eds.) (1997). *Neighborhood poverty: Context and consequences for children.* New York: Russell Sage Foundation.

Brosschot, J. F., & Janssen, E. (1998). Continuous monitoring of affective-autonomic response dissociation in repressors during negative emotional stimulation. *Personality and Individual Differences, 25,* 69–84.

Broughton, J. (1978). Development of concepts of self, mind, reality, and knowledge. *New Directions for Child Development, 1,* 75–100.

Brown, A., Bransford, J., Ferrara, R., & Campione, J. (1983). Learning, remembering, and understanding. In E. M. Markman & J. H. Flavell (Eds.), *Carmichael's manual of child psychology* (Vol. III). New York: John Wiley.

Brown, A. S., Cohen, P., Greenwald, S., & Susser, E. (2000a). Nonaffective psychosis after prenatal exposure to rubella. *American Journal of Psychiatry, 157,* 438–443.

Brown, A. S., van Os, J., Driessens, C., Hoek, H. W., & Susser, E. S. (2000b). Further evidence of relation between prenatal famine and major affective disorder. *American Journal of Psychiatry, 157,* 190–195.

Brown, G., Bhrolchain, M., & Harris, T. (1975). Social class and psychiatric disturbance among women in an urban poulation. *Sociology, 9,* 225–254.

Brown, G. W., Andrews, B., Harris, T. O., & Adler, Z. (1986). Social support, self-esteem, and depression. *Psychological Medicine, 16,* 813-831.

Brown, G. W., Birley, J. L., & Wing, J. K. (1972). Influence of family life on the course of schizophrenic disorders: A replication. *British Journal of Psychiatry, 121,* 241-258.

Brown, G. W., & Harris, T. O. (1978). *Social origins of depression: A study of psychiatric disorder in women.* New York: Free Press.

Brown, G. W., & Harris, T. O. (1989). Depression. In G. W. Brown & T. O. Harris (Eds.), *Life events and illnesses.* New York: Guilford Press.

Brown, G. W., Harris, T. O., & Hepworth, C. (1994). Life events and endogenous depression: A puzzle reexamined. *Archives of General Psychiatry, 51,* 525–534.

Brown, J., & Smart, S. A. (1991). The self and social conduct: Linking self-representations to prosocial behavior. *Journal of Personality and Social Psychology, 60,* 368–375.

Brown, J. B. (1991). Staying fit and staying well: Physical fitness as a moderator of life stress. *Journal of Personality and Social Psychology, 61,* 555–561.

Brown, N. O. (1959). *Life against death: The psychoanalytic meaning of history.* Middleton, CT: Wesleyan University Press.

Brown, P. K., & Wald, G. (1964). Visual pigments in single rods and cones in the human retina. *Science, 144,* 45–52.

Brown, R. (1973). *A first language: The early stages.* Cambridge, MA: Harvard University Press.

Brown, R., & Kulik, J. (1977). Flashbulb memories. *Cognition, 5,* 73-99.

Brown, R., & Fraser, C. (1963). The acquisition of syntax. In C. N. Cofer & B. Musgrave (Eds.), *Verbal behavior and learning: Problems and processes* (pp. 158–201). New York: McGraw-Hill.

Brown, R. W., Galanter, E., Hess, D., & Mandler, G. (1962). *New directions in psychology.* New York: Holt.

Brown, R. W., & McNeill, D. (1966). The tip-of-the- tongue phenomenon. *Journal of Verbal Learning and Verbal Behavior, 5,* 325–337.

Brown, S. L. (1985). Two adolescents at risk for schizophrenia: A family case study: Discussion. *International Journal of Family Therapy, 7,* 149–154.

Brown, T. A., Chorpita, B. F., & Barlow, D. H. (1998) Structural relationships among dimensions of the DSM-IV anxiety and mood disorders and dimensions of negative affect, positive affect, and autonomic arousal. *Journal of Abnormal Psychology, 107,* 179–192.

Brownell, K. D., & Rodin, J. (1994). The dieting maelstrom: Is it possible and advisable to lose weight? *American Psychologist, 49,* 781–791.

Brubaker, R. G., & Wickersham, D. (1990). Encouraging the practice of testicular self-examination: A field application of the theory of reasoned action. *Health Psychology, 9,* 154–163.

Bruce, D., & Bahrick, H. P. (1992). Perceptions of past research. *American Psychologist, 47,* 319–328.

Bruch, H. (1970). Eating disorders in adolescence. *Proceedings of the American Psychopathology Association, 59,* 181–202.

Bruch, H. (1973). *Eating disorders: Obesity, anorexia nervosa, and the person within.* New York: Basic Books.

Bruder, G., Kayser, J., Tenke, C., Amador, X., Friedman, M., Sharif, Z., & Gorman, J. (1999). Left temporal lobe dysfunction in schizophrenia: Event-related potential and behavioral evidence from phonetic and tonal dichotic listening tasks. *Archives of General Psychiatry. 56,* 267–276.

Bruner, J. S. (1992). Another look at New Look 1. *American Psychologist, 47,* 780–783.

Bruyer, R. (1991). Covert face recognition in prosopagnosia: A review. *Brain and Cognition, 15,* 223–235.

Bryant, F. B., Yarnold, P. R., & Grimm, L. G. (1996). Toward a measurement model of the Affect Intensity Measure: A three-factor structure. *Journal of Research in Personality, 30,* 223-247.

Bryant, P. E., & Trabasso, T. (1971). Transitive inferences and memory in young children. *Nature, 232,* 456–458.

Bucci, W. (1997). *Psychoanalysis and cognitive science: A multiple code theory.* New York: Guilford Press.

Buchanan, G. M., & Seligman, M. E. P. (Eds.) (1995). *Explanatory style.* Hillsdale, NJ: Lawrence Erlbaum.

Buck, R. (1986). The psychology of emotion. In J. E. LeDoux and W. Hirst (Eds.), *Mind and brain: Dialogues in cognitive neuroscience.* New York: Cambridge University Press.

Bugental, D. B., & Goodnow, J. J. (1998). Socialization processes. In W. Damon (Ed. in Chief) and N. Eisenberg (Vol. Ed.), *Handbook of child psychology* (Vol. 3, pp. 389–462). New York: John Wiley.

Buhrich, N., Bailey, J. M., Martin, N. G. (1991). Sexual orientation, sexual identity, and sex-dimorphic behaviors in male twins. *Behavior Genetics, 21,* 75–96.

Buhrmester, D. (1990). Intimany of friendship, interpersonal competence, and adjustment during preadolescence and adolescence. *Child Development, 61,* 1101–1111.

Bukatko, D., & Daehler, M. W. (2004). *Child development* (5th ed.). New York: Houghton Mifflin.

Bukowski, W., Gauze, C., Hoza, B., & Newcomb, A. (1993). Differences and consistency beween same-sex and other-sex peer relationships during early adolescence. *Developmental Psychology, 29,* 255–263.

Bunge, S. A., Klingberg, T., Jacobsen, R. B., & Gabrieli, J. D. E. (2000). A resource model of the neural basis of executive working memory. *Proceedings of the National Academy of Science, U.S.A., 97,* 3573–3578.

Burgess, N., & Hitch, G. J. (1999). Memory for serial order: A network model of the phonological loop and its timing. *Psychological Review 106,* 551–581.

Buri, J., Louiselle, P., Misukanis, T., & Mueller, R. (1988). Effects of parental authoritarianism on self-esteem. *Personality and Social Psychology Bulletin, 14,* 271–282.

Burke, W., & Cole, A. M. (1978). Extra-retinal influences on the lateral geniculate nucleus. *Review of Physiology, Biochemistry, and Pharmacology, 80,* 105–166.

Burks, B. (1938). On the relative contributions of nature and nurture to average group differences in intelligence. *Proceedings of the National Academy of Sciences, U.S.A 24,* 276–282.

Burks, B. S. (1928). The relative influence of nature and nurture upon mental development: A comparative study of foster parent-foster child resemblance and true parent-true child resemblance. *27th Yearbook of the National Society for the Study of Education, 27,* 219–316.

Burnstein, E., Crandall, C., & Kitayama, S. (1994). Some neo-Darwinian decision rules for altruism: Weighing cues for inclusive fitness as a function of the biological importance of the decision. *Journal of Personality & Social Psychology, 67,* 773–789.

Bushman, B. J. (1995). Moderating role of trait aggressiveness in the effects of violent media on aggression. *Journal of Personality & Social Psychology, 69,* 950–960.

Bushman, B. J. (1997). Effects of alcohol on human aggression: Validity of proposed explanations. In M. Galanter (Ed.). *Recent developments in alcoholism, Vol. 13. Alcohol and violence: Epidemiology, neurobiology, psychology, family issues* (pp. 227–243). New York: Plenum Press.

Bushman, B. J. (1998). Priming effects of media violence on the accessibility of aggressive constructs in memory. *Personality and Social Psychology Bulletin, 24,* 537–545.

Bushman, B. J., & Anderson, C. A. (2001). Media violence and the American public: Scientific facts versus media misinformation. *American Psychologist, 56,* 477–489.

Bushman, B. J., & Baumeister, R. F. (1998). Threatened egotism, narcissism, self-esteem, and direct and displaced aggression: Does self-love or self-hate lead to violence? *Journal of Personality and Social Psychology, 75,* 219–229.

Bushman, B. J., & Baumeister, R. F. (2002). Does self-love or self-hate lead to violence? *Journal of Research in Personality, 36,* 543–545.

Bushman, B. J., & Cooper, H. M. (1990). Effects of alcohol on human aggression: An integrative research review. *Psychological Bulletin, 107,* 341–354.

Buss, D. M. (1991). Evolutionary personality psychology. *Annual Review of Psychology, 42,* 459–492.

Buss, D. M. (1999). Human nature and individual differences: The evolution of human personality. In L. A. Pervin & O. P. John (Eds.), *Handbook of personality: Theory and research* (2nd ed., pp. 31–56). New York: Guilford Press.

Buss, D. M. (2000). The evolution of happiness. *American Psychologist, 55,* 15–23.

Buss, D. M., & Angleitner, A. (1989). Mate selection preferences in Germany and the United States. *Personality & Individual Differences, 10,* 1269–1280.

Buss, D. M., & Kenrick, D. T. (1998). Evolutionary social psychology. In D. T. Gilbert, S. T. Fiske, et al. (Eds.), *The handbook of social psychology,* (Vol. 2, 4th ed., pp. 982–1026). Boston, MA: McGraw-Hill.

Buss, D. M., Larsen, R. J., Westen, D., & Semmelroth, J. (1992). Sex differences in jealousy: Evolution, physiology, and psychology. *Psychological Science, 3,* 251–255.

Buss, D. M., & Schmitt, D. P. (1993). Sexual strategies theory: An evolutionary perspective on human mating. *Psychological Review, 100,* 1–29.

Buss, D. M., & Shackelford, T. K. (1997). Human aggression in evolutionary psychological perspective. *Clinical Psychology Review, 17,* 605-619.

Bussey, K. (1999). Children's categorization and evaluation of different types of lies and truths. *Child Development, 70,* 1338–1347.

Butler, A. B., & Hodos, W. (1996). *Comparative vertebrate neuroanatomy: Evolution and adaptation.* New York: Wiley-Liss.

Butler, C. A. (1976). New data about female sexual response. *Journal of Sex and Marital Therapy, 2,* 40–46.

Butler, R. N. (1969). Ageism: Another form of bigotry. *Gerontologist, 9,* 243–246.

Butler, R. N. (1975). *Why survive? Being old in America.* New York: Harper & Row.

Butler, R. N. (1984). Senile dementia: Reversible and irreversible. *Counseling Psychology, 12,* 75–79.

Butt, A., Testylier, G., & Dykes, R. (1997). Acetylcholine release in rat frontal and somatosensory cortex is enhanced during lactile discrimination learning. *Psychobiology, 25,* 18–33.

Butters, N., Heindel, W. C., & Salmon, D. (1990). Dissociation of implicit memory in dementia: Neurological implications. *Bulletin of the Psychonomic Society, 28,* 359–366.

Butterworth, A. (1978). A review of a primer of infant development. *Perception, 17,* 363–364.

Butzlaff, R. L., & Hooley, J. M. (1998). Expression emotion and psychiatric relapse: A meta-analysis. *Archives of General Psychiatry, 55,* 547–552.

Buunk, B. P., Angleitner, A., Oubaid, V., & Buss, D. M. (1996). Sex differences in jealousy in evolutionary and cultural perspective: Tests from the Netherlands, Germany, and the United States. *Psychological Science, 7,* 359–363.

Bynum, C. W. (1987). *Holy feast and holy fast.* Berkeley: University of California Press.

Byrne, D., et al. (1968). The effects of physical attractiveness, sex, and attitude similarity on interpersonal attraction. *Journal of Personality, 36,* 259–271.

Byrne, D., & Murnen, S. (1988). Maintaining loving relationships. In R. Sternberg & M. L. Barnes (Eds.), *The psychology of love* (pp. 293–310). New Haven, CT: Yale University Press.

Cacioppo, J. T., Ernst, J. M., Burleson, M. H., McClintock, M. K., Malarkey, W. B., Hawkley, L. C., Kowalewski, R. B., Paulsen, A., Hobson, J. A., Hugdahl, K., Spiegel, D., & Berntson, G. G. (2000). Lonely traits and concomitant physiological processes: The MacArthur social neuroscience studies. *International Journal of Psychophysiology, 35,* 143–154.

Cacioppo, J. T., & Gardner, W. L. (1999). Emotions. *Annual Review of Psychology, 50,* 191-214.

Cacioppo, J. T., Gardner, W. L., & Berntson, G. G. (1997). Beyond bipolar conceptualizations and measures: The case of attitudes and evaluative space. *Personality and Social Psychology Review, 1,* 3–25.

Cadoret, R. J., O'Gorman, T. W., Troughton, E., & Heywood, E. (1985). Alcoholism and antisocial personality. *Archives of General Psychiatry, 42,* 161–167.

Cadoret, R. J., Yates, W. R., Troughton, E., Woodworth, G., & Stewart, M. A. (1995). Genetic- environmental interaction in the genesis of aggressivity and conduct disorders. *Archives of General Psychiatry, 52,* 916–924.

Caggiula, A. R., Epstein, L. H., Antelman, S., Seymour, M., & Taylor, S. S. (1991). Conditioned tolerance to the anorectic and corticosterone- elevating effects of nicotine. *Pharmacology, Biochemistry, and Behavior, 40,* 53–59.

Cahill, L., Prins, B., Weber, M., & McGaugh, J. L. (1994). !b-Adrenergic activation and memory for emotional events. *Nature, 371,* 702-704.

Calhoun, K. S., Moras, K., Pilkonis, P. A., & Rehm, L. P. (1998). Empirically supported treatments: Implications for training. *Journal of Consulting & Clinical Pshcology, 66,* 151–162.

Cameron, L. D., Leventhal, H., & Love, R. R. (1998). Trait anxiety, symptom perceptions, and illness-related responses among women with breast cancer in remission during a Tamoxifen clinical trial. *Health Psychology, 17*: p. 459–469.

Camp, B. W., & Bash, M. A. S. (1981). *Think aloud: Increasing social and cognitive skills—a problem solving program for children (primary level).* Champaign, IL: Research Press.

Campbell, D. T., & Stanley, J. C. (1963). *Experimental and quasi-experimental designs for research.* Chicago: Rand McNally.

Campbell, J. D. (1986). Similarity and uniqueness: The effects of attribute type, relevance, and individual differences in self-esteem and depression. *Journal of Personality and Social Psychology, 50,* 281–294.

Campbell, S. B. (1985). Hyperactivity in preschoolers: Correlates and prognostic implications. *Clinical Psychology Review, 5,* 405–428.

Campbell, W. K., & Sedikides, C. (1999). Self-threat magnifies the self-serving bias. A meta-analytic integration. *Reviews of General Psychology, 3,* 23–43.

Campfield, L., Arthur, S., Francoise, J., Rosenbaum, M., & Hirsch, J. (1996). Human eating: Evidence for a physiological basis using a modified paradigm. Special Issue: Society for the Study of Ingestive Behavior, Second Independent Meeting. *Neuroscience & Biobehavioral Reviews, 20,* 133–137.

Campfield, L., Brandon, P., & Smith, F. J. (1985). On-line continuous measurement of blood glucose and meal pattern in free-feeding rats: The role of glucose in meal initiation. *Brain Research Bulletin, 14,* 605–617.

Campione, J. C., Brown, A. L., & Ferrara, R. A. (1982). Mental retardation and intelligence. In R. J. Sternberg (Ed.), *Handbook of human intelligence* (pp. 393–490). New York: Cambridge University Press.

Campos, J. J., Barrett, K. C., Lamb, M. E., Goldsmith, H. H., & Stenberg, C. (1983). Socioemotional development. In P. H. Mussen (Ed.), *Handbook of child psychology: Vol. II. Infancy and developmental psychobiology.* New York: John Wiley.

Campos, J. J., Bertenthal, B. I., & Kermoian, R. (1992). Early experience and emotional development: The emergence of wariness and heights. *Psychological Science, 3,* 61-64.

Cancer prevention and early detection facts and figures. (2002). American Cancer Society.

Candy, T. R., Crowell, J. A., & Banks, M. S. (1998). Optical, receptoral, and retinal constraints on foveal and peripheral vision in the human neonate. *Vision Research, 38,* 3857-3870.

Canivez, G. L., & Watkins, M. W. (1998). Long-term stability of the *Wechsler Intelligence Scale for Children, third edition. Psychological Assessment, 10,* 285–291.

Cannon, T. D., Kaprio, J., Lönnqvist, J., Huttunen, M., & Koskenvuo, M. (1998). The genetic epidemiology of schizophrenia in a Finnish twin cohort: A population-based modeling study characterization of psychotic conditions. *Archives of General Psychiatry, 55,* 67–74.

Cannon, W. B. (1927). The James-Lange theory of emotions: A critical examination and an alternative theory. *American Journal of Psychiatry, 39,* 106–124.

Cannon, W. B. (1932). *The wisdom of the body.* New York: W.W. Norton.

Cantor, N. (1990). From thought to behavior: Having and doing in the study of personality and cognition. *American Psychologists, 45,* 735–750.

Cantor, N., & Blanton, H. (1996). Effortful pursuit of personal goals in daily life. In P. M. Gollwitzer, J. A. Bargh, et al. (Eds.), *The psychology of action: Linking cognition and motivation to behavior* (pp. 338–359). New York: Guilford Press.

Cantor, N., & Harlow, R. (1994). Personality, strategic behavior, and daily-life problem solving. *Current Directions in Psychologial Science 3,* 169–172.

Cantor, N., & Kihlstrom, J. F. (1987). Personality and social intelligence. Englewood Cliffs, NJ: Prentice-Hall.

Capaldi, E., & VandenBos, G. (1991). Taste, food exposure, and eating behavior. *Hospital and Community Psychiatry, 42,* 787–789.

Caplan, D., & Waters, G. S. (1990). Short-term memory and language comprehension: A critical review of the neuropsychological literature. In G. Vallar and T. Shallice (Eds.), *Neuropsychological impairments of short-term memory* (pp. 337–389). Cambridge: Cambridge University Press.

Caplan, P. J., Crawford, M., Hyde, J. S., & Richardson, J. T. E. (1997). *Gender differences in human cognition.* London: Oxford University Press.

Caporael, L. R., & Baron, R. M. (1997). Groups as the mind's natural environment. In J. A. Simpson & D. T. Kenrick (Eds.), *Evolutionary social psychology.* (pp. 317–344). Mahwah, NJ: Lawrence Erlbaum.

Cardno, A. G., Bowen, T., Guy, C. A., Jones, L. A., McCarthy, G., Williams, N. M., Murphy, K. C., Spurlock, G., Gray, M., Sanders, R. D., Craddock, N., McGuffin, P., Owen, M. J., & O'Donovan, M. C. (1999). CAG repeat length in the hKCa3 gene and symptom dimensions in schizophrenia. *Biological Psychiatry, 45,* 1592–1596.

Cardno, A. G., Marshall, E. J., Coid, B., Macdonald, A. M., Ribchester, T. R., Davies, N. J., Venturi, P., Jones, L. A., Lewis, S. W., Sham, P. C., Gottesman, I. I., Farmer, A. E., McGuffin, P., Reveley, A. M., & Murray, R. M. (1999). Heritability estimates for psychotic disorders: The Maudsley Twin Psychosis Series *Archives of General Psychiatry, 56,* 162–168.

Cardozo, B. L., Vergara, A., Agani, F., & Gotway, C. A. (2000). 162–168. Mental health, social functioning, and attitudes of Kosovar Albanians following the War in Kosovo. *Journal of the American Medical Association, 284,* 569–577.

Carey, G. (1990). Genes, fears, phobias, and phobic disorders. *Journal of Counseling and Development, 68,* 628–632.

Carey, M. P., & Vanable, P. A. (2003). AIDS/HIV. In A. M. Nezu, C. M. Nezu, & P. A. Geller (Eds.), *Handbook of psychology: Health psychology* (Vol. 9, pp. 219–244). Hoboken, NJ: John Wiley & Sons.

Carlsmith, J. M., & Anderson, C. A. (1979). Ambient temperature and the occurrence of collective violence: A new analysis. *Journal of Personality and Social Psychology, 37,* 337–344.

Carlson, E. A. (1998). A prospective longitudinal study of attachment disorganization/disorientation. *Child Development, 69,* 1107–1128.

Carlson, E. B., & Rosser-Hogan, R. (1991). Trauma experiences, posttraumatic stress, dissociation, and depression in Cambodian refugees. *American Journal of Psychiatry, 148,* 1548–1551.

Carlson, N. R. (1999). *Foundations of physiological psychology* (4th ed.). New York: Allyn & Bacon.

Carlson, S., Pertovaara, A., & Tanila, H. (1987). Late effects of early binocular visual deprivation on the function of Brodmann's area 7 of monkeys. *Developmental Brain Research, 33,* 101-111.

Carmagnani, A., & Carmagnani, E.-F. (1999). Biofeedback: Present state and future possibilities. *International Journal of Mental Health, 28,* 83–86.

Carolsfeld, J., Tester, M., Kreiberg, H., & Sherwood, N. M. (1997). Pheromone-induced spawning of Pacific herring: I. Behavioral characterization. *Hormones & Behavior, 31,* 256–268.

Carone, B. J., Harrow, M., & Westermeyer, J. F. (1991). Posthospital course and outcome in schizophrenia. *Archives of General Psychiatry, 48,* 247–253.

Carpenter, K. M., Hasin, D. S., Allison, D. B., & Faith, M. S. (2000). Relationship between obesity and DSM-IV major depressive disorder, suicide ideation, and suicide attempts: Results from a general population study. *American Journal of Public Health, 90,* 251–257.

Carpenter, P. A., Miyaka, A., & Just, M. A. (1995). Language comprehension: Sentence and discourse processing. *Annual Review, 46,* 91–120.

Carroll, J. B. (1993). *Human cognitive abilities: A survey of factor-analytic studies.* New York: Cambridge University Press.

Carroll, J. M., & Russell, J. A. (1996). Do facial expressions signal specific emotions? Judging emotion from the face in context. *Journal of Personality & Social Psychology, 70,* 205–218.

Carskadon, M. A., & Dement, W. (1982). Nocturnal determinants of daytime sleepiness, *Sleep, 5,* 73–81.

Carter, F. A., McIntosh, V. V. W., Joyce, P. R., Sullivan, P. F., & Bulik, C. M. (2003). Role of exposure with response prevention in cognitive-behavioral therapy for bulimia nervosa:

Three year follow-up results. *International Journal of Eating Disorders, 33,* 127–135.

Cartwright, R. D. (1996). Dreams and adaptation to divorce. In D. Barrett (Ed.), *Trauma and dreams* (pp. 179–185). Cambridge, MA: Harvard University Press.

Carver, C. S. (1998). Resilience and thriving: Issues, models, and linkages. *Journal of Social Issues, 54,* 245–266.

Carver, C. S., & Scheier, M. F. (2000). *Perspectives on personality* (4th ed.). Boston: Allyn & Bacon.

Carver, C. S., Scheier, M. F., & Weintraub, J. K. (1989). Assessing coping strategies: A theoretically based approach. *Journal of Personality and Social Psychology, 56,* 267–283.

Carver, L. J., Dawson, G., Panagiotides, H., Meltzoff, A. N., McPartland, J., Gray, J., & Munson, J. (2003). Age-related differences in neural correlates of face recognition during the toddler and preschool years. *Developmental Psychobiology, 42,* 148–159.

Case, R. (1984). The process of stage transitions: A neo-Piagetian view. In R. J. Sternberg (Ed.), *Mechanisms of cognitive development.* New York: Freeman.

Case, R. (1992). Neo-Piagetian theories of child development. In R. J. Sternberg & C. A. Berg, *Intellectual development* (pp. 161–196). New York: Cambridge University Press.

Case, R. (1998). The development of conceptual structures. In W. Damon (Ed. in Chief) and N. Eisenberg (Vol. Ed.), *Handbook of child psychology* (Vol. 2, pp. 745–800). New York: John Wiley.

Casey, M. B., Nuttall, R. L., & Pezaris, E. (1997). Mediators of gender differences in mathematics college entrance test scores: A comparison of spatial skills with internalized beliefs and anxieties. *Development Psychology, 33,* 669–680.

Cash, T. F., Gillen, B., & Burns, D. S. (1977). Sexism and "beautyism" in personnel consultant decision making. *Journal of Applied Psychology, 62,* 301–310.

Cashmore, J. A., & Goodnow, J. J. (1986). Influences on Australian parents' values: Ethnicity versus socioeconomic status. *Journal of Cross-Cultural Psychology, 17,* 441–454.

Casper, R. C., Hedeker, D., & McClough, J. F. (1992). Personality dimensions in eating disorders and their relevance for subtyping. *Journal of the American Academy of Child and Adolescent Psychiatry, 31,* 830–840.

Caspi, A. (1998). Personality development across the lifespan. In W. Damon (Ed.), *Handbook of child psychology: Vol. 3. Social, emotional, and personality development* (N. Eisenberg, Vol. Ed.) (pp. 311–388). New York: John Wiley & Sons.

Caspi, A. (2000). The child is father of the man: Personality continuities from childhood to adulthood. *Journal of Personality and Social Psychology, 78,* 158–172.

Caspi, A., Elder, G. E., & Herbener, E. (1990). Childhood personality and the prediction of life-course patterns. In L. N. Robins & M. Rutter (Eds.), *Straight and devious pathways from childhood to adulthood* (pp. 13–35). New York: Cambridge University Press.

Caspi, A., Lynam, D., Moffitt, T., & Silva, P. (1993). Unraveling girls' delinquency: Biological, dispositional, and contextual contributions to adolescent misbehavior. *Developmental Psychology, 29,* 19–30.

Cassidy, J., Kirsh, S. J., Scolton, K., & Parke, R. D. (1996). Attachment and representations of peer relationships. *Developmental Psychology, 32,* 892–904.

Cassidy, J., & Shaver, P. R. (Eds.). (1999). *Handbook of attachment: Theory, research, and clinical applications.* New York: Guilford Press.

Castle, D. J., & Ames, F. R. (1996). Cannabis and the brain. *Australian & New Zealand Journal of Psychiatry, 30,* 179–183.

Cattell, R. B. (1957). *Personality and motivation: Structure and measurement.* Yonkers-on-Hudson, New York: World Book Co.

Cattell, R. B. (1990). Advances in Cattellian personality theory. In L. Pervin (Ed.), *Handbook of personality: Theory and research* (pp. 101–110). New York: Guilford Press.

Cave, C. B. (1997). Very long-lasting priming in picture naming. *Psychological Science, 8,* 322–325.

Ceci, S. J. (1990). Framing intellectual assessment in terms of a person-process-context model. *Educational Psychologist, 25,* 269–291.

Ceci, S. J., & Bronfenbrenner, U. (1991). On the demise of everyday memory:"The rumors of my death are much exaggerated"(Mark Twain). *American Psychologist, 46,* 27–31.

Centers for Disease Control. (1980). *Ten leading causes of death in the United States 1977.* Washington, DC: U.S. Government Printing Office.

Centers for Disease Control. (2002). Annual smoking-attributable mortality, years of potential life lost, and economic costs—United States, 1995–1999, *MMWR, 51.*

Centers for Disease Control. (2003a). HIV/AIDS update.

Centers for Disease Control. (2003b). Overweight prevalence. National Center for Health Statistics. Retrieved June 13, 2003: http://www.cdc.gov/nchs/fastats/overwt.htm

Cervantes, C. A., & Callahan, M. (1998). Labels and explanations in mother-child emotion talk: Age and gender differentiation. *Developmental Psychology, 34,* 88–98.

Chaiken, M. L., Gentner, T. Q., & Hulse, S. H. (1997). Effects of social interaction on the development of startling song and the perception of these effects by conspecifics. *Journal of Comparative Psychology, 111,* 379–392.

Chaiken, S. (1980). Heuristic versus systematic information processing and the use of source versus message cues in persuasion. *Journal of Personality and Social Psychology, 39,* 752–766.

Chaiken, S. R., Kyllonen, P. C., & Tirre, W. C. (2000). Organization and components of psychomotor ability. *Cognitive Psychology, 40,* 198–226.

Chamberlain, J. (2001, June). Court appearances can stem teen smoking, study finds. *Monitor on Psychology, 32,* 59.

Chambless, D. C., & Gillis, M. M. (1993). Cognitive therapy of anxiety disorders. *Journal of Consulting and Clinical Psychology, 61,* 248–260.

Chambless, D. L., & Hollon, S. D. (1998). Defining empirically supported therapies. *Journal of Consulting & Clinical Psychology, 66,* 7–18.

Chambless, D. L., & Steketee, G. (1999). Expressed emotion and behavior therapy outcome: A prospective study with obsessive-compulsive and agoraphobic outpatients. *Journal of Consulting and Clinical Psychology, 67,* 658–665.

Chamove, A. S. (1978). Therapy of isolate rhesus: Different partners and social behavior. *Child Development, 49,* 43–50

Champion, V. L. (1990). Breast self-examination in women 35 and older: A prospective study. *Journal of Behavioral Medicine, 13,* 523–538.

Champion, V. L. (1994). Strategies to increase mammography utilization. *Medical Care, 32,* 118–129.

Champoux, M., & Suomi, S. J. (1994). Behavioral and adrenocortical responses of rhesus macaque mothers to infant separation in an unfamiliar environment. *Primates, 35,* 191–202.

Chance, P. (1988). *Learning and behavior.* (2nd ed.). Belmont, CA: Wadsworth.

Chandler, L. S., Richardson, G. A., Gallagher, J. D., & Day, N. L. (1996). Prenatal exposure to alcohol and marijuana: Effects on motor development of preschool Children. *Alcoholism: Clinical & Experimental Research, 20,* 455–461.

Chen, J., & Gardner, H. (1997). Alternative assessment from a multiple intelligences theoretical perspective. In D. P. Flanagen, J. L. Genshaft, and P. L. Harrison (Eds.) *Contemporary intellectual assessment: Theories, tests, and issues* (pp. 105–121). New York: Guilford Press.

Chen, S., & Chaiken, S. (1999). The heuristic-systematic model in its broader context. In S. Chaiken & Y. Trope (Eds.), *Dual-process theories in social psychology.* (pp. 73–96). New York: Guilford Press.

Cherry, E. C. (1953). Some experiments on the recognition of speech, with one and with two ears. *Journal of the Acoustical Society of America, 25,* 975–979.

Chess, S., & Thomas, A. (1986). *Temperament in clinical practice.* New York: Guilford Press.

Chess, S., & Thomas, A. (1987). *Origins and evolution of behavior disorders: From infancy to early adult life.* Cambridge, MA: Harvard University Press.

Cheyette, S. R., & Cummings, J. L. (1995). Encephalitis lethargica: Lessons for contemporary neuropsychiatry. *Journal of Neuropsychiatry & Clinical Neurosciences, 7,* 125–134.

Chi, M. T. H. (1978). Knowledge structures and memory development. In R. Siegler (Ed.), *Children's thinking: What deficits?* Hillsdale, NJ: Lawrence Erlbaum.

Chi, M. T. H., Glaser, R., & Rees, E. (1982). Expertise in problem solving. In R. J. Sternberg (Ed.), *Advances in the psychology of human intelligence,* (Vol. 1, pp. 7–76). Hillsdale, NJ: Lawrence Erlbaum.

Choi, I., Dalal, R., Kim, P., & Park, H. (2003). Culture and judgment of causal relevance. *Journal of Personality and Social Psychology, 84,* 46–59.

Choi, I., Nisbett, R. E., & Norenzayan, A. (1999). Causal attribution across cultures: Variation and universality. *Psychological Bulletin, 125,* 47–63.

Chomsky, N. (1957). *Syntactic structures.* The Hague: Mouton.

Chomsky, N. (1959). Review of Skinner's Verbal Behavior. *Language, 35,* 26–58.

Chomsky, N. (1965). *Aspects of the theory of syntax.* Oxford: M. I. T. Press.

Chomsky, N. (1986). *Knowledge of language: Its nature, origins, and use.* New York: Praeger.

Christenfeld, N. (1997). Memory for pain and the delayed effects of distraction. *Health Psychology, 16,* 327–330.

Christensen, A., & Heavey, C. L. (1999). Interventions for couples. *Annual Review of Psychology, 50,* 165–190.

Christianson, S. A. (1992). Emotional stress and eyewitness memory: A critical review. *Psychological Bulletin, 112(2)Z,* 284–309.

Chrobak, J. J., & Buzsaki, G. (1994). Selective activation of deep layer (V–VI) retrohippocampal cortical neurons during hippocampal sharp waves in the behaving rat. *Journal of Neuroscience, 14,* 1660–1670.

Chung, K. K. K., Martinez, M., & Herbert, J. (2000). c-fos expression, behavioural, endocrine and autonomic responses to acute social stress in male rats after chronic restraint: Modulation by serotonin. *Neuroscience, 95,* 453–463.

Church, A. T. (2000). Culture and personality: Toward an integrated cultural trait psychology. *Journal of Personality, 68,* 651–703.

Church, A. T. (2001). Personality measurement in cross-cultural perspective. *Journal of Personality, 69,* 955–978.

Church, A. T., & Lonner, W. J. (1998). The cross-cultural perspective in the study of personality: Rationale and current research. *Journal of Cross-Cultural Psychology, 29,* 32–62.

Cialdini, R. B. (1993). *Influence* (3rd ed.). New York: Harper Collins.

Cialdini, R. B., Borden, R. J., Thorne, A., Walker, M. R., Freeman, S., & Sloan, L. R. (1976). Basking in reflected glory: Three (football) field studies. *Journal of Personality and Social Psychology, 34,* 366–375.

Cialdini, R. B., & Kenrick, D. T. (1976). Altruism as hedonism: A social development perspective on the relationship of negative mood state and helping. *Journal of Personality and Social Psychology, 34,* 907–914.

Cialdini, R. B., & Trost, M. R. (1998). Social influence: Social norms, conformity, and compliance. In D. T. Gilbert & S. T. Fiske (Eds.), *The handbook of social psychology* (Vol. 2, pp. 151-192). New York: McGraw-Hill.

Cialdini, R. B., Vincent, J. E., Lewis, S. K., Catalan, J., Wheeler, D., & Darby, B. L. (1975). Reciprocal concessions procedure for inducing compliance: The door-in- the-face technique. *Journal of Personality and Social Psychology, 31,* 206–215.

Ciraulo, D. A., & Renner, J. A. (1991). Alcoholism. In D. A. Ciraulo & R. I. Shader (Eds.) *Clinical manual of chemical dependence.* Washington, DC: American Psychiatric Press.

Clader, R. (2002). The humoral theory: How the world was fooled. http://www.cranford-schools.org/chs/scholars/2002/17c/clader.html

Clancy, S. A., Schacter, D. L., McNally, R. J., & Pitman, R. K. (2000). False recognition in women reporting recovered memories of sexual abuse. *Psychological Science, 11,* 26–31.

Clark, A. S., & Goldman-Rakic, P. (1989). Gonadal hormones influence the emergence of cortical function in nonhuman primates. *Behavioral Neuroscience, 103,* 1287–1295.

Clark, D. A., Beck, A. T., & Alford, B. A. (1999). *Scientific foundations of cognitive theory and therapy of depression.* New York: John Wiley.

Clark, D. M. (1994). Cognitive therapy for panic disorder. In B. E. Wolfe, J. D. Maser, et al. (Eds.), *Treatment of panic disorder: A consensus development conference* (pp. 121–132). Washington, DC: American Psychiatric Press.

Clark, K. E., & Ladd, G. W. (2000). Connectedness and autonomy support in parent-child relationships: Links to children's socioemotional orientation and peer relationships. *Developmental Psychology, 36,* 485–498.

Clark, M. S., & Pataki, S. (1995). Interpersonal processes influencing attraction and relationships. In A. Tesser (Ed.), *Advanced social psychology.* New York: McGraw-Hill.

Claustrat, B., Brun, J., David, M., et al. (1992). Melatonin and jet lag: Confirmatory result using a simplified protocol. *Biological Psychiatry, 32,* 705–711.

Clayton, S. (1991). Gender differences in psychosocial determinants of adolescent smoking. *Journal of School Health, 61,* 15–120.

Cleare, A., & Bond, A. (1997). Does central oserotonergic function correlate inversely with aggression? A study using *d*-fenfluramine in healthy subjects. *Psychiatry Research, 69,* 89–95.

Cleghorn, J. M., Peterfy, G., Pinter, E. J., & Pattee, C. J. (1970). Verbal anxiety and the beta adrenergic receptors: A facilitating mechanism? *Journal of Nervous and Mental Disease, 151,* 266–272.

Clifford, M. M., & Walster, E. (1973). The effect of physical attractiveness on teacher expectations. *Sociological Education, 46,* 248–258.

Clinchy, B. M., & Norem, J. K. (1998). (Eds.) *The gender and psychology reader.* New York: New York University Press.

Cloninger, C. R. (1998). The genetics and psychobiology of the seven factor model of personality. In K. R. Silk (Ed.), *Biology of personality disorders. Review of psychiatry series* (pp. 63-92). Washington, DC: American Psychiatric Association.

Cloninger, C. R., Bohman, M., & Sigvardsson, S. (1981). Inheritance of alcohol abuse. *Archives of General Psychiatry, 38,* 861–868.

Cobb, S. (1976). Social support as a moderator of life stress. *Psychosomatic Medicine, 38,* 300–314.

Cody, H., & Kamphaus, R. W. (1999). Down syndrome. In S. Goldstein, C. R. Reynolds, et al.

(Eds.), Handbook of neurodevelopmental and genetic disorders in children (pp. 385–405). New York: Guilford Press.

Cohen, D. (1983). *Piaget: Critique and reassessment.* New York: St. Martin's Press.

Cohen, D., & Nisbett, R. E. (1997). Field experiments examining the culture of honor: The role of institutions in perpetuating norms about violence. *Personality and Social Psychology Bulletin, 23,* 1188–1199.

Cohen, D., Nisbett, R. E., Bowdle, B. F., & Schwarz, N. (1996). Insult, aggression, and the southern culture of honor: An "experimental ethnography." *Journal of Personality & Social Psychology, 70,* 945–960.

Cohen, D., & Strayer, J. (1996). Empathy in conduct-disordered and comparison youth. *Developmental Psychology, 32,* 988–998.

Cohen, J. D., Schooler, J. W. (1997). *Scientific approaches to consciousness.* Mahwah, NJ: Lawrence Erlbaum.

Cohen, L. B., Diehl, R. L., Oakes, L. M., & Loehlin, J. L. (1992). Infant perception of /aba/ versus /apa/: Building a quantitative model of infant categorical discrimination. *Developmental Psychology, 28,* 261–272.

Cohen, R. M., Gross, M., Nordahl, T., Semple, W., Oren, D., & Rosenthal, N. (1992). Preliminary data on the metabolic brain pattern of patients with Winter seasonal affective disorder. *Archives of General Psychiatry, 49,* 545–552.

Cohen, S., & Herbert, T. B. (1996). Health psychology: Psychological factors and physical disease from the perspective of human psychoneuroimmunology. *Annual Review of Psychology, 47,* 113–142.

Cohen, S., Tyrrell, D. A. J., & Smith, A. P. (1991). Psychological stress and susceptibility to the common cold. *New England Journal of Medicine, 325,* 606–612.

Cohen, S., & Williamson, G. M. (1991). Stress and infectious disease in humans. *Psychological Bulletin, 109,* 5–24.

Cohen, S., & Wills, T. A. (1985). Stress, social support, and the buffering hypothesis. *Psychological Bulletin, 98,* 310–357.

Colby, A., & Kohlberg, L. (1984). Invariant squence and internal consistency in moral judgment stages. In W. M. Kurtines & J. L. Gewirtz (Eds.), *Morality, moral behavior and moral development.* New York: John Wiley.

Cole, D. A., Martin, J. M., Peeke, L. A., Seroczynski, A. D., & Fier, J. (1999). Children's over- and underestimation of academic competence: A longitudinal study of gender differences, depression, and anxiety. *Child Development, 70,* 459–473.

Cole, M. (1975). An ethnographic psychology of cognition. In R. Brislin, et al. (Eds.), *Cross-cultural perspectives on learning.* New York: Sage Publications.

Cole, M., Gay, J., Glick, J. A., & Sharp, D. W. (1971). *The cultural context of learning and thinking.* New York: Basic Books.

Cole, P. M., Zahn-Waxler, C., Fox, N. A., & Usher, B. A. (1996). Individual differences in

emotion regulation and behavior problems in preschool children. *Journal of Abnormal Psychology, 105,* 518–529.

Coleman, M. J., Levy, D. L., Lenzenweger, M. F., & Holzman, P. S. (1996). Thought disorder, perceptual aberrations, and schizotypy. *Journal of Abnormal Psychology, 105,* 469-473.

Collett, T. S., & Baron, J. (1994). Biological compasses and the coordinate frame of landmark memories in honeybees. *Nature, 368,* 137–140.

Colley, A., Ball, J., Kirby, N., Harvey, R., & Vingelen, I. (2002). Gender-linked differences in everyday memory performance: Effort makes the difference. *Sex Roles, 47,* 577–582.

Collier, G., Johnson, D. F., & Berman, J. (1998). Patch choice as a function of procurement cost and encounter rate. *Journal of the Experimental Analysis of Behavior, 69,* 5–16.

Collings, S., & King, M. (1994). Ten-year followup of 50 patients with bulimia nervosa. *British Journal of Psychiatry, 164,* 80–87.

Collins, A., & Loftus, E. F. (1975). A spreading-activation theory of semantic processing. *Psychological Review, 82,* 407–428.

Collins, A. M., & Quillian, M. R. (1969). Retrieval time from semantic memory. *Journal of Verbal Learning and Verbal Behavior, 8,* 240-247.

Collins, B. (1981). Rivals at Flushing Meadows. *The New York Times Magazine,* August 30, p. 70.

Collins, R. L., Lapp, W. M., Emmons, K. M., & Isaac, L. M. (1990). Endorsement and strength of alcohol expectancies. *Journal of Studies on Alcohol, 51,* 336–342.

Collins, W. A., & Gunnar, M. R. (1990). Social and personality development. *Annual Review of Psychology, 41,* 387–416.

Collins, W. A., Maccoby, E. E., Steinberg, L., Hetherington, E. M., & Bornstein, M. H. (2000). Contemporary research on parenting: The case for nature and nurture. *American Psychologist, 55,* 218–232.

Cologer-Clifford, A., Simon, N., & Jubilan, B. (1992). Genotype, uterine position, and testosterone sensitivity in older female mice. *Physiology and Behavior, 51,* 1047–1050.

Colvin, C. R. (1993). Judgable people: Personality, behavior, and competing explanations. *Journal of Personality and Social Psychology, 64,* 861–873.

Colvin, C. R., Block, J., & Funder, D. C. (1995). Overly positive self-evaluations and personality: Negative implications for mental health. *Journal of Personality & Social Psychology, 68,* 1152–1162.

Comaroff, J. (1980). Healing and the cultural order: The case of the Barolong boo Ratshidi of Southern Africa. *American Ethnologist, 7,* 637–657.

Compas, B., Hinden, B. R., & Gerhardt, C. (1995). Adolescent development: Pathways and processes of risk and resilience. *Annual Review of Psychology, 46,* 265–293.

Compton, W. M., Helzer, J., Hai-Gwo, H., Eng-Kung, Y., McEvoy, L., Tipp, J., & Spitznagel, E. (1991). New methods in cross-cultural psychiatry: Psychiatric illness in Taiwan and the United States. *American Journal of Psychiatry, 148,* 1697–1704.

Conger, R., Conger, K., Elder, G., Lorenz, F., Simons, R., & Whitbeck, L. (1993). Family economic stress and adjustment of early adolescent girls. *Developmental Psychology, 29,* 206–219.

Conklin, H. M., Curtis, C. E., Katsanis, J., & Iacono, W. G. (2000). Verbal working memory impairment in schizophrenia patients and their first-degree relatives: Evidence from the Digit Span Task. *American Journal of Psychiatry, 157,* 275–277.

Conway, L. G., Schaller, M., Tweed, R. G., & Hallett, D. (2001). The complexity of thinking across cultures: Interactions between culture and situational context. *Social Cognition, 19,* 228–250.

Conway, M. A. (1995). *Flashbulb memories.* Hillsdale, NJ: Lawrence Erlbaum Associates.

Cooley, C. H. (1902). *Human nature and the social order.* New York: Scribners.

Coombs, C., & Lehner, P. E. (1984). Conjoint design and analysis of the bilinear model: An application to judgments of risk. *Journal of Mathematical Psychology, 28,* 1–42.

Cooper, J., & Fazio, R. H. (1984). A new look at dissonance theory. *Advances in experimental social psychology, 17,* 229–266.

Cooper, L. A. (1976). Demonstration of a mental analog of an external rotation. *Perception and Psychophysics, 19,* 296–302.

Cooper, L. A., & Shepard, R. N. (1973). Chronometric studies of the rotation of mental images. In W. G. Chase (Ed.), *Visual information processing.* New York: Academic Press.

Coopersmith, S. (1967). *The antecedents of self-esteem.* San Francisco: Freeman.

Cork, R. C. (1996). Implicit memory during anesthesia. In S. R. Hameroff, A. W. Kaszniak, & A. C. Scott (Eds.), *Toward a science of consciousness: The first Tucson discussions and debates. Complex adaptive systems* (pp. 295–302). Cambridge, MA: MIT Press.

Cornblatt, B. A., & Kelip, J. G. (1994). Impaired attention, genetics, and the pathophysiology of schizophrenia. *Schizophrenia Bulletin, 20,* 31–46.

Corr, P. J., Pickering, A. D., & Gray, J. A. (1995). Personality and reinforcement in associative and instrumental learning. *Personality & Individual Differences, 19,* 47–71.

Corsica, J. A., & Perri, M. G. (2003). Obesity. In A. M. Nezu, C.M. Nezu, & P. A. Geller (Eds.), *Handbook of psychology: Health psychology* (Vol. 9, pp. 121–146). Hoboken, NJ: John Wiley & Sons.

Coryell, W., Endicott, J., & Winokur, G. (1992). Anxiety syndromes as epiphenomena of primary major depression: Outcome and familial psychopathology. *American Journal of Psychiatry, 149,* 100–107.

Cosmides, L. (1989). The logic of social exchange: Has natural selection shaped how humans reason? Studies with the Wason selection task. *Cognition, 31,* 187–276.

Cosmides, L., & Tooby, J. (1995). From evolution to adaptations to behavior. Toward an integrated evolutionary psychology. In R. Wong, et al. (Eds.), *Biological perspectives on motivated activities* (pp. 11–74). Norwood: Ablex Publishing.

Cosmides, L., & Tooby, J. (1999). Toward an evolutionary taxonomy of treatable conditions. *Journal of Abnormal Psychology, 108,* 453–464.

Costa, P. T., & McCrae, R. (1977). Age differences in personality structure revisited: Studies in validity, stability, and change. *International Journal of Aging and Human Development, 8,* 261–275.

Costa, P. T., Jr., & McCrae, R. R. (1988). Personality in adulthood: A six-year longitudinal study of self-reports and spouse ratings on the NEO Personality Inventory. *Journal of Personality and Social Psychology, 54,* 853–863.

Costa, P. T., Jr., & McCrae, R. R. (1990). Personality: Another "hidden factor" in stress research. *Psychological Inquiry, 1,* 22–24.

Costa, P. T., Jr., & McCrae, R. R. (1997). Stability and change in personality assessment: The Revised NEO Personality Inventory in the Year 2000. *Journal of Personality Assessment, 68,* 86–94.

Coull, J. T., & Sahakian, B. J. (2000). Psychopharmacology of memory. In G. E. Berrios & J. R. Hodges (Eds.). *Memory disorders in psychiatric practice.* (pp. 75–98). New York: Cambridge University Press.

Courtenay, W. H., McCreary, D. R., & Merighi, J. R. (2002). Gender and ethnic differences in health beliefs and behavior. *Journal of Health Psychology, 7,* 219–231.

Courtney, S. M., et al. (1998). An area specialized for spatial working memory in human frontal cortex. *Science, 279,* 1347–1351.

Courtney, S. M., Ungerleider, L. G., Keil, K., & Haxby, J. V. (1997). Transient and sustained activity in a distributed neural system for human working memory. *Nature, 386,* 608–611.

Cousins, S. (1989). Culture and self-perception in Japan and the United States. *Journal of Personality and Social Psychology, 56,* 124–131.

Cowan, C. P., & Cowan, P. A. (1992). *When partners become parents.* New York: Basic Books.

Cowan, N. (1994). Mechanisms of verbal short-term memory. *Current Directions in Psychological Science, 3,* 185–189.

Cowdry, R. W., & Gardner, D. L. (1988). Pharmacotherapy of borderline personality disorder: Alprazolam, carbamazepine, trifluoperazine, and tranylcypromine. *Archives of General Psychiatry, 45,* 111–119.

Cowgill, D. O., & Holms, L. D. (1972). *Aging and modernization.* New York: Appleton-Century Crofs.

Cowley, G. (2003, May 5). How progress makes us sick. *Newsweek,* 33–35.

Coyle, J. (1991). Molecular biological and neurobiological contributions to our understanding of Alzheimer's disease. In A. Tasman & S. Goldfinger, (Eds.), *American psychiatric press review of psychiatry* (Vol. 10, pp. 515–527). Washington, DC: American Psychiatric Press.

Coyne, J. C., Thompson, R., Klinkman, M. S., & Nease, D. E., Jr. (2002). Emotional disorders in primary care. *Journal of Consulting and Clinical Psychology, 70,* 798–809.

Craig, A. D., Reiman, E. M., Evans, A., & Bushnell, M. C. (1996). Functional imaging of an illusion of pain. *Nature, 384,* 258–260.

Craig, J. C., & Rollman, G. B. (1999). Somesthesis. *Annual Review of Psychology, 50,* 305–331.

Craik, F., & Lockhart, R. (1972). Levels of processing: A framework for memory research. *Journal of Verbal Learning and Verbal Behavior, 11,* 671–684.

Craik, F. I. M., Govoni, R., Naveh-Benjamin, M., & Anderson, N. D. (1996). The effects of divided attention on encoding and retrieval processes in human memory. *Journal of Experimental Psychology: General, 125,* 159–180.

Craik, F. I. M., & Salthouse, T. A. (2000). *The handbook of aging and cognition* (2nd ed.). Mahwah, NJ: Lawrence Erlbaum.

Crair, M. C., Gillespie, D. C., & Stryker, M. P. (1998). The role of visual experience in the development of columns in cat visual cortex. *Science, 279,* 566–570.

Cramer, P. (1996). *Storytelling, narrative, and the Thematic Apperception Test.* New York: Guilford Press.

Crandall, C. (1994). Prejudice against fat people: Ideology and self-interest. *Journal of Personality and Social Psychology, 66,* 882–894.

Crandall, C. S. (1995). Do parents discriminate against their heavyweight daughters? *Personality and Social Psychology Bulletin, 21,* 724–735.

Crawford, M., & Unger, R. (2000). *Women and gender: A feminist psychology.* New York: McGraw-Hill.

Crews, F. C. (1998). *Unauthorized Freud: Doubters confront a legend.* New York: Viking Penguin, Inc.

Crick, F., & Koch, C. (1998). Consciousness an neuroscience. *Cerebral Cortex, 8,* 97–107.

Crick, F., & Mitchison, G. (1983). The function of dream sleep. *Nature, 304,* 111–114.

Crick, N. R., & Dodge, K. A. (1994). A review and reformulation of social information-processing mechanisms in children's social adjustment. *Psychological Bulletin, 115,* 74–101.

Critchley, H., Daly, E., Phillips, M., Brammer, M., Bullmore, E., Williams, S., Amelsvoort, T. V., Robertson, D., David, A., & Murphy, D. (2000). Explicit and implicit neural mechanisms for processing of social information from facial expressions: A functional magnetic resonance imaging study. *Human Brain Mapping, 9,* 93–105.

Crits-Christoph, P. (1992). The efficacy of brief dynamic psychotherapy: A meta-analysis. *American Journal of Psychiatry, 149,* 151–158.

Crook, T. H., Youngjohn, J., Larrabee, G., & Salama, M. (1992). Aging and everyday memory. *Neuropsychology, 6,* 123–136.

Cross, S. E., & Markus, H. (1999). The cultural constitution of personality. In L. Pervin & O. John (Eds.), *Handbook of personality: Theory and research,* (2nd ed., pp. 378–396). New York: Guilford Press.

Crow, T. J. (1980). Molecular pathology of schizophrenia: More than one disease process? *British Medical Journal, 280,* 66–68.

Crowder, R. (1993). Systems and principles in

memory theory: Another critique of pure memory. In A. F. Collins, S. Gathercole, M. A. Conway, & P. E. Morris (Eds.), *Theories of memory* (pp. 139–161). Hillsdale, NJ: Lawrence Erlbaum.

Crowell, J. A., & Feldman, S. S. (1991). Mothers' working models of attachment relationships and mother and child behavior during separation and reunion. *Developmental Psychology, 27,* 597–605.

Crowne, D. P., & Marlow, D. (1964). *The approval motive: Studies in evaluative dependence.* New York: John Wiley.

Csikszentmihalyi, M., & Larson, R. (1984). *Being adolescent: Conflict and growth in the teenage years.* New York: Basic Books.

Culos-Reed, S. N., Brawley, L. R., Martin, K. A., & Leary, M. R. (2002). Self-presentation concerns and health behaviors among cosmetic surgery patients. *Journal of Applied Social Psychology, 32,* 560–569.

Cummins, R. A., Livesey, P. J., & Evans, J. G. M. (1977). A developmental theory of environmental enrichment. *Science, 197,* 692–694.

Cunningham, M. R., Roberts, A. R., Barbee, A. P., Druen, P. B., et al. (1995)."Their ideas of beauty are, on the whole, the same as ours": Consistency and variability in the cross-cultural perception of female physical attractiveness. *Journal of Personality & Social Psychology, 68,* 261–279.

Curran, J. P., & Lippold, S. (1975). The effects of physical attraction and attitude similarity on attraction in dating dyads. *Journal of Personality and Social Psychology, 43,* 528–539.

Curtiss, S. (1977). *Genie: A psycholinguistic study of a modern-day wild child.* New York: Academic Press.

Curtiss, S. (1989). The independence and task-specificity of language. In A. Bornstein & J. Bruner (Eds.), *Interaction in human development.* Mahwah, NJ: Lawrence Erlbaum.

D'Amico, E. J., & Fromme, K. (1997). Health risk behaviors of adolescent and young adult siblings. *Health Psychology, 16,* 426–432.

D'Andrade, R. G. (1992). Cognitive anthropology. In T. Schwartz, G. M. White, et al. (Eds.), *New directions in psychological anthropology.* Publications of the Society for Psychological Anthropology (Vol. 3, pp. 47–58). Cambridge: Cambridge University Press.

D'Esposito, M., Detre, J., Aquirre, G., Stallcup, M., Alsop, D., Tippet, L., & Farah, M. (1997). A functional MRI study of mental image generation. *Neuropsychologia, 35,* 725–730.

D'Zurilla, T., & Sheedy, C. (1991). Relation between social problem-solving and subsequent level of psychological stress in college students. *Journal of Personality and Social Psychology, 61,* 841–846.

Daley, S. E., Hammen, C., Burge, D., Davila, J., Paley, B., Lindberg, N., & Herzberg, D. S. (1999). Depression and Axis II symptomatology in an adolescent community sample: Concurrent and longitudinal associations. *Journal of Personality Disorders, 13,* 47–59.

Dalgleish, T., & Power, M. J. (1999). *Handbook of cognition and emotion.* Chichester, England: John Wiley & Sons Ltd.

Dalton, K. (1987). Should premenstrual syndrome be a legal defense? In B. E. Ginsburg & B. F. Carter (Eds.), *Premenstrual syndrome: Ethical and legal implications in a biomedical perspective* (pp. 287–300). New York: Plenum Press.

Daly, M., & Wilson, M. (1988). Evolutionary social psychology and family homicide. *Science, 242,* 519–524.

Damasio, A. R. (1994). *Descartes' error: Emotion, reason, and the human brain.* New York: Grosset/Putnam.

Damasio, H., Bechara, A., & Damasio, A. R. (2002). Do somatic markers mediate decisions on the gambling task?: Reply. *Nature Neuroscience, 5,* 1104.

Damon, W. (1977). *The social world of the child.* San Francisco: Jossey-Bass.

Damon, W., & Hart, D. (1988). Self-understanding in childhood and adolescence. New York: Cambridge University Press.

Daneman, M., & Merikle, P. (1996). Working memory and language comprehension: A meta-analysis. *Psychonomic Bulletin and Review, 3,* 422–433.

Daniel, M., Rowley, K. G., McDermott, R., Mylvaganam, A., & O'Dea, K. (1999). Diabetes incidence in an Australian aboriginal population: An 8-year follow-up. *Diabetes Care, 22,* 1993.

Danziger, E. (1998). Getting here from there: The acquisition of "point of view" in Mopan Maya. *Ethos, 26,* 48-72.

Darley, J. M., & Latané, B. (1968). When will people help in a crisis? *Psychology Today, 2,* 54–57, 70–71.

Darley, J. M., & Shultz, T. R. (1990). Moral rules: Their content and acquisition. *Annual Review of Psychology, 41,* 525–556.

Darwin, C. (1872). *The expression of the emotions in man and animals.* London: John Murray/Julian Friedmann, 1979.

Dasen, P. (1975). Concrete operational development in three cultures. *Journal of Cross-Cultural Psychology, 6,* 156–172.

Dasen, P., & Heron, A. (1981). Cross-cultural tests of Piaget's theory. In H. C. Triandis & A. Heron (Eds.), *Handbook of cross-cultural psychology: Vol. 4. Developmental psychology.* Boston, MA: Allyn & Bacon.

Davanloo, H. (1985). Short-term dynamic psychotherapy. In H. I. Kaplan & B. J. Sadock (Eds.), *Comprehensive textbook of psychiatry* (4th ed.). Baltimore, MD: Williams & Wilkins.

Davidson, D. (1996). The role of schemata in children's memory. In H. W. Reese (Ed.), *Advances in child development and behavior* (pp. 35–58). San Diego, CA: Academic Press.

Davidson, L. M., & Baum, A. (1986). Chronic stress and posttraumatic stress disorders. *Journal of Consulting and Clinical Psychology, 54,* 303–308.

Davidson, R. (1992). Emotion and affective style: Hemispheric substrates. *Psychological Science, 3,* 39–43.

Davidson, R. (1995). Cerebral asymmetry, emotion and affective style. In R. J. Davidson & K. Hugdahl (Eds.), *Brain asymmetry* (pp. 361–387). Cambridge, MA: MIT Press.

Davis, D. L., & Whitten, R. G. (1987). The cross-cultural study of human sexuality. *Annual Review of Anthropology, 16,* 69–98.

Davis, H. (1996). Underestimating the rat's intelligence. *Cognitive Brain Research, 3,* 291–298.

Davis, H., & Perusse, R. (1988). Numerical competence in animals: Definitional issues, current evidence, and a new research agenda. *Behavioral and Brain Sciences, 11,* 561–615.

Davis, J. M. (1985). Minor tranquilizers, sedatives, and hypnotics. In H. I. Kaplan, & B. J. Sadock (Eds.), *Comprehensive textbook of psychiatry* (4th ed.). Baltimore, MD: Williams & Wilkins.

Davis, S. (1990). Men as success objects and women as sex objects: A study of personals advertisements. *Sex Roles, 23,* 43–50.

Davidson, L. M., & Baum, A. (1986). Chronic stress and posttraumatic stress disorders. *Journal of Consulting and Clinical Psychology, 54,* 303–308.

Davison, K. P., Pennebaker, J. W., & Dickerson, S. S. (2000). Who talks? The social psychology of illness support groups. *American Psychologist, 55,* 205–217.

Dawes, R. (1997). Judgment, decision making, and interference. In D. Gilbert, S. Fiske, & G. Lindzey (Eds.), *Handbook of social psychology* (pp. 497–549). Boston, MA: McGraw-Hill.

Day, N. L., Richardson, G. A., Goldschmidt, L., & Cornelius, M. D. (2000). Effects of prenatal tobacco exposure on preschoolers' behavior. *Journal of Developmentsl and Behavioral Pediatrics, 21,* 180–188.

Deacon, T. W. (1996). *The making of language.* Edinburgh: Edinburgh University Press.

Deak, G. O., Flom, R. A., & Pick, A. D. (2000). Effects of gesture and target on 12- and 18-month-olds' joint visual attention to objects in front of or behind them. *Developmental Psychology, 36,* 511–523.

Deater-Deckard, K., Dodge, K. A., Bates, J. E., & Pettit, G. S. (1996). Physical discipline among African American and European American mothers: Links to children's externalizing behaviors. *Developmental Psychology, 32,* 1065–1072.

de Castro, J., & Brewer, M. (1992). The amount eaten in meals by humans is a power function of the number of people present. *Physiology and Behavior, 51,* 121–125.

de Castro, J. M. (1993). Genetic influences on daily intake and meal patterns of humans. *Physiology & Behavior, 53,* 777–782.

Deci, E. L., Koestner, R., & Ryan, R. M. (1999). A meta-analytic review of experiments examining the effects of extrinsic rewards on intrinsic motivation. *Psychological Bulletin, 125,* 627–668.

Deglin, V. L., & Kinsbourne, M. (1996). Divergent thinking styles of the hemispheres: How syllogisms are solved during transitory hemisphere suppression. *Brain & Cognition, 31,* 285–307.

deGonzague, B., Receveur, O., Wedll, D., & Kuhnlein, H. V. (1999). Dietary intake and body mass index of adults in 2 Ojibwe communities. *Journal of the American Dietetic Association, 99,* 710–726.

DeKay, T. (1998). *An evolutionary-computational approach to social cognition: Grandparental investment as a test case.* Unpublished doctoral dissertation, University of Michigan.

DeLander, G. E., & Wahl, J. (1991). Descending systems activated by morphine (ICV) inhibit kainic acid (IT)-induced behavior. *Pharmacology, Biochemistry, and Behavior, 39,* 155-159.

De La Ronde, C., & Swann, W. B., Jr. (1998). Partner verification: Restoring shattered images of our intimates. *Journal of Personality and Social Psychology, 75,* 374–382.

Delfour, F., & Marten, K. (2001). Mirror image processing in three marine mammal species: Killer whales (*Orchinus orca*), false killer whales (*Pseudorca crassidens*) and California sea lions (*Zalophus californianus*). *Behavioural Processes, 53,* 181–190.

Del Monte, M. M. (2001). Fact or fantasy? A review of recovered memories of childhood sexual abuse. *Irish Journal of Psychological Medicine, 18,* 99–105.

DeLoache, J. S., Miller, K. F., & Rosengren, K. S. (1997). The credible shrinking room: Very young children's performance with symbolic and nonsymbolic relations. *Psychological Science, 8,* 308–313.

DeLongis, A., Folkman, S., & Lazarus, R. S. (1988). The impact of daily stress on health and mood: Psychological and social resouces as mediators. *Journal of Personality and Social Psychology, 54,* 486–495.

Dembroski, T. M., & Costa, P. T. (1987). Coronary prone behavior: Components of the Type A pattern and hostility. *Journal of Personality, 55,* 211–235.

Demorest, A. P., & Siegel, P. F. (1996). Personal influences on professional work: An empirical case study of B. F. Skinner. *Journal of Personality, 64,* 243–261.

Demorest, M. E. (1986). Problem solving: Stages, strategies, and stumbling blocks. *Journal of Academic Rehabilitation Audiology, 19,* 13–26.

Dempster, F. N. (1996). Distributing and managing the conditions of encoding and practice. In E. L. Bjork & R. A. Bjork (Eds.), *Memory. Handbook of perception and cognition* (2nd ed., pp. 317–344). San Diego, CA: Academic Press.

DeMulder, E. K., Denham, S., Schmidt, M., & Mitchell, J. (2000). Q-sort assessment of attachment security during the preschool years: Links from home to school. *Developmental Psychology, 36,* 274–282.

Denham, S., & Holt, R. W. (1993). Preschoolers' likability as cause or consequence of their social behavior. *Developmental Psychology, 29,* 271–275.

De Pascalis, V., & Perrone, M. (1996). EEG asymmetry and heart rate during experience of hypnotic analgesia in high and low hypnotizables. International *Journal of Psychophysiology, 21,* 163–175.

DePaulo, B. M., & Friedman, H. S. (1998). Nonverbal communication. In D. T. Gilbert, S. T. Fiske, & G. Lindzey (Eds.), *The handbook of social psychology* (4th ed.). New York: Mc- Graw-Hill.

Deregowski, J. B. (1970). Effect of cultural value of time upon recall. *British Journal of Social and Clinical Psychology, 9,* 37–41.

DeRosier, M., & Kupersmidt, J. (1991). Costa Rican children's perceptions of their social networks. *Developmental Psychology, 27,* 656–662.

de St. Aubin, E., McAdams, D. P., & Kim, T. C. (2004). (Eds.) *The generative society: Caring for future generations.* Washington, DC: American Psychological Association.

DeSteno, D. A., & Salovey, P. (1996). Genes, jealousy, and the replication of misspecified models. *Psychological Science, 7,* 376–377.

Deutsch, J. A., & Gonzalez, M. E. (1980). Gastric nutrient content signals satiety. *Behavioral and Neural Biology, 30,* 113–116.

DeValois, R. L., & DeValois, K. (1975). Neural coding of color. In E. C. Carterette & M. P. Friedman (Eds.), *Handbook of perception.* New York: Academic Press.

Devine, P. (1989). Stereotypes and prejudice: Their automatic and controlled components. *Journal of Personality and Social Psychology, 56,* 5–18.

Devine, P., Monteith, M., Zuwerink, J., & Elliot, A. (1991). Prejudice with and without compunction. *Journal of Personality and Social Psychology, 60,* 817–830.

Devine, P. G., & Monteith, M. J. (1993). The role of discrepancy-associated affect in prejudice reduction. In D. M. Mackie, D. L. Hamilton, et al. (Eds.), *Affect, cognition and stereotyping: Interactive processes in group perception* (pp. 317–344). San Diego, CA: Academic Press.

Devine, P. G., Plant, E. A., Amodio, D. M., Harmon-Jones, E., & Vance, S. L. (2002). The regulation of explicit and implicit race bias: The role of motivations to respond without prejudice. *Journal of Personality and Social Psychology, 82,* 835–848.

Devlin, M. J., Yanovski, S. Z., & Wilson, G. T. (2000). Obesity: What mental health professionals need to know. *American Journal of Psychiatry, 157,* 854–866.

DeVos, G., & Suarez-Orozco, M. M. (1986). Child development in Japan and the United States: Prospectives of cross-cultural comparisons. In H. W. Stevenson & H. Azuma (Eds.), *Child development and education in Japan* (pp. 289–298). New York: W. H. Freeman.

de Waal, F. (1989). *Peacemaking among primates.* Cambridge, MA: Harvard University Press.

de Wijk, R. A., Schab, F. R., & Cain, W. S. (1995). Odor identification. In F. R. Schab, R. G. Crowder, et al. (Eds.), *Memory for odors* (pp. 21–37). Mahwah, NJ: Lawrence Erlbaum.

Dewis, L. M., Kirkby, K. C., Martin, F., Daniels, B. A., Gilroy, L. J., & Menzies, R. G. (2001). Computer-aided vicarious exposure versus live graded exposure for spider phobia in children. *Journal of Behavior Therapy and Experimental Psychiatry, 32,* 17–27.

De Witte, P. (1996). The role of neurotransmitters in alcohol dependence: Animal research. *Alcohol and Alcoholism, 31,* 13–16.

De Wolff, M., & van Ijzendoorn, M. H. (1997). Sensitivity and attachment: A meta-analysis on parental antecedents of infant attachment. *Child Development, 68,* 571-591.

Dews, P. B. (1959). Some observations on an operant in the octopus. *Journal of the Experimental Analysis of Behavior, 2,* 57–63.

Diamond, M. C. (1978). The aging brain: Some enlightening and optimistic results. *American Psychologist, 66,* 66–71.

Diaz-Guerrero, R. (1979). The development of coping style. *Human Development, 2,* 320–331.

Di Blas, L., & Forzi, M. (1999). Refining a descriptive structure of personality attributes in the Italian language: The abridged big three circumplex structure. *Journal of Personality and Social Psychology, 76,* 451–481.

Di Chiara, G., Acquas, E., & Tanda, G. (1996). Ethanol as a neurochemical surrogate of conventional reinforcers: The dopamine-opioid link. *Alcohol, 13,* 13–17.

Dick, D. M., Rose, R. J., Viken, R. J., & Kaprio, J. (2000). Pubertal timing and substance use: Associations between and within families across late adolescence. *Developmental Psychology, 36,* 180–189.

Diener, E. (2000). Subjective well-being: The science of happiness and a proposal for a national index. *American Psychologist, 55,* 34–43.

Diener, E., & Suh, M. E. (1998). Subjective well-being and age: An international analysis. In K. W. Schaie & M. P. Lawton (Eds.), *Annual review of genontology and geriatrics, Vol 17: Focus on emotion and adult development* (pp. 304-324). New York: Springer.

Dies, R. (1992). The future of group therapy. *Psychotherapy, 29,* 58–64.

Dietz, W. H. (1998). Health consequences of obesity in youth: Childhood predictors of adult disease. *Pediatrics, 101,* 518–526.

Difede, J., & Hoffman, H. G. (2002). Virtual reality exposure therapy for World Trade Center post-traumatic stress disorder: A case report. *CyberPsychology and Behavior, 5,* 529–535.

Dil, N. (1984). Noverbal communication in young children. *Topics in Early Childhood Special Education, 4,* 82–99.

DiLalla, L. F. (2002). Behavior genetics of aggression in children: Review and future directions. *Developmental Review, 22,* 593–622.

Dion, K., Berscheid, E., & Walster, E. (1972). What is beautiful is good. *Journal of Personality and Social Psychology, 24,* 285–290.

Dion, K. K. (2002). Cultural perspectives on physical attractiveness. In G. Rhodes & L. A. Zebrowitz (Eds.), *Facial attractiveness: Evolutionary, cognitive, and social perspectives. Advances in visual cognition* (Vol. 1, pp. 239–259). Westport, CT: Ablex Publishing.

Dion, K. K., & Berscheid, E. (1974). Physical attractiveness and peer perception among children. *Sociometry, 37,* 1–12.

Dion, K. K., & Dion, K. L. (1996). Cultural perspectives on romantic love. *Personal Relationships, 3,* 5–17.

Dion, K. L., & Dion, K. K. (1988). Romantic love: Individual and cultural perspectives. In R. Sternberg and M. Barnes (Eds.), *The psychology of love.* New Haven, CT: Yale University Press.

Dipboye, R. L. (1997). Organizational barriers to implementing a rational model of training. In M. A. Quinones and A. Ehrenstein (Eds.), *Training for a rapidly changing workplace: Applications of psychological research.* (pp. 31–60). Washington: American Psychological Association.

DiPietro, J. A., Hodgson, D. M., Costigan, K. A., & Johnson, T. R. B. (1996). Fetal antecedents of infant temperament. *Child Development, 67,* 2568–2583.

Dittes, J. E. (1959). Effect of changes in self-esteem upon impulsiveness and deliberation in making judgments. *Journal of Abnormal Social Psychology, 53,* 100–107.

Dixit, A. R., & Crum, R. M. (2000). Prospective study of depression and the risk of heavy alcohol use in women. *American Journal of Psychiatry, 157,* 751–758.

Dixon, N. F. (1971). *Subliminal perception: The nature of a controversy.* New York: McGraw-Hill.

Dixon, N. F. (1981). *Preconscious processing.* New York: John Wiley.

Doane, J. A., et al. (1981). Parental communication deviance and affective style: Predictors of subsequent schizophrenia spectrum disorders in vulnerable adolescents. *Archives of General Psychiatry, 38,* 679–685.

Dobson & Teller (1978). Visual acuity in human infants: A review and comparison of behavioral and electrophysiological studies. *Visual Research, 18,* 1469–1483.

Dodd, B. (1979). Lip reading in infants: Attention to speech presented in- and out-of-synchrony. *Cognitive Psychology, 11,* 478–484.

Dodge, K., Lochman, J., Harnish, J., Bates, J. E., & Pettit, G. (1997). Reactive and proactive aggression in school chidlren and psychiatrically impaired chronically assaultive youth. *Journal of Abnormal Psychology, 106,* 37–51.

Dodge, K., Pettit, G., Bates, J. E., & Valente, E. (1995). Social information-processing patterns partially mediate the effect of early physical abuse on later conduct problems. *Journal of Abnormal Psychology, 104,* 632–643.

Doi, T. (1992). On the concept of amae. *Infant Mental Health Journal, 13,* 7–11.

Dollard, J., Doob, L., Miller, N. E., Mowrer, O., & Sears, R. (1939). *Frustration and aggression.* New Haven, CT: Yale University Press.

Dollard, J., & Miller, N. (1950). *Personality and psychotherapy: An analysis in terms of learning, thinking, and culture.* New York: McGraw-Hill.

Domhoff, G. W. (1996). *Finding meaning in dreams: A quantitative approach.* New York: Plenum Press.

Doty, R. L., Green, P. A., Ram, C., & Tandeil, S. L. (1982). Communication of gender from human breath odors: Relationship to perceived intensity and pleasantness. *Hormones and Behavior, 16,* 13–22.

Douvan, E., & Adelson, J. (1966). *The adolescent experience.* New York: John Wiley.

Dovidio, J., & Gaertner, S. (1993). Stereotypes and evaluative intergroup bias. In D. Mackie & D. Hamilton (Eds.), *Affect, cognition, and stereotyping: Interactive processes in group perception.* San Diego, CA: Academic Press.

Dovidio, J. F., & Gaertner, S. L. (1998). On the nature of contemporary prejudice: The causes, consequences, and challenges of aversive racism. In J. L. Eberhardt & S. T. Fiske (Eds.), *Confronting racism: The problem and the response* (pp. 3–32). Thousand Oaks, CA: Sage.

Dovidio, J. F., Kawakami, K., & Gaertner, S. L. (2000). Reducing contemporary prejudice: Combating explicit and implicit bias at the individual and intergroup level. In S. Oskamp (Ed.), *Reducing prejudice and discrimination. 'The Claremont Symposium on Applied Social Psychology* (pp. 137–163). Mahwah, NJ: Lawrence Erlbaum.

Downey, G., Freitas, A. L., Michaelis, B., & Khouri, H. (1998). The self-fulfilling prophecy in close relationships: Rejection sensitivity and rejection by romantic partners. *Journal of Personality and Social Psychology, 75,* 545–560.

Dozier, M., & Kobak, R. (1992). Psychophysiology in attachment interviews: Converging evidence for deactivating strategies. *Child Development, 63,* 1473–1480.

Draguns, J. G. (1990). Normal and abnormal behavior in cross-cultural perspective: Specifying the nature of their relationship. In J. J. Beeman (Ed.), *Cross-Cultural perspectives. Current theory and research in motivation.*

Drasdo, N. (1977). The neural representation of visual space. *Nature, 266,* 554–556.

Drepper, J., Timmann, D., Kolb, F. P., & Diener, H. C. (1999). Non-motor associative learning in patients with isolated degenerative cerebellar disease. *Brain, 122,* 87–97.

Dryer, D. C., & Horowitz, L. M. (1997). When do opposites attract? Interpersonal complementarity versus similarity. *Journal of Personality & Social Psychology, 72,* 592–603.

DuBois, C. (1944). *The people of Alor: A social psychological study of an East Indian.* Minneapolis: University of Minnesota Press.

Duckitt, J. (1992). Psychology and prejudice: A historical analysis and integrative framework. *American Psychologist, 47,* 1182–1197.

Dudley, R. (1991). IQ and heritability. *Science, 252,* 191–192.

Duggal, H. S., Berezkin, G., & John, V. (2002). PTSD and TV viewing of World Trade Center. *Journal of the American Academy of Child and Adolescent Psychiatry, 41,* 494–495.

Duman, R. S., Heninger, G. R., & Nestler, E. J. (1997). A molecular and cellular theory of depression. *Archives of General Psychiatry, 54,* 597–606.

Dumaret, A. (1985). I.Q., scholastic performance and behavior of sibs raised in contrasting environments. *Journal of Child Psychology and Psychiatry and Allied Disciplines, 26,* 553–580.

Duncan, G., & Brooks, G. J. (2000). Family poverty, welfare reform, and child development. *Child Development, 71,* 188–196.

Duncan, J., Seitz, R., Kolodny, J., et al. (2000). A neural basis for general intelligence. *Science, 289,* 457–460.

Duncker, K. (1946). On problem solving. *Psychological Monographs, 158,* 5, #270.

Dunifon, R., & Duncan, G. J. (1998). Long-run effects of motivation on labor-market success. *Social Psychology Quarterly, 61,* 33–48.

Dunn, J., Bretherton, I., & Munn, P. (1987). Conversations about feeling states between mothers and their young children. *Developmental Psychology, 23,* 132–139.

Dunn, J., & McGuire, S. (1992). Sibling and peer relationships in childhood. *Journal of Child Psychology and Psychiatry, 33,* 67–105.

Durkheim, E. (1915). *The elementary forms of the religious life.* New York: Free Press.

Dutton, D. G. (1996). *The domestic assault of women.* Vancouver: University of British Columbia Press.

Duval, F., Mokrani, M. C., Monreal, J., Bailey, P., Valdebenito, M., Crocq, M. A., & Macher, J. P. (2003). Dopamine and serotonin function in untreated schizophrenia: Clinical correlates of the apomorphine and *d*-fenfluroamine tests. *Psychoneuroendocrinology, 28,* 627–642.

Dweck, C. (1975). The role of expectations and attributions in the alleviation of learned helplessness. *Journal of Personality and Social Psychology, 31,* 674–685.

Dweck, C. (1986). Motivational processes affecting learning. *American Psychologist, 41,* 1040–1048.

Dworkin, R. H., Hartsetin, G., Rosner, H., Walther, R., Sweeney, E. W., & Brand, L. (1992). A high-risk method for studying psychosocial antecedents of chronic pain: The prospective investigation of herpes zoster. *Journal of Abnormal Psychology, 101,* 200–205.

Eagly, A., Ashmore, R., Makhijani, M., & Longo, L. (1991). What is beautiful is good, but: A meta-analytic review of research on the physical attractiveness stereotype. *Psychological Bulletin, 110,* 109–128.

Eagly, A., & Chaiken, S. (1992). *The psychology of attitudes.* San Diego, CA: Harcourt Brace.

Eagly, A. H. (1978). Sex differences in influenceability. *Psychological Bulletin, 85,* 86–116.

Eagly, A. H. (1983). Gender and Social Influence: A social psychological analysis. *American Psychologist, 38,* 971–981.

Eagly, A. H. (1995). The science and politics of comparing men and women. *American Psychologist, 50,* 145–158.

Eagly, A. H., & Carli, L. L. (1981). Sex of researchers and sex-typed communications as determinants of sex differences in influenceability: A meta-analysis of social influence studies. *Psychological Bulletin, 90,* 1–20.

Eagly, A. H., & Chaiken, S. (1998). Attitude structure and function. In D. T. Gilbert, S. T. Fiske, et al. (Eds.), *The handbook of social psychology* (Vol. 2, 4th ed., pp. 269–322). Boston, MA: McGraw-Hill.

Eagly, A. H., & Crowley, M. (1986). Gender and

helping behavior: A meta-analytic review of the social psychological literature. *Psychological Bulletin, 100,* 283–308.

Eagly, A., & Steffen, V. (1986). Gender and aggressive behavior: A meta-analytic review of the social psychological literature. *Psychological Bulletin, 100,* 309–330.

Eagly, A. H., & Wood, W. (1999). The origins of sex differences in human behavior: Evolved dispositions versus social roles. *American Psychologist, 54,* 408–423.

Eaton, S. B., & Konner, M. (1985). Paleolithic nutrition: A consideration of its nature and current implications. *The New England Journal of Medicine, 312,* 283–289.

Ebbesen, E. B., Kjos, G. L., & Konecni, V. J. (1976). Spatial ecology: Its effect on the choice of friends and enemies. *Journal of Experimental Social Psychology, 12,* 505–518.

Ebbinghaus, H. (1885). *Memory.* New York: Columbia University/Dover, 1964.

Eckensberger, L. H. (1994). Moral development and its measurement across cultures. In W. J. Lonner & R. Malpass (Eds.), *Psychology and culture.* Needham Heights, MA: Allyn & Bacon.

Eder, R. (1990). Uncovering young children's psychological selves: Individual and developmental differences. *Child Development, 61,* 849–863.

Edelman, G. M. (1989). *The remembered present: A biological theory of consciousness.* New York: Basicbooks.

Edwards, C. P., & Whiting, B. B. (1983). Differential socialization of girls and boys in light of cross-cultural research. In W. Damon (Ed.), *Social and personality development: Essays on the growth of the child.* New York: W.W. Norton.

Edwards, D. A., & Einhorn, L. C. (1986). Preoptic and midbrain control of sexual motivation. *Physiology and Behavior, 37,* 329–335.

Edwards, W. (1977). How to use multiattribute utility measurement for social decision making. *IEEE Transactions in Systems Man and Cybernetics, 17,* 326–340.

Edwards, W., & Newman, J. R. (1986). Multiattribute choice. In H. R. Arkes & K. R. Hammond (Eds.), *Judgment and decision making: An interdisciplinary reader.* Cambridge: Cambridge University Press.

Egger, M. D., & Flynn, J. P. (1963). Effect of electrical stimulation of the amygdala on hypothalamically elicited attack behavior in cats. *Journal of Neurophysiology, 26,* 705–720.

Ehlers, A., & Breuer, P. (1992). Increased cardiac awareness in panic disorder. *Journal of Abnormal Psychology, 101,* 371–382.

Ehrman, R., Ternes, J., O'Brien, C. P., & McLellan, A. T. (1992). Conditioned tolerance in human opiate addicts. *Psychopharmacology, 108,* 218–224.

Eichenbaum, H. (1997). Declarative memory: Insights from cognitive neurobiology. *Annual Review, 48,* 547–572.

Eimas, P. D., Siqueland, E. R., Jusczyk, P., & Vigorito, J. (1971). Speech perception in infants. *Science, 171,* 303–306.

Eimas, P. D. (1985). The equivalence of cues in the perception of speech by infants. *Infant Behavior and Development, 8,* 125-138.

Einstein, G. O., & McDaniel, M. A. (1990). Normal aging and prospective memory. *Journal of Experimental Psychology: Learning, Memory, & Cognition, 16,* 717–726.

Einstein, G. O., Smith, R. E., McDaniel, M. A., & Shaw, P. (1997). Aging and prospective memory: The influence of increased task demands at encoding and retrieval. *Psychology & Aging, 12,* 479–488.

Eisenberg, N. (2000). Emotion, regulation, and moral development. *Annual Review of Psychology, 51,* 665-697.

Eisenberg, N., Fabes, R. A., & Murphy, B. C. (1996). Parent's reactions to children's negative emotions: Relations to children's social competence and comforting behavior. *Child Development, 67,* 2227–2247.

Eisenberg, N., Miller, P. A., Shell, R., McNalley, S., & Shea, C. (1991). Prosocial development in adolescence: A longitudinal study. *Developmental Psychology 27,* 849–857.

Eisenberg, N., & Zhou, Q. (2000). Regulation from a developmental perspective. *Psychological Inquiry, 11,* 166–171.

Ekman, P. (1971). Universals and cultural differences in facial expression. In J. K. Cole (Ed.), *Nebraska symposium on motivation.* Lincoln: University of Nebraska Press.

Ekman, P. (1977). Biological and cultural contributions to body and facial movement. In J. Blacking (Ed.), *The anthropology of the body.* A.S.A. Monograph 15. London: Academic Press.

Ekman, P. (1992). An argument for basic emotions. *Cognition and Emotion, 6,* 169-200.

Ekman, P. (1992). Facial expressions of emotion: New findings, new questions. *Psychological Science, 3,* 34–38.

Ekman, P. (1999). Facial expressions. In T. Dalgleish & M. Power (Eds.), *The handbook of cognition and emotion* (pp. 301–320). New York: John Wiley & Sons.

Ekman, P., & Davidson, R. J. (1993). Voluntary smiling changes regional brain activity. *Psychological Science, 4,* 342–345.

Ekman, P., & Friesen, W. V. (1975). *Unmasking the face: A guide to recognizing emotions from facial cues.* Englewood Cliffs, NJ: Prentice-Hall.

Ekman, P., & Keltner, D. (1997). Universal facial expressions of emotion: An old controversy and new findings. In U. C. Segerstrale & P. Molnar (Eds.), *Nonverbal communication: Where nature meets culture* (pp. 27-46). Hillsdale, NJ: Lawrence Erlbaum.

Ekman, P., Levenson, R. W., & Friesen, W. V. (1983). Autonomic nervous system activity distinguishes among emotions. *Science, 221,* 1208-1210.

Ekman, P., & Oster, H. (1979). Facial expressions of emotion. *Annual Review of Psychology, 30,* 527-554.

Elder, G. H., Jr. (1998). The life course as developmental theory. *Child Development, 69,* 1–12.

Eldridge, L., Knowlton, B., & Engel, S. (2000). *Hippocampus selectively encodes episodic memories.* Unpublished manuscript, UCLA.

Elias, M., Elias, J., & Elias, P. (1990). Biological and health influences on behavior. In J. Birren & K. W. Schaie (Eds.), *Handbook of the psychology of aging* (3rd ed., pp. 80–102). New York: Academic Press.

Elias, M. F., Beiser, A., Wolf, P. A., Au, R., White, R. F., & D'Agostino, R. B. (2000). The preclinical phase of Alzheimer disease: A 22-year prospective study of the Framingham cohort. *Archives of Neurology, 57,* 808-813.

Elkin, I., Shea, M. T., Watkins, J., & Imber, S. (1989). National Institute of Mental Health Treatment of Depression Collaborative Research Program: General effectiveness of treatments. *American Journal of Psychiatry, 46,* 971–982.

Elkind, D. (1981). Children's discovery of the conservation of mass, weight, and volume: Piaget replications studies II. *Journal of Genetic Psychology, 98,* 37–46.

Elkins, I. J., Mcgue, M., & Iacono, W. G. (1997). Genetic and environmental influences on parent- son relationships: Evidence for increasing genetic influence during adolescence. *Developmental Psychology, 33,* 351–363.

Elkis, H., Friedman, L., Wise, A., & Meltzer, H. Y. (1995). Meta-analyses of studies of ventricular enlargement and cortical sulcall prominence in mood disorders: Comparisons with controls or patients with schizophrenia. *Archives of General Psychiatry. 52,* 735–746.

Ellicott, A., Hammen, C., Gitlin, M., Brown, G., & Jamison, K. (1990). Life events and the course of bipolar disorder. *American Journal of Psychiatry, 147,* 1194–1198.

Elliot, A. J., & Church, M. A. (1997). A hierarchical model of approach and avoidance achievement motivation. *Journal of Personality & Social Psychology, 72,* 218–232.

Elliot, A. J., & Harackiewicz, J. M. (1996). Approach and avoidance achievement goals and intrinsic motivation: A mediational analysis. *Journal of Personality and Social Psychology, 70,* 461–475.

Elliott, J. (1977). The power and pathology of prejudice. In P. G. Zimbardo & F. L. Ruch (Eds.), *Psychology and life* (9th ed.). Glenview, IL: Scott, Foresman.

Ellis, A. (1962). *Reason and emotion in psychotherapy.* New York: Lyle Stuart.

Ellis, A. (1977). The basic clinical theory of rational- emotive therapy. In A. Ellis & R. Grieger (Eds.), *Handbook of rational-emotive therapy.* New York: Springer.

Ellis, A. (1984). Rational-emotive therapy. In R. J. Corsini (Ed.), *Current psychotherapies* (2nd ed.). Itasca, IL: Peacock Publishers.

Ellis, A. (1987). Cognitive therapy and rational-emotive therapy: A dialogue. *Journal of Cognitive Psychotherapy, 1,* 205–255.

Ellis, A. (1989). *Inside rational-emotive therapy: A critical appraisal of the theory and therapy of Albert Ellis.* New York: Academic Press.

Ellis, A. (1999). Why rational-emotive therapy to rational emotive behavior therapy? *Psychotherapy, 36,* 154–159.

Ellis, A. (2002a). *Overcoming resistance: A rational emotive behavior therapy integrated approach* (2nd ed.). New York: Springer.

Ellis, A. (2002b). The role of irrational beliefs in perfectionism. In G. L. Flect & P. L. Hewitt (Eds.), *Perfectionism: Theory, research, and treatment* (pp. 217–229). Washington, DC: American Psychological Association.

Ellis, B. J., & Garber, J. (2000). Psychosocial antecedents of variation in girls' pubertal timing: Maternal depression, stepfather presence, and marital and family stress. *Child Development, 71,* 485-501.

Ellis, L., & Ames, M. A. (1987). Neurohormonal functioning and sexual orientation: A theory of homosexuality-heterosexuality. *Psychological Bulletin, 101,* 233–258.

Emery, R. E., Waldron, M., Kitzmann, K. M., & Aaron, J. (1999). Delinquent behavior, future divorce or nonmarital childbearing, and externalizing behavior among offspring: A 14-year prospective study. *Journal of Family Psychology, 13,* 568–579.

Emmons, R., & King, L. A. (1988). Conflict among personal strivings: Immediate and long-term implications for psychological and physical well-being. *Journal of Personality and Social Psychology, 54,* 1040–1048.

Endo, Y., Heine, S. J., & Lehman, D. R. (2000). Culture and positive illusions in close relationships: How my relationships are better than yours. *Personality and Social Psychology Bulletin, 26,* 1571–1586.

Engel, S., Zhang, X., & Wandell, B. (1997). Colour tuning in human visual cortex measured with functional magnetic resonance imaging. *Nature, 388,* 68–71.

Engen, T. (1982). *The perception of odors.* New York: Academic Press.

Engle, R. W. (2001). What is working memory capacity? In H. L. Roediger & J. S. Nairne (Eds.), *The nature of remembering: Essays in honor of Robert G. Crowder* (pp. 297-314). Washington, DC: American Psychological Association.

Epley, N., & Dunning, D. (2000). Feeling "holier than thou": Are self-serving assessments produced by errors in self or social prediction? *Journal of Personality and Social Psychology, 79,* 861–875.

Epley, N., & Gilovich, T. (1999). Just going along: Nonconscious priming and conformity to social pressure. *Journal of Experimental Social Psychology, 35,* 578–589.

Epstein, S. (1979). The stability of behavior: On predicting most of the people much of the time. *Journal of Personality and Social Psychology, 37,* 1097–1126.

Epstein, S. (1986). Does aggregation produce spuriously high estimates of behavior stability? *Journal of Personality and Social Psychology, 50,* 1199–1210.

Epstein, S. (1992). Coping ability, negative self-evaluation, and overgeneralization: Experiment and theory. *Journal of Personality and Social Psychology, 62,* 826–836.

Epstein, S. (1994). Integration of the cognitive and the psychodynamic unconscious. *American Psychologist, 49,* 709–724.

Epstein, S. (1997). This I have learned from over 40 years of personality research. *Journal of Personality, 65,* 3–32.

Epstein, S. (1998). Cognitive-experiential self-theory. In D. F. Barone, M. Hersen, et al. (Eds.), *Advanced personality. The Plenum series in social/clinical psychology* (pp. 211–238). New York: Plenum Press.

Era, P., Jokela, J., & Heikkinen, E. (1986). Reaction and movement times in men of different ages: A population study. *Perceptual and Motor Skills, 63,* 111–130.

Erdelyi, M. H. (1985). *Psychoanalysis: Freud's cognitive psychology.* New York: Freeman.

Erdmann, G., & Van Lindern, B. (1980). The effects of beta-adrenergic stimulation and beta-adrenergic blockade on emotional reactions. *Psychophysiology, 17,* 332–338.

Erhardt, A. A., & Baker, S. W. (1974). Fetal androgens, human central nervous system differentiation, and behavior sex differences. In R. C. Friedman, R. M. Richart, & R. L. Vande Wiele (Eds.), *Sex differences in behavior.* New York: John Wiley.

Ericsson, K. A., & Kintsch, W. (1995). Long-term working memory. *Psychological Review, 102,* 211-245.

Erikson, E. (1963). *Childhood and society.* New York: W.W. Norton.

Erikson, E. (1968). *Identity: Youth and crisis.* New York: W.W. Norton.

Erikson, E. (1969). *Gandhi's truth: On the origin of militant nonviolence.* New York: W.W. Norton.

Erlenmeyer K. L., Adamo, U. H., Rock, D., Roberts, S. A., Bassett, A. S., Squires-Wheeler, E., et al. (1997). The New York High-Risk Project Prevalence and Comorbidity of Axis I Disorders in Offspring of Schizophrenic Parents at 25-Year Follow-up. *Archives of General Psychiatry, 54,* 1096–1102.

Escobedo, L. G., & Peddicord, J. P. (1996). Smoking prevalence in U.S. birth cohorts: The influence of gender and education. *American Journal of Public Health, 86,* 231–236.

Estes, W. K. (1994). *Classification and cognition.* New York: Oxford University Press.

Euler, H. A., & Weitzel, B. (1996). Discriminative grandparental solicitude as reproductive strategy. *Human Nature, 7,* 39–59.

Evans, G. W., Palsane, M. N., & Carrere, S. (1987). Type A behavior and occupational stress: A cross-cultural study of blue-collar workers. *Journal of Personality and Social Psychology, 52,* 1002–1007.

Evans-Pritchard, E. E. (1956). *Nuer religion.* Oxford: Clarendon Press. Even after having an STD, many teenagers do not adopt safer-sex practices. *Perspectives on Sexual and Reproductive Health, 35,* 103–104.

Everson, C. A. (1997). Sleep deprivation and the immune system. In M. R. Pressman, & W. C. Orr (Eds.), *Understanding sleep: The evaluation and treatment of sleep disorders. Application and practice in health psychology* (pp. 401–424).

Washington, DC: American Psychological Association.

Eysenck, H. (1987a). The growth of a unified scientific psychology: Ordeal by quakery. In A. Staats & L. Mos (Eds.), *Annals of theoretical psychology,* (Vol. 5, pp. 91–113). New York: Plenum Press.

Eysenck, H. (1987b). *Theoretical foundations of behavior therapy.* New York: Plenum Press.

Eysenck, H. J. (1952). The effects of psychotherapy: an evaluation. *Journal of Consulting Psychology, 16,* 319–324.

Eysenck, H. J. (1953). *The structure of human personality.* New York: John Wiley.

Eysenck, H. J. (1964). Psychotherapy or behaviour therapy. *Indian Psychological Review, 1,* 33-41.

Eysenck, H. J. (1982). Development of a theory. In H. J. Eysenck (Ed.), *Personality, genetics and behavior: Selected papers.* (pp. 593–595). New York: Praeger.

Eysenck, H. J. (1983a). Human learning and individual differences: The genetic dimension. *Educational Psychology, 3,* 169–188.

Eysenck, H. J. (1983b). The roots of creativity: Cognitive ability or personality trait? *Roeper Review, 5,* 10–12.

Eysenck, H. J. (1990). Biological dimensions of personality. In L. A. Pervin (Ed.), *Handbook of personality: Theory and research* (pp. 244–276). New York: Guilford Press.

Eysenck, H. J. (1993). Creativity and personality: Suggestions for a theory. *Psychological Inquiry, 4,* 147–178.

Fabrega, H. (1994). International systems of diagnosis in psychiatry. *Journal of Nervous & Mental Disease, 182,* 256–263.

Fagot, B. I. (1985). Changes in thinking about early sex role development. *Developmental Review, 5,* 83–98.

Fagot, B. I., & Patterson, G. R. (1969). An in vivo analysis of reinforcing contingencies for sex-role behaviors in the preschool child. *Developmental Psychology.*

Fairburn, C. G., Cooper, Z., Doll, H. A., & Welch, S. L. (1999). Risk factors for anorexia nervosa: Three integrated case-control comparisons. *Archives of General Psychiatry, 56,* 468–476.

Faith, M. S., Rha, S. S., Neale, M. C., & Allison, D. B. (1999). Evidence for genetic influences on human energy intake: Results from a twin study using measured observations. *Behavior Genetics, 29,* 145–154.

Fancher, R. E. (2004). The concept of race in the life and thought of Francis Galton. In A. S. Winston (Ed.), *Defining difference. Race and racism in the history of psychology* (pp. 49-75). Washington, DC: American Psychological Association.

Fanselow, M. S. (1998). Pavlovian conditioning, negative feedback, and blocking: Mechanisms that regulate association formation. *Neuron, 20,* 625–627.

Fanselow, M. S., & LeDoux, J. E. (1999). Why we think plasiticity underlying Pavlovian fear conditioning occurs in the basolateral amygdala. *Neuron, 23,* 229–232.

Fantz, R. L., Fagan III, J. F., & Miranda, S. B. (1975). Early visual selectivity. In L. B. Cohen & P. Salapatek (Eds.), *Infant perception: From sensation to cognition: Vol. I. Basic visual processes.* New York: Academic Press.

Farah, M. J. (2000). *The cognitive neuroscience of vision.* Malden, MA: Blackwell Publishers.

Faraone, S. V., Biederman, J., Feighner, J. A., & Monuteaux, M. C. (2000). Assessing symptoms of attention deficit hyperactivity disorder in children and adults: Which is more valid? *Journal of Consulting and Clinical Psychology, 68,* 830–842.

Faraone, S. V., Biederman, J., & Milberger, S. (1995). How reliable are maternal reports of their children's psychopathology? One-year recall of psychiatric diagnoses of ADHD children. *Journal of the American Academy of Child & Adolescent Psychiatry, 34,* 1001–1008.

Farber, N. B., Newcomer, J. W., & Olney, J. W. (1999). Glycine agonists: What can they teach us about schizophrenia? *Archives of General Psychiatry, 56,* 13–17.

Farmer, C. M., O'Donnell, B. F., Niznikiewicz, M. A., Voglmaier, M. M., McCarley, R. W., & Shenton, M. E. (2000). Visual perception and working memory in schizotypal personality disorder. *American Journal of Psychiatry, 157,* 781–786.

Farmer, I. P., Meyer, P. S., Ramsey, D. J., & Goff, D. C. (1996). Higher levels of social support predict greater survival following acute myocardial infarction: *Corpus Christi Heart Project. Behavioral Medicine, 22,* 59–66.

Fass, P. S. (1980). The I.Q.: A cultural and historical framework. *American Journal of Education,* 431–458.

Faw, B. (2003). Pre-frontal executive committee for perception, working memory, attention, long-term memory, motor control, and thinking: A tutorial review. *Consciousness and Cognition: An International Journal, 12,* 83–139.

Fazio, R. (1990). Multiple processes by which attitudes guide behavior: The MODE model as an integrative framework. In L. Berkowitz (Ed.), *Advances in Experimental Social Psychology, 23,* 75–109.

Fazio, R., Jackson, J. R., Dunton, B., & Williams, C. J. (1995). Variability in automatic activation as an unobtrusive measure of racial attitudes: A bona fide pipeline? *Journal of Personality and Social Psychology, 69,* 1013–1027.

Fazio, R., & Zanna, M. (1981). Direct experience and attitude-behavior consistency. In L. Berkowitz (Ed.), *Advances in experimental social psychology* (Vol. 14). New York: Academic Press.

Fazio, R. H. (1986). How do attitudes guide behavior? In R. M. Sorrentino & E. T. Higgins (Eds.), *The handbook of motivation and cognition: Foundations of social behavior.* New York: Guilford Press.

Fazio, R. H. (1995). Attitudes as object-evaluation associations: Determinants, consequences, and correlates of attitude accessibility. In R. E. Petty,

J. A. Krosnick, et al. (Eds.), *Attitude strength: Antecedents and consequences.* Ohio State University series on attitudes and persuasion (Vol. 4, pp. 247–282). Mahwah, NJ: Lawrence Erlbaum.

Fazio, R. H., Ledbetter, J. E., & Towles-Schwen, T. (2000). On the costs of accessible attitudes: Detecting that the attitude object has changed. *Journal of Personality and Social Psychology, 78,* 197–210.

Fears, T. R., & Scotto, J. (1982). Changes in skin cancer morbidity between 1971–1972 and 1977–1978. *Journal of the National Cancer Institute, 69,* 365–370.

Fehm-Wolfsdorf, G., Soherr, U., Arndt, R., Kern, W., et al. (1993). Auditory reflex thresholds elevated by stress-induced cortisol secretion. *Psychoneuroendocrinology, 18,* 579–589.

Feingold, A. (1988). Matching for attractiveness in romantic partners and same-sex friends: A meta-analysis and theoretical critique. *Psychological Bulletin, 104,* 226–235.

Feingold, A. (1992). Good-looking people are not what we think. *Psychological Bulletin, 111,* 304–341.

Feingold, A. (1994). Gender differences in personality: A meta-analysis. *Psychological Bulletin, 116,* 429–456.

Feldman, D. E., Brainard, M. S., & Knudsen, E. I. (1996). Newly learned auditory responses mediated by NMDA receptors in the owl inferior colliculus. *Science, 271,* 525–528.

Feldman, M. D., & Ford, C. V. (1994). *Patient or pretender: Inside the strange world of factitious disorders.* Oxford: John Wiley & Sons.

Feng, A. S., & Ratnam, R. (2000). Neural basis of hearing in real-world situations. *Annual Review of Psychology, 51,* 699–725.

Ferguson, E. D. (2000). *Motivation: A biosocial and cognitive integration of motivation and emotion.* New York: Oxford University Press.

Fernald, A., & Kuhl, P. (1987). Acoustic determinants of infant preference for motherese speech. *Infant Behavior and Development, 10,* 279–293.

Ferro, T., Verdeli, H., Pierre, F., & Weissman, M. M. (2000). Screening for depression in mothers bringing their offspring for evaluation or treatment of depression. *American Journal of Psychiatry, 157,* 375–379.

Ferster, C. B., & Skinner, B. F. (1957). *Schedules of reinforcement.* East Norwalk, CT: Appleton-Century-Crofts.

Ferster, D., & Miller, K. D. (2000). Neural mechanisms of orientation selectivity in the visual cortex. *Annual Review of Neuroscience, 23,* 441–471.

Festinger, L. (1957). *A theory of cognitive dissonance.* New York: Harper & Row.

Festinger, L. (1962). Cognitive dissonance. *Scientific American, 107,* 409–415.

Festinger, L., & Carlsmith, J. M. (1959). Cognitive consequences of forced compliance. *Journal of Abnormal and Social Psychology, 58,* 203–210.

Festinger, L., Schachter, S., & Back, K. (1950). *Social pressures in informal groups: A study of human factors in housing.* New York: Harper Bros.

Fiedler, F. E. (1978). The contingency model and the dynamics of the leadership process. In L. Berkowitz (Ed.), *Advances in experimental social psychology* (Vol. 12, pp. 59-112). New York: Academic Press.

Fieder, F. E. (1981). Leadership effectiveness. *American Behavioral Scientist, 24,* 619-632.

Field, A. E., Camargo, C. A., Jr., Taylor, C. B., Berkey, C. S., Frazier, L., Gillman, M. W., & Colditz, G. A. (1999). Overweight, weight concerns, and bulimic behaviors among girls and boys. *Journal of the American Academy of Child and Adolescent Psychiatry, 38,* 754–760.

Fincham, F. D. (1998). Child development and marital relations. *Child Development, 69,* 543–574.

Fincham, F. D., & Beach, S. R. H. (1999). Conflict in marriage: Implications for working with couples. *Annual Review of Psychology, 50,* 47–77.

Finkelhor, D. (1994). The international epidemiology of child sexual abuse. *Child Abuse & Neglect, 18,* 409–417.

Finkelhor, D., Hotaling, G., Lewis, I. A., & Smith, C. (1990). Sexual abuse in a national survey of adult men and women: Prevalence, characteristics, and risk factors. *Child Abuse & Neglect, 14,* 19–28.

Finlay, B. L., & Darlington, R. (1995). Linked regularities in the development and evolution of mammalian brains. *Science, 268,* 1578–1583.

Finlay-Jones, R., & Brown, G. W. (1981). Types of stressful life event and the onset of anxiety and depressive disorders. *Psychological Medicine, 11,* 803–815.

Finn, P. R., Sharkansky, E. J., Brandt, K. M., & Turcotte, N. (2000). The effects of familial risk, personality, and expectancies on alcohol use and abuse. *Journal of Abnormal Psychology, 109,* 122–133.

Fiore, M. C., Bailey, W. C., Cohen, S. J., Dorfman, S. F., Fox, B. J., Goldstein, M. G., et al. (2000). *Treating tobacco use and dependence: Clinical practice guideline.* Rockville, MD: U.S. Department of Health and Human Service.

Fischer, A. H. (Ed.) (2000). *Gender and emotion: Social psychological perspectives.* New York: Cambridge University Press

Fischer, K. W. (1980). A theory of cognitive development: The control and construction of hierarchies of skills. *Psychological Review, 87,* 477–531.

Fischer, K. W., Shaver, P. R., & Carnochan, P. (1990). How emotions develop and how they organize development. *Cognition and Emotion, 4,* 81–127.

Fiset, P., Paus, T., Daloze, T., Plourde, G., Meuret, P., Bonhomme, V., Hajj-Ali, N., Backman, S. B., & Evans, A. C. (1999). Brain mechanisms of propofol-induced loss of consciousness in humans: A positron emission tomographic study. *Journal of Neuroscience, 19,* 5506–5513.

Fishbein, M., & Ajzen, I. (1974). Attitudes towards objects as predictors of single and multiple behavioral criteria. *Psychologial Review, 81,* 59–74.

Fisher, S., & Greenberg, R. (1985). *The scientific*

credibility of Freud's theories and therapy. New York: Columbia University Press.

Fisher, S., & Greenberg, R. P. (1996). *Freud scientifically reappraised: Testing the theories and therapy.* New York: John Wiley & Sons.

Fishkin, J., Keniston, K., & MacKinnon, C. (1973). Moral reasoning and political ideology. *Journal of Personality and Social Psychology, 27,* 109–119.

Fiske, A. P., Kitayama, S., Markus, H. R., & Nisbett, R. E. (1998). The cultural matrix of social psychology. In D. T. Gilbert & S. T. Fiske (Eds.). *The handbook of social psychology, Vol. 2* (4th ed., pp. 915–981). Boston, MA: McGraw-Hill.

Fiske, S. (1992). Thinking is for doing: Portraits of social cognition from daguerreotype to laserphoto. *Journal of Personality and Social Psychology, 63,* 877–889.

Fiske, S. (1995). Social cognition. In A. Tesser (Ed.), *Constructing social psychology.* New York: McGraw-Hill.

Fiske, S. T. (1993). Social cognition and social perception. *Annual Review of Psychology, 44,* 155–194.

Fiske, S. T. (1998). Stereotyping, prejudice, and discrimination. In D. T. Gilbert, S. T. Fiske, et al. (Eds.), *The handbook of social psychology* (Vol. 2, 4th ed., pp. 357–411). Boston, MA: McGraw-Hill.

Fiske, S. T., & Taylor, S. E. (1991). *Social cognition* (2nd ed.) New York: McGraw-Hill.

Flanagan, J. C. (1978). A research approach to improving our quality of life. *American Psychologist, 33,* 138-147.

Flanagan, J. C. (1978). A research approach to improving our quality of life. *American Psychologist, 33,* 138-147.

Flavell, J., Green, F. L., Flavell, E., & Grossman, J. B. (1997). The development of children's knowledge about inner speech. *Child Development, 68,* 39–47.

Flavell, J. H. (1977). (Ed.) *Cognitive development.* Oxford: Prentice-Hall.

Flavell, J. H. (1996). Piaget's legacy. *Psychological Science, 7,* 200-203.

Flavell, J. H. (1982). Structures, stages, and sequences in cognitive development. In W. A. Collins (Ed.), *The concept of development* (Vol. 15). Hillsdale, NJ: Lawrence Erlbaum.

Flavell, J. H. (1992). Perspectives on perspective taking. In H. Beilin & P. B. Pufall (Eds.), *Piaget's theory: Prospects and possibilities. The Jean Piaget symposium series.* (pp. 107–139). Hillsdale, NJ: Lawrence Erlbaum.

Flavell, J. H. (1999). Cognitive development: Children's knowledge about the mind. *Annual Review of Psychology, 50,* 21–45.

Flavell, J. H., Botkin, P. T., Fry, C. L., Jr., Wright, J. W., & Jarvis, P. E. (1968). *The development of role-taking and communications skills in children.* New York: John Wiley.

Flavell, J. H., Friedrichs, A. G., & Hoyt, J. D. (1970). Developmental changes in memorization processes. *Cognitive Psychology, 1,* 324–340.

Flavell, J. H., Green, F. L., Flavell, E. R., & Grossman, J. B. (1997). The development of

children's knowledge about inner speech. *Child Development, 68,* 39–47.

Flavell, J. H., Green, F. L., Flavell, E. R., & Lin, N. T. (1999). Development of children's knowledge about unconsciousness. *Child Development, 70,* 396–412.

Flavell, J. H., & Miller, P. H. (1998) Social cognition. In W. Damon (Ed. in Chief) and N. Eisenberg (Vol. Ed.), *Handbook of child psychology* (Vol. 2, pp. 851–898). New York: John Wiley.

Flavell, J. H., & Wellman, H. M. (1977). Metamemory. In R. V. Kail, Jr. & J. W. Hagen (Eds.). *Perspectives on the development of memory and cognition.* Hillsdale, NJ: Lawrence Erlbaum.

Fleming, J. H., & Rudman, L. A. (1993). Between a rock and a hard place: Self-concept regulating and communicative properties of distancing behaviors. *Journal of Personality and Social Psychology, 64,* 44–59.

Fletcher, G. O., Simpson, J. A., Thomas, G., & Giles, L. (1999). Ideals in intimate relationships. *Journal of Personality and Social Psychology, 76,* 72–89.

Flor, H., Haag, G., & Turl, D. C. (1986). Long-term efficacy of EMG biofeedback for chronic rheumatic back pain. *Pain, 27,* 195–202.

Flynn, J. R. (1987). Massive IQ gains in 14 nations: What IQ tests really measure? *Psychological Bulletin, 101,* 171–191.

Flynn, J. R. (1999). Searching for justice: The discovery of IQ gains over time. *American Psychologist, 54,* 5–20.

Foa, E. B., Dancu, C. V., Hembree, E. A., Jaycox, L. H., Meadows, E. A., & Street, G. P. (1999). A comparison of exposure therapy, stress inoculation training, and their combination for reducing posttraumatic stress disorder in female assault victims. *Journal of Consulting and Clinical Psychology, 67,* 194–200.

Fodor, J. (1983). *The modularity of mind.* Cambridge, MA: MIT Press.

Fogel, A., Melson, G. F., & Mistry, J. (1986). Conceptualizing the determinants of nurturance: A reassessment of sex differences. In A. Fogal & G. F. Melson (Eds.), *Origins of nurturance.* Hillsdale, NJ: Lawrence Erlbaum.

Folkman, S., & Lazarus, R. S. (1980). An analysis of coping in a middle-aged community sample. *Journal of Health and Social Behavior, 21,* 219-239.

Folkman, S., & Moskowitz, J. T. (2000). Positive affect and the other side of coping. *American Psychologist, 55,* 647–654.

Fonagy, P., Steele, H., & Steele, M. (1991). Maternal representations of attachment during pregnancy predict the organization of infant–mother attachment at one year of age. *Child Development, 62,* 891–905.

Ford, M. (1979). The construct validity of egocentrism. *Psychological Bulletin, 86,* 1169–1188.

Foreyt, J. P. (1987). Issues in the assessment and treatment of obesity. *Journal of Consulting and Clinical Psychology, 55,* 677–684.

Foreyt, J. P., & Goodrick, G. D. (1995). The ultimate triumph of obesity. *Lancet, 346,* 134–135.

Forgas, J. P. (1995). Mood and judgment: The af-

fect infusion model (AIM). *Psychological Bulletin, 117,* 39–66.

Forsyth D. R. (1990). *Group Dynamics,* (2nd ed.), Pacific Grove, CA: Brooks/Cole.

Foster, G. (1965). Peasant society and the image of limited good. *American Anthropologist, 67,* 293–315.

Foster, M. A., Jurkovic, G. J., Ferdinand, L. G., & Meadows, L. A. (2002). The impact of the genogram on couples: A manualized approach. *Family Journal Counseling and Therapy for Couples and Families, 10,* 34–40.

Foulkes, D. (1993). Data constraints on theorizing about dream function. In A. Moffitt & M. Kramer (Eds.), *The functions of dreaming* (pp. 11-20). Albany, NY: State University of New York Press.

Fowles, D. C. (1992). Schizophrenia: Diathesis–stress revisited. *Annual Review of Psychology, 43,* 303–336.

Fox, N. (1991b). If it's not left, it's right: Electroencephalograph asymmetry and the development of emotion. *American Psychologist, 46,* 863–872.

Fox, N. A., Rubin, K. H., Calkins, S. D., Marshall, T. R., Coplan, R. J., Porges, S. W., et al. (1995). Frontal activation asymmetry and social competence at four years of age. *Child Development, 66,* 1770–1784.

Fozard, J. (1990). Vision and hearing in aging. In J. Birren & K. W. Schaie (Eds.), *Handbook of the psychology of aging* (3rd ed.). New York: Academic Press.

Fraiberg, S. (1975). The development of human attachments in infants blind from birth. *Merrill-Palmer Quarterly, 21,* 315–334.

Fraley, R. C., & Shaver, P. R. (1998). Airport separations: A naturalistic study of adult attachment dynamics in separating couples. *Journal of Personality & Social Psychology, 75,* 1198–1212.

Frank, E., Anderson, B., Reynolds, C. F., Ritenour, A., & Kupfer, D. J. (1994). Life events and the research diagnostic criteria endogenous subtype: A confirmation of the distinction using the Bedford College methods. *Archives of General Psychiatry, 51,* 519–524.

Frank, E., Swartz, H. A., Mallinger, A. G., Thase, M. E., Weaver, E. V., & Kupfer, D. J. (1999). Adjunctive psychotherapy for bipolar disorder: Effects of changing treatment modality. *Journal of Abnormal Psychology, 108,* 579–587.

Frank, J. D. (1978). *Psychotherapy and the human predicament: A psychosocial approach.* New York: Schocken.

Frankl, V. (1959). *Man's search for meaning: An introduction to logotherapy.* New York: Pocket Books.

Franklin, J., Donohew, L., Dhoundiyal, V., & Cook, P. L. (1988). Attention and our recent past: The scaly thumb of the reptile. *American Behavioral Scientist, 31,* 312–326.

Franks, V. (1986). Sex stereotyping and the diagnosis of psychopathology. In D. Howard (Ed.), *The dynamics of feminist therapy* (pp. 219–232). New York: Haworth Press.

Franz, C., McClelland, D., & Weinberger, J. (1991). Childhood antecedents of conventional social accomplishment in midlife adults: A 36-year prospective study. *Journal of Personality and Social Psychology, 60,* 586–595.

Free, M., & Beekhuis, M. (1985). A successful adaptation of systematic desensitization in the treatment of a phobia of babies. *Behaviour Change, 2,* 59–64.

Freedman, J. L., & Fraser, S. C. (1966). Compliance without pressure: The foot-in-the-door technique. *Journal of Personality and Social Psychology, 4,* 195–202.

Freedman, M. A. (2002). Quality of life and menopause: The role of estrogen. *Journal of Women's Health, 11,* 703–718.

Freedman, N., Hoffenberg, J. D., Vorus, N., & Frosch, A. (1999). The effectiveness of psychoanalytic psychotherapy: The role of treatment duration, frequency of sessions, and the therapeutic relationship. *Journal of the American Psychoanalytic Association, 47,* 741–772.

Freeman, W. (1959). Psychosurgery. In S. Aneti (Ed.), *American handbook of psychiatry II.* New York: Basic Books.

Freud, A. (1936). *The ego and the mechanisms of defense.* New York: International Universities Press.

Freud, A. (1958). Adolescence. *Psychoanalytic Study of the Child, 13,* 255–278.

Freud, S. (1900). *The interpretation of dreams.* New York: Avon, 1965.

Freud, S. (1912). The dynamics of transference. In J. Strachey (Ed., Trans.), *The standard edition of the complete psychological works of Sigmund Freud,* (Vol. 12, pp. 97–108). London: Hogarth, 1958.

Freud, S. (1915). The unconscious. In P. Rieff (Ed.), *Freud: General psychological theory.* New York: Collier, 1963.

Freud, S. (1917). Mourning and melancholia. In P. Reiff (Ed.), *Freud: General psychological theory.* New York: Collier, 1963.

Freud, S. (1923). *The ego and the id.* New York: W. W. Norton.

Freud, S. (1928). *The Future of an Illusion. International psychoanalytical library, no. 15.* New York: Liveright.

Freud, S. (1933). *New introductory lectures on psychoanalysis.* New York: W.W. Norton, 1965.

Fried, C. B., & Aronson, E. (1995). Hypocrisy, misattribution, and dissonance reduction. *Personality and Social Psychology Bulletin, 21,* 925–933.

Fried, P. A. (1995). The Ottawa Prenatal Prospective Study (OPPS): Methodological issues and findings: It's easy to throw the baby out with the bath water. Special Issue: 1994 International Symposium on Cannabis and the Cannabinoids: Developmental effects. *Life Sciences, 56,* 2159–2168.

Friedman, J. M. (2000). Obesity in the new millennium. *Nature, 404,* 632–634.

Friedman, L. S., Lichtenstein, E., & Biglan, A. (1985). Smoking onset among teens: An empirical analysis of initial situations. *Addictive Behaviors, 10,* 1–13.

Friedman, M., & Rosenman, R. H. (1959). Association of specific overt behavior pattern with blood and cardiovascular findings—blood cholesterol level, blood clotting time, incidence of arcus senilis, and clinical coronary heart disease. *Journal of the American Medical Association, 162,* 1286–1296.

Friedman, M. A., & Brownell, K. D. (1995). Psychological correlates of obesity: Moving to the next research generation. *Psychological Bulletin, 117,* 3–20.

Frieze, I. H., & Browne, A. (1989). Violence in marriage. In L. Ohlin & M. Tonry (Eds.), *Family violence.* Chicago: University of Chicago Press.

Frith, C., & Dolan, R. (1996). The role of the prefrontal cortex in higher cognitive functions. *Cognitive Brain Research, 5,* 175–181.

Fromkin, V., Krashen, S., Curtiss, S., Rigler, D., & Rigler, M. (1974). The development of language in Genie: A case of language acquisition beyond the critical period. *Brain and Language, 1,* 81–107.

Fromm, E. (1955). *The sane society.* Greenwich, CT: Fawcett Books.

Fry, A. F., & Hale, S. (1996). Processing speed, working memory, and fluid intelligence: Evidence for a developmental cascade. *Psychological Science, 7,* 237–241.

Funder, D., & Colvin, C. R. (1991). Explorations in behavioral consistency: Properties of persons, situations, and behaviors. *Journal of Personality and Social Psychology, 60,* 773–794.

Furman, W., & Buhrmester, D. (1992). Age and sex differences in perceptions of networks of personal relationships. *Child Development, 63,* 103–115.

Fussel, S. R., & Krauss, R. M. (1992). Coordination of knowledge in communication: Effects of speakers' assumptions about what others know. *Journal of Personality and Social Psychology, 62,* 378–391.

Fuster, J. (1989). *The prefrontal cortex* (2nd ed.). New York: Raven.

Fuster, J. M. (1997). Network memory. *Trends in Neurosciences, 20,* 451-459.

Fyer, A. J., Mannuzza, S., Chapman, T. F., Martin, L. Y., & Klein, D. F. (1995). Specificity in familial aggregation of phobic disorders. *Archives of General Psychiatry, 52,* 564–573.

Gabbard, G. (1992). Psychodynamic psychiatry in the "decade of the brain." *American Journal of Psychiatry, 149,* 991–998.

Gabbard, G. O., & Atkinson, S. D. (1996). (Eds.) *Synopsis of treatments for psychiatric disorders* (2nd ed.) Washington, DC: American Psychiatric Association.

Gabbay, F. (1992). Behavior-genetic strategies in the study of emotion. *Psychological Science, 3,* 50–55.

Gable, S. L., & Reis, H. T. (1999). Now and then, them and us, this and that: Studying relationships across time, partner, context, and person. *Personal Relationships, 6,* 415–432.

Gabrieli, J. D., Desmond, J. E., Demb, J. B., Wagner, A. D., Stone, M. V., Vaidya, C. J., & Glover, G. H. (1996). Functional magnetic resonance imaging of semantic memory processes in the frontal lobes. *Psychological Science, 7,* 278–283.

Gabrieli, J. D. (1998). Cognitive neuroscience of human memory. *Annual Review of Psychology, 49,* 87–115.

Gadow, K., & Sprafkin, J. (1993). Television violence and children with emotional and behavioral disorders. *Journal of Emotional and Behavioral Disorders, 1,* 54–63.

Gaensbauer, T., Chatoor, I., Drell, M., Siegel, D., et al. (1995). Traumatic loss in a one-year old girl. *Journal of the American Academy of Child and Adolescent Psychiatry, 34,* 520–528.

Galinsky, A. D., & Moskowitz, G. B. (2000). Perspective-taking: Decreasing stereotype expression, stereotype accessibility, and in-group favoritism. *Journal of Personality and Social Psychology, 78,* 708–724.

Gallistel, C. R., & Gibbon, J. (2000). Time, rate, and conditioning. *Psychological Review, 107,* 289-344.

Gallup, G. H. (1972). It's done with mirrors: Chimps and self-concept. *Psychology Today, 4,* 58-61.

Gamsa, A. (1990). Is emotional disturbance a precipitator or a consequence of chronic pain? *Pain, 42,* 183–195.

Gangestad, S. W., & Snyder, M. (2000). Self-monitoring: Appraisal and reappraisal. *Psychological Bulletin, 126,* 530–555.

Ganley, R. (1989). Emotion and eating in obesity: A view of the literature. *International Journal of Eating Disorders, 8,* 343–361.

Gannon, P. J., Holloway, R. L., Broadfield, D. C., & Braun, A. R. (1998). Asymmetry of chimpanzee planum temporale: Human-like pattern of Wernicke's brain language, area homolog. *Science, 279,* 220–222.

Garb, H. N. (1984). The incremental validity of information used in personality assessment. *Clinical Psychological Review, 40,* 641–655.

Garcia, J. (1979). I.Q.: The conspiracy. In J. B. Maas (Ed.), *Readings in psychology today* (4th ed., pp. 198–202). New York: Random House.

Garcia, J., & Garcia y Robertson, R. (1985). Evolution of learning mechanisms. In B. L. Hammonds (Ed.), *The Master lecture series* (Vol. 4). Washington, DC: American Psychological Association.

Garcia, J., & Koelling, R. (1966). Relation of cue to consequence in avoidance learning. *Psychonomic Science, 4,* 123–124.

Garcia, J., Lasiter, P., Bermudez-Rattoni, & Deems, D. (1985). A general theory of aversion learning. *Annals of the New York Academy of Sciences, 443,* 8–21.

Gardner, B. T., & Gardner, R. A. (1975). Evidence for sentence constituents in the early utterances of child and chimpanzee. *Journal of Experimental Psychology: General, 104,* 244–267.

Gardner, H. (1975). *The shattered mind.* New York: Alfred A. Knopf.

Gardner, H. (1983). *Frames of mind: The theory of multiple intelligences.* New York: Basic Books.

Gardner, H. (1985). *The mind's new science: A history of the cognitive revolution.* New York: Basic Books.

Gardner, H. (1999). *Intelligence reframed: Multiple*

intelligences for the 21st century. New York: Basic Books.

Gardner, H. (2000). The giftedness matrix: A developmental perspective. In R. C. Friedman, B. M. Shore, et al. (Eds.), *Talents unfolding: Cognition and development* (pp. 77–88). Washington, DC: American Psychological Association.

Garfield, C. (1986). *Peak performers: The new heroes of American business.* New York: Morrow.

Garner, D. M., & Garfinkel, P. E. (1979). The Eating Attitudes Test: An index of the symptoms of anorexia nervosa. *Psychological Medicine, 9,* 273–279.

Garner, D. M., & Wooley, S. (1991). Confronting the failure of behavioral and dietary treatments for obesity. *Clinical Psychology Review, 11,* 729–780.

Garver, D. L. (1997). The etiologic heterogeneity of schizophrenia. *Harvard Review of Psychiatry, 4,* 317–327.

Gaudreau, D., & Peretz, I. (1999). Implicit and explicit memory for music in old and young adults. *Brain & Cognition, 40,* 126–129.

Gauthier, J. G., Ivers, H., & Carrier, S. (1996). Nonpharmacological approaches in the management of recurrent headache disorders and their comparison and combination with pharmacotherapy. *Clinical Psychology Review, 16,* 543–571.

Gazzaniga, M. (1967). The split brain in man. *Scientific American, 217,* 24–29.

Ge, X., Conger, R. D., & Elder, G. (1996). Coming of age too early: Pubertal influences on girls' vulnerability to psychological distress. *Child Development, 67,* 3386–3400.

Geary, D. C., Rumsey, M., Bow-Thomas, C. C., & Hoard, M. K. (1995). Sexual jealousy as a facultative trait: Evidence from the pattern of sex differences in adults from China and the United States. *Ethology & Sociobiology, 16,* 355–383.

Gebhard, P. H. (1971). Human sexual behavior: A summary statement. In D. S. Marshall & R. C. Suggs (Eds.), *Human sexual behavior: Variations in the ethnographic spectrum.* New York: Basic Books.

Geen, R. G. (1995). Human aggression. In A. Tesser (Ed.), *Advanced social psychology.* New York: McGraw-Hill.

Geen, R. G. (1998). Aggression and antisocial behavior. In D. T. Gilbert, S. T. Fiske, et al. (Eds.), *The handbook of social psychology* (Vol. 2, 4th ed., pp. 317–356). Boston, MA: McGraw-Hill.

Geen, R. G. (2001). *Human aggression* (2nd ed.) New York: Taylor & Francis.

Geertz, C. (1963). The integrative revolution: Primordial sentiments and civil politics in the new states. In C. Geertz (Ed.), *Old societies and new states.* New York: Free Press.

Geertz, C. (1974). From the natives' point of view. *American Academy of Arts and Sciences Bulletin, 28,* 26–43.

Geldard, G. A. (1972). *The human senses* (2nd ed.). New York: John Wiley.

Gelinas, D. J. (1983). The persisting negative effects of incest. *Psychiatry, 46,* 312–332.

Gelman, R., & Baillargeon, R. (1983). A review of Piagetian concepts. In J. H. Flavell & E. M. Markman (Eds.), *Handbook of child psychology: Cognitive development* (Vol. 3). New York: John Wiley.

Gentner, D. (1983). Structure-mapping: A theoretical framework for analogy. *Cognitive Science, 7,* 155-170.

Gentner, D., & Holyoak, K. J. (1997). Reasoning and learning by analogy: Introduction. *American Psychologist, 52,* 32–34.

Gentner, D., & Markman, A. B. (1997). Structure mapping in analogy and similarity. *American Psychologist, 52,* 45–46.

George, D., Carroll, P., Kersnick, R., & Calderon, K. (1998). Gender-related patterns of helping among friends. *Psychology of Women Quarterly, 22,* 685–704.

George, M. S., Lisanby, S. H., & Sackeim, H. A. (1999). Transcranial magnetic stimulation: Applications in neuropsychiatry. *Archives of General Psychiatry, 56,* 300–311.

Gerken, L., & McIntosh, B. J. (1993). Interplay of function morphemes and prosody in early language. *Developmental Psychology, 29,* 448–457.

Gershon, S., & Soares, J. C. (1997). Current therapeutic profile of lithium. *Archives of General Psychiatry, 54,* 16–20.

Gerstner, C., & Day, D. V. (1994). Cross-cultural comparison of leadership prototypes. *Leadership Quarterly, 5,* 121–134.

Gest, S. D. (1997). Behavioral inhibition: Stability and associations with adaptation from childhood to early adulthood. *Journal of Personality and Social Psychology, 72,* 467–475.

Gibbs, R. W., Jr. (1981). Your wish is my command: Convention and context in interpreting indirect requests. *Journal of Verbal Learning and Verbal Behavior, 20,* 431–444.

Gibson, E. J. (1969). *Principals of perceptual learning and its development.* Englewood-Cliffs, NJ: Prentice- Hall.

Gibson, E. J. (1984). Perceptual development from the ecological approach. In M. E. Lamb, A. L. Brown, & B. Rogoff (Eds.), *Advances in developmental psychology* (Vol. 3).

Gibson, E. J., & Walk, R. D. (1960). The "visual cliff." *Scientific American, 202,* 64–71.

Gibson, H. B. (1996). Sexual functioning in later life. In R. T. Woods, et al. (Eds.), *Handbook of the clinical psychology of ageing* (pp. 183–193). Chichester, England: John Wiley & Sons.

Gibson, J. J. (1966). *The senses considered as perceptual systems.* Boston, MA: Houghton Mifflin.

Gibson, J. J. (1979). *The ecological approach to visual perception.* Boston, MA: Houghton Mifflin.

Giesler, R. B., Josephs, R. A., & Swann, W. B., Jr. (1996). Self-verification in clinical depression: The desire for negative evaluation. *Journal of Abnormal Psychology, 105,* 358–368.

Gigerenzer, G., & Goldstein, D. G. (1996). Reasoning the fast and frugal way: Models of bounded rationality. *Psychological Review, 103,* 650–669.

Gilbert, D. (1989). Thinking lightly about others: Automatic components of the social inference process. In J. S. Uleman & J. A. Bargh (Eds.), *Unintended thought* (pp. 189–211). New York: Guilford Press.

Gilbert, L. (1995). The articulation of circumstance and causal understandings. In D. Sperber & D. Premack (Eds.), *Causal cognition: A multidisciplinary debate* (pp. 557-576). New York: Oxford University Press.

Gilbert, D. T., Fiske, S. T., & Lindzey, G. (1998). *The handbook of social psychology* (Vol. 1, 4th ed.). Boston, MA: McGraw-Hill.

Gilbert, D. T., Pinel, E. C., Wilson, T. C., Blumberg, S. J., & Wheatley, T. P. (1998). Immune neglect: A source of durability bias in affective forecasting. *Journal of Personality and Social Psychology, 75,* 617–638.

Gilbert, P. L., Harris, M. J., McAdams, L. A., & Jeste, D. V. (1995). Neuroleptic withdrawal in schizophrenic patients: A review of the literature. *Archives of General Psychiatry, 52,* 173–188.

Gilboa, E., & Gotlib, I. H. (1997). Cognitive biases and affect persistence in previously dysphoric and never-dysphoric individuals. *Cognition & Emotion, 11,* 517–538.

Gilert, D. T., & Malone, P. S. (1995). The correspondence bias. *Psychological Bulletin, 117,* 21–38.

Gilhooly, K. J. (1989). Human and machine problem solving: Toward a comparative cognitive science. In K. J. Gilhooly (Ed.), *Human and machine problem solving.* New York: Plenum Press.

Gill, M. (1982). *The analysis of transference: Vol. 1. Theory and technique. Psychological Issues, Monograph,* No. 53.

Gilleard, C. J. (2000). Is Alzheimer's disease preventable? A review of two decades of epidemiological research. *Aging & Mental Health, 4,* 101–118.

Gilligan, C. (1982). *In a different voice.* Cambridge, MA: Harvard University Press.

Gilligan, J. (1996). Exploring shame in special settings: A psychotherapeutic study. In C. Cordess, M. Cox, et al. (Eds.), *Forensic psychotherapy: Crime, psychodynamics and the offender patient, Vol. 2: Mainly practice. Forensic focus series, No. 1* (pp. 475–489). London: Jessica Kingsley Publishers.

Gilmore, R. O., & Johnson, M. H. (1995). Working memory in infancy: Six-month-olds' performance on two versions of the oculomotor delayed response task. *Journal of Experimental Child Psychology, 59,* 397–418.

Gladue, B. A., Green, R., & Hellman, R. E. (1984). Neuroendocrine response to estrogen and sexual orientation. *Science, 225,* 1496–1499.

Gladwin, T. (1970). *East is a big bird.* Cambridge, MA: Belknap Press.

Glantz, S. A., & Parmley, W. W. (1991). Passive smoking and heart disease: Epidemiology, physiology, and biochemistry. *Circulation, 83,* 1–12.

Glass, G. V., & Smith, M. L. (1980). Ask not for whom the bell tolls. *American Psychologist, 35,* 223.

Glassman, N., & Andersen, S. (1997). *Activating transference without consciousness: Using signifi-*

cant- other representations to go beyond the sub-liminally given information. Unpublished manuscript, Department of Psychology, New York University.

Gleason, T. R. (2002). Social provisions of real and imaginary relationships in early childhood. *Developmental Psychology, 38,* 979–992.

Gleason, T. R., Sebanc, A. M., & Hartup, W. W. (2000). Imaginary companions of preschool children. *Developmental Psychology, 36,* 419–428.

Gleitman, L. R., Gleitman, H., Landau, B., & Warner, E. (1988). Where learning begins: Initial representations for language learning. In F. Newmeyer (Ed.), *Linguistics: The Cambridge survey. Vol. III. Language: Psychological and biological aspects.* Cambridge: Cambridge University Press.

Gluck, M. A., & Myers, C. E. (1997). Psychobiological models of hippocampal function in learning and memory. *Annual Review, 48,* 481–514.

Godden, D. R., & Baddeley, A. D. (1975). Context- dependent memory in two natural environments: On land and underwater. *British Journal of Psychology, 66,* 325–331.

Godin, G., Gagne, C., Maziade, J., Moreault, L., Beaulieu, D., & Morel, S. (2001). Breast cancer: The intention to have a mammography and clinical breast examination—application of the theory of planned behavior. *Psychology and Health, 16,* 423–441.

Goff, D. C., Bagnell, A. L., & Perlis, R. H. (1999). Glutamatergic augmentation strategies for cognitive impairment in schizophrenia. *Psychiatric Annals, 29,* 649–654.

Gogate, L. J., Bahrick, L. E., & Watson, J. D. (2000). A study of multimodal motherese: The role of temporal synchrony between verbal labels and gestures. *Child Development, 71,* 878-894.

Gold, J. M., Carpenter, C., Randolph, C., Goldberg, T. E., & Weinberger, D. E. (1997). Auditory working memory and Wisconsin card sorting test performance in schizophrenia. *Archives of General Psychiatry, 54,* 159–165.

Gold, M. S., & Pearsall, H. R. (1983). Hypothyroidism —or is it depression? *Psychosomatics, 24,* 646–656.

Goldberg, L. R. (1981). Language and individual differences: The search for universals in personality lexicons. In L. Wheeler (Ed.), *Review of personality and social psychology.* Beverly Hills, CA: Sage.

Goldberg, L. R. (1993). The structure of phenotypic personality traits. *American Psychologist, 48,* 26–34.

Golden, R. M., & Rumelhart, D. E. (1993). A parallel distributed processing model of story comprehension and recall. *Discourse Processes, 16,* 203–237.

Goldfield, B. A., & Snow, C. E. (1989). Individual differences in language acquisition. In J. Berko Gleason (Ed.), *The development of language* (2nd ed.). Columbus, OH: Merrill.

Goldfried, M. R., & Davison, G. C. (1994). *Clinical behavior therapy* (2nd ed.). New York: John Wiley & Sons.

Goldfried, M. R., & Wolfe, B. E. (1998). Toward a more clinically valid approach to therapy research. *Journal of Consulting and Clinical Psychology, 66,* 143-150.

Goldman-Rakic, P. (1995). Cellular basis of working memory. *Neuron, 14,* 477–485.

Goldman-Rakic, P. (1996). Regional and cellular fractionation of working memory. *Proceedings of the National Academy of Sciences, U.S.A., 93,* 13473–13476.

Goldner, E. M., Srikameswaran, S., Schroeder, M. L., Livesley, W. J., & Birmingham, C. L. (1999). Dimensional assessment of personality pathology in patients with eating disorders. *Psychiatry Research, 85,* 151–159.

Goldsmith, H. H., & Alansky, J. A. (1987). Maternal and infant temperamental predictors of attachment: A meta-analytic review. *Journal of Consulting and Clinical Psychology, 55,* 805–816.

Goldsmith, S. K., Shapiro, R. M., & Joyce, J. N. (1997). Disrupted pattern of D2 dopamine receptors in the temporal lobe in schizophrenia: A postmortem study. *Archives of General Psychiatry, 54,* 649–658.

Goldsmith, T. H. (1994). Ultraviolet receptors and color visions: Evolutionary implications and a dissonance of paradigms. *Vision Research, 34,* 1479–1487.

Goldstein, A. J., & Chambless, D. J. (1978). A re-analysis of agoraphobia. *Behavior Therapy, 9,* 47–59.

Goldstein, E. B. (1989). *Sensation and perception.* Belmont, CA: Wadsworth.

Goldstein, J. M., Goodman, J. M., Seidman, L. J., Kennedy, D. N., Makris, N., Lee, H., Tourville, J., Caviness, V. S., Faraone, S. V., & Tsuang, M. T. (1999). Cortical abnormalities in schizophrenia identified by structural magnetic resonance imaging. *Archives of General Psychiatry, 57,* 537–547.

Goldstein, M. J. (1988). The family and psychopathology. *Annual Review of Psychology, 39,* 283–299.

Goldstein, R. B., Wickramaratne, P. J., Horwath, E., & Weissman, M. M. (1997). Familial aggregation and phenomenology of "early"-onset (at or before age 20 years) panic disorder. *Archives of General Psychiatry, 54,* 271–278.

Goldstone, R. L., & Kersten, A. (2003). Concepts and categorization. In A. F. Healy & R. W. Proctor (Eds.), *Handbook of psychology: Experimental psychology* (Vol. 4, pp. 599–621). New York: John Wiley & Sons.

Goleman, D. (1995). *Emotional intelligence.* New York: Bantam Books.

Golomb, A., Ludolph, P., Westen, D., Block, M. J., et al. (1994). Maternal empathy, family chaos, and the etiology of borderline personality disorder. *Journal of the American Psychoanalytic Association, 42,* 525–548.

Gomez, A., & Gomez, R. (2002). Personality traits of the behavioral approach and inhibition systems: Association with processing of emotional stimuli. *Personality and Individual Differences, 32,* 1299–1316.

Good, B. J., & Kleinman, A. M. (1985). Culture and anxiety: Cross-cultural evidence for the patterning of anxiety disorders. In A. H. Tuma & J. D. Maser (Eds.), *Anxiety and the anxiety disorders* (pp. 297-323). Hillsdale, NJ: Lawrence Erlbaum Associates.

Goodenough, B., & Gillam, B. (1997). Gradients as visual primitives. *Journal of Experimental Psychology: Human Perception and Performance, 23,* 370–387.

Goodman, G. S., Ghetti, S., Quas, J. A., Edelstein, R. S., Alexander, K. W., Redlich, A.D., Cordon, I. M., & Jones, D. P. H. (2003). A prospective study of memory for child sexual abuse: New findings relevant to the repressed-memory controversy. *Psychological Science, 14,* 113–118.

Goodman, L., Koss, M., Fitzgerald, L., Russo, N., & Keita, G. (1993). Male violence against women: Current research and future directions. *American Psychologist, 48,* 1054–1058.

Goodman, S. H. (1997). The parental discipline–child behavior problems puzzle: Some new pieces. *Psychological Inquiry, 8,* 192–194.

Goodnow, J. J. (1976). The nature of intelligent behavior: Questions raised by cross-cultural studies. In L. B. Resnick (Ed.), *The nature of intelligence* (pp. 169–188). Hillsdale, NJ: Lawrence Erlbaum.

Goodwin, C. J. (1999). *A history of modern psychology.* New York: John Wiley & Sons.

Goodwin, F. K., & Ghaemi, S. N. (1997). Future directions in mood disorder research. In A. Honig & H. M. van Praag (Eds.), *Depression: Neurobiological, psychopathological and therapeutic advances. Wiley series on clinical and neurobiological advances in psychiatry* (Vol. 3, pp. 627–643). New York: John Wiley & Sons.

Goodwin, F. K., & Ghaemi, S. N. (1998). Understanding manic-depressive illness. *Archives of General Psychiatry, 55,* 23–25.

Goodwin, F. K., & Roy-Byrne, P. (1987). Treatment of bipolar disorders. In A. J. Frances and R. E. Hales (Eds.), *Psychiatric Update Annual Review* (Vol. 6).

Goodwyn, S. W., & Acredolo, L. P. (1998). Encouraging symbolic gestures: A new perspective on the relationship between gesture and speech. In J. M. Iverson & S. Goldin-Meadow (Eds.), *The nature and functions of gesture in children's communication. New directions for child development,* No. 79 (pp. 71-73). San Francisco: Jossey-Bass.

Goodwyn, S. W., Acredolo, L. P., & Brown, C. A. (2000). Impact of symbolic gesturing on early language development. *Journal of Nonverbal Behavior, 24,* 81–103.

Goody, J. (1977). *The domestication of the savage mind.* Cambridge: Cambridge University Press.

Gopnik, A. (1993). How we know our minds: The illusion of first-person intentionality. *Behavioral and Brain Sciences, 16,* 1–14.

Gordis, E. (1996). Alcohol research: At the cutting edge. *Archives of General Psychiatry, 53,* 199–201.

Gordon, M., & Shankweiler, P. J. (1971). Different equals less: Female sexuality in recent marriage manuals. *Journal of Marriage and the Family, 33,* 459–466.

Gorman, J. M., Kent, J. M., Sullivan, G. M., & Coplan, J. D. (2000). Neuroanatomical hypothesis of panic disorder, revised. *American Journal of Psychiatry, 157,* 493–505.

Gorn, G. J. (1982). The effects of music in advertising on choice behavior: A classical conditioning approach. *Journal of Marketing, 46,* 94–100.

Gorski, R. A., & Barraclough, C. A. (1963). Effects of low dosages of androgen on the differentiation of hypothalamic regulatory control of ovulation in the rat. *Endocrinology, 73,* 210–216.

Gortmaker, S. L., Must, A., Perrin, J. M., Sobol, A. M., & Dietz, W. H. (1993). Social and economic consequences of overweight in adolescence and young adulthood. *The New England Journal of Medicine, 329,* 1008–1012.

Goschke, T., & Kuhl, J. (1993). Representations of intentions: Persisting activation in memory. *Journal of Experimental Psychology: Learning, Memory, and Cognition, 19,* 1211–1226.

Goschke, T., & Kuhl, J. (1996). Remembering what to do: Explicit and implicit memory for intentions. In M. Brandimonte, G. Einstein, & M. McDaniel (Eds.), *Prospective memory: Theory and applications* (pp. 53-91). Mahwah, NJ: Lawrence Erlbaum Associates.

Goto, H. (1971). Auditory perception by normal Japanese adults of the sounds "I" and "r." *Neuropsychologia, 9,* 317–323.

Gottesman, I. I. (1991). *Schizophrenia genesis: The origins of madness.* New York: Freeman.

Gottesman, I. I., & Bertelsen, A. (1989). Confirming unexpressed genotypes for schizophrenia: Risks in the offspring of Fischer's Danish identical and fraternal discordant twins. *Archives of General Psychiatry, 50,* 527–540.

Gottlieb, G. (1991). Experiential canalization of behavioral development: Theory. *Developmental Psychology, 27,* 4–13.

Gottlieb, J. P., Kusunoki, M., & Goldberg, M. E. (1998). The representation of visual salience in monkey parietal cortex. *Nature, 391,* 481–484.

Gottman, J. (1998). Psychology and the study of marital processes. *Annual Review of Psychology, 49,* 169–197.

Gould, E., Tanapat, P., McEwen, B. S., Flugge, G., & Fuchs, E. (1998). Proliferation of granule cell precursors in the dentate gyrus of adult monkeys is diminished by stress. *Proceedings of the National Academy of Sciences, U.S.A., 95,* 3168–3171.

Gould, S. J. (1981). *The mismeasure of man.* New York: W.W. Norton.

Gould, S. J. (1984). Human equality is a contingent fact of history. *Natural History, 92,* 26–33.

Gracely, R., Lynch, S., & Bennett, G. J. (1992). Painful neuropathy: Altered central processing maintained dynamically by peripheral input. *Pain, 51,* 175–194.

Graesser, A. C., Millis, K. K., & Zwaan, R. (1997). Discourse comprehension. *Annual Review of Psychology, 48,* 163–189.

Graf, P., & Schacter, D. L. (1987). Selective effects of interference on implicit and explicit memory for new associations. *Journal of Experimental Psychology: Learning, Memory, & Cognition, 13,* 45–53.

Graham, K. S., Patterson, K., & Hodges, J. R. (1999). Episodic memory: New insights from the study of semantic dementia. *Current Opinion in Neurobiology, 9,* 245–250.

Graugaard, P., & Finset, A. (2000). Trait anxiety and reactions to patient-centered and doctor-centered styles of communication: An experimental study. *Psychosomatic Medicine, 62,* 33–39.

Gray, J. A. (1987). *The psychology of fear and stress* (2nd ed.). New York: Cambridge University Press.

Gray, J. A. (1990). Brain systems that mediate both emotion and cognition. *Cognition and Emotion, 4,* 269–288.

Gray, J. A. (1994). Framework for a taxonomy of psychiatric disorder. In S. H. M. van Goozen & N. E. Van de Poll (Eds.), *Emotions: Essays on emotion theory.* (pp. 29–59). Hillsdale, NJ: Lawrence Erlbaum.

Graybeal, A., Sexton, J. D., & Pennebaker, J. W. (2002). The role of story-making in disclosure writing: The psychometric properties of narrative. *Psychology and Health, 17,* 571–581.

Graziadei, P. P. C. (1969). The ultra-structure of vertebrate taste buds. In C. Pfaffman (Ed.), *Olfaction and taste,* (Vol. 3). New York: Rockefeller University Press.

Green, L., & Freed, D. E. (1993). The substitutability of reinforcers. *Journal of the Experimental Analysis of Behavior, 60,* 141–158.

Green, R. (1987). *The "sissy boy" syndrome and the development of homosexuality.* New Haven, CT: Yale University Press.

Greenberg, J., Pyszczynski, T., Solomon, S., Simon, L., et al. (1994). Role of consciousness and accessibility of death-related thoughts in mortality salience effects. *Journal of Personality & Social Psychology, 67,* 627–637.

Greenberg, L. S., & Safran, J. D. (1990). Emotional-change processes in psychotherapy. In R. Plutchik & H. Kellerman, Henry (Eds.), *Emotion, psychopathology, and psychotherapy. Emotion: Theory, research, and experience* (Vol. 5, pp. 59–85). San Diego, CA: Academic Press.

Greene, D. M., & Swets, J. A. (1966). *Signal detection theory and psychophysics.* New York: Wiley.

Greeno, C. G., & Wing, R. R. (1994). Stress-induced eating. *Psychological Bulletin, 115,* 444–464.

Greeno, J. G. (1978). Natures of problem-solving abilities. In W. K. Estes (Ed.), *Handbook of learning and cognitive processes* (Vol. 5). Hillsdale, NJ: Lawrence Erlbaum.

Greenough, W. T. (1991). Experience as a component of normal development: Evolutionary considerations. *Developmental Psychology, 27,* 14–17.

Greenwald, A. G. (1980). The totalitarian ego: Fabrication and revision of personal history. *American Psychologist, 35,* 603–618.

Greenwald, A. G., & Banaji, M. (1995). Implicit social cognition: Attitudes, self-esteem, and stereotypes. *Psychological Review, 102,* 4–27.

Greenwald, A. G., Banaji, M. R., Rudman, L. A., Farnham, S. D., Nosek, B. A., & Mellott, D. S. (2002). A unified theory of implicit attitudes, stereotypes, self-esteem, and self-concept. *Psychological Review, 109,* 3–25.

Greenwald, A. G., McGhee, D. E., & Schwartz, J. L. K. (1998). Measuring individual differences in implicit cognition: The implicit association test. *Journal of Personality and Social Psychology, 74,* 1464–1480.

Gregory, R. (1978). *Eye and brain: The psychology of seeing* (3rd ed.). New York: McGraw-Hill.

Gregory, R. I. (1970). *The intelligent eye.* New York: McGraw-Hill.

Grencavage, L. M., & Norcross, J. C. (1990). Where are the commonalities among the therapeutic common factors? *Professional Psychology: Research and Practice, 21,* 372–378.

Grice, H. P. (1975). Logic and conversation. In P. Cole & J. L. Morgan (Eds.), *Syntax and semantics: Speech acts* (pp. 41–58). San Diego, CA: Academic Press.

Griffith, E. E., Young, J. L., & Smith. (1984). An analysis of the therapeutic elements in a Black church service. *Hospital and Community Psychiatry, 35,* 464–469.

Griffitt, W. (1987). Females, males, and sexual responses. In K. Kelley (Ed.), *Females, males, and sexuality: Theories and research.* Albany: State University of New York Press.

Griggs, R. A., & Cox, J. R. (1982). The elusive thematic-materials effect in Wason's selection task. *British Journal of Psychology, 73,* 407–420.

Grimshaw, G. M., Bryden, M. P., & Finegan, J. K. (1995). Relations between prenatal testosterone and cerebral lateralization in children. *Neuropsychology, 9,* 68–79.

Grob, C., & Dobkin de Rios, M. (1992). Adolescent drug use in cross-cultural perspective. *Journal of Drug Issues, 22,* 121–138.

Grob, G. N. (1983). Historical origins of deinstitutionalization. *New Directions for Mental Health Services, 17,* 15–29.

Gross, J. J. (1998). Antecedent- and response-focused emotion regulation: Divergent consequences for experience, expression, and physiology. *Journal of Personality & Social Psychology, 74,* 224–237.

Gross, J. J. (1999). Emotion regulation: Past, present, future. *Cognition and Emotion, 13,* 551-573.

Group for the Advancement of Psychiatry (GAP) Committee on Alcoholism and the Addictions. (1991). Substance abuse disorders: A psychiatric priority. *American Journal of Psychiatry, 148,* 1291–1300.

Grunbaum, A. (1984). *The foundations of psychoanalysis: A philosophical critique.* Berkeley: University of California Press.

Gruneberg, M. M., Morris, P. E., & Sykes, R. N. (1988). (Eds.) *Practical aspects of memory: Current research and issues, Vol. 1: Memory in everyday life.* Oxford: John Wiley & Sons.

Grusec, J. E., & Goodnow, J. J. (1994). Summing up and looking to the future. *Developmental Psychology, 30,* 29–31.

Guarnaccia, P. J., & Rogler, L. H. (1999). Research on culture-bound syndromes: New directions. *American Journal of Psychiatry, 156,* 1322–1327.

Gumperz, J. J., & Levinson, S. C. (Eds.). (1996). *Rethinking linguistic relativity.* Cambridge: Cambridge University Press.

Gunderson, J. G. (1986). Pharmacotherapy for patients with borderline personality disorder. *Archives of General Psychiatry, 43,* 698–700.

Gunter, B., & McAleer, J. (1990). *Children and television: The one eyed monster?* London: Routledge.

Gur, R. E., Cowell, P. E., Latshaw, A., Turetsky, B. I., Grossman, R. I., Arnold, S. E., Bilker, W. B., & Gur, R. C. (2000). Reduced dorsal and orbital prefrontal gray matter volumes in schizophrenia. *Archives of General Psychiatry, 57,* 761–768.

Gur, R. E, Turetsky, B. I., Bilker, W. B., & Gur, R. C. (1999). Reduced gray matter volume in schizophrenia. *Archives of General Psychiatry, 56,* 905–911.

Gurevich, E. V., Bordelon, Y., Shapiro, R. M., Arnold, S. E., Gur, R. E., & Joyce, J. N. (1997). Mesolimbic dopamine D3 receptors and use of antipsychotics in patients with schizophrenia: A postmortem study. *Archives of General Psychiatry, 54,* 225–232.

Gust, D., Gordon, T., Brodie, A., & McClure, H. (1994). Effect of a preferred companion in modulating stress in adult female rhesus monkeys. *Physiology and Behavior, 4,* 681–684.

Gustavson, C. R., Kelly, D. J., Sweeny, M., & Garcia, J. (1976). Prey-lithium aversions: I: Coyotes and wolves. *Behavioral Biology, 17,* 61–72.

Guzowski, J. F., Lyford, G. L., Stevenson, G. D., Houston, F. P., McGaugh, J. L., Worley, P. F., & Barnes, C. A. (2000). Inhibition of activity-dependent arc protein expression in the rat hippocampus impairs the maintenance of long-term potentiation and the consolidation of long-term memory. *Journal of Neuroscience, 20,* 3993–4001.

Haaga, D. A. F., & Stiles, W. B. (2001). Randomized clinical trials in psychotherapy research: Methodology, design, and evaluation. In C. R. Snyder & R. E. Ingram (Eds.), *Handbook of psychological change: Psychotherapy processes and practices for the 21st century* (pp. 14-39). New York: John Wiley & Sons.

Hagan, M. M., Castaneda, E., Sumaya, I. C., Fleming, S. M., Galloway, J., & Moss, D. E. (1998). The effect of hypothalamic peptide YY on hippocampal acetylcholine release in vivo: Implications for limbic function in binge-eating behavior. *Brain Research, 805,* 20–28.

Hagger, M. S., Chatzisarantis, N., Biddle, S. J. H., & Orbell, S. (2001). Antecedents of children's physical activity intentions and behaviour: Predictive validity and longitudinal effects. *Psychology and Health, 16,* 391–407.

Hahlweg, K., Fiegenbaum, W., Frank, M., Schroeder, B., & von Witzleben, I. (2001). Short- and long-term effectiveness of an em-pirically supported treatment for agoraphobia. *Journal of Consulting and Clinical Psychology, 69,* 375–382.

Hahn, C., Pawlyk, A. C., Whybrow, P. C., Gyulai, L., & Tejani-Butt, S. M. (1999). Lithium administration affects gene expression of thyroid hormone receptors in rat brain. *Life Sciences, 64,* 1793–1802.

Hahn, S. E., & Smith, C. S. (1999). Daily hassles and chronic stressors: Conceptual and measurement issues. *Stress Medicine, 15,* 89–101.

Halasz, P. (1993). Arousals without awakening: Dynamic aspect of sleep. *Physiology & Behavior, 54,* 795–802.

Hale, S., Bronik, M., & Fry, A. (1997). Verbal and spatial working memory in school-age children: Differences in susceptibility to interference. *Developmental Psychology, 33,* 364–371.

Haley, J. (1971). Family therapy: A radical change. In J. Haley (Ed.), *Changing families: A family therapy reader.* New York: Grune & Stratton.

Haley, J. (1976). *Problem-solving therapy.* San Francisco: Jossey-Bass.

Halford, G. (1989). Reflections on 25 years of Piagetian cognitive developmental psychology, 1963–1988. *Human Development, 32,* 325–357.

Hall, G. S. (1904). *Adolescence: Its psychology and its relations to physiology, anthropology, sociology, sex, crime, religion, and education* (Vols. 1–2.). New York: Appleton-Century-Crofts.

Halmi, K. A. (1999). Eating disorders: Defining the phenotype and reinventing the treatment. *American Journal of Psychiatry, 156,* 1673–1675.

Hamermesh, D. S., & Biddle, J. E. (1994). Beauty and the labor market. *American Economic Review, 84,* 1174–1195.

Hamida, B. S., Mineka, S., & Bailey, J. M. (1998). Sex differences in perceived controllability of mate value: An evolutionary perspective. *Journal of Personality and Social Psychology, 75,* 953-966.

Hamilton, D., & Sherman, J. (1994). Stereotypes. In R. S. Wyer, Jr., & T. K. Srull (Eds.), *Handbook of social cognition: Vol. 1. Basic processes* (2nd ed., pp. 1–68). Hillsdale, NJ: Lawrence Erlbaum.

Hamilton, R. H., & Pascual-Leone, A. (1998). Cortical plasticity associated with Braille learning. *Trends in Cognitive Neuroscience, 2,* 168–174.

Hamilton, W. D. (1964). The genetical theory of social behavior. *Journal of Theoretical Biology, 6,* 1–52.

Hanin, B., Sprour, N., Margolin, J., & Braun, P. (1993). Electroconvulsive therapy in mania: Successful outcome despite short duration of convulsions. *Convulsive Therapy, 9,* 50–53.

Hanna, J. (1989, September 25). Sexual abandon: The condom is unpopular on the campus. *Maclean's,* p. 48.

Hannigan, S. L., & Tippens-Reinitz, M. (2001). A demonstration and comparison of two types of inference-based memory errors. *Journal of Experimental Psychology: Learning, Memory, and Cognition, 27,* 931–940.

Hansen, W. B., & O'Malley, P. M. (1996). Drug use. In R. J. DiClemente, W. B. Hansen, et al. (Eds.), *Handbook of adolescent health risk behav-ior. Issues in clinical child psychology* (pp. 161–192). New York: Plenum Press.

Harari, H., Harari, O., & White, R. V. (1985). The reaction to rape by American male bystanders. *Journal of Social Psychology, 125,* 653–658.

Hardeman, W., Johnston, M., Johnston, D. W., Bonetti, D., Wareham, N. J., & Kinmonth, A. L. (2002). Application of the theory of planned behaviour in behaviour change interventions: A systematic review. *Psychology and Health, 17,* 123–158.

Harkness, S., & Super, C. M. (2002). Culture and parenting. In M. H. Bornstein (Ed.), *Handbook of parenting: Vol. 2: Biology and ecology of parenting* (2nd ed., pp. 253-280). Mahwah, NJ: Lawrence Erlbaum Associates.

Harlow, H. F., & Zimmerman, R. R. (1959). Affectional responses in the infant monkey. *Science, 130,* 421–432.

Harlow, R., & Cantor, N. (1994). Personality as problem solving: A framework for the analysis of change in daily-life behavior. *Journal of Personality Integration, 4,* 355–386.

Harmon-Jones, E., & Allen, J. J. B. (1998). Anger and frontal brain activity: EEG asymmetry consistent with approach motivation despite negative affective valence. *Journal of Personality & Social Psychology, 74,* 1310–1316.

Harris, B. (1979). Whatever happened to little Albert? *American Psychologist, 34,* 151–160.

Harris, C. R., & Christenfeld, N. (1996). Gender, jealousy, and reason. *Psychological Science, 7,* 364–366.

Harris, J. E. (1980). Memory aids people use: Two interview studies. *Memory and Cognition, 8,* 31–38.

Harris, J. R. (1998). *The nurture assumption: Why children turn out the way they do.* New York: Free Press.

Harris, J. R. (2000). The outcome of parenting: What do we really know? *Journal of Personality, 68,* 625–637.

Harris, M. B., Walters, L. C., & Waschull, S. (1991). Gender and ethnic differences in obesity- related behaviors and attitudes in a college sample. *Journal of Applied Social Psychology, 21,* 1545–1566.

Harris, Y. H. (1995). *The opportunity for romantic love among hunter-gatherers.* Paper presented at the annual convention of the Human Behavior and Evolution Society, June, Santa Barbara, CA.

Hart, B., & Risley, T. (1992). American parenting of language-learning children: Persisting differences in family-child interactions observed in natural home environments. *Developmental Psychology, 28,* 1096–1105.

Hart, E. A., Leary, M. R., & Rejeski, W. J. (1989). The measurement of social physique anxiety. *Journal of Sport and Exercise Psychology, 11,* 94–104.

Harter, S. (1998). The development of self-representations. In W. Damon (Ed. in Chief) and N. Eisenberg (Vol. Ed.), *Handbook of child psychology* (Vol. 3, pp. 553–618). New York: John Wiley & Sons.

Harter, S. (1999). *The construction of the self: A de-*

velopmental perspective. New York: Guilford Press.

Harter, S., & Monsour, A. (1992). Development analysis of conflict caused by opposing attributes in the adolescent self-portrait. *Developmental Psychology, 28,* 251–260.

Harter, S., Waters, P., & Whitesell, N. R. (1998). Relational self-worth: Differences in perceived worth as a person across interpersonal contexts among adolescents. *Child Development, 69,* 756–766.

Hartline, H. K. (1938). The response of single optic nerve fibers of the vertebrate eye to illuminate of the retina. *American Journal of Physiology, 121,* 400–415.

Hartmann, H. (1939). *Ego psychology and the problem of adaptation.* New York: International Universities Press.

Hartup, W. (1989). Social relationships and their developmental significance. *American Psychologist, 44,* 120–126.

Hartup, W. W. (1977). Aggression in childhood: Developmental perspectives. In M. Hertherington and D. Ross (Eds.), *Contemporary readings in child psychology.* New York: McGraw-Hill.

Hartup, W. W. (1996). The company they keep: Friendships and their developmental significance. *Child Development, 67,* 1–13.

Hartup, W. W. (1998). Cooperation, close relationships, and cognitive development. In W. M. Bukowski, A. F. Newcomb, et al. (Eds.), *The company they keep: Friendship in childhood and adolescence. Cambridge studies in social and emotional development* (pp. 213–237). New York: Cambridge University Press.

Harway, M. (2000). Families experiencing violence. In W. C. Nichols & M. A. Pace-Nichols (Eds.), *Handbook of family development and intervention. Wiley series in couples and family dynamics and treatment.* (pp. 391–414). New York: John Wiley & Sons.

Harwood, R. L., Schoelmerich, A., Schulze, P. A., & Gonzalez, Z. (1999). Cultural differences in maternal beliefs and behaviors: A study of middle-class Anglo and Puerto Rican mother–infant pairs in four everyday situations. *Child Development, 70,* 1005–1016.

Harwood, R. L., Schoelmerich, A., Ventura-Cook, E., Schulze, P. A., & Wilson, S. P. (1996). Culture and class influence on Anglo and Puerto Rican mothers' beliefs regarding long-term socialization goals and child behavior. *Child Development, 67,* 2446–2461.

Hasselquist, D., & Bensch, S. (1991). Trade-off between mate guarding and mate attraction in the polygynous great reed warbler. *Behavioral Ecology and Sociobiology, 28,* 187–193.

Hatfield, E. (1988). Passionate and companionate love. In R. J. Sternberg & M. L. Barnes (Eds.), *The psychology of love* (pp. 191–217). New Haven, CT: Yale University Press.

Hatfield, J. S., Ferguson, L. R., & Alpert, R. (1967). Mother-child interaction and the socialization process. *Child Development, 38,* 365–414.

Haugtvedt, C., & Petty, R. (1992). Personality and persuasion: Need for cognition moderates the persistence and resistance of attitude changes. *Journal of Personality and Social Psychology, 63,* 308–319.

Hauser, S. T., & Safyer, A. W. (1994). Ego development and adolescent emotions. *Journal of Research on Adolescence, 4,* 487–502.

Hay, D. F., Caplan, M., Castle, J., & Stimson, C. A. (1991). Does sharing become increasingly "rational" in the second year of life? *Developmental Psychology, 27,* 987–993.

Hayes, S. C., & Wilson, K. (1994). Acceptance and commitment therapy: Altering the verbal support for experiential avoidance. Special section: Clinical behavior analysis. *Behavior Analysis, 17,* 289–303.

Hazan, C., & Diamond, L. M. (2000). The place of attachment in human mating. *Review of General Psychology, l 4,* 186–204.

Hazan, C., & Shaver, P. (1987). Romantic love conceptualized as an attachment process. *Journal of Personality and Social Psychology, 57,* 731–739.

Health risks and benefits of alcohol consumption. (2000). *Alcohol Research and Health, 24,* 5–11.

Healy, A. F., & McNamara, D. S. (1996). Verbal learning and memory: Does the modal model still work? *Annual Review, 47,* 143–172.

Healy, S. D. (1996). Ecological specialization in the avian brain. In C. F. Moss, S. J. Shettleworth, et al. (Eds.), *Neuroethological studies of cognitive and perceptual processes* (pp. 84–110). Boulder, CO: Westview Press.

Heath, A. C., & Madden, P. A. F. (1995). Genetic influences on smoking behavior. In J. R. Turner & L. R. Cardon (Eds.), *Behavior genetic approaches in behavioral medicine* (pp. 45–66). New York: Plenum Press.

Hebb, D. O. (1949). *The organization of behavior: A neuropsychological theory.* New York: John Wiley.

Hebl, M. R., & Heatherton, T. F. (1998). The stigma of obesity in women: The difference is black and white. *Personality & Social Psychology Bulletin, 24,* 417–426.

Hebl, M. R., & Mannix, L. M. (2003). The weight of obesity in evaluating others: A mere proximity effect. *Personality and Social Psychology Bulletin, 29,* 28–38.

Heckers, S., Goff, D., Schacter, D. L., Savage, C. R., Fischman, A. J., Alpert, N. M., & Rauch, S. L. (1999). Functional imaging of memory retrieval in deficit vs nondeficit schizophrenia. *Archives of General Psychiatry, 56,* 1117–1123.

Hedricks, C. A. (1994). Female sexual activity across the human menstrual cycle. *Annual Review of Sex Research, V,* 122–172.

Hegarty, J., Baldessarini, R., Tohen, M., Waternaux, C., & Oepen, G. (1994). One hundred years of schizophrenia: A meta-analysis of the outcome literature. *American Journal of Psychiatry, 151,* 1409–1416.

Heider, F. (1958). *The psychology of interpersonal relations.* New York: John Wiley.

Heine, S. J., & Lehman, D. R. (1997). Culture, dissonance, and self-affirmation. *Personality & Social Psychology Bulletin, 23,* 389–400.

Heishman, S. J. (1999). Behavioral and cognitive effects of smoking: Relationship to nicotine addiction. *Nicotine & Tobacco Research, 1,* S143–S147.

Heller, D. (1986). *The children's God.* Chicago: University of Chicago Press.

Helmholtz, H. von. (1863). *Die Lehre von den tonempfindungen als physiolgisdne grundlage fur die theorie der musik.* Brunswick: Vierweg-Verlag.

Helson, R., & Klohnen, E. C. (1998). Affective coloring of personality from young adulthood to midlife. *Personality & Social Psychology Bulletin, 24,* 241–252.

Henderson, N. D. (1982). Human behavior genetics. *Annual Review of Psychology, 33,* 403–440.

Henninger, P. (1992). Conditional handedness: Handedness changes in multiple personality disordered subject reflect shift in hemispheric dominance. *Consciousness and Cognition, 1,* 265–287.

Herdt, G. (1997). *Same sex, different cultures: Gays and lesbians across cultures.* Boulder, CO: Westview Press.

Herdt, G. H. (Ed.). (1984). *Ritualized homosexuality in Melanesia.* Berkeley: University of California Press.

Hering, E. (1878). *Zur Lehre vom Lichtsinne.* Vienna: Gerold.

Hering, E. (1920). *Grundzuge, der Lehr vs. Lichtsinn.* Berlin: Springer.

Heritch, A., Henderson, K., & Westfall, T. (1990). Effects of social isolation on brain catecholamines and forced swimming in rats. *Journal of Psychiatric Research, 24,* 251–258.

Herman, J., Perry, J. C., & Van der Kolk, B. A. (1989). Childhood trauma in borderline personality disorder. *American Journal of Psychiatry, 146,* 490–495.

Herman, J. L. (1992). *Trauma and recovery: The aftermath of violence—from domestic violence to political terror.* New York: Basic Books.

Herold, E. S. (1981). Contraceptive embarrassment and contraceptive behavior among young single women. *Journal of Youth and Adolescence, 10,* 233–242.

Herrigel, E. (1953). *Zen in the art of archery.* New York: Vintage Books.

Herrmann, D., McEvoy, C., Hertzod, C., Hertel, P., & Johnson, M. K. (Eds.) (1996). *Basic and applied memory research* (Vols. 1–2). Mahwah, NJ: Lawrence Erlbaum.

Herrmann, D. J., Crawford, M., & Holdsworthy, M. (1992). Gender-linked differences in everyday memory performance. *British Journal of Psychology, 83,* 221–231.

Herrnstein, R. J. (1970). On the law of effect. *Journal of the Experimental Analysis of Behavior, 13,* 243–266.

Hersen, M., & Bellack, A. S. (Eds.). (1999). *Handbook of comparative interventions for adult disorders* (2nd ed.). New York: John Wiley & Sons.

Hersey, P., & Blanchard, K. (1982). *Management of organizational behavior: Utilizing human resources* (2nd ed.). Englewood Cliffs, NJ: Prentice-Hall.

Herz, M. I., Lamberti, J. S., Mintz, J., Scott, R.,

O'Dell, S. P., McCartan, L., & Nix, G. (2000). A program for relapse prevention in schizophrenia: A controlled study. *Archives of General Psychiatry, 57,* 277-283.

Herzog, D. B., Dorer, D. J., Keel, P. K., Selwyn, S. E., Ekeblad, E. R., Flores, A. T., Greenwood, D. N., Burwell, R. A., & Keller, M. B. (1999). Recovery and relapse in anorexia and bulimia nervosa: A 7.5-year follow-up study. *Journal of the American Academy of Child & Adolescent Psychiatry, 38,* 829–837.

Hick, K. M., & Katzman, D. K. (1999). Self-assessment of sexual maturation in adolescent females with anorexia nervosa. *Journal of Adolescent Health, 24,* 206–211.

Hicks, R. A., & Pelligrini, R. (1991). The changing sleep habits of college students. *Perceptual & Motor Skills, 72,* 631–636.

Higgins, E. T. (1987). Self-discrepancy: A theory relating self and affect. *Psychological Review, 94,* 319–340.

Higgins, E. T. (1999). Self-discrepency: A theory relating self and affect. In R. F. Baumeister (Ed.), *The self in social psychology. Key readings in social psychology* (pp. 150–181). Philadelphia: Psychology Press/Taylor & Francis.

Higgins, E. T., & Bargh, J. A. (1987). Social cognition and social perception. *Annual Review of Psychology, 38,* 369–425.

Higgins, R. L., Snyder, C. R., & Berglas, S. (Eds.) (1990). *Self-handicapping: The paradox that isn't.* New York: Plenum Press.

Higley, J., Mehlman, P., Taub, D., Higley, S., Suomi, S., Linnoila, M., & Vickers, J. H. (1992). Cerebrospinal fluid momoamine and adrenal correlates of aggression in free-ranging rhesus monkeys. *Archives of General Psychiatry, 49,* 436–441.

Hilgard, E. R. (1986). *Divided consciousness: Multiple controls in human thought and action.* New York: John Wiley.

Hill, A. (1999). Phantom limb pain: A review of the literature on attributes and potential mechanisms. *Journal of Pain and Symptom Management, 17,* 125–412.

Hill, J. O., & Peters, J. C. (1998). Environmental contributions to the obesity epidemic. *Science, 280,* 1371–1374.

Hillhouse, J. J., Stair III, A. W., & Adler, C. M. (1996). Predictors of sunbathing and sunscreen use in college undergraduates. *Journal of Behavioral Medicine, 19,* 543–562.

Hilliard, R. B., Henry, W. P., & Strupp, H. H. (2000). An interpersonal model of psychotherapy: Linking patient and therapist developmental history, therapeutic process, and types of outcome. *Journal of Consulting and Clinical Psychology, 68,* 125–133.

Hinde, R. (1982). *Ethology: Its nature and relations with other sciences.* New York: Oxford University Press.

Hingson, R., & Howland, J. (1993). Alcohol and non-traffic unintended injuries. *Addiction, 88,* 877–883.

Hirsch, J. (1997). Some history of heredity-vs-environment, genetic inferiority at Harvard (?), and the (incredible) Bell curve. *Genetica, 99,* 207–224.

Hirsch, J., & Knittle, J. L. (1970). Cellularity of obese and nonobese human adipose tissue. *Federation Proceedings, 29,* 1516–1521.

Hirshberg, L. M. (1990). When infants look to their parents: II. Twelve-month-olds' response to conflicting parental emotional signals. *Child Development, 61,* 1187–1191.

Hirst, W. (1994). The remembered self in amnesics. In U. Neisser & R. Fivush (Eds.), *The remembering self: Construction and accuracy in self-narrative* (pp. 252–277). New York: Cambridge University Press.

Hirt, E. R., Zillmann, D., Erickson, G. A., Kennedy, C. (1992). Costs and benefits of allegiance: Changes in fans' self-ascribed competencies after team victory versus defeat. *Journal of Personality & Social Psychology, 63,* 724–738.

Hittner, J. B. (1997). Alcohol-related outcome expectancies: Construct overview and implications for primary and secondary prevention. *Journal of Primary Prevention, 17,* 297–314.

Hobfoll, S. E., Schwarzer, R., & Chon, K. K. (1998). Disentangling the stress labyrinth: Interpreting the meaning of the term stress as it is studied in a health context. *Anxiety, Stress, and Coping, 11,* 181–212.

Hobson, J. A. (1988). *The dreaming brain.* New York: Basic Books.

Hobson, J. A., & McCarley, R. W. (1977). The brain as a dream state generator: An activation-synthesis hypothesis of the dream process. *American Journal of Psychiatry, 134,* 1335–1348.

Hochbaum, G. (1958). *Public participation in medical screening programs* (DHEW Publication No. 572, Public Health Service). Washington, DC: U.S. Government Printing Office.

Hock, E., Eberly, M., Bartle-Haring, S., Ellwanger, P., & Widaman, K. F. (2001). Separation anxiety in parents of adolescents: Theoretical significance and scale development. *Child Development, 72,* 284–298.

Hodges, E. V. E., & Perry, D. G. (1999). Personal and interpersonal antecedents and consequences of victimization by peers. *Journal of Personality & Social Psychology, 76,* 677–685.

Hoek, H. W. (1993). Review of the epidemiological studies of eating disorders. *International Review of Psychiatry, 5,* 61–74.

Hoff-Ginsberg, E. (1990). Maternal speech and the child's development of syntax: A further look. *Journal of Child Language, 17,* 85–99.

Hoffman, H. G., Doctor, J. N., Patterson, D. R., Carrougher, G. J., & Furness, T. A. (2000). Virtual reality as an adjunctive pain control during burn wound care in adolescent patients. *Pain, 85,* 305–309.

Hoffman, L. (1981). *Foundations of family therapy.* New York: Basic Books.

Hoffman, L. (1991). A reflexive stance for family therapy. *Journal of Strategic and Systemic Therapies, 10,* 4–17.

Hoffman, M. A., & Levy-Shiff, R. (1994). Coping and locus of control: Cross-generational transmission between mothers and adolescents. *Journal of Early Adolescence, 14,* 391–405.

Hoffman, M. L. (1978). Psychological and biological perspectives on altruism. *International Journal of Behavioral Development, 1,* 323–339.

Hoffman, M. L. (1982). Development of prosocial motivation: Empathy and guilt. In N. Eisenberg (Ed.), *The development of prosocial behavior.* New York: Academic Press.

Hoffman, M. L. (1998). Varieties of empathy-based guilt. In J. Bybee (Ed.), *Guilt and children* (pp. 91-112). San Diego, CA: Academic Press.

Hoffman, M. L., & Saltzstein, H. D. (1967). Parent discipline and the child's moral development. *Journal of Personality and Social Psychology, 5,* 45–47.

Hoffman, P. (1997). The endorphin hypothesis. In W. P. Morgan, et al. (Eds.), *Physical activity and mental health. Series in health psychology and behavioral medicine* (pp. 163–177). Washington, DC: Taylor & Francis.

Hofmann, S., & DiBartolo, P.M. (Eds.) (2001). *From social anxiety to social phobia: Multiple perspectives.* Boston, MA: Allyn & Bacon.

Hogan, R. (1983). What every student should know about personality psychology. In A. M. Rogers & J. Scheirer (Eds.), *G. Stanley Hall lecture series,* (Vol. 6). Washington, DC: American Psychological Association.

Hogan, R. (1987). Personality psychology: Back to basics. In J. Aronoff, et al. (Eds.), *The emergence of personality.* New York: Springer.

Hogan, R., Curphy, G., & Hogan, J. (1994). What we know about leadership: Effectiveness and personality. *American Psychologist, 49,* 493–304.

Hohmann, G. W. (1966). Some effects of spinal cord lesions on experienced emotional feelings. *Psychophysiology, 3,* 143–156.

Holahan, C. K., & Holahan, C. J. (1999). Being labeled as gifted, self-appraisal, and psychological well-being: A life span developmental perspective. *International Journal of Aging and Human Development, 48,* 161–173.

Holden, C. (1980). Identical twins reared apart. *Science, 207,* 1323–1325.

Holland, A. J., & Oliver, C. (1995). Down's syndrome and the links with Alzheimer's disease. *Journal of Neurology, Neurosurgery & Psychiatry, 59,* 111–114.

Holland, J., Holyoak, K., Nisbett, R., & Thagard, P. (1986). *Induction: Processes of inference, learning, and discovery.* Cambridge, MA: MIT Press.

Holland, R. W., Verplanken, B., & van Knippenberg, A. (2002). On the nature of attitude-behavior relations: The strong guide, the weak follow. *European Journal of Social Psychology, 32,* 869–876.

Hollis, K. L. (1997). Contemporary research on Pavlovian conditioning: A "new" functional analysis. *American Psychologist, 52,* 956–965.

Hollon, S. (1988). Cognitive therapy. In Lyn Y. Abramson (Ed.), *Social cognition and clinical psychology: A synthesis* (pp. 204–253). New York: Guilford Press.

Hollon, S. D., & Beck, A. T. (1994). Cognitive and cognitive-behavioral therapies. In A. E. Bergh & S. L. Garfield (Eds.), *Handbook of psychotherapy and behavior change* (4th ed.) (pp. 428-466). Oxford: John Wiley & Sons.

Hollon, S. D., Shelton, R. C., & Davis, D. D. (1993). Cognitive therapy for depression: Conceptual issues and clinical efficacy. *Journal of Consulting & Clinical Psychology, 61,* 270–275.

Holmes, D. (1990). The evidence for repression: An examination of sixty years of research. In J. L. Singer (Ed.), *Repression and dissociation: Implications for personality theory, psychopathology, and health* (pp. 85–102). Chicago: University of Chicago Press.

Holmes, T. H., & Rahe, R. H. (1967). The social readjustment rating scale. *Journal of Psychosomatic Research, 11,* 213–218.

Holmgren, R. A., Eisenberg, N., & Fabes, R. A. (1998). The relations of children's situational empathy-related emotions to dispositional prosocial behavior. International *Journal of Behavioral Development, 22,* 169–193.

Holscher, C., Anwyl, R., & Rowan, M. J. (1997). Stimulation on the positive phase of hippocampal theta rhythm induces long-term potentiation that can be depotentiated by stimulation on the negative phase in area C1 in vivo. *Journal of Neuroscience, 17,* 6470–6477.

Holt, R. (1976). Drive or wish? A reconsideration of the psychoanalytic theory of motivation. In M. Gill & P. Holzman (Eds.), *Psychology vs. metapsychology: Psychoanalytic essays in memory of George Klein. Psychological Issues,* Monograph 36, Vol. 9, No. 4.

Holt, R. R. (1985). The current status of psychoanalytic theory. *Psychoanalytic Psychology, 2,* 289–315.

Holyoak, K. J., & Simon, D. (1999). Bidirectional reasoning in decision making by constraint satisfaction. *Journal of Experimental Psychology: General, 128,* 3–31.

Holyoak, K. J., & Spellman, B. A. (1993). Thinking. *Annual Review of Psychology, 44,* 265–315.

Holyoak, K. J., & Thagard, P. (1995). *Mental leaps: Analogy in creative thought.* Cambridge, MA: MIT Press.

Homans, G. (1961). *Social behavior: Its elementary forms.* London: Routledge & Kegan Paul.

Honeybourne, C., Matchett, G., & Davey, G. (1993). Expectancy models of laboratory preparedness effects: A UCS-expectancy bias in phylogenetic and ontogenetic fear-relevant stimuli. *Behavior Therapy, 24,* 253–264.

Hooks, M. S., Jones, G. H., Juncos, J. L., Neill, D. B., et al. (1994). Individual differences in schedule-induced and conditioned behaviors. *Behavioural Brain Research, 60,* 199–209.

Hooley, J., & Teasdale, J. D. (1989). Predictors of relapse in unipolar depressives: Expressed emotion, marital distress and perceived criticism. *Journal of Abnormal Psychology, 98,* 229–235.

Hooley, J. M. (1998). Expressed emotion and locus of control. *Journal of Nervous & Mental Disease, 186,* 374–378.

Hooley, J. M., & Hiller, J. B. (1998). Expressed emotion and the pathogenesis of relapse in schizophrenia. In M. F. Lenzenweger & R. H. Dworkin (Eds.), *Origins and development of schizophrenia: Advances in experimental psychopathology* (pp. 447–468). Washington, DC: American Psychological Association.

Horn, J. (1998). A basis for research on age differences in cognitive capabilities. In J. J. McArdle & R. W. Woodcock (Eds.). *Human cognitive abilities in theory and practice.* (pp. 57–91). Mahwah, NJ: Lawrence Erlbaum.

Horn, J. C., & Meer, J. (1987). The vintage years. *Psychology Today, 21,* 76–90.

Horn, J. L. (1968). Organization of abilities and the development of intelligence. *Psychological Review, 75,* 242–259.

Horn, J. L., & Cattell, R. B. (1967). Age differences in fluid and crystallized intelligence. *Acta Psychologica, 26,* 107–129.

Horn, J. L., & Hofer, S. M. (1992). Major abilities and development in the adult period. In R. J. Sternberg & C. A. Berg (Eds.), *Intellectual development* (pp. 44–99). New York: Cambridge University Press.

Horn, J. L., & Noll, J. (1997). Human cognitive capabilities: gf-gc theory. In D. P. Flanagen, J. L. Genshaft & P. L. Harrison (Eds.), *Contemporary intellectual assessment: Theories, tests and issues* (pp. 53–91). New York: Guilford Press.

Horn, J. M., Loehlin, J. C., & Willerman, L. (1979). Intellectual resemblance among adoptive and biological relatives: The Texas Adoption Project. *Behavior Genetics, 9,* 177–207.

Horn, J. M., Loehlin, J. C., & Willerman, L. (1982). Aspects of the inheritance of intellectual abilities. *Behavioral Genetics, 12,* 479-516.

Horner, T. M., & Chethik, L. (1986). Conversation attentiveness and following in 12- and 18-week-old infants. *Infant Behavior and Development, 9,* 203–213.

Horney, K. (1926). The flight from womanhood. *International Journal of Psychoanalysis, 7,* 324-339.

Horowitz, M. (1988). *Introduction to psychodynamics: A synthesis.* New York: Basic Books.

House, J. S., Landis, K. R., & Umberson, D. (1988a). Social relationships and health. *Science, 241,* 540–545.

Hovland, C. (1937). The generalization of conditioned responses: IV. The effects of varying amounts of reinforcement upon the degree of generalization of conditioned responses. *Journal of General Psychology, 21,* 261–276.

Hovland, C. I., & Janis, I. (1959). *Personality and persuasibility.* New Haven, CT: Yale University Press.

Howard, K. I., Kopta, S. M., Krause, M. S., & Orlinsky, D. E. (1986). The dose–effect relationship in psychotherapy. *American Psychologist, 41,* 159–164.

Howard, K. I., Orlinsky, D. E., & Lueger, R. J. (1994). Clinically relevant outcome research in individual psychotherapy: New models guide the researcher and clinician. *British Journal of Psychiatry, 165,* 4–8.

Howe, M. L. (2000). *The fate of early memories: Developmental science and the retention of childhood experiences.* Washington, DC: American Psychological Association.

Howes, C., & Hamilton, C. E. (1992). Children's relationships with child care teachers: Stability and concordance with parental attachments. *Child Development, 63,* 867–878.

Howes, C., Hamilton, C. E., & Philiopsen, L. C. (1998). Stability and comorbidity of child-caregiver and child-peer relationships. *Child Development, 69,* 418–426.

Hsu, F. L. K. (1981). *Americans and Chinese: Passage to difference* (3rd ed.). Honolulu: University Press of Hawaii.

Hsu, L. K. G. (1989). The gender gap in eating disorders: Why are the eating disorders more common among women. *Clinical Psychology Review, 9,* 393–407.

Hubel, D. H., & Wiesel, T. N. (1959). Receptive fields of single neurons in the cat's striate cortex. *Journal of Physiology, 148,* 574–591.

Hubel, D. H., & Wiesel, T. N. (1963). Single-cell responses in striate cortex of kittens deprived of vision in one eye. *Journal of Neuropsychology, 26,* 1003–1009.

Hubel, D. H., & Wiesel, T. N. (1979). Brain mechanisms of vision. *Scientific American, 241,* 150–162.

Huesmann, L. R. (1998). The role of social information processing and cognitive schema in the acquisition and maintenance of habitual aggressive behavior. In R. G. Geen & E. Donnerstein (Eds.), *Human aggression: Theories, research, and implications for policy* (pp. 73–109). New York: Academic Press.

Hulka, B. S., & Meirik, O. (1996). Research on the menopause. *Maturitas, 23,* 109–112.

Hull, C. L. (1943). *Principles of behavior: An introduction to behavior theory.* New York: Oxford University Press.

Hull, C. L. (1952). *A behavior system: An introduction to behavior theory concerning the individual organism.* New Haven, CT: Yale University Press.

Hull, J. G. (1987). Self-awareness model. In H. T. Blane & K. E. Leonard (Eds.), *Psychological theories of drinking and alcoholism* (pp. 272–304). New York: Guilford Press.

Hull, J. G., & Bond, C. F. (1986). Social and behavioral consequences of alcohol consumption and expectancy: A meta-analysis. *Psychological Bulletin, 99,* 347–360.

Hulme, C., Maughan, S., & Brown, G. D. A. (1991). Memory for familiar and unfamiliar words: Evidence for a long-term memory contribution to short-term memory span. *Journal of Memory and Language, 30,* 685–701.

Hultsch, D., & Dixon, R. (1990). Learning and memory in aging. In J. Birren & K. W. Schaie (Eds.), *Handbook of the psychology of aging* (3rd ed.). New York: Academic Press.

Humphreys, K., & Klaw, E. (2001). Can targeting nondependent problem drinkers and providing Internet-based services expand access to assistance for alcohol problems? A study of the moderation management self-help/mutual aid organization. *Journal of Studies of Alcohol, 62,* 528–532.

Humphreys, M. S., & Kashima, Y. (2002). Connectionism and self: Distributed representational systems and their implications for self and identity. In Y. Kashima & M. Foddy (Eds.), *Self and identity: Personal, social, and symbolic* (pp. 27–54). Mahwah, NJ: Lawrence Erlbaum.

Hundleby, J. D., Pawlik, K., & Cattell, R. B. (1965). *Personality factors in objective test devices: A critical integration of a quarter of a century's research*. San Diego, CA: Knapp.

Hunt, E., & Agnoli, F. (1991). The Whorfian hypothesis: A cognitive psychology perspective. *Psychological Review, 98,* 377–389.

Hupka, R. B., Zaleski, Z., Otto, J., Reidl, L., et al. (1997). The colors of anger, envy, fear, and jealousy: A cross-cultural study. *Journal of Cross-Cultural Psychology, 28,* 156–171.

Hurvich, L. M., & Jameson, D. (1957). An opponent- process of color vision. *Psychological Review, 64,* 384–404.

Huselid, B. F., & Cooper, M. L. (1994). Gender roles as mediators of sex differences in expression of pathology. *Journal of Abnormal Psychology, 103,* 595–603.

Huston, A. C. (1983). Sex-typing. In M. Hetherington (Ed.), *Handbook of child psychology: Vol. 4. Social and personality development.* New York: John Wiley.

Huston, T. L. (1973). Ambiguity of acceptance, social desirability, and dating choice. *Journal of Experimental Social Psychology, 9,* 32–42.

Huston, T. L. (1994). Courtship antecedents of marital satisfaction and love. In R. Erber, R. Gilmour, et al. (Eds.), *Theoretical frameworks for personal relationships* (pp. 43–65). Hillsdale, NJ: Lawrence Erlbaum.

Hyde, J. S. (1990). Meta-analysis and the psychology of gender differences. *Signs, 16,* 55–73.

Idle, J. R. (1990). Titrating exposure to tobacco smoke using cotinine: A minefield of misunderstandings. *Journal of Clinical Epidemiology, 43,* 313–317.

Ilardi, S. S., & Craighead, W. E. (1999). The relationship between personality pathology and dysfunctional cognitions in previously depressed adults. *Journal of Abnormal Psychology, 108,* 51–57.

Inciardi, J. A., Surratt, H. L., & Saum, C. A. (1997). *Cocaine-exposed infants: Social, legal, and public health issues.* Thousand Oaks, CA: Sage.

Inglehart, M. R. (1991). *Reactions to critical life events: A social psychological analysis.* New York: Praeger.

Inhelder, B., & Piaget, J. (1958). *The growth of logical thinking from childhood to adolescence.* New York: Basic Books.

Inkeles, A., & Smith, D. H. (1974). *Becoming modern: Individual change in six developing countries.* Cambridge, MA: Harvard University Press.

Innis, N. K. (1992). Early research on the inheritance of the ability to learn. *American Psychologist, 47,* 190–197.

Insko, C. A. (1964). Primacy versus recency in persuasion as a function of the timing of arguments and measures. *Journal of Abnormal and Social Psychology, 69,* 381–391.

Insko, C. A., Arkoff, A., & Insko, V. M. (1965). Effects of high and low fear-arousing communications upon opinions toward smoking. *Journal of Experimental Social Psychology, 1,* 156–266.

Irwin, M., Schafer, G., & Fieden, C. (1974). Emic and unfamiliar category sorting of Mano farmers and U.S. undergradutes. *Journal of Cross-Cultural Psychology, 5,* 407–423.

Isaacowitz, D. M., & Seligman, M. E. P. (2001). Is pessimism a risk factor for depressive mood among community dwelling older adults? *Behavior Research and Therapy, 39,* 255–272.

Isen, A. (1984). Toward understanding the role of affect in cognition. In R. S. Wyer, Jr. & T. K. Srull (Eds.), *Handbook of social cognition* (Vol. 3). Hillsdale, NJ: Lawrence Erlbaum.

Isen, A. (1993). Positive affect and decision making. In M. Lewis & J. M. Haviland (Eds.), *Handbook of emotions* (pp. 261–277). New York: Guilford Press.

Ishai, A., Ungerleier, L. G., Martin, A., Schouten, J. L., & Haxby, J. V. (1999). Distributed representation of objects in the human ventral visual pathway. *Proceedings of the National Academy of Science, U.S.A., 96,* 9379–9384.

Islam, M. R., & Hewstone, M. (1993). Intergroup attributions and affective consequences in majority and minority groups. *Journal of Personality and Social Psychology, 64,* 936–950.

Ismail, B., Cantor-Graae, E., & McNeil, T. F. (1998). Minor physical anomalies in schizophrenic patients and their siblings. *American Journal of Psychiatry, 155,* 1695–1702.

Iyengar, S. S., & Lepper, M. R. (1999). Rethinking the value of choice: A cultural perspective on intrinsic motivation. *Journal of Personality & Social Psychology, 76,* 349–366.

Izard, C. (1990). Facial expressions and the regulation of emotions. *Journal of Personality and Social Psychology, 58,* 487–498.

Izard, C. E. (1971). *The face of emotion.* New York: Appleton.

Izard, C. E. (1977). *Human emotions.* New York: Plenum Press.

Izard, C. E. (1997). *Emotions and facial expressions: A perspective from differential emotions theory.* New York: Cambridge University Press.

Izard, C. E., & Buechler, S. (1980). Aspects of consciousness and personality in terms of differential emotions theory. In R. Plutchik & H. Kellerman (Eds.), *Emotion: Theory, research, and experience: Vol. I. Theories of emotion.* New York: Academic Press.

Izquierdo, I., & Medina, J. H. (1997). The biochemistry of memory formation and its regulation by hormones and neuromodulators. *Psychobiology, 25,* 1–9.

Jablenski, A. (1989). Epidemiology and cross-cultural aspects of schizophrenia. *Psychiatric Annals, 19,* 516–524.

Jackendoff, R. (1996). The architecture of the linguistic- spatial interface. In P. Bloom, M. A. Peterson, et al. (Eds.), *Language and space. Language, speech, and communication* (pp. 1–30). Cambridge, MA: MIT Press.

Jacklin, C. (1989). Female and male: Issues of gender. *American Psychologist, 44,* 127–133.

Jackson, J. L., & Kroenke, K. (2001). The effect of unmet expectations among adults presenting with physical symptoms. *Annals of Internal Medicine, 134,* 889–897.

Jackson, S. W. (1986). *Melancholia and depression: From Hippocratic times to modern times.* New Haven, CT: Yale University Press.

Jacobs, T. J., & Charles, E. (1980). Life events and the occurrence of cancer in children. *Psychosomatic Medicine, 42,* 11–24.

Jacobson, E. (1964). The self and the object world. *Psychoanalytic Study of the Child, 9,* 75–127.

Jacobson, J. L., Jacobsen, S. W., Sokol, R. J., & Martier, S. S. (1993). Teratogenic effects of alcohol on infant development. *Alcoholism: Clinical and Experimental Research, 17,* 174–183.

Jacobson, N. S., Christensen, A., Prince, S. E., Cordova, J., & Eldridge, K. (2000). Integrative behavioral couple therapy: An acceptance-based, promising new treatment for couple discord. *Journal of Consulting and Clinical Psychology, 68,* 351–355.

Jacoby, L. L., & Kelley, C. M. (1987). Unconscious influences of memory for a prior event. *Personality and Social Psychology Bulletin, 13,* 314–336.

Jacques, E. (1965). Death and the mid-life crisis. *International Journal of Psychoanalysis, 46,* 502–514.

Jaffee, S., & Hyde, J. S. (2000). Gender differences in moral orientation: A meta-analysis. *Psychological Bulletin, 126,* 703–726.

Jahoda, M. (1988). Opening address: The range of convenience of personal construct psychology —an outsider's view. In F. Fransella & L. F. Thomas (Eds.), *Experimenting with personal construct psychology.* (pp. 1–14). London: Routledge & Kegan Paul.

James, W. (1884). What is emotion? *Mind, 19,* 188–205.

James, W. (1890). *Principles of psychology* (Vol. 1). New York: Henry Holt.

James, W. (1902). *Varieties of religious experience.* New York: American Library, 1958.

Jang, K. L., McCrae, R., Angleitner, A., Reimann, R., & Livesley, W. J. (1998). Heritability of facet-level traits in a cross-cultural twin sample: Support for a hierarchical model of personality. *Journal of Personality and Social Psychology, 74,* 1556–1575.

Jangid, R. K., Vyas, J. N., & Shukla, T. R. (1988). The effects of the transcendental meditation programme on the normal individuals. *Journal of Personality and Clinical Studies, 4,* 145–149.

Janoff-Bulman, R. (1992). *Shattered assumptions: Towards a new psychology of trauma.* New York: Free Press.

Janowitz, H. D., & Grossman, M. I. (1949). Some factors affecting the food intake of normal dogs and dogs with esophagostomy and gastric fistula. *American Journal of Physiology, 159,* 143–148.

Jarvis, W. B. G., & Petty, R. E. (1996). The need to evaluate. *Journal of Personality and Social Psychology, 70,* 172–194.

Jasmos, T. M., & Hakmiller, K. I. (1975). Some effects of lesion level, and emotional cues of affective expression in spinal cord patients. *Psychological Reports, 37,* 859–870.

Jeffery, K. J. (1997). LTP and spatial learning—where to next? *Hippocampus, 7,* 95–110.

Jemmott III, J. B., Boryseko, J. Z., Borysenko, M., McClelland, D. C., Chapman, R., Meyer, D., & Benson, H. (1983). Academic stress, power motivation, and decrease in salivary secretory immunoglobulin A secretion rate. *Lancet, 1,* 1400–1402.

Jencks, C. (1998). Racial bias in testing. In C. Jencks & M. Phillips (Eds.), *The Black-White test score gap* (pp. 55–85). Washington, DC: Brookings Institution.

Jencks, C., & Phillips, M. (1998). *The Black-White test score gap.* Washington, DC: Brookings Institution.

Jenike, M., Baer, L., Ballantine, T., & Martuza, R. (1991). Cingulotomy for refractory obsessive-compulsive disorder: A long-term follow-up of 33 patients. *Archives of General Psychiatry, 48,* 548–555.

Jenike, M. A. (1983). Obsessive compulsive disorder. *Comprehensive Psychiatry, 24,* 99–111.

Jenkins, J. H., & Karno, M. (1992). The meaning of expressed emotion: Theoretical issues raised by cross-cultural research. *American Journal of Psychiatry, 149,* 9–21.

Jenner, E. A., Watson, P. W. B., Miller, L., Jones, F., & Scott, G. M. (2002). Explaining hand hygiene practice: An extended application of the Theory of Planned Behavior. *Psychology, Health, and Medicine, 7,* 311–326.

Jensen, A. R. (1969). How much can we boost IQ and scholastic achievement? *Harvard Educational Review, 39,* 1–123.

Jensen, A. R. (1973). *Educability and group differences.* New York: Harper & Row.

Jensen, A. R. (1998). Jensen on "Jensenism." *Intelligence, 26,* 181–208.

Jewesbury, E. C. O. (1951). Insensitivity to pain. *Brain, 74,* 336–353.

Jockin, V., McGue, M., & Lykken, D. (1996). Personality and divorce: A genetic analysis. *Journal of Personality and Social Psychology, 71,* 288–299.

John, O., & Robins, R. (1994). Accuracy and bias in self-perception: Individual differences in self-enhancement and the role of narcissism. *Journal of Personality and Social Psychology, 66,* 206–219.

John, O. P. (1990). The big five factor taxonomy: Dimensions of personality in the natural language and in questionnaires. In L. Pervin (Ed.), *Handbook of personality: Theory and research* (pp. 66–100). New York: Guilford Press.

John, O. P., & Srivastava, S. (1999). The Big Five Trait taxonomy: History, measurement, and theoretical perspectives. In L. A. Pervin & O. P. John (Eds.), *Handbook of personality: Theory and research* (2nd ed., pp. 102–138). New York: Guilford Press.

Johnson, J. V., Stewart, W., Hall, E. M., Fredlund, P., et al. (1996). Long-term psychosocial work environment and cardiovascular mortality among Swedish men. *American Journal of Public Health, 86,* 324–331.

Johnson, K. O., & Lamb, G. H. (1981). Neural mechanisms of spatial tactile discrimination: Neural patterns evoked by Braille-like dot patterns in the monkey. *Journal of Physiology, 310,* 117–144.

Johnson, R., & Murray, F. (1992). Reduced sensitivity of penile mechanoreceptors in aging rats with sexual dysfunction. *Brain Research Bulletin, 28,* 61–64.

Johnson, S. L., & Jacob, T. (2000). Sequential interactions in the marital communication of depressed men and women. *Journal of Consulting & Clinical Psychology, 68,* 4–12.

Johnson, S. L., & Miller, I. (1997). Negative life events and time to recovery from episodes of bipolar disorder. *Journal of Abnormal Psychology, 106,* 449–457.

Johnson-Laird, P. N. (1995). Mental models, deductive reasoning, and the brain. In M. S. Gazzaniga et al. (Eds.), *The cognitive neurosciences* (pp. 999–1008). Cambridge, MA: MIT Press.

Johnson-Laird, P. N. (1996). The process of deduction. In D. Steier & T. M. Mitchell (Eds.), *Mind matters: A tribute to Allen Newell. Carnegie Mellon Symposia on cognition* (pp. 363–399). Hollsdale, NJ: Lawrence Erlbaum.

Johnson-Laird, P. N. (1999). Deductive reasoning. *Annual Review of Psychology, 50,* 109–135.

Johnson-Laird, P. N., Legrenzi, P., Girotto, V., & Legrenzi, M. S. (2000). Illusions in reasoning about consistency. *Science, 288,* 531–532.

Johnson-Laird, P. N., Legrenzi, P., & Legrenzi, M. S. (1972). Reasoning and a sense of reality. *British Journal of Psychology, 63,* 395–400.

Joiner, T. E. (2000). Depression's vicious scree: Self-propagating and erosive processes in depression chronicity. *Clinical Psychology—Science and Practice, 7,* 203–218.

Jolicoeur, P., Gluck, M. A., & Kosslyn, S. M. (1984). Pictures and names: Making the connection. *Cognitive Psychology, 16,* 243-275.

Jonas, E., Schimel, J., Greenberg, J., & Pyszczynski, T. (2002). The scrooge effect: Evidence that mortality salience increases prosocial attitudes and behavior. *Personality and Social Psychology Bulletin, 28,* 1342–1353.

Jonas, K., Diehl, M., Bromer, P. (1997). Effects of attitudinal ambivalence on information processing and attitude-intention consistency. *Journal of Experimental Social Psychology, 33,* 190–210.

Jones, E. E., & Berglas, S. (1978). Control of attributions about the self through self-handicapping strategies: The appeal of alcohol and the role of underachievement. *Personality and Social Psychology Bulletin, 4,* 200–206.

Jones, E. G. (2000). Cortical and subcortical contributions to activity-dependent plasticity in primate somatosensory cortex. *Annual Review of Neuroscience, 23,* 1–37.

Jones, J. L., & Leary, M. R. (1994). Effects of appearance-based admonitions against sun exposure on tanning intentions in young adults. *Health Psychology, 13,* 86–90.

Jones, K. L., Smith, D. W., Ulleland, C. N., & Streissguth, A. (1973). Pattern of malformation in offspring of chronic alcoholic mothers. *Lancet, 1,* 1267–1271.

Josephson, B. R., Singer, J. A., & Salovey, P. (1996). Mood regulation and memory: Repairing sad moods with happy memories. *Cognition & Emotion, 10,* 437–444.

Julien, R. M. (1998). *A primer on drug action.* New York: Freeman.

Jusczyk, P. W., Houston, D. M., & Newsome, M. (1999). The beginnings of word segmentation in English-learning infants. *Cognitive Psychology, 39,* 159–207.

Just, M. A., & Carpenter, P. A. (1992). A capacity theory of comprehension: Individual differences in working memory. *Psychological Review, 99,* 122–149.

Kaas, J. H. (1987). Somatosensory cortex. In G. Adelman (Ed.), *Encyclopedia of neuroscience* (Vol. 2). Boston, MA: Birkhauser.

Kafetsios, K., & Nezlek, J. B. (2002). Attachment styles in everyday social interaction. *European Journal of Social Psychology, 32,* 719–735.

Kagan, J. (1976). Emergent themes in human development. *American Scientist, 64,* 186–196.

Kagan, J. (1983). Stress and coping in early development. In N. Garmezy & M. Rutter (Eds.), *Stress, coping, and development in children.* New York: McGraw-Hill.

Kagan, J. (1984). *The nature of the child.* New York: Basic Books.

Kagan, J. (1989). Temperamental contributions to social behavior. *American Psychologist, 44,* 668–674.

Kagan, J., Kearsley, R. B., & Zelazo, P. R. (1978). *Infancy: Its place in human development.* Cambridge, MA: Harvard University Press.

Kagan, J., & Zentner, M. (1996). Early childhood predictors of adult psychopathology. *Harvard Review of Psychiatry, 3,* 341–350.

Kahn, R. S., Davidson, M., & Davis, K. L. (1996). Dopamine and schizophrenia revisted. In S. J. Watson et al. (Eds.), *Biology of schizophrenia and affective disease.* (pp. 369–391). Washington, DC: American Psychiatric Press.

Kahn, S., Zimmerman, G., Csikszentmihalyi, M., & Getzels, J. (1985). Relations between identity in young adulthood and intimacy at midlife. *Journal of Personality and Social Psychology, 49,* 1316–1322.

Kahneman, D., & Tversky, A. (1979). Prospect theory: An analysis of decision under risk. *Econometrica, 47,* 263–291.

Kahneman, D., & Tversky, A. (1982). The simulation heuristic. In D. Kahneman, P. Slovic, & A. Tversky (Eds.), *Judgment under uncertainty: Heuristics and biases* (pp. 201-208). New York: Cambridge University Press.

Kail, R. (1991a). Developmental change in speed of processing during childhood and adolescence. *Psychological Bulletin, 109,* 490–501.

Kail, R. (1991b). Processing time declines exponentially during childhood and adolescence. *Developmental Psychology, 27,* 259–266.

Kail, R. (2000). Speed of information processing: Developmental change and links to intelligence. *Journal of School Psychology, 38,* 51–61.

Kail, R., & Pellegrino, J. W. (1985). *Human intelligence: Perspectives and prospects.* New York: Freeman.

Kamen, L. P., & Seligman, M. E. P. (1987). Explanatory style and health. *Current Psychological Research & Reviews, 6,* 207–218.

Kamil, A. C., & Jones, J. E. (1997). The seed-storing corvid Clark's nutcracker learns geometric relationships among landmarks. *Nature, 390,* 276–279.

Kamin, L. J. (1969). Predictability, surprise, attention, and conditioning. In B. A. Campbell & R. M. Church (Eds.), *Punishment and aversive behavior.* New York: Appleton-Century-Crofts.

Kamin, L. J. (1974). *The science and politics of I.Q.* Hillsdale, NJ: Lawrence Erlbaum.

Kaminer, Y., & Hrecznyj, B. (1991). Lysergic acid diethylamide-induced chronic visual disturbances in an adolescent. *Journal of Nervous and Mental Disease, 179,* 173–174.

Kampe, K. K. W., Frith, C. D., Dolan, R. J., & Frith, U. (2001). Reward value of attractiveness and gaze. *Nature, 416,* 589.

Kandel, E. R. (1998). A new intellectual framework for psychiatry. *American Journal of Psychiatry, 155,* 457–469.

Kandel, E. R. (1999). Biology and the future of psychoanalysis: A new intellectual framework for psychiatry revisited. *American Journal of Psychiatry, 156,* 505–524.

Kane, M. J., & Engle, R. W. (2002). The role of prefrontal cortex in working memory capacity, executive attention, and general fluid intelligence: An individual- differences perspective. *Psychonomic Bulletin and Review, 9,* 637–671.

Kanizsa, G. (1976). Subjective contours. *Scientific American, 234,* 48–52.

Kanner, A. D., Coyne, J. C., Schaefer, C., & Lazarus, R. S. (1981). Comparison of two modes of stress measurement: Daily hassles and uplifts versus major life events. *Journal of Behavioral Medicine, 491,* 1–39.

Kanwisher, N., McDermott, J., & Chun, M. M. (1997). The fusiform face area: A module in human extrastriate cortex specialized for face perception. *Journal of Neuroscience, 17,* 4302–4311.

Kaplan, J. S., & Sue, S. (1997). Ethnic psychology in the United States. In D. F. Halpern & A. E. Voiskounsky (Eds.), *States of mind: American and post-Soviet perspectives on contemporary issues in psychology.* (pp. 342–369). New York: Oxford University Press.

Kapur, S., Tulving, E., Cabeza, R., & McIntosh, A. R. (1996). The neural correlates of intentional learning of verbal materials: A PET study in humans. *Cognitive Brain Research, 4,* 243–249.

Kapur, S., Zipursky, R., Jones, C., Remington, G., & Houle, S. (2000). Relationship between dopamine D-sub-2 occupancy, clinical response, and side effects: A double-blind PET study of first-episode schizophrenia. *American Journal of Psychiatry, 157,* 514–520.

Kardiner, A. (1945). *The psychological frontiers of society.* New York: Columbia University Press.

Karney, B. R., & Bradbury, T. N. (2000). Attributions in marriage: State or trait? A growth curve analysis. *Journal of Personality & Social Psychology, 78,* 295–309.

Kassin, S., & Kiechel, K. (1996). The social psychology of false confessions: Compliance, internationalization, and confabulation. *Psychological Science, 7,* 125–128.

Katahn, M., & McMinn, M. (1990). Obesity: A biobehavioral point of view. *Annals of the New York Academy of Arts and Sciences, 602,* 189–204.

Katigbak, M., Church, A. T., & Akamine, T. (1996). Cross-cultural generalizability of personality dimensions: Relating indigenous and imported dimensions in two cultures. *Journal of Personality and Social Psychology, 70,* 99–114.

Katz, H., & Beilin, H. (1976). A test of Bryant's claims concerning the young children's understanding of quantitative invariance. *Child Development, 47,* 877–880.

Katz, I., & Hass, R. (1988). Racial ambivalence and American value conflict: Correlational and priming studies of dual cognitive structures. *Journal of Personality and Social Psychology, 55,* 893–905.

Katz, J., & Melzack, R. (1990). Pain "memories" in phantom limbs: Review and clinical observations. *Pain, 43,* 319–336.

Kaufman, L., & Rock, I. (1989). The moon illusion thirty years later. In M. Hershenson (Ed.), *The moon illusion* (pp. 193–234). Hillsdale, NJ: Lawrence Erlbaum.

Kawakami, K., Dovidio, J. F., Moll, J., Hermsen, S., & Russin, A. (2000). Just say no (to stereotyping): Effects of training in the negation of stereotypic associations on stereotype activation. *Journal of Personality and Social Psychology, 78,* 871–888.

Kaye, W. H., Gendall, K., & Strober, M. (1998). Serotonin neuronal function and selective serotonin reuptake inhibitor treatment in anorexia and bulimia nervosa. *Biological Psychiatry, 44,* 825–838.

Kazdin, A. E., & Tuma, A. H. (1982). *Single-case research designs.* San Francisco: Jossey-Bass.

Keefe, F. J., Buffington, A. L. H., Studts, J. L., & Rumble, M. E. (2002). Behavioral medicine: 2002 and beyond. *Journal of Consulting and Clinical Psychology, 70,* 852–856.

Keel, P. K., & Mitchell, J. E. (1997). Outcome in bulimia nervosa. *American Journal of Psychiatry, 154,* 313–321.

Keller, L. S., & Butcher, J. N. (1991). Assessment of chronic pain patients with the MMPI-2. Minneapolis: University of Minnesota Press.

Kelley, H. H. (1950). The warm-cold variable in first impressions of persons. *Journal of Personality, 18,* 431–439.

Kelley, H. H. (1973). The process of causal attribution. *American Psychologist, 28,* 107–128.

Kelley, H. H. (1979). *Personality relationships.* Hillsdale, NJ: Lawrence Erlbaum.

Kelley, H. H. (1992). Common-sense psychology and scientific psychology. *Annual Review of Psychology, 43,* 1–23.

Kelley, H. H., & Thibaut, J. W. (1978). *Interpersonal relations: A theory of interdependence.* New York: Wiley.

Kelley, J. E., Lumley, M. A., & Leisen, J. C. C. (1997). Health effects of emotional disclosure in rheumatoid arthritis patients. *Health Psychology, 16,* 331–340.

Kelley, S. A., Brownell, C. A., & Campbell, S. B. (2000). Mastery motivation and self-evaluative affect in toddlers: Longitudinal relations with maternal behavior. *Child Development, 71,* 1061–1071.

Kelly, G. A. (1955). *Psychology of personal constructs.* New York: W.W. Norton.

Kelly, J. A. (1995). *Changing HIV risk behavior: Practical strategies.* New York: Guilford Press.

Keltner, D., & Bonanno, G. A. (1997). A study of laughter and dissociation: Distinct correlates of laughter and smiling during bereavement. *Journal of Personality and Social Psychology, 73,* 687–702.

Keltner, D., Kring, A. M., & Bonanno, G. A. (1999). Fleeting signs of the course of life: Facial expression and personal adjustment. *Current Directions in Psychological Science, 8,* 18–22.

Kemeny, M. E., & Laudenslager, M. L. (1999). Beyond stress: The role of individual difference factors in psychoneuroimmunology. *Brain, Behavior and Immunity, 13,* 73–75.

Kenardy, J., Evans, L., & Tian, P. (1992). The latent structure of anxiety symptoms in anxiety disorders. *American Journal of Psychiatry, 149,* 1058–1061.

Kendall, P. C. (1993). Treating anxiety disorders in children: Results of a randomized clinical trial. *Journal of Consulting and Clinical Psychology, 62,* 100–110.

Kendall, P. C. (1998). Empirically supported psychological therapies. *Journal of Consulting & Clinical Psychology, 66,* 3–6.

Kendall, P. C. (1999). Clinical significance. *Journal of Consulting and Clinical Psychology, 67,* 283–284.

Kendall, P. C., Marrs-Garcia, A., Nath, S. R., & Sheldrick, R. C. (1999). Normative comparisons for the evaluation of clinical significance. *Journal of Consulting and Clinical Psychology, 67,* 285–299.

Kendler, K. S. (1995). Adversity, stress and psychopathology: A psychiatric genetic perspective. *International Journal of Methods in Psychiatric Research, 5,* 163–170.

Kendler, K. S., & Gardner, C. O., Jr. (1998). Boundaries of major depression: An evaluation of DSM-IV criteria. *American Journal of Psychiatry, 155,* 172–177.

Kendler, K. S., Gardner, C. O., & Prescott, C. A. (1999a). Clinical characteristics of major depression that predict risk of depression in relatives. *Archives of General Psychiatry, 56,* 322–327.

Kendler, K. S., Karkowski, L. M., Neale, M. C., & Prescott, C. A. (2000a). Illicit psychoactive substance use, heavy use, abuse and dependence in a U.S. population-based sample of male twins. *Archives of General Psychiatry, 57,* 261–269.

Kendler, K. S., Karkowski, L. M., & Prescott, C. A. (1999b). Causal relationship between stressful life events and the onset of major depression. *American Journal of Psychiatry, 156,* 837–848.

Kendler, K. S., MacLean, C., Neale, M., Kessler, R., Heath, A., & Eaves, L. (1991). The genetic epidemiology of bulimia nervosa. *American Journal of Psychiatry, 148,* 1627–1637.

Kendler, K. S., Myers, J. M., O'Neill, F. A., Martin, R., Murphy, B., MacLean, C. J., Walsh, D., & Straub, R. E. (2000b). Clinical features of schizophrenia and linkage to chromosomes 5q, 6p, 8p, and 10p in the Irish Study of High Density Schizophrenia Families. *American Journal of Psychiatry, 157,* 402–408.

Kendler, K. S., Neale, M., Kessler, R., Heath, A., & Eaves, L. (1992b). The genetic epidemiology of phobias in women: The interrelationship of agoraphobia, social phobia, situational phobia, and simple phobia. *Archives of General Psychiatry, 49,* 273–281.

Kendler, K. S., Neale, M. C., Heath, A. C., Kessler, R. C., & Eaves, L. J. (1994). A twin-family study of alcoholism in women. *American Journal of Psychiatry, 151,* 707–715.

Kendler, K. S., Neale, M. C., Kessler, R. C., & Heath, A. C. (1993). A longitudinal twin study of 1-year prevalence of major depression in women. *Archives of General Psychiatry, 50,* 843-852.

Kendler, K. S., Neale, M. C., Kessler, R.C., & Heath, A. C. (1993). A test of the equal-environment assumption in twin studies of psychiatric illness. *Behavior Genetics, 23,* 21–27.

Kendler, K. S., Prescott, C., Neale, M. C., & Pedersen, N. L. (1997). Temperance Board registration for alcohol abuse in a national sample of Swedish male twins, born 1902 to 1949. *Archives of General Psychiatry, 54,* 178–184.

Kendler, K. S., Walters, E. E., Neale, M. C., & Kent, P. (2003). The cradle of thought. *Psychoanalytic Psychotherapy, 17,* 181–183.

Kenealy, P. M. (1997). Mood-state-dependent retrieval: The effects of induced mood on memory reconsidered. *Quarterly Journal of Experimental Psychology: Human Experimental Psychology, 50,* 290–317.

Kenrick, D., Groth, G., Trost, M., & Sadalla, E. (1993). Integrating evolutionary and social exchange perspectives on relationships: Effects of gender, self-appraisal, and involvement level on mate selection criteria. *Journal of Personality and Social Psychology, 64,* 951–969.

Kenrick, D., & Keefe, R. (1992). Age preferences in mates reflect sex differences in human reproductive strategies. *Behavioral and Brain Sciences, 15,* 75–113.

Kenrick, D. T., & Stringfield, D. O. (1980). Personality traits and the eye of the beholder: Crossing some traditional philosophical boundaries in the search for consistency in all of the people. *Psychological Review, 87,* 88–104.

Kent, P. (2003). The cradle of thought. *Psychoanalytic Psychotherapy, 17,* 181–183.

Kernberg, O. (1975). *Borderline conditions and pathological narcissism.* New York: Aronson.

Kernberg, O. (1984). *Severe personality disorders: Psychotherapeutic strategies.* New Haven, CT: Yale University Press.

Kernberg, O. F., Selzer, M. A., Koenigsberg, H. W., Carr, A. C., & Appelbaum, A. H. (1989). *Psychodynamic psychotherapy of borderline patients.* New York: Basic Books.

Kessler, R. C., Heath, A. C., & Eaves, L. J. (1995). The structure of the genetic and environmental risk factors for six major psychiatric disorders in women: Phobia, generalized anxiety disorder, panic disorder, bulimia, major depression, and alcoholism. *Archives of General Psychiatry, 52,* 374–383.

Kessler, R. C., House, J. S., & Turner, J. B. (1987a). Unemployment and health in a community sample. *Journal of Health and Social Behavior, 28,* 51–59.

Kessler, R. C., McGonagle, K. A., Zhao, S., Nelson, C. B., Hughes, M., Eshleman, S., Wittchen, H., & Kendler, K. S. (1994). Lifetime and 12-month prevalence of DSM-III-R psychiatric disorders in the United States. *Archives of General Psychiatry, 51,* 8–19.

Kessler, R. C., Price, R. H., & Wortman, C. B. (1985). Social factors in psychopathology: Stress, social support, and coping processes. *Annual Review of Psychology, 36,* 531–572.

Kessler, R. C., Sonnega, A., Bromet, E., & Hughes, M. (1995). Posttraumatic stress disorder in the National Comorbidity Study. *Archives of General Psychiatry, 52,* 1048-1060.

Kessler, R. C., Stein, M. B., & Berglund, P. (1998). Social phobia subtypes in the National Comorbidity Survey. *American Journal of Psychiatry, 155,* 613–619.

Kessler, R. C., Turner, J. B., & House, J. S. (1989). Unemployment, reemployment, and emotional functioning in a community sample. *American Sociological Review, 54,* 648–657.

Kessler, R. C., Zhao, S., Katz, S. J., Kouzis, A. C., Frank, R. G., Edlund, M., & Leaf, P. (1999). Past-year use of outpatient services for psychiatric problems in the National Comorbidity Survey. *American Journal of Psychiatry, 156,* 115–123.

Kety, S. S., Rosenthal, D., Wender, P. H., Schulsinger, F., & Jacobsen, B. (1975). Mental illness in the biological and adoptive families of adopted individuals who have become schizophrenic: A preliminary report based on psychiatric interviews. In Fieve, Rosenthal, & Brill (Eds.), *Genetic research in psychiatry.* Baltimore, MD: Johns Hopkins University Press.

Khaleque, A., & Rohner, R. P. (2002). Perceived parental acceptance-rejection and psychological adjustment: A meta-analysis of cross-cultural and intracultural studies. *Journal of Marriage and Family, 64,* 54–64.

Kiecolt-Glaser, J. K., Glaser, R., Shuttleworth, E. C., & Dyer, C. S. (1987). Chronic stress and immunity in family caregivers of Alzheimer's disease victims. *Psychosomatic Medicine, 49,* 523-535.

Kiecolt-Glaser, J. K., McGuire, L., Robles, T. F., & Glaser, R. (2002). Psychoneuroimmunology: Psychological influences on immune function and health. *Journal of Consulting and Clinical Psychology, 70,* 537–547.

Kiewitz, C., & Weaver III, J. B. (2001). Trait aggressiveness, media violence, and perceptions of interpersonal conflict. *Personality and Individual Differences, 31,* 821–835.

Kihlstrom, J. F. (1987). The cognitive unconscious. *Science, 237,* 1445–1452.

Kihlstrom, J. F. (1996). Unconscious processes in social interaction. In S. R. Hameroff, A.W. Kasniak, & A. C. Scott (Eds.), *Toward a science of consciousness: The first Tucson discussions and debates. Complex adaptive systems* (pp. 93–104). Cambridge, MA: MIT Press.

Kihlstrom, J. F., & Cantor, N. (2000). Social intelligence. In R. J. Sternberg (Ed.), *Handbook of intelligence* (pp. 359–379). New York: Cambridge University Press.

Kim, H., & Markus, H. R. (1999). Deviance or uniqueness, harmony or conformity? A cultural analysis. *Journal of Personality and Social Psychology, 77,* 785–800.

Kim, J. J., & Fanselow, M. S. (1992). Modality-specific retrograde amnesia of fear. *Science, 256,* 675–677.

Kim, J. M. S., Andreasen, N. C., O'Leary, D. S., Watkins, G. L., Ponto, L. L. B., & Hichwa, R. D. (2000). Regional neural dysfunctions in chronic schizophrenia studied with positron emission tomography. *American Journal of Psychiatry, 157,* 542–548.

Kimura, D. (1987). Are men's and women's brains really different? *Canadian Psychology, 28,* 133–148.

King, A. J., & Carlile, S. (1995). Neural coding for auditory space. In M. S. Gazzaniga et al. (Eds.), *The cognitive neurosciences* (pp. 279–293). Cambridge, MA: MIT Press.

King, F. A. (1991). Animal research: Our obligation to educate. In M. A. Novak & A. J. Petto (Eds.), *Through the looking glass: Issues of psychological well-being in captive nonhuman primates* (pp. 212-220). Washington, DC: American Psychological Association.

King, H. E. (1961). Psychological effects of excitation in the limbic system. In D. E. Sheer (Ed.), *Electrical stimulation of the brain.* Austin: University of Texas Press.

Kinney, D. K., Holzman, P. S., Jacobsen, B., Jansson, L., Faber, B., Hildebrand, W., et al. (1997). Thought disorder in schizophrenic and control adoptees and their relatives. *Archives of General Psychiatry, 54,* 475–479.

Kinomura, S., Larsson, J., Gulyas, B., & Roland, P. E. (1996). Activation of attention by the human reticular formation and thalamic intralaminar nuclei. *Science, 271,* 512–515.

Kinsbourne, M., & Smith, W. L. (1974). *Hemispheric disconnection and cerebral function.* Springfield, IL: Charles C. Thomas.

Kinsey, A. C., Pomeroy, W. B., & Martin, C. E. (1948). *Sexual behavior in the human male.* Philadelphia: W. B. Saunders.

Kinsey, A. C., Pomeroy, W. B., Martin, C. E., & Gebhard, P. (1953). *Sexual behavior in the human female.* Philadelphia: W. B. Saunders.

Kintsch, W., & Greeno, J. G. (1985). Understanding and solving word arithmetic problems. *Psychological Review, 92,* 109–129.

Kintsch, W., & van Dijk, T. A. (1978). Toward a model of text comprehension and production. *Psychological Review, 85,* 363-394.

Kirsch, I., & Lynn, S. J. (1998). Social-cognitive alternatives to dissociation theories of hypnotic involuntariness. *Review of General Psychology, 2,* 66–80.

Kirsch, I., Montgomery, G., & Sapirstein, G. (1995). Hypnosis as an adjunct to cognitive behavioral psychotherapy: A meta-analysis. *Journal of Consulting & Clinical Psychology, 63,* 214–220.

Kisker, E. E. (1985). Teenagers talk about sex, pregnancy, and contraception. *Family Planning Perspectives, 17,* 83–90.

Kitayama, S., & Markus, H. R. (Eds.). (1994). *Emotion and culture: Empirical studies of mutual influence.* Washington, DC: American Psychological Association.

Kitayama, S., Markus, H. R., Matsumoto, H., & Norasakkunkit, V. (1997). Individual and collective processes in the construction of the self: Self-enhancement in the United States and self-criticism in Japan. *Journal of Personality and Social Psychology, 72,* 1245-1267.

Klaczynski, P. (1997). Bias in adolescents' everyday reasoning and its relationship with intellectual ability, personal theories, and self-serving motivation. *Developmental Psychology, 33,* 273–283.

Klaczynski, P. (2000). Motivated scientific reasoning biases, epistemological beliefs, and theory polarization: A two-process approach to adolescent cognition. *Child Development, 71,* 1347–1366.

Klayman, J., & Ha, Y. (1989). Hypothesis testing in rule discovery: Strategy, structure, and content. *Journal of Experimental Psychology: Learning, Memory, and Cognition, 15,* 596–604.

Klein, C. T. F., & Helweg-Larsen, M. (2002). Perceived control and the optimistic bias: A meta-analytic review. *Psychology and Health, 17,* 437–446.

Klein, D. N., Schwartz, J. E., Rose, S., & Leader, J. B. (2000). Five-year course and outcome of dysthymic disorder: A prospective, naturalistic follow-up study. *American Journal of Psychiatry, 157,* 931–939.

Kleinke, C. L., Peterson, T. R., & Rutledge, T. R. (1998). Effects of self-generated facial expressions on mood. *Journal of Personality & Social Psychology, 74,* 272–279.

Kleinman, A. (1988). *Rethinking psychiatry: From cultural category to personal experience.* New York: Macmillan.

Klesges, R. C., & Klesges, L. M. (1988). Cigarette smoking as a dietary strategy in a university population. *International Journal of Eating Disorders, 7,* 413–417.

Kleven, M., & Seiden, L. (1991). Repeated injection of cocaine potentiates methamphetamine-induced toxicity to dopamine-containing neurons in rat striatum. *Brain Research, 557,* 340–343.

Kling, K. C., Hyde, J. S., Showers, C. J., & Buswell, B. N. (1999). Gender differences in self-esteem: A meta-analysis. *Psychological Bulletin, 125,* 470–500.

Klinger, M. R., & Greenwald, A. G. (1994). Preferences need no inferences? The cognitive basis of unconscious mere exposure effects. In P. M. Niedenthal, S. Kitayama, et al. (Eds.), *The heart's eye: Emotional influences in perception and attention* (pp. 67–85). San Diego, CA: Academic Press.

Klinnert, M. D., Campos, J. J., Sorce, J. F., Emde, R. R., & Svejda, M. (1983). Emotions as behavior regulators: Social reference in infancy. In R. Plutchik & H. Kellerman (Eds.), *Emotion: Theory, research, and experience: Vol. 2. Emotions in early development.* San Diego, CA: Academic Press.

Kluckhohn, F., & Strodtbeck, F. (1961). *Variations in value orientations.* Evanston, IL: Row, Peterson.

Kluger, A., & DeNisi, A. (1996). The effects of feedback interventions on performance: A historical review, a meta-analysis, and a preliminary feedback intervention theory. *Psychological Bulletin, 119,* 254–284.

Kluver, H., & Bucy, P. (1939). Preliminary analysis of functions of the temporal lobe in monkeys. *Archives of Neurology and Psychiatry, 42,* 979–1000.

Knott, R., & Marlsen-Wilson, W. (2001). Does the medial temporal lobe bind phonological memories? *Journal of Cognitive Neuroscience, 13,* 593–609.

Knowles, E. A., Morris, M. W., Chiu, C., & Hong, Y. (2001). Culture and the process of person perception: Evidence for automaticity Among East Asians in correcting for situational influence on behavior. *Personality and Social Psychology Bulletin, 27,* 1344–1356.

Knowlton, B. J., Mangels, J. A., & Squire, L. R. (1996). A neostriatal habit learning system in humans. *Science, 273,* 1399–1402.

Knupfer, G. (1991). Abstaining for foetal health: The fiction that even light drinking is dangerous. *British Journal of Addiction, 86,* 1063–1073.

Kochanska, G. (1997). Multiple pathways to conscience for children with different temperaments: From toddlerhood to age 5. *Developmental Psychology, 33,* 228-240.

Kochanska, G., Murray, K. T., & Harlan, E. T. (2000). Effortful control in early childhood: Continuity and change, antecedents, and implications for social development. *Developmental Psychology, 36,* 220–232.

Koerner, K., & Linehan, M. M. (2000). Research on dialectical behavior therapy for patients with borderline personality disorder. *Psychiatric Clinics of North America, 23,* 151–167.

Koestner, R., Weinberger, J., & McClelland, D. C. (1991a). Task-intrinsic and social-extrinsic sources of arousal for motives assessed in fantasy and self-report. *Journal of Personality, 59,* 57–82.

Koestner, R., Zuroff, D., & Powers, T. (1991b). Family origins of adolescent self-criticism and

its continuity into adulthood. *Journal of Abnormal Psychology, 100,* 191–197.

Kohlberg, L. (1963). The development of children's orientations toward a moral order. I. Sequence in the development of moral thought. *Vita Humana, 6,* 11–33.

Kohlberg, L. (1976). Moral stages and moralization: The cognitive-developmental perspective. In T. Lickona (Ed.), *Moral development and behavior: Theory, research, and social issues.* New York: Holt, Rinehart & Winston.

Kohlberg, L., & Kramer, R. (1969). Continuities and discontinuities in childhood and adult moral development. *Human Development, 12,* 93–120.

Kohlberg, L. A. (1966). A cognitive-developmental analysis of children's sex-role concepts and attitudes. In E. E. Maccoby (Ed.), *The development of sex differences.* Stanford, CA: Stanford University Press.

Kohlenberg, R. J., & Tsai, M. (1994). Improving cognitive therapy for depression with functional analytic psychotherapy: Theory and case study. *Behavior Analyst, 17,* 305–319.

Kohler, W. (1925). *The mentality of apes.* New York: Harcourt Brace.

Kohut, H. (1971). *The analysis of the self: A systematic approach to the treatment of narcissistic personality disorders.* New York: International Universities Press.

Kohut, H. (1977). *The restoration of the self.* New York: International Universities Press.

Kokko, K., & Pulkkinen, L. (1997). Economical and psychological well-being of the unemployed. *Psykologia, 32,* 349-359.

Kolb, B., & Whishaw, I. Q. (1996). *Fundamentals of neuropsychology.* New York: Freeman.

Kolb, B., & Whishaw, I. Q. (2001). *An introduction to brain and behavior.* New York: Worth.

Konishi, M. (1995). Neural mechanisms of auditory image formation. In M. S. Gazzaniga et al. (Eds.), *The cognitive neurosciences* (pp. 269–277). Cambridge, MA: MIT Press.

Konner, M. (1991). Universals of behavioral development in relation to brain myelination. In K. R. Gibson & A. C. Petersen (Eds.), *Brain maturation and cognitive development: Comparative and cross-cultural perspectives.* New York: Aldine de Gruyter.

Konrad, A. M., Ritchie, J., Edgar, J., Lieb, P., Corrigall, E. (2000). Sex differences and similarities in job attribute preferences: A meta-analysis. *Psychological Bulletin, 126,* 593–641.

Kopelman, P. G. (2000). Obesity as a medical problem. *Nature, 404,* 635–643.

Kopp, C. B. (1989). Regulation of distress and negative emotions: A developmental view. *Developmental Psychology, 25,* 343–354.

Korfine, L., & Hooley, J. M. (2000). Directed forgetting of emotional stimuli in borderline personality disorder. *Journal of Abnormal Psychology, 109,* 214–221.

Koriat, A., Goldsmith, M., & Pansky, A. (2000). Toward a psychology of memory accuracy. *Annual Review of Psychology, 51,* 481–537.

Korn, J. H., Davis, R., & Davis, S. F. (1991). Historians' and chairpersons' judgments of eminence among psychologists. *American Psychologist, 46,* 789–792.

Korten, A. E., Henderson, A. S., Christensen, H., Jorm, A. F., et al. (1997). A prospective study of cognitive function in the elderly. *Psychological Medicine, 27,* 919–930.

Koss, M. (1993). Rape: Scope, impact, interventions, and public policy responses. *American Psychologist, 48,* 1062–1069.

Kosslyn, S. M. (1983). *Ghosts in the mind's machine.* New York: W.W. Norton.

Kosslyn, S. M., Alpert, N. M., Thompson, W. L., Maljokovic, V., et al. (1993). Visual imagery activates topographically organized visual cortex: PET investigations. *Journal of Cognitive Neuroscience, 5,* 263–287.

Kosslyn, S. M., Thompson, W. L., Costantini-Ferrando, M. F., Alpert, N. M., & Spiegel, D. (2000). Hypnotic visual illusion alters brain color processing. *American Journal of Psychiatry, 157.*

Kosslyn, S. M., Thompson, W. L., Kim, I. J., & Alpert, N. M. (1995). Topographical representations of mental images in primary visual cortex. *Nature, 378,* 496–498.

Kouri, E., Pope, H. G., Yurgelun-Todd, D., & Gruber, S. (1995). Attributes of heavy vs. occasional marijuana smokers in a college population. *Biological Psychiatry, 38,* 475–481.

Kourtzi, Z., & Kanwisher, N. (2000b). Activation in human MT/MST by static images with implied motion. *Journal of Cognitive Neuroscience, 12,* 48–55.

Kovacs, D. M., Parker, J. G., & Hoffman, L. W. (1996). Behavioral, affective, and social correlates of involvement in cross-sex friendship in elementary school. *Child Development, 67,* 2269–2286.

Kowalski, R. M. (1997). (Ed.) *Aversive interpersonal behaviors.* New York: Plenum Press.

Kowalski, R. M. (2001). (Ed.) *Behaving badly: Aversive behaviors in interpersonal relationships.* Washington, DC: American Psychological Association.

Kowalski, R. M., & Bodenlos, J. (2003). Psychosocial predictors of organ donation. Manuscript under review.

Kowalski, R. M., & Brown, K. (1994). Psychosocial barriers to cervical cancer screening: Effects of self-presentation and social evaluation. *Journal of Applied Social Psychology, 24,* 941–958.

Kowalski, R. M., Ellis, M., Hamby, M., Ritchie, J., & Starkovich, E. (2002). Perceptions of pet peeves in our relationships with close friends and strangers. Paper presented at the meeting of the Society for Personality and Social Psychology, Savannah, GA.

Kowalski, R. M., & Wolfe, R. (1994). Collective identity orientation, patriotism, and reactions to national outcomes. *Personality and Social Psychology Bulletin, 20,* 533–540.

Kraaij, V., & Garnefski, N. (2002). Negative life events and depressive symptoms in late life: Buffering effects of parental and partner bonding? *Personal Relationships, 9,* 205–214.

Kraemer, G. (1992). A psychobiological theory of attachment. *Behavioral and Brain Sciences, 15,* 493–541.

Kramer, L., & Gottman, J. (1992). Becoming a sibling: "With a little help from my friends." *Developmental Psychology, 28,* 685–699.

Kramer, L., Perozynski, L. A., & Chung, T. (1999). Parental responses to sibling conflict: The effects of development and parent gender. *Child Development, 70,* 1401–1414.

Kramer, P. (1993). *Listening to Prozac.* New York: Viking Press.

Kraus, N., Malmfors, T., & Slovic, P. (1992). Intuitive toxicology: Expert and lay judgments of chemical risks. *Risk Analysis, 12,* 215–232.

Kraus, S. J. (1995). Attitudes and the prediction of behavior: A meta-analysis of the empirical literature. *Personality & Social Psychology Bulletin, 21,* 58–75.

Kremen, A. M., & Block, J. (1998). The roots of ego-control in young adulthood: Links with parenting in early childhood. *Journal of Personality & Social Psychology, 75,* 1062–1075.

Kring, A. M., & Gordon, A. H. (1998). Sex differences in emotion: Expression, experience, and physiology. *Journal of Personality & Social Psychology, 74,* 686–703.

Kripke, D., Simons, R. N., Garfinkel, L., & Hammond, E. C. (1979). Short and long sleep and sleeping pills. *Archives of General Psychiatry, 36,* 103–116.

Krueger, R. F. (2000). Phenotypic, genetic, and nonshared environmental parallels in the structure of personality: A view from the Multidimensional Personality Questionnaire. *Journal of Personality and Social Psychology, 79,* 1057–1067.

Kruesi, M., Hibbs, E., Zahn, T., & Keysor, C. (1992). A 2-year prospective follow-up study of children and adolescents with disruptive behavior disorders: Prediction by cerebrospinal fluid 5-hydroxyindoleacetic acid, homovanillic acid, and autonomic measures? *Archives of General Psychiatry, 49,* 429–435.

Krystal, A. D., Dean, M. D., Weiner, R. D., Tramontozzi, L. A., Connor, K. M., Lindahl, V. H., & Massie, R. W. (2000). ECT stimulus intensity: Are present ECT devices too limited? *American Journal of Psychiatry, 157,* 963–967.

Kuhl, P. K., & Meltzoff, A. N. (1988). Speech and an intermodal object of perception. In A. Tonas (Ed.), *Minnesota symposium on child psychology: Vol. 20. Perceptual development in infancy.* Hillsdale, NJ: Lawrence Erlbaum.

Kuhlmeier, V. A., Boysen, S. T., & Mukobi, K. L. (1999). Scale-model comprehension by chimpanzees *(Pan troglodytes). Journal of Comparative Psychology, 113,* 396–402.

Kuhn, T. S. (1970). *The structure of scientific revolutions* (2nd ed.). Chicago: University of Chicago Press.

Kuiper, N. A., & Derry, P. A. (1982). Depressed and nondepressed content self-reference in mild depression. *Journal of Personality, 50,* 67–79.

Kuiper, N. A., Olinger, L. J., MacDonald, M. R.,

& Shaw, B. F. (1985). Self-schema processing of depressed and nondepressed content: The effects of vulnerability on depression. *Social Cognition, 3,* 77–93.

Kunda, Z. (1990). The case for motivated reasoning. *Psychological Bulletin, 108,* 480–498.

Kunda, Z., & Thagard, P. (1996). Forming impressions from stereotypes, traits, and behaviors: A parallel-constraint-satisfaction theory. *Psychological Review, 103,* 284–308.

Kunz, P. R., & Woolcott, M. (1976). Season's greetings: From my status to yours. *Social Science Research, 5,* 269–278.

Kunzendorf, R. G., Spanos, N. P., & Wallace, B. (Eds.). (1996). *Hypnosis and imagination. Imagery and human development series.* New York: Baywood Publishing Co.

Kuo-shu, Y., & Bond, M. H. (1990). Exploring implicit personality theories with indigenous or imported constructs: The Chinese case. *Journal of Personality and Social Psychology, 58,* 1087–1095.

Kurzban, R., & Leary, M. R. (2001). Evolutionary origins of stigmatization: The functions of social exclusion. *Psychological Bulletin, 127,* 187-208.

Kushner, M. G., Abrams, K., & Borchardt, C. (2000). The relationship between anxiety disorders and alcohol use disorders: A review of major perspectives and findings. *Clinical Psychology Review, 20,* 149–171.

Kvavilashvili, L. (1987). Remembering intention as a distinct form of memory. *British Journal of Psychology, 78,* 507–518.

LaBar, K. S., & LeDoux, J. E. (1996). Partial disruption of fear conditioning in rats with unilateral amygdala damage: Correspondence with unilateral temporal lobectomy in humans. *Behavioral Neuroscience, 110,* 991–997.

Labarre, W. (1966). The Aymaya: History and world view. *Journal of American Folklore, 79,* 130–144.

Labouvie-Vief, G., & Schell, D. A. (1982). Learning and memory in late life. In B. B. Wolman (Ed.), *Handbook of developmental psychology.* Englewood Cliffs, NJ: Prentice-Hall.

Ladd, G. W. (1999). Peer relationships and social competence during early and middle childhood. *Annual Review of Psychology, 50,* 333–359.

Ladd, G. W., & Mize, J. (1983). A cognitive-social learning model of social skill training. *Psychological Review, 90,* 127–157.

LaFreniere, P. J., & Sroufe, L. A. (1985). Profiles of peer competence in the preschool: Interrelations between measures, influences of social ecology, and relation to attachment history. *Developmental Psychology, 21,* 56–69.

Laing, D. G., Prescott, J., Bell, G. A., & Gilmore, R. (1993). A cross-cultural study of taste discrimination with Australians and Japanese. *Chemical Senses, 18,* 161–168.

Lakoff, G. (1985). *Women, fire, and dangerous things.* Chicago: University of Chicago Press.

Lakoff, G. (1989). A suggestion for a linguistics with connectionist foundations. In D. Touretzky, G. E. Hinton, et al. (Eds.), *Proceedings of the*

1988 Connectionist Models Summer School. (pp. 301–314). San Mateo, CA: Morgan Kaufmann.

Lakoff, G. (1997). How unconscious metaphorical thought shapes dreams. In D. J. Stein (Ed.), *Cognitive science and the unconscious. Progress in psychiatry* (No. 52, pp. 89–120). Washington, DC: American Psychiatric Press.

Lalumiere, M. L., Blanchard, R., & Zucker, K. J. (2000). Sexual orientation and handedness in men and women: A meta-analysis. *Psychological Bulletin, 126,* 575–592.

Lamb, M. E. (1987). Introduction: The emergent American father. In M. E. Lamb (Ed.), *The father's role: Cross-cultural perspective.* Hillsdale, NJ: Lawrence Erlbaum.

Lamb, M. E., Easterbrooks, M. A., & Holden, G. (1980). Reinforcement and punishment among preschoolers: Characteristics and correlates. *Child Development, 51,* 1230–1236.

Lamb, M. E., & Roopnarine, J. L. (1979). Peer influences on sex-role development in preschoolers. *Child Development, 50,* 1219–1222.

Lambert, M J., & Bergin, A. E. (1994). The effectiveness of psychotherapy. In A. E. Bergin, & S. L. Garfield (Eds.), *Handbook of psychotherapy and behavior change* (4th ed., pp. 143-189). Oxford: John Wiley & Sons.

Lambert, M. J., Shapiro, D. A., & Bergin, A. E. (1986). The effectiveness of psychotherapy. In S. L. Garfield and A. E. Bergin (Eds.), *Handbook of psychotherapy and behavior change.* New York: John Wiley.

Lame Deer, J., & Erdoes, R. (1972). *Lame Deer, seeker of visions.* New York: Simon & Schuster.

Landau, E., & Weissler, K. (1993). Parental environment in families with gifted and nongifted children. *Journal of Psychology, 127,* 129–142.

Landman, J. T., & Dawes, R. M. (1982). Psychotherapy outcome: Smith and Glass' conclusions stand up under scrutiny. *American Psychologist, 37,* 504–516.

Landy, D., & Aronson, E. (1969). The influence of the character of the criminal and his victim on the decisions of simulated jurors. *Journal of Experimental Social Psychology, 5,* 141–152.

Lane, C., & Hobfoll, S. E. (1992). How loss affects anger and alienates potential supporters. *Journal of Consulting and Clinical Psychology, 6,* 935–942.

Lane, R. D., Reiman, E. M., Bradley, M. M., Lang, P. J., Ahern, G. L., Davidson, R. J., & Schwartz, G. E. (1997). Neuroanatomical correlates of pleasant and unpleasant emotion. *Neuropsychologia, 35,* 1437-1444.

Lang, P. (1995). The emotion probe: Studies of motivation and attention. *American Psychologist, 50,* 372–385.

Lang, P. J. (1994). The varieties of emotional experience: A meditation on James-Lange theory. *Psychological Review, 101,* 212–221.

Lange, C. G. (1885). The emotions: A psychophysiological study, Trans. I. A. Haupt. In C. G. Lange & W. James (Eds.), *Psychology classics,* (Vol. I). Baltimore, MD: Williams & Wilkins, 1922.

Langer, E. J. (1978). Rethinking the role of thought in social interaction. In J. H. Harvey, W. I. Ickes, & R. F. Kidd (Eds.), *New directions in attribution research* (Vol. 2, pp. 35–58). Hillsdale, NJ: Lawrence Erlbaum.

Langlois, J., Ritter, J. M., Roggman, L., & Vaughn, L. S. (1991). Facial diversity and infant preferences for attractive faces. *Developmental Psychology, 27,* 79–84.

Langlois, J. H., & Downs, A. C. (1980). Mothers, fathers, and peers as socialization agents of sex-typed play behaviors in young children. *Child Development, 51,* 1217–1247.

Lanzetta, J. T., Cartwright-Smith, J., & Kleck, R. E. (1976). Effects of nonverbal dissimulation on emotional experience and autonomic arousal. *Journal of Personality and Social Psychology, 33,* 354–370.

Laroi, F. (2003). The family systems approach to treating families of persons with brain injury: A potential collaboration between family therapist and brain injury professional. *Brain Injury, 17,* 175–187.

Larose, H., & Standing, L. (1998). Does the halo effect occur in the elderly? *Social Behavior & Personality, 26,* 147–150.

Larsen, R. J., Billings, D. W., & Cutler, S. E. (1996). Affect intensity and individual differences in informational style. *Journal of Personality, 64,* 185-207.

Larson, R. W. (1997). The emergence of solitude as a constructive domain of experience in early adolescence. *Child Development, 68,* 80–93.

Larson, R. W., Richards, M. H., Moneta, G., Holmbeck, G., & Duckett, E. (1996). Changes in adolescents' daily interactions with their families from ages 10 to 18: Disengagement and transformation. *Developmental Psychology, 32,* 744–754.

Larzelere, R. E., Schneider, W. N., Larson, D. B., & Pike, P. L. (1996). The effects of discipline responses in delaying toddler misbehavior recurrences. *Child & Family Behavior Therapy, 18,* 35–57.

Lasswell, H. D. (1948). The structure and function of communication in society. In L. Bryson (Ed.), *Communication of ideas.* New York: Harper-Collins.

Latimer, P. R. (1979). The behavior treatment of self-excoriation in a twelve-year-old girl. *Journal of Behavioral Therapy and Experimental Psychiatry, 10,* 349–352.

Laub, J. B., & Sampson, R. J. (1995). The long-term effect of punitive discipline. In J. McCord (Ed.), *Coercion and punishment in long-term perspectives* (pp. 247–258). New York: Cambridge University Press.

Lavie, P. (1996). *The enchanted world of sleep* (A. Berris, Trans.). New Haven, CT: Yale University Press.

Lawrence, C. B., Turnbull, A. V., & Rothwell, N. J. (1999). Hypothalamic control of feeding. *Current Opinion in Neurobiology, 9,* 778–783.

Lazarus, R. (1981). The stress and coping paradigm. In C. Eisdorfer, D., Cohen, A. Kleinman, & P. Maxim (Eds.), *Models for clinical psychopathology.* New York: Spectrum.

Lazarus, R. S. (1993). From psychological stress to the emotions: A history of changing outlooks. *Annual Review of Psychology, 44,* 1–21.

Lazarus, R. S. (1999a). *Stress and emotion: A new synthesis.* New York: Springer.

Lazarus, R. S. (1999b). The cognition-emotion debate: A bit of history. In T. Dalgleish & M. Power (Eds.), *The handbook of cognition and emotion* (pp. 3–20). New York: John Wiley & Sons.

Leaper, C., Anderson, K. J., & Sanders, P. (1998). Moderators of gender effects on parents' talk to their children: A meta-analysis. *Developmental Psychology, 34,* 3–27.

Leary, M. R. (1995). *Self-presentation: Impression management and social behavior.* Duguque, IA: Brown & Benchmark.

Leary, M. R. (1999). The scientific study of personality. In V. J. Derlega, B. A., Winstead, & W. H. Jones (Eds.), *Personality: Contemporary theory and research* (pp. 3–26). Chicago: Nelson-Hall.

Leary, M. R. (Ed.) (2001). *Interpersonal rejection.* London: Oxford University Press.

Leary, M. R., Britt, T. W., Cutlip, W. D., & Templeton, J. D. (2002). Social blushing. *Psychological Bulletin, 112,* 446–460.

Leary, M. R., & Jones, J. L. (1993). The social psychology of tanning and sunscreen use: Self-presentational motives as a predictor of health risk. *Journal of Applied Social Psychology, 23,* 1390–1406.

Leary, M. R., & Kowalski, R. M. (1990). Impression management: A literature review and two-component model. *Psychological Bulletin, 107,* 34–47.

Leary, M. R., Tchividjian, L. R., & Kraxberger, B. E. (1994). Self-presentation can be hazardous to your health: Impression management and health risk. *Health Psychology, 13,* 461–470.

Lecky, P. (1945). *Self-consistency: A theory of personality.* New York: Island Press.

LeDoux, J. (1995). Emotion: Clues from the brain. *Annual Review of Psychology, 46,* 209–235.

LeDoux, J. (1998). Fear and the brain: Where have we been, and where are we going? *Biological Psychiatry, 44,* 1229–1238.

LeDoux, J. E. (1989). Cognitive-emotional interactions in the brain. *Cognition and Emotion, 3,* 267–289.

LeDoux, J. E. (2000). Emotion circuits in the brain. *Annual Review of Neuroscience, 23,* 155–184.

LeDoux, J. E., Wilson, D. H., & Gazzinaga, M. S. (1977). Manipulo-spatial aspects of central lateralization. *Neuropsychologia, 15,* 743–750.

Lee, D. (1950). The conception of the self among the Wintu Indians. In D. Lee (Ed.), *Freedom and culture.* Englewood Cliffs, NJ: Prentice-Hall, 1959.

Lee, E. (1951). Negro intelligence and selective migration: A Philadelphia test of Klineberg's hypothesis. *American Sociological Review, 61,* 227–233.

Lee, Y., & Seligman, M. E. P. (1997). Are Americans more optimistic than the Chinese? *Personality & Social Psychology Bulletin, 23,* 32–40.

Lehman, D. R., Wortman, C. B., & Williams, A. F. (1987). Long-term effects of losing a spouse or child in a motor vehicle crash. *Journal of Personality and Social Psychology, 52*, 218–231.

Lehmann, H. E. (1985). Affective disorders: Clinical features. In H. I. Kaplan & B. J. Sadock (Eds.), *Comprehensive textbook of psychiatry* (4th ed.), Baltimore, MD: Williams & Wilkins.

Lehrman, D. S. (1956). On the organization of maternal behavior and the problem of instinct. In *L'instinct dans le Comportement des Animaux et de l'homme.* Paris: Masson et Cie.

Lempers, J. D., Flavell, E. R., & Flavell, J. H. (1977). The development in very young children of tacit knowledge concerning visual perception. *Genetic Psychology Monographs, 95,* 3–53.

Lenneberg, E. (1967). *The biological foundations of language.* New York: John Wiley.

Lenzenweger, M. F., Loranger, A. W., Korfine, L., & Neff, C. (1997) Detecting personality disorders in a nonclinical population: Application of a 2-stage for case identification. *Archives of General Psychiatry, 54*, 345–351.

Leonard, B. E., & Song, C. (2002). Changes in the immune system in rodent models of depression. *International Journal of Neuropsychopharmacology, 5*, 345-356.

Lepore, S. J. (1997). Expressive writing moderates the relation between intrusive thoughts and depressive symptoms. *Journal of Personality and Social Psychology, 73*, 1030–1037.

Lepore, S. J., & Greenberg, M. A. (2002). Mending broken hearts: Effects of expressive writing on mood, cognitive processing, social adjustment, and health following a relationship breakup. *Psychology and Health, 17*, 547–560.

Lepper, M. R., Greene, D., & Nisbett, R. E. (1996). Undermining children's intrinsic interest with extrinsic reward: A test of the "overjustification" hypothesis. In F. Fein, Steven, and S. Spencer (Eds.), *Readings in social psychology: The art and science of research.* (pp. 10-18). Boston, MA: Houghton Mifflin.

Lerman, C., Caporaso, N. E., Audrain, J., Main, D., Bowman, E. D., Lockshin, B., et al. (1999). Evidence suggesting the role of specific genetic factors in cigarette smoking. *Health Psychology, 18*, 14-20.

Lerman, C., Hughes, C., Benkendorf, J. L., Biesecker, B., Kerner, J., Willison, J., Eads, N., Hadley, D., & Lynch, J. (1999). Racial differences in testing motivation and psychological distress following pretest education for BRCA 1 gene testing. *Cancer Epidemiology, Biomarkers, and Prevention, 8*, 361–368.

Lerner, R. (1991). Changing organism-context relations as the basic process of development: A developmental contextual perspective. *Developmental Psychology, 27*, 27–32.

Lerner, J. S., & Keltner, D. (2000). Beyond valence: Toward a model of emotion-specific influences on judgment and choice. *Cognition and Emotion, 14*, 473-493.

LeVay, S. (1991). A difference in hypothalamic structure between heterosexual and homosexual men. *Science, 253*, 1034–1037.

Levenson, J. L., & Bemis, C. (1991). The role of psychological factors in cancer onset and progression. *Psychosomatics, 32*, 124–132.

Levenson, R., & Ruef, A. (1992). Empathy: A physiological substrate. *Journal of Personality and Social Psychology, 63*, 234–246.

Levenson, R. W. (1992). Autonomic nervous system differences among emotions. *Psychological Science, 3*, 23–27.

Levenson, R. W., Ekman, P., & Friesen, W. (1990). Voluntary facial action generates emotion- specific autonomic nervous system activity. *Psychophysiology, 27*, 363–385.

Levenson, R. W., Ekman, P., Heider, K., & Friesen, W. V. (1992). Emotion and autonomic nervous system activity in the Minangkabau of West Sumatra. *Journal of Personality and Social Psychology, 62*, 972–988.

Leventhal, E. A., Leventhal, H., Shacham, S., & Easterling, D. V. (1989). Active coping reduces reports of pain from childbirth. *Journal of Consulting and Clinical Psychology, 57*, 365–371.

Leventhal, H., & Leventhal, E. A. (1993). Affect, cognition, and symptom perception. In C. R. Chapman & K. M Foley, (Eds.), *Current and emerging issues in cancer pain: Research and practice. Bristol-Myers Squibb Symposium on Pain Research series.* (pp. 153–173). New York: Raven.

Leventhal, H., & Tomarken, A. J. (1986). Emotion: Today's problems. *Annual Review of Psychology, 37*, 565–610.

Levine, L. J., & Burgess, S. L. (1997). Beyond general arousal: Effects of specific emotions on memory. *Social Cognition, 15*, 157–181.

LeVine, R. (1982). *Culture, behavior, and personality* (2nd ed.). Chicago: Aldine.

LeVine, R. A., & LeVine, B. B. (1963). Nyasongo: A Gusii community in Kenya. In B. Whiting (Ed.), *Six cultures: Studies in child rearing* (pp. 19–202). New York: John Wiley.

Levine, R. V., Martinez, T., Brase, G., & Sorenson, K. (1994). Helping in 36 U.S. cities. *Journal of Personality and Social Psychology, 67*, 69–82.

Levinger, G. (1976). Social psychological perspectives on marital dissolution. *Journal of Social Issues, 32*, 21–47.

Levinson, D. (1978). *The seasons of a man's life.* New York: Ballantine Books.

Levinson, D. J., Darrow, C. N., Klein, E. B., Levinson, M. H., & McKee, B. (1978). *The seasons of a man's life.* New York: Alfred A. Knopf.

Levkovitz, Y., Caftori, R., Avital, A., & Richter, L. G. (2002). The SSRI's drug Fluoxetine, but not the noradrenergic tricyclic drug Desipramine, improves memory performance during acute major depression. *Brain Research Bulletin, 58*, 345–350.

Lewicki, P. (1986). *Nonconscious social information processing.* New York: Academic Press.

Lewin, K. (1939). Field theory and experiment in social psychology: Concepts and methods. *American Journal of Sociology, 44*, 868–897.

Lewinsohn, P. M., Allen, N. B., Seeley, J. R., & Gotlib, I. H. (1999). First onset versus recurrence of depression: Differential processes of psychosocial risk. *Journal of Abnormal Psychology, 108*, 483–489.

Lewinsohn, P. M., Gotlibm, I. H., Lewinsohn, M., Seeley, J. R., & Allen, N. B. (1998). Gender differences in anxiety disorders and anxiety symptoms in adolescents. *Journal of Abnormal Psychology, 107*, 109–117.

Lewinsohn, P. M., Solomon, A., Seeley, J. R., & Zeiss, A. (2000). Clinical implications of "subthreshold" depressive symptoms. *Journal of Abnormal Psychology, 109*, 345–351.

Lewis, D. A. (2000). Distributed disturbances in brain structure and function in schizophrenia. *American Journal of Psychiatry, 157*, 1–2.

Lewis, D. O., Yeager, C. A., Swica, Y., Pincus, J. H., & Lewis, M. (1997a). Objective documentation of child abuse and dissociation in 12 murderers with dissociative identity disorder. *American Journal of Psychiatry, 154*, 1703–1710.

Lewis, J. W. (1990). Premenstrual syndrome as a criminal defense. *Archives of Sexual Behavior, 19*, 425–441.

Lewis, M., & Bendersky, M. (1995). *Mothers, babies, and cocaine: The role of toxins in development.* Hillsdale, NJ: Lawrence Erlbaum.

Lewis, M., Feiring, C., & Rosenthal, S. (2000). Attachment over time. *Child Development, 71*, 707–720.

Lewis, N., & Brooks-Gunn, J. (1979). *Social cognition and the acquisition of self.* New York: Plenum Press.

Lewkowicz, D. J. (2000). The development of intersensory temporal perception: An epigenetic systems/limitations view. *Psychological Bulletin, 126*, 281–308.

Li, Z., Kim, C. H., Ichikawa, J., & Meltzer, H. Y. (2003). Effect of repeated administration of phencyclidine on spatial performance in an eight-arm radial maze with delay in rats and mice. *Pharmacology, Biochemistry, and Behavior, 75*, 335-340.

Liberman, A., & Chaiken, S. (1992). Defensive processing of personally relevant health messages. *Journal of Experimental Social Psychology.*

Liberman, N., & Trope, Y. (1998). The role of feasibility and desirability conditions in near and distant future decisions: A test of temporal construal theory. *Journal of Personality and Social Psychology, 75*, 5-18.

Lichtenberg, J. (1983). *Psychoanalysis and motivation.* Hillsdale, NJ: Analytic Press.

Lickliter, R., & Bahrick, L. E. (2000). The development of infant intersensory perception: Advantages of a comparative convergent-operations approach. *Psychological Bulletin, 126*, 260–280.

Lieberman, M., Doyle, A., & Markiewicz, D. (1999). Developmental patterns in security of attachment to mother and father in late childhood and early adolescence: Associations with peer relations. *Child Development, 70*, 202–213.

Lieberman, M. D. (2000). Intuition: A social cognitive neuroscience approach. *Psychological Bulletin, 126*, 109–136.

Lieberman, M. D., Ochsner, K. N., Gilbert, D. T., & Schacter, D. L. (2001). Do amnesics exhibit cognitive dissonance reduction? The role of explicit memory and attention in attitude change. *Psychological Science.*

Lieberman, S. (1956). The effects of changes in roles on the attitudes of role occupants. *Human Relations, 9,* 385–402.

Lierman, L. M., Kasprzyk, D., & Benoliel, J. Q. (1991). Understanding the adherence to breast self-examination in older women. *Western Journal of Nursing Research, 13,* 46–66.

Lierman, L. M., Young, H. M., Kasprzyk, D., & Benoliel, J. Q. (1990). Predicting breast self-examination using the theory of reasoned action. *Nursing Research, 39,* 97–101.

Lifton, R. J. (1963). *Thought reform and the psychology of totalism: A study of brainwashing in China.* New York: W.W. Norton.

Limongelli, L., Boysen, S. T., & Visalberghi, E. (1995). Comprehension of cause-effect relations in a tool-using task by chimpanzees *(Pan troglodytes). Journal of Comparative Psychology, 109,* 18–26.

Lin, E. H., & Peterson, C. (1990). Pessimistic explanatory style and response to illness. *Behaviour Research and Therapy, 28,* 243-248.

Lindberg, M. (1980). Is knowledge base development a necessary and sufficient condition for memory development? *Journal of Experimental Child Psychology, 30,* 401–410.

Lindemann, C. G. (Ed). (1996). *Handbook of the treatment of the anxiety disorders* (2nd ed.). Northvale, NJ: Jason Aronson.

Lindley, R. H., & Smith, W. R. (1992). Coding tests as measures of IQ: Cognitive or motivation? *Personality and Individual Differences, 13,* 25–29.

Linehan, M. (1987a). Dialectical behavior therapy for borderline personality disorder: Theory and method. *Bulletin of the Menninger Clinic, 51,* 261–276.

Linehan, M. M. (1987b). Dialectical behavioral therapy: A cognitive behavioral approach to parasuicide. *Journal of Personality Disorders, 1,* 328–333.

Linehan, M. M. (1993). *Cognitive-behavioral treatment of borderline personality disorder.* New York: Guilford Press.

Linehan, M. M. (2000). Behavioral treatments of suicidal behaviors: Definitional obfuscation and treatment outcomes. In R. W. Maris & S. S. Canetto (Eds.), *Review of suicidology, 2000.* (pp. 84–111). New York: Guilford Press.

Lisspers, J., & Ost, L. (1990). Long-term follow-up of migraine treatment: Do the effects remain up to six years? *Behaviour Therapy and Research, 28,* 313–322.

Litt, M., Babor, T., DelBoca, F., Kadden, R., & Cooney, N. (1992). Types of alcoholics, II: Application of an empirically derived typology to treatment matching. *Archives of General Psychiatry, 49,* 609–614.

Litt, M. D., Kadden, R. M., Cooney, N. L., & Kabela, E. (2003). Coping skills and treatment outcomes in cognitive-behavioral and interactional group therapy for alcoholism. *Journal of Consulting and Clinical Psychology, 71,* 118–128.

Little, A. (1987). Attributions in cross-cultural context. *Genetic, Social, and General Psychology Monographs, 113,* 61-79.

Livesley, W. J., & Bromley, D. B. (1973). *Person perception in childhood and adolescence.* London: John Wiley.

Livingstone, M., & Hubel, D. H. (1988). Segregation of form, color, movement, and depth: Anatomy, physiology, and perception. *Science, 240,* 740–749.

Locke, E., & Latham, G. (1990). *A theory of goal-setting and task performance.* Englewood Cliffs, NJ: Prentice-Hall.

Locke, E. A. (1991). Goal theory vs. control theory: Contrasting approaches to understanding work motivation. *Motivation and Emotion, 15,* 9–27.

Locke, E. A. (1996). Motivation through conscious goal setting. *Applied and Preventive Psychology, 5,* 117–124.

Lockhart, R. S., & Craik, F. (1990). Levels of processing: A retrospective commentary on a framework for memory research. *Canadian Journal of Psychology, 44,* 87–112.

Loeb, R. C., Horst, L., & Horton, P. J. (1980). Family interaction patterns associated with self-esteem in preadolescent girls and boys. *Merrill-Palmer Quarterly, 26,* 203–217.

Loehlin, J. (1992). *Genes and environment in personality development.* New York: Guilford Press.

Loehlin, J. C., Horn, J. M., & Willerman, L. (1989). Modeling IQ change: Evidence from the Texas Adoption Project. *Child Development, 60,* 993–1004.

Loehlin, J. C., Horn, J. M., & Willerman, L. (1997). Heredity, environment and IQ in the Texas Adoption Project. In R. J. Sternberg, E. L. Grigorenko, et al. (Eds.), *Intelligence, heredity, and environment* (pp. 105–125). New York: Cambridge University Press.

Loehlin, J. C., Willerman, L., & Horn, J. M. (1988). Human behavior genetics. *Annual Review of Psychology, 39,* 101–133.

Loevinger, J. (1976). *Ego development.* San Francisco: Jossey-Bass.

Loevinger, J. (1985). Revision of the sentence completion test for ego development. *Journal of Personality and Social Psychology, 48,* 420–427.

Loewenstein, W. R. (1960). Biological transducers. *Scientific American,* 98–108.

Loftus, E. (1993). The reality of repressed memories. *American Psychologist, 48,* 518–537.

Loftus, E. (1997a). Creating false memories. *Scientific American, 277,* 70–75.

Loftus, E. (1997b). Memory for a past that never was. *Current Directions in Psychological Science, 6,* 60–65.

Loftus, E. F., Levidow, B., & Duensing, S. (1992). Who remembers best? Individual differences in memory for events that occurred in a science museum. *Applied Cognitive Psychology, 6,* 93–107.

Loftus, E. F., & Palmer, J. C. (1974). Reconstruction and automobile destruction. An example of the interaction between language and memory. *Journal of Verbal Learning and Verbal Behavior, 13,* 585–589.

Loftus, E. F., Polonsky, S., & Fullilove, M. T. (1994). Memories of childhood sexual abuse: Remembering and repressing. *Psychology of Women Quarterly, 18,* 67–84.

Loftus, E. F., & Zanni, G. (1975). Eyewitness testimony: The influence of the wording of a question. *Bulletin of the Psychonomic Society, 5,* 86–88.

Logie, R. (1996). The seven ages of working memory. In J. T. E. Richardson, R. W. Engle, L. Hasher, R. Logie, E. Stoltzfus, & R. Zacks (Eds.), *Working memory and human cognition* (pp. 31–65). New York: Oxford University Press.

Lohman, T. G. (2002). Body composition. In K. D. Brownell & C. G. Fairburn (Eds.), *Eating disorders and obesity: A comprehensive handbook* (2nd ed., pp. 62–66). New York: Guilford Press.

Lonner, W., & Malpass, R. (Eds.) (1994a). *Readings in psychology and culture.* Boston, MA: Allyn & Bacon.

Lonner, W. J., & Malpass, R. (1994b). *Psychology and Culture.* Needham Heights, MA: Allyn & Bacon.

Lopez, A., Atran, S., Coley, J. D., Medin, D. L., & Smith, E. E. (1997). The tree of life: Universal and cultural features of folkbiological taxonomies and inductions. *Cognitive Psychology, 32,* 251–295.

Lore, R., & Schultz, L. A. (1993). Control of human aggression: A comparative perspective. *American Psychologist, 48,* 16–25.

Lorenz, K. (1935). The companion in the bird's world. The fellow-member of the species as releasing factor of social behavior. *Journal fuer Ornithologie, 83,* 137–213.

Lorenz, K. (1937). Ueber den Begriff der Instinkthandlung. / The concept of instinctive action. *Folia Biotheoretica, 2,* 17–50.

Lorenz, K. (1966). *On aggression.* New York: Harcourt, Brace & World.

Lorenz, K. (1979). *King Solomon's ring.* New York: Harper-Collins.

Lott, A., & Lott, B. (1974). The role of reward in the formation of positive interpersonal attitudes. In T. Huston (Ed.), *Foundations of interpersonal attraction.* New York: Academic Press.

Louw, F., & Straker, G. (2002). An integration of cognitive therapy and psychodynamic therapy. *Journal of Psychotherapy Integration, 12,* 190–217.

Lovaas, O. I. (1977). *The autistic child.* New York: John Wiley.

Lovaas, O. I. (1987). Behavioral treatment and normal educational and intellectual functioning in young autistic children. *Journal of Consulting and Clinical Psychology, 55,* 3–9.

Low, B. S. (1989). Cross-cultural patterns in the training of children: An evolutionary perspective. *Journal of Comparative Psychology, 103,* 311–319.

Lu, C., Shaikh, M. B., & Siegel, A. (1992). Role of NMDA receptors in hypothalamic facilitation of feline defensive rage elicited from the midbrain pariaqueductal gray. *Brain Research, 581,* 123–132.

Lubart, T. I. (2003). In search of creative intelligence. In R. J. Sternberg J. Lautrey, et al. (Eds.), *Models of intelligence: International perspectives* (pp. 279–292). Washington, DC: American Psychological Association.

Luborsky, L. (1985). Therapist success and its determinants. *Archives of General Psychiatry, 42,* 602–611.

Luborsky, L., Barber, J. P., & Crits-Christoph, P. (1990). Theory-based research for understanding the process of dynamic psychotherapy. *Journal of Consulting and Clinical Psychology, 58,* 281–287.

Luborsky, L., & Crits-Christoph, P. (1990). *Understanding transference: The core conflictual relationship theme method.* New York: Basic Books.

Luborsky, L., Docherty, J. P., Miller, N. E., & Barber, J. P. (1993). What's here and what's ahead in dynamic therapy research and practice? In N. E. Miller, L. Luborsky, et al. (Ed.), *Psychodynamic treatment research: A handbook for clinical practice* (pp. 536–553). New York: Basic Books.

Luborsky, L., McLellan, A. T., Diguer, L., Woody, G., & Seligman, D. A. (1997). The psychotherapist matters: Comparison of outcomes across twenty-two therapists and seven patient samples. *Clinical Psychology-Science & Practice, 4,* 53–65.

Lubow, R. E., & Gewirtz, J. C. (1995). Latent inhibition in humans: Data, theory, and implications for schizophrenia. *Psychological Bulletin, 117,* 87–103.

Luchins, A. (1957). Primacy-recency in impression formation. In C. Hovland (Ed.), *The order of presentation in persuasion* (pp. 33–61). New Haven, CT: Yale University Press.

Ludolph, P. S., Westen, D., Misle, B., Jackson, A., et al. (1990). The borderline diagnosis in adolescents: Symptoms and developmental history. *American Journal of Psychiatry, 147,* 470–476.

Lumer, E. D., & Rees, G. (1999). Covariation of activity in visual and prefrontal cortex associated with subjective visual perception. *Proceedings of the National Academy of Science, U.S.A., 96,* 1669–1673.

Lundh, L., Wikstrom, J., Westerlund, J., & Ost, L. (1999). Preattentive bias for emotional information in panic disorder with agoraphobia. *Journal of Abnormal Psychology, 108,* 222–232.

Luria, A. R. (1973). *The working brain.* Harmondsworth, UK: Penguin.

Luthar, S. S., Cicchetti, D., & Becker, B. (2000). Research on resilience: Response to commentaries. *Child Development, 71,* 573–575.

Lyketsos, C. G., Chen, L., & Anthony, J. C. (1999). Cognitive decline in adulthood: An 11.5-year follow-up of the Baltimore Epidemiologic Catchment Area Study. *American Journal of Psychiatry, 156,* 58–65.

Lykken, D. T., Bouchard, T. J., McGue, M., & Tellegen, A. (1993). Heritability of interests: A twin study. *Journal of Applied Psychology, 78,* 649–661.

Lykken, D. T., McGue, M., Tellegen, A., & Bouchard, T. J. (1992). Emergenesis: Genetic traits that may not run in families. *American Psychologist, 47,* 1565–1577.

Lynch, O. M. (1990). The social construction of emotion in India. In O. M. Lynch (Ed.), *Divine passions: The social construction of emotion in India* (pp. 3–34). Berkeley: University of California Press.

Lynd-Stevenson, R. M. (1999). Expectancy-value theory and predicting future employment status in the young unemployed. *Journal of Occupational and Organizational Psychology, 72,* 101–106.

Lynn, S. J., Lock, T., Myers, B., & Payne, D. G. (1997). Recalling the unrecallable: Should hypnosis be used to recover memories in psychotherapy? *Current Directions in Psychological Science, 6,* 79–83.

Lyons, A. S., & Petrucelli III, R. J. (1978). *Medicine: An illustrated history.* New York: Harry Abrams.

Lyons, M. J., Eisen, S. A., Goldberg, J., True, W., Lin, N., Meyer, J. M., et al. (1998). A registry-based twin study of depression in men. *Archives of General Psychiatry, 55,* 468–472.

Lyons, M. J., True, W. R., Eisen, S. A., & Goldberg, J. (1995). Differential heritability of adult and juvenile antisocial traits. *Archives of General Psychiatry, 52,* 906–915.

Lyons-Ruth, K., Connell, D., Grunebaum, H., & Botein, S. (1990). Infants at social risk: Maternal depression and familiy support services as mediators of infant development and security of attachment. *Child Development, 61,* 85–98.

Lyons-Ruth, K., Easterbrooks, M. A., & Cibelli, C. D. (1997). Infant attachment strategies, infant mental lag, and maternal depressive symptoms. Predictors of internalizing and externalizing problems at age 7. *Developmental Psychology, 33,* 681–692.

Lytton, H. (1990). Child and parent effects in boys' conduct disorder: A reinterpretation. *Developmental Psychology, 26,* 683–697.

Maccoby, E. (1992). The role of parents in the socialization of children: An historical overview. *Developmental Psychology, 28,* 1006–1017.

Maccoby, E. E., & Jacklin, C. N. (1974). *The psychology of sex differences.* Stanford, CA: Stanford University Press.

Maccoby, E. E., & Jacklin, C. N. (1980). Sex differences in aggression: A rejoinder and reprise. *Child Development, 51,* 964–980.

MacCoun, R. J. (1998). Biases in the interpretation and the use of research results. *Annual Review of Psychology, 49,* 259–287.

MacDonald, A. W., Cohen, J. D., Stenger, V. A., & Carter, C. S. (2000). Dissociating the role of the dorsolateral prefrontal and anterior cingulate cortex in cognitive control. *Science, 288,* 1835–1838.

Mace, R. (1996). Biased parental investment and reproductive success in *Gabbra pastoralists. Behavioral Ecology & Sociobiology, 38,* 75–81.

Macfie, J., Toth, S. L., Rogosch, F. A., Robinson, J., Emde, R. N., & Cicchetti, D. (1999). Effect of maltreatment on preschoolers' narrative representations of responses to relieve distress and of role reversal. *Developmental Psychology, 35,* 460–465.

MacKinnon, D. F., Jamison, K. R., & DePaulo, J. R. (1997). Genetics of manic-depressive illness. *Annual Review of Neuroscience, 20,* 355-373.

MacKinnon-Lewis, C., Starnes, R., Volling, B., & Johnson, S. (1997). Perceptions of parenting as predictors of boys' sibling and peer relations. *Developmental Psychology, 33,* 1024–1031.

Mackintosh, N. J. (1998). *IQ and human intelligence.* New York: Oxford University Press.

Macklin, M. L., Metzger, L. J., Litz, B. T., McNally, R. J., Lasko, N. B., Orr, S. P., & Pitman, R. K. (1998). Lower precombat intelligence is a risk factor for posttraumatic stress disorder. *Journal of Consulting & Clinical Psychology, 66,* 323–326.

MacLean, P. D. (1982). On the origin and progressive evolution of the triune brain. In E. Armstrong & D. Falk, (Eds.), *Primate brain evolution.* New York: Plenum Press.

MacLean, P. D. (1990). A reinterpretation of memorative functions of the limbic system. In E. Goldberg, et al. (Eds.), *Contemporary neuropsychology and the legacy of Luria. Institute for research in behavioral neuroscience.* (pp. 127–154). Hillsdale, NJ: Lawrence Erlbaum.

Macrae, C. N., & Bodenhausen, G. V. (2000). Social cognition: Thinking categorically about others. *Annual Review of Psychology, 51,* 93–120.

Macrae, C. N., Bodenhausen, G. V., & Milne, A. B. (1998). Saying no to unwanted thoughts: Self-focus and the regulation of mental life. *Journal of Personality & Social Psychology, 74,* 578–589.

Macrae, C. N., Milne, A. B., & Bodenhausen, G. (1994). Stereotypes as energy-saving devices: A peek inside the cognitive toolbox. *Journal of Personality and Social Psychology, 66,* 37–47.

MacWhinney, B. (1998). Models of the emergence of language. *Annual Review of Psychology, 49,* 199–227.

Madden, P. A. F., Heath, A. C., Rosenthal, N. E., & Martin, N. G. (1996). Seasonal changes in mood and behavior: The role of genetic factors. *Archives of General Psychiatry, 53,* 47–55.

Magee, W. J., Eaton, W. W., Wittchen, H., McGonagle, K. A., & Kessler, R. C. (1996). Agoraphobia, simple phobia, and social phobia in the National Comorbidity Survey. *Archives of General Psychiatry, 53,* 159–168.

Maguire, E. A., Frackowiak, R. S. J., & Frith, C. D. (1997). Recalling routes around London: Activation of the right hippocampus in taxi drivers. *Journal of Neuroscience, 17,* 7103-7110.

Maguire, E. A., Mummery, C. J., & Buechel, C. (2000). Patterns of hippocampal-cortical interaction dissociate temporal lobe memory subsystems. *Hippocampus, 10,* 475-482.

Mahler, M., Pine, F., & Bergman, A. (1975). *The psychological birth of the human infant: Symbiosis and individualization.* New York: Basic Books.

Mahoney, D. P. (1997, December). Virtual therapy nets real results. *Computer Graphics World, 20.*

Maier, S. F. (2003). Bi-directional immune-brain communication: Implications for understanding stress, pain, and cognition. *Brain, Behavior, and Immunity, 17,* 69-85.

Main, M. (1990). Cross-cultural studies of attachment organization: Recent studies, changing methodologies, and the concept of conditional strategies. *Human Development, 33,* 48–61.

Main, M. (1995). Recent studies in attachment: Overview, with selected implications for clinical work. In S. Goldberg, R. Muir, et al. (Eds.). *Attachment theory: Social, developmental, and cinical perspectives.* (pp. 407–474). Hillsdale, NJ: Analytic Press.

Main, M., Kaplan, N., & Cassidy, J. (1985). Security in infancy, childhood, and adulthood: A move to the level of representation. In I. Bretherton & E. Waters (Eds.), Growing points of attachment theory and research. *Monographs of the Society for Research in Child Development, 50* (No. 1–2), 67–104.

Main, M., & Solomon, J. (1986). Discovery of a new, insecure-disorganized/disoriented attachment pattern. In T. Brazelton & M. Yogman, (Eds.), *Affective development in infancy* (pp. 95–124). Norwood, NJ: Ablex.

Maj, M., Veltro, F., Pirozzi, R., Lobrace, S., & Magliano, L. (1992). Pattern of recurrence of illness after recovery from an episode of major depression: A prospective study. *American Journal of Psychiatry, 149,* 795–800.

Major, B., Zubek, J. M., Cooper, M. L., Cozzarelli, C., et al. (1997). Mixed messages: Implications of social conflict and social support within close relationships for adjustment to a stressful life event. *Journal of Personality & Social Psychology, 72,* 1349–1363.

Malamuth, N. M., & Donnerstein, E. (1982). The effects of aggressive-pornographic mass media stimuli. In L. Berkowitz (Ed.) *Advances in Experimental Social Psychology,* Vol. 15. New York: Academic Press.

Malpass, R. S., & Devine, P. G. (1980). Realism and eyewitness identification research. *Law and Human Behavior, 4,* 347–358.

Malt, B., & Smith, E. E. (1984). Correlated properties in natural categories. *Journal of Verbal Learning and Verbal Behavior, 23,* 250–269.

Maltby, N., Kirsch, I., Mayers, M., & Allen, G. J. (2002). Virtual reality exposure therapy for the treatment of fear of flying: A controlled investigation. *Journal of Consulting and Clinical Psychology, 70,* 1112–1118.

Mandler, G. (1997). *Human nature explored.* New York: Oxford University Press.

Maner, J. K., Luce, C. L., Neuberg, S. L., Cialdini, R. B., Brown, S., & Sagarin, B. J. (2002). The effects of perspective taking on motivations for helping: Still no evidence for altruism. *Personality and Social Psychology Bulletin, 28,* 1601–1610.

Mangelsdorf, S., Gunnar, M., Kestenbaum, R., Lang, S., & Andreas, D. (1990). Infant proneness- to-distress temperament, maternal personality, and mother-infant attachment: Associations and goodness of fit. *Child Development, 61,* 820–831.

Manji, H. K., Chen, G., Shimon, H., Hsiao, J. K., Potter, W. Z., & Belmaker, R. H. (1995). Guanine nucleotide-binding proteins in bipolar affective disorder: Effects of long-term lithium

treatment. *Archives of General Psychiatry, 52,* 135–144.

Mann, J. (1982). *A casebook in time-limited psychotherapy.* New York: McGraw-Hill.

Mann, J. J., Huang, Y., Underwood, M. D., Kassir, S. A., Oppenheim, S., Kelly, T. M., Dwork, A. J., & Arango, V. (2000). A serotonin transporter gene promoter polymorphism (5-HTTLPR) and prefrontal cortical binding in major depression and suicide. *Archives of General Psychiatry, 57,* 729–738.

Manne, S. (2003). Coping and social support. In A. M. Nezu, C. M. Nezu, et al. (Eds.), *Handbook of psychology: Health psychology* (Vol. 9, pp. 51–74). Hoboken, NJ: John Wiley & Sons.

Mannuzza, S., Klein, R. G., Bessler, A., Malloy, P., & Lpadula, M. (1998). Adult psychiatric status of hyperative boys grown up. *American Journal of Psychiatry, 155,* 493–498.

Manuck, S. B., Flory, J. D., Ferrell, R. E., Dent, K. M., Mann, J. J., & Muldoon, M. F. (1999). Aggression and anger-related traits associated with a polymorphism of the tryptophan hydroxylase gene. *Biological Psychiatry, 45,* 603–614.

Maquet, P., Peters, J., Aerts, J., & Delfiore, G. (1996). Functional neuroanatomy of human rapid-eye-movement sleep and dreaming. *Nature, 383,* 163–166.

Marcia, J. (1987). The identity status approach to the study of ego identity development. In T. Honess & K. Yardley (Eds.), *Self and identity: Perspectives across the lifespan* (pp. 161–171). Boston, MA: Routledge & Kegan Paul.

Marcia, J. E. (1999). Representational thought in ego identity, psychotherapy, and psychosocial developmental theory. In I. E. Sigel (Ed.), *Development of mental representation: Theories and applications* (pp. 391–414). Mahwah, NJ: Lawrence Erlbaum.

Marcotte, A., & Morere, D. (1990). Speech lateralization in deaf populations: Evidence for a developmental critical period. *Brain & Language, 39,* 134–152.

Marcus, D. E., & Overton, W. E. (1978). The development of cognitive gender constancy and sex role preferences. *Child Development, 49,* 434–444.

Marengo, J., Harrow, M., Sands, J., & Galloway, C.. (1991). European versus U.S. data on the course of schizophrenia. *American Journal of Psychiatry, 148,* 606–611.

Margolskee, R. (1995). Receptor mechanisms in gustation. In R. L. Doty (Ed.), *Handbook of olfaction and gustation.* New York: Marcel Dekker.

Marian, V., & Neisser, U. (2000). Language-dependent recall of autobiographical memories. *Journal of Experimental Psychology: General, 129,* 361-368.

Marino, L. (2002). Convergence of complex cognitive abilities in cetaceans and primates. *Brain, Behavior, and Evolution, 59,* 21–32.

Marks, D. F., Sykes, C. M., & McKinley, J. M. (2003). Health psychology: Overview and professional issues. In A. M. Nezu, C. M. Nezu, & P. A. Geller (Eds.), *Handbook of psychology:*

Health psychology (Vol. 9, pp. 5–26). Hoboken, NJ: John Wiley & Sons.

Marks, I. M. (1969). *Fears and phobias.* New York: Academic Press.

Markus, H. (1977). Self-schemata and processing information about the self. *Journal of Personality and Social Psychology, 35,* 63–78.

Markus, H., & Cross, S. (1990). The interpersonal self. In L. Pervin (Ed.), *Handbook of personality: Theory and research* (pp. 576–608). New York: Guilford Press.

Markus, H., & Kitayama, S. (1991). Culture and the self: Implications for cognition, emotion, and motivation. *Psychological Review, 98,* 224–253.

Markus, H. R., & Kitayama, S. (2001). The cultural construction of self and emotion: Implications for social behavior. In W. G. Parrott (Ed.), *Emotions in social psychology: Essential readings* (pp. 119-137). New York: Psychology Press.

Markus, H., & Nurius, P. (1986). Possible selves. *American Psychologist, 41,* 954–969.

Markus, H., & Wurf, E. (1987). The dynamic self-concept: A social psychological perspective. *Annual Review of Psychology, 38,* 299–337.

Marlatt, G. A., & Baer, J. S. (1988). Addictive behaviors: Etiology and treatment. *Annual Review of Psychology, 39,* 223–252.

Marsh, R. L., Hiscks, J. L., & Bink, M. L. (1998). Activation of completed, uncompleted, and partially completed intentions. *Journal of Experimental Psychology: Learning, Memory and Cognition, 24,* 350–361.

Marshall, D. A., & Moulton, D. G. (1981). Olfactory sensitivity to a-ionone in humans and dogs. *Chemical Senses, 6,* 53–61.

Martikainen, P., & Valkonen, T. (1996). Mortality after the death of a spouse: Rates and causes of death in a large Finnish cohort. *American Journal of Public Health, 86,* 1087–1093.

Martin, C. L., & Ruble, D. N. (1997). A developmental perspective of self-construals and sex differences: Comment on Cross and Madson (1997). *Psychological Bulletin, 122,* 45–50.

Martin, C. L., Ruble, D. N., & Szkrybalo, J. (2002). Cognitive theories of early gender development. *Psychological Bulletin, 128,* 903-933.

Martin, D. J., Garske, J. P., & Davis, M. K. (2000). Relation of the therapeutic alliance with outcome and other variables: A meta-analytic review. *Journal of Consulting and Clinical Psychology, 68,* 438–450.

Martin, J., & Sugarman, J. (1999). *The psychology of human possibility and constraint.* Albany: State University of New York Press.

Martin, J. A., Maccoby, E. E., Baran, K. W., & Jacklin, C. N. (1981). Sequential analysis of mother-child interaction at 18 months: A comparison of microanalytic methods. *Developmental Psychology, 17,* 146-157.

Martin, K. A., & Leary, M. R. (2001). Self-presentational determinants of health risk behavior among college freshmen. *Psychology and Health, 16,* 17–27.

Martin, K. A., Leary, M. R., & O'Brien, J. (2001). Role of self-presentation in the health practices of a sample of Irish adolescents. *Journal of Adolescent Health, 28,* 259–262.

Martin, M. A. (1985). Students' applications of self-questioning study techniques: An investigation of their efficacy. *Reading Psychology, 6,* 69–83.

Martinez, J. L., & Derrick, B. E. (1996). Long-term potentiation and learning. *Annual Review, 47,* 173–203.

Maslach, C. (1979). Negative emotional biasing of unexplained arousal. *Journal of Personality and Social Psychology, 37,* 953–969.

Masling, J. M., & Bornstein, R. F. (Eds.). (1994). *Empirical perspectives on object relations theory.* Washington, DC: American Psychological Association.

Maslow, A. H. (1962). *Toward a psychology of being.* Princeton, NJ: Van Nostrand.

Maslow, A. H. (1970). *Motivaiton and personality* (2nd ed.). New York: Harper & Row.

Mason, E. (1970). Obesity in pet dogs. *Veterinary Record, 86,* 612–616.

Masserman, J. H., Wechkin, S. & Terris, W. (1964). "Altruistic" behavior in rhesus monkeys. *American Journal of Psychiatry, 121,* 584–585.

Masters, W., & Johnson, V. (1966). *Human sexual response.* Boston, MA: Little, Brown.

Masterson, J. F., & Rinsley, D. B. (1975). The borderline syndrome: The role of the mother in the genesis and psychic structure of the borderline personality. *International Journal of Psychoanalysis, 56,* 163–177.

Matarazzo, J. D. (1980). Behavioral health and behavioral medicine: Frontiers for a new health psychology. *American Psychologist, 35,* 807–817.

Mathews, A., & Macleod, C. (1994). Cognitive approaches to emotion. *Annual Review of Psychology, 45,* 25–50.

Matsumoto, D., Kasri, F., & Kooken, K. (1999). American-Japanese cultural differences in judgements of expression intensity and subjective experience. *Cognition and Emotion, 13,* 201–218.

Matsuoka, S. (1990). Theta rhythms: State of consciousness. *Brain Topography, 3,* 203–208.

Matthews, K. A. (1992). Myths and realities of the menopause. *Psychosomatic Medicine, 54,* 1–9.

Mauro, R., Sato, K., & Tucker, J. (1992). The role of appraisal in human emotions: A cross-cultural study. *Journal of Personality and Social Psychology, 62,* 301–317.

Mavissakalian, M., & Perel, J. (1992). Protective effects of imipramine maintenance treatment in panic disorder with agoraphobia. *American Journal of Psychiatry, 149,* 1053–1057.

May, R. (1953). *Man's search for himself.* New York: Signet Books.

May, R., Angel, E., & Ellenberger, H. F. (1958). *Existence: A new dimension in psychiatry and psychology.* New York: Basic Books.

Mayberry, R., & Eichen, E. B. (1991). The long-lasting advantage of learning sign language in childhood: Another look at the critical period for language acquisition. *Journal of Memory and Language, 30,* 486–512.

Mayer, J., Gasche, Y., Braverman, D., & Evans, T. (1992). Mood-congruent judgment is a general effect. *Journal of Personality and Social Psychology, 63,* 119–132.

Mayer, J. D., & Salovey, P. (1997). What is emotional intelligence? In P. Salovey & D. Sluyter (Eds.), *Emotional development and emotional intelligence: Implications for educators.* New York: Basic Books.

Mayer, J. D., Salovey, P., & Caruso, D. (2000). Models of emotional intelligence. In R. J. Sternberg (Ed.), *Handbook of intelligence* (pp. 396–420). New York: Cambridge University Press.

McAdams, D. (1992a). The five-factor model in personality: A critical appraisal. *Journal of Personality, 60,* 329–361.

McAdams, D., & Vaillant, G. (1982). Intimacy motivation and psychosocial adjustment: A longitudinal study. *Journal of Personality Assessment, 46,* 586–593.

McAdams, D., & West, S. G. (1997). Introduction: Personality psychology and the case study. *Journal of Personality, 65,* 757–783.

McAdams, D. P. (1999). Motives. In V. J. Derlega, B. A. Winstead, et al. (Eds.), *Personality: Contemporary theory and research. Nelson-Hall series in psychology* (2nd ed., pp. 162–194). Chicago: Nelson-Hall.

McAdams, D. P., & de St. Aubin, E. (1998). *Generativity and adult development: How and why we care for the next generation.* Washington, DC: American Psychological Association.

McAdams, D. P., de St. Aubin, E., & Logan, R. L. (1993). Generativity among young, midlife, and older adults. *Psychology and Aging, 8,* 221-230.

McAdams, D. P., Hart, H. M., & Maruna, S. (1998). The anatomy of generativity. In D. P. McAdams & E. de St. Aubin (Eds.), *Generativity and adult development: How and why we care for the next generation.* (pp. 7–43). Washington, DC: American Psychological Association.

McAdams, D. P., Hoffman, B. J., Mansfield, E. D., & Day, R. (1996). Themes of agency and communion in significant autobiographical scenes. *Journal of Personality, 64,* 339–377.

McAndrew, F. T. (2002). New evolutionary perspectives on altruism: Multilevel- selection and costly-signaling theories. *Current Directions in Psychological Science, 11,* 79–82.

McCaul, K. D., & Malott, J. M. (1984). Distraction and coping with pain. *Psychological Bulletin, 95,* 516–533.

McClelland, D. C. (1978). Managing motivation to expand human freedom. *American Psychologist, 33,* 201–210.

McClelland, D. C. (1985). *Human motivation.* Glenview, IL: Scott, Foresman.

McClelland, D. C., Atkinson, J. W., Clark, R. A., & Lowell, E. L. (1953). *The achievement motive.* New York: Appleton-Century-Crofts.

McClelland, D. C., Koestner, R., & Weinberger, J. (1989). How do self-attributed and implicit motives differ? *Psychological Review, 96,* 690–792.

McClelland, D. C., & Pilon, D. A. (1983). Sources of adult motives in patterns of parent behavior in early childhood. *Journal of Personality and Social Psychology, 44,* 564–554.

McClelland, D. C., & Winter, D. G. (1969). *Motivating economic achievement.* New York: Free Press.

McClelland, J. L. (1995). Constructive memory and memory distortions: A parallel-distributed processing approach. In D. L. Schacter (Ed.), *Memory distortions: How minds, brains, and societies reconstruct the past* (pp. 69–90). Cambridge, MA: Harvard University Press.

McClintock, M. K. (1971). Menstrual synchrony and suppression. *Nature, 229,* 244–245.

McCloskey, M., & Macaruso, P. (1995). Representing and using numerical information. *American Psychologist, 50,* 351–363.

McCloskey, M., Wible, C. G., & Cohen, N. J. (1988). Is there a special flashbulb-memory mechanism? *Journal of Experimental Psychology: General, 117,* 171–181.

McClure, J. (1998). Discounting causes of behavior: Are two reasons better than one? *Journal of Personality and Social Psychology, 74,* 7-20.

McComb, K., Packer, C., & Pusey, A. (1994). Roaring and numerical assessment in contests between groups of female lions, Panthera leo. *Animal Behaviour, 47,* 379–387.

McConaghy, N. (1979). Maternal deprivation: Can its ghost be laid? *Australian and New Zealand Journal of Psychiatry, 13,* 209–217.

McConahay, J., & Hough, J. (1976). Symbolic racism. *Journal of Social Issues, 32,* 23–45.

McConkey, K. M. (1995). *Hypnosis, memory, and behavior in criminal investigation.* New York: Guilford Press.

McCrae, R. R. (1996). Social consequences of experiential openness. *Psychological Bulletin, 120,* 323–337.

McCrae, R. R., & Costa, P. T. (1990). *Personality in adulthood.* New York: Guilford Press.

McCrae, R. R., & Costa, P. (1997). Personality trait structure as a human universal. *American Psychologist, 52,* 509–516.

McCrae, R. R., Costa, P., del Pilar, G., Rolland, J.-P., & Parker, W. D. (1998a). Cross-cultural assessment of the five-factor model: The revised NEO Personality Inventory. *Journal of Cross-Cultural Psychology, 29,* 171–188.

McDaniel, M. A. (1995). Prospective memory: Progress and processes. In D. L. Medin (Ed.), *The psychology of learning and motivation: Advances in research and theory* (Vol. 33, pp. 191-227). San Diego, CA: Academic Press.

McDaniel, M. A., Robinson-Riegler, B., & Einstein, G. O. (1998). Prospective remembering: Perceptually driven or conceptually driven processes? *Memory and Cognition, 26,* 121–134.

McDonald, J. L. (1997). Language acquisition: The acquisition of linguistic structure in normal and special populations. *Annual Review of Psychology, 48,* 215–241.

McEvoy, G. M., & Cascio, W. F. (1989). Cumulative evidence of the relationship between employee age and job performance. *Journal of Applied Psychology, 74,* 11–17.

McEwan, B. S. (1999). Stress and hippocampal plasticity. *Annual Review of Neuroscience, 22,* 105–122.

McEwen, B. S. (2003). Stress and neuroendocrine function: Individual differences and mechanisms leading to disease. In O. M. Wolkowitz & A. J. Rothschild (Eds.), *Psychoneuroendocrinology: The scientific basis of clinical practice* (pp. 513-546). Washington, DC: American Psychiatric Press.

McEwen, B. S., Alves, S.E., Bulloch, K., & Weiland, N. G. (1998). Clinically relevant basic science studies of gender differences and sex hormone effects. *Psychopharmacology Bulletin, 34,* 251-259.

McGaugh, J. L. (2000). Memory: A century of consolidation. *Science, 287,* 248–251.

McGlynn, F. D., Mealies, W. L., Jr., & Landau, D. L. (1981). The current status of systematic desensitization. *Clinical Psychology Review, 1,* 149–179.

McGue, M., Bacon, S., & Lykken, D. (1993). Personality stability and change in early adulthood: A behavior genetic analysis. *Developmental Psychology, 29,* 96–109.

McGue, M., & Bouchard, T. J. (1998). Genetic and environmental influences on human behavioral differences. *Annual Review of Neuroscience, 21,* 1–24.

McGue, M., Pickens, R. W., & Svikis, D. (1992). Sex and age effects on the inheritance of alcohol problems: A twin study. *Journal of Abnormal Psychology, 101,* 3–17.

McGuire, F. L. (1982). Treatment of the drinking driver. *Health Psychology, 1,* 137–152.

McGuire, S., Manke, B., Saudino, K. J., Reiss, D., Hetherington, E. M., & Plomin, R. (1999). Perceived competence and self-worth during adolescence: A longitudinal behavioral genetic study. *Child Development, 70,* 1283–1296.

McGuire, W. (1986). The myth of massive media impact: Savagings and salvagings. In G. Comstock (Ed.), *Public communication and behavior* (Vol. 1). New York: Academic Press.

McGuire, W. J. (1961). The effectiveness of supportive and refutational defenses in immunizing and restoring beliefs against persuasion. *Sociometry, 24,* 184–197.

McGuire, W. J. (1985). Attitudes and attitude change. In G. Lindzey & E. Aronson (Eds.), *Handbook of Social Psychology.* Reading, MA: Addison-Wesley.

McGuire, W. J., & Papageorgis, D. (1962). Effectiveness of forewarning in developing resistance to persuasion. *Public Opinion Quarterly, 26,* 24–34.

McHale, S. M., Crouter, A. C., & Tucker, C. J. (1999). Family context and gender role socialization in middle childhood: Comparing girls to boys and sisters to brothers. *Child Development, 70,* 990–1004.

McKelvie, S. J. (1997). The availability heuristic: Effects of fame and gender on the estimated frequency of male and female names. *Journal of Social Psychology, 137,* 63-78.

McKoon, G., & Ratcliff, R. (1998). Memory-based language processing: Psycholinguistic research in the 1990s. *Annual Review of Psychology, 49,* 25–42.

McLoyd, V. (1989). Socialization and development in a changing economy: The effects of paternal job and income loss on children. *American Psychologist, 44,* 293–302.

McNally, R. (1987). Preparedness and phobias: A review. *Psychologial Bulletin, 101,* 283–303.

McNeil, T. F., Cantor-Graae, E., & Weinberger, D. R. (2000). Relationship of obstetric complications and differences in size of brain structures in monozygotic twin pairs discordant for schizophrenia. *American Journal of Psychiatry, 157,* 203–212.

Mead, M. (1928). *Coming of age in Samoa: A psychological study of primitive youth for Western civilization.* New York: Morrow & Co.

Meaney, M., & McEwen, B. (1986). Testosterone implants into the amygdala during the neonatal period masculinize the social play of juvenile female rats. *Brain Research, 398,* 324–328.

Medin, D. L., & Heit, E. (1999). Categorization. In B. M. Bly & D. E. Rumelhart (Eds.), *Cognitive science: Handbook of perception and cognition* (2nd ed., pp. 99–143). San Diego, CA: Academic Press.

Medin, D. L., Lynch, E. B., Coley, J. D., & Atran, S. (1997). Categorization and reasoning among tree experts: Do all roads lead to Rome? *Cognitive Psychology, 32,* 49–96.

Medin, D. L., Lynch, E. B., & Solormon, K. O. (2000). Are there kinds of concepts? *Annual Review of Psychology, 51,* 121–147.

Medin, D. L., Ross, N., Atran, S., Burnett, R. C., & Blok, S. V. (2002). Categorization and reasoning in relation to culture and expertise. In B. H. Ross (Ed.), *The psychology of learning and motivation: Advances in research and theory* (Vol. 41, pp. 1–41). San Diego, CA: Academic Press.

Medin, D. L., & Schaffer, M. M. (1978). Context theory of classification learning. *Psychological Review, 85,* 207-238.

Medin, D. L., & Smith, E. E. (1981). Strategies and classification learning. *Journal of Experimental Psychology: Human Learning and Memory, 7,* 241–253.

Meichenbaum, D. (1977). *Cognitive-behavior modification: An integrative approach.* New York: Plenum Press.

Meichenbaum, D. (1990). Cognitive perspective on teaching self-regulation. *American Journal of Mental Retardation, 94,* 367–369.

Mellers, B., Schwartz, A., & Cooke, A. D. J. (1998). Judgment and decision making. *Annual Review of Psychology, 49,* 447–477.

Mellers, B., Schwartz, A., Ho, K., & Ritov, I. (1997). Decision affect theory: Emotional reactions to the outcomes of risky options. *Psychological Science, 8,* 423–429.

Mellers, B., Schwartz, A., & Ritov, I. (1999). Emotion-based choice. *Journal of Experimental Psychology: General, 128,* 332–345.

Meltzoff, A. (1990). Towards a developmental cognitive science: The implications of cross-modal matching and imitation for the development of representation and memory in infancy. *Annals of the New York Academy of Sciences, 608,* 1–7.

Meltzoff, A. N. (1995). What infant memory tells us about infantile amnesia: Long-term recall and deferred imitation. Special Issue: Early memory. *Journal of Experimental Child Psychology, 59,* 497–515.

Meltzoff, A. N., & Borton, R. W. (1979). Intermodal matching by human neonates. *Nature, 282,* 403–404.

Meltzoff, A. N., & Moore, M. K. (1977). Imitation of facial and manual gestures by human neonates. *Science, 198,* 75–78.

Melzack, R. (1970). Phantom limbs. *Psychology Today,* 63–68.

Melzack, R. (1993). Pain: Past, present and future. *Canadian Journal of Experimental Psychology, 47,* 615–629.

Melzack, R., & Wall, P. D. (1983). *The challenge of pain.* New York: Basic Books.

Menard, M. T., Kosslyn, S., Thompson, W. L., Alpert, N. M., et al. (1996). Encoding words and pictures: A positron emission tomography study. *Neuropsychologia, 34,* 185–194.

Mendlowicz, M. V., & Stein, M. B. (2000). Quality of life in individuals with anxiety disorders. *American Journal of Psychiatry, 157,* 669–682.

Mendola, J. D., Dale, A. M., Fischl, B., Liu, A. K., & Tootell, R. B. H. (1999). The representation of illusory and real contours in human cortical visual areas revealed by functional magnetic resonance imaging. *Journal of Neuroscience, 19,* 8560–8572.

Mendoza, S. P., & Mason, W. A. (1997). Attachment relationships in New World primates. In C. S. Carter, I. I. Lederhendler, & B. Kirkpatrick (Eds.), *The integrative neurobiology of affiliation* (Vol. 807, pp. 203–209). New York: New York Academy of Sciences.

Menon, T., Morris, M. W., Chiu, C., & Hong, Y. (1999). Culture and the construal of agency: Attribution to individual versus group dispositions. *Journal of Personaity and Social Psychology, 76,* 701–717.

Merikangas, K. R., Dierker, L. C., & Szamari, P. (1998). Psychopathology among offspring of parents with substance abuse and/or anxiety disorders: A high risk study. *Journal of Child Psychology & Psychiatry & Allied Disciplines, 39,* 711–720.

Merriam, A. P. (1971). Aspects of sexual behavior among the Bala (Basongye). In D. S. Marshall & R. C. Suggs (Eds.), *Human sexual behavior: Variations in the ethnographic spectrum.* New York: Basic Books.

Merriman, W. E., Marazita, J. M., Jarvis, L. H., Evey-Burkey, J. A., & Biggins, M. (1996). What can be learned from something's not being named. *Child Development, 66,* 1890-1908.

Merton, R. K. (1957). *Social theory and social structure.* Glencoe, IL: Free Press.

Mervis, C. B., & Rosch, E. (1981). Categorization of natural objects. *Annual Review of Psychology, 32,* 89–115.

Mesquita, B., Frijda, N. H., & Scherer, K. R. (1997). Culture and emotion. In J. W. Berry & P.

R. Dasen (Eds.), *Handbook of cross-cultural psychology, Vol. 2: Basic processes and human development* (2nd ed.; pp. 255-297.

Messer, S., Sass, L. H., & Woolfolk, R. L. (Eds.). (1988). *Hermeneutics and psychologial theory.* New Brunswick, NJ: Rutgers University Press.

Messer, S., & Winokur, M. (1980). Some limits to the integration of psychodynamic and behavior therapy. *American Psychologist, 35,* 818–827.

Metcalfe, J. (2000). Metamemory: Theory and data. In E. Tulving & F. I. Craik (Eds.). *The Oxford handbook of memory.* (pp. 197–211). New York: Oxford University Press.

Metcalfe, J., & Shimamura, A. P. (1994). (Eds.) *Megacognition: Knowing about knowing.* Cambridge, MA: MIT Press.

Mezzacappa, E. S., Katkin, E. S., & Palmer, S. N. (1999). Epinephrine, arousal, and emotion: A new look at two-factor theory. *Cognition and Emotion, 13,* 181–199.

Mezzich, J. E., Kirmayer, L. J., Kleinman, A., Fabrega, H., Parron, D. L., Good, B. J., Lin, K., & Manson, S. M. (1999). The place of culture in DSM-IV. *Journal of Nervous & Mental Disease, 187,* 457–464.

Mezzich, J. E., Kleinman, A., Fabrega, H., & Parron, D. L. (1996). Culture and psychiatric diagnosis: A DSM-IV perspective. Washington, DC: American Psychiatric Press.

Michelson, D., Bancroft, J., Targum, S., Kim, Y., & Tepner, R. (2000). Female sexual dysfunction associated with antidepressant administration: A randomized, placebo-controlled study of pharmacologic intervention. *American Journal of Psychiatry, 157,* 239–243.

Mickelson, K. D., Kessler, R. C., & Shaver, P. R. (1997). Adult attachment in a nationally representative sample. *Journal of Personality & Social Psychology, 73,* 1092–1106.

Mikulincer, M., & Florian, V. (1997). Are emotional and instrumental supportive interactions beneficial in times of stress? The impact of attachment style. *Anxiety, Stress & Coping: an International Journal, 10,* 109–127.

Mikulincer, M., Florian, V., & Hirschberger, G. (2003). The existential function of close relationships: Introducing death into the science of love. *Personality and Social Psychology Review, 7,* 20–40.

Mikulincer, M., Florian, V., & Weller, A. (1993). Attachment styles, coping strategies, and posttraumatic psychological distress: The impact of the Gulf War in Israel. *Journal of Personality and Social Psychology, 64,* 817–826.

Milberger, S., Biederman, J., Faraone, S. V., Chen, L., & Jones, J. (1996). Is maternal smoking during pregnancy a risk factor for attention deficit hyperactivity disorder in children? *American Journal of Psychiatry, 153,* 1138–1142.

Milewski-Hertlein, K. A. (2001). The use of a socially constructed genogram in clinical practice. *American Journal of Family Therapy, 29,* 23–38.

Milgram, S. (1963). Behavioral study of obedience. *Journal of Abnormal and Social Psychology, 67,* 371–378.

Milgram, S. (1965). Some conditions of obedience and disobedience to authority. *Human Relations, 18,* 57–76.

Milgram, S. (1969). *Obedience to authority.* New York: Harper & Row.

Milgram, S. (1974). *Obedience to authority: An experimental view.* New York: Harper & Row.

Millar, M. G., & Millar, K. U. (1996). The effects of direct and indirect experience on affective and cognitive responses and the attitude-behavior relation. *Journal of Experimental Social Psychology, 32,* 561–579.

Miller, C. T., & Downey, K. T. (1999). A meta-analysis of heavyweight and self-esteem. *Personality and Social Psychology Review, 3,* 68–84.

Miller, C. T., Rothblum, E. D., Barbour, L., & Brand, P. A. (1990). Social interactions of obese and nonobese women. *Journal of Personality, 58,* 365–380.

Miller, D. T., & Ratner, R. K. (1998). The disparity between the actual and assumed power of self-interest. *Journal of Personality and Social Psychology, 74,* 53-62.

Miller, G. A. (1956). The magical number seven, plus or minus two: Some limits in our capacity for processing information. *Psychological Review, 63,* 81–97.

Miller, G. A., Galanter, E., & Pribram, K. H. (1960). *Plans and the structure of behavior.* New York: Holt, Rinehart & Winston.

Miller, I. J., Jr. (1995). Anatomy of the peripheral taste system. In R. L. Doty (Ed.), *Handbook of olfaction and gustation.* New York: Marcel Dekker.

Miller, J. G. (1994). Cultural diversity in the morality of caring: Individually oriented versus duty-based interpersonal moral codes. *Cross-Cultural Research, 28,* 3–39.

Miller, J. G. (1997). A cultural-psychology perspective on intelligence. In R. J. Sternberg & E. L. Grigorenko (Eds.), *Intelligence, heredity, and environment* (pp. 269–302). New York: Cambridge University Press.

Miller, J. L., & Eimas, P. (1995). Speech perception: From signal to word. *Annual Review of Psychology, 46,* 467–492.

Miller, L. T., & Vernon, P. A. (1997). Developmental changes in speed of information processing in young children. *Developmental Psychology, 33,* 549–554.

Miller, N., & Campbell, D. T. (1959). Recency and primacy in persuasion as a function of the timing of speeches and measurement. *Journal of Abnormal and Social Psychology, 59,* 1–9.

Miller, N. E. (1985). The value of behavioral research on animals. *American Psychologist, 40,* 423-440.

Miller, P. A., Eisenberg, N., Fabes, R., & Shell, R. (1996). Relations of moral reasoning and vicarious emotion to young children's prosocial behavior toward peers and adults. *Developmental Psychology, 32,* 210–219.

Miller, T. W., & Kraus, R. F. (1990). An overview of chronic pain. *Hospital and Community Psychiatry, 41,* 433–440.

Miller, W. A., Ratliff, F., & Hartline, H. K. (1961). How cells receive stimuli. *Scientific American, 222–238.*

Miller, W. R., & Hester, R. K. (1980). Treating the problem drinker: Modern approaches. In W. R. Miller (Ed.), *The addictive behaviors: Treatment of alcoholism, drug abuse, smoking, and obesity.* New York: Pergamon.

Mills, J., & Clark, M. S. (1994). Communal and exchange relationships: Controversies and research. In R. Erber, R. Gilmour, et al. (Eds.), *Theoretical frameworks for personal relationships* (pp. 29–42). Hillsdale, NJ: Lawrence Erlbaum.

Mills, M. (1995). *Characteristics of personals ads differ as a function of publication readership SES.* Paper presented at the annual convention of the Human Behavior and Evolution Society, June, Santa Barbara, CA.

Milner, B., Corkin, S., & Teuber, H. L. (1968). Further analysis of the hippocampal amnesic syndrome: Fourteen year follow-up study of H.M. *Neuropsychologia, 6,* 215–234.

Milner, P. (1991). Brain-stimulation reward: A review. *Canadian Journal of Psychology, 45,* 1–36.

Mineka, S., & Sutton, S. K. (1992). Cognitive biases and the emotional disorders. *Psychological Science, 3,* 65–69.

Mineka, S., Watson, D., & Clark, L. A. (1998). Comorbidity of anxiety and unipolar mood disorders. *Annual Review of Psychology, 49,* 377–412.

Minsky, M. (1975). A framework for representing knowledge. In P. H. Winston (Ed.), *The psychology of computer vision.* New York: McGraw-Hill.

Minuchin, S. (1974). *Families and family therapy.* Cambridge, MA: Harvard University Press.

Miranda, A. O., & Fraser, L. D. (2002). Culture-bound syndromes: Initial perspectives from individual psychology. *Journal of Individual Psychology, 58,* 422–433.

Mirsky, A. F., & Duncan, C. C. (1986). Etiology and expression of schizophrenia: Neurobiological and psychosocial factors. *Annual Review of Psychology, 37,* 291–319.

Mischel, W. (1968). *Personality and assessment.* New York: John Wiley.

Mischel, W. (1973). Toward a cognitive social learning reconceptualization of personality. *Psychological Review, 39,* 351–364.

Mischel, W. (1979). On the interface of cognitive and personality: Beyond the person-situation debate. *American Psychologist, 34,* 740–754.

Mischel, W. (1990). Personality dispositions revisited and revised: A view after three decades. In L. A. Pervin (Ed.), *Handbook of personality: Theory and research* (pp. 111-134). New York: Guilford.

Mischel, W., & Mischel, H. N. (1976). A cognitive social-learning approach to morality and self-regulation. In T. Lickona (Ed.), *Moral development and behavior: Theory, research, and social issues.* New York: Holt, Rinehart & Winston.

Mischel, W., & Shoda, Y. (1995). A cognitive-affective system theory of personality: Reconceptualizing situations, dispositions, dynamics, and invariance in personality structure. *Psychological Review, 102,* 246–268.

Mischel, W., & Shoda, Y. (1998). Reconciling processing dynamics and personality dispositions. *Annual Review of Psychology, 229–258.*

Mishra, R. C. (1997). Cognition and cognitive development. In J. W. Berry, P. R. Dasen, & T. S. Swanaswathi (Eds.), *Handbook of cross-cultural psychology: Vol. 2. Basic processes and human development* (2nd ed., pp. 143–175). Boston, MA: Allyn & Bacon.

Mistry, J., & Rogoff, B. (1985). A cultural perspective on the development of talent. In F. D. Horowitz & M. O'Brien (Eds.), *The gifted and talented: Developmental perspectives* (pp. 125–144). Washington, DC: American Psychological Association.

Misumi, J., & Peterson, M. F. (1985). The performance- maintenance (PM) theory of leadership: Review of a Japanese research program. *Administrative Science Quarterly, 30,* 198–223.

Mitchell, S. A. (1988). *Relational concepts in psychoanalysis: An integration.* Cambridge, MA: Harvard University Press.

Mitchell, S. A., & Aron, L. (1999). (Eds.) *Relational psychoanalysis: The emergence of a tradition.* Hillsdale, NJ: Analytic Press.

Modestin, J. (1992). Multiple personality disorder in Switzerland. *American Journal of Psychiatry, 149,* 88-92.

Moeller, G., & Applezweig, M. M. (1957). A motivational factor in conformity. *Journal of Abnormal Social Psychology, 55,* 114–120.

Moffit, T. E., Caspi, A., Dickson, N., Silva, P., & Stanton, W. (1996). Childhood-onset versus adolescent-onset antisocial conduct problems in males: Natural history from ages 3 to 18 years. *Development & Psychopathology, 8,* 399–424.

Mogil, J. S., Yu, L., & Basbaum, A. I. (2000). Pain genes? Natural variation and transgenic mutants. *Annual Review of Neuroscience, 23,* 777–811.

Mokdad, A. H., Serdula, M. K., Dietz, W. H., Bowman, B. A., Marks, J. S., & Koplan, J. P. (1999). The spread of the obesity epidemic in the United States. *Journal of the American Medical Association, 282,* 1519–1522.

Moloney, D. P., Bouchard, T., & Segal, N. (1991). A genetic and environmental analysis of the vocational interests of monozygotic and dizygotic twins reared apart. *Journal of Vocational Behavior, 39,* 76–109.

Money, J. (1987). Sin, sickness, or status? Homosexual gender identity and psychoneuroendocrinology. *American Psychologist, 42,* 384–399.

Money, J., & Ehrhardt, A. A. (1972). *Man and woman. Boy and girl.* Baltimore, MD: Johns Hopkins University Press.

Money, J., Schwartz, M., & Lewis, V. G. (1984). Adult heterosexual status and fetal hormonal masculinization and demasculinization. *Psychoneuroendocrinology, 9,* 405–414.

Monk, T. H. (1997). Shift work. In M. R. Pressman & W. C. Orr (Eds.), *Understanding sleep: The evaluation and treatment of sleep disorders. Application and practice in health psychology* (pp. 249–266). Washington, DC: American Psychological Association.

Monroe, S. M., & Simons, A. D. (1991). Diathesis– stress theories in the context of life stress research: Implications for the depressive disorders. *Psychological Bulletin, 110,* 406–425.

Montano, D. E., Thompson, B., Taylor, V. M., & Mahloch, J. (1997). Understanding mammography intention and utilization among women in an inner city public hospital clinic. *Preventive Medicine, 26,* 817–824.

Montemayor, R., & Eisen, M. (1977). A developmental sequence of self-conceptions from childhood to adolescence. *Developmental Psychology, 13,* 314–319.

Montgomery, S. (1994a). Long-term treatment of depression. *British Journal of Psychiatry, 165,* 31–36.

Montgomery, S. A. (1994b). Antidepressants in long-term treatment. *Annual Review of Medicine, 45,* 447–457.

Moore, C.C., & Mathews, H. F. (2001). (Eds.) *The psychology of cultural experience.* New York: Cambridge University Press.

Moos, R. H., & Billings, A. G. (1982). Conceptualizing and measuring coping resources and processes. In L. Goldberger & S. Breznitz (Eds.), *Handbook of stress.* New York: Macmillan.

Moos, R. H., & Schaefer, J. A. (1986). Life transitions and crises. In R. H. Moos & J. A. Schaefer (Eds.), *Coping with life crises: An integrated approach.* New York: Plenum Press.

Moreland, R. L. (1985). Social categorization and the assimilation of new group members. *Journal of Personality and Social Psychology, 48,* 1173–1190.

Morelli, G., Rogoff, B., Oppenheim, D., & Goldsmith, D. (1992). Cultural variation in infants' sleeping arrangements: Questions of independence. *Developmental Psychology, 28,* 604–613.

Moretti, M. M., & Higgins, E. T. (1999). Own versus other standpoints in self-regulation. Developmental antecedents and functional consequences. *Review of General Psychology, 3,* 188–223.

Morgan, C. D., & Murray, H. H. (1935). A method for investigating fantasies: The thematic apperception test. *Archives of Neurology and Psychiatry, 34,* 289-306.

Morgan, J. (1986). *From simple input to complex grammar.* Cambridge, MA: MIT Press.

Mori, D., Chaiken, S., & Pliner, P. (1987). "Eating lightly" and the self-presentation of femininity. *Journal of Personality and Social Psychology, 53,* 693–702.

Morling, B., & Epstein, S. (1997). Compromises produced by the dialectic between self-verification and self-enhancement. *Journal of Personality & Social Psychology, 73,* 1268–1283.

Morris, J. S., Frith, C. D., Perrett, D. I., Rowland, D., Young, A. W., Calder, A. J., & Dolan, R. J. (1996). A differential neural response in the human amygdala to fearful and happy facial expressions. *Nature, 383,* 812–815.

Morris, J. S., Oehman, A., & Dolan, R. J. (1998). Conscious and unconscious emotional learning in the human amygdala. *Nature, 393,* 467–470.

Morris, R. G., & Baddeley, A. D. (1988). Primary and working memory functioning in Alzheimer-type dementia. *Journal of Clinical and Experimental Neuropsychology, 10,* 279–296.

Morse, J. M., & Park, C. (1988). Differences in cultural expectations of the perceived painfulness of childbirth. In K. Michaelson (Ed.), *Childbirth in America: Anthropological perspectives.* South Hadley, MA: Bergin & Garvey.

Movie stars who smoke linked to teens lighting up. (2003, June 9). *The Greenville News.*

Mowrer, O. H. (1960). *Learning theory and behavior.* New York: John Wiley.

Moyer, K. E. (1983). The physiology of motivation: Aggression as a model. In C. James Scheirer & Anne M. Rogers (Eds.), *G. Stanley Hall Lecture Series* (Vol. 3). Washington, DC: American Psychological Association.

Mroczek, D. K., & Kolarz, C. M. (1998). The effect of age on positive and negative affect: A developmental perspective on happiness. *Journal of Personality and Social Psychology, 75,* 1333–1349.

Mueller, T. I., Leon, A. C., Keller, M. B., Solomon, D. A., Endicott, J., Coryell, W., Warshaw, M., & Maser, J. D. (1999). Recurrence after recovery from major depressive disorder during 15 years of observational follow-up. *American Journal of Psychiatry, 156,* 1000–1006.

Mulligan, R. (1996). Dental pain. In J. Barber (Ed.), *Hypnosis and suggestion in the treatment of pain: A clinical guide* (pp. 185–208). New York: W.W. Norton.

Mumaw, R., & Pellegrino, J. (1984). Individual differences in complex spatial processing. *Journal of Educational Psychology, 76,* 920–939.

Mumford, D. B. (1993). Eating disorders in different cultures. *International Review of Psychiatry, 5,* 109–113.

Munk, M., Roelfsema, P., Konig, P., Engel, A. K., & Singer, W. (1996). Role of reticular activation in the modulation of intracortical synchronization. *Science, 272,* 271–274.

Murphy, G. L., & Medin, D. L. (1985). The role of theories in conceptual coherence. *Psychological Review, 92,* 289–316.

Murphy, J. M. (1976). Psychiatric labeling in cross-cultural perspective. *Science, 191,* 1019–1028.

Murray, S. L., & Holmes, J. G. (1997). A leap of faith? Positive illusions in romantic relationships. *Personality and Social Psychology Bulletin, 23,* 586–604.

Murray, S. L., & Holmes, J. G. (1999). The (mental) ties that bind: Cognitive structures that predict relationship resilience. *Journal of Personality and Social Psychology, 77,* 1228–1244.

Murray, S. L., Holmes, J. G., & Griffin, D. W. (2000). Self-esteem and the quest for felt security: How perceived regard regulates attachment processes. *Journal of Personality and Social Psychology, 78,* 478–498.

Murray, S. L., Holmes, J. G., MacDonald, G., & Ellsworth, P. C. (1998). Through the looking glass darkly? When self-doubts turn into relationship insecurities. *Journal of Personality and Social Psychology, 75,* 1459–1480.

Murrey, G. J., Cross, H. J., & Whipple, J. (1992). Hypnotically created pseudomemories: Further investigation into the "memory distortion or response bias" question. *Journal of Abnormal Psychology, 101*, 75–77.

Myers, D. (2001). *Psychology*. New York: Worth.

Myers, D. G. (2000). The funds, friends, and faith of happy people. *American Psychologist, 55*, 56–67.

Myers, D. G., & Diener, E. (1995). Who is happy? *Psychological Science, 6*, 10–19.

Myers, L. B., & Vetere, A. (2002). Adult romantic attachment styles and health-related measures. *Psychology, Health, and Medicine, 7*, 175–180.

NAAFA. NAAFA kid's project. Retrieved 6-13-2003: http://www.naafa.org/kids/html

Nadel, L., Samsonovich, A., Ryan, L., & Moscovitch, M. (2000). Multiple trace theory of human memory: Computational, neuroimaging, and neuropsychological results. *Hippocampus, 10*, 352-368.

Nader, K., & van der Kooy, D. (1997). Deprivation state switches the neurobiological substrates mediating opiate reward in the ventral tegmental area. *Journal of Neuroscience, 17*, 383–390.

Nakao, M., Nomura, S., Shimosawa, T., Fujita, T., & Kuboki, T. (1999). Blood pressure biofeedback treatment, organ damage and sympathetic activity in mild hypertension. *Psychotherapy and Psychosomatics, 68*, 341–347.

Nakao, M., Nomura, S., Shimosawa, T., Yoshiuchi, K., Kumano, H., Kuboki, T., et al. (1997). Clinical effects of blood pressure biofeedback treatment on hypertension by auto-shaping. *Psychosomatic Medicine, 59*, 331–338.

Narita, K., Sasaki, T., Akaho, R., Okazaki, Y., Kusumi, I., Kato, T., Hashimoto, O., Fukuda, R., Koyama, T., Matsuo, K., Okabe, Y., Nanko, S., Hohjoh, H., & Tokunaga, K. (2000) Human leukocyte antigen and season of birth in Japanese patients with schizophrenia. *American Journal of Psychiatry, 157*, 1173–1175.

Nash, M. R. (1988). Hypnosis as a window on regression. *Bulletin of the Menninger Clinic, 52*, 383–403.

Nathan, P. E. (1998). *The DSM-IV and its antecedents: Enhancing syndromal diagnosis. Making diagnosis meaningful: Enhancing evaluation and treatment of psychological disorders.* J. W. Barron (Ed). (pp. 3–27). Washington, DC: American Psychological Association.

Nathans, J. (1987). Molecular biology of visual pigments. *Annual Review of Physiology, 10*, 163–194.

National Center for Health Statistics. (2000). Healthy people 2002 review, 1998– 1999. *National Vital Statistics Report, 47*, 5. (Series 19: Data from the National Vital Statistics System).

National Highway Traffic Safety Administration (NHTSA). (2002). Facts about: Drinking and driving. U.S. Department of Commerce.

National Institute for Allergy and Infectious Diseases. (1999, July). An introduction to sexually transmitted diseases. Retrieved 6-6-2003 from http://www.niaid.nih.gov/factsheets/std-info.htm.

Naylor, M. R., Helzer, J. E., Naud, S., & Keefe, F. J. (2002). Automated telephone as an adjunct for the treatment of chronic pain: A pilot study. *Journal of Pain, 3*, 429–438.

Negandhi, A. R. (1973). *Management and economic development: The case of Taiwan.* The Hague: Martinus Nijhoff.

Neher, A. (1991). Maslow's theory of motivation: A critique. *Journal of Humanistic Psychology, 31*, 89–112.

Neisser, U. (1967). *Cognitive psychology.* New York: Appleton-Century-Crofts.

Neisser, U. (1976a). *Cognition and reality.* San Francisco: Freeman.

Neisser, U. (1991). A case of misplaced nostalgia. *American Psychologist, 46*, 34–36.

Neisser, U., Boodoo, G., Bouchard, T. J., Boykin, A. W., Brody, N., Ceci, S. J., Halpern, D. F., Loehlin, J. C., Perloff, R., Sternberg, R. J., & Urbina, S. (1998a). Intelligence: Knowns and unknowns. In M. E. Hertzig & E. A. Farber (Eds.), *Annual progress in child psychiatry and child development: 1997* (pp. 95–133). Bristol, PA: Brunner/Mazel.

Neisser, U., & Harsch, N. (1992). Phantom flashbulbs: False recollections of hearing the news about *Challenger.* In E. Winograd & U. Neisser (Eds.), *Affect and accuracy in recall: Studies of "flashbulb" memories.* New York: Cambridge University Press.

Neisser, U., et al. (Eds.) (1998b) *The rising curve: Long-term gains in IQ and related measures.* Washington, DC: American Psychological Association.

Nelson, C. A. (1995). The ontogeny of human memory: A cognitive neuroscience perspective. *Developmental Psychology, 31*, 723–738.

Nelson, D. A., & Crick, N. R. (1999). Rose-colored glasses: Examining the social information-processing of prosocial young adolescents. *Journal of Early Adolescence, 19*, 17–38.

Nesbitt, E. B. (1973). An escalator phobia overcome in one session of flooding in vivo. *Journal of Behavior Therapy and Experimental Psychiatry, 4*, 405–406.

Nestadt, G., Samuels, J., Riddle, M., Bienvenu, J., Liang, K., LaBuda, M., Walkup, J., Grados, M., & Hoehn-Saric, R. (2000). A family study of obsessive-compulsive disorder. *Archives of General Psychiatry, 57*, 358–363.

Nettelbeck, T., & Wilson, C. (1997). Speed of information processing and cognition. In W. E. MacLean, Jr. (Ed.), *Ellis' handbook of mental deficiency, psychological theory and research* (3rd ed., pp. 245–274). Hillsdale, NJ: Lawrence Erlbaum.

Neugarten, B. L. (1977). Personality and aging. In J. E. Birren & K. W. Schaie (Eds.), *Handbook of the psychology of aging.* New York: Academic Press.

Neutra, M., & Leblond, C. P. (1969). The Golgi apparatus. *Scientific American*, 100–107.

Newcomb, P. A., & Carbone, P. P. (1992). The health consequences of smoking. Cancer. *Medical Clinics of North America, 76*, 305–331.

Newcomb, T. M. (1956). The predictions of interpersonal attraction. *American Psychologist, II*, 575–586.

Newcomb, T. M. (1961). *The acquaintance process.* New York: Holt, Rinehart & Winston.

Newcombe, N., Drummey, A. B., & Lie, E. (1995). Children's memory for early experience. Special issue: Early memory. *Journal of Experimental Child Psychology, 59*, 337–342.

Newell, A. (1969). Heuristic programming: Ill-structured problems. In J. Aronofsky (Ed.), *Progress in operations research* (Vol. 3). New York: John Wiley.

Newell, A., & Simon, H. A. (1972). *Human problem solving.* Englewood Cliffs, NJ; Prentice-Hall.

Newman, H. G., Freeman, F. N., & Holzinger, K. J. (1937). *Twins: A study of heredity and environment.* Chicago: University of Chicago Press.

Newman, J. (1995). Thalamic contributions to attention and consciousness. *Consciousness and Cognition, 4*, 172–193.

Newman, L. S., Duff, K., & Baumeister, R. (1997). A new look at defensive projection: Thought suppression, accessibility, and biased person perception. *Journal of Personality and Social Psychology, 72*, 980–1001.

Newport, E. L. (1990). Maturational constraints on language learning. *Cognitive Science, 14*, 11–28.

Newport, E. L., Gleitman, H., & Gleitman, L. R. (1977). Mother, I'd rather do it myself: Some effects and noneffects of maternal speech style. In C. Snow & C. A. Ferguson (Eds.), *Talking to children: Language input and acquisition.* Cambridge: Cambridge University Press.

Newsome, W. T., Britten, K. H., & Moushon, J. A. (1989). Neuronal correlates of a perceptual decision. *Nature, 341*, 52–54.

Nickerson, R. S. (1998). Confirmation bias: A ubiquitous phenomenon in many guises. *Review of General Psychology, 2*, 175–220.

Niedenthal, P., Setterlund, M., & Wherry, M. B. (1992). Possible self-complexity and affective reactions to goal-relevant evaluation. *Journal of Personality and Social Psychology, 63*, 5–16.

Nielsen, D. A., Jenkins, G. L., Stefanisko, K. M., Jefferson, K. K., & Goldman, G. (1997). Sequence, splice site, and population frequency distribution analyses of polymorphic human tryptophan hydroxylase intron 7. *Molecular Brain Research, 45*, 145–148.

Nigg, J. T., & Goldsmith, H. H. (1994). Genetics of personality disorders: Perspectives from personality and psychopathology research. *Psychological Bulletin, 115*, 346–380.

Nigg, J. T., Lohr, N. E., Westen, D., Gold, L. J., & Silk, K. (1992). Malevolent object representations in borderline personality disorder and major depression. *Journal of Abnormal Psychology, 101*, 61–67.

Nisbett, R. E., Peng, K., Choi, I., Norenzayan, A. (2001). Culture and systems of thought: Holistic versus analytic cognition. *Psychological Review, 108*, 291-310.

Nisbett, R. E., & Ross, L. (1980). *Human inference: Strategies and shortcomings of social judgment.* Englewood Cliffs, NJ: Prentice-Hall.

Nisbett, R. E., & Wilson, T. D. (1977). Telling more than we can know: verbal reports on mental processes. *Psychological Review, 84,* 231–259.

Nolde, S. F., Johnson, M. K., & Raye, C. L. (1998). The role of prefrontal cortex during tests of episodic memory. *Trends in Cognitive Sciences, 2,* 399–406.

Nolen-Hoeksema, S., Girgus, J. S., & Seligman, M. E. (1992). Predictors and consequences of childhood depressive symptoms: A 5-year longitudinal study. *Journal of Abnormal Psychology. 101,* 405–422.

Norcross, J., Karg, R., & Prochaska, J. (1997). Clinical psychologists in the 1990s: Part 1. *Clinical Psychologist, 50,* 4–8.

Norenzayan, A., & Nisbett, R. E. (2000). Culture and causal cognition. *Current Directions in Psychological Science, 9,* 132–135.

Norman, W. T. (1963). Toward an adequate taxonomy of personality attributes: Replicated factor structure in peer nomination personality ratings. *Journal of Abnormal and Social Psychology, 66,* 574–583.

Norton, R. N., & Morgan, M. Y. (1989). The role of alcohol in mortality and morbidity from interpersonal violence. *Alcohol, 24,* 565–576.

Novak, M. A., & Harlow, H. F. (1975). Social recovery of monkeys isolated for the first year of life: Rehabilitation and therapy. *Developmental Psychology, 11,* 453–465.

Nowak, R. (1994). Nicotine research. Key study unveiled – 11 years late. *Science, 264,* 196–197.

Nussbaum, R. L., & Ellis, C. E. (2003). Alzheimer's disease and Parkinson's disease. *New England Journal of Medicine, 348,* 1356–1364.

Nyberg, L. (1998). Mapping episodic memory. *Behavioral Brain Research, 90,* 107–114.

Nyborg, H., & Jensen, A. R. (2000). Black-white differences on various psychometric tests: Spearman's hypothesis tested on American armed services veterans. *Personality and Individual Differences, 28,* 593–599.

Oakhill, J., Johnson-Laird, P. N., & Garnham, A. (1989). Believability and syllogistic reasoning. *Cognition, 31,* 117–140.

Oatley, K., & Jenkins, J. M. (1992). Human emotion: Function and dysfunction. *Annual Review of Psychology, 43,* 55–85.

O'Brien, T. B., & DeLongis, A. (1996). The interactional context of problem-, emotion-, and relationship- focused coping: The role of the Big Five personality factors. *Journal of Personality, 64,* 775–813.

Ochsner, K. N. (2000). Are affective events richly recollected or simply familiar? The experience and process of recognizing feelings past. *Journal of Experimental Psychology: General, 129,* 242–261.

Ochsner, K. N., & Schacter, D. L. (2000). A social cognitive neuroscience approach to emotion and memory. In J. C. Borod, et al. (Eds.), *The neuropsychology of emotion* (pp. 163–193). New York: Oxford University Press.

O'Connor, T. G., McGuire, S., Reiss, D., Hetherington, E. M., & Plomin, R. (1998). Co-occurrence of depressive symptoms and antisocial behavior in adolescence: A common genetic liability. *Journal of Abnormal Psychology, 107,* 27–37.

O'Connor, T. G., Rutter, M., Beckett, C., Keaveney, L., Kreppner, J., & the English and Romanian Adoptees Study Team. (2000). The effects of global severe privation on cognitive competence: Extension and longitudinal follow- up. *Child Development, 71,* 376–390.

Oehman, A., & Mineka, S. (2001). Fears, phobias, and preparedness: Toward an evolved module of fear and fear learning. *Psychological Review, 108,* 483–522.

Oettingen, G., Little, T. D., Lindenberger, U., & Baltes, P. B. (1994). Causality, agency, and control beliefs in East versus West Berlin children: A natural experiment on the role of context. *Journal of Personality and Social Psychology, 66,* 579–595.

Oettingen, G., & Seligman, M. (1990). Pessimism and behavioral signs of depression in East versus West Berlin. *European Journal of Social Psychology, 20,* 207–220.

Offer, D., & Offer, J. (1975). *From teenage to young manhood: A psychological study.* New York: Basic Books.

Offer, D., Ostrov, E., Howard, K., & Atkinson, R. (1990). Normality and adolescence. *Psychiatric Clinics of North America, 13,* 377–388.

Ogata, N., Voshii, M., & Narahashi, T. (1989). Psychotropic drugs block voltage-gated ion channels in neuroblastoma cells. *Brain Research, 476,* 140–144.

Ogbu, J. (1991). Minority coping responses and school experience. *Journal of Psychohistory, 18,* 434–456.

Ohman, A., Esteves, F., & Soares, J. F. (1995). Preparedness and preattentive associative learning: Electrodermal conditioning to masked stimuli. *Journal of Psychophysiology, 9,* 99–108.

Ohman, A., Fredrikson, M., Hugdahl, K., & Rimmon, P. (1976). The premise of equipotentiality in human classical conditioning. *Journal of Experimental Psychological General, 105,* 313–337.

Ohman, A., & Mineka, S. (2001). Fears, phobias, and preparedness: Toward an evolved module of fear and fear learning. *Psychological Review, 108,* 483–522.

Okasha, A., El Akabaw, A. S., Snyder, K. S., Wilson, A. K., Youssef, I., & El Dawla, A. S. (1994). Expressed emotion, perceived criticism, and relapse in depression: A replication. *American Journal of Psychiatry, 151,* 1001–1005.

Oldenburg, B. (2002). Preventing chronic disease and improving health: Broadening the scope of behavioral medicine research and practice. *International Journal of Behavioral Medicine, 9,* 1–16.

Olds, J., & Milner, P. (1954). Positive reinforcement produced by electrical stimulation of septal areas and other regions of rat brains. *Journal of Comparative and Physiological Psychology, 47,* 419–427.

O'Leary, A. (1992). Self-efficacy and health: Behavioral and stress-physiological mediation. *Cognitive Therapy & Research, 16,* 229–245.

O'Leary, A., Brown, S., & Suarez-Al-Adam, M. (1997). Stress and immune function. In T. W. Miller (Ed.), *Clinical disorders and stressful life events* (pp. 181–215). Madison, CT: International Universities Press.

Oliner, S., & Oliner, P. (1988). *The altruistic personality: Rescuers of Jews in Nazi Europe.* New York: Free Press.

Oliner, S. P. (2002). Extraordinary acts of ordinary people: Faces of heroism and altruism. In S. G. Post, L. G. Underwood, J. P. Scholss, & W. B. Hurlbut (Eds.). *Altruism and altruistic love: Science, philosophy, & religion in dialogue* (pp. 123–139). London: Oxford University Press.

Olson, D. (1985). Circumplex model VII: Validation and FACES III. *Family Process, 25,* 337–351.

Olson, D. H. (2000). Circumplex model of marital and family systems. *Journal of Family Therapy, 22,* 144–167.

Olson, G. B. (1981). Perception of melodic contour through intrasensory matching and intersensory transfer by elementary school students. *Journal of Educational Research, 74,* 358–362.

Olson, J. M., & Zanna, M. (1993). Attitudes and attitude change. *Annual Review of Psychology, 44,* 117–154.

Olson, J. M., Vernon, P. A., Harris, J. A., & Jang, K. L. (2001). The heritability of attitudes: A study of twins. *Journal of Personality and Social Psychology, 80,* 845-860.

Olster, D. H., & Blaustein, J. D. (1989). Development of progesterone-facilitated lordosis in female guinea pigs: Relationship to neural estrogen and progestin receptors. *Brain Research, 484,* 168–176.

Olweus, D. (1980). Familial and temperamental determinants of aggressive behavior in adolescent boys: A causal analysis. *Developmental Psychology, 16,* 644–666.

Olweus, D. (1988). Environmental and biological factors in the development of aggressive behavior. In W. Buikhuisen & S. A. Mednick (Eds.), *Explaining criminal behaviour: Interdisciplinary approaches* (pp. 90-120). Leiden, Netherlands: E. J. Brill.

Olweus, D., Mattsson, A., Schalling, D., & Loew, H. (1980). Testosterone, aggression, physical, and personality dimensions in normal adolescent males. *Psychosomatic Medicine, 42,* 253–269.

O'Neill, R. M., Greenberg, R. P., & Fisher, S. (1992). Humor and anality. *Humor: International Journal of Humor Research, 5,* 283–291.

Oppenheim, D., Nir, A., Warren, S., & Emde, R. N. (1997). Emotion regulation in mother-child narrative co-construction: Associations with children's narratives and adaptation. *Developmental Psychology, 33,* 284–294.

Oprah: A heavenly body? (March 31, 1997) *U. S. News & World Report,* p. 18.

Orne, M. T., Sheehan, P. W., & Evans, F. J. (1968). Occurrence of posthypnotic behavior outside the experimental setting. *Journal of Personality and Social Psychology, 9,* 189–196.

Ornstein, R. E. (1986). *The psychology of consciousness.* (2nd ed.). NewYork: Penguin.

Ortony, A., Clore, G. L., & Collins, A. (1988). *The cognitive structure of emotions.* NewYork: Cambridge University Press.

Ortony, A., & Turner, T. J. (1990). What's basic about basic emotions? *Psychological Review, 97,* 315–331.

Oskamp, S. (1991). Factors influencing household recycling behavior. *Environment & Behavior, 23,* 494–519.

Ost, L. (1991). Acquisition of blood and injection phobia and anxiety response patterns in clinical patients. *Behavior Research and Therapy, 29,* 323–332.

Otto, M. W., Reilly-Harrington, N., & Sachs, G. S. (2003). Psychoeducational and cognitive-behavioral strategies in the management of bipolar disorder. *Journal of Affective Disorders, 73,* 171–181.

Ouellette, J. A., & Wood, W. (1998). Habit and intention in everyday life: The multiple processes by which past behavior predicts future behavior. *Psychological Bulletin, 124,* 54–74.

Overholser, J. C. (2002). Cognitive-behavioral treatment of social phobia. *Journal of Contemporary Psychotherapy, 32,* 125–144.

Owens, K., & King, M. C. (1999). Genomic views of human history. *Science, 286,* 451-453.

Ozgen, E., & Davies, I. R. L. (2002). Acquisition of categorical color perception: A perceptual learning approach to linguistic relativity hypothesis. *Journal of Experimental Psychology: General, 131,* 477–493.

Packwood, J., & Gordon, B. (1975). Steropsis in normal domestic cat, Siamese cat, and cat raised with alternating monocular occlusion. *Journal of Neurophysiology, 38,* 1485–1499.

Page, S. (1977). Effects of the mental illness label in attempts to obtain accommodation. *Canadian Journal of Behavioural Science, 9,* 85–90.

Page, S. (1999). Accomodating persons with AIDS: Acceptance and rejection in rental situations. *Journal of Applied Social Psychology, 29,* 261–270.

Paivio, A. (1991). Dual coding theory: Retrospect and current status. *Canadian Journal of Psychology, 45,* 255–287.

Paivio, S. C., & Greenberg, L. S. (1995). Resolving "unfinished business"; efficacy of experimental therapy using empty-chair dialogue. *Journal of Consulting and Clinical Psychology, 63,* 419–425.

Palme, G., & Palme, J. (1999). Personality characteristics of female seeking treatment for obesity, bulimia nervosa and alcoholic disorders. *Personality and Individual Differences, 26,* 255–263.

Papez, J. W. (1937). A proposed mechanism of emotion. *Archives of Neurology and Psychiatry, 38,* 725–743.

Pargament, K. I., & Park, C. L. (1995). Merely a defense? The variety of religious means and ends. *Journal of Social Issues, 51,* 13–32.

Park , D. C., Smith, A. D., Lautenschlager, G., & Earles, J. L. (1996). Mediators of long-term memory performance across the life span. *Psychology & Aging, 11,* 621–637.

Park, D. C., & Schwarz, N. (2000). *Cognitive aging: A primer.* Philadelphia, PA: Psychology Press/Taylor & Francis.

Park, D. C., Smith, A. D., Lautenschlager, G., & Earles, J. L. (1996). Mediators of long-term memory performance across the life span. *Psychology & Aging, 11,* 621–637.

Park, S., & Holzman, P. S. (1993). Association of working memory deficit and eye tracking dysfunction in schizophrenia. *Schizophrenia Research, 11,* 55–61.

Parke, R. D., & Buriel, R. (1998). Socialization in the family: Ethnic and ecological perspectives. In W. Damon (Ed. in Chief) and N. Eisenberg (Vol. Ed.), *Handbook of Child Psychology,Vol. 3.* (pp. 463–552). NewYork: John Wiley.

Parker, J. G., & Asher, S. R. (1987). Peer relations and later personal adjustment: Are low-accepted children at risk? *Psychological Bulletin, 102,* 357–389.

Parkin, A. J., & Java, R. I. (1999). Deterioration of frontal lobe function in normal aging: Influences of fluid intelligence versus perceptual speed. *Neuropsychology, 13,* 539–545.

Parkin, A. J., Walter, B. M., & Hunkin, N. M. (1995). Relationships between normal aging, frontal lobe function, and memory for temporal and spatial information. *Neuropsychology, 9,* 304–312.

Parloff, M. B., London, P., & Wolfe, B. (1986). Individual psychotherapy and behavior change. *Annual Review of Psychology, 37,* 321–349.

Parsons, T. (1951). *The social system.* Glencoe, IL: Free Press.

Pascual-Leone, A., & Torres, F. (1993). Plasticity of the sensorimotor cortex representations of the reading finger in Braille. *Brain.*

Pascual-Leone, A., Walsh, V., & Rothwell, J. (2000). Transcranial magnetic stimulation in cognitive neuroscience—virtual lesion, chronometry, and functional connectivity. *Current Opinion in Neurobiology, 10,* 232–237.

Passaro, K. T., & Little, R. E. (1997). Childbearing and alcohol use. In R. W. Wilsnack & S. C. Wilsnack (Eds.), *Gender and alcohol: Individual and social perspectives* (pp. 90–113). Rutgers, NJ: Rutgers Center of Alcohol Studies.

Passig, D., & Eden, S. (2003). Cognitive intervention through virtual environments among deaf and hard-of-hearing children. *European Journal of Special Needs Education, 18,* 173–182.

Pattatucci, A., & Hamer, D. (1995). Development and familiarity of sexual orientation in females. *Behavior Genetics, 25,* 407–420.

Patterson, D. R., Everett, J. J., Burns, G. L., & Marvin, J. A. (1992). Hypnosis for the treatment of burn pain. *Journal of Consulting & Clinical Psychology, 60,* 713–717.

Patterson, D. R., & Ptacek, J. T. (1997). Baseline pain as a moderator of hypnotic analgesia for burn injury treatment. *Journal of Consulting & Clinical Psychology, 65,* 60–67.

Patterson, G. R., & Bank, L. (1986). Bootstrapping your way in the nomological thicket. *Behavioral Assessment, 8,* 49–73.

Paulesu, E., Frith, U., Snowling, M., Gallagher, A., Morton, J., Frackowiak, R. S. J., & Frith, C. D. (1996). Is developmental dyslexia a disconnection syndrome? Evidence from PET scanning. *Brain, 119,* 143–157.

Paunonen, S. V., Jackson, D. N., Trzebinski, J., & Forsterling, F. (1992). Personality structure across cultures: A multimethod evaluation. *Journal of Personality and Social Psychology, 62,* 447–456.

Pause, B. M., Bernfried, S., Krauel, K., Fehm-Wolfsdorf, G., & Ferstl, R. (1996). Olfactory information processing during the course of the menstrual cycle. *Biological Psychology, 44,* 31–54.

Pavlov, I. P. (1927). *Conditioned reflexes.* New York: Oxford University Press.

Pavone, L., Meli, C., Nigro, F., Lisi, R., et al. (1993). Late diagnosed phenylketonuria patients: Clinical presentation and results of treatment. *Developmental Brain Dysfunction, 6,* 184–187.

Payne, D. G., Neuschatz, Lampien, J., & Lynn, S. J. (1997). Compelling memory illusions: The qualitative characteristics of false memories. *Current Directions in Psychological Science, 6,* 56–60.

Pedersen, D. M., & Wheeler, J. (1983). The Muller-Lyer illusion among Navajos. *Journal of Social Psychology, 121,* 3–6.

Pederson, D. R., Moran, G., Sitko, C., Campbell, K., Ghesquire, K., & Acton, H. (1990). Maternal sensitivity and the security of infant-mother attachment: A q-sort study. *Child Devleopment, 61,* 1974–1983.

Peele, S. (1986). Implications and limitations of genetic models of alcoholism and other addictions. *Journal of Studies on Alcohol, 47,* 63–73.

Pelham, B. W., Mirenberg, M. C., & Jones, J. T. (2002). Why Susie sells seashells by the seashore: Implicit egotism and major life decisions. *Journal of Personality and Social Psychology, 82,* 469–487.

Penfield, W., & Rasmussen, T. (1950). *The cerebral cortex of man: A clinical study of localization of function.* Oxford: Macmillan.

Peng, D., & Nisbett, R. E. (1999). Culture, dialectics, and reasoning about contradiction. *American Psychologist, 54,* 741–754.

Pennebaker, J., Colder, M., & Sharp, L. K. (1990). Accelerating the coping process. *Journal of Personality and Social Psychology, 58,* 528–537.

Pennebaker, J. W. (1997a). *Opening up: The healing power of expressing emotions* (rev. ed.). New York: Guilford Press.

Pennebaker, J. W. (1997b). Writing about emotional experiences as a therapeutic process. *Psychological Science, 8,* 162–166.

Pennebaker, J. W. (1990). *Opening up.* NewYork: Guilford Press.

Pennebaker, J. W., Barger, S. D., & Tiebout, J. (1989). Disclosure of traumas and health among Holocaust survivors. *Psychosomatic Medicine, 51,* 577–589.

Pennebaker, J. W., Kiecolt-Glaser, J., & Glaser, R. (1988). Disclosure of traumas and immune function: Health implications for psychotherapy. *Journal of Consulting and Clinical Psychology, 56,* 239–245.

Pennebaker, J. W., Mayne, T. J., & Francis, M. E. (1997). Linguistic predictors of adaptive bereavement. *Journal of Personality & Social Psychology, 72,* 863–871.

Pennebaker, J. W., & Seagal, J. D. (1999). Forming a story: The health benefits of narrative. *Journal of Clinical Psychology, 55,* 1243–1254.

Perdue, C., & Gurtman, M. (1990). Evidence for the automaticity of ageism. *Journal of Experimental Social Psychology, 26,* 199–216.

Perlman, D. N., Clark, M. A., Rakowski, W., & Ehrich, B. (1999). Screening for breast and cervical cancers: The importance of knowledge and perceived cancer survivability. *Women's Health, 28,* 93–112.

Perlmutter, M. (1983). Learning and memory through adulthood. In M. W. Riley, B. B. Hess, & K. Bond (Eds.), *Aging in society: Selected reviews of recent research.* Hillsdale, NJ: Lawrence Erlbaum.

Perlmutter, M., Dams, C., Berry, J., Kaplan, M., Pearson, D., & Verdonik, J. (1990). Aging and memory. *Annual Review of Gerontology and Geriatrics, 7,* 57–92.

Perls, F. S. (1969). *Ego, hunger and aggression: The beginning of Gestalt therapy.* New York: Random House.

Perls, F. S. (1989). Theory and technique of personality integration. *TACD Journal, 17,* 35–52.

Perris, E. E., Myers, N. A., & Clifton, R. K. (1990). Long-term memory for a single infancy experience. *Child Development, 61,* 1796–1807.

Perruchet, P. (1989). The effect of spaced practice on explicit and implicit memory. *British Journal of Psychology, 80,* 113–130.

Perry, E., Walker, M., Grace, J., & Perry, R. (1999). Acetylcholine in mind: A neurotransmitter correlate of consciousness? *Trends in Neurosciences, 22,* 273–280.

Perry, G. D., & Bussey, K. (1979). The social learning theory of sex differences: Imitation is alive and well. *Journal of Personality and Social Psychology, 37,* 1699–1712.

Pervin, L. A. (2003). *The science of personality* (2nd ed.). New York: Oxford.

Peskin, J. (1992). Ruse and representations: On children's ability to conceal information. *Developmental Psychology, 28,* 84–89.

Peterson, C. (1988). Explanatory style as a risk factor for illness. *Cognitive Therapy and Research, 12,* 119–132.

Peterson, C. (1995). Explanatory style and health. In G. M. Buchanan, M. E. P. Seligman, et al. (Eds.), *Explanatory style* (pp. 233–246). Hillsdale, NJ: Lawrence Erlbaum.

Peterson, C. (2000). The future of optimism. *American Psychologist, 55,* 44–55.

Peterson, G. W., & Peters, D. F. (1985). The socialization values of low-income Appalachian White and rural Black mothers: A comparative study. *Journal of Comparative Family Studies, 16,* 75-91.

Peterson, C., & Seligman, M. E. P. (1984). Causal explanations as a risk factor for depression: Theory and evidence. *Psychological Review, 91,* 347–374.

Peterson, C., Seligman, M., & Vaillant, G. (1988). Pessimistic explanatory style is a risk factor for physical illness: A thirty-five-year longitudinal study. *Journal of Personality & Social Psychology, 55,* 23–27.

Peterson, C. B., & Mitchell, J. E. (1999). Psychosocial and pharmacological treatment of eating disorders: A review of research findings. *Journal of Clinical Psychology, 55,* 685–697.

Petrinovich, L. F. (1999). *Darwinian dominion: Animal welfare and human interests.* Cambridge, MA: MIT Press.

Petry, N. M., Martin, B., Cooney, J. L., & Kranzler, H. R. (2000). Give them prizes and they will come: Contingency management for treatment of alcohol dependence. *Journal of Consulting and Clinical Psychology, 68,* 250–257.

Pettigrew, T. (1958). Personality and socio-cultural factors in intergroup attitudes: A cross-national comparison. *Journal of Conflict Resolution, 2,* 29–42.

Pettigrew, T. F., & Meertens, R. W. (1995). Subtle and blatant prejudice in western Europe. *European Journal of Social Psychology, 25,* 57–75.

Pettit, G. S. (1997). The developmental course of violence and aggression: Mechanisms of family and peer influence. *Psychiatric Clinics of North America, 20,* 283–299.

Petty, F. (1995). GABA and mood disorders: A brief review and hypotheses. *Journal of Affective Disorders, 34,* 275–281.

Petty, R., & Cacioppo, J. (1981). *Attitudes and persuasion: Classic and contemporary approaches.* Dubuque, IA: W. C. Brown.

Petty, R., & Cacioppo, J. (1986a). *Communication and persuasion: Central and peripheral routes to attitude change.* New York: Springer-Verlag.

Petty, R., & Cacioppo, J. T. (1986b). The elaboration likelihood model of persuasion. *Advances in Experimental Social Psychology, 19,* 123–205.

Petty, R., & Krosnick, J. (1994). *Attitude strength: Antecedents and consequences.* Hillsdale, NJ: Lawrence Erlbaum.

Petty, R. E., & Wegener, D. T. (1998). Matching versus mismatching attitude functions: Implications for scrutiny of persuasive messages. *Personality & Social Psychology Bulletin, 24,* 227–240.

Petty, R. E., & Wegener, D. T. (1999). The elaboration likelihood model: Current status and controversies. In S. Chaiken & Y. Trope (Eds.), *Dual process theories in social psychology* (pp. 7–72). New York: Guilford Press.

Petty, R. E., Wegener, D. T., & Fabrigar, L. R. (1997). Attitudes and attitude change. *Annual Review of Psychology, 48,* 609–648.

Pezdek, K., & Banks, W. P. (1996). (Eds.) *The recovered memory/false memory debate.* San Diego, CA: Academic Press.

Phelps, E. A., O'Connor, K. J., Cunningham, W. A., Funayama, E. S., Gatenby, J. C., Gore, J. C., & Banaji, M. (2000). Performance on indirect measures of race evaluation predicts amygdala activation. *Journal of Cognitive Neuroscience, 12,* 729–738.

Phillips, D. P., Ruth, T. E., & Wagner, L. M. (1993). Psychology and survival. *Lancet, 342,* 1142–1145.

Phillips, M. L., Young, A. W., Senior, C., Brammer, M., Andrews, C., Calder, A. J., et al. (1997). A specific neural substrate for perceiving facial expressions of disgust. *Nature, 389,* 495–498.

Piaget, J. (1926). *The language and thought of the child.* New York: Humanities Press, 1951.

Piaget, J. (1932). *The moral judgment of the child* (M. Gabrain, Trans.). New York: Free Press.

Piaget, J. (1965). *The moral judgment of the child.* New York: Free Press.

Piaget, J. (1970). Piaget's theory. In P. Mussen, (Ed.), *Carmichael's manual of child psychology.* New York: John Wiley.

Piaget, J. (1972). Development and learning. In C. S. Lavatelli & F. Stendler (Eds.), *Readings in child behavior and development* (3rd ed.). New York: Harcourt Brace Jovanovich.

Piaget, J., & Inhelder, B. (1956). *The child's conception of space* (F. J. Langdon & J. L. Lunzer, Trans.). London: Routledge & Kegan Paul.

Piaget, J., & Inhelder, B. (1969). *The psychology of the child.* New York: Basic Books.

Pickens, R., Svikis, D., McGue, M., Lykken, D., Heston, L., & Clayton, P. (1991). Heterogeneity in the inheritance of alcoholism: A study of male and female twins. *Archives of General Psychiatry, 48,* 19–28.

Piers, G., & Singer, M. (1953). *Shame and guilt: A psychoanalytic and a cultural study.* Springfield, IL: Charles C. Thomas.

Pihl, R., Peterson, J., & Finn, P. (1990). Inherited predisposition to alcoholism: Characteristics of sons of male alcoholics. *Journal of Abnormal Psychology, 99,* 291–301.

Pilkington, C. J., Tesser, A., & Stephens, D. (1991). Complementarity in romantic relationships: A self-evaluation maintenance perspective. *Journal of Social & Personal Relationships, 8,* 481–504.

Pillard, R. C., Poumadere, J., & Carretta, R. A. (1981). Is homosexuality familial? A review, some data, and a suggestion. *Archives of Sexual Behavior, 10,* 465–473.

Pillard, R. C., Poumadere, J., & Carretta, R. A. (1982). A family study of sexual orientation. *Archives of Sexual Behavior, 11,* 511–520.

Pillemer, D. B. (1984). Flashbulb memories of the assassination attempt on President Reagan. *Cognition, 16,* 63–80.

Pinel, E. C., & Swann, W. B., Jr. (2000). Finding the self through others: Self-verification and social movement participation. In S. Stryker & T. J. Owens (Ed.), *Self, identity, and social movements. Social movements, protest, and contention, Vol. 13.* (pp. 132–152). Minneapolis: University of Minnesota Press.

Pinel, J. P., Assanand, S., & Lehman, D. R. (2000). Hunger, eating, and ill health. *American Psychologist, 55,* 1105-1116.

Pingitore, R., Dugoni, B. L., Tindale, R. S., & Spring, B. (1994). Bias against overweight job applicants in a simulated employment interview. *Journal of Applied Psychology, 79,* 909–917.

Pinker, S. (1994). *The language instinct: How the mind creates language.* New York: Harper-Collins.

Piper, W. E., Ogrodniczuk, J. S., Joyce, A. S., McCallum, M., Rosie, J. S., O'Kelly, J. G., & Steinberg, P. I. (1999). Prediction of dropping out in time-limited, interpretive individual psychotherapy. *Psychotherapy, 36,* 114–122.

Pi-Sunyer, F. X. (1999). Co-morbidities of overweight and obesity: Current evidence and research issues. *Medicine and Science in Sports and Exercise, 31* (Suppl. 11), S602–S608.

Pliner, P., & Chaiken, S. (1990). Eating, social motives, and self-presentation in women and men. *Journal of Experimental Social Psychology, 26,* 240–254.

Plomin, R. (1997). Identifying genes for cognitive abilities and disabilities. In R. J. Sternberg & E. L. Grigorenko (Eds.), *Intelligence, heredity, and environment* (pp. 89-104). New York: Cambridge University Press.

Plomin, R. (1999). Genetics and general cognitive ability. *Nature, 402* (Suppl, 6761), C25-C29).

Plomin, R., & Caspi, A. (1999). Behavioral genetics and personality. In L. Pervin & O. John (Eds.), *Handbook of personality: Theory and research* (2nd ed., pp. 251–276). New York: Guilford Press.

Plomin, R., Chipuer, H., & Loehlin, J. C. (1990). Behavioral genetics and personality. In L. Pervin (Ed.), *Handbook of personality: Theory and research* (pp. 225–243). New York: Guilford Press.

Plomin, R., & DeFries, J. (1980). Genetics and intelligence: Recent data. *Intelligence, 4,* 15–24.

Plomin, R., DeFries, J. C., McClearn, G. E., & Rutter, R. (1997). *Behavioral genetics* (3rd ed.), New York: Freeman.

Plomin, R., Defries, J. C., McGuffin, P. (2001). *Behavioral genetics* (4th ed.), New York: Worth.

Plomin, R., Reiss, D., Hetherington, E. M., & Howe, G. W. (1994). Nature and nurture: Genetic contributions to measures of the family environment. *Developmental Psychology, 30,* 32–43.

Plomin, R., Willerman, L., & Loehlin, J. C. (1976). Resemblance in appearance and the equal environments assumption in twin studies of personality. *Behavior Genetics, 6,* 43–52.

Plous, S. (1996). Attitudes toward the use of animals in psychological research and education: Results from a national survey of psychologists. *American Psychologist, 51,* 1167-1180.

Plutchik, R. (1980). *Emotions: A psychoevolutionary synthesis.* New York: Harper & Row.

Plutchik, R. (1997). The circumplex as a general model of the structure of emotions and personality. In R. Plutchik, H. R. Conte, et al. (Eds.). *Circumplex models of personality and emotions* (pp. 17–45). Washington,DC: American Psychological Association.

Poldrack, R. A., Desmond, J. E., Glover, G. H., & Gabrieli, J. D. E. (1998). The neural basis of visual skill learning: An fMRI study of mirror reading. *Cerebral Cortex, 8,* 1–10.

Pollen, D. A. (1999). On the neural correlates of visual perception. *Cerebral Cortex, 9,* 4–19.

Pollock, V. E., Briere, J., Schneider, L., Knop, J., Mednick, S., & Goodwin, D. W. (1990). Childhood antecedents of antisocial behavior: Parental alcoholism and physical abusiveness. *American Journal of Psychiatry, 147,* 1290–1293.

Ponds, R., Brouwer, W., & Van Wolffelaar, P. (1988). Age differences in divided attention in a simulated driving task. *Journal of Gerontology, 43,* 151–156.

Poon, L., Clayton, P. M., Martin, P., Johnson, M. A., Courtenay, B., Sweaney, A., Merriam, S., Pless, B. S., & Thielman, S. (1992). The Georgia Centenarian study. *International Journal of Aging and Human Development, 34,* 1–17.

Pope, H. G., Gruber, A. J., & Yurgelun-Todd, D. (1995). The residual neuropsychological effects of cannabis: The current status of research. *Drug & Alcohol Dependence, 38,* 25–34.

Porath, M. (2000). Social giftedness in childhood: A developmental perspective. In R. C. Friedman, B. M. Shore, et al. (Eds.), *Talents unfolding: Cognition and development.* (pp. 195–215). Washington, DC: American Psychological Association.

Porkka-Heiskanen, T., Strecker, R. E., Thakkar, M., & Bjorkum, A. A. (1997). Adenosine: A mediator of the sleep-induced effects of prolonged wakefulness. *Science, 276,* 1265–1268.

Posner, M. I. (1995). Attention in cognitive neuroscience: An overview. In M. S. Gazzaniga, et al. (Eds.), *The cognitive neurosciences* (pp. 615–624). Cambridge, MA: MIT Press.

Posner, M. I., & DiGirolamo, G. J. (2000). Attention in cognitive neuroscience: An overview. In M. S. Gazzaniga (Ed.), *The new cognitive neurosciences* (2nd ed., pp. 623–631). Cambridge, MA: MIT Press.

Posner, N. I., & Raichle, M. E. (1996). Precis of image and mind. *Behavioral and Brain Sciences, 18,* 327–383.

Posner, R. M., Boies, S., Eichelman, W. H., & Taylor, R. L. (1969). Retention of visual and name codes of single letters. *Journal of Experimental Psychology, 79,* 1-16.

Pospisil, L. (1963). *Kapauka Papuan political economy.* New Haven, CT: Yale University Publications in Anthropology, No. 67.

Postle, B. R., & D'Esposito, M. (1999). "What"–then–"where" in visual working memory: An event-related fMRI study. *Journal of Cognitive Neuroscience, 11,* 585–597.

Povinelli, D., & Simon, B. B. (1998). Young children's understanding of briefly versus extremely delayed images of the self: Emergence of the autobiographical stance. *Developmental Psychology, 34,* 188–194.

Pratkanis, A. R., Eskenazi, J., & Greenwald, A. G. (1994). What you expect is what you believe (but not necessarily what you get): A test of the effectiveness of subliminal self-help audiotapes. *Basic & Applied Social Psychology, 15,* 251– 276.

Premack, A. J., & Premack, D. (1972). Teaching language to an ape. *Scientific American, 227,* 92–99.

Premack, D. (1962). Reversibility of the reinforcement relation. *Science, 136,* 235–237.

Premack, D. (1965). *Reinforcement theory.* In D. Levine (Ed.), *Nebraska symposium on motivation* (Vol. 3, pp. 123–180). Lincoln: University of Nebraska Press.

Prescott, C. A., & Kendler, K. S. (1999). Genetic and environmental contributions to alcohol abuse and dependence in a population-based sample of male twins. *American Journal of Psychiatry, 156,* 34–40.

Preti, G., Cutler, W. B., Garcia, G. R., Huggins, M., & Lawley, J. J. (1986). Human axillary secretions influence women's menstrual cycles: The role of donor extract from females. *Hormones and Behavior, 20,* 474–482.

Pribram, K. H. (1980). The biology of emotions and other feelings. In R. Plutchik & H. Kellerman (Eds.), *Emotion: Theory, research, and experience: Vol. I. Theories of emotion.* New York: Academic Press.

Price, R. A., Charles, M. A., Pettitt, D. J., & Knowler, W. C. (1993). Obesity in Pima Indians: Large increases among post-World War II birth cohorts. *American Journal of Physical Anthropology, 92,* 473–480.

Price-Williams, D. (1981). Concrete and formal operations. In R. H. Munroe, R. L. Munroe, & B. D. Whiting (Eds.), *Handbook of cross-cultural human development.* New York: Garland Press.

Price-Williams, D., Gordon, W., & Ramirez, M. (1969). Skill and conservation: A study of pottery- making children. *Developmental Psychology, 1,* 769.

Price-Williams, D. R. (1985). In G. Lindzey and E. Aronson (Eds.), *Handbook of social psychology.* Reading, MA: Addison-Wesley.

Priester, J. R. (2002). Sex, drugs, and attitudinal ambivalence: How feelings of evaluative tension influence alcohol use and safe sex behaviors. In W. D. Crano & M. Burgoon (Eds.), *Mass media and drug prevention: Classic and contemporary theories and research* (pp. 145–162). Mahwah, NJ: Lawrence Erlbaum.

Priester, J. R., & Petty, R. E. (1996). The gradual threshold model of ambivalence: Relating the positive and negative bases of attitudes to subjective ambivalence. *Journal of Personality & Social Psychology, 71,* 431–449.

Prochaska, J. D. (1984). *The transtheoretical approach: Crossing traditional boundaries of therapy.* Homewood, IL: Dow Jones-Irwin.

Puce, A., Allison, T., Asgari, M., Gore, J. C., & McCarthy, G. (1996). Differential sensitivity of human visual cortex to faces, letterstrings, and textures: A functional magnetic resonance imaging study. *Journal of Neuroscience, 16,* 5205–5215.

Puce, A., Allison, T., Bentin, S., Gore, J. C., & McCarthy, G. (1998). Temporal cortex activation in humans viewing eye and mouth movements. *Journal of Neuroscience, 18,* 2188–2199.

Putnam, F. W. (1991). Dissociative disorders in children and adolescents: A developmental perspective. *Psychiatric Clinics of North America, 14,* 519–531.

Putnam, F. W. (1995). Rebuttal of Paul McHugh. *Journal of the American Academy of Child and Adolescent Psychiatry, 34,* 963.

Putnam, H. (1973). Reductionism and the nature of psychology. *Cognition, 2,* 131–146.

Quay, L. C. (1974). Language, dialect, age, and intelligence-test performance in disadvantaged Black children. *Child Development, 45,* 463-468.

Quitkin, F. M., Rabkin, J. G., Gerald, J., Davis, J. M., & Klein, D. F. (2000). Validity of clinical trials of antidepressants. *American Journal of Psychiatry, 157,* 327–337.

Rachlin, H., Green, L., Kagel, J. H., & Battalio, R. C. (1976). Economic demand theory and psychological studies of choice. In G. H. Bower (Ed.), *The psychology of learning and motivation* (Vol. 10, pp. 129–154). New York: Academic Press.

Rafalovich, A. (2001). Psychodynamic and neurological perspectives on ADHD: Exploring strategies for defining a phenomenon. *Journal for the Theory of Social Behaviour, 31,* 397–418.

Raine, A., & Venables, P. H. (1984). Electrodermal nonresponding, antisocial behavior, and schizoid tendencies in adolescents. *Psychophysiology, 21,* 424–433.

Raine, A., Lenez, T., Bihrle, S., LaCasse, L., & Colletti, P. (2000). Reduced prefrontal gray matter volume and reduced autonomic activity in antisocial personality disorder. *Archives of General Psychiatry, 57,* 119–127.

Rallison, M. (1986). *Growth disorders in infants, children, and adolescents.* New York: John Wiley.

Ralston, D., Gustafson, D., Elsass, P., & Cheung, F. (1992). Eastern values: A comparison of managers in the United States, Hong Kong, and the People's Republic of China. *Journal of Applied Psychology, 77,* 664–671.

Ramachandran, V. S., & Hirstein, W. (1998). The perception of phantom limbs: The D. O. Hebb lecture. *Brain, 121,* 1603–1630.

Ramirez-Amaya, V., & Bermudez-Rattoni, F. (1999). Conditioned enhancement of antibody production is disrupted by insular cortex and amygdala but not hippocampal lesions. *Brain, Behavior and Immunity, 13,* 46–60.

Ramos, A., Berton, O., Mormede, P., & Chaouloff, F. (1997). A multiple-test study of anxiety-related behaviours in six inbred rat strains. *Behavioural Brain Research, 85,* 57–69.

Ramus, F., Hauser, M., Miller, C., Morris, D., & Mehler, J. (2000). Language discrimination by human newborns and by cotton-top tamarin monkeys. *Science, 288,* 349–351.

Rand, C. S., & Kuldau, J. M. (1990). The epidemiology of obesity and self-defined weight problem in the general population: Gender, race, age, and social class. *International Journal of Eating Disorders, 9,* 329–343.

Randhawa, B. (1991). Gender differences in academic achievement: A closer look at mathematics. *Alberta Journal of Educational Research, 37,* 241–257.

Rao, S. C., Rainier, G., & Miller, E. K. (1997). Integration of what and where in the primate prefrontal cortex. *Science, 276,* 821–824.

Rao, S. M., Huber, S. J., & Bornstein, R. A. (1992). Emotional changes with multiple sclerosis and Parkinson's disease. *Journal of Consulting and Clinical Psychology, 60,* 369–378.

Rapee, R. (1991). Generalized anxiety disorder: A review of clinical features and theoretical concepts. *Clinical Psychology Review, 11,* 419–440.

Rapee, R. M., Brown, T. A., Antony, M., & Barlow, D. (1992). Response to hyperventilation and inhalation of 5.5% carbon dioxide-enriched air across the DSM-III-R anxiety disorders. *Journal of Abnormal Psychology, 101,* 538–552.

Rashidy-Pour, A., Motaghed-Larijani, Z., & Bures, J. (1995). Reversible inactivation of the medial septal area impairs consolidation but not retrieval of passive avoidance learning in rats. *Behavioural Brain Research, 72,* 185–188.

Rawsthorne, L. J., & Elliot, A. J. (1999). Achievement goals and intrinsic motivation: A meta-analytic review. *Personality and Social Psychology Review, 3,* 326–344.

Rea, C. P., & Modigliani, V. (1988). Educational implications of the spacing effect. In M. M. Gruneberg, P. E. Morris, et al. (Eds.), *Practical aspects of memory: Current research and issues: Vol. 1. Memory in everyday life* (pp. 402–406). New York: John Wiley & Sons.

Read, S. J., Vanman, E. J., & Miller, L. C. (1997). Connectionism, parallel constraint satisfaction processes, and Gestalt principles: (Re)introducing cognitive dynamics to social psychology. *Personality and Social Psychology Review, 1,* 26–53.

Reber, A. S. (1989). Implicit learning and tacit knowledge. *Journal of Experimental Psychology: General, 118,* 219–235.

Reber, A. S. (1992). The cognitive unconscious: An evolutionary perspective. *Consciousness and Cognition, 1,* 93–133.

Reber, A. S. (1993). *Implicit learning and tacit knowledge: An essay on the cognitive unconscious.* New York: Oxford University Press.

Recanzone, G. H., Schreiner, C. E., & Merzenich, M. M. (1993). Plasticity in the frequency representation in the primary auditory cortex following discontinuous training in adult owl monkeys. *Journal of Neuroscience.*

Reder, L. M., & Schunn, C. D. (1996). Metacognition does not imply awareness: Strategy choice is governed by implicit learning and memory. In L. M. Reder (Ed.), *Implicit memory and metacognition* (pp. 45–77). Mahwah, NJ: Lawrence Erlbaum.

Rees, G., Frackowiak, R., & Firth, C. (1997). Two modulatory effects of attention that mediate object categorization in human cortex. *Science, 275,* 835–838.

Regan, D., & Fazio, R. (1977). On the consistency between attitudes and behavior: Look to the method of attitude formation. *Journal of Experimental Social Psychology, 13,* 28–45.

Regan, P. C. (1996). Rhythms of desire: The association between menstrual cycle phases and female sexual desire. *Canadian Journal of Human Sexuality, 5,* 145–215.

Regan, T. (1997). The rights of humans and other animals. *Ethics and Behavior, 7,* 103–111.

Reifman, A., Larrick, R., & Fein, S. (1991). Temper and temperature on the diamond: The heat-aggression relationship in major league baseball. *Personality & Social Psychology Bulletin, 17,* 580–585.

Reiman, E. M. (1997). The application of positron emission tomography to the study of normal and pathologic emotions. *Journal of Clinical Psychiatry, 58,* 4–12.

Reiman, P., & Chi, M. T. H. (1989). Human expertise. In K. J. Gilhooly (Ed.), *Human and machine problem solving.* New York: Plenum Press.

Reinisch, J. M. (1981). Prenatal exposure to synthetic progestins increases potential for aggression in humans. *Science, 211,* 1171–1173.

Reis, H. J., & Shaver, P. (1988). Intimacy as an interpersonal process. In S. Duck (Ed.), *Handbook of personal relationships: Theory, relationships and interventions.* New York: John Wiley.

Reis, H. T., Nezlek, J., & Wheeler, L. (1980). Physical attractiveness in social interaction. *Journal of Personality and Social Psychology, 38,* 604-617.

Reisberg, D. (1997). *Cognition: Exploring the science of the mind.* New York: W.W. Norton.

Reisenzein, R. (1983). The Schachter theory of emotion: Two decades later. *Psychological Bulletin, 94,* 239–264.

Repacholi, B., & Gopnik, A. (1997). Early reasoning about desires: Evidence from 14- and 18-month-olds. *Developmental Psychology, 33,* 12–21.

Rescorla, R. A. (1973). Second order conditioning: Implications for theories of learning. In F. J. McGuigan and D. B. Lumsden (Eds.), *Contemporary approaches to conditioning and learning.* New York: John Wiley.

Rescorla, R. A. (1988). Pavlovian conditioning: It's not what you think it is. *American Psychologist, 43,* 151–160.

Rescorla, R. A. (1999). Partial reinforcement reduces the associative change produced by nonreinforcement. *Journal of Experimental Psychology: Animal Behavior, 25,* 403–414.

Rescorla, R. A., & Holland, P. C. (1982). Behavioral studies of associative learning in animals. *Annual Review of Psychology, 33,* 265–308.

Rescorla, R. A., & Wagner, A. R. (1972). A theory of Pavlovian conditioning: Variations in the effectiveness of reinforcement and non-reinforcement. In A. H. Black & W. F. Prokasy (Eds.), *Classical conditioning: II. Current research and theory.* New York: Appleton.

Rest, J. R. (1983). Morality. In J. H. Flavell & E. M. Markman (Eds.), *Handbook of child psychology: Vol. 3. Cognitive development.* New York: John Wiley.

Reuter-Lorenz, P. A., & Stanczak, L. (2000). Differential effects of aging on the functions of the corpus callosum. *Developmental Neuropsychology, 18,* 113–137.

Reynolds, A. J., Mehana, M., & Temple, J. A. (1995). Does preschool intervention affect children's perceived competence? *Journal of Applied Development Psychology, 16,* 211–230.

Rhee, S. H., Waldman, I. D., Hay, D. A., & Levy, F. (1999). Sex differences in genetic and environmental influences on DSM-III-R attention-deficit/ hyperactivity disorder. *Journal of Abnormal Psychology, 108,* 24–41.

Rholes, W. S., Simpson, J. A., Blakely, B. S., Lanigan, L., & Allen, E. A. (1997). Adult attachment styles, the desire to have children, and working models of parenthood. *Journal of Personality, 65,* 357–385.

Richards, B. J. (1990). *Language development and individual differences: A study of auxiliary verb learning.* Cambridge: Cambridge University Press.

Richards, J. B., Sabol, K. E., & Freed, C. R. (1990). Conditioned rotation: A behavioral analysis. *Physiology and Behavior, 47,* 1083–1087.

Richards, J. M., & Gross, J. J. (2000). Emotion regulation and memory: The cognitive costs of keeping one's cool. *Journal of Personality and Social Psychology.*

Richards, M. H., Crowe, P. A., Larson, R., Swarr, A (1998). Developmental patterns and gender differences in the experience of peer companionship during adolescence. *Child Development, 69,* 154-163.

Richards, R., Kinney, D., Lunde, I., Benet, M., & Merzel, A. (1988). Creativity in manic-depressives, cyclothymes, and their normal relatives, and control subjects. *Journal of Abnormal Psychology, 97,* 281–288.

Richardson, J. T. E. (1996a). Evolving concepts of working memory. In J. T. E. Richardson, R. W. Engle, L. Hasher, R. Logie, E. Stoltzfus, & R. Zacks (Eds.), *Working memory and human cognition* (pp. 3–29). New York: Oxford University Press.

Richardson, J. T. E. (1996b). Evolving issues in working memory. In J. T. E. Richardson, R. W. Engle, L. Hasher, R. Logie, E. S. Stoltzfus, & R. Zacks (Eds.), *Working memory and human cognition* (pp. 121–152). New York: Oxford University Press.

Richardson, S. A., & Koller, H. (1996). *Twenty-two years: Causes and consequences of mental retardation.* Cambridge: Harvard University Press.

Rickard, T. C., Romero, S. G., Basso, G., Wharton, C., Flitman, S., & Grafman, J. (2000). The calculating brain: An fMRI study. *Neuropsychologia, 38,* 325-335.

Ricks, M. H. (1985). The social transmission of parental behavior: Attachment across generations. In I. Bretherton & E. Waters (Eds.), *Growing points of attachment theory and research. Monographs of the Society for Research in Child Development, 50,* (1–2, Serial No. 209), 211–227.

Riesen, A. H. (1960). The effects of stimulus deprivation on the development and atrophy of the visual sensory system. *American Journal of Orthopsychiatry, 30,* 23–36.

Riley, A. J. (1991). Sexuality and the menopause. *Sexual and Marital Therapy, 6,* 135–145.

Rinn, W. E. (1984). The neuropsychology of facial expression: A review of the neurological and psychological mechanisms for producing facial expressions. *Psychological Bulletin, 95,* 52–77.

Rips, L. (1990). Reasoning. *Annual Review of Psychology, 41,* 321–353.

Rips, L. J. (1995). Deduction and cognition. In E. E. Smith, D. N. Osherson, et al. (Eds.), *Thinking: An invitation to cognitive science: Vol. 3. An invitation to cognitive science* (2nd ed., pp. 297–343). Cambridge: MIT Press.

Ritov, I., & Baron, J. (1990). Reluctance to vaccinate: Omission bias and ambiguity. *Journal of Behavioral Decision-Making, 3,* 263-277.

Robben, H. S., Webley, P., Weigel, R., & Warneryd, K.-E. (1990). Decision frame and opportunity as determinants of tax cheating: An international experimental study. *Journal of Economic Psychology, 11,* 341–364.

Robbins, T. W. (1997). Arousal systems and attentional processes. *Biological Psychology, 45,* 57–71.

Robbins, T. W., & Everitt, B. J. (1999). Interaction of the dopaminergic system with mechanisms of associative learning and cognition: Implications for drug abuse. *Psychological Science, 10,* 199–202.

Roberts, W. A. (1995). Simultaneous numerical and temporal processing in the pigeon. *Current Directions in Psychological Science, 4,* 47–51.

Robertson, D., Davidoff, J., & Braisby, N. (1999). Similarity and categorization: Neuropsychological evidence for a dissociation in explicit categorization tasks. *Cognition, 71,* 1–42.

Robertson, D., Davidoff, J., & Shapiro, L. (2003). Squaring the circle: The cultural relativity of good shape. *Journal of Cognition and Culture, 2,* 29–51.

Robertson, L. C., & Rafal, R. (2000). Disorders of visual attention. In M. S. Gazzaniga (Ed.), *The new cognitive neurosciences* (2nd ed., pp. 633–649). Cambridge, MA: MIT Press.

Robin, A. A. (1958). A controlled study of the effects of leucotomy. *Journal of Neurology, Neurosurgery and Psychiatry, 21,* 262–269.

Robin, N., & Holyoak, K. (1995). Relational complexity and the functions of the prefrontal cortex. In M. Gazzaniga (Ed.), *The cognitive neurosciences* (pp. 987–997). Cambridge, MA: MIT Press.

Robins, R. W., & Beer, J. S. (2001). Positive illusions about the self: Short-term benefits and long-term costs. *Journal of Personality & Social Psychology, 80,* 340–352.

Robinson, B. W., et al. (1969). Dominance reversal resulting from aggressive responses evoked by brain telestimulation. *Physiology and Behavior, 4,* 749–752.

Robinson, D., Woerner, M. G., Alvir, J. M. J., Bilder, R., Goldman, R., Geisler, S., Koreen, A., Sheitman, B., Chakos, M., Mayerhoff, D., & Lieberman, J. A. (1999). Predictors of relapse following response from a first episode of schizophrenia or schizoaffective disorder. *Archives of General Psychiatry, 56,* 241–247.

Robinson, F. P. (1961). *Effective study.* New York: Harper & Row.

Robinson, G. (1996). Cross cultural perspectives on menopause. *The Journal of Nervous and Mental Disease, 184,* 453–458.

Robinson, K. J., & Roediger III, H. L. (1997). Associative processes in false recall and false recognition. *Psychological Science, 8,* 231–237.

Robinson, T. N. (1999). Reducing children's television viewing to prevent obesity a randomized controlled trial. *Journal of the American Medical Association, 282,* 1561–1567.

Rodin, J., Elias, M., Silberstein, L. R., & Wagner, A. (1988). Combined behavioral and pharmacologic treatment for obesity: Predictors of successful weight maintenance. *Journal of Consulting and Clinical Psychology, 56,* 399–404.

Rodin, J., Schank, D., & Striegel-Moore, R. (1989). Psychological features of obesity. *Medical Clinics of North America, 73,* 47–66.

Rodkin, P., Farmer, T. W., Pearl, R., & Van Acker, R. (2000). Heterogeneity of popular boys: Antisocial and prosocial configurations. *Developmental Psychology, 36,* 14–24.

Rodman, H. R. (1997). Temporal cortex. In G. Adelman & B. Smith (Eds.), *Encyclopedia of Neuroscience.* Amsterdam: Elsevier.

Rodman, H. R., & Albright, T. D. (1989). Single-unit analysis of pattern-motion selective properties in the middle temporal visual area (MT). *Experimental Brain Research, 75,* 53–64.

Roediger, H. L. (1990). Implicit memory: Retention without remembering. *American Psychologist, 45,* 1043–1056.

Roediger, H. L., & McDermott, K. B. (1995). Creating false memories: Remembering words not presented in lists. *Journal of Experimental Psychology: Learning, Memory, and Cognition, 21,* 803–814.

Rogan, M. T., Staeubli, U. V., & LeDoux, J. E. (1997). AMPA receptor facilitation accelerates fear learning without altering the level of conditioned fear acquired. *Journal of Neuroscience, 17,* 5928–5935.

Roger, T. B., Kuiper, N. A., & Kirker, W. S. (1977). Self-reference and the encoding of personal information. *Journal of Personality and Social Psychology, 35,* 677–688.

Rogers, C. (1959). A theory of therapy, personality, and interpersonal relationships, as developed in the client-centered framework. In S. Koch (Ed.), *Psychology: A study of a science,* (Vol. 3). New York: McGraw-Hill.

Rogers, C. R. (1951). *Client-centered therapy: Its current practice, implications, and theory.* Boston, MA: Houghton Mifflin.

Rogers, C. R. (1961). *On becoming a person: A therapist's view of psychotherapy.* Boston, MA: Houghton Mifflin.

Rogers, C. R. (1980). *A way of being.* Boston, MA: Houghton Mifflin.

Rogers, C. R., & Sanford, M. A. (1985). Client-centered psychotherapy. In H. I. Kaplan & B. J. Sadock (Eds.), *Comprehensive textbook of psychiatry* (4th ed.). Baltimore, MD: Williams & Wilkins.

Rogler, L. H., Cortes, D. E., & Malgady, R. G. (1991). Acculturation and mental health status among hispanics: Convergence and new directions for research. *American Psychologist, 46,* 585–592.

Rogoff, B., & Lave, J. (Eds.), (1984). *Everyday cognition: Its development in social context.* Cambridge, MA: Harvard University Press.

Rohner, R. (1975a). Parental acceptance-rejection and personality development: A universalist approach to behavioral science. In R. W. Brislin et al. (Eds.), *Cross-cultural perspectives on learning* (pp. 251–269). New York: Sage.

Rohner, R. (1975b). *They love me, they love me not.* New Haven, CT: HRAF Press.

Rohner, R. P. (1986). *The warmth dimension: Foundations of parental acceptance-rejection theory.* Beverly Hills, CA: Sage.

Rohner, R. P., & Britner, P. A. (2002). Worldwide mental health correlates of parental acceptance-rejection: Review of cross-cultural and intracultural evidence. *Cross-Cultural Research: The Journal of Comparative Social Sciences, 36,* 15–47.

Ronis, D. L. (1992). Conditional health threats: Health beliefs, decisions, and behaviors among adults. *Health Psychology, 11,* 127–134.

Rosch, E. (1973). On the internal structure of perceptual and semantic categories. In T. E. Moore (Ed.), *Cognitive development and the acquisition of language.* New York: Academic Press.

Rosch, E. (1978). Principles of categorization. In E. Rosch & B. Lloyd (Eds.), *Cognition and categorization.* New York: John Wiley.

Roseman, I. J., Dhawan, N., Rettek, S. I., Naidu, R. K., et al. (1995). Cultural differences and cross-cultural similarities in appraisals and emotional responses. *Journal of Cross-Cultural Psychology, 26,* 23–48.

Rosen, A. B., & Rozin, P. (1993). Now you see it, now you don't: The preschool child's conception of invisible particles in the context of dissolving. *Developmental Psychology, 29,* 300–311.

Rosen, J. C., & Gross, J. (1987). The prevalence of weight reducing and weight gaining in adolescent girls and boys. *Health Psychology, 6,* 131–147.

Rosen, K. S., & Rothbaum, F. (1993). Quality of parental caregiving and security of attachment. *Developmental Psychology, 29,* 358–367.

Rosenberg, M. (1979). *Conceiving the self.* New York: Basic Books.

Rosenberg, R. N. (2003). Advances in molecular and genetic basis of Alzheimer's disease. In M. F. Weiner & A. M. Lipton (Eds.), *The dementias: Diagnosis, treatment, and research* (3rd ed., pp. 433–452). Washington, DC: American Psychiatric Publishing.

Rosenberg, S. D., Rosenberg, H. J., & Farrell, M. P. (1999). The midlife crisis revisited. In S. L. Willis & J. D. Reid (Eds.), *Life in the middle: Psychological and social development in middle age.* (pp. 25–45, 47–73). San Diego, CA: Academic Press.

Rosenblatt, A., Greenberg, J., Solomon, S., Pyszczynski, T., & Lyon, D. (1989). Evidence for terror management theory: I. The effects of mortality salience on reactions to those who violate or uphold cultural values. *Journal of Personality and Social Psychology, 57,* 681–690.

Rosenblum, G. D., & Lewis, M. (1999). The relations among body image, physical attractiveness, and body mass in adolescence. *Child Development, 70,* 50–64.

Rosenhan, D. L. (1973). On being sane in insane places. *Science, 179,* 252–258.

Rosenheck, R., Dunn, L., Peszke, M., Cramer, J., Xu, W., Thomas, J., & Charney, D. (1999). Impact of clozapine on negative symptoms and on the deficit syndrome in refractory schizophrenia. *American Journal of Psychiatry, 156,* 88–93.

Rosenstock, I. M. (1966). Why people use health services. *Milbank Memorial Fund Quarterly, 44,* 94ff.

Rosenthal, D. (1970). *Genetic theory and abnormal behavior.* New York: McGraw-Hill.

Rosenthal, R., & Jacobson, L. (1966). Teachers' expectancies: Determinants of pupils' IQ gains. *Psychological Reports, 19,* 115–118.

Rosenwald, G. (1988). The multiple case study method. *Journal of Personality, 56,* 239–264.

Rosenzweig, M. R., Bennett, E. L., & Diamond, M. C. (1972). Brain changes in response to experience. *Scientific American, 226,* 22–29.

Ross, C. A., Anderson, G., Fleisher, W., & Norton, G. R. (1991). The frequency of multiple personality disorder among psychiatric inpatients. *American Journal of Psychiatry, 148,* 1717–1720.

Ross, L. (1977). The intuitive psychologist and his shortcomings: Distortions in the attribution process. In L. Berkowitz (Ed.), *Advances in Experimental Social Psychology, 10,* 84.

Ross, M., & Sicoly, F. (1979). Egocentric biases in availability and attribution. *Journal of Personality and Social Psychology, 37,* 322–336.

Ross, M., Xun, W. Q. E., & Wilson, A. E. (2002). Language and the bicultural self. *Personality and Social Psychology Bulletin, 28,* 1040–1050.

Ross, S. M., & Ross, L. E. (1971). Comparison of trace and delay classical eyelid conditioning as a function of interstimulus interval. *Journal of Experimental Psychology, 91,* 165–167.

Rosso, I. M., Cannon, T. D., Huttunen, T., Huttunen, M. O., Loennqvist, J., & Gasperoni, T. L. (2000). Obstetric risk factors for early-onset schizophrenia in a Finnish birth cohort. *American Journal of Psychiatry, 157,* 801–807.

Roth, A., Fonagy, P., Parry, G., & Target, M. (1996). *What works for whom? A critical review of psychotherapy research.* New York: Guilford Press.

Roth, M. (1978). Epidemiological studies. In R. Katzman, R. D.Terry, & K. L. Bick (Eds.), *Alzheimer's disease: Senile dementia and related disorders.* New York: Raven.

Rothbaum, B. O., Hodges, L. F., Kooper, R., Opdyke, D., Williford, J., & North, M. M. (1995). Effectiveness of computer-generated (virtual reality) graded exposure in the treatment of acrophobia. *American Journal of Psychiatry, 152,* 626–628.

Rothbaum, B. O., Hodges, L. F., Ready, D., Graap, K., & Alarcon, R. D. (2001). Virtual reality exposure therapy for Vietnam veterans with posttraumatic stress disorder. *Journal of Clinical Psychiatry, 62,* 617–622.

Rothbaum, B. O., Hodges, L., Smith, S., Lee, J. H., & Price, L. (2000). A controlled study of virtual reality exposure therapy for the fear of flying. *Journal of Consulting and Clinical Psychology, 68,* 1020–1026.

Rothbaum, B. O., & Schwartz, A. C. (2002). Exposure therapy for posttraumatic stress disorder. *American Journal of Psychotherapy, 56,* 59–75.

Rothbaum, F., Pott, M., Azuma, H., Miyake, K., & Weisz, J. (2000). The development of close relationships in Japan and the United States: Paths of symbiotic harmony and generative tension. *Child Development, 71,* 1121–1142.

Rothblum, E. D. (1983). Sex-role stereotypes and depression in women. In V. Franks & E. D. Rothblum (Eds.), *The stereotyping of women: Its effects on mental health* (pp. 83–111). New York: Springer.

Rothblum, E. D. (1992). The stigma of women's weight: Social and economic realities. *Feminism and Psychology, 2,* 61-73.

Rothgerber, H. (1997). External intergroup threat as an antecedent to perceptions in in-group and out-group homogeneity. *Journal of Personality & Social Psychology, 73,* 1206–1212.

Rotter, J. (1971). External control and internal control. *Psychology Today,* June, 40–45.

Rotter, J. B. (1954). *Social learning and clinical psychology.* New York: Prentice-Hall.

Rotter, J. B. (1966). Generalized expectancies for internal versus external control of reinforcement. *Psychological Monographs* (Whole No.609).

Rotter, J. B. (1990). Internal versus external control of reinforcement: A case history of a variable. *American Psychologist, 45,* 489–493.

Rotton, J., & Cohn, E. G. (2000). Violence is a curvilinear function of temperature in Dallas: A replication. *Journal of Personality and Social Psychology, 78,* 1074–1081.

Rotton, J., et al. (1979). The air pollution experience and physical aggression. *Journal of Applied Social Psychology, 9,* 397–442.

Rovee-Collier, C. (1990). The "memory system" of prelinguistic infants. In A. Diamond (Ed.), *Development and neural bases of higher cognitive functions* (pp. 517–542). New York: New York Academy of Sciences Press.

Rowe, D. C. (1999). Heredity. In V. J. Derlega, B. A. Winstead, & W. H. Jones (Eds.), *Personality: Contemporary theory and research* (pp. 66–100). Chicago: Nelson-Hall.

Rowe, D. C., Jacobson, K. C., & Van den Oord, E. J. C. G. (1999). Genetic and environmental influences on vocabulary IQ: Parental education level as moderator. *Child Development, 70,* 1151–1162.

Rowe, D.C., & Rodgers, J. L. (2002). Expanding variance and the case of historical changes in IQ means: A critique of Dickens and Flynn (2001). *Psychological Review, 109,* 759–763.

Rowe, J. W., & Kahn, R. L. (1997). Successful aging. *Gerontologist, 37,* 433–440.

Rubin, D. C. (1995). *Memory in oral traditions: The cognitive psychology of epic, ballads, and countingout rhymes.* New York: Oxford University Press.

Rubin, D. C., & Kozin, M. (1984). Vivid memories. *Cognition, 16,* 81–95.

Rubin, D. C., Rahhal, T. A., & Poon, L. W. (1998). Things learned in early childhood are remembered best. *Memory and Cognition, 26,* 3–19.

Ruble, D. N., & Martin, C. L. (1998) Gender development. In W. Damon (Ed. in Chief) and N. Eisenberg (Vol. Ed.), *Handbook of child psychology* (Vol. 3, pp. 933–1016). New York: John Wiley.

Rudman, L. A., Greenwald, A. G., Mellott, D. S., & Schwartz, J. L. K. (1999). Measuring the automatic components of prejudice: Flexibility and generality of the Implicit Association Test. *Social Cognition, 17,* 437–465.

Ruffman, T. (1999). Children's understanding of logical inconsistency. *Child Development, 70,* 872–886.

Rumbaugh, D. M. (1992). Learning about primates' learning, language, and cognition. In G. G. Brannigan & M. R. Merrens (Eds.), *The undaunted psychologist: Adventures in research.* New York: McGraw-Hill.

Rumbaugh, D. M., & Gill, T. V. (1977). Lana's acquisition of language skills. In D. M. Rumbaugh (Ed.), *Language learning by a chimpanzee: The Lana project* (pp. 165–192). New York: Academic Press.

Rumelhart, D. (1984). Schemata and the cognitive system. In R. S. Wyer & T. K. Srull (Eds.), *Handbook of social cognition* (Vol. 1). Hillsdale, NJ: Erlbaum.

Rumelhart, D. E., McClelland, J. L., & the PDP Research Group. (1986). *Parallel distributed processing: Explorations in the microstructure of cognition.* Cambridge, MA: MIT Press.

Runyan, W. M. (1984). *Life histories and psychobiography: Explanations in theory and method.* New York: Oxford University Press.

Rusbult, C. E., & Van Lange, P. A. M. (2003). Interdependence, interaction, and relationships. *Annual Review of Psychology, 54,* 351–375.

Rusbult, C. E., Verette, J., Whitney, G. A., Slovik, L. F., & Lipkus, I. (1991). Accomodation processes in close relationships: Theory and preliminary empirical evidence. *Journal of Personality and Social Psychology, 60,* 53–78.

Rushton, W. A. H. (1962). Visual pigments in man. *Scientific American,* 120–132.

Russell, J. A. (1991). Culture and the categorization of emotions. *Psychological Bulletin, 110,* 426-450.

Russell, J. A. (1994). Is there universal recognition of emotion from facial expression? A review of the cross-cultural studies. *Psychological Bulletin, 115,* 102–141.

Russell, J. D., & Roxanas, M. (1990). Psychiatry and the frontal lobes. *Australian and New Zealand Journal of Psychiatry, 24,* 113–132.

Russell, M. J. (1976). Human olfactory communication. *Nature, 260,* 520–522.

Russo, R., & Parkin, A. J. (1993). Age differences in implicit memory: More apparent than real. *Memory and Cognition, 21,* 73–80.

Rutter, M., Quinton, D., & Liddle, C. (1983). Parenting in two generations: Looking backwards and looking forwards. In N. Madge (Ed.), *Families at risk* (pp. 60–98). London: Heineman.

Ryan, J. J., Sattler, J. M., & Lopez, S. J. (2000). Age effects on Wechsler Adult Intelligence Scale-III subtests. *Archives of Clinical Neuropsychology, 15,* 311–317.

Ryan, R. M., & Deci, E. L. (2000). Intrinsic and extrinsic motivations: Classic definitions and new directions. *Contemporary Educational Psychology, 25,* 54–67.

Ryner, J., WIlson, R., & Ballard, K. (2003). Making decisions about hormone replacement therapy. *British Medical Journal, 326,* 322–326.

Rypma, B., & D'Esposito, M. (2000). Isolating the neural mechanisms of age-related changes in human working memory. *Nature Neuroscience, 3,* 509–515.

Saarni, C. (1998). Issues of cultural meaningfulness in emotional development. *Developmental Psychology, 34,* 647–652.

Sacks, O. (1973). *Awakenings.* London: Duckworth.

Sacks, O. (1993). A neurologist's notebook: To see and not see. *New Yorker,* May 10, 59–73.

Saegert, S., & Winkel, G. H. (1990). Environmental psychology. *Annual Review of Psychology, 41,* 441–477.

Saffran, J., Aslin, R., & Newport, E. (1996). Statistical learning by 8-month-old infants. *Science, 274,* 1926–1928.

Sagi, A. (1990). Attachment theory and research from a cross-cultural perspective. *Human Development, 33,* 10–22.

Sagi, A., van IJzendoorn, M. H., Aviezer, O., Donnell, F., & Mayseless, O. (1994). Sleeping out of the home in a kibbutz communal arrangement: It makes a difference for infant-mother attachment. *Child Development, 65,* 971–991.

Sahraie, A., Weiskrantz, L., Barbur, J. L., Simmons, A., Williams, S. C., & Brammer, M. J. (1997). Pattern of neuronal activity associated with conscious and unconscious processing of visual signals. *Proceedings of the National Academy of Sciences, U.S.A., 94,* 9406–9411.

Sakurai, T., et al. (1998). Orexins and orexin receptors: A family of hypothalamic neuropeptides and g protein-coupled receptors that regulate feeding behavior. *Cell, 92,* 573–585.

Salkovskis, P. M., Jones, D. R., & Clark, D. M. (1986). Respiratory control in the treatment of panic attacks: Replication and extension with concurrent measurement of behavior and PCPs. *British Journal of Psychiatry, 148,* 526–532.

Sallis, J. F., Prochaska, J. J., Taylor, W. C., Hill, J. O., & Geraci, J. C. (1999). Correlates of physical activity in a national sample of girls and boys in grades 4 through 12. *Health Psychology, 18,* 410–415.

Salovey, P., Mayer, J., & Caruso, D. (2002). The positive psychology of emotional intelligence. In C. R. Snyder & S. J. Lopez (Eds.), *Handbook of positive psychology* (pp. 159–171). London: Oxford University Press.

Salovey, P., Mayer, J. D., & Rosenhan, D. L. (1991). Mood and healing: Mood as a motivator of helping and helping as a regulator of mood. In M. S. Clark (Ed.), *Prosocial behavior.* Newbury Park, CA.: Sage.

Salovey, P., Rothman, A. J., & Rodin, J. (1998). Health behavior. In D. T. Gilbert, S. T. Fiske, et al. (Eds.), *The handbook of social psychology,* (Vol. 2, 4th ed., pp. 633–683). Boston, MA: McGraw-Hill.

Salthouse, T. (1992). The information-processing perspective on cognitive aging. In R. Sternberg & C. Berg (Eds.), *Intellectual development.* Cambridge: Cambridge University Press.

Salthouse, T. A. (1996). General and specific speed mediation of adult age differences in memory. *Journals of Gerontology Series B- Psychological Sciences and Social Sciences, 51B,* P30–P42.

Salthouse, T. A. (2000). Item analyses of age relations on reasoning tests. *Psychology & Aging, 15,* 3–8.

Salthouse, T. A. (2000). Pressing issues in cognitive aging. In D. C. Park & N. Schwarz (Eds.). *Cognitive aging: A primer.* (pp. 43–54). Philadelphia: Psychology Press/Taylor & Francis.

Sameroff, A., Seifer, R., Baldwin, A., & Baldwin, C. (1993). Stability of intelligence from preschool to adolescence: The influence of social and family risk factors. *Child Development, 64,* 80–97.

SAMHSA (Substance Abuse and Mental Health Services Administration). (2001). 2001 National Household Survey on Drug Abuse. Retrieved 6-12-2003 from http://www.samhsa.gov

Samudra, K., & Cantwell, D. P. (1999). Risk factors for attention-deficit/hyperactivity disorder. In H. C. Quay & A. E. Hogan (Eds.), *Handbook of disruptive behavior disorders* (pp. 199-220). Dordrecht, Netherlands: Kluwer.

Sandler, J., & Rosenblatt, B. (1962). The concept of the representational world. *Psychoanalytic Study of the Child, 17,* 128–145.

Sanfilipo, M., Lafargue, T., Rusinek, H., Arena, L., Loneragan, C., Lautin, A., Feiner, D., Rotrosen, J., & Wolkin, A. (2000). Volumetric measure of the frontal and temporal lobe regions in schizophrenia: Relationship to negative symptoms. *Archives of General Psychiatry, 57,* 471–480.

Sanger, T. M., Lieberman, J. A., Tohen, M., Grundy, S., Beasley, C., & Tollefson, G. D. (1999). Olanzapine versus haloperidol treatment in first-episode psychosis. *American Journal of Psychiatry, 156,* 79–87.

Sapir, E. (1949). *Culture, language and personality.* Berkeley: University of California Press.

Sapolsky, R. M. (1996). Stress, glucocorticoids and damage to the nervous system: The current state of confusion. *Stress: The International Journal on the Biology of Stress, 1,* 1-19.

Sarafino, E. P. (2002). *Health psychology: Biopsychosocial interactions* (4th ed.). Hoboken, NJ: John Wiley & Sons.

Sarason, B. R., Sarason, I. G., & Gurung, R. A. R. (1997). Close personal relationships and health outcomes: A key to the role of social support. In S. Duck et al. (Eds.), *Handbook of personal relationships: Theory, research and inter-*

ventions (2nd ed., pp. 547–573). Chichester, England: John Wiley & Sons.

Saraswathi, T., & Dutta, R. (1988). Current trends in developmental psychology: A life span perspective. In J. Pandey (Ed.), *Psychology in India: The state-of-the-art:* Vol. 1. *Personality and mental processes* (pp. 93–152). London: Sage.

Sarnat, H. B., & Netsky, M. G. (1974). *Evolution of the nervous system.* New York: Oxford University Press.

Sartre, J. P. (1971). Being and nothingness: An essay in phenomenological ontology (H. E. Barnes, Trans.). New York: Citadel Press.

Sass, C. (2003, May). Childhood obesity seen even in preschool. Paper presented at the meeting of the Pediatric Academic Societies Annual Meeting, Seattle.

Satel, S. L., Southwick, S. M., & Gawin, F. H. (1991). Clinical features of cocaine-induced paranoia. *American Journal of Psychiatry, 148,* 495–498.

Saucier, G., & Goldberg, L. R. (2001). Lexical studies of indigenous personality factors: Premises, products, and prospects. *Journal of Personality, 69,* 847–879.

Sauerwein, K. (1992, October 21). Too scared to be safe: Teens know they need condoms if they're going to have sex, but they're too freaked out to buy them. *Los Angeles Times.*

Saundino, K. (1997). Moving beyond the heritability question: New directions in behavioral genetic studies of personality. *Current Directions in Psychological Science, 6,* 86–89.

Savage-Rumbaugh, E. S., McDonald, K., Sevcik, R., Hopkins, W., & Rupert, E. (1986). Spontaneous symbol acquisition and communicative use by pygmy chimpanzees (*pan paniscus*). *Journal of Experimental Psychology: General, 115,* 211–235.

Savage-Rumbaugh, E. S., Pate, J. L., Lawson, J., Smith, S. T., & Rosenbaum, S. (1983). Can a chimpanzee make a statement? *Journal of Experimental Psychology: General, 112,* 457–492.

Savage-Rumbaugh, E. S., Rumbaugh, D. M., & Boysen, S. (1978). Symbolic communication between two chimpanzees. *Science, 201,* 641–644.

Savin-Williams, R. C., & Small, S. A. (1986). The timing of puberty and its relationship to adolescent and parent perceptions of family interactions. *Developmental Psychology, 22,* 342–347.

Scarr, S., & Carter-Saltzman, L. (1982). Genetics and intelligence. In R. J. Sternberg (Ed.), *Handbook of human intelligence* (pp. 792–896). New York: Cambridge University Press.

Scarr, S., Pakstis, A. J., Katz, S. H., & Barker, W. B. (1977). The absence of a relationship between degree of white ancestry and intellectual skills within a black population. *Human Genetics, 39,* 69–86.

Scarr, S., & Weinberg, R. A. (1976). IQ test performance of black children adopted by white families. *American Psychologist, 31,* 726–739.

Scarr, S., & Weinberg, R. A. (1983). The Minnesota adoption studies: Genetic differences

and malleability. *Child Development, 54,* 260–267.

Schab, F. R., & Crowder, R. G. (1995). Odor recognition memory. In F. R. Schab, F. R. G. Crowder, et al. (Eds.), *Memory for odors* (pp. 9–20). Mahwah, NJ: Lawrence Erlbaum.

Schachter, F. F., Shore, E., Hodapp, R., Chalfin, S., & Bundy, C. (1978). Do girls talk earlier? Mean length of utterance in toddlers. *Developmental Psychology, 14,* 388–392.

Schachter, S., & Singer, J. (1962). Cognitive, social, and physiological determinants of emotional state. *Psychological Review, 69,* 379–399.

Schacter, D. (1995a). Implicit memory: A new frontier for cognitive neuroscience. In M. Gazzaniga (Ed.), *The cognitive neurosciences* (pp. 815–824). Cambridge, MA: MIT Press.

Schacter, D. (1995b). *Memory and distortion: How minds, brains, and societies recollect the past.* Cambridge, MA: Harvard University Press.

Schacter, D. (1997). False recognition and the brain. *Current Directions in Psychological Science, 6,* 65–70.

Schacter, D., Cooper, L. A., & Valdiserri, M. (1992). Implicit and explicit memory for novel visual objects in older and younger adults. *Psychology and Aging, 7,* 299–308.

Schacter, D. L. (1999). The seven sins of memory: Insights from psychology and cognitive neuroscience. *American Psychologist, 54,* 182–203.

Schacter, D. L., & Buckner, R. L. (1998). Priming and the brain. *Neuron, 20,* 185–195.

Schacter, D. L., Verfaellie, M., Anes, M., & Racine, C. (1998). When true recognition suppresses false recognition: Evidence from amnesic patients. *Journal of Cognitive Neuroscience.*

Schafe, G. E., & Bernstein, I. L. (1996). Taste aversion learning. In E. D. Capaldi (Ed.), *Why we eat what we eat: The psychology of eating* (pp. 31–51). Washington, DC: American Psychological Association.

Schaie, K. W. (1988). Ageism in psychological research. *American Psychologist, 43,* 179–183.

Schaie, K. W. (1990). Intellectual development in adulthood. In J. E. Birren & K. W. Schaie (Eds.), *Handbook of the psychology of aging* (3rd ed.). New York: Van Nostrand Reinhold.

Schaie, K. W. (1994). The course of adult intellectual development. *American Psychologist, 49,* 304–313.

Schatzberg, A. F. (2000). New indications for antidepressants. *Journal of Clinical Psychiatry, 61,* 9–17.

Schauble, L., & Glaser, R. (1990). Scientific thinking in children and adults. *Contributions to Human Development, 21,* 9–27.

Scheff, T. J. (1970). Schizophrenia as ideology. *Schizophrenia Bulletin, 1,* 15–20.

Scheier, M., & Carver, C. (1993). On the power of positive thinking: The benefits of being optimistic. *Current Directions in Psychological Science, 2,* 26–30.

Scheier, M. F., Matthews, K. A., Owens, J., Magovern, G. J., Lefebvre, R. C., Abbott, R., & Carver, C. S. (1989). Dispositional optimism and recovery from coronary artery bypass

surgery: The beneficial effects on physical and psychological well-being. *Journal of Personality and Social Psychology, 57,* 1024–1040.

Scheper-Hughes, N. (1979). *Saints, scholars, and schizophrenics: Mental illness in rural Ireland.* Berkeley: University of California Press.

Scher, S., & Cooper, J. (1989). Motivational basis of the dissonance: The singular role of behavioral consequences. *Journal of Personality and Social Psychology, 56,* 899–906.

Scherer, K., & Wallbott, H. (1994). Evidence for universality and cultural variation of differential emotion response patterning. *Journal of Personality & Social Psychology, 66,* 310–328.

Scherer, K. R. (1997). Profiles of emotion-antecedent appraisal: Testing theoretical predictions across cultures. *Cognition & Emotion, 11,* 113–150.

Scherer, K. R. (1999). Appraisal theory. In T. Dalgleish & M. Power (Eds.), *The handbook of cognition and emotion* (pp. 637–664). New York: John Wiley & Sons.

Schiavi, R. C., Schreiner-Engle, P., Mandeli, J., Schanzer, H., et al. (1990). Healthy aging and male sexual function. *American Journal of Psychiatry, 147,* 766–771.

Schiavi, R. C., Schreiner-Engel, P., White, D., & Mandeli, J. (1991). The relationship between pituitary-gonadal function and sexual behavior in healthy aging men. *Psychosomatic Medicine, 53,* 363–374.

Schiff, M., Duyme, M., Dumaret, A., & Tomkiewicz, S. (1982). How much could we boost scholastic achievement and IQ scores? A direct answer from a French adoption study. *Cognition, 12,* 165–196.

Schiffman, H. R. (1996). *Sensation and perception* (4th ed.). New York: John Wiley.

Schlegel, A., & Barry III, H. (1991). *Adolescence: An anthropological inquiry.* New York: Free Press.

Schlenker, B. R., & Forsyth, D. R. (1977). On the ethics of psychological research. *Journal of Experimental Social Psychology, 13,* 369–396.

Schlesser, M. A., & Altshuler, K. Z. (1983). The genetics of affective disorder: Date, theory, and clinical applications. *Hospital and Community Psychiatry, 34,* 415–422.

Schmidt, F. L., & Hunter, J. E. (1998). The validity and utility of selection methods in personnel psychology: Practical and theoretical implications of 85 years of research findings. *Psychological Bulletin, 124,* 262–274.

Schmidt, N. B., Lerew, D. R., & Trakowski, J. H. (1997a). Body vigilance in panic disorder: Evaluating attention to bodily perturbations. *Journal of Consulting and Clinical Psychology, 65,* 214–220.

Schmidt, N. B., Trakowski, J. H., & Staab, J. P. (1997b). Extinction of a panicogenic effects of a 3% CO2 challenge in patients with panic disorder. *Journal of Abnormal Psychology, 106,* 630–640.

Schnapf, J., Kraft, T., Nunn, B., & Baylor, D. (1989). Transduction in primate cones. *Neuroscience Research,* Suppl. 10, 9–14.

Schneider, M. L., Roughton, E. C., Koehler, A. J., & Lubach, G. R. (1999). Growth and development following prenatal stress exposure in primates: An examination of ontogenetic vulnerability. *Child Development, 70,* 263–274.

Schneider, M. L., Roughton, E. C., & Lubach, G. R. (1997). Moderate alcohol consumption and psychological stress during pregnancy induce attention and neuromotor impairments in primate infants. *Child Development, 68,* 747–759.

Schraw, G., Dunkle, M. E., & Bendixen, L. D. (1995). Cognitive processes in well-defined and ill-defined problem solving. *Applied Cognitive Psychology, 9,* 523–538.

Schreiber, F. R. (1973). *Sybil.* Chicago: Regnery.

Schreiner, C. E., Read, H. L., & Sutter, M. L. (2000). Modular organization of frequency integration in primary auditory cortex. *Annual Review of Neuroscience, 23,* 501–529.

Schuckit, M. (1984). Relationship between the course of primary alcoholism in men and family history. *Journal of Studies on Alcohol, 45,* 334–338.

Schuckit, M. A. (1994). Low level of response to alcohol as a predictor of future alcoholism. *American Journal of Psychiatry, 151,* 184–189.

Schultz, T., & Schliefer, M. (1983). Towards a refinement of attribution concepts. In J. Jaspars, F. Fincham, & M. Hewstone (Eds.), *Attribution theory and research: Conceptual, developmental, and social dimensions* (pp. 37–62). New York: Academic Press.

Schultz, W. (1998). Predictive reward signal of dopamine neurons. *Journal of Neurophysiology, 80,* 1–27.

Schultz, W., Dayan, P., & Montague, P. R. (1997). A neural substrate of prediction and reward. *Science, 275,* 1593–1599.

Schurr, P. P., Ford, J. D., Friedman, M. J., Green, B. L., Dain, B. J., & Sengupta, A. (2000). Predictors and outcomes of posttraumatic stress disorder in World War II veterans exposed to mustard gas. *Journal of Consulting and Clinical Psychology, 68,* 258-268.

Schuster, D. T. (1990). Fulfillment of potential, life satisfaction, and competence: Comparing four cohorts of gifted women at midlife. *Journal of Educational Psychology, 82,* 471–478.

Schwarz, N. (1999). Self-reports: How the questions shape the answers. *American Psychologist, 54,* 93–105.

Schwartz, D., Dodge, K. A., Pettit, G. S., & Bates, J. E. (2000). Friendship as a moderating factor in the pathway between early harsh home environment and later victimization in the peer group. *Developmental Psychology, 36,* 646–662.

Schwartz, G. E. (1987). Personality and health: An integrative health science approach. In V. P. Makosky (Ed.), *The G. Stanley Hall Lecture Series* (Vol. 7). Washington, DC: American Psychological Association.

Science historian predicts a billion deaths from tobacco by end of the century. (2002). *Bulletin of the World Health Organization, 80,* 80.

Scott, J. (2001). Cognitive therapy as an adjunct to medication in bipolar disorder. *British Journal of Psychiatry, 178,* s164–s168.

Scott, S. K., Young, A. W., Calder, A. J., & Hellawell, D. J. (1997). Impaired auditory recognition of fear and anger following bilateral amygdala lesions. *Nature, 385,* 254–257.

Scoville, W. B., & Milner, B. (1957). Loss of recent memory after bilateral hippocampal lesions. *Journal of Neurology, Neurosurgery, and Psychiatry, 20,* 11–21.

Scribner, S. (1986). Thinking in action: Some characteristics of practical thought. In R. J. Sternberg & R. K. Wagner (Eds.), *Practical intelligence: Nature and origins of competence in the everyday world* (pp. 13–40). New York: Cambridge University Press.

Scroppo, J. C., Drob, S. L., Weinberger, J. L., & Eagle, P. (1998). Identifying dissociative identity disorder: A self-report and projective study. *Journal of Psychology, 107,* 272–284.

Searle, J. R. (2000) Consciousness. *Annual Review of Neuroscience, 23,* 557–578.

Sears, D. O. (1986). College sophomores in the laboratory: Influences of a narrow data base on social psychological view of human nature. *Journal of Personality and Social Psychology, 51,* 515–530.

Sears, R. R. (1977). Sources of life satisfactions of the Terman gifted men. *American-Psychologist, 32,* 119–128.

Seelinger, G., & Schuderer, B. (1985). Release of male courtship display in *Periplaneta americana*: Evidence for female contact sex pheromone. *Animal Behaviour, 33,* 599–607.

Segal, M. W. (1974). Alphabet and attraction: An unobtrusive measure of the effect of propinquity in a field setting. *Journal of Personality and Social Psychology, 30,* 654–657.

Segal, N. L. (1997). Same-age unrelated siblings: A unique test of within-family environmental influences on IQ similarity. *Journal of Educational Psychology, 89,* 381–390.

Segal, N. L. (2000). Virtual twins: New findings on within-family environmental influences on intelligence. *Journal of Educational Psychology, 92,* 442-448.

Segall, M. H. (1988). Cultural roots of aggressive behavior. In M. H. Bond (Ed.), *The cross-cultural challenge to social psychology.* Newbury Park, CA: Sage.

Segall, M. H., Campbell, D. T., & Herskovitz, M. J. (1966). *Influence of culture on visual perception.* New York: Bobbs-Merrill.

Segall, M. H., Dasen, P. R., Berry, J. W., & Poortinga, Y. H. (1990). *Human behavior in global perspective: An introduction to cross-cultural psychology.* New York: Pergamon.

Seger, C. A. (1994). Implicit learning. *Psychological Bulletin, 115,* 163–196.

Seidenberg, M. S. (1997). Language acquisition and use: Learning and applying probabilistic constraints. *Science, 275,* 1599–1603.

Seidenberg, M. S., & Petitto, L. A. (1987). Communication, symbolic communication, and language: Comment on Savage-Rumbaugh, McDonald, Sevcik, Hopkins, & Rupert (1986). *Journal of Experimental Psychology: General, 116,* 279–287.

Seidman, S. N., & Rieder, R. O. (1994). A review of sexual behavior in the United States. *American Journal of Psychiatry, 151,* 330-341.

Seifer, R., Schiller, M., Sameroof, A., et al. (1996). Attachment, maternal sensitivity, and infant temperament during the first year of life. *Developmental Psychology, 32,* 12–25.

Sekuler, R., & Blake, R. (1994). *Perception* (3rd ed.). New York: McGraw-Hill.

Seligman, L. (1975). Skin potential as an indicator of emotion. *Journal of Counseling Psychology, 22,* 489–493.

Seligman, M. E. P. (1971). Phobias and preparedness. *Behavior Therapy, 193,* 323–325.

Seligman, M. E. P. (1995). The effectiveness of psychotherapy: The Consumer Reports study. *American Psychologist, 50,* 965–974.

Selkoe, D. J. (2002). Alzheimer's disease is a synaptic failure. *Science, 298,* 789-791.

Selman, R. L. (1980). *The growth of interpersonal understanding.* New York: Academic Press.

Selye, H. (1936). A syndrome produced by diverse nocuous agents. *Nature, 138,* 32.

Selye, H. (1976). *The stress of life.* New York: McGraw-Hill.

Serpell, L., Treasure, J., Teasdale, J., & Sullivan, V. (1999). Anorexia nervosa: Friend or foe? *International Journal of Eating Disorders, 25,* 177–186.

Serpell, R. (1989). Dimensions endogenes de l'intelligence chez les A-chewa et autres peuples africans. In J. Retschitzky, M. Bossel-Lagos, & P. Dasen (Eds.), *La recherche interculturelle.* Paris: L'Harmattan.

Sethi, S., & Seligman, M. (1993). Optimism and fundamentalism. *Psychological Science, 4,* 256–259.

Sewall, L., & Wooten, B. R. (1991). Stimulus determinants of achromatic constancy. *Journal of the Optical Society of America, 8,* 1794–1809.

Shallice, T., & Warrington, E. K. (1970). Independent functioning of verbal memory stores: A neuropsychological study. *Quarterly Journal of Experimental Psychology, 22,* 261-273.

Shantz, C. U. (1983). Social cognition. In J. H. Flavell & E. M. Markman (Eds.), *Handbook of child psychology: Vol. 3. Cognitive Development.* New York: John Wiley.

Shapley, R. (1995). Parallel neural pathways and visual function. In M. S. Gazzaniga et al. (1995), *The cognitive neurosciences* (pp. 315–324). Cambridge, MA: MIT Press.

Shaver, P., Hazan, C., & Bradshaw, D. (1988). Love as attachment. In R. J. Sterberg & M. L. Barnes, *The psychology of love.* New Haven, CT: Yale University Press.

Shaver, P., Schwartz, J., Kirson, D., & O'Connor, G. (1987). Emotion knowledge: Further exploration of a prototype approach. *Journal of Personality and Social Psychology, 52,* 1061–1086.

Shaver, P. R., Collins, N., & Clark, C. L. (1996). Attachment styles and internal working models of self and relationship partners. In G. O. Fletcher, J. Fitness, et al. (Eds.), *Knowledge structures in close relationships: A social psychological approach* (pp. 25–61). Mahwah, NJ: Lawrence Erlbaum.

Shaywitz, B. A., Shaywitz, S. E., Pugh, K. R., Constable, R. T., et al. (1995). Sex differences in the functional organization of the brain for language. *Nature, 373,* 607–609.

Shaywitz, S., Shaywitz, B., Pugh, K. R., Fulbright, R. K., Constable, R. T., Mencl, W. E., et al. (1998). Functional disruption in the organization of the brain for reading in dyslexia. *Proceedings of the National Academy of Science, U.S.A., 95,* 2636–2641.

Shea, M., Glass, D., Pilkonis, P., Watkins, J., & Docherty, J. (1987). Frequency and implications of personality disorders in a sample of depressed outpatients. *Journal of Personality Disorders, 1,* 27–42.

Shea, M. T., Elkin, I., Imber, S., & Sotsky, S. (1992). Course of depressive symptoms over follow-up: Findings from the National Institute of Mental Health Treatment of Depression Collaborative Research Program. *Archives of General Psychiatry, 49,* 782–787.

Shedler, J., & Block, J. (1990). Adolescent drug use and psychological health: A longitudinal inquiry. *American Psychologist, 45,* 612–630.

Shedler, J., Mayman, M., & Manis, M. (1993). The illusion of mental health. *American Psychologist, 48,* 1117–1131.

Sheehy, G. (1976). *Passages.* New York: E. P. Dutton.

Shefler, G., Dasberg, H., & Ben-Shakhar, G. (1995). A randomized controlled outcome and follow-up study of Mann's time-limited psychotherapy. *Journal of Consulting and Clinical Psychology, 63,* 585–593.

Sheline, Y. I. (2003). *American Journal of Psychiatry* (in press).

Sheline, Y. I, Mittler, B. L., & Mintum, M. A. (2002). The hippocampus and depression. *European Psychiatry, 17,* 300s–305s.

Sheperis, C. J., Renfro-Michel, E. L., & Doggett, R. A. (2003). In-home treatment of reactive attachment disorder in a therapeutic foster care system: A case example. *Journal of Mental Health Counseling, 25,* 76–88.

Shepher, J. (1978). Reflections on the origins of human pair-bonds. *International Journal of Social and Biological Structures, 1,* 253–264.

Sher, K. J., Bartholow, B. D., & Nanda, S. (2001). Short- and long-term effects of fraternity and sorority membership on heavy drinking: A social norms perspective. *Psychology of Addictive Behaviors, 15,* 42–51.

Sherif, M., et al. (1961). *Intergroup conflict and cooperation: The Robber's Cave experiment.* Norman: University of Oklahoma Press.

Sherif, M., & Sherif, C. W. (1979). Research on intergroup relations. In W. G. Austin & S. Worchel (Eds.), *The social psychology of intergroup relations.* Monterey, CA: Brooks/Cole.

Sherman, R. L. (1994). The rock ceiling: A study of African-American women managers' experiences and perceptions of barriers restricting advancement in the corporation. Dissertation Abstracts International Section A. *Humanities & Social Sciences, 54,* 3226.

Sherwin, B. (1993). *Menopause myths and realities.* Washington, DC: American Psychiatric Press.

Shettleworth, S. J. (1988). Foraging as operant behavior and operant behavior as foraging: What have we learned? In G. H. Bower et al. (Eds.), *The psychology of learning and motivation: Advances in research and theory* (Vol. 22, pp. 1–49). San Diego, CA: Academic Press.

Shevrin, H., Bond, J., Brakel, L., Hertel, R., & Williams, W. J. (1996). *Conscious and unconscious processes: Psychodynamic, cognitive, and neurophysiological convergences.* New York: Guilford Press.

Shields, J. (1962). *Monozygotic twins brought up apart and brought together.* London: Oxford University Press.

Shimamura, A. P. (1995). Memory and frontal lobe function. In M. S. Gazzaniga, et al. (Eds.), *The cognitive neurosciences.* (pp. 803–813). Cambridge, MA: MIT Press.

Shimizu, H., & LeVine, R. A. (Eds.). (2001). *Japanese frames of mind: Cultural perspectives on human development.* New York: Cambridge University Press.

Shiner, R. L. (2000). Linking childhood personality with adaptation: Evidence for continuity and change across time in late adolescence. *Journal of Personality and Social Psychology, 78,* 310-325.

Shultz, T. R., & Lepper, M. R. (1995). Cognitive dissonance reduction as constraint satisfaction. *Psychological Review, 103,* 219–240.

Shweder, R. A. (1980). Scientific thought and social cognition. In W. A. Collins (Ed.), *Development of cognition, affect, and social relations: Minnesota Symposium on Child Development* (Vol. 13). Hillsdale, NJ: Lawrence Erlbaum.

Shweder, R. A. (1999). Why cultural psychology? *Ethos, 27,* 62–73.

Shweder, R. A., & Bourne, E. J. (1982). Does the concept of the person vary cross-culturally? In A. J. Marsella & G. M. White (Eds.), *Cultural conceptions of mental health and therapy.* Boston, MA: D. Reidel.

Siegel, A., Roeling, T. A. P., Gregg, T. R., & Kruk, M. R. (1999). Neuropharmacology of brain-stimulation-evoked aggression. *Neuroscience and Biobehavioral Reviews, 23,* 359–389.

Siegel, R. K. (1990). *Intoxication.* New York: Pocket Books.

Siegel, S. (1984). Pavlonian conditioning and heroin overdose: Reports by overdose victims. *Bulletin of the Psychonomic Society, 22,* 428–430.

Siegfried, Z., Berry, E. M., Hao, S., & Avraham, Y. (2003). Animal models in the investigation of anorexia. *Physiology and Behavior. 79,* 39–45.

Siegler, I. C., Bastian, L. A., Steffens, D. C., Bosworth, H. B., & Costa, P. T. (2002). Behavioral medicine and aging. *Journal of Consulting and Clinical Psychology, 70,* 843–851.

Siegler, R. S. (1991). *Children's thinking* (2nd ed.). Englewood Cliffs, NJ: Prentice-Hall.

Siegler, R. S. (1996). *Emerging minds: The process of change in children's thinking.* New York,: Oxford University Press.

Siegler, R. S. (2000). Unconscious insights. *Current Direction in Psychological Science, 9,* 79–83.

Siegler, R. S., & Ellis, S. (1996). Piaget on childhood. *Psychological Science, 7,* 211–215.

Siegman, A. W. (1994). From Type A to hostility to anger: Reflections on the history of coronary-prone behavior. In A. W. Siegman, T. W. Smith, et al. (Eds.). *Anger, hostility, and the heart* (pp. 1–21). Hillsdale, NJ: Lawrence Erlbaum.

Siever, L. J., & Davis, K. L. (1991). A psychobiological perspective on the personality disorders. *American Journal of Psychiatry, 148,* 1647-1658.

Sifneos, P. (1973). The prevalence of alexithymic characteristics in psychosomatic patients. *Psychotherapy and Psychosomatics, 22,* 255–262.

Sifneos, P. (1987). *Short-term dynamic psychotherapy: Evaluation and technique* (2nd ed.). New York: Plenum Press.

Sigall, H., Page, R., & Brown, A. C. (1971). Effort expenditure as a function of evaluation and evaluator attractiveness. *Representative Research in Social Psychology, 2,* 19–25.

Sillars, A. L., & Zietlow, P. (1993). Investigations of marital communication and lifespan development. In N. Coupland & J. Nussbaum (Eds.), *Discourse and lifespan identity: Language and language behaviors* (Vol. 4, pp. 237–261). Newbury Park, CA: Sage.

Simmons, L. W. (1990). Pheromonal cues for the recognition of kin by female field crickets, *Gryllus bimaculatus. Animal Behaviour, 40,* 192–195.

Simmons, R. (2002). *Odd girl out.* New York: Harcourt.

Simon, D., & Holyoak, K. J. (2002). Structural dynamics of cognition: From consistency theories to constraint satisfaction. *Personality and Social Psychology Review, 6,* 283–294.

Simon, H. (1990). Invariants of human behavior. *Annual Review of Psychology, 41,* 1–19.

Simon, H. A. (1978). Information-processing theory of human problem solving. In W. K. Estes (Ed.), *Handbook of learning and cognitive processes.* Hillsdale, NJ: Lawrence Erlbaum.

Simonoff, E., Bolton, P., & Rutter, M. (1998). Genetic perspectives on mental retardation. In J. A. Burack, R. M. Hodapp, et al. (Eds.), *Handbook of mental retardation and development* (pp. 41–79). New York: Cambridge University Press.

Simons, H. W., Berkowitz, N. N., & Moyer, R. J. (1970). Similarity, credibility, and attitude change: A review and a theory. *Psychological Bulletin, 73,* 1–16.

Simonton, D. K. (1994). *Greatness: Who makes history and why?* New York: Guilford Press.

Simonton, D. K. (1997). Creative productivity: A predictive and explanatory model of career trajectories and landmarks. *Psychological Review, 104,* 66–89.

Simpson, J., Gangestad, S., & Lerma, M. (1990). Perception of physical attractiveness: Mechanisms involved in the maintenance of romantic relationships. *Journal of Personality and Social Psychology, 59,* 1192–1201.

Singer, J. L. (1990). *Repression and dissociation: Implications for personality theory, psychopathology, and health.* Chicago: University of Chicago Press.

Singer, J. L., & Singer, D. G. (1981). *Television, imagination, and aggression: A study of preschoolers,* Hillsdale, NJ: Lawrence Erlbaum.

Skal, D. J. (1993). *The monster show: A cultural history of horror.* New York: W.W. Norton.

Skeels, H. M. (1966). Adult states of children with contrasting early life experiences: A follow-up study. *Monographs of the Society for Research in Child Development, 31* (serial No. 105), 70.

Skinner, B. F. (1938). *The behavior of organisms.* New York: Appleton-Century-Crofts.

Skinner, B. F. (1948). *Walden Two.* New York: Macmillan.

Skinner, B. F. (1951). How to teach animals. *Scientific American, 185,* 26–29.

Skinner, B. F. (1953). *Science and human behavior.* New York: Macmillan.

Skinner, B. F. (1974). *About behaviorism.* New York: Vintage Books.

Skinner, B. F. (1977). Hernstein and the evolution of behaviorism. *American Psychologist, 32,* 1006–1012.

Skinner, B. F. (1990). Can psychology be a science of mind? *American Psychologist, 45,* 1206–1210.

Skodak, M., & Skeels, H. M. (1949). A final follow- up study of one hundred adopted children. *Journal of Genetic Psychology, 75,* 85–125.

Skoog, G., & Skoog, I. (1999). A 40-year followup of patients with obsessive-compulsive disorder. *Archives of General Psychiatry, 56,* 121– 127.

Skowronski, J. J., & Lawrence, M. A. (2001). A comparative study of the implicit and explicit gender attitudes of children and college students. *Psychology of Women Quartely, 25,* 155–165.

Slaby, R. G., & Frey, K. S. (1976). Development of gender constancy and selective attention to same-sex models. *Child Development, 46,* 849–856.

Slade, L. A., & Rush, M. C. (1991). Achievement motivation and the dynamics of task difficulty choices. *Journal of Personality and Social Psychology, 60,* 165–172.

Sloboda, J. A., Hermelin, B., & O'Connor, N. (1985). An exceptional music memory. *Music Perception, 3,* 155–169.

Slochower, J. (1987). The psychodynamics of obesity: A review. *Psychoanalytic Psychology, 4,* 145–159.

Slutske, W. S., Heath, A. C., Kinwiddie, S. H., Madden, P. A. F., Buholz, K. K., Dunne, M. P., et al. (1997). Modeling genetic and environmental influences in the etiology of conduct disorder: A study of 2682 adult twin pairs. *Journal of Abnormal Psychology, 106,* 266–279.

Smith, C. (1985). Sleep states and learning: A review of the animal literature. *Neuroscience and Biobehavioral Review, 9,* 157–168.

Smith, C., & Lloyd, B. (1978). Maternal behavior and perceived sex of infant: Revisited. *Child Development, 49,* 1263–1265.

Smith, C. A., & Ellsworth, P. (1985). Patterns of cognitive appraisal in emotion. *Journal of Personality and Social Psychology, 48,* 813–838.

Smith, D. E., & Seymour, R. B. (1994). LSD: History and toxicity. *Psychiatric Annals, 24,* 145–147.

Smith, E. E. (1995). Concepts and categorization. In E. E. Smith, D. N. Osherson, et al. (Eds.), *Thinking: An invitation to cognitive science: Vol. 3. An invitation to cognitive science* (2nd ed., pp. 3–33). Cambridge, MA: MIT Press.

Smith, E. E. (2000). Neural bases of human working memory. *Current Directions in Psychological Science, 6,* 45–49.

Smith, E. E., Jonides, J., & Koeppe, R. A. (1996). Dissociating verbal and spatial working memory using PET. *Cerebral Cortex, 6,* 11-20.

Smith, E. E., Patalano, A. L., & Jonides, J. (1998). Alternative strategies of categorization. *Cognition, 65,* 167–196.

Smith, E. R. (1998). Mental representation and memory. In D. T. Gilbert, S. T. Fiske, et al. (Eds.), *The handbook of social psychology,* (Vol. 2, 4th ed., pp. 391–445). Boston, MA: McGraw-Hill.

Smith, J. A., Hauenstein, N. M. A., & Buchanan, L. B. (1996). Goal setting and exercise performance. *Human Performance, 9,* 141–154.

Smith, K. (1984). Drive: In defence of a concept. *Behaviorism, 12,* 71–114.

Smith, L. T. (1991). The search for the world of light: Maori perspectives on research in education. In J. R. Morss & T. Linzey (Eds.), *Growing up: The politics of human learning* (pp. 46-55). Auckland, New Zealand: Longman Paul Limited.

Smith, M. B. (1978). Perspectives on self-hood. *American Psychologist, 33,* 1053–1063.

Smith, M. B. (1988). Can there be a human science? *Symposium of the American Psychological Association,* Atlanta, GA.

Smith, M. B. (1994). Selfhood at risk: Postmodern perils and the perils of postmodernism. *American Psychologist, 49,* 405–411.

Smith, M. L., & Glass, G. V. (1977). Meta-analysis of psychotherapy outcome studies. *American Psychologist, 32,* 752–760.

Smith, M. L., Glass,G. V., & Miller, R. L. (1980). *The benefits of psychotherapy.* Baltimore: John Hopkins University Press.

Smith, M. T., & Layton, R. (1989, Jan/Feb). Still human after all these years. *Sciences, 29,* 10-13.

Smith, M. W., Sharit, J., & Czaja, S. J. (1999). Aging, motor control, and the performance of computer mouse tasks. *Human Factors, 41,* 389–396.

Smith, P. K., & Daglish, L. (1977). Sex differences in parent and infant behavior. *Child Development, 48,* 1250–1254.

Smith, R. E. (2003). The cost of remembering to remember in event-based prospective memory: Investigating the capacity demands of delayed intention performance. *Journal of Experimental Psychology: Learning, Memory, and Cognition, 29,* 347–361.

Smith, R. E., & Swinyard, W. R. (1983). Attitude-behavior consistency: The impact of product trial versus advertising. *Journal of Marketing Research, 20,* 257–267.

Smith, S. L., & Donnerstein, E. (1998). Harmful effects of exposure to media violence: learning of aggression, emotional desensitization, and fear. In R. G. Geen & E. Donnerstein (Eds.), *Human aggression: Theories, research, and implications for social policy* (pp. 167–202). San Diego, CA: Academic Press.

Smith, S. M., & Petty, R. E. (1995). Personality moderators of mood congruency effects on cognition: The role of self-esteem and negative mood regulation. *Journal of Personality and Social Psychology, 68,* 1092–1107.

Smolensky, P. (1988). On the proper treatment of connectionism. *Behavioral and Brain Sciences, 11,* 1-74.

Smotherman, W. P., & Robinson, S. R. (1996). The development of behavior before birth. *Developmental Psychology, 32,* 425–434.

Snyder, D. K., Wills, R. M., & Grady-Fletcher, A. (1991). Long-term effectiveness of behavioral versus insight-oriented marital therapy: A 4-year follow-up study. *Journal of Consulting and Clinical Psychology, 59,* 138–141.

Snyder, M. (1974). Self-monitoring of expressive behavior. *Journal of Personality and Social Psychology, 30,* 526–537.

Snyder, M., & Cantor, N. (1979). Testing hypotheses about other people: The use of historical knowledge. *Journal of Experimental Social Psychology, 15,* 330–342.

Snyder, M., & Ickes, W. (1985). In G. Lindzey and E. Aronson (Eds.), *Handbook of social psychology,* Reading, MA: Addison-Wesley.

Snyder, M., Tanke, E. D., & Berscheid, E. (1977). Social perception and interpersonal behavior: On the self-fulfilling nature of social stereotypes. *Journal of Personality and Social Psychology, 35* 656–666.

Sobal, J., & Stunkard, A. (1989). Socioeconomic status and obesity: A review of the literature. *Psychological Bulletin, 105,* 260–275.

Sobol, R. K. (2003, June 9). The art of listening. *U. S. News & World Report, 134.*

Sohlberg, S., & Strober, M. (1994). Personality in anorexia nervosa: An update and a theoretical integration. *Acta Psychiatrica Scandinavica, 89* (Suppl 37), 16.

Solomon, D. A., Keller, M. B., Leon, A. C., Mueller, T. I, Lavori, P. W., Shea, M. T., Coryell, W., Warshaw, M., Turvey, C., Maser, J. D., & Endicott, J. (2000). Multiple recurrences of major depressive disorder. *American Journal of Psychiatry, 157,* 229–233.

Solomon, D. A., Keller, M. B., Leon, A. C., Mueller, T. I., Shea, M. T., Warshaw, M., et al. (1997). Recovery from major depression: A 10-year prospective follow-up across multiple episodes. *Archives of General Psychiatry, 54,* 1001–1006.

Solomon, L. Z., Solomon, H., & Maiorca, J. (1982). The effects of bystander's anonymity, situational ambiguity, and victim's status on helping. *Journal of Social Psychology, 117,* 285–294.

Solomon, S., Greenberg, J., & Pyszczynski, T. (1991). A terror management theory of social behavior: The psychological functions of self-esteem and cultural worldviews. In L. Berkowitz (Ed.), *Advances in Experimental Social Psychology, 24,* 93–159.

Somer, O., & Goldberg, L. (1999). The structure of Turkish traits—descriptive adjectives. *Journal of Personaity and Social Psychology, 76,* 431–450.

Sommer, R., & Sommer, B. A. (1983). Mystery in Milwaukee: Early intervention, I.Q., and psychology textbooks. *American Psychologist, 38,* 982–985.

Sorensen, P. W. (1996). Biological responsiveness to pheromones provides fundamental and unique insight into olfactory function. *Chemical Senses, 21,* 245–256.

Sorrentino, R. M., & Higgins, E. T. (Eds.). (1996). *Handbook of motivation and cognition:* Vol. 3. *The interpersonal context.* New York: Guilford Press.

Souchay, C., Isingrini, M., & Espagnet, L. (2000). Aging, episodic memory feeling-of-knowing, and frontal functioning. *Neuropsychology, 14,* 299–309.

Spain, D. (Ed.). (1992). *Psychoanalytic anthropology after Freud.* New York: Psyche Press.

Spanos, N. P., Burgess, C. A., Wallace-Capretta, S., & Ouaida, N. (1996). Simulation, surreptitious observation and the modification of hypnotizability: Two tests of the compliance hypothesis. *Contemporary Hypnosis, 13,* 161–176.

Spanos, N. P., Stenstrom, R. J., & Johnston, J. C. (1988). Hypnosis, placebo, and suggestion in the treatment of warts. *Psychosomatic Medicine, 50,* 245–260.

Spearman, C. (1904). General intelligence, objectively determined and measured. *American Journal of Psychology, 15,* 201–293.

Spearman, C. (1927). *The abilities of man: Their nature and measurement.* New York: Macmillan.

Speicher, B. (1994). Family patterns of moral judgement during adolescence and early adulthood. *Developmental Psychology, 30,* 624–632.

Spelke, E., Hirst, W., & Neisser, U. (1976). Skills of divided attention. *Cognition, 4,* 215–230

Spellman, B. A., & Holyoak, K. (1992). If Saddam is Hitler then who is George Bush? Analogical mapping between systems of social roles. *Journal of Personality and Social Psychology, 62,* 913–933.

Spence, A. P. (1989). *Biology of human aging.* Englewood Cliffs, NJ: Prentice-Hall.

Spence, S. A., Liddle, P. F., Stefan, M. D., Hellewell, J. S. E., Sharma, T., Friston, K. J., Hirsch, S. R., Frith, C. D., Murray, R. M., Deakin, J. F. W., & Grasby, P. M. (2000). Functional anatomy of verbal fluency in people with schizophrenia and those at genetic risk: Focal dysfunction and distributed disconnectivity reappraised. *British Journal of Psychiatry, 176,* 52–60.

Spencer, M. B., & Markstrom-Adams, C. (1990). Identity processes among racial and ethnic minority children in America. *Child Development, 61,* 290–310.

Spencer, S. J., Steele, C. M., & Quinn, D. M. (2002). Stereotype threat and women's math performance. In A. E. Hunter & C. Forden (Eds.), *Readings in the psychology of gender: Exploring our differences and commonalities* (pp. 54–68). Needham Heights, MA: Allyn & Bacon.

Sperling, G. (1960). The information available in brief visual presentations. *Psychological Monographs, 74,* 1–29.

Sperry, R. (1984). Consciousness, personal identity and the divided brain. *Neuropsychologia, 22,* 661–673.

Spiegel, D. (1999). Healing words - Emotional expression and disease outcome. *Journal of the American Medical Association, 281,* 1328–1329.

Spiegel, D., & Kato, P. M. (1996). Psychological influences on cancer incidence and progression. *Harvard Review of Psychiatry, 4,* 10–26.

Spillman, L. (1994). The Mermann grid illusion: A tool for studying human perceptive field organization. *Perception, 23,* 691–708.

Spirduso, W., & MacRae, P. (1990). Motor performance and aging. In J. E. Birren & K. W. Schaie (Eds.), *Handbook of the psychology of aging* (3rd ed.). New York: Van Nostrand Reinhold.

Spiro, M. (1965). *Context and meaning in cultural anthropology.* New York: Free Press.

Spitz, R. A. (1945). Hospitalism: An inquiry into the genesis of psychiatry conditions in early childhood. *Psychoanalytic Study of the Child, 1,* 53–74.

Spitzer, R., Williams, J. B. W., Gibbon, M., & First, M. (1992). The structured clinical interview for DSM-III-R (SCID) I: History, rationale, and description. *Archives of General Psychiatry, 49,* 624–629.

Spitzer, R. L. (1985). DSM-III and the politics-science dichotomy syndrome: A response to Thomas E. Schacht's "DSM-III and the politics of truth." *American Psychologist, 40,* 522–526.

Sporer, S., Malpass, R., & Koehnken, G., (Eds.). (1996). *Psychological issues in eyewitness identification.* Mahwah, NJ: Lawrence Erlbaum.

Sprecher, S., & Regan, P. C. (2002). Liking some things (in some people) more than others: Partner preferences in romantic relationships and friendships. *Journal of Social and Personal Relationships, 19,* 463–481.

Squire, L. R. (1986). Mechanisms of memory. *Science, 232,* 1612–1619.

Squire, L. R. (1989). On the course of forgetting in very long-term memory. *Journal of Experimental Psychology: Learning, Memory, and Cognition, 15,* 241–245.

Squire, L. R. (1992). Declarative and nondeclarative memory: Multiple brain systems supporting learning and memory. *Journal of Cognitive Neuroscience, 4,* 232–243.

Squire, L. R. (1995). Memory and brain systems. In R. D. Broadwell, et al. (Eds.), *Neuroscience, memory, and language. Decade of the brain,* (Vol. 1, pp. 59–75). Washington, DC: U.S. Government Printing Office.

Squire, L. R., & Zola-Morgan, S. (1991). The medial temporal lobe memory system. *Science, 253,* 1380–1386.

Srinivas, K., Breedin, S. D., Coslett, H. B., & Saffran, E. M. (1997). Intact perceptual priming in a patient with damage to the anterior inferior temporal lobes. *Journal of Cognitive Neuroscience, 9,* 490–511.

Srivastava, A., Borries, C., & Sommer, V. (1991). Homosexual mounting in free-ranging female langurs *(Presbytis entellus-R). Archives of Sexual Behavior, 20,* 487–512.

Sroufe, L. A., & Waters, E. (1977). Heart rate as a convergent measure in clinical and developmental research. *Merrill Palmer Quarterly, 23,* 3-27.

Staal, W. G., Hulshoff Pol, H. E., Schnack, H. G., Hoogendoorn, M. L. C., Jellema, K., & Kahn, R. S. (2000). Structural brain abnormalities in patients with schizophrenia and their healthy siblings. *American Journal of Psychiatry, 157,* 416–421.

Stacy, A. W. (1997). Memory activation and expectancy as prospective predictors of alcohol and marijuana use. *Journal of Abnormal Psychology, 106,* 61–73.

Stadler, M. A., & Frensch, P. A. (1998). *Handbook of implicit learning.* London: Sage.

Stallings, M., Hewitt, J., Cloninger, C. R., Heath, A. C., & Eaves, L. J. (1996). Genetic and environmental structure of the Tridimensional Personality Questionnaire: Three or four temperament dimensions? *Journal of Personality and Social Psychology, 70,* 127–140.

Stanley, M. A., Beck, J. G., Novy, D. M., Averill, P. M., Swann, A. C., Diefenbach, G. J., & Hopko, D. R. (2003). Cognitive-behavioral treatment of late-life generalized anxiety disorder. *Journal of Consulting and Clinical Psychology, 71,* 309–319.

Stattin, H., & Magnusson, D. (1989). The role of early aggressive behavior in the frequency, seriousness, and types of later crime. *Journal of Consulting and Clinical Psychology, 57,* 710–718.

Steele, C., & Aronson, J. (1995). Stereotype threat and the intellectual test performance of African Americans. *Journal of Personality and Social Psychology, 69,* 797–811.

Steele, C. M. (1988). The psychology of self-affirmation: Sustaining the integrity of the self. In L. Berkowitz (Ed.), *Advances in experimental social psychology, Vol. 21: Social psychological studies of the self: Perspectives and programs.* (pp. 261–302). San Diego, CA: Academic Press.

Steele, C. M. (1997). A threat in the air: How stereotypes shape intellectual identity and performance. *American Psychologist, 52,* 613–629.

Steele, H., Steele, M., & Fonagy, P. (1996). Associations among attachment classifications of mothers, fathers, and their infants. *Child Development, 67,* 541–555.

Stein, B. E., & Meredith, M. A. (1990). Multisensory integration: Neural and behavioral solutions for dealing with stimuli from different sensory modalities. *Annals of the New York Academy of Sciences, 608,* 51–70.

Stein, H. F. (2000). Disposable youth: The 1999 Columbine High School massacre as American metaphor. *Journal for the Psychoanalysis of Culture and Society, 5,* 217–236.

Stein, T. S., & Kwan, J. (1999). Thriving in a busy practice: Physician- patient communication training. *Effective Clinical Practice, 2,* 63–70.

Steinberg, L., Lamborn, S. D., Darling, N., & Mounts, N. S. (1994). Over-time changes in adjustment and competence among adolescents from authoritative, authoritarian, indulgent, and neglectful families. *Child Development, 65*, 754–770.

Steiner, I. D. (1972). *Group processes and productivity.* New York: Academic Press.

Steinhausen, H. C., Willms J., & Spohr, H. L. (1993). Long-term psychopathological and cognitive outcome of children with fetal alcohol syndrome. *Journal of the American Academy of Child and Adolescent Psychiatry, 32*, 990–994.

Stephan, W. G. (1987). The contact hypothesis in intergroup relations. In C. Hendrick (Ed.), *Group processes and intergroup relations. Review of personality and social psychology* (Vol. 9, pp. 13–40). Beverly Hills, CA: Sage.

Stephens, D. W., & Krebs, J. R. (1986). *Foraging theory.* Princeton: Princeton University Press.

Stephens, R. S., Roffman, R. A., & Curtin, L. (2000). Comparison of extended versus brief treatments for marijuana use. *Journal of Consulting and Clinical Psychology, 68*, 898–908.

Stepper, S., & Strack, F. (1993). Proprioceptive determinants of emotional and nonemotional feelings. *Journal of Personality & Social Psychology, 64*, 211–220.

Stern, D. (1985). *The interpersonal world of the infant.* New York: Basic Books.

Stern, K., & McClintock, M. K. (1998). Regulation of ovulation by human pheromones. *Nature, 392*, 177–179.

Sternbeger, R. J., Forsythe, G. B., Hedlund, et al. (2000). *Practical intelligence in everyday life.* New York: Cambridge University Press.

Sternberg, R. J. (Ed.). (1984). *Mechanisms of cognitive development.* New York: Freeman.

Sternberg, R. J. (1985). *Beyond IQ: A triarchic theory of human intelligence.* New York: Cambridge University Press.

Sternberg, R. J. (1987). *The triangle of love: Intimacy, passion, commitment.* New York: Basic Books.

Sternberg, R. J. (1988). Triangulating love. In R. Sternberg & M. L. Barnes (Eds.), *The psychology of love.* New Haven, CT: Yale University Press.

Sternberg, R. J. (1996). Costs of expertise. In K. A. Ericsson (Ed.), *The road to excellence: The acquisition of expert performance in the arts and sciences, sports, and games* (pp. 347–354). Hinsdale, NJ: Lawrence Erlbaum.

Sternberg, R. J. (1997a). *Satisfaction in close relationships.* New York: Guilford Press.

Sternberg, R. J. (1997b). The triarchic theory of intelligence. In D. P. Flanagan, J. L. Genshaft, & P. L. Harrison (Eds.), *Contemporary intellectual assessment: Theories, tests, and issues* (pp. 92–104). New York: Guilford Press.

Sternberg, R. J. (1997c). Construct validation of a triangular love scale. *European Journal of Social Psychology, 27*, 313–335.

Sternberg, R. J. (1998). *Handbook of creativity.* New York: Cambridge University Press.

Sternberg, R. J. (1998a). *Cupid's arrow: The course of love through time.* New York: Cambridge University Press.

Sternberg, R. J. (1998b). *Love is a story: A new theory of relationships.* London: Oxford University Press.

Sternberg, R. J. (1999). Looking back and looking forward on intelligence: Toward a theory of successful intelligence. In M. Bennett, et al. (Eds.), *Developmental psychology: Achievements and prospects.* (pp. 289–308). Philadelphia: Psychology Press/Taylor & Francis.

Sternberg, R. J. (2000a). *Handbook of intelligence.* New York: Cambridge University Press.

Sternberg, R. J. (2000b). The concept of intelligence. In R. J. Sternberg (Ed.), *Handbook of intelligence* (pp. 3–15). New York: Cambridge University Press.

Sternberg, R. J. (2002). Beyond g: The theory of successful intelligence. In R. J. Sternberg & E. L. Grigorenko (Eds.), *The general factor of intelligence: How general is it?* (pp. 447–479). Mahwah, NJ: Lawrence Erlbaum.

Sternberg, R. J., Hojjat, M., & Barnes, J. L. (2001). Empirical tests of aspects of a theory of love as a story. *European Journal of Personality, 15*, 199–218.

Sternberg, R. J., & O'Hara, L. A. (2000). Intelligence and creativity. In R. J. Sternberg (Ed.), *Handbook of intelligence* (pp. 611–630). New York: Cambridge University Press.

Sternberg, S. (1975). Memory scanning: New findings and current controversies. *Quarterly Journal of Experimental Psychology, 27*, 1-32.

Stevens, A., & Coupe, P. (1978). Distortions in judged spacial relations. *Cognitive Psychology, 10*, 422–437.

Stevens, B., & Fields, R. D. (2000). Response of Schwann cells to action potentials in development. *Science, 287*, 2267-2271.

Stevens, C. F. (1979). The neuron. *Scientific American, 241*, 54–65.

Stevens, S. S. (1956). The direct estimation of sensory magnitudes—loudness. *American Journal of Psychology, 69*, 1-25.

Stevens, S. S. (1961). Psychophysics of sensory function. In W. Rosenblith (Ed.), *Sensory communication* (pp. 1–33). Cambridge, MA: MIT Press.

Stevens, S. S. (1975). *Psychophysics: Introduction to its perceptual, neural, and social prospects.* New York: John Wiley.

Stevens, S. S., & Newman, E. B. (1934). The localization of pure tone. *Proceedings of the National Academy of Sciences, U.S.A., 20*, 593–596.

Stevenson-Hinde, J., & Verschueren, K. (2002). Attachment in childhood. In P. K. Smith & C. H. Hart (Eds.), *Blackwell handbook of childhood social development* (pp. 182–204). Malden, MA: Blackwell.

Stewart, D. E., & Robinson, G. E. (1997). *A clinician's guide to menopause.* Washington, DC: Health Press International.

Stewart, W. A. (1969). On the use of Negro dialect in the teaching of reading. In J. C. Baratz & R. W. Schuy (Eds.), *Teaching black children to read* (pp. 156–219). Washington, DC: Center for Applied Linguistics.

Stice, E., & Barrera, M. (1995). A longitudinal examination of the reciprocal relations between perceived parenting and adolescents' substance use and externalizing behaviors. *Developmental Psychology, 31*, 322–334.

Stickgold, R. (1998). Sleep: Off-line memory reprocessing. *Trends in Cognitive Sciences, 2*, 484–492.

Stoff, D. M., Breiling, J., & Maser, J. D. (Eds.), (1997). *Handbook of antisocial behavior.* New York: John Wiley.

Stogdill, R., & Coons, A. (1957). *Leader behavior: Its description and measurement.* Columbus, OH: Ohio State University Bureau of Business Research.

Stone, J. (2002). Battling doubt by avoiding practice: The effects of stereotype threat on self-handicapping in white athletes. *Personality and Social Psychology Bulletin, 28*, 1667–1678.

Stoolmiller, M. (1999). Implications of the restricted range of family environments for estimates of heritability and nonshared environment in behavior-genetic adoption studies. *Psychological Bulletin, 125*, 392–409.

Storms, M. D. (1973). Videotape and the attribution process: Reversing actors' and observers' points of view. *Journal of Personality and Social Psychology, 27*, 165–175.

Stowell, J. R., McGuire, L., Robles, T., Glaser, R., & Kiecolt-Glaser, J. K. (2003). Psychoneuroimmunology. In A. M. Nezu, C. M. Nezu, & P. A. Geller (Eds.) *Handbook of psychology: Health psychology* (Vol. 9, pp. 75–95). Hoboken, NJ: John Wiley & Sons.

Strang, D. J. (1972). Conformity, ability, and self-esteem. *Representative Research in Social Psychology, 3*, 97–103.

Straub, R. O. (2002). *Health psychology.* New York: Worth.

Strauman, T. (1992). Self-guides, autobiographical memory, and anxiety and dysphoria: Toward a cognitive model of vulnerability to emotional distress. *Journal of Abnormal Psychology, 101*, 87–95.

Strauman, T., Lemieux, A., & Coe, C. (1993). Self-discrepancy and natural killer cell activity: Immunological consequences of negative self-evaluation. *Journal of Personality and Social Psychology, 64*, 1042–1052.

Straus, A. S. (1977). Northern Cheyenne ethnopsychology. *Ethos, 5*, 326–357.

Straus, A. S. (1982). The structure of the self in Northern Cheyenne culture. In B. Lee (Ed.), *Psychosocial theories of the self.* New York: Plenum Press.

Straus, M. A., & Kantor, G. K. (1994). Corporal punishment of adolescents by parents: A risk factor in the epidemiology of depression, suicide, alcohol abuse, child abuse, and wife beating. *Adolescence, 29*, 543-561.

Straus, M. A., & Mouradian, V. E. (1998). Impulsive corporal punishment by mothers and antisocial behavior and impulsiveness of children. *Behavioral Sciences and the Law, 16*, 353–374.

Strauss, C., & Quinn, N. (1997). *A cognitive theory of cultural meaning.* New York: Cambridge University Press.

Strauss, D. H., Spitzer, R. L., & Muskin, P. R. (1990). Maladaptive denial of physical illness: A proposal for DSM-IV. *American Journal of Psychiatry, 147*, 1168–1172.

Strauss, J., Carpenter, W. T., & Bartko, J. (1974). The diagnosis and understanding of schizophrenia, III: Speculations on the processes that underlie schizophrenic symptoms and signs. *Schizophrenia Bulletin, 1,* 61–69.

Strauss, J., & Ryan, R. M. (1987). Autonomy disturbances in subtypes of anorexia nervosa. *Journal of Abnormal Psychology, 96,* 254–258.

Strayer, J. (1993). Children's concordant emotions and cognitions in response to observed emotions. *Child Development, 64,* 188–201.

Strayer, J., & Roberts, W. (1997). Facial and verbal measures of children's emotions and empathy. *International Journal of Behavioral Development, 20,* 627–649.

Streissguth, A., Barr, H., Johnson, M. D., & Kirchner, G. (1985). Attention and distraction at age 7 years related to maternal drinking during pregnancy. *Alcoholism: Clinical and experimental research, 9,* 195.

Streissguth, A., Sampson, P., & Barr, H. (1989). Neurobehavioral dose-response effects of prenatal alcohol exposure in humans from infancy to adulthood. *Annals of the New York Academy of Sciences, 562,* 145–158.

Stricker, G. (1996). Empirically validated treatment, psychotherapy manuals, and psychotherapy integration. *Journal of Psychotherapy Integration, 6,* 217–226.

Stricker, G., & Healey, B. J. (1990). Projective assessment of object relations: A review of the empirical literature. *Psychological Assessment, 2,* 219–230.

Striegel-Moore, R. H., Dohm, F. A., Kraemer, H. C., Taylor, C. B., Daniels, S., Crawford, P. B., & Schreiber, G. B. (2003). Eating disorders in White and Black women. *American Journal of Psychiatry, 160,* 1326–1331.

Striegel-Moore, R. H., Silberstein, L. R., & Rodin, J. (1986). Toward an understanding of risk factors for bulimia. *American Psychologist, 41,* 246–263.

Strober, M., Freeman, R., Lampert, C., Diamond, J., & Kaye, W. (2000). Controlled family study of anorexia nervosa and bulimia nervosa: Evidence of shared liability and transmission of partial syndromes. *American Journal of Psychiatry, 157,* 393–401.

Stromme, P., & Magnus, P. (2000). Correlations between socioeconomic status, IQ and aetiology in mental retardation: A population-based study of Norwegian children. *Social Psychiatry and Psychiatric Epidemiology, 35,* 12–18.

Stromswold, K. (1995). The cognitive and neural bases of language acquisition. In M. S. Gazzaniga (Ed.), *The cognitive neurosciences.* (pp. 855–870). Cambridge, MA: MIT Press.

Stroud, L. R., Salovey, P., & Epel, E. S. (2002). Sex differences in stress responses: Social rejection versus achievement stress. *Biological Psychiatry, 52,* 318–327.

Strough, J., & Marie-Covatto, A. (2002). Context and age differences in same- and other-gender peer preferences. *Social Development, 11,* 346–361.

Strupp, H., & Binder, J. L. (1984). *Psychotherapy in a new key: A guide to time-limited dynamic psychotherapy.* New York: Basic Books.

Stucke, T. S., & Sporer, S. L. (2002). When a grandiose self-image is threatened: Narcissism and self-concept clarity as predictors of negative emotions and aggression following ego threat. *Journal of Personality, 70,* 509–532.

Stumpf, H. (1993). The factor structure of the Personality Research Form: A cross-national evaluation. *Journal of Personality, 61,* 1–26.

Stunkard, A. J., Harris, J. R., Pedersen, N. L., & McClearn, G. E. (1990). The body mass index of twins who have been reared apart. *New England Journal of Medicine, 322,* 1483–1487.

Stuss, D., Picton, T. W., & Alexander, M. P. (2001). Consciousness, self-awareness, and the frontal lobes. In S. P. Salloway & P. F. Malloy (Eds.), *The frontal lobes and neuropsychiatric illness* (pp. 101-109). Washington, DC: American Psychiatric Publishing.

Suarez-Orozco, M., Spindler, G., & Spindler, L. (1994). *The making of psychological anthropology II.* Fort Worth, TX: Harcourt Brace Jovanovich.

Suedfeld, P., & Granatstein, J. L. (1995). Leader complexity in personal and professional crises: Concurrent and retrospective information processing. *Political Psychology, 16,* 509–544.

Suedfeld, P., & Pennebaker, J. W. (1997). Health outcomes and cognitive aspects of recalled negative life events. *Psychosomatic Medicine, 59,* 172–177.

Sullivan, H. S. (1953). *The interpersonal theory of psychiatry.* New York: W.W. Norton.

Suls, J., David, J. P., & Harvey, J. H. (1996). Personality and coping: Three generations of research. *Journal of Personality, 64,* 711–735.

Suls, J., Green, P., & Hillis, S. (1998). Emotional reactivity to everyday problems, affective inertia, and neuroticism. *Personality & Social Psychology Bulletin, 24,* 127–136.

Suomi, S. J. (1999). Behavioral inhibition and impulsive aggressiveness: Insights from studies with rhesus monkeys. In L. Balter & C. S. Tamis-LeMonda (Eds.), *Child psychology: A handbook of contemporary issues.* (pp. 510–525). Philadelphia: Psychology Press/Taylor & Francis.

Suomi, S. J. (2000). A biobehavioral perspective on developmental psychopathology: Excessive aggression and serotonergic dysfunction in monkeys. In A. J. Sameroff & M. Lewis (Eds.), *Handbook of developmental psychopathology* (2nd Ed., pp. 237–256) New York: Kluwer Academic/ Plenum Publishers.

Super, C. M. (1981). Cross-cultural research on infancy. In H. C.Triandis & A. Heron (Ed.), *Handbook of cross-cultural psychology: Vol. 4. Developmental psychology.* Boston, MA: Allyn & Bacon.

Super, C. M., & Harkness, S. (1980). *Anthropological perspectives on child development.* San Francisco: Jossey-Bass.

Susser, E., Neugebauer, R., Hoek, H. W., Brown, A. S., Lin, S., Labovitz, D., & Gorman, J. M. (1996). Schizophrenia after prenatal famine further evidence. *Archives of General Psychiatry, 53,* 25–31.

Sutker, P., Winstead, D., Galina, Z., & Allai, A. (1991). Cognitive deficits and psychopathology among former prisoners of war and combat veterans of the Korean conflict. *American Journal of Psychiatry, 148,* 67–72.

Sutton, S. K., & Davidson, R. J. (1997). Prefrontal brain asymmetry: A biological substrate of the behavioral approach and inhibition systems. *Psychological Science, 8,* 204–210.

Sutton, S. R. (1989). Smoking attitudes and behavior: Applications of Fishbein and Ajzen's theory of reasoned action to predicting and understanding smoking decisions. In T. Ney & A. Gale (Eds.), *Smoking and human behavior* (pp. 289–312). Chichester, England: Wiley.

Swain, I., Zelano, P., & Clifton, R. K. (1993). Newborn infants'memory for speech sounds retained over 24 hours. *Developmental Psychology, 29,* 312–323.

Swain, S. A., Polkey, C. E., Bullock, P., & Morris, R. G. (1998). Recognition memory and memory for order in script-based stories following frontal lobe excisions. *Cortex, 34,* 25–45.

Swan, G. E., Hudmon, K. S., & Khroyan, T. V. (2003). Tobacco dependence. In A. M. Nezu, C. M. Nezu, & P. A. Geller (Eds.), *Handbook of psychology: Health psychology* (Vol. 9, pp. 147–168). Hoboken, NJ: John Wiley & Sons.

Swann, W. (1990). To be adored or to be known: The interplay of self-enhancement and selfverification. In R. M. Sorrentino & E. T. Higgins (Eds.), *Handbook of motivation and cognition.* (Vol. 2, pp. 408–448). New York: Guilford Press.

Swann, W., Griffin, J., Predmore, S., & Gaines, B. (1987). The cognitive-affective crossfire: When self-consistency confronts self-enhancement. *Journal of Personality and Social Psychology, 52,* 881–889.

Swann, W., Stein-Seroussi, A., & Giesler, R. B. (1992a). Why people self-verify. *Journal of Personality and Social Psychology, 62,* 392–401.

Swann, W., Wenzlaff, R., Krull, D. S., & Pelham, B. (1992b). Allure of negative feedback: Self-verification strivings among depressed persons. *Journal of Abnormal Psychology, 101,* 293–306.

Swann, W. B. (1997). The trouble with change: Self-verification and allegiance to the self. *Psychological Science, 8,* 177–180.

Sweet, R. A., Mulsant, B. H., Gupta, B., Rifai, A. H., Pasternak, R. E., McEachran, A., & Zubenko. (1995). Duration of neuroleptic treatment and prevelence of tardive dyskinesia in late life. *Archives of General Psychiatry, 52,* 478–486.

Swets, J. A. (1992). The science of choosing the right decision threshold in high-stakes diagnostics. *American Psychologist, 47,* 522–532.

Swim, J. K., Aikin, K. J., Hall, W. S., & Hunter, B. A. (1995). Sexism and racism: Old-fashioned and modern prejudices. *Journal of Personality and Social Psychology, 68,* 199–214.

Szasz, T. (1974). *The myth of mental illness: Foundations of a theory of personal conduct,* (rev. ed.). New York: Harper & Row.

Szeszko, P. R., Robinson, D., Alvir, J. M. J.,

Bilder, R. M., Lencz, T., Ashtari, M., Wu, H., & Bogerts, B. (1999). Orbital frontal and amygdala volume reductions in obsessive-compulsive disorder. *Archives of General Psychiatry, 56,* 913–919.

Szymusiak, R., Iriye, T., & McGinty, D. (1989). Sleep-walking discharge of neurons in the posterior lateral hypothalamic area of cats. *Brain Research Bulletin, 23,* 111–120.

Tagiuri, R., Blake, R. R. , & Bruner, J. S. (1953). Some determinants of the perception of positive and negative feelings in others. *Journal of Abnormal and Social Psychology, 48,* 585–592.

Tajfel, H. (1981). *Human groups and social categories: Studies in social psychology.* Cambridge: Cambridge University Press.

Tajfel, H. (1982). *Social identity and intergroup relations.* New York: Cambridge University Press.

Tamminga, C., Thaker, G., Buchanon, R., Kirkpatrick, B., Alpha, L., Chase, T., & Carpenter, W. T. (1992). Limbic system abnormalities identified in schizophrenia using positron emission tomography with fluorodeoxyglucose and neocortical alterations with deficit syndrome. *Archives of General Psychiatry, 49,* 522–530.

Tan, C. C. (1991). Occupational health problems among nurses. *Scandinavian Journal of Work, Environment, and Health. 17,* 221–230.

Tanaka, J. W., & Taylor, M. (1991). Object categories and expertise: Is the basic level in the eye of the beholder? *Cognitive Psychology, 23,* 457–482.

Tandberg, E., Larsen, J. P., Aarsland, D., & Cummings, J. L. (1996). The occurrence of depression in Parkinson's disease: A community-based study. *Archives of Neurology, 53,* 175–179.

Tanner, J. E., & Byrne, R. W. (1996). Representation of action through iconic gesture in a captive lowland gorilla. *Current Anthropology, 37,* 162–173.

Tarr, M. J., Buelthoff, H. H., Zabinski, M., & Blanz, V. (1997). To what extent do unique parts influence recognition across changes in viewpoint? *Psychological Science, 8,* 282–289.

Tassinary, L. G., & Cacioppo, J. (1992). Unobservable facial actions and emotion. *Psychological Science, 3,* 28–33.

Tavris, C., & Wade, C. (2001). *Psychology in perspective.* Upper Saddle River, NJ: Prentice-Hall.

Taylor, J. G. (2002). Paying attention to consciousness. *Trends in Cognitive Sciences, 6,* 206–210.

Taylor, G. J., & Taylor, H. L. (1997). Alexithymia. In M. McCallum, and W. E. Piper (Eds.), *Psychological mindedness: A contemporary understanding. The LEA series in personality and clinical psychology.* (pp. 77–104). Mahwah, NJ: Lawrence Erlbaum.

Taylor, S. (1991). *Health psychology* (2nd ed.). New York: McGraw-Hill.

Taylor, S., & Crocker, J. (1980). Schematic bases of social information processing. In E. T. Higgins, P. Herman, & M. Zanna (Eds.), *Social cognition: The Ontario Symposium.* Hillsdale, NJ: Lawrence Erlbaum.

Taylor, S. E. (2003). *Health psychology* (5th ed.). New York: McGraw-Hill.

Taylor, S. E., & Armor, D. A. (1996). Positive illusions and coping with adversity. *Journal of Personality, 64,* 873–898.

Taylor, S. E., & Brown, J. D. (1988). Illusion and well-being: A social psychological perspective on mental health. *Psychological Bulletin, 103,* 193–210.

Taylor, S. E., Kemeny, M. E., Reed, G. M., Bower, J. E., & Gruenewald, T. L. (2000). Psychological resources, positive illusions, and health. *American Psychologist, 55,* 99–109.

Taylor, S. E., Pham, L., Rivkin, I., & Armor, D. (1998). Harnessing the imagination: Mental stimulation, self-regulation, and coping. *American Psychologist, 53,* 429–439.

Taylor, S. E., Repetti, R. L., & Seeman, T. (1997). Health psychology: What is an unhealthy environment and how does it get under the skin? *Annual Review of Psychology, 48,* 411–448.

Tedeschi, J. T., Schlenker, B. R., & Bonoma, T. V. (1971). Cognitive dissonance: Private ratiocination or public spectacle? *American Psychologist, 26,* 685–695.

Teitelbaum, P. (1961). Disturbances in feeding and drinking behavior after hypothalamic lesions. *Nebraska Symposium on Motivation, 39–68.*

Tellegen, A., Lykken, D. T., Bouchard, T. J., Jr., Wilcox, K. J., & Rich, S. (1988). Personality similarity in twins reared apart and together. *Journal of Personality and Social Psychology, 54,* 1031–1039.

Terman, L. M. (1916). *The measurement of intelligence.* Boston: Houghton Mifflin.

Terman, L. M. (1925). *Genetic studies of genius: Vol. 1. Mental and physical traits of a thousand gifted children.* Stanford, CA: Stanford University Press.

Terman, L. M., & Oden, M. H. (1947). *Genetic studies of genius: Vol. 4. The gifted child grows up: Twenty-five years' follow-up of a superior group.* Stanford, CA: Stanford University Press.

Terman, L. M., & Oden, M. H. (1959). *Genetic studies of genius: Vol. 5. The gifted group at midlife.* Stanford, CA: Stanford University Press.

Terman, M., Terman, J. S., & Ross, D. C. (1998) A controlled trial of timed bright light and negative air ionization for treatment of winter depression. *Archives of General Psychiatry, 55,* 875–882.

Terrace, H. S. (1979). How Nim Chimsky changed my mind. *Psychology Today, 3,* 65–76.

Terry, D. J., & Hogg, M. A. (2001). Attitudes, behavior, and social context: The role of norms and group membership in social influence processes. In J. P. Forgas & K. D. Williams (Eds.), *Social influence: Direct and indirect processes* (pp. 253–270). Philadelphia: Psychology Press.

Tesser, A. (1993). On the importance of heritability in psychological research: The case of attitudes. *Psychological Review,100,* 129–142.

Tesser, A., Whitaker, D., Martin, L., & Ward, D. (1998). Attitude heritability, attitude change and physiological responsivity. *Personality and Individual Differences, 24,* 89-96.

Tetlock, P., & Levi, A. (1982). Attributional bias: On the inconclusiveness of the cognitive-motivation debate. *Journal of Experimental Social Psychology, 18,* 68–88.

Tetlock, P. E. (1989). Structure and function in political belief systems. In A. R. Pratkanis, S. J. Breckler, et al. (Eds.), *Attitude structure and function. The third Ohio State University volume on attitudes and persuasion* (pp. 129–151). Hillsdale, NJ: Lawrence Erlbaum.

Thase, M., Simons, A. D., Cahalane, J., McGeary, J., & Harden, T. (1991). Severity of depression and response to cognitive behavior therapy. *American Journal of Psychiatry, 148,* 784–789.

Thase, M. E. (2000). Relapse and recurrence of depression: An updated practical approach for prevention. In K. J. Palmer (Ed.), *Drug treatment issues in depression.* (pp. 35–52). Kwai Chung, Hong Kong: Adis International Publications.

Thase, M. E., & Kupfer, D. J. (1996). Recent developments in the pharmacotherapy of mood disorders. *Journal of Consulting & Clinical Psychology, 64,* 646–659.

Thelen, E. (1995). Motor development: A new synthesis. *American Psychologist, 50,* 79–95.

Thelen, E., & Smith, L. B. (1994). *A dynamic systems approach to the development of cognition and action.* Cambridge University: The MIT Press.

Thigpen, C. H., & Cleckley, H. (1954). *The three faces of Eve.* Kingsport, TN: Kingsport Press.

Thomas, D. G., & Lykins, M. S. (1995). Event-related potential measures of 24-hour retention in 5-month-old infants. *Developmental Psychology, 31,* 946–957.

Thompson, D. A., & Campbell, R. G. (1977). Hunger in humans induced by 2-deoxy-D-glucose: Clucoprivic control of taste preference and food intake. *Science, 198,* 1065–1068.

Thompson, V. A., & Paivio, A. (1994). Memory for pictures and sounds: Independence of auditory and visual codes. *Canadian Journal of Experimental Psychology, 48,* 380–398.

Thompson, V. A., Striemer, C. L., Reikoff, R., Gunter, R. W., & Cambell, J. I. D. (2003). Syllogistic reasoning time: Disconfirmation disconfirmed. *Psychonomic Bulletin & Review, 10,* 184–189.

Thorndike, E. L. (1898). Animal intelligence: An experimental study of the associative processes in animals. *Psychological Review Monograph Supplement, 2* (Whole No. 8).

Thorndike, E. L. (1911). *Animal intelligence: Experimental studies.* New York: Macmillan.

Thurstone, L. L. (1938). Primary mental abilities. *Psychometric Monographs* (Vol. 1). Chicago: Chicago University Press.

Thyer, B. A. (1980). Prolonged in vivo exposure therapy with a 70-year-old woman. *Journal of Behavior Therapy and Experimental Psychiatry, 11.*

Tienari, P. (1991). Interaction between genetic vulnerability and family environment: The Finnish adoptive family study of schizophrenia. *Acta Psychiatrica Scandinavica, 84,* 460–465.

Timberlake, W., Farmer, D., & Valeri, A. (1991). Reinforcement of applied settings: Figuring out ahead of time what will work. *Psychological Bulletin, 110,* 379–391.

Tinbergen, N. (1951). *The study of instinct.* Oxford: Clarendon Press.

Titone, D. A. (2002). Memories bound: The neuroscience of dreams. *Trends in Cognitive Sciences, 6,* 4–5.

Tizard, B., & Hodges, J. (1978). The effects of early institutional rearing on the development of eight-year old children. *Journal of Child Psychology and Psychiatry, 19,* 99–108.

Tolliver, L. M. (1983). Social and mental health needs of the aged. *American Psychologist, 38,* 316–318.

Tolman, E. C. (1948). Cognitive maps in rats and men. *Psychological Review, 55,* 189–208.

Tolman, E. C., & Honzik, C. H. (1930). Insight in rats. *University of California Publications in Psychology, 4,* 215–232.

Tomarken, A. J., Davidson, R. J., Wheeler, R. E., & Doss, R. C. (1992). Individual differences in anterior brain asymmetry and fundamental dimensions of emotion. *Journal of Personality & Social Psychology, 62,* 676–687.

Tomkins, S. S. (1962). *Affect, imagery, consciousness: Vol. 1. The positive affects.* New York: Springer.

Tomkins, S. S. (1980). Affect as amplification: Some modifications in theory. In R. Plutchik & H. Kellerman (Eds.), *Emotion: Theory, research, and experience: Vol. I. Theories of emotion.* New York: Academic Press.

Tomkins, S. S. (1986). Script theory. In J. Aronoff, A. I. Radin, & R. Zucker (Eds.), *The emergence of personality* (pp. 147–216). New York: Springer.

Tomlinson-Keasey, C., & Little, T. D. (1990). Predicting educational attainment, occupational achievement, intellectual skill, and personal adjustment among gifted men and women. *Journal of Educational Psychology, 82,* 442–455.

Tonigan, J. S., Miller, W. R., & Connors, G. J. (2000). Project MATCH client impressions about Alcoholics Anonymous: Measurement issues and relationship to treatment outcome. *Alcoholism Treatment Quarterly, 18,* 25–41.

Tooby, J., & Cosmides, L. (1992). The psychological foundations of culture. In J. H. Barkow, L. Cosmides, & J. Tooby (Eds.), *The adapted mind: Evolutionary psychology and the generation of culture* (pp. 19–136). New York: Oxford University Press.

Tootell, R. B. H., Reppas, J. B., Dale, A. M., & Look, R. B. (1995a). Visual motion aftereffect in human cortical area MT revealed by functional magnetic resonance imaging. *Nature, 375,* 139–141.

Tootell, R. B. H., Reppas, J. B., Kwong, K. K., & Malach, R. (1995b). Functional analysis of human MT and related visual cortical area using magnetic resonance imaging. *Journal of Neuroscience, 15,* 3215–3230.

Tootell, R. B. H., Silverman, M. S., Switkes, E., & De Valois, R. L. (1982). Deoxyglucose analysis of retinotopic organization in primate striate cortex. *Science, 218,* 902–904.

Toppino, T. C., & Schneider, M. A. (1999). The mix-up regarding mixed and unmixed lists in spacing-effect research. *Journal of Experimental Psychology: Learning, Memory, & Cognition, 25,* 1071–1076.

Torrey, E. F. (1986). *Witchdoctors and psychiatrists: The common roots of psychotherapy and its future.* New York: Jason Aronson.

Traiwick, M. (1990). The ideology of love in a Tamil family. In O. M. Lynch (Ed.), *Divine passions: The social construction of emotion in India.* Berkeley: University of California Press.

Triandis, H. (Ed.). (1980). *Handbook of cross-cultural psychology* (6 vols.). Boston, MA: Allyn & Bacon.

Triandis, H. (1989). The self and social behavior in differing cultural contexts. *Psychological Bulletin, 96,* 506–520.

Triandis, H. (1994). *Culture and social behavior.* New York: McGraw-Hill.

Triesman, A. (1986). Properties, parts and objects. In K. Boff, L. Kaufman, & J. Thomas (Eds.), *Handbook of perception and human performance* (Vol. 2, pp. 3501–3570). New York: John Wiley.

Triplett, N. (1898). The dynamogenic factors in pacemaking and competition. *American Journal of Psychology, 9,* 507–533.

Trivers, R. (1972). Parental investment and sexual selection. In B. Campbell (Ed.), *Sexual selection and the descent of man: 1871–1971* (pp. 136–179). Chicago: Aldine.

Trivers, R. L. (1971). The evolution of reciprocal altruism. *Quarterly Review of Biology, 46,* 35–57.

Tronick, E., Morelli, G., & Ivey, P. (1992). The Efe forager infant and toddler's pattern of social relationships: Multiple and simultaneous. *Developmental Psychologist, 28,* 568–577.

Trope, Y., & Liberman, A. (1996). Social hypothesis testing: Cognitive and motivational mechanisms. In E. T. Higgins, W. Kruglanski, et al. (Eds.), *Social psychology: Handbook of basic principles* (pp. 239–270). New York: Guilford Press.

Tsuang, M. T., Lyons, M. J., Meyer, J. M., Doyle, T., Eisen, S. A., Goldberg, J., True, W., Lin, N., Toomey, R., & Eaves, L. (1998). Co-occurrence of abuse of different drugs in men: The role of drug-specific and shared vulnerabilities. *Archives of General Psychiatry, 55,* 967–972.

Tuckey, M. R., & Brewer, N. (2003). The influence of schemas, stimulus ambiguity, and interview schedule on eyewitness memory over time. *Journal of Experimental Psychology, 9,* 101–118.

Tuddenham, R. D. (1962). The nature & measurement of intelligence. In L. Postman (Ed.), *Psychology in the making: Histories of selected research problems* (pp. 469–525). New York: Alfred A. Knopf.

Tulving, E. (1972). Episodic and semantic memory. In E. Tulving and W. Donaldson (Eds.), *Organization of memory* (pp. 381–403). New York: Academic Press.

Tulving, E. (1987). Multiple memory systems and consciousness. *Human Neurobiology, 6*(2), 67–80.

Tulving, E., Schachter, D. L., & Stark, H. A. (1982). Priming effects in word-fragment completion are independent of recognition memory. *Journal of Experimental Psychology: Learning, Memory, and Cognition, 8,* 336-342.

Tulving, E., & Thomson, D. M. (1973). Encoding specificity and retrieval processes in episodic memory. *Psychological Review, 80,* 359–380.

Turiel, E. (1998). The development of morality. In W. Damon (Ed.), *Handbook of child psychology: Vol. 3. Social, emotional, and personality development* (N. Eisenberg, Vol. Ed.) (pp. 863–932). New York: John Wiley & Sons.

Turkheimer, E. (1991). Individual and group differences in adoption studies of IQ. *Psychological Bulletin, 110,* 392–405.

Turner, S. M., Beidel, D. C., Long, P. J., & Greenhouse, J. (1992b). Reduction of fear in social phobics: An examination of extinction patterns. *Behavior Therapy, 23,* 389–403.

Turner, V. (1969). *The ritual process.* Chicago: Aldine.

Turner, V. W. (1967). *A forest of symbols: Aspects of Ndembu ritual.* Ithaca, NY: Cornell University Press.

Tversky, A. (1977). Features of similarity. *Psychological Review, 84,* 327–352.

Tversky, A., & Kahneman, D. (1973). Availability: A heuristic for judging frequency and probability. *Cognitive Psychology, 5,* 207–232.

Tversky, A., & Kahneman, D. (1974). Judgment under uncertainty: Heuristics and biases. *Science, 185,* 1124–1131.

Tversky, A., & Kahneman, D. (1981). Extensional vs. intuitive reasoning: The conjunction fallacy in probability judgment. *Psychological Review, 90,* 293–315.

Udry, J. R., Billy, J. O. G., Morris, N. M., Groff, T. R., & Raj, J. H. (1985). Serum androgenic hormones motivate sexual behavior in adolescent boys. *Fertility and Sterility, 43,* 90–94.

Ullman, S. (1989). Aligning pictorial descriptions: An approach to object recognition. *Cognition, 32,* 193–254.

Ullman, S. (1995). The visual analysis of shape and form. In M. S. Gazzaniga, et al. (Eds.), *The cognitive neurosciences.* (pp. 339–350). Cambridge, MA: MIT Press.

Ulrich, R. E. (1991). Animal rights, animal wrongs, and the question of balance. *Psychological Science, 2,* 197–201.

Ulrich, R. S. (1984). View through a window may influence recovery from surgery. *Science, 224,* 420–421.

Unger, R. K. (1979). *Female and male: Psychological perspectives.* New York: Harper & Row.

Ungerleider, L. G., & Haxby, J. V. (1994). "What" and "where" in the human brain. *Current Opinion in Neurobiology, 4,* 157–165.

U.S. Bureau of the Census. (1998a). *Current Population Reports, P23-194, Population Profile of the United States: 1997.* Washington, DC: U.S. Government Printing Office.

U.S. Bureau of the Census. (1998b). *Statistical Abstract of the United States.* Washington, DC: U.S. Census Bureau.

U.S. Bureau of the Census. (1999). *Statistical Abstracts of the United States: 2001.* Retrieved 6-12-2003 from http://www.census.gov

U.S. Census Bureau. (2002, September). Health insurance coverage: 2001. U.S. Department of Commerce.

U.S. Department of Health and Human Services (1994). *Preventing tobacco use among young people: A report of the Surgeon General.* Atlanta, GA: U.S. Department of Health and Human Services.

U.S. Department of Health and Human Services (2000). *Healthy people 2010: Understanding and improving health.* Washington, DC: Author.

U. S. Department of Health and Human Services. (2001). *National Household Survey on Drug Abuse.* Washington, DC: Author.

Vaillant, C., & Vaillant, L. M. (1998). The role of ego mechanisms of defense in the diagnosis of personality disorders. In J. Barron (Ed.), *Making diagnosis meaningful* (pp. 139–158). Washington, DC: American Psychological Association.

Vaillant, G. (1977). *Adaptation to life.* Boston, MA: Little, Brown.

Vaillant, G. (Ed.). (1992). *Ego mechanisms of defense: A guide for clinicians and researchers.* Washington, DC: American Psychiatric Association Press.

Vaillant, G., & Perry, J. C. (1985). Personality disorders. In H. I. Kaplan & B. J. Sadock (Eds.), *Comprehensive textbook of psychiatry* (4th ed.). Baltimore, MD: Williams & Wilkins.

Vaillant, G., & Vaillant, C. (1990). Natural history of male psychology health: XII. A 45-year study of predictors of successful aging at age 65. *American Journal of Psychiatry, 147,* 31–37.

Vaillant, G. E. (1992). The historical origins and future potential of Sigmund Freud's concept of the mechanisms of defence. *International Review of Psycho-Analysis, 19,* 35–50.

Vaillant, G. E. (1996). A long-term follow-up of male alcohol abuse. *Archives of General Psychiatry, 53,* 243–249.

Vaillant, G. E., & Hiller-Sturmhofel, S. (1996). The natural history of alcoholism. *Alcohol Health and Research World, 20,* 152–153.

Valenstein, E. S. (1986). *Great and desperate cures.* New York: Basic Books.

Valenstein, E. S. (1988). The history of lobotomy: A cautionary tale. *Michigan Quarterly, 27,* 417–437.

Vance, E. B., & Wagner, N. N. (1976). Written descriptions of orgasm: A study of sex differences. *Archives of Sexual Behavior, 5,* 87–98.

van der Staay, F. J., & Blokland, A. (1996). Behavioral differences between outbred Wistar, inbred Fischer 344, Brown Norway, and hybrid Fischer 344 Brown Norway rats. *Physiology & Behavior, 60,* 97–109.

van Duijn, C. M. (1996). Epidemiology of the dementias: Recent developments and new approaches. *Journal of Neurology, Neurosurgery & Psychiatry, 60,* 478–488.

Van Essen, D. C., Anderson, C. H., & Felleman, D. J. (1992). Information processing in the primate visual system: An integrated systems perspective. *Science, 255,* 419–423.

van Ijzendoorn, M. (1995). Adult attachment representations, parental responsiveness, and infant attachment: A meta-analysis on the predictive validity of the Adult Attachment Interview. *Psychological Bulletin, 117,* 387–403.

van Ijzendoorn, M., & Kroonenberg, P. (1988). Cross-cultural patterns of attachment: A meta-analysis of the strange situation. *Child Development, 59,* 147–156.

van Ijzendoorn, M. H., & Bakermans-Kranenburg, M. J. (1996). Attachment representations in mothers, fathers, adolescents, and clinical groups: A meta-analytic search for normative data. *Journal of Consulting & Clinical Psychology, 64,* 8-21.

van Ijzendoorn, M. H., & De Wolf, M. S. (1997). In search of the absent father—Meta-analyses of infant-father attachment: A rejoinder to our discussants. *Child Development, 68,* 604–609.

Van Overwalle, F., & Van Rooy, D. (2001). How one cause discounts or augments another: A connectionist account of causal competition. *Personality and Social Psychology Bulletin, 27,* 1613–1626.

Van Thiel, D. H. (1996). Liver transplantation for alcoholics with terminal liver disease. *Alcohol Health & Research World, 20,* 261–266.

Varia, I., & Rauscher, F. (2002). Treatment of generalized anxiety disorder with citalopram. *International Clinical Psychopharmacology, 17,* 103–107.

Varley, C. K. (1984). Attention deficit disorder (the hyperactivity syndrome): A review of selected issues. *Developmental and Behavioral Pediatrics, 5,* 254–258.

Vasquez, K., Durik, A. M., & Hyde, J. S. (2002). Family and work: Implications of adult attachment styles. *Personality and Social Psychology Bulletin, 28,* 874–886.

Vaughn, B. E., Stevenson-Hinde, J., Waters, E., & Kotsaftis, A. (1992). Attachment security and temperament in infancy and early childhood: Some conceptual clarifications. *Developmental Psychology, 28,* 463–473.

Velez-Blasini, C. J. (1997). A cross-cultural comparison of alcohol expectancies in Puerto Rico and the United States. *Psychology of Addictive Behaviors, 11,* 124–141.

Venables, P. H. (1996). Schizotypy and maternal exposure to influenza and to cold temperature: The Mauritius Study. *Journal of Abnormal Psychology, 105,* 53–60.

Veneziano, R. A., & Rohner, R. P. (1998). Perceived paternal acceptance, paternal involvement, and youths' psychological adjustment in a rural, biracial southern community. *Journal of Marriage & the Family, 60,* 335–343.

Ventis et al. (2001). humor and systematic desensitization.

Vernon, P. A., & Weese, S. E. (1993). Predicting intelligence with multiple speed of information-processing tests. *Personality and Individual Differences, 14,* 413–419.

Verschueren, K., & Marcoen, A. (1999). Representation of self and socioemotional competence in kindergartners: Differential and combined effects of attachment to mother and father. *Child Development, 70,* 183–201.

Vierikko, E., Pulkkinen, L., Kaprio, J., Viken, R., & Rose, R. J. (2003). Sex differences in gentic and environmental effects on aggression. *Aggressive Behavior, 29,* 55–68.

Viinamaeki, H., Koskela, K., & Niskanen, L. (1996). Rapidly declining mental well being during unemployment. *European Journal of Psychiatry, 10,* 215–221.

Viken, R. J., Rose, R. J., Kaprio, J., & Koskenvuo, M. (1994). A developmental genetic analysis of adult personality: Extraversion and neuroticism from 18 to 59 years of age. *Journal of Personality and Social Psychology, 66,* 722–730.

Vinogravdov, S., & Yalom, I. (1989). *Concise guide to group psychotherapy.* Washington, DC: American Psychiatric Press.

Vinter, A., & Perruchet, P. (2000). Implicit learning in children is not related to age evidence from drawing behavior. *Child Development, 71,* 1223–1240.

Vitaro, F., Tremblay, R. E., Kerr, M., Pagani, L., & Bukowski, W. M. (1997). Disruptiveness, friends' characteristics, and delinquency in early adolescence: A test of two competing models of development. *Child Development, 68,* 676–689.

Vogel, G. (2003, April 11). The problem with cloning primates. *Science Now,* p. 1.

Von Senden, M. (1960). *Space and sight.* Public Health transcript. New York: Free Press.

Vormbrock, J. (1993). Attachment theory as applied to wartime and job-related marital separation. *Psychological Bulletin, 114,* 122–144.

Vygotsky, L. (1978). *Mind in society: The development of higher psychological processes,* M. Cole, V. John-Steiner, S. Scribner, & E. Souberman (Eds.). Cambridge, Cambridge University Press.

Wachtel, P. (1977). *Psychoanalysis and behavior therapy: Toward an integration.* New York: Basic Books.

Wachtel, P. (1993). *Therapeutic communication.* New York: Guilford Press.

Wachtel, P. (1997). *Psychoanalysis, behavior therapy, and the relational world.* Washington, DC: American Psychological Association Press.

Wachtel, P. L. (1984). On theory, practice, and the nature of integration. In H. Arkowitz & S. B. Messer (Eds.), *Psychoanalytic therapy and behavior therapy: Is integration possible?* (pp. 31–52). New York: Plenum Press.

Wadden, T. A., Brownell, K. D., & Foster, G. D. (2002a). Obesity: Responding to the global epidemic. *Journal of Consulting and Clinical Psychology, 70,* 510–525.

Wadden, T. A., Womble, L. G., Stunkard, A. J., & Anderson, D. A. (2002b). Psychsocial consequences of obesity and weight loss. In T. A. Wadden & A. J. Stunkard (Eds.), *Handbook of obesity treatment* (pp. 144–169). New York: Guilford Press.

Wagner, A. D., Schacter, D. L., Rotte, M., Koutstaal, Maril, A., Dale, A. M., Rosen, B. R., & Buckner, R. L. (1998). Building memories: Remembering and forgetting of verbal experiences as predicted by brain activity. *Science, 281,* 1188–1191.

Wagner, A. W., & Linehan, M. (1999). Facial expression recognition ability among women with borderline personality disorder: Implications for emotion regulation. *Journal of Personality Disorders, 13*, 329–344.

Wagstaff, G. F. (1984). The enhancement of witness memory by "hypnosis": A review and methodological critique of the experimental literature. *British Journal of Experimental and Clinical Hypnosis, 2*, 3–12.

Wahlbeck, K., Cheine, M., Essali, A., & Adams, C. (1999). Evidence of clozapine's effectiveness in schizophrenia: A systematic review and meta-analysis of randomized trials. *American Journal of Psychiatry, 156*, 990–999.

Wakeling, A. (1996). Epidemiology of anorexia nervosa. *Psychiatry Research, 62*, 3–9.

Walker, E. F., & Diforio, D. (1997). Schizophrenia: A neural diathesis-stress model. *Psychological Review, 104*, 667–685.

Wallace, A. F. C. (1956). Revitalization movements. *American Anthropologist, 58*, 264–281.

Wallace, A. F. C. (1959). Cultural determinants of response to hallucinatory experiences. *Archives of General Psychiatry, 1*, 58–69.

Wallace, B. (1993). Day persons, night persons, and variability in hypnotic susceptibility. *Journal of Personality and Social Psychology, 64*, 827–833.

Wallace, P. (1977). Individual discrimination of humans by odor. *Physiology and Behavior, 19*, 577–579.

Waller, N., Kojetin, B., Bouchard, T., & Lykken, D. (1990). Generic and environmental influences on religious interests, attitudes, and values: A study of twins reared apart and together. *Psychological Science, 1*, 138–142.

Waller, N. G., & Ross, C. A. (1997). The prevalence and biometric structure of pathological dissociation in the general population: Taxometric and behavior genetic findings. *Journal of Abnormal Psychology, 106*, 499–510.

Wallerstein, J. S., & Corbin, S. B. (1999). The child and the vicissitudes of divorce. In R. M. Galatzer-Levy, L. Kraus, et al. (Eds.), *The scientific basis of child custody decisions* (pp. 73–95). New York: John Wiley & Sons.

Wallerstein, R. S. (1988b). One psychoanalysis or many? *International Journal of Psycho-Analysis, 69*, 5–22.

Wallerstein, R. S. (1989). The psychotherapy research project of the Menninger Foundations: An overview. *Journal of Consulting and Clinical Psychology, 57*, 195–205.

Walsh, J. K., & Lindblom, S. S. (1997). Psychophysiology of sleep deprivation and disruption. In M. R. Pressman, W. C. Orr, et al. (Eds.), *Understanding sleep: The evaluation and treatment of sleep disorders. Application and practice in health psychology* (pp. 73–110). Washington, DC: American Psychological Association.

Walster, E., Aronson, V., Abrahams, D., & Rottman, L. (1966). The importance of physical attractiveness in dating behavior. *Journal of Personality and Social Psychology, 4*, 508–516.

Walter, H. J., & Vaughan, R. D. (1993). AIDS risk reduction among a multiethnic sample of urban high school students. *Journal of the American Medical Association, 270*, 725–730.

Walters, J. M., & Gardner, H. (1986). The theory of multiple intelligences: Some issues and answers. In R. J. Sternberg & R. K. Walters (Eds.), *Practical intelligence: Nature and origins of competence in the everyday world.* New York: Cambridge University Press.

Wang, Q., & Leichtman, M. D. (2000). Same beginnings, different stories: A comparison of American and Chinese children's narratives. *Child Development, 71*, 1329–1346.

Warner, L. A., Kessler, R. C., Hughes, M., Anthony, J. C., & Nelson, C. B. (1995). Prevalence and correlates of drug use and dependence in the United States: Results from the national comorbidity survey. *Archives of General Psychiatry, 52*, 219–229.

Warwick, Z. S., Hall, W. G., Pappas, T. N., & Schiffman, S. S. (1993). Taste and smell sensations enhance the satiating effect of both a high-carbohydrate and a high-fat meal in humans. *Physiology and Behavior, 53*, 553–563.

Wason, P. C. (1960). On the failure to eliminate hypotheses in a conceptual task. *Quarterly Journal of Experimental Psychology, 12*, 129–140.

Wason, P. C. (1968). Reasoning about a rule. *Quarterly Journal of Experimental Psychology, 20*, 273–281.

Wasserman, E. A., & Miller, R. R. (1997). What's elementary about associative learning? *Annual Review, 48*, 573–607.

Watanabe, T., Sasaki, Y., Miyauchi, S., et al., (1998). Attention-regulated activity in human primary visual cortex. *Journal of Neurophysiology, 79*, 2218–2221.

Waters, E., Hamilton, C. E., & Weinfield, N. S. (2000a). The stability of attachment security from infancy to adolescence and early adulthood: General introduction. *Child Development, 71*, 678–683.

Waters, E., Merrick, S., Treboux, D., Crowell, J., & Albersheim, L. (2000b). Attachment security in infancy and early adulthood: A twenty-year longitudinal study. *Child Development, 71*, 684–689.

Waters, E. Wippman, J., & Sroufe, J. A. (1979). Attachment, positive affect, and competence in the peer group: Two studies of construct validation. *Child Development, 50*, 821–829.

Watkins, L. R., & Maier, S. F. (2000). The pain of being sick: Implications of immune-to-brain communication for understanding pain. *Annual Review of Psychology, 29*, 57.

Watson, D. (2000). *Mood and temperament.* New York: Guilford Press.

Watson, D., & Clark, L. A. (1992). Affects separable and inseparable: On the hierarchical arrangement of the negative affects. *Journal of Personality and Social Psychology, 62*, 489–505.

Watson, D., & Tellegen, A. (1985). Toward a consensual structure of mood. *Psychological Bulletin, 98*, 219–225.

Watson, J. (1925). *Behaviorism.* New York: W.W. Norton, 1970.

Watson, J., & Rayner, R. (1920). Conditioned emotional reactions. *Journal of Experimental Psychology, 3*, 1–14.

Watson, M. W., & Getz, K. (1990). The relationship between Oedipal behaviors and children's family role concepts. *Merrill-Palmer Quarterly, 36*, 487–505.

Waugh, N. C., & Norman, D. A. (1965). Primary memory. *Psychological Review, 72*, 89-104.

Weale, R. (1982). *Focus on vision.* Cambridge, MA: Harvard University Press.

Webb, W. B., & Cartwright, R. D. (1978). Sleep and dreams. *Annual Review of Psychology, 29*, 223–252.

Wechsler, D. (1939). *Measurement of adult intelligence.* Baltimore: Williams & Wilkins.

Wechsler, D. (1997). *WAIS-III: Administration and scoring manual.* Psychological Corporation.

Wedekind, C., & Milinski, M. (2000). Cooperation through image scoring in humans. *Science, 288*, 850–852.

Wegesin, D. J. (1998). A neuropsychologic profile of homosexual and heterosexual men and women. *Archives of Sexual Behavior, 27*, 91–108.

Wegner, D. (1992). You can't always think what you want: Problems in the suppression of unwanted thoughts. *Advances in Experimental Social Psychologyt, 25*, 193–225.

Wegner, D., Shortt, J., Blake, A. W., & Page, M. S. (1990). The suppression of exciting thoughts. *Journal of Personality and Social Psychology, 58*, 409–418.

Wegner, D. M., & Bargh, J. A. (1998). Control and automaticity in social life. In D. Gilbert, S. T. Fiske, & G. Lindzey (Eds.), *Handbook of social psychology* (4th ed., pp. 446–496). New York: McGraw-Hill.

Wegner, D. M., & Wheatley, T. (1999). Apparent mental causation: Sources of the experience of will. *American Psychologist, 54*, 480–492.

Weinberg, R. A. (1989). Intelligence and IQ: Landmark issues and great debates. *American Psychologist, 44*, 98–104.

Weinberg, R. A., Scarr, S., & Waldman, I. D. (1992). The Minnesota Transracial Adoption Study: A follow-up of IQ test performance at adolescence. *Intelligence, 16*, 117–135.

Weinberger, D. A. (1990). The construct validity of the repressive coping style. In J. L. Singer (Ed.), *Repression and dissociation: Implications for personality, psychopathology and health.* Chicago: University of Chicago Press.

Weinberger, J. (1995). Common factors aren't so common: The common factors dilemma. *Clinical Psychology—Science and Practice, 2*, 45–69.

Weiner, B. (1974). *Achievement motivation and attribution theory.* Morristown, NJ: General Learning Press.

Weiner, H. (1985). The psychobiology and pathophysiology of anxiety and fear. In A. H. Tuma & J. D. Maser (Eds.), *Anxiety and the anxiety disorders* (pp. 333-354). Hillsdale, NJ: Lawrence Erlbaum Associates.

Weiner, M. J. (1980). The effect of incentive and control over outcomes upon intrinsic motivation and performance. *Journal of Social Psychology, 112*, 247–254.

Weiner, R. D., & Coffey, C. E. (1988). Indications for use of electroconvulsive therapy. In A. J. Frances & R. E. Hales (Eds.), *Review of Psychiatry* (Vol. 7). Washington, DC: American Psychiatric Press.

Weinfield, N. S., Sroufe, L. A., & Egeland, B. (2000). Attachment from infancy to early adulthood in a high-risk sample: Continuity, discontinuity, and their correlates. *Child Development, 71,* 695–702.

Weinhardt, L. S., Carey, M. P., Carey, K. B., Maisto, S. A., & Gordon, C. M. (2001). The relation of alcohol use to sexual HIV risk behavior among adults with a severe and persistent mental illness. *Journal of Consulting and Clinical Psychology, 69,* 77–84.

Weinstein, N. D. (1980). Unrealistic optimism about future life events. *Journal of Personality and Social Psychology, 39,* 306–320.

Weinstein, N. D., & Klein, W. M. (1996). Unrealistic optimism: Present and future. *Journal of Social and Clinical Psychology, 15,* 1–8.

Weisberg, P., & Waldrop, P. R. (1972). Fixed-interval work habits of Congress. *Journal of Applied Behavior Analysis, 5,* 93–97.

Weiskrantz, L. (1997). *Consciousness lost and found: A neuropsychological exploration.* England: Oxford University Press.

Weiskrantz, L., Warrington, E., Sanders, M. D., & Marshall, J. (1974). Visual capacity in the hemianopic field following a restricted occipital ablation. *Brain, 97,* 709–728.

Weiss, B., Dodge, K., Bates, J., & Pettit, G. (1992). Some consequences of early harsh discipline: Child aggression and a maladaptive social information processing style. *Child Development, 63,* 1321–1335.

Weiss, G., Hechtman, L., Milroy, T., & Perlman, T. (1985). Psychiatric status of hyperactives as adults: A controlled prospective 15-year follow-up of 63 hyperactive children. *Journal of the American Academy of Child Psychiatry, 24,* 211–220.

Weiss, L. H., & Schwarz, J. C. (1996). The relationship between parenting types and older adolescents' personality, academic achievements, adjustment, and substance use. *Child Development, 67,* 2101–2114.

Weiss, R. S. (1986). Continuities and transformations in social relationships from childhood to adulthood. In W. W. Hartup & Z. Rubin (Eds.), *Relationships and development* (pp. 95–110). Hillsdale, NJ: Lawrence Erlbaum.

Weiss, V. (1992). Major genes of general intelligence. *Personality and Individual Differences, 13,* 1115–1134.

Weisse, C. S. (1992). Depression and immunocompetence: A review of the literature. *Psychological Bulletin, 111,* 475–489.

Weissman, M. M., Bland, R. C., Canino, G. J., Faravelli, C., Greenwald, S., Hwu, H., et al. (1997). The cross-national epidemiology of panic disorder. *Archives of General Psychiatry, 54,* 305–309.

Wentzel, K. R., & Asher, S. R. (1995). The academic lives of neglected, rejected, popular, and controversial children. *Child Development, 66,* 754–763.

Werker, J. F., & Tees, R. C. (1984). Cross-language speech perception: Evidence for perceptual reorganization during the first year of life. *Infant Behavior and Development, 7,* 49–63.

Werner, H. (1948). *Comparative psychology of mental development* (rev. ed.). Chicago: Follett.

Wertenbaker, L. (1981). *The eye: Window to the world.* Washington, DC: U.S. News books.

Wertheimer, M. (1961). Psychomotor coordination of auditory and visual space at birth. *Science, 134,* 1692.

Wertsch, J., & Kanner, B. (1992). A sociocultural approach to intellectual development. In R. Sternberg & C. A. Berg (Eds.), *Intellectual development* (pp. 328–349). New York: Cambridge University Press.

Wesley, F., & Sullivan, E. (1986). *Human growth and development: A psychological approach* (2nd ed.). New York: Human Sciences Press.

West, R. L. (1996). An application of prefrontal cortex function theory to cognitive aging. *Psychological Bulletin, 120,* 272–292.

Westen, D. (1985). *Self and society: Narcissism, collectivism, and the development of morals.* New York: Cambridge University Press.

Westen, D. (1991). Social cognition and object relations. *Psychological Bulletin, 109,* 429–455.

Westen, D. (1992). The cognitive self and the psychoanalytic self: Can we put our selves together? *Psychological Inquiry, 3,* 1–13.

Westen, D. (1994). Toward an integrative model of affect regulation: Applications to social-psychological research. *Journal of Personality, 62,* 641–647.

Westen, D. (1995). A clinical-empirical model of personality: Life after the Mischelian ice age and the Neolithic era. *Journal of Personality, 63,* 495–524.

Westen, D. (1998). The scientific legacy of Sigmund Freud: Toward a psychodynamically informed psychological science. *Psychological Bulletin, 124,* 333–371.

Westen, D. (2000). Integrative psychotherapy: Integrating psychodynamic and cognitive-behavioral theory and technique. In C. R. Snyder & R. E. Ingram (Eds.), *Handbook of psychology change: Psychotherapy processes and practices for the 21st century* (pp. 217-242). New York: John Wiley & Sons.

Westen, D., & Chang, C. (2000). Personality pathology in adolescence: A review. In A. H. Esman, L. T. Flaherty, & Lois T. (Eds.). *Adolescent psychiatry: Developmental and clinical studies, Vol 25. The Annals of the American Society for Adolescent Psychiatry.* (pp. 61–100). Hillsdale, NJ: Analytic Press.

Westen, D., & Feit, A. (1999). All the President's women: Cognitive and emotional constraint satisfaction in ambiguous social cognition. Unpublished manuscript, Boston University.

Westen, D., & Gabbard, G. (1999). Psychoanalytic approaches to personality. In L. Pervin & O. John (Eds.), *Handbook of personality: Theory and research* (2nd ed., pp. 57–101). New York: Guilford Press.

Westen, D., & Harnden-Fischer, J. (2001). Classifying eating disorders by personality profiles: Bridging the chasm between Axis I and Axis II. *American Journal of Psychiatry.*

Westen, D., Klepser, J., Ruffins, S., Silverman, M., Lifton, N., & Boekamp, J. (1991). Object relations in childhood and adolescence: The development of working representations. *Journal of Consulting and Clinical Psychology, 59,* 400–409.

Westen, D., Lohr, N., Silk, K., Gold, L., & Kerber, K. (1990). Object relations and social cognition in borderlines, major depressives, and normals: A TAT analysis. *Psychological Assessment: A Journal of Consulting and Clinical Psychology, 2,* 355–364.

Westen, D., & Morrison, K. (2001). A meta-analytic investigation of empirically supported treatments for depression, anxiety, and generalized anxiety disorder. Unpublished manuscript, Boston University.

Westen, D., Muderrisoglu, S., Fowler, C., Shedler, J., & Koren, D. (1997). Affect regulation and affective experience: Individual differences, group differences, and measurement using a Q-sort procedure. *Journal of Consulting and Clinical Psychology, 65,* 429–439.

Westen, D., & Shedler, J. (1999). Revising and assessing axis II, Part II: Toward an empirically based and clinically useful classification of personality disorders. *American Journal of Psychiatry, 156,* 273-285.

Wetherick, N. (1975). The role of semantic information in short-term memory. *Journal of Verbal Learning and Verbal Behavior, 14,* 471–480.

Wheeler, L., & Kim, Y. (1997). What is beautiful is culturally good: The physical attractiveness stereotype has different content in collectivistic cultures. *Personality and Social Psychology Bulletin, 23,* 795–800.

Wheeler, M. A., Stuss, D. T., & Tulving, E. (1995). Frontal lobe damage produces episodic memory impairment. *Journal of the International Neuropsychological Society, 1,* 525–533.

Wheeler, M. A., Stuss, D. T., & Tulving, D. (1997). Toward a theory of episodic memory: The frontal lobes and autonoetic consciousness. *Psychological Bulletin, 121,* 331–354.

Whipple, B., Josimovich, J. B., & Komisaruk, B. R. (1990). Sensory thresholds during the antepartum, intrapartum and postpartum periods. *International Journal of Nursing Studies, 27,* 213–221.

Whitam, F., & Mathy, R. (1991). Childhood cross-gender behavior of homosexual females in Brazil, Peru, the Philippines, and the United States. *Archives of Sexual Behavior, 20,* 151–170.

Whitbourne, S. K. (2001). *Adult development and aging: Biopsychosocial perspectives.* New York: John Wiley & Sons.

Whitbourne, S. K., & Hulicka, I. (1990). Ageism in undergraduate psychology texts. *American Psychologist, 45,* 1127–1136.

Whitbourne, S. K., Zuschlag, M. K., Elliot, L. B., & Waterman, A. S. (1992). Psychosocial development in adulthood: A 22-year sequential study. *Journal of Personality & Social Psychology, 63,* 260–271.

White, K. M., Hogg, M., & Terry, D. J. (2002). Improving attitude-behavior correspondence through exposure to normative support from a salient ingroup. *Basic and Applied Social Psychology, 24,* 91–103.

White, R. W. (1959). Motivation reconsidered: The concept of competence. *Psychological Review, 66,* 297–333.

Whitfield, K. E., Weidner, G., Clark, R., & Anderson, N. B. (2003). Cultural aspects of health psychology. In A. M. Nezu, C. M. Nezu, & P. A. Geller (Eds.), *Handbook of psychology: Health psychology* (Vol. 9, pp. 545–568). Hoboken, NJ: John Wiley & Sons.

Whiting, B. B., & Edwards, C. P. (1988). *Children of different worlds: The formation of social behavior.* Cambridge, MA: Harvard University Press.

Whiting, B. B., & Whiting, J. W. M. (1975). *Children of six cultures: A psychocultural analysis.* Cambridge, MA: Harvard University Press.

Whiting, J. (1964). The effects of climate on certain cultural practices. In W. Goodenough (Ed.), *Explorations in cultural anthropology: Essays in honor of George Peter Murdock* (pp. 511–544). New York: McGraw-Hill.

Whiting, J. W. M., & Child, I. L. (1953). *Child training and personality: A cross-cultural study.* New Haven, CT: Yale University Press.

Whiting, J. W. M., & Whiting, B. B. (1973). Altruistic and egoistic behavior is six cultures. In L. Nader & T. W. Marekzki (Eds.), *Cultural illness and helath: Essays in human adaptation.* Washington, DC: American Anthropological Association.

Whitt, E. J., Edison, M. I., Pascarella, E. T., Nora, A., & Terenzini, P. T. (1999). Women's perceptions of a "chilly climate" and cognitive outcomes in college: Additional evidence. *Journal of College Student Development, 40,* 163–177.

WHO. (1995). *World health report: Bridging the gaps.* Geneva: Author.

WHO. (1998). *Obesity: Preventing and managing the global epidemic. Report of a WHO consultation on obesity.* Geneva: Author.

WHO. (1999). *World health report: Making a difference.* Geneva: Author.

Whorf, B. L. (1956). *Language, thought, and reality.* Cambridge, MA: MIT Press.

Wicker, A. W. (1969). Attitudes versus action: The relationship of verbal and overt behavioral responses to attitude objects. *Journal of Social Issues, 25,* 41–78.

Widiger, T. A., & Sankis, L. M. (2000). Adult psychopathology: Issues and controversies. *Annual Review of Psychology, 51,* 377–404.

Wiesel, T. N. (1982). Postnatal development of the visual cortex and the influence of environment. *Nature, 299,* 583–591.

Wiesel, T. N., & Hubel, D. H. (1960). Receptive fields of ganglion cells in the cat's retina. *Journal of Physiology, 153,* 583–594.

Wieselquist, J., Rusbult, C. E., Foster, C. A., & Agnew, C. R. (1999). Commitment, pro-relationship behavior, and trust in close relation-

ships. *Journal of Personality and Social Psychology, 77,* 942–966.

Wigfield, A., & Eccles, J. S. (2000). Expectancy-value theory of achievement motivation. *Contemporary Educational Psychology, 25,* 68–81.

Wilke, M. (2001). Changing standards: Condom advertising on American television. *Kaiser Daily Reproductive Health Report.*

Wilkins, M. C. (1982). The effect of changed material on ability to do formal syllogistic reasoning. *Archives of Psychology, 16,* 1–83.

Wilkinson, S. C. (1993). WISC-R profiles of children with superior intellectual ability. *Gifted Child Quarterly, 37,* 84–91.

Wilkinson-Ryan, T., & Westen, D. (2000). Identity disturbance in borderline personality disorder: An empirical investigation. *American Journal of Psychiatry, 157,* 528–541.

Williams, C., & Bybee, J. (1994). What do children feel guilty about? Developmental and gender differences. *Developmental Psychology, 30,* 617–623.

Williams, C. D. (1959). The elimination of tantrum behavior by extinction procedures. *Journal of Abnormal and Social Psychology, 59,* 269.

Williams, J. (2003). Dementia and genetics. In R. Plomin, J. C. DeFries, et al. (Eds.), *Behavioral genetics in the postgenetic era* (pp. 503–527). Washingon, DC: American Psychological Association.

Williams, J. E., & Best, D. L. (1982). *Measuring sex stereotypes: A thirty-nation study.* Beverly Hills, CA: Sage.

Williams, J. E., & Best, D. L. (1990). *Measuring sex stereotypes: A multination study.* Newbury Park, CA: Sage.

Williams, J. H. (1983). The emergence of gender differences. In W. Damon (Ed.), *Social and personality development.* New York: W.W. Norton.

Williams, K. B. (2001). *Ostracism: The power of silence.* New York: Guilford Press.

Williams, K. B., Harkins, S., & Latane, B. (1981). Identifiability as a deterrent to social loafing: Two cheering experiments. *Journal of Personality and Social Psychology, 40,* 303–311.

Williams, L. M. (1994). Recall of childhood trauma: A prospective study of women's memories of child sexual abuse. *Journal of Consulting and Clinical Psychology, 62,* 1167–1176.

Williams, R. L. (1974). Scientific racism and IQ: The silent mugging of the black community. *Psychology Today,* 32–41.

Williams, W. M., & Ceci, S. J. (1997). Are Americans becoming more or less alike? Trends in race, class, and ability differences in intelligence. *American Psychologist, 52,* 1226–1235.

Wills, T. A. (1981). Downward comparison principles in social psychology. *Psychological Bulletin, 90,* 245–271.

Wilson, E. O. (1975). *Sociobiology: A new synthesis.* Cambridge, MA: Harvard University Press.

Wilson, E. O., & Bossert, W. H. (1996). Chemical communication among animals. In L. D. Houck & L. C. Drickamer (Eds.), *Foundations of animal behavior: Classic papers with commentaries* (pp. 602–645). Chicago: University of Chicago Press.

Wilson, M. A., & McNaughton, B. L. (1994). Reactivation of hippocampal ensemble memories during sleep. *Science, 265,* 676–679.

Wilson, S. L. (2001). Attachment disorders: Review and current status. *Journal of Psychology, 135,* 37–51.

Wilson, T., Lisle, D., Schooler, J., & Hodges, S. (1993). Introspecting about reasons can reduce post-choice satisfaction. *Personality & Social Psychology Bulletin, 19,* 331–339.

Wilson, T. D., Lindsey, S., & Schooler, T. Y. (2000). A model of dual attitudes. *Psychological Review, 107,* 101–126.

Wilson, T. D., Wheatley, T., Meyers, J. M., Gilbert, D. T., & Axsom, D. (2000b). Focalism: A source of durability bias in affective forecasting. *Journal of Personality and Social Psychology, 78,* 821–836.

Winn, P. (1995). The lateral hypothalamus and motivated behavior: An old syndrome reassessed and a new perspective gained. *Current Directions in Psychological Science, 4,* 182–187.

Winner, E. (2000). The origins and ends of giftedness. *American Psychologist 55,* 159–169.

Winograd, E., & Neissier, U. (Eds.). (1993). *Affect and accuracy in recall: Studies of "flashbulb" memories.* New York: Cambridge University Press.

Winokur, G., & Tanna, V. L. (1969). Possible role of X-linked dominant factor in manic depressive disease. *Diseases of the Nervous System, 30,* 89-94.

Winson, J. (1985). *Brain and psyche: The biology of the unconscious.* New York: Anchor.

Winter, D. (1993). Power, affiliation, and war: Three tests of a motivational model. *Journal of Personality and Social Psychology, 65,* 532–545.

Winter, D. G. (1987). Enhancement of an enemy's power motivation as a dynamic of conflict escalation. *Journal of Personality and Social Psychology, 42,* 41–46.

Winterbottom, M. R. (1953). *The relation of childhood training in independence to achievement motivation.* Unpublished doctoral dissertation, Univerisity of Michigan, Ann Arbor.

Wispe, L. G., & Drambarean, N. C. (1953). Physiological need, word frequency, and visual deviation thresholds. *Journal of Experimental Psychology, 46,* 25-31.

Witelson, S. F., Kigar, D. L., & Harvey, T. (1999). The exceptional brain of Albert Einstein. *Lancet, 353,* 2149–2153.

Wixom, J., Ludolph, P., & Westen, D. (1993). Quality of depression in borderline adolescents. *Journal of the American Academy of Child & Adolescent Psychiatry, 32,* 1172–1177.

Wixted, J., & Ebbesen, E. (1991). On the form of forgetting. *Psychological Science, 2,* 409–415.

Woike, B., & Aronoff, J. (1992). Antecedents of complex social cognitions. *Journal of Personality and Social Psychology, 63,* 97–104.

Woike, B., Gershkovich, I., Piorkowski, R., & Polo, M. (1999). The role of motives in the content and structure of autobiographical memory. *Journal of Personality & Social Psychology, 76,* 600–612.

Wolf, A. M., & Colditz, G. A. (1998). Current estimates of the economic costs of obesity in the United States. *Obesity Research, 6,* 97–106.

Wolfe, J., Erickson, D. J., Sharkansky, E. J., King, D. W., & King, L. A. (1999). Course and predictors of posttraumatic stress disorder among Gulf War veterans: A prospective analysis. *Journal of Consulting and Clinical Psychology, 67,* 520–528.

Wolpe, J. (1958). *Psychotherapy by reciprocal inhibition.* Stanford, CA: Stanford University Press.

Wolpe, J. (Ed.). (1964). *The conditioning therapies: The challenge in psychotherapy.* New York: Holt, Rinehart & Winston.

Woo, J., Ho, S. C., Yuen, Y. K., Yu, L. M., & Lau, J. (1998). Cardiovascular risk factors and 18-month mortality and morbidity in an elderly Chinese population aged 70 years and over. *Gerontology, 44,* 51–55.

Wood, J. M., Lilienfeld, S. O., Garb, H. N., & Nezworski, M. T. (2000). "The Rorschach test in clinical diagnosis": A critical review, with a backward look at Garfield (1947). *Journal of Clinical Psychology, 56,* 395–430.

Wood, J. V., & Lockwood, P. (1999). Social comparisons in dysphoric and low self-esteem people. In R. M. Kowalski & M. R. Leary (Eds.), *The social psychology of dysfunctional behavior* (pp. 97–136). Washington, DC: American Psychological Association.

Wood, R., & Bandura, A. (1989). Impact of conceptions of ability on self-regulatory mechanisms and complex decision-making. *Journal of Personality and Social Psychology, 56,* 407-415.

Wood, R., & Bandura, A. (1989). Social cognitive theory of organizational management. Special issue: Theory development forum. *Academy of Management Review, 14,* 361–384.

Wood, W. (2000). Attitude change: Persuasion and social influence. *Annual Review of Psychology, 51,* 539–570.

Wood, W., Wong, F., & Chachere, J. G. (1991). Effects of media violence on viewers' aggression in unconstrained social interaction. *Psychologial Bulletin, 109,* 371–383.

Woodruff, S. I., Edwards, C. C., Conway, T. L., & Elliott, S. P. (2001). Pilot test of an Internet virtual world chat room for rural teen smokers. *Journal of Adolescent Health, 29,* 239–243.

Woods, S. C., Schwartz, M. W., Baskin, D. G., & Seeley, R. J. (2000). Food intake and the regulation of body weight. *Annual Review of Psychology, 51,* 255-277.

Woodward, A. L., & Sommerville, J. A. (2000). Twelve-month-old infants interpret action in context. *Psychological Science, 11,* 73–77.

Worthington, E. L., Jr., Martin, G. A., Shumate, M., & Carpenter, J. (1983). The effect of brief Lamaze training and social encouragement on pain endurance in a cold pressor tank. *Journal of Applied Social Psychology, 13,* 223–233.

Wright, I. C., Rabe-Hesketh, S., Woodruff, P. W. R., David, A. S., Murray, R. M., & Bullmore, E. T. (2000). Meta-analysis of regional brain volumes in schizophrenia. *American Journal of Psychiatry, 157,* 16–25.

Wright, L. B., Treiber, F. A., Davis, H., & Strong, W. B. (1996). Relationship of John Henryism to cardiovascular functioning at rest and during stress in youth. *Annals of Behavioral Medicine, 18,* 146–150.

Wulff, D. M. (1997). *Psychology of religion: Classic and contemporary* (2nd ed.). New York: John Wiley & Sons.

Wyatt, G. E., Peters, S. D., & Guthrie, D. (1988a). Kinsey revisited: I. Comparisons of the sexual socialization and sexual behavior of White women over 33 years. *Archives of Sexual Behavior, 17,* 201–239.

Wyatt, G. E., Peters, S. D., & Guthrie, D. (1988b). Kinsey revisted: II. Comparisons of the sexual socialization and sexual behavior of Black women over 33 years. *Archives of Sexual Behavior, 17,* 289–332.

Wyatt, R. J. (1996). Neurodevelopmental abnormalities and schizophrenia: A family affair. *Archives of General Psychiatry, 53,* 11–18.

Wynne, L. C. (1961). The study of intrafamilial alignments and splits in exploratory family therapy. In N. Ackerman, et al. (Eds.), *Exploring the base for family therapy.* New York: Family Service Association of America.

Yadin, E., & Thomas, E. (1996). Stimulation of the lateral septum attenuates immobilization-induced stress ulcers. *Physiology & Behavior, 59,* 883–886.

Yager, J. (2000). Weighty Perspectives: Contemporary challenges in obesity and eating disorders. *American Journal of Psychiatry, 157,* 851–853.

Yahne, C. E., & Miller, W. R. (1999). Enhancing motivation for treatment and change. In B. S. McCrady & E. E. Epstein (Eds.), *Addictions: A comprehensive guidebook* (pp. 235–249). New York: Oxford University Press.

Yalom, I. D. (1995). *The theory and practice of group psychotherapy* (4th ed.). New York: Basic Books.

Yalon, I., Brown, S., & Bloch, S. (1975). The written summary as a group psychotherapy technique. *Archives of General Psychiatry, 32,* 605–613.

Yamamoto, D., Ito, H., & Fujitani, K. (1996). Genetic dissection of sexual orientation: Behavioral, cellular, and molecular approaches in *Drosophila melanogaster. Neuroscience Research, 26,* 95–107.

Yaniv, I., & Meyer, D. (1987). Activation and metacognition of inaccessible stored information: Potential bases for incubation effects in problem solving. *Journal of Experimental Psychology: Learning, Memory, and Cognition, 13,* 187–205.

Yassa, R., Nair, N., Iskandar, H., & Schwartz, G. (1990). Factors in the development of severe forms of tardive dyskinesia. *American Journal of Psychiatry, 147,* 1156–1163.

Yoon, C. K. (2003, June 17). The evolving peppered moth gains a furry counterpart. *The New York Times,* Section F, p. 3.

Young, A. J., MacLeod, H. A., & Lawrence, A. B. (1994). Effect of manipulation design on operant responding in pigs. *Animal Behavior, 47,* 1488–1490.

Young, A. W. (1994). Face recognition. In G. d'Ydewalle, P. Eelen, et al. (Eds.), *International perspectives on psychological science: Vol. 2. The state of the art.* (pp. 1–27). Hove, UK: Lawrence Erlbaum.

Young, D. R., Miller, K. W., Wilder, L. B., Yanek, L. R., & Becker, D. M. (1998). Physical activity patterns of urban African Americans. *Journal of Community Health, 23,* 99–112.

Younger, B. A., & Fearing, D. D. (1999). Parsing items into separate categories: Developmental change in infant categorization. *Child Development, 70,* 291–303.

Youniss, J., & Haynie, D. (1992). Friendship in adolescence. *Developmental and Behavioral Pediatrics, 13,* 59–66.

Yu, B., Zhang, W., Jing, Q., Peng, R., Zhang, G., & Simon, H. A. (1985). STM capacity for Chinese and English language materials. *Memory and Cognition, 13,* 202–207.

Zahn-Waxler, C., Radke-Yarrow, M., Wagner, E., & Chapman, M. (1992a). Development of concern for others. *Developmental Psychology, 28,* 126–136.

Zahn-Waxler, C., Robinson, J., & Emde, R. (1992b). The development of empathy in twins. *Developmental Psychology, 28,* 1038–1047.

Zajonc, R. B. (1965). Social facilitation. *Science, 149,* 269–274.

Zajonc, R. B. (1968). The attitudinal effects of mere exposure. *Journal of Personality and Social Psychology, 9,* 1–27.

Zajonc, R. B. (1980). Feeling and thinking: Preferences need no inferences. *American Psychologist, 35,* 151–175.

Zajonc, R. B. (1998). Emotions. In D. T. Gilbert, S. T. Fiske, et al. (Eds.), *The handbook of social psychology* (Vol. 2, 4th ed., pp. 591–632). Boston, MA: McGraw-Hill.

Zajonc, R. B., & Markus, H. (1985). Must all affect be mediated by cognition? *Journal of Consumer Research, 12,* 363-364.

Zanarini, M. C. (Ed.). (1997). *Role of sexual abuse in the etiology of borderline personality disorder.* Washington, DC: American Psychiatric Press.

Zanarini, M. C., Gunderson, J. G., Marino, M. F., Schwartz, E. D., & Frankenberg, F. R. (1989). Childhood experience of borderline patients. *Comprehensive Psychiatry, 30,* 18–25.

Zanarini, M., Gunderson, J., Marino, M., Schwartz, E., & Frankenburg, F. (1990). Psychiatric disorders in the families of borderline outpatients. In P. Links (Ed.), *Family environment and borderline personality disorder* (pp. 69–84). Washington, DC: American Psychiatric Press.

Zanna, M. P., & Cooper, J. (1974). Dissonance and the pill: An attribution approach to studying the arousal properties of dissonance. *Journal of Personality and Social Psychology, 9,* 703–709.

Zaragosta, M., & Mitchell, K. J. (1996). Repeated exposure to suggestion and the creation of false memories. *Psychological Science, 7,* 294–300.

Zatzick, D. F., & Dimsdale, J. E. (1990). Cultural variations in response to painful stimuli. *Psychosomatic Medicine, 52,* 544–557.

Zeanah, C. H., & Zeanah, P. D. (1989). Intergenerational transmission of maltreatment: Insights from attachment theory and research. *Psychiatry, 52,* 177–196.

Zechmeister, E. B., & Shaughnessy, J. J. (1980). When you know that you know and when you think that you know but you don't. *Bulletin of the Psychonomic Society, 15,* 41-44.

Zeki, S., Aglioti, S., McKeefry, D., & Berlucchi, G. (1999). The neurological basis of conscious color perception in a blind patient. *Proceedings of the National Academy of Science, U.S.A., 96,* 14124–14129.

Zervas, I. M., Augustine, A., & Fricchione, G. L. (1993). Patient delay in cancer: A view from the crisis model. *General Hospital Psychiatry, 15,* 9–13.

Zhao, L., Kirkmeyer, S. V., & Tepper, B. J. (2003). A paper screening test to assess genetic taste sensitivity to 6-*n*-propylthiouracil. *Physiological Behavior, 78,* 625–633.

Zeigarnik, B. (1967). On finished and unfinished tasks. In W. D. Ellis (Ed.), *A source book of Gestalt psychology* (pp. 300-314). London: Routledge and Kegan Paul.

Zigler, E., & Styfco, S. J. (2000). Pioneering steps (and fumbles) in developing a federal preschool intervention. *Topics in Early Childhood Special Education, 20,* 67-70, 78.

Zillman, D., Baron, R. A., & Tamborini, R. (1981). Special costs on smoking: Effects of tobacco smoke on hostile behavior. *Journal of Applied Social Psychology, 11,* 548–561.

Zimbardo, P. G. (1972). Pathology of imprisonment. *Society,* 4–8.

Zimbardo, P. G. (1975). Transforming experimental research into advocacy for social change. In M. Deutsch and H. A. Hornstein (Eds.), *Applying social psychology: Implications for research, practice, and training.* Hillsdale, NJ: Lawrence Erlbaum.

Zinbarg, R. E., & Barlow, D. H. (1996). Structure of anxiety and the anxiety disorders: A hierarchical model. *Journal of Abnormal Psychology, 105,* 181–193.

Zinbarg, R., Barlow, D., Brown, T., & Hertz, R. (1992). Cognitive-behavioral approaches to the nature and treatment of anxiety disorders. *Annual Review of Psychology, 43,* 235–267.

Zinbarg, R. E., Barlow, D. H., Liebowitz, M., & Street, L. (1994). The DSM-IV field trial for mixed anxiety-depression. *American Journal of Psychiatry, 151,* 1153–1162.

Zipursky, R. B., Lambe, E. K., Kapur, S., & Mikulis, D. J. (1998). Cerebral gray matter volume deficits in first episode psychosis. *Archives of General Psychiatry, 55,* 540–546.

Zornberg, G. L., Buka, S. L., & Tsuang, M. T. (2000). Hypoxic-ischemia-related fetal/neonatal complications and risk of schizophrenia and other nonaffective psychoses: A 19-year longitudinal study. *American Journal of Psychiatry, 157,* 196–202.

Zuckerman, M. (1994). *Behavioral expression and biosocial bases of sensation seeking.* New York: Cambridge University Press.

Zuckerman, M., Koestner, R., DeBoy, T., Garcia, T., Maresca, B., & Sartois, J. (1988). To predict some of the people some of the time. A reexamination of the moderator variable approach in personality theory. *Journal of Personality and Social Psychology, 54,* 1006–1019.

Photo Credits

Images. Page 283 (bottom): ©Getty Images. Page 286: ©Dag Sundberg/The Image Bank/Getty Images. Page 287 (top): ©Maks Product/The Image Bank/Getty Images. Page 287 (bottom): ©Renee Lynn/Stone/Getty Images.

Chapter 9 Opener: John Armstrong, Dreaming Head, 1938. ©Tate Gallery, London/Art Resource. Page 292: ©Alberto Incrocci/The Image Bank/Getty Images. Page 295: ©Laura Dwight/Corbis Images. Page 296: ©SW Productions/PhotoDisc, Inc./Getty Images. Page 297: ©Kwame Zikomo/Superstock. Page 305: ©Ed Young/Photo Researchers. Page 309: ©Index Stock. Page 310: ©David Parker/Photo Researchers. Page 312: ©Joe Raedle/Getty Images News and Sport Services. Page 316 (top): ©Michael Nichols/Magnum Photos, Inc. Page 316 (bottom): ©Greenlar/The Image Works.

Chapter 10 Opener: ©Ong/Superstock. Page 320: ©Digital Vision/Getty Images. Page 321: ©Roger Lemayne/Getty Images News and Sport Services. Page 322: ©Lew Merrin/Photo Researchers. Page 324: ©AP/WideWorld Photos. Page 327: © Theirry Falise/Getty Images News and Sport Services. Page 328 (left): ©Carolina Biological/Phototake. Page 328 (right): ©RNT Productions/Corbis Images. Page 329: ©Topham/The Image Works. Page 330: ©Stohehill//Masterfile. Page 335: Courtesy Neal E. Miller. Page 336: ©Chet Gordon/The Image Works. Page 337 (left): ©Giraudon/Art Resource. Page 337 (center): ©Topham/The Image Works. Page 337 (right): Jim Smeal/Ron Galella Ltd. Page 339 (top): ©Steve Weinberg/Stone/Getty Images. Page 339 (bottom): ©Shaitil/ Rozinski/Index Stock. Page 340: ©Gary Gladstone/The Image Bank/Getty Images. Page 341: ©Jon Feingersh/Masterfile. Page 342: ©Steve Liss/Corbis Sygma. Page 345: ©Michael Newman/PhotoEdit. Page 351 (top): ©Getty Images News and Sport Services. Page 351 (bottom) & 353: P. Ekman, Human Interaction Lab, University of California San Francisco. Page 354: ©Jason Nethreington/The Image Bank/Getty Images. Page 355: © Douglas Kirkland/Corbis Images. Page 360: Courtesy Drew Westen. Page 363 (top): ©Art Wolf/Stone/Getty Images. Page 363 (center): ©Joe McDonald/Bruce Coleman, Inc. Page 363 (bottom): ©Tom Hussey/The Image Bank/Getty Images.

Chapter 11 Opener: Edvard Munich, Ashes, 1894. ©ARS, NY Ashes. 1894. National Gallery, Oslo. Photo credit: Scala/Art Resource. Page 369: ©Bettmann/CORBIS IMAGES. Page 370: Courtesy of San Diego Museum of Man. Page 371 (left): ©Bettmann/CORBIS IMAGES. Page 371 (right): ©A. Ramey/PhotoEdit. Page 372: ©Bettman/Corbis Images. Page 376: ©Howard Grey/Stone/Getty Images. Page 380 (top): Tsuni/Gamma-Presse, Inc. Page 380 (bottom left): ©Thinkstock/Getty Images. Page 380 (bottom right): ©PhotoDisc, Inc./Getty Images. Page 381: Photo by Marty Hale-Evans courtesy of Mary McGhee, A Place At The Table Project, SeaFATtle <http://www.seafattle.org/APATT/apatt.htm. Page 384 (top): ©AP/WideWorld Photos. Page 384 (bottom): ©Mark Mainz/Getty Images News and Sport Services. Page 385: ©The NewYorker Collection 2001 Michael Shaw from the cartoonbank.com. Page 387: ©MichaelNewman/PhotoEdit. Page 388: ©Bettmann/Corbis Images. Page 390 (top): ©Royalty-Free/Corbis Images. Page 390 (bottom): ©Phototake. Page 393 (top): Courtesy Dr. James W. Hanson, University of Iowa Hospital and Clinics. Page 393 (bottom): ©The NewYorker Collection 2000 Lee Lorenz from the cartoonbank.com. Page 399 (left): Peter Poulides/Stone/Getty Images. Page 399 (right): ©Cheng Yu/Taxi/Getty Images. Page 404 (top): ©AP/WideWorld Photos. Page 404 (bottom): ©Brooks Kraft/Corbis Images. Pages 405 & 406: ©AP/WideWorld Photos. Page 407: ©Joseph Rodriquez/Black Star. Page 408: ©Getty Images News and Sport Services. Page 411: Tommy Hindley/Professional Sport/The Image Works. Page 414: ©Stuart Cohen/Index Stock. Page 415: ©Daniel J. Cox/Stone/Getty Images. Page 418: ©AP/WideWorld Photos.

Chapter 12 Opener: ©Byford/Superstock. Page 421: ©Lewis Agrell/Stock Illustration Source/Images.com. Page 424 (top): ©Photo Researchers. Page 424 (bottom): ©Bettmann/Corbis Images. Page 426: ©John Running/Stone/Getty Images. Page 427: ©Andy Saks/Stone/Getty Images. Page 428 (top): ©The Image Bank/Getty Images. Page 428 (bottom): ©Pierre Tremblay/Masterfile. Page 430: ©Sandra Lousada/Woodfin Camp. Page 432 (top): ©1921, Rorschach: Psychodiagnostics, Hans Huber Medical publisher, Bern. Page 433: ©Sidney Harris. Page 437: ©John-Marshall Mantel/Corbis Images. Page 439 (left): ©Bettman/Corbis Images. Page 439 (right): ©Dr. Scott T. Grafton/Visuals Unlimited. Page 444 (top): Courtesy Prof. Walter Mischel. Page 444 (bottom): Courtesy Jerome Kagan, Harvard University. Page 445: ©Will Waldron/The Image Works. Page 454: Lippa di Dalmasio, The Madonna of Humility. Courtesy The National Gallery, London. Page 455: Courtesy NewYork Public Library Picture Collection.

Chapter 13 Opener: Rufino Tamayo, The Family, 1987. ©COll. Olga Tamayo, Mexico City, D.F., Mexico. Photo credit: Schalkwijk/Art Resource. Page 459: ©Gail Mooney/Corbis Images. Page 461: From Carlson, 1980 p.189 International Journal of

Neuroscience, courtesy The Gordon and Breach Publishers, Switzerland. Reproduced with permission. Page 462: ©Don Smetzer/PhotoEdit. Page 466 (left): ©Stone/Getty Images. Page 466 (center): ©Neil Harding/Stone/Getty Images. Page 466 (right): ©Petit Format/Photo Researchers. Page 469: ©Camille Tokerud/Stone/Getty Images. Page 470: ©Tom Raymond/Stone/Getty Images. Page 472: ©Elie Bernager/Stone/Getty Images. Page 473: From A. N. Meltzoff & M. K. Moore, Science, 1977, 198, 75-78. Page 476: Courtesy Wayne Behling,Ypsilanti Press, Miehigan. Page 477: ©Jeffrey W. Myers/ Stock Boston. Page 479: ©Elizabeth Crews. Page 480: ©Andy Sacks/Stone/Getty Images. Page 482: ©Donna Day/Stone/Getty Images. Page 484: ©Tony Freeman/PhotoEdit. Page 485 (left): ©UPI/Corbis Bettman. Page 485 (right): ©Jeff Markowitz/Corbis Sygma. Page 486: ©Corbis Images. Page 487: ©B. Stitzer/PhotoEdit. Page 490: ©Jose Polleross/The Image Works. Page 492: ©D Greco/The Image Works.

Chapter 14 Opener: ©P.J. Cook/The Bridgeman Art Library/Getty Images. Page 496: ©Rick Raymond/Stone/Getty Images. Page 497: ©Mary Evans Picture Library. Page 498: ©Life Magazine, copyright Time, Inc. Page 500 (left): ©Tom Mc Hugh/Photo Researchers. Page 500 (right): ©Stephanie Maze/Woodfin Camp & Associates. Page 504: Courtesy of David Pelzer. Page 508: Courtesy Cora du Bois: The People of Alor: A Social- Psychological Study of and East Indian Island, University of Minnesota Press, 1944. Reproduced with permission. Page 510: ©Tom Raymond/Stone/Getty Images. Page 511: ©Owaki - Kulla/Corbis Images. Page 512: Courtesy Robin Kowalski. Page 513 (left): ©Jeff Greenberg/The Image Works. Page 513 (right): Tom & Dee Ann McCarthy/Corbis Stock Market. Page 517: ©The NewYorker Collection 1997 William Seig from the cartoonbank.com. All Rights Reserved. Page 518: ©AP/WideWorld Photos. Page 520: ©Jason Szenes/Corbis Sygma. Page 523: ©David Kennerly/ UP/Corbis Images. Page 526: ©Greg Smith/Corbis SABA. Page 527: ©UPI//Corbis Images. Page 533 (left): ©Andy Berhaut/Photo Researchers. Page 533 (center): ©Bill Strode/Woodfin Camp & Associates, Inc. DC. Page 533 (right): ©Don Smetzer/Stone/Getty Images. Page 535: ©Ron Dahlquest/Stone/Getty Images.

Chapter 15 Opener: Rufino Tamayo, Today, 1988. ©Coll. Olga Tamayo, Mexico City, D.F., Mexico. Photo Credit: Schalkwijk/Art Resource. Page 539: ©Superstock. Page 541: ©Tony Arruza/Corbis Images. Page 545: ©Penny Tweedie/Stone/Getty Images. Page 556: ©Anthony Marland/Stone/Getty Images. Page 559: Courtesy Monte Buschbaum, MD, Mt. Sinai Medical Center. Reproduced with permission. Page 560: From Lieberman et al, The American Journal of Psychiatry, 1992, Copyright 1998, The American Psychiatric Association. Reprinted by permission. Page 567: ©David Butow/Black Star. Page 569: ©Leverett Bradley/Stone/Getty Images. Page 570: ©1993 Jennifer Berman, Humerus Cartoons. Page 571: ©Peter Marlow/Magnum Photos, Inc. Page 576: ©Jacques Pavlovsky/Corbis Images.

Chapter 16 Opener: ©John Martin/Stock Illustration Source/Images.com. Page 582: ©Zubin Shroff/Stone/Getty Images. Page 584: ©Sidney Harris. Page 586: ©PhotoDisc, Inc./Getty Images. Page 588: ©Sidney Harris. Page 590: ©AP/WideWorld Photos. Page 591: Courtesy of theVirtual Reality Medical Center. Page 595: Courtesy Les Greenberg. Page 597 (top): ©Hank Morgan/Photo Researchers. Page 597 (bottom): ©DavidYoung/PhotoEdit. Page 599: ©The Cover Story/Corbis Images. Page 606: ©Tony Freeman/PhotoEdit. Page 607 (top): Will McIntyre/Photo Researchers. Page 607 (bottom): Renato M.E. Sabbatini, Brain & Mind Magazine, June 1997.

Chapter 17 Opener: Alberto Giacometti, City Square (La Place), 1948. Digital Image ©The Museum of Modern Art/Licensed by SCALA/Art Resource, NY. Page 615: ©Royalty-Free/Corbis Images. Page 620 (left): ©Anna Flyn/Stock Boston. Page 620 (right): ©ITN/FSP/Liaison Agency, Inc./Getty Images. Page 624: Robert Ayers/UNC Pembroke Photo. Page 625: ©Reuters NewMedia Inc./Corbis Images. Page 626: ©Bettman/Corbis Images. Page 627: ©AP/WideWorld Photos. Page 628: ©Alan Klehr/Stone/Getty Images. Page 630: ©Jeff Greenberg/Peter Arnold, Inc. Page 635: ©Corbis Stock Market. Page 637: ©Joel Rogers/Corbis Images. Page 642: ©Gabe Palmer/Corbis Stock Market. Page 651: Courtesy Selz/Seabolt communications, Inc.

Chapter 18 Opener: ©Malcah Zeldis, Brighton Beach, Art Resource. Page 654: ©Keystone Paris/Corbis Sygma. Page 657: ©Masterfile. Page 659: ©David C. Tomlinson/Stone/Getty Images. Page 661: ©Callahan/Levin Represents. Page 665: ©Phil Schermeister/Corbis Images. Page 667: ©Edward Hasneur/New York Times Pictures. Page 671: ©Wesley Bocxe/Photo Researchers. Page 672 (top): Sidney Baldwin/Photofest. Page 672 (bottom): ©Carl S. Sams II/Peter Arnold, Inc. Page 678: ©John Barr/Liaison Agency, Inc./Getty Images. Page 680:Yale Interaction Library,Yale University. Page 682: Courtesy William Vandivert. Page 684: Courtesy Prof. Philip G. Zimbardo, Dept. of Psychology, Stanford University. Page 690: ©Paul Griffin/Stock Boston.

Illustration and Text Credits

Chapter 1 Figure 1.3: From Cave, C. B. (1997). Long-lasting priming in picture naming. *Psychological Science*, 8, 322-325. Copyright © 1997. Reprinted with the permission of Blackwell Science, Inc. Figure 1.6: Based on DeKay,T. (1988). An evolutionary-computational approach to social cognition: Grandparental investment as a test case. Unpublished doctoral dissertation, University of Michigan.

Chapter 2 Figure 2.1: From Pennebaker, J., Colder, M., & Sharp, L. K. (1990). Accelerating the coping process. *Journal of Personality and Social Psychology*, 58, 528-537. Copyright © 1990 by the American Psychological Association. Reprinted and adapted with the permission of the APA and the authors. Figure 2.6: From Bower, G. H. (1981). Mood and memory. *American Psychologist*, 36, 129-148. Copyright © 1981 by the American Psychological Association. Reprinted with the permission of the APA and the author. Table 2.5: Adapted from R. L. Shiner (2000). Linking childhood personality with adaptation: Evidence for continuity and change across time in late adolescence. *Journal of Personality and Social Psychology*, 78, p. 316. Copyright © 2000 by the American Psychological Association. Reprinted and adapted with the permission of the APA and the author.

Chapter 3 Figure 3.16 From *Fundamentals of Human Neuropsychology* by B. Kolb & I. Q. Whishaw. © 1996 by W. H. Freeman and Company. Used with permission of Worth Publisher. Figure 3.12: From Penfield,W., & Rasmussen,T. (1950). *The Cerebral Cortex of Man*. Copyright © 1978 by the Gale Group. Reprinted by permission of The Gale Group. Figure 3.13a: From Gazzaniga, M. S. (August 1967). The split brain in man. Scientific American. Illustration by Eric O. Mose. Copyright 1967. Reprinted and adapted by permission of Eric H. Mose.

Chapter 4 Figure 4.3c: From Stevens, S. S. (1961). Psychophysics of sensory function. In W. Rosenblith (ed.), *Sensory Communication*, 1-33. Cambridge, MA: MIT Press. Used with permission. Figures 4.8, 4.13, and 4.21: From Sekuler, R., & Blake, R. (1994). Perception, 3rd Edition. New York: McGraw-Hill, Inc. Copyright © 1994, 1990, 1985 by McGraw-Hill, Inc. Reprinted and adapted with the permission of the publisher. Figure 4.26: From Ramachandran,V. S., & Hirstein,W. (1998). The perception of phantom limbs. *The D. O. Heff Lecture. Brain 121*, 1612. Used with permission of the publisher. Figure 4.29e: From Kanisza, G. (April 1976). Subjective contours. *Scientific American*, 234, 48. Copyright © 1976 by Scientific American, Inc. Reprinted with the permission of the publisher. Figure 4.30: From Biederman, I. (1990). Higher level vision. In D. N. Osherson et al. (eds.), *An Invitation to Cognitive Science*,Volume 2. Copyright © 1990 by the Massachusetts Institute of Technology. Reprinted with the permission of The MIT Press. Figure 4.31: From Biederman, I. (1987). Recognition by components. *Computer Visions, Graphics, and Image Processing*, 32, 29-73. Copyright © 1985 by Academic Press, Inc. Reprinted with the permission of the publisher and the author. Table 4.1: From Brown, R., Galanter, E., & Hess, E. H. (1962). *New Directions in Psychology*. New York: Harcourt Brace & Co. Reprinted with the permission of Roger W. Brown, Harvard University.

Chapter 5 Figure 5.2: From Pavlov, I. P. (1927). *Conditioned Reflexes*. New York: Oxford University Press. Copyright 1927. Reprinted with the permission of Oxford University Press, Ltd. Figure 5.6: From Garcia, J. and Koelling, R. (1966). Relation of cue to consequence in avoidance learning. *Psychonomic Science*, 4, 123-124. Copyright © 1966. Reprinted with the permission of Psychonomic Society, Inc. Figure 5.11: From Gray, J .A. (1988)."Gray's Three Behavioral Systems" from *The Psychology of Fear and Stress, 2nd Edition*. New York: Cambridge University Press. Copyright ©

1988. Reprinted with the permission of Cambridge University Press and the author. Figure 5.13: From Rotter, J. (1971, June). External control and internal control: Locus of control. *Psychology Today*, 42. Copyright © 1971 by Sussex Publisher, Inc. Reprinted with the permission of Psychology Today Magazine. Figure 5.14: From Bandura, A. (1967). In *The Young Child: Reviews of Research*,W. Hartup and N. Smothergill (eds.).Washington, DC: National Association for the Education of Young Children. Copyright © 1967 by NAEYC. Reprinted with permission from the National Association for the Education of Young Children.

Chapter 6 Figure 6.4: From Atkinson, R. C., & Shiffrin, R. N. (1968). Human memory: A proposed system and its control processes. In K. W. Spence & J. T. Spence (Eds.), The psychology of learning and motivation (Vol. 2). Copyright © 1968 by Academic Press, Inc. Reprinted with the permission of the publisher. Figure 6.5. From Baddeley, A. (1986). *Working memory*. New York: Oxford University Press, Inc. Copyright © 1986 Oxford University Press, Inc. Reprinted with the permission of the publisher. Figure 6.6: From Logie, R. (1996). The seven ages of working memory. In J.T. E. Richardson et al., *Working Memory and Human Cognition*. New York: Oxford University Press. Copyright © 1996 Oxford University Press, Inc. Reprinted with the permission of the publisher. Figure 6.7b: From Courtney et al. (1997).Transient and sustained activity in a distributed neural system for human working memory. *Nature, 386*, (6625), p. 610. Copyright © 1997 by Macmillan Magazines Ltd. Reprinted with the permission of *Nature* and the authors. Figure 6.10: From Hermann, D. J., Crawford, M., & Holdsworth, M. (1992). Gender-linked differences in everyday memory performance. *British Journal of Psychology*, 83, 221-231. Copyright © 1992. Reprinted with the permission of the British Psychological Society. Figure 6.11: From Bahrick, et al. (1993). Maintenance of foreign language vocabulary and the spacing effect. Psychological Science, 4, p. 319. Copyright © 1993. Reprinted with the permission of Blackwell Science, Inc. Figure 6.16: Adapted from Bahrick, et al. (1996). Accuracy and distortion in memory for high school grades. Psychological Science, 7, p. 266. Copyright © 1996. Reprinted with the permission of Blackwell Science, Inc.

Chapter 7 Figure 7.1: Adapted from Cooper, L. A., & Shepard, R. N. (1973). The manipulation of visual representations. *Memory and Cognition*, 1, (3), 246-250. Copyright © 1973. Reprinted with the permission of the Psychonomic Society, Inc. Figure 7.4: From Wason, P. C. (1968). Reasoning about a rule. *Quarterly Journal of Experimental Psychology*, 20, 273-281. Copyright © 1968. Reprinted with the permission of Lawrence Erlbaum Associates, Ltd., Hove, UK, and the author. Figure 7.5: Adapted from Griggs, R. A., & Cox, J. R. (1982). The elusive thematic-materials effect in Watson's selection task. *British Journal of Psychology*, 73, 407-420, extract. Reprinted and adapted with the permission of the British Psychological Society and the authors. Figure 7.9: Adapted from Rumelhart, D. (1984). Schemata and the cognitive system. In R. S.Wyler & T. K. Strull (eds.), *Handbook of social cognition*,Vol. 1. Hillsdale, New Jersey: Erlbaum. Copyright © 1984. Reprinted and adapted with the permission of Lawrence Erlbaum Associates and the author. Figure 7.12: From Frith & Dolan (1996). The role of the prefrontal cortex in higher cognitive functions. *Cognitive Brain Research, 5*, 178. Copyright © 1996. Reprinted with the permission of Elsevier Science Limited. Figure 7.13: From Damasio, A. (1994). DescartesÕerror: Emotion, reason and the human brain, p. 210. Copyright © 1994 by Antonio R. Damasio. Reprinted with the permission of the author. Figure 7.16: From Premack, A. J., & Premack, D. (October 1972). Teaching language to an ape. *Scientific American, 227*, 92-99. Copyright © 1972 by Scientific American, Inc. All rights reserved. Reprinted with permission. Figure 7.18: Adapted from Pinker, S. (1994). *The language instinct: How the mind creates language*. Copyright © 1994 by Stephen Pinker. Reprinted with the permission of HarperCollins Publishers, Inc. Table 7.1: Adapted from Irwin, M., Schafer, G., & Feiden, C. (1974). Emic and unfamiliar category sorting of Mano farmers and U.S. undergraduates. *Journal of Cross-Cultural Psychology, 5*, 407-423. Copyright © 1974 by Sage Publications, Inc. Reprinted and adapted with the permission of the publisher. Tables 7.3 and 7.4: Adapted from Edwards, W. (1977). How to use multiattribute utility measurement for social decision making. *IEEE Transactions in Systems, Man and Cybernetics, 17*, 326-340. Copyright © 1977 by IEEE. Reprinted with the permission of the publisher.

Chapter 8 Figure 8.3: Excerpted and adapted with permission from Duncan, J., Seitz, R., Kolodny, J., Bor, D., Herzog, H., Ahmed, A., Newell, F. N., & Emslie, H. (2000). A neural basis for general intelligence. *Science 289*, 457-460. Figure 8.4: From J. Horn and J. Noll (1997). Human cognitive capacity: Gf - Gc theory. In D. P. Flanagan, J. L. Gershaft, & P. L. Harrison (eds.), *Contemporary Intellectual Assessment.* Copyright © 1997. Reprinted with the permission of The Guilford Press. Figure 8.5: From Mumaw, R., & Pellegrino, J. (1984). Individual differences in complex spatial processing. *Journal of Educational Psychology, 76*, 920-939. Copyright © 1984 by the American Psychological Association. Reprinted with the permission of the APA and the authors. Figure 8.6: From Sameroff, A., Baldwin, A., & Baldwin, C. (1993). Stability of intelligence from preschool to adolescence: The influence of social and family risk factors. *Child Development, 64*, 89. Copyright © 1993 by the Society for Research in Child Development. Reprinted and adapted with permission of the Society for Research in Child Development. Table 8.1: Simulated items similar to those in Wechsler Adult Intelligence Scale, Third Edition. Copyright © 1997 by The Psychological Corporation. Reproduced by permission. All rights reserved. "Wechsler Adult Intelligence Scale" and "WAIS" are trademarks of the Psychological Corporation registered in the United States of America and/or other jurisdictions. Table 8.3: Adapted from Henderson, N. D. (1982). Correlations in IQ for pairs of people with varying degrees of genetic relatedness and shared environment. *Annual Review of Psychology, 33*, 219-243. Copyright © 1982 by Annual Reviews, Inc. Reprinted and adapted with the permission of the author and the publisher.

Chapter 9 Figure 9.5: Adapted from Squire, L. R. (1986). Priming effects in amnesia. *Science, 232*, 1612-1619. Copyright © 1986 by American Association for the Advancement of Science. Reprinted and adapted with the permission of the publisher and the author. Figure 9.9: Adapted from Kripke, D. F, Simons, R. N., Garfinkel, L., & Hammond, E. C. (1979). Short and long sleep and sleeping pills: Is increased mortality associated? *Archives of General Psychiatry, 36*, 103-116. Copyright © 1979 by the American Medical Association. Reprinted and adapted with permission. Figure 9.11: From Cartwright, R. D. (1978). *A primer on sleep and dreaming*. Reading: Addison-Wesley, Inc. Copyright © 1978 by R. D. Cartwright. Reprinted with the permission of the author. Table 9.1: Adapted from Lavie, P. (1996). *In the enchanted world of sleep* (pp. 176-177), translated by A. Berris. New Haven, CT: Yale University Press. Copyright © 1996 by Yale University. Reprinted with the permission of Yale University Press.

Chapter 10 Figure 10.3: Adapted from Simmons, L.W. (1990). Pheromonal cues for the recognition of kin by female field crickets, *Gryllus bimaculutus*. *Animal Behavior, 40*, 194. Copyright © 1990 by Academic Press Inc. Reprinted and adapted with the permission of the publisher. Figure 10.4: Adapted from Lyengar, S., & Lepper,M. (1999). Rethinking the value of choice: A cultural perspective on intrinsic motivation. *Journal of Personality and Social Psychology, 76*, 349-366. Copyright © 1999 by the American Psychological Association. Reprinted with the permission of the APA and the authors. Figure 10.6: From Thompson, D. A., & Campbell, R. G. (1977). Hunger in humans induced by 2 deoxy-d glucose: Glucoprivic control of taste preference and food intake. *Science, 198*, 1065-1068. Copyright © 1977 by the American Association for the Advancement of Science. Reprinted with the permission of *Science*. Figure 10.8: From Masters,W. H., & Johnson,V. E. (1966). *Human Sexual Response*, p. 5. Boston: Little, Brown and Company. Copyright © 1966 by the Masters and Johnson Institute. Reprinted with permission. Figure 10.9: From Butler, C.A. (1976). New data about female sexual response. *Journal of Sex and Marital Therapy, 10*, 42. Copyright © 1976 by Taylor & Francis, Inc. Reprinted with the permission of Taylor & Francis, Inc., http://www.routledge-ny.com, and the author. Figure 10.10: From Gladue, B. A., Green, R., & Hellman, R. E. (1984). Neuroendocrine response to estrogen and sexual orientation. *Science, 225*, 1496. Copyright © 1984 by American Association for the Advancement of Science. Reprinted with the permission of *Science*. Figure 10.13: From Myers, D., & Diener, E. (1995). Who is happy? *Psychological*

Science, 6, no. 1, 13. Copyright © 1995. Reprinted with the permission of the publisher. Figure 10.15: From Ekman, P., et al. (1983). Autonomic nervous system activity distinguishes among emotions. *Science, 221*, 1209. Copyright © 1984 by the American Association for the Advancement of Science. Reprinted with the permission of the publisher and the author. 10.19: Adapted from Tomarken, A., Davidson, R.J., Wheeler, R. E., & Doss, R. C. (1992). Individual difference in interior brain asymmetry and fundamental dimensions of emotion. *Journal of Personality and Social Psychology, 62*, 681. Copyright © 1992 by the American Psychological Association. Reprinted and adapted with the permission of the APA and the authors. Figure 10.22: From Buss, D. M., Larsen, R.,Westen, D., & Semmelroth, J. (1992). Sex differences in jealousy: Evolution, Physiology and Psychology. *Psychological Science, 3*, 251-255. Copyright © 1992. Reprinted with the permission of the publisher and Dr. David M. Buss, Department of Psychology, The University of Michigan. Table 10.1: Adapted from McClelland, D. C., Atkinson, J.W., Clark, R. A., & Lowell, E. L. (1953). *The Achievement Motive*, p. 294. New York: Irvington Publisher. Copyright 1953 by Appleton Century Crofts. Reprinted and adapted with the permission of Ardent Media, Inc. Table 11.2: Excerpt from Holmes,T. H., & Rahe, R. E. (1967). The social readjustment rating scale. *Journal of Psychosomatic Research, 11*, 213-218. Copyright © 1967 by Elsevier Science, Inc. Reprinted with the permission of the publisher.

Chapter 11 Figure 11.5: From Gortmaker, S. L., et al. (1993). Social and economic consequences of overweight in adolescence and young adulthood. *The New England Journal of Medicine, 329*, 1008-1012. Copyright © 1993 by The Massachusetts Medical Society. Reprinted with the permission of the publisher. Figure 11.6: Hebl, M. R., & Mannix, L. M. (2003). The weight of obesity in evaluating others: A mere proximity effect. *Personality and Social Psychology Bulletin, 29*, 28-38. Copyright © by Sage Publications. Reprinted with the permission of the publisher. 11.8: From Friedman, J. M. Obesity in the new millenium. *Nature*, vol. 404, pp 632-334. Copyright © 2000 by the Nature Publishing Group. Reprinted with the permission of the publisher. Figure 11.10: From Tobacco use in the United States, 1900-1998 (Figure 1A). American Cancer Society, Surveillance Research. Copyright by The American Cancer Society. Reprinted with the permission of The American Cancer Society. Figure 11.14: Courtenay, W. H., McCreary, D. R., & Merighi, J. R. (2002). Gender and ethnic differences in health beliefs and behavior. *Journal of Health Psychology, 7*, 219-231. Copyright © Sage Publications. Reprinted with the permission of the publisher. Figure 11.16: From Taylor et al. (1997). *Annual Review of Psychiatry, 148*, 411-448. Copyright © 1997 by Annual Reviews. Figure 11.17: From Adams, P. R., & Adams, G. R. (1984). Mount Saint Helens's ashfall: Evidence for a disaster stress reaction. *American Psychologist, 39* (3), 257. Copyright © 1984 by the American Psychological Association. Reprinted with the permission of the APA and the authors. Figure 11.18: Adapted from Cohen, S., & Williamson, G. M. (1991). Stress and infectious diseases in humans. *Psychological Bulletin, 109*, 5. Copyright © 1991 by the American Psychological Association. Reprinted and adapted with the permission of the APA and the authors. Figure 11.19: From Brown, J. B. (1991). Staying fit and staying well: Physical fitness as a moderator of life stress. *Journal of Personality and Social Psychology, 61*, 559. Copyright © 1991 by American Psychological Association. Reprinted and adapted with the permission of the APA and the author. Figure 11.20: From Cohen, S,Ytrrell, P. A. J., & Smith, A. P. (1991). Psychological stress and susceptibility to the common cold. *New England Journal of Medicine, 325*, 609-610. Copyright © 1991 by Massachusetts Medical Society. Reprinted with the permission of The New England Journal of Medicine and the authors. Figure 11.21: Pennebaker, J. W., Kiecolt-Glaser, J., & Glaser, R. (1988). Disclosure of traumas and immune function: Health implications for psychotherapy. *Journal of Consulting and Clinical Psychology, 56*, 239-245. Copyright © 1988 by the American Psychological Association. Reprinted and adapted with the permission of the APA and the authors. Table 11.4: Excerpt from Holmes,T. H., & Rahe, R. E. (1967). The social readjustment rating scale. *Journal of Psychosomatic Research, 11*, 213-218. Copyright © 1967 by Elsevier Science, Inc. Reprinted with the permission of the publisher. Table 11.5: From Martikainen P., & Valkonen,T. (1996). Mortality after the death of a spouse: Rates and causes of death in a large Finnish cohort. *American Journal of Public Health, 86*, 1090. Copyright © 1996. Reprinted with the permission of American Public Health Association.Text:

Chapter 12 Figure 12.5: From Wood, R., & Bandura, A. (1989). Impact of conceptions of ability on self-regulatory mechanisms and complex decision making. *Journal of Personality and Social Psychology, 56*, 411-413. Copyright © 1988 by the American Psychological Association. Reprinted with the permission of the APA and the authors. Figure 12.7: Adapted from Eysenck, H. J. (1953). *The Structure of Human Personality*, p. 13. London: Methuen & Co. Copyright 1953. Reprinted with the permission of the publisher. Figure 12.8: From Bouchard, T. J., & McGue, M. (1981).

psychotherapy outcome studies. *American Psychologist, 32,* 754. Copyright © 1977 by the American Psychological Association. Reprinted with the permission of the APA and the authors. Figure 16.10: From Seligman, M. E P. (1995). The effectiveness of psychotherapy. *American Psychologist, 12,* 968. Copyright © 1995 by American Psychological Association. Reprinted with the permission of the APA and the author.

Chapter 17 Figure 17.1: From Steele, C. M. (1997). A threat in the air: How stereotypes shape intellectual identity and performance. *American Psychologist, 52,* 621. Copyright © 1997 by the American Psychological Association. Reprinted with the permission of the APA and the author. Figure 17.2: From Luchins, A .S. (1957). Primacy-recency in impression formation. In C. I. Hovland (ed.), *The Order of Presentation in Persuasion,* pp. 34-35. New Haven, CT: Yale University Press. Copyright © 1957 by Yale University Press. Reprinted with permission. Figure 17.3: Adapted from Kunda, Z., & Thagard, P. (1996). Forming impressions from stereotypes, traits and behaviors: A parallel-constraint-satisfaction theory. *Psychology Review, 303,* 286. Copyright © 1996 by the American Psychological Association. Reprinted with the permission of the APA and the authors. Figure 17.4: Adapted from Macrae, C. N, Bodenhausen, G.V., & Milne, A. B. (1998). Saying no to unwanted thoughts: Self-focus and the regulation of mental life. *Journal of Personality and Social Psychology, 74,* 585. Copyright © 1998 by the American Psychological Association. Reprinted with the permission of the APA and the authors. Figure 17.5: From Woike, B., & Aronoff, J. (1992). Complexity of social cognition. *Journal of Personality and Social Psychology, 63,* 102. Copyright © 1992 by the American Psychological Association. Reprinted and adapted with the permission of the APA and the authors. Figure 17.7: From Heine, S. J., & Lehman, D. (1997). Culture, dissonance and self-affirmation. *Personality and Social Psychology Bulletin, 23,* 396. Copyright © 1997. Reprinted with the permission of Sage Publications, Inc. and the authors. Figure 17.7: From Kihlstrom, J. F & Cantor, N. (1983). Mental representations of the self. In L.

Berkowitz (ed.), *Advances in Experimental Social Psychology, 15.* Copyright © 1983 by Academic Press, Inc. Reprinted with the permission of the publisher and the authors. Figure 17.9: Adapted from Strauman, T. Lemieux, A., & Coe, C. (1993). Self-discrepancy and natural killer cell activity. *Journal of Personality and Social Psychology, 64,* 1049. Copyright © 1993 by the American Psychological Association. Reprinted and adapted with the permission of the APA and the authors.

Chapter 18 Figure 18.2: From R. J. Sternberg (1987). The triangle of love: Intimacy, passion, commitment. New York: Basic Books. Copyright © 1987 by Basic Books. Reprinted with the permission of the publisher. Figure 18.3: From Buss, D. M., & Schmitt, D. P. (1993). Sexual strategies theory: An evolutionary perspective on human mating. *Psychology Review, 100(2),* 204-232. Copyright © 1993 by the American Psychological Association. Reprinted with the permission of the APA and the authors. Figure 18.5: Adapted from Darley, J. M., & Latane, B. (December 1968). When will people help in a crisis? *Psychology Today,* 70-71. Copyright © 1968 by Sussex Publisher, Inc. Reprinted with the permission of *Psychology Today Magazine.* Figure 18.6: From Cohen, D., Nisbett, R., Bowdle, B., & Schwarz, N. (1996). Insult, aggression, and the Southern culture of honor: An experimental ethnography. *Journal of Personality and Social Psychology, 70,* 945-960. Copyright © 1996 by the American Psychological Association. reprinted with the permission of the APA and the authors. Figure 18.8: From Anderson, C. (1989). Temperature and aggression: Ubiquitous effects of heat on occurrence of human violence. *Psychological Bulletin, 106,* 74-96. © 1989 by the American Psychological Association. Reprinted with the permission of the APA and the authors. Figure 18.12: From Milgram, S. (1965). Some conditions of obedience and disobedience to authority. *Human Relations, 18,* 63. Copyright © 1965. Reprinted with the permission of Alexandra Milgram. Figure 18.13 and 18.14: From Asch, S. E. (November 1955). Opinions and social pressure. *Scientific American, 193,* (6), 193. Copyright © 1955 by the Estate of Sara Love.

Name Index

Subject Index